COUNTY COLLEGE OF MORRIS LIBRARY

Dictionary of Literary Biography

1. *The American Renaissance in New England,* edited by Joel Myerson (1978)
2. *American Novelists Since World War II,* edited by Jeffrey Helterman and Richard Layman (1978)
3. *Antebellum Writers in New York and the South,* edited by Joel Myerson (1979)
4. *American Writers in Paris, 1920-1939,* edited by Karen Lane Rood (1980)
5. *American Poets Since World War II,* 2 parts, edited by Donald J. Greiner (1980)
6. *American Novelists Since World War II, Second Series,* edited by James E. Kibler Jr. (1980)
7. *Twentieth-Century American Dramatists,* 2 parts, edited by John MacNicholas (1981)
8. *Twentieth-Century American Science-Fiction Writers,* 2 parts, edited by David Cowart and Thomas L. Wymer (1981)
9. *American Novelists, 1910-1945,* 3 parts, edited by James J. Martine (1981)
10. *Modern British Dramatists, 1900-1945,* 2 parts, edited by Stanley Weintraub (1982)
11. *American Humorists, 1800-1950,* 2 parts, edited by Stanley Trachtenberg (1982)
12. *American Realists and Naturalists,* edited by Donald Pizer and Earl N. Harbert (1982)
13. *British Dramatists Since World War II,* 2 parts, edited by Stanley Weintraub (1982)
14. *British Novelists Since 1960,* 2 parts, edited by Jay L. Halio (1983)
15. *British Novelists, 1930-1959,* 2 parts, edited by Bernard Oldsey (1983)
16. *The Beats: Literary Bohemians in Postwar America,* 2 parts, edited by Ann Charters (1983)
17. *Twentieth-Century American Historians,* edited by Clyde N. Wilson (1983)
18. *Victorian Novelists After 1885,* edited by Ira B. Nadel and William E. Fredeman (1983)
19. *British Poets, 1880-1914,* edited by Donald E. Stanford (1983)
20. *British Poets, 1914-1945,* edited by Donald E. Stanford (1983)
21. *Victorian Novelists Before 1885,* edited by Ira B. Nadel and William E. Fredeman (1983)
22. *American Writers for Children, 1900-1960,* edited by John Cech (1983)
23. *American Newspaper Journalists, 1873-1900,* edited by Perry J. Ashley (1983)
24. *American Colonial Writers, 1606-1734,* edited by Emory Elliott (1984)
25. *American Newspaper Journalists, 1901-1925,* edited by Perry J. Ashley (1984)
26. *American Screenwriters,* edited by Robert E. Morsberger, Stephen O. Lesser, and Randall Clark (1984)
27. *Poets of Great Britain and Ireland, 1945-1960,* edited by Vincent B. Sherry Jr. (1984)
28. *Twentieth-Century American-Jewish Fiction Writers,* edited by Daniel Walden (1984)
29. *American Newspaper Journalists, 1926-1950,* edited by Perry J. Ashley (1984)
30. *American Historians, 1607-1865,* edited by Clyde N. Wilson (1984)
31. *American Colonial Writers, 1735-1781,* edited by Emory Elliott (1984)
32. *Victorian Poets Before 1850,* edited by William E. Fredeman and Ira B. Nadel (1984)
33. *Afro-American Fiction Writers After 1955,* edited by Thadious M. Davis and Trudier Harris (1984)
34. *British Novelists, 1890-1929: Traditionalists,* edited by Thomas F. Staley (1985)
35. *Victorian Poets After 1850,* edited by William E. Fredeman and Ira B. Nadel (1985)
36. *British Novelists, 1890-1929: Modernists,* edited by Thomas F. Staley (1985)
37. *American Writers of the Early Republic,* edited by Emory Elliott (1985)
38. *Afro-American Writers After 1955: Dramatists and Prose Writers,* edited by Thadious M. Davis and Trudier Harris (1985)
39. *British Novelists, 1660-1800,* 2 parts, edited by Martin C. Battestin (1985)
40. *Poets of Great Britain and Ireland Since 1960,* 2 parts, edited by Vincent B. Sherry Jr. (1985)
41. *Afro-American Poets Since 1955,* edited by Trudier Harris and Thadious M. Davis (1985)
42. *American Writers for Children Before 1900,* edited by Glenn E. Estes (1985)
43. *American Newspaper Journalists, 1690-1872,* edited by Perry J. Ashley (1986)
44. *American Screenwriters, Second Series,* edited by Randall Clark, Robert E. Morsberger, and Stephen O. Lesser (1986)
45. *American Poets, 1880-1945, First Series,* edited by Peter Quartermain (1986)
46. *American Literary Publishing Houses, 1900-1980: Trade and Paperback,* edited by Peter Dzwonkoski (1986)
47. *American Historians, 1866-1912,* edited by Clyde N. Wilson (1986)
48. *American Poets, 1880-1945, Second Series,* edited by Peter Quartermain (1986)
49. *American Literary Publishing Houses, 1638-1899,* 2 parts, edited by Peter Dzwonkoski (1986)
50. *Afro-American Writers Before the Harlem Renaissance,* edited by Trudier Harris (1986)
51. *Afro-American Writers from the Harlem Renaissance to 1940,* edited by Trudier Harris (1987)
52. *American Writers for Children Since 1960: Fiction,* edited by Glenn E. Estes (1986)
53. *Canadian Writers Since 1960, First Series,* edited by W. H. New (1986)
54. *American Poets, 1880-1945, Third Series,* 2 parts, edited by Peter Quartermain (1987)
55. *Victorian Prose Writers Before 1867,* edited by William B. Thesing (1987)
56. *German Fiction Writers, 1914-1945,* edited by James Hardin (1987)
57. *Victorian Prose Writers After 1867,* edited by William B. Thesing (1987)

58 *Jacobean and Caroline Dramatists*, edited by Fredson Bowers (1987)

59 *American Literary Critics and Scholars, 1800-1850*, edited by John W. Rathbun and Monica M. Grecu (1987)

60 *Canadian Writers Since 1960, Second Series*, edited by W. H. New (1987)

61 *American Writers for Children Since 1960: Poets, Illustrators, and Nonfiction Authors*, edited by Glenn E. Estes (1987)

62 *Elizabethan Dramatists*, edited by Fredson Bowers (1987)

63 *Modern American Critics, 1920-1955*, edited by Gregory S. Jay (1988)

64 *American Literary Critics and Scholars, 1850-1880*, edited by John W. Rathbun and Monica M. Grecu (1988)

65 *French Novelists, 1900-1930*, edited by Catharine Savage Brosman (1988)

66 *German Fiction Writers, 1885-1913*, 2 parts, edited by James Hardin (1988)

67 *Modern American Critics Since 1955*, edited by Gregory S. Jay (1988)

68 *Canadian Writers, 1920-1959, First Series*, edited by W. H. New (1988)

69 *Contemporary German Fiction Writers, First Series*, edited by Wolfgang D. Elfe and James Hardin (1988)

70 *British Mystery Writers, 1860-1919*, edited by Bernard Benstock and Thomas F. Staley (1988)

71 *American Literary Critics and Scholars, 1880-1900*, edited by John W. Rathbun and Monica M. Grecu (1988)

72 *French Novelists, 1930-1960*, edited by Catharine Savage Brosman (1988)

73 *American Magazine Journalists, 1741-1850*, edited by Sam G. Riley (1988)

74 *American Short-Story Writers Before 1880*, edited by Bobby Ellen Kimbel, with the assistance of William E. Grant (1988)

75 *Contemporary German Fiction Writers, Second Series*, edited by Wolfgang D. Elfe and James Hardin (1988)

76 *Afro-American Writers, 1940-1955*, edited by Trudier Harris (1988)

77 *British Mystery Writers, 1920-1939*, edited by Bernard Benstock and Thomas F. Staley (1988)

78 *American Short-Story Writers, 1880-1910*, edited by Bobby Ellen Kimbel, with the assistance of William E. Grant (1988)

79 *American Magazine Journalists, 1850-1900*, edited by Sam G. Riley (1988)

80 *Restoration and Eighteenth-Century Dramatists, First Series*, edited by Paula R. Backscheider (1989)

81 *Austrian Fiction Writers, 1875-1913*, edited by James Hardin and Donald G. Daviau (1989)

82 *Chicano Writers, First Series*, edited by Francisco A. Lomelí and Carl R. Shirley (1989)

83 *French Novelists Since 1960*, edited by Catharine Savage Brosman (1989)

84 *Restoration and Eighteenth-Century Dramatists, Second Series*, edited by Paula R. Backscheider (1989)

85 *Austrian Fiction Writers After 1914*, edited by James Hardin and Donald G. Daviau (1989)

86 *American Short-Story Writers, 1910-1945, First Series*, edited by Bobby Ellen Kimbel (1989)

87 *British Mystery and Thriller Writers Since 1940, First Series*, edited by Bernard Benstock and Thomas F. Staley (1989)

88 *Canadian Writers, 1920-1959, Second Series*, edited by W. H. New (1989)

89 *Restoration and Eighteenth-Century Dramatists, Third Series*, edited by Paula R. Backscheider (1989)

90 *German Writers in the Age of Goethe, 1789-1832*, edited by James Hardin and Christoph E. Schweitzer (1989)

91 *American Magazine Journalists, 1900-1960, First Series*, edited by Sam G. Riley (1990)

92 *Canadian Writers, 1890-1920*, edited by W. H. New (1990)

93 *British Romantic Poets, 1789-1832, First Series*, edited by John R. Greenfield (1990)

94 *German Writers in the Age of Goethe: Sturm und Drang to Classicism*, edited by James Hardin and Christoph E. Schweitzer (1990)

95 *Eighteenth-Century British Poets, First Series*, edited by John Sitter (1990)

96 *British Romantic Poets, 1789-1832, Second Series*, edited by John R. Greenfield (1990)

97 *German Writers from the Enlightenment to Sturm und Drang, 1720-1764*, edited by James Hardin and Christoph E. Schweitzer (1990)

98 *Modern British Essayists, First Series*, edited by Robert Beum (1990)

99 *Canadian Writers Before 1890*, edited by W. H. New (1990)

100 *Modern British Essayists, Second Series*, edited by Robert Beum (1990)

101 *British Prose Writers, 1660-1800, First Series*, edited by Donald T. Siebert (1991)

102 *American Short-Story Writers, 1910-1945, Second Series*, edited by Bobby Ellen Kimbel (1991)

103 *American Literary Biographers, First Series*, edited by Steven Serafin (1991)

104 *British Prose Writers, 1660-1800, Second Series*, edited by Donald T. Siebert (1991)

105 *American Poets Since World War II, Second Series*, edited by R. S. Gwynn (1991)

106 *British Literary Publishing Houses, 1820-1880*, edited by Patricia J. Anderson and Jonathan Rose (1991)

107 *British Romantic Prose Writers, 1789-1832, First Series*, edited by John R. Greenfield (1991)

108 *Twentieth-Century Spanish Poets, First Series*, edited by Michael L. Perna (1991)

109 *Eighteenth-Century British Poets, Second Series*, edited by John Sitter (1991)

110 *British Romantic Prose Writers, 1789-1832, Second Series*, edited by John R. Greenfield (1991)

111 *American Literary Biographers, Second Series*, edited by Steven Serafin (1991)

112 *British Literary Publishing Houses, 1881-1965*, edited by Jonathan Rose and Patricia J. Anderson (1991)

113 *Modern Latin-American Fiction Writers, First Series*, edited by William Luis (1992)

114 *Twentieth-Century Italian Poets, First Series*, edited by Giovanna Wedel De Stasio, Glauco Cambon, and Antonio Illiano (1992)

115 *Medieval Philosophers*, edited by Jeremiah Hackett (1992)

116 *British Romantic Novelists, 1789-1832*, edited by Bradford K. Mudge (1992)

117 *Twentieth-Century Caribbean and Black African Writers, First Series*, edited by Bernth Lindfors and Reinhard Sander (1992)

118 *Twentieth-Century German Dramatists, 1889-1918*, edited by Wolfgang D. Elfe and James Hardin (1992)

119 *Nineteenth-Century French Fiction Writers: Romanticism and Realism, 1800-1860*, edited by Catharine Savage Brosman (1992)

120 *American Poets Since World War II, Third Series*, edited by R. S. Gwynn (1992)

121 *Seventeenth-Century British Nondramatic Poets, First Series*, edited by M. Thomas Hester (1992)

122 *Chicano Writers, Second Series*, edited by Francisco A. Lomelí and Carl R. Shirley (1992)

123 *Nineteenth-Century French Fiction Writers: Naturalism and Beyond, 1860-1900*, edited by Catharine Savage Brosman (1992)

124 *Twentieth-Century German Dramatists, 1919-1992*, edited by Wolfgang D. Elfe and James Hardin (1992)

125 *Twentieth-Century Caribbean and Black African Writers, Second Series*, edited by Bernth Lindfors and Reinhard Sander (1993)

126 *Seventeenth-Century British Nondramatic Poets, Second Series*, edited by M. Thomas Hester (1993)

127 *American Newspaper Publishers, 1950-1990*, edited by Perry J. Ashley (1993)

128 *Twentieth-Century Italian Poets, Second Series*, edited by Giovanna Wedel De Stasio, Glauco Cambon, and Antonio Illiano (1993)

129 *Nineteenth-Century German Writers, 1841-1900*, edited by James Hardin and Siegfried Mews (1993)

130 *American Short-Story Writers Since World War II*, edited by Patrick Meanor (1993)

131 *Seventeenth-Century British Nondramatic Poets, Third Series*, edited by M. Thomas Hester (1993)

132 *Sixteenth-Century British Nondramatic Writers, First Series*, edited by David A. Richardson (1993)

133 *Nineteenth-Century German Writers to 1840*, edited by James Hardin and Siegfried Mews (1993)

134 *Twentieth-Century Spanish Poets, Second Series*, edited by Jerry Phillips Winfield (1994)

135 *British Short-Fiction Writers, 1880-1914: The Realist Tradition*, edited by William B. Thesing (1994)

136 *Sixteenth-Century British Nondramatic Writers, Second Series*, edited by David A. Richardson (1994)

137 *American Magazine Journalists, 1900-1960, Second Series*, edited by Sam G. Riley (1994)

138 *German Writers and Works of the High Middle Ages: 1170-1280*, edited by James Hardin and Will Hasty (1994)

139 *British Short-Fiction Writers, 1945-1980*, edited by Dean Baldwin (1994)

140 *American Book-Collectors and Bibliographers, First Series*, edited by Joseph Rosenblum (1994)

141 *British Children's Writers, 1880-1914*, edited by Laura M. Zaidman (1994)

142 *Eighteenth-Century British Literary Biographers*, edited by Steven Serafin (1994)

143 *American Novelists Since World War II, Third Series*, edited by James R. Giles and Wanda H. Giles (1994)

144 *Nineteenth-Century British Literary Biographers*, edited by Steven Serafin (1994)

145 *Modern Latin-American Fiction Writers, Second Series*, edited by William Luis and Ann González (1994)

146 *Old and Middle English Literature*, edited by Jeffrey Helterman and Jerome Mitchell (1994)

147 *South Slavic Writers Before World War II*, edited by Vasa D. Mihailovich (1994)

148 *German Writers and Works of the Early Middle Ages: 800-1170*, edited by Will Hasty and James Hardin (1994)

149 *Late Nineteenth- and Early Twentieth-Century British Literary Biographers*, edited by Steven Serafin (1995)

150 *Early Modern Russian Writers, Late Seventeenth and Eighteenth Centuries*, edited by Marcus C. Levitt (1995)

151 *British Prose Writers of the Early Seventeenth Century*, edited by Clayton D. Lein (1995)

152 *American Novelists Since World War II, Fourth Series*, edited by James and Wanda Giles (1995)

153 *Late-Victorian and Edwardian British Novelists, First Series*, edited by George M. Johnson (1995)

154 *The British Literary Book Trade, 1700-1820*, edited by James K. Bracken and Joel Silver (1995)

155 *Twentieth-Century British Literary Biographers*, edited by Steven Serafin (1995)

156 *British Short-Fiction Writers, 1880-1914: The Romantic Tradition*, edited by William F. Naufftus (1995)

157 *Twentieth-Century Caribbean and Black African Writers, Third Series*, edited by Bernth Lindfors and Reinhard Sander (1995)

158 *British Reform Writers, 1789-1832*, edited by Gary Kelly and Edd Applegate (1995)

159 *British Short-Fiction Writers, 1800-1880*, edited by John R. Greenfield (1996)

160 *British Children's Writers, 1914-1960*, edited by Donald R. Hettinga and Gary D. Schmidt (1996)

161 *British Children's Writers Since 1960, First Series*, edited by Caroline Hunt (1996)

162 *British Short-Fiction Writers, 1915-1945*, edited by John H. Rogers (1996)

163 *British Children's Writers, 1800-1880*, edited by Meena Khorana (1996)

164 *German Baroque Writers, 1580-1660*, edited by James Hardin (1996)

165 *American Poets Since World War II, Fourth Series*, edited by Joseph Conte (1996)

166 *British Travel Writers, 1837-1875*, edited by Barbara Brothers and Julia Gergits (1996)

167 *Sixteenth-Century British Nondramatic Writers, Third Series*, edited by David A. Richardson (1996)

168 *German Baroque Writers, 1661-1730*, edited by James Hardin (1996)

169 *American Poets Since World War II, Fifth Series*, edited by Joseph Conte (1996)

170 *The British Literary Book Trade, 1475-1700*, edited by James K. Bracken and Joel Silver (1996)

171 *Twentieth-Century American Sportswriters*, edited by Richard Orodenker (1996)

172 *Sixteenth-Century British Nondramatic Writers, Fourth Series*, edited by David A. Richardson (1996)

173 *American Novelists Since World War II, Fifth Series*, edited by James R. Giles and Wanda H. Giles (1996)

174 *British Travel Writers, 1876-1909*, edited by Barbara Brothers and Julia Gergits (1997)

175 *Native American Writers of the United States*, edited by Kenneth M. Roemer (1997)

176 *Ancient Greek Authors*, edited by Ward W. Briggs (1997)

177 *Italian Novelists Since World War II, 1945-1965* edited by Augustus Pallotta (1997)

178 *British Fantasy and Science-Fiction Writers Before World War I*, edited by Darren Harris-Fain (1997)

179 *German Writers of the Renaissance and Reformation, 1280-1580*, edited by James Hardin and Max Reinhart (1997)

Documentary Series

1 *Sherwood Anderson, Willa Cather, John Dos Passos, Theodore Dreiser, F. Scott Fitzgerald, Ernest Hemingway, Sinclair Lewis*, edited by Margaret A. Van Antwerp (1982)

2 *James Gould Cozzens, James T. Farrell, William Faulkner, John O'Hara, John Steinbeck, Thomas Wolfe, Richard Wright*, edited by Margaret A. Van Antwerp (1982)

3 *Saul Bellow, Jack Kerouac, Norman Mailer, Vladimir Nabokov, John Updike, Kurt Vonnegut*, edited by Mary Bruccoli (1983)

4 *Tennessee Williams*, edited by Margaret A. Van Antwerp and Sally Johns (1984)

5 *American Transcendentalists*, edited by Joel Myerson (1988)

6 *Hardboiled Mystery Writers: Raymond Chandler, Dashiell Hammett, Ross Macdonald*, edited by Matthew J. Bruccoli and Richard Layman (1989)

7 *Modern American Poets: James Dickey, Robert Frost, Marianne Moore*, edited by Karen L. Rood (1989)

8 *The Black Aesthetic Movement*, edited by Jeffrey Louis Decker (1991)

9 *American Writers of the Vietnam War: W. D. Ehrhart, Larry Heinemann, Tim O'Brien, Walter McDonald, John M. Del Vecchio*, edited by Ronald Baughman (1991)

10 *The Bloomsbury Group*, edited by Edward L. Bishop (1992)

11 *American Proletarian Culture: The Twenties and The Thirties*, edited by Jon Christian Suggs (1993)

12 *Southern Women Writers: Flannery O'Connor, Katherine Anne Porter, Eudora Welty*, edited by Mary Ann Wimsatt and Karen L. Rood (1994)

13 *The House of Scribner, 1846–1904*, edited by John Delaney (1996)

14 *Four Women Writers for Children, 1868–1918*, edited by Caroline C. Hunt (1996)

Yearbooks

1980 edited by Karen L. Rood, Jean W. Ross, and Richard Ziegfeld (1981)

1981 edited by Karen L. Rood, Jean W. Ross, and Richard Ziegfeld (1982)

1982 edited by Richard Ziegfeld; associate editors: Jean W. Ross and Lynne C. Zeigler (1983)

1983 edited by Mary Bruccoli and Jean W. Ross; associate editor: Richard Ziegfeld (1984)

1984 edited by Jean W. Ross (1985)

1985 edited by Jean W. Ross (1986)

1986 edited by J. M. Brook (1987)

1987 edited by J. M. Brook (1988)

1988 edited by J. M. Brook (1989)

1989 edited by J. M. Brook (1990)

1990 edited by James W. Hipp (1991)

1991 edited by James W. Hipp (1992)

1992 edited by James W. Hipp (1993)

1993 edited by James W. Hipp, contributing editor George Garrett (1994)

1994 edited by James W. Hipp, contributing editor George Garrett (1995)

1995 edited by James W. Hipp, contributing editor George Garrett (1996)

1996 edited by Samuel W. Bruce and L. Kay Webster, contributing editor George Garrett (1997)

Concise Series

Concise Dictionary of American Literary Biography, 6 volumes (1988-1989): *The New Consciousness, 1941-1968; Colonization to the American Renaissance, 1640-1865; Realism, Naturalism, and Local Color, 1865-1917; The Twenties, 1917-1929; The Age of Maturity, 1929-1941; Broadening Views, 1968-1988.*

Concise Dictionary of British Literary Biography, 8 volumes (1991-1992): *Writers of the Middle Ages and Renaissance Before 1660; Writers of the Restoration and Eighteenth Century, 1660-1789; Writers of the Romantic Period, 1789-1832; Victorian Writers, 1832-1890; Late Victorian and Edwardian Writers, 1890-1914; Modern Writers, 1914-1945; Writers After World War II, 1945-1960; Contemporary Writers, 1960 to Present.*

Dictionary of Literary Biography® • Volume One Hundred Seventy-Nine

German Writers of the Renaissance and Reformation 1280–1580

Dictionary of Literary Biography® • Volume One Hundred Seventy-Nine

German Writers of the Renaissance and Reformation 1280–1580

Edited by
James Hardin
University of South Carolina
and
Max Reinhart
University of Georgia

A Bruccoli Clark Layman Book
Gale Research
Detroit, Washington, D.C., London

Advisory Board for
DICTIONARY OF LITERARY BIOGRAPHY

John Baker
William Cagle
Patrick O'Connor
George Garrett
Trudier Harris

Matthew J. Bruccoli and Richard Layman, Editorial Directors
C. E. Frazer Clark Jr., Managing Editor
Karen Rood, Senior Editor

Printed in the United States of America

The paper used in this publication meets the minimum requirements
of American National Standard for Information Sciences–Permanence
Paper for Printed Library Materials, ANSI Z39.48-1984. ∞ ™

This publication is a creative work fully protected by all applicable copyright laws, as well as by misappropriation, trade secret, unfair competition, and other applicable laws. The authors and editors of this work have added value to the underlying factual material herein through one or more of the following: unique and original selection, coordination, expression, arrangement, and classification of the information.

All rights to this publication will be vigorously defended.

Copyright © 1997 by Gale Research
835 Penobscot Building
Detroit, MI 48226

All rights reserved including the right of reproduction in
whole or in part in any form.

Library of Congress Cataloging-in-Publication Data

German writers of the Renaissance and Reformation, 1280-1580 / edited by Max Reinhart and
   James Hardin.
   p. cm.–(Dictionary of literary biography; v. 179)
"A Bruccoli Clark Layman book."
Includes bibliographical references and index.
ISBN 0-7876-1068-2 (alk. paper)
1. German literature–Early modern, 1500-1700–Bio-bibliography. 2. German literature–Middle High
German, 1050-1500–Bio-bibliography. I. Reinhart, Max, 1946– . II. Hardin, James N. III. Series.
PT241. G47 1997
830.9   97-2716
[B]–DC21   CIP

---

10 9 8 7 6 5 4 3 2 1

For Hans-Gert Roloff and Eckhard Bernstein: Scholars and Teachers of German Humanism

Contents

Plan of the Series xiii
Introduction xv

Hermann Bote (circa 1460–circa 1520) 3
  Priscilla A. Hayden-Roy

Sebastian Brant (1457–1521) 14
  John Van Cleve

Conrad Celtis (1459–1508) 23
  David Price

Albrecht Dürer (1471–1528) 34
  David Price

Elisabeth von Nassau-Saarbrücken
  (after 1393–1456) 42
  Albrecht Classen

Albrecht von Eyb (1420–1475) 48
  John L. Flood

Johann Fischart
  (1546 or 1547–1590 or 1591) 55
  Stephen L. Wailes

Hans Folz (between 1435 and 1440–1513) 63
  Joe G. Delap

Sebastian Franck (1499–1542) 70
  Priscilla A. Hayden-Roy

Nicodemus Frischlin (1547–1590) 83
  Richard E. Schade

Argula von Grumbach (1492–after 1563?) 89
  Hermina Joldersma

Eobanus Hessus (1488–1540) 97
  Harry Vredeveld

Ulrich von Hutten (1488–1523) 111
  James V. Mehl

Petrus Lotichius Secundus (1528–1560) 124
  Wanda Merchant

Peter Luder (circa 1415–1472) 129
  Frank Baron

Martin Luther (1483–1546) 135
  Jeffrey Jaynes

Niklaus Manuel (Niklaus Manuel Deutsch)
  (circa 1484–1530) 152
  Glenn Ehrstine

Philipp Melanchthon (1497–1560) 166
  Derk Visser

Olympia Fulvia Morata (1526–1555) 178
  John L. Flood

Thomas Murner (1475–1537) 184
  Linda L. Gaus

Oswald von Wolkenstein (1376 or 1377–1445) .198
  Albrecht Classen

Paracelsus (Philippus Aureolus Theophrastus
  Bombastus von Hohenheim)
  (1493–1541) 206
  Gerhild Scholz Williams

Caritas Pirckheimer (1467–1532) 212
  Paula Datsko Barker

Willibald Pirckheimer (1470–1530) 218
  Eckhard Bernstein

Paul Rebhun (circa 1500–1546) 226
  Paul F. Casey

Johannes Reuchlin (1455–1522) 231
  David Price

Hans Sachs (1494–1576) 241
  Eckhard Bernstein

Joannes Sapidus (Hans Witz)
  (1490–1561) 253
  Peter Schaeffer

Paul Melissus Schede (1539–1602) 260
  David Price

Heinrich Seuse (Henry Suso)
  (1295?–1366) 265
  Debra L. Stoudt

Contents

Heinrich Steinhöwel (1411/1412-1479) 276
Albrecht Classen

Johannes Tauler (circa 1300-1361) 281
David Blamires

Johannes von Tepl (Johannes von Saaz)
(circa 1350-1414/1415) 287
Anne Winston-Allen

Joachim Vadianus (Joachim Von Watt)
(1484-1551) 293
Peter Schaeffer

Burkhard Waldis (circa 1490-1556?) 303
Joe G. Delap

Georg Wickram (circa 1505-circa 1561) 309
Elisabeth Wåghäll

Jakob Wimpfeling (1450-1528) 317
James H. Overfield

Heinrich Wittenwiler
(before 1387-circa 1414?) 326
Albrecht Classen

Niklas von Wyle (circa 1415-1479) 332
John L. Flood

Huldrych Zwingli (1484-1531) 338
J. Wayne Baker

Checklist of Further Readings 349
Contributors 353
Cumulative Index 357

Plan of the Series

... Almost the most prodigious asset of a country, and perhaps its most precious possession, is its native literary product – when that product is fine and noble and enduring.

Mark Twain*

The advisory board, the editors, and the publisher of the *Dictionary of Literary Biography* are joined in endorsing Mark Twain's declaration. The literature of a nation provides an inexhaustible resource of permanent worth. We intend to make literature and its creators better understood and more accessible to students and the reading public, while satisfying the standards of teachers and scholars.

To meet these requirements, *literary biography* has been construed in terms of the author's achievement. The most important thing about a writer is his writing. Accordingly, the entries in *DLB* are career biographies, tracing the development of the author's canon and the evolution of his reputation.

The purpose of *DLB* is not only to provide reliable information in a convenient format but also to place the figures in the larger perspective of literary history and to offer appraisals of their accomplishments by qualified scholars.

The publication plan for *DLB* resulted from two years of preparation. The project was proposed to Bruccoli Clark by Frederick C. Ruffner, president of the Gale Research Company, in November 1975. After specimen entries were prepared and typeset, an advisory board was formed to refine the entry format and develop the series rationale. In meetings held during 1976, the publisher, series editors, and advisory board approved the scheme for a comprehensive biographical dictionary of persons who contributed to North American literature. Editorial work on the first volume began in January 1977, and it was published in 1978. In order to make *DLB* more than a reference tool and to compile volumes that individually have claim to status as literary history, it was decided to organize volumes by topic, period, or genre. Each of these freestanding volumes provides a biographical-bibliographical guide and overview for a particular area of literature. We are convinced that this organization – as opposed to a single alphabet method – constitutes a valuable innovation in the presentation of reference material. The volume plan necessarily requires many decisions for the placement and treatment of authors who might properly be included in two or three volumes. In some instances a major figure will be included in separate volumes, but with different entries emphasizing the aspect of his career appropriate to each volume. Ernest Hemingway, for example, is represented in *American Writers in Paris, 1920-1939* by an entry focusing on his expatriate apprenticeship; he is also in *American Novelists, 1910-1945* with an entry surveying his entire career. Each volume includes a cumulative index of the subject authors and articles. Comprehensive indexes to the entire series are planned.

The series has been further augmented by the *DLB Yearbooks* (since 1981) which update published entries and add new entries to keep the *DLB* current with contemporary activity. There have also been *DLB Documentary Series* volumes which provide biographical and critical source materials for figures whose work is judged to have particular interest for students. One of these companion volumes is entirely devoted to Tennessee Williams.

We define literature as the *intellectual commerce of a nation:* not merely as belles lettres but as that ample and complex process by which ideas are generated, shaped, and transmitted. *DLB* entries are not limited to "creative writers" but extend to other figures who in their time and in their way influenced the mind of a people. Thus the series encompasses historians, journalists, publishers, book collectors, and screenwriters. By this means readers of *DLB* may be aided to perceive literature not as cult scripture in the keeping of intellectual high priests but firmly positioned at the center of a nation's life.

DLB includes the major writers appropriate to each volume and those standing in the ranks behind them. Scholarly and critical counsel has been sought in deciding which minor figures to include and how full their entries should be. Wherever possible, useful references are made to figures who do not warrant separate entries.

Each *DLB* volume has an expert volume editor responsible for planning the volume, selecting the figures for inclusion, and assigning the entries. Volume editors are also responsible for preparing, where appropriate, appendices surveying the major periodicals and literary and intellectual movements for their volumes, as well as lists of further readings. Work on the series as a whole is coordinated at the Bruccoli Clark Layman editorial center in Columbia, South Carolina, where the editorial staff is responsible for accuracy and utility of the published volumes.

One feature that distinguishes *DLB* is the illustration policy – its concern with the iconography of literature. Just as an author is influenced by his surroundings, so is the reader's understanding of the author enhanced by a knowledge of his environment. Therefore *DLB* volumes include not only drawings, paintings, and photographs of authors, often depicting them at various stages in their careers, but also illustrations of their families and places where they lived. Title pages are regularly reproduced in facsimile along with dust jackets for modern authors. The dust jackets are a special feature of *DLB* because they often document better than anything else the way in which an author's work was perceived in its own time. Specimens of the writers' manuscripts and letters are included when feasible.

Samuel Johnson rightly decreed that "The chief glory of every people arises from its authors." The purpose of the *Dictionary of Literary Biography* is to compile literary history in the surest way available to us – by accurate and comprehensive treatment of the lives and work of those who contributed to it.

The *DLB* Advisory Board

Introduction

The beginning of the period covered by *DLB 179: German Writers of the Renaissance and Reformation, 1280–1580* is known as the late Middle Ages. It is often contrasted unfavorably with the preceding High Middle Ages, the period from roughly 1170 to 1280, which was notable for its many enduring contributions to history and culture: the rise of the Holy Roman Empire under the Hohenstaufens; Gothic architecture; monastic culture; the Thomistic synthesis of Aristotelian and Christian thought; and the first golden age of German literature with the courtly epic and *Minnesang* (courtly love poetry). Until well into the twentieth century historians tended to characterize the late Middle Ages as a downhill slide from an optimistic, aristocratic, courtly culture into a pessimistic, middle-class urban society—a slide accompanied by intellectual decline, political disintegration, and increasing spiritual malaise.

While recent scholarship provides a more judicious view of the late Middle Ages and its transition into the early modern age, the emphasis on crisis still obtains. An air of fin-de-siècle anxiety caused many at the beginning of the period to anticipate earth-shattering change; but if to some minds the coming crisis adumbrated catastrophe, to others it promised salvation. The visionary Joachim of Fiore had predicted prior to 1200 that the long-prophesied Third Age, the Age of the Spirit, a time of love and brotherhood, would arrive in the late thirteenth century, after a period of testing and strife. Heiko Oberman finds support in this worldview for his thesis in *The Dawn of the Reformation* (1986) that the crises of the late Middle Ages were the "birthpangs of the modern era."

A tectonic shift took place about 1250 that definitively changed the face of European society. The period treated in this volume begins in shock: on the heels of the Great Interregnum, the period from 1250 to 1273 when no emperor could be selected, Europe found itself caught in a horrifying tide of the Black Death when the bubonic plague broke out in 1347. The period's two great institutions, the church and the empire, were in profound transition; conflict and change would characterize them for the next three centuries.

The end of the Hohenstaufen dynasty in 1254 provided the feudal lords with the opportunity to assert their claims against a central seat of power; the empire never recovered its unchallenged sovereignty over the German princes, even after the rise of the Hapsburgs in the late thirteenth century. The *Goldene Bulle* (Golden Bull), a document promulgated in 1356 by Emperor Charles IV, recognized the territorial autonomy of the princes and led to the rise of independent-minded German city councils and territorial princes capable of negotiating new alliances and forming new allegiances. The success of the Protestant Reformation would result, in part, from this development. With the Ottoman conquest of Constantinople (today Istanbul, Turkey) in 1453 a fear of Turkish invasion gripped the empire, as can be seen in the seemingly endless barrage of anti-Turk polemics produced during the next two centuries, and kept the imperial government in Vienna constantly on its guard and off balance. By the end of the fifteenth century, anarchy had become widespread; the empire was unable to carry out its plans except by borrowing money, at high interest rates, from wealthy urban families; in 1499 the Swiss Confederation broke with the empire; and unevenly distributed economic growth led to unrest that culminated in the bloody suppression of the peasants in 1524–1525. Through a series of strategic marriages the Hapsburg Empire had extended its rule so widely that, it was said, the sun never set on Charles V's lands; but its financial and political indebtedness to electors, financiers, and territorial allies sapped its strength and opened the door for the competing claims of France to imperial hegemony on the Continent.

But no development had greater consequences for political changes in the empire than the movement for church reform in the first half of the sixteenth century. The controversy over the limits of the church's role in the world had come to a head in the first quarter of the fourteenth century with the conciliar movement, which called for separation of ecclesiastical and imperial powers. Pope Boniface VIII's bull *Unam sanctam ecclesiam* (One Holy Church, 1302), adapting Saint Thomas Aquinas's principle that grace perfects nature to claim that all things temporal should be subject to ecclesiastical authority, was refuted by the *Defensor pacis* (Defender of Peace, 1324) of Marsilius of Padua. Marsilius, one of a new breed of royal apologists trained at the University of Paris, argued that temporal sovereignty is granted by the people to the emperor, and that the role of the church on earth is limited to spiritual succor. Marsilius's argument would influence northern Reformist thought in the sixteenth century, from Martin Luther in Germany to Huldrych Zwingli in Switzerland and Thomas Cromwell in England. The church's public humiliation in the so-called Babylonian Captivity–the removal of the papacy from Rome to Avignon between 1305 and 1377–occasioned intense internal scrutiny and calls for reform. The mystic Meister Eckhart condemned the materialism of the Roman *Mauerkirche* (church of walls) and, long before Luther, called for a priesthood of all believers, insisting that the kingdom of God is within the individual. Eckhart's teachings were condemned as heresy in 1329 by Pope John XXII, notorious for his loathing of everything German. By the middle of the fifteenth century the church, having long since rejected the argument that it should imitate Christ's poverty, was occupying itself with the pursuit of wealth by many means–including the sale of indulgences and ecclesiastical offices–to support its massive hierarchy, ambitious building program, and international interests. The resulting movement for reform led to two events of particular gravity: Luther's rejection of papal in favor of princely jurisdiction over the Protestant church; and the right of princes, legislated in the Peace of Augsburg (1555), to determine the legal religion in their respective territories. The resulting particularism would determine the political face of Germany for the following two and a half centuries.

In German literature the transition from the High Middle Ages to the late Middle Ages becomes visible around the middle of the thirteenth century, more or less contemporaneously with the political crisis in the empire. The work that is often cited as representing the turning point between the older and newer social cultures is the narrative poem *Helmbrecht,* written between around 1265 and 1280 by Wernher der Gartnaere. This coarse work provides evidence that aristocratic social standards were under fire: the elegant style of the courtly era was yielding to blunt humor, heavy-handed didacticism, and the use of realistic language. Casually applied or less-elevated forms, amoral tales and adventures, satiric anecdotes, fables, and burlesque Shrovetide plays became commonplace, though not without a struggle. Popular preachers such as Berthold von Regensburg denounced the trend, and a generation later a great mystical movement would arise and urge a return to inner piety. A literature of fools flourished; the subtle artistry and individualism of the *Minnesinger,* the high-medieval singers of courtly love, gave way to the more formalized versification of urban-dwelling, rote-trained Meistersinger. The trend toward realism in art that manifested itself after the decline of high-medieval literature accelerated in the fifteenth century. Heinrich Wittenwiler's poem *Der Ring* (circa 1410), a hyperbolic allegory employing an eclectic range of genres, relentlessly satirizes all social classes. The Low German translation of the Netherlandic fable *Reineke Fuchs* (Reynard the Fox, 1498) cynically mirrors a world run amok in stupidity and immorality. The knightly poet Oswald von Wolkenstein burst the traditional limits of *Minnesang* by filling it with realistic elements from his own turbulent life. One of the most prevalent forms was the folk song, which was used for a wide range of themes from love to piracy, thereby anticipating the versatility of the later *Kunstballade* (art ballad).

Meanwhile, a process was occurring that is known in German as *Verbürgerlichung* (the growth of the urban bourgeoisie), and a middle-class mentality was insinuating itself into the cultural and educational spheres. Between the tenth and fifteenth centuries the number of cities increased nearly twentyfold, and the cities replaced the feudal courts as social centers. Trade and manufacture on an ever-larger scale supplanted the rural cottage industries, and middle-class money began to acquire properties that had formerly been in the hands of the nobility and the church. Wealthier cities, such as those along the overland trade routes–Leipzig, Nuremberg, Strasbourg, and Augsburg–purchased their independence from the empire and became free imperial cities; economic and military alliances were formed between cities and territories. Wealthy burgher families, such as the Fuggers and the Welsers in Augsburg, capitalized on the emperor's need for cash to finance his increasingly expensive ventures. This change is reflected in literature in the introduction of a new kind of hero: as the network of commercial centers expanded, the symbolic importance of the gallant-knight figure began to fade, while the experiences of the wandering merchant became the subject of much of the new burgher literature.

This change did not happen at once, of course. The courtly tradition continued, though in a way that often resembled parody–as in the works of the knightly poets Wolkenstein and Hugo von Montfort. The courtly epic, in particular, found its imitation in a new anonymous *Nibelunger Lied* (Song of the Nibelungs, circa 1485), a somewhat prosaic reworking of the anonymous heroic epic, the *Nibelungenlied,* of around 1200. In various locations there was a resurgence of aristocratic culture: at the court at Rotten-weil, near Stuttgart; at Innsbruck; at Vienna under Maximilian I; and at Saarbrücken with the prose adaptations of French novels by Elisabeth von Nassau-Saarbrücken.

It would be wide of the mark to identify the growth of the bourgeois art forms and worldview solely with the trend toward greater realism, as though realism somehow conflicted with "higher" formal and spiritual ideals—a position taken by many literary historians as late as the 1970s. In fact, the development of a European middle class was strongly encouraged by humanistic ideas from northern Italy that, by the fifteenth century, were finding currency north of the Alps. The image that most inspired the educated segment of the rising middle class was the ancient ideal of *vera nobilitas* (true nobility). Here, in embryonic form, is the German concept of *Bildung* (cultivation; education in the broadest sense): by turning one's mind to noble aspirations, one can become not only self-reliant but intellectually and spiritually noble. The most immediate manifestation of this ideal was the founding of universities: Prague in 1348, Vienna in 1365, Heidelberg in 1386, Cologne in 1388, Erfurt in 1389, Rostock in 1419, Basel in 1460, Ingolstadt in 1472, Tübingen in 1477, and Wittenberg in 1502. The impact of the concept of Bildung on the development of modern German thought and society is incalculable.

Embattled though they were, church and empire continued to provide Europe with its two great pillars of unity. Although the centrifugal forces of medieval feudalism acted against centralization, they could not entirely escape the pull of the church on one side and the empire on the other. Only when the respective unifying forces of these two institutions on nations and peoples are taken into account is it possible to appreciate the degree of unity amid diversity that existed in greater "Germania."

The church continued to order peoples' lives through rituals that transcended particularistic conditions, and it constituted the geopolitical and spiritual center for the majority of Europeans during much of the period from 1280 to 1580. Correspondingly, the place of the church in urban literature remained strong throughout. Late-medieval religious poetry focused on iconographic representations of the exemplary life and death of Christ. The religious drama, with burgher actors directed by clerics and staged in the town or cathedral square, adapted the themes of the Nativity, the Passion, Marian laments, or the Last Judgment, arousing believers to deeper devotion and sinners to repentance. Collections of hagiography and calendar meditations on the church year were popular. Movements of popular piety gained momentum from a special affection for some religious figure, such as Mary, or cultic fascination with a certain concept, such as death. In the empire, with Rudolf of Hapsburg's election as emperor in 1273, a political dynasty came to power that would rule Europe for more than half a millennium. Despite the shift toward territorial autonomy that occurred after the reign of Charles IV, the empire continued to function not only as the highest secular power but also as the representation of a grand idea: the ultimate embodiment of human potential. No other single institution had such power to effect universal change as did the empire.

Additional forces of unity, less concrete but no less real, speak for a common European conceptualization of thought and culture in the late medieval and early modern ages. Two are essential for a proper understanding of the German literature of the period: a heightened expectation, beginning with the revival of republican political theory in quattrocento Italy, of the renewal of ancient greatness, an expectation that could be expressed either in chiliastic or in optimistically visionary language; and a concomitant nationalism that led not only to political uprisings throughout the empire but also to ambitious attempts to create great literature in the vernacular. In this light it becomes apparent that Luther's translation of the Bible into German was an act of patriotism.

The most important unifying factor for European literature was the massive storehouse of motifs and rhetorical devices from which all national literatures drew until well into the eighteenth century. The scores of lexica and other handbooks produced from the time of Donatus, a fourth-century commentator on Virgil, through the Middle Ages and beyond demonstrate that the literature written at the threshold of the modern age was nourished by an ancient tradition, a tradition that was guaranteed by the medieval Scholastic compilations. That tradition is inventoried in Ernst Robert Curtius's *Europäische Literatur im Lateinischen Mittelalter* (1948; translated as *European Literature and the Latin Middle Ages,* 1953), a work that is indispensable for any student of medieval and early modern literature. Differences in philosophy notwithstanding, the humanistic "new learning" of the Renaissance took place within the continuous arc of learning that extended from late antiquity to the Middle Ages.

Humanism represents a major link between the medieval and early modern periods. Humanism's roots ran deep in that conservative tradition of medieval thought, beginning with the end of the Roman Empire, to which is owed the preservation of the heritage of classical Greek and Latin literature. This aspect of humanism is characterized by a belief in the superiority of antiquity over modernity and a desire to effect a renewal or rebirth—a "Renaissance"—of ancient values. The humanists proposed to accomplish this renewal by returning *ad fontes* (to the sources), and they believed that the restoration of the venerable would inevitably lead to reform of the major institutions of society. Thus, a utopian dynamic permeates humanism from Dante Alighieri's *De Monarchia* (On Monarchy, 1313) through Thomas More's *Utopia* (1516), to Tommasso Campanella's *Città del Sole* (City of the Sun, 1623).

Humanism originated in the trecento as part of the Italian national movement in the northern cities. Its first proponents were intellectuals who looked to the ancient Roman Republic as a political model and seized on the lives and writings of Cicero and Seneca as ethical models. By the mid quattrocento their successors had forged a political ideology that was based on an idealized version of ancient republican virtues and of the highly educated civil servant, fervently devoted to the republic. The education—the new learning—of the "civic humanist" consisted in the mastery of secular skills indispensable to running an efficient government; the most important disciplines for this purpose were rhetoric, history, and moral philosophy. These three fields were the bedrock of what Leonardo Bruni, the most eloquent Renaissance proponent of Ciceronian style and thought, called the *studia humanitatis,* the goal of which was to perfect and adorn the human being. The personal and mental qualities necessary for the *vir bonus dicendi peritus* (good man skilled in public speaking) provide the key to understanding much of the literature produced in Germany from the fourteenth to the seventeenth centuries.

The history of German humanism may be divided roughly into five phases: protohumanism, from around 1350 to around 1400; early humanism, from around 1440 to around 1480; high humanism, from around 1480 to around 1530; humanism and the Reformation, from around 1520 to around 1555; and late humanism, from around 1555 to 1600 and beyond. It is important to note that the term *German* in *German humanism* denotes a larger geographical area than that of today's Germany, although it is a matter of contention among scholars just how far that boundary may legitimately be extended. In the early modern age Germania reached from the Alpine areas of the south, including present-day Austria and parts of Switzerland, to the Low Countries and the Baltic region.

Humanism made preliminary inroads in the German-speaking lands through Charles IV, emperor from 1346 to 1378. An admirer of Italian life and art, Charles had, by midcentury, turned Prague into a respectable cultural center that was home to the first university in the German-speaking world, the first northern botanical garden, and many of the leading minds in Europe, including the Italian theorist of the new Roman Law, Bartolo Sassoferrato. German jurists who went to study in Italy enthusiastically embraced the new learning and became mediators in its dissemination north of the Alps. Charles's *Goldene Bulle,* named after the imperial golden seal and composed in Latin, was based on the new law; it regulated the election of the emperor by a college of electoral princes, thereby establishing the relationship between the empire and the states that endured until the empire was abolished by Napoleon in 1806. The Italian Cola di Rienzi arrived in Prague with the ecstatic vision of Charles as the restorer of ancient Rome; the sober emperor ignored the fiery Rienzi but embraced the Renaissance style of Rienzi's countryman, the poet Petrarch (Francesco Petrarca). The chancery language thus created was the first imperial model for a standard written language. Under the administration of Chancellor Johannes von Neumarkt civil servants began to be instructed in this style, not only in Latin but also in its German equivalent. The first German masterpiece composed in this style, representing the beginning stage of New High German as a written language, was *Der Ackermann aus Böhmen* (The Plowman of Bohemia, 1401), by the lawyer Johannes von Tepl. *Der Ackermann aus Böhmen* rejects contempt for the world and pleads with Petrarchan elegance for the dignity of humanity and the right to enjoy the beauty and pleasures of this world.

Most scholars characterize this first humanist flowering not as humanism proper but as prehumanism or protohumanism. Its early end may have been the result of the violent measures taken against the Hussites in Prague between 1410 and 1420, which chilled reformist initiatives. Over the next several decades, however, many German writers traveled to Italy and returned to Germany professing the new learning. At least three factors proved decisive for the full return of humanism to German soil. First, the ecclesiastical reform councils of Constance, from 1414 to 1418, and of Basel, from 1431 to 1449, brought over the Alps many Italian humanists who made a lasting impression on northern intellectuals and princes. Second, the Brethren of the Common Life offered a model of simple piety that suited the humanists' moderate approach to religious reform; like the humanists, the Brethren were devoted to classical learning and the reconstruction of original texts. Third, movable type, presumably invented by Johannes Gutenberg in 1436, became one of the humanists' primary tools once they understood its implications for the dissemination of knowledge.

German early humanism was launched in the early 1440s when Emperor Frederick III hired the eminent Italian humanist Enea Silvio Piccolomini (later Pope Pius II) to direct the chancery in the new imperial seat of Vienna. This "apostle of humanism to Germany" taught the Germans about their own country and its history in his *De ritu, situ, moribus et conditione Germaniae* (On the Customs, Geography, Habits, and Condition of Germany, 1457), a work of unprecedented range and insight into Germany as a unique nation and culture. What made the book a sensation was its popularization among the early humanists of Tacitus, the ancient Roman historian of Germany. No other single figure so captured the imagination of Germans during the entire early modern period as did Tacitus. Tacitus's praise in his *Germania,* which had been rediscovered around 1420, of the Germanic virtues of modesty, generosity, honesty, loyalty, freedom, perseverance, courage, genius, and nobility provided the Germans with a powerful set of ideological tools in their cultural war with Rome over the next century.

The usefulness of these elegant writers and speakers of Latin attracted the attention of secular princes. On a less grand scale, to be sure, than the renowned patrons of Renaissance Italy, many German princes supported humanists through employment either at court or at universities they had endowed, such as those of Vienna and Heidelberg. The University of Vienna led the way with lectures on Terence, Virgil, Juvenal, Horace, and the art of rhetoric, as well as on modern astronomical theories. The phenomenon of the "wandering humanist," the modern counterpart of the medieval *ordo vagorum* (errant order) of wandering monks, contributed to the cross-pollenization of knowledge throughout the network of courtly, academic, and urban centers of humanism. Peter Luder, after studying in Italy, circulated among Heidelberg (where, in 1456, he introduced into Germany the term *studia humanitatis*), Ulm, Erfurt, Leipzig, Basel, Padua, and Vienna. Wherever three or four humanists gathered, a *sodalitas* (intellectual society) arose. The most notable, Heidelberg's Sodalitas litteraria rhenana, was founded by Conrad Celtis and cultivated by Johann von Dalberg, court chancellor and bishop of Worms. This society attracted leading humanist personalities, including Johannes Reuchlin and Rudolf Agricola. Other important *sodalitates* emerged in Augsburg around Konrad Peutinger, in Ingolstadt and Vienna around Celtis, in Nuremberg around Willibald Pirckheimer, in Erfurt around Eobanus Hessus, and in Gotha around Mutianus Rufus. A direct line can be traced from these societies to the *Sprachgesellschaften* (language and literary societies) of seventeenth-century Germany and the pan-European *respublica litterata* (republic of letters). All shared the ideal, created in the cradle of humanism by Dante, Giovanni del Vergilio, Petrarch, and Giovanni Boccaccio, of perfecting language, thought, and manners for the sake of the nation and of humanity.

German humanism was dominated by male authors, as was every period of German literary history up to the late twentieth century. What is surprising is that some women, who lacked the freedom of men to travel to the major centers of learning, became masterful poets and attained to a degree of scholarship equivalent to their male counterparts. They include Argula von Grumbach, a champion of the Reformation; Olympia Morata, a correspondent of humanists; and Caritas Pirckheimer, scholarly abbess and sister of Willibald Pirckheimer. The high regard in which these learned women were held by humanists is suggested in Desiderius Erasmus's *Colloquium Abbatis et Eruditae* (Conversation between an Abbot and a Learned Woman, 1526), in which an educated woman refutes the arguments of a boorish clergyman.

The working language of the republic of letters was Latin—or, as it is called, Neo-Latin; this fact has sometimes led to the relegation of humanist writers to stepchild status in histories of German literature. But as Johann Wolfgang von Goethe would later say, "der Deutsche [bleibt] sich treu, und wenn er auch mit fremden Zungen spricht" (the German [remains] true to himself, even when he speaks in foreign tongues). The expressive range of Neo-Latin expanded on a track distinct from that of most vernacular composition in the fifteenth and sixteenth centuries. The consequence of this continuing refinement in Neo-Latin literature was that the learned German composition that appeared in the seventeenth century was already on an advanced level of formal quality.

One activity of the early humanists that had important consequences for German letters and manners was the translation of choice works from classical and other highly evolved literary and technical languages. The reliance of the Germans at various periods in history on external models has been disparaged as manneristic ersatz culture, but gifted translators such as Niclas von Wyle, Heinrich Steinhöwel, and Albrecht von Eyb abetted the improvement of a vernacular prose style as they elevated the art of translation to an act of co-creation. At a time when written German was not yet sufficiently mature to attempt composition at the level of complexity and subtlety of Augustan Latin, Renaissance Italian, or Neo-Latin, the *Übersetzer* (translators) became the mediators of the best writings and most progressive social and political ideas in Europe. An example is the Swiss humanist Leo Jud's 1521 German translation of Erasmus's work of Christian pacifism, *Querela Pacis* (1521; translated into English as *The Complaint of Peace,* 1559). They also made possible the cultivation over the next several decades of adapted genres, particularly the drama. Eyb's translations of comedies by Plautus inspired the revival of classical drama in German; the quality of his translations would be unmatched until J. M. R. Lenz's adaptations in the eighteenth century. It is impossible to determine the extent to which the translators may have affected the decision of others to compose in the vernacular, but by the late fifteenth century the phenomenon is conspicuously visible in Sebastian Brant's *Das Narrenschiff* (The Ship of Fools, 1494) and in technical works, especially atlases, chronicles, and almanacs. Translation in the opposite direction sometimes occurred, as well: Jakob Lochner's Latin translation of Brant's work as *Stultifera Navis* (1497) became a European best-seller.

By 1500, therefore, literary Germany was bilingual. For much of the early modern period, up to the language reform led by Martin Opitz in the early seventeenth century, a recriminative *querelle des anciens et modernes* (quarrel of the ancients and the moderns) raged over the issue of whether Latin or German was the superior linguistic instrument for education and technology. The choice often boiled down to the pragmatic consideration of which language was more appropriate for a given work or occasion or whether one sought to reach a national or a European audience. In general, the humanists did not oppose the trend toward a wider reading audience. One of the most widely circulated documents of the sixteenth century was the *Constitutio Criminalis Carolina* (Carolinian Code of Criminal Law, 1532), a corpus of legal and penal doctrine written in German by jurists of Charles V's court and intended for consumption by the modestly educated laity.

Three traits may be said to be central to humanism. The first is individualism. As the human being was drawn into the center of humanist observations, the so-called Renaissance man, the *uomo universale,* emerged as the ideal. A universal genius such as Leonardo da Vinci best represents this ideal of the perfected individual. Baldassare Castiglione's *Il Libro del Cortegiano* (The Book of the Courtier, 1528; translated as *The Cortyer,* 1561) made the ideal accessible at least to the affluent section of the population by describing the proper learning and decorum of the well-bred man. In the German-speaking lands one thinks of such personalities as the renowned polymath Paracelsus (Philippus Aureolus Theophrastus Bombastus von Hohenheim) or Erasmus of Rotterdam. No one embodied this ideal more than Rudolf Agricola. Scholar, musician, poet, painter, and sportsman, Agricola would be immortalized by Jacob Burckhardt in his *Die Kultur der Renaissance in Italien* (1859; translated as *The Civilization of the Period of the Renaissance in Italy,* 1878). The individual life, even of modestly successful persons, became the focus of several new or revived genres, such as autobiography; biographical appreciation, frequently taking the form of eulogy, is one of the most useful kinds of documents for reconstructing the psychological, social, and cultural milieu of the time. German painters, with their fascination with portraiture, contributed to the early modern phenomenon of self-representation. Albrecht Dürer's interest in the human body led to his revolutionary study of perspective and proportion, and he raised artistic self-awareness to a new level with his many self-portraits—especially the famous one of 1500. Matthias Grünewald's awe-filled crucifixions exaggerate the human form into expressionistic anguish. Hans Holbein the Younger's portraits of royal and aristocratic English personalities combine elements of sensuousness, realism, and monumentality.

The printing press played an indispensable role in the rise of the personality. By 1500 the implications of mechanical reproduction were clear. Unlike the manuscript, often anonymous and circulating in a few laboriously hand-reproduced copies, hundreds of copies of a printed book could be disseminated rapidly, each boldly bearing the name of the author. Printing created the potential for greater personal influence and engendered a more self-conscious style. Prodigious private libraries were compiled by wealthier humanists, such as Willibald Pirckheimer. Vast stores of knowledge were at the individual's fingertips; the world itself seemed within the grasp of historians, geographers, and explorers.

A second main trait of humanism was patriotism. Motivated by Piccolomini's cultural-geographical history and the Tacitean image of a common German fatherland, a wave of nationalist sentiment swept across Germany. Celtis was the chief evangelist of the concept of *renovatio imperii* (the empire restored) as applied to Germany. His discovery and publication of high-quality medieval German writings aroused interest in a quest for the true history of Germany. The next fifty years mark the first high point in the production of cultural-political historiography in Germany. Notable examples are *Germa-*

nia (1501), by the Strasbourg humanist Jakob Wimpfeling, and *Kosmographey* (1544), by Sebastian Münster. Celtis's inaugural *Oratio* in 1492 at the University of Ingolstadt is a programmatic appeal to Germany to wield the weapon of its own intellectual and moral heritage against the onslaught of "foreign"–that is, Roman–influence; its echo can be heard in Opitz's *Aristarchus* (1617) and as late as Johann Gottlieb Fichte's *Reden an die deutsche Nation* (Orations to the German Nation, 1808). To Celtis, that program meant opposing the monopolistic claim of Italy to cultural and political authority. His appeal to Apollo (1486) to move to Germany is motivated by reasons no less patriotic than aesthetic:

linque delectos Helicona, Pindum et,
ac veni in nostras vocitatus oras
    carmine grato.

(Leave fair Helicon and depart your Pindus,
and by pleasant song designated, hasten
    to these our borders.
                    (translated by George Schoolfield)

Ulrich von Hutten was uniquely open to Celtis's call. His Latin dialogue *Arminius*, composed about 1519, presents a German national hero, a composite of the Apollonian poet in Celtis and the Germanic virtues described by Tacitus, to forge a powerful weapon in the Germanic cultural war against the Romanist claim on Western civilization. The proliferation of sixteenth-century commentaries on Tacitus offered an endless rehearsal of the alleged Germanic virtues. Hutten's unparalleled self-assertiveness carried over to his patriotic decision to write in German as well as in Latin. Many other humanists, both in literature and in the natural sciences, followed Hutten in this decision, one that sometimes required moral courage. Paracelsus had to flee Basel in 1528 for holding medical lectures in German; the botanist Hieronymus Bock dared to correct errors in the field through his herbal study in German (1539). The attitude of these men is symptomatic of the will for reform that had evolved in the humanists by the early sixteenth century and reflects their opinion that reform was possible only in the mother tongue, for only thus could larger numbers of people be enlisted. It only remained for Luther to provoke the Roman authorities with a public act of disobedience.

A third major trait of humanism is critique. The appearance of the word *critique* and such cognates as *critic* and *critical* as technical terms can be dated to Angelo Poliziano's use of the Latin term *criticus* in 1492 to characterize the new *eruditi* (learned men) in their struggle against the coalition of Scholastic philosophers and theologians. A phenomenal outpouring of critical writings occurred in the early modern period; in the German lands it began with the conciliar theories sparked by Marsilius and others, including the Germans Conrad of Gelnhausen and Nicholas of Cusa; the Lollard writings of John Wyclif, which inspired the Hussites' Four Articles of Prague (1420); the remonstrations against and defenses of Luther; the ubiquitous pamphlet and broadsheet literature; and the dozens of conduct manuals, manifestos, debates, and complaints. The literature of fools has an honorable place in critical literature. Among its most distinguished examples are Brant's *Das Narrenschiff*, Erasmus's *Moriae encomium* (1511; translated as *The Praise of Folie*, 1569), and Kaspar Scheidt's five-thousand-line German translation (1551) of Friedrich Dedekind's *Grobianus* (Mr. Boor, 1549). It reached a high point with the publication of the devastating *Epistolae obscurorum virorum* (Letters of Obscure Men, 1516; revised, 1517), an anonymously published attack on the benighted opponents of the new learning: in scores of invented letters the vices and stupidity of the clergy and other unlearned types are lampooned by a handful of humanists, including Crotus Rubeanus and Hutten. No other work or event so symbolized the crisis at which the old order had arrived.

Popular myth has it that ecclesiastical reform began with Luther's nailing of his ninety-five theses to the door of the Wittenberg Castle Church on 31 October 1517 (in Germany, 31 October is known as *Reformationstag* [Reformation Day]). Many scholars question whether Luther posted his theses or distributed them by other means. However that may be, eminent minds within the church were grappling with the issue of reform by the early fourteenth century; it turned into a burning concern when the church suffered the Great Schism of 1378. Reformist ideas produced concrete solutions in the conciliar movement over the next two centuries, but opinions divided sharply over whether rule in this world should be according to secular or theocratic principles and whether church government should proceed directly from the Pope (the Roman Church) or Christ (the Universal Church). The papacy lost power and influence in this period up to the Council of Basel in the 1430s, and the councils themselves fell into schismatic camps the more they extended their prerogatives to negotiate with heretics, grant indulgences, and absolve sins. The German councillor Nicolas of Cusa called for concord and a renewal of consent to the Pope's authority. But hopes of returning to medieval unity dimmed as secular and civilian control of religious matters increased–a move justified by the growing awareness of the inefficiency and corruption of the clergy—and a new institution of spiritual identity, the national church, arose.

Luther's actual reforms were probably more radical than he originally intended, for as late as 1518 he was still attempting to work within the structure of the Catholic Church. But with the papal interdiction that year he began a hastily assembled program of reform that was largely complete by 1520. Basing his argument on Holy Scripture, he flatly asserted the moral and spiritual failings of the Roman Church, declared the Pope to be the Antichrist, and called for the Pope's power to be distributed into the hands of secular princes as emergency bishops. In the "Reformation Year" 1520, amid a flurry of propagandistic broadsheets that struck at the heart of papal authority and abusive financial practices, Luther published his three best-known Reform works: *An den christlichen Adel deutscher Nation* (To the Christian Nobility of the German Nation), *Von der babylonischen Gefangenschaft der Kirche* (On the Babylonian Captivity of the Church), and *Von der Freiheit eines Christenmenschen* (On the Liberty of a Christian Individual). These works galvanized the Protestant movement; Hutten was inspired to compose his only German-language poem, "Ain new lied" (A New Song, 1521). In a single stroke, Luther had established the phenomenon of the public sphere through a literature whose purpose is to serve truth by agitating the public into action. At this time, too, the printing press reached its maturity: four thousand copies of *An den christlichen Adel deutscher Nation* alone appeared in August and were sold out within days; twelve more printings followed in rapid succession.

Although Luther remained the chief spokesman for the Reformation until his death, the cause took on a life of its own, spreading widely and splintering into factions. Great diversity of ideas of reform and renewal characterized the movement over the following half decade. The "radical Reformers" called for extreme action. The imperial knights Hutten and Franz von Sickingen acted to appropriate church real estate by force; Andreas Karlstadt urged the dissolution of monasteries, encouraged monks and nuns to reject their vows of celibacy, and incited *Bilderstürmerei* (iconoclasm), the destruction of church iconography; in the Peasants' War of 1524–1525 Thomas Münzer led a movement of peasants toward a visionary *ecclesia futura* (future church) that ended in a terrible slaughter of innocents. Sectarian communities of Anabaptists, Moravian Brethren, and others sprang up in the cracks between the dominant confessions. In Switzerland an independent reform movement, more moderate in nature, grew up around Zwingli and found its most distinguished leader in his French disciple John Calvin.

While many historians emphasize the influence of Scholasticism on Luther at the expense of humanism, others see it the other way around. Certainly, the stamp of the new learning on him is indelible, even if, perhaps, it is not always obvious in his politics, theology, and literary work. Like Erasmus and the best of the Renaissance philologists, Luther looked ad fontes, to the Hebrew and Greek texts of the Bible, not simply to the later Vulgate Latin as previous translators had. But his true genius lay in his ability to make the biblical word accessible to the common German-speaking man and woman, as he explains in his *Sendbrief vom Dolmetschen* (Treatise on Translating, 1530). His translation of the Bible was first published in its entirety in 1534, though it continued to undergo revision in consultation with Philipp Melanchthon and other philologists, until the final version appeared in 1546. Luther's linguistic innovations made German a greater instrument of expressive power than it had been since the High Middle Ages. His Early New High German, based on East Middle German dialect and Saxon chancery usage, still lagged behind contemporary English, French, Italian, and Spanish as a stylistic and formal medium, however. The task of turning German into a genuine literary language was reserved for the language reformers of the seventeenth century and the writers of the German Enlightenment, Sturm und Drang, and Weimar Classicism.

The Reformation touched all aspects of life and letters between about 1520 and 1555. There are few if any writings in German of the period, whether *Flugschrift* (broadsheet), drama, treatise, polemic, song, poem, fable, emblem, anecdote, or epic, that do not relate directly to this seminal event. In the literature of the Reformation content overwhelms form: the song is either a church hymn or has some other edifying purpose; the drama is a stage for the enactment or adaptation of biblical stories; even the carnivalesque Shrovetide play, frowned on by Luther, often proceeds toward a final moral on a favorite Reformation theme. The Flugschrift is the bludgeon of Reformation genres: typically a single-page flyer, though often much longer, it hammers home a propagandistic message. A late-sixteenth-century translation-adaptation by Johann Spreng of Homer's *Iliad,* published posthumously in 1610, depicts its heroes as good Protestant citizens. Luther–or, encouraged by Luther, Melanchthon or another humanist authority–frequently provided the rationale in epistles, directives, quasi-theoretical theses, or personal visitations for making profitable use of literary inventions.

By contrast, the practitioners of Neo-Latin literature continued to cultivate secular themes; but even here, much of what they wrote was undertaken in the spirit of camaraderie in a struggle against a common opponent. Brant, Hutten, and Thomas Murner wrote in both Latin and German or used Latin with the intention of serving the German cause. Hutten's declaration in his poem "Clag und Vormahnung" (Complaint and Warning, 1520), that he would compose henceforth in his mother tongue did not mean that he was abandoning Latin—indeed, he continued to write almost exclusively in that language—but signaled his solidarity with the Germans against the Roman Church. From Johannes Reuchlin to Celtis, Erasmus, Beatus Rhenanus, and Sebastian Franck, Latin played a militant role in the cause of reform. As a rule, German served the local or national interest, Latin the cosmopolitan. But writing in Latin also granted a measure of freedom to pursue worldly forms such as the erotic poem, the eclogue, and the epigram. The rediscovery of Plautus and Terence gave new impulse to the restoration of the classical theater through creative modern imitations that were possible only in Latin; the few imitations in German generally fall short of the mark. Historical and philological scholarship flourished in Latin, especially in the second half of the sixteenth century. Perhaps most important, Latin functioned as the conduit to the world of European letters.

The desire of the humanists for moral and social reform made them natural allies of Luther. As a group, the humanists were deeply pious and favored a return to a purer form of Christian discipleship, much like that proposed in *De Imitatione Christi* (On the Imitation of Christ, 1427) by the German monk Thomas à Kempis. They served the Reformation well, particularly in its formative years, by exposing and satirizing the corruption of the church. But their inherent conservatism caused most humanists to balk at, and finally to reject, the movement in the early 1520s as it moved past intellectual dissent into open rebellion and outright destruction. A deeper philosophical division soon became clear, as well; Luther himself saw it coming as early as 1517, when he predicted that Erasmus would become a foe. In 1524 Erasmus published *De libero arbitrio diatribe* (A Disquisition on Free Will), demonstrating a profound incompatibility between Luther's view of the human being as helplessly fallen and his own view of human participation in the act of grace. Thus, a rift developed between convinced Reformers and humanists over this fundamental question of human volition, as well as over such issues as human educability and the proper method of reforming institutions. Nevertheless, most humanists continued to serve the Reformation's cause in ways that suited their temperament and philosophy. Preeminent among them was Melanchthon, whose tireless devotion to educational reform, brilliant distillation of Protestant theology in his *Loci communes* (1521; revised, 1535; revised again, 1544; revised again, 1559), and statement of the articles of Protestant faith in the *Augsburg Confession* (1530) helped to guarantee credibility and longevity for the tenets of the Reformation.

After Luther's death in 1546, civil wars erupted all over Germany, sparked in large part by rival claims to authority over religious practice. In 1555 the Peace of Augsburg provided a legal solution: according to the principle *cuius regio eius religio* (whose region, his religion), princes were permitted to determine confessional practices in their respective territories. Lutheranism predominated in the north and the east, while the majority of southern and western lands remained Catholic. The Augsburg settlement held until 1648, when the Peace of Westphalia established different guidelines.

Reformist tendencies within the Catholic Church continued throughout the period of the Protestant Reformation at a hastened pace, culminating in the Council of Trent from 1545 to 1563. Repudiating key Lutheran doctrines, such as justification by faith and the supremacy of the Bible, the council reaffirmed the validity of traditional Catholic doctrines and practices. But reform was instituted, especially in the areas of education and behavior of the clergy; significantly, greater use of the vernacular in sermons was also urged. It was in the spirit of reform that Ignatius Loyola established the Society of Jesus in 1534. This society succeeded beyond all expectations in recapturing some of the influence that had been lost to the Protestants. The Jesuits established first-rate schools for both clergy and civil officials, were dauntless in their missionary efforts, and did not hesitate to borrow Lutheran strategies, such as the use of the school drama for religious and moral instruction. By the end of the sixteenth century the order was a formidable moral and social force. Edifying tracts in the Spanish mystical style attracted many people back into the fold, and anti-Lutheran pamphlets circulated, unanswered, in many places.

The second half of the sixteenth century in Germany, as in the rest of Europe, was full of cruelty, seen most ignominiously in the witch hunts in Bavaria and elsewhere that were inspired by a malignant interpretation of Exod. 22:18. Against such excesses a "Second Reformation" was conceived; it was based on the Erasmian politics of conciliation and led by moderate Lutherans and Calvinists associated with the Heidelberg court of Elector Friedrich III. Their foremost achievement was the Heidelberg Catechism of 1563, which avoided as much as possible the contentious doctrinal issues and constituted a key plank in Friedrich's program of reform. Adherents of the new reform, among them many later humanists, were said to belong to the Reform Church. A doctrine of irenicism (peace) found expression in the works of men such as Zacharias Ursinus and Caspar Olevianus. The *Irenicum* (1614) of Ursinus's disciple David Pareus laid the groundwork for a possible reunification of Lutherans and Calvinists. The spirit of irenicism is everywhere in evidence in the cultural reform movement of the seventeenth century and is especially visible in the literary society Fruchtbringende Gesellschaft (Fruit-bringing Society).

German literature between 1280 and 1580 falls into spiritual and worldly categories. With respect to poetry there is a strong tendency toward the song, for lyrical production of the time commonly arises in response to, or for the sake of, some social occasion and is meant to be collectively experienced. In the late medieval period devotional rituals, church festivals, pilgrimages, and praises of Mary were typical occasions. Others arose as history dictated; for instance, with the outbreak of the Black Death in 1347 scourge songs came into existence. The melodies were usually borrowed from familiar secular songs, a practice known as contrafacture. Most authors of spiritual lyrics were anonymous.

The late-medieval worldly lyric derived from two traditions: *Volkslied* (folk song) and Minnesang. Volkslied exhibits a more primitive, less formalized quality than Minnesang. It was transmitted orally; occasionally a printed edition appeared, such as the Augsburg compilation by Klara Hätzlerin in 1471. Folk song provides a useful register of themes and sentiments for analyzing the self-understanding of the emerging burgher class. The historical ballad, or lay, became one of its most significant variations after 1300, celebrating military victories, telling of bloody pirate exploits, chronicling church councils, or reinventing heroic epics (the anonymous new *Hildebrandslied* [Lay of Hildebrand] of the late fourteenth century, unlike the original of around 820, has a happy ending). Elements of Minnesang continued to inform late-medieval love poetry, but the verse is typically wooden and the thought dull by comparison with the fluid lines and subtle imagery of a Heinrich von Morungen. The female presence is no longer the "edeliu schoene frouwe reine" (noble, lovely lady pure) but "liebes Elselein" (dear little Else). Love is sentimental and often consummated: *hôhe minne* (exalted love) steps down to *nidere minne* (humble love), corresponding to the preference for realism of the rising burgher society.

Minnesang joined the *Spruchdichtung* (aphoristic poetry) of the wandering minstrels to form *Meistersang*, which is already discernible in some of the later poetry of Walther von der Vogelweide in the early thirteenth century. In the hands of the new urban Meistersinger, however, the form became standardized as a type of poetic-musical craft attainable by any industrious journeyman. Books of rules, known as tabulatures, described the procedure by which one might progress from *Schüler* (pupil) to *Schulfreund* (school friend) to *Singer* to *Dichter* (poet). The first printed systematization, an elucidation of twenty-four principles, was made by Adam Puschmann in 1571. Meistersang flourished in the fifteenth century in the hands of such poets as Hans Folz and arrived at its golden age with the masters of sixteenth-century Nuremberg: Peter Probst and, especially, Hans Sachs, who composed some four thousand songs in the style. The first history of Meistersang, by Cyriacus Spangenberg, appeared in Strasbourg in 1598. Richard Wagner immortalized the great era of Meistersang in his comic opera *Die Meistersinger von Nürnberg* (1867; translated as *The Master-Singers of Nuremberg*, 1892).

Most secular poetry written in German during the early modern period failed to progress formally beyond its late-medieval counterpart and suffered from a growing tension between content and form. While other national poetries were developing sophisticated forms adequate to the changes in human experience, German-language poetry remained quite inflexible. This situation began to change only late in the sixteenth century with, for instance, the Psalm translations (1572) of Paul Melissus Schede and the *Teutsche Lieder* (German Songs, 1576–1580) of the Viennese poet Jakob Regnart, both transitional figures on the way to the Opitzian reform.

Spiritual song in the sixteenth century is synonymous with the *Kirchenlied* (hymn). The new polyphonic character of the Lutheran hymn helped elevate it to a position of liturgical prominence matched only by the vernacular sermon itself. As such, it became a powerful weapon in the Protestant arsenal, particularly in Germany; Luther's opponent Müntzer used hymns to great effect, as well, as did Zwingli in Zurich and, in the Calvinist cause, Michael Weisse and Johann Fischart. The Jesuits also learned to exploit the hymn on behalf of the

Counter-Reformation, though only later and not with comparable effectiveness. Nikolaus Beutner's *Catholisch Gesang-Buch* (Catholic Song Book, 1602) was one of the most successful Jesuit compilations. Whereas Luther based his compositions mainly on the Psalms, the Catholic hymn reestablished the link with medieval folk song. Both Luther and Müntzer also appropriated some powerful Latin hymns in the Patristic tradition, such as the Advent hymn *Veni redemptor gentium* (Come, Savior of the Nations), itself a product of Saint Ambrose's struggle against Arianism. The years 1523 and 1524 represent the high point in Protestant hymn production, for in those years Luther and Müntzer wrote the majority of their hymns and offered theoretical remarks on them that are important for hymnology. Of Luther's thirty-six hymns, twenty-four appeared in 1524 in the *Chorgesangbüchlein* (Choir Songbook).

The hymn was not the only form of spiritual lyric. Sachs, for example, contributed an impressive amount of verse of lasting spiritual beauty and power; among his finest are his lyrical epitaph for Luther and the *Wittenbergisch Nachtigall* (Nightingale of Wittenberg, 1523), which promoted the introduction of the Reformation in Nuremberg. And Dürer, who is generally known solely as a great artist, was an accomplished spiritual lyricist, as well.

Medieval religious drama was spoken in Latin and bound to the church year and its ritualistic themes. While the medieval church was aware of classical theater, it allowed Plautus and Terence only to be read, not performed. The anti-Terence martyr dramas of Hrotsvit of Gandersheim are indicative of the church's mistrust of the pagan effect on young minds. (Even Hrotsvit's plays were suspect; they came to public attention only with Celtis's rediscovery and printed edition of them in 1501.) A loosening of the liturgical character of medieval drama began in the thirteenth century, when it underwent a transformation from spectacle to play. First, the Easter, Christmas, or Passover scene was removed from its strict liturgical context. Later, plays started to be performed beyond the confines of the church, and there was a gradual introduction of vernacular songs to accompany the spectacle as it processed through town. Plays performed in the market square used a large raised *Simultanbühne* (simultaneous stage) on which fixed boxes at the back allowed more than one action to take place at the same time. Original extrapolations were added in late-medieval Easter plays, such as the salve-purchase and Resurrection scenes in the anonymous *Innsbrucker Osterspiel* (Innsbruck Easter Play, 1391). By 1450 laypersons and city officials were assuming greater responsibility for the productions.

Major dramatic celebrations became common, lasting for several days and involving a broader range of themes from salvation history. Religious drama achieved full development in the fourteenth and fifteenth centuries; the anonymous *Rheinisches Osterspiel* (Rhineland Easter Play) of 1456 is considered the first real German drama in the technical sense. Successful productions of religious dramas are reported in various places, for example, the Künzelsau Corpus Christi play of 1479 and the Frankfurt am Main Passion play of 1493.

Almost all Reformation drama is middle class, though not all middle-class drama is Reformational. It is also strongly didactic, even pedagogical, and frequently tendentious (*Tendenzdrama*). Actually, the designation *Reformation drama*, while useful, is rather too broad. Drama moved toward secularization as it moved away from liturgical constraints; as it came into contact with secular forms, such as the Shrovetide play; and as it felt the impact of the humanists' rediscovery and appropriation of Plautus and Terence. Catholic drama, on the other hand, remained essentially unchanged until around 1600, when Jesuit dramatists introduced spectacular innovations. The history of German drama from late medieval to pre-Baroque is, therefore, almost exclusively the domain of the Protestant Reformers, on the one hand, and the humanists, on the other.

The staging of biblical events (*Bibeldrama*) enjoyed its height of popularity in the Reformation, along with plays depicting such allegorical figures as Justice, Truth, and Wisdom and their opposites. In 1534 Luther recommended staging the apocryphal books of Judith for "tragedy" and Tobias for "comedy," but many other biblical figures were dramatized, as well. Burkhart Waldis's Low German *De Parabell vam vorlorn Szohn* (Parable of the Prodigal Son, 1527) is a model of Lutheran dogma and instruction. The Prodigal Son here represents the sinner who receives unmerited grace—justification through faith—while his hardworking brother represents the alleged Catholic view of justification through works. Citizens of Colmar performed Georg Wickram's version of the parable, *Ein schönes und evangelisches Spil von dem verlornen Sun* (A Beautiful and Evangelical Play about the Prodigal Son), in 1540. Sixt Birck in Basel adapted the apocryphal story of Susanna in 1532 both as a portrayal of an ideal Christian wife and as a protest against unmarried clergy. In Saxony in 1535 Paul Rebhun adapted the same material, making Susanna an ideal type of incorruptible wife and mother. Thiebolt Gart's *Joseph* (1540) is the finest of the many dramatic treatments of the Old Testament title figure. Several important Protestant plays were also produced in

Latin, including the Dutchman Gulielmus Gnaphäus's version of the Prodigal Son, *Acolastus* (1529), and the highly regarded *Pammachius* (1538) of Thomas Naogeorgus, a bellicose drama that presents the Pope as the Antichrist.

In contrast with the medieval religious practice of portraying types, the humanists had an interest in presenting human beings as individuals. Donatus's commentary on Terence, rediscovered in 1433 by Johann Arispa, became the official authority for the humanists. A play by Terence was first staged in Germany in 1500. The standard version of Terence's works in Germany was Melanchthon's edition of 1516; Melanchthon considers Terence the model of the burgher mentality. The Terentian drama is seamlessly organized in three parts: protasis, epitasis, catastrophe; its orations are founded on Quintilian and Ciceronian rhetoric; and there is a moral message. The Terentian stage offered an important technical advance: the undramatic simultaneous-booth concept of medieval drama is energized by curtained houses that open up for entrances into a single-action scene, thus producing a succession of scenes that drive the drama toward conclusion. Erasmus noted that the Terentian drama was absolutely essential for perfecting Latin, a point that figured prominently in its appropriation by the academy. Some Germans began to write original Latin plays in imitation; early examples of special note are Wimpfeling's *Stylpho* (1480), the first German humanist play, which represents the transition from the dialogue to the dramatic play, and Reuchlin's highly successful comedy in five acts of two scenes each, *Henno* (1497), which became the model for the later school drama (it went through thirty-one editions between 1498 and 1523). Celtis's university productions in Vienna in 1502–1503 of works by Plautus and other ancient playwrights assured their further reception in Germany. His Ingolstadt inaugural oration of 1492 includes a statement about the value to the Germans of staging good plays. Eyb, a Plautus enthusiast, is of singular importance as a theoretician of humanist drama, as can be seen, in particular, in the introduction to his play *Menaechmi* (The Twins, 1511). Eyb's comments on drama translation are also valuable: he was a confident translator who strove for the sense rather than the literal meaning of the word.

The chief center for humanist *Schuldrama* (school drama) in the sixteenth century was Strasbourg, with its scholars of classical literature and excellent playhouse. Among the most important dramas to be performed in Strasbourg was Naogeorgus's *Mercator* (1540), a type of Everyman play. One of the most gifted of all Protestant dramatists was the Tübingen professor of poetry Nicodemus Frischlin, the "Terentius Christianus" (Christian Terence) of Germany, who possessed the rare ability to infuse his characters with individual traits, as in his biblical dramas *Rebecca* (1576) and *Susanna* (1578) and his historical drama *Fraw Wendelgard* (1580). Later in the century Netherlandic humanist drama became a model, especially for the tragedy, and inspired imitations and adaptations in Germany well into the seventeenth century. The Latin Everyman play of the Catholic Georg Macropedius, *Hecastus* (1539), for example, derives from a Latin adaptation of the original anonymous Dutch version, *Elckerlijk* (1495). The purposes of the student performances were to perfect the students' Latin elocution and to inculcate into them the alleged exemplary behavior found in classical drama; the latter purpose often required bowdlerizing the material. Luther recognized the potential dividend of Schuldrama for the Reformation, and in 1524 he addressed the issue in his directive *An die Ratsherren aller Städte deutsches Lands, daß sie christliche Schulen aufrichten und halten sollen* (To the Councilors of All Cities in Germany, That They Should Establish and Maintain Christian Schools). The same practical thrust would inform Christian Weise's training of young men for an active civic and political life through school drama in the late seventeenth century. Not all school drama was written in Latin; Birck and Dedekind were among those who offered German-language plays for the academy. In Strasbourg, the general public was regularly invited to school productions.

The other major dramatic genre was the *Fastnachtspiel* (Shrovetide play). Its origins are not entirely reconstructible, though some scholars believe that it arose as a way of venting pent-up emotions and desires repressed by the church. The genre tends to fall into two types: one that stresses moral instruction and one with greater farcical content. The patrician city of Lübeck apparently required these plays to emphasize the virtues; Nuremberg, a city for which the carnival event was largely an artisan affair, allowed greater hilarity, even vulgarity. The *Fastnachtspiel* is intimately associated with the latter city. It first flowered there in conjunction with the Meistersinger plays of the mid fifteenth century; around the 1450s Hans Rosenplüt made use of both literary and political themes (for example, the Turkish threat) in his clever but plodding pieces. His more talented successor was Folz, whose cunning-peasant plays of around 1480 demonstrate mature dialogue and technical self-confidence. Pamphilus Gengenbach, a Swiss, gives added moral depth with his *Spiel von den zehn Altern dieser Welt* (Play about the Ten Ages of This World, 1515).

The typical Fastnachtspiel has an uncomplicated, revuelike structure. An *Einschreier* (herald; literally, "in-crier") introduces the play; the drama proceeds, usually for about three hundred lines in doggerel couplets, and entails a series of loosely related episodes ending with a moral; an *Ausschreier* (out-crier) dismisses everyone. They were performed in homes, inns, or streets, depending on where the troupe could find or gather an audience. The nature of the play is often rough-and-tumble and involves familiar conflicts of conscience—a kind of middle-class psychomachia between broadly painted vices and virtues. The greatest and most prolific writer of Fastnachtspiel was the Nuremberg cobbler Sachs. His characters are more fully drawn and are exceptionally memorable—the student in Paradise, the pregnant farmer—than those in most other such plays, and contrast figures are introduced. He also added elements from humanist drama and was the first to structure the Fastnachtspiel in acts.

Fastnachtspiel, like most other genres, was often employed in the service of the Reformation and is, in those instances, similar to Bibeldrama. Waldis's *De Parabell vam vorlorn Szohn* is one example. Gengenbach's *Die Gouchmatt der Buhler* (The Meadow of Enamored Fools, 1521) satirizes libidinous love as practiced by members of several social classes. The Swiss Protestant Niklas Manuel composed two virulent attacks on the Catholic Church: *Vom Papst und seiner Priesterschaft* (On the Pope and His Priesthood, 1524), based on Gengenbach's *Die Totenfresser* (The Corpse Eaters, 1521), and a work on the sale of indulgences, *Der Ablaßkrämer* (The Indulgence Merchant, 1525), aimed at winning over the conservative agricultural population around Bern. These plays show Manuel to be a pioneer in religious-political satire, a use of drama rare before this time.

The history of German narrative after the High Middle Ages concerns primarily, though not exclusively, the evolution of prose. The process began with the vernacular sermons of the Franciscans David von Augsburg and his disciple Berthold von Regensburg and continued in the areas of jurisprudence—the codification of German laws—and historiography, for which verse was proving less and less suitable. Early precedents include the *Sachsenspiegel* (Code of Saxon Law, circa 1230) of Eike von Repgow and the first chronicle to be written in German prose, the *Sachsenchronik* (Saxon Chronicle, 1237). Jansen Enikel of Vienna produced a rather crude *Weltchronik* (World Chronicle) in 1276 in mixed verse that reads much like prose. A German translation of a French prose romance exists from about 1300.

The greatest composer of literary prose in late-medieval Germany was the Dominican monk Meister Eckhart. A severe ascetic who removed himself from the artificialities of ecclesiastical culture, Eckhart crafted with his mystical writings between 1295 and 1327 a speculative prose style capable of incisive criticism. His thought anticipated the critical nominalism—the idea that nothing is universal except contractual agreements formed in human language, a concept that contributed to the erosion of the aura of authority—of the "modernists," such as William of Occam. Eckhart's disciples Johannes Tauler and Heinrich Seuse promoted and developed his legacy and exercised a significant impact on Luther's thought. The early-modern religious-political tract can be traced directly to Eckhart and his school. The mystics made particular use of the epistle and the aphorism, infusing them with spiritual ardor and impassioned rhythms. The double influence of mystical feeling and high-medieval courtly sensibility is present in the *Sprüche und Lieder* (Aphorisms and Songs, circa 1318) of Heinrich von Meißen. Other kinds of German prose types prior to the importation of the Petrarchan style include sagas, such as the *Karlmeinet* (Small Carl, 1320); lives of saints and martyrs, such as the *Märterbuch* (Book of Martyrs, circa 1340); epistles, such as the correspondence between Heinrich von Nördlingen and Margarete Ebner between 1332 and 1350; protonovellas, such as the *Edelstein* (Precious Gem, 1350), which the Swiss monk Ulrich Boner adapted from Latin sources; and sermons, particularly those of Seuse and Tauler.

The initial flowering of the Petrarchan *ars scribendi* (art of writing) was intense but short-lived. It was also, for reasons of state, bilingual. Chancellor Neumarkt wrote his formularies in both Latin and German; his instructions on official epistolary style circulated throughout the empire in many manuscripts under the title *Summa Cancellariae Caroli IV.* (Chancery Formulary of Charles IV, after 1364). He also produced a beautifully wrought translation, *Das buch der liepkozung* (Book of Adoration, undated), of meditational soliloquies ascribed to Saint Augustine. As a literary work it cannot compare, however, with Tepl's *Der Ackermann aus Böhmen,* which combines highly learned rhetorical elegance with deep personal emotion to create a work of world literature. While Tepl did consult models, among them Petrarch's *De remediis utriusquae fortunae* (1478?; translated as *Physicke against Fortune,* 1579) and Pope Innocent III's treatise *De contemptu mundi* (On Contempt for the World, circa 1200–1210), *Der Ackermann aus Böhmen* remains an original work of genius.

The main course of German prose in the early modern age, however, was separate from this protohumanist experience in Prague. Other lines extend from medieval sources. Among the most important are mysticism (Seuse's autobiography, circa 1362, the first in German; Rulman Merswin's populist writings, circa 1382), moral satire (Wittenwiler's *Der Ring*), legends and lives (Hans Mair von Nördlingen's adaptation of the *Iliad*, 1392; Johannes Hartlieb's *Alexander*, 1444), farce and anecdote (Heinrich Kaufringer's burlesque anecdotes, circa 1400; Philipp Frankfurter's *Der Pfaffe vom Kalenberg* [The Pastor of Kalenberg, 1473]; Hieronymus Rauscher's *Päpistische Lügen* [Popish Lies, 1562]; the folk book *Eulenspiegel*, 1515), prose translation (Elisabeth von Nassau-Saarbrücken's translation of *Loher und Maller* and others from the French in the 1430s; Eleonore von Vorderösterreich's *Pontus und Sidonia* from the French, circa 1456; Thüring von Ringoltingen's *Melusine* from the French, 1456–a source for Goethe's novella "Die neue Melusine" [The New Melusine], inserted in his novel *Wilhelm Meisters Wanderjahre oder Die Entsagenden* [1821; translated as *Wilhelm Meister's Travels; or, The Renunciants*, 1827]), Bible translation (the *Wenzelbibel*, Old Testament only, circa 1400; the *Mentel-Bibel*, the first printed German Bible, 1466).

The translators of the second half of the fifteenth century cultivated a humanist-model German prose, just as they did for drama. That meant, in the first place, the translation of Italian literature of the trecento and quattrocento. The translators were especially fond of the fable and the novella, which in their brevity and artfulness constituted an ideal exercise for imitation and emulation. The most important translation of fables is Steinhöwel's *Das selb leben Esopi* (The Life of Aesop, 1477/1478), which includes translations of farcical writings by the Italian humanist Gian Francesco Poggio Bracciolini. In the novella, Boccaccio's "Tancredi," via Bruni's Latin translation (circa 1415) of *The Decameron* (1348-1353) provided the model for Eyb's "Guiscardus und Sigismunda" (1472); the Nuremberg translator Heinrich Schlüsselfelder attempted, with only moderate success, a German version of *The Decameron* in 1472. Petrarch's "Griseldis" (1373), a Latin translation of Boccaccio's Italian novella, became a popular German folk story in the version by Steinhöwel and was dramatized by Sachs in 1546. Historically, the most important contribution of the Übersetzer was the Swiss-born Wyle's *Translatzen* (Translations, 1478), an anthology of eighteen pieces from the Latin or Italian of Petrarch, Boccaccio, Piccolomini, and others. Gotthold Ephraim Lessing would later declare Wyle and Steinhöwel to be the originators of German printed literature.

It is common in the sixteenth century to find both Neo-Latin and German vernacular versions of a common source. Thus, the Tübingen professor Heinrich Bebel's Latin *Facetiae* (Farces, 1508-1514), based on the collection of the same name by Poggio Bracciolini (written circa 1430, published posthumously in 1471), was translated into German in 1558; meanwhile, the Franciscan monk Johannes Pauli published his own German version of Poggio Bracciolini's farces in 1522 under the title *Schimpf und Ernst* (Mischief and Morality). The humanist version moralizes in an elegant and moderate fashion; the vernacular displays local color and sauciness. Vernacular versions of humanist models were sometimes undertaken with the purpose of spreading the message of the Reformation to a popular audience. An outstanding example is the collection *Deutsche Sprüchwörter* (German Proverbs, 1534) by the staunch Lutheran Johannes Agricola, which he modeled on the *Adagia* (Adages, 1500) of Erasmus.

It was natural that the *Streitgespräch* (disputation) and other polemical forms, such as the Flugschrift, *Manifest* (manifesto), or *Traktat* (treatise), should flourish during times of confessional strife. There are too many examples to detail, and they include forms not commonly associated with dispute, such as the epistle or song. The early-sixteenth-century humanists, for example, turned the epistle to militant ends, as in the *Epistolae obscurorum virorum*, in their battle with their orthodox opponents. The humanists could draw on a long tradition of argumentation summarized in the rhetorical handbooks and perfected in the courts. *Der Ackermann aus Böhmen* is technically a Streitgespräch between the Plowman and Death before the divine seat of justice and is replete with legal allusions and emotion-arousing figures. The speculative prose of Eckhart provided another model for ecclesio-political criticism during the Reformation. Both influences are visible in works as diverse as Hutten's *Clagschrift* (Complaint, 1520), Müntzer's *Manifest an die Mansfelder Bergknappen* (Manifesto to the Mansfield Miners, 1525), and Sebastian Franck's *Paradoxa* (1534). Not to be forgotten is the widely circulated and anonymous *Karsthans* (Hans Hoe, 1521), a Protestant-favoring dispute among a peasant, Luther, and others, in which key issues leading up to the Peasants' War are aired. A related form is the dialogue. This tendentious genre was employed by Hutten in his *Gesprächbüchlein* (Book of Dialogues, 1521), a translation of four of his Latin dialogues that polemicize on contemporary political themes, and by Sachs in his

Dialoge (1524), a propagandistic effort to get Nuremberg to adopt the Reformation.

During the fifteenth and sixteenth centuries German also made advances as an instrument of technical, scientific, and other specialized forms of writing. For example, in geography and cartography there were Hartmann Schedel's *Weltchronik* (Chronicle of the World, 1493), Brant's *Chronik über Deutschland* (Chronicle of Germany, after 1521), Franck's *Weltbuch* (World Book, 1534), and Münster's *Kosmographey,* the first large-scale German historical geography. In art there was Dürer's study *Von menschlicher Proportion* (On Human Proportion, 1528); in metaphysics *Das Buch der Erkanntnus* (The Book of Knowledge, circa 1534), by Paracelsus; in botany Bock's *Kräuterbuch* (Book of Herbs, 1539). German also took a step toward representational literature in the elevation of the individual through public praise. These works were primarily lyrical contributions modeled on recent humanist epicedia by Willibald Pirckheimer, Joachim Camerarius, and Hessus on the occasion of Dürer's death; prose versions appeared in the form of funeral sermons and, more important, literary appreciations such as Melanchthon's funeral oration for Luther, translated anonymously as *Oratio, Uber der Leich des Ehrwiridigen D. M. Luthers* (Oration over the Corpse of the Honorable Dr. Martin Luther, 1546).

A *Narrenliteratur* (literature of fools) flourished from the Middle Ages until the Reformation. This literature had roots in the classical *stultitia-sapientia* (foolishness-wisdom) tradition, on the one hand, and in the late-medieval didactic tradition of the *tôr* (fool), on the other. While it is particularly associated with the Fastnachtspiel, the literature of fools reached a vehement climax in the late fifteenth century with Brant's *Das Narrenschiff*, which has as its premise that the basic selfishness of the human being must be met by self-knowledge gained through reason and morality. Much fools' literature represents a conservative impulse to reverse the perceived revolutionary changes occurring in society, and most writers of such works opposed the Reformation as excessively libertarian. Two works by Murner–*Narrenbeschwörung* (Fools' Exorcism, 1512), a verse satire, and *Von dem großen lutherischen Narren* (On the Great Lutheran Fool, 1522)–respond with the horrified realization that Brant's vision of fools has become diabolical reality. In his *Moriae encomium* the humanist Erasmus turns the concept of foolishness in the direction of Christian paradox: to the eyes of an irrational and spiritually blind world, faith appears as foolishness. One of the most popular works of the post-Reformation period was Dedekind's highly entertaining satire on vulgar manners, *Grobianus,* translated into German by Scheidt. Scheidt's pupil in Worms, Fischart, with his great command of the rhetoric of satire, directed his barbs against the Jesuits and other perceived evils.

The few attempts at epic verse during the period are largely disappointing. The anonymous *Der Große Alexander* (Alexander the Great, 1397) is composed in repetitive couplets and is purely adventurous in intent. *Das Buch der Abenteuer* (The Book of Adventure, circa 1475), also anonymous, is a long anthology of popular knightly epics more or less in the style of the late-thirteenth-century *Jüngere Titurel* (The Young Titurel). A more successful verse epic is the *Teuerdank* (1517), written by Melchior Pfintzing on the instructions of Maximilian I, which is important not least for its many autobiographical details about the emperor; the elaborately ornamented artifact itself represents a decisive moment in the history of bookmaking. An interesting if rather belated political-satiric epic in support of the Reformation was written in 1595 by the preacher and educator Georg Rollenhagen: *Der Froschmeuseler* is a parody of the pseudo-Homeric *Battle of the Frogs and Mice*. The *Knittelvers* (rhymed-couplet) translation of the *Iliad* by the Augsburg schoolmaster Spreng is tedious and given to moral strictures. Fischart's most popular publication, *Das glückhafft Schiff von Zürich* (The Happy Ship from Zurich, 1576), is the story of a voyage taken by a group of Zurich citizens to Strasbourg for a shooting festival; it is the finest work of its kind in the early modern period.

The medieval tradition of *Teufelliteratur* (devil literature) enjoyed a revival in the sixteenth century, especially in northern and middle Germany; Catholic authorities prohibited its publication in Bavaria and other areas they controlled. Starting with Matthäus Friedrich's *Sauffteufel* (Boozer Devil) in 1552, it dealt with every kind of demon, reaching its peak with the story of Faust's deal with the devil in the anonymous *Historia von D. Johann Fausten* (History of Dr. Johann Faust, 1587). While usually playful, devil literature occasionally became deadly serious. Even as freethinking a satirist as Fischart was swept away for a time in his zealous translation of the French jurist Jean Bodin's *De la démonomanie des sorciers* (1580) as *De Daemonomania Magorum: Vom auß gelaßnen wütigen Teuffelsheer allerhand Zauberen, Hexen und Hexenmeistern* (On the Diabolical Madness of Witches: On the Furiously Unrestrained Satanic Horde of Sundry Magicians, Witches, and Sorcerers, 1581).

It was in the longer prose narrative that perhaps the most innovative work took place. Until the mid sixteenth century Germans had been content to imitate the French prose novel; after that time indigenous folk books gained a wide readership, most famously the *Historia von D. Johann Fausten,* a cautionary tale in the tradition of Murner against overweening human pride. The sophisticated Alsatian *Lalebuch* (The Lale Folk, 1597; also published as the *Schildbürger* [Citizens of Schilda, 1598]) tells about the foolishly wise citizens of the town of Schilda in a kind of magical realism that anticipates Gottfried Keller's *Leute von Seldwyla* (The People of Seldwyla, 1856). In the 1550s the Colmar official Wickram sewed together material from the lives of middle-class citizens in a manner distinctly German. His *Der Goldtfaden* (1557; translated as *The Golden Thread,* 1991), with its well-developed plot and structure, is the first original German work worthy of the designation *novel* and represents a clear step beyond the medieval epic in the direction of the modern social novel. Wickram also wrote anecdotal farce in the manner of Pauli. His *Rollwagenbüchlein* (Carriage Booklet, 1555) entertains without moralizing; it belongs to a subgenre of the novel known as travel literature. Many collections of anecdotes of various kinds appeared around this time; among the most popular were those by Jakob Frey, Martin Montanus, Michael Lindner, and Hans Wilhelm Kirchhoff. Fischart's *Geschichtklitterung* (Narrative Scribbling, 1582), a massive, ingenious, idiosyncratic translation of the first book of François Rabelais's *Gargantua et Pantagruel* (1532–1564), seems an appropriate conclusion to an age that was awash in confessional-political disarray and a transition into one known for its own formal and ideological excesses.

Obviously, it is not possible to treat all the writers in this long span who might well be justifiably included. We have made an attempt to include all the most significant figures and a generous sampling of lesser lights whose works and lives are illustrative of the thought and zeitgeist of the period. Some decisions had to be made regarding nationalities of writers dealt with in this volume, and it was decided that recent national claims to these writers should be honored. For that reason we did not include Erasmus, a Dutchman, or Nikolaus Copernicus, a Pole, and so forth.

As in preceding *DLB* volumes treating German literature the attempt has been made to avoid the use of terms that are not comprehensible to the general reader. For that reason the titles of works appearing in the text have been translated into English the first time they occur. The works cited in the Checklist of Further Readings at the end of this volume by Eckhard Bernstein, Bruno Boesch, Konrad Burdach, Heinz Otto Burger, Xenja von Ertzdorff, Hans Georg Kemper, Steven Ozment, Josef Schmidt, and Ingeborg Spriewald were especially useful in the writing of this introduction.

—Max Reinhart with James Hardin

Acknowledgments

This book was produced by Bruccoli Clark Layman, Inc. Karen L. Rood is senior editor for the *Dictionary of Literary Biography* series. Philip B. Dematteis was the in-house editor.

Administrative support was provided by Ann M. Cheschi and Brenda A. Gillie.

Bookkeeper is Joyce Fowler.

Copyediting supervisor is Laurel M. Gladden Gillespie. The copyediting staff includes Phyllis A. Avant, Patricia Coate, Jeff Miller, William L. Thomas Jr., and Allison Trussell.

Editorial associate is L. Kay Webster.

Layout and graphics staff includes Marie L. Parker and Janet E. Hill.

Office manager is Kathy Lawler Merlette.

Photography editors are Julie E. Frick and Margaret Meriwether. Photographic copy work was performed by Joseph M. Bruccoli.

Production manager is Samuel W. Bruce.

Software specialist is Marie L. Parker.

Systems manager is Chris Elmore.

Typesetting supervisor is Kathleen M. Flanagan. The typesetting staff includes Pamela D. Norton and Patricia Flanagan Salisbury. Freelance typesetters include Melody W. Clegg and Delores Plastow.

Walter W. Ross, Steven Gross, and Mark McEwan did library research. They were assisted by the following librarians at the Thomas Cooper Library of the University of South Carolina: Linda Holderfield and the interlibrary-loan staff; reference-department head Virginia Weathers; reference librarians Marilee Birchfield, Stefanie Buck, Stefanie DuBose, Rebecca Feind, Karen Joseph, Donna Lehman, Charlene Loope, Anthony McKissick, Jean Rhyne, Kwamine Simpson, and Virginia Weathers; circulation-department head Caroline Taylor; and acquisitions-searching supervisor David Haggard.

The publishers acknowledge the generous assistance of William R. Cagle, director of the Lilly Library, Indiana University, and his staff, who provided many of the illustrations in this volume. Their work represents the highest standards of librarianship and research.

Dictionary of Literary Biography® • Volume One Hundred Seventy-Nine

German Writers of the Renaissance and Reformation 1280–1580

Dictionary of Literary Biography

Hermann Bote
(circa 1460 – circa 1520)

Priscilla A. Hayden-Roy
University of Nebraska–Lincoln

MAJOR WORKS: *Dat boek von veleme rade* (Lübeck: Arndes, circa 1493);

Weltchronik (1493-1502)
   Manuscript: Brunswick manuscript, formerly referred to as the Hetling or Halberstadt manuscript; autograph, in Stadtarchiv Braunschweig (H VI 1, no. 28).
   First publication: Excerpts in *Sammlung etlicher noch nicht gedruckten alten Chroniken,* edited by Caspar Abel (Brunswick: Schröder, 1732), pp. 27-220;

Weltchronik (1502-1518)
   Manuscript: Hannover manuscript, autograph, in Niedersächsische Landesbibliothek Hannover (XI 669).
   First publication: Excerpts in *Auswahl aus den Werken von Hermann Bote,* edited by Gerhard Cordes, Texte zur deutschen Philologie und Literaturgeschichte, no. 1 (Wolfenbüttel: Wolfenbütteler Verlagsanstalt, 1948), pp. 19-28;

Dat tollenboyck (1503-1507)
   Manuscripts: Autograph, in Stadtarchiv Braunschweig (B I 9, No. 57); two later copies of this manuscript have survived, both in the Stadtarchiv Braunschweig: one from the eighteenth century (B I 9, No. 58) and one from the nineteenth century (H V, No. 277).
   First publication: Excerpts in "Die Heerstraßen auf Braunschweig um 1500," edited by Werner Spieß, *Studien und Vorarbeiten zum Historischen Atlas Niedersachsens,* 16 (1937): 118-124;

Ein kurtzweilig Lesen von Dil Ulenspiegel, geboren uß dem Land zu Brunßwick: Wie er sein Leben volbracht hatt: xcvi. seiner geschichten (Strasbourg: Grüninger, 1510 or 1511; revised, 1515; revised, 1519); translated, probably by Laurence Andrewe [title unknown] (Antwerp: Jan Van Doesborgh, 1518);

Dat Schichtboick (1510-1514)
   Manuscripts: Autograph, in the Herzog August Bibliothek Wolfenbüttel (Cod. Guelf. 120 Extravag.). Three additional manuscript copies from the seventeenth century have been preserved: one is in the Herzog August Bibliothek Wolfenbüttel (107 Blankenburg), and two are in the Stadtarchiv Braunschweig (H III 2, 44 2° and H III 2, 19 2°). The Brunswick theologian and schoolteacher Andreas Schoppius (1538-1614) incorporated nearly the entire *Schichtboick* into his *Chronikon der Stadt brunswiek* (Chronicle of the City of Brunswick), which has been preserved in more than twenty manuscript copies from the sixteenth and seventeenth centuries in Brunswick and Wolfenbüttel.
   First publication: *Shigt-Bôk der Stad Brunswyk: Zur Ergänzung von G. G. Leibnitii Scriptores rerum Brunsvicensium,* edited by Karl F. A. Scheller (Brunswick: Waisenhaus, 1829).
   Standard edition: *Die Chroniken der niedersächsischen Städte: Braunschweig,* volume 2, edited by Ludwig Hänselmann, Die Chroniken der deutschen Städte vom 14. bis ins 16. Jahrhundert, volume 16 (Leipzig: Salomon Hirzel, 1880; reprinted edition, Göttingen: Vandenhoeck & Ruprecht, 1962), pp. 299-468.
   Editions in modern German: *Das Schichtbuch: Geschichten von Ungehorsam und Aufruhr in Braunschweig 1292-1514: Nach dem Niederdeutschen des Zollschreibers Hermann Bothen und anderen Überlieferungen bearbeitet von L. H.,* adapted

by Hänselmann (Brunswick: Goeritz & zu Putlitz, 1866; reprinted edition, Hannover: Hirschheydt, 1979); *Zwei Kapitel aus dem Schichtbuch: Mittelniederdeutsch mit neuhochdeutscher Übersetzung*, edited and translated by Herbert Blume, Bibliophile Schriften der Literarischen Vereinigung Braunschweig, volume 32 (Brunswick: Literarische Vereinigung, 1985), pp. 11-43; "Ein Städtischer Aufruhr wird unterdrückt," in *Das Mittelalter: Ein Lesebuch aus Texten und Zeugnissen des 6. bis 16. Jahrhunderts*, edited by Hartmut Boockmann (Munich: Beck, 1988), pp. 289-300;

Van der pagemunte (1510-1513)
Manuscript: Appended to the autograph of *Dat Schichtboik*.
First publication and standard edition: *Die Chroniken der niedersächsischen Städte: Braunschweig*, volume 2, pp. 409-450;

Kirchen- und Klösterverzeichnis (1514-1516)
Manuscript: Appended to the autograph of *Dat Schichtboick*.
Standard edition: *Die Chroniken der niedersächsischen Städte: Braunschweig*, volume 2, pp. 469-477.
Edition in modern German: Translated by Eberhard Rohse as "Hermann Bote: Kirchen- und Klösterverzeichnis der Stadt Braunschweig, aus Dat schicht boick, Bl. 177-187," in *Kirchen, Klöster, Heilige: Vorreformatorische Kirchengeschichte Braunschweigs im Werk Hermann Botes: Begleitheft zur gleichnamigen Ausstellung*, edited by Jürgen Diestelmann (Brunswick: Kuhle, 1988), pp. 16-23;

Wappenbuch (1514-1516)
Manuscript: Appended to the autograph of *Dat Schichtboick*.
First publication and standard edition: In *Die Chroniken der niedersächsischen Städte: Braunschweig*, volume 2, pp. 478-493;

Totentanz (1518)
Manuscript: Autograph, appended to the *Weltchronik*, Hannover manuscript.
First publication: In "Ein prosaischer norddeutscher Totentanz des 16. Jahrhunderts," edited by Conrad Borchling, *Niederdeutsches Jahrbuch*, 28 (1902): 25-31.
Edition in modern German: "Anhang zu Botes Hannoverscher Weltchronik: Abbildung mit Edition und Übersetzung von Heinz-Lothar Worm," in *Hermen Bote: Braunschweiger Autor zwischen Mittelalter und Neuzeit*, edited by Detlev Schöttker and Werner Wunderlich, Wolfenbütteler Forschungen, no. 37 (Wiesbaden: Harrassowitz, 1987), pp. 48-65–includes facsimile and transcription of original;

De Koker (1520?)
Manuscript: Original no longer extant.
First publication: In *Reineke de Vos, mit dem Koker*, edited by Friedrich August Hackmann (Wolfenbüttel: Frytag, 1711), pp. 301-380.
Standard edition: *Der Köker: Mittelniederdeutsches Lehrgedicht aus dem Anfang des 16. Jahrhunderts*, edited by Gerhard Cordes, Altdeutsche Textbibliothek, no. 60 (Tübingen: Niemeyer, 1963).
Edition in modern German: *De Koker: Der Köcher*, edited and translated into modern German by Heinz-Lothar Worm, Litterae, volume 111 (Göppingen: Kümmerle, 1989)–includes facsimile of original.
Edition in English: "Bote's *De Koker:* An English Prose Translation with Philological Analysis and Annotations," translated by June Lillian Sherif, dissertation, New York University, 1979.

Editions: *Ein kurtzweilig Lesen von Dil Ulenspiegel: Nach dem Druck von 1515 mit 87 Holzschnitten*, edited by Wolfgang Lindow (Stuttgart: Reclam, 1966; revised, 1968; revised, 1975; revised, 1978);

Ein kurzweiliges Buch von Till Eulenspiegel aus dem Lande Braunschweig: Wie er sein Leben vollbracht hat: Sechsundneunzig seiner Geschichten, edited and translated by Siegfried H. Sichtermann (Frankfurt am Main: Insel, 1978);

Ein kurtzweilig lesen von Dil Ulenspiegel, facsimile of 1519 edition, edited by Anneliese Schmitt (Leipzig: Insel, 1979);

Dyl Vlenspiegel: In Abbildung des Drucks von 1515 (S 1515), edited by Werner Wunderlich, Litterae, volume 96 (Göppingen: Kümmerle, 1982);

Hermen Botes Radbuch: In Abbildung des Druckes L ca. 1492/93: Mit dem Text nach Herman Brandes und mit einer Übersetzung von Heinz-Lothar Worm, edited by Wunderlich, Litterae, volume 105 (Kümmerle: Göppingen, 1985).

Editions in English: *Here beginneth a merye Jest of a man that was called Howle glas and of many meruaylous thynges and Jestes that he dyd in his lyfe, in Eastland and in many other places*, translated anonymously (London: Copland, before 1557?);

Till Eulenspiegel: His Adventures, translated by Paul Oppenheimer (New York & London: Garland, 1991).

OTHER: "Lied von der 'Katzenteilung'" (1488), attributed to Bote, in Herbert Blume, "Hermann

Botes Ludeke-Holland-Lieder und ihre Überlieferung," *Braunschweigisches Jahrbuch,* 66 (1985): 64-67;

"Anno dusent verhundert acht und achtig jar" (1491), in Rochus von Liliencron, *Die historischen Volkslieder der Deutschen vom 13. bis ins 16. Jahrhundert,* 4 volumes (Leipzig: Vogel, 1865-1869; reprinted edition, Hildesheim: Olms, 1966), II: 216-221; also in Blume, 67-70;

"De katte und de hund" (1491), in Liliencron, II: 213-214; in Blume, 71-74;

"Nach Christj gebhurt 1488 Jhar" (1491 or later), attributed to Bote, also in Blume, 74-75;

"Von den Hensesteden im brunswigischen und luneborger lande" (1492 or 1493), in Liliencron, II: 315-320;

"Nu horet und market ut ganzem flit" (1519), in *Die Stiftsfehde: Erzählungen und Lieder,* edited by Hermann Adolf Lüntzel, Zeitschrift des Museums zu Hildesheim: Abteilung für Geschichte und Kunst, no. 1 (Hildesheim: Gerstenberg, 1846), pp. 201-204; also in Liliencron, III: 280-283;

"Frunde, market jung und old" (1519), in *Die Stiftsfehde,* pp. 208-212; also in Liliencron, III: 287-291.

Hermann Bote, as depicted in his Dat boek von veleme rade

Hermann Bote, one of the great masters of Low German, has acquired an increasingly visible place within literary history since the end of the nineteenth century as researchers have identified him as the author of a growing list of works. All except one of these works—which include political songs; a volume of rhymed verse on social stations; two world chronicles and a city chronicle; a collection of proverbs; several works on specialized topics such as taxation, economics, and heraldry; and the most recent and sensational attribution, the early prose novel *Ein kurtzweilig Lesen von Dil Ulenspiegel* (An Entertaining Reading about Till Eulenspiegel, 1510 or 1511; translated, 1518)—were written or published anonymously. Only two were printed during Bote's lifetime; the remaining works were circulated as manuscripts, and several of them have never been published in their entirety. Most of his works are in Bote's native Middle Low German (Eastphalian) dialect, which is largely incomprehensible to readers of modern German. These factors have contributed to Bote's obscurity and kept his works inaccessible to most students of German literature. This problem has been alleviated to some degree with the recent publication of several of Bote's works with parallel translations into modern German; the critical edition of Bote's works now being planned will open his entire oeuvre to a much wider audience. Scholarly interest in Bote has surged since the early 1980s: three Bote colloquiums were held in Germany between 1981 and 1988, and the published proceedings present an overview of the most recent Bote scholarship as well as extensive bibliographies. Interest in Bote is markedly interdisciplinary: beyond his considerable contributions to the literature of the early modern period, his writings offer important insights into a wide range of political, social, economic, and theological issues as seen through the eyes of an official in the early modern city of Brunswick.

Little is known about Bote's life; what is known has been gleaned chiefly from archival records or from references to himself in his own works. Born in Brunswick, probably in the 1460s, he was the son of Arnt Bote, a master smith and member of the council of one of the boroughs of the city. Bote did not follow his father into the smiths' guild; some scholars have speculated, on the basis of designations of Bote as "Her Umpenplump" (Mr. Hobblebobble) and "amechtig humpeller" (powerless hobbler) in two political songs directed against him, that he was physically handicapped and for this reason chose the more sedentary job of *tollenschriver* (tax and customs secretary) for the city of Brunswick. In his *Dat boek von veleme rade* (The Book of Many Wheels or Book of Much Counsel—the title is intentionally ambiguous, circa 1493) Bote calls himself an "unbelerde knecht" (uneducated servant), but this is to some degree a rhetorical gesture. His writings indicate that although he had only a rudimentary grasp of Latin and certainly was not humanistically educated, he had acquired an impressive breadth of knowledge. His chronicles demonstrate wide-ranging familiarity with history and geography; his specialized works show knowledge of economics and heraldry; and in terms of literary form, his works draw widely on medieval traditions such as the *Schwank* (jest), satire, allegory, rhymed verse, and the chronicle.

Bote's hometown of Brunswick was a member of the Hanseatic League, a trading federation of northern German cities with proud traditions of independent governance. By the late fifteenth century many of these cities, including Brunswick, were in decline, their independence threatened by encroaching territorial princes. Bote was an ardent supporter of Brunswick's rights and privileges, which, he believed, were divinely ordained and could be preserved only if the citizens and the city council maintained concord among themselves for the common good. As tollenschriver, a high and sensitive post in the city administration, Bote acquired intimate familiarity with the workings of the city council and with the economic structure of the city. His writings about the city are superbly informed and vigorously engaged with their subject.

The earliest work attributed to Bote appeared in 1488 in the aftermath of a successful uprising led by the head of the furriers' guild, Ludeke Hollant. Bote was a vociferous opponent of any who threatened the old order, and this song parodies the form of a testament: a cat is dismembered and its parts bequeathed to the various guilds. As the cat was the symbol of the furriers' guild, the song's reference to Hollant was transparent. This sort of disrespect would not be tolerated by the new regime; Bote was subjected to house arrest and relieved of his duties as tollenschriver. Bote mentions these events in his chronicle of Brunswick's uprisings, *Dat Schichtboick* (The History Book or Book of Uprisings, 1510–1514), but does not include this or the other songs he wrote relating to this event. Herbert Blume believes that he has found the text of the dismembered-cat song in several of the manuscript copies of the *Chronikon der Stadt brunswiek* (Chronicle of the City of Brunswick), by the Brunswick theologian and schoolteacher Andreas Schoppius. These manuscripts represent the primary source for all of Bote's political songs.

While Hollant and his party ruled Brunswick, Bote appears to have served as *hogreve* (magistrate or judge) in Rötgesbüttel, a village north of Brunswick in the district of Papenteich. In 1491 Hollant's regime collapsed and he fled the city. During that year Bote wrote two or three political songs mocking the deposed leader: "Anno dusent verhundert acht und achtig jar" (In the Year 1488), "De katte und de hund" (The Cat and the Dog), and, perhaps, "Nach Christj gebhurt 1488 Jhar" (A.D. 1488). These, too, are recorded in the Schoppius manuscripts. Schoppius, who died in 1614, recorded these texts in High German, so their presumed original form in Bote's Eastphalian dialect has been lost. Blume's 1985 edition of Bote's songs relating to the Hollant uprising presents the texts as they appear in the oldest Schoppius manuscripts. Rochus von Liliencron's edition (1865–1869) of historical German folk songs from the thirteenth to the sixteenth centuries attempts a reconstruction of the original dialect and, consequently, offers a less reliable text.

During his exile from Brunswick Bote also wrote *Dat boek von veleme rade,* usually referred to as the *Radbuch* (Wheel Book), which was published in Lübeck in 1492 or 1493. (The single copy of this edition known to remain is owned by the Metropolitan Museum of Art in New York.) The work, written in rhymed couplets, describes the social stations through the analogy of wheels. Thus, the mill wheel represents the Pope and ecclesiastical princes; the cogwheel, the emperor and the electors; the winch, the nobility; the wagon wheel, the burghers; and the plow wheel, the peasants. Five additional wheels potentially disrupt the first five: the driving wheel (women), the spinning wheel (children), the wheel of fortune (the devil's wheel), the spur wheel (fools), and the broken wheel (thieves). Each section is illustrated with a woodcut depicting the wheel and its representatives; Matthias Brandis was probably the artist who executed most of the woodcuts. The *Radbuch* was published anonymously; its author was identified in the late nineteenth century through the discovery of an acrostic constructed from the beginning initials of chapters 2 through 11, which spell *HERMEN BOTE.* The work stands in the tradition of medieval didactic verse; its conception of divinely ordained social order is also traditional. But Bote's work is written from the perspective of a city burgher, with the city's interests shaping the responsibilities and duties of all social stations. Bote's urgent appeal to live according to one's station, his criticism of discord as the root of all social evil, his appeal to the emperor to protect the rights of cities, and his *Fürstenangst* (fear of the territorial princes) are typical of this perspective and of Bote's work in general.

In 1493 Bote was back in Brunswick, serving as manager of one of the city's beer cellars. Recent scholarship indicates that this work was related to his former job in the customs booth—although it was clearly a lower office—insofar as both involved the collection of taxes for the city. Bote mentions this position in a political song written in 1492 or 1493, "Von den Hensesteden im brunswigischen und luneborger lande" (On the Hanseatic Cities in the Lands of Brunswick and Lüneburg).

By 1497 Bote was again serving as tollenschriver, a position he would hold until 1513. This period was one of considerable literary activity for Bote. In 1493 he had begun work on his first world chronicle—referred to as the *Weltchronik,* Brunswick manuscript, since its acquisition by the Brunswick City Archives. The work, nearly 450 pages long, covers the history of the world from its beginning through 1438, where the manuscript breaks off in midsentence. The *Weltchronik* mentions the death of "Ullenspeygel" from the plague in 1350 in the city of Mölln—the only extant report of Till Eulenspiegel in a chronicle from the period. Bote worked on the chronicle until 1502, when he began a second world chronicle. Referred to as the *Weltchronik,* Hannover manuscript, this second chronicle is more than 450 pages in length. Its first part is a condensation of the first chronicle into 160 pages. The second part begins with a history of the popes, moves on to the German bishoprics (excluding those in south Germany), and then discusses the European countries and the most important territories of the Holy Roman Empire, with emphasis on north Germany. Bote essentially completed the Hannover *Weltchronik* in 1504, but he continued to update it with current events until 1518. No more than excerpts have been published from either of Bote's world chronicles, but both offer a grand overview of secular and ecclesiastical history as it was understood at that time.

According to the register at the beginning of the Hannover *Weltchronik,* eight additional texts were appended to the chronicle; they were concerned largely with religious subjects and were probably written in 1518. Three have survived and are relatively intact. One of these texts, a prose adaptation of *Totentanz* (Dance of Death) that had been published in Lübeck in 1489, has attracted particular scholarly interest. The complete appendix, including the *Totentanz,* was published in 1987, with

Page from the Hannover manuscript copy of Bote's second Weltchronik *(Niedersächsische Landesbibliothek, ms. XI 669, folio 12ʳ)*

a modern German translation by Heinz-Lothar Worm.

Between 1503 and 1507 Bote wrote *Dat tollenboyck* (Customs Book). Commissioned by the city council, this reference manual outlines the tax and customs policies in Brunswick, at the same time giving an overview of Bote's work as tollenschriver. *Dat tollenboyck* is the only work signed by Bote, and its handwriting provided the basis for identifying works written in his hand.

In 1973 the Swiss lawyer and bibliophile Peter Honegger published a study that argued for Bote's authorship of the anonymously published novel *Ein kurtzweilig Lesen von Dil Ulenspiegel*. In his examination of the beginning initials of the episodes he discovered not only a series of alphabetic acrostics—a technique favored by Bote—but also, at the beginning of episodes 90 through 95, the initials *ERMAN B.* Honegger also argued that Bote was bilingual and that Bote himself wrote the High German version printed in Strasbourg in 1510 or 1511. Philological studies have, however, refuted the latter contention. It seems most probable that Bote wrote and published a Low German version, no longer extant,

Page from the first edition of the early prose novel Till Eulenspiegel, *recently attributed to Bote*

which was translated into High German by a native of Strasbourg (hence the presence of Alsatian dialect forms in the Strasbourg edition) whose identity remains unknown. Until and unless the Low German original is found, scholars face important questions regarding Bote's presumed authorship: which of the episodes in the Strasbourg edition were written by Bote? Which were added in Strasbourg? Its flaws notwithstanding, Honegger's study made plausible the most sensational addition to Bote's oeuvre and has given tremendous impetus to Bote scholarship. (Bote's authorship has not been universally accepted by scholars. The most vocal opponent, the historian Bernd Ulrich Hucker, who originally supported Honegger's thesis, has come to oppose it, basing his arguments on an unfinished study by Edward Schröder.)

The earliest edition of *Ein kurtzweilig Lesen von Dil Ulenspiegel* was printed in 1510 or 1511 and exists only in two fragments, both published by Grüninger in Strasbourg. It was republished in 1515–the first complete extant edition–and in at least five more editions by the same publisher by 1543; sixteenth-century editions from many other German cities have also survived. During the sixteenth century it was translated into Danish, Dutch, English, French, Latin, Polish, and Yiddish. The popularity of the book was certainly assisted by its woodcuts, which, from the earliest editions, illustrate each episode. The original woodcuts, which vary greatly in quality, were made by several artists, including Hans Baldung Grien.

Ein kurtzweilig Lesen von Dil Ulenspiegel belongs to a group of works referred to as early prose novels, a loosely defined body of literature that in the fifteenth and sixteenth centuries supplanted the medieval courtly verse epic and preceded the novel as it emerged in the seventeenth and eighteenth centuries. The older designation, *Volksbuch* (folk book), rests on historical misconceptions and is not favored among Germanists. *Ein kurtzweilig Lesen von Dil Ulenspiegel* draws on the tradition of the medieval Schwank: Der Stricker's *Die Schwänke des Pfaffen Amîs* (The Merry Tales of Parson Amîs, after 1225–circa 1250?) and Philipp Frankfürter's *Des pfaffen geschicht und histori vom Kalenberg* (The Story and History of the Pastor of Kalenberg, 1473) were among the vernacular jest cycles that provided Bote with material for several of the Eulenspiegel episodes.

In writing the novel Bote compiled legends that were circulating about a real person, the man whose death he had recorded in the Brunswick *Weltchronik;* but the historical events mentioned in the book as having occurred during Till's lifetime actually span a period of nearly five hundred years, so Bote's intention is at least partly humorous. The work relates Eulenspiegel's life from birth to death in ninety-six brief *Historien* (in the sixteenth century a *Historie* could refer either to a fictional narrative or a factual one). Till's early years take place in and around Brunswick. His travels take him to places as distant as Poland, Prague, Antwerp, and Rome; but he repeatedly returns to northern Germany, and he dies in Mölln, a small town just south of Lübeck. Many of the episodes take place in Hanseatic League cities–not surprising, given Bote's Hanseatic allegiance. Each episode relates a prank played by Till; his victims come from the entire spectrum of society, including those within the traditional social stations–the peasants, artisans, nobility, university professors, and clergymen (among the latter, even the Pope)–and those outside the traditional stations, such as Jews and beggars. This interest in the whole sweep of society bears similarity to Bote's *Radbuch*. Although Till is a vagabond lacking rank or station, he is able to insinuate himself into the highest and lowest social settings by means of his wit and his ability to present himself as qualified to those interested in his services as an artisan's assistant, sacristan, doctor, and so forth. It is important to note that Till does not appear in the woodcuts dressed as a fool, nor is there any indication in the text that he is outwardly identifiable as a rogue. On the contrary, it is his ability to conceal his true identity through appropriate disguise and language that enables him to infiltrate society undetected. Many of Till's pranks are scatological, and many are shockingly destructive; nevertheless, they are funny.

Interpreting *Till Eulenspiegel* presents a great challenge to scholars, particularly given the tremendous mutability of this figure through the centuries—from the celebrated national hero of Charles De Coster's novel *La légende d'Ulenspiegel et de Lamme Goedsak au pays de Flandres et Ailleurs* (1868; translated as *The Glorious Adventures of Tyl Ulenspiegl*, 1943) to the harmless prankster of modern children's books to the Marxist protorevolutionary in Christa and Gerhard Wolf's *Till Eulenspiegel: Erzählung für den Film* (Till Eulenspiegel: Filmscript, 1972). Studies of the reception of *Till Eulenspiegel* in the sixteenth century indicate that from the outset the work has given rise to various, frequently contradictory, interpretations. As a portrayal of vice and its consequences, *Till Eulenspiegel* served a didactic, admonitory function. Contemporary authors such as Hans Sachs and Johann Fischart adapted Eulenspiegel histories in this manner. Not infrequently Till's pranks are conceived as retribution for a fault or vice on the part of his victim. In this case Till functions as a "wise fool," mirroring the faults of society to his readers. Heinz-Günter Schmitz has argued (in *Hermann Bote* [1991], edited by Blume and Eberhard Rohse) that entertaining works such as *Till Eulenspiegel* were understood to have the medicinal effect of driving away melancholy. But these tales of destruction and disrespect also aroused suspicion; the work was roundly condemned by contemporary theologians of both the Protestant and Roman Catholic camps and was placed on an index of forbidden books published in Antwerp in 1569. The inherent ambiguity of the Eulenspiegel tales has given the novel its longevity, but it also raises historical questions regarding the nature and function of the jest novel in the early modern period.

Between 1510 and 1514 Bote wrote a third historical work, *Dat Schichtboick*, a history of six uprisings that occurred in Brunswick between 1293 and 1514. The title, like that of the *Radbuch*, is ambiguous: *schicht* means both "history" and "violent uprising" in Bote's Low German. Considered Bote's historical masterpiece, the work offers lively, extremely readable, albeit highly partisan accounts of the social, political, and economic tensions and their historical repercussions in medieval Brunswick. The work is unique among late-medieval city chronicles, which generally follow the organization of universal chronicles. Instead, Bote's work focuses only on the six uprisings. Each is introduced with an animal analogy, which compresses into a didactic fable the central lesson to be gleaned from the uprising. For example, Bote begins his account of the 1488 uprising by admonishing the ass, who foolishly raises a cat (representing Hollant) onto the throne, rather than honoring its legitimate ruler, the lion (the city council; the lion also traditionally represents the city of Brunswick). He concludes the analogy with a warning that is repeated throughout the work: "Hirumme wes vorsichtich in dynen dingen unde hot deck vor twidracht" (So be careful in all your matters and avoid discord). The histories illustrate the importance of maintaining concord among the various factions within the city, so that the "common good"—the traditional rights and privileges of Hanseatic Brunswick and the wealth and strength they bring the city—might be preserved.

Bote followed the Hollant schicht with *Van der pagemunte* (On Currency, 1510–1513), a brief history of Brunswick's currency between 1412 and 1510. This text, which includes detailed illustrations of coins, was featured in an exhibit held in 1988 at the Brunswick City Museum, "City and Museum in the Late Middle Ages." Matthias Puhle argues that *Van der pagemunte* supplies a necessary economic explanation of the Hollant schicht, and should not be viewed as an unrelated appendix. Bote initially completed *Dat Schichtboick* in 1513, but in the following year he recorded the events involved in a sixth schicht, which occurred between 1512 and 1514. Bote was an eyewitness of the last two uprisings in *Dat Schichtboick*, and his account includes references to himself, in the third person, which at times provide the only source of biographical information we have on Bote. Following the sixth schicht are appended two further texts, only tangentially related to the material in *Dat Schichtboick*: a *Kirchen- und Klösterverzeichnis* (Index of Churches and Monasteries), a register of ecclesiastical properties in Brunswick; and the richly illustrated *Wappenbuch* (Book of Heraldry). Both were written between 1514 and 1516. The *Kirchen- und Klosterverzeichnis* was the center of an exhibit held in 1988 in Brunswick on pre-Reformation church history as reflected in Herman Bote's writings.

Dat Schichtboick has enjoyed a surprisingly wide dissemination over the centuries, first through Schoppius's *Chronikon der Stadt brunswiek*, which exists in more than twenty manuscript copies from the

First page of the manuscript for Bote's history of uprisings in Brunswick (Herzog August Bibliothek Wolfenbüttel, Cod. Guelf. 120 Extravag.)

sixteenth and seventeenth centuries. In the nineteenth century Brunswick city archivist Ludwig Hänselmann, who was responsible for the early identifications of Bote's works and who also produced the standard edition of *Dat Schichtboick,* brought this work to a wider audience through his *Schichtbuch,* a modern German adaptation that combines *Dat Schichtboick* with several other Brunswick chronicles, and his novella, *Hans Dilien der Türmer,* which borrows passages from *Dat Schichtboick.*

In 1513 Bote was once again victimized by an uprising in his native Brunswick. In a conflict known as the *Aufruhr der Armut* (Uprising of the Poor), the events of which Bote related in the sixth and final schicht of *Dat Schichtboick,* the guilds protested a series of fees imposed by the council and demanded that they be rescinded and all those responsible for them removed from office. Their anger turned on the tollenschriver, Bote, who hid in a Franciscan cloister, only to be found by the mob, dragged out, beaten, imprisoned, and threatened with execution. Only through the intervention of city officials was Bote's life spared, but it appears that he was never reinstated to his position in the customs booth.

From 1516 to 1520 Bote appears to have been

the director of a municipal brickyard. In 1519, again responding to political events, he wrote two songs that have survived: "Nu horet und market ut ganzem flit" (Now hear and listen carefully) and "Frunde, market jung und old" (Friends, listen, young and old). They depict the events of the *Hildesheimer Stiftsfehde* (Feud of the Hildesheim Diocese), a territorial war fought among local lords and bishops that resulted in great loss of life in the Battle at Soltau on 29 June 1519. Two songs from the opposing party also have survived; they include the references to Bote that suggest that he was crippled. Bote's songs about the Hildesheimer Stiftsfehde have been analyzed by Matthias Nix, who maintains that they express sympathy for the cause of the Brunswick dukes, rather than following the strict policy of neutrality advocated by Brunswick's city council.

Probably in 1520 Bote wrote his last work, *De Koker* (The Quiver), a collection of more than two thousand lines of gnomic verse with interlocking rhymes—the last line of one gnome, or proverb, rhymes with the first line of the next. Here, too, Bote uses the acrostic: the beginning initials of each section follow the alphabet. The original text of *De Koker* has been lost. Scholars believe that it existed in manuscript form when its first editor, Friedrich August Hackmann, published it with a Low German version of *Reineke de Vos* (The Fox) in 1711. Published anonymously, it was definitively attributed to Bote in the 1930s.

In the introduction to *De Koker* the author explains the title: the book is a quiver full of arrows (the proverbs) meant to supply the archer (the reader) with verbal weaponry against the destruction and senseless vicissitudes of the world:

> Wey wyl dagegen straffen efde schelden
> Alle dat eme hyrynne wedderfart?
> Wyl nü eyn dem andern in den bart
> Warpen efte scheyten eyne klyven,
> Den spyet myt speyheyt verdryven,
> Deme kumt düsse Koker wol even
> Dar mach he de pyle uthheven,
> De da gud syn to synem bogen.
>
> (Who wants to condemn or complain
> About one's fortune?
> If someone wants to throw or shoot a burr
> Into another's beard,
> And drive off scorn with clever mockery,
> This quiver will serve that purpose.
> From it he can take the arrows
> That are well suited to his bow.)

Though Bote concedes his impotence in the face of misfortune—here he shares the pessimistic worldview of the late medieval age—the humorous proverbs protect the self, as if by laughing at his fate the individual is, in some sense, preserved.

The proverbs, which for the most part are Bote's inventions, spring from one topic to another with no ordering principle aside from the acrostic organization of the section initials. They treat such disparate topics as human character, social behavior, women, the church, the household, food, war, disease, and filth. The tone varies: many proverbs are heavily ironic; others are sheer nonsense. The work is unique in its composition, its artful and engaging rhyme, and the breadth of its scope; it represents an admirable culmination of Bote's literary career. In 1520 his name disappears from the records; it is assumed that this was the year he died.

There has been considerable dispute among Bote scholars as to whether his oeuvre should be extended to include additional works. A case has been made for the *Cronecken der Sassen* (Chronicle of the Saxons), printed in Mainz by Peter Schöffer in 1492, which has been attributed to the Brunswick goldsmith Cord (Conrad) Bothe. Analysis of the work's language demonstrates considerable similarity to Bote's. Otherwise, nothing points definitively to him as the author; the editors of the forthcoming critical edition of Bote's works plan to include it as a supplemental volume, without asserting his authorship. Far more shaky are the claims made for Bote's authorship of *Dat narren schyp* (The Ship of Fools, 1497), the Low German version of Sebastian Brant's *Das Narrenschiff* (1494), and of *Reynke de vos,* 1498), both of which were published in Lübeck. Some have suggested that Bote moved to Lübeck to work in the printing trade around the time of Hollant's regime in Brunswick. To date, convincing evidence has not been put forward to support either Bote's authorship of these works or of his stay in Lübeck, although both theses have found their way into many scholarly studies on Bote. Timothy Sodmann (in *Hermann Bote,* edited by Blume and Rohse) has provided an overview of research on the question, and he maintains that arguments for Bote's authorship of *Reynke de vos* are unfounded. Even without these works, Hermann Bote must be ranked among the outstanding writers of the late medieval/early modern period. The controversies surrounding his work are still being debated, and in many respects Bote scholarship is still in its infancy.

Bibliographies:

Herbert Blume and Werner Wunderlich, eds., *Hermen Bote: Bilanz und Perspektiven der Forschung,* Beiträge zum Hermen-Bote-Kolloquium vom 3. Oktober 1981 in Braunschweig (Göppingen: Kümmerle, 1982), pp. 133-154;

Walter Hinz, ed., *Till Eulenspiegel: Katalog der Bücher, Zeitschriften und Manuskripte des Eulenspiegel-Museums zu Schöppenstedt* (Schöppenstedt: Freundeskreis Till Eulenspiegels, 1984);

Detlev Schöttker and Werner Wunderlich, eds., *Hermen Bote: Braunschweiger Autor zwischen Mittelalter und Neuzeit,* Wolffenbütteler Forschungen, no. 37 (Wiesbaden: Harrassowitz, 1987), pp. 245–255;

Blume and Eberhard Rohse, eds., *Hermann Bote: Städtisch-hansischer Autor in Braunschweig 1488-1988: Beiträge zum Braunschweiger Bote-Kolloquium 1988* (Tübingen: Niemeyer, 1991), pp. 365–371.

References:

David Blamires, "Reflections on Some Recent 'Ulenspiegel' Studies," *Modern Language Review,* 77 (1982): 351–360;

Herbert Blume, "Bote, Hermann," in *Literatur-Lexikon: Autoren und Werke deutscher Sprache,* volume 2, edited by Walther Killy (Munich: Bertelsmann Lexikon Verlag, 1989), pp. 128–130;

Blume, "Hermann Bote–Autor des *Eulenspiegel-Buches?* Zum Stand der Forschung," *Eulenspiegel Jahrbuch,* 34 (1994): 11–32;

Blume, "Hermann Botes Ludeke-Holland-Lieder und ihre Überlieferung," *Braunschweigisches Jahrbuch,* 66 (1985): 57–77;

Blume and Eberhard Rohse, eds., *Hermann Bote: Städtisch-hansischer Autor in Braunschweig 1488-1988: Beiträge zum Braunschweiger Bote-Kolloquium 1988* (Tübingen: Niemeyer, 1991);

Blume and Werner Wunderlich, eds., *Hermen Bote: Bilanz und Perspektiven der Forschung,* Beiträge zum Hermen-Bote-Kolloquium vom 3. Oktober 1981 in Braunschweig (Göppingen: Kümmerle, 1982);

Georg Bollenbeck, *Till Eulenspiegel: Der dauerhafte Schwankheld. Zum Verhältnis von Produktions- und Rezeptionsgeschichte* (Stuttgart: Metzler, 1985);

Jörgen Bracker, *Die Hanse: Lebenswirklichkeit und Mythos,* 2 volumes (Hamburg: Museum für Hamburgische Geschichte, 1989);

Friedrich W. D. Brie, *Eulenspiegel in England,* Palaestra, no. 27 (Berlin: Mayer & Müller, 1903);

Gerhard Cordes, "Die Weltchroniken von Hermann Bote," *Braunschweigisches Jahrbuch,* 34 (1953): 75–101;

Thomas Cramer, ed., *Till Eulenspiegel in Geschichte und Gegenwart* (Bern: Peter Lang, 1978);

Charles De Coster, *La légende d'Ulenspiegel et de Lamme Goedsak au pays de Flandres et Ailleurs* (Paris, 1868); translated by Allan Ross Macdougall as *The Glorious Adventures of Tyl Ulenspiegl* (New York: Pantheon, 1943);

Jürgen Diestelmann, ed., *Kirchen, Klöster, Heilige: Vorreformatorische Kirchengeschichte Braunschweigs im Werk Hermann Botes. Begleitheft zur gleichnamigen Ausstellung* (Brunswick: Kuhle, 1988);

Ludwig Hänselmann, *Hans Dilien der Turner: Eine braunschweigische Geschichte a.d. 14. Jahrhundert* (Wolfenbüttel: Zwiszler, 1918);

Priscilla Hayden-Roy, "The Masquerade of History: Hermann Bote's *Schichtboik*," *Daphnis: Zeitschrift für Mittlere Deutsche Literatur,* 22 (1993): 561–580;

Hayden-Roy, "Till Eulenspiegel's Transgressions against Convention: Interpreting the Parasite," *Daphnis: Zeitschrift für Mittlere Deutsche Literatur,* 20 (1991): 7–31;

Peter Honegger, *Ulenspiegel: Ein Beitrag zur Druckgeschichte und zur Verfasserfrage* (Neumünster: Wachholtz, 1973);

Bernd Ulrich Hucker, "Bote, Hermen," in *Lexikon des Mittelalters,* volume 2, edited by Jens P. Aegidius (Munich & Zurich: Artemis, 1983), cols. 482–484;

Hucker, "Eulenspiegel, Til," in *Enzyklopädie des Märchens,* volume 4, edited by Kurt Ranke (Berlin & New York: De Gruyter, 1984), cols. 538–555;

Cord Meckseper, ed., *Stadt im Wandel: Kunst und Kultur des Bürgertums in Norddeutschland 1150–1650,* Landesausstellung Niedersachsen 1985, 4 volumes (Stuttgart-Bad Cannstadt: Cantz, 1985), I: 563–572;

Jan-Dirk Müller, "Volksbuch/Prosaroman im 15./16. Jahrhundert–Perspektiven der Forschung," in *Internationales Archiv für Sozialgeschichte der deutschen Literatur, 1. Sonderheft: Forschungsreferate,* edited by Wolfgang Frühwald, Georg Jäger, and Alberto Martino (Tübingen: Niemeyer, 1985), pp. 1–128;

Matthias Nix, " 'Ick prise di, Brunswike!': Hermann Botes Lieder zur Hildesheimer Stiftsfehde," *Braunschweigisches Jahrbuch,* 74 (1993): 27–65;

Matthias Puhle, *Stadt und Geld im ausgehenden Mittelalter: Zur Münzgeschichte 'Van der Pagemunte' des Braunschweiger Autors Hermen Bote (ca. 1450–1520),* Städtisches Museum Braunschweig, Arbeitsberichte, no. 58 (Brunswick: Städtisches Museum, 1988);

Werner Röcke, *Die Freude am Bösen: Studien zu einer Poetik des deutschen Schwankromans im Spätmittelalter* (Munich: Fink, 1987);

George C. Schoolfield, "Herman Bote: An Introductory Essay," in *Germanic Studies in Honor of Otto*

Springer, edited by Stephen J. Kaplowitt (Pittsburgh: K & S Enterprises, 1978), pp. 281–303;

Detlev Schöttker and Wunderlich, eds., *Hermen Bote: Braunschweiger Autor zwischen Mittelalter und Neuzeit,* Wolffenbütteler Forschungen, volume 37 (Wiesbaden: Harrassowitz, 1987);

Edward Schröder, *Untersuchungen zum Volksbuch von Eulenspiegel, nach dem unvollendeten Manuskript von etwa 1936,* edited by Hucker and Wolfgang Virmond, Abhandlungen der Akademie der Wissenschaften in Göttingen, Philologisch-Historische Klasse, Dritte Folge, no. 159 (Göttingen: Vandenhoeck & Ruprecht, 1988);

Brigitte Schulte, "Hermen Botes Prosa-Totentanz und sein Verhältnis zur Lübecker Vorlage," *Korrespondenzblatt des Vereins für niederdeutsche Sprachforschung,* 88 (1981): 15–22;

Wolfgang Virmond, *Eulenspiegel und seine Interpreten* (Berlin: Arbeitsstelle für Hermen-Bote- und Eulenspiegel-Forschung, 1981);

Stephen L. Wailes, "The Childishness of Till: Hermen Bote's *Ulenspiegel,*" *German Quarterly,* 64 (1991): 127–137;

Christa Wolf and Gerhard Wolf, *Till Eulenspiegel: Erzählung für den Film* (East Berlin: Edition Neue Texte, 1972);

Wunderlich, "Hermen Botes Radbuch: Eine allegorische Ständedidaxe um 1500," *Colloquia Germanica,* 19 (1986): 119–137;

Wunderlich, *"Till Eulenspiegel"* (Munich: Fink, 1984);

Wunderlich, ed., *Eulenspiegel heute: Kulturwissenschaftliche Beiträge zu Geschichtlichkeit und Aktualität einer Schalksfigur* (Neumünster: Wachholtz, 1988);

Wunderlich, ed., *Eulenspiegel-Interpretationen: Der Schalk im Spiegel der Forschung 1807–1977* (Munich: Fink, 1979).

Sebastian Brant
(1457 – 10 May 1521)

John Van Cleve
Augsburg College

BOOKS: *Expositiones sive declarationes admodum necessarie ac perutiles omnium titulorum legalium exacta repetitaque opera ac diligentia interpretatorum* (Basel: Printed by Michael Furter for Andreas Helmut, 1490);

In laudem gloriose virginis Marie multorumque sanctorum. Varii generis carmina Sebastiani Brant. utriusque juris doctoris famosissimi (Basel: Johann Bergmann von Olpe, 1494);

Das Narren Schyff (Basel: Johann Bergmann von Olpe, 1494); translated by Alexander Barclay as *This Present Boke named the Shyp of folys of the worlde was translated in the College of Saynt Mary Otery in the counte of Deuonshyre: out of Laten, Frenche, and Doche into the Englysshe tonge* (London: Richard Pynson, 1509);

De Origine et conversatione bonorum Regum: et laude Civitatis Hierosolymae: cum exhortatione eiusdem recuperandae (Basel: Johann Bergmann von Olpe, 1495);

Liber Faceti docens mores hominum: praecipue Iuvenum, in supplementum illorum, qui a Cathone erant omissi: per Sebastianum Brant in vulgare noviter translatus (Basel: Johann Bergmann von Olpe, 1496);

Varia Sebastiani Brant Carmina. Ad nobilem et splendidissimum virum dominum Heinricum de Büno (Basel: Johann Bergmann von Olpe, 1498).

Edition: *Narrenschiff,* edited by Friedrich Zarncke (Leipzig: Wigand, 1854).

Editions in English: *The Ship of Fools, by Sebastian Brant. Translated into Rhyming Couplets, with Introduction and Commentary,* translated by Edwin H. Zeydel (New York: Columbia University Press, 1944; New York: Dover, 1962);

The Ship of Fools, translated by William Gillis (London: Folio Society, 1971).

OTHER: Gratianus, *Decretum Gratiani summo studio elaboratum: correctum et cum libris Biblie accurate concordatum,* edited by Brant (Basel: Johann Froben, 1493);

Engraving by Jakov van der Heyden after a painting by Hans Baldung Grien

Jean Baptiste de Gasalupis, *De modo studendi in utroque Jure: cum nominibus omnium scribentium in iure,* edited by Brant (Basel: Michael Furter, 1500);

Anicius Manlius Severinus Boethius, *Boetius de Philosophico consolatu sive de consolatione philosophiae: cum figuris ornatissimis noviter expolitum,* edited by Brant (Strasbourg: Johannes Grüninger, 1501);

Der heiligen leben nüw mit vil me Heilegen, und darzu der Passion, edited by Brant (Strasbourg: Johannes Grüninger, 1502);

Virgilii opera, edited by Brant (Strasbourg: Johannes Grüninger, 1503);

Der Freidanck, edited by Brant (Strasbourg: Johannes Grüninger, 1508);

"Die Freiheitstafel," in *Das Narrenschiff von Dr. Sebastian Brant, nebst dessen Freiheitstafel,* edited by Adam Walther Strobel (Quedlinburg & Leipzig: Basel, 1839), pp. 301-312.

Title page for Brant's masterpiece

The name Sebastian Brant is inextricably tied to *Das Narrenschiff* (The Ship of Fools, 1494), by far his best-known work. The identities of author and work are so interdependent that literary histories regularly ignore the rest of Brant's not insubstantial oeuvre. The first German literary work to demonstrate the mass-market potential of the new printing technology, *Das Narrenschiff* achieved such unprecedented domestic and international popularity that it has been called the most famous work of German literature before the time of Johann Wolfgang von Goethe. It provided the archetype for the "Literature of Fools," a genre closely associated with the pedagogical mission of humanism that includes such noted works as the *Moriae encomium* (1511; translated as *The Praise of Folie,* 1549), by Desiderius Erasmus, and the *Epistolae obscurorum virorum* (The Letters of Obscure Men, 1516), by Crotus Rubeanus, Ulrich von Hutten, and others. During the nineteenth century and for much of the twentieth, literary scholarship offered little positive evaluation of the work. The complex nature of the reaction to *Das Narrenschiff* makes for an interesting study in itself, and since the 1960s the analysis of and response to that reaction have prompted a reevaluation of the work.

Brant was born in Strasbourg in 1457. His father, Diebold Brant, owned and operated the inn at the sign of the Golden Lion with his wife and at least three sons, of whom Sebastian was the oldest. The marginal success of the family establishment contrasted sharply with the accomplishments of Diebold Brant's father, a member of the wine merchant's guild who had been elected to the Great City Council for eight terms. When Diebold died in January 1468, the combined duties of parent and breadwinner fell to his widow, Barbara Picker Brant.

Scholarship has made much of the influence exerted by Barbara Brant on her firstborn, and there can be no doubt that it was considerable. When the great philologist Friedrich Zarncke theorized in the introduction to his 1854 edition of *Narrenschiff* that the active, assertive mother left the stamp of "womanish" sensitivity on her son, he set a pattern that was followed for decades by scholars–including Edwin H. Zeydel as recently as 1967. But no cogent evidence has been adduced to support such a theory, and it is reasonable to suspect nineteenth-century sexism as the source of an explanation for an adult personality that was sensitive to criticism, emotionally dependent on friends, and morally judgmental.

The unfortunately traditional characterization of a man raised in the absence of a father appears all the more mean-spirited in light of the great effort expended by Barbara Brant to ensure that Sebastian would have the opportunity to make the most of what she deemed to be his sizable talents. His education probably began at a local parish school or at one in nearby Baden. As he outstripped the abilities of his teachers, his mother engaged private tutors and thus placed a strain on the tight family budget. In Brant's part of Europe new, rigorous schools had opened under the aegis of humanism, but there is no evidence that Brant attended one.

Strasbourg did not yet have a university, so in 1475 Brant was sent off to the new University of Basel. Basel had been an exciting center of intellectual life since the convocation of the Church Council there in 1431. Although little came of the council's attempts to reform the administration of the church, the delegates had represented the cream of humanism. Aeneas Sylvius (later Pope Pius II), Nicolaus Cusanus, Giuliano Cesarini, and Louis d'Allemand had rubbed shoulders with a constant procession of prelates and imperial officials. One incentive to hold the council in Basel had been the presence there of the Carthusian monastery with its excellent library. Intellectual activity had continued with the development of a small but active printing industry. Brant enrolled in the Humanistic Faculty, which provided a core curriculum of logic, philosophy, physics, and classical rhetoric on which later studies would be based. Canonical works of Greek and Latin literature were studied as part of the instruction in philosophy and rhetoric. In addition, Brant was tutored in ancient Greek and Latin by the redoubtable scholar Johannes Reuchlin. To help pay his expenses Brant worked as the famulus (household servant) of Jacob Hugonis, a professor who was open to the new studies of humanism.

As a student Brant lived in a bursa, an academic hall that served as dormitory, dining room, and classroom building. Each bursa had its own character, somewhat on the order of the colleges of British universities. Aristotelian logic was the pet study at Brant's bursa. He practiced his Latin in a favorite venue of the time, lyric poetry, and developed a small reputation in Basel for his verse. He studied manuscripts at the Carthusian monastery and developed friendships with Reuchlin, Johannes Heynlin von Stein, and Ludwig Moser.

The university, founded in 1460, had immediately become embroiled in a debate that in the late Middle Ages had split Scholasticism, the movement that had dominated Western philosophy and theology since the ninth century. By Brant's time most students of theology belonged to one of two camps, the realists and the nominalists. The former held that universal concepts had a real existence outside the mind, the latter that such concepts existed only as names. The Dominican order championed realism; the Franciscans, nominalism. Brant's mentor, Heynlin, was a leading realist. A theologian with a special interest in Aristotelian philosophy, Heynlin had studied and taught at the University of Paris before arriving in Basel to influence the placement of realists in the humanistic faculty. He had become the dean of the faculty but had soon gone back to Paris to promote the establishment of a new printing industry there. When he returned to Basel, it was as a preacher, although he also gathered a group of younger scholars around him.

Heynlin was a humanist in a specific, limited sense. Not at all characterized by the exuberant joie de vivre of a Conrad Celtis, he cultivated a spartan scholarship and a limpid Latinity through the study of the ancient writers. Their language, not their message, was his first concern. His interest in printing also allied him with the humanists, as did his preference for the new studies. But as he grew older, Heynlin became increasingly concerned about what he took to be the rise of worldliness and the decline of morality. To his devoted follower Brant he passed on his aversion for the corruption of the "city of man." Fully consistent with the development of Heynlin's analysis of society was his ultimate withdrawal from the world into the austere Carthusian order with its rules of contemplation and silence. As a preacher and teacher Heynlin exerted a profound influence on Johannes Trithemius, Jakob Wimpfeling, and the charismatic Strasbourg preacher Geiler von Kaisersberg; but Brant was his true intellectual offspring.

Brant took his baccalaureate degree after just two years, an indication that his preparation in Strasbourg had been thorough. In 1484 he received a license to teach and practice law in Basel, and he quickly built a reputation as an effective and inspiring instructor. In 1485 he married Elisabeth Burg. Two years later he was teaching Latin literature in the Humanistic Faculty; one of his students was Jacob Locher, who in 1497 would translate *Das Narrenschiff* into Latin verse. Brant was awarded his doctorate of law in 1489.

The books Brant wrote and edited at this time in his life were intended to support his efforts in the classroom. His *Expositiones sive declarationes admodum necessarie ac perutiles omnium titulorum legalium exacta repititaque oepra ac diligentia interpretatorum* (Expositions or Explanations of All Divisions of Law, Civil as Well as Canon, 1490), a compendium of precedents, is a textbook for his law students that went through many editions. He edited *Decretum Gratiani summo studio elaboratum: correctum et cum libris Biblie accurate concordatum* (The Canonical Rules of Gratianus Carefully Worked out and Coordinated with the Bible, 1493), a work on canon law for students. He also translated a set of lectures to prepare students for the rigors of legal study, Jean Baptiste de Gasalupis's *De modo studendi in utroque jure* (How to Study Both Civil and Criminal Law, 1500). His pedagogical writings testify to his dedication to the new humanist approach to higher education.

Brant was also active in the publishing trade. He worked with the major publishers in Basel—Johann Amerbach, Johann Froben, Michael Furter, Michael Kesler, Johann Bergmann von Olpe, Johann

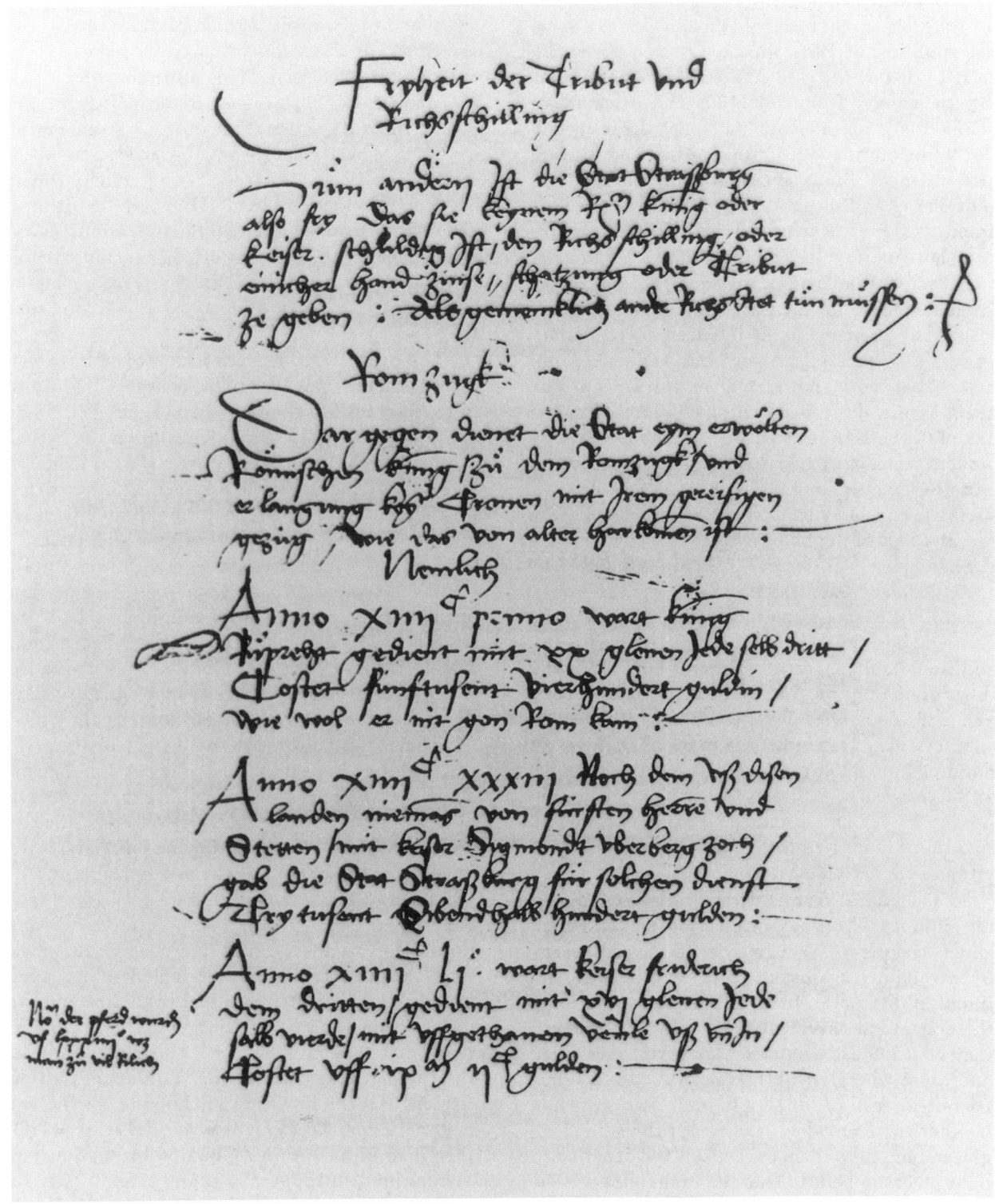

Page from the autograph manuscript for Brant's "Freiheitstafel" (Strasbourg City Archives)

Petri, Johann Wenssler, and Thomas Wolff—selecting and editing manuscripts, determining reliable texts in cases of variations, and writing introductions and dedications.

Some of Brant's early Latin and German verse was published as *Varia Sebastiani Brant Carmina* (Diverse Lyric Poems, 1498). The stiff, pretentious occasional poetry from the 1480s and early 1490s marks floods on the Rhine, a solar eclipse, a hailstorm, the coronation of Maximilian, and his capture at Bruges. Brant versifies the principles of elegant dining and those of ethical behavior. A long hymn to Mary, "Ave praeclara" (Hail, illustrious one), mirrors Heynlin's devotion to the Virgin.

Brant's scholarship, his poetry, and his indefatigable labors for the Basel publishing industry secured him renown in the intellectual community well before the publication of *Das Narrenschiff*. But it was that work that propelled him into prominence as one of the major writers of humanism and one of the best-known German writers of the early modern age. *Das Narren Schyff* was published by Johann Bergmann von Olpe in 1494. It consists of a prologue and 112 chapters, all in verse couplets. In the first half of the book each chapter begins on a left-hand page, with a three-line motto, followed by a woodcut, and the first four lines of the text proper. Most of the chapters conclude with thirty-four lines on the opposing recto; but some chapters have two additional full pages of text and conclude with thirty-four lines on the second recto. The second half of the book is less precise in its composition: the chapters vary from thirty-four to more than two hundred lines in length, and beginning with chapter 48, "Eyn gesellen schiff" (A Journeyman's Ship), the literary conceit, or sustained allegory, of a ship occurs much more frequently. Still, the work is by no means a connected narrative.

The typical chapter decries a kind of folly that the author presents as lamentably common. For example, chapter 3, "Von gytikeit" (Of Greed), begins by inveighing against the fool who lives for the things of this world. Brant attacks those who forget the ephemeral nature of the money and property they hoard, those who waste what they have saved, and those who give all their property to imagined friends instead of looking to their own salvation. Neither their so-called friends nor their heirs will give a thought to them once they have departed for their places in hell. In contrast Brant cites the wise man who knows that he should spend his time not gathering wealth but developing self-knowledge. In the closing lines the poet buttresses his argument with examples from classical antiquity before concluding with a couplet that promises degradation to those who pile up worldly goods. Many chapters feature such a movement from a prolonged—even repetitive—and bitingly sarcastic observation of contemporary life to a short contrast with the wise man and then to references to the Bible, ancient Greece and Rome, or classical mythology.

The work lacks not only a sustained narrative but also any obvious logical movement from one type of folly to another. One obvious arrangement would have been to begin with lesser vices and proceed to deadly sins. Instead, "Von gytikeit" comes between "Von guten reten" (Of Good Councilors) and "Von nuwen funden" (Of Innovations). And while chapters 102 through 112 do constitute a unit in which more-serious follies are treated, chapter 101 is titled "Von oren blosen" (Of Blowing into Ears).

The title was the poet's idea. Zeydel cites several uses in the same vein of the concepts of fool and folly before 1494, among them Nigel Wireker's *Speculum stultorum* (Mirror of Fools) from the twelfth century and John Lydgate's *Order of Fools* from the fifteenth. It cannot be determined whether Brant was familiar with his predecessors in the literature of folly, and the provenance of the ship metaphor has also proved elusive. The ship of revelers was a traditional image in Brant's part of Europe. His friend and fellow humanist Wimpfeling had presided over a meeting in Heidelberg at which a comical address was given by Jodocus Gallus from a lecture platform shaped like a ship; the address had to do with a ship that could fly through the air.

Several chapters vary so substantially from the rest that they have been made the basis of theories about the structure of the poem. In chapter 22, "Die ler der wisheit" (The Teaching of Wisdom), the allegorical Wisdom addresses humanity directly, warning against the pursuit of riches and claiming a direct relationship with God; the wise, Wisdom says, will find eternal salvation, the foolish, utter damnation. Beat Mischler argues that chapter 22 constituted the centerpiece in an original plan for a poem of forty-seven chapters but that Brant bowed to requests from the printer, Bergmann von Olpe, to lengthen the book. That theory would account for the summarizing chapter 46, "Von dem gwalt der narren" (Of the Power of Fools), and for the anagogical chapter 47, "Von dem weg der sellikeit" (On the Road of Salvation). Chapter 48, "A Journeyman's Ship," introduces a second ship of fools; the remaining chapters might have been intended as descriptions of those passengers.

The concluding unit of eleven chapters relies more heavily on the ship conceit than do the earlier ones. Most striking is chapter 103, "Vom endkrist"

(Of the Antichrist). The woodcut shows the battered hulk of the foundering ship used as a throne by the Antichrist. His crown is a winged demon. His orb is a purse; his sword is a flail. At the base of the cut Saint Peter uses his key to draw a boatload of penitent passengers to shore as, all around, fools drown in the waves.

The woodcuts for *Das Narrenschiff* were executed by several artists working in one Basel shop. Stylistic analysis has determined that Albrecht Dürer, then a journeyman learning his vocation, led the effort. Some of the illustrations represent the general message of their chapters; others are more closely related to the three-line mottoes that precede them. A few are still not completely understood. The cuts attributed to Dürer show an attention to realism and a sense of perspective associated with the developing Northern Renaissance. Some of the cuts by the other illustrators are crude by comparison.

There are several measures of the enormous success of *Das Narrenschiff*. Six authorized and seven pirated editions were printed during the poet's lifetime. During the following century and a quarter twenty-nine editions and reprints appeared. Such numbers were unheard of at the time, as was the international reception of a work from a national tradition that was virtually unknown beyond German-speaking Europe. Translations and adaptations began appearing in 1497 in most of the major European languages; Latin, Dutch, English, and Low German versions were soon available, and there were three French versions before 1500. The poem can be seen as the first international best-seller in the history of German literature, and the only such best-seller until the appearance of young Goethe's *Die Leiden des jungen Werthers* (translated as *The Sorrows of Werther*, 1779) in 1774.

Throughout the nineteenth century and until the final third of the twentieth, German scholars approached *Das Narrenschiff* with ambivalence. Proud of the work's success—and, during periods of nationalistic fervor, eager to trumpet the poem's ringing defense of Maximilian and the imperial idea—scholars nevertheless felt obliged to point out what they considered serious aesthetic deficiencies: there was no apparent organizing principle; the verse was wooden; the message was preachy. The lack of enthusiasm stemmed in part from the long-held judgment that German literature reached a low point during the fifteenth and sixteenth centuries, that Latin language literature was derivative, and that the vernacular tradition was not just unschooled but coarse. The only writings of genuine interest were religious tracts that supposedly fell outside the purview of Germanics.

Title page for Brant's edition of the works of Virgil

The scholarship of Ulrich Gaier in the mid 1960s radically altered the consensus on Brant, and particularly on *Das Narrenschiff*, by demonstrating previously neglected or undetected aesthetic systems within which the poet worked. Gaier showed that the poem is a sophisticated exercise in classical rhetoric and an attempt to rejuvenate the Roman satire of Horace and Juvenal. Since Gaier's rehabilitation of the poem as literature, Brant research has experienced a substantial surge. One product of that research, and of the rekindled interest in the literature of the fifteenth and sixteenth centuries generally, has been far greater sophistication in the analysis of audience and literary reception during the Age of Luther. Maximilian Lorenz Baeumer, for example, has demonstrated the oral nature of any literary work whose author was not content to address only the tiny community of humanists: at a time of widespread illiteracy, vernacular literature, in particular, had to be suitable for reading aloud; with its couplets, short chapters, and illustrations (the pictures were held up and shown to the audience), *Das Narrenschiff* was tailor-made for such performance. It was, therefore, able to appeal to the uneducated at the same time that it held out to the university-trained reader the attractions of classical allusions, genre experimentation, and rhetorical virtuosity.

Brant was never to repeat this simultaneous appeal to two audiences. During the rest of the 1490s he focused his energies on traditional academic pursuits, on writings that addressed his fellow intellectuals, and on his deep concerns about the health and the future of the Holy Roman Empire of the German Nation. A year after *Das Narrenschiff* appeared, Bergmann von Olpe published *De Origine et conversatione bonorum Regum: et laude Civitatis Hierosolymae: cum exhortatione eiusdem recuperandae* (On the Origin and Conversion of Good Kings and in Praise of the State of Jerusalem: With an Exhortation to Reconquer It). Written in Latin prose, the work was meant for the educated and, in particular, for the emperor. It surveys the history of Jerusalem from its founding, through the days of Christ, to the Muslim occupation. Islam is shown as the infidel enemy, hostile to all that is true and holy. The work, which incorporates references to a panoply of authorities, concludes with an address to Maximilian, calling on him to gather his princes and root out the Turks.

In 1496, when Heynlin lay dying in the monastery, the only friend allowed to attend him was Brant. After Heynlin's death Brant wrote an epigram addressed to the deceased in which the poet refers to himself as Heynlin's little son.

Humanism was a movement based on friendships; as a new and constantly evolving approach to the great questions of existence, it required the mutual support of the like-minded. Geiler von Kaisersberg was such a friend to Brant. An older student at Basel when Brant arrived, Geiler departed in 1476 and soon built a reputation as a charismatic preacher in Strasbourg. Geiler was a conservative, a defender of the prerogatives of church and empire. His homilies borrowed heavily from the sayings and the dialect of Alsace so that he could reach every member of his audience, regardless of educational attainment. In 1498–1499 he gave a long series of sermons based on chapters of *Das Narrenschiff*. That he could adapt it so readily to his purposes constitutes another testament to his friend's broad appeal.

During the later 1490s Brant undertook a series of diplomatic assignments for the bishop of Basel. In 1498 he published a collection of his lyric poems, *Varia Sebastiani Brant Carmina,* on diverse religious and nonreligious topics. Many of the poems are of mediocre quality, and none has sparked interest since the poet's death.

In 1499 Maximilian's attempt to force the Swiss cantons to join the empire went down to defeat at the Battle of Dorneck. Peace negotiations at Basel led to the dissolution of all ties and to the establishment of the independent Swiss Confederation. Brant saw the developments as a particularly grievous link in the unbroken chain of imperial decline.

Brant had maintained close friendships in Strasbourg, and his mother and several other relatives still lived there. When the post of legal adviser to the city government came open, he applied. His precise reasons for wanting to leave Basel have not been ascertained, but the city's decision to join the Swiss Confederation doubtless played a role. Geiler wrote a letter of recommendation, and the city council offered Brant the position. His duties commenced in January 1501, six months before Basel was to join the confederation. In 1503 he was promoted to the position of municipal secretary. His duties included offering legal opinions, editing the minutes of council meetings, drafting transactions and resolutions, maintaining official correspondence, and acting as municipal censor. He no longer participated in university life, and his connections with the Basel publishers suffered; but he seems to have found the move eminently satisfactory. Strasbourg was a prosperous free imperial city with an extensive hinterland, so that its role in the affairs of the southwestern empire was substantial. The council was well pleased with Brant's work and gave him several written commendations.

In 1502 Emperor Maximilian invited Brant to Innsbruck to render private opinions on matters of state. Maximilian later referred to him as the "dear, loyal Sebastian Brandt." In 1508 the emperor summoned him for advice pertaining to a dispute with the city of Venice. At least one other private audience has been documented. Brant used his status as a favorite to plead Strasbourg's case, usually with success. But he never succeeded in goading Maximilian to take up arms against the Turks.

Brant's editorial labors continued unabated in Strasbourg. A Latin edition of Boethius's *De consolatione Philosophiae* (The Consolation of Philosophy, circa 524) appeared in 1501, followed a year later by *Der heilġien leben nüw mit vil me Heilġien, und darzu der Passion* (Lives of the Saints, New and with Many More Saints, and in Addition the Passion, 1502). The latter work went through several editions. Brant also edited the works of Virgil for the Strasbourg publisher Johannes Grüninger. Brant's 1508 edition of the *Bescheidenheit* (Wisdom, circa 1215–1230) of Freidank effectively saved that thirteenth-century Swabian poet from obscurity. In its aphoristic style the work has much in common with *Das Narrenschiff*. Brant felt compelled to add supporting passages from the Bible and from classical antiquity.

Relatively soon after his return to his native city Brant wrote "Die Freiheitstafel" (The Tablets of Freedom). It is a description of the murals in a meeting room in the Strasbourg city hall. The poem's observations concerning political ethics and appurtenant virtues are delivered in fifty-three strophes.

Brant's fame meant that he risked being drawn into the disputes that periodically raged in academe. When the Freiburg professors Ulrich Zasius and Locher engaged in a bitter quarrel, Brant sided with Zasius and against his former student; but he did so in a fashion that allowed him to remain close to Locher. By 1505 Brant had learned to curb his temper.

But he occasionally had to take uncomfortable public stands. As city censor Brant banned Wimpfeling's book on education, *Diatriba,* in 1510. He found it rife with unacceptable invective against monks, especially Dominicans. Similarly, he withheld his approval for the publication of Thomas Murner's *Die Gäuchmatt* (usually translated as The Fool's Meadow, 1519). The manuscript, which had been accepted by the Strasbourg publisher Matthias Hupfuff, was found to have scurrilous references to the emperor and the Swiss.

Letters in Strasbourg were greatly cultivated by a literary society founded by Wimpfeling with the aid of Brant. It provided a forum for the discussion of new works, including unpublished manuscripts. Visiting writers were feted and sometimes boarded as members' guests. In 1514 Erasmus paid such a visit to Strasbourg and met Brant, whom he later praised in a letter to Wimpfeling.

As a staunch German patriot and a friend of Maximilian, Brant was the natural choice to represent Strasbourg in paying homage to the new emperor, Charles V, in 1520. Although he had been seriously ill the preceding year, Brant made the trip to Ghent, where he saw Erasmus again and delivered a congratulatory address to Charles. During the journey Dürer painted a portrait of Brant.

The last year of Brant's life was marked by bitterness. The lack of order in the empire that had disturbed him for so many years seemed even more apparent. The church was rife with insupportable practices, and the Turks still menaced eastern Europe. Fearing a calamity that would annihilate civilization, Brant suffered what Zeydel calls a nervous breakdown. The old man's pessimism stands in stark contrast to the optimism of the German who was then changing the very foundations of Western society, Martin Luther. By the time Brant died on 10 May 1521, the world had passed him by.

Portrait of Brant by Albrecht Dürer (1520)

Sebastian Brant's place in German literary history is guaranteed by the innovations present in *Das Narrenschiff*. Its use of the fool motif, its reliance on humor and common sense, its appeal to an audience that did not know Latin, its use of illustrations, and its appearance as a printed book available for purchase in the new publishing market made it a milestone in European letters. If his limitations mean that Brant will probably never be considered one of Germany's great writers, his one striking accomplishment is Germany's first work of modern world literature.

Bibliographies:

Joachim Knape and Dieter Wuttke, *Sebastian-Brant-Bibliographie: Forschungsliteratur von 1800 bis 1985* (Tübingen: Niemeyer, 1990);

Thomas Wilhelmi, *Sebastian Brant: Bibliographie* (Bern: Peter Lang, 1990).

Biography:

Charles Schmidt, *Histoire littéraire de l'Alsace a la fin de XVe et au commencement du XVIe siècle* (Paris: Sandoz & Fischbacher, 1879).

References:

Maximilian Lorenz Baeumer, *Die Reformation als Revolution und Aufruhr* (Frankfurt am Main & Bern: Peter Lang, 1991);

Gerhard Dünnhaupt, "Sebastian Brant: *The Ship of Fools*," in *The Renaissance and Reformation in Germany: An Introduction,* edited by Gerhart Hoffmeister (New York: Ungar, 1977), pp. 69–81;

Ulrich Gaier, *Satire: Studien zu Neidhart, Wittenwiler, Brant und zur satirischen Schreibart* (Tübingen: Niemeyer, 1967);

Gaier, *Studien zu Brants Narrenschiff* (Tübingen: Niemeyer, 1966);

William Gilbert, "Sebastian Brant: Conservative Humanist," *Archiv für Reformationsgeschichte,* 46 (1955): 145–167;

E. L. Harrison, "Virgil, Sebastian Brant, and Maximilian I," *Modern Language Review,* 76, no. 1 (1981): 99–115;

Barbara Könneker, *Sebastian Brant: Das Narrenschiff* (Munich: Oldenbourg, 1966);

Klaus Manger, *Das "Narrenschiff": Entstehung, Wirkung und Deutung* (Darmstadt: Wissenschaftliche Buchgesellschaft, 1983);

Beat Mischler, *Gliederung und Produktion des "Narrenschiffes" (1494) von Sebastian Brant* (Bonn: Bouvier, 1981);

Fr. Aurelius Pompen, *The English Versions of "The Ship of Fools": A Contribution to the History of the Early French Renaissance in England* (London: Longmans & Green, 1925);

John Van Cleve, *Sebastian Brant's "The Ship of Fools" in Critical Perspective, 1800–1991* (Columbia, S.C.: Camden House, 1993);

Friedrich Winkler, *Dürer und die Illustrationen zum Narrenschiff: Die Baseler und Straßburger Arbeiten des Künstlers und der altdeutsche Holzschnitt* (Berlin: Deutscher Verein für Kunstwissenschaft, 1951);

Edwin H. Zeydel, *Sebastian Brant* (New York: Twayne, 1967).

Papers:

Sebastian Brant's papers are at the libraries of the University of Basel and the University of Strasbourg, and in the city archives of Strasbourg.

Conrad Celtis
(1 February 1459 - 4 February 1508)

David Price
University of Texas at Austin

BOOKS: *Ars versificandi et carminum* (Leipzig: Konrad Kachelofen, circa 1486);

Proseuticum poeticum ad dei genitricem (Leipzig: Martin Landsberg, circa 1487);

Proseuticum ad Fridericum III. pro laurea apollinari (Nuremberg: Friedrich Creussner, 1487);

Epitoma in utramque Ciceronis rhetoricam cum arte memorativa nova et modo epistolandi utilissimo (Ingolstadt: Johann Kachelofen, 1492);

Panegyris ad duces Bavarie.... Oratio in gymnasio Ingolstadensi habita (Augsburg: Erhard Ratdolt, 1492);

In vitam divi Sebaldi carmen (Basel: Johann Bergmann von Olpe, circa 1494);

Ad divam dei genitricem sublevatis aegritudinibus gratiarum actio (Vienna: Johann Winterburg, 1498);

Oeconomia (Vienna: Johann Winterburg, circa 1499);

Septenaria sodalitas litteraria Germaniae (Vienna: Johann Winterburg, 1500);

Ludus Dianae (Nuremberg: Hieronymus Höltzel, 1501);

Quatuor libri amorum secundum quatuor latera Germaniæ (Nuremberg, 1502);

Divo Maximiliano Augusto Conradi Celtis ῥαπσωδια (Augsburg: Johannes Otmar, 1505);

Libri odarum quatuor, cum Epodo, et sæculari carmine, compiled by Thomas Resch, Joachim Vadianus, and others (Strasbourg: Schürer, 1513);

Fünf Bücher Epigramme von Konrad Celtes, edited by Karl Hartfelder (Berlin: Calvary, 1881; reprinted, Hildesheim: Olms, 1963);

Conrad Celtis und sein Buch über Nürnberg, edited by Albert Werminghoff (Freiburg: Julius Bolze, 1921);

Oratio in Gymnasio in Ingelstadio publice recitata, cum carminibus ad Orationem pertinentibus, edited by Hans Rupprich (Leipzig: Teubner, 1932);

Quattuor libri Amorum secundum quattuor latera Germaniae. Germania generalis, edited by Felicitas Pindter (Leipzig: Teubner, 1934);

Libri odarum quattuor. Liber epodon. Carmen saeculare, edited by Pindter (Leipzig: Teubner, 1937);

Ludi scaenici (Ludus Dianae, Rhapsodia), edited by Pindter (Leipzig: Teubner, 1945);

Conradi Celtis quae Vindobonae prelo subicienda curavit opuscula, edited by Adel (Leipzig: Teubner, 1966)–includes "Episodia sodalitatis," "Ad Divam Dei Genetricem," "Oeconomia," "De situ et moribus Germaniae," selections from "Norimberga," "Septenaria sodalitas litteraria Germaniae," and "Carmen saeculare."

Editions: "The *Ludus Dianae* of Conrad Celtis," edited by Virginia Gingerich, *Germanic Review*, 15 (1940): 159-180;

"Unbekannte Celtis-Epigramme zum Lobe Dürers," edited by Dieter Wuttke, *Zeitschrift für Kunstgeschichte*, 30 (1967): 321-325.

Editions in English: *Selections from Conrad Celtis, 1459-1508*, edited and translated by Leonard Forster (Cambridge: Cambridge University Press, 1948);

An Anthology of Neo-Latin Poetry, edited and translated by Fred J. Nichols (New Haven: Yale University Press, 1979), pp. 436-461.

OTHER: Seneca, *Lucy anei senece cordubensis hercules furens tragoedia prima incipit, etc.*, edited by Celtis (N.p., after 13 February 1487)–comprises *Hercules furens* and *Thyestis*;

Apuleius, *Lucij Apulei Platonici et Aristotelici philosophi epitoma divinum de mundo seu cosmographia ductu Conradi Celtis*, edited by Celtis (Vienna: Winterburg, circa 1497);

Tacitus, *Cornelii Taciti de origine et situ Germanorum liber*, edited by Celtis (N.p., circa 1500);

Nicholas of Cusa, *Propositiones domini cardinalis Nicolai Cuse de Li non aliud*, edited by Celtis (Vienna: Winterburg, circa 1500-1501)–includes "Carmen saeculare," by Celtis;

Hrotsvit of Gandersheim, *Opera Roswithae illustris virginis et monialis Germaniae, gente Saxonica ortae, nvper a Conrado Celte inventa*, edited by

Conrad Celtis presenting his edition of the works of Hrotsvit of Gandersheim to Elector Friedrich of Saxony. This woodcut, which is attributed to Albrecht Dürer, was published in that book.

Celtis (Nuremberg: Hieronymus Höltzel, 1501).

On 18 April 1487 Emperor Friedrich III crowned Conrad Celtis *poeta laureatus,* making him the first German to receive the distinction so coveted by humanists. David Friedrich Strauß designated him the *Erzhumanist* (archhumanist), an enduring sobriquet that conveys both Celtis's role as harbinger of and his dedication to the humanist movement. He devoted his life entirely to the cause of spreading humanist studies in Germany and, most important, to writing humanist poetry.

Celtis's birth date, 1 February 1459, is known from his elegy Amores 1.1, in *Quatuor libri amorum* (Four Books of Amores, 1502); otherwise, little can be said with confidence about the circumstances of his birth and youth. He seems to have been born in Wipfeld, a small village in the vicinity of Würzburg. That origin would accord with his frequent self-characterization as a Franconian. Early sources record that he had his first training in Latin from an older brother who had taken holy orders. The *Vita* published posthumously with his *Odes* in 1513 claims that his father was a vintner who was opposed to his study of letters and that Celtis had to run away from home, floating down the Main River on a raft, to enroll at the University of Cologne. Dieter Wuttke, however, doubts that Celtis's break with his family was that drastic. For example, in 1482, before he had had significant employment, he possessed the means to engage a Greek student as his personal secretary.

The name Celtés (which is sometimes spelled *Celtes*) is a Latin translation of the German *Pickel,* a small hoe used especially by vintners. Matriculation records at the University of Cologne list him as both Pyckell and Bickel. He later added a Greek equivalent for *Pickel,* which created a Roman-sounding tripartite name: Conradus Celtis Protucius. His device included the letters *CCPP,* which stood for "Conradus Celtis Protucius Poeta," arranged as a ligature on an escutcheon with three stars. His motto was "παρεστο φρονησις" (May prudence be present).

The matriculation register places Celtis at the University of Cologne between 14 October 1478 and 1 December 1479, the latter being the date he received the B.A. He then began the curriculum in theology, although he ceased those studies around 1480 or 1481 without taking a degree. His later writings—particularly Ode 3.21, to Wilhelm Mommerloch—reveal mixed feelings about the university. He expresses respect for the grand tradition of theological and philosophical studies at Cologne (especially the works of Albertus Magnus) but objects to the dominance of scholasticism and, above all, the absence of humanist studies.

After several journeys, one of which involved an extended stay at the court of King Matthias Corvinus in Budapest, he continued his studies in Heidelberg. University records indicate that he was there at least from 13 December 1484 until 20 October 1485. Heidelberg was known in 1484 as a university that was receptive to humanist studies. Rudolf Agricola, widely considered one of the most accomplished northern humanists of his generation, had recently gone there, drawn by Johann Dalberg, Bishop of Worms, and Elector Philipp of the Palatinate, both of whom encouraged humanist learning. It was almost certainly Agricola's presence that attracted Celtis. Celtis later claimed that he learned the rudiments of Hebrew and Greek under Agricola's tutelage, but it is unlikely that he did so because Agricola, who died on 27 October 1485, was not in residence at Heidelberg for much of Celtis's tenure there. Furthermore, Celtis's knowledge of Hebrew was negligible, although he occasionally used a Hebrew flourish in his writings (usually nothing more than the title of a book of the Hebrew Bible). Celtis eventually acquired an adequate command of Greek, and a distinctive element of his future peregrinations would be the encouragement of Greek studies at several universities.

After receiving the M.A.–the usual terminal degree for a professor of the arts–in October 1485, Celtis taught in Erfurt, Rostock, and Leipzig. His first publications were textbooks for his courses. *Ars versificandi et carminum* (The Art of Versification and of Poems) was published for a poetics course at the University of Leipzig, probably in 1486. The work, which is mostly a list of technical terms in prosody and a series of metrical schemes, includes an often-cited passage outlining the remarkably broad domain Celtis accorded poetry: it is the *officium* (duty) of poetry to represent "customs, deeds, accomplishments, places, peoples, lands, rivers, courses of stars, the nature of things, and the emotions of minds and souls." In accordance with this statement of purpose, history, geography, and scientific-philosophical topics were prominent in his verse, even though he is now remembered principally as a poet of love. The *Ars versificandi* also includes, as its last item, Celtis's sapphic poem "Ad Apollinem" (To Apollo). The hymn urges the god, as an allegory for classical culture, to leave Italy for Germany to propagate the humanist style of poetry: "Sic velis nostras rogitamus oras / Italas ceu quondam aditare terras; / Barbarus sermo fugiatque, ut atrum / Subruat omne" (Thus we beseech you / That you might wish to come to our shores, as you once went to Italy; / And that barbarian speech be put to flight and / All darkness be swept away). In a slightly revised form the poem was republished as "Ode 4.5." He also published for his courses an edition of Seneca's *Hercules furens* and *Thyestes* in 1487.

In 1487 Celtis was crowned poet laureate at Nuremberg. The honor seems to have intensified his interest in Horace, the Roman poet who created the concept of the poet crowned with laurel. Immediately after his coronation Celtis published *Proseuticum ad Fridericum III* (The Request to Friedrich III), which describes the ceremony and in-

Celtis presenting his Quatuor libri amorum *to Emperor Maximilian I. The woodcut, attributed to Albrecht Dürer, appears in that book.*

cludes several panegyric odes to the emperor. Celtis composed two odes for this work based on Horace's *Odes* 1.1 and 1.2 and an epode loosely based, according to Eckart Schäfer, on Horace's *Epode* 1. Later Celtis would structure some of his poetry collections to correspond to Horace's oeuvre. Like Horace, he organized four books of odes and one of epodes, and he wrote "Carmen saeculare" (Poem for the Seculum), on the putative dawn of a new age–Celtis's was a commemoration of the year 1500, Horace's of the Augustan era. While Celtis is probably mostly responsible for the final organization of his odes, they–along with the epodes and "Carmen saeculare"–were not published until 1513, after his death.

The coronation also marks the beginning of what Celtis called his *decennalis peregrinatio* (ten years of wandering). Before undertaking a trip through Italy, he appears to have returned briefly to Leipzig, where he was publicly criticized for plagiarism. The most egregious case was his publication of a poem, "Virgo, decus caeli" (The Virgin, the Glory of Heaven), by Gregorius Tyfernas, without any credit given the author, in an anthology of four poems to Mary titled *Proseuticum poeticum ad dei genitricem* (Poetic Entreaty to the Mother of God, circa 1487). The scandal would be remembered at least once later in his career, but it did no real damage to his reputation in Germany.

In Italy, Celtis visited the important humanist centers of Venice, Padua, Bologna, Florence, and Rome. He would remain in contact with several Italian humanists throughout his life—most notably with the scholar-printer Aldus Manutius. He was involved in unsuccessful plans to support a move of the Aldine press to Vienna, and he tried unsuccessfully to have his own Greek grammar published by Aldus. (It never was published, but it survives in a manuscript in Nuremberg.) While in Italy he is known to have studied under or associated with Marcus Sambellicus, Baptista Guarinus, Philippus Beroaldus the Elder, Marsilio Ficino, and Pomponius Laetus. Laetus or Ficino may have been the inspiration for his *sodalitates*, the literary-scholarly societies he would subsequently establish in the north. Ficino was unquestionably an important source for Celtis's Neoplatonism, which, in turn, informed the philosophical outlook of the sodalities. Celtis often expressed an interest in astrology and, in particular, in Pythagorean numerology, subjects he would have explored in Italy.

In his writings Celtis tended to complain about Italy, but his attitude may indicate only that the Italians were not as impressed with him as his fellow Germans had been. Several epigrams record Celtis's displeasure with Italy. Perhaps the best known is Epigram 3.40, "De puella Romae reperta" (Concerning a Girl Found at Rome), which claims, somewhat predictably, that if an ancient girl were to be resurrected to the present day, she would be unable to see anything of Rome's past grandeur and piety. Celtis's German patriotism and support of the House of Habsburg lie at the core of Epigram 2.48, "De osculo Caesaris et Papae" (Concerning the Kiss of the Emperor and of the Pope), on an audience (perhaps fictional) with Pope Innocent VIII:

> Cum dederas, Caesar Friderice, coronam,
>   Figebas nostris oscula blanda genis.
> Ast ego dum Romae vidissem tecta Nocentis,
>   Oscula ferre suo iusserat ille pedi.
> Oscula prona dedi, sed me mage Caesaris ora
>   Delectant, nocuo quam dare labra pedi.

(Emperor Friedrich, when you gave me the sacred crown, you placed a gentle kiss on my cheeks. But when I visited the palace of Pope Nocent at Rome, he ordered me to kiss his foot. I gave the kiss, bent down, but the emperor's lips delight me more than kissing that nocent foot.)

After roughly two years in Italy, Celtis moved on to Poland. There he continued his studies at the University of Kraków from 1489 to 1491, mainly under the astronomer Albert Brudzewski. He also taught courses in Aristotelian philosophy and letter writing. Among his most important students was Laurentius Corvinus, who was to organize some of the earliest productions of Roman drama in the Holy Roman Empire (an exercise Celtis himself would later conduct in Vienna). He visited Prussia, and after his stay in Kraków he spent time in Breslau (today Wrocław, Poland) and Prague.

It is likely that Celtis's ideas about poetry and humanist studies crystallized during this time. Kraków is the principal setting for his first book of *Amores*, in which many of the poems are addressed to a woman named Hasilina. Also, his mathematical and astronomical studies, however thin his knowledge in these areas may have been, bespeak the polymathic goals he connected to humanist literary-cultural studies.

Celtis's experiences in eastern Europe formed the topic of the first book of *Amores* and also served as an organizing principle for the first book of odes that he was planning to publish. According to his account in Amores 1.3, he received his poetic mission when, in a manner reminiscent of Saint Paul's conversion, he was thrown from his horse as he approached Kraków during a storm. But it was a pagan god, Apollo, who revived Celtis from apparent death:

> "Surge!"—ait,—"et priscum capiant tua membra vigorem,
>   Ut patriae fines quattuor ipse canas,
> Turgidus Eois quam claudit Vistula ab oris,
>   Sed latus austrinum maximus Hister habet,
> Rhenus ab occiduis limes sed dicitur oris
>   Et boreae partem gens Codonea tenet.
> Hinc quicquid mediis Germania continet oris,
>   Carmine Phoebeo nota sub orbe dabis.
> Sed patiens varias tolerabis, Celtis, aerumnas,
>   Orbe decennalis dum peregrinus eris."

(He [Apollo] said: "Rise! And may your limbs receive their old vigor so that you can sing of the four regions of your country, which the swollen Vistula closes from the eastern lands; but the great Danube holds the southwest side; the Rhine is called the border on the west; and the

Septenaria sodalitas Litteraria Germanie

Septem castrensis Danubianus

Si clara grecie recenseo lumina
Erraticos septem globos vincencia
Vicinitatis rite munus exequor
Seruant eoas gratus et gete plagas
Qua pontico septem hostijs hister mari
Illabitur septemplici haud nilo minor
Hinc nomen est septem datum castrensibus

Dantiscanus Vistulanus

Vnita septem est Rhoma collibus sacris
Quos inter edibus superbis arduus
Suum potens tarpeius extulit caput
Musis palatinus sacer: cauum incolunt
Aues auentinum: cupido celium
Sed exquilinus et quirinalis pium
Iouem vident in viminalis vertice

Pomeranus Codoneus

Metropolitanas ferox alemania
Vrbes habet septem vt domus thomulea
In collibus septena templa condidit
Treueris vetusta et dicior colonia
Et saxonum terris madeburgum nobile
Et littorales arcticum prope circulum
Premensis et rigensis vrbs sauromatum

Albinus Luneburganus

Superba cecropis bifrontis patria
Fecunda que artis edidit septem sacras
Septem sophie gloriatur lumina
Habete: quis septena mundi triplicis
Stupenda cedant plurimum miracula

Page from the poem in which Celtis outlined his idea of establishing seven sodalities, or literary societies, throughout Germany. He founded two such societies and inspired the formation of several others (courtesy of the Lilly Library, Indiana University).

Woodcut Sterbebild *(death picture) of Celtis executed by Hans Burgkmaier in 1507, the year before the poet's death*

Baltic people hold the northern part. Then, whatever Germany contains in the middle, you will celebrate in song under Apollo's orb. But Celtis, you will suffer and endure much hardship while you travel across the orb for ten years.")

This poem more or less describes the organization of his four books of *Amores*, each of which combines amatory poems about a woman from an area of Germany with other poems about the area or about Celtis's experiences there. By the time Celtis published the *Amores* in 1502 he had complicated the scheme by adding to each section a stage of life; for example, he called the first book "Liber I. qui Hasilina vel pubertas vel vistula et latus Germaniae orientale inscribitur" (The First Book, Which Is Entitled Hasilina, or Puberty, or the Vistula, or the Eastern Border of Germany). The women of the other books are Elsula of Regensburg, Ursula of Mainz, and Barbara of Lübeck.

Because of the presumed immediacy of the poetry, scholars have accepted Celtis's account of his experiences with Hasilina as autobiographical.

This limitation of real experience to the Hasilina poems is odd, however, because all of the love poems are written as if expressing actual events and emotions of people; Elsula is even said to have died in an outbreak of plague. The poetry about Hasilina, furthermore, is no less conventional and no more original than that about the other lovers. Celtis did, however, include a letter purporting to be from Hasilina in a collection of letters he was probably compiling for publication. Ursula Hess has shown that it cannot possibly be an authentic letter by a woman of the Polish nobility. She also notes that the name Hasilina means little more than "darling" and was never used in Czech (the language of the letter and the language used in court circles at Kraków) as an actual name. Moreover, Hasilina's full name, Hasilina z Rzytonic a na Kepsstaynie, may sound aristocratic but is, according to Hess, a sophomorically obscene designation for genitalia. Celtis dated the bogus letter as having been written in 1500, before the publication of the *Amores;* but the letter is a complaint from Hasilina about a reading of one of his poems about her at an inn in Kraków. Celtis's humor, then, derives from the very idea of fictionality, since the letter shows how a woman could be compromised by the imminent publication of his poetry.

After returning to Germany, Celtis resided at first in Nuremberg, where he knew several prominent residents: Sebald Schreyer, Willibald Pirckheimer, Caritas Pirckheimer, and Albrecht Dürer. An attempt was made to have him appointed to the faculty of a proposed humanist school there, but without success. He would return to the city often in later years, and he actively tried to curry favor with the city council by writing an encomiastic description of the city, "Norimberga," which would be published in 1502 in *Quatuor libri amorum*. In 1494 he published a poetic tribute to Saint Sebald, the patron saint of the city; and he seems to have been engaged to revise Hartmann Schedel's *Weltchronik* (1493), customarily known in English as the *Nuremberg Chronicle*. The revision, however, was never carried out.

At the end of 1491 Celtis was in Ingolstadt, where he received a special appointment from Duke George of Bavaria-Landshut to lecture on poetry. In gratitude for his new position he published "Panegyris ad duces Bavarae" (Panegyric to the Dukes of Bavaria) together with his "Oratio in gymnasio Ingolstadensi habita" (Inaugural Address at the University of Ingolstadt) as *Panegyris ad duces Bavarie . . . Oratio in gymnasio Ingol-*

stadensi habita in 1492; the panegyric is yet another endorsement of humanist studies. In his biography of Celtis, Lewis W. Spitz generously says that "the *Oratio*, too, makes a studied effort, and a successful one, to avoid any logical structure or ordered reasoning" as a stylistic counterpoint to syllogistic writing. The appearance of a casual organization was also a stylistic goal in Celtis's elegies, although the disorder and especially the repetitiveness of the inaugural address are glaring. Celtis's speech is effective, however, because of its enthusiasm. To convince Germans to embrace humanist studies he praises Germany for its intellectual past and vividly portrays the arrogance of Italian humanism, which tended to scorn the accomplishments of the northerners. More important, Celtis stresses the usefulness of humanist studies for government, claiming that civilizations are controlled "linguae viribus" (by the power of language). He proposes the study of "philosophia," by which he means universal knowledge, and of "eloquentia," meaning rhetoric. The speech has a strongly polemical quality: it rudely dismisses Scholasticism and, most emphatically, the use of nonhumanist Latin. The modesty topos of the proem, in which Celtis speaks of the limitations of his Latin style, hardly diminishes the force of his critique of university studies. This combativeness is typical of early humanists, though it is especially pronounced in Celtis. The published version of the speech included an ode, "Ad Sigismundum Fusilium, de his quod futurus philosophus scire debeat" (To Sigmund Fusilius, on Those Things the Future Philosopher Ought to Know).

Celtis posted an invitation to students to attend his lectures at Ingolstadt, the wording of which would not have fostered good relations with his colleagues: "quosdam audimus incontinue et insuaviter pariter omnem artem et dicendi legem cathedris velut anseres instrepere" (we hear certain ones who squawk like geese from the lecterns without fluency or elegance against all art and law of speech). One of the courses announced would probably have used his recently published *Epitoma in utramque Ciceronis rhetoricam* (An Epitome of Each Rhetoric by Cicero, 1492), an epitome of the anonymous *Rhetorica ad Herennium* (The Rhetoric to Herennius), then thought to be a work by Cicero, and of Cicero's *De inventione*. *Epitoma in utramque Ciceronis rhetoricam* included the first edition of his frequently republished tract on letter writing, which contains a model love letter addressed to a woman named Hasilina.

Celtis's memorial tablet in the Saint Stephen's Cathedral, Vienna

Celtis's appointment at Ingolstadt was for a half year. He then held a rectorship at the cathedral school in Regensburg in the winter of 1492–1493. During his tenure at Regensburg he discovered in the library of the Saint Emmeran monastery a manuscript (now in the Bavarian State Library) of the works of the tenth-century canoness Hrotsvit of Gandersheim. Celtis was permitted to take the manuscript from the monastery (he seems never to have returned it), and he circulated it among some colleagues throughout Germany before publishing it in 1501 in a sumptuous edition with woodcuts attributed to Dürer and epigrams by members of the Rhenish Sodality. He dedicated the volume to the elector Friedrich III of Saxony; Hrotsvit had been a Saxon with close ties to the Ottonian court. Hrotsvit's works, especially her dramas, were something of an answer to Celtis's patriotic prayers because he was able to hold them up to Italian humanists as an example of a rich Latin liter-

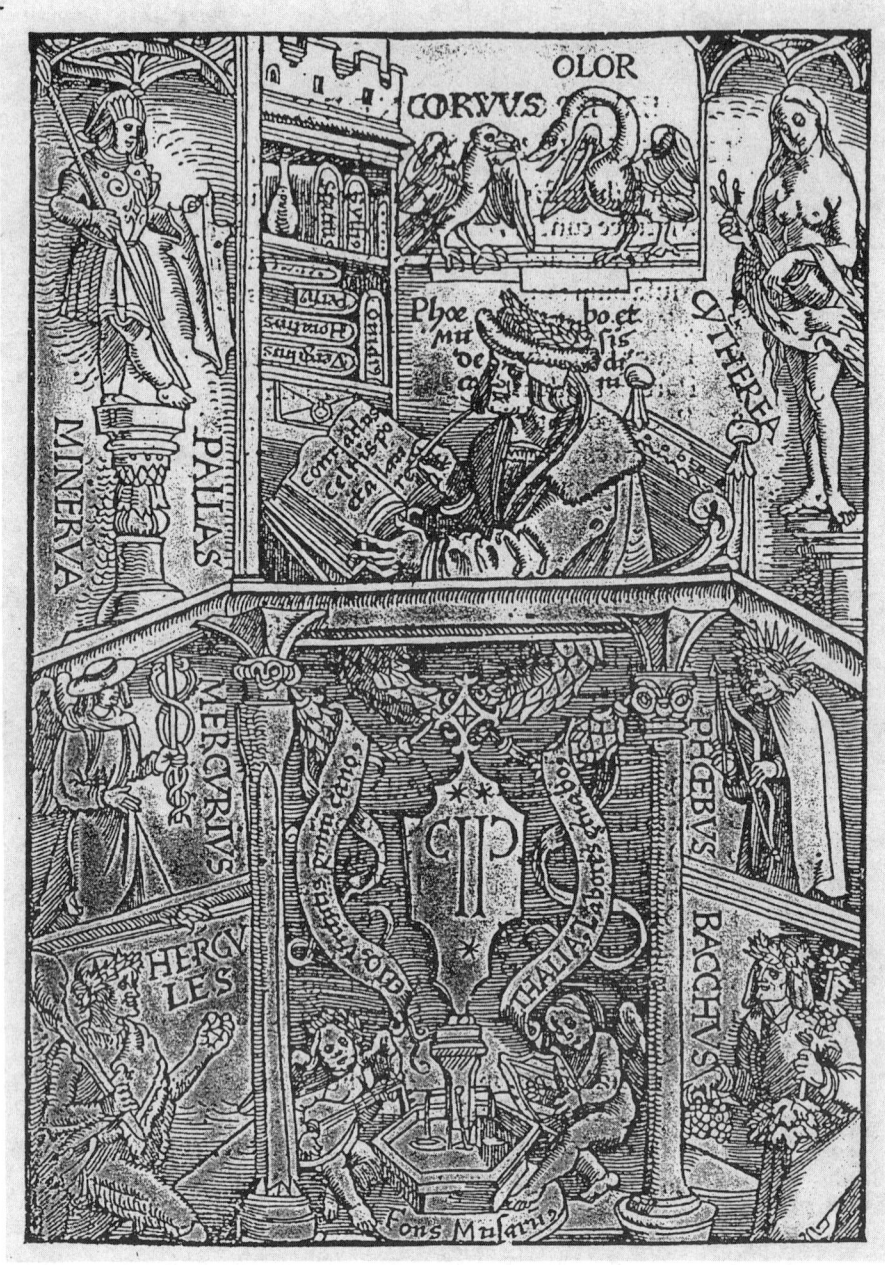

Woodcut, attributed to Hans Baldung Grien, showing Celtis writing. The illustration appears in the posthumous edition of Celtis's odes, epodes, and "Carmen saeculare."

ary history in Germany. (One of the strangest episodes in the scholarly reception of Celtis's works was the unsuccessful attempt by Joseph Aschbach to prove that Celtis fabricated Hrotsvit and composed the works himself.) In the monastery at Ebrach, Celtis discovered Gunther of Pairis's twelfth-century work *Ligurinus,* an epic tribute to Friedrich Barbarossa. He wanted to publish this work, too, as a document of German literary culture; the Sodality of Augsburg, under the direction of Conrad Peutinger, finally published it in 1507. Celtis also turned up the only Roman road map known to have survived; it is now referred to as the *Tabula Peutingeriana* because Celtis bequeathed it to Peutinger. He almost certainly "borrowed" it from a monastery library.

In 1494, following the resignation of Johannes Riedner, a professor of the arts whom Celtis had often called incompetent, Celtis was appointed to a regular faculty position at Ingolstadt. He traveled often during his tenure there—an indication, perhaps, that he was looking for a position elsewhere. (He would later mock the residents of Ingolstadt as beer-swilling beet eaters.) An outbreak of plague that closed the university in the summer semester of 1495 gave him the opportunity for a lengthy residence in Heidelberg, where he served as tutor to the children of Elector Philipp.

During his stay at Heidelberg he founded the Sodalitas Rhenana (Rhenish Sodality), the most successful literary society he was to establish. With his considerable prestige he was able to attract to the society many intellectual luminaries, the most prominent of whom were Johannes Reuchlin, Bishop Johann von Dalberg, and Abbot Trithemius of Sponheim. The sodality was loosely organized, with no known membership requirements, and included members from beyond the borders of the Palatinate. Dalberg was designated its leader, which certainly contributed to the sodality's success. According to Celtis's enthusiastic accounts, members were to be committed to the study of the three sacred languages—Latin, Greek, and Hebrew—and to philosophy, principally Neoplatonism. With the exception of Reuchlin, none of the members achieved the ideal of trilingualism; most hardly knew any Greek at this time, let alone Hebrew.

In 1497 Maximilian I, an important patron of humanism, approved a special appointment for Celtis at the University of Vienna. A charter from Maximilian, dated 31 October 1501, established in Vienna the Collegium Poetarum et Mathematicorum, a small humanist institute to be directed by Celtis. Celtis's teaching and publications were diverse, ranging from the usual humanist fare of poetry and rhetoric to more-distinctive topics, such as editions of Apuleius's Latin version of the pseudo-Aristotelian *De mundo* (On the World, circa 1497), of Tacitus's *Germania* (circa 1500), and of the twenty propositions of Nicholas of Cusa's *De non aliud* (Concerning the Not-Other, circa 1500–1501). Celtis rarely published only a single work in a volume. The edition of Tacitus includes two geographical works by Celtis: "De situ et moribus Germaniae" (Geography and Customs of Germany), a set of seven poems praising Germany; and an extract from "Norimberga," his prose tribute to Nuremberg, which was intended, in part, as an example of what he wanted to accomplish in a monumental "Germania illustrata," a project he often discussed but never finished. The Nicholas of Cusa volume includes the first edition of Celtis's "Carmen saeculare," an astrological plea for the good fortune of Germany in the new age that would begin with the turn of the century. The poem ends with a reference to God that is striking for its ambiguity: "Quisquis es, curas habeas benignas / Rebus Alemanis! tibi multa fumant / Templa per urbes" (Whoever you are, grant favor to the endeavors of Germany! Many temples throughout our cities burn offerings for you).

Celtis had established the Sodalitas Danubiana (Danube Sodality) on his arrival in Vienna. The *Episodia,* a set of epigrammatic tributes to Celtis by the members of the sodality, indicates that the *princeps* (leader) of the society was Johannes Vitez, bishop of Veszprim, and that the society included diverse and well-respected scholars. The Rhenish and Danube sodalities inspired the formation of groups elsewhere, including Augsburg, Leipzig, Linz, and Strasbourg. Celtis indicates in *Epigrams* 1.1 that he hoped to organize humanists into four regional sodalities, although his poem *Septenaria sodalitas litteraria Germaniae* (The Seven-Part Literary Society of Germany, 1500) sets the ideal number at seven. There are also references—for example in the edition of Hrotsvit's works—to a single sodality of German humanists as an ideal.

Celtis repeatedly published tributes to Maximilian. In 1502 the first edition of the *Amores* included an extravagant dedication to the emperor. More significantly, Celtis wrote two dramas, *Ludus Dianae* (Play of Diana, 1501) and ῥαπσωδια (Rhapsody, 1505), for celebrations at the imperial court. Celtis was familiar with Roman drama—in addition to his edition of Seneca's plays, he produced Terence's *Eunuchus* and Plautus's *Aulularia* in the winter semester of 1502–1503—but the lack of plot in his own works makes them starkly different from those of the ancients. *Ludus Dianae* is a series of panegyrics to Maximilian and, especially in the first act, to his second wife, Maria Bianca Sforza. In addition to five acts with speeches of praise, the play includes four polyphonic odes as interludes. ῥαπσωδια, first performed by students at the Collegium Poetarum et Mathematicorum in 1504, celebrates Maximilian's victory over Bohemian troops at the Battle of Wenzenbach during the Bavarian War of Succession. The play includes a series of tributes to the emperor from the nine Muses. Each play also portrays the crowning of a poet laureate by the emperor. It is not possible to identify the source of the music for the plays, although it was a crucial aspect of the courtly entertainment. An accomplished musician, Celtis always stressed the importance of music for poetry. Under his direction Petrus Tritonius published music for twenty-two meters, especially those used by Horace and Celtis, in a work titled *Melopoiae* (1507). Celtis instructed his students to sing Horatian odes in different melodies for the different strophic schemes.

Though he continued to be remarkably productive as a poet and scholar, Celtis suffered from premature aging and general physical deterioration during the final decade of his life. He was one of the first Germans to fall victim to syphilis, with his earliest outbreak occurring around 1495 and a serious episode following in 1498. When the disease went into remission he proclaimed himself cured and, in accordance with a vow, made a pilgrimage to the shrine of the Holy Virgin at Altötting, Bavaria, in thanksgiving. He published *Ad divam dei genitricem* (To the Holy Mother of God, 1498), a collection of four poems, to commemorate the pilgrimage.

Celtis died on 4 February 1508. He wrote an epitaph for himself that includes the assurance of a humanist kind of immortality: "Mortuus ille quidem, sed longum vivus in aevum / Colloquitur doctis per sua scripta viris" (He is, it is true, dead, but living into an advanced age he speaks to learned people through his writings). After a funeral procession of members of the university he was laid to rest in Saint Stephen's Cathedral in Vienna, where a memorial tablet commemorates him, more conventionally, with an image of the cross and the word *vivo,* indicating his eternal life in Christ.

Celtis's will requested that Peutinger supervise the editing of the works that Celtis had not managed to have printed during his lifetime, but for unknown reasons Peutinger did not publish any of Celtis's works. In 1513 several of Celtis's students and followers, including Thomas Resch and Joachim Vadianus, edited and published in one volume four books of his odes, one book of epodes, and the "Carmen saeculare." Many of the poems had already appeared in print, although it is clear that Celtis had planned to shape the odes into a collection similar to the amores. This edition includes the first biography of Celtis, "Conradi Celtis per sodalitatem litterariam Rhenanam vita" (The Life of Conrad Celtis, by the Rhenish Sodality). A surviving manuscript shows that Celtis had been compiling a collection of his epigrams; he had completed four books and begun a fifth. Like the poems, many of the epigrams had been published during his lifetime. Celtis's compilation was not published until 1881, when it was edited by Karl Hartfelder; this edition, however, adds many pieces that are not in Celtis's manuscript.

Celtis's fame was considerable throughout the sixteenth century, but his works did not exert much influence on other poets. Similarly, the blossoming of German poetry in the seventeenth century, which owed much to humanist Latin poetry, did not use Celtis as a direct source. Modern scholarship has focused on him to a greater extent than on any other Latin poet of his generation, but it has been concerned primarily with his position in the history of humanism in Germany; analysis of his poetry has been neglected in favor of biographical and historical studies.

Letters:

Der Briefwechsel des Konrad Celtis, edited by Hans Rupprich (Munich: Beck, 1934).

Bibliographies:

Der Gesamtkatalog der Wiegendrucke, edited by the Kommission für den Gesamtkatalog der Wiegendrucke, volume 6 (Stuttgart: Hiersemann, 1968), entries 6460-6470;

Verzeichnis der im deutschen Sprachbereich erschienenen Drucke des XVI. Jahrhunderts, edited by the Bavarian State Library in Munich, volume 4 (Stuttgart: Hiersemann, 1985), entries C-1897-1935.

Biographies:

Harald Drewinc, *Vier Gestalten aus dem Zeitalter des Humanismus* (Saint Gall: Zollikofer, 1946);

Lewis Spitz, *Conrad Celtis: The German Arch-Humanist* (Cambridge, Mass.: Harvard University Press, 1957);

Dieter Wuttke, "Conradus Celtis Protucius," in *Deutsche Dichter der frühen Neuzeit,* edited by Stephan Füssel (Berlin: Erich Schmidt, 1993), pp. 173-199.

References:

Klaus Arnold, "Konrad Celtis und sein Buch über Nürnberg," in *Acta Conventus Neolatini Guelpherbytani 1985,* edited by Stella Revard, Fidel Rädle, and Mario Di Cesare (Binghamton, N.Y.: Medieval and Renaissance Texts and Studies, 1988), pp. 7-15;

Joseph Aschbach, *Roswitha und Conrad Celtis,* second edition (Vienna: Braumüller, 1868);

Gedeon Borsa, "Drei weitere unbekannte Einblattdrucke aus dem XV. Jahrhundert in der österreichischen Nationalbibliothek," *Gutenberg Jahrbuch* (1960): 55-61;

Theodor Geiger, *Conrad Celtis in seinen Beziehungen zur Geographie* (Munich: Wolf, 1896);

Günter Hess, "Von der Kunst zu überleben: Die Scheltrede des Conrad Celtis an den Rat von Nürnberg," in *Handbuch der Literatur in Bayern,* edited by Albrecht Weber (Regensburg: Pustet, 1987), pp. 163-174;

Ursula Hess, "Erfundene Wahrheit: Autobiographie und literarische Rolle bei Conrad Celtis," in *Bildungsexklusivität und volksprachliche Literatur: Literatur vor Lessing–nur für Experten?,* edited by Klaus Grubmüller und Günter Hess (Tübingen: Niemeyer, 1986), pp. 136-147;

Jürgen Leonardt, "Niccolo Perotti und die *Ars versificandi* von Conrad Celtis," *Humanistica Lovaniensia,* 30 (1981): 13-18;

Felicitas Pindter, "Die Lyrik des Conrad Celtis," dissertation, University of Vienna, 1930;

Karl Leopold Preiss, "Konrad Celtis und der italienische Humanismus," dissertation, University of Vienna, 1952;

David Price, "Desiring the Barbarian: Latin, German and Women in the Poetry of Conrad Celtis," *German Quarterly,* 65 (1992): 159-167;

Jacques Ridé, "Un grand projet patriotique 'Germania illustrata,'" in *Humanisme allemand 1480-1540* (Munich: Fink / Paris: Vrin, 1979), pp. 99-112;

Lawrence Ryan, "Conrad Celtis and the Mystique of Number," in *From Wolfram and Petrarch to Goethe and Grass: Studies in Literature in Honour of Leonard Forster,* edited by D. H. Green, L. P. Johnson, and Dieter Wuttke (Baden-Baden: Koerner, 1982), pp. 181-192;

Ryan, "Conrad Celtis' *Carmen saeculare:* Ode for a New German Age," in *Acta Conventus Neo-Latini Bononiensis 1979,* edited by R. J. Schoeck (Binghamton, N.Y.: Medieval and Renaissance Texts and Studies, 1985), pp. 592-606;

Eckart Schäfer, "Conrad Celtis' Ode an Apoll," in *Gedichte und Interpretationen,* edited by Volker Meid (Stuttgart: Reclam, 1982), pp. 81-93;

Schäfer, *Deutscher Horaz: Conrad Celtis, Georg Fabricius, Paul Melissus, Jacob Balde: Die Nachwirkungen des Horaz in der neulateinischen Dichtung Deutschlands* (Wiesbaden: Steiner, 1976), pp. 1-38;

Lewis W. Spitz, *The Religious Renaissance of the German Humanists* (Cambridge, Mass.: Harvard University Press, 1963), pp. 81-109;

Stephen Wailes, "The Literary Relationship of Conrad Celtis and Caritas Pirckheimer," *Daphnis: Zeitschrift für Mittlere Deutsche Literatur,* 17 (1988): 423-440;

Franz Josef Worstbrock, "Die *Ars versificandi et carminum* des Konrad Celtis," in *Studien zum städtischen Bildungswesen des späten Mittelalters und der frühen Neuzeit,* edited by Bernd Moeller, Hans Patze, and Karl Stackmann (Göttingen: Vandenhoeck & Ruprecht, 1983), pp. 462-498;

Worstbrock, "Die Brieflehre des Conrad Celtis: Textgeschichte und Autorschaft," in *Philologie als Kulturwissenschaft: Studien zur Literatur und Geschichte des Mittelalters,* edited by Ludger Grenzmann, Hubert Herkommer, and Dieter Wuttke (Göttingen: Vandenhoeck & Ruprecht, 1987), pp. 242-269;

Dieter Wuttke, "Dürer und Celtis: Von der Bedeutung des Jahres 1500 für den deutschen Humanismus: Jahrhundertfeier als symbolische Form," *Journal of Medieval and Renaissance Studies,* 10 (1980): 72-129;

Wuttke, "Textkritisches Supplement zu Hartfelders Edition der Celtis-Epigramme," in *Renatae litterae: Studien zum Nachleben der Antike und zur europäischen Renaissance,* edited by Klaus Heitmann and Eckhart Schroeder (Frankfurt am Main: Athenaeum, 1973), pp. 105-130;

Wuttke, "Zur griechischen Grammatik des Konrad Celtis," in *Silvae: Festschrift für Ernst Zinn zum 60. Geburtstag,* edited by Michael von Albrecht and Eberhard Heck (Tübingen: Niemeyer, 1970), pp. 289-303.

Albrecht Dürer
(21 May 1471 – 6 April 1528)

David Price
University of Texas at Austin

BOOKS: *VNderweysung der messung, mit dem zirckel vnd richtscheyt, in Linien ebnen vnnd gantzen corporen* (Nuremberg: Printed by Hieronymus Formschneider, 1525; enlarged, 1538); translated by Walter L. Strauss as *The Painter's Manual: A Manual of Measurement of Lines, Areas, and Solids by Means of Compass and Rule* (New York: Abaris, 1977);

Etliche vnderricht, zu befestigung der Stett, Schlosz, vnd flecken (Nuremberg: Hieronymus Formschneider, 1527);

HIerinn sind begriffen vier Bücher von menschlicher Proportion (Nuremberg: Hieronymus Formschneider, 1528);

Dürer: Schriftlicher Nachlaß, 3 volumes, edited by Hans Rupprich (Berlin: Deutscher Verein für Kunstwissenschaft, 1956–1969).

Editions: *Vier Bücher von menschlicher Proportion . . . Faksimile der Erstausgabe* (London: Wagner, 1970);

Etliche Underricht zu Befestigung der Stett, Schloss und Flecken, introduction by Martin Biddle (Farnsborough, U.K.: Gregg International, 1972).

Editions in English: *Literary Remains of Albrecht Dürer,* translated by William Martin Conway (Cambridge: Cambridge University Press, 1889);

Records of Journeys to Venice and the Low Countries, translated by Rudolph Tombo, edited by Roger Fry (Boston: Merrymount, 1913; republished, New York: Dover, 1995).

OTHER: *Die heimlich offenbarung iohannis,* woodcuts by Dürer (Nuremberg: Anton Koberger for Albrecht Dürer, 1498); published in Latin as *Apocalypsis cum Figuris* (Nuremberg: Anton Koberger for Albrecht Dürer, 1498);

Benedictus Chelidonius, *Epitome in divae parthenices Mariae historiam,* woodcuts by Dürer (Nuremberg: Hieronymus Höltzel for Albrecht Dürer, 1511);

Albrecht Dürer; self-portrait in oil on panel, 1500 (Alte Pinakothek, Munich)

Chelidonius, *Passio Christi,* woodcuts by Dürer (Nuremberg: Hieronymus Höltzel for Albrecht Dürer, 1511);

Chelidonius, *Passio Domini nostri Jesu,* woodcuts by Dürer (Nuremberg: Hieronymus Höltzel for Albrecht Dürer, 1511).

If one judges according to the level of both general and scholarly interest, no artist in the history of German culture has achieved greater significance than Albrecht Dürer. As a painter, he was the first of the Northern Renaissance artists whose

The Four Horsemen of the Apocalypse, *one of Dürer's full-page woodcuts for his* Apocalypse, *published in German and Latin editions in 1498*

works stood comparison with those of the Italian masters. It was, however, in the "lesser art" of graphics—woodcuts, engravings, and etchings—that he achieved international and historical greatness. Perhaps inspired by his early work in the printing industry, or perhaps attracted by the prestige enjoyed by Italian and German humanist writers, Dürer also expended a great deal of energy on his writings. In the sixteenth century he was highly regarded for his work on geometry and perspective, and he still has a considerable reputation for the elegance and creativity of his prose. Erwin Panofsky claims that Dürer's theoretical books constitute "the birth of German scientific writing." Dürer's oeuvre also includes important examples of early modern German autobiographical and epistolary writing. After a false start attempting to learn versification (an effort that he recorded with humorous self-effacement), he eventually succeeded; some twenty poems survive from his hand, several of which he published on broadsides accompanied by images.

Dürer was born on 21 May 1471 in Nuremberg, the son of Albrecht Dürer, a goldsmith who had emigrated from Hungary, and Barbara Holper Dürer, the daughter of a Nuremberg master goldsmith. After early training in the craft of his father and maternal grandfather, Dürer convinced his father to allow him to study painting instead. In 1486 he was apprenticed to Michael Wolgemut, whose workshop was distinguished for its collaborations with printers; among its productions was Hartmann Schedel's *Weltchronik* (Nuremberg Chronicle, 1493), the most lavishly illustrated printed book of the fifteenth century. In the spring of 1490, after completing his apprenticeship, Dürer began traveling as a journeyman—perhaps as far north as the Low Countries, perhaps to Strasbourg, and certainly to Colmar, where he hoped to meet Martin Schongauer, a master of the art of engraving. Schongauer, however, died in February 1491, somewhat before Dürer's arrival. Most of Dürer's time as a journeyman was probably spent in Basel, a major printing center. The earliest woodcut that can be firmly attributed to him is an image of Saint Jerome in his study, published as the title page to a 1492 Basel edition of Jerome's letters. He seems to have worked for the printer Johann Amerbach, with whom he later corresponded, and, most significantly, for Johann Bergmann von Olpe, the publisher of Sebastian Brant's *Das Narrenschiff* (Ship of Fools, 1494). Most experts agree that Dürer designed many of the woodcuts for *Das Narrenschiff*.

Dürer returned to Nuremberg in May 1494. On 7 July he married Agnes Frey, the daughter of a goldsmith; the marriage was childless. On the basis of a spiteful letter by Dürer's lifelong friend Willibald Pirckheimer, many biographers have imagined the Dürers to have been a deeply incompatible couple. There is, however, no testimony from Dürer or his wife that their marriage was unsatisfactory to them. Dürer almost certainly spent the winter of 1494–1495 in Italy; nothing is known about the trip except that Dürer, according to a letter of 7 February 1506, had admired artwork in Venice eleven years previously that no longer impressed him.

By 1500 Dürer had developed a style of representation that, as Panofsky says, "marked the beginning of the Renaissance style in the North." Among his early masterpieces was a printed book in separate German and Latin editions, titled *Die heimlich offenbarung iohannis* (The Secret Revelation of John, 1498) and *Apocalypsis cum Figuris* (The Apocalypse with Illustrations), respectively, and commonly known as *Dürer's Apocalypse* or *Book of Revelation*. A series of fifteen full-page woodcuts accompanying the text of the biblical Book of Revelation, it is often said to be the first book ever designed and published by an artist. A relatively early masterpiece in the medium of engraving, *Adam and Eve* (1504) was informed by his study of classical proportions, an important topic of his later writings, and is now regarded as one of the supreme visual representations of the ideals of northern European Christian humanism.

Dürer's renown, in particular for his graphic works, smoothed the way for his second trip to Italy, begun around the end of the summer of 1505. Although in his letters he mentions difficulties with some Italian artists and with guild regulations, he also records his general success and, in particular, the flattering attentions Giovanni Bellini accorded him. Dürer spent most of his time in Venice, where he completed *Feast of the Rose Garland,* which, according to Dürer, established his reputation as a painter: "jch hab awch dy moler all geschtilt, dy do sagten, jm stechen wer jch gut, aber jm molen west jch nit mit farben vm zw gen" (I have silenced all those painters who said I was a good engraver but did not know how to handle colors in painting).

Ten letters to Pirckheimer, dated between 6 January and 13 October 1506, survive from Dürer's stay in Venice. Pirckheimer played an important role in Dürer's life as the artist's connection to the highest level of Nuremberg society and to the humanist movement. In addition to quotidian matters such as arranging loans for his family back in Nuremberg and discussing purchases he was making for Pirckheimer and others, Dürer reports regularly on his artistic progress. The letters also indicate Dürer's

Knight, Death, and the Devil *(1513), one of Dürer's three* Meisterstiche *(master engravings)*

desire for social status; on 13 October, just before his return to Nuremberg, he writes, "Hÿ pin jch ein her, doheim ein schmarotzer" (Here I am a gentleman, at home a parasite). The letters, which are cast in an unusually—sometimes startlingly—familiar tone, include quite a few satiric and sarcastic passages. In the eighth letter (8 September) he ironizes such a seemingly important topic as Pirckheimer's rhetorical acumen; and in several places he mocks Pirckheimer's sexual interests, claiming in the tenth letter that Pirckheimer's "*bulen*" (lovemaking) is as incongruous as a shaggy dog playing with a kitten. One of Dürer's macaronic (Italian-German) salutations even ironizes Pirckheimer's high social standing, although it is at the same time a self-mockery of his own poor command of Italian. Self-irony occurs in other places, as in such exaggerated gestures as having his new fancy coats send greetings to Pirckheimer in the eighth and ninth (23 September) letters.

Despite his concerns, Dürer returned to Nuremberg to enjoy a level of prestige unprecedented for a German artist. Nine letters, dated between 28 August 1507 and 12 October 1509, to Jakob Heller of Frankfurt am Main demonstrate rhetorical elegance, persistence, and boldness in his approach to business. The letters report on Dürer's progress on the *Heller Altar Piece* (whose central panel would be destroyed by fire in 1729) and argue for a sales price higher than that originally agreed on. In 1509 Dürer acquired the now-famous house in the Zisselgasse and became a member of the Large Council of Nuremberg. He received important commissions from Emperor Maximilian I, including one for the *Portenn der Eeren* (Triumphal Arch, 1512), a commemoration of the emperor and the House of Hapsburg created from 192 separate woodcuts by Dürer and other artists. Beginning in 1515, by Maximilian's order, he was paid a yearly stipend of one hundred florins out of Nuremberg's imperial tax assessment. The intensity and accomplishment of Dürer's graphic works were unprecedented. In 1513 and 1514 he completed what are now known as the three *Meisterstiche* (master engravings): *Knight, Death and the Devil*, *Melencolia I*, and *Saint Jerome in His Study*, works that are routinely ranked among the most important ever produced in the medium.

An important topic that has been neglected by scholars is Dürer's activity as a designer and publisher of humanist books. In 1511 he republished the *Book of Revelation*—although, perhaps as an indication of his international, humanist orientation, only in Latin. That same year he published three books of humanist devotional poems by Benedictus Chelidonius with full-page woodcut illustrations by Dürer: *Epitome in divae parthenices Mariae historiam* (The Life of the Virgin), *Passio Christi* (The Small Passion), and *Passio Domini nostri Jesu* (The Large Passion). The intricate interaction of poetry and image in the three works intensifies the emotional force of the Passion by making it an experience of the present rather than a historical event and by trying to make that experience penitential. At the beginning of the *Small Passion*, for example, Christ says to the reader, "O cessa culpis me cruciare novis" (Oh, stop crucifying me with your new sins). In the *Small Passion*, in an amazing tour de force of Horatian style, Chelidonius uses no fewer than twenty different classical meters.

Dürer's own poems, which he also published with woodcut images, serve devotional purposes similar to Chelidonius's. They do not evince a humanist style—that is, they are not grounded in Greco-Roman poetic conventions—although some were published together with humanist poems on the same topics. (The Latin poems are anonymous but are usually attributed to Chelidonius.) While, to the detriment of Dürer's reputation, scholarly attention has focused mainly on a ridiculously awkward poem sent to Pirckheimer and a resulting exchange of humorous poems between Dürer and Lazarus Spengler, the other poems are more accomplished and more germane to a study of his art. Several are brief rhyming prayers addressed to saints, intended to augment the religious impact of devotional images. Prayers addressed to Saint Catherine and the Virgin were printed with woodcuts designed, perhaps, by Hans Baldung Grien or another artist in Dürer's workshop.

Three of Dürer's poems were printed as broadsides with woodcuts by Dürer; all three woodcuts have the date 1510: *Die sieben Tagzeiten* (The Seven Canonical Hours), *Tod und der Landsknecht* (Death and the Soldier), and *Der Schulmeister* (The Schoolmaster). *Der Schulmeister* and *Tod und der Landsknecht*, with their combination of moral didacticism and satire, recall the pious appeals to various social groups found in the medieval Dances of Death and in Brant's *Das Narrenschiff*. Dürer expresses thoroughly orthodox ideas of salvation, though, like Brant, he also expresses anxiety over religious degeneration. In *Tod und der Landsknecht* he endorses acts of faith and charity but denies the efficacy of fiscal practices such as the endowment of masses. *Die sieben Tagzeiten* condenses the canonical hours into a brief poem. As in monastic observances and in medieval Books of Hours, the seven canonical hours symbolize moments of Christ's Passion. Matins, for example, represents the betrayal of Christ; compline, his burial in the tomb of Joseph of Arimathea. Dürer based the poem on a hymn, "Patris sapientia veritas divina" (The Father's Wisdom, the Divine Truth), which was sung at Friday services in Nuremberg's Saint Sebald Church. The poem is cast in part as a prayer to be recited by the laity; along with the simple woodcut, it encourages identification with Christ's Passion and with the Virgin's reverential steadfastness.

In addition to his letters, which extend from 1506 until 1528, Dürer wrote several accounts of events in his life. A one-page fragment of a document known as the *Gedenkbuch* (Book of Memory) survives, in which he describes the deaths of his father in 1502 and his mother in 1513, as well as a curiosity that he characterizes as "daz grost wunderwerck, daz jch all mein dag gesehen hab" (the greatest miracle I ever saw): crucifixes that fell from heaven and left marks on people's clothing. Dürer sketched one in watercolor onto the surviving page of the "Gedenkbuch," showing Christ on the cross with Mary and Saint John at his sides. In 1524 Dürer wrote an annalistic summary of his family's history; now called the *Familienchronik*, it begins with a brief account of his father's origins in Hungary and continues, with terse entries, to describe events up to the end of 1523.

One of the most valuable of Dürer's writings to survive is the diary of his trip to the Low Countries; the entries cover the period from 12 July 1520 to 15 July 1521. The purpose of the journey was to secure the reinstatement of his stipend from Maximilian I's successor, Charles V, but Dürer also used the trip (and apparently planned it as such) to meet artists and establish other contacts in the Netherlands. The entries record gifts and sales of many prints and several paintings. Among the events described are his disagreeable encounter with Lady Margaret, regent of the Low Countries, who disliked and refused Dürer's portrait of Maximilian I; his near death in a strange boating accident; and his fascination with Aztec art on exhibition in Brussels. The diary also includes the "Lutherklage" (Lament for Luther), the entry for 17 May 1521 that records his reaction to the false report that Martin Luther had been murdered after the Diet of Worms. It expresses fervent support for Luther's movement, as well as his wish, in a lengthy apostrophe, that Desiderius Erasmus would assume intellectual leadership of Luther's cause.

Dürer devoted considerable energy to composing books for artists. He may have started these projects shortly before his second trip to Italy, but he worked in earnest on them after his return in 1507. Manuscript fragments survive from as early as 1513 of a work titled "Speiss für Malerknaben" (Nourishment for Apprentice Painters). It was not until 1525, however, that he published his first tract, *UNderweysung der messung* (Manual of Measurement). This comprehensive study of geometry and perspective was informed by Dürer's study of the works of ancient, Italian, and German scholars. He translated parts of Euclid's geometry into German, using the Latin translation by Bartolommeo Zamberti as his source; he probably consulted with the Bolognese mathematician Luca Pacioli and also relied on the German scholar Johannes Werner, as well as the anonymously published *Geometria deutsch* (German Geometry). *UNderweysung der messung* deals with linear, plane, and solid geometry, which prepare the way for Dürer's well-known discussion of perspective in book 4. Book 3 includes his often reproduced geometric rationalizations of lettering of both antiqua and textura.

In 1527 Dürer published a work on fortification, *Etliche underricht zu befestigung der Stett, Schlosz, und flecken* (Some Instruction for the Fortification of Cities, Castles, and Lands), which he dedicated to Charles V's brother, the future Emperor Ferdinand I. It proposes architectural solutions for the new problem of building fortifications to withstand artillery attack. Although a minor study, it is the first

Title page for The Small Passion, *a book of devotional poems by Benedictus Chelidonius with illustrations by Dürer*

publication on the topic in German.

By 1513 Dürer had finished what would become the first book of *HIerinn sind begriffen vier Bücher von menschlicher Proportion* (Herein Are Contained Four Books on Human Proportion); but the complete work would not be published until October 1528, several months after his death. It is an extensive study of the human body, using Vitruvius's canon, the system of Leon Battista Alberti, and Dürer's own measurements of variations in bodily proportions. The remarkable diversity of human proportions casts considerable doubt on the notion that there is an ideal proportion. He concludes book 3 with a general discussion of beauty that is now known as the "Aesthetic Discourse," in which he proposes the impossibility, for humans, of understanding or perceiving an absolute ideal of beauty. In a passage he referred to as the "seltsame Red" (the unusual statement) he attributes value to representations of humanity that are not intended to be ideal or perfectly harmonious. Book 4 deals with proportions of parts of bodies depicted in motion.

As indicated by the "Lutherklage," Lutheranism played an important role in Dürer's final years. In a letter to Georg Spalatin from early 1520 he describes Luther as someone "der mir aws grossen engsten gehollfen hat" (who helped me overcome great anxieties). A list in Dürer's handwriting indicates that he owned several books by Luther. He probably was among the earliest adherents to Luther's movement, and there is no evidence that he returned to the Catholic fold, as was to be the case with Pirckheimer. One of his greatest woodcuts, *Last Supper* (1523), is often associated with Protestant utraquism (the demand that the laity also receive the cup of the Eucharist). His last major work, *Four Apostles* (1526), a painting on two panels, uses four passages from Luther's translation of the New Testament, published in September 1522, at the base of the panels. The apostle John is even depicted as reading from the beginning of his gospel in Luther's translation.

Dürer died in Nuremberg on 6 April 1528. The cause of death is not known, although there are indications that he had had spells of bad health since his journey to the Low Countries. He was mourned by such important intellectual figures as Erasmus, Luther, and Philipp Melanchthon. Several notable poets, including Hans Sachs and Eobanus Hessus, published epicedia for him. Pirckheimer, who saw *HIerinn sind begriffen vier Bücher von menschlicher Proportion* through the press for Agnes Dürer, also published a few memorial poems, including the inscription that was used for Dürer's tombstone. Despite his Catholicism and his bitterness over Nuremberg's embrace of Lutheranism, Pirckheimer wrote a lengthy tribute that expressed hope for Dürer's salvation in terms that would have been largely unobjectionable to the various parties in the ecclesiastical disputes. It concludes with a touching apostrophe to his Protestant friend: "felix interea somno requiesce beato, / dormit enim in Christo vir bonus, haud moritur" (Fortunate Albrecht, rest for now in blessed sleep. / For the good man who slumbers in Christ does not die).

The existing body of Dürer scholarship uses his writings almost exclusively as sources for establishing facts about his life and for discussing his artistic views. In view of his towering stature among visual artists, this emphasis is understandable. Nonetheless, his major accomplishment as a writer of scientific German prose and his success as a poet and author of autobiography, diary, and letters need much more analysis.

Bibliographies:

Matthias Mende, *Dürer-Bibliographie* (Wiesbaden: Harrassowitz, 1971);

Bavarian State Library, ed., *Verzeichnis der im deutschen Sprachbereich erschienenen Drucke des XVI. Jahrhunderts,* volume 5 (Stuttgart: Hiersemann, 1985), entries D2853–D2861.

Biographies:

Moriz Thausing, *Dürer: Geschichte seines Lebens und seiner Kunst,* 2 volumes (Leipzig: Seemann, 1884);

Erwin Panofsky, *The Life and Art of Albrecht Dürer* (Princeton: Princeton University Press, 1955);

Jane Campbell Hutchison, *Albrecht Dürer* (Princeton: Princeton University Press, 1990);

Kurt Löcher, "Albrecht Dürer," in *Deutsche Dichter der frühen Neuzeit (1450–1600),* edited by Stephan Füssel (Berlin: Erich Schmidt, 1993), pp. 270–280.

References:

Albrecht Dürer 1471–1528: Ausstellung des Germanischen Nationalmuseums Nürnberg 1971 (Munich: Prestel, 1971);

Fedja Anzelewsky, *Albrecht Dürer: Das malerische Werk* (Berlin: Deutscher Verlag für Kunstwissenschaft, 1971);

Jan Białostocki, *Dürer and His Critics, 1500–1971* (Baden-Baden: Koerner, 1986);

Białostocki, "Dürer und die Humanisten," in *Pforzheimer Reuchlinpreis 1955–1993: Die Reden der Preisträger* (Heidelberg: Winter, 1994), pp. 200–216;

Max Dvořák, *The History of Art as the History of Ideas,* translated by John Hardy (London: Routledge, 1984);

Ernst Gombrich, "The Evidence of Images," in *Interpretation: Theory and Practice,* edited by Charles S. Singleton (Baltimore: Johns Hopkins University Press, 1969), pp. 35–104;

Stephen Greenblatt, "Murdering Peasants: Status, Genre, and the Representation of Rebellion," in *Representing the English Renaissance,* edited by Greenblatt (Berkeley: University of California Press, 1988), pp. 1–29;

Mechtild Habermann and Peter O. Müller, "Zur Wortbildung bei Albrecht Dürer: Ein Beitrag zum Nürnberger Frühneuhochdeutschen um 1500," *Zeitschrift für deutsche Philologie,* 106 (1987): 117–137;

Dwight E. Langston, "A Linguistic Analysis of Albrecht Dürer's *Ein Vnder Richt Alle Mas Zw Endern,*" dissertation, Tulane University, 1973;

Joseph Meder, *Dürer-Katalog* (Vienna: Gilhofer & Rauschburg, 1932);

Erwin Panofsky, "Albrecht Dürer and Classical Antiquity," in his *Meaning in the Visual Arts* (Chicago: University of Chicago Press, 1955), pp. 236-285;

David Price, "Albrecht Dürer's Representations of Faith: The Church, Lay Devotion and Veneration in the *Apocalypse* (1498)," *Zeitschrift für Kunstgeschichte,* 57 (1994): 688-696;

Hans Rupprich, *Die deutsche Literatur vom späten Mittelalter bis zum Barock: 1. Teil, 1370-1520* (Munich: Beck, 1970), pp. 682-697;

Herbert Schade, ed., *Albrecht Dürer: Kunst einer Zeitenwende* (Regensburg: Pustet, 1971);

Peter Strieder, *Albrecht Dürer,* translated by Nancy M. Gordon and Walter L. Strauss (New York: Abaris, 1982);

Ernst Ullmann, Günter Grau, and Rainer Behrends, eds., *Albrecht Dürer: Zeit und Werk* (Leipzig: Karl-Marx-Universität, 1971);

Verein für Geschichte der Stadt Nürnberg und von der Senatskommission für Humanismus-Forschung der Deutschen Forschungsgemeinschaft, ed., *Albrecht Dürers Umwelt: Festschrift zum 500. Geburtstag Albrecht Dürers am 21. Mai 1971* (Nuremberg: Selbstverlag des Vereins für Geschichte der Stadt Nürnberg, 1971);

Friedrich Winkler, *Dürer und die Illustrationen zum Narrenschiff* (Berlin: Deutscher Verein für Kunstwissenschaft, 1951);

Dieter Wuttke, "Dürer und Celtis: Von der Bedeutung des Jahres 1500 für den deutschen Humanismus: Jahrhundertfeier als symbolische Form," *Journal of Medieval and Renaissance Studies,* 10 (1980): 72-129.

Elisabeth von Nassau-Saarbrücken
(after 1393 – 17 January 1456)

Albrecht Classen
University of Arizona

MAJOR WORKS: *Loher und Maller* (before 1437)
Manuscripts: Ms. H, Hamburg, Staats- und Universitätsbibliothek, cod. 11 in scrinio, between 1455 and 1472; ms. K, Cologne, Historisches Archiv, cod. W*337, fol. 1^r–149^r, fifteenth century; ms. P, Burg Krivoklát/Pürglitz (Czech Republic), cod. I a 3, 1483; ms. W, Vienna, Österreichische Nationalbibliothek, cod. 2816, written in 1493.
First publication: *Loher und Maller* (Strasbourg: Johannes Grüninger, 1514).
Standard edition: *Loher und Maller: Ritterroman,* edited by Karl Simrock (Stuttgart: Cotta, 1868).
Edition: *Lother und Maller: Eine Rittergeschichte aus einer ungedruckten Handschrift,* edited and translated into modern German by Dorothea Schlegel (Frankfurt am Main: Wilmans, 1805).

Herpin (circa 1437)
Manuscripts: The work is found in three manuscripts titled "Lewen buch von Burges in Berrye": ms. A, Berlin, Staatsbibliothek, Mgf 464, 1487; ms. B, Wolfenbüttel, Herzog August Bibliothek, Cod. Guelf. 46 Novissimi 2°, between 1455 and 1472; ms. C, Heidelberg, Universitätsbibliothek, Cpg 152, circa 1475; another ms., Erlangen, Universitätsbibliothek, was lost before 1826.
First publication: *Herpin* (Strasbourg: Johannes Grüninger, 1514).
Standard edition: "Elisabeth von Nassau-Saarbrücken: Der weiße Ritter oder Geschichte von Herzog Herpin von Bourges und seinem Sohne Löw," in *Die deutschen Volksbücher,* volume 11, edited by Karl Simrock (Basel: Schwabe, 1886), pp. 213–445.
Edition: *Historie von Herzog Herpin: Übertragen aus dem Französischen von Elisabeth von Nassau-Saarbrücken.* Heidelberg, Universitätsbibliothek, Cod. Pal. Germ. 152, critical introduction and description of the manuscripts by Ute von Bloh, Codices illuminati medii aevi, no. 17 (Munich: Lengenfelder, 1990).

Sibille (circa 1437)
Manuscript: Hamburg, Staats- und Universitätsbibliothek, cod. 12 in scrinio, fol. 58^r–76^v.
Standard edition: *Der Roman von der Königin Sibille in drei Prosafassungen des 14. und 15. Jahrhunderts,* edited by Hermann Tiemann (Hamburg: Hauswedell, 1977).

Huge Scheppel (1437)
Manuscript: Hamburg, Staats- und Universitätsbibliothek, cod. 12 in scrinio, fol. 1^r–51^v, written between 1455 and 1472.
First publication: *Hug Schapler,* edited by Conrad Heyndörffer (Strasbourg: Printed by Johann Grüninger, 1500).
Standard editions: "Hug Schapler," in *Volksbücher vom sterbenden Rittertum,* edited by Heinz Kindermann (Weimar & Leipzig: Böhlau, 1928), pp. 23–114, 285; *Hug Schapler, ein lieplichs lesen und ein wahrhafftige Hystorij,* epilogue by Marie-Luise Linn (Hildesheim & New York: Olms, 1974); "Hug Schapler," in *Romane des 15. und 16. Jahrhunderts,* edited by Jan-Dirk Müller (Frankfurt am Main: Deutscher Klassiker Verlag, 1990), pp. 177–381.

The annals of medieval German literature include virtually no woman writer who composed secular works—although there were many religious women writers, such as Mechthild von Magdeburg and Gertrud the Great. This situation changed in the fifteenth century, when several noblewomen translated courtly romances and similar texts from French into German. These works are not, however, simple translations but adaptations, contributions to German literature in their own right. Both Eleonore of Austria and Elisabeth von Nassau-Saarbrücken had enough literary sensitivity to imbue the translated works with new values, ideas, and styles. These texts found wide appeal and were soon printed and sold on the book markets as chapbooks, or, more precisely, early prose novels.

Elisabeth von Nassau-Saarbrücken was the most important representative of her sex in fifteenth-century German literature, and her novels contributed to the transformation of the late Middle Ages into the early Modern Age in Germany. Although Elisabeth's original literary intent was simply to familiarize the aristocratic circles of western Germany with courtly tales from northeastern France, her translations of these verse romances into prose demonstrated the high level of literary genius in Germany, as well.

Elisabeth was born in Vézélize sometime after 1393 to Frederick V of Lorraine, the younger brother of Charles I, the duke of Lorraine, and Margarethe of Vaudémont-Joinville. Elisabeth's father exerted considerable political influence in France and Germany and was heavily involved in national and international activities. He died in the Hundred Years' War at the Battle of Agincourt in 1415, when English longbowmen destroyed the French army.

In 1405 Elisabeth's mother commissioned a copy of the French chansons de geste, a collection of verse narratives about Charlemagne, his court, and related characters. According to a note in the epilogue to Elisabeth's novel *Loher und Maller* (before 1437), Elisabeth used this manuscript to translate four of the texts into German prose. In the 1450s Elisabeth obtained a new copy of the chansons de geste and revised her translations. Other connections to French literature existed through Elisabeth's brother Anton, who belonged to the circle of poet friends of Duke Charles d'Orléans.

On 11 August 1412 Elisabeth married Count Philipp I of Nassau-Saarbrücken, the great-grandson of the German king Adolf von Nassau, who held considerable power in the western region of the empire. He also held the territory of Commercy as a fiefdom from the king of France and was a member of the advisory grand council. Elisabeth and Philipp had three children: Philipp II, born in 1418; Johann III, born in 1423; and Margarethe, born in 1426. After her husband's death in 1429, Elisabeth assumed control of the government on behalf of her oldest son and maintained the family's rule over its lands despite serious political conflicts after 1431 concerning the inheritance of Lorraine. In 1430 she married Count Henry IV of Blamont, who died in 1441. Philipp II assumed rulership of the Rhine valley territories in 1437, and Johann III received the earldom of Saarbrücken as his inheritance in 1442.

Elisabeth had many contacts with literary-oriented courts in Germany and France. Her uncle, Duke Charles I of Lorraine, was a dedicated humanist. His wife, Margarethe, established personal contacts between Elisabeth and the highly cultured court at Heidelberg, in particular with Countess Mechthild von Rottenburg, daughter of King Ruprecht III of the Palatinate. Elisabeth began her translation work after officially stepping down as the crowned head of her family in 1437. She wanted to provide the German readers at her court and elsewhere with access to the French chansons de geste; she dedicated her chapbooks, however, solely to her son Johann III of Nassau-Saarbrücken. *Herpin* (composed circa 1437; published, 1514) concerns three generations of a ducal family that is in opposition to the emperor Charlemagne. *Sibille* (composed circa 1437) introduces his grandson Ludwig; in *Loher und Maller* Ludwig's brother is the central figure; *Huge Scheppel* (Hugo Capet, composed 1437; published as *Hug Schapler*, 1500), finally, describes the marriage of Ludwig's daughter to the title character. Elisabeth's authorship of *Loher und Maller* and *Huge Scheppel* is confirmed through explicit references in their forewords; the other two novels have been attributed to her because of stylistic criteria and the fact that the four novels together constitute a continuous narrative. The manuscripts of the works commissioned by Count Johann III are similar and have uniform illustrations. Scholars have not been able to establish with certainty the order in which the translations were made.

Elisabeth's novels describe the rise and fall of the Carolingian dynasty between the eighth and the tenth centuries, although they rely much more on medieval legend than on historic fact; they also include references to nobility from the Saarbrücken area. In *Herpin* the narrative commences with false accusations against an innocent member of the court, Duke Herpin of Bourges, who escapes to the woods with his pregnant wife. Charlemagne emerges as a weak character, subject to political manipulations from evil counselors who hate the good duke. The refugees evade several attempts to murder them and successfully fend for themselves in the woods. After the duchess gives birth to a boy, however, the three are separated. A lioness abducts the deserted baby and feeds him in its cave until a knight discovers him. The knight takes Löw (Lion), as he will be called later, and gives him a proper education.

Meanwhile, the duchess kills a giant; then, disguised as a man, she kills the leader of the army that is besieging Toledo and thereby decides the outcome of the war. The king of Toledo's daughter falls in love with "him," forcing the duchess to reveal her true identity. But now the king wants to marry her. A divine voice tells her to leave the court and search for her husband and son.

Illustrations from the manuscript for Elisabeth von Nassau-Saarbrücken's Huge Scheppel *(Hamburg, Staats- und Universitätsbibliothek, cod. 12 in scrinio)*

Löw marries a king's daughter and has two sons by her, Ölbaum and Wilhelm. He regains the paternal inheritance of Bourges, which leads to a war with Charlemagne. A divine voice tells Charlemagne to acknowledge Löw as the lord of Bourges. Löw's parents are allowed to return, but they die violent deaths. Löw's sons go out into the world and find wives: Ölbaum marries Fröhlich, and Wilhelm marries Grassien and both marriages result in children. They return to their father's court, but they, too, die violent deaths. Finally, the next generation comes of age and avenges their parents.

The title character of *Sibille,* which was probably Elisabeth's second translation, is a Byzantine princess who is wooed by Charlemagne and finally promised to him. She is not happy at the prospect of leaving her parents and country behind; but she follows her future husband to France, where they are married. An ugly dwarf pursues the queen and tries to sleep with her but gets a beating from her instead. To avenge himself, he sneaks into the royal bedroom and crawls into bed with her while the king is in church. On his return Charlemagne is confronted with the seeming adultery and orders Sibille to be burned at the stake, even though she is pregnant and the accusation is blatantly false. He finally permits Sibille to be spared death by fire, expelling her from the country instead and throwing the dwarf into the flames. After escaping an attempted rape by a courtier, Sibille finds a haven in a city, has her baby, and lives there for many years. Eventually Sibille returns to Constantinople; her father welcomes her home, then marches with his army to France to force his son-in-law to take Sibille back.

After many complications, which show Charlemagne to be subject to the advice of evil counselors, Sibille's friends convince him that he acted unjustly and that the queen's enemies deserve to die.

Thematically, Loher und Maller is similar to the two previous novels: a noble family is subjected to slander, unfair persecutions, and murderous attacks, but its members persevere because of their good character, high moral standards, and chivalric ideals. Loher is the youngest son of Sibille and Charlemagne, born after the couple had reunited. His friend Maller is the son of King Galien and Queen Rosemunde. Loher has too much success among the ladies at court to suit the knights, who complain to Loher's brother Ludwig; he reports the matter to their father, who had forbidden Loher any further amorous adventures. Charlemagne bans Loher from the country for seven years but provides him with an entourage and with sufficient gold to embark on a life of chivalry so that he can gain experience and a reputation.

On the way to Constantinople, Loher and Maller strike up a friendship with Prince Ott of Pavia, who turns out to be an evil competitor for the favor of the Byzantine emperor Orscher—like Charlemagne, a poor judge of character. But Loher overcomes all hindrances, marries Orscher's daughter, and becomes the successor to the throne of Constantinople. Some years later Ludwig's evil counselors ambush Loher in Paris and castrate him. Loher, Maller, and Loher's cousin Isinbart begin a brutal war against their opponents, and Loher's son, Marfone, joins their forces with his own army. They win the war and punish the traitors at Ludwig's court. Loher and Ludwig make peace, and Loher moves to Rome where the Pope had also given him the imperial crown. Maller becomes a hermit; later he is mortally wounded when Loher throws a knife at him. Before he dies he forgives Loher but warns his friend that his relatives will seek revenge. Although Loher begs Maller's family for forgiveness, they go to war against him, which ends in a peace settlement. Afterward Loher becomes a hermit, and Ludwig goes back to Paris. More wars involving family members follow; in the course of describing them the author mentions Huge Scheppel, Ludwig's son-in-law, and thus establishes a direct link to her next novel.

Loher und Maller was reprinted often in the fifteenth and sixteenth centuries. In 1805 Dorothea Schlegel, the wife of the Romantic writer Friedrich Schlegel, translated it into modern German and published it in an abridged edition as Lother und Maller.

Huge Scheppel proved to be Elisabeth's most popular work, perhaps because it idealizes the romantic notion that in an aristocratic society the best person will become the leader of the country, irrespective of his social background: although Huge is a butcher's son, he becomes the successor to the French king Louis the Pious because of his excellent character. In fact, the historical Hugh Capet, king of France from 987 to 996, was the son of Hugues le Grand (Hugh the Great), duke of the Franks and count of Paris, who was the virtual ruler of France from the death of Louis IV in 954 until his own death in 956.

Huge Scheppel thus gives a fictionalized account of the origin of the Capetian dynasty. The prologue says that Charlemagne's son Ludwig—known in France as Louis I, "the Pious"—left behind only a daughter, Merie. She was entitled to the throne, but war broke out among suitors for her hand in marriage. For that reason, the rule that women could follow in the royal line was later abandoned.

The story begins with Huge, as a youth in Paris, squandering his deceased father's money on amorous adventures that result in the births of ten bastard sons. He flees Paris to avoid imprisonment but continues his erotic pursuits. When he rescues a virgin from being raped and returns her to her father, the latter showers him with money and knightly trappings. He returns to Paris, where the young Queen Merie is beleaguered by the grand lords of France who want her to marry one of their sons. Hugh overcomes them all in a series of battles, the brutality of which is more typical of the nature of warfare in the fifteenth century than in the tenth. In particular, the protagonist demonstrates considerable skill in trickery. At one point he enters the enemy's camp and kills two of their leaders in their own tent. The queen knights him and grants him the dukedom of Orléans as a reward for his achievements.

In another series of battles the queen's relatives from Venice and Hungary and Hugh's ten grown sons fight yet another wooer, Duke Frederick, who has threatened to destroy Paris and burn the queen at the stake. Duke Frederick is finally captured, and Hugh is offered the queen's hand and the French throne. He makes the prisoner swear peace and respect for the crown and withdraws to Orléans with his wife. When he goes on a tour of his kingdom, leaving his pregnant wife behind, Frederick and his friend Duke Asselin attack Orléans. They take the city and the castle, except for a tower where the queen has found refuge. The queen's mother is, however, in his power, and he

Elisabeth's grave in the Collegiate Church of Saint Arnual, Saarbrücken

threatens to burn her unless Merie capitulates. To save her mother, the queen gives herself up to Frederick, who takes her to his territory. Meanwhile, Huge is ambushed and barely escapes death. In the guise of a hermit he sneaks back into Orléans and meets secretly with his court constable, Dammartin. On Huge's instructions Dammartin advises Frederick to marry the queen in a public ceremony, which will give Huge the opportunity to fight his opponent and win his wife back. The final battle takes place in the church; all of Frederick's and Asselin's men are killed, and the two dukes are taken prisoner. Later they are beheaded.

The last chapter briefly describes Huge's successful crusade against the Muslims and other events of his reign as the king of France. When he dies his oldest son, Ruprecht, succeeds him; the dynasty of the Capetians has been established. The novel was republished well into the eighteenth century; in the later editions the original brutality and violence were increasingly replaced by elements of civility.

Elisabeth von Nassau-Saarbrücken died on 17 January 1456 and was entombed in the Collegiate Church of Saint Arnual near Saarbrücken. Her four translations provided her audience with access to French courtly literature and also demonstrated that German women could write popular prose novels.

References:

Ute von Bloh, "Information–Appell–Dokument: Die Briefe in den Heldenepen der Elisabeth von Nassau-Saarbrücken," *Zeitschrift für Literaturwissenschaft und Linguistik,* 23 (1993): 24–49;

Bernhard Burchert, *Die Anfänge des Prosaromans in Deutschland: Die Prosaerzählungen der Elisabeth von Nassau-Saarbrücken* (Frankfurt am Main, Bern & New York: Peter Lang, 1987);

Burchert, "Auf dem Wege zum Roman: Anmerkungen zu der Gattungskontroverse um den 'Hug Schapler,'" *Zeitschrift für deutsche Philologie,* 107 (1988): 400–410;

Albrecht Classen, *The German Volksbuch: A Critical History of a Late-Medieval Genre* (New York: Mellen, 1995);

Classen, "Women in Fifteenth-Century Literature: Protagonists (Melusine), Poets (Elisabeth von Nassau-Saarbrücken), and Patrons (Mechthild von Österreich)," in *"Der Buchstab tödt–der Geist macht lebendig": Festschrift zum 60. Geburtstag von Hans-Gert Roloff,* volume 1, edited by James Hardin and Jörg Jungmayr (Bern & Berlin: Peter Lang, 1992), pp. 431–458;

Wolfgang Haubrichs, "'Die kraft von franckrich wappen': Königsgeschichte und genealogische Motivik in den Prosahistorien der Elisabeth von Nassau-Saarbrücken," *Deutschunterricht,* 43, no. 4 (1991): 4–19;

Ralf Konczak, *Studien zur Druckgeschichte zweier Romane Elisabeths von Nassau-Saarbrücken: "Loher und Maller" und "Herpin"* (Frankfurt am Main: Peter Lang, 1991);

Ursula Liebertz-Grün, "Höfische Autorinnen: Von der karolingischen Kulturreform bis zum Humanismus," in *Deutsche Literatur von Frauen,* volume 1: *Vom Mittelalter bis zum Ende des 18. Jahrhunderts,* edited by Gisela Brinker-Gabler (Munich: Beck, 1988), pp. 39–64;

Wolfgang Liepe, *Elisabeth von Nassau-Saarbrücken: Entstehung und Anfänge des Prosaromans in Deutschland* (Halle an der Saale: Niemeyer, 1920);

Irmela von der Lühe, "Die Anfänge des Prosaromans: 'Hug Schapler' und 'Fortunatus,'" in *Einführung in die deutsche Literatur des 12. bis 16. Jahrhunderts,* volume 3: *Bürgertum und Fürstenstaat: 15./16. Jahrhundert,* edited by Winfried

Frey and others (Opladen: Westdeutscher Verlag, 1981), pp. 69-91;

Jan-Dirk Müller, "Held und Gemeinschaftserfahrung: Aspekte der Gattungstransformation im frühen deutschen Prosaroman am Beispiel des 'Hug Schapler,' " *Daphnis: Zeitschrift für Mittlere Deutsche Literatur,* 9 (1980): 393-426;

Müller, "Späte chanson-de-geste-Rezeption und Landesgeschichte: Zu den Übersetzungen der Elisabeth von Nassau-Saarbrücken," *Wolfram-Studien,* 11 (1989): 206-226;

Hans-Gert Roloff, "Anfänge des deutschen Prosaromans," in *Handbuch des deutschen Romans,* edited by Helmut Koopmann (Düsseldorf: Bagel, 1983), pp. 54-79, 596-600;

G. Sauder, "Elisabeth und ihre Prosaromane," in *Saarländische Lebensbilder,* volume 1 (Saarbrücken: Saarbrücker Druckerei & Verlag, 1982), pp. 31-56;

Hans Hugo Steinhoff, "Elisabeth von Nassau-Saarbrücken," in *Die deutsche Literatur des Mittelalters: Verfasserlexikon,* volume 2, fascicle 1-2, second revised edition, edited by Kurt Ruh and others (Berlin & New York: De Gruyter, 1978), cols. 482-488;

Norbert Thomas, *Handlungsstruktur und dominante Motivik im deutschen Prosaroman des 15. und frühen 16. Jahrhunderts* (Nuremberg: Carl, 1971);

Kurt Wais, "Märchen und chanson de geste: Themengeschichtliches zu Robert le Diable, Berte aus grans pies, Loher und Maller," in *Festgabe für Julius Wilhelm zum 80. Geburtstag,* edited by Hugo Laitenberger (Wiesbaden: Steiner, 1977), pp. 120-138;

Karl A. Zaenker, "Elisabeth of Nassau-Saarbrücken," in *An Encylopedia of Continental Women Writers,* volume 1, edited by Katharina M. Wilson (New York & London: Garland, 1991), pp. 368-369.

Albrecht von Eyb
(24 August 1420 – 23 or 24 July 1475)

John L. Flood
University of London Institute of Germanic Studies

WORKS: *Speculum poetrie* (1449)
> **Manuscript:** Gotha, Forschungs- und Landesbibliothek, Ms. 217;

Tractatus de speciositate Barbarae puellulae (1451-1452)
> **Manuscripts:** Munich, Bayerische Staatsbibliothek, Clm 504, fol. 348, and Clm 6717, fol. 69; Bern Stadtbibliothek, Cod. Bern. 506, fols. 6^v–9^v; all date from the fifteenth century.
>
> **Standard edition:** "Tractatus de speciositate Barbarae puellulae," in *Albrecht von Eyb und die Frühzeit des deutschen Humanismus,* by Max Herrmann (Berlin: Weidmann, 1893), pp. 100-102;

Appellacio mulierum Bambergensium (1451-1452)
> **Manuscript:** Munich, Bayerische Staatsbibliothek, Clm 504, fols. 349^r–350^r, fifteenth century.
>
> **Standard edition:** "Appellacio mulierum Bambergensium," in *Albrecht von Eyb und die Frühzeit des deutschen Humanismus,* pp. 104-107;

Ad laudem et commendationem Bambergae civitatis oratio (1451-1452)
> **First publication:** In *Margarita poetica* (Nuremberg: J. Sensenschmidt, 1472).
>
> **Standard edition:** "Ad laudem et commendationem Bambergae civitatis oratio," edited by William Hammer, in his "Albrecht von Eyb, Eulogist of Bamberg," *Germanic Review,* 17 (1942): 14-19;

Clarissimarum feminarum laudacio (24 November 1459)
> **Manuscripts:** Munich, Bayerische Staatsbibliothek, Clm 650, fols. 27^r–72^r; Eichstätt Stadtbibliothek, Cod. 186, fols. 269^r–289^r; both from the fifteenth century;

Invectiva in lenam (27 November 1459)
> **Manuscripts:** Munich, Bayerische Staatsbibliothek, Clm 650, fols 27^r–72^r; Eichstätt Stadtbibliothek, Cod. 186, fols. 269^r–289^r; both from the fifteenth century;

An viro sapienti uxor sit ducenda (1459-1460)
> **Manuscripts:** Munich, Bayerische Staatsbibliothek, Clm 650, fols. 27^r–72^r (according to Herrmann, a copy authorized by Eyb himself and one that formerly belonged to Hartmann Schedel [1440-1514]); Munich, Bayerische Staatsbibliothek, Clm 522 fols. 259^r–271^v, fifteenth century; Eichstätt Stadtbibliothek, Cod. 186, fols. 269^r–289^r, fifteenth century; Eichstätt, Episcopal Archive (manuscript with no pressmark);

Margarita poetica (Nuremberg: J. Sensenschmidt, 1472);

Ob einem manne sey zunemen ein eelichs weyb oder nicht (Nuremberg: A. Koberger, 1472);

Albrecht von Eyb; woodcut from the first edition of his Spiegel der Sitten *(1511)*

German poems (circa 1475)
> **Manuscript:** Munich, Bayerische Staatsbibliothek, Clm 5185, fols. 1ʳ–19ᵛ, fifteenth century;

Spiegel der Sitten (Augsburg: Johann Otmar, 1511);

"Albrecht von Eyb's 'Grisardis': A Transcription of the Early New High German Narrative with Annotation," edited by John Christian Weber, dissertation, New York University, 1979.

Editions: *Albrecht von Eybe's Ehestandsbüchlein,* translated into modern German (omitting the legend of Albanus) by Karl Müller (Sonderhausen: Fassheber, 1879);

Albrecht von Eyb: Deutsche Schriften, 2 volumes, edited by Max Herrmann (Berlin: Weidmann, 1890);

Albrecht von Eyb, Ehebüchlein: Faksimile der Originalausgabe von Anton Koberger, Nürnberg, 1472, edited by Elisabeth Geck (Wiesbaden: Pressler, 1966);

Albrecht von Eyb, "Ob einem manne sey zunemen ein eelichs weyb oder nicht," edited by Helmut Weinacht (Darmstadt: Wissenschaftliche Buchgesellschaft, 1982);

Albrecht von Eyb, Spiegel der Sitten, edited by Gerhard Klecha, Texte des späten Mittelalters und der frühen Neuzeit, no. 34 (Berlin: Erich Schmidt, 1989).

OTHER: "Praecepta artis rhetoricae," misattributed to Pope Pius II (Enea Silvio Piccolomini), in Pius's *Opera omnia* (Basel: J. Amerbach, circa 1488);

Die Plautus-Übersetzungen des Albrecht von Eyb, edited by Peter Andreas Litwan (Bern, Frankfurt am Main & New York: Peter Lang, 1984).

Albrecht von Eyb is regarded as one of the earliest German humanists. Max Herrmann called him the first German humanist to embrace not only the external form (*Gestalt*) but also the inner spirit (*Gehalt*) of the new learning. Joseph Anthony Hiller, on the other hand, regarded him as a "literary, medieval moralist, a medieval thinker, rather than a 'humanist,'" a view that has not found much favor. The truth probably lies somewhere between these two positions: in some respects Eyb was, indeed, a latter-day medieval moralist, but his encounter with the *studia humanitatis* of fifteenth-century Italy left an indelible mark on much of his writing. Helmut Weinacht, while preferring to attach no labels, would, if pressed, call him a Christian humanist. Today he is remembered above all for his translations of plays by Titus Maccius Plautus, but his views on marriage are also attracting renewed scholarly interest.

Eyb was born into an ancient Franconian noble family at Schloss Sommersdorf, near Ansbach, Bavaria, on 24 August 1420. The third son of Ludwig von Eyb and Margaretha von Wolmershausen, he was destined for the church. From 1436 to 1438 he studied at the University of Erfurt, but after the death of his father in the latter year, his elder brother Ludwig insisted that he continue his education at the Latin school at Rothenburg ob der Tauber. He returned to Erfurt in 1443. In 1444 he became canon at the cathedral in Eichstätt. That same year he went to Italy, where he was to spend all but one of the next fifteen years. He studied in Pavia from 1444 to 1447; in Bologna in 1447–1448; and in Padua from 1448 to 1451. He spent the year 1451–1452 in Bamberg to fulfill his obligations and draw his emoluments as a canon of the cathedral there, then went back to Bologna. In 1455 he returned to Pavia, where, on 7 February 1459, he was admitted to the degree of doctor of canon and civil law. His law teachers at Pavia included Cato Sacco, whom he frequently mentions in his *Spiegel der Sitten* (Mirror of Morals, 1511); Gasparino Barzizza, mentioned in *Margarita poetica* (Poetic Pearl, 1472); and Baldassare Rasino, who had a profound effect on him. At Bologna he was influenced by Baptista de St. Petro and Giovanni Lamola. He also become acquainted with Maffeo Vegio, Lorenzo Valla, and Francesco Filelfo.

On his return to Germany in 1459, Eyb became involved in ecclesiastical and political affairs, serving as legal adviser to various cities and princes in Franconia but specializing in representing women in matrimonial cases. His income from this work, together with the proceeds of the various benefices he held—in addition to his canonries at Eichstätt and Bamberg, he became canon at Würzburg in 1462; he was also archdeacon of Iphofen and *cubicularius* (chamber-servant) to Pope Pius II—enabled him to devote himself almost entirely to literary pursuits in later life. Between 1448 and 1459 he built up a substantial library.

The earliest of Eyb's works, which has never been printed, was *Speculum poetrie* (Mirror of Poetry, 1449). It is nothing but a moralizing assemblage of literary quotations, thematically arranged, foreshadowing his *Margarita poetica*.

Eyb's earliest original works, composed in Bamberg in 1451–1452, are invectives and eulogies on the humanistic model. The first, influenced by the *Eurialus and Lucretia* (1444) of Enea Silvio Piccolomini (the future Pius II), was *Tractatus de speciositate Barbarae puellulae* (In Praise of the Beauty of the Young Girl Barbara); it is a free, but

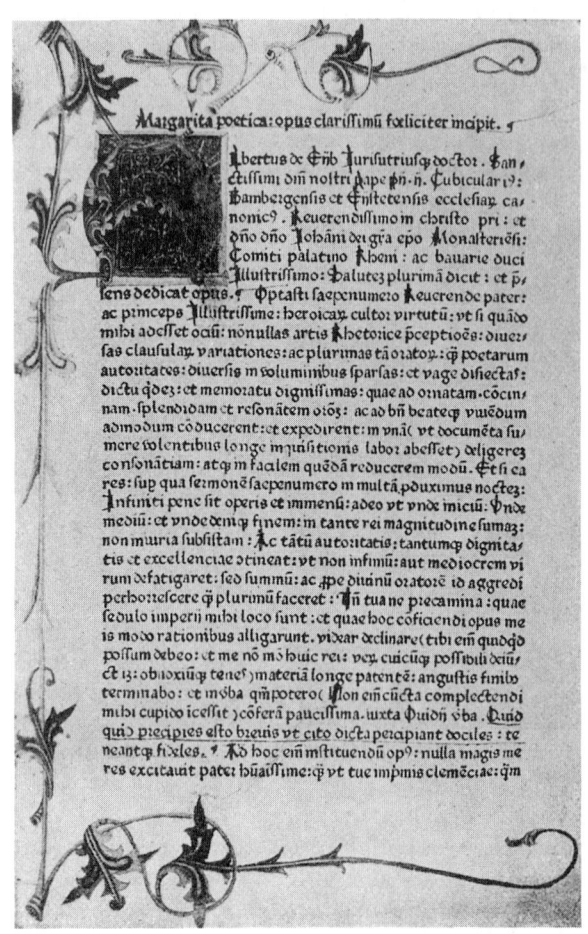

First page of Eyb's *Margarita poetica*

not vulgar, description of the title figure's physical attractions—whether Barbara was real or fictitious is not clear. *Appellacio mulierum Bambergensium* (Addressing the Women of Bamberg), inspired by Leonardo Bruni's *Oratio Heliogabali* (1408), is a clever satire on the supposedly lax morals of Bamberg women. It was followed by *De commendatione dignissimi et divinissimi Eucharistiae sacramento oratio* (Commendation of the Most Worthy and Divine Sacrament of the Eucharist) and *Ad laudem et commendationem Bambergae civitatis oratio* (In Praise and Commendation of the City of Bamberg). The latter two pieces appeared as "oratio 1" and "oratio 16," respectively, in *Margarita poetica*.

Margarita poetica, probably compiled in Italy in 1459, was Eyb's first important work. It is an attempt at writing a humanistic handbook on rhetoric, letters, and orations. In essence, it is an anthology of humanistic texts in which the mass of textual examples soon swamps any theoretical considerations. The first part subsumes his own "Praecepta artis rhetoricae" (Precepts of the Art of Rhetoric), written around 1457 and printed not later than 1488 in the collected works of Pius II, to whom it was erroneously attributed. It comprises excerpts of stylistic interest from Roman writers and Italian humanists and concludes with thirty orations intended to serve as models of humanistic style; among them are pieces by Antonio Beccadelli, Bessarion, Giovanni Lamola, and Gian Francesco Poggio Bracciolini, and four (numbers 1, 16, 17, and 30) by Eyb himself. The concluding speech, which functions as an epilogue, includes a defense of humanistic ideals of learning in which Eyb draws heavily on Bruni's *De studiis et litteris liber* (Studying Literature, 1422–1429). He regards Cicero as the supreme stylist and quotes extensively from his works. Lactantius, "the Christian Cicero" much admired by Italian humanists, is another favorite of Eyb's: he cites Lactantius's *Divinae Institutiones* (Divine Institutions), *De Opificio Dei* (On God's Creation), and *De Ira* (On Anger). Other writers extensively quoted, and on whom he had attended lectures in Italy, include Valerius Maximus, Terence, and Plautus (eighteen of Plautus's plays are cited); but Julius Caesar, Apuleius, and Macrobius are also represented, whereas patristic writers (apart from Lactantius and Orosius) scarcely figure. Among medieval writers he makes significant reference only to the fourteenth-century *De vita et moribus philosophorum* (The Lives and Manners of the Philosophers) of Walter Burley (which, however, he attributes to Diogenes Laertius). From the Renaissance, Petrarch is quoted extensively. The wide range of places—Nuremberg, Rome, Paris, Strasbourg, Venice, Toulouse, and Basel—in which it was published indicates that *Margarita poetica* was recognized as a useful collection of humanistic writings, at least until the complete texts became more readily accessible. The growth of printing made Eyb's compilation redundant, and it was not republished after 1503.

Of three short pieces written in Eichstätt in 1459–1460 the first, *An viro sapienti uxor sit ducenda* (Whether a Wise Man Should Marry), is, in effect, a Latin draft for his first treatise in the vernacular, *Ob einem manne sey zunemen ein eelichs weyb oder nicht* (Whether a Man Should Take a Wife or Not, 1472). It stands in the tradition of (yet tellingly does not cite) *De re uxoria* (On Property in Marriage), written by Francesco Barbaro on the occasion of the marriage of Lorenzo Medici in 1415. The other two, *Clarissimarum feminarum laudacio* (Praise of Famous Ladies) and *Invectiva in lenam* (Invective against the Procuress), also deal with the subject of women. The former, whose title reflects the influence of Giovanni Boccaccio's *De claris mulieribus* (On Famous Women, 1361–1362)—a work much read in southern Germany at the time (Michael Dallapiazza records twenty-seven manuscripts of it in Germany, and it was one of the earliest books printed at Ulm [1473])—presents the great deeds of historical women as models for others; Eyb aims to show that women have been of great service to the world in matters moral, literary, and social. *Invectiva in lenam,* written three days after *Clarissimarum feminarum laudacio,* sets out the wicked qualities of women. Since it is dedicated to the canons of Eichstätt, it is possible that Eyb wrote the piece after they objected to his one-sided glorification of women in the *Clarissimarum feminarum laudacio.*

Ob einem manne sey zunemen ein eelichs weyb oder nicht, generally known as Eyb's *Ehebüchlein* (Little Book on Marriage), is dedicated to the city council of Nuremberg on New Year's Day 1472. The subject of marriage is treated with dignity and refinement in a clear, concise, and fluent prose that has often been held up as among the best of the period. Taking theological, moral, and legal considerations into account, Eyb considers the pros and cons of marriage from the point of view of the *honestum* (honorable) and *utile* (useful) as well as the *dulce* (agreeable) and comes down decisively in favor of the institution, with a few reservations. The divine order requires marriage for the propagation of humanity, and it should be contracted for God's glory. Marriage is essential for morality; without it human society would collapse. Though married life may be beset with many difficulties, it offers the recompense of companionship and of joy in offspring. To illustrate his views Eyb includes in the work translations of two Renaissance novellas: "Marina" and "Guiscardus und Sigismunda" (the latter after Bruni's Latin version of Boccaccio's *Decameron* IV, 1)—two of the best German translations of the period. The second part of the book comprises the chapters "Das lob der Ee" (In Praise of Marriage) and "Das lob der frawen" (In Praise of Women), in which he gathers together all the arguments he has advanced earlier. The third part is only loosely related to the first two: after dealing with the organization of weddings, Eyb reflects on the transience and sinfulness of human life, then counters this pessimistic tone with a translation of the medieval legend of Albanus under the heading "Das kein sunder verzweyfeln solle" (Lest the sinner despair). All in all, Hiller and Weinacht are right to say that Eyb is in no way a forerunner of Martin Luther, as some, including Herrmann, have claimed: he does not deny the sacramental status of marriage; and, even though he dedicated the work to the Nuremberg city council, there is no evidence that he envisaged marriage as passing into the control of the civil authorities.

Eyb's second work in German, *Spiegel der Sitten,* was completed in May 1474, but he was unable to see it into print before his death on 23 or 24 July 1475. It remained unpublished until his nephew, Prince-Bishop Gabriel von Eyb, commissioned the Eichstätt canon Johann Huff to prepare it for press. Huff arranged with the Augsburg publisher Johannes Rynmann to have it printed by Johann Otmar in that city in September 1511. Eyb's aim in this work was to set forth not only the virtues but also the vices, for a person could avoid the latter only if attention was drawn to them. The book falls into two parts, both of which are thematically arranged: the first fifty-four chapters deal with the four cardinal virtues, the seven deadly sins, attitudes to death, and the Last Things. The last forty-one chapters discuss all sorts and conditions of people, from kings and princes to merchants and peasants, widows and virgins, rich and poor. The individual chapters consist largely of quotations from ancient authors, loosely strung together and drawn largely from the same florilegia and late-medieval scholastic texts that Eyb used for *Margarita poetica.* He endeavored to reconcile medieval views with those of Italian humanism by augmenting the patristic and medieval material with quotations from classical and humanist authors. He relied on manuscripts from his own library and also on sources that may not have been available in his own collection, such as the *Communiloquium* (Collection of Quotations, thirteenth century) of Johannes Guallensis, the *Pharetra doctorum* (Quiver of Doctors, thirteenth century), Vincent of Beauvais's *Speculum doctrinale* (Mirror of Doctrine, thirteenth century), works by Johannes Nider and Nikolaus von Dinkelsbühl, and Johannes Herolt's *Promptuarium exemplorum* (A Storehouse of Exempla, circa 1440). The final part of Eyb's work comprises his translation of Plautus's *Menaechmi* and *Bacchides,* and of the *Philogenia* of Ugolino Pisani. (Eyb had not included the *Bacchides* in *Spiegel der Sitten;* it was added by Huff.) Breathing the air of classical antiquity, Plautus's plays had to be thoroughly reworked. Eyb's aim was not to acquaint his readers with life in classical Rome but to re-create the works in the context of the cultural and moral conditions of fifteenth-century Germany. He replaced the classical names with homely German ones (thus, in *Bacchides* Chrysalus, Nicobus, Philoxenus, and Parasitus become Pentz, Utz, Kuntz, and Fritz, respectively), excised mythological references, and re-

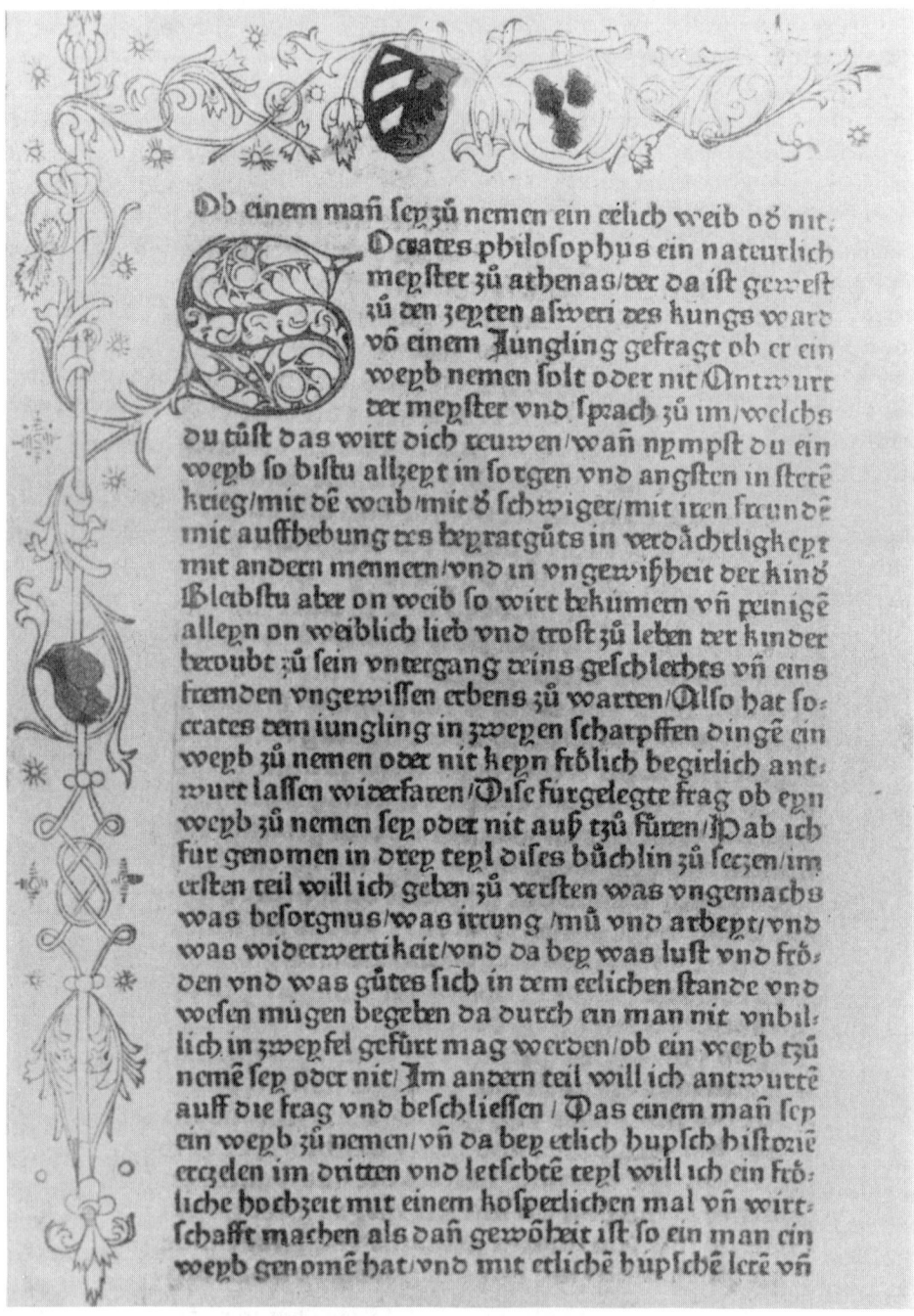

Page from Eyb's Ehebüchlein, *his first work in German*

placed Latin proverbs with German equivalents. Of the three plays, *Bacchides* is the closest to the Latin original. In the prefatory material to *Spiegel der Sitten* Eyb writes that the reader should admire "die hübschait vnd süssigkait der wörter vnd die swärlichait der synnen vnd red vnd nit die fröhlichait vnd wollust der Comedien" (the beauty and sweetness of the words [a Petrarchan echo] and the seriousness of the meaning and the dialogue but not the merriment or pleasure the comedies afford). The translations attracted attention in the sixteenth century: Hans Sachs wrote a verse version of *Menaechmi* in 1540, and Martin Glaser based a Shrovetide play on *Philogenia* that was printed in 1552. Eyb is important as a translator because he translates freely—as he puts it in the prefatory material, "nit als gar von worten zu worten ... sunder nach dem synn vnd mainung der materien als sy am verstendlichisten vnd besten lauten mügen" (not word for word ... but according to the sense and meaning of the matter in the way that they sound most intelligible and best). It is his striving after intelligibility and his command of popular idiom (which set him off markedly from his contemporary Niklas von Wyle) that have earned him the reputation of being one of the best German prose writers before Luther.

Eyb has been credited with authorship of an anonymous version of Boccaccio's story of Griselda (*Decameron*, X, 10) that is probably based on Erhard Gross's *Grisardis* (1436). Eyb's possible authorship of the work was the subject of controversy between Max Herrmann and Philipp Strauch; in his 1979 dissertation John Christian Weber edited the text, from a manuscript at the University of Pennsylvania, under Eyb's name.

Though Eyb's German works undeniably include medieval elements, which led Hiller to reject Herrmann's classification of him as a humanist, it is precisely the mingling of medieval and humanist traditions that is characteristic of early humanism in Germany. Yet Hiller's assessment of Eyb is, perhaps, not wholly inappropriate: "As a lawyer he wanted justice, as a writer, morality, as a cleric, sanctity." Full appreciation of Albrecht von Eyb's status as a scholar and writer is hampered, however, by the parlous situation regarding editions of his works: apart from the encomium on Bamberg, none of his Latin works is available in a modern edition, and, for all their importance—not least in the history of translation—even his German writings have been edited only in a piecemeal fashion.

References:

Eckhard Bernstein, "Albrecht von Eyb," in *Deutsche Dichter der frühen Neuzeit (1450–1600): Ihr Leben und Werk,* edited by Stephan Füssel (Berlin: Erich Schmidt, 1993), pp. 96–110;

Bernstein, *Die Literatur des deutschen Frühhumanismus* (Stuttgart: Metzler, 1978), pp. 62–75;

K. O. Conrady, "Zu den deutschen Plautusübertragungen," *Euphorion,* 48 (1954): 373–396;

Murray Aiken Cowie, *Proverbs and Proverbial Phrases in the German Works of Albrecht von Eyb* (Chicago: University of Chicago Press, 1942);

Michael Dallapiazza, *Die Boccaccio-Handschriften in den deutschsprachigen Ländern* (Bamberg: Wendel, 1988);

Alan R. Deighton, "Zwei unbekannte Handschriften des 'Ehebüchleins' Albrechts von Eyb," *Zeitschrift für deutsches Altertum,* 116 (1987): 134–140;

Irene Erfen-Hänsch, *Historia Sigismunde: Abbildungen zu einer Boccaccio-Novelle im deutschen Frühdruck. Leonardo Bruni, Arigo, Niklas von Wyle, Albrecht von Eyb* (Göppingen: Kümmerle, forthcoming, 1997);

Erfen-Hänsch, *Historia Sigismunde: Zur Rezeption einer Boccaccio-Novelle im deutschen Frühhumanismus. Leonardo Bruni, Arigo, Niklas von Wyle, Albrecht von Eyb* (Göppingen: Kümmerle, forthcoming, 1997);

Monika Fink-Lang, "Das Ehebüchlein des Albrecht von Eyb," in *Nürnberg und Italien: Begegnungen, Einflüsse und Ideen,* edited by Volker Kapp and Frank-Rutger Hausmann (Tübingen: Stauffenburg, 1991), pp. 169–180;

Goswin Gailhofer, "Der Humanist Albrecht von Eyb," *Sammelblatt des historischen Vereins Eichstätt,* 42 (1927): 28–71;

William Hammer, "Albrecht von Eyb, Eulogist of Bamberg," *Germanic Review,* 17 (1942): 1–19;

Reinhard K. Hennig, "Albrecht von Eybs 'Lob der Ehe' und seine Vorlage," *Journal of English and Germanic Philology,* 84 (1985): 364–373;

Max Herrmann, *Albrecht von Eyb und die Frühzeit des deutschen Humanismus* (Berlin: Weidmann, 1893);

Herrmann, "Die lateinische Marina," *Vierteljahrsschrift für Literaturgeschichte,* 3 (1890): 1–27;

Joseph Anthony Hiller, *Albrecht von Eyb: A Medieval Moralist* (Washington, D.C.: Catholic University of America, 1939);

Rudolf Hirsch, "Printing and the Spread of Humanism in Germany: The Example of Albrecht von Eyb," in his *The Printed Word: Its Impact and*

Diffusion (London: Variorum, 1978), pp. 24-37;

Gerhard Klecha, "Albrecht von Eyb," in *Die deutsche Literatur des Mittelalters: Verfasserlexikon,* volume 1, second edition, edited by Kurt Ruh (Berlin & New York: De Gruyter, 1978), cols. 180-186;

William Melczer, "Albrecht von Eyb (1420-75) et les racines italiennes du premier humanisme allemand," in *L'humanisme allemand (1480-1540): Colloque international de Tours,* edited by Joël Lefebvre and Jean-Claude Margolin (Munich: Fink, 1979), pp. 31-44;

Karin Morvay, *Die Albanuslegende: Deutsche Fassungen und ihre Beziehungen zur lateinischen Überlieferung* (Munich: Fink, 1977), pp. 126-150;

Agostini Sottili, "An uxor viro sapienti sit ducenda: Zum Stemma codicum von Albrecht von Eybs lateinischer Eheschrift," *Wolfenbütteler Renaissance-Mitteilungen,* 4 (1980): 81-87;

Philipp Strauch, *Die Grisardis des Erhard Gross nach der Breslauer Handschrift* (Halle: Niemeyer, 1931);

Helmut Weinacht, "Albrecht von Eyb," in *Fränkische Klassiker: Eine Literaturgeschichte in Einzeldarstellungen,* edited by Wolfgang Buhl (Nuremberg: Nürnberger Presse, 1971), pp. 170-182;

Weinacht, "Die Bamberger Traktate Albrechts von Eyb," *Frankenland,* new series 29 (1977): 284-289, 315-322;

Gianni Zippel, "Gli inizi dell'Umanesimo tedesco e l'Umanesimo italiano nel XV secolo," *Bollettino dell'Istituto Storico Italiano per il Medio Evo,* 75 (1963): 345-389.

Johann Fischart
(1546 or 1547 – 1590 or 1591)

Stephen L. Wailes
Indiana University

BOOKS: *Nacht Rab oder Nebelkräh: Von dem vberauß Jesuwidrischen geistlosen Schreiben vnnd Leben des Hans Jacobs Gackels, der sich nennet Rab?* (Strasbourg, 1570);

Der Barfüsser Secten und Kuttenstreit (Strasbourg: Bernhard Jobin, circa 1570–1571; revised, 1577);

Von S. Dominici des Predigermünchs vnd S. Francisci Barfüssers artlichem Leben und grossen Greweln (Ober-Ursel: Nicolaus Henricus, 1571);

Eulenspiegel Reimensweiß: Eine neue Beschreibung und Legendt des kurtzweiligen Lebens und seltsamen Thaten Thyll Eulenspiegels (Frankfurt am Main: Hieronymus Feyerabend & Bernhard Jobin, 1572);

Aller Praktik Großmutter: Ein dickgeprockte neuwe und trewe, laurhaffte und immerdaurhaffte Procdick, auch possierliche, doch nit verführliche Pruchnasticatz (Strasbourg: Bernhard Jobin, 1572; revised, 1574);

Onomastica II. I. Philosophicum, Medicum, Synonymum ex variis vulgaribusque linguis. II. Theophrasti Paracelsi: hoc est, earum vocum, quarum in scriptis eius solet usus esse, explicatio, by Fischart and Michael Schütz (Strasbourg: Bernhard Jobin, 1574);

Neue künstliche Figuren biblischer Historien, grüntlich von Tobia Stimmer gerissen. Vnd zu Gotsförchtiger Ergetzung andächtiger Hertzen mit artigen Reimen begriffen durch J.F.G.M. (Basel: Thomas Gwarin, 1576);

Das Glückhafft Schiff von Zürich: Ein Lobspruch, vonn der Glücklichen und Wolfertigen Schiffart, einer Burgerlichen Geselschafft auß Zürich, auf das außgeschriben Schiessen gehn Straßburg den 21. Junij des 76. Jars, nicht vil erhörter weis vollbracht (Strasbourg: Bernhard Jobin, 1577);

Flöh Hatz, Weiber Tratz: Der wunderunrichtige und spotwichtige Rechtshandel der Flöh mit den Weibern (Strasbourg: Bernhard Jobin, 1577);

Die wunderlichst unerhörtest Legend und Beschreibung des abgeführten, quartirten, gevierten und viereckechten Vierhörnigen Hütleins (Strasbourg: Bernhard Jobin, 1580);

Johann Fischart

Gantz gedenkwürdige und eygentliche Verzeichnuß wie die mächtig und prächtig von vielen Jahren her zugerüste Spanische Armada zu Ende nechst verschienenen Sommers dieses 1588. Jahrs umb Bezwingung der Niderlanden und Einnemmung des Königreiches Engelland abgefahren (Strasbourg: Bernhard Jobin, 1588);

Ordenliche Beschreibung, welches gestalt die Nachbarliche Bündnuß und Verain der dreyen Löblichen Freien Stätt Zürich, Bern und Straßburg, dieses gegenwärtigen 1588. Jars, im Monat Maio ist ernewert, bestättiget und vollzogen worden (Strasbourg: Bernhard Jobin, 1588);

Catalogus Catalogorum perpetuo durabilis. Das ist: Ein Ewigwerende, Gordianischer, Pergamenischer und Tiraninonischer Bibliothecken gleichwichtige und richtige Verzeichnuß und Registratur (Strasbourg: Bernhard Jobin, 1590).

Editions and Collections: *Dichtungen von Johann Fischart, genannt Menzer,* edited by Karl Goedeke (Leipzig: Brockhaus, 1880);

Johann Fischarts Werke: Eine Auswahl. Teil 1–3, 3 volumes, edited by Adolf Hauffen (Stuttgart: Union Deutsche Verlagsgesellschaft, 1892–1895);

Flöh Hatz, Weiber Tratz, edited by Alois Haas (Stuttgart: Reclam, 1967);

Das Glückhafft Schiff von Zürich, edited by Haas (Stuttgart: Reclam, 1967);

Catalogus Catalogorum perpetuo durabilis. Das ist: Ein Ewigwerende, Gordianischer, Pergamenischer und Tiraninonischer Bibliothecken gleichwichtige und richtige Verzeichnuß und Registratur, edited by Michael Schilling (Tübingen: Niemeyer, 1993);

Johann Fischart: Sämtliche Werke, 1 volume published, edited by Hans-Gert Roloff, Ulrich Seelbach, and W. Eckehart Spengler (Bern: Peter Lang, 1993–).

OTHER: "Ein artliches Lob der Lauten," in *Das erste Buch newerleßener fleißiger ettlicher viel schöner Lautenstück,* edited by Bernhard Jobin (Strasbourg: Bernhard Jobin, 1572), fols. 2ᵇ–6ᵃ;

Das sechste Buch, der Historien vom Amadis auß Franckreich, auch seinen Nachkommen und Söhnen: Gantz nützlich von guten Lehren und lieplich von Geschichten zulesen. Auss frantzösischer Sprach newlich in Teutsche durch J.F.G.M. gebracht, translated by Fischart (Frankfurt am Main: Feyerabend, 1572);

Psalmen, geistliche Lieder und Kirchengesänge: D. Mar. Luthers. Auch viler anderer gotseliger Mäner, contributions by Fischart (Strasbourg: Bernhard Jobin, 1573; revised, 1576);

"Ein nothwendige Anweisung und Vorbericht in Lesung folgender lieblicher Histori von stäter Lieb des Ismenii und der Ismene, was daraus zu lehrnen, und wie das regiment der Liebe zuerkennen," in *Ismenius: Oder, Ein vorbild Stäter Liebe,* by Eustathius Makrembolites, translated by Joh. Christ. Artopeus (Strasbourg: Bernhard Jobin, 1573), fols. 104–108;

François Rabelais, *Affenteurliche und vngeheurliche Geschichtschrift vom Leben, Rhaten vnd Thaten der for langen Weilen vollenwolbeschraiten Helden und Herrn Grandgusier, Gargantoa, vnd Pantagruel, Königen inn Vtopien und Ninenreich,* translated and adapted by Fischart (Strasbourg: Bernhard Jobin, 1575); revised as *Affentheurlich naupengeheurliche Geschichtklitterung, von Thaten vnd rhaten der . . . Helden . . . Grandgusier, Gorgantoa vnd Pantagruel* (Strasbourg: Bernhard Jobin, 1582); edited by Ute Nyssen as *Geschichtklitterung (Gargantua): Text der Ausgabe letzter Hand von 1590,* 2 volumes (Düsseldorf: Rand, 1963, 1964);

Johannes Carnarius and Willibald Pirckheimer, *Podagrammisch Trostbüchlein: Innhaltend zwo artlicher SchuzReden von herlicher Ankonft, Geschlecht, Hofhaltung, Nuzbarkeit und tiefgesuchtem Lob des hochgeehrten, gliedermächtigen und zarten Fräuleins Podagra,* translated by Fischart (Strasbourg: Bernhard Jobin, 1577);

Plutarch and Desiderius Erasmus, *Das philosophisch Ehezuchtbüchlein: Oder, Des berühmtesten und hocherleuchtesten griechischen Philosophi oder natürlicher Weisheit Erkündigers und Lehrers Plutarchi naturgescheide eheliche Gesaz oder vernunftgemäße Ehegebot,* translated and edited, with contributions, by Fischart (Strasbourg: Bernhard Jobin, 1578);

Philipp von Marnix, *BinenKorb des Heyl. Römischen Imenschwarms, seiner Hummelszellen (oder Himmelszellen) Hurrnaußnäster, Brämengeschwürm und Wäspengetöß,* translated and enlarged by Fischart (Strasbourg: Bernhard Jobin, 1579);

Merkliche frantzösische Zeitung, von den herrlichen Solenniteten und Ceremonien, so bei dem erst neugestiffteten RitterOrden vom H. Geyst gebraucht vnd gehalten. Samt den Namen der Ritter vnd Herrn, welche inn solchen neuen Orden, den ersten dises 79. Jars getretten vnd aufgenommen werden. Darzu eyne notwendige Anleytung, den geheymnussen dises vergeysteten Ordens etlicher masen nachzusinnen, ist vorgethan worden. Auß Frantzösischem treulich inns Teutsch gebracht, translated, with concluding poem, by Fischart (N.p., 1579);

"Fürtreffliches artliches Lob, deß Landlustes, Mayersmut und lustigen Feldbaumans Leben, aus des Horatii Epodo, Beatus ille, etc. gezogen und verteutschet," in *Siben Bücher von dem Feldbau und vollkommener Bestellung eines ordentlichen Mayershofs oder Landguts,* by Charles Estienne, translated by Melchior Sebisch (Strasbourg: Bernhard Jobin, 1579);

Ricardus Anglicus, *Correctorium Alchymiae Richardi Anglici,* edited by Fischart (Strasbourg: Bernhard Jobin, 1581);

Jean Bodin, *De Daemonomania Magorum: Vom außgelaßnen wütigen Teuffelsheer der unsinnigen Hexen und Hexenmeyster,* translated by Fischart (Strasbourg: Bernhard Jobin, 1581); republished as *De Magorum Daemonomania* (Strasbourg: Bernhard Jobin, 1586);

Malleorum quorundam maleficarum tam veterum quam recentiorum autorum tomi duo, 2 volumes, edited by Fischart (Frankfurt am Main: Nikolaus Bassäus, 1582);

John Calvin, *Der heilig Brotkorb der H. Römischen Reliquien oder Würdigen Heiligthumbs procken: Das ist Johannis Calvini Notwendige Vermanung von der Papisten Heiligthumb,* revised by Fischart (Strasbourg: Bernhard Jobin, 1583);

Kurtze Beschreibung des Lottringischen vnd Guisischen Feindlichen einfals in die Graueschafft Mümpelgart, welcher zu endt des abgeloffenen 1587. Jahrs, vnd Eingang dieses 1588. beschehen, edited, with introduction and concluding verses, by Fischart (N.p., 1588).

Johann Fischart was the most important writer of German in the last third of the sixteenth century. His many works in prose and verse, representing various literary genres and types, engage important political and religious issues of the day as well as answer the need of a cultured elite for entertainment. His virtuosity with language is rooted in a native fascination with phonology, morphology, etymology, borrowings, and lendings but is disciplined by a thorough training in rhetoric and poetics. The density and difficulty of his style, combined with the topicality of many of his subjects and allusions, give his work little appeal to modern readers. Fischart is not widely known in English-speaking countries.

Born in Strasbourg in 1546 or 1547, Fischart often placed the initials *G. M.,* for *genannt Menzer* (called "From Mainz"), after his own to form a pen name indicating his family's place of origin. Because of the strong education in the liberal arts and the zealous Protestantism he displayed when he began to write for publication in his twenties, one infers that he attended the well-known Strasbourg gymnasium directed by the Protestant humanist Johann Sturm. In 1562, after the death of his father, Johann, a prosperous spice merchant, Fischart was sent to Worms and placed under the supervision of the noted humanist author and teacher Kaspar Scheidt, a close family friend and perhaps a cousin. In 1565, his schooling finished, he traveled to the Netherlands, France, and Italy, and possibly to England. During this trip he studied law in Siena; later, in 1574, he would acquire a doctorate in civil and canon law in Basel.

Fischart's career as an author is linked to the marriage in 1567 of his eldest sister to the Swiss printer Bernhard Jobin. In 1570 Jobin opened in Strasbourg what was to prove to be a highly successful printery. That same year Fischart's first published work appeared; although the printer's name does not appear on the title page, it may well have been printed by Jobin. *Nacht Rab oder Nebelkräh* (Night Raven; or, Fog Crow) is an anti-Catholic polemic in nearly nineteen hundred rhymed couplets; special

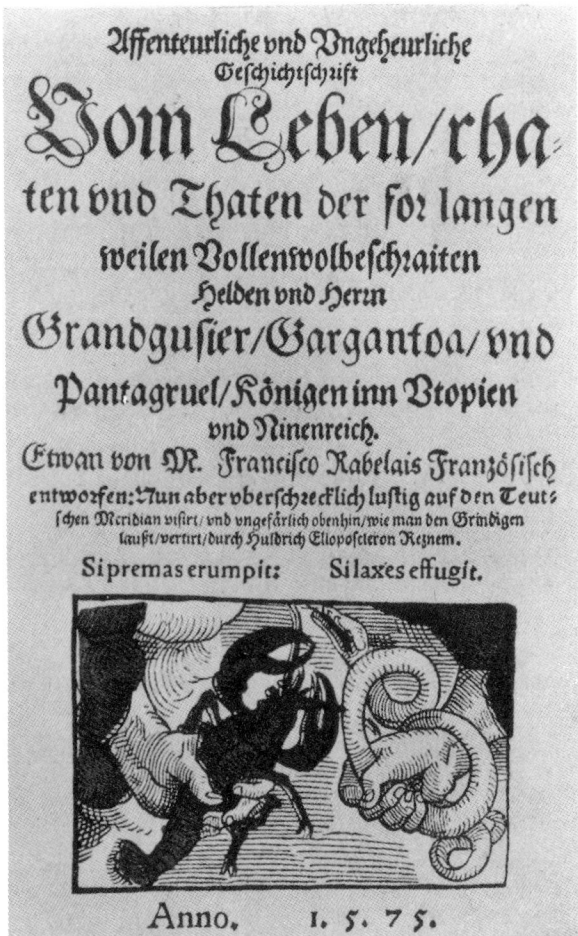

Title page for Fischart's adaptation of the first book of François Rabelais's Gargantua et Pantagruel

objects of attack are the Jesuits, the Catholic push for religious power in Strasbourg, and the Catholic controversialist Johann Jakob Rabe. Rabe's name inspired Fischart to endless puns and wordplay in the course of the loosely structured attack. That year or the next Fischart's brother-in-law printed his broadside *Der Barfüsser Secten und Kuttenstreit* (On Franciscan Sects and Disputes). In 1571 Fischart extended his polemical efforts with a forty-seven-hundred-line harangue against the mendicant orders, *Von S. Dominici des Predigermünchs und S. Francisci Barfüssers artlichem Leben* (The Life of Saint Dominic the Preaching Friar and Saint Francis the Barefoot Friar).

Fischart was open to literary ventures other than religious polemics. In 1572 he published an adaptation into verse of the popular chapbook *Til Eulenspiegel* (1510–1511), a work that has been attributed to Hermann Bote. Fischart greatly expanded the work to include barbs aimed at Catholic

Title page in the work for which Fischart is best known today

targets and to promote a comprehensive bourgeois morality not found in his source. His parody of the almanac form, *Aller Praktik Großmutter* (The Grandmother of All Almanacs), appeared the same year, as did his translation from the French of the sixth book of the best-selling fifteenth-century prose romance *Amadís de Gaula* (Amadís of Gaul), a huge treasury of chivalric adventures.

Fischart contributed sixteen songs and a rhymed preface to a collection of Protestant church music, *Psalmen, geistliche Lieder und Kirchengesänge* (Psalms, Hymns and Church Songs), published by Jobin in 1573. When the collection was revised in 1576 five of Fischart's contributions were omitted, but twenty others appeared for the first time. His texts, adapted to familiar melodies, thus made up 31 of the 177 pieces in the revised edition, almost as many as those by Martin Luther. Fischart never again published sacred songs; he supported himself by his writing, and he apparently chose his subjects and forms as much on the basis of the marketplace as on that of personal inclination or conviction. He seems to have been responding here, as elsewhere, to a particular opportunity. In 1574 he collaborated with Michael Schütz (known as Michael Toxites) on *Onomastica II* (Two Onomastics), lexica for the study of Paracelsus's scientific and medical tracts.

Often marketplace and personal factors pointed the same way, and such was probably the case for the work on which his reputation for originality and stylistic bravura mainly rests: his adaptation of the first book of François Rabelais's *Gargantua et Pantagruel* (1532–1564), published in 1575 as *Affenteurliche und ungeheurliche Geschichtschrift vom Leben, Rhaten und*

Thaten der for langen Weilen vollenwolbeschraiten Helden und Herrn Grandgusier, Gargantoa, und Pantagruel, Königen inn Utopien und Ninenreich (Momentous, Monstrous History of the Lives and Times of the Erstwhile Celebrated Lords and Heroes Gargantua and Pantagruel, Kings of Utopia) and revised in 1582 as *Affentheurlich naupengeheurliche Geschichtklitterung* (Adventuresome Narrative Scribbling). This extraordinary undertaking is a close translation of Rabelais's work, to the extent that the original is followed at all; Fischart adds much new material, including whole chapters, and amplifies his translation throughout. In the 1575 edition the original is expanded threefold, and even more material is added in the revision. The expansion is achieved largely through incessant verbal innovations and variations in the smallest components of style. Fischart indulges his passion for linguistic manipulations on the basis of sound, sense, and sight; one term generates another, one thought brings forth variants, one phrase or verbal figure spawns progeny that themselves reproduce. In his preface Fischart begs indulgence for the book's mannerisms with the old argument that he is presenting a negative example, "ein verwirrtes ungestaltes Muster der heut verwirrten und ungestalten Welt" (a confused and formless illustration of today's confused and formless world), in the hope of leading the reader away from this flux, which is presided over by the devil. Critical evaluation of the book has been mixed. It is difficult reading even for the specialist; while granting that a current of vital force energizes and unifies it, not all critics believe that it has philosophical or artistic coherence or that it promotes a set of values or a vision of life. As interest has grown in literature that undermines or deconstructs models and conventions, scholars have found Fischart's "scribbling" more and more intriguing.

"The German Rabelais," as Fischart has been called, continued to write in various forms and styles. He collaborated with the prominent artist Tobias Stimmer on *Neue künstliche Figuren biblischer Historien* (New Artistic Pictures of Biblical Stories, 1576), contributing five or six lines of verse for each of Stimmer's 170 woodcuts. He kept the poems doctrinally neutral so that they would not impede the volume's sales. In 1577 (a putative printing of 1576 is lost) appeared *Das Glückhafft Schiff von Zürich* (The Fortunate Ship from Zurich), the only work by Fischart known to general readers today and the only one that has enjoyed a consistently positive reception. In about six hundred couplets it celebrates the exploits of twenty-four men from Zurich who rowed down the Limmat, Aare, and Rhine Rivers to Strasbourg in a single day in June 1576 to participate in a shooting match.

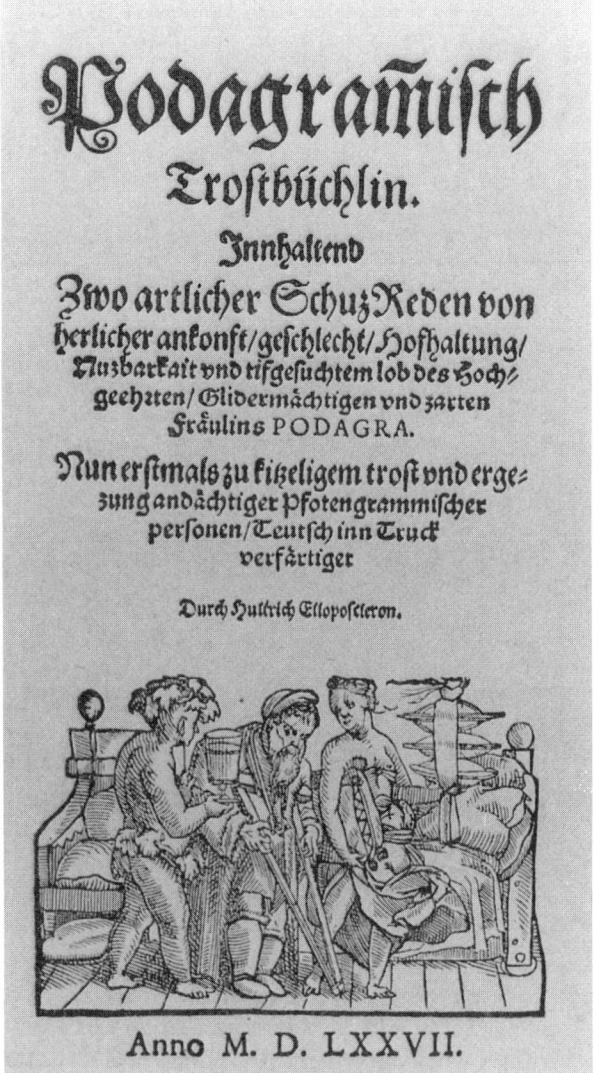

Title page for Fischart's free translation of two satiric encomiums to gout, originally written in Latin by Johannes Carnarius and Willibald Pirckheimer

Fischart treats this event as an adventure of modern argonauts. He embellishes his narrative rhetorically yet tastefully, keeping his style simple and accessible (by the standards of the period), and finds in his subject a demonstration both of social solidarity and of the bourgeois virtues of hard work and perseverance. The poem is written with wit and elegance; it promotes common virtues and civic pride. Admirers of Fischart like to think that *Das Glückhafft Schiff von Zürich* reveals something of the author's real person, but its isolation in his oeuvre argues that it was simply another literary project whose characteristics were determined by the subject and the prospective purchasers.

From 1577 to 1581 Fischart published a series of books appealing to contemporary tastes. *Flöh*

Fischart's bookplate; woodcut by Jost Ammann

Hatz, Weiber Tratz (Hunting of Fleas, Defiance of Women, 1577) adds to the rich tradition of "flea literature," works in which the vehicle of fleas' complaints about persecution by women enabled authors to make humorous observations on women's bodies, hygiene, and dress. Characteristically, Fischart's *Flöh Hatz, Weiber Tratz* was more than twice the length of Jobin's first volume with this title, written by Matthias Holtzer and published in 1573. In 1577 also appeared Fischart's free translation of two satiric encomiums, written in Latin by Johannes Carnarius and Willibald Pirckheimer, about the gout. *Podagrammisch Trostbüchlein* (Consolations of Gout) stands in a long line of literary entertainments centered on this affliction of the well-to-do, who could afford to buy the works. Fischart's *Das philosophisch Ehezuchtbüchlein* (Philosophical Treatise on Marital Discipline, 1578) combines free translations from the works of Plutarch and Desiderius Erasmus with his own large collection of proverbs, anecdotes, and exempla. Marriage literature was highly popular; Fischart's contribution is conventional in outlook and speaks to the interests of the natural consumers of the product, the patriarchal, Protestant bourgeoisie. Returning to religious controversy, Fischart translated and expanded an anti-Catholic polemic by the Netherlander Philipp von Marnix; the work was published by Jobin in 1579 as *BinenKorb des Heyl. Römischen Imenschwarms* (The Hive of the Holy Roman Swarm). Starting from the conceit that the three-tiered papal tiara resembles a man-made beehive, Marnix and Fischart attack the dogma of the Roman Church and the morality of its many organizational groups. Just as harsh, but narrower in scope, is Fischart's 1580 diatribe against the Jesuits, *Die wunderlichst unerhörtest Legend und Beschreibung des abgeführten, quartirten, gevierten und viereckechten Vierhörnigen Hütleins* (The Strangest and Most Shocking Legend and Description of the Four-Cornered Hat). In 1581 he edited, with clear sympathy, a collection of alchemical writings, *Correctorium Alchymiae Richardi Anglici* (The Alchemical Correctorium of Ricardus Anglicus).

This decade of feverish literary production ended in 1580, when Fischart gained a position in Speyer as a lawyer attached to the imperial high court. Such positions were a kind of practicum in imperial law, which the incumbents hoped would lead to full appointments elsewhere. Fischart's ambition to achieve economic security and social recognition is reflected not only in this career change but also in the dedications of his published works. In 1577 he had dedicated his *Podagrammisch Trostbüchlein* to Egenolf III. von Rappoltstein, one of the most powerful noblemen in Upper Alsace; in 1581 he dedicated to Egenolf *De Daemonomania Magorum* (On the Diabolical Madness of Witches), his translation of the distinguished French political theorist Jean Bodin's *Démonomanie des Sorciers* (1580). In the latter dedication he praises Egenolf's dedication to divine and human justice as well as the nobleman's devotion to humane studies. Such praise, of course, is a form of self-recommendation. Fischart's interest in appealing not only to the general public's obsession with witchcraft but also to the practical needs of those in authority may lie behind his work on a new edition (1582) of the handbook for Dominican inquisitors in witch trials, the infamous *Malleus Maleficarum* (Hammer for Witches). His role in this collaboration was to edit the texts and to supply Latin summaries of supplemental writings in the vernacular.

On 11 November 1583 Fischart married Anna Elisabeth Hertzog, from a prosperous family. Their son, Hans Bernhard, was born in 1584 and their daughter, Anna Elisabeth, in 1588. In the year of his marriage Fischart attained the kind of appointment he had been seeking, that of *Amtmann* (prefect) in Forbach, a community in the German part of Lorraine. His duties were administrative and judicial, including the collection of taxes, duties, and fines; presiding in court; supervising the police and forest workers; and, generally, representing the interests of the feudal lords vis-à-vis the commoners. Although there is no direct evidence that he served as Amtmann after 1586, it is likely that he held the office until his death in 1590 or early 1591. If so, Fischart, who had published a second edition of his translation of Bodin's *Démonomanie* in 1586, would have presided at the witch trials in Forbach and nearby villages in September 1587. The trials probably led to executions, since in 1595 a ducal privy councillor and judge reported that in Lorraine nine hundred persons had been in the recent past executed for sorcery. Thus, it seems that Fischart, who belonged to the cultural elite, had a superior intelligence and education, and was a fierce critic of ecclesiastical superstitions and human foibles, actively collaborated in one of the darker chapters of religious and social history in the age of the Counter Reformation.

From 1580 until his death Fischart published relatively little. He revised and edited *Der heilig Brotkorb* (The Sacred Breadbasket, 1583), a German translation of a work by John Calvin on the Catholic cult of relics; and, in overlapping roles as author, translator, and editor, he published *Gantz gedenkwürdige und eygentliche Verzeichnuß wie die mächtig und prächtig von vielen Jahren her zugerüste Spanische Armada zu Ende nechst verschienenen Sommers dieses 1588. Jahrs umb Bezwingung der Niderlanden und Einnemmung des Königreiches Engelland abgefahren* (A Memorable Account of How the Mighty Spanish Armada Set out Last Summer to Subdue the Netherlands and Conquer England, 1588). When Strasbourg entered into a political alliance with Zurich and Bern in 1588 to forestall aggression by imperial Catholic powers, Fischart celebrated the event in print as *Ordenliche Beschreibung, welches gestalt die Nachbarliche Bündnuß und Verain der dreyen Löblichen Freien Stätt Zürich, Bern und Straßburg, dieses gegenwärtigen 1588. Jars, im Monat Maio ist ernewert, bestättiget und vollzogen worden* (A Proper Description of the Renewal and Completion of the Federation among Zurich, Bern, and Strasbourg in May 1588). His last work appeared not long before his death: *Catalogus Catalogorum* (Catalogue of Catalogues, 1590) is a satire on traditional forms of learning, as well as on the published catalogues of the annual Frankfurt book exhibitions. In the preface and epilogue Fischart acknowledged his debt to Rabelais, who in book 2, chapter 7 of *Gargantua et Pantagruel* gives a list of 140 books supposedly in the cloister library of Saint Victor in Paris that were especially pleasing to Pantagruel.

The thrust of Rabelais's catalogue of authentic and fictive titles and authors is to attack musty scholasticism, church abuses, chicaneries of doctors and lawyers, and so forth. Characteristically, Fischart expanded this conception to a list of 527 works, some closely adapted from Rabelais, others of his own invention. To decipher the wit and satiric message of the entries requires a knowledge of ancient and modern languages and familiarity with late-sixteenth-century European culture comparable to that of the author. The *Catalogus Catalogorum* is, thus, an epitome of Fischart as writer: witty, elegant, topical, erudite, recondite, and almost entirely consigned to academic specialists.

It is difficult to reach a conclusion regarding Fischart's importance and stature as an author. There can be no doubt of his learning, linguistic and stylistic gifts, and fecund imagination in adapting, expanding, and elaborating a model; less clear is his ability to conceive and execute a large literary design – here the study of *Affentheurlich naupengeheurliche Geschichtklitterung* may benefit his reputation. The strength of his personal devotion to the causes he promoted as a writer remains uncertain, for although he was clearly a convinced Protestant, none of his writings bespeaks deep religious faith. His denunciations of Catholic institutions and practices seem to be linked to a powerful animus against Catholic individuals such as Rabe. Fischart's twenty years of authorship divide evenly between a period in which he supported himself by writing, usually in collaboration with his brother-in-law Jobin (1570 to 1580), and a period of occasional writing while he practiced professions based on his legal training (1581 to 1590). While the products of these periods do not contradict each other, neither do they coalesce into an intellectual and spiritual portrait such as one gains from study of the lawyer and man of letters Sebastian Brant, who was active approximately a century before Fischart.

It would be anachronistic to try to draw lines between Fischart's activities in translating, paraphrasing, adapting, compiling, editing, and expanding, on the one hand, and what one would now call "writing," on the other. Consensus even on the Fischart canon is not easy to achieve – Ulrich Seelbach lists forty-seven titles, while Wilhelm Kühlmann numbers his works as "mehr als siebzig" (more than seventy). Fischart's fondness for pen names and anonymity, and his predilection for revising and collaborating on works, severely vex this question. It is symptomatic that no full-length study of the man and his work has appeared since Adolf Hauffen's of 1921 and 1922. If the critical edition now underway makes good progress, a successor to Hauffen's book may appear even before its centennial is observed.

Bibliography:

Christian Hoffmann, "Bücher und Autographen von Johann Fischart," *Daphnis,* 25, no. 2-3 (1996): 489-579.

Biography:

Adolf Hauffen, *Johann Fischart: Ein Literaturbild aus der Zeit der Gegenreformation,* 2 volumes (Berlin & Leipzig: De Gruyter, 1921, 1922).

References:

Pia Holenstein, *Der Ehediskurs der Renaissance in Fischarts Geschichtklitterung* (Bern: Peter Lang, 1991);

Stefan Janson, *Jean Bodin – Johann Fischart: De la Démonomanie des Sorciers – Vom Außgelaßnen wütigen Teuffelsheer (1581) und ihre Fallberichte* (Frankfurt am Main: Peter Lang, 1980);

Erich Kleinschmidt, "Gelehrtentum und Volkssprache in der frühneuzeitlichen Stadt: Zur literaturgesellschaftlichen Funktion Johann Fischarts in Straßburg," in *Politik und Dichtung vom Mittelalter bis zur Neuzeit,* edited by Wolfgang Haubrichs (Göttingen: Vandenhoeck & Ruprecht, 1980), pp. 128-147;

Wilhelm Kühlmann, "Johann Fischart," in *Deutsche Dichter der frühen Neuzeit (1450-1600),* edited by Stephan Füssel (Berlin: Erich Schmidt, 1993), pp. 589-612;

Christoph Mühlemann, *Fischarts "Geschichtklitterung" als manieristisches Kunstwerk: Verwirrtes Muster einer verwirrten Welt* (Bern & Frankfurt am Main: Peter Lang, 1972);

Jan-Dirk Müller, "Von der Subversion frühneuzeitlicher Ehelehre: Zu Fischarts 'Ehezuchtbüchlein' und 'Geschichtklitterung,' " in *The Graph of Sex and the German Text: Gendered Culture in Early Modern Germany 1500-1700,* edited by Lynne Tatlock (Amsterdam & Atlanta: Rodopi, 1994), pp. 121-156;

Gerhard Schank, *Etymologie und Wortspiel in Johann Fischarts "Geschichtklitterung,"* second edition (Freiburg im Breisgau: Burg, 1978);

Ulrich Seelbach, "Projektbericht: Johann Fischart, Kritische Gesamtausgabe der Werke," in *Probleme der Edition von Texten der frühen Neuzeit,* edited by Lothar Mundt and others (Tübingen: Niemeyer, 1992), pp. 205-211;

Dieter Seitz, *Johann Fischarts Geschichtklitterung: Untersuchungen zur Prosastruktur und zum grobianischen Motivkomplex* (Frankfurt am Main: Athenäum, 1974);

Walter Eckehart Spengler, *Johann Fischart gen. Mentzer: Studie zur Sprache und Literatur des ausgehenden 16. Jahrhunderts* (Göppingen: Kümmerle, 1969);

Florence Weinberg, *Gargantua in a Convex Mirror: Fischart's View of Rabelais* (New York: Peter Lang, 1986).

Hans Folz
(between 1435 and 1440 – January 1513)

Joe Delap
Kansas Wesleyan University

BOOKS: *Zu wissen sei allen christen die sich zu der osterlichen zeit* (Nuremberg: Hans Folz, 1479); republished as *Diß büchlin in wyset wie sich ein jecklicher christen mönsch schicken soll zü einer gantzen volkomenen und gemeyner bycht* (N.p., 1497);

Drei törichte Fragen (Nuremberg: Hans Folz, 1479);

Item von eim fauln hürn sun der sich auff püberey leyt die lewt vm gelt zu betriegen (Nuremberg: Hans Folz, 1479); republished as *Die worper* (Nuremberg: Hans Folz, circa 1483);

Von einem krichischen arczat der sich aus gab all krankheit am prüen zu erkennen (Nuremberg: Hans Folz, 1479);

Item ein krieg den der dichter dises spruchs gehapt hat wider einen iuden mit dem er wandret und wie er im all sein frag verantwurt (Nuremberg: Hans Folz, 1479);

Item von einem purger von straßpurg der gen rom zoch (Nuremberg: Hans Folz, 1479); republished as *Item ein fast abenteurischen spruch von einem kauffman von straßpurg der gen rom zoch* (Nuremberg: Hans Folz, circa 1480);

Zv wissen das her nach folget ein teutsch worhaftig poetische ystory von wannen das heylig römische reich seinen vrsprung erstlich hab (Nuremberg: Hans Folz, 1479);

Item von dreyen studenten die vm ein aller schönste wirtin pulten doch keiner von dem andern wissend (Nuremberg: Hans Folz, 1480);

Item wie adam und eua nach dem vnd sie aus dem paradis verdriben worden sein ir gancz leben verschlyssen haben (Nuremberg: Hans Folz, 1480);

Item von einem reichen kargen oder vngenugigen man der eins vastags einen armen zu haws lud (Nuremberg: Hans Folz, 1480); republished as *Der kargenspigel: Ein schöner spruch von einem Reichen kargen und einem Arme durfftigen, dar innen angezaigt, welcher standt der selligkit nehenner sey* (Nuremberg: Stefan Hamer, 1534);

Item von dreyen weyben die einen porten funden (Nuremberg: Hans Folz, 1481);

Item ein pulschafft von einer pawrn meyt und von einem iungen gesellen (Nuremberg: Hans Folz, 1481);

Charcoal drawing thought to be a portrait of Hans Folz, circa 1520; drawing attributed to Hans Schwarz (Ehemals Staatliche Museen Berlin-Dahlem)

Item von dem pfarrer im loch dom man zallt tausent fier hundert vnd im dem süben vnd firczig iar gescheen (Nuremberg: Hans Folz, 1481);

Item fast abenteurisch Klopfan auff allerley art (Nuremberg: Hans Folz, 1481);

Item ein fast köstlicher spruch von der pestilencz (Nuremberg: Hans Folz, 1482); revised as *Hie nach folget vast ein kostlicher Vnnd gruntlicher spruch von der pestilencz* (Augsburg: Johann Bämler, 1483);

Die pehemisch irrung (Nuremberg: Hans Folz, 1483);

Die Gedicht Peycht (Nuremberg: Hans Folz, between 1483 and 1488);

Ein köler der sein weib einß goltsmids weib vnd sein meit schlug (Nuremberg: Hans Folz, between 1483 and 1488);

Uon einem kü dip (Nuremberg: Hans Folz, between 1483 and 1488);

Der pachen dip (Nuremberg: Hans Folz, between 1483 and 1488);

Dreyer Paurn Frag (Nuremberg: Hans Folz, between 1483 and 1488);

Der Neü Güllden Traum (Nuremberg: Hans Folz, between 1483 and 1488);

Uon Allem Haußrot (Nuremberg: Hans Folz, between 1483 and 1488);

Uitas patrum vel liber colacionum. Zu teutsch Confect Puch (Nuremberg: Hans Folz, between 1483 and 1488);

In frankenreich ein künig sas . . . (Nuremberg: Hans Folz, between 1483 and 1488);

Die frech: vnd die still (Nuremberg: Hans Folz, between 1483 and 1488); republished as *Von zweyer frawen krig* (Nuremberg: Johann Stüchs, n.d.);

Ein freyheit swach in kalter zeyt (Nuremberg: Hans Folz, between 1483 and 1488);

Von der Jüden Messias (Nuremberg: Hans Folz, between 1483 and 1488);

Uon dem obersten Richter in der wellt (Nuremberg: Hans Folz, between 1483 and 1488); republished as *Nun volgt hernach ain spruch oder red Vom obersten richtter* (Nuremberg, n.d.);

Ein fasnacht spil von pulern den fraw venus ein vrteil fellt (Nuremberg: Hans Folz, between 1483 and 1488);

Ein fasnacht spil von den die sich die weiber nerren laßen (Nuremberg: Hans Folz, between 1483 and 1488);

Eyn liet genant der pöß rauch. In der flam weis (Nuremberg: Hans Folz, between 1483 and 1488);

Ein neü lied in prenbergers thon (Nuremberg: Hans Folz, between 1483 and 1488);

Ein Faßnacht spil von einem pawrn gericht (Nuremberg: Johann Stüchs, between 1483 and 1488);

Von dem kunig Salomon vnd Marckolffo vnd einem narrn ein hübsch Faßnacht spil new gemacht (Nuremberg: Johann Stüchs, between 1483 and 1488);

Liber collationum (Nuremberg: Johann Sensenschmidt, 1485);

Uon Einem Puler (Nuremberg: Hans Folz, 1488);

Uon Eynem Spiler (Nuremberg: Hans Folz, circa 1488);

Von Eynem Füller (Nuremberg: Hans Folz, circa 1488);

Ein gar suptil rechnung Ruprecht Kolpergers von dem Gsuchs der Juden (Nuremberg: Peter Wagner, 1491);

Von der collacion vnsers aller gnedigsten hern vnd romischen kunigs maximilian in nurenperg zu gericht (Nuremberg: Peter Wagner, circa 1491);

Dises puchlein saget vnß von allen paten die von natur heiß sein (Nuremberg: Peter Wagner, circa 1491); republished as *Dyß puchlein hat gemacht vnnd erfarn Mayster Clement von Gracz von allen paden dye von natur hayss sint* (Brünn: Conrad Stahel & Mathias Preunlein, 1495);

Von allem hausrot (Bamberg: Marx Ayrer, 1493);

Wem der geprant wein nutz sey oder schad vnd wie er gerecht oder falschlich gemacht sey (Bamberg: Marx Ayrer, 1493);

Ein hübsch faßnacht spil von einer gar pewrischen pawrn heyrat seer kurtzweylig vnd gut zu lachen (Nuremberg: Jobst Gutknecht, 1521);

Wie man den pranten wein erkent ob er valsch oder gerecht gemachet sey (N.p., n.d.).

Editions: *Fastnachtspiele aus dem fünfzehnten Jahrhundert,* 4 volumes, edited by Adelbert von Keller (volumes 1-3, Stuttgart: Literarischer Verein, 1853; volume 4, Stuttgart: Literarischer Verein, 1858; reprinted, Darmstadt: Wissenschaftliche Buchgesellschaft, 1965-1966)—includes Folz's *Die alt und neu ee, Herzog von Burgund, Die zwölf buhlerischen Bauern,* and *Kaiser Constantinus;*

Die Reimpaarsprüche, edited by Hanns Fischer (Munich: Beck, 1961);

Die Meisterlieder des Hans Folz: Aus der Münchener Originalhandschrift und der Weimarer Handschrift Q. 566 mit Ergänzungen aus anderen Quellen, edited by August L. Mayer (Dublin: Weidmann, 1970).

The celebrated sixteenth-century Nuremberg poet and playwright Hans Sachs spoke highly of the late-medieval writer and publisher Hans Folz, calling him a "durchleuchtig" (luminous) poet and including him among the twelve grand old masters of *Meistergesang* or *Meisterlieder,* poetry set to music by the guild members known as Meistersinger. Folz was a founder of the Nuremberg *Singschule* (singing school). He was also the first publisher of plays in the German language. As a writer Folz left behind a generous contribution to early modern German literature, especially in the area of polemic verse, much of which was printed on his own press.

Little is known about Folz's early years. Most scholars infer from his calling himself "hans von

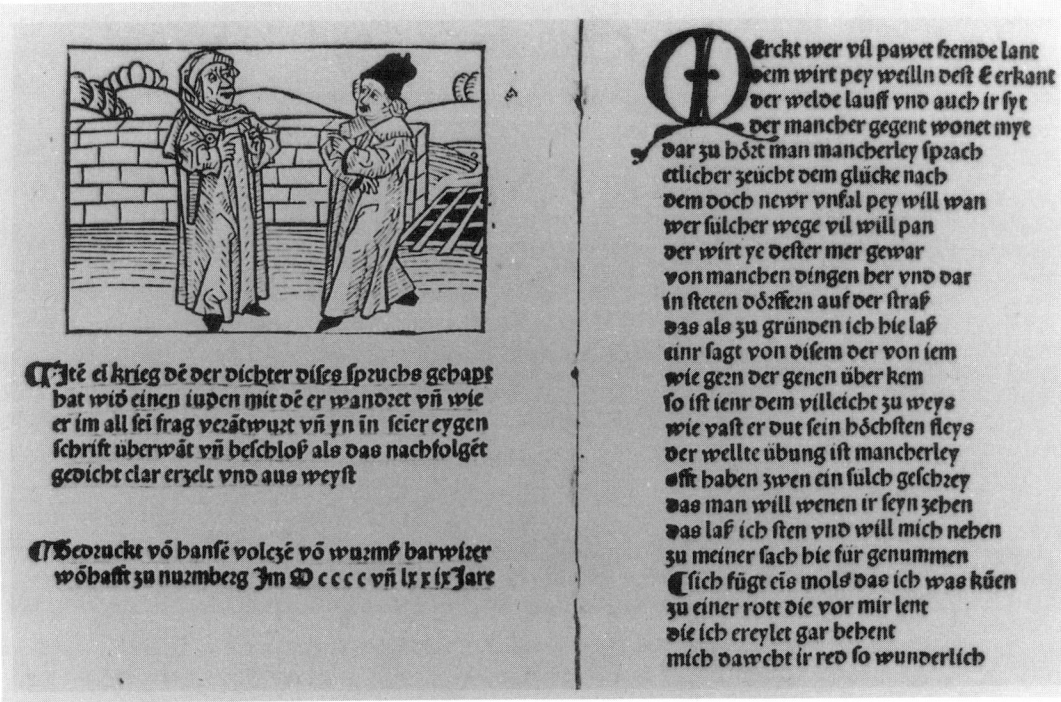

First two pages of Folz's anti-Semitic work Christ und Jude

wurmß" that he was born in Worms, but there is little documentary evidence for this assumption. Estimates of the year of his birth range from 1435 to 1440, based on the fact that Folz was able to pay the one hundred gulden necessary to apply for Nuremberg citizenship in 1459; the amount indicates that Folz had attained the rank of master barber, which would have occurred when he was between twenty and twenty-five. It is likely that he received sophisticated training at an early age; it is doubtful that, as some scholars have suggested, he taught himself to read and write both German and Latin. Folz did not attend a university but was trained in Worms as a *barbirer* or *barwirer* (barber), the early modern German equivalent of a *Wundarzt* (surgeon). As an apprentice barber he traveled as far as southern France or Spain and settled for a short time in Augsburg. Finally, he set up his surgical and barber practice in Nuremberg. He was married at least twice; the earliest record of his having a wife is dated 1493, when he would have been more than fifty years old. One wife, Agnes, died in 1499; later Folz married a woman named Elsbeth. It is not known whether Folz had children.

Recent scholarship has emphasized that Folz's literary works conformed to the tastes and norms of his fellow citizens—as Rüdiger Krohn puts it, in an apt metaphor for a surgeon, he had his hand on the pulse of his times and public. This portrayal of Folz as a conformist writer contradicts earlier assessments of him as a rebellious spirit among the Meistersinger. It is doubtful that, as some nineteenth-century critics claimed, Folz was banned from Worms for rejecting the traditional melodies of the Meistergesang in favor of a reform in the genre introduced by Nestler of Speyer. Those who maintain that Folz was involved in this controversy must be unaware that all of his work on Meistergesang dates from well after he left Worms for Nuremberg; nearly a quarter of his works in the genre were begun in the second half of the 1470s, and the rest were produced after 1480. Folz's intensive development of his style—he invented seventeen melodies, fourteen of which can be found in his own songs—was more than likely perfected only after his arrival in Nuremberg and, therefore, after the uproar surrounding Nestler's innovations in the Meistergesang. It is also doubtful that Folz, as a novice Meistersinger who kept strictly to the rules for creating new tunes, would help fuel the fires of Nestler's literary revolt. In addition, recent studies have raised doubt as to whether Folz even wrote the six Meisterlieder, today in the Staatsbibliothek in Berlin, that employ the so-called unknown melody on which the reform of the genre was supposedly based. Even if he were the creator of the new melody, he would only be the latest in a series of Meistersinger who had carried out similar reforms ear-

Page from a manuscript in Folz's handwriting (Thüringer Landesbibliothek Weimar, Hs. Q. 566, folio 15ʳ)

lier in the fifteenth century. Finally, Folz's printed works, including his later mostly religious Meisterlieder, display strictly conformist attitudes. Thus, the myth of his rebellious nature is easily dispelled.

In 1479, employing his own printing press, Folz began publishing rhymed verses such as *Zu wissen sei allen christen die sich zu der osterlichen zeit* (Be It Known to All Christians at Eastertime), known as the *Beichtspiegel* (Confessional Mirror), condemning those who write secular songs and Shrovetide plays, along with other grievous sinners. Some scholars consider the *Beichtspiegel* Folz's first published work because the year 1473 appears in its lines, but there is no other evidence that it appeared before the four other works that bear the same year of publication. The issue of which work came first pales in significance next to Folz's feat of publishing German verse a full decade before it was common to do so.

Also noteworthy from this period is Folz's *Item ein krieg den der dichter dises spruchs gehapt hat wider einen iuden mit dem er wandret und wie er im all sein frag verantwurt,* known as *Christ und Jude* (Christian and Jew, 1479). This work, which was probably written around 1473, during the city council's first efforts to expel the Jews from Nuremberg, represents an early attempt by Folz to reflect—perhaps to promote—in print the anti-Semitism that was on the rise in the city. Folz's polemics against the Nuremberg Jews would appear throughout the city's twenty-five-year struggle against two emperors over the right to expel Jewish residents and seize their property. (The expulsion of the Jews from Nuremberg finally came about in 1498–1499, long after Folz had ceased to publish his own writings.)

In 1488 Folz, for unknown reasons, ceased using his own press, despite the apparent success of his publications. His publication of German verse during this period is of great literary-historical significance, for although German prose incunabula enjoyed broad popularity from about 1470 onward, German verse publications were rare before 1490.

To appeal to the broadest possible audience Folz composed the majority of his works in easily recitable rhymes rather than in prose, which is more difficult to commit to memory. Judging from the frequent and favorable references to the common folk in his writings, this group apparently constituted a considerable portion of his audience. Such people would have consumed Folz's works mostly by hearing them sung, as the poor were generally illiterate and, in any case, could not afford to buy books. His audience was unlikely to have included country folk, who are often the subject of his ridicule. *Item ein fast köstlicher spruch von der pestilencz* (Likewise a Most Delightful Dictum on the Plague, 1482), a verse tract on the plague that Folz reworked and published in prose as *Hie nach folget vast ein kostlicher Unnd gruntlicher spruch von der pestilencz* (Hereupon Follows a Most Delightful and Profound Dictum on the Plague, 1483), was evidently intended for well-to-do readers, who would have been accustomed to reading lengthy prose literature—mostly romance novels—in the vernacular. The work is dedicated to his

Title page for a Shrovetide play by Folz

"besundern guten freunt" (especially good friend) Anton Haller, a highly respected Nuremberg citizen (though not a member of the patrician Haller family).

In addition to being one of the first printers of early modern German verse, Folz was the first to publish plays in German; and again, much of what he published was his own work. He wrote his *Fastnachtspiele* (Shrovetide plays) between the early 1470s and the early 1490s, but they were republished well into the sixteenth century. Although his authorship cannot be proven in all cases, it is estimated that Folz wrote approximately thirty Shrovetide plays—more than a quarter of all such plays written in Nuremberg during the fifteenth century. The plays have been criticized not only for their lack of originality but also for their anti-Jewish tone and content. *Kaiser Constantinus* (Emperor Constantine) and *Von dem kunig Salomon und Marckolffo und einem narrn ein hübsch Faßnacht spil new gemacht* (Of King Solomon and Markolf and a Fool: A New

Shrovetide Play, between 1483 and 1488) are usually mentioned as early examples, both of which remained unpublished until Adelbert von Keller's editions of 1853 and 1858, but the dates of which may be estimated from records of their performances. The anti-Semitic polemics are especially strong in his later play *Herzog von Burgund* (Duke of Burgundy). Eckehard Catholy points out that Shrovetide plays cannot be construed as the expressions of the sentiments of the authors, but David Price has shown that exceptions must be made for certain of Folz's plays. While Folz borrows themes from earlier medieval plays, he gives them new vigor through his interpretations of them.

Recurring topics in Folz's works include domestic and social problems (how to run one's home, refrain from adultery, or avoid abusing alcohol), religious issues (Christianity versus Judaism, indiscretions of the clergy, praise for the Virgin Mary or the Trinity), medicine (potions, baths, avoiding the ravages of the plague), and humorous situations (usually involving peasants fighting, marrying, or displaying ignorance in a manner that a city dweller might find amusing). Folz seems to have understood the effectiveness of humor, even in dealing with serious subjects. His *Die Gedicht Peycht* (Confessional Poem, between 1483 and 1488), for example, is a parody of the *Beichtspiegel,* his earlier, earnest text on the same subject. At the same time, his works tend to be inflammatory; *Die alt und neu ee* (The Old and New Marriage) and *Von uberwindung der Juden in ihr Talmut* (On the Conquest of the Jews in Their Talmud) are two conspicuous examples of the anti-Semitic works that have attracted more scholarly attention in recent years than have any other aspect of Folz's writing. According to Rüdiger Krohn, as early as the nineteenth century his ruthless attacks on the Jews were called "hateful."

After Folz gave up his publishing business, he continued to place his writings into the hands of readers with the help of another Nuremberg publisher, Peter Wagner. Only a handful of first editions appeared after 1490, however. Among these, *Ein gar suptil rechnung Ruprecht Kolpergers von dem Gsuchs der Juden,* otherwise known as *Jüdischer Wucher* (Jewish Usury, 1491), stands out as a parting shot against the Jews shortly before their expulsion from Nuremberg. Another text from this period, *Von der collacion vnsers aller gnedigsten hern vnd romischen kunigs maximilian in nurenperg zu gericht* (On the Gathering of Our Most Gracious Lord and Roman King Maximilian in Nuremberg for the Diet, circa 1491), portrays the festivities surrounding Emperor Maximilian I's visit for the convening of the imperial diet. Finally, *Dises puchlein saget vnß von allen paden die von natur heiß sein* (This Booklet Tells of All Baths That Are Hot by Nature, circa 1491) is useful for the insight it provides into contemporary social norms and Folz's travel experiences. He probably wrote little after 1491, as no new works of his appear from this point on: it is difficult to believe that Folz, always the entrepreneur, would have written something in these later years without attempting to have it published. He died in Nuremberg in January 1513.

Folz's earlier works continued to be published well into the sixteenth century. In Nuremberg, Hans Stüchs, Jobst Gutknecht, and Stefan Hamer are three of the publishers who brought Folz's works back to life during the 1520s and 1530s; Valentin Holl of Augsburg is also known to have reproduced texts that Folz had printed earlier. Several of Foltz's works were republished in the nineteenth century. None of his writings has been translated into English.

In contrast to Sachs's admiration for Folz's works, Karl Goedeke in the nineteenth century found Folz's writings to epitomize what he considered to be the moral decay of German literature of the late medieval era. Goedeke derides Folz as a "blumendüftelnder Meistersänger, Schmutziger Schwankdichter und Verfasser lasciver Faßnachtspiele" (a perfume-wafting Meistersinger, author of dirty stories, and writer of lascivious Shrovetide plays). Although Goedeke takes his scorn for Folz's style, which he characterizes as both opulent and decadent, to the point of refusing even to try to analyze Folz's poetry, he admits that Folz's writings were popular in their day and became widespread through print at an early point in that medium's development. Whereas Goedeke finds Folz's style and choice of topics so distasteful as to make his works unworthy of study, late-twentieth-century scholars consider these same aspects of his writing to be of considerable literary and cultural significance. Catholy says that Folz, by virtue of his technical and literary merits, belongs more to the sixteenth century than to the Middle Ages—a claim he cannot make for other fifteenth-century Meistersinger, such as Hans Rosenplüt. Other assessments of Folz's works view his publications as for financial gain: pandering to a newly found reading public. Before Folz's publication of his own works there were few, if any, writers with a similar orientation toward publishing for financial gain.

Folz met a vital need among the Nuremberg reading public by providing humorous and instructive verse. He will, however, be remembered as an author who sometimes sacrificed good taste for the sake of popularity (as when he ridiculed peasants and clergy) and of conformity with municipal authorities (by promoting hatred of the Jews). He was one of the first German writers to realize the full potential of the new print medium and also one of the first to test its limits.

Bibliography:

Ingeborg Spriewald, "Hans Folz–Dichter und Drucker," *Beiträge zur Geschichte der deutschen Sprache und Literatur,* 83 (1961): 242–277.

References:

David Blamires, "Hans Folzen 'Die Wahrsagebeeren' als Quelle für Ulenspiegel," *Zeitschrift für deutsches Altertum und deutsche Literatur,* 111 (1982): 53–60;

Eckehard Catholy, *Das Fastnachtspiel des Spätmittelalters: Gestalt und Funktion* (Tübingen: Metzler, 1961), pp. 48–49;

Hanns Fischer, "Hans Folz: Altes und Neues zur Geschichte seines Lebens und seiner Schriften," *Zeitschrift für deutsches Altertum und deutsche Literatur,* 95 (1966): 212–236;

Karl Goedeke, "Burkard Waldis," in his *Grundriß zur Geschichte der deutschen Dichtung aus den Quellen,* volume 1, second edition (Dresden: Ehlermann, 1884), pp. 329–333;

Walter Hinck, *Handbuch des deutschen Dramas* (Düsseldorf: Bebel, 1980), p. 31;

Johannes Janota, "Folz, Hans," in *Die deutsche Literatur des Mittelalters: Verfasserlexikon,* volume 2, edited by Kurt Ruh, second edition (Berlin: De Gruyter, 1977), pp. 769–793;

Wilhelm Kosch, "Folz, Hans," in *Deutsches Literatur-Lexikon,* edited by Kosch, third edition (Bern: Francke, 1978), pp. 296–305;

Rüdiger Krohn, "Hans Folz," in *Deutsche Dichter der frühen Neuzeit (1450–1600): Ihr Leben und Werk,* edited by Stephan Füssel (Berlin: Schmidt, 1993), pp. 111–124;

Fritz Langensiepen, *Tradition und Vermittlung: Literaturgeschichtliche und didaktische Untersuchungen zu Hans Folz* (Berlin: Schmidt, 1980);

Brian Murdoch, *Hans Folz and the Adam-Legends: Texts and Studies* (Amsterdam: Rodopi, 1977);

David Price, "Hans Folz's Anti-Jewish Carnival Plays," *Fifteenth Century Studies,* 19 (1992): 209–228;

Edith Wenzel, "Zur Judenproblematik bei Hans Folz," *Zeitschrift für deutsche Philologie,* 101 (1982): 79–104;

Elisabeth Wunderle, "Folz, Hans," in *Literaturlexikon: Autoren und Werke deutscher Sprache,* volume 3, edited by Walter Killy (Gütersloh: Bertelsmann, 1989), pp. 427–429.

Papers:

Hans Folz's manuscripts are distributed among several locations. Among them are the Munich manuscript, Heidelberg Manuscript 109, Weimar Manuscript Q. 566, and Berlin Manuscript 4. germ. 414.

Sebastian Franck
(1499 – 1542)

Priscilla A. Hayden-Roy
University of Nebraska at Lincoln

WORKS: *Von dem greüwlichen laster der trunckenhayt, so inn disen letsten zeytten erst schier mit den Frantzosen aufkommen, was füllerey, sauffen, vnd zutrincken, für jammer und vnrath, schade der seel vnd deù leibs, auch armut vnd schedlich not anricht, vnd mit sich bringt. Vnd wie dem vbel zuraten wer, gründtlicher bericht vnd rathschlag, auù götlicher geschrifft* (Augsburg: Heinrich Steiner, 1528);

Chronica, Zeÿtbuch vnd geschychtbibel von anbegyn biù inn diù gegenwertig M.D.xxxj. jar. Darinn beide Gottes vnd der welt lauff, hendel, art, wort, werck, thun, lassen, kriegen, wesen, vnd leben ersehen vnd begriffen wirt. Mit vil wunderbarlichen gedechtniùwürdigen worten vnd thatten, guten vnd bösen Regimenten, Decreten . . . Durch Sebastianum Francken von Wörd, vormals in teütscher zungen nie gehört noch gelesen (Strasbourg: Balthasar Beck, 1531; revised edition, Ulm: Hans Varnier the Elder, 1536);

Weltbuch: spiegel vnd bildtniù des gantzen erdbodens von Sebastiano Franco Wördensi in vier bücher, nemlich in Asiam, Aphricam, Europam, vnd Americam, gestelt vnd abteilt, Auch aller darinn begriffner Länder, nation, prouintzen vnd Inseln, gelegenheit, grösse, weite, gewächù, eygentschafft . . . Auch etwas von new gefundenen welten vnd Inseln, nitt auss Beroso, Joanne de monte villa, S. Brandons Histori, vnd dergleichen fabeln, sunder auss angenummnen, glaubwirdigen erfarnen, weltbeschreibern, müselig zuhauff tragen vnd auù vilen weitleüffigen büchern in ein handtbuch eingeleibt vnd verfaùt, vormals dergleichen in Teütsch nie auùgangen (Tübingen: Ulrich Morhart the Elder, 1534);

Paradoxa ducenta octoginta, das ist, CCLXXX. Wunderred vnd gleichsam Räterschafft, auù der H. Schrifft, so vor allem fleysch vngleublich vnd vnwar sind, doch wider der gantzen Welt wohn vnd achtung, gewiù vnd waar. Item aller in Got philosophierenden Christen, rechte, götliche Philosophei, vnd Teütsche Theologei, voller verbogener Wunderred vnd gehaimnuù . . . entdeckt, auùgefürt, vnd an den tag geben (Ulm: Hans Varnier the Elder, 1534); translated by E. J. Furcha as *280 Paradoxes or*

Sebastian Franck

Wondrous Sayings, Texts and Studies in Religion, volume 26 (Lewiston, N.Y. & Queenston, Ont.: Mellen, 1986);

Das Gott das ainig ain, vnd höchstes gut, sein almechtigs, wars, lebendigs wort, will, kunst, gesatz, Sun, sinn, Caracter, liecht, leben, Bild, Reich, arm, gayst, krafft, hand, Christus, der New mensch, vnd des weybs Som, neben der Schlangen somen, in aller menschen hertz sey . . . Item das wort, Christus, der new mensch, werde dann in vnns wie empfunden vnd empfanngen, also geboren, gewiùt, gelesen, gebraucht, vnd angelegt (Augsburg: Silvan Otmar, 1534);

Des Grossen Nothelffers vnnd Weltheiligen Sant Gelts, oder S. Pfennings Lobgesang durch ein Ironey vnd Spotlob Schimpflich gedicht (Ulm: Sebastian Franck, 1537);

Wie man Beten vnnd Psallieren soll, Ein Wolgedichter, Schriftreicher Psalm, sampt seiner Vorred, Auùlegung, vnd anzeygung waher er genomen (Ulm: Sebastian Franck, 1537);

Die Guldin Arch darein der kern vnnd die besten hauptsprüch, der Heyligen schrifft, alten Lerer vnd Väter der kirchen, Auch der erleuchten Heyden vnd Philosophen, für vnd vber die gmein stell der schrifft (Augsburg: Heinrich Steiner, 1538);

Germaniae Chronicon. Von des gantzen Teutschlands, aller Teutschen Völcker herkommen, Namen, Händeln, guten und bösen Thaten, Reden, Räthen, Kriegen, Sigen, Niderlagen, Stifftungen, Veränderungen der Sitze, Reich, Länder, Religion, Gesetze, Policei, Spraach, Völker und Sitten, vor vnd nach Christi Geburt, von Noe biù auf Carolum V. (Frankfurt am Main: Christian Egenolff, 1538);

Das verbüthschiert mit siben Sigeln verschlossen Buch, das recht niemandt auffthun, verstehen, oder lesen kan, dann das lamb, vnd die mit dem Thaw bezaichnet, das lamb angehören, sampt einer vorred von den siben Sigeln, was die seyen, vnd wie die auffthon werden (Augsburg: Heinrich Steiner, 1539);

Handbüchlin siben haubt puncten auù der Bibel gezogen vnd zusamen bracht, darinn angezeygt ist, leben vnd todt, Himel vnnd Hell, was Gott gebeüt vnd verbeüt, lont vnd strafft, mit allem thun vnnd lassen, das Gott von vns begert, für eyn jeden menschen nützlich zu wissen (Frankfurt am Main: Printed by Cyriacus Jacob, 1539);

Was gesagt sei: Der Glaub thuts alles: Vnd warumb jm die Rechtfertigung alleyn werde zugeschriben, Auùzogen grundtlicher bericht vnd vrteyl auù der schrifft, as Felix Frei (Tübingen: Ulrich Morhart the Elder, 1539);

Das Krieg büchlin. des frides. Ein krieg des frides, wider alle lermen, auffrür vnd vnsinnigkait zu kriegen, mit gründlicher anzaigung, auù wichtigen eehafften vrsachen, auù gründtlichen argumenten der Hailigen Schrifft, as Friedrich Wernstreyt (Augsburg: Heinrich Steiner, 1539);

Schrifftliche vnd gantz gründtliche auùlegung, des LXIIII. Psalm, Die Falschen Zungen, Propheten, Leerer, Lieger, Trieger, Gottsfeind, vnd Eerabschneider, betreffende, wie, vnd mit was kunst sie sich vnderston vnd üben, Christum vnd seine glider, auùzureütten vnd züuertilgen, wie fern sie es bringen, vnd wie sie sich selbs schädigen, vnd in jr eygne gegrabne grub vnnd strick fällen, on all menschliche gloù vnd Affect auùgefürt. So klar nie an tag bracht (Tübingen: Ulrich Morhart the Elder, 1539);

Sprichwörter, Schöne, Weise, Herrliche Clügreden, vnnd Hoffsprüch: Darinnen der alten vnd nachkommen, aller Nationen vnnd Sprachen gröste vernunfft vnnd klugheit. Was auch zu ewiger vnnd zeitlicher Weissheyt, Tugent, Zucht, Kunst, Hausshaltung vnnd wesen dienet, gespürt vnnd begriffen würt. Zusamentragen in ettlich Tausent, Inn lustig höflich Teutsch beküurtzt, Beschriben vnnd auùgeleget (Frankfurt am Main: Printed by Christian Egenolff, 1541);

Von dem Kindertauff, Bestendiger vnd klarer Gegenbericht, wider das vngegründtes büchlein eines Widertäuffers . . . Item zween Sendbrieff Sebastiani Francken, von auffhebungen aller Kirchen ordnungen vnd policey, vor nie in Truck auùgangen. Mit einer einfeltiger warer Widerlegung der selbigen . . . An eine Gotsfürchtige Iungfraw vom Adel geschrieben (N.p., 1563);

Von vier zwieträchtigen Kirchen, deren jede die ander verhasset vnnd verdammet (1596)

Manuscript: In *Liederhandschrift*, by Daniel Sudermann (1596), Staatsbibliothek zu Berlin, p. 256.

First publication: In *Das deutsche Kirchenlied von der ältesten Zeit bis zu Anfang des 17. Jahrhunderts*, volume 3, edited by Philipp Wackernagel (Leipzig: Teubner, 1870), pp. 817–818;

Van Het Rycke Christi. Een stichtelijck Tractaet, allen eenvoudighen Christenen tot onderwijsinghe . . . door den verlichteden ende van Gott-gheleerden Sebastiaen Franck van Werdt, translated into Dutch by Herbold Thombergen (Gouda: Jasper Tournay, 1611);

Een stichtelijck Tractaet, van de Werelt, des Duyvels Rijck. Hier by ghevoecht de Ghemeynschap der Heylighen. Beschreven door den verlichteden Sebastiaen Franck van Wordt, translated into Dutch by Thombergen (Gouda: Printed by Jasper Tournay for Andries Burier, 1618);

Theologia, vulgo Germanica vocata et an te annos ab huius seculi phoenice quodam Teutonici ordinis Germano germanice conscripta latinitate donata, et vbi author paulo obscurior, vel spiritu scientie altitudine sublimior, per paraphrasim aucta et explicata fusius (date unknown)

Manuscript: From the sixteenth or seventeenth century, in Amsterdam University Library.

First publication: Excerpts in *Sebastian Francks lateinische Paraphrase der Deutschen Theologie und seine holländisch erhaltenen Traktate*, by Alfred Hegler (Tübingen: G. Schnürlen, 1901).

Editions and collections: *Paradoxa*, translated into modern German, with introduction by Siegfried Wollgast (Berlin: Akademie, 1966);

Sämtliche Werke: Kritische Ausgabe mit Kommentar, 3 volumes published, edited by Hans-Gert Roloff and others (Berlin: Peter Lang, 1992–).

Edition in English: "A Letter to John Campanus by Sebastian Franck," in *Spiritual and Anabaptist Writers: Documents Illustrative of the Radical Reformation*, edited by George Huntston Williams (Philadelphia: Westminster, 1962), pp. 145-160.

OTHER: Valentin Krautwald, *Von der gnaden Gottes, jrem ordentlichen gang, vnd schnellen lauff, Das sie an die Sacrament nit gebunden, noch an etwas eüsserliches gehäfftet sei*, edited by Caspar Schwenckfeld, foreword and afterword by Franck (Ulm: Hans Varnier the Elder, 1535);

Krautwald, *Epistola Ministri Cuivsdam Verbi, ad Qvendam Symnistam, De Ecclesia, Clauibus, Sacramentis, Veráq; Ministrorum spiritus electione*, afterword by Franck (Ulm: Hans Varnier the Elder, 1535);

Georg Birckeymer, *Von dem auffrichtigen wandel, leben vnd gutten gewissen der glaubigen, was ein recht gläubiger Christen man, Vnd new geporner vergotteter mensch sei, mit dem pensel der schrifft entworffen*, summary by Franck (Frankfurt am Main: Cyriacus Jacob, between 1539 and 1543);

"Die Gelehrten die Verkehrten," attributed to Franck, edited by Johannes Bolte, in *Sitzungsberichte der preussischen Akademie der Wissenschaften, Philosophisch-historische Klasse* (1925): 108-114.

TRANSLATIONS: Andreas Althammer, *Diallage, das ist, vereynigung der streytigen sprüch, welche im ersten anplick scheynen wider einander zu sein*, translated, with a foreword, by Franck (Nuremberg: Printed by Friedrich Peypus for Lienhard zur Aich, 1528);

Simon Fish, *Klagbrieff oder supplication der armen dürfftigen in Engenlandt, an den König daselbs gestellet, wider die reychen geystlichen bettler* (Nuremberg: Friedrich Peypus, 1529);

Georgius de Hungaria, *Chronica vnnd beschreibung der Türckey mit yhrem begriff, ynnhalt, prouincien, völckern, ankunfft, kriegen, reysen, glauben, religionen, gesatzen, sytten, geperden, weis, regimenten, frümkeyt, vnnd boùheiten, von eim Sibenbürger xxij. jar darinn gefangen gelegen yn Latein beschrieben, verteütscht Mit eyner schönen Vorrhed. zehen oder aylff Nation vnd Secten der Christenheyt*, translated, with interlinear commentary and afterword, by Franck (Nuremberg: Friedrich Peypus, 1530); republished, with new foreword and without afterword (Augsburg: Heinrich Steiner, 1530);

Filippo Beroaldo, *Ein künstlich höflich Declamation vnd hefftiger wortkampff, zanck vnnd hader dreyer brüder vor gericht, Nämlich eins Sauffers, Hürers, vnd Spilers, vnder welchen der ergest aù seines vatters geschäfft vnd Testament enterbt sein soll, Dero keiner der böst will sein* (Nuremberg: Friedrich Peypus, 1531);

Desiderius Erasmus, *Das Theür vnd Künstlich Büchlin Morie Encomion das ist. Ein Lob der Thorhait, von Erasmo Roterodamo schimpfflich gespilt, zu lesen nit weniger nützlich, dann lieblich, verteütscht*, translated, with interlinear commentary, by Franck (Ulm: Hans Varnier the Elder, 1534)—volume also includes Heinrich Cornelius Agrippa of Nettisheim, "Von der Hayloßigkaitt: Eytellkaytt: vnd vngewißhait aller Menschlichen Künst vnd weyßhait, Zu ende mit angehefft. Ein Lob des Esels, auß Heinrico Cornelio Agrippa, De Vanitate. etc. verteütscht," translated by Franck; "Von dem Bam deß wißens Gutz vnd böß Dauon Adam den Todt hat gessen, vnd noch heüt alle Menschen den Todt essen, Was der sei, vnd wie er noch heüt iedermann verbotten. Was dargegen der Bawm des Lebens sei," by Franck; and "Encomium: Ein Lob des Thorechten Götlichen Worts, Was das sei, von des selben Maiestät, vnd was für vnderschaid zwisschen der Schrifft, eüssern vnd innern Worts sei. Alles zum tail verteütscht zum tail beschrieben," by Franck; "Von dem Bam deß wißens" translated by John Everard as *The Forbidden Fruit. Or A Treatise of the Tree of Knowledge of Good & Evill, of which Adam the first, & as yet all Mankind doe eate death* (London?, 1640);

Sebastian Münster, *Sechshundert Dreyzehen Gebot vnd Verpot der Juden. Von der selben Rabi auù dem Grossen Propheten Mose zu samen zogen, mit einer gar kurtzen auùlegung der Hebreischen Rabin, mit welch anhang vnd zusatz, sy die Gebot Gottes haben zenicht gemacht, wie sie diù Christus beschuldiget, vnd von jn zeugt vnd clagt*, translated, with a foreword, by Franck (Ulm: Sebastian Franck, 1537);

Johannes Trithemius, *Chronica Ein überauù lustig warhafftig Histori, von der Franckeu [sic] ankunfft, narung auffwachsung*, translated, with a foreword, by Franck (Ulm: Hans Varnier the Elder, 1539).

Sebastian Franck is generally counted among the members of the "radical" Reformation, which includes a wide range of religious dissenters of the sixteenth and seventeenth centuries who believed that Martin Luther, Huldrych Zwingli, and John Calvin had stopped short of a thorough reform of the church. The group embraced such disparate figures as the Anabaptist Menno Simons, the social reformer Thomas Müntzer, the anti-Trinitarian Mi-

Title page for the revised edition of Franck's "History Bible"

chael Servetus, and Franck, who inveighed against all outward manifestations of religion and insisted on the purely spiritual, invisible nature of God, God's Word, and the Church. Perhaps in no other early modern European does one find the consequences of the spiritualist position so clearly and drastically expressed and lived out as in Franck.

True to his convictions, Franck founded no sect and cultivated no following. His views have been preserved through his writings, most of which Franck, an ardent supporter of the new technology, printed on his own press. He left behind a sizable corpus that includes histories, theological writings, translations, polemical works, a collection of proverbs, a few poems, and some forewords and shorter pieces. Most of Franck's longer works are not original but are massive compilations of passages from other sources—histories, the Bible, biblical commentaries, and the works of ancient philosophers—interspersed with Franck's commentary. Efforts to systematize his thought have foundered on the inconsistencies that arise from his compiling method; recent studies have focused on the method itself as an expression of Franck's nonpartisan stance. All of Franck's published works were written in German; the only longer work written in Latin, a paraphrase of the fifteenth-century *Theologia Deutsch* (German Theology), has never been published. Franck's preference for the vernacular is linked to his theological views—his skepticism about formal learning and his belief that true wisdom lay in simple hearts—but also reflects his linguistic strengths: a mediocre Latin stylist, Franck was, despite his frequently distracting volubility, a master of the German idiom; he has been ranked second only to Luther among German prose writers of the sixteenth century. Franck wrote with energy and conviction, using a rich vocabulary and wide range of expression; he could enliven the most abstract discourse with vibrant images and an unfailing reservoir of popular sayings and proverbs. An opponent of all forms of religious coercion, an advocate of nonsectarianism, and a man who spoke out against the atrocities of war, Franck has been seen to anticipate modern doctrines of religious tolerance, freedom of conscience, and pacifism.

It is assumed, on the basis of a 22 May 1539 letter in which Franck said that he was forty, that he was born in 1499. His place of birth was Donauwörth, a relatively small imperial city in southwestern Germany. It is not known who his parents were, although some have speculated that his father was a weaver; in any case, the evidence indicates that Franck was not born into wealth. He may have gone to school in Donauwörth or in nearby Nördlingen, where there was a Latin school and where his uncle ran an inn. The first record of Franck can be found in the matriculation lists of the University of Ingolstadt, where he enrolled in 1515; he paid the poor students' fee of one groschen. It is likely that Franck's interest in humanism and history was awakened in Ingolstadt, although he was not there long enough to receive a thorough grounding in humanistic learning; his grasp of Latin was adequate, but he had only limited knowledge of Greek. He received a bachelor of arts in 1517.

In 1518 Franck began studies for the priesthood at the Dominican college in Heidelberg. He may have witnessed Luther's Heidelberg Disputation on 16 April 1518; this event might have marked the beginning of Franck's interest in the Reformation and his disaffection with the Roman Catholic Church. It is certain that he met the future reformers Johannes Brenz, Martin Bucer, and Martin Frecht, who were also students at the Dominican college. Bucer and Frecht would become Franck's bitter opponents in the 1530s.

In the first half of the 1520s Franck served as a priest in the bishopric of Augsburg. During this period he accepted the doctrines of the Reformation, although the circumstances of his conversion are undocumented. Between 1525 and 1526 he served as Protestant pastor in Buchenbach; the village was within the territory of Nuremberg, a city that had aligned itself with Luther's teachings. In 1528 he assumed pastoral duties in nearby Gustenfelden, and in March of that year he married Ottilie Beham. She is generally assumed to be the sister of two of the three so-called godless painters of Nuremberg, Barthel and Sebald Beham, who were disciplined by the Nuremberg City Council because of their heterodox views. It was possibly through the brothers or through Ottilie that Franck was introduced to the writings of Hans Denck, an influential spiritualist whose thought bears considerable similarity to that of the mature Franck.

The year 1528 also marks the beginning of Franck's literary activities. He began with a translation from the Latin of Andreas Althammer's *Diallage* (1527), a tract against Denck written from the perspective of the Lutheran camp. Franck added a foreword berating those who live un-Christian lives while claiming to base their faith on Scripture; the criticism was aimed at Denck, but Franck would soon turn it against the Lutherans themselves. He would later adopt the structural principle of Althammer's work—the presentation of apparently conflicting Scripture passages—in his *Paradoxa ducenta octoginta* (280 Paradoxes, 1534) and *Das verbüthschiert mit siben Sigeln verschlossen Buch* (The Book Sealed with Seven Seals, 1539).

Franck's first original work, *Von dem greüwlichen laster der trunckenhayt* (On the Dreadful Vice of Drunkenness, 1528), went through seventeen additional editions, including translations into Low German, Dutch, Czech, and Hungarian. Franck's insistence in the book that there can be no faith without good works is something of a shift of emphasis in the Lutheran doctrine of *sola fide* (by faith alone). He urges that public vice be punished by the church with the ban and by the princes with the sword and the law. Widespread drunkenness, he says, is a sign of the end times; this eschatological perspective informs Franck's oeuvre as a whole and was widespread among his contemporaries, as well (the most notable example being Luther). Franck's skill as a writer, combining stridency with an engagingly colloquial German, is already evident in this early work. The agitated, impatient tone of the book suggests the frustration he may have experienced in his work as a pastor.

In late 1528 or early 1529 Franck and his wife

"Der Geschichtsschreiber" (The Historiographer): woodcut on the title page of
Franck's Germaniae Chronicon

moved to the imperial city of Nuremberg, where he worked as a translator. His translation of Simon Fish's *A Supplicacyon for the Beggars,* a seminal tract of the English Reformation that satirizes the English clergy, was published in 1529, the same year as the original. Patrick Hayden-Roy has suggested that Franck may have had access to a manuscript for the Latin translation of this work, which was published in 1530, since there is no evidence that Franck knew English. Franck then turned to a chronicle by a man from Transylvania, now believed to be Georgius de Hungaria, who had been enslaved by the Turks for twenty-two years. Franck interpolates his own convictions into the text, so that the result is less a translation than an adaptation. Franck included a foreword that Luther had written for a Latin edition of the work, but Franck's interpolations indicate that by this time he had come to embrace a different theological viewpoint. The merely outward faiths professed by Lutherans, Zwinglians, and Baptists will be superseded by a truly spiritual faith that "alle eusserlich predig, Ceremoni, Sacrament, ban, beruff, als unnötig, wil auß dem weg raumen, und glat ein unsichtpar geystlich kirchen in ainigkeit des geyst und glauben versamlet, unter allen völckern, und allein durchs ewig unsichtbar wort, von Got on ainich eusserlich mittel regiert wil anrichten" (will dispose of all outward preaching, ceremony, sacrament, ban, vocation as unnecessary and will establish an invisible, spiritual church in the unity of the spirit and faith, gathered together from all peoples solely through the eternal, invisible Word, ruled by God without any external means). This spiritualist understanding of the church would remain fundamental to all of Franck's subsequent works and would create considerable problems for him. In the second edition of the work, published in Augsburg in 1530, Franck replaced Luther's foreword with one of his own.

Around 1530 the Francks moved to Strasbourg, a thriving imperial city with an active printing trade and a reputation for leniency toward religious heterodoxy. In a 4 February 1531 letter to the religious dissident Johannes Campanus (translated 1962), Franck outlines his beliefs and pays tribute to one of his Strasbourg contacts, the spiritualist Johannes Bünderlin. He also expresses agreement with the anti-Trinitarian views of Servetus, a Spanish dissident whom he might also have met in Strasbourg.

Franck's first book to appear after he moved to Strasbourg was *Ein künstlich höflich Declamation* (An Artful, Polite Declamation, 1531); the work is a translation of *Declamatio Lepidissima Ebriosi Scortatoris Aleatoris de uitiositate Disceptantium* (A Pleasant Declamation of a Drunk, a Fornicator, and a Gambler Disputing Vice, 1499), a short satire by the Italian humanist Filippo Beroaldo that was widely disseminated in Europe in the sixteenth century both in Latin and in translations into various vernaculars. (The first translation into German had been by Jakob Wimpfeling in 1513.) The "Argument" preceding the text gives the premise of the work: a father stipulates on his deathbed that the worst of his three sons—one is a gambler, another a whoremonger, and the third a drunk—will be disinherited. The text relates the three brothers' statements before a jury: each marshals biblical and ancient sources in arguing for the depravity of his brothers' vices while citing examples of great men of the past who shared his own failing. The jury's verdict is not given. Beroaldo's satire would have appealed to Franck for several reasons: it expresses the moral concerns Franck had voiced in *Von dem greüwlichen laster der trunckenhayt*; it exemplifies one of his favorite themes, how learning can be put to perverse uses; and its open-ended form makes the reader the arbiter, a technique Franck would favor in his historical and theological writings. Franck dedicated the translation to his uncle, the innkeeper Michael Franck in Nördlingen. The dedication describes the temptations facing innkeepers, particularly in these "dangerous last days," to become facilitators of their customers' vices for pecuniary gain.

Also in 1531 Franck published one of his most significant works, *Chronica, Zeÿtbuch und geschychtbibel* (Chronicle, Book of Time, and History Bible). The book, which runs to more than 530 folio leaves, is divided into three sections: the history of the world from Adam to Christ; a secular history from imperial Rome to 1531 focused on a "Kaiserchronik" (Chronicle of the Emperors); and a discussion of the Popes and of spiritual matters. Franck's work is a compilation of many sources but expresses a view of history that is unique to its age. He calls the book a "geschychtbibel" because in history he finds divine truth in living form, rather than in the dead letter of books: "Also lebt die Histori andere schrifft aber leer stuck und gesatz bücher leren allein und seind seel[l]os und todt gegen den lebendigen Historien, darinn Got gesehen, dort allein gehört wirdt" (Thus, history lives, while other writings, teachings, and books of law merely instruct; they are without soul and dead to the living histories in which God is seen and where alone he is heard). Truth cannot be captured by the dogmatic formulas of written texts but becomes visible to the spiritually minded who contemplate the works of God in history—a radical departure from the teachings of both Luther and the Roman Church. Franck's task as historian is to compile the experience of the ages in a nonpartisan manner, leaving his reader to discover the divine truth therein: "[Will] auch nit, was ich glaub, oder von yemand hatte, anzeigen, und mein urteil, zu sich setzen, sonder bloß . . . eines yeden geschicht erzelen, und dem leser zu urteiln auffopffern" (I do not wish to present what I believe or have from somebody else, or add my judgment, but rather merely tell every story and offer it to the reader to judge). There is no single message to be gleaned from the "History Bible"—such an imposition of his own judgment on the material would reduce it to mere dogmatic letter, rather than living history. Yet certain themes are reiterated: skepticism toward all forms of power and toward all church institutions; pessimism regarding the ways of the world; expectation of imminent divine judgment; and sympathy with those who suffer as the true witnesses of the spirit.

Despite Franck's nonpartisan stance, *Chronica, Zeÿtbuch und geschychtbibel* caused a scandal that would have disastrous results for the young writer. In the foreword to his chronicle of the emperors, Franck, drawing on material found in Desiderius Erasmus's *Adagiorum chiliades* (1515; translated as *Proverbes or Adagies with Newe Addicions Gathered out of the Chiliades of Erasmus*, 1539), discusses the eagle as an apt representation of the royal ruler: he robs, murders, and is bloodthirsty and hostile to peace. While Erasmus had qualified his words by excluding the good and pious princes from his description, Franck made no such diplomatic gesture; the passage was taken as a bald insult to the emperor's majesty. Nor did Franck's tactlessness stop there: he also managed to offend Erasmus—whom he highly esteemed—by bestowing on him the dubious honor of being included in the "Chronica der Römischen ketzer" (Chronicle of the Roman Heretics), the best-known section of the *Chronica, Zeÿtbuch und geschychtbibel*. An important precursor of Gottfried Arnold's *Unpartheyische Kirchen- und Ketzerhistorie* (Impartial History of the Church and of Heretics, 1699-1700), the "Chronica der Römischen ketzer" finds truth in many of the teachings condemned as heterodox by the Roman Catholic Church. For nearly ten pages Franck points out passages in Erasmus's writings that Rome would deem heretical but with which Franck is in sympathy. To distance himself from this incriminating description Erasmus sent an angry letter to the Strasbourg City Council attacking not only Franck but also the council for allowing such a work to be published. City officials were additionally provoked by Franck's allegation in the *Chronica, Zeÿtbuch und geschychtbibel* that Strasbourg's religious reform remained Zwinglian, rather than Lutheran: early in 1531 Strasbourg had been accepted into the Smalkaldic League, a federation of Lutheran territories and cities, on the basis of the city's rejection of the Zwinglian view of the Eucharist in favor of the Lutheran view. The Strasbourg officials had adopted this position in the hope of placating the emperor, who was willing to make a temporary peace with the Lutheran camp while maintaining adamant opposition to the "Sacramentarians" in Zwinglian Switzerland. Franck's offensive portrayal of the emperor, his remarks about Strasbourg's persistent Zwinglianism, and Erasmus's complaint combined to force the city council to take action. In December 1531 Franck was incarcerated, and all copies of the *Chronica, Zeÿtbuch und geschychtbibel* were confiscated; later that same month he was expelled from the city.

After his expulsion Franck resided briefly in Kehl, across the Rhine from Strasbourg, while he unsuccessfully petitioned the authorities to reverse their decision. In the fall of 1532 he moved to the imperial city of Esslingen, where he made his living selling soap. In the fall of 1533 he applied to the imperial city of Ulm for citizenship, which was granted to him in October 1534. After working for the Ulm printer Hans Varnier, he established himself as an independent printer. Some of the works he printed are his own translations, and to several of these he added a foreword. Four of his own works appeared in 1534: the *Weltbuch* (Book of the World), a geography conceived as the fourth part of the *Chronica, Zeÿtbuch und geschychtbibel;* a book generally referred to as the *Vier Kronbüchlin* (Four Crown Booklets), which includes both original works and translations; the *Paradoxa ducenta octoginta;* and a short tract, *Das Gott das ainig ain, und höchstes güt, sein* (That God Is the Single One and Highest Good). Of these, the *Vier Kronbüchlin* and the *Paradoxa ducenta octoginta* are of particular literary interest.

Franck chose to publish the *Vier Kronbüchlin* under the title of his German translation of Erasmus's *Moriae encomium* (1511; translated as *The Praise of Folie*, 1549), possibly to avoid problems with Ulm's censor. Franck's is the first complete translation of the *Moriae encomium* into German, but the work assumes new character and meaning through its al-

Title page for Franck's collection of contradictory Bible passages

terations of the original, through its commentary, and through its position relative to the three other texts in the volume. Franck uses a broad range of rhetorical strategies to make Erasmus's work clearer, more vibrant, and less abstract, thereby making it more accessible to a less educated readership. His interlinear commentary also simplifies the work, as the dizzying irony of the original gives way to simple inner-versus-outer antitheses. The commentary also expresses Franck's spiritualist concerns and takes aim at the theology of the Reformation.

The second part of the *Vier Kronbüchlin* is Franck's German translation of excerpts from Heinrich Cornelius Agrippa of Nettisheim's *De incertitudine et vanitate scientiarum* (On the Uncertainty and Vanity of Knowledge, 1530), showing the folly of all learning. The third and fourth pieces are essays by Franck: "Von dem Bam deß wißens Gutz und böß" (translated as *The Forbidden Fruit. Or A Treatise of the Tree of Knowledge of Good & Evill, of which Adam the first, & as yet all Mankind doe eate death*, 1640) argues that all learning derives from original sin and is mere outer flesh; "Encomium: Ein Lob des

Thorechten Götlichen Worts" (Encomium: In Praise of the Foolish Divine Word) insists that the Word of God is not bound to the letter but speaks immediately to the inner person. The four works taken together form a single argument, as Franck claims in his foreword: they demonstrate the folly of human knowledge and plead for spiritual rebirth. Given Franck's tendency toward long-windedness, this book stands out as a relatively succinct statement of his theological concerns; it also offers fine examples of his ability as a translator.

The most comprehensive statement of Franck's spiritualist views is found in *Paradoxa ducenta octoginta*, a massive collection of paradoxical passages from the Bible and other sources, each of which is followed by a commentary by Franck. A much-loved form of the Renaissance, the paradox has a long tradition in mysticism, where it serves as a linguistic marker of the ineffable—the mystery of the godhead or the union with God experienced by the mystic. Franck's familiarity with Christian Neoplatonic mysticism is evident in his references in *Paradoxa ducenta octoginta* to Dionysius the Areopogite (the Pseudo-Dionysius), Meister Eckart, Johannes Tauler, and the *Theologia deutsch*. Franck's object, however, is not to convey the mystical experience; rather, the paradox mirrors his view of a bifurcated reality, the eternal contradiction between the spiritual and fleshly realms:

> Dann durch aus alle ding ist anders in der warhait, dann es von aussen an zu sehen ist nach dem schein. Gott hält immer zu in allen dingen mit der Welt widerpart, unnd urtailt das widerspil, Darumb wie die Welt ain ding hält, nennet, glaubt, redt, wil etc. so ergreiff du das widerspil, und gegen urtail, so has tu Gottes wort, weyßhait, und willen ergrieffen.

> (For everything is different in truth, than when viewed from outside according to appearance. In all things God always takes the opposite side from the world, and judges according to the opposite. Therefore, as the world holds, names, believes, speaks, wills one thing, so when you grasp the opposite and counterjudgment, you have grasped God's Word, wisdom, and will.)

Throughout the work Franck begins with a paradoxical or apparently false phrase or statement, such as "Der Welt herrschafft, die gröst knechtschafft" (The world's dominion, the greatest servitude), "Got ist der welt Teüffel" (God is the world's devil), or "Die gottlosen sindt der Welt hailig" (The godless are holy to the world). In his commentary he resolves the contradiction by showing how the judgments of the world directly oppose those of the spirit. Over hundreds of pages this format makes for rather tedious reading, but one must admire the consistency with which Franck lays out his spiritualist faith and does not shy away from a thoroughgoing condemnation of all institutionalized religion. The true Church, he maintains, is an invisible body, not bound to any place or time; the Word of God is not fixed by letter or dogma but speaks directly through the spirit to the inner person. Certainly Arnold was correct in noting in his *Kirchen- und Ketzerhistorie* that Franck's *Paradoxa ducenta octoginta* is rife with heresy.

Initially, however, Franck's writings created fewer problems for him in Ulm than did his old Strasbourg enmities. Bucer wrote to Philipp Melanchthon requesting that Melanchthon inform the influential Lutheran prince Philipp of Hesse of Franck's noxious presence in Ulm. Melanchthon obliged, and Philipp of Hesse responded by writing a letter on 31 December 1534 urging the Ulm City Council to expel Franck. Franck's appeals to the city council were successful, at least for a time, because he was able to exploit the tensions between the council and the clergy in Ulm: Patrick Hayden-Roy has argued that Franck's advocacy of a purely spiritual church found resonance among some members of the city council insofar as it placed responsibility for matters of discipline and order in the hands of the temporal authorities.

During the appeal process Franck was allowed to remain in Ulm and continue his printing trade, but he had to agree not to publish any of his own works without submitting them for review to the city censor. In 1536 he published a revised edition of the *Chronica, Zeÿtbuch und geschychtbibel;* although he added an apology for the section in the "Kaiserchronik" that had given such offense, he—incredibly—republished the section unchanged in the new edition. There was no immediate protest against the work, however. To avoid the censor, Franck published three new works outside Ulm: *Die Guldin Arch* (The Golden Ark, 1538) in Augsburg, the *Germaniae Chronicon* (Chronicle of Germany, 1538) in Frankfurt am Main, and *Das verbüthschiert mit siben Sigeln verschlossen Buch* in Augsburg in 1539. He published two additional works pseudonymously in 1539: the short theological tract *Was gesagt sei: Der Glaub thuts alles* (What Is Meant by: Faith Does It All) in Tübingen and *Das Krieg büchlin. des frides* (The War Booklet of Peace) in Augsburg.

Die Guldin Arch is another compilation: Scripture passages are organized under thematic rubrics and supplied with related passages from the church fathers and even from some ancient philosophers, including Cicero and Seneca. It is noteworthy that the "erleuchten Heyden und philosophen" (enlightened heathens and philosophers) are granted equal footing with the Christians. The emphasis is on mystical and spiritual themes. Franck's foreword includes a restatement of his theological convictions and a denunciation of the theology of the day; he says that he hopes his book will be used as a concordance, enabling Scripture to perform exegesis on itself. The lengthy *Germaniae Chronicon* is a compilation from the writings of various historians, interspersed with Franck's observations, focusing on the political history of the German Empire up to the time of Charles V. Hans Sachs was a particular admirer of this work, which expresses pride in the land, resources, and culture of "Germania."

Related to *Die Guldin Arch* but radically different in its organization is *Das verbüthschiert mit siben Sigeln verschlossen Buch*. With his reference in the title to the sealed book mentioned in chapter 5 of Revelation, Franck suggests that the Bible itself is unsealed only to the spiritually reborn. The work presents not only thematically related passages but also a "Schrifftkrieg" (Scripture battle) of contradictory passages: each *Schrifft* (text) is supplied with a *Gegenschrifft* (countertext). The technique is similar to that used in the *Paradoxa ducenta octoginta,* but here the contradictions are gleaned only from the Bible. Franck's intention was to point out the danger of accepting scriptural authority unquestioningly, as he believed Luther and his followers had, instead of going within oneself to find the true sense of God's Word. Franck concludes the work with an apology for it and for his other writings, in which he puts forward again his understanding of spiritual truth and makes a plea for religious tolerance. He has communicated his *gab* (gift), he argues, not to be taken as an article of faith but "der gemein gottes zu gut" (for the good of God's community), so that others would hold to what speaks to their hearts. Just as he does not force his opinions on anyone, so he expects that others will not make themselves masters of his faith or force him to be the servant of their minds. His heart, he claims, is not divided against anyone; he finds "brüder" (brothers) among the Turks, the Papists, the Jews, and all other sects and peoples.

Franck published his *Das Krieg büchlin. des frides* under the pseudonym Friderich Wernstreyt. Both names relate to his theme: *Friderich* means "peace[ful] kingdom," *Wernstreyt* means "oppose conflict." The work assumes an important place in the body of antiwar literature written in early modern Germany, which includes, most prominently, Erasmus's *Querela pacis* (Complaint of Peace, 1517). Franck borrows heavily from Erasmus's work in his discussion, although he does not share its optimistic humanist view of peace as a natural state achievable through reason and education. For Franck, peace is an inner condition that exists, paradoxically, in the midst of the struggles and wars that inevitably occupy the perverted outer world. Like the true church, peace resides on the spiritual side of Franck's division between the flesh and the spirit; but his condemnation of war is thorough and includes a powerful indictment of all those, including the institutional church, who are occupied with the "vihisch" (bestial) and "teuffelisch" (devilish) business of war. Franck's eschatological perspective is evident in this work: he considers war a sign of the end times and of God's imminent judgment.

While in Ulm, Franck also wrote many poems, several of which were published. *Des Grossen Nothelfers unnd Weltheiligen Sant Gelts, oder S. Pfennings Lobgesang* (A Song in Praise of the Great Helper in Time of Need, Saint Penny), published in 1537 by Franck's press, comprises more than five hundred intricately rhymed lines. The poem's antithetical argument is familiar from Franck's other works: money is the god of this deluded world and, at the same time, the instrument of the devil and of the Antichrist. In 1537 Franck published his own psalm, *Wie man Beten unnd Psallieren soll* (How One Should Pray and Sing Psalms), followed by his own interpretation. The poem of more than one hundred lines follows the meter of Luther's "Aus tiefer Not schrei ich zu dir" (From Depths of Woe I Cry to Thee, 1524); it establishes an opposition between the mere noise of fleshly psalms and true singing "im geist" (in the spirit). Another satiric poem by Franck, "Von vier zwiträchtigen Kirchen" (On the Four Discordant Churches), is preserved in a manuscript of songs compiled by Daniel Sudermann in the late sixteenth century. It follows the meter of "Mag ich unglück nit widerstan" (Should I Not Withstand Misfortune) and provides a critique of the Roman, Lutheran, Zwinglian, and Anabaptist sects, as he calls them. The true Christian, he maintains, looks to Christ alone, though he or she may be despised by all the world. Scholars have argued that Johann Fischart incorporated material from two additional songs believed to have been written into his lengthy poem *Bewärung und Erklärung des Uralten gemeynen Sprüchworts: Die Gelehrten die Verkehrten* (Proof and Explanation of the Ancient Common Saying: The Learned [Are] the Perverted, 1584). A text for the first of these, "Die Gelehrten die Verkehrten," was found in a Berlin manuscript by Johannes Bolte; he published it in 1925, with an attribution to Franck. Whether Fischart also had a model by Franck for the "Vom Glaubenszwang" (On Forcing Faith) section of his poem is uncertain; in any case, no such poem by Franck has been found. Carlos Gilly has argued, in an article in *Se-*

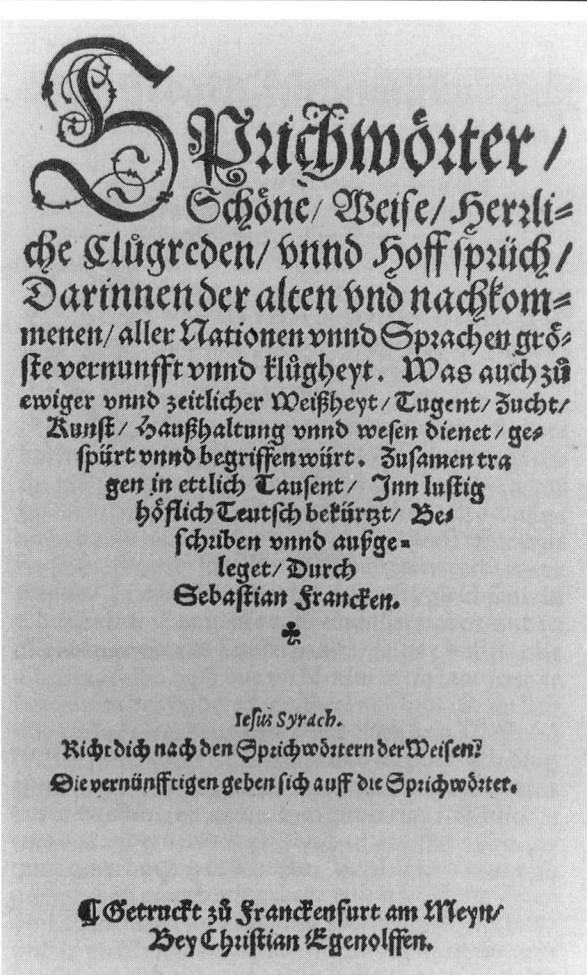

Title page for Franck's collection of German proverbs

bastian Franck (1499–1542) (1993), edited by Jan-Dirk Müller, that this second "original" may never have existed but was composed for the first time by Fischart. He has also questioned the attribution of the first poem to Franck.

When *Die Guldin Arch* appeared, the city pastor, Frecht, Franck's former fellow student at the Dominican college, complained to the Ulm City Council. Franck consistently went behind the backs of the censors in publishing his works, Frecht claimed; through his printing and writing he was causing offense and bringing the city into disrepute. Franck's spiritualism and skeptical view of outward displays of religion could not be tolerated in a city that was struggling to institute a new ecclesiastical order, and in the summer of 1539 Franck was ordered to leave Ulm. He, his wife, and their six children—one of whom was only two months old—set out for Basel. Ottilie Franck was in ill health and died en route.

Franck's fortunes improved in Basel. He obtained citizenship, as well as guild membership, and worked with the printer Nicolaus Brylinger, with whom he put out such works as a parallel Greek and Latin Bible based on Erasmus's 1516 edition. In 1541 he married Margarete (Barbara) Beck in Strasbourg; she was the stepdaughter of Balthasar Beck, the printer of the original edition of Franck's *Chronica, Zeÿtbuch und geschychtbibel*.

Franck's most popular work, *Sprichwörter, Schöne, Weise, Herrliche Clügreden, unnd Hoffsprüch* (Proverbs, Lovely, Wise, Glorious Clever Sayings and Adages), was printed in Frankfurt am Main in 1541. The work went through twelve further editions between 1545 and 1615, although in these the material was reorganized, and much of Franck's commentary was deleted; beginning with the 1548 edition his name was omitted from the title page. One of the most comprehensive collections of German proverbs ever published, the work is still consulted as a source. For Franck, the proverb was closely related to his theology of the inner word: it is a kernel of divine wisdom planted within the hearts of all people. He says in the dedication: "Darinnen zu sehen, was weißheyt, kunst, verstand, religion, und verborgner gheym in der alten Teutschen, Latiner, Griechen und Hebreer Sprichwörtern steckt ... und dergleichen selbs im Herrn nachzudencken, als einem festen wort Gots, das Gott in aller menschen hertz unnd mund geschriben unnd gelegt hat, wie in der außlegung ettlicher Sprichwörter ersehen würt" (In [the proverbs] one can see what wisdom, art, understanding, religion, and hidden mystery reside in the old German, Latin, Greek, and Hebrew proverbs ... and consider them in the Lord as a solid Word of God, which God has written and placed in every person's heart and mouth, as will be seen in the interpretation of several of the proverbs). Erasmus expressed a similarly high view of the proverb in *Adagiorum chiliades,* which Franck consulted in writing his work. For both men the proverb was evidence that divine truth was to be found in nature and in all peoples, not merely in the Bible and church dogma. Here lies the connection to Franck's historical works: both look to the realm of experience to find God's revelation.

Franck died in the fall of 1542; the inventory of his goods indicates that he was relatively well off. After his death several works that Franck had never published began to circulate in Holland: three letters, including the one to Campanus; the manuscript for a paraphrase of the *Theologia Deutsch,* the only longer work Franck wrote in Latin; and two shorter theological tracts that have survived only in Dutch translations, *Van Het Rycke Christi* (On the Kingdom of Christ, 1611) and *Een stichtelijck Tractaet, van de Werelt*

(An Edifying Tract on the World, 1618).

The reception of Franck's work has undergone many transformations over the centuries. There was some interest in him among religious dissenters in the Low Countries in the late sixteenth and early seventeenth centuries, and several of his published works were translated into Dutch. The 1640 English translation of "Von dem Bam deß wißens Gutz und böß" may have circulated among the radical sects of the English Civil War period. But, generally speaking, Franck fell into obscurity in the seventeenth and eighteenth centuries because he left behind no following to cultivate his memory and because his theological views had been anathematized by the leaders of the Reformation. The most notable exception to this ignoring of Franck is Arnold's brief discussion of him in *Unpartheyische Kirchen- und Ketzerhistorie;* but, contrary to what one might expect, Arnold's account is less than enthusiastic. Not until the mid nineteenth century would Franck find admirers, and then it would be among historians who discovered in his writings a peculiarly modern voice, a precursor of developments in eighteenth-century German philosophy. Wilhelm Dilthey's much-quoted comment, "In hundert Rinnsalen fliessen die Ideen Francks der modernen Zeit entgegen" (Franck's ideas flow in a hundred rivulets into the modern age), written in 1892, captures the spirit of this "Franck renaissance." The interest in Franck in the nineteenth century led to a scouring of the archives for documents relating to him, many of which were published; on the basis of these documents a good deal of Franck's biography was reconstructed, and several excellent studies were produced. Alfred Hegler's *Geist und Schrift bei Sebastian Franck* (Spirit and Letter in Sebastian Franck, 1892), the first work to exploit this material, remains the most incisive analysis of Franck's thought. The Marxist historian Siegfried Wollgast placed Franck in a tradition of "materialistischer pantheismus" (materialistic pantheism) that he traced from the medieval German mystics through Franck to Gotthold Ephraim Lessing, Immanuel Kant, Johann Gottfried Herder, Johann Wolfgang von Goethe, and finally Ludwig Feuerbach. This interpretation, however, as well as earlier attempts—such as Dilthey's—to draw lines from Franck to Kant rely on anachronistic schemas. Franck scholarship has been advanced by Klaus Kaczerowsky's meticulous 1976 bibliography, and a critical edition of Franck's collected works has been underway since 1992.

Bibliographies:

Philip Kintner, "Sebastian Franck: An American Library Finding List," *Archiv für Reformationsgeschichte,* 55 (1954): 48–55;

Klaus Kaczerowsky, *Sebastian Franck Bibliographie: Verzeichnisse von Francks Werken, der von ihm gedruckten Bücher sowie der Sekundär-Literatur. Mit einem Anhang: Nachweise von Francks Briefwechsel und der Archivalien zu seinem Leben* (Wiesbaden: Pressler, 1976);

Christoph Dejung, "Sebastian Franck," in *Bibliotheca Dissidentium,* volume 7, edited by André Séguenny (Baden-Baden: Koerner, 1986), pp. 39–119.

Biographies:

Will-Erich Peuckert, *Sebastian Franck: Ein deutscher Sucher* (Munich: Piper, 1943);

Eberhard Teufel, *"Landräumig": Sebastian Franck, ein Wanderer am Donau, Neckar und Rhein* (Neustadt an der Aisch: Degener, 1954);

Patrick Hayden-Roy, *The Inner Word and the Outer World: A Biography of Sebastian Franck* (New York: Peter Lang, 1994).

References:

Gottfried Arnold, *Unpartheyische Kirchen- und Ketzer-Historie, vom Anfang des Neuen Testaments biù auf das Jahr Christi 1688,* 4 volumes (Frankfurt am Main: Fritsch, 1699–1700);

Johannes Bolte, "Zwei satirische Gedichte von Sebastian Franck," in *Sitzungsberichte der preussischen Akademie der Wissenschaften Philosophisch-historische Klasse* (1925): 89–114;

Wilhelm Dilthey, *Weltanschauung und Analyse des Menschen seit Renaissance und Reformation,* edited by Georg Misch (Stuttgart: Teubner, 1957), pp. 80–89;

Julius Endriß, *Sebastian Francks Ulmer Kämpfe* (Ulm: Höhn, 1935);

Alfred Hegler, *Geist und Schrift bei Sebastian Franck: Eine Studie zur Geschichte des Spiritualismus in der Reformationszeit* (Freiburg im Breisgau: Mohr, 1892);

Hegler, *Sebastian Francks lateinische Paraphrase der Deutschen Theologie und seine holländisch erhaltenen Traktate* (Tübingen: Schnürlen, 1901);

Hegler and Walther Köhler, eds., *Beiträge zur Geschichte der Mystik in der Reformationszeit* (Berlin: Schwetschke, 1906);

Hans J. Hillerbrand, *A Fellowship of Discontent* (New York: Harper & Row, 1967), pp. 31–64;

Rufus M. Jones, *Spiritual Reformers of the 16th and 17th Centuries* (London: Macmillan, 1914);

Philip Kintner, "Studies in the Historical Writings of Sebastian Franck (1499–1542)," dissertation, Yale University, 1958;

Peter Klaus Knauer, *Der Buchstabe lebt: Schreibstrategien bei Sebastian Franck* (Bern: Peter Lang, 1993);

Jan-Dirk Müller, "Buchstabe, Geist, Subjekt: Zu einer frühneuzeitlichen Problemfigur bei Sebastian Franck," *Modern Language Notes,* 106 (1991): 648–674;

Müller, ed., *Sebastian Franck (1499–1542)* (Wiesbaden: Harrassowitz, 1993);

Steven Ozment, *Mysticism and Dissent: Religious Ideology and Social Protest in the Sixteenth Century* (New Haven: Yale University Press, 1973), pp. 137–167;

Ozment, "Sebastian Franck: Critic of the 'New Scholastics,' " in *Profiles of Radical Reformers: Biographical Sketches from Thomas Müntzer to Paracelsus* (Kitchener, Ont. & Scottdale, Pa.: Herald, 1982), pp. 226–233;

Eugene Peters, "Sebastian Franck's Theory of Religious Knowledge," *Mennonite Quarterly Review,* 35 (1961): 267–281;

Bruno Quast, *Sebastian Francks 'Kriegbüchlin des Frides': Studien zum radikalreformatorischen Spiritualismus* (Tübingen: Francke, 1993);

Rudolf Stadelmann, *Vom Geist des ausgehenden Mittelalters: Studien zur Geschichte der Weltanschauung von N. Cusanus bis S. Franck,* Deutsche Vierteljahrsschrift für Literaturwissenschaft und Geistesgeschichte, Buchreih, no. 15 (Halle: Niemeyer, 1929);

Horst Weigelt, *Sebastian Franck und die lutherische Reformation* (Gütersloh: Mohn, 1972);

Franz Weinkauff, "Sebastian Franck von Donauwerd," *Alemannia,* 5 (1877): 131–147; 6 (1878): 49–86; 7 (1879): 1–66;

Stephen C. Williams, " 'Türkenchronik': Ausdeutende Übersetzung: Georgs von Ungarn 'Tractatus de moribus, condictionibus et nequicia Turcorum' in der Verdeutschung Sebastian Francks," in *Reisen und Welterfahrung in der deutschen Literatur des Mittelalters,* edited by Dietrich Huschenbett and John Margetts (Würzburg: Königshausen & Neumann, 1991), pp. 185–195;

Siegfried Wollgast, *Der deutsche Pantheismus im 16. Jahrhundert* (Berlin: Akademie-Verlag, 1972).

Nicodemus Frischlin
(22 September 1547 – 29 November 1590)

Richard E. Schade
University of Cincinnati

BOOKS: *Stipendium Tubingense* (Tübingen: V. Morhard's widow, 1569);

Carmen De Astronomico Horologio Argentoratensi (Strasbourg: Nicolaus Wyriot, 1575);

Rebecca, comoedia nova et sacra (Frankfurt am Main: Andreas Wechel, 1576); translated into German by Jacob Frischlin as *Rebecca* (Frankfurt am Main: Johann Spiess, 1589);

De nuptijs illustrissimi Principis, ac Domini, D. Lvdovici, Dvcis Wirtembergici & Teccij etc., comitis mompeligardii, &c. cum illustrissima Principe ac Domina, D. Dorothea Vrsvla, Marchionissa Badensi, &c. Stuccardiae, anno 1575. Mense Novembri celebratis. Libri Septem, versv heroico (Tübingen: Georg Gruppenbach, 1577); translated into German by Karl C. Beyer as *Sieben Bücher, Von der Fürstlichen Würtembergischen Hochzeit, Des Durchleuchtigen Hochgebornen Fürsten vnd Herrn, Herrn Ludwigen, Hertzogen zu Würtemberg vnd Theck mit der Durchleuchtigen vnd Hochgebornen Fürstin vnd Fräwle Dorothea Ursula, geborner Marggräffin von Baden, etc. zu Stutgart, Anno, etc. 1575. im Monat Nouember gehalten* (Tübingen: Georg Gruppenbach, 1578);

Susanna, comoedia nova (Tübingen: Alexander Hock, 1578); translated into German by Jacob Frischlin as *Susanna* (Frankfurt am Main: Johann Spiess, 1589);

Hildegardis Magna, comedia nova (Tübingen: Georg Gruppenbach, 1579);

Fraw Wendelgardt, ein new Comedie oder Spil (Tübingen: Alexander Hock, 1580);

Priscianvs Vapvlans. Nicodemi Frishlini alemanni comoedia lepida, faceta & vtilis (Strasbourg: Bernhard Jobin, 1580);

Oratio de vita rustica (Tübingen: Alexander Hock, 1580);

Dido. Tragoedia nova ex quarto libro Virgilianæ Æneidos (Tübingen: Alexander Hock, 1581);

Iulius Redivivus: Comoedia, in lavdem Germaniae & Germanorum scripta (Strasbourg: Bernhard Jobin, 1585); translated into German by Jacob Frischlin as *Julius Redivivus*

Nicodemus Frischlin (University of Tübingen)

(Speyer: Dalbin, 1585);

Operum poeticorum Nicodemi Frischlini poetae, oratoris et philosophi, pars scenica (Strasbourg: Bernhard Jobin, 1585; revised, 1589);

De secundis nuptijs illvstrissimi Principis ac domini, D. Ludovici, Dvcis Wirtembergici ac Teccensis &c. cum illustrissima Duce ac domina, D. Vrsvla, duce bauariae, Comite Palatina Rheni, &c. praeterito Maio, huius 1585 anni celebratis Stuccardiae, libri qvatvor: Versv conscripti heroico (Tübingen: Georg Gruppenbach, 1585);

Grammatice Latina (Frankfurt am Main: Johann Spiess, 1586);

Aristophanes, veteris comoedia princeps (Frankfurt am

Main: Johann Spiess, 1586);

De Astronomicæ Artis cum Doctrina cælesti et Naturali Philosophia Congruentia (Frankfurt am Main: Johann Spiess, 1586);

Helvetio-Germani. Comoedia nova (Helmstedt: Jacob Lucius, 1589);

Phasma: Hoc est; Comædia Posthvma, Nova et Sacra (Strasbourg, 1592); translated into German by Arnold Glaser as *Phasma: Das ist, ein newe, geistliche, nachgehndig Comœdie* (Greifswald: Ferber, 1593);

Hebræis (Strasbourg: Bernhard Jobin, 1599);

Operum poeticorum Nicodemi Frischlini poetae, oratoris et philosophi, pars elegiaca (Strasbourg: Bernhard Jobin's heirs, 1601);

Operum poeticorum Nicodemi Frischlini poetae, oratoris et philosophi, pars paraphrastica (Frankfurt am Main: Johann Spiess, 1602);

Rhetorica: seu institvtionvm oratoriarvm libri duo (Leipzig: Michael Lantzenberger, 1604);

Orationes (Strasbourg: Karl, 1605);

Deutsche Dichtungen von Nicodemus Frischlin, Theils zum Erstenmal aus den Handschriften, Theils nach Altendrucken herausgegeben, edited by David Friedrich Strauß (Stuttgart: Litterarischer Verein, 1857).

Editions: *Fraw Wendelgard,* edited by Alfred Kuhn and Eugen Weidmann (Stuttgart: Grüninger, 1908);

Fraw Wendelgardt: Eine deutsche Komödie von Nikodemus Frischlin, 1580. Neudruck mit Einleitung, edited by Paul Rothweiler (Ellwangen: Ipf- und Jagst-Zeitung, 1912);

Julius Redivivus, edited by Walther Janell (Berlin: Weidmann, 1912);

Aristophanes, veteris comoedia princeps (Hildesheim: Olms, 1982);

Julius Redivivus, edited by Richard E. Schade (Stuttgart: Reclam, 1983).

In his day Nicodemus Frischlin was probably the most influential Neo-Latin writer in the German territories. He adapted the classical imagination to late-sixteenth-century concerns, whether literary or curricular, religious or political. His contemporaries regarded him as a latter-day Terence, and even a century after his death schoolmasters stipulated that his dramas be performed. While his reputation as a man of letters dimmed thereafter, his person remained unforgotten. His tumultuous life still fascinates scholars and recently has led to a reevaluation of his accomplishments as an important representative of the late Renaissance in Germany.

The Protestant Reformation was still young when Philipp Nicodemus Frischlin was born on 22 September 1547 in Balingen, a small walled city dominated by a centrally situated church and the modest half-timbered residence of the Hohenzollern dynasty. His father, Jakob Frischlin, was a Lutheran clergyman and, as such, a person of some importance in the community of artisans, tradespeople, and peasants; his mother, Agnes née Ruoff, was the daughter of an artisan. She would outlive Nicodemus and all but one of the eight children she bore her husband. Frischlin's schooling began at age seven or eight at the local Latin school, an institution that prepared pupils for university study (as opposed to the German school, with its focus on vocational skills). In 1558 he was sent to nearby Tübingen for additional elementary schooling, moving on to more advanced preparatory work in Königsbronn in 1560 and in Bebenhausen in 1562. By the age of fifteen Frischlin was conversant in Latin, Greek, and Hebrew, the so-called holy languages of the Old and New Testaments; that is, he possessed the essential linguistic skills for following in his father's footsteps as a pastor.

Frischlin enrolled at the University of Tübingen on 12 November 1562. He and the other students who were totally supported by the duchy for training Lutheran clergy lived in a converted monastery, the Tübinger Stift (Tübingen Institute). In addition to theology they studied Cicero's orations, Philipp Melanchthon's influential book on rhetoric, Aristotelian ethics and physics, classical languages, astronomy, mathematics, geometry, and medicine under renowned scholars. By 1565 Frischlin had earned an M.A. He continued his studies in theology, but his academic career took an abrupt turn when he was offered a position as an "extraordinary" professor of poetry and history before completion of his doctorate. On 9 June 1568 the twenty-year-old Frischlin held a ceremonial introductory lecture on the value and uses of literature. His first published work, *Stipendium Tubingense* (The Tübingen Institute, 1569), a poetic encomium to his old school, was dedicated to Ludwig, heir to the duchy of Württemberg. And even his marriage in 1568 to Margarete Brenz, the granddaughter of the Lutheran reformer of Württemberg, Johann Brenz, seemed motivated by professional ambition.

Frischlin's teaching duties included lecturing on Cicero, Horace, Julius Caesar, and Virgil's *Aeneid;* his dramatic dialogue *Dido* (1581), based on Virgil's tale of the legendary queen who founded Carthage, and his comedy *Helvetio-Germani* (The Swiss-Germans, 1589), based on Caesar's *Commentaries on the Gallic War* (58-44 B.C.), would result from these pedagogical activities. He also explicated the principles of astronomy, and for seven years he was responsible for overseeing the weekly disputation exercises.

In 1575 Frischlin published *Carmen De Astronomico Horologio Argentoratensi*, a detailed laudatory verse description of a great clock that had recently been installed in the Strasbourg cathedral. The work documents the author's consummate Latinity and reveals a clever strategy of praise: Strasbourg, the home of great teachers, Protestant scholars, and influential merchants, is shown to be equally progressive in the mechanical arts, and its sponsorship of the complex project attests to the vision of the city council.

The epic *De nuptiis illustrissimi Principis, ac Domini, D. Ludovici, Ducis Wirtembergici & Teccii etc., comitis mompeligardii, &c. cum illustrissima Principe ac Domina, D. Dorothea Ursula, Marchionissa Badensi, &c. Stuccardiae, anno 1575. Mense Novembri celebratis. Libri Septem, versu heroico* (Seven Books in Heroic Verse concerning the Wedding of the most noble Prince and Lord Ludwig, Duke of Württemberg and Teck, Count of Montbeliard etc. with the most noble Princess and Lady Dorothea Ursula, Margravine of Baden, etc. Celebrated November 1575 in Stuttgart, 1577) cemented Frischlin's position in the ducal city of Stuttgart. Court festivals were elaborate affairs involving tightly scripted pomp and circumstance, much of it with allegorical overtones, and Ludwig's nuptials in November 1575 were no exception. In Frischlin's poetic account every noble guest had to be named, the glorious table ornamentation detailed, the ceremonial jousts documented, the untold beauty of Dorothea Ursula of Baden praised. The work reflects Frischlin's mastery of Latinity and of classical models: Ludwig is stylized both as Virgil's noble hero Aeneas and benefactor Maecenas. The author of the court festival description was, it followed, the Virgil of Württemberg.

His play *Rebecca*, first performed at Ludwig's wedding and published in 1576, was inspired by chapter 24 of Genesis. It is imitative of the language, scenes, and characters of the Romans Plautus and Terence, but literary imitation was, at the time, considered a mark of excellence: it demonstrated the author's ability to adapt ancient texts to modern sensibilities. Frischlin was unrelenting in his currying of the powerful, and the Holy Roman Emperor Rudolph II crowned him poet laureate in 1576 and subsequently elevated him to the lower nobility as a *Pfalzgraf* (palatine count). Less than a decade into his career Frischlin had outstripped many of his former teachers and university colleagues.

Like *Rebecca*, Frischlin's play *Susanna* (1578), based on a story from the Apocrypha, represents an attempt to conjoin Christian topics with pagan liter-

Woodcut by Tobias Stimmer for Frischlin's satiric drama Priscianus Vapulans

ary forms. Such works earned the playwright the reputation of a Christian Terence.

Frischlin's status as the self-styled Stuttgart court poet, as well as his patent of nobility, did not ingratiate him with his university colleagues. Also, he termed himself a doctor, even though he had not earned the degree. Furthermore, his notions about instruction in grammar, the keystone in the arch of humanist pedagogy, flew in the face of tradition. His satiric drama *Priscianus Vapulans* (The Beaten Priscian, 1580), performed at the university's centenary celebrations, audaciously called for the replacement of Priscian's time-honored grammar text with more progressive ones by Melanchthon and Desiderius Erasmus. Another play, *Phasma* (The Vision), first performed in 1580 but published posthumously in 1592, took on topics of Roman Catholicism and Protestant sectarianism in the context of the crucial debates surrounding the adoption of articles of Lutheran orthodoxy. While Frischlin came down decisively on the side of Lutheranism, treating the topic onstage was risky. Frischlin's pronounced and highly public convictions and his unapologetic self-confidence could not but grate on the sensibilities of his Tübingen colleagues.

The final straw was Frischlin's oration on Virgil's notions of rural life, held in 1580. The topic was innocuous enough—a discussion of pastoral poetry extolling the virtues of the simple life in tune with nature—but Frischlin used it as the vehicle for a less-than-veiled critique of urban life and the landed nobility. When he sought ducal permission to publish the talk, it came to the attention of Württemberg's aristocracy. The nobles made the speech a cause célèbre. The campaign against Frischlin was merciless, especially since the author was not one to avoid a fight. By 1582 his situation had become un-

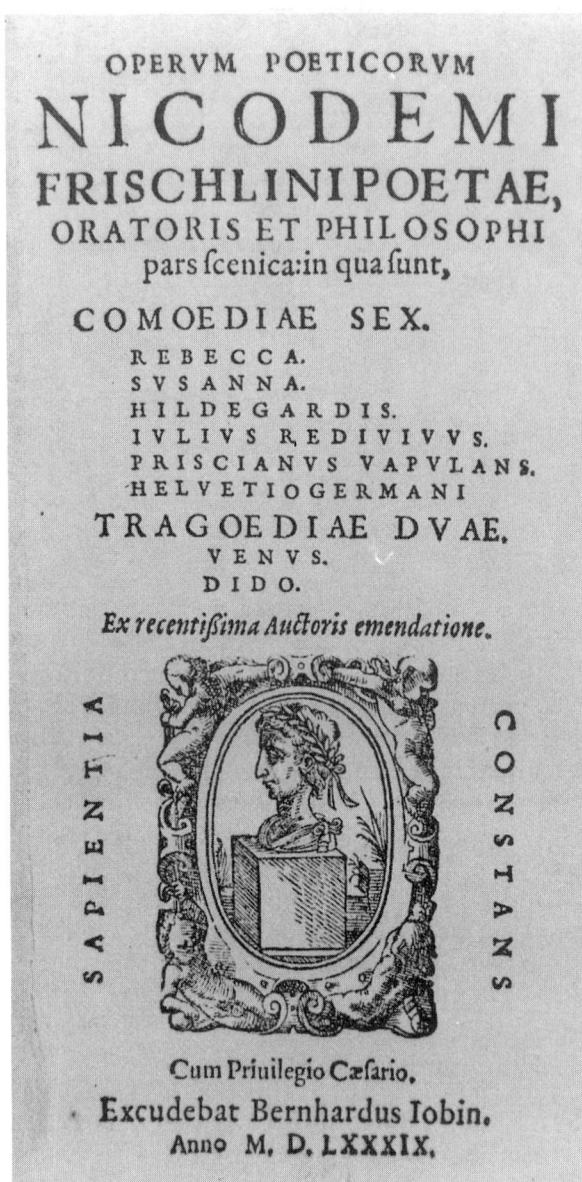

Title page for the collected edition of Frischlin's plays

on the poet's return he was placed under house arrest in his Tübingen residence. He was banished from Ludwig's territory forever in July 1586.

Ludwig's decision had not come easily. The duke recognized the playwright's genius, and Frischlin had made every effort to rehabilitate himself. For the duke's second marriage the poet had produced another massive court festival book, *De secundis nuptiis illustrissimi Principis ac domini, D. Ludovici, Ducis Wirtembergici ac Teccensis &c. cum illustrissima Duce ac domina, D. Ursula, duce bavarise, Comite Palitina Rheni, &c. praeterito Maio, huius 1585 anni celebratis Stuccardiae, libri quatuor: Versu conscripti heroico* (Four Books written in Heroic Verse concerning the Second Marriage of the most noble Prince and Lord Ludwig Duke of Württemberg and Teck etc. with the most noble Princess and Lady Ursula, Bavarian Princess and Countess of the Rhenish Palatine etc. Celebrated in May of 1585 in Stuttgart, 1585), and he had performed in his own celebratory drama, *Julius Redivivus* (Revivified Julius, 1585), which was staged at the festivities. In the comedy he depicts himself as the German Neo-Latin poet Eobanus Hessus engaged in conversation with Julius Caesar, the representative of the practical arts, and with Cicero, the exemplar of the speech arts. The two Romans have been conjured up from the underworld to sixteenth-century Germany to marvel at and critique the best that Württemberg and the empire had to offer. Frischlin's tactic was to flatter his duke both as a latter-day Caesar and as a sponsor of Ciceronian principles in the rhetorical and literary arts.

Banished forever from Württemberg, Frischlin vainly sought appointments in Prague, the capital of the empire, and Wittenberg, the symbolic capital of Lutheranism. He briefly gained employment in Brunswick as director of a secondary school. Typically, however, he became embroiled in local theological disputes and was dismissed. He went on to the Hessian court in Kassel, to the university town of Marburg (where his model Hessus had once taught), and to the publishing center Frankfurt am Main. In Frankfurt he sought to establish his own press, since few publishers would have risked their reputations printing new titles by the recently banished scholar and poet. Out of funds, he requested money from his wife's estate in Württemberg. When support was denied him, he fired off an invective at Stuttgart's ducal chancellors in March 1590, an act that led to his arrest in Mainz on grounds of defamation of state. By May he was incarcerated in the hilltop fortress in Urach. He fell to his death while attempting to escape through a chimney vent on 29 November.

tenable, and Ludwig saw to it that he was exiled to the nether regions of the empire as the director of a Lutheran secondary school in Ljubljana in present-day Slovenia.

Frischlin instituted major pedagogical reforms in Ljubljana and published seminal works on grammar theory that were at odds with the less progressive views of his former colleagues. When he sought to regain a foothold in Tübingen in 1584 he was accused of Roman Catholic sympathies—a cardinal sin in ultraorthodox Lutheran Württemberg—and was attacked, with some justification, for adulterous affairs. Frischlin fled Tübingen without the duke's permission. This act incited the ire of Ludwig, and

Remarkably, Frischlin's years of exile had been a period of literary creativity. He published important essays on humanist pedagogy and pamphlets on issues in rhetoric and grammar, and he revised editions of his plays; he also wrote laudatory occasional verse and countless letters. Even in prison he worked on a massive epic, biblical dramas, and various historical works, seeking to assure Ludwig and others of his contrition. After he plunged to his death his rivals jeered, but not without a modicum of respect. A Latin epigram by Martin Crusius, a Tübingen adversary, sums up the sentiment: "Frischlinus jacet hic, celsa qui decidit arce: / Ingenio clarus, mente sed ater erat" (Frischlinus lieth here, dashed badly by the fall; / A mind so very good, misused, after all).

Frischlin's life is well documented because of his altercations with the authorities: large collections of letters, petitions, and directives exist in Stuttgart and Tübingen. His biography is instructive, because his predicaments presage those of German writers in the seventeenth century, when most literati were at the beck and call of princely benefactors. That he was the most influential German playwright prior to Andreas Gryphius is made apparent by the frequent reprinting of his Latin plays and the translations of them into German by his younger brother Jakob Frischlin, a schoolmaster. He was cited in poetic handbooks, and school theaters performed his dramas as part of their curricular program well into the next century. A curious commemorative piece celebrating his years in Braunschweig enjoyed currency a century after his death, and his life story was often told in the eighteenth century. David Friedrich Strauß, the biographer of Ulrich von Hutten and Jesus Christ, put Frischlin scholarship on firm footing with his *Leben und Schriften des Dichters und Philologen Nicodemus Frischlin* (Life and Writings of the Writer and Philologist Nicodemus Frischlin, 1856). Strauß depicts his subject as a martyr.

Frischlin was indebted to the imitative techniques of humanism; he sought to spark the ancient forms with language and substance pertinent to the sixteenth century. In that regard he was typical of late-Renaissance Neo-Latinists in preabsolutist Germany. It was for that reason, however, that Frischlin had a limited impact on later literary culture in the German lands. A generation after his death Andreas Gryphius and Martin Opitz, consummate Neo-Latinists in their own right, went beyond Frischlin by favoring the vernacular and by seeking their models as much in contemporary European literatures as in the traditions of classical antiquity. They

Contemporary engraving of Frischlin

are regarded as standing at the threshold of modern German literature, while Frischlin is seen as fulfilling the potential of Renaissance humanism.

Biographies:

Karl P. Conz, *Nikodem Frischlin der unglükliche Wirtembergische Gelehrte und Dichter* (Königsberg, 1792);

David Friedrich Strauß, *Leben und Schriften des Dichters und Philologen Nicodemus Frischlin: Ein Beitrag zur deutschen Culturgeschichte in der zweiten Hälfte des sechzehnten Jahrhunderts* (Frankfurt am Main: Literarische Anstalt, 1856);

Walther Hauff, "Frischlin als Mensch," in Frischlin's *Julius Redivivus*," edited by Walther Janell (Berlin: Weidmann, 1912), pp. lix-lxxiii;

Richard E. Schade, "Nicodemus Frischlin," in *Deutsche Dichter: Leben und Werk deutschsprachiger Autoren*, edited by Gunter E. Grimm and Frank R. Max (Stuttgart: Reclam, 1988), pp. 112-117;

Adalbert Elschenbroich, "Nicodemus Frischlin," in *Literatur Lexikon*, volume 4, edited by Walter Killy (Munich: Bertelsmann, 1989), pp. 37-39;

Hedwig Röckelein and Casimir Bumiller, *. . . ein un-*

ruhig Poet, Nicodemus Frischlin 1547–1590 (Balingen: Stadtarchiv, 1990);

Schade, "Philipp Nicodemus Frischlin," in *Deutsche Dichter der frühen Neuzeit (1450–1600): Ihr Leben und Werk,* edited by Stephan Füssel (Berlin: Erich Schmidt, 1993), pp. 613–625.

References:

Wilfried Barner, *Barockrhetorik: Untersuchungen zu ihren geschichtlichen Grundlagen* (Tübingen: Niemeyer, 1970), pp. 418–425;

Adalbert Elschenbroich, "Imitatio und Disputatio in Nikodemus Frischlins Religionskomödie Phasma," in *Stadt–Schule–Universität: Buchwesen und die deutsche Literatur im 17. Jahrhundert,* edited by Albrecht Schöne (Munich: Beck, 1976), pp. 335–370;

Elschenbroich, "Eine textkritische Nikodemus Frischlin-Ausgabe: Vorüberlegungen," *Jahrbuch für Internationale Germanistik,* 12 (1980): 179–195;

Donald Hamilton, "Nicodemus Frischlin's Festival Book on the First Wedding of Ludwig II of Württemberg (1575)," dissertation, University of Cincinnati, 1993;

Sabine Holtz and Dieter Mertens, eds., *Nicodemus Frischlin (1547–1590): Poetische und prosaische Praxis unter den Bedingungen des konfessioneller Zeitalters* (Stuttgart: Fromann-Hulzboog, 1997);

David Price, "Nicodemus Frischlin's Rhetoric," in *Acta Conventus Neo-Latini Guelpherbytani,* edited by Stella P. Revard (Binghamton: State University of New York, 1988), pp. 531–539;

Price, *The Political Dramaturgy of Nicodemus Frischlin: Essays on Humanist Drama in Germany* (Chapel Hill: University of North Carolina Press, 1990);

Fidel Rädle, "Einige Bemerkungen zu Frischlins Dramatik," in *Acta Conventus Neo-Latini Guelpherbytani,* pp. 289–298;

Jacques Ridé, "Der Nationalgedanke im 'Julius Redivivus' von Nicodemus Frischlin," *Daphnis,* 9 (1980): 719–741;

Richard E. Schade, "Court Festival in Stuttgart: Nicodemus Frischlin's *Würtembergische Hochzeit* (1575)," *Daphnis,* 23 (1994): 371–407;

Schade, "Frischlin's *Julius Redivivus* (1585): Comedy, Court and Personal Politics," in his *Studies in Early German Comedy 1500–1650* (Columbia, S.C.: Camden House, 1988), pp. 97–122;

Schade, "Komödie und Konfession: Eine Dokumentation zu Frischlins 'Phasma' (1592)," *Euphorion,* 86 (1992): 284–318;

Samuel Wheelis, "Publish and Perish: On the Martyrdom of Philip Nicodemus Frischlin," *Neophilologus,* 58 (1974): 42–51.

Papers:

The Universitätsbibliothek Tübingen and the Staatsarchiv in Stuttgart hold voluminous files of letters to and from, and petitions from, Nicodemus Frischlin.

Argula von Grumbach
(1492 – after 1563?)

Hermina Joldersma
University of Calgary

BOOKS: *Wie eyn Christliche fraw des Adels jn Beiern durch jren jn Gotlicher schrift wolgegründten Sendtbryeffe die Hohenschuol zuo Ingoldstat, vmb das sie einen Euangelischen Jüngling, zuo wydersprechung des wort Gottes, betrangt haben, straffet* (Nuremberg: Friedrich Peypus, 1523); translated by Peter Matheson as "The Account of a Christian Woman of the Bavarian Nobility whose open letter, with arguments based on divine Scripture, criticises the University of Ingolstadt for compelling a young follower of the gospel to contradict the word of God," in *Argula von Grumbach. A woman's Voice in the Reformation,* edited by Matheson (Edinburgh: Clark, 1995), pp. 72-91;

Ein Christennliche schrifft einer erbarn frawen vom Adel darinn sie alle Christenliche stendt vnd obrikeiten ermant Bey der warheit vnd dem wort gottes zuopleiben vnd solchs auù Christlicher pflicht zum ernstlichsten zuo handthabend (Bamberg: Georg Erlinger, 1523); translated by Matheson as "A Christian Writing by an honourable noblewoman in which she exhorts all Christian estates and authorities to remain true to the truth and to the word of God and to take most earnestly their Christian duty in this regard," in *Argula von Grumbach,* pp. 100-112;

An ain Ersamen Weysen Radt der stat Jngolstat, ain sandt brieff, von Fraw Argula von grunbach geborne von Stauffen (Augsburg: Philipp Ulhart the Elder, 1523); translated by Matheson as "To the honourable, wise Council of the town of Ingolstadt, an open letter from Argula von Grunbach, née von Stauffen," in *Argula von Grumbach,* pp. 117-122;

Ermanung an den Durchleuchtigen hochgebornen fürsten vnnd hern herren Johannsen Pfaltzgrauen bey Reyn Hertzogen in Bayrn vnd Grauen zu Spanheim et cetera. Das seyn F.G. ob dem wort gottis halten woell. Von einer erbaren frawen vom Adel seinn gnaden zugeschickt (Bamberg: Georg Erlinger, 1523); translated by Matheson as "To his eminence the noble Prince and Lord Johann, Count Palatine of the Rhine, Duke of Bavaria, Count of Spanheim . . . my most gracious lord," in *Argula von Grumbach,* pp. 125-128;

Dem Durchleuchtigisten Hochgebornen Fürsten vnd herren, Herrnn Friderichen, Hertzogen tzuo Sachssen, Des heiligen Roemischen Reychs Ertzmarschalck vnnd Chürfursten, Landtgrauen yn Düringen, vnnd Marggrauen tzuo Meyssen, meynem Gnedigisten herren (Erfurt: Wolfgang Stürmer, 1523); translated by Matheson as "To his eminence, the noble Prince and Lord, Frederick, Duke of Saxony, Supreme Marshall and Elector of the Holy Roman Empire, Count of Thüringen, Margrave of Meissen, my most gracious lord," in *Argula von Grumbach,* pp. 131-134;

An den Edlen vnd gestrengen herren, Adam von Thering der Pfaltzgrauen stathalter zuo Newburg et cetera. Ain sandtbrieff von fraw Argula von Grunbach geborne von Stauffen (Augsburg: Philipp Ulhart the Elder, 1523); translated by Matheson as "To the noble and honourable Adam von Thering, the Count Palatine's Administrator in Neuburg . . . , an open letter from Argula von Grunbach, née von Stauff," in *Argula von Grumbach,* pp. 141-149;

Ein Sendbrieff der edeln Frawen Argula Staufferin An die von Regenùburg. M.D.XXiiij. von fraw Argula von Grumbach, geborne von Stauffen (Nuremberg: Hans Hergot, 1524); translated by Matheson as "An open letter by the Noblewoman, Argula von Stauff to the People of Regensburg," in *Argula von Grumbach,* pp. 154-159;

Eyn Antwort in gedichtùweiù, ainem auù der hohen Schul zu Ingolstat auff ainen spruch, newlich von jm auùgangen, welcher hynden dabey getruckt steet. Anno. M.D.XXiiij. Argula von Gruombach geboren von Stauff. (Eyn Spruch von der Staufferin jres Disputierens halben) (Nuremberg: Hieronymus Höltzel, 1524); translated by Matheson as "An Answer in verse to a member of the University of Ingolstadt in response to a recent utterance of his which is printed below. The year of our Lord 1524," in *Argula von Grumbach,* pp. 173-195.

Argula von Grumbach was, for a brief time, an important voice in the debate over the Reformation; she was also one of few women to express an opinion on contemporary events through the new medium of print. Her participation, for about a year, in the pamphlet wars of the time brought her popularity with supporters of the new teaching and notoriety with its opponents. That her first publication—a denunciation of the Ingolstadt University theological faculty's treatment of a young colleague with pro-Reformation leanings—was inspired by a local event with an identifiably human element, rather than by abstract principle, is typical of the way women participated in the debate. That in her subsequent publications she addressed more far-ranging issues, even taking it upon herself to instruct rulers in their business, establishes Grumbach's place in a long tradition of women who justified their interference in the affairs of men by an appeal to what Martin Luther called the "priesthood of all believers"—the divine inspiration that gave even women the right to criticize the actions of princes on the basis of principles derived from Scripture. That she was largely ignored by those whom she addressed—or, if noticed, was attacked not on the basis of her arguments but because of her sex—shows the limited effect women could have. Nevertheless, Grumbach's defense of the Reformation is rational and eloquent, and her passionate rhetoric is among the most persuasive examples of pro-Reformation writing in the early sixteenth century.

Born in 1492 in the castle Ernfels near the village of Beratzhausen, northwest of Regensburg, Argula von Stauff was one of at least eight children of Bernhardin von Stauff and the former Katharina von Törring (or Thering). From 1508 until her marriage in 1516 she served as maid-in-waiting to Duchess Kunigunde, the mother of Duke Albert and sister of Emperor Maximilian, at the Bavarian court. The deaths of both of her parents of the plague within five days of each other in 1509 and the execution of her uncle and guardian Hieronymus von Stauff for treason in 1516 seem to have instilled a certain fearlessness in her. In a published letter (December 1523) to her cousin Adam von Törring, the governor of Neuberg, she says: "hab mich darein gesetzt, alles zu verlieren, ja Leib und Leben" (I have reconciled myself to losing everything, even life and limb). Her husband, Friedrich von Grumbach, a member of the lower Franconian nobility, was not particularly sympathetic to the Reformation, and it is not surprising that she did not always use his name on her publications: four have some version of "Argula von Grumbach née von Stauff," while the others give her maiden name alone.

After their marriage the Grumbachs moved to Lenting, near Ingolstadt, a property the Grumbach family had acquired in 1503. Duke Ludwig of Bavaria had appointed Friedrich von Grumbach governor of Dietfurt in Altmühtal the year before; though it was a lucrative position and carried substantial legal and judicial power, it gave the duke leverage to demand that Friedrich stop his wife's pro-Reformation activity.

It is through Martin Luther's letters that scholars know of Grumbach's early intense interest in the Reformation and of her correspondence with such leading reformers as Paul Speratus, cathedral preacher in Würzburg until he was forced to flee to Iglau in Mähren in 1521; Georg Spalatin, humanist and court preacher to Elector Frederick the Wise of Saxony; Andreas Osiander, preacher at the Saint Lorenz church in Nuremberg; and with Luther himself. From Spalatin she requested and received a recommended list of reformational titles, and in her letter of 20 September 1523 to the faculty at Ingolstadt she reported that she had read all of Luther's German-language works—despite a Munich court decree of 5 March 1523 forbidding Bavarian subjects to own or discuss reformational literature. Because Luther's enemies could interpret his correspondence with a woman as licentiousness, Grumbach was compelled to write to him through intermediaries; nevertheless, in a 13 June 1522 letter Luther tells Speratus that he had answered her briefly. (All direct correspondence between Luther and Grumbach has been lost.) From Luther's letters it is known that Grumbach traveled to Coburg to visit Luther in 1530; over supper they seem to have discussed personal matters as well as theological ones, for Luther passed on to his wife Grumbach's advice on weaning a child.

It was her boldly worded letter of 20 September 1523 to the notoriously conservative theological faculty at the University of Ingolstadt that made Grumbach the best-known female adherent of the Lutheran Reformation of her day and the first of only a few women in the sixteenth century who joined the fray through publications under their own names. The controversy that aroused Grumbach's ire was the case of Arcasius Seehofer, a young faculty member who had studied with Philipp Melanchthon in Wittenberg and had professed some sympathy with the Reformation in his lectures at Ingolstadt. When banned reformist publications were found in his quarters, he was imprisoned and threatened with execution; only through his father's intervention was he permitted to renounce publicly

Title page for Argula von Grumbach's pamphlet denouncing the Ingolstadt University theology faculty for its treatment of a young colleague

his heretical leanings and accept virtual imprisonment in a nearby cloister. Grumbach's letter of protest, *Wie eyn Christliche fraw des Adels in Beiern durch iren in Gotlicher schrifft wolgegründten Sendtbryeffe die Hohenschuol zuo Ingoldstat, umb das sie einen Evangelischen Jüngling, zuo wydersprechung des wort Gottes, betrangt haben, straffet* (translated as "The Account of a Christian Woman of the Bavarian Nobility whose open letter, with arguments based on divine Scripture, criticizes the University of Ingolstadt for compelling a young follower of the gospel to contradict the word of God," 1995), dated 20 September 1523 and probably published in early November of that year, is all the more remarkable considering that women were entirely excluded from university affairs and that her own education was limited to what she may have received from Duchess Kunigunde at the Bavarian court. (To be sure, Grumbach seems to have had more contact with learning and educational institutions than many members of the nobility, since her brother Marcellus had enrolled at the University of Ingolstadt on 24 November 1522 and five Grumbachs are recorded as having attended the university.) She justifies her right to join in the discussion not only theologically—she is a Christian before she is a woman—but also politically: the university is a publicly funded institution, and the faculty's actions are bringing the university an unwelcome notoriety.

Grumbach begins the letter with a characteristic juxtaposition of biblical quotations and her own annotations applying the passages to

Front and back of a medal that was long thought to depict Grumbach. Modern scholaòship has cast doubt on that belief (Staatliche Münzsammlung, Munich).

current issues. Though this style is common to much of the debate over the Reformation, her writing is uncommonly direct and clear, addressing the reader at an emotional level without resorting to the name-calling in which some of her contemporaries, including Luther, indulged. The letter opens with a theological justification of her action:

> Der Herr sagt Johannis am zwölfften, Ich Licht komme in die Welt, daß ein jeglicher, der an mich glaubet, nicht bleibe in der Finsterniß. Welches Licht ich hertzlich wünsch uns allen beizuwohnen, und zu erleuchten, alle erstockte und erblindete Herzen Amen. Ich finde einen Spruch Matthäi am 10. also lautende: Wer mich bekennet vor den Menschen, den bekenne ich auch vor meinem himlischen Vater. Und Lucä am 9. Wer sich meiner schämet und meiner Wort, dessen werde ich mich auch schämen, so ich komme in meiner Majestät. Etc. Solche Wort, von Gott selbs geredt, sind mir allezeit vor meinen Augen, dann es werden weder Frauen noch Mann darinnen ausgeschlossen. Aus diesem werde ich gedrungen euch zu schreiben.

> (The Lord says in John 12, "I have come as light into the world, that whoever believes in me may not remain in darkness." It is my fervent wish that this light will attend us all and illuminate all stubborn and blinded hearts, Amen. I find a passage in Matthew 10 which reads: "So everyone who acknowledges me before men, I also will acknowledge before my Father who is in heaven." And Luke 9: "For whoever is ashamed of me and of my words, of him will I be ashamed when I come in my glory etc." These words, spoken by God himself, are constantly before my eyes, for in them neither women nor men are excluded. And on account of these words I feel pressed to write to you.)

Grumbach's understanding of the political aspects of the various translations of the Bible is highly astute. Challenging the theological faculty at Ingolstadt to a debate, she anticipates the criticism that her ideas are tainted by their dependence on Luther's translation and proposes to use a German edition published thirty years earlier (probably the illustrated Coburg Bible of 1481 that had been given to her by her father when she was ten with instructions to study it diligently). Equally astute is her assertion that she knows no Latin. Instead, she takes up the reformist defense of German as an acceptable—in fact, preferable—language of religious discourse: "Ich kann kein Latein, aber ihr könnt teutsch, in dieser Zung gebohren und erzogen" (I know no Latin, but you know German, for you have been born and raised in this tongue). She roundly condemns the violence with which secular and, especially, church courts treat those accused of heresy: "Es ist leicht disputirt, so man nicht Schrifft, sondern Gewalt brauchet, in solcher Disputation siehe ich nichts anders, dann daß der züchtiger der gelehrtest ist" (Disputation is a simple thing, if one appeals to force rather than to Scripture; I cannot understand such disputations in any other way than that the torturer has the greatest knowledge).

Though Grumbach's letter is dated only thirteen days after Seehofer's recantation, she did not act hastily. Before sending it she traveled to Nuremberg to consult with Osiander, who expressed amazement at her knowledge of Scripture. Handwritten copies of the letter circulated for some time before it was printed, and Duke Wilhelm IV of Bavaria, the elector Frederick the Wise, and the mayor and city council of Ingolstadt first saw her missive in this form. In its printed version the letter became a best-selling pamphlet.

Well aware of the intimate connection between religious and secular authority, Grumbach addressed a second letter, also dated 20 September 1523, to Duke Wilhelm IV, drawing his attention to the Seehofer affair. Often mistaken, because of its misleading title, for a pamphlet addressed to "alle Christenliche stendt und obrikeiten" (all Christian estates and authorities), it is, rather, the first of Grumbach's publications admonishing the secular authorities to ensure that the true gospel is preached and that wrongs in the church are addressed. But the letter to the duke includes more wide-ranging—and likely unwelcome—advice: not only does Grumbach call on him to censure the faculty action against this "achtzehen jähriges Kind" (eighteen-year-old child), but she also encourages him to promote clerical marriage and suggests that he tax the church to support his campaign against the Turks, since "der arme Mann" (the poor man) is already overburdened.

In a letter of 15 October 1523 to his brother Ludwig, Wilhelm expressed his dismay over "solche ungeschickte schreiben" (such unseemly writing) being directed at himself and the university, and he ordered Ludwig to dismiss Grumbach's husband as governor for permitting her to write the letters. There were exaggerated tales of further recommended punishments: on 13 November 1523, for example, Hans von der Planitz wrote Frederick the Wise that Wilhelm and Ludwig had advised Friedrich von Grumbach to cut off two of his wife's fingers, or even to strangle her, if necessary, without fear of reprisal. Still, Argula von Grumbach wrote her cousin Törring that her husband was doing his best "daß er Christum in mir verfolgt" (to persecute Christ in me); she seems to imply that Törring himself had suggested that Friedrich wall her up as one might an anchoress.

Grumbach's subsequent letters are variations on Reformation themes. In a letter dated 28 October 1523 she urged the mayor and city council of Ingolstadt to consider the Seehofer matter in the light of Scripture and to examine the state of their own souls. She says in closing, "Bittet Gott für mich, deßgleichen will ich Gott auch für euch bitten" (Pray to God for me, and in the same way I will pray to God for you). Her letters of 1 December 1523 to Count Palatine Johann von Simmern and Frederick the Wise encourage them to be true to their reformist sympathies by furthering evangelical reform at the upcoming Diet of Nuremberg. On the count palatine's invitation Grumbach traveled to Nuremberg to discuss her views with him; in the letter to her cousin she criticizes the frivolous and extravagant behavior of the princes attending the Diet, concluding: "Ich habe selbs zu Nürnberg gesehen, ein solches kindisch Wesen der Fürsten, das mir, dieweil ich leb, vor Augen ist" (As long as I live, I'll never forget what I saw in Nuremberg, the princes behaving like a bunch of kids).

By February 1524 Friedrich von Grumbach had lost his position as governor; later that spring, after a brief stay in the Rhineland, Argula von Grumbach and her four children moved back to Lenting. She was not deterred from supporting the reformist cause publicly: in a letter of 29 June 1524 to the city council of Regensburg she sharply condemns the council's decision to move against the Protestants. Her last publication was a long poem, written in late summer 1524, responding to a satire on her by "Johannes Landshut"—a pseudonym for an Ingolstadt student. "Landshut" claimed that she defended Seehofer because she was in love with him and his curly hair. Grumbach replies that Landshut must not have been worth a learned opponent, as God sent a mere woman to counter him, and she compares herself to such female leaders from the Old Testament as Judith and Deborah. She challenges her opponent to a debate, as, in her first letter, she had challenged the Ingolstadt faculty; perhaps because she was a woman, her challenge was never taken up. All of her writing received only indirect and personal, never direct and public, reaction.

Letters to a moneylender in Regensburg named Mosse, indicate that the Grumbachs were in somewhat straitened circumstances in the latter half of the 1520s; the couple seems to have lived apart for several years, during which time she administered their estates. Friedrich died in the second half of 1530; Argula married a Count von Schlick, who seems to have been relatively reform-minded, around 1533 and was widowed again in 1535. All of her children were from her first marriage, and at least three predeceased her: Georg died in 1539, Hans Georg in 1544, and Apollonia in 1539; Gottfried may have survived her. She maintained businesslike relations with several of her erstwhile opponents, such as Johann Eck and Leonhard von Eck. Leonhard von Eck, who had urged Duke Wilhelm to suppress her writings, even intervened on her behalf in a legal case to regain the castle Ernfels; it had been taken from her by force by her

Title page for Grumbach's second pamphlet (courtesy of the Lilly Library, Indiana University)

nephew Ruprecht, the son of her former guardian, Hieronymus von Stauff.

The controversy surrounding the date of Grumbach's death forms a fitting conclusion to her unusual life. Wigulaeus Hund entered 1554 in his Bavarian family chronicle of 1586, and his other entries have proven accurate. But in 1563 there was some intriguing correspondence among Duke Albrecht V of Bavaria and members of the Munich City Council: letters of 5 and 11 August discuss measures to be taken against "ein alltes erlebts ... unverstendigs weib" (a worn-out ... senile old woman) of the Stauff family who has been inciting simple folk in the surrounding villages to rebellion against the Catholic Church. The actions ascribed to this woman, however, such as organizing conventicles and officiating at funerals, are far more radical than Grumbach's published protestations of the 1520s. On the other hand, in 1563 Grumbach would have been seventy-one, not necessarily too old for such actions and, perhaps, old enough not to consider consequences. Also, several Schlicks were among the friends and relatives who sought leniency for the old woman, and it seems almost too much of a coincidence that two women named Stauff could have been reformist agitators. The matter will probably never be resolved.

There are two purported visual depictions of Grumbach: one is constituted by two versions of a portrait medal; the other is the woodcut on the title page of her pamphlet to the faculty at Ingolstadt. Silke Halbach, however, has shown conclusively that the link between the medal and Grumbach was made in the 1860s by the copyist Philipp Sommer. Sommer created a copy of a medal that was then, as now, in the Germanisches Nationalmuseum in Nuremberg; neither the original medal nor the portrait sketch accompanying it identifies the person pictured, but Sommer added to the front of his copy, in a circle around the outer edge, the words "ARGVLA * VON * GRVNBACH * EIN * GEBORNE * VON * STAVFFEN." He also rearranged the inscription on the back from five rather messy lines to four beautifully symmetrical ones: "*VERLOGEN * VND * / * NEYDISCH * ZVNGEN * / *HAN * MICH * ZV * LEID * VND * / *SCHMERCZ* GEDRVNGEN*" (Lying and envious tongues have compelled me to sorrow and pain). The woodcut, on the other hand, is not intended as a likeness but as a representation of how Grumbach's actions were perceived during her time. On the left, a decorously dressed woman holds a book in her left hand; facing her, on the right, are five men (in another edition there are eight) in academic robes—clearly, the faculty at Ingolstadt. The men carry no books; rather, there are two books lying on the ground in the space between the two parties, and an elevated window in the background, more on the woman's half of the woodcut, is a physical manifestation of the light of God illuminating the debate. The most striking feature of the representation is the imbalance between the lone woman and the male hierarchy.

The reception of Grumbach's writings up to the mid twentieth century was divided along confessional lines: critics who agreed with her theological stance, such as the Reformer Johann Eberlin von Günsburg, admired her, while those who disagreed, such as the Jesuit Jakob Gretser, did not. Recent research with a feminist orientation has begun to try to understand what it might have meant for a woman to be an author in the early sixteenth century. Clearly, Argula von Grumbach, a remarkable woman whose courageous writing was inspired by her faith, constitutes an important part of that picture.

Biographies:
Georg Cunrad Rieger, *Das Leben Argulae von Grumbach, gebohrner von Stauffen, als einer Juengerin Jesu, Zeugin der Warheit und Freundin Lutheri, samt eingemengter Nachricht von Arsatio Seehofern* (Stuttgart: Metzler & Erhardt, 1737);

Felix Joseph Lipowsky, *Argula von Grumbach, gebohrne Freiinn von Stauffen, eine historische mit Urkunden belegte Abhandlung* (Munich: Joseph Lindauer, 1801);

Hermann Alexander Pistorius, *Frau Argula von Grumbach, geborene von Stauffen, und ihr Kampf mit der Universität zu Ingolstadt* (Magdeburg: Falckenberg, 1845);

Eduard Engelhardt, *Argula von Grumbach, die bayerische Tabea: Ein Lebensbild aus der Reformationszeit für den christlichen Leser dargestellt* (Nuremberg: Raw, 1860);

Erich Bauer, "Argula von Grumbach und ihre Flugschriften: Untersuchungen zu Leben und Wirken einer Standesfrau zu Beginn der Reformation," dissertation, Salzburg University, 1987;

Silke Halbach, *Argula von Grumbach als Verfasserin reformatorischer Flugschriften* (Frankfurt am Main: Peter Lang, 1992);

Peter Matheson, ed., *Argula von Grumbach: A Woman's Voice in the Reformation* (Edinburgh: Clark, 1995).

References:
Roland H. Bainton, "Argula von Grumbach," in his *Women of the Reformation in Germany and Italy* (Minneapolis: Augsburg, 1971), pp. 97–109;

Barbara Becker-Cantarino, "Argula von Grumbach (ca. 1492-1563) und die Reformation in Bayern," in *Deutsche Literatur von Frauen,* volume 1: *Vom Mittelalter bis zum Ende des 18. Jahrhunderts,* edited by Gisela Brinker-Gabler (Munich: Beck, 1988), pp. 155-159;

Becker-Cantarino, "Religiöse Streiterinnen: Katharina Zell und Argula von Grumbach," in her *Der lange Weg zur Mündigkeit* (Stuttgart: Metzler, 1987), pp. 96-110;

Irmgard Bezzel, "Argula von Grumbach und Johannes aus Landshut: Zu einer Kontroverse des Jahres 1524," *Gutenberg Jahrbuch,* 61 (1986): 201-207;

Bezzel, "Der Sendbrief Argula von Grumbach an die Universität Ingolstadt (1523) in zwei redaktionellen Bearbeitungen," *Gutenberg Jahrbuch,* 62 (1987): 166-173;

Albrecht Classen, "Argula von Grumbach," in *An Encyclopedia of Continental Women Writers,* volume 1, edited by Katharina M. Wilson (New York & London: Garland, 1991), pp. 497-498;

Classen, "Footnotes to the German Canon: Maria von Wolkenstein and Argula von Grumbach," in *The Politics of Gender in Early Modern Europe,* edited by Jean R. Brink, Allison P. Coudert, and Maryanne C. Horowitz (Kirksville, Mo.: Sixteenth Century Journal Publishers, 1989), pp. 131-147;

Classen, "Woman Poet and Reformer: The 16th-Century Feminist Argula von Grumbach," *Daphnis,* 20 (1991): 167-197;

K. A. Deubner, "Das Leben der Argula von Grumbach," *Die Wartburg,* 29 (1930): 73-80;

Ernst Dorn, "Argula von Grumbach, die Schloßfrau von Lenting bei Ingolstadt," *Bayerische Diasporablätter,* 1 (1902): 102-105;

Maria Heinsius, "Argula von Grumbach," in her *Das Unüberwindliche Wort: Frauen in der Reformationszeit* (Munich: Kaiser, 1951), pp. 134-159;

Heinsius, *Das Bekenntnis der Argula von Grumbach* (Munich, 1928);

A. Heuschel, "Frau Argula von Grumbach, geboren von Stauffen," *Der alte Glaube,* 12 (1911): 738-741;

Theodor Kolde, "Arsacius Seehofer und Argula von Grumbach," *Beiträge zur bayerischen Kirchengeschichte,* 11 (1905): 49-77, 97-124, 149-188;

Georg Christian Lehms, "Argula von Grumbach," in his *Teutschlands galante Poetinnen* (Frankfurt am Main: Verlegung des Autoris, 1715), pp. 71-73;

Elke Reese, "Eine Streiterin für die Reformation. Argula von Grumbach (1492-1568)," *Lutherische Monatshefte,* 22 (1983): 303-310;

Paul Russell, "Common People and the Future of the Reformation in the Pamphlet Literature of Southwestern Germany to 1525," *Archiv für Reformationsgeschichte,* 74 (1983): 122-140;

Russell, "Female Pamphleteers–the Housewives Strike Back," in his *Lay Theology in the Reformation: Popular Pamphleteers in Southwest Germany 1521-1525* (Cambridge: Cambridge University Press, 1986), pp. 185-211;

H. Saalfeld, "Argula von Grumbach, die Schlossherrin von Lenting," *Sammelblatt des historischen Vereins Ingolstadt,* 69 (1960): 42-53;

Angelika Schmid-Biesalski, "Bayerische Reformation, Argula von Grumbach," in her *Lust, Liebe und Verstand: Protestantische Frauen aus fünf Jahrhunderten* (Gelnhausen, Berlin & Stein: Burckhardthaus-Laetare, 1981), pp. 19-44;

Kurt Erich Schöndorf, "Argula von Grumbach: Eine Verfasserin von Flugschriften in der Reformationszeit," in *Frauen und Frauenbilder: Dokumentiert durch 2000 Jahre,* edited by Jorunn Valgard and Elsbeth Wessel, Osloer Beiträge zur Germanistik, volume 8 (Oslo: Universitetet i Oslo Germanistisk instituut, 1983), pp. 182-202;

J. M. Söltl, "Argula von Grumbach," *Neue Jahrbücher der Geschichte und Politik,* 10 (1847): 270-276;

Georg R. Spohn, "Widmungsexemplare Ulrichs von Hutten und ein Sendschreiben Argulas von Grumbach an Pfalzgraf Johann II von Pfalz-Simmern," *Archiv für Mittelrheinische Kirchengeschichte,* 23 (1971): 141-146;

Robert Stupperich, "Die Frau in der Publizistik der Reformation," *Archiv für Kulturgeschichte,* 37 (1955): 204-233;

Leonhard Theobald, "Das Sendschreiben der Stauferin Argula von Grumbach an Kammerer und Rat von Regenburg," *Zeitschrift für bayerische Kirchengeschichte,* 11 (1936): 53-56;

Merry Wiesner, "Women's Response to the Reformation," in *The German People and the Reformation,* edited by Ronnie Po-Chia Hsi (Ithaca, N.Y. & London: Cornell University Press, 1988), pp. 148-171;

Alice Zimmerli-Witschi, "Frauen in der Reformationszeit," dissertation, University of Zurich, 1981.

Papers:
Papers of Argula von Grumbach are in the Bavarian State Archive, Munich.

Eobanus Hessus
(6 January 1488 – 4 October 1540)

Harry Vredeveld
Ohio State University

BOOKS: *De pungna* [sic] *studentum Erphordiensium cum quibusdam coniuratis nebulonibus Eobani Hessi Francobergii carmen* (Erfurt: Wolfgang Stürmer, 1506);

De recessu studentum ex Erphordia tempore pestilenciae Eobani Hessi Francobergii carmen heroicum extemporaliter concinnatum (Erfurt: Wolfgang Stürmer, 1506);

De laudibus et praeconiis incliti atque tocius Germaniae celebratiss. Gymnasii litteratorii apud Erphordiam Eobani Hessi Francobergii, eiusdem litterariae commanipulationis alumnuli, iuvenis ephebi carmen succisivis horis deductum (Erfurt: Wolfgang Stürmer, 1507);

De amantium infoelicitate, contra Venerem, de Cupidinis impotentia et versu et soluta oratione opusculum Erphordiense (Erfurt: Hans Knappe the Elder, 1508);

Bucolicon (Erfurt: Hans Knappe the Elder, 1509); revised as *Bucolicorum idyllia XII, nuper anno demum decimooctavo a prima aeditione recognita ac dimidia plus parte vel aucta vel concisa atque in ordinem alium redacta. His accessere ex recenti aeditione idyllia quinque* (Hagenau: Johann Setzer, 1528);

Encomium nuptiale divo Sigismundo, regi Poloniae, scriptum anno Christiani calculi M.D.XII Magistri Eobani Hessi diligentia (Kraków: Johann Haller, 1512);

Sylvae duae nuper aeditae: Prussia et Amor (Leipzig: Melchior Lotter the Elder, 1514);

Heroidum Christianarum epistolae, opus novitium nuper aeditum anno M.D.xx.iiii (Leipzig: Melchior Lotter the Elder, 1514); revised as *Heroidum libri tres, nuper ab authore recogniti et ab aeditionis prioris iniuria vindicati* (Hagenau: Johann Setzer, 1532);

Hymnus paschalis nuper ex Erphurdiensi Gymnasio Christianae victoriae acclamatus (Erfurt: Hans Knappe the Elder, 1515);

De vera nobilitate et priscis Germanorum moribus. Ad Georgium Spalatinum libellus carmine elegiaco (Erfurt: Matthes Maler, 1515?);

Eobanus Hessus in 1526; drawing by Albrecht Dürer (British Museum)

Oratio sive praelectio in auspicio Officiorum M. Tullii Ciceronis et M. Accii Plauti comoediarum in Academia Erphurdiensi per Magistrum Eobanum Hessum in eadem Academia bonas litteras publice profitentem habita M.D.XV (Erfurt: Hans Knappe the Elder, 1515?);

De vitanda ebrietate elegia, additis super eadem re aliquot epigrammatis (Erfurt: Matthes Maler, 1516);

Quae in hoc libello nova habentur: Epistola Italiae ad divum Maximilianum Caes. Aug. Ulricho Hutteno Equite Germano autore. Responsio Maximiliani Aug. Helio Eobano Hesso autore. Addita sunt Hutteni de eadem re epigrammata aliquot nuper ex urbe Roma missa, sumpto ex his temporum motibus argumento, by Hessus and Ulrich von Hutten (Erfurt: Matthes Maler, 1516);

Victoria Christi ab inferis carmine heroico (Erfurt: Matthes Maler, 1517);

A profectione ad Des. Erasmum Roterodamum hodoeporicon carmine heroico. Eiusdem ad eundem epistola elegiaca. Eiusdem Virgini Matri votum car. elegiaco. Erasmi Roterodami ad Mutianum Rufum, Iudocum Ionam, Eobanum Hessum, Ioan. Draconem, Henricum Bemingum epistolae (Erfurt: Matthes Maler, 1519);

Oratio de studiorum instauratione in inclyta schola Erphurd. omnium ordinum consessu frequentissimo auditorio ab Eob. Hesso habita 1519 m. Sept. (Erfurt: Matthes Maler, 1520);

Praefatio in epistolas divi Pauli Apostoli ad Corynthios Erphurdiae ad Christianae philosophiae studiosorum ordinem habita ab eximio viro D. Iodoco Iona Northusiano, iurium designato, D. canonico ibidem apud divi Severi, cum epistola Petri Mosellani ad eundem. Huic addita est non multum dissimili argumento Eobani Hessi praefaciuncula in Enchiridion Christiani militis, by Hessus and Jodocus Jonas (Erfurt: Matthes Maler, 1520);

In Eduardum Leeum quorundam e sodalitate literaria Erphurdiensi Erasmici nominis studiosorum epigrammata, by Hessus and others (Erfurt: Hans Knappe the Elder, 1520);

Habes hic, lector: In evangelici Doctoris Martini Lutheri laudem defensionemque elegias IIII. Ad Iodocum Ionam Northusanum cum eodem a Caesare redeuntem elegiam I. Ad Udalricum Huttenum Equitem Germanum ac poetam nobilissimum de causa Lutheriana elegiam I. In Hieronymum Emserum Lutheromastiga conviciatorem invectivam elegiam I (Erfurt: Matthes Maler, 1521);

Ecclesiae afflictae epistola ad Lutherum (Hagenau: Johann Setzer, 1523);

De non contemnendis studiis humanioribus futuro theologo maxime necessariis aliquot clarorum virorum ad Eobanum Hessum epistolae. D. Martini Lutheri una, Philippi Melanchthonis duae, Petri Mosellani una, Iodoci Ionae una, Ioannis Draconis duae, Hessi una ad magnificum D. Georgium Sturtz, rectorem Gymnasii. Eiusdem de contemptu studiorum ode una. Eiusdem ad magnificum Senatum Erphurdiensem παράκχησις carmine elegiaco, cum quibusdam aliis, by Hessus, Martin Luther, Philip Melanchthon, Peter Mosellanus, Justus Jonas, and Johannes Drach (Erfurt: Matthes Maler, 1523);

Ad illustrissimum Principem Guilielmum, Ducem Brunsvigensem etc., apud hostes captivum Eobani Hessi consolatio (Erfurt?: Matthes Maler?, 1523);

Eobani Hessi in poetam Sarmatam Germanos ignaviae insimulantem invectiva (Erfurt: Matthes Maler, 1523);

Dialogi tres, Melaenus, Misologus, Fugitivi, studiorum et veritatis causa nuper aediti (Erfurt: Matthes Maler, 1524);

Bonae valetudinis conservandae praecepta ad magnificum D. Georgium Sturtiaden per Eobanum Hessum. Medicinae laus ad Martinum Hunum per eundem. Musaeum Sturtianum per eundem. Tabula differentiarum omnis generis febrium per D. Georgium Sturtiaden. Tabula cognoscendorum secundum communes et planetares horas humorum per Henricum Grammataeum (Erfurt: Johann Loersfelt, 1524); revised as *Bonae valetudinis conservandae rationes aliquot. Simplicium ciborum facultates quaedam. Medicinae encomion. Chorus illustrium medicorum. Novem Musae* (Frankfurt am Main: Johann Petreius?, 1531);

Scribendorum versuum maxime compendiosa ratio, in schola Nurenbergae nuper instituta pueris proposita (Nuremberg: Friedrich Peypus, 1526);

Ad illustrissimum Principem Ioannem Fridericum, Ducem Saxoniae, elegia. Epicedia duo: In mortem divi Friderici, Principis Electoris, Ducem [sic] Saxoniae; In Guilielmum Nesenum qui in traiectu Albis periit. Cur hoc tempore studia literarum tanto contemptu habeantur, idyllion ad Philippum Melanchthonem (Nuremberg: Friedrich Peypus, 1526);

Elegiae tres. De schola Norica, ad Barptholomeum Bacchium. In auspicio scholae propositum carmen. In invidum quo intentatae calumniae respondet (Nuremberg: Friedrich Arthemisius, 1526);

Ex idylliis Eobani Hessi encomia duo, Urbis Norenbergae et illustr. Philippi Hessorum principis (Nuremberg: Johann Petreius, 1527);

In hypocrisim vestitus monastici ἐκφῴγησις. Psalmi quatuor ex Davidicis carmine redditi. Ad R.P.D. Fridericum abbatem divi Aegidii apud inclytam Nurenbergam (Nuremberg: Johann Petreius, 1527);

Venus triumphans, ad Ioachimum Cam. Qu. Ioachimi Camerarii querela, qua superiori carmini respondet. In nuptiis Ioachimi Cam. epithalamion seu ludus Musarum, per Eob. Eiusdem ad eundem in Hispanias abeuntem propemticon. Ex schola Norica anno M.D.XXVII, by Hessus and Joachim Camerarius (Nuremberg: Johann Petreius, 1527);

Epicedion in funere Alberti Dureri Nurenbergensis, aetatis suae pictorum omnium facile principis, dictum. Somnium de eodem. Epithaphia et alia quaedam, Helio Eobano Hesso authore. De eodem monodia Thomae Venatorii et epitaphia duo, by Hessus and Thomas Venatorius (Nuremberg: Friedrich Peypus, 1528);

De tumultibus horum temporum querela. Priscorum temporum cum nostris collatio. Omnium regnorum Europae mutatio. Bellum servile Germaniae. Haec omnia carmine heroico. Ad Germaniam afflictam consolatio paraenetica, elegia una. Roma capta, elegiae duae (Nuremberg: Friedrich Peypus, 1528);

In P. Virgilii Maronis Bucolica ac Georgica adnotationes, ac loci omnes maxime Theocriti, tum etiam Hesiodi quidam, quibus usus est Virgilius, Latine redditi (Hagenau: Johann Setzer, 1529);

Divo ac invicto Imp. Caes. Carolo V. Augusto Germaniam ingredienti urbis Norimbergae gratulatoria acclamatio. Ad eundem de bello contra Turcas suscipiendo adhortatio, per H. Eobanum Hessum. In adventum eiusdem urbis Francofurdii gratulatio, per Iacobum Micyllum, by Hessus and Jacob Micyllus (Nuremberg: Johann Petreius, 1530);

Illustrium ac clarorum aliquot virorum memoriae scripta epicedia per Helium Eobanum Hessum. Epithaphia epigrammata composita ab Ioachimo Camerario Bombergensi [sic], by Hessus and Camerarius (Nuremberg: Friedrich Peypus, 1531);

Urbs Noriberga illustrata carmine heroico (Nuremberg: Johann Petreius, 1532);

In funere clariss. quondam viri, D. Hieronymi Ebneri, Urbis Noribergae aerario praefecti supremi etc., per Helium Eobanum Hessum anno M.D.XXXII mense Augusto dictum (Nuremberg: Johann Petreius, 1532);

De victoria Wirtembergensi, ad illustrem et inclytum heroa Philippum, Hessorum omnium ac finitimarum aliquot gentium principem, gratulatoria acclamatio (Erfurt: Melchior Sachse, 1534);

Sylvarum libri VI, nuper primum aediti anno M.D.XXXIII (Hagenau: Peter Braubach, 1535);

In funere clariss. et incomparabilis eruditionis viri, D. Erasmi Roterodami, epicedion (Marburg: Eucharius Cervicornus, 1537);

Elegia, recens scripta, de Calumnia (Marburg: Eucharius Cervicornus?, 1538);

Descriptio Calumniae, ad doctissisimum [sic] *virum Philippum Melanthonem. Ad optimum virum M. Philippum Nidanum, in morte Barbarae uxoris consolatio, eodem authore. Naenia in obitum Barbarae, Philippi Pistorii Nidani coniugis, et epistola ad Helium Eobanum Hessum poetam, autore Ioanne Draconite* (Marburg: Christian Egenolph, 1539);

Epithalamion, seu ludus gratulatorius in nuptiis et receptione insigniorum Doctoratus Iurium humanissimi et eruditissimi viri, D. Iusti Studaei (Frankfurt am Main: Christian Egenolph, 1539);

Operum Helii Eobani Hessi farragines duae, nuper ab eodem qua fieri potuit diligentia contractae et in hanc, quam vides, formam coactae, quibus etiam non parum multa accesserunt, nunc primum et nata et aedita (Schwäbisch Hall: Peter Braubach, 1539);

Helii Eobani Hessi, poetae Germani, operum flores ac sententiae insigniores, commodo studiosorum selecti, edited by Christophorus Aulaeus (Frankfurt am Main: Christian Egenolph, 1551);

Explicatio H. Eobani Hessi, poetae excellentissimi, in Iohan. Murmelii tabulas de ratione faciendorum versuum, edited by Michael Lindener (Nuremberg: Johann Petreius, 1552).

Collection: *Dichtungen der Jahre 1528–1537,* edited and translated by Harry Vredeveld (Bern, Frankfurt am Main, New York & Paris: Peter Lang, 1990).

OTHER: Johann Lang, *Ioannis Langi Erphurdiensis epistola ad excellentiss. D. Martinum Margaritanum, Erphurdiensis Gymnasii rectorem, pro literis sacris et seipso,* edited by Hessus (Erfurt: Matthes Maler, 1521);

Ulrich von Hutten, *De arte versificandi carmen heroicum per Hulderichum Huttenum. Item* ΟΥΤΙΣ. *Nemo. Item exegoria in ebrietatem per Eobanum Hessum,* edited by Hessus (Nuremberg: Johann Petreius, 1531);

Marco Girolamo Vida, *Marci Hieronymi Vidae Cremonensis poetae clarissimi de arte poetica libri III, nuper in usum studiosorum in lucem aediti,* edited by Hessus (Nuremberg: Friedrich Artemisius, 1531).

TRANSLATIONS: *Psalmus CXVIII ex ipsius M. Lutheri scholiis, praeterea sedecim alii Latino carmine redditi per Helium Eobanum Hessum. Eiusdem de fructu lectionis Psalmorum elegia. Epistola M. Lutheri. Epistola Ph. Melanchthonis. Iacobi Micylli psalmi duo. . . . E schola Norica, mense Februario M.D.XXX* (Nuremberg, 1530);

Theocritus, *Idyllia triginta sex, Latino carmine reddita* (Hagenau: Johann Setzer, 1531);

Salomonis Ecclesiastes carmine redditus per Helium Eobanum Hessum, bonas literas apud inclytam Norinbergam profitentem, illustriss. Principi Ioanni Friedericho, Sacri Ro. Imp. Electori, Duci Saxoniae etc., inscriptus, cum elegia ad eundem olim scripta in fine adiecta (Nuremberg: Johann Petreius, 1532);

Homer, *Homericae aliquot icones insigniores, Latinis versibus redditae* (Nuremberg: Friedrich Peypus, 1533);

Colluthus, Theocritus, and Moschus, *Coluthi Lycopolitae Thebani vetusti admodum poetae de raptu Helenes ac iudicio Paridis poema, nunc primum ab Helio Eobano Hesso Latino carmine redditum. Epithalamion Helenes ex Theocrito. Moschi Amor fugitivus eodem interprete* (Erfurt: Melchior Sachse, 1534);

Jodocus Hessus, *Ludus de podagra, in quo eius affectionis natura, commoda iuxta ac incommoda recensentur, e vulgari Germanico in Latinum carmen coacta* (Mainz: Peter Schoeffer the Younger, 1537);

Psalterium universum carmine elegiaco redditum atque explicatum ac nuper in schola Marpurgensi aeditum (Marburg: Eucharius Cervicornus, 1537; revised and enlarged edition, Schwäbisch Hall: Peter Braubach, 1538);

Homer, *Poetarum omnium seculorum longe principis Homeri Ilias, hoc est, de rebus ad Troiam gestis descriptio, iam recens Latino carmine reddita* (Basel: Robert Winter, 1540).

Eobanus Hessus was the foremost Latin poet of the German Renaissance, the heart and soul of Erfurt humanism in its heyday. Mutianus Rufus (Konrad Muth) hailed him as "Pindarus neotericoterus" (a modern Pindar); Desiderius Erasmus dubbed him "Christianus Ovidius" (a Christian Ovid); and Johannes Reuchlin, half in jest, crowned him "the king" of poets (ἐσσήν; rex). His star blazed resplendent for more than a century after his death—as long as Latin continued to be read as a living language and prized more than his native tongue. Besides a brilliant style and classical learning he brought to his work an uncommonly wide range of themes; a warm, engaging tone; and a refreshing boldness in pioneering new genres on German soil. His *Bucolicon* (Bucolic Poem, 1509) introduced the allegorical eclogue cycle to German literature, while his *Heroidum Christianarum epistolae* (Letters of Christian Heroines, 1514) originated the genre of the sacred heroic epistle. No less memorable is his elegant *Urbs Noriberga illustrata carmine heroico* (Nuremberg Glorified in Heroic Verse, 1532), which vividly depicts the city's scenic, artistic, and cultural splendors. He was just as much at home in the medical field, as one can see by his enormously successful *Bonae valetudinis conservandae praecepta* (Precepts for Keeping in Good Health, 1524). But though works such as these had long since made Hessus a household name throughout the republic of letters, his fame was capped by a splendid verse paraphrase of the entire Psalter—a book that remained a best-seller for many decades and earned him another sobriquet: "Hessicus David" (the Hessian David). Likewise, his verse translations of Theocritus's *Idylls* (1531) and Homer's *Iliad* (1540) continued to be read and admired until the rise of vernacular literature finally pushed humanist poetry into the shadows and forced Hessus's star to set.

The eldest son of poor parents, Hessus was born in the village of Halgehausen near Frankenberg, Hesse. As he liked to point out, it was in his stars to become a poet, for the day of his birth—6 January 1488—coincides with the rising of the constellation Lyre. His father, Hans Koch, who came from the neighboring county of Wittgenstein, worked for the Cistercian abbey of Haina as a farmhand or, less likely, as a cook; his mother, Katharina, was a native of Gemünden on the Wohra. Hessus received his elementary education from Abbot Dietmar in Haina. Unlike his younger brother, who was made an apprentice, he showed so much intellectual promise that he was sent to live with relatives in Gemünden so that he could attend the classes of his kinsman Johann Mebes. In 1502 he moved to Frankenberg, where the gifted teacher Jakob Horle, a recent graduate of the University of Erfurt, had just opened a grammar school. Quickly spotting his pupil's genius, Horle took Hessus under his wing and taught him the principles of Latin versification. Hessus would recall that moment in the letter to Posterity that concludes the *Heroidum Christianarum epistolae*:

> . . . ut autem
> Nunc etiam vates vivere certus eram,
> Sorduit humanas quicquid sibi subdere mentes,
> Displicuit posset quicquid amare puer.
> Obtulit in triviis quendam fortuna magistrum,
> Qui numeris certum diceret esse modum.
> Hunc colui supplex, illi tantisper adhesi,
> Dum didici certis legibus ire pedes.
> Sponte sua influxit brevibus mihi Musa diebus,
> Et mihi iam puero non leve nomen erat.

> (Now as soon as I found out that there were poets alive even today,
> I loathed everything that other people put their minds to
> and took a dislike to what normal boys regard as fun.
> As luck would have it, I found a teacher in grammar school
> who one day remarked that verses had rhythmical patterns.
> I respectfully besieged him with questions and clung to him
> for as long as it took to learn the rules of prosody.
> Spontaneously the Muse streamed into me in just a few days,
> and even as a youth I enjoyed no mean fame.)

In the autumn of 1504 Eoban enrolled at the University of Erfurt, giving his name as Eobanus Coci Francobergius (Eoban, Koch's son, of Frankenberg). Two years later he dropped the surname Coci and began styling himself Eobanus Hessus Francobergius to pay tribute to his native land of Hesse. Among his teachers at Erfurt were Ludwig Christiani of Frankenberg, Ludwig Platz of Melsungen, Laurentius Arnoldi of Usingen, and Maternus Pistoris of Ingweiler. His true mentor, however, was the renowned humanist Mutianus, who had studied in Deventer, Erfurt, Bologna, Rome, and Ferrara and was then a canon at Gotha in what he called his "Beata tranquillitas" (Blessed Tranquillity). Georg Spalatin, Johannes Crotus Rubianus, Ulrich von Hutten, Justus Jonas, Peter Eberbach, and Herbord von der Marthen were among the disciples Mutianus attracted. Like others who had gotten to know Hessus, Mutianus predicted a great future for him, telling him in a letter of August 1506: "Hesse, puer, sacri gloria fontis eris" (Hessus, young man, you're bound to be Helicon's pride).

No trace of Hessus's earliest verse has survived. One first meets him as an apprentice poet in two narrative poems of 1506 that draw on his experiences as a student at Erfurt. *De pungna [sic] studentum Erphordiensium cum quibusdam coniuratis nebulonibus* (The Battle between the Students of Erfurt and a Mob of Sworn Scoundrels) gives an account of a street battle that occurred on 9 August 1505. *De recessu studentum ex Erphordia tempore pestilenciae* (The Departure of the Students from Erfurt during a Time of Plague) tells how an outbreak of plague later that month forced the faculty and students to flee for their lives. Hessus was among those who followed a group of teachers to Melsungen in Hesse; but one of the students came down with the plague and touched off an epidemic in the town, and the group had to take to the road again. In Frankenberg they rented a large house next to the church, where they spent a productive winter before returning to Erfurt in the spring. Hessus received his B.A. in 1506.

In the category of apprentice works one may also place *De laudibus et praeconiis incliti atque tocius Germaniae celebratiss. Gymnasii litteratorii apud Erphordiam* (A Panegyric Extolling the Renowned University of Erfurt, the Most Renowned in All Germany, 1507), to which Hutten contributed an elegy, "In Eobanum Hessum vivacissimi ingenii adolescentem" (On That Most High-spirited and Talented Youth, Eobanus Hessus). The book was dedicated to Hessus's patron, the suffragan bishop Johannes Bonemilch of Laasphe, who thereupon appointed Hessus headmaster of the cathedral school of Saint Severus and granted him free meals at the bishop's house. The following spring, while enjoying a semester break from his "molestissimis ludi literatorii laboribus" (terribly wearisome teaching duties), Hessus wrote a satire in prose with an admixture of verse, *De amantium infoelicitate, contra Venerem, de Cupidinis impotentia* (On the Wretchedness of Lovers, Against Venus, On the Mad Fury of Cupid, 1508). In the work Fronto Fundinus (Peter Eberbach), a poetically gifted friend of Hessus's, has fallen in love with a prostitute, but after he squanders his patrimony on her, she callously throws him out of her house. Mad with unrequited passion and shame, the heartbroken gallant pines away in the woods. Hessus, on one of his walks in the country, encounters Fundinus and learns what has happened. Finally, Hessus cures him with the Muses' aid.

While it found favor with the reading public—it was reprinted in Wittenberg in 1515—the satire, with its occasionally obscene language, did nothing to enhance its author's reputation with Bonemilch, who withdrew his patronage and forced Hessus to step down as headmaster. Penniless but glad to be rid of this burden, Hessus plunged back into his studies. In 1509 he earned his M.A. from Erfurt and published the *Bucolicon*, a cycle of eclogues on which he had been working for some years. The title page brims with self-confident pride:

Rustica quem Siculi delectat musa poetae,
   Cui placet ex nostris pastor uterque Maro,
Sive quid ulterius, vates Germane, requiris,
   Me quoque fer Latii ruris habere locum.
Primus Teutonico pavi pecus orbe Latinum,
   Sive ea fama aliquid, sive ea fama nihil.

(If the rustic muse of the Sicilian poet delights you,
   if you, fellow countrymen, take pleasure in the bucolics of the two Virgils,
Or if any of you German bards are hankering for something else,
   put up with me as I too take my place in the Latin countryside.
I am the first to pasture a Latin flock on German soil,
   whether that counts for something or not.)

To many readers, this achievement did indeed count for much. In a survey of German writers published in 1510, Hutten hails his friend as Germany's greatest living poet.

The masters to whom Hessus alludes in his introductory epigram are Theocritus (the first seven of whose idylls he read in the translation by Martino Filetico), Virgil, and Baptista Mantuanus, known in his day as the Christian Virgil. They may be taken to stand for the three levels of pastoral recapitulated in the *Bucolicon*. The first, and to the Christian mind the lowest, level is literal pastoral, exemplified in Theocritus's idylls. Here the herdsman is a shepherd pure and simple, an emblem of the natural man. On a deeper level, represented by Virgil's bucolics, the shepherd is a convenient mask for the poet and his friends and patrons. On the deepest level, however, the eclogue gains a tropological dimension, confronting the reader with questions of good and evil. This is the level that was pioneered by Mantuanus—William Shakespeare's "good old

Mantuan"–in his incredibly popular *Adulescentia* (Youth, 1498).

Each of these models comes to the fore in the *Bucolicon*. In imitation of Theocritus, Hessus has his shepherds talk about everyday concerns or debate the merits of their flocks. But literal pastoral is nearly everywhere overshadowed by veiled allusions to the poet and his circle of friends. On this allegorical level Hessus recounts how Ludwig Christiani prodded him to leave Frankenberg, then goes on to depict university life in Erfurt. He praises Mutianus, Spalatin, Jonas, and Crotus Rubianus and sings a pastoral elegy on the death of Landgrave Wilhelm II of Hesse. In other eclogues he satirizes the disastrous political conditions in Erfurt; lampoons a rival poet, Riccardo Sbruglio; and expresses his disappointment at not receiving the laurel crown that lesser lights had so readily obtained. But the *Bucolicon* is also a moral-religious work. Its underlying theme is the story of Hessus's inner growth: in the first eclogue he is a callow if precocious youth, piping songs of innocence in his native Hesse; but no sooner does he reach Erfurt than he metamorphoses into a lusty swain ogling the "mammosae Veneres et Phillides" (large-breasted Venuses and Phyllises) and desperately falling in love. In the latter half of the book Hessus comes of age: a mature twenty-one-year-old, he embraces Mutianus's ideal of tranquillity and eschews passionate love. The cycle of ten eclogues concludes with praise of the Virgin Mary, the goddess and guiding light of all good shepherds.

In the autumn of 1509 Hessus left Erfurt, reappearing in Riesenburg (today Prabuty, Poland) as secretary to Hiob von Dobeneck, bishop of Pomesania. A great favorite of the bishop's, Hessus often accompanied his lord on hunts and on embassies abroad. In February 1512, for example, he traveled to Kraków to attend the wedding of King Sigismund I of Poland with Barbara Zapolya of Hungary; for the occasion he hastily composed *Encomium nuptiale divo Sigismundo, regi Poloniae* (Encomium Celebrating the Nuptials of the Godlike Sigismund, King of Poland). His travels throughout the region are also reflected in a verse letter that he sent to Mutianus, probably in 1510: "Generalis Prussiae descriptio" (General Description of Prussia). Together with "Illiciti amoris antidotarium" (A Batch of Antidotes to Illicit Love), written for the priest Theodor Collucius (Temonius), the elegy was first printed in *Sylvae duae nuper aeditae: Prussia et Amor* (Two Poems on Diverse Topics, Hot from the Press: Prussia and Love, 1514). This book marks the first time that Hessus used the name Helius Eobanus Hessus–*Helius*, because he was born on a Sunday and because the sun-god Helios (Apollo) is the patron of poets.

But as he lived the courtier's life, Hessus became a heavy drinker. His alcoholism, according to his friend Joachim Camerarius, resulted from pride in his abilities and in his athlete's physique:

> Putavit enim se etiam inter poculorum certamina, quae maxime tum in aulis certabantur et a nobilitate frequentabantur, non vinci ab altero oportere. Advehuntur in illa loca etiam vina plenissima. Sed potus coquitur cum alibi tum maxime Gedani is qui cerebro infestior sit fumis suis quam vini cuiuscunque ingurgitatio. Ac est ille quidem hoc quoque consecutus, ut de palma in isto genere cum Eobano contendere vellet nemo. Sed brevi tempore repletione nimia iuvenile corpus graviter afflixit et vires nonnihil enervavit.

> (For he believed that even at the drinking bouts that were so popular just then at the courts and among many of the nobility he should not allow himself to be defeated by anyone else. In that region they import very full-bodied wines too. But in many places and especially at Gdansk they brew that drink that with its vapors impairs the brain far more than the guzzling of any wine whatsoever. And yet he proved so accomplished even here that nobody wanted to compete with Eobanus for the palm in this kind of contest. Still, it was not long before his immoderate tippling gravely weakened his youthful body and seriously undermined his health.)

In the spring of 1513 the bishop sent Hessus to the newly founded University of Frankfurt an der Oder to study law. The intention was to prepare him for a career as chancellor and ambassador, but no sooner had he left the episcopal court than the poet in him resurfaced. He sold his law books and, in the autumn of the same year, moved to Leipzig. There he made a great impression on the young Camerarius:

> Erat iuvenis ille pulcherrimus, corpore firmo et procero et membris elegantibus, facie plane virili et ore severo, barbaque conspicua ac profunda genae totae vestiebantur. Neque ego facile existimo fuisse quenquam a primo ortu cuius habitus atque constitutio ac species cum Eobanico corpore conferri, nedum huic ut illa praeferri possent.

> (He was an unusually handsome young man, of sturdy build and tall stature, with well-proportioned limbs, a thoroughly manly face, and a grave demeanor, and his cheeks were entirely covered with a conspicuous, thick beard. I can hardly imagine there has ever been anyone who in physical condition and constitution and appearance could compare with Eobanus, let alone surpass him in these things.)

This account tallies with Hessus's self-description in his letter to Posterity in the *Heroidum Christianarum epistolae*:

Corpus erat membrisque decens patiensque laborum,
  Robore firma suo brachia, crura, latus.
Forma virum decuisse potest, sine labe decensque;
  Frons diversa, animi spiritus altus erat.

(My body was good-looking in all its members and able to endure hard labor;
  arms, legs, and trunk were strong and well-built.
My features were manly, unblemished, and handsome;
  broad was my forehead, high-minded my soul.)

It was in Leipzig that Hessus published the *Heroidum Christianarum epistolae*, his most important and original work to that time. The first fifteen letters had been written in Prussia; many of them had been composed on horseback, he says, while he was riding out to hunt or traveling with the bishop. He had finished the remaining nine in Frankfurt an der Oder and hurriedly revised the others, for he was never one to labor long at polishing his style. As he explains in the dedicatory letter to the bishop:

[Non] ea . . . ingenii foelicitate praeditu[s sum], ut more Rhomani Homeri versus ursino more pariam, sed primo statim partu, licet infoeliciter alioqui et minus belle, qualitercunque tamen absolvam, admodumque rarenter mihi usu venit, ut rudia quaedam atque indigesta quasi mortario conteram.

(The fact is that I am not endowed with that felicity of mind that would let me produce verses the way the Roman Homer [Virgil] was able to do–by licking them into shape in the manner of a she-bear. My method of composition, rather, is to let the words stand exactly as I first wrote them down, be they ever so infelicitous or less than agreeable otherwise, without regard to their quality. Only rarely do I find myself pounding down on a shapeless and disorderly mass, in a mortar, as it were.)

The genre of the heroic epistle is modeled on Ovid's *Heroides*, a set of twenty-one fictitious letters, mostly by mythological heroines who appeal to their beloveds to come back to them or requite their love; of these epistles the last six are love letters by men that are answered by the heroines. Hessus has such a pair of letters at the start of his book: Emmanuel (Christ) writes to the Virgin Mary to announce the Incarnation, and Mary humbly accepts God's plan. The voice of a male suitor is heard again at the book's end, where Hessus declares his love for the personified Posterity and tells her about his life and aspirations. The remaining twenty-one letters are by female saints of history and legend who write to Jesus or to their beloveds in Christ. Mary Magdalene, for example, appeals to the risen Jesus to show himself to her on Easter Morning. Catherine of Alexandria addresses herself to her bridegroom, Christ. Elizabeth of Hungary fears for the life of her husband, Ludwig IV of Thuringia, who is away on a crusade with Emperor Frederick II. Helen writes her son Constantine that she has found the True Cross. Cunegund urges her husband, Heinrich, to let her prove her faithfulness to him by walking barefoot over hot coals. Monica exhorts her son, Augustine, to become a Christian. The courtesan Thais begs her confessor, Paphnutius, to release her from the dark cell in which she has been doing penance for three years. The widowed Paula wants Jerome to know that she and her daughter are on their way to live with him in Bethlehem.

The work, Hessus's masterpiece, made him famous throughout Europe. Accordingly, when he returned to Erfurt in the summer of 1514, he quickly established himself as the undisputed head of the local humanists. Reuchlin, punning on *Hessus* and the Greek *hessên* (king), nicknamed him the king of poets. These were happy and productive years for Hessus. He married Katharina Spater at the end of 1514, an occasion that was celebrated in an epithalamium by his friend Euricius Cordus (1515). Although a professorship would elude him for several more years, he was able to eke out a living by teaching literature privately–but then, who needs money when one is young and impassioned, first among equals in Erfurt, and filled with patriotic fervor at the sight of a humanistic Germany awakened from its medieval slumber and defeating the forces of entrenched obscurantism?

This pride and optimism are reflected in the patriotic themes that enter Hessus's poetic repertoire at this time. In his elegy *De vera nobilitate et priscis Germanorum moribus* (On True Nobility and the Good Old Morals of the Ancient Germans, 1515?) he attacks the degenerate ways of modern-day German noblemen as compared with the heroic virtues of their forebears and endorses the genuine nobility that he and his fellow humanists are striving to achieve: the nobility of the soul. When you look around in today's Germany, he continues, you can still find great heroes to celebrate–Emperor Maximilian, for instance, who is valiantly battling the Venetians, or Frederick the Wise of Saxony, who recently founded the University of Wittenberg. Hessus, moreover, was closely associated with the *Epistolae obscurorum virorum* (Letters of Obscure Men, 1515), the devastating satire largely composed by Crotus Rubianus that made Reuchlin's enemies–the Dominicans and the theologians of Cologne–the laughingstock of Europe. And in his elegy "Maximilianus Augustus Italiae" (Emperor Maximilian's Reply to Italia, 1516) Hessus gives a stylish, upbeat response to Hutten's heroic letter from the hard-pressed Italia (Italy), who pleads with the emperor to come to her aid and throw out her oppressors.

The exultation that Reuchlin's struggle against the "obscure men" aroused among the German humanists shows up in other poems of Hessus's. One can sense something of it in his sapphic *Hymnus paschalis* (1515), the subtitle of which proclaims that the "Paschal Hymn" was written as an acclamation of the "Christianae victoriae" (Christian victory). If this hint should prove too subtle for the conservative dunces to grasp, Hessus appends several epigrams, including:

> Monstrorum domitor toto, Iove natus, ab orbe
>   Nobile, virtutum praemia, nomen habet.
> Gloria Capnioni non est minor. Ille nec Hydra
>   Nec reliquis vicit monstra minora feris.
> Qualia iam nemo quaerit–nisi forsitan esse
>   Incipis ignotus, bardocuculle, tibi!

> (The son of Jupiter who overcame monsters throughout the world
>   earned enormous fame for his heroic deeds.
> Reuchlin's fame is in no way smaller [than Hercules']. He has conquered monsters
>   every bit as ferocious as the Hydra and those other wild beasts.
> Nobody asks any more what kind of ogres they were–unless you perhaps, monk's cowl,
>   have grown blind to yourself!)

Equally triumphant in mood and theme is the narrative poem *Victoria Christi ab inferis* (Christ's Victory in the Underworld, 1517). The models for this work were Macarius Mutius's epyllion on the same subject, *De triumpho Christi* (The Triumph of Christ, 1499), and–most curiously–a little-known poem, "Triumphus Christi heroicus" (The Heroic Triumph of Christ), that has been attributed to the early Christian writer Juvencus but more probably dates from the late Middle Ages. Many verses from the latter poem reappear verbatim in Hessus's work.

In July 1518 Hessus was appointed professor of poetics and rhetoric at the University of Erfurt, and he soon established himself as the institution's brightest star. Flush with success, he decided to visit his hero, Erasmus, who was then living in Louvain. Accompanied by a young nobleman, Johann von Werter, he set out on foot on 28 September 1518. After stopping in Gotha to see Mutianus, the two reached Frankfurt am Main on 6 October and from there traveled by boat down the Rhine, intending to go as far as Cologne. But hearing that that city was in the grip of the plague, they disembarked at Bonn and once more struck out on foot. By mid October they were in Louvain. That evening Hessus sent Erasmus an extemporaneous letter in verse, introducing himself and asking for a meeting the following day. The Dutch humanist, still convalescing from illness and eager to resume his philological work on the New Testament, gave Hessus a cool reception at first but warmed to him before long. At his departure on 20 October Hessus could take with him letters from Erasmus to some of his Erfurt friends and for Mutianus, as well as a stirring letter in praise of himself that opened with the lines:

> Iam arbitrabar mihi probe cognitam Germaniam, et quicquid esset insignium ingeniorum pervestigatum. Adamabam ingenium Beati Renani; exosculabar indolem Philippi Melanchtonis; suspiciebam Capnionis maiestatem; capiebar Hutteni daeliciis. Et ecce de repente Hessus, quod antehac in singulis vel amabam vel mirabar, unus universum exhibuit. Quid enim aliud Heroides tuae quam Christianum Ovidium referunt? Cui vel in oratione soluta contigit ea facilitas quae tibi in omni carminis genere? Eloquentiam aequat eruditio; et utrunque decorat Christiana pietas. Iam in oratione prosa talis es ut alienus a carmine videri possis. O venam ingenii vere auream! Nec a stilo mores abhorrent, quibus nihil candidius, nihil simplicius, nihil potest esse purius. Rara avis, eximia doctrina sine supercilio. Quid superest optandum, mi doctissime Hesse, nisi ut egregiis tuis dotibus, quas partim tuis vigiliis, partim coelo debes, fortuna respondeat?

(I thought I knew my Germany well and had sought out all its distinguished minds. I was devoted to the abilities of Beatus Rhenanus, found Philip Melanchthon's character delightful, admired Reuchlin's dignity, and was much taken with Hutten's charming conversation. And here is Hessus all of a sudden, uniting in himself all I had previously loved or admired in others separately. What does one think of in your *Heroides* but a Christian Ovid? Who is so happy in plain prose as you are in verse of every kind? Your learning balances your gifts of expression, and your Christian piety enhances both. In prose you are already so successful that one would think you had no poetry in you. Yours is a truly golden vein of talent. And your character matches your style: nothing could be more frank, more simple, more unspoilt. A rare bird indeed is learning untouched by arrogance. What more can one hope for, my learned Hessus, except that your great gifts, which you owe partly to hard work and partly to heaven, should be answered by good fortune? [Translation by R. A. B. Mynors and D. F. S. Thomson])

Overjoyed by Erasmus's tribute, Hessus published this letter and most of the others as an appendix to his delightful *A profectione ad Des. Erasmum Roterodamum hodoeporicon* (My Journey to Desiderius Erasmus of Rotterdam), printed in Erfurt in 1519 and reprinted in Louvain at Erasmus's instigation. That same year he lectured on the latter's *Enchiridion militis Christiani* (Dagger of the Christian Soldier, 1503), publishing a "Praefaciuncula" (Short Preface) to this "plane divinum opus" (absolutely divine work) in August 1520. And when Erasmus called on his supporters in Erfurt to help him silence the English theologian Edward Lee, who had disparaged his philological work on the Greek New Testament, it was Hessus who led the charge with a barrage of epigrams against Lee, *In Eduardum Leeum . . . epigrammata* (1520).

The epigrams against Lee and the preface to the *Enchiridion militis Christiani* represent the highwater mark of Hessus's zeal for Erasmus. Though he never ceased to admire the great man, his fervor waned markedly during the next decade and a half; and Erasmus, for his part, distanced himself more and more from the Protestant Hessus. The reason was Martin Luther. In early April 1521, on his way to the Diet of Worms, Luther had spent a few days in Erfurt. Profoundly moved by the reformer's personality and preaching, Hessus composed *In evangelici Doctoris Martini Lutheri laudem defensionemque elegias IIII* (Four Elegies in Praise and Defense of the Evangelical Doctor Martin Luther, 1521). The first two elegies hail Luther as he approaches Erfurt and tell how Rector Crotus Rubianus, Hessus, and many other faculty members rode out to welcome him to the city. The third poem describes the enthusiasm that Luther's sermon kindled in everyone's heart, while the fourth praises him on his departure and wishes him godspeed. To these elegies Hessus added three others that are set a few weeks later. The first lauds Jonas, who had boldly accompanied Luther to Worms; the next is an appeal to Hutten to rise up in arms for Luther and defend German freedom from the "strygibus papistis" (papist vampires); the third is an invective directed at Luther's antagonist Hieronymus Emser. The Protestant ardor that informs these poems also blazes up in *Ecclesiae afflictae epistola ad Lutherum* (Letter from the Sorely Afflicted Church to Luther, 1523), an elegy in which the church appeals to Luther to liberate her from the bonds of papal tyranny.

The tones of lament in this elegy may be attributed to the rapidly deteriorating situation in Erfurt. There, as in so many other German cities, the Reformation had led to popular unrest and rebellion against ecclesiastical and civic authority. The radical preachers, openly contemptuous of humanistic learning, advocated a return to an evangelically simple life; and the university itself, losing students to internal dissension, social disorder, a renewed outbreak of the plague, and the drawing power of Wittenberg, was rapidly collapsing. By 1526 only fourteen students were still enrolled. As head of the humanistic faction, Hessus could not stand idly by as the obscurantists gutted the university and the liberal arts. As a first salvo he published *De non contemnendis studiis humanioribus futuro theologo maxime necessariis aliquot clarorum virorum ad Eobanum Hessum epistolae* (Letters of Some Illustrious Men to Eobanus Hessus Concerning Humanistic Studies, Which, Far from Being Contemptible, Are Absolutely Indispensable for the Budding Theologian, 1523), a collection of letters by Luther, Melanchthon, Jonas, Peter Mosellanus, and Johannes Drach about the value of studies in Latin and Greek, particularly for students of theology. He added several poems of his own, among them an ode deploring the contempt in which the humanities were held and an urgent appeal to the city council for help. The next year he published the satiric *Dialogi tres* (Three Dialogues), in which he defends the study of medicine against evangelical critics who claimed that good health depended on faith alone and flails at the preachers and runaway monks who, in his view, had brought the university to the brink of ruin.

Hessus was defending medicine because, reduced to poverty by the lack of students, he had been obliged to look for a more lucrative source of income. At the urging of his friends, he had followed the example of Cordus and had enthusiastically taken up medical studies in 1523. Though he never became a physician—in large part because he could not afford the expenses associated with the degree—he turned his knowledge of dietetics into a superb poem, *Bonae valetudinis conservandae praecepta*. Based on many ancient, medieval, and modern sources—in particular Paul of Aegina, the eleventh- or twelfth-century *Regimen sanitatis Salernitanum* (Salernitan Regimen of Health), and Marsilio Ficino's *De vita* (On Life, 1489)—the book was a huge success, going through more than two dozen reprints, receiving several commentaries by physicians, and being translated into German by Johannes Episcopius (1576). In an accompanying "Medicinae laus" (Praise of Medicine) Hessus versified the salient points of Erasmus's *Encomium medicinae* (Encomium of Medicine, 1518) and so managed to deliver another shot at the Lutheran preachers.

In 1526 Hessus went to Nuremberg to teach at the Gymnasium of Saint Aegidius, a humanistic school that had just been founded by Melanchthon. His relief at escaping the misery of Erfurt and his high hopes for the future are palpable in *Elegiae tres* (Three Elegies, 1526), a work he wrote to advertise the new school. It was at this time that the most productive phase of his career began. He wrote a denunciation of monasticism, *In hypocrisim vestitus monastici* ἐκφώνησις (Against the Hypocrisy of the Monk's Cowl), which was printed together with a verse paraphrase of several Psalms in 1527. That same year he composed and published together two poems celebrating Camerarius's marriage to Anna Truchsess: "Venus triumphans" (Venus Triumphant) and "In nuptiis Ioachimi Camerarii epithalamion" (An Epithalamium on the Occasion of Joachim Camerarius's Wedding), the latter in imitation of Erasmus's epithalamium for Pieter Gillis (1524). He also produced textbooks for his students: a guide to versification (1526), an edition of Virgil's *Bucolics* and *Georgics* with detailed notes on their Greek sources (1529), as well as editions of Hutten's *De arte versificandi* (The Art of Versification, 1531) and Marco Girolamo Vida's *De arte poetica* (The Art of Poetry, 1531). His lectures on Johannes Murmellius's *Tabulae in artis componendorum versuum rudimenta* (The Rudiments of Versification, circa 1515) were published posthumously by his former pupil Michael Lindener in 1552.

With Camerarius's help Hessus also pursued his studies in Greek, concentrating on Theocritus. The first fruit of this work was a thoroughgoing revision of the *Bucolicon* with an eye to turning the eclogues into "idylls." Some of the original pastorals were split in half and put into a different context so as to highlight the literal, Theocritan level and de-emphasize the moralizing tone of the earlier version; the eleventh eclogue, in praise of the Virgin Mary, was dropped altogether. Enriched with five new idylls, the book was published in 1528 as *Bucolicorum idyllia*.

Some of the newly added idylls–a word Hessus understood to mean "little pictures"–are, indeed, poems after Theocritus's own heart. One is an adaptation of the ancient poet's eleventh idyll, in which the Cyclops cures himself of his passionate love for Galatea through the power of song. Another, an encomium of Landgrave Philip of Hesse, has its counterpart in Theocritus's panegyric of Ptolemy (seventeenth idyll). A third poem offers an encomiastic description of Nuremberg. The two remaining "little pictures" date back to the end of Hessus's Erfurt period. As one might expect, they are anything but idyllic: they deplore the contempt in which liberal studies are held and place the blame squarely on the Protestant preachers.

Other works of Hessus's also focus on the cultural and political disasters that plagued the 1520s, specifically the Peasants' Revolt of 1524 to 1526 and the sack of Rome in 1527. In a series of poems published as *De tumultibus horum temporum querela* (Laments on the Tumults of These Times, 1528) he compares the present with all previous ages and finds his own to be the worst. But he adds a poem of consolation, reminding his countrymen of their former greatness and urging them to stand together so that they may rise again to preeminence in Europe. And in his elegies "Caes. Carolo V. Augusto Germaniam ingredienti urbis Norimbergae gratulatoria acclamatio" (Congratulatory Acclamation by the City of Nuremberg to Emperor Charles V on His Entry into Germany) and "Ad eundem de bello contra Turcas suscipiendo adhortatio" (An Exhortation to the Emperor to Undertake a War against the Turks), published together in 1530, he ventures to address Charles V at the diet of Augsburg, calling on him to heal the religious divisions in Germany and mount an attack on the common enemy, the Turks.

A year before he left Nuremberg for good, Hessus, debt-ridden as always, presented the city fathers with a masterful encomium of their town, *Urbs Noriberga illustrata carmine heroico,* which draws both on his own observations and on Conrad Celtis's prose description (1502). Toward the end of his poem Hessus praises the councilors for their wisdom in founding and maintaining a school devoted to the ancient languages. The city council showed its gratitude for this magnificent work by giving him forty guilders and discharging him of the debts he had accumulated. They did nothing, however, to shore up the Gymnasium of Saint Aegidius, which by then had fallen on hard times.

And so, with a growing family to feed, the spendthrift Hessus found himself chronically burdened with financial cares. He remained productive throughout the 1530s; but as the decade wore on he devoted himself less and less to original writing and more and more to verse translations, poetic paraphrases of biblical texts, and collecting and reworking earlier efforts. Thus, he published the first complete verse translation of Theocritus's *Idylls*–the culmination of three years of hard, if often interrupted work–in 1531 and a verse paraphrase of the Book of Ecclesiastes in 1532. The eulogies he had composed for such men as Hutten, Mutianus, Reuchlin, Frederick the Wise, Albrecht Dürer, and Willibald Pirckheimer were gathered under the title *Illustrium ac clarorum aliquot virorum memoriae scripta epicedia* (Epicedia Written in Memory of Some Illustrious and Famous Men, 1531). Later he published tributes to the city councilor Hieronymus Ebner (1532) and Erasmus (1537). He also brought together many of the occasional poems he had written over the years and published them in 1535 as *Sylvarum libri VI* (Six Books of Medleys), augmented in the *Operum farragines duae* (1539) with three new books.

In the same year that he published his *Ecclesiastes* and *Urbs Noriberga illustrata carmine heroico* Hessus also completed a long-planned overhaul of the *Heroidum Christianarum epistolae*. Titled *Heroidum libri tres*

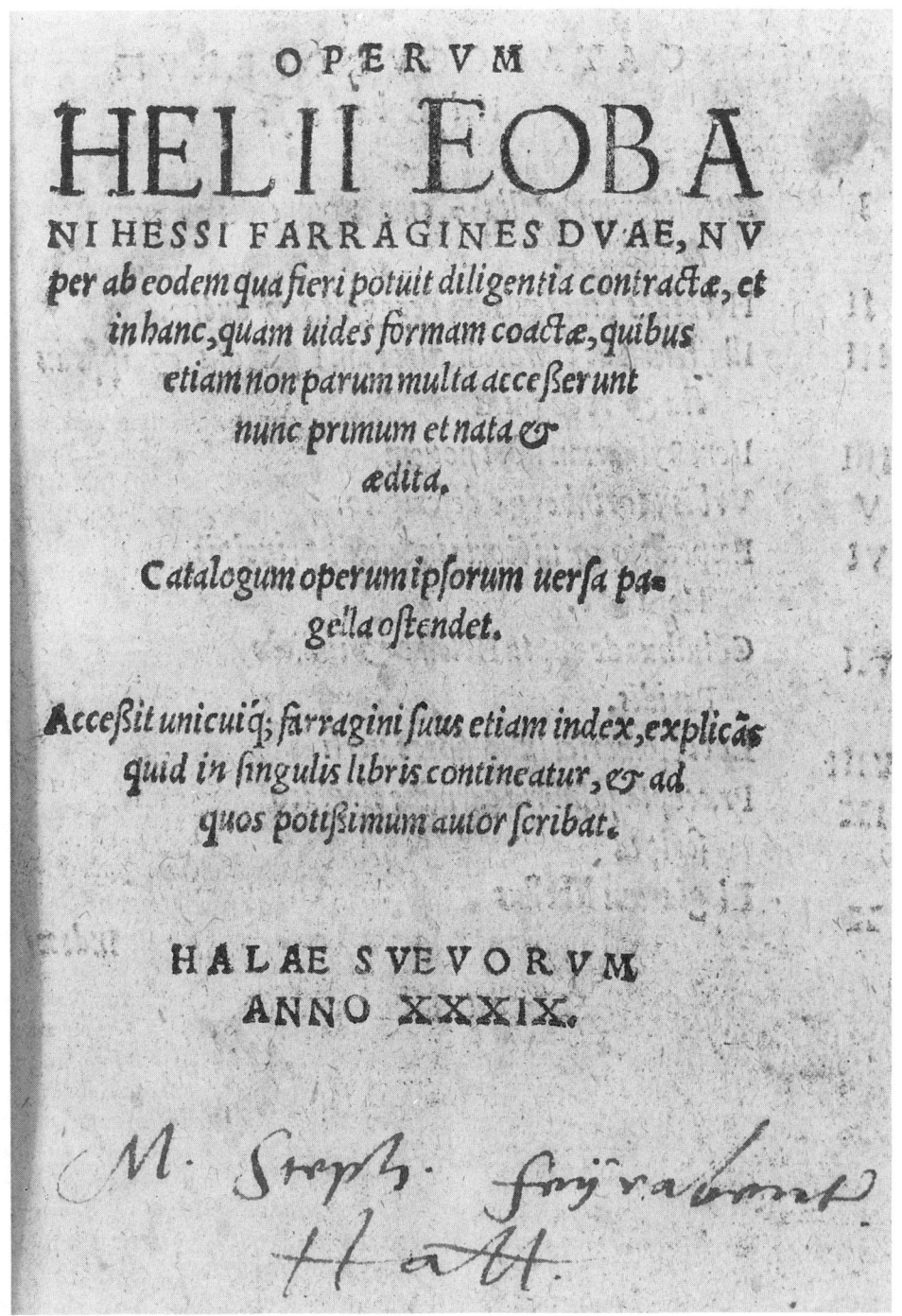

Title page for Hessus's revised edition of his collected works (courtesy of the Lilly Library, Indiana University)

(Three Books of Heroic Epistles, 1532), the new work reflects not just his improved ear for Latin style but also his Protestant sensibilities regarding the medieval legends. Gone are such extravagant stories as the Eleven Thousand Virgins and Saint George and the Dragon. Other letters are rewritten from top to bottom, sometimes by eliminating objectionable materials, sometimes by replacing legendary heroines with more-acceptable ones. And to make it plain that more than half the work deals with biblical and historical subjects, Hessus organized the poems into three categories. The first book consists of six letters drawn from the New Testament. The second comprises five letters based on history (Helen's discovery of the True Cross and Monica's admonitions to Augustine, for example), as well as two taken from legend (the miraculous birth of the Virgin Mary and Saint Martha's exploits in Provence). The third book contains purely legendary themes: letters by eight saints, including Catherine, Cunegund, and Thais. As in the original version, Hessus's letter to Posterity brings up the rear. (In 1539, in the edition of his collected works, Hessus appended to the book the *Ecclesiae afflictae epistola ad Lutherum* of 1523.)

Lured by the promise of a professorship and by nostalgia for the good old days, Hessus returned to Erfurt in May 1533. There he completed verse translations of "Coluthi de raptu Helenes ac iudicio Paridis poema" (Colluthus's "The Rape of Helen and the Judgment of Paris"), "Epithalamion Helenes ex Theocrito" ("Helen's Epithalamium," from Theocritus), and "Moschi Amor fugitivus" (Moschus's "Runaway Amor"), which were published together in 1534. He also translated a German work by his friend Jodocus Hessus, which he titled *Ludus de podagra* (Play about Gout, 1537), and toiled at a verse paraphrase of the entire Psalter. But if he had harbored any illusions about the state of affairs at Erfurt University, he was soon disabused. Setting his mind on returning to his native Hesse, therefore, he began angling for an invitation to teach at the new University of Marburg. An opportunity to impress the Hessians came in 1534. Landgrave Philip had just won an almost bloodless victory at Lauffen in Württemberg and restored his Protestant kinsman Duke Ulrich I to power. Hessus responded with a grandiloquent poem, *De victoria Wirtembergensi* (The Victory in Württemberg), in which he described Philip's triumph and compared the landgrave to the Homeric heroes and Alexander the Great. The work proved popular in Hesse and quickly sold out. Hessus was invited to present a copy of his book to Philip and went back to Erfurt, as he reported to Johannes Meckbach in a letter of 8 November 1534, "donatu[s] liberaliter et oneratu[s] magna spe" (rich in presents and laden with great hope).

Finally, in 1536, after much negotiation, he was appointed professor of history at the University of Marburg; in 1538 he was elected its rector. Thus, it was at Marburg that he published the verse paraphrase of the Psalter (1537) that he had begun in earnest three years before at Erfurt. Dedicated to Landgrave Philip, the work drew high praise from Luther and went on to become a best-seller, especially after Hessus added versified arguments for each Psalm (1538). By the end of the century there were some fifty reprints, often in combination with his paraphrase of the book of Ecclesiastes. At the request of Melanchthon, whom some were suspecting of Catholic leanings, Hessus also published a poetic attack on Calumny (1538). He had it reprinted in 1539, along with a consolation for Philip Pistorius of Nidda on the death of his wife. More important, he gathered up and revised his major works in *Operum Helii Eobani Hessi farragines duae* (Two Farragoes of the Works of Helius Eobanus Hessus, 1539). His last book, the admirable verse translation of the *Iliad*, came out in September 1540, a few weeks before his death.

Hessus had just started work on a poetic description of the Christian calendar when he died on 4 October 1540. He left behind his wife, four sons (Hieronymus, Julius, Heliodorus, and Callimachus; another son, Anastasius, had died young in 1532), a daughter (Norica), no worldly fortune to speak of, but an enormous reputation as the king of poets. Drach delivered the eulogy, taking as his text 1 Thess. 4:13–18, on the certainty of the Resurrection; it was published in 1541 as *Ein Trostpredigt von der aufferstehung* (A Sermon of Consolation about the Resurrection). Poetic epitaphs poured in from friends and colleagues and were published in *Epitaphia aliquot epigrammata in mortem clarissimi poetae Helii Eobani Hessi* (Some Epitaphs on the Death of that Most Illustrious Poet Helius Eobanus Hessus, 1540). Jacob Micyllus, Hessus's student during the latter's heyday in Erfurt and the leading poet of the younger generation, composed a long epicedion for his idol that was printed at Wittenberg in 1542 and reprinted at the head of Drach's edition of Hessus's correspondence in 1543. Another admirer, Christophorus Aulaeus, culled quotations from Hessus's collected works in *Helii Eobani Hessi, poetae Germani, operum flores ac sententiae insigniores, commodo studiosorum selecti* (Flowers and Especially Memorable Maxims from the Works of the German Poet Helius Eobanus Hessus, Selected for the Benefit of Students, 1551). And in a beautifully crafted biography (1553) and four collections of letters (1553, 1557, 1561, and 1568) Camerarius completed the picture of his dear friend's life and work.

With Hessus's death the glory days of the Renaissance in Germany were over. Henceforth the Reformation and Counterreformation would absorb the creative energies of northern Europe and slowly but inexorably eclipse the fame of Hessus and his fellow humanists. But as the sixteenth century drew to a close and a new era of vernacular literature, worthy of its Neo-Latin predecessors, started to dawn, one German dramatist looked back in awe at the achievements of the previous age. And as he proudly showed off his Germany to the astonished Caesar and Cicero, resurrected from the underworld for that purpose, he chose as his spokesman the paragon of modern German culture: Eobanus Hessus. The playwright was Nicodemus Frischlin, the play *Julius redivivus* (Julius Brought Back to Life, 1585).

Letters:

Helii Eobani Hessi, poetae excellentiss., et amicorum ipsius epistolarum familiarium libri XII, quibus non modo vita illius, sed et aliarum rerum descriptiones pulcherr. scituque digniss. continentur, edited by Johannes Drach (Marburg: Christian Egenolph, 1543);

Narratio de H. Eobano Hesso, comprehendens mentionem de compluribus illius aetatis doctis et eruditis viris, composita a Ioachimo Camerario Pabebergensi. Epistolae Eobani Hessi ad Camerarium et alios quosdam, familiari in genere, cum lepidae ac facetae, tum eruditae et literatae, cum quibusdam Camerarii et aliorum scriptis, quorum nihil ante hunc diem ad hunc modum editum fuit, edited by Joachim Camerarius (Nuremberg: Johann Montan & Ulrich Neuber, 1553);

Libellus alter, epistolas complectens Eobani et aliorum quorundam doctissimorum virorum necnon versus varii generis atque argumenti, edited by Camerarius (Leipzig: Valentin Bapst, 1557);

Tertius libellus epistolarum H. Eobani Hessi et aliorum quorundam virorum, autoritate, virtute, sapientia, doctrinaque excellentium, edited by Camerarius (Leipzig: Ernst Voegelin, 1561);

Libellus novus, epistolas et alia quaedam monumenta doctorum superioris et huius aetatis complectens, edited by Camerarius (Leipzig: Johann Rambau, 1568), signatures B1^r–D1^v;

Celebrium virorum cum Norimbergensium tum aliorum quoque epistolae ineditae LX, edited by Bernhard F. Hummel (Nuremberg: Bauer, 1777), pp. 55–72;

Virorum clarorum saeculi XVI et XVII epistolae selectae e codicibus manuscriptis Gottingensibus, edited by Ernest Weber (Leipzig: Teubner, 1894), pp. 19–25.

Biographies:

Joachim Camerarius, *Narratio de H. Eobano Hesso, comprehendens mentionem de compluribus illius aetatis doctis et eruditis viris* (Nuremberg: Johann Montan & Ulrich Neuber, 1553);

Kaspar Friedrich Lossius, *Helius Eoban Hesse und seine Zeitgenossen: Ein Beitrag zur Erfurthischen Gelehrten- und Reformationsgeschichte* (Gotha: Perthes, 1797); republished as *Anfang und Fortgang der Reformation; oder Helius Eobanus Hesse und seine Zeitgenossen* (Gotha: Perthes, 1817);

Wigand Lauze, "Von des erleuchten und hoch begabten Poeten Helii Eobani hessi leben und absterben," *Zeitschrift des Vereins für hassische Geschichte und Landeskunde,* second supplement, volume 1 (1841): 426–441;

Martin Hertz, *Helius Eoban Hesse: Ein Lehrer- und Dichterleben aus der Reformationszeit* (Berlin: Hertz, 1860);

Gotthold Schwertzell, *Helius Eobanus Hessus, ein Lebensbild aus der Reformationszeit* (Halle: Niemeyer, 1874);

Karl Krause, *Helius Eobanus Hessus, sein Leben und seine Werke: Ein Beitrag zur Cultur- und Gelehrtengeschichte des 16. Jahrhunderts,* 2 volumes (Gotha: Perthes, 1879);

Ingeborg Gräßer-Eberbach, *Helius Eobanus Hessus: Der Poet des Erfurter Humanistenkreises* (Erfurt: Verlagshaus Thüringen, 1993).

References:

Clemens M. Bruehl, "Zwei unbekannte Briefe von Erasmus," *Quaerendo,* 16 (1986): 243–258;

Otto Clemen, "Bibliographisches zu Helius Eobanus Hessus und Biblio-Biographisches zum Verfasser der 'Katzipori,'" *Archiv für Schreib- und Buchwesen,* 3 (1929–1930): 7–10;

Heinrich Dörrie, *Der heroische Brief: Bestandsaufnahme, Geschichte, Kritik einer humanistisch-barocken Literaturgattung* (Berlin: De Gruyter, 1968);

Georg Ellinger, *Geschichte der neulateinischen Literatur Deutschlands im sechzehnten Jahrhundert,* 3 volumes (Berlin & Leipzig: De Gruyter, 1929–1933), II: 3–23;

Heinz Entner, "Helius Eobanus Hessus und die lutherische Reformation in Erfurt 1521–1525," in *Weltwirkung der Reformation: Internationales Symposium anläulich der 450-Jahr-Feier der Reformation in Wittenberg vom 24. bis 26. Oktober 1967,* 2 volumes, edited by Max Steinmetz and Gerhard Brendler (Berlin: VEB Deutscher Verlag der Wissenschaften, 1969), II: 472–484;

W. Leonard Grant, *Neo-Latin Literature and the Pastoral* (Chapel Hill: University of North Carolina Press, 1965), pp. 164–169, 427;

Erich Kleineidam, *Universitas Studii Erffordensis: Überblick über die Geschichte der Universität Erfurt,* 3 volumes (Leipzig: St. Benno, 1964–1980), II: 173–268;

Karl Krause, "Eine neu aufgefundene Schrift des Eobanus Hessus," *Centralblatt für Bibliothekswesen,* 11 (1894): 163–169;

Kurt Romeick, "Eobanus Hessus über die Zustände in Erfurt im Jahre 1525," *Aus der Vergangenheit der Stadt Erfurt,* 1 (1955): 82–92;

Eckart Schäfer, "Der deutsche Bauernkrieg in der neulateinischen Literatur," *Daphnis,* 9 (1980): 1-31;

Wolfgang Schmid, "Antike Motive im Epicedion des Eobanus Hessus auf den Tod Dürers: Über eine humanistische Motivkontamination u.a. aus dem Epitaphios Bionos," in *Philomathes: Studies and Essays in the Humanities in Memory of Philip Merlan,* edited by Robert B. Palmer and Robert Hamerton-Kelly (The Hague: Nijhoff, 1971), pp. 508-521;

R. W. Scribner, "The Erasmians and the Beginning of the Reformation in Erfurt," *Journal of Religious History,* 9 (1976): 3-31;

Hugo Steiger, "Eobanus Hesse und Albrecht Dürer," *Bayerische Blätter für das Gymnasial-Schulwesen,* 66 (1930): 72-81;

Winfried Trillitzsch, "Humanismus und Reformation: Der Erfurter Humanist und 'Dichterkönig' Helius Eobanus Hessus," *Wissenschaftliche Zeitschrift, Friedrich-Schiller-Universität Jena,* Gesellschaftswissenschaftliche Reihe, no. 33 (1984): 343-357;

Harry Vredeveld, "The *Bucolicon* of Eobanus Hessus: Three Versions of Pastoral," in *Acta Conventus Neo-Latini Guelpherbytani: Proceedings of the Sixth International Congress of Neo-Latin Studies, Wolfenbüttel 12 August to 16 August 1985,* edited by Stella P. Revard, Fidel Rädle, and Mario A. Di Cesare (Binghamton: Medieval and Renaissance Texts and Studies, 1988), pp. 375-382;

Vredeveld, "A Forgotten Poem by Eobanus Hessus to Mutianus Rufus," in *"Der Buchstab tödt—der Geist macht lebendig": Festschrift zum 60. Geburtstag von Hans-Gert Roloff von Freunden, Schülern und Kollegen,* 2 volumes, edited by James Hardin and Jörg Jungmayr (Bern, Berlin, Frankfurt am Main, New York, Paris & Vienna: Peter Lang, 1992), I: 1067-1083;

Vredeveld, "*Helii Eobani Hessi Heroidum Libri Tres,*" dissertation, Princeton University, 1970;

Vredeveld, "Helius Eobanus Hessus' *Bonae valetudinis conservandae rationes aliquot:* An Inquiry into Its Sources," *Janus,* 72 (1985): 83-112;

Vredeveld, "Der heroische Brief 'Maria Magdalena Iesu Christo' aus den 'Heroidum Libri Tres' des Helius Eobanus Hessus (1488-1540)," *Daphnis,* 6 (1977): 65-90;

Vredeveld, "Mittelalterliche Legende in ovidischer Form: Wege der Worte in den *Heroidum Christianarum Epistolae* des Helius Eobanus Hessus, am Beispiel des Briefes 'Maria Aegyptia Zozimae,' " in *Wege der Worte: Festschrift für Wolfgang Fleischhauer,* edited by Donald C. Riechel (Cologne & Vienna: Böhlau, 1978), pp. 237-262;

Vredeveld, "A Neo-Latin Satire on Love-Madness: The Third Eclogue of Eobanus Hessus' *Bucolicon* of 1509," *Daphnis,* 14 (1985): 673-719;

Vredeveld, "Pastoral Inverted: Baptista Mantuanus' Satiric Eclogues and their Influence on the *Bucolicon* and *Bucolicorum Idyllia* of Eobanus Hessus," *Daphnis,* 14 (1985): 461-496;

Vredeveld, "Traces of Erasmus' Poetry in the Work of Helius Eobanus Hessus," *Humanistica Lovaniensia,* 35 (1986): 48-59;

Vredeveld, "The Unsuspected Source of Eobanus Hessus's *Victoria Christi ab Inferis,*" in *Acta Conventus Neo-Latini Sanctandreani: Proceedings of the Fifth International Congress of Neo-Latin Studies, St Andrews 24 August to 1 September 1982,* edited by I. D. McFarlane (Binghamton: Medieval and Renaissance Texts and Studies, 1986), pp. 293-297.

Ulrich von Hutten
(21 April 1488 – 29 August 1523)

James V. Mehl
Missouri Western State College

BOOKS: *Nemo* (Erfurt: Sebaldus Striblita, 1510); revised as *ÖYTIΣ Nemo* (Augsburg: Johann Miller, 1518);

Equestris ordinis poetae in Vuedegum Loetz Consulem Gripesualdensem im Pomerania et filium eius Hennigum Vtr: Juris doctorem Querelarum libri duo pro insigni quadam iniuria sibi ab illis facta (Frankfurt an der Oder: Johann Hanau, 1510);

De Arte Versificandi Liber vnus Heroico carmine ad Ioannem et Alexandrum Osthenios Pomeranos Equites (Leipzig: Wolfgang Stöckel, 1511);

Ad divvm Maximilianvm Caesa. Aug. F. P. bello in Venetos euntem, Vlrici Hutteni Equitis, Exhortatio (Vienna: Hieronymus Victor & Johann Singriener, 1512); revised as *Exhortatorium* (Augsburg: Johann Miller, 1519);

Ex equestri ordine Adolesentis Carmen emunctissimum mores hominum admodum iucunde complectens cui Titulus vir bonus (Erfurt: Hans Knappe, 1513);

Baptisati cuiusdam iudaei Ioannis Pepercorni Hallis oppido Magdburgensis diocesis: ante arcem divi Mauritii: in Coemeterio iudaeorum lento igni assati (Mainz: Johann Schöffer, 1514);

In lavdem reverendissimi Alberthi Archepiscopi Mogvntini Vlrichi de Hutten Equitis Panegyricus (Tübingen: Thomas Anshelm, 1515);

Epistola ad Maximilianum Caesarem Italiae fictitia (Strasbourg: Matthias Schürer, 1516);

Epistolae obscurorum virorum ad Venerabilem virum magistrum Ortuinum Gratium Dauentriensem Coloniae agrippinae bonas litteras docentem: varijs et locis et temporibus missae ac demum in volumen coactae, by Hutten, Crotus Rubeanus, Hermannus Buschius, and others (Speyer: Jakob Schmidt, 1516; revised, 1517); translated by Francis Griffin Stokes as *Epistolae obscurorum virorum* (London: Chatto & Windus, 1909); translation republished as *On the Eve of the Reformation: "Letters of Obscure Men"* (New York: Harper & Row, 1964);

Phalarismvs Dialogvs Hvttenicvs (Mainz: Johann Schöffer, 1517);

Ulrich von Hutten

Epistola ad illvstrem virvm Hermannvm de Nevenar Hvtteniana, qva contra Capnionis aemvlos confirmatvr (Mainz: Johann Schöffer, 1518);

Avla. Dialogvs (Augsburg: Sigmund Grimm & Marx Wirsung, 1518);

Ad Principes Germaniae, vt bellum Turcis inuehant. Exhortatoria (Augsburg: Sigmund Grimm & Marx Wirsung, 1518);

Ad Bilibaldum Pirckheymer Patricium Norimbergensem Epistola vitae suae rationem exponens (Augsburg: Sigmund Grimm & Marx Wirsung, 1518);

Triumphus Doc. Reuchlini habes studiose lector, Ioannis Capnionis viri praestantissimi Encomion. Triumphanti illi ex deuictis Obscuris viris, Id est Theologistis Coloniensis & Fratribus de Ordine Praedicatorum, ab Eleutherio Byzeno decantatum, by Hutten and others (Hagenau: Thomas Anshelm, 1518);

Febris. Dialogus Huttenicus (Mainz: Johann Schöffer, 1519);

De Guaiaci medicina et morbo gallico liber unus (Mainz: Johann Schöffer, 1519); translated by Thomas Paynel as *Of the wood called guaiacum, that healeth the Fr[ench]e Poc[kes] and also helped the goute in the feete, the stoone, the palsey, lepree, dropsy, fallynge euyll, and other dyseases* (London: Thomas Berthelet, 1536);

Hoc in volumine haec continentur Ulrichi Hutteni Equ. Super interfectione propinqui sui Ioannis Hutteni Equ. Deploratio. Ad Ludouichum Huttenum super interemptione filij Consolatoria. In Ulrichum Vuirtenpergensem orationes V. In eundem Dialogus, cui titulus Phalarismus. Apologia pro Phalarismo, & aliquot ad amicos epistolae. Ad Franciscum Galliarum regem epistola ne causam Vuirtenpergensem tueatur exhortatoria (Mainz: Johann Schöffer, 1519);

Hulderichi Hutteni eq. Germ. Dialogi. Fortuna. Febris prima. Febris secunda. Trias Romana. Inspicientes (Mainz: Johann Schöffer, 1520); translated into German by Hutten as *Gespräch büchlin herr Ulrichs von Hutten. Feber das Erst. Feber das Ander. Wadiscus. oder die Römische dreyfaltigkeit* (Strasbourg: Johann Schott, 1521);

Epistola Ulrichi de Hutten Equitis, ad D. Martinum Lutherum Theologum. Vuittembergae (Wittenberg: Melchior Lotter the Younger, 1520);

Hoc in libello haec continentur: Ulrichi De Hutten, Equitis Germani, ad Carolum Imperatorem, aduersus intentatam sibi a Romanistis vim & iniuriam, Conquestio. Eiusdem alia ad Principes, ac viros Germaniae, de eadem re conquestio. Eiusdem ad Albertum Brandepurgensem, & Fridericum Saxonum Ducem, Principes Electores, aleaeque ad alios Epistolae (Strasbourg: Johann Schott, 1520); translated into German by Hutten as *In dißem Buchlin findet man Hern Wlrichs von Hutten Vber und gegen vorgwaltigung des Bapsts, vnnd der Romanisten, klagschrifft an Keyserliche maiestat* (Strasbourg: Johann Schott, 1520);

Ein Clagschrift des Hochberumten und Ernuestem herrn Ulrichs von Hutten gekroeneten Poeten vnd Orator an alle stend Deütscher nation (Strasbourg: Martin Flach, 1520);

Clag vnd vormanung gegen dem übermaessigen vnchristlichen gewalt des Bapsts zu Rom vnd der vngeistlichen geistlichen (Strasbourg: Johann Schott, 1520);

In incendium Lutherianum Exclamatio Ulrichi Hutteni Equitis (Wittenberg: Johann Rhau-Grunenberg, 1521);

Eyn Klag über den Luterischen Brandt zu Mentz (Worms: Hans Werlich von Erfurt, 1521);

Enndtschüldigung Ulrichs von Hutten Wyder etlicher vnwarhafftiger auß geben von ym als solt er wider alle geystlicheit vnd priesterschafft sein mit erklaerung etlicher seiner geschrifften (Worms: Hans Werlich von Erfurt, 1521);

Gesprechbiechlin Neüw Karsthans, by Hutten, Martin Bucer, and others (Strasbourg: Matthias Schürer, 1521);

Dialogi Huttenici noui, perquam festiui. Bulla, uel Bullicida. Monitor primus. Monitor secundus. Praedones (Strasbourg: Johann Schott, 1521);

In Hieronymum Aleandrum, & Marinum Caracciolum Oratores Leonis X. apud Vormaciam Inuectiuae singulae (Paris: Printed by Pierre Vidoué for Konrad Resch, 1521);

Anzoeig Wie allwegen sich die Roemischen Bischoeff od' Baepst gegen den teütschen Kayßeren gehalten haben uff die kürtzst vß Chronicken und Historien gezogen K. maiestaet fürzubringen (Strasbourg: Johann Schott, 1521);

Duae ad Martinum Lutherum Epistolae Ulrici ab Hutten (Wittenberg, 1521);

Hoc in libello haec continentur Helii Eobani Hessi, ad Hulderichum Huttenum, ut Christianae Veritatis caussam, & Lutheri iniuriam armis contra Romanistas prosequatur, Exhortatorium. Hulderichi Hutteni ad Helium Eobanum Hessum pro eadem re responsorium (Strasbourg: Johann Schott, 1521);

Ain new lied (Schlettstadt: Nikolaus Küffer, 1521);

Das ist der hoch thuren Babel, id est Confusio Pape darinn Doctor Luther gefangen ist (Strasbourg: Matthias Schürer, 1521);

Vormanung an die freien vnd reich Stette teutscher nation (Strasbourg: Johann Knobloch, 1522);

Ein demütige ermanung an ein gemeyne statt Wormbß von Vlrich von Hutten zugeschrieben (Speyer: Jakob Schmidt, 1522);

Ulrichi ab Hutten cum Erasmo Roterodamo, Presbytero, Theologo, Expostulatio (Strasbourg: Johann Schott, 1523); translated by Randolph J. Klawiter as "Expostulation of Ulrich von Hutten with Erasmus of Rotterdam, Priest and Theologian," in *The Polemics of Erasmus of Rotterdam and Ulrich von Hutten*, edited by Klawiter (Notre Dame & London: University of Notre Dame Press, 1977), pp. 59–126;

Arminius Dialogus Huttenicus, Quo homo patriae amantissimus, Germanorum laudem celebrauit (Hagenau: Johann Setzer, 1529).

Collections: *Vlrichi Hvtteni equitis Germani opera qvæ reperiri potvervnt omnia,* 7 volumes, edited by Eduard Böcking (Leipzig: Teubner, 1859-1870);

Ulrichs von Hutten Deutsche Schriften, edited by Siegfried Szamatólski (Strasbourg: Trübner, 1891);

Deutsche Schriften, edited by Peter Ukena (Munich: Winkler, 1970);

Deutsche Schriften, 2 volumes, edited by Heinz Mettke (Leipzig: VEB Bibliographisches Institut, 1972, 1974).

Edition in English: "The remarkable medicine guaiacum and the cure of the Gallic disease by Ulrich von Hutten, German knight," translated by Clarence W. Mendell, *Archives of Dermatology and Syphilology,* 23 (1931): 409-428, 681-704, 1045-1063.

OTHER: Livy, *T. Livius Patavinvs Historicvs. Dvobvs libris avctvs cvm L. Flori Epitome. et annotatis in libros VII Belli maced,* with a preface by Hutten (Mainz: Peter Schöffer, 1518 or 1519);

Lorenzo Valla, *De donatione Constantini quid ueri habeat, eruditorum quorundam iudicium, ut in uersa pagella uidebis,* preface and commentaries by Hutten (Basel: Andreas Cratander, 1519 or 1520); translated as *A treatyse of the donation or gyfte and endowment of possessyons, gyuen and graunted vnto Siluester, pope of Rhome, by Constantyne, emperour of Rome* (London: Printed by Thomas Godfray, circa 1534);

De vnitate ecclesiae conservanda, et schismate, quod fuit inter Henrichum IIII. imp. & Gregorium VII. Pont. Max. cuiusdam eius temporis theologi liber, in uetustiss. Fuldensi bibliotheca ab Huttenno inuentus nuper, edited by Hutten (Mainz: Johann Schöffer, 1520);

De schismate extingvendo, et vere ecclesiastica libertate adserenda epistolae aliqvot mirvm in modvm liberae, et veritatis stvdio strenvae, edited by Hutten (Mainz: Johann Schöffer, 1520);

Pope Leo X, *Bvlla Decimi Leonis, contra errores Martini Lutheri, & sequacium,* glosses by Hutten (Strasbourg: Johann Schott, 1520);

Concilia wie man die halten sol. Vnd von verleyhung geystlicher lehenpfrunden. Antzoeig damit der Baepst Cardinaelen vnd aller Curtisanen list vrsprung vnd handel bitz vff diß zeit. Ermanung das ein yeder bey dem rechten alten Christlichen glauben bleiben vnnd sich zu keiner newerung bewegen lassen soll durch herr Cunrat zärtlin in 76 artickel veruas, βt, edited by Hutten (Strasbourg: Johann Schott, 1521);

Marcus Tullius Cicero, *Des hochberumpten Marci Tullii Ciceronis buechlein von dem Alter dürch herr Johan

Title page for the revised edition of Hutten's autobiographical poem

Neuber Caplan zu Schwartzenberg vß dem latein inn Teütsch gebracht,* translated by Hutten (Augsburg: Sigmund Grimm, 1522);

Sallust, *C. Salvstii et Q. Cvrtii Flores, selecti per Hulderichum Huttenum equitem, eiusdemque scholijs non indoctis illustrati,* edited by Hutten (Strasbourg: Johann Herwagen, 1528);

Sallust, *C. Crispi Salvstii Historici clasissimi L. Sergij Catilinae coniuratio, Bellum Iugurthinum, In M.T. Ciceronem inuectiua. . . . Cum alphabetico flosculorum Salustianorum ab Huldericho Hutteno selectorum indice,* edited by Hutten (Paris: Simon Colines, 1530).

In a well-known letter of 25 October 1518 to the Nuremburg patrician and humanist Willibald Pirckheimer, Ulrich von Hutten expressed his personal optimism and his hope for the humanist cause: "O seculum! O literae! Iuvat vivere, etsi quiescere nondum iuvat, Bilibalde. Vigent studia, florent ingenia" (Oh century! Oh letters! It is a joy to be alive. It is not a time to keep quiet, Willibald. Studies thrive and minds flourish). Hutten cited the achievements of his humanist friends–Desiderius Erasmus, Johannes Oekolampadius, Guillaume Budé, Jacques Lefèvre d'Étaples, Guillaume Cop, and Joannes Ruellius –as evidence for the impending victory over their Scholastic opponents. Hutten's own accomplishments as a humanist had been recognized the previous year, when he was crowned poet laureate of the empire. But Hutten was shifting his literary efforts from humanism to the promotion of Martin Luther's religious reform. In April 1519 Erasmus sent Hutten a cautionary letter, praising his courageous spirit and his genius as a writer but also advising that he keep himself safe for the Muses. Rejecting Erasmus's plea for circumspection and moderation, Hutten soon became a leading propagandist for the evangelical cause. These events suggest that Hutten's significance as a German literary figure can be judged primarily in terms of his contributions to humanism and to the Reformation, to poetics and to religious polemic, during the early sixteenth century.

Hutten was born on 21 April 1488 in the castle of Steckelberg, near Fulda on the border of Franconia and Hesse. He was the descendant of a large clan of Franconian knights. His father, also named Ulrich, and his mother, Ottilie, née von Eberstein, were members of the minor nobility, a class that was experiencing serious economic and political decline by the late fifteenth century. His pious parents intended their son for the religious life, sending him at the age of eleven to the monastic school in Fulda. Hutten, however, left the school in 1505, explaining in later years that he believed that he could better serve God and the world through another calling. Thus, at the age of seventeen, without the blessing of his family and nearly destitute, Hutten began his wanderings from university to university.

As an adult Hutten would see himself primarily as a German knight, in quest of the truth and a defender of causes. But he was never provided the formal training of a knight and lacked the military skills needed for success on the battlefield. He was further hampered by a small physique: his body was exhumed in the twentieth century and found to have been five feet, one inch in height. During his university years he contracted syphilis, which weakened him physically and emotionally and would contribute to his death at the age of thirty-five. Although Hutten often threatened to wield his knight's sword, in practice he used his pen and the printing press in waging his battles.

Hutten studied briefly at the Universities of Cologne and Erfurt and received a B.A. from the University of Frankfurt an der Oder in 1507. It was at Erfurt in 1506 that he first came into contact with Mutianus Rufus (Konrad Muth), whose home in nearby Gotha was a meeting place for some of the younger German humanists. They included Eobanus Hessus and Crotus Rubeanus (Johannes Jäger), with whom Hutten would maintain lifelong friendships. These humanists revived ancient literary forms, including poetry and satire, as a means of attacking Scholasticism and corruption in the church. There is no evidence that Hutten was influenced by the Neoplatonic theism, derived from the Italians Marsilio Ficino and Pico della Mirandola, that so interested Mutianus. Hutten was never concerned with issues of speculative philosophy; rather, it was the wandering humanist poet Johannes Rhegius Aesticampianus who had the greatest impact on him during these early years. Also important were Aesticampianus's lectures on Tacitus's *Germania*, which Ulrich attended at Leipzig in 1508. Aesticampianus also encouraged Hutten's literary efforts by including several of the younger man's poems in his own publications. Hutten's first published writings were short introductory poems, or elegies, composed according to rules that he outlines in one of his earliest complete works, *De Arte Versificandi* (On the Art of Poetry, 1511). The *De Arte Versificandi* would be reprinted sixty-six times before 1560 and was used as a textbook throughout Europe.

Hutten's difficulties and disappointments during his student years, along with his humanistic interests, are reflected in several of his earliest publications. In his poem *Vir bonus* (The Good Man), composed between 1506 and 1507 and published in 1513, he identifies ethical principles, taken largely from ancient Greek and Roman authors, that contribute to a morally correct life. Between 1507 and 1509 he composed a longer poem, *Nemo* (Nobody, 1510); a revised version, ΟΥΤΙΣ *Nemo,* was completed in 1515 and published in 1518. *Nemo* is one of Hutten's most important works because of its highly autobiographical orientation. In the first version Hutten adopts the persona of a prodigal son, alone and destitute, and identifies himself with Homer's hero Odysseus. The later version is a more complex mock encomium, in the manner of Erasmus's *Moriae encomium* (1511; translated as *The Praise of Folie,* 1549). Nemo becomes both narrator and main figure, expanding the linguistic possibilities for self-irony and expressing Hutten's yearning for a sense of identity.

Hutten enrolled at the University of Greifswald in the fall of 1510 and found lodging with the burgermeister, Wedeg Lötz, and his lawyer son, Henning. In December, Hutten moved out after a quarrel with his landlords; as he made his way across the frozen landscape he was assaulted and robbed by servants of the Lötzes. After making his way to Rostock, where students from the university provided him a place to stay, the embittered Hutten composed *Equestris ordinis poetae in Vuedegum Loetz Consulem Gripesualdensem im Pomerania et filium eius Hennigum Vtr: Juris doctorem Querelarum libri duo pro insigni quadam iniuria sibi ab illis facta* (Two Books of Complaints, by a Knight-Poet, in Return for Certain Injustices Brought on by Wedeg Lötz, a Burgermeister of Greifswald in Pomerania, and His Son Henning, a Doctor of Law, 1510) as a series of elegies dedicated to his humanist friends. The poems include attacks on the Lötzes, mocking their middle-class pretensions and greed and ridiculing Henning's legal profession. In the second book Hutten dedicates a poem to the German poets in which he describes a fictional journey through the towns and cities of the empire and mentions fifty poets by name; he was attempting to create the myth of a unified humanist movement in Germany. The young Hutten identified himself closely with the humanists: he had demonstrated his ability to challenge enemies with his pen.

Rejecting his family's advice that he either return to the monastery or pursue a degree in law, in 1511 Hutten traveled to Vienna. There he was welcomed by the humanist circle originally organized by Conrad Celtis. In 1512 he published a book of poems, *Ad divum Maximilianum Caesa. Aug. F. P. bello in Venetos euntem, Vlrici Hutteni Equitis, Exhortatio* (Exhortation by the Knight Ulrich Hutten to the Emperor Maximilian to Continue the War against Venice). The subjects and treatment of these poems indicate the impact of the cultural and political views of such patriotic humanists as Celtis, Aesticampianus, and Heinrich Bebel. In one of the poems, "Quod ab illa antiquitus Germanorum claritudine nondum degeneraverint nostrates" (Why the Germans Are Not Degenerate in Comparison with Former Times), Hutten maintained that Germany was entering a period of peaceful prosperity following a period of internal warfare and political strife. Evidence of the cultural renewal could be seen in the flourishing arts and scholarship, as well as in the inventions of gunpowder and printing. The imperial troops led by Maximilian were victorious on the battlefield and were feared by both the Turks and the French; Hutten saw his own knightly class playing a leading role in the new imperium, and his humanism took a more patriotic and nationalist turn. Realizing that his chances for an appointment at court depended on further studies, he traveled across the Alps to Italy in 1512.

Shortly after Hutten began his studies of Roman law at the University of Pavia there was a siege

Full-page woodcut of the Vir bonus, *from Hutten's work with that title*

of the city, during which he was locked in his room by the French soldiers because of his loyalty to the emperor. Sick and fearing for his life, Hutten wrote his own epitaph. He escaped through bribery and traveled to Bologna, but his academic pursuits there were thwarted by illness and by poverty, which forced him to join Maximilian's army. During the summer and fall of 1513 he took part in military campaigns in northern Italy. During this time he composed several short poems that he dedicated to Maximilian; they would be published in a revised edition of *Ad divum Maximilianum Caesa. Aug. F. P. bello in Venetos euntem, Vlrici Hutteni Equitis, Exhortatio*, titled *Exhortatorium* (Exhortation), in 1519. His approach in these epigrams is that of a war correspondent, and his support for Maximilian and the imperial effort is clearly evident. Hutten also wrote several poems depicting Julius II, the warrior pope whom he criticized for involvement in Italian politics, as the Antichrist. In February 1514 he returned to Germany with a contingent of German troops, destitute and continuing to search for his identity.

Rejected by his father, Hutten was supported by two patrons in Mainz: a relative, Frowin von Hutten; and Eitelwolf von Stein. Both men were educated knights who supported the humanist cause. Stein accepted a post at the court of Albert of Brandenburg, who was soon to be installed as archbishop-elector. Hutten was hopeful that Albert, a patron of artists and men of letters, would become a leader of the humanist effort among the German princes. It was at Eitelwolf's suggestion that Hutten composed a *Panegyricus* (Panegyric, 1515) in honor of Albert's accession to the see of Mainz, a position that also made him primate of the German bishops and chancellor of the empire. In thirteen hundred Latin hexameters Hutten eulogizes his subject with historical references and rhetorical flourishes; the poem is a model of courtly verse. In recognition of this accomplishment Albert paid Hutten the substantial sum of two hundred gulden, which was intended to provide financial support for continued legal studies in Italy; he was promised a position at Albert's court on the completion of those studies. The poet had little interest, however, in either Roman law or the life of a courtier. Before returning to Italy, Hutten took up two causes that redirected his literary energies.

First, he played a leading role in defending the humanist Johann Reuchlin, who wanted to preserve Hebrew books for scholarly purposes, against the attacks of Johann Pfefferkorn, a Jew who had converted to Christianity, and the Scholastic theologians who called for the destruction of the books. Among Reuchlin's major opponents were the Dominican inquisitor Jacob Hoogstraten, Conrad Köllin, Arnold Tongern, and the conservative arts professor Ortwin Gratius, all at the University of Cologne. Reuchlin's supporters included Erasmus, Crotus and other humanists in the circle of Mutianus, Hermannus Buschius, and the Cologne patrician Hermann von Neuenahr. In March 1514 Reuchlin had published *Clarorum virorum epistolae* (Letters of Famous Men), a collection of letters written in his support. That same month George, count Palatine and bishop of Speyer, who had been asked to adjudicate the case, had ruled in favor of Reuchlin. So, in August, when Hutten, Reuchlin, and Buschius had a festive meeting with Erasmus, who had stopped over in Mainz on his way to Basel, there was reason for optimism among the humanists.

But Reuchlin's cause still needed literary defense, and Hutten conspired with Buschius, Crotus, and others in the production of two satires dealing with the affair: *Epistolae obscurorum virorum* (Letters of Obscure Men, 1516; translated, 1909) and *Triumphus Doc. Reuchlini* (Triumph of Reuchlin, 1518). Hutten's exact role in these projects is not known, since they were planned secretly and published anonymously. Through textual analysis and other evidence, scholars have determined that Hutten wrote the first letter, along with an appendix of seven letters, in the first edition of *Epistolae obscurorum virorum;* it is generally agreed that he was also responsible for most of the letters in the second series, which appeared in an enlarged edition of the work in 1517. Most of his letters were written during his second trip to Italy. All of them are mimic satire, a literary style that allowed Reuchlin's opponents to mock themselves with their own words. In letter after letter the obscurantist correspondents reveal their academic pretensions, intellectual shallowness, and moral corruption. Whereas most of the letters in the first series have completely fictional characters, except for the addressee, Gratius, Hutten introduced the names of actual persons, including Erasmus, into the second series. The satire of the later letters is more strident and confrontational, creating the illusion of opposing camps of humanists and Scholastics. The work was reprinted many times and is regarded as the first modern satire in Germany.

The first draft of *Triumphus Doc. Reuchlini,* directed mainly at Hoogstraten, may have been written by Buschius, but Hutten is generally considered the author of the longer final version. This edition included a large foldout woodcut, "Reuchlin's Triumph," with the knight Hutten leading a cart carrying Reuchlin. Another work expressing Hutten's support of Reuchlin, *Epistola ad illustrem virum Hermannum de Neuenar* (Letter to Count Hermann von Neuenahr), also appeared in 1518.

Hutten saw the Reuchlin case as an opportunity to promote the cultural and political cause of humanism in Germany by attacking and castigating the Scholastic theologians and their defenders. His defense of Reuchlin did not mean, however, that Hutten approved of Jews or of Judaism. In the fall of 1514, at the same time he was conspiring with Crotus, Buschius, and the other humanists, his lurid account of the burning of another Johann Pfefferkorn in Halle was published in Mainz.

In the spring of 1515, while attempting to cure his syphilis at the baths in Ems in preparation for his journey to Italy, Hutten received word of two deaths. His patron Stein had died of natural causes, and his cousin, Hans von Hutten, had been brutally murdered by Duke Ulrich of Württemberg because of the duke's desire for Hans's young, attractive wife. The large Hutten clan demanded justice, and Ulrich was happy to lend his support to the family cause. His major literary contribution to the dispute was *Phalarismus* (Tyranny in the Manner of Phalaris), a dialogue that he completed in Italy and published in Mainz in 1517. It is Hutten's first use of the dialogue form, a style that he borrowed from the Greek author Lucian. In his dialogue of the dead, Hutten identifies Duke Ulrich with Phalaris, the ancient tyrant of Agrigent. In a series of works that were collected as *Deploratio* (Lament, 1519) Hutten continued to call on the German nobles, especially the princes, to bring justice to the murderous duke.

In October 1515 Hutten began his second journey to Italy to study law. As during the first trip, his academic pursuits were thwarted by a series of misadventures. He reached Rome in the spring of 1516, and letters provided by Erasmus gave him entrée into humanist circles. A worsening of his syphilis during the summer led him to travel to Viterbo for a cure. At an inn there he got into an altercation with five Frenchmen, one of whom was killed. Hutten later claimed that the Frenchmen had insulted the emperor and that he was defending the national honor; it is possible that this story of patriotic fervor was invented to lend nobility to what was essentially a barroom brawl. In any case, the incident forced him to leave Rome. He enrolled again at the University of Bologna, where he became a leader of the German students. When a violent feud broke out between the German and Lombard student groups, he was compelled to leave the city. He traveled to Ferrara and then to Venice, where two cousins tried to persuade him to join them on a pilgrimage to the Holy Land; but, with introductions from Erasmus, he had been welcomed by the humanists in Venice and was embarrassed to go on the pilgrimage. He returned to Germany in the summer of 1517 without a law degree.

Despite his problems, Hutten had continued his literary activities in Italy. He had maintained his support of the Reuchlinist cause, completing most of his letters for *Epistolae obscurorum virorum;* and he had revised *Phalarismus.* He had also become more intensely interested in promoting German nationalism and attacking the papacy. There is evidence that he renewed his study of Tacitus's *Annals* while in Italy, a study that resulted in his dialogue *Arminius*, which would be published posthumously in 1529. Tacitus's favorable treatment of the German hero Arminius against the declining and corrupted forces of Rome led Hutten to promote Arminius as a model for German cultural and political renewal; his work marked the beginning of the Arminius cult in Germany. While visiting Johannes Cochlaeus in June 1517 Hutten found a copy of Lorenzo Valla's work proving that the Donation of Constantine, granting temporal power to the papacy, was a forgery. After returning to Germany, Hutten wrote a preface to Valla's work, dedicating it sarcastically to Pope Leo X, and added critical commentaries on the fraudulent Donation. The work was printed in late 1519 or early 1520 as *De donatione Constantini quid ueri habeat, eruditorum quorundam iudicium, ut in uersa pagella uidebis* (translated as *A treatyse of the donation or gyfte and endowment of possessyons, gyuen and graunted unto Siluester, pope of Rhome, by Constantyne, emperour of Rome,* circa 1534).

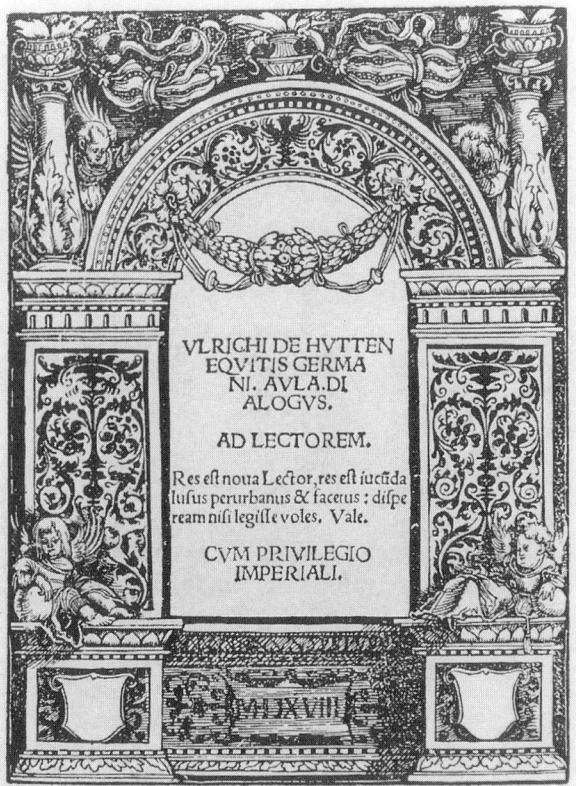

Title page for Hutten's dialogue Aula, *in which he satirizes courtly life*

Hutten was met favorably on his return to Germany. He stayed initially with the humanist Conrad Peutinger, the city secretary of Augsburg. Peutinger procured an audience for Hutten with the aging Emperor Maximilian, and on 12 July 1517 Maximilian crowned Hutten poet laureate. Hutten soon received the promised position of counselor at the court of Archbishop Albert in Mainz, and in December he was sent on a diplomatic mission to ratify a treaty between the elector and the French king,

Title page for Hutten's collection of five of his dialogues (courtesy of the Lilly Library, Indiana University)

Francis I. In Paris he met the leading French humanists, including Budé and Lefèvre d'Étaples, thereby broadening his humanist contacts. Life at court did not agree with Hutten, however, and he satirized the pretensions and shallowness of the courtiers in his dialogue *Aula* (Courtly Life, 1518). The main character in the dialogue is Misaulus (Court Hater), obviously a reference to the author. Hutten wrote *Aula,* perhaps as an amusement, in August 1518 while attending the Diet of Augsburg.

The diet, which met from July to September, renewed Hutten's interest in imperial reform. In the months preceding the diet he wrote an *Exhortatoria* (Exhortation, 1518) that he intended to deliver as a speech during the deliberations at Augsburg. As a supporter of Maximilian's policy, he challenged the German princes to engage in a war against the Turks. He strenuously objected, however, to the Pope's intention of levying a tax on the Germans as a means of financing the crusade; Hutten saw the crusade as a way of promoting imperial power, and thereby the German national cause, over the authority of Rome. During the proceedings Hutten, who was in the entourage of Duke Albert, observed with great interest the role of the papal legate, Cardinal Cajetan (Thomas de Vio). As he was about to leave Augsburg in November, Hutten directed a frontal attack, titled *Febris* (Fever, 1519), against Cajetan, along with the latter's courtiers, the nobility, and the merchants, for their luxurious lifestyles. For Hutten, the cardinal symbolized the corruption of the Roman court, a corruption that threatened not only German freedom but also the effectiveness of imperial leadership. Hutten wished a fever on Cajetan because he had come to take the Germans' gold. No doubt Hutten had in mind the fever that was a symptom of his own syphilitic condition.

Hutten's syphilis had grown progressively worse. It produced severe swelling and bone deformation in his left ankle, which, in turn, caused major muscle deterioration in his left leg; he was also plagued with ruptured lesions and periodic fevers. By 1518 he was in the tertiary stage of the disease. Before leaving Augsburg he had undergone a month-long treatment for the illness in which he had been confined to a room and placed on a rigid diet; his only liquid was a brew made from the dried wood of the guaiac tree, imported from the Caribbean island of Santo Domingo. The purpose of the drink was to cause sweating and a general purging of the body. Hutten was so pleased with the results that he wrote an account of the disease and the cure, *De Guaiaci medicina et morbo gallico liber unus* (A Book on the Guaiac Cure and the French Disease, 1519; translated as *Of the wood called guaiacum, that healeth the Fr[ench]e Poc[kes] and also helped the goute in the feete, the stoone, the palsey, lepree, dropsy, fallynge evyll, and other dyseases,* 1536). The book traces the entry of syphilis into Europe, describes its symptoms, and details the treatment Hutten underwent in Augsburg. It was reprinted many times in Latin and was translated into German by Thomas Murner in 1519, as well as into English and French.

On his return to Mainz, Hutten sent Erasmus copies of *Febris* and *Phalarismus*. His treatment in Augsburg had left him feeling well enough to seek a bride; his overtures to Arnold von Glauberg for the hand of Glauberg's daughter, however, proved fruitless. Hutten's more optimistic attitude is reflected in several letters to Pirckheimer during these months, conveying his frustrations with the courtly life and his desire for more-active pursuits. Pirckheimer encouraged Hutten to renew his commitment to the humanist cause.

Taking advantage of the political vacuum created by the death of Emperor Maximilian in January 1519, Duke Ulrich of Württemberg had occupied the imperial city of Reutlingen. Still outraged by the duke's killing of his cousin, Hutten joined the army of the Swabian League that battled Ulrich in March and April. During the war Hutten became close friends with his cousin, Franz von Sickingen, the most powerful and influential of the imperial knights. On 6 April the League took Stuttgart, allowing Hutten and Sickingen to visit Reuchlin. Both knights pledged to protect the embattled scholar. On his return to Mainz, Hutten was instructed by Elector Albert to send a silver-gilt cup as a present to Erasmus. In a gesture of appreciation, Erasmus addressed to Hutten his famous letter of 23 July 1519 about Thomas More. That summer Hutten attended the election in Frankfurt am Main at which Charles of Hapsburg became the new emperor. Hutten's commission at the court of Elector Albert came to an end at this time, although he continued to receive a pension.

Believing that Germany's future under renewed imperial leadership depended on the military defeat of the Roman Catholic Church—a view that was shared by Sickingen—Hutten traveled to Brussels to gain the approval and assistance of Archduke Ferdinand for his plan to declare war on the Vatican. On the way he met with Erasmus in Louvain; Erasmus objected to Hutten's impractical proposal but provided him with a letter of introduction to Ferdinand. The archduke found the plan ludicrous and dangerous. Hutten was forced to flee to Steckelberg and then to Sickingen's castle, the Ebernburg. Pope Leo X instructed Elector Albert to investigate the case and send Hutten to Rome for prosecution for promoting a military defeat of the Roman Church; even Hutten's Mainz printer, Johann Schöffer, was arrested. In the meantime Hutten printed, without authorization, a letter that Erasmus had sent to Albert on 19 October 1519 showing sympathy for Luther. Erasmus's anger over Hutten's action placed further strains on their relationship.

Hutten's collection *Deploratio* (Lament), which includes his dialogue *Phalarismus* and five orations against Duke Ulrich, was published in September 1519. That fall he discovered an eleventh-century manuscript in the Fulda library, which he edited and published the next year as *De unitate ecclesiae conservanda, et schismate* (On Schism and Preserving the Unity of the Church). His dedicatory preface called on Archduke Ferdinand and the newly elected emperor to support his plan for freeing Germany from the Roman yoke. He published a similar manuscript, *De schismate extinguendo* (On Ending the Schism), at about the same time. Both of these historical documents illustrated, for Hutten, the strong imperial leadership against the Roman popes during the late-medieval schism in the church. An important collection, *Dialogi* (Dialogues), which included "Fortuna" (Fortune), "Febris prima" (Fever I), "Febris secunda" (Fever II), "Trias Romana" (Roman Trinity), and "Inspicientes" (Observers), also appeared in early 1520. In "Fortuna," the most philosophical and autobiographical of the dialogues, Hutten discusses the whims of fortune and one's ability to direct the course of one's life. "Febris prima" and "Inspicientes" attack Cajetan. In "Febris secunda" Hutten criticizes the degenerate and immoral lifestyles of the clergy, proposing sarcastically that this new fever could be cured by providing them with concubines. "Trias Romana," probably the most creative and interesting of his dialogues, satirizes the religious establishment by constantly repeating the metaphor of the Trinity. In Rome, for example, there are always three activities under way: the salvation of souls, the reconstruction of churches, and the crusade against the Turks. The pilgrim to Rome comes away with three things: biased knowledge, a bad stomach, and an empty purse. German freedom could be restored only by declaring war against the Pope and his supporters.

During the next several years Hutten devoted his political and literary energies almost entirely to the defeat of the Catholic Church and the victory of Luther. Although he had little direct contact with the Reformer and little understanding of or interest in Luther's theology, Hutten became one of Luther's most ardent supporters. He saw Luther's proposals as he had seen Reuchlin's case earlier: as a political issue that could be used to advance the cause of German freedom. Early in 1520, as Luther was coming under increasing censure from Rome, Hutten and Sickingen pledged their personal support to the Reformer. Hutten's stand for evangelical reform was made public with the appearance in June of that year of *Epistola Ulrichi de Hutten Equitis, ad D. Martinum Lutherum Theologum. Wuittembergae* (Letter of Ulrich Hutten, Knight, to Doctor Martin Luther, Theologian at Wittenberg). Hutten's actions were reported to the Roman curia by Johann Eck and other Catholic partisans. When the papal legate Jerome Aleander was sent to Germany in the summer to circulate the ban against Luther, he was also authorized to burn Hutten's "Tria Romana" and similar writings. Hutten interpreted this response as proof of Rome's intent to undermine German liberty.

From the fall of 1520 through 1522 Hutten confined himself mainly to the Ebernburg and other castles under Sickingen's control. Along with Sickingen and Hartmut von Cronburg, Hutten served as one of the most important lay propagandists during the early Reformation. Assisted by Martin Bucer, he

Title page for the German version of Hutten's Dialogi, *translated by the author and Martin Bucer*

translated his Latin *Dialogi* into the vernacular *Gespräch büchlin* (A Pamphlet of Dialogues, 1521) to reach a wider audience. In September Hutten addressed a series of petitions, titled "Conquestiones" (Complaints), to Emperor Charles, to the German princes and the estates, to Elector Albert, and to Frederick the Wise, elector of Saxony, asking for their support in his legal case with Rome. The petitions were collected and published in Latin in 1520 and were translated, mostly by Bucer, as *In dißem Buchlin findet man Hern Wlrichs von Hutten Über und gegen vorgwaltigung des Bapsts, unnd der Romanisten, klagschrifft an Keyserliche maiestat* (Writings of Complaint to the Emperor: One Finds in This Little Book Ulrich von Hutten's "Over and Against the Power of the Pope and the Romanists," 1520). The translations are rather literal, with clauses following one another as in the Latin. In addition, Hutten wrote critical glosses for the papal bull, *Exsurge domine,* that had been issued against Luther in June; the texts of the bull and the glosses were published as *Bulla Decimi Leonis, contra errores Martini Lutheri* (The Bull of Leo X against the Errors of Martin Luther). In November, Hutten observed a public burning of Luther's books in Cologne orchestrated by the papal legate Aleander; he responded with a short poem, *In incendium Lutherianum Exclamatio* (A Protest against the Burning of Luther's Books, 1521). It was followed quickly by a similar work, *Ein Klag über den Luterischen Brandt zu Mentz* (A Complaint against the Lutheran Bonfire at Mainz, 1521), after another public burning.

Hutten wrote several important pamphlets in 1520. They include his first pamphlet written only in German, *Clag und vormanung gegen dem übermaessigen vnchristlichen gewalt des Bapsts zu Rom und der vngeistlichen geistlichen* (Complaint and Warning Against the Presumptious Unchristian Power of the Pope in Rome and the Unspiritual Spiritual Estate, 1520). In this 1,578-line poem Hutten says that he wants to tell the *Teutschen* (German people) the *Warheit* (truth). The "complaint" is about Hutten's personal difficulties with the church; the "warning" is a call for a general uprising against the Pope and his immoral courtiers, who are fleecing the innocent Germans. Since November 1520 Hutten had also been working on a new collection of Latin dialogues; it appeared in 1521 as *Dialogi Huttenici novi* (New Dialogues by Hutten). "Bulla vel Bullicida" (Bull or Bull Killer) is an obvious play on the bull *Exsurge domine* against Luther: Sickingen will lead the Germans in a struggle against the papal bull killers. In "Monitor primus" (Admonisher I) Erasmus tells Luther that he, Erasmus, is going to Rome to become a cardinal because the political conditions have become too dangerous in the North; in "Monitor secundus" (Admonisher II) Sickingen wins over an admonisher for his war to reform the empire and the church. Finally, in "Praedones" (Robbers) Sickingen leads the battle against the true robbers of Germany: the monks, priests, and courtiers; Hutten calls on the burghers of the German towns to support Sickingen and the knights in this conflict. These themes are repeated in a vernacular pamphlet, *Enndtschüldigung Ulrichs von Hutten Wyder etlicher unwarhafftiger außgeben von ym als solt er wider alle geystlicheit und priesterschafft sein mit erklaerung etlicher seiner geschrifften* (Ulrich von Hutten's Apology Against Some False Reports as if He Was Against All Clergy and Priests, with an Explanation of Some of His Works, 1521). In another vernacular pamphlet, *Anzoeig Wie allwegen sich die Roemischen Bischoeff od' Baepst gegen den teütschen Kayßeren gehalten haben uff die kürtzst uß Chronicken und Historien gezogen K. maiestaet fürzubringen* (Disclosure How the Roman Bishops or Popes Have Always Behaved toward the German Emperors, Briefly Extracted from Chronicles and Histories, Done [for the Benefit of] the Imperial Majesty, 1521), Hutten informs the Germans about how the popes had opposed the emperors, from the time of Otto I. This pamphlet would be reprinted ten times by 1560.

Hutten did not attend the Diet of Worms in early 1521, but he quickly responded to the diet's condemnation of and imperial ban against Luther. In his *Invectivae* (Invectives, 1521) Hutten attacked the two papal representatives at the diet, Aleander and Marinus Caracciolus. In a short poem, *Ain new Lied* (A New Song, 1521), which later commentators have described as the most significant German verse written between the time of Walther von der Vogelweide and that of Johann Wolfgang von Goethe, Hutten declares his personal war against the Catholic clergy. At about this same time Hutten was portrayed in a large woodcut attached to the anonymous *Triumphus veritatis* (Triumph of Truth, 1524) as a hero leading a captured band of cardinals, bishops, canons, monks, and theologians. In real life, however, Hutten's *Pfaffenkrieg* (war against the clergy) was quixotic. He never actually wielded his sword; his only military success against the Romanists was an extortion of two thousand gulden from the Strasbourg Carthusians.

Hutten saw his immediate future as bound up with that of his friend Sickingen. Despite the new imperial policy opposing Luther, Sickingen remained loyal to Charles V and fought with him in the war against France. Following a military defeat Sickingen returned to Germany and, unable to pay his troops, resigned his imperial commission. In September, Sickingen retired to the Ebernburg, where he led a small group of knights, including Hutten, in following the reform preached by Luther. This was only the third such group in Germany; Hutten referred to it as the "Asylum of Justice." These knights were especially active in producing pamphlets as religious propaganda for the Lutheran cause. Hutten's contributions to this effort in 1522 included *Vormanung an die freien und reich Stette teutscher nation* (Warning to the Free and Imperial Cities of the German Nation) and *Ein demütige ermanung an ein gemeyne statt Wormbß* (A Humble Exhortation to the Entire City of Worms), which called on the nobles and towns to oppose the German princes. These tracts contributed to the provocation of the Knights' Revolt of 1522-1523, in which, in August 1522, Sickingen's knights attacked the archbishop of Trier. Hutten was too ill to participate in these battles. The united forces of the princes repulsed Sickingen, capturing his men and his castles, and Sickingen was killed.

Hutten fled the Ebernburg in November and went to Basel, a safe haven in Switzerland, where Erasmus was in residence. His relationship with the famous humanist, however, had seriously deterio-

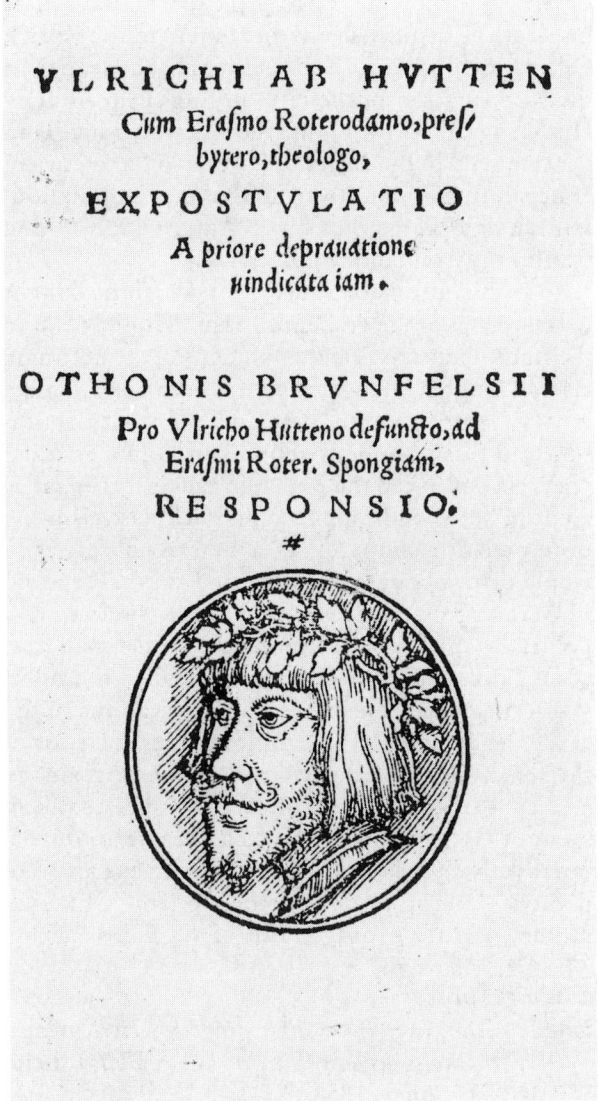

Title page for Hutten's attack on Desiderius Erasmus for failing to support the Reformation (courtesy of the Lilly Library, Indiana University)

rated. He was granted temporary asylum by the city council, but Erasmus refused to see him. He was expelled from the city in January and traveled to Mühlhausen, in Alsace, where he attacked Erasmus in *Ulrichi ab Hutten cum Erasmo Roterodamo, Presbytero, Theologo, Expostulatio* (translated as "Expostulation of Ulrich von Hutten with Erasmus of Rotterdam, Priest and Theologian," 1977). While recognizing his old friend's positive qualities, Hutten criticized Erasmus for remaining neutral in the Lutheran dispute. Erasmus's refusal to show public support for the Reformer was, in Hutten's view, a betrayal of Germany and of Hutten himself. Erasmus's response, *Spongia* (Sponge), accused Hutten of betraying his own humanist cause. Hutten never saw

Spongia, which appeared in print several days after his death. Erasmus also wrote letters to the Zurich City Council and to Ulrich Zwingli, the leader of the Reformation in the city, urging them to deny Hutten's request for refuge there. Zwingli had Hutten removed to the island of Ufenau in Lake Zurich, concealing his identity from the local population. Hutten died of syphilis on 29 August 1523. A pen was his only remaining possession.

In his quest for causes, for which he fought with great courage and enthusiasm, Hutten reflects the traditional biases and limitations of the declining class of knights into which he had been born. Unlike most knights, however, he had a university education and was a committed humanist and a talented poet. He embraced the Reuchlin cause, treating it as a battle between humanism and Scholasticism; he promoted the emperor as a new Arminius who would bring about the political and cultural renewal of Germany; and he supported Luther's reform as a political war against the Romanists for German freedom. In the end, however, Hutten failed to understand the deeper meanings and implications of the causes he defended. His significance lies in his use of the pen, rather than the sword, as a humanist author and as a religious pamphleteer. For his advancement of German liberty Hutten became an important symbol for later German nationalists and Romantics—among them Goethe, Johann Gottfried Herder, and the propagandists of the Third Reich.

Bibliographies:

Eduard Böcking, *Index bibliographicvs Hvttenianvs; Verzeichniss der schriften Ulrichs von Hutten* (Leipzig: Teubner, 1858);

Josef Benzing, *Ulrich von Hutten und seine Drucker: Eine Bibliographie der Schriften Huttens im 16. Jahrhundert* (Wiesbaden: Harrassowitz, 1956);

Helmut Spelsberg, "Veroffentlichungen Ulrichs von Hutten," in *Ulrich von Hutten: Ritter, Humanist, Publizist 1488–1523; Katalog zur Ausstellung des Landes Hessen anläßlich des 500. Geburtstages,* edited by Peter Laub (Kassel: Hessischer Museumsverband, 1988), pp. 412–441.

Biographies:

David Friedrich Strauß, *Ulrich von Hutten,* 3 volumes (Leipzig: Brockhaus, 1858–1860); translated by Jane Sturge as *Ulrich von Hutten: His Life and Times* (London: Daldy, Isbister, 1874);

Hajo Holborn, *Ulrich von Hutten and the German Reformation,* translated by Roland H. Bainton (New Haven: Yale University Press, 1937);

Heinrich Grimm, *Ulrich von Hutten: Wille und Schicksal* (Göttingen: Musterschmidt, 1971);

Eckhard Bernstein, *Ulrich von Hutten* (Reinbek bei Hamburg: Rowohlt, 1988).

References:

Thomas G. Benedek, "The Influence of Ulrich von Hutten's Medical Descriptions and Metaphorical Use of Medicine," *Bulletin of the History of Medicine,* 66 (1992): 355–375;

Eckhard Bernstein, "Creating Humanist Myths: Two Poems by Ulrich von Hutten," in *Acta Conventus Neo-Latini Torontonensis,* edited by Alexander Dalzell and others (Binghamton, N.Y.: Medieval & Renaissance Texts and Studies, 1991), pp. 249–260;

Thomas W. Best, *The Humanist Ulrich von Hutten: A Reappraisal of His Humor* (Chapel Hill: University of North Carolina Press, 1969);

Miriam Usher Chrisman, *Conflicting Visions of Reform: German Lay Propaganda Pamphlets, 1519–1530* (Atlantic Highlands, N.J.: Humanities Press, 1996), pp. 65–89;

Robert Herndon Fife, "Ulrich von Hutten as a Literary Problem," *Germanic Review,* 23 (1948): 18–29;

Heinrich Grimm, *Ulrichs von Hutten Lehrjahre an der Universität Frankfurt und seine Jugenddichtungen* (Frankfurt an der Oder: Trowitzsch, 1938);

Wolfgang Hardtwig, "Ulrich von Hutten: Überlegungen zum Verhältnis von Individuum, Stand und Nation in der Reformationszeit," *Geschichte in Wissenschaft und Unterricht,* 35 (1984): 191–206;

Volker Honemann, "Der deutsche Lukian: Die volkssprachigen Dialoge Ulrichs von Hutten," *Pirckheimer-Jahrbuch,* 4 (1988): 37–55;

Lewis Jillings, "The Aggression of the Cured Syphilitic: Ulrich von Hutten's Projection of His Disease as Metaphor," *German Quarterly,* 68 (1995): 1–18;

Jillings, "Ulrich von Hutten's Self-Stylisation as Odysseus: The Conservative Use of Myth," *Colloquia Germanica,* 23 (1993): 93–107;

Werner Kaegi, "Hutten und Erasmus: Ihre Freundschaft und ihr Streit," *Historische Vierteljahrsschrift,* 22 (1924–1925): 200–278, 461–514;

Paul Kalkoff, *Ulrich von Hutten und die Reformation* (Leipzig: Verein für Reformationsgeschichte, 1920);

Barbara Könneker, "Ulrich von Hutten," in *Contemporaries of Erasmus,* 3 volumes, edited by Peter G. Bietenholz (Toronto: University of Toronto Press, 1985–1987), II: 216–220;

Könneker, "Vom Poeta Laureatus zum Propagandisten: Die Entwicklung Huttens als Schriftsteller in seinen Dialogen von 1518 bis 1521," in *L'Humanisme Allemand (1480-1540): XVIIIe Colloque International de Tours*, edited by Joël Lefèbvre and Jean-Claude Margolin (Munich: Fink / Paris: Vrin, 1979), pp. 303-319;

Wilhelm Kreutz, *Die Deutschen und Ulrich von Hutten: Rezeption von Autor und Werk seit dem 16. Jahrhundert* (Munich: Fink, 1984);

Wilhelm Kühlmann, "Edelmann-Höfling-Humanist: Zur Behandlung epochaler Rollenprobleme in Ulrich von Huttens Dialog 'Aula' und in seinem Brief an Willibald Pirckheimer," in *Höfischer Humanismus,* edited by August Buck (Weinheim: VCH Acta Humaniora, 1989), pp. 161-182;

Peter Laub, ed., *Ulrich von Hutten–Ritter, Humanist, Publizist 1488-1523: Katalog zur Ausstellung des Landes Hessen anläßlich des 500. Geburtstages* (Kassel: Hessischer Museumsverband, 1988);

Jean-Claude Margolin, "Le *Nemo* d'Ulrich von Hutten: Crise du langage, crise de conscience, crise de société?," in *Virtus et Fortuna: Zur Deutschen Literatur zwischen 1400 und 1720,* edited by Joseph P. Strelka and Jörg Jungmayr (Bern, Frankfurt am Main & New York: Peter Lang, 1983), pp. 118-163;

James V. Mehl, "Characterizations of the 'Obscure Men' of Cologne: A Study in Pre-Reformation Collective Authorship," in *The Rhetorics of Lifewriting in Early Modern Europe: Forms of Biography from Cassandra Fedele to Louis XIV,* edited by Thomas F. Mayer and D. R. Woolf (Ann Arbor: University of Michigan Press, 1995), pp. 163-185;

C. A. Melin, " 'Ich sprich, sie habents nimmer Fug': Propaganda and Poetry in Ulrich von Hutten's *Klag und Vormahnung*," *Modern Language Studies,* 15 (1985): 50-59;

Manfred Meyer, "Hutten und Luther," in *450 Jahre Reformation,* edited by Leo Stern and Max Steinmetz (Berlin: VEB Deutscher Verlag der Wissenschaften, 1967), pp. 102-117;

James H. Overfield, *Humanism and Scholasticism in Late Medieval Germany* (Princeton: Princeton University Press, 1984), pp. 247-297;

Michael Peschke, *Ulrich von Hutten (1488-1523) als Kranker und als medizinischer Schriftsteller* (Cologne: Forschungsstelle des Instituts für die Geschichte der Medizin, 1985);

Volker Press, "Ulrich von Hutten, Reichsritter und Humanist 1488-1523," *Nassauische Annalen,* 85 (1974): 71-86;

Helmut Scheuer, "Ulrich von Hutten: Kaisertum und deutsche Nation," *Daphnis,* 2 (1973): 133-157;

Ernst Schubert, "Ulrich von Hutten (1488-1523)," *Fränkische Lebensbilder,* 9 (1980): 93-123;

Lewis W. Spitz, *The Religious Renaissance of the German Humanists* (Cambridge, Mass.: Harvard University Press, 1963), pp. 110-129;

Sam Wheelis, "Ulrich von Hutten: Representative of Patriotic Humanism," in *The Renaissance and Reformation in Germany,* edited by Gerhart Hoffmeister (New York: Ungar, 1977), pp. 111-127;

Peter Ziegler, "Ulrich von Hutten (1499-1523)," in *Ufnau–die Klosterinsel im Zürichsee,* edited by Ziegler and Ulrich Gut (Zurich: Gut, 1971), pp. 125-132.

Petrus Lotichius Secundus
(2 November 1528 – 7 November 1560)

Wanda Merchant
University of Texas at Austin

BOOKS: *Petri Lotichii Secundi Elegiarum Liber. Eiusdem Carminum libellus* (Paris: Michel Vascosan, 1551);

Petri Lotichii Elegiarum Liber II. Eiusdem Venator (Lyons: Johannes Tornaes, 1553);

Petri Lotichii Secundi Carminum Libellus (Bologna: Anselm Giaccarello, 1556);

De obitu clarissimi vir Iacobi Micylli, ad D. Philippvm Melanthonem, P. Lotichii Secundi. Elegia (Heidelberg: Jòannis Carbonis, 1558);

In obitvm . . . Philippi Melanthonis, ad D. Georgivm Cracouium iureconsultum, Illustris. Principis Augusti ducis Saxoniae . . . P. Loyichii Secvndi elegia (Wittenberg: Johannes Crato, 1560);

Poemata . . . Petri Lotichii Secundi . . . Quae Passim Edita Hoc Libello Compraehensa Sunt et Nunc Primum Ista Forma Expressa (Leipzig: Ernst Voegelin, 1561);

Poemata Petri Lotichii Secundi Solitariensis, edited by Christian Lotichius (Leipzig: Ernst Voegelin, 1563);

Poemata Petri Lotichii II Solitariensis cum Praefatione, edited by Joachim Camerarius (Leipzig: Johannes Steinmann, 1576);

Petri Lotichii Secundi Opera Omnia. Quibus accessit Vita eiusdem, edited by Camerarius, with biography of Lotichius by Johann Hagius (Leipzig: Johannes Steinmann, 1586).

Editions in English: "Petrus Lotichius Secundus Elegiarum liber primus," edited, with introduction, translation, and commentary, by Katherine Anne O'Rourke Fraiman, dissertation, Columbia University, 1973;

An Anthology of Neo-Latin Poetry, edited by Fred J. Nichols (New Haven & London: Yale University Press, 1979), 546–567.

OTHER: "De Fructu Danielis Prophetae," in *Commentarius in Danielem ex Ebraco versum,* by Johannes Draconites (Marburg: Andreas Kolbe, 1545).

Petrus Lotichius Secundus

Petrus Lotichius Secundus was considered by his Renaissance contemporaries to be one of the greatest Latin poets of his time, and he remains an important figure in literary studies in Germany. In the sixteenth and seventeenth centuries he was routinely ranked among the leading European poets, with his accomplishment as a love poet often compared to those of such luminaries as Janus Secundus and Pierre Ronsard. Martin Opitz, in *Buch von der Deutschen Poeterey* (Book of German Poetry, 1624), called Lotichius "unser *Lotichius,* der Fürst aller Deutschen Poeten" (our *Lotichius,* the prince of all German poets), translated one of his poems into German, and named him one of the masters of elegy along with Ovid, Propertius, Tibullus, Jacopo Sannazaro, and Janus Secundus. Lotichius owes his reputation to the simplicity and elegance of his style and to the sympathy and humanity with which he writes about everyday life, nature, love, war, and death.

Lotichius was born on 2 November 1528 in Niederzell, a small village near Schlüchtern, about fifty miles northeast of Frankfurt am Main in the duchy of Hanau. He was the second child and first son of Johannes, a small farmer, and Elizabeth Lotz. In addition to his sister, Elizabeth, Petrus Lotichius had two brothers. While the younger of the brothers died in childhood, the older, Christian, born in 1530 or 1531, would also become a poet and would publish his own and his brother's poems after Lotichius's death.

Lotichius was named for his paternal uncle, Peter Lotz, a reform-minded clergyman and the most prominent member of the family. The uncle took the Latin name Petrus Lotichius when he became abbot of the Schlüchtern monastery in 1534. As the founder of the monastery school, the elder Petrus Lotichius was responsible for the future poet's earliest education. To introduce the new humanistic learning to his students and to the monks, the abbot brought well-known scholars to the school as instructors; among them was Johannes Pedioneus Rhetus, who would later become professor of rhetoric and poetry at the University of Ingolstadt. These attempts to establish a reputable school at the monastery met with some success, although few of the teachers remained there for long; when no teacher was available, the students were forced to attend other schools in the area. While Lotichius's early education was interrupted by these travels from Schlüchtern to nearby towns, he was able to achieve a sufficient foundation for his subsequent scholarly achievements.

In 1542 Lotichius was sent by his uncle to the school of Jakob Micyllus in Frankfurt am Main. Micyllus had studied at Erfurt and Wittenberg and was a member of the humanist circles of the poet Eobanus Hessus in Erfurt and of Philipp Melanchthon in Wittenberg. In Frankfurt, Lotichius studied Latin and Greek and began to write poetry in imitation of the classics.

On the advice of his uncle, who by this time had been excommunicated for attempting to introduce reforms at the Schlüchtern monastery, Lotichius entered the University of Marburg in 1544. In Marburg, Lotichius lived with theology professor Johannes Draconites, who published the first two of Lotichius's poems to appear in print. The first, "Ad Gulielmum inclytum Hessorum Principis filium, patriae decus," was supposedly an addendum to an oration written and published by Draconites. It has been lost. The second, "De Fructu Danielis Prophetae," was included in Draconites's *Commentarius in Danielem ex Ebraeo versum,* which was published in 1545. In 1544 Lotichius wrote an epithalamium for his sister's marriage to the pastor of Schlüchtern; in this poem the main influences appear to have been Horace, Martial, and Ovid. In Marburg, Lotichius began his friendship with Johann Hagius, whose biography of Lotichius would appear in a collection of the poet's works twenty-six years after Lotichius's death.

After Marburg, Lotichius's uncle suggested further study with noted humanist scholars. Accordingly, Lotichius went to Wittenberg, which had become a center of the humanist movement, to study poetry and theology with Melanchthon and with Joachim Camerarius, a prominent classical scholar, poet, and Lutheran theologian. Lotichius arrived in Wittenberg in the spring of 1546. The political situation in the city had become increasingly tense since the death of Martin Luther in February of that year. The emperor Charles V's attempts to eliminate his main opposition, the Protestant princes who had banded together as the Schmalkaldic League, had culminated in what became known as the Schmalkaldic War; hostilities had begun in southern Germany earlier in 1546 but were gradually encroaching on Wittenberg. In November, when imperial forces invaded Protestant lands in Saxony, the faculty and students were dismissed from the university and urged to flee to Magdeburg, a bastion of Lutheranism. While Melanchthon was forced to retreat further, to Halle, Lotichius and many of his friends remained in Magdeburg and enlisted in the forces of Johann Friedrich, the Protestant elector of Saxony. Lotichius remained in the service of the Protestant forces in Magdeburg until the end of the war in 1547.

After his seven months in Magdeburg, during which he suffered from a severe illness, Lotichius continued his studies in Erfurt and then returned to Wittenberg, where he completed his M.A. in 1548. During this time he wrote *carmina* (lyric poems) about love, drinking, and friends; the erotic poems, in particular, are imbued with an intensity that is unusual for a German Neo-Latin humanist. While several poems laud fictional women characters, three praise a real woman he met in Wittenberg. His letters to friends during this period verify that she was his lover, although the name he gave her–Claudia–is probably an allusion to Clodia, the lover of Catullus. Hagius omits this love affair, which ended unhappily for Lotichius, from his story of the poet's life but writes that "Sic scilicet Amor . . . qui Lotichium fecit Poetam, fecit Philosophum, fecit Medicum" (Love . . . made Lotichius a poet, a philosopher, and a doctor).

In great distress over losing his love, Lotichius returned to Schlüchtern to visit his family near the end of 1549. He remained there for more than a month while he recovered from another illness. In the meantime his uncle's political difficulties had worsened, and it was obvious that the instability of Charles V's Augsburger Interim—a provisional settlement of the religious conflict—was leading to an even greater conflict. Lotichius decided to leave Germany, and on the recommendation of Camerarius he was invited to accompany the nephews of Daniel Stiebar, the canon of Würzburg, on a trip to France. In exchange for tutoring and chaperoning his nephews Lotichius received the patronage of Stiebar.

In 1550 Lotichius and his wards traveled to Paris. The following year Lotichius's first book, *Petri Lotichii Secundi Elegiarum Liber. Eiusdem Carminum libellus* (Petrus Lotichius Secundus's First Book of Elegies and His Short Book of Poems), dedicated to Stiebar and comprising revised elegies from the Schmalkaldic War period and various carmina, was published in Paris by Michel Vascosan. The book's depiction of the grave political situation in Germany, with its apparent opposition to the power of Charles V, appealed to the French publisher. No printer in Germany, except perhaps in Magdeburg, would have defied the emperor by publishing such a condemnation of the imperial forces. Although Lotichius spent at least a year in Paris, his thoughts apparently remained with his homeland: most of the poems he wrote during this period concern the pain of his unhappy love affair with "Claudia" or the increasingly tense political situation in Germany.

His military experience is the setting of the eleven elegies in the book, which reveal a lonely, disillusioned, and ill young man. The elegies, which include an introductory poem and an epilogue, are laments on war and on military service, expressions of grief for the loss of loved ones, and depictions of the poet's sickness and depression. The poems move through pessimism, interrupted by occasional moments of hope, to anticipation of the war's end and the return to family, friends, and a life as a poet rather than as a soldier. The most striking of the elegies, "Ad Ioachimum Camerarium Pabenbergensem. De obsidione urbis Magdeburgensis" (To Joachim Camerarius of Bamberg. On the Siege of the City of Magdeburg), which describes the siege and condemns the brutality of the imperial forces, reveals a profound understanding of the political context into which the events fit. When Magdeburg was pillaged and burned by an imperial army on 20 May 1631, during the Thirty Years' War, many read the elegy as a prophecy of the city's destruction; it continued to be interpreted as such well into the eighteenth century, although, as later scholars have pointed out, Lotichius's elegy ends with the salvation of the city.

In 1551 Lotichius moved on to the University of Montpellier, France's most renowned school of medicine, where he studied under Guillaume Rondelet. Poems written during his stay in Montpellier, many dedicated to Rondelet, show a shift to happier content and tone. His second volume of poems, *Petri Lotichii Elegiarum Liber II. Eiusdem Venator* (Petrus Lotichius's Second Book of Elegies), published in Lyons in 1553 and comprising elegies and songs written in France, reflect the joy of student life and love; much of the latter part of the book is devoted to describing Montpellier's landscape. Lotichius praises the verdant countryside and the peaceful safety of the city in contrast to the cold and conflict of northern Germany. The love poems describe the poet's complicated intertwining of new love for a woman to whom he gives the pseudonym Callirrhoe and renewed love for Claudia.

Early in 1554 Lotichius returned to Wittenberg, stopping for several months in Avignon on the way. In Baden-Baden he visited his patron, Stiebar, who was gravely ill. Accompanied by his friend Hagius, Lotichius traveled over the Alps to Padua in the fall of 1554. At the University of Padua he resumed his study of botany and medicine and visited the grave of Petrarch in the hills nearby. In 1555 an outbreak of plague forced him to flee to Bologna, which he praised as the city of muses and graces, the city of all cities. His third collection of poetry, *Petri Lotichii Secundi Carminum Libellus* (Petrus Lotichius Secundus's Small Book of Poems), published in Bologna in 1556, includes elegies and songs depicting his travels, his studies, and his life in Italy. He modeled the work on *Hodoeporicon Itineris Italici* (Poem Describing the Journey to Italy, 1533), by Georg Sabinus, a friend to whom he dedicated one of the elegies. He chronicles his return to Wittenberg in 1554 in an elegy in which he recounts his anticipation at coming home and his disappointment at arriving in the midst of a civil war. Themes from his previous work reappear in new ways, reflecting his experiences in Italy: while it does not hold a central place, war always looms in the background as his reason for remaining in what he refers to as exile; sorrow over the death of a friend returns in an elegy written on the death of Stiebar in August 1555; and death and love combine in a poem concerning the imagined death of Callirrhoe. Sickness and depression, so movingly described in the sixth elegy of the first book, recur in the ninth elegy of the third book, which is subtitled "Cum gravissimo morbo laboraret Bononiae" (As He Suffers from a Very Severe Sickness in Bologna). In spite of his medical training, he downplays the physical side of the illness, instead describing its mental and emotional consequences.

According to Hagius, the illness that afflicted Lotichius in Bologna began when the poet mistakenly drank a love potion meant for a companion. Scholars have doubted the story, but it is known that Lotichius was confined to bed with a high fever. He finally recovered, but the illness left him weakened and demoralized. A sense of his own mortality added to his sadness over the death of his patron, and financial worries resulting from the loss of Stiebar's support prompted him to finish his medical degree as soon as possible.

Lotichius received his M.D. in May 1556 and returned to Schlüchtern. There he regained much of his mental vigor in the company of his family and friends. During the winter of 1556–1557 he solicited letters of support for his candidacy for a position on the medical faculty at the University of Heidelberg, and in 1557 Prince Otto Heinrich, elector of the palatinate, appointed him professor of medicine and botany there. Lotichius and his friend Micyllus became involved in a reform movement at Heidelberg that resulted in a charter, adopted in December 1558: the final step in moving the university away from the medieval Scholastic system of education, the charter completed the work begun by the great German humanists Johann Dalberg, Peter Luder, and Conrad Celtis and made Heidelberg one of the most prominent centers of humanist learning in Germany. It also officially established the university as a purely Protestant institution. Lotichius became a member of the academic senate and sat on a commission that made recommendations for improving the arts college of the university.

During the last few years of his life Lotichius confined his poetic work to the revision of his previous writings and to occasional poems such as the *epicedia* (funeral poems) he composed for Micyllus in 1558 and for Melanchthon in 1560. A letter to Carolus Clusius dated 11 September 1560 refers to an extensively revised edition of his three published books of elegies and carmina that he has been preparing. Failing health and sadness at the deaths of his friends Micyllus and Melanchthon finally took their toll on Lotichius, and he died in Heidelberg on 7 November 1560, five days after his thirty-second birthday. He was attended at his death by his favorite student, Johannes Posthius, who also arranged for the funeral. Lotichius was buried near Micyllus in Saint Peter's Church in Heidelberg, under a marker donated by his supporter Erasmus Neustetter. Neustetter wrote the inscription for the stone:

Hoc situs est tumulo Lotichius ille Secundus,
  Carmine qui primus, primus et eloquio.
Virtus, ingenium, multa experientia, si quid
  Carmina docta valent; vivere dignus erat.
Sed quia cuncta rapit fatum, pia membra quiescant
  Molliter, ipse animus astra petita tenet.

(In this tomb lies that Lotichius Secundus,
  Who is first in song and first in eloquence.
If his virtues, his genius, his great experience,
  And his learned songs are worth anything, he deserved to live.
But since fate carries away everyone, may his pious limbs rest
  Softly; his spirit itself is in the stars he strove for.)

Although Lotichius's death ended his plan of publishing a revised edition of his works, two collections did appear posthumously, at the urging of Camerarius. The first, in 1561, included all of Lotichius's previously published poems, except for those in the Lyons edition of 1553, as well as a few poems that had not appeared in print before and that were probably furnished by Camerarius. The second collection, assembled by Christian Lotichius from manuscripts left to him by his brother and published in 1563, became the definitive version. It consists of four books of elegies, three books of carmina, and six eclogues, and it incorporates the author's final revisions. The poems offer a chronicle of Lotichius's life from his service in the Schmalkaldic War (book 1), through his sojourns in France (book 2) and Italy (book 3), to his years in Heidelberg (book 4). His fame and importance as a writer of Neo-Latin verse rest principally on these four books of elegies.

The eighteen editions of Lotichius's work published between 1561 and 1842–including the 1586 collection, edited by Camerarius and including the life of Lotichius by Hagius–bear witness to the continued esteem in which his poetry was held. Poets and scholars of the baroque period, such as Opitz, considered him the greatest German poet of his time. His influence began to wane in the seventeenth century, as more writers began to write exclusively in German; but that his works continued to be read can be seen by the reaction to the destruction of Magdeburg in 1631, when many were reminded of Lotichius's "prophetic" elegy. Georg Ellinger regarded Lotichius as the most important modern lyricist before Friedrich Gottlieb Klopstock and as the precursor to the great German lyrical poets of the eighteenth century. While no extensive commentaries on his works were published until the twentieth century, his place in the literary history of the early modern period is indisputable: he remains one of the greatest masters of Neo-Latin lyrical poetry.

Bibliography:

Bavarian State Library in Munich, *Verzeichnis der im deutschen Sprachbereich erschienenen Drucke des XVI. Jahrhunderts,* volume 11 (Stuttgart: Hiersemann, 1991), entries 2856-L2873, pp. 571-573.

Biographies:

August Ebrard, *Petrus Lotichius der Jüngere: Sein Leben und eine Auswahl seiner Gedichte metrisch ins Deutsch übertragen* (Gütersloh: Bertelsmann, 1883);

Josef Dünninger, "Zu Petrus Lotichius Secundus," *Fränkische Lebensbilder,* 5 (1973): 135-148;

Stephen Zon, *Petrus Lotichius Secundus, Neo-Latin Poet* (Bern: Peter Lang, 1983);

Bernhard Coppel, "Petrus Lotichius Secundus," in *Deutsche Dichter der frühen Neuzeit,* edited by Stephan Füssel (Berlin: Erich Schmidt, 1993), pp. 529-544.

References:

Bernhard Coppel, "Bericht über Vorarbeiten zu einer neuen Lotichius-Edition," *Daphnis,* 7 (1978): 55-106;

Coppel, "Lotichius in Italien–Das Italienerlebnis deutscher Humanisten," *Unsere Heimat: Mitteilungen des Heimatbundes für Heimatschutz und Heimatpflege im Kreise Schlüchtern,* 9 (1993): 167-183;

Coppel, "Marginalien zu Dichterischen Berührungspunkten zwischen Petrus Lotichius Secundus und C. Valerius Catullus," in *ACTA Conventus Neo-Latini Lovaniensis,* edited by Jozef IJsewijn (Munich: Fink, 1973), pp. 159-170;

Georg Ellinger, *Geschichte der neulateinischen Literatur Deutschlands im 16. Jahrhundert,* volume 2 (Berlin: De Gruyter, 1929), pp. 340-411;

Ellinger, "Zu Petrus Lotichius Secundus," *Zeitschrift für deutsche Philologie,* 63 (1938): 251-254;

August Heimpel, "Das Neueste von der Lotichius-Forschung," *Unsere Heimat: Mitteilungen des Heimatbundes für Heimatschutz und Heimatpflege im Kreise Schlüchtern,* 21 (1929): 50-53;

Heimpel, *Stammbuch der Lotichier aus Schlüchtern* (Frankfurt am Main: Bechtold, 1902);

Walter Ludwig, "Petrus Lotichius Secundus and the Roman Elegists–Prolegomena to a Study of Neo-Latin Elegy," in *Classical Influences on European Culture A.D. 1500-1700,* edited by R. R. Bolgar (Cambridge: Cambridge University Press, 1976): 171-190;

Eckart Schäfer, "Das Acis-Gedicht des Lotichius," *Unsere Heimat: Mitteilungen des Heimatbundes für Heimatschutz und Heimatpflege im Kreise Schlüchtern,* 9 (1993): 154-166;

Schäfer, "Zwischen deutschem Volkslied und römischer Elegie: Imitatio und Selbstfindung in Lotichius' 'De Puella infelici,' " in *Gedichte und Interpretationen,* volume 1, edited by Volker Meid (Stuttgart: Reclam, 1982), pp. 94-110;

Hermann Wiegand, "Krieg und Frieden im Werk des Petrus Lotichius Secundus," *Unsere Heimat: Mitteilungen des Heimatbundes für Heimatschutz und Heimatpflege im Kreise Schlüchtern,* 9 (1993): 131-153.

Papers:

Petrus Lotichius Secundus's papers are scattered. No definitive collections exist.

Peter Luder
(circa 1415 – 1472)

Frank Baron
University of Kansas

MAJOR WORKS: Correspondence, lectures, speeches, and poems, edited by Wilhelm Wattenbach, in his "Peter Luder, der erste humanistische Lehrer in Heidelberg," *Zeitschrift für die Geschichte des Oberrheins,* 22 (1869): 33–127;

"Peter Luders Lobrede auf Pfalzgraf Friedrich den Siegreichen," edited by Wattenbach, *Zeitschrift für die Geschichte des Oberrheins,* 23 (1871): 21–38;

"Elegia Petri Luder poeta[ae] clarissimi ad Panphilam amicam suam singularem" and "Ad Mavortium virum Fridericum Principem Rheni gloriosissimum," edited by Frank Baron, in his "The Beginnings of German Humanism: The Life and Work of the Wandering Humanist Peter Luder," dissertation, University of California, Berkeley, 1966, pp. 207–213;

Die Metrikvorlesung des Frühhumanisten Peter Luder, edited by Eske Bockelmann, Gratia, Bamberger Schriften zur Renaissanceforschung, volume 14 (Bamberg: Kaiser, 1984).

Although the historic achievements of Renaissance humanism in Germany around 1500 are rightfully attached to such names as Conrad Celtis, Johannes Reuchlin, and Ulrich von Hutten, the pioneering work occurred decades earlier. In Italy the rediscovery of forgotten aspects of the ancient world had produced a critical reevaluation of the prevalent modes of thought and a recognition of the severe limitations of the existing educational system; in the middle of the fifteenth century the Italian humanist movement, which resulted from these changes, began to have an influence in Germany. Peter Luder played a key role in this earliest phase of German humanism but was totally forgotten until 1869, when Wilhelm Wattenbach discovered his long-neglected manuscripts.

Born around 1415 in the village of Kislau in the diocese of Speyer, Luder registered at the University of Heidelberg for the winter semester of 1430–1431. Because he was poor, he did not have to pay the registration fee. As a student of the philosophy faculty Luder was exposed to the monolithic Scholastic system of education, which was built around the study of logic as prescribed by Aristotle and his medieval interpreters. These studies, which ignored such subjects as literature and history, did not inspire Luder, and, without getting a degree, he left for Italy.

He would stay away from Germany for more than twenty years, traveling throughout Italy and visiting Greece. At the University of Ferrara he studied under Guarino da Verona, whose courses treated the languages and literature of ancient Greece and Rome and ignored the Scholastic curriculum. Guarino shunned abstract philosophy and logic and denied the authority of Aristotle in all areas except ethics. Luder said later that "verum et infallibile fundamentum mihi ponerem, ad studia humanitatis, historiographos, oratores scilicet et poetas toto me mentis ardore converti" (in order to establish a true and infallible foundation for all fields, I applied myself with all my heart to the humanistic studies, to the historians, orators, and poets).

In 1444 Luder was in Venice as a scribe in the service of Doge Francisco Foscari. In this position he was able to observe at first hand the privileged position humanistic studies enjoyed at the courts of Italy. In the 1450s Luder began the study of medicine at the University of Padua, but he maintained his interest in humanism. He finally returned to Germany in 1456, filled with hope that German universities and courts would grant humanistic studies the same importance and respect that they enjoyed on the other side of the Alps.

On his return Luder secured a teaching position at the University of Heidelberg, audaciously announcing that he had accepted the task of restoring the Latin language, which had lapsed into a state of barbarism. Initially, he appeared to have wide support for his program from Pfalzgraf (Count of the Palatinate) Friedrich I, der Siegreiche (the Victorious), and among the faculties of theology, medicine, and law. As Luder prepared to deliver his inaugural lecture, however, opposition developed in the philosophical faculty, which was responsible for the basic course of Scholastic studies.

Luder expounded on his concept of studia humanitatis in his inaugural lecture, which he probably delivered in almost identical form at all the universities where he taught. History, rhetoric, and poetry were at the core of Luder's program: "Historia enim fida est preceptorum ac veritatis magistra" (History is the trustworthy teacher of maxims and truth). For Luder, history was an essential means of communicating ideas and, thus, was an extension of philosophy: "adveniente autem historia, ubi fides comparatur et res ipsa a clarissimis iam sic gesta viris ostenditur, numquid animum unius cuiusque ad imitationis studia eadem sic peragere invitat, incendit, inflammat?" (If history comes to the aid, however, trustworthiness is established by comparison, and if an action, performed by very illustrious men, becomes manifest, does it not invite, inspire, and inflame every mind to imitation, in order to carry out similar actions?). Luder goes on to cite examples of historical actions that are worthy of imitation. Stressing the usefulness of a knowledge of history for the conduct of civil affairs, he points out that wisdom and maturity can be acquired by learning from the experience of entire centuries. He quotes Cicero: "Historia enim testis est temporum, lux veritatis, via memoriae, magistra vitae, nuntia vetustatis" (For history is the witness of time, the light of truth, the path of recollection, the teacher of life, the messenger of antiquity).

Proceeding to a discussion of rhetoric, Luder says that orators

> nos laudare benefacta et detestari facinora docent. Ab hiis quoque oratoribus quam facillime auditores nostros hinc quidem ad indignationem, ad odium, ad tritstitiam, ad lacrimas, hinc vero ad misericordiam, ad amorem, ad gaudium, ad risus et impellere et provocare docemur.

> (teach us to praise brave deeds and to renounce criminal ones. They teach us to inspire our listeners most easily to indignation, hatred, sadness, and tears, as well as to compassion, to love, to praise and to laughter.)

God gave human beings alone, according to Luder, the sublime ability to speak so that they could express their emotions more powerfully. He quotes from the *Aeneid* to show the power of rhetoric: speaking of Neptune's calming the seas, Virgil compares the god to an orator who addresses a furious crowd intent on insurrection, and, with his words, controls their passions and calms their hearts. Luder asserts: "Ceterae enim artes sine praeceptis rhetoricae et eius exercitatione nudae, inornatae ac prorsus elingues, vix in publicum prodire audent" (Without the precepts of rhetoric and their use the other arts are naked, disordered, and utterly mute).

Finally, Luder turns to poetry:

> Neque enim quisquam perfecte aut syllabarum aut verborum enuntiationem, soni quoque elegantiam, aut concinnam orationis venustatem scire poterit, qui poetas contempnendo non legerit. Haec enim poesis non verba solum et sillabas, sed et tropos et figuras omnemque ornatum ac orationis suavitatem nobis aperit atque ostendit.

> (He who has not read poets because of contempt for them will not be able to comprehend completely the pronunciation of syllables or words, the elegance of sound, or the harmonious beauty of a speech. For poetry reveals and demonstrates to us not only the words and syllables, but also the tropes, figures, and the entire construction and attractiveness of a speech.)

He cites Terence and Virgil as poets he admires. He argues at length that the study of pagan and secular poetry is justified, in spite of the frequent charge that it is immoral. He urges his listeners to be selective, to pick the roses from among thorns—a procedure that is necessary, he points out, even in reading the Bible. Finally, he cites the fourth eclogue of Virgil's *Bucolica* as a prediction of the coming of Christ.

At Heidelberg, Luder lectured on Horace, Terence, Seneca, Ovid, Virgil, and Valerius Maximus; gave courses on rhetoric; taught the art of letter writing; and treated metrics. He considered creative effort a natural result of the humanist's studies, and some of his own poems have survived. In most of his teaching and in his literary work Luder depended on his Italian teachers and on ancient texts; most of his formal writings are mosaics of quotations. Like his teacher Guarino, he could quote many literary texts from memory. He carried the humanistic method of *imitatio* to an extreme: the passages in his inaugural lecture that describe the disciplines of history, rhetoric, and poetry are taken, without substantial change, from lectures of Guarino.

Luder dedicated most of his historical works and poems to Friedrich I. A speech on the historical background of the Palatinate promotes the count's aggressive expansionist policies; a lengthy poem combines autobiographical elements with effusive praise for Luder's patron. Luder is, however, important primarily because of his pioneering accomplishments as a teacher rather than for his work as a historian or poet. Stephan Hoest, one of his students in Heidelberg, later became a theologian and a prominent member of the Heidelberg faculty; Jakob Wimpfeling, the most influential Heidelberg humanist before the Reformation, in turn, revered Hoest as his most valued teacher. Hoest's lectures and other writings reveal his acquaintance with literary texts Luder had introduced in Heidelberg and show that the studia humanitatis had taken a firm foothold at the university. Poetry, rhetoric, and history had by then become respected subjects that seriously challenged the monopoly of Scholastic philosophy.

In Luder's time, however, this process was only beginning. It soon became evident to him that financial resources were unavailable for new subjects. Although Luder wrote poetry and historical texts with the hope of gaining financial support from Friedrich, the count was involved in military campaigns and did not consider a court humanist a necessity. Luder was forced to rely on tutoring to support himself.

He explored possibilities at other universities, teaching at Erfurt and Leipzig between 1460 and 1462. How Luder introduced himself is apparent from a lecture announcement he posted on a bulletin board at the University of Leipzig; it was preserved by Hartmann Schedel, one of Luder's students there. To prevent people unsympathetic to his program from tearing down the announcement, Luder warned that a guard was hiding nearby. The announcement is written in a clear humanistic hand, in stark contrast to the Gothic script generally employed at that time in Germany. The key sentence reads: "Petrus Luder poesim professus . . . faciet orationem publicam, qua argumentis rationibusque firmissimis ostendet studia humanitatis, hystoriagraphos, oratores scilicet et poetas omnibus fore capessanda" (Peter Luder, professor of poetry . . . will hold a public oration, in which he will present the humanistic studies, [that is,] historians, orators, and poets, with most compelling arguments and reasons why everyone should be engaged with them).

Propagating humanistic studies was no more profitable at these schools than it had been in Heidelberg, even when eminent members of the universities supported his work. The universities were structured to promote the Scholastic system and did not provide many opportunities for humanistic teachers. Therefore, Luder returned to Italy and resumed his medical studies in 1462. In 1464 he went to Basel and, with his newly acquired doctorate, became a professor of medicine and a practicing physician. This sound financial basis enabled him to continue his humanistic activities. After four years in Basel, he briefly entered diplomatic service; a

Medal depicting Guarino da Verona, Peter Luder's teacher at the University of Ferrara

speech he wrote to deliver to the king of France for Archduke Sigismund of Tirolia has survived.

Luder taught at all the universities in German-speaking central Europe. Records show that a certain Peter, a doctor of arts and medicine, was invited to become a member of the faculty of a university that was established in Pressburg, Hungary, in 1469; but there is no indication that Luder went there, and the University of Pressburg was dissolved soon after its founding. From 1470 to 1472, the final two years of his life, Luder lived in Vienna, where he continued to lecture on the studia humanitatis.

Luder's most important student was, unquestionably, Schedel, the author of the *Weltchronik* (Nuremberg Chronicle, 1493). Schedel was already a master of arts and an instructor when Luder came to Leipzig. By that time he had certainly heard of Luder: his uncle, Hermann Schedel, had tried to attract Luder to teach in Augsburg. Hartmann Schedel followed Luder to Padua and, like him, took up the study of medicine there. In Padua he maintained his newly acquired interest in humanistic studies, and there is evidence that he did so under Luder's tutelage: Schedel's lecture notes on Ovid, which originated at this time, identify Luder as the teacher who delivered the lectures in Padua. An extraordinarily diligent and meticulous student, Schedel obtained or copied all the literary, philosophical, and scientific texts he encountered in Germany and in Italy; Luder's lectures formed an important part of his collection.

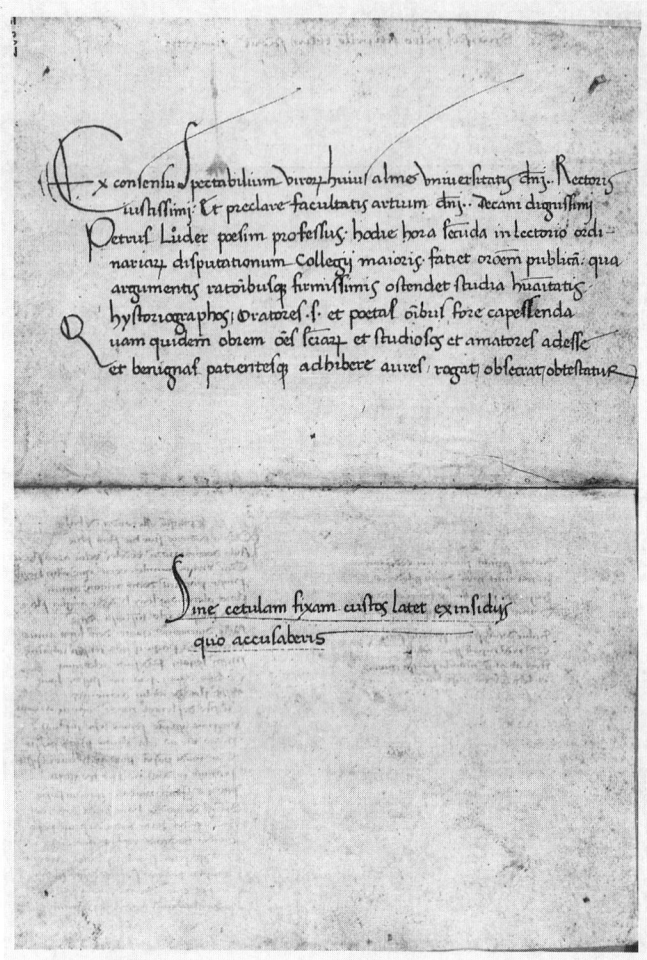

Announcement of a lecture on humanistic studies by Luder (Bayerische Staatsbibliothek, Munich, Hartmann Schedel Collection, clm 466, folio 285ʳ)

Schedel's *Weltchronik* reflects the influence of Italian humanism and, indirectly, is evidence that his teacher had opened up completely new areas of literary activity to him. The chronicle assigns great prominence to geography and, in particular, to the graphic depiction of European cities. It is also a comprehensive biographical dictionary, in which Schedel's treatment of the fourteenth and fifteenth centuries reveals new developments in intellectual history: the scholars Schedel discusses include the great names of Renaissance humanism. These biographies constitute a contemporary history of the movement.

The dependence of German humanists such as Luder and Schedel on Italian models does not earn them praise for originality, but it is valuable as an indication of the lines of influence from Italy to Germany. Paradoxically, the tendency of humanists to borrow and imitate was not without innovative dimensions: in Germany, Luder's program represented something new; and his work introduced into German universities the fields of history, rhetoric, and poetry, which the Scholastic system had almost totally neglected. The humanists helped to establish historical narration and the literary imagination as legitimate areas of study and of creative activity, and Schedel's impressive *Weltchronik* shows originality that goes beyond its sources. The intellectual energies of humanism transformed the texts of the past in new and creative ways.

Noting Luder's death in 1472 in his diary, Schedel refers to Luder as his first humanistic teacher. Although Luder was not alone in bringing the ideas of humanism to Germany, he has emerged in recent literary histories and criticism as the central figure among the pioneering fifteenth-century German humanists.

References:

Klaus Arnold, "Stephan Hoest," in *Die Deutsche Lit-*

eratur des Mittelalters: Verfasserlexikon (Berlin: De Gruyter, 1983), volume 4, columns 79-81;

Wilfried Barner, "Studia toto amplectenda pectore," in *Respublica Guelpherbytana: Festschrift für Paul Raabe,* edited by August Buck and Martin Bircher, *Chloe:* Beihefte zum *Daphnis,* volume 6 (Amsterdam: Rodopi, 1987), pp. 227-251;

Frank Baron, "Peter Luder," in *Die Deutsche Literatur des Mittelalters: Verfasserlexikon* (Berlin: De Gruyter, 1985), volume 5, columns 954-959;

Baron, *Stephan Hoest: Reden und Briefe. Quellen zur Geschichte der Scholastik und des Humanismus im 15. Jahrhundert* (Munich: Fink, 1971);

Gustav Bauch, *Die Universität Erfurt im Zeitalter des Frühhumanismus* (Breslau: Marcus, 1904), pp. 43-50;

Eckhard Bernstein, *German Humanism* (Boston: Twayne, 1983), pp. 12-16;

Bernstein, *Die Literatur des deutschen Frühhumanismus* (Stuttgart: Metzler, 1978), pp. 34-38;

Ludwig Bertalot, "Humanistische Vorlesungsankündigungen im Deutschland im 15. Jahrhundert," in his *Studien zum italienischen und deutschen Humanismus,* volume 1, edited by Paul Oskar Kristeller (Rome: Edizioni di storia e letteratura, 1975), pp. 219-250;

Albert Büchi, ed., *Albrecht von Bonstetten: Briefe und ausgewählte Schriften* (Basel: Huber, 1893);

Maximilian Buchner, "Humanistische Lobrede (Peter Luders?) auf Kilian von Bibra, der spätere Würzburger Domprobst (+1494)," *Archiv des historischen Vereins für Unterfranken und Aschaffenburg,* 49 (1907): 201-222;

Buchner, "Die Stellung des kurpfälzischen Kanzlers Mathias Ramung (+1478) zum geistigen Leben seiner Zeit," *Neue Heidelberger Jahrbücher,* 16 (1909): 81-94;

Heinz Otto Burger, *Renaissance, Humanismus, Reformation: Deutsche Literatur im europäischen Kontext* (Bad Homburg: Gehlen, 1969), pp. 140-142, 154-155, 169-170;

Mihály Császár, *Az Academia Istropolitana. Matyas Kiraly Pozsonyi Egyeteme* (Pressburg: Eder, 1914), p. 105:

Heinz Entner, *Frühhumanismus und Schultradition im Leben und Werk des Wanderpoeten Samuel Karoch von Lichtenberg* (Berlin: Akademie, 1968): 1-9;

Karl Grossmann, "Die Frühzeit des Humanismus in Wien bis zu Celtis' Berufung," *Jahrbuch für Landeskunde von Niederösterreich,* 22 (1929): 150-325;

Heinrich Hammer, "Literarische Beziehungen und musikalisches Leben des Hofes Herzog Siegmunds von Tirol," *Zeitschrift des Ferdinandeums,* 3 (1899): 71-107;

Karl Hartfelder, "Matthias von Kemnat," *Forschungen zur deutschen Geschichte,* 22 (1882): 331-349;

Beatrice Hernad, *Die Graphiksammlung des Humanisten Hartmann Schedel* (Munich: Prestel, 1990);

Paul Joachimsen, "Frühhumanismus in Schwaben," *Württembergische Vierteljahrshefte für Landesgeschichte,* new series 5 (1896): 63-126, 257-291;

Joachimsen, ed., *Hermann Schedels Briefwechsel (1452-1478)* (Tübingen: Litterarischer Verein, 1893);

Rudolf Kettemann, *Heidelberg im Spiegel seiner ältesten Beschreibung* (Heidelberg: Palatium, 1986), pp. 5-16;

Kettemann, "Peter Luder (um 1415-1472): Die Anfänge der humanistischen Studien in Deutschland," in *Humanismus im deutschen Südwesten,* edited by Paul Gerhard Schmidt (Sigmaringen: Thorbecke, 1993), pp. 13-34;

Jan-Dirk Müller, "Der siegreiche Fürst im Entwurf der Gelehrten: Zu den Anfängen eines höfischen Humanismus in Heidelberg," in *Höfischer Humanismus,* edited by August Buck (Weinheim: VCH, 1989);

Müller, ed., *Wissen für den Hof: Der spätmittelalterliche Verschriftungsprozeß am Beispiel Heidelberg im 15. Jahrhundert,* Münstersche Mittelalter-Schriften, volume 67 (Munich: Fink, 1994);

Karl Müllner, "Acht Inauguralreden des Veronesers Guarino und seines Sohnes Battista," *Wiener Studien,* 18 (1896): 283-306;

Veit Probst, *Petrus Antonius de Clapis (ca. 1440-1512): Ein italienischer Humanist im Dienste Friedrichs des Siegreichen von der Pfalz* (Paderborn: Schöningh, 1989), pp. 4-37;

Helmut Reinalter, "Der Wanderhumanist Peter Luder und seine Beziehungen zu Herzog Sigmund von Tirol," *Mitteilungen des österreichischen Staatsarchivs,* 26 (1973): 148-167;

Gerhard Ritter, "Aus dem geistigen Leben der Heidelberger Universität," *Zeitschrift für die Geschichte des Oberrheins,* new series 37 (1922): 1-32;

Ritter, "Aus dem Kreise der Hofpoeten Pfalzgraf Friedrich I," *Zeitschrift für die Geschichte des Oberrheins,* 38 (1923): 109-123;

Ritter, *Die Heidelberger Universität* (Heidelberg: Winter, 1936), pp. 464-500;

Steven Rowan, "Chronicle as Cosmos: Hartmann Schedel's Nuremberg Chronicle, 1493," *Daphnis,* 15 (1986): 375-407;

Elisabeth Rücker, *Die Schedelsche Weltchronik: Das größte Buchunternehmen der Dürer-Zeit* (Munich: Prestel, 1988);

Agostino Sottili, "Peter Luders medizinische Promotion," *Wolfenbüttler Renaissance Mitteilungen,* 9 (1987): 118;

Wolfgang Stammler, *Von der Mystik zum Barock,* second edition (Stuttgart: Metzler, 1950), pp. 525, 537–538;

Georg Voigt, *Die Wiederbelebung des classischen Alterthums,* 2 volumes (Berlin: Reimer, 1893), II: 263–482;

Wilhelm Wattenbach, "Hartmann Schedel als Humanist," *Forschungen zur deutschen Geschichte,* 11 (1871): 351–374;

Wattenbach, "Nachträgliches über Peter Luder," *Zeitschrift für die Geschichte des Oberrheins,* 27 (1875): 95–99;

Wattenbach, "Sigismund Gossembrot als Vorkämpfer der Humanisten und seine Gegner," *Zeitschrift für die Geschichte des Oberrheins,* 25 (1873): 36–69.

Papers:

Peter Luder's correspondence and manuscripts for his lectures, speeches, and poetry are in the Österreichische Nationalbibliothek in Vienna (cod. vindob. 3244, 4323, 7288) and in the Hartmann Schedel collection at the Bayerische Staatsbibliothek in Munich (clm 382, 418, 459, 466, 663, 3586, 4393, 7080, 22403).

Martin Luther
(10 November 1483 – 18 February 1546)

Jeffrey Jaynes
Methodist Theological School in Ohio

SELECTED BOOKS: *Disputatio D. Martini Luther Theologi, pro declaratione virtutis indulgentiarum* (Basel: Adam Petri, 1517);

Eynn Sermon von dem Ablasz vnnd Gnade (Wittenberg: Johann Grunenberg, 1518);

Resolutiones disputationem de Indulgentiarum virtute (Wittenberg: Johann Rhau-Grunenberg, 1518);

Eyn Sermon von der Bereytung zum Sterbenn (Wittenberg: Johann Rhau-Grunenberg, 1519);

Eyn Sermon von den Wucher (Wittenberg: Johann Rhau-Grunenberg, 1519);

Eyn Sermon von dem Bann (Wittenberg: Johann Rhau-Grunenberg, 1520);

An den Christlichen Adel deutscher Nation: von des Christlichen Standes Besserung (Wittenberg: Melchior Lotter the Younger, 1520);

De captivate babylonica ecclesiae, præludium (Wittenberg: Melchior Lotter the Younger, 1520);

Von der Freyheyt einiß Christen menschen (Wittenberg: Johann Rhau-Grunenberg, 1520);

De votis monasticis (Wittenberg: Johann Rhau-Grunenberg, 1521);

Eyn trew Vormanung Martini Luther tzu allen Christen. Sich tzu vorhuten fur auffruhr vnnd Emporung (Wittenberg: Melchior Lotter the Younger, 1522);

Eyn bett buchlin der tzehen gepott. Des glawbens. Des vatter vnßers und des Ave Maria (Wittenberg: Johann Rhau-Grunenberg, 1522);

Das eyn Christliche Versamlung odder Gemeyne: recht und macht habe: alle lere tzu urteylen und lerer tzu berufen, ein- und abzusetzen (Wittenberg: Lucas Cranach the Elder & Christian Döring, 1523);

Uon welltlicher vberkeytt, wie weytt man yhr gehorsam schuldig sey (Wittenberg: Nickel Schirlentz, 1523);

Formula missae et communionis pro Eccelsia Vuitembergensi (Wittenberg: Nickel Schirlentz, 1523);

Ordenung eyns gemeynen kastens (Wittenberg: Lucas Cranach the Elder & Christian Döring, 1523);

Das Ihesus Christus eyn geborner Iude sey (Wittenberg: Lucas Cranach the Elder & Christian Döring, 1523);

Martin Luther in 1526; portrait by Lucas Cranach the Elder (Lutherhalle, Wittenberg)

An die Radherrn aller stedte deutsches lands: das sie christliche Schulen auffrichten vnd hallten sollen (Wittenberg: Lucas Cranach the Elder & Christian Döring, 1524);

Von Kauffshandlung vnd wucher (Wittenberg: Hans Lufft, 1524);

Geystliche Gesangk Buchlein (Wittenberg: Joseph Klug, 1524);

Ermanunge zum fride auff die zwelff artikel der Bawrschafft ynn Schwaben (Wittenberg: Joseph Klug, 1525);

Wider die rewbischen vnnd mördischen rotten der anderen bawren (Erfurt: Melchior Sachse, 1525);

De servo arbitrio Mar. Lutheri ad D. Erasmum Roterodamum (Wittenberg: Hans Lufft, 1525);

Widder die hymelischen propheten, von den bildern vnd Sacrament (Wittenberg: Lucas Cranach the Elder & Christian Döring, 1525);

Deudsche Messe vnd ordnung Gottis dienstes (Wittenberg: Melchior Lotter, 1526);

Das diese Worte Christi (Das ist mein leib etce) noch fest stehen widder die Schwerm geister (Wittenberg: Melchior Lotter, 1527);

Vnterricht der Visitatoren an die Pfarhern ym Kurfurstenthum zu Sachsen, by Luther and Philipp Melanchthon (Wittenberg: Nickel Schirlentz, 1528);

Vom abendmahl Christi, Bekendnis (Wittenberg: Melchior Lotter, 1528);

Enchiridion. Der kleine Catechismus für die gemeine Pfarher vnd Prediger, gemehret vnd verbessert (Wittenberg: Nickel Schirlentz, 1529);

Deudsch Catechismus (Wittenberg: Georg Rhau, 1529);

Vom kriege widder die Türken (Wittenberg: Hans Weiß, 1529);

Eine Heerpredigt widder die Türken (Wittenberg: Nickel Schirlentz, 1529);

Vermanung an die geistlichen versamlet auf dem Reichstag zu Augsburg (Wittenberg: Hans Lufft, 1530);

Warnunge D. Martini Luther, An seine lieben Deudschen (Wittenberg: Hans Lufft, 1531);

Ein sendbrieff D. M. Lutthers. Vom Dolmetzschen vnd Fürbit der heiligenn (Nuremberg: Georg Rottmaier, 1531);

Eine einfeltige weise zu Beten, für einen guten Freund (Wittenberg: Hans Lufft, 1535);

Beelzebub an die Heilige Bepstliche Kirche (Wittenberg: Nickel Schirlentz, 1537);

Artickel, so da hetten sollen auffs Concilion zu Mantua, oder wo es würde sein, vberantwortet werden (Wittenberg: Hans Lufft, 1538);

Ein Brieff D. Mart. Luther wider die Sabbather an einen guten Freund (Wittenberg: Nickel Schirlentz, 1538);

Von den Concilijs vnd Kirchen (Wittenberg: Hans Lufft, 1539);

Der Erste Teil der Bücher D. Mart. Luth. vber etliche Epistel der Aposteln (Wittenberg: Hans Lufft, 1539);

Wider Hans Worst (Wittenberg: Hans Lufft, 1541);

Vermanunge zum Gebet, Wider den Türeken (Wittenberg: Nickel Schirlentz, 1541);

Der XXIX. Psalm ausgelegt, durch Doctor Iohan Bugenhagen . . . Ein trost D. Martini Luthers den Weibern, welchen es vngerade gegangen ist mit Kindergeberen (Wittenberg: Joseph Klug, 1542);

New Zeitung vom Rhein (Wittenberg: Hans Lufft, 1542);

Von den Iüden vnd jhren Lügen (Wittenberg: Hans Lufft, 1543);

Haußpostil D. Martin Luther (Nuremberg: Johann vom Berg & Ulrich Neuber, 1544);

Wider das Bapstum zu Rom vom Teuffel gestifft (Wittenberg: Hans Lufft, 1545);

Tomvs Primus Omnivm Opervm . . . Martini Lutheri (Wittenberg: Hans Lufft, 1545);

Tomvs Secvndvs Omnivm Opervm . . . Martini Lutheri (Wittenberg: Hans Lufft, 1546);

Der ander Teil der Bücher D. Mart: Luth: Darin alle Streitschriften, sampt etlichen Sendbrieuen, an Fürsten vnd Stedte (Wittenberg: Hans Lufft, 1548);

Tomvs Tertivs Omnivm Opervm . . . Martini Lutheri (Wittenberg: Hans Lufft, 1549);

Der Dritte Teil der bücher des . . . Martini Lutheri, darin zusamen gebracht sind christliche vnd tröstliche Erklerung vnd auslegung der furnemesten Psalmen (Wittenberg: Hans Lufft, 1550);

Der Vierdte Teil der Bücher des . . . Mart. Luth. darin . . . Christliche vnd tröstliche erklerung vnd auslegung vber etliche fürneme Capitel vnd Sprüche aus göttlicher Schrifft (Wittenberg: Hans Lufft, 1551);

Der Fünffte Teil der Bücher des . . . Martini Lutheri, darinnen . . . die Auslegung vber das erste Buch, vnd folgend vber etliche Capitel der andern Bücher Mose (Wittenberg: Hans Lufft, 1552);

Tomvs Qvartvs Omnivm Opervm . . . Martini Lutheri (Wittenberg: Hans Lufft, 1552);

Der Sechste teil der Bücher des . . . Martini Lutheri, darinnen begriffen etliche auslegung der heiligen Schrifft im newen Testament, auch die Bücher vom Ehestand, Kauffshendel vnd Wucher, Vermanung vnd Trostschifften (Wittenberg: Hans Lufft, 1553);

Der Siebend Teil der bücher des . . . Mart. Lutheri, Darinnen begriffen, die Bücher vom Christlichen stand, wider den Bapst, vnd die Bischoue . . . Item, von der Kirchen vnd den Concilijs (Wittenberg: Hans Lufft, 1554);

Tomvs Qvintvs Omnivm Opervm . . . Martini Lutheri (Wittenberg: Hans Lufft, 1554);

Tomvs Sextvs Omnivm Opervm . . . Martini Lutheri (Wittenberg: Peter Seitz's heirs, 1555);

Der Achte teil der Bücher des . . . Martini Lutheri: darinnen die verdeutschte Auslegunge begriffen vber die Psalmos graduum, vnd den 110 Psalm, Das fünffte buch Mose, vnd dies Propheten (Wittenberg: Hans Lufft, 1556);

Der Neundte Teil der Bücher des—Martini Lutheri: darinnen die Propositiones vom Ablas . . . samt vielen Sendbrieun an Bapst, Keiser, Fürstn vnd Bischoue, vnd andern schrifften von dem 17. bis in das 33. jar (Wittenberg: Hans Lufft, 1557);

Tomvs Septimvs Omnivm Opervm . . . Martini Lutheri (Wittenberg: Thomas Klug, 1557);

Der Zehende Teil der Bücher des . . . Martini Lutheri, Nemlich, die herrliche Auslegung vber das Erste Buch Mosi (Wittenberg: Thomas Klug, 1558);

Der Eilffte Teil der Bücher des . . . Martini Lutheri, Nemlich die herrliche Auslegung vber das Erste Buch Mosi (Wittenberg: Thomas Klug, 1558);

Der Zwelffte vnd letzte Teil der Bücher des . . . Mart. Lutheri: Nemlich die erste Auslegung vber die Epistel an die Galater, Ecclesiastes oder Prediger Salomonis, sampt etlichen Trostschriften, Sendbrieuen vnd handlungen (Wittenberg: Hans Lufft, 1559);

Tischreden, oder colloquia Doct. Mart. Luthers, so er in vielen Jaren gegen gelarten leuten auch frembden Gesten, und seinen Tischgesellen gefüret, edited by Johannes Aurifaber (Eisleben: Urban Gaubisch, 1566); translated by Henri Bell as *Dris. Martini Lutheris colloquia mensalia; or . . .divine discourses at his table* (London: William Du Gard, 1652).

Collections: *Dr. Martin Luthers sämmtliche Schriften*, 23 volumes, edited by Johann Georg Walch (Saint Louis: Concordia, 1880–1910);

D. Martin Luthers Werke: Kritische Gesamtausgabe, 104 volumes (Weimar: Böhlau, 1883–1984).

Editions in English: *Watchwords for the Warfare of Life*, translated by Mrs. Elizabeth Charles (New York: Dodd, 1868);

The First Principles of the Reformation: The 95 Theses and the Three Primary Works, translated by Henry Wace (London: Murray, 1883);

Luther's Works, edited by Jaroslav Pelikan and Helmut T. Lehmann (Philadelphia: Fortress, 1955–);

Martin Luther: Selections from His Writings, edited by John Dillenberger (Garden City, N.Y.: Doubleday, 1961);

Selected Writings of Martin Luther, edited by Theodore G. Tappert (Philadelphia: Fortress, 1967);

Martin Luther, edited by E. G. Rupp and Benjamin Drewery (New York: Saint Martin's Press, 1970).

OTHER: *Eyn geystlich edles Buchleynn. von rechter vnderscheyd vnd vorstand. was der alt vnd new mensche sey. Was Adams vnd gottis kind sey. vnd wie Adam ynn vns sterben vnnd Christus ersteen sall*, introduction by Luther (Wittenberg: Johann Rhau-Grunenberg, 1516);

Sylvester de Prierio, *Epitoma responsionis ad Martinvm Lvtherum*, introduction and critical glosses by Luther (Wittenberg: Melchior Lotter the Younger, 1520);

Das Newe Testament Deutzsch, translated by Luther (Wittenberg: Melchior Lotter, 1522; revised, 1522);

Das Allte Testament deutsch, translated by Luther (Wittenberg: Melchior Lotter the Younger, 1523);

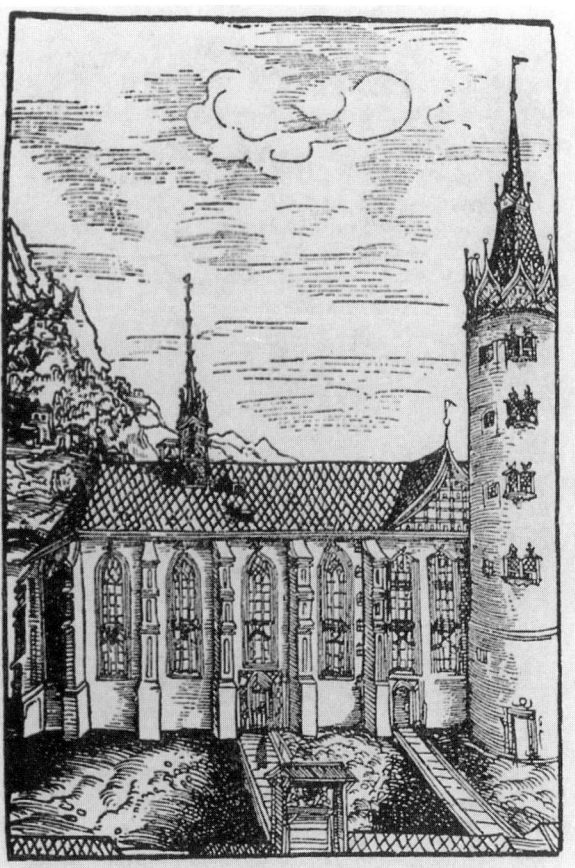

The Castle Church in Wittenberg; the door on which Luther is popularly believed to have nailed his Ninety-five Theses is in the center.

Der Psalter teutsch (Strasbourg: Johann Knobloch, 1524);

Das tauffbuchlin verdeudscht, auffs new zu gericht, translated and revised by Luther (Wittenberg: Hans Weiß, 1526)

Biblia: das ist, die gantze Heilige Schrifft Deudsch, translated by Luther (Wittenberg: Hans Lufft, 1534; revised, 1541);

Aesop, *Hundert Fabeln aus Esopo*, translated by Luther and others, edited by Nathan Chytraeus (Rostock: Jacob Lucius, 1571).

Early in the 1520s Hans Holbein, the great German artist and illustrator, depicted Martin Luther as *Hercules Germanicus*. In this image the vigorous Luther, clothed in his Augustinian cowl and wielding a deadly club, stands triumphant over several vanquished proponents of Scholastic theology. It is appropriate that Luther should be associated with the mythology of antiquity, since his life and influence have been so susceptible to characterizations of mythical proportions. Champion of German liberties, reviler of the Jews,

Title page for Luther's pamphlet calling on the German princes to take the lead in reforming the church

source of modern High German, seed of dogmatic intolerance, herald of the Protestant Reformation, heretic of the Catholic Church, friend of God and foe of the devil—these and countless other descriptions embrace some aspect of the man. Regardless of personal perspective, however, one would have to judge Luther's efforts in publishing and his literary achievements as truly herculean: from 1516 to 1546 he wrote a treatise nearly every other week—some sixty thousand printed pages that today fill the 104 volumes published thus far in the Weimar edition (1883) of his works. It has been estimated that Luther's writings account for 20 percent of all the literature printed in Germany from 1500 to 1530. The breadth of his literary accomplishments is also impressive, as his works include theological tracts, hymns, poetry, liturgies, sermons, *postillae* (preaching aids), commentaries, translations, and polemics. Luther may have written more than any of his predecessors, and more has probably been written about him than about almost any other religious figure in history.

Despite his accomplishments, Luther came from modest origins—a fact that he never ceased to mention. He was born in Eisleben in the county of Mansfeld on 10 November 1483. His father, Hans, rose from the status of copper miner to become a *Hüttenmeister* (copper smelter) and owner of a few small mines. These mining interests led him to move his family in 1484 from Eisleben to the town of Mansfeld, where he parlayed his business success into a position on the town council in 1508. Luther's mother, Margareta, née Lindemann, came from a burgher family that was well established in the Thuringian city of Eisenach.

After completing his primary Latin education in the Mansfeld town school, Luther moved in 1497 to Magdeburg, where he lived and studied at a foundation school established by the Brethren of the Common Life. He completed his pre-university education in Eisenach, living in the vicinity of his mother's family, and boarding with the family of Heinrich Schalbe. The quasi-monastic lifestyle of the Brethren in Magdeburg, and his experience with an informal collegium in Eisenach, introduced Luther to life in a religious community. Next, encouraged by his father, Luther enrolled at the University of Erfurt: the university matriculation register for May 1501, listing "Martinus Ludher ex Mansfeldt," is the first documented reference to the Reformer. Humanist influence was strong at Erfurt; although Luther's accomplishments as a classical scholar would never rival those of such humanist luminaries as Conrad Celtis, Ulrich von Hutten, Mutianus Rufus, Eobanus Hessus, and Crotus Rubeanus, he would retain a commitment to original languages and sources that reflected their agenda.

The prevailing philosophical tradition at Erfurt, however, was nominalism, and it was in this context that Luther learned to think about the nature of the world and of God. The nominalist *via moderna* (modern way), in contrast to the realist *via antiqua* (ancient way) of Thomas Aquinas and Duns Scotus, emphasized personal experience and observation as opposed to speculation on abstract universal truths. Nominalist preachers such as Gabriel Biel of Strasbourg argued that God will not deny grace to one who makes a sincere effort. Jodokus Trutfetter and Bartholomaeus Arnoldi von Usingen, Luther's instructors in the arts faculty at Erfurt, were aligned with the nominalist tradition. Luther received his bachelor of arts in 1502 and his masters in 1505, graduating near the top of his class.

Erfurt was the scene of the first pivotal crisis in Luther's life. Plagued by spiritual doubts and by what he called *Anfechtungen* (moral trials), he abandoned his intention of pursuing studies in law. During a thun-

Luther burning the papal bull of excommunication on 10 December 1520

derstorm on the Feast Day of the Visitation of Mary he vowed to Anne, patron saint of miners, to become a monk. He subsequently entered the order of the Observant Augustinians at the Black Cloister in Erfurt. Johann von Staupitz, vicar general of the order in Germany, sought to provide spiritual consolation to the scrupulous friar in the midst of his Anfechtungen; but Staupitz was frequently exasperated by Luther's confessions, characterizing them as "Humpelwerk und Puppensünden" (weak excuses and play sins). Luther found little comfort in the exercise of his religious office after he was ordained a priest in 1507, trembling in terror as he celebrated the Mass. At Staupitz's instigation, however, he began to study the Scriptures, and he found cosolation there. Luther had seen his first Bible as a twenty-year-old university student in Erfurt, and he received one during the year of his novitiate. In addition to his Bible studies, Luther continued his training as a theologian and began to lecture on the *Sententiae libri quatuor* (Four Books of Sentences, circa 1160) of Peter Lombard. In 1508 he lectured on moral philosophy at Elector Friedrich's recently established University of Wittenberg, using Aristotle's *Nichomachean Ethics* as his text. He dabbled in mystical theology, reading works by Bridget of Sweden and Saint Bonaventura and, eventually, the early-fifteenth-century *Theologia Deutsch* (German Theology). Luther's exceptional level of commitment at the Erfurt cloister was recognized by his peers, and in the winter of 1510 they sent him to Rome as their representative in negotiating a settlement between rival factions of the Augustinian order. Luther returned from his trip disillusioned by the religious laxity that he encountered in Rome, where seven masses could be crammed into an hour, and disappointed over his failure to gain recognition for his faction.

Tensions in the Erfurt cloister encouraged Luther to follow Staupitz to the University of Wittenberg in the fall of 1511. With Staupitz's retirement as professor of theology in 1512, Luther began to lecture on the subject, and he was promoted to doctor of theology in October of that year. In Wittenberg, Luther resided with the other canons in the Augustinian monastery that would later be presented to him and his family as a gift from the elector. In 1513 Staupitz insisted that Luther assume duties as preacher at the city church in Wittenberg.

At the university Luther lectured on the Psalms from 1513 to 1515, Paul's Epistles to the Romans in 1515-1516, and the Epistle to the Galatians in 1516-1517. Rejecting his nominalist training, he came to a new understanding of God's righteousness. His first significant published work was a short introduction to a new edition of the *Theologia Deutsch* in 1516. The following year he prepared a series of theses against scholastic theology for his student Franz Günther to defend at a disputation on 4 September. Shortly afterward Luther presented a series of arguments that would eventually shatter the medieval Church Catholic: on 31 October 1517 he dispatched his *Diputatio pro declaratione virtutis indulgentiarum* (Disputation on the Declaration Concerning the Power of Indulgences), better known as his Ninety-five Theses, to Albrecht of Brandenburg, archbishop of Mainz and German elector, calling for a debate on the practice of selling indulgences–conditional promises of divine forgiveness and of diminished time in purgatory. (Much later, Philipp Melanchthon would claim that Luther posted the theses on the door of the Castle Church in Wittenberg.) Luther was incensed with the way indulgences were being hawked by the Dominican preacher Johann Tetzel with the jingle "Sobald als das Geld im koffer klingt, sofort die Seele aus dem Fegefeur springt" (As soon as coin in the money box clings, the soul from purgatory springs); this sort of inappropriate extension of the sacrament of penance had been condemned at the Sorbonne in 1482. Even though a debate never occurred, Luther attracted the attention of an influential German audience. He expanded his discussion of the issue in his *Resolutiones disputationem de Indulgentiarum virtute* (Resolutions on the Disputation Concerning the Power of Indulgences, 1518).

In 1518 Luther was invited to defend his developing theology before a gathering of fellow Augustinians in Heidelberg. In the "Disputatio Heidelberg habita" (Theses of the Heidelberg Disputation), published in the first volume of his collected Latin works (1545), he did not refer to the matter of indulgences, but, in what he believed represented the spirit of Saint Augustine, he appealed to divine grace and branded his nominalist heritage as a Pelagian error leading to damnation. While Luther won over many supporters at Heidelberg, including the Dominican Martin Bucer of Strasbourg and the educator Georg Simmler of Heidelberg, he also alienated many and found himself embroiled in a growing series of controversies. The Dominican Sylvester Prierias's *In Praesumptuosas Martini Lutheri conclusiones de potestate Papae dialogus* (Dialogue against the Presumptuous Conclusions of Martin Luther Concerning the Authority of the Pope, 1518) argued that Luther's position on indulgences threatened the Pope's authority and must be rejected. That same year the papal legate, Cardinal Cajetan (Tommaso de Vio), summoned Luther to the Diet of Augsburg to make the same point. The following year, at a debate in Leipzig, the theologian Johannes Eck not only forced Luther to acknowledge his defiance of the authority of the bishop of Rome but got Luther to equivocate on the authority of ecclesiastical councils. For Luther, Scripture was the final authority; for Eck, this position was tantamount to spiritual anarchy.

Luther was making enemies; but he was also gaining friends through the publication of his sermons, which dealt with a wide range of controversial social and religious topics. *Eynn Sermon von dem Ablasz unnd Gnade* (A Sermon on Indulgences and Grace, 1518) was a popular restatement of his condemnation of indulgences; *Eyn Sermon von der Bereytung zum Sterbenn* (A Sermon on Preparation for Dying, 1519) contributed to the literature of *ars moriendi* (the art of dying); *Eyn Sermon von den Wucher* (A Sermon on Usury, 1519) attacked economic inequality; and *Eyn Sermon von dem Bann* (A Sermon on the Ban, 1520) defended church discipline but rejected papal excommunication.

In 1520 Luther, learning that a papal bull of excommunication, *Exsurge Domine,* had been issued against him, published *An den christlichen Adel deutscher Nation: von des Christlichen Standes Besserung* (To the Christian Nobility of the German Nation: Concerning the Improvement of the Christian Estate). The work calls on the princes to serve as *Nötbishofe* (emergency bishops) and make the cause of church reform a concern of the German nation. Luther blasts what he identifies as the three *Mauer* (walls) of papal tyranny–the separation of the clerical from the lay estates and the exclusive authority of the Pope to interpret Scripture and to call a council–and argues for what would come to be called the priesthood of all believers. He also calls for reducing ecclesiastical revenues, forbidding pilgrimages to Rome, and eliminating masses for the dead. In *De captivate babylonica ecclesiae* (On the Babylonian Captivity of the Church, 1520) Luther insists that the church's sacramental practices have no sound scriptural basis and serve only the interests of the hierarchy; he concludes that only baptism and the Eucharist should be practiced as sacraments, for they alone had both the mandate of Scripture (the Word of promise) and a visible sign. In *Von*

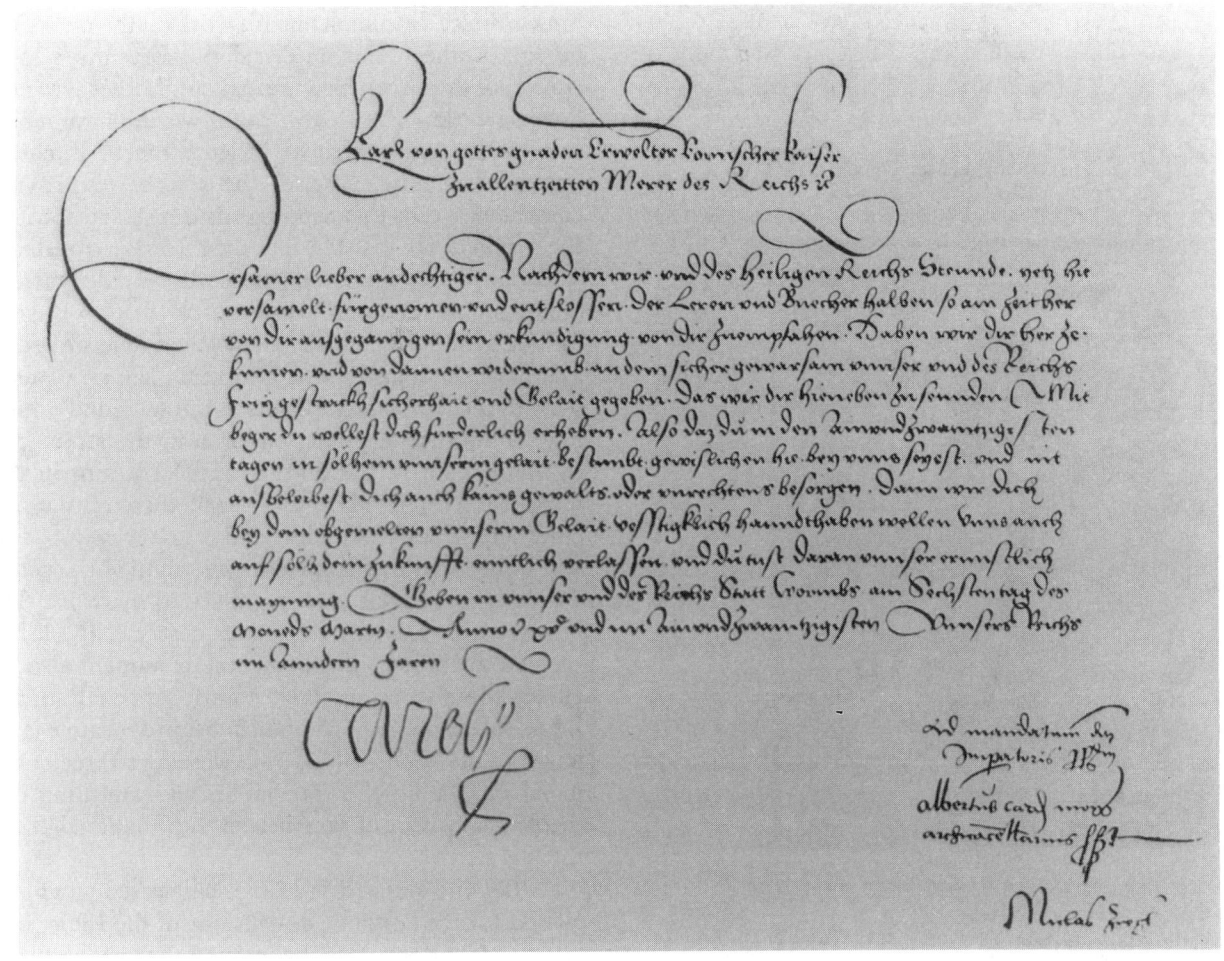

Order from Emperor Charles V summoning Luther to appear at the imperial diet in Worms in 1521 (from Gerhard Brendler, Martin Luther: Theology and Revolution, *1991)*

der Freyhey einiß Christen menschen (On the Freedom of a Christian, 1520) Luther offers his clearest statement to that time on the principle of justification by faith, arguing that no amount of good works can make a person righteous before God; righteousness comes as a gift of divine grace through faith. Nevertheless, Luther maintains, the needs of the outer person for moral restraints and the need to live in a loving relationship to one's neighbor require one to live as servant as well as lord. Law and Gospel belong together, and good works should proceed naturally from a faith that makes one righteous *coram deo* (before God).

On the morning of 10 December 1520 Luther marked the expiration of his sixty-day grace period for responding to the papal bull of excommunication by gathering with Melanchthon and several university students to burn the bull, along with the writings of several Scholastic theologians and a copy of the *Corpus Iuris Canonici* (Body of Canon Law). In January 1521 Luther was excommunicated in Rome, and in April he was summoned to appear before Emperor Charles V at the Die of Worms. The emperor had one request: recant. Luther's response was equally straightforward: he would retract nothing unless convinced to do so by the Word of God or by reasonable argument. In contrast to the popular image of the Augustinian friar standing defiant before the emperor at Worms, Luther reported that he was so shaken by the experience that he was nauseated nearly to the point of incapacitation. Luther was guaranteed safe passage to return home, but Elector Friedrich decided that he would be safer in Friedrich's castle at the Wartburg, outside Eisenach. Meanwhile, in Augsburg, Charles V issued the Edict of Worms, calling for Luther's arrest and banning his writings. Enforcement of the edict, however, was nearly impossible because of the myriad political entities into which the empire was divided.

Although he resented the isolation from his Wittenberg associates, the Wartburg proved to be a productive and invigorating environment for Luther. In this setting he expanded his critical assault on the institutions of the Roman Church with the attack on the whole structure of monastic life, *De votis monasticis* (On Monastic Vows, 1521). Here he holds that monastic

Woodcut by Cranach for Luther's translation of the New Testament (the "Septembertestament")

vows violate the principles of Christian freedom and rejects the traditional monastic counsels of perfection, insisting on a uniform Christian estate. By 1523 he would be calling for the closing of monasteries and convents. He also turned his attention to a project that would consume the rest of his life: the translation of the Bible into German. During this exile period he devoted himself to the translation of the New Testament, completing the task in less than three months by averaging some fifteen hundred words a day. The resulting *Das Newe Testament Deutzsch* was published in Wittenberg in September 1522, thereby coming to be known as the *Septembertestament;* it was followed by a slightly modified *Dezembertestament* when the three thousand copies of the first edition sold out almost immediately. Subsequently Luther would translate the rest of the Bible, providing a translation of the Psalms in 1524 and completing the rest of the Old Testament in 1534; in the latter year Luther's entire German Bible was published. He would continue to revise his translation until his death.

His work was, indeed, one of translation; it was no mere paraphrase or modification of the Vulgate but was based on the best available Greek and Hebrew sources. In completing his work on the New Testament, Luther relied on Desiderius Erasmus's 1519 edition of the Greek New Testament. Luther was not, however, content with a word-for-word, literal rendition of the text, which he called a mere "Buchstabieren" (spelling exercise); he sought to provide equivalent words that captured the sense and spirit of the original. He insisted that the effective translator "mus die mutter jhm hause, die kinder auff der gassen, den gemeinen man auff dem marckt drumb fragen, und den selbigen auff das maul sehen, wie sie reden und darnach dolmetzschen, so verstehen sie es auch und mercken, das man Deutsch mit jn redet" (must ask the mother at home, children in the street, the common man in the market and look him in the mouth, and listen to how they speak, then translate accordingly. They will understand it that way, too, and will notice that one is speaking German with them). There is a rustic or earthy quality to his work that hearkens back to the peasant ancestry that Luther seemed to cherish. The Septembertestament also includes some stunning illustrations, especially in the Book of Revelation; one of the most provocative is an image of the Whore of Babylon wearing a three-tiered papal tiara. Luther's translation was anything but theologically neutral, whether for the unlettered or for the literate.

Beyond simplicity, Luther cultivated an appreciation for the aesthetic dimensions of the Bible. In a letter to Georg Spalatin he insisted that people must learn that German nightingales can sing as beautifully as Roman goldfinches. Nowhere is his elegance of expression more evident than in his translation of the Psalms, based on the Hebrew texts. In Psalm 51 he has King David confess:

Gott sey mir gnedig, nach deiner Güte
Und tilge meine Sünde, nach deiner grossen Barmhertzigkeit ...
An dir allein hab ich gesündiget
Und übel fur dir gethan.
Auff das du recht behaltest in deinen worten,
Und rein bleibest, wenn du gerichtet wirst.

(God be gracious to me, according to thy goodness;
And blot out my sins, according to your great mercy ...
Against thee alone have I sinned
And done this evil in thy sight.
That thou might be justified when thou speakest
And remain pure when thou judgest.)

Here Luther has retained the parallelism of the Hebrew text, yet he has couched this penitential outburst of the fallen king in language that would be clear to any German. The translators of the King James Bible in the next century would draw much of their inspiration from Luther's German text, especially from the

Psalms, as they attempted to match gracious speech with economy of expression. Moreover, Luther's Psalms would provide inspiration to Johann Sebastian Bach, whose many oratorios and cantatas would give the language of the *Lutherbibel* a permanent place in German culture.

Luther's Bible also played a pivotal role in the linguistic evolution of Modern High German. Early-modern Germany was a hodgepodge of principalities, ecclesiastical territories, and imperial free cities with a confusing array of regional and territorial dialects, but the court speech of Saxony was emerging as a universal diplomatic language because it could be generally understood from the Low Countries to Switzerland and Bohemia. Luther realized the advantage living in Wittenberg gave him: "Ich red nach der sächsischen Canzeley, welcher nachfolgen alle fürsten und könige im teutsch lande" (I speak the language of the Saxon chancellery that all the princes and kings of Germany seek to imitate). Luther had no interest in replicating the frivolities of court speech, but he wanted to employ language that would be comprehensible to the largest number of people. Thus, Luther took the modified German of the princes to the people, and the vast dissemination of the *Lutherbibel* gave permanence to this linguistic form as literary New High German.

Luther's passion for the text of the Bible should not be misconstrued as a worship of the Bible. In his preface to the translation of the New Testament he indicates that he does not regard all of the books to be of equal worth. He recognizes the Gospel of John, Paul's letters to the Romans, and the first letter of Peter as exceptionally valuable, but he says that the book of James is full of straw and has serious questions about the canonical authority of Revelations. Thus Luther brought his own critical judgments to the Scriptures, a reflection of his humanist heritage. He expected and hoped that ordinary people would read the Scriptures frequently, even daily, and his later interest in education was inspired by a desire to expand this literate audience. Moreover, the prefaces Luther wrote for the various books of the Bible were meant as guides for the common folk. Yet he would always maintain that the text was insufficient without the proclamation of the Word through preaching. Therefore, he spent much time during his stay at the Wartburg in composing postillae.

Luther's absence from Wittenberg afforded him the opportunity to think, write, and translate, but he was aware of what his absence meant to the tumultuous movement that was beginning to surface at home. Melanchthon could provide adequate intellectual leadership to the cause of Reform, as was evident in his *Loci communes rerum theologicarum* (1521; translated as *The Loci Communes of Philip Melanchthon,* 1944), a work that Luther praised as the best systematic theology of its time. Melanchthon did not, however, possess the personal force necessary to rally public sentiment. The most popular Wittenberg leader during Luther's exile was Andreas Karlstadt, dean of the theology faculty and Luther's companion in the Leipzig disputation. Yet in Luther's mind, Karlstadt introduced ecclesiastical innovations, such as dispensing with the Mass, advocating clerical marriage, and offering two kinds of Communion, merely for the sake of fomenting rebellion. Receiving permission from the elector to return home, Luther gave a series of sermons in March 1522 that restored order to the community.

Luther understood that introducing reform measures too rapidly could unravel social constraints that he wanted to preserve. Accordingly, he composed a treatise against sedition, *Eyn trew vormanung Martini Luther tzu allen Christen. Sich tzu vorhuten fur auffruhr unnd Emporung* (A Faithful Admonition from Martin Luther to All Christians to Guard Themselves against Insurrection and Disorderliness, 1522). He followed it with a more extensive treatise on his understanding of the proper relationship between church and state, *Von welltlicher uberkeytt, wie weytt man yhr gehorsam schuldig sey* (On Secular Authority: To What Extent It Should Be Obeyed, 1523). Luther maintains the Augustinian distinction between the Kingdom of God (the divine realm) and the Kingdom of the World (the secular realm), but he goes further than Augustine in laying out specific duties for secular rulers. He defends the right of secular authorities to wield the sword in the midst of a wicked world, but he chastises princes who "vermessen auch ynn Gottis Stuel zu setzen, und die gewissen und glauben zu meisten, und nach yherm tollen gehyrn, den helige geist zur schulen furren" (put themselves in the place of God, lord it over conscience and faith, and put the Holy Spirit to school according to their mad brains). Duke Georg's prohibition of the printing of Luther's German New Testament in Albertine Saxony was the kind of trangression that, according to Luther, confused the proper spheres of secular and spiritual authorities.

Practical issues of Reform began to consume more of Luther's attention. In *Formula missae et communionis* (Form of the Mass and Communion, 1523) he retained the traditional Latin vocabulary but eliminated references to the mass as a sacrifice and offered two kinds of communion to the laity. Vernacular liturgical resources appeared in his guide for personal prayer and confession, *Eyn bett buchlin der tzehen gepott. Des glawbens. Des vatter vnßers und des Ave Maria* (A Little Prayer Book on the Ten Commandments, the Creed, the Lord's Prayer, and the Hail Mary, 1522) and in his *Das tauffbuchlin verdeudscht* (The German Baptism

Title page for Luther's attack on the rebellious peasantry

Book, 1526). Sharing with his humanist supporters the conviction that any significant changes, whether social or religious, must be undergirded by sufficient learning, Luther issued an appeal for universal public education in *An die Radherrn aller stedte deutsches lands: das sie christliche Schulen auffrichten und hallten sollen* (To the Councillors of All Cities in Germany: That They Should Establish and Maintain Christian Schools, 1524). In regard to relief for the poor, he recommended community action in *Ordenung eyns gemeynen kastens* (Community Chest Order, 1523). His preface to these regulations makes an explicit connection between *gottes dienst* (service to God, or worship) and service to one's needy neighbor.

On 13 June 1525 Luther, who had set aside his Augustinian cowl the previous October, married a former Cistercian nun, Katherine von Bora, sixteen years his junior. Their first child, Johannes—named after Johannes Bugenhagen, the Wittenberg city pastor who had performed the marriage ceremony— was born the next summer and was followed by five more children: Elisabeth in 1527, Magdelena in 1529, Martin in 1531, Paul in 1533, and Margarete in 1534. Katherine ran their household in the former cloister with efficiency and even managed a small pig farm.

The year of his marriage brought one of the greatest intellectual challenges Luther would ever experience: the need to respond to Erasmus's treastise *De libero arbitrio* (On the Freedom of the Will, 1524). In his *De servo arbitrio* (On the Bondage of the Will, 1525) Luther rightly observed that "Unus tu et solus cardinem rerum uidisti, et iugulum petisti" (You and you alone [Erasmus] have seen to the heart of the matter and seized the jugular). The disputants marshaled many scriptural passages to support their respective positions, Erasmus defending human freedom and Luther claiming that the fallen condition of humankind resulted in the loss of freedom. Above all, Luther insisted on the certainty of theological assertions for "Spiritus sanctus non est Scepticus" (the Holy Spirit is not a skeptic). The contrast between the cautious Erasmus and the dogmatic Luther is symptomatic of the gap that was growing between humanist and Protestant Reformers in this generation.

Beyond the rhetoric of the debate, Erasmus believed that Luther's grace-laden theology sacrificed moral resposibility, undercut ethics, and was at least partially responsible for the social tragedies that erupted in the Peasants' War of 1524–1525. The message of Christian liberty had obvious social as well as spiritual implications, and whether intended or not by the theologians, it affirmed the longings of many for a different kind of reformation. *Gemeindereformationen* (communal Reform movements) capitalized on the climate of religious discontent to argue for local control of ecclesiastical affairs. Luther's own treatise *Das eyn Christliche Versamlung odder Gemeyne: recht und macht habe: alle lere tzu urteylen und lerer tzu berufen, ein- und abzusetzen* (That a Christian Assembly Has the Right and Authority to Judge All Teaching and to Call, Appoint, and Dismiss Teachers, 1523) identified a central element of this communal reform: the right to call a pastor. Luther's response to the early stages of the peasant rebellion in 1524, *Ermanunge zum fride auff die zwelff artikel der Bawrschafft ynn Schwaben* (Admonitions on Peace from the Twelve Articles of the Swabian Peasantry, 1525), urged both peasants and princes to exercise restraint. But when a more full-scale revolution broke out in the spring of 1525 Luther, in his *Wider die Rewbischen unnd mördischen rotten der anderen bawren* (Against the Robbing and Murdering Hordes of Other Peasants, 1525), called on the princes to crush the rebels; they did so with great ferocity.

The events of 1525 fueled the magisterial, as opposed to the popular, wing of the Reformation, and the meeting of the imperial diet at Speyer in 1526 set the stage for the *landesherrliche Kirchenregiment* (territorial church system). Since Charles V's issuance of the Edict of Worms, Lutheranism had technically been a renegade movement. After the diet at Speyer, however, the estates of the empire were allowed to proceed with their own programs of reform in anticipation of the convening of a general church council. The process of implementing reform assumed a more official posture as princes and their advisers sought to introduce ecclesiastical changes. In Luther's Saxony, as in many other German territories, teams of clergy and lay authorities designated by the prince visited the parishes; in Saxony they used the visitation protocols drafted by Melanchthon. After the preliminary round of visitations was completed, Luther and Melanchthon collaborated on a summary set of instructions, *Unterricht der Visitatoren an die Pfarhern ym Kurfürstenthum zu Sachsen* (Instructions for the Parish Visitors to the Congregations in Electoral Saxony, 1528), that was adopted as the first church ordinance for Electoral Saxony. Reforms in worship were one important element of this visitation process, and Luther's vernacular *Deudsche Messe und ordnung Gottis diensts* (German Mass and Order of Service, 1526) was introduced as the norm for Saxony.

An important consequence of these early rounds of visitations was Luther's commitment to providing basic instruction in Christian faith in the form of a catechism. In his preface to his *Enchiridion. Der kleine Katechismus für die gemeine Pfarher und Prediger, gemehret und verbessert* (Handbook: Small Catechism for the Common Pastor and Preacher, Expanded and Improved, 1529), Luther explained the urgency of the task after hearing the reports of the visitors: "Hilf, lieber Gott, wie manchen Jammer habe ich gesehen, daß der gemeine Mann doch so garnichts weiß von der christliche Lehre, sonderlich auf den Dörfen" (Good God, what wretchedness I beheld! The common people, especially those who live in the country, have no knowledge whatsoever of Christian teaching). The Small Catechism, first published as a broadsheet, sought to address this deficiency with an emphasis on belief over religious practice. As Luther discussed the prescriptions of the Ten Commandments, he focused on faith, placing each commandment in the context of a relationship with the divine: "Wir sollen Gott fürchten, lieben und vertrauen, daß . . . " (We should fear, love and trust God, so that . . .). His discussions of the Lord's Prayer and the Apostles' Creed and his explanations of the sacraments of Communion and baptism maintained this accent on what one should know as opposed to what one should do. The Small Catechism was designed for simple family instruction; Luther's subsequent *Deudsch Catechismus* (German Catechism, 1529), known as the *Großer Katechismus* (Large Catechism), provided more elaborate explanations of basic Christian doctrines for pastors and teachers.

Another aid to Reform at the popular level were

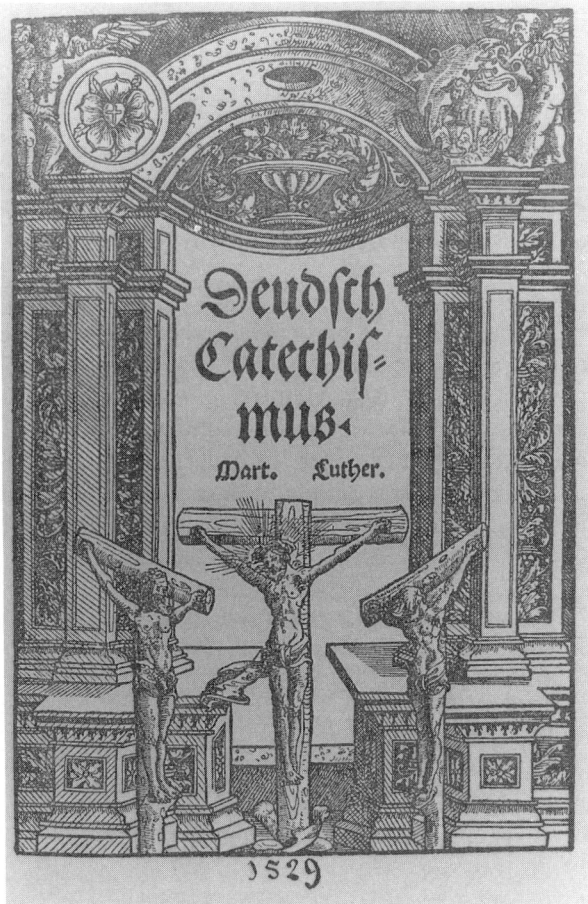

Title page for Luther's Large Catechism

the many hymns that Luther composed or edited. The first of his hymnbooks, the *Geystliche Gesangk Buchlein* (Spiritual Hymn Book), appeared in 1524; it was followed by nearly one hundred other collections over the course of his life. Luther's hymns were effective because their melodies captured the soul of the simple folk and their texts expressed the depths of his theological insights. In "Vom himmel hoch" (From Heaven on High) Luther marvels at the majesty and simplicity of the Incarnation:

Ach Herr, du Schöpfer aller Ding,
wie bist du worden so gering,
daß du da liegt auf dürrem Gras
davon ein Rind und Esel aß.

(Ah Lord and Creator of all,
How art thou become so small
lying there on withered grass,
whereof ate a cow and ass).

The hymn "Nun freut euch lieben Christen gmein" (Rejoice Now, Beloved Christian Congregation) recalls his dispute with Erasmus over free will:

> Dem Teufel ich gefangen lag
> im Tod war ich verloren,
> mein Sund mich quälte Nacht und Tag,
> darin ich war geboren.
>
> (I lay captured by the Devil,
> lost in death,
> my sinfulness tormented me day and night,
> in which I was born.)

The pervasive battle for Luther was with the devil and cosmic evil. Hymns provided him the opportunity to exult in victories already won, even though the comfort proved personally elusive as he continued to struggle with his Anfechtungen. The familiar stanzas of his "Ein feste Burg is unser Gott" (A Mighty Fortress Is Our God) recognize this demonic opposition yet affirm the power of the divine Word:

> Und wenn die Welt voll Teufel wär
> und wolt uns gar verschlingen
> so fürchten wir uns nicht so sehr
> es soll uns doch gelingen.
> Die fürst dieser Welt
> wie saur er sich stellt
> tut er uns doch nicht
> das macht, er ist gericht
> ein Wörtlein kann ihn fällen.
>
> (And though this world with devils filled,
> should threaten to undo us,
> We will not fear for God has willed,
> his truth to triumph through us,
> the prince of darkness grim,
> we tremble not for him.
> His rage we can endure,
> for lo his doom is sure,
> one little word shall fell him.)

These powerful hymns and the simple teaching of the Small Catechism may represent Luther's most enduring and universal religious contributions.

In 1529 the imperial diet, meeting again in Speyer, suspended previously granted concessions to the evangelical—that is, Lutheran—states. This action resulted in an official protest by representatives of the cities and territories, and, hence, to the generic title *Protestant* for these estates of the empire. When it came to negotiating territorial arrangements, Luther was a terrible politician. His participation in the colloquy that Landgrave Philip of Hesse sponsored at his castle in Marburg in 1529 demonstrates his disdain for political expediency and unswerving commitment to theological positions. These meetings with the south German and Swiss representatives, the most important of whom was Huldrych Zwingli of Zurich, foundered on an issue Luther regarded as critical: the understanding of Christ's presence in the Eucharist. Luther had addressed this matter on countless occasions, beginning with *Widder die hymelischen propheten, von den bildern und Sacrament* (Against the Heavenly Prophets in the Matter of Images and Sacraments, 1525), then again in his *Das diese Worte Christi (Das ist mein leib etce) noch fest stehen widder die Schwerm geister* (That the Words of Christ [This Is My Body, etc.] Still Stand Firm against the Fanatics, 1527). Moreover, in his *Vom abendmahl Christi, Bekendnis* (Confession on the Lord's Supper, 1528) Luther had again made the point that insisting on the real presence of Christ distinguished his thinking from the errors he associated with Zwingli and Johann Oecolampadius. When the parties met at Marburg agreement was reached on every article except the one on Christ's presence in the Eucharist. This doctrine alone was sufficient to separate the Swiss "Reformed" movement from the German Lutherans.

The next summer the imperial diet convened again, this time in Augsburg. The emperor was present, but Luther was not; he remained close to the proceedings but safe at Coburg Castle, trusting Melanchthon to carry out the critical negotiations at the diet. He communicated with the participants in *Vermanung an die geistlichen versamlet auf dem Reichstag zu Augsburg* (Admonition to the Clergy Assembled at Augsburg, 1530), outlining his doctrinal proposals and calling on the clergy to heed the Gospel. In Coburg, Luther continued to work on his lectures on the Psalms and completed a series of translations of Aesop's fables that would be published in 1571. The most important consequence of the Diet of Augsburg for Luther was the completion of *Confessio fidei exhibita invictissimo Imperatori Carolo V.* (1531; translated as *The confessyon of the fayth of the Germaynes exhibited to . . . Emperour Charles the v in the councell . . . holden at Augusta 1530*, 1536)—the Augsburg Confession—submitted by Melanchthon on 25 June but written under Luther's supervision. The Catholic and imperial response to the confession, the *Confutatio* (Confutation of the Augsburg Confession), defended the orthodox positions of Rome and labeled the Protestants theologically deviant. The Augsburg Confession, however, remains the definitive expression of the Lutheran Reformation.

After Augsburg a foreboding, even apocalyptic, tone would characterize many of Luther's writings. It is evident in *Warnunge D. Martini Luther, An seine lieben Deudschen* (Address of Dr. Martin Luther to His Beloved Germans, 1531), in which he expresses disgust at the outcome of the diet, argued that he would never counsel rebellion, and made it clear that he believed that conflict was imminent and that the Protestants would offer resistance. Furthermore, Luther insisted, "Man muß nicht alles auffrürisch sein lassen, was die

Title page for, and illustration from, the first edition of Luther's complete translation of the Bible. The illustration shows God blessing his creation, with Adam and Eve in the center.

bluthunde auffrürisch schelten" (One cannot take for rebellion everything that the bloodhounds designate as rebellion). The treatise reveals an important shift in Luther's thinking: hitherto he had opposed any attempt to legitimize resisting the emperor, but now he was willing to support the rights of a defensive alliance. Luther's arguments bore fruit in the formation of the Protestant Schmalkaldic league in 1531.

The simple caricatures of "old man" Luther—boorish, dogmatic, bigoted, constipated, and outdated, have been challenged as scholars have turned greater attention to the later stages of his career. Luther continued to be prolific as a writer, although the freshness of his ideas and the vigor of his presence had begun to wane. Students and Wittenberg associates such as Veit Dietrich, Georg Rörer, and Conrad Cordatus began to collect anecdotes of the lives of Luther and his family in 1531 and continued doing so until the year before his death; for some, the crude and satiric Luther who was captured in these *Tischreden* (Table Talks, 1566; translated as *Dris. Martini Lutheris colloquia mensalia, . . divine discourses at his table*, 1652) had an almost endearing quality. Luther could also be conciliatory in the continual attempts to secure political alliances through confessional negotiations. His 1536 meeting with the Strasbourg representatives Bucer and Wolfgang Capito produced the Wittenberg Concord, in which the parties compromised on their understandings of the Lord's Supper. Moreover, linking the south Germans with Saxony provided an important partner in the network of the Schmalkaldic estates. The following year Luther composed his own confession of faith, *Artickel, so da hetten sollen auffs Concilion zu Mantua, oder wo es würde sein, uberantwortet werden* (Articles that Should Have Been Addressed Either at the Council of Mantua or Wherever It Might Be, 1538), generally known as *Die Schmalkaldischen Artikel* (The Schmalkaldic Articles), in response to an urgent request from Elector Johann Friedrich. Pope Paul III's Council of Mantua was scheduled to meet during 1537, and the elector and other German Protestant leaders wanted a concise expression of their faith to offer at it. Although the council was never convened, it provided Luther the opportu-

Luther's grave in the Wittenberg Castle church

nity to outline clearly where he would and would not compromise with the Church of Rome. Luther still had the capacity to offer lucid theological arguments, and the Lutheran church incorporated the Schmalkaldic Articles into the *Book of Concord* (1580), the foundational document of the church.

Nevertheless, there is something to the observation that the later Luther was known more by his enemies than by his friends. Of particular concern to Luther was an unholy trinity of the Turks, the Jews, and the Pope and his allies. To the Christian citizens of the German Empire the Turk was a terrifying "other" whose armies had besieged Vienna in 1529 and whose alleged atrocities made for frightening bedtime tales. Beginning with the military advances of the Ottoman Empire in the early 1520s, polemical pamphlets known collectively as the *Türkenbücher* circulated throughout the German Empire. These writings tended to wax and wane, depending upon the perceived imminence of a Turkish invasion. Luther contributed directly to this literature on a couple of occasions. His initial writings, *Vom kriege widder die Türken* (On War against the Turks, 1529) and *Eine Heerpredigt widder die Türken* (A Military Sermon against the Turks, 1529) concerned the propriety of a military response. Later he wrote *Vermanunge zum Gebet, Wider den Türcken* (An Admonition to Pray against the Turk, 1541), in which he describes the Turks both as a demoniacal agent of God's wrath and as a schoolmaster sent to stimulate honorable worship. Luther's real purpose in writing these works was to shame lax German Christians into obedient service to God.

While the Turks were an alien outsider, the Jews were an alien insider—at least in those territories that had not driven them into exile. Luther's early thinking about the Jews demonstrates guarded optimism: he believed that the emancipation of the Gospel and of true preaching would result in the salvation—that is, the conversion—of the Jews. In *Das Ihesus Christus eyn geborner Iude sey* (That Jesus Christ Was Born a Jew, 1523) he argued that Jews should be treated in a friendly fashion so that many of them would become true Christians and return to the faith of their fathers, the prophets and patriarchs. This fanciful thinking about Jewish conversions to Christianity was not, of course, borne out in reality, and Luther became increasingly bitter about what he regarded as this lost opportunity for the Jews. His exasperation is evident in *Ein Brieff D. Mart. Luther wider die Sabbather an einen guten Freund* (A Letter of Dr. Martin Luther against the Sabbatarians, to a Good Friend, 1538), in which he seeks to demonstrate the error of the false Jewish hopes for a Messiah and to make the case for the fulfillment of Old Testament prophecies in Christ. The pamphlet is generally cordial and self-confident, and occasionally rude.

Luther's harshest comments were reserved for his scandalous *Von den Iüden und ihren Lügen* (On the Jews and Their Lies, 1543). In this treatise Luther abandons the treatment of the Jews in a friendly fashion for a rather different response: "Wir müssen mit gebet und Gottes furcht eine scharffe barmhertzigkeit uben, ob wir doch etliche aus der flammen und glut erretten kündten" (We must, with prayer and the fear of God, exercise a harsh mercy, in hopes that we can save some from the flames and embers). He goes on to argue that those Jews who remain obstinate in their religious tradition should have their schools and synagogues burned and razed, their houses destroyed, their books confiscated, and their livelihoods stripped away. Although some have argued that Luther should be considered religiously intolerant rather than anti-Semitic, these belligerent statements represent the most negative aspect of his legacy.

Luther's final assaults on the papacy and affiliated parties contained nothing new; they were simply expressed in a more comical or coarse fashion. For pure invective and ad hominem attack Luther never surpassed his reply to Duke Heinrich of Brunswick, *Wider Hans Worst* (Against Hans Wurst, 1541). The treatise is a farce based on Hans Wurst, a clownish character who appeared at fairs and marketplaces with a sausage around his neck. For Luther, Duke Heinrich was the fool Hans Wurst; in addition, he referred to the duke as a devil, an archprostitute, and a harem guard. For any who might differ with Luther's assessment, he had a suggestion: "so thut in die Bruch und hengt sie an den hals, und macht davon euch ein galreden und fresset ir groben Esel und Sewe" (so do it in your pants, and hang it around your neck and make it into a sausage, then gobble it down like the gross asses and sows you are). Although scatalogical language was an element of Luther's rhetoric throughout his life, this mode of expression seemed to occur more often in his later works. Duke Heinrich was an adversary of the Saxon elector and the Hessian landgrave and a persecutor of faithful Lutherans in his territory; thus, Luther's assault was motivated by religious concerns, however difficult that dimension may be to discern in this particular exchange. When it came to attacking the papacy directly, Luther still preferred the appropriately colorful language of Scripture that spoke of Antichrists and Great Whores of Babylon. One of Luther's last published treatises was this kind of work, *Wider das Bapstum zu Rom vom Teuffel gestifft* (Against the Papacy at Rome, Founded by the Devil, 1545). He was shocked and dismayed when he learned that Pope Paul III had taken upon himself the responsibility of delaying the first meeting of the church council scheduled to open in Trent. For Luther, it was but one final example that the authority of Rome was entirely out of proportion.

Luther's battles with an array of foes, and his struggles with his personal Anfechtungen, concluded on 18 February 1546. Luther's life ended where it began, in the town of Eisleben in the county of Mansfeld. He had been summoned there to aid the counts in their dispute regarding the division of their territory. He should not have made the journey, given the state of his health, but he believed that it was important to attempt to mediate in this situation. His body was returned to Wittenberg for the funeral service on 20 February. His pastor Bugenhagen preached the funeral sermon, and Melanchthon offered the eulogy. Luther was buried in front of the pulpit of the Castle Church.

The year before his death Luther had provided a preface to the complete edition of his Latin writings (1545-1547). He refers to the controversies and experiences that surrounded his earliest works—the debate over indulgences; the battles with Tetzel, Cajetan, and Eck; and his increasing alienation from the Roman Church. He describes a theological breakthrough that later came to be called his *Turmerlebnis* (tower experience), when he felt as though "apertis portis in ipsam paradisum intrasse" (he had entered into paradise itself with the gates flung open). Luther's life, however, had manifested many breakthroughs as he abandoned one system of philosophical and religious commitments and developed a theology and a church suitable to his new understanding. The literary output that accompanied this feat was truly staggering and remains an accomplishment with few if any rivals. In the Latin preface Luther offers a more humble assessment: "cupiebam omnes libros meos perpetua oblivione sepultos, ut melioribus esset locus" (I wished that all my books were consigned to perpetual oblivion, so that better ones could take their place). Luther's writings, hymns, translations, sermons, and liturgies, however, continue to inform religious practice throughout the Christian community, both Protestant and Catholic. Luther's own caution is appropriate: too much can be and has been made of his influence. Yet the language of his Bible, and the literature he addressed to so many different audiences of his day, make it impossible to overlook his contributions.

Bibliographies:

Josef Benzing and Helmut Claus, *Lutherbibliographie: Verzeichnis der gedruckten Schriften Martin Luthers bis zu dessen Tod* (Baden-Baden: Heitz, 1966);

Herbert Wolf, *Germanistische Luther-Bibliographie: Martin Luthers deutsches Sprachschaffen im Spiegel des internationalen Schrifttums der Jahre 1880-1980* (Heidelberg: Winter, 1985).

Biographies:

Julius Köstlin, *Martin Luther the Reformer* (London: Cassell, 1883);

Preserved Smith, *The Life and Letters of Martin Luther* (Philadelphia: Lutheran Publication Society, 1913);

Paul J. Reiter, *Martin Luther: Umwelt, Charakter und Psychose* (Copenhagen: Levin & Munksgaard, 1937);

Heinrich Boehmer, *Road to Reformation: Martin Luther to the Year 1521,* translated by John W. Doberstein and Theodore G. Tappert (Philadelphia: Muhlenberg, 1946);

Roland Herbert Bainton, *Here I Stand: A Life of Martin Luther* (New York: Abingdon-Cokesbury, 1950);

Erik H. Erikson, *Young Man Luther: A Study in Psychoanalysis and History* (New York: Norton, 1958);

John Murray Todd, *Martin Luther: A Biographical Study* (New York: Paulist Press, 1964);

Erwin Iserloh, *Luther zwischen Reform und Reformation: Der Thesenanschlag fand nicht statt* (Münster: Aschendorff, 1966);

A. G. Dickens, *Martin Luther and the Reformation* (London: English Universities Press, 1967);

James Atkinson, *Martin Luther and the Birth of Protestantism* (Baltimore: Penguin, 1968);

Hartmann Grisar, *Martin Luther: His Life and Work*, tranlsated and adapted by Frank J. Eble (New York, AMS, 1971);

Heinrich Bornkamm, *Martin Luther in der Mitte seines Lebens: Das Jahrzehnt zwischen dem Wormser und dem Augsburger Reichstag*, edited by Karin Bornkamm (Göttingen: Vandenhoeck & Ruprecht, 1979); translated by E. Theodore Bachman as *Luther in Mid-Career, 1521–1530* (Philadelphia: Fortress, 1983);

H. G. Haile, *Luther: An Experiment in Biography* (Garden City, N.Y.: Doubleday, 1980);

Bernhard Lohse, *Martin Luther: Eine Einführung in sein Leben und sein werk* (Munich: Beck, 1981);

Peter Manns, *Martin Luther: An Illustrated Biography*, translated by Michael Shaw (New York: Crossroad, 1982);

James Arne Nestingen, *Martin Luther: His Life and Teachings* (Philadelphia: Fortress, 1982);

Wilhelm Fleschendranger, *Martin Luther: Bildbiographie* (Leipzig: Bibliographisches Institut, 1982);

John Todd, *Luther: A Life* (New York: Crossroad, 1982);

Eric W. Gritsch, *Martin—God's Court Jester: Luther in Retrospect* (Philadelphia: Fortress, 1983);

Helmar Junghans, ed., *Leben und Werk Martin Luthers von 1526 bis 1546: Festgabe zu seinem 500. Geburtstag*, 2 volumes (Göttingen: Vandenhoeck & Ruprecht, 1983);

Marc Lienhard, *Martin Luther: Un Temps, une Vie, un Message* (Geneva: labor et Fides, 1983);

Joachim Rogge, *Martin Luther: Sein Leben, Seine Zeit, sein Wirkungen* (Berlin: Evangelische Verlagsanstalt, 1983);

Martin Brecht, *Martin Luther*, 3 volumes, translated by James L. Schaff (Philadelphia: Fortress, 1985–1992);

James Kittelson, *Luther the Reformer: The Story of the Man and His Career* (Minneapolis: Augsburg, 1986);

Heiko Oberman, *Luther: Man between God and the Devil*, translated by Eileen Walliser-Schwarzbart (New Haven: Yale University Press, 1989);

Albrecht Beutel, *Martin Luther* (Munich: Beck, 1991).

References:

Kurt Aland, *Hilfsbuch zum Lutherstudium*, third edition (Wittenberg: Luther-Verlag, 1970);

Paul Althaus, *The Ethics of Martin Luther*, translated by Robert C. Schultz (Philadelphia: Fortress, 1972);

Althaus, *The Theology of Martin Luther* (Philadelphia: Fortress, 1966);

David V. N. Bagchi, *Luther's Earliest Opponents: Catholic Controversialists, 1518–1525* (Minneapolis: Fortress, 1991);

Oswald Bayer, *Promissio: Die Geschichte der reformatorischen Wende in Luthers Theologie* (Göttingen: Vandenhoeck & Ruprecht, 1971);

Ernest Bizer, *Fides ex Auditu: Eine Untersuchung über die Entdeckung der Gerechtigkeit Gottes durch Martin Luther* (Neukirchen: Kreis Moers, 1958);

Bizer, *Studien zur Geschichte des Abendmahlstreits in 16. Jahrhundert* (Gütersloh: Bertelsmann, 1940);

Peter Blickle, *Communal Reformations: The Quest for Salvation in Sixteenth Century Germany* (Atlantic Highlands, N.J.: Humanities, 1992);

Heinz Bluhm, *Martin Luther, Creative Translator* (Saint Louis: Concordia, 1965);

Heinrich Bornkamm, *Thesen and Thesenanschlag Luthers: Geschehen und Bedeutung* (Berlin: Topelmann, 1967);

Thomas A. Brady, "Settlements: The Holy Roman Empire," in *Handbook of European History 1400–1600*, edited by Brady, Heiko A. Oberman, and James D. Tracy (Leiden: Brill, 1995), pp. 349–384;

Martin Brecht, *Luther als Schriftsteller* (Stuttgart: Calwer, 1990);

A. G. Dickens, *The German Nation and Martin Luther* (New York: Harper & Row, 1974);

Gerhard Dünnhaupt, ed., *Martin Luther Quincentennial* (Detroit: Wayne State University Press, 1984);

Gerhard Ebeling, *Luther: An Introduction to His Thought* (Philadelphia: Fortress, 1970);

Mark U. Edwards, *Luther and the False Brethren* (Stanford, Cal.: Stanford University Press, 1975);

Edwards, "Luther's Biography," in *Reformation Europe: A Guide to Research, 2*, edited by William S. Maltby (Saint Louis: Center for Reformation Studies, 1992), pp. 5–20;

Edwards, *Luther's Last Battles: Politics and Polemics, 1531–1546* (Ithaca, N.Y.: Cornell University Press, 1983);

Edwards, *Printing, Propaganda, and Martin Luther* (Berkeley: University of California Press, 1994);

Stephen Fischer-Galati, *Ottoman Imperialism and German Protestantism, 1521–1555* (Cambridge, Mass.: Harvard University Press, 1959);

George W. Forell, *Faith Active in Love: An Investigation of the Principles Underlying Luther's Social Ethics* (Minneapolis: Augsburg, 1954);

Leif Grane, *Martinus Noster: Luther in the German Reform Movement, 1518–1521* (Mainz: Zabern, 1994);

Grane, *Modus loquendi Theologicus: Luthers Kampf um die Erneuerung der Theologie* (Leiden: Brill, 1975);

H. G. Haile, "The Great Martin Luther Spoof," *Yale Review,* 65 (1976): 43-57;

Haile, "Luther and Literacy," *PMLA,* 49 (1976): 816-828;

Haile, "Martin Luther and the Art of the Gloss," *Georgia Review,* 24 (Summer 1980): 323-333;

Scott Hendrix, *Ecclesia in Via: Ecclesiological Developments in the Medieval Psalms Exegesis and the Dictata super Psalterium (1513-1515) of Martin Luther* (Leiden: Brill, 1974);

Erwin Iserloh, *The Theses Were Not Posted: Luther between Reform and Reformation,* translated by Jared Wicks (Boston: Beacon Press, 1968);

Helmar Junghans, *Der junge Luther und die Humanisten* (Göttingen: Vandenhoeck & Ruprecht, 1985);

Steffen Kjeldgaard-Pedersen, *Gesetz, Evangelium, und Buße: Theologiegeschichtliche Studien zum Verhältnis zwischen dem jungen Johann Agricola (Eisleben) und Martin Luther* (Leiden: Brill, 1983);

Walter Köhler, *Zwingli und Luther: Ihr Streit über das Abendmahl nach seinen politischen und religiösen Beziehungen,* 2 volumes, Quellen und Forschungen zur Reformationsgeschichte, volumes 6-7 (Volume 1, Leipzig: Heinsius, 1924; volume 2, Gütersloh: Bertelsmann, 1953);

Hans-Walter Krumwiede, *Zur Entstehung des landesherrlichen Kirchenregiments in Kursachsen und in Braunschweig-Wolfenbüttel* (Göttingen, 1967);

Kurt Löcher, ed., *Martin Luther und die Reformation in Deutschland* (Schweinfurt: Weppert, 1988);

Bernard Lohse, *Mönchtum und Reformation: Luthers Auseinandersetzung mit dem Mönchsideal des Mittelalters* (Göttingen: Vandenhoeck & Ruprecht, 1963);

Joseph Lortz and Erwin Iserloh, *Kleine Reformationsgeschichte: Ursachen, Verlauf, Wirkung* (Freiburg im Breisgau: Herder, 1969);

Martin E. Marty, ed., *The Place of Trust: Martin Luther on the Sermon on the Mount* (San Francisco: Harper & Row, 1983);

Alistair E. McGrath, *Luther's Theology of the Cross: Martin Luther on Justification, 1509-1519* (London: Blackwell, 1985);

Karl Heinz zur Mühlen, *Nos extra Nos: Luthers Theologie zwischen Mystik und Scholastik* (Tübingen: Mohr, 1972);

Gerhard Müller, *Causa Reformationis: Beiträge zur Reformationsgeschichte und zur Theologie Martin Luthers* (Gütersloh: Mohn, 1989);

Heiko A. Oberman, *The Roots of Anti-Semitism in the Age of the Renaissance and Reformation* (Philadelphia: Fortress, 1984);

Daniel Olivier, *Le procès luther* (Paris: Fayard, 1971);

Steven Ozment, *When Fathers Ruled: Family Life in Reformation Europe* (Cambridge, Mass.: Harvard University Press, 1983);

Otto Pesch, *Hinführung zu Luther* (Mainz: Matthias-Grünewald, 1982);

Gordon Rupp, *The Righteousness of God* (London: Hodder & Stoughton, 1953);

Heinz Schilling, "Confessional Europe," in *Handbook of European History, 1400-1600,* edited by Thomas A. Brady, Heiko A. Oberman, and James D. Tracy (Leiden: Brill, 1995);

Robert W. Scribner, *For the Sake of Simple Folk: Popular Propaganda for the German Reformation* (Oxford: Clarendon Press, 1994);

David C. Steinmetz, *Luther and Staupitz: An Essay in the Intellectual Origins of the Protestant Reformation* (Durham, N.C.: Duke University Press, 1980);

Gerald Strauss, *Luther's House of Learning: Indoctrination of the Young in the German Reformation* (Baltimore: Johns Hopkins University Press, 1978);

Jared Wicks, *Cajetan Responds: A Reader in Reformation Controversy* (Washington, D.C.: Catholic University of America Press, 1978);

Herbert Wolf, *Martin Luther: Eine Einführung in germanistische Luther-Studien* (Stuttgart: Metzler, 1980);

Eike Wolgast, *Die Wittenberger Theologie und die Politik der evangelischen Stände: Studien zu Luthers Gutachten in politischen Fragen* (Gütersloh: Mohn, 1977).

Niklaus Manuel
(Niklaus Manuel Deutsch)
(circa 1484 - 28 April 1530)

Glenn Ehrstine
University of Iowa

WORKS: *Sprüche zum Totentanz* (circa 1516-1519)

Manuscript: Verses accompanying Manuel's *Totentanz* mural, painted on a wall of the Dominican monastery in Bern, razed in 1660.

First publication and standard edition: In *Niklaus Manuel*, edited by Jakob Baechtold, Bibliothek älterer Schriftwerke der deutschen Schweiz und ihres Grenzgebietes, series 1, volume 2 (Frauenfeld: Huber, 1878), pp. 1-20;

Ein seltsamer wunderschöner Traum, attributed to Manuel (circa 1521-1522)

Manuscript: Staats- und Universitätsbibliothek Hamburg, cod. ms. germ. 28–also includes fragments of Manuel's 1523 carnival plays.

First publication: Fritz Burg, "Dichtungen des Niclaus Manuel: Aus einer Handschrift der Hamburger Stadtbibliothek," in *Neues Berner Taschenbuch auf das Jahr 1897,* edited by Heinrich Türler (Bern: Wyss, 1896), pp. 1-136;

Bicoccalied (1522)

Manuscript: Fragment in the hand of Aegidus Tschudi, circa 1550, Zentralbibliothek Zurich, Ms. T. 447.

First publication: *Ein hüpsch nüw lied vnd verantwortung desz Sturms halb beschähen zuo Piggoga, in der wyß wie das Paffier Lied* (Bern: Benjamin Ulman, circa 1590).

Standard edition: In *Niklaus Manuel*, edited by Baechtold, pp. 21-28;

Ein fasznacht spyl, so zuo Bern vff der hern fasznacht, in dem M.D.XXII. iare, von Burgersönen offenlich gemacht ist, Darinn die warheit in schimpfs wysz vom pabst, vnd siner priesterschafft gemeldet würt. Item ein ander spyl, daselbs vff der alten fasznacht darnach gemacht, anzeigend grossen vnderscheid zwischen dem Papst, vnd Christum Jesum vnserm seligmacher (Zurich: Christoph Froschauer, 1524);

Der Ablßakrämer (1525)

Manuscript: In the author's own hand,

Self-portrait of Niklaus Manuel (from Günther Müller, Deutsche Dichtung von der Renaissance bis zum Ausgang des Barock, 1927)

Bürgerbibliothek Bern, Mss. Hist. Helv. XVI 159.

First publication: In *Niklaus Manuel*, edited by Baechtold, pp. 112-132.

Standard edition: *Der Ablaßkrämer*, edited by Paul Zinsli, Altdeutsche Übungstexte, no. 17 (Bern: Francke, 1960);

Barbali Ein Gespräch Kvrtzwylig wie ein muoter wolt Dz jr tochter in ein kloster solt Die muoter selb hie ouch zuohört Wie jr tochter die pfaffen lert (Zurich: Christoph Froschauer, 1526);

Ein hüpsch lied in schilers hoff thon, Meyster gsang, jnnhaltende ein gespräch, des Fabers vnd Eggen Badenfart betreffende (Zurich: Christoph Froschauer, 1526);

Ein kleglichе Botschafft dem Bapst zuo komen, antreffend des gantzen Bapsthuombs weydung, nit des viechs, sonder des zartten völcklins, vnd was syn heydischeyt darzuo geantwurt vnd than hatt (N.p., 1528);

Die ordnung vnd letster will der Messz, so da die gantz Pfaffheyt, gesöygt, erneert, vnd beschirmet hat wie ein muoter ein kind (N.p., 1528).

Editions and collections: "Bicoccalied," in *Die historischen Volkslieder der Deutschen vom 13. bis 16. Jahrhundert,* volume 3, edited by Rochus von Liliencron (Leipzig: Vogel, 1867), pp. 406-409;

Niklaus Manuel, edited by Jakob Baechtold, Bibliothek älterer Schriftwerke der deutschen Schweiz und ihres Grenzgebietes, series 1, volume 2 (Frauenfeld: Huber, 1878);

Niklaus Manuels Spiel evangelischer Freiheit "Die Totenfresser," edited by Ferdinand Vetter, Die Schweiz im deutschen Geistesleben, no. 16 (Leipzig: Haessel, 1923);

"Vom Papst und seiner Priesterschaft," in *Deutsche Spiele und Dramen des 15. Und 16. Jahrhunderts,* edited by Hellmut Thomke, Bibliothek deutscher Klassiker, no. 136 (Frankfurt am Main: Deutscher Klassiker Verlag, 1996), pp. 139-209.

Niklaus Manuel was one of the most colorful figures of the Swiss Reformation. Though by trade a painter, he was multitalented and succeeded as a playwright, poet, magistrate, and mercenary, leading his nineteenth-century editor, Jakob Baechtold, to compare him to the quintessential *uomo universale* of the Renaissance, Leonardo da Vinci. Following the redating of Manuel's first plays and the discovery of new sources, later scholars have been quick to temper Baechtold's praise of his subject's originality. Nevertheless, even for the modern reader Manuel's plays, songs, and dialogues have lost little of the vitality that made them some of the most widely circulated Protestant pamphlets. Above all, the success of his carnival plays *Vom Papst und seiner Priesterschaft* (The Pope and His Priests) and *Von Papsts und Christi Gegensatz* (The Difference between the Pope and Christ), performed in 1523 and published together in 1524, makes Manuel, along with Thomas Murner and Thomas Naogeorgus, one of the Reformation's outstanding polemicists.

No record of Manuel's birth exists; several noncontemporary sources give his age at his death in 1530 as forty-six, so that he was probably born around 1484. According to a 1509 marriage agreement between Manuel and Katharina Frisching—the only surviving document that offers clues to the identities of his parents—his mother was Margaretha Vogt, née Fricker, the daughter of Thüring Fricker, city chancellor of Bern. The document gives the groom's name as Niclaus Alleman; therefore, his father was probably not Hans Vogt, who was Margaretha's husband in 1484, but Emanuel Alleman or de Alamanis, a druggist whose grandfather, Jacobus de Alamanis, had come to Bern from Chieri, near Turin in northern Italy. No other document gives the name Alleman; apparently, at some time after 1509 Manuel adopted his father's first name as his own surname; a document of 1512 lists him as Niclaus Emanuel. Still later he dropped the *E* from Emanuel. Furthermore, Manuel often signed his artworks with the monogram *NMD*, in which the final initial represents *Deutsch* (German)—a translation of his father's last name. Art historians often refer to him as Niklaus Manuel Deutsch, and it is wise to check under both *Deutsch* and *Manuel* in indexes when searching for information on the painter-poet. All of his children, however, carried the last name Manuel: Margaretha, born in 1516; Hieronymus, born in 1520; Hans-Rudolf, born in 1525; Niklaus, born in 1528; and Magdalena, who was born in 1524 and died young. Hans-Rudolf would take after his father as an artist and a playwright, producing woodcuts and the carnival play *Das Weinspiel* (The Wine Play, 1548).

Little is known concerning Manuel's education. Earlier assumptions that Manuel's learned grandfather Fricker provided him with a humanist education in the Latin school of Heinrich Wölfflin, making him a possible schoolmate of Huldrych Zwingli, are pure conjecture. In fact, nothing in Manuel's artistic or literary production suggests that he had any exposure to Latin or even to French, the lingua franca for dealings with Bern's western neighbors. Similarly, attempts to place Manuel as an apprentice or journeyman with Hans Fries in neighboring Fribourg, Hans Burgkmair in Augsburg, or Albrecht Dürer in Nuremberg have remained speculative. The existence of a thriving stained-glass industry in Bern at the turn of the century and the fact that Manuel's earliest extant drawings are designs for stained-glass windows indicate that he probably learned his trade in a local workshop.

Manuel's dated works fall into the period 1515 to 1529; all of his early drawings, however, are undated, while his later works were sporadic, so that

Copies of two panels from Manuel's mural Totentanz, *depicting the Pope, a cardinal, an abbot, and a canon (Bern Historical Museum)*

his career as artist mainly spanned the years 1507 to 1522. In all, approximately ninety drawings, thirty paintings, and ten woodcuts survive. Moreover, copies exist of two murals that have been destroyed: *Salomons Götzendienst* (Solomon's Idolatry, 1518), on the house of Antoni Noll on Bern's Cathedral Square (removed in 1758); and the monumental *Totentanz* (Dance of Death), painted from around 1516 to 1519 on a courtyard wall of the local Dominican monastery. In 1517 Manuel painted the ceiling of the newly completed choir of the Bernese cathedral, and between 1522 and 1524 he helped to design its Renaissance choir stalls, the first of their kind in Switzerland. Several of his paintings are altarpieces commissioned by local churches, indicating that his talent was in high demand in Bern; but he also stood in at least indirect contact with some of the most prominent artists in northern Europe, including Hans Baldung Grien, Urs Graf, and, possibly, Dürer. Indeed, several of his unsigned works were earlier considered to be products of these contemporaries, and his artistic oeuvre is worthy of comparison with the best of his age.

The *Totentanz*, considered by many to be Manuel's masterpiece, was simultaneously his debut as a poet. Four rhymed quatrains accompany twenty-two of the mural's twenty-four panels; panels 2 and 24 have three quatrains and three irregular stanzas, respectively. Twenty-one panels record Death's exchange with representatives of the clergy, the nobility, or a trade. While the Pope and other members of the church hierarchy retain some dignity in the mural itself, the verses are unabashedly anticlerical and prophetic of later Protestant charges of Catholic corruption. This feature has led to speculation that Manuel had already adopted the new faith by 1519 or that his original text was revised during renovations following the local introduction of the Reformation. Portrayals of the Dance of Death, however, traditionally criticize the clergy, and the prominent Bernese citizens portrayed in the mural and the local Dominicans would have certainly objected if Manuel had exploited the piece for Protestant propaganda. Though a few of the lines may be post-Reformation additions, the criticism of the church does not exceed the limits acceptable at the time. Moreover, the majority of the verses are unquestionably Manuel's; they are composed in the direct, unaffected language that is the hallmark of his later works.

Beyond these verses, however, several aspects of Manuel's art indicate that he was becoming increasingly interested in language, and especially the theater. Early inscriptions on Manuel's paintings and drawings are cryptic, jumbled collections of letters whose meaning was known only to the artist and, perhaps, to the works' commissioners. His drawings, especially, occasionally contain three- or four-letter abbreviated maxims that complement iconographic cues as to the works' meaning but themselves require interpretation: *SNE, NRG, NISM, GGVG, NKAW, SASD, HDNM,* and *GWSP*. Some of these abbreviations appear in some drawings; others in other drawings. Scholars have been able to decipher only two of these abbreviations, which are spelled out in drawings that have to do with the uncertain nature of love: *GGVG* is "Gott geb uns Glück" (May God give us good fortune), and *NKAW* is "Niemand kann alles wissen" (No one can know everything). Around 1517, however, Manuel's inscriptions become clear, straightforward explanations of his works' allegorical content. In *Das Urteil des Paris* (The Judgment of Paris, circa 1517–1518) Cupid and Venus are unambiguously labeled; Paris is "Der Torecht" (the foolish one); and infrared photography has revealed that Juno was originally identified as "Ivno ein Götin der uberwindung inn. Strits" (Juno, a goddess of overcoming inner[?] conflict). Figures in another work are labeled Gerechtigkeit (justice), Rosendorn (rose thorn), Richter (judge), Töchterli (daughter), and Bettler (beggar). Several of these figures interact as if they were actors, and the series in which they appear bears the name *Schauspielfiguren* (stage figures); it was most likely created to illustrate an edition of a play, which, judging from the apparent financial transactions depicted, may have dealt with bribery.

Manuel's interest in the theater, however, is best represented by the mural *Salomons Götzendienst*: framed by an arch with Renaissance ornaments, the biblical account of Solomon's submission to his wives' idolatrous will unfolds in the foreground while a host of contemporary Swiss figures populates a raised platform that resembles a stage. The figures' gestures and, above all, the depiction of a fool in an apparent exegetical function suggest that the mural depicts a carnival play. The mural also contains a lengthy explanatory inscription, and it is possible that Manuel's later tendency to label figures in his art developed in conjunction with his exposure to the dramatic roles of local plays. Regardless of the ultimate cause, Hans Christoph von Tavel notes that "Die kunstlerische Entwicklung Manuels läßt sich verallgemeinernd mit den folgenden schlagwörtern charakterisieren: Von der anschauung zur lesbarkeit, von Raum zum Zeichen, vom Bild zum Wort" (Manuel's artistic development can be generally characterized with the following catchwords: from perception to legibility, from perspective to sign, from image to word)—a development that eventually led to the neglect of his original profession. Manuel did not, however, abandon his art, as some scholars have suggested: the 1527 stained-glass window designs *Christus und die Ehebrecherin* (Christ and the Adulteress) and *König Josia läßt die Götzenbilder zerstören* (King Josiah Orders the Idols Destroyed) indicate that he was well aware of the "Protestant" art of the Lukas Cranach school, and other drawings made after 1522 survive. His motivation was perhaps partly financial, for in 1522 he unsuccessfully applied for the vacant position of *Großweibel* (sergeant at arms) of Bern, citing his inability to support his family from his income as a painter.

Manuel's writings are known for their bold and belligerent tone, which probably derives from his experience as a *Reisläufer* (Swiss mercenary) during the Italian campaigns of the early sixteenth century. Following the victories at Grandson and Murten over Charles the Bold of Burgundy in 1476 and the defeat of imperial forces at the Battle of Dornach in 1499, the Swiss enjoyed a reputation as the best troops in Europe. The emperor, the French king, and even the Pope were willing to pay handsomely for their services, and the Swiss grew rich as these rulers struggled for control of northern Italy. Manuel may have joined the French campaign of 1516 for Milan: his name is conspicuously absent from the Easter roll of Bern's Great Council, of which he had become a member in 1510 and which, together with the more powerful Small Council, governed Bernese affairs; moreover, a letter to the council from Bernese troops in Milan is written in what appears to be Manuel's hand. There is no question, however, that he participated in the 1522 campaign, which resulted in a humiliating defeat for the French and their Swiss allies against papal and imperial forces at Bicocca. Manuel himself, in a letter now lost, wrote to his wife that he received a small wound in his left hand during the Battle of Novara, and the chronicler Valerius Anshelm reports that Manuel took part in the subsequent plundering of the city by victorious Swiss troops. Manuel appears to have been an able tactician, for he assumed a high rank in Protestant military actions following the Bernese Reformation. As *Bannerhauptmann* (captain of the banner) he was third in command during the quelling of the part religious, part economic Oberland uprising of October 1528, and in June 1529 he assumed the same rank among the troops of the Bernese Tanners' Guild in the First War of Kappel. During the Protestant grain embargo of September 1529 he commanded Bernese troops while holding the rank of *Lütiner* (second in command).

The Swiss defeat at Bicocca was the impulse for Manuel's *Bicoccalied* (Song of Bicocca, 1522). The Reisläufer had a long-standing rivalry with the emperor's *Landsknechte* (German mercenaries), and each side mocked the other's military prowess in caustic songs written to popular melodies. The Landsknechte celebrated their victory at Bicocca with such a song, now lost, and Manuel returned their ridicule in twenty-five eight-line stanzas. As a participant in the battle, he portrays the ebb and flow of the fighting in great detail, taunting the imperial troops with the claims that they avoided hand-to-hand combat in a cowardly fashion and that they owed their victory to superior artillery. The language is the raw speech of soldiers (though crass idioms were not at all unusual for the polemic literature of the time): referring to the artillery, he says, "Möcht ich so vil vorteil han, mit iteligen huoren wölt ich üch allsampt bestan" (If I could have such an advantage, I could lick you all with vain whores).

Manuel's Das Urteil des Paris *(Museum of Fine Arts, Basel)*

The song appears to have circulated widely, provoking a response in turn from the German rivals. The *Bicoccalied* does not survive in a contemporary imprint; but it has been transmitted anonymously in an imprint from the end of the sixteenth century, and an earlier manuscript fragment exists in the hand of the sixteenth-century Swiss chronicler Aegidus Tschudi. As Manuel does not "sign" the song at the end with his *Schwytzerdegen* (Swiss dagger)—his artist's device and the final word of his carnival plays and his dialogue *Barbali* (1526)—it is not clearly identified as his work. He is known to be the author, however, from the Reformation chronicle of Heinrich Bullinger, Zwingli's successor in Zurich, who also records several of the later stanzas.

There is less information concerning the authorship of *Ein seltsamer wunderschöner Traum* (A Strange and Wondrous Dream, circa 1521–1522), a fragmentary work of 863 verses discovered in Hamburg in 1895 by Fritz Burg. Told in the first person, the poem relates the dream of a soldier in the field to whom the eschatological context of contemporary events is suddenly revealed. The Pope is depicted as the Antichrist, and he and his corrupt followers do everything in their power to hinder the Reformation spread of the gospel. After his death the Pope arrives in heaven but is turned away by Saint Peter: the Pope's keys cannot unlock the heavenly gates, nor do his indulgences gain him entrance; but he is welcomed in hell. The dreamer beholds a vision of the Virgin Mary in heaven before he is rudely awakened by the cock's crow. Burg dated the work between the death of Pope Leo X in December 1521 and the election of Hadrian VI in August 1522, and he attributed it to Manuel for two main reasons: it is written, along with fragments of Manuel's *Vom Papst und seiner Priesterschaft* and *Von Papsts und Christi Gegensatz,* on Bernese paper produced between 1521 and 1523; and, in a letter to Zwingli of 12 August 1529, Manuel requests the return of several pamphlets he had loaned the Zurich Reformer, including *Ein aplasz kremer* (An Indulgence Peddler), *ein korgricht* (The Morality Court), and *ein troumm* (A Dream). Burg hypothesized that *ein troumm* is identical with the work he had just discovered; and, since it is mentioned in conjunction with *Der Ablaßkrämer* (The Indulgence Peddler, 1525), which is known to have been written by Manuel, it appeared likely that Manuel was its author, as well. Influential scholars, including Ferdinand Vetter, Conrad-André Beerli, and Jean-Paul Tardent, adopted Burg's assessment, with Tardent treating *Ein seltsamer wunderschöner Traum* as a biographical document indicative of an existential crisis experienced by Manuel following the Swiss defeat at Bicocca. In 1979, however, Paul Zinsli pointed to linguistic and stylistic elements in the work that are highly atypical for Manuel, such as non-Bernese dialect forms and a tone of passive resignation. The matter has not been resolved; it is still possible that Manuel wrote the original version of *Ein seltsamer wunderschöner Traum* but that a scribe, possibly from Saint Gall, altered it during the process of transcription, resulting in the work's present form.

The Hamburg manuscript also includes large sections of *Vom Papst und seiner Priesterschaft* and *Von Papsts und Christi Gegensatz,* an indication of the enormous popularity of these works in pre-Reformation Bern; Anshelm devotes a whole section of his Bernese chronicle to an account of the plays and of their success in converting local citizens to the new faith. By comparing the Hamburg fragments with the faulty 1524 and 1525 printings of the plays printed by Christoph Froschauer in Zurich, Vetter reconstructed the probable original version of *Vom Papst und seiner Priesterschaft* and published it as *Die Totenfresser* (The Corpse Eaters, 1923), the title by which Anshelm refers to the play. In Vetter's edition the play comprises 1,770 lines in seven major sections. Also, based on references in the plays to events of late 1522, including the Turkish siege of Rhodes, Vetter demonstrated that the plays must have been performed during the carnival of 1523–not that of 1522, as recorded by both Anshelm and the Froschauer printings. This dating seems all the more plausible because Manuel was fighting in Italy during the early months of 1522 and would have been unable to participate in a performance.

In 1521 Matthew Cardinal Schiner had complained to Bernese troops imprisoned in Milan about a carnival play recently performed in Bern that had ridiculed papal military policy. After the Swiss defeat by papal and imperial troops at Bicocca the Pope was even less popular in Bern, and Manuel played to this sentiment by adding a generous dose of Protestant polemic to his ridicule of militant clergy in *Vom Papst und seiner Priesterschaft*. In the first scene of the play, which was performed on 15 February, mourners carry in a coffin containing the body of a rich farmer and announce their intention to spare no expense in establishing masses and benefices for the deceased. The church hierarchy, from the Pope on down, rejoices in finding yet another wealthy scapegoat whose death will finance their extravagant lifestyle. They praise indulgences, canon law, and taxes on priestly concubines (the tax was a source of revenue to the clergy, who were exempt from paying it) but curse Protestantism because it deprives them of their income. While the necrophagous clergy of this section had appeared in an earlier work titled *Die Totenfresser* (1521), printed and possibly written by Pamphilus Gengenbach, the remainder of the play is Manuel's work alone and portrays the Pope as especially bellicose. In the second section a raucous Swiss Guard praises the Pope's generosity; in the third section a knight of Rhodes arrives to request the Pope's financial and military aid in repelling the Turkish siege of the island, begun in July 1522. The Pope, however, is too busy with his wars in Italy, and the knight laments that the leader of the Catholic Church would rather fight Christians than heathens. In the fourth section the Protestant preacher Lüpolt Schüchnit (Lüpolt Fears-Nothing) encourages some peasants to speak out against indulgences and church corruption. Saints Peter and Paul step forward in the next section to contrast the Pope's pomp and greed to the humility and brotherly love of the original bishop of Rome, Peter himself. Peter speaks of his own poverty and faith and says that he would never have placed the present Pope on the apostolic throne. In the sixth and seventh sections the mustered mercenaries of the Pope, intent on spoils and plunder, contrast starkly with the humble prayer of Lüpolt Schüchnit, who entreats the audience to place its faith in Christ alone. In the much shorter (214 lines) *Von Papsts und Christi Gegensatz,* performed on 22 February, two peasants discuss the contrast between the entry of Christ and his disciples into Jerusalem, as related in the Bible, to the papal entourage that is passing by on the opposite side of the street; Christ's peaceable humility stands out against the militant fanfare of the Pope. By placing an affirmation of secular authority in the mouths of his anticlerical peasants Manuel apparently avoided the censure of the still largely Catholic Small Council, which reimbursed the players for their expenses and later appointed Manuel steward of Erlach, a small Bernese territory on Lake Bienne.

Von Papsts und Christi Gegensatz was most likely inspired by Cranach's *Passional Christi und Antichristi* (The Passion of Christ and the Antichrist, 1521), a series of twenty-six woodcuts contrasting Christ's hardships with papal luxury. Indeed, many elements of Manuel's carnival plays reveal that he conceived them with the eye of a painter. Because the medieval "simultaneous stage" could depict several localities at once, Manuel could physically translate the antithetical principle behind much Protestant art, such as Cranach's *Passional Christi und Antichristi* or *Gesetz und Gnade* (The Law and the Gospel) altarpieces, into two opposing sections of the stage, one reserved for the Pope and his followers, the other for the adherents of the new faith. The audience could readily identify a speaker's confession according to where he or she appeared on the stage. In *Vom Papst und seiner Priesterschaft* Manuel reserved yet another section of the stage for the apostles Peter and Paul. From their vantage point, which most likely was at the back of the stage, they could offer visual cues as to compatibility of characters and their statements with Scripture. Manuel had already created contrastive locations for biblical and contemporary figures in *Salomons Götzendienst,* and, just as the mural resembles a carnival stage, *Vom Papst und seiner Priesterschaft* and *Von Papsts und Christi Gegensatz* resemble Reformation broadsheets in their combination of image and exegesis.

Though the exact date of Manuel's appointment to office in Erlach is unknown, he first appears as steward in surviving documents on 18 September 1523; his tenure lasted through September 1528, following his election to the Bernese Small Council on 14 April of that year. His father-in-law had been steward in Erlach before him and may have given him advice on carrying out his duties. Several of Manuel's letters to the Small Council demonstrate that he was as concerned for the well-being of the local inhabitants as he was for the interests of his superiors. He traveled regularly to Bern for the meetings

Manuel's stained-glass window design König Josia läßt die Götzenbilder zerstören

of the Great Council, of which he was still a member, and he is assumed to have been one of the leading proponents of the new faith there. He was apparently just as active in Erlach: when Bern surveyed its thirty-four territories in 1526 to ascertain their attitude toward the Reformation, Erlach was one of only two who supported the movement.

Manuel composed five Protestant pamphlets during his time as steward; they document the continuing spread of the Reformation in Bern and Switzerland. *Der Ablaßkrämer* of 1525, perhaps Manuel's most powerful carnival play, portrays in 558 lines the violent humiliation of Richardus Hinderlist (Richard Deceitful). This corrupt cleric is traditionally assumed to be a caricature of Bernhardin Sanson, a Franciscan monk who sold indulgences in Bern in 1518 and who is also referred to—though not by name—in *Vom Papst und seiner Priesterschaft*. When Hinderlist returns to a village the inhabitants, who are now adherents of the new faith, demand their money back from his earlier sales. When he refuses, they hang him by his arms until he confesses his misdeeds, which include not only the hawking of worthless indulgences but also the sale of counterfeit relics and the seduction of women during confession. The locals then divide his money among themselves but take only as much as they had originally given, donating the rest to a crippled beggar. This closing act of Christian charity refutes the suggestion, still made by many critics, that *Der Ablaßkrämer* paints a negative picture of peasants following the uprisings of 1525. Their unruliness is, rather, part of the play's carnival license; they differ from the peasants of *Vom Papst und seiner Priesterschaft* only in that they enact on the clergy what the rustics of the former carnival play had simply wished to do. Still, in 1525 the portrayal of popular insurrection was a volatile undertaking. Though *Der Ablaßkrämer* survives as a manuscript in Manuel's own hand, no printing of it is known to exist, suggesting that the contemporary political situation was too unstable to allow for its publication. Nonetheless, internal evidence implies that the play was performed, and it is likely that Manuel intended his carefully transcribed manuscript, together with an accompanying drawing, to be published.

His next work was the rhymed dialogue *Barbali*, written in 1526. Baechtold's 1878 edition, based on a 1526 Froschauer printing, has 1,940 verses; the lengths of the seven other known contemporary printings are somewhat less, as their biblical passages are not versified. All eight printings are anonymous, but Manuel unmistakably marked the work with his Schwytzerdegen. Like the carnival plays, the dialogue is critical of church corruption; yet its scathing polemic gives way to a calmer portrayal of Protestant theology's social implications. The work begins on the day following Barbali's tenth birthday. Her mother wants to place her in a convent to assure a good life for her, but Barbali asks for a year to think about the matter. During this time she eagerly reads the New Testament; and, when her mother asks for her decision a year later, she announces that monasticism has no basis in Scripture and that she would prefer to live a life of honest work according to God's will, including the raising of a family in holy matrimony. Her mother, distraught, calls for the local priest, but neither he nor five other clerics can persuade Barbali to change her mind. She calmly parries their arguments with quotes from the Bible and even converts one of them. The others leave, cursing her as a heretic who will soon be burned. Her mother, however, is convinced that her daughter has been moved by the Holy Ghost, and she happily abandons her earlier plan to place Barbali in a convent. In this dialogue Manuel may have drawn on *Ein Vermanung aller Christen, das sie sich erbarmen uber die Klosterfrawen* (An Admonishment to All Christians to Take Pity on Nuns), the third pamphlet in Johann Eberlin von Günzburg's series *Die fünfzehn Bundsgnossen* (The Fifteen Confederates, 1521) and one that also treats the suffering of women forced into convents by well-intentioned parents. *Barbali*, however, appeared at a time when monasteries and convents in Bernese territory had already begun losing occupants to the Reformation. In 1523 the Small Council had granted the nuns of Königsfelden the right to leave the convent and marry. In 1525 the nuns of Fraubrunnen became disobedient, and discipline everywhere was a constant problem. Barbali's comments were thus not new but reflected a growing crisis within monastic institutions.

As it gained adherents, the Reformation threatened to divide the Helvetian Confederacy. The inner cantons—Uri, Schwyz, Unterwalden, Zug, and Lucerne—remained staunchly Catholic and reacted with dismay when Basel and Bern were unwilling to isolate Zurich following its Zwinglian reform of 1523. By 1526 Bern's own government was bitterly divided; and when, on Whitmonday, 21 May 1526, the Catholic majority resolved to renew the alliance with the inner cantons by taking a solemn oath never to forsake the old faith, several members of the Protestant minority, including Manuel, left the Great Council in protest. This event coincided with the beginning of the Baden Disputation, which lasted until 9 June and was to decide the question of reform for all cantons. Among the Catholic representatives were Johann Eck, Mar-

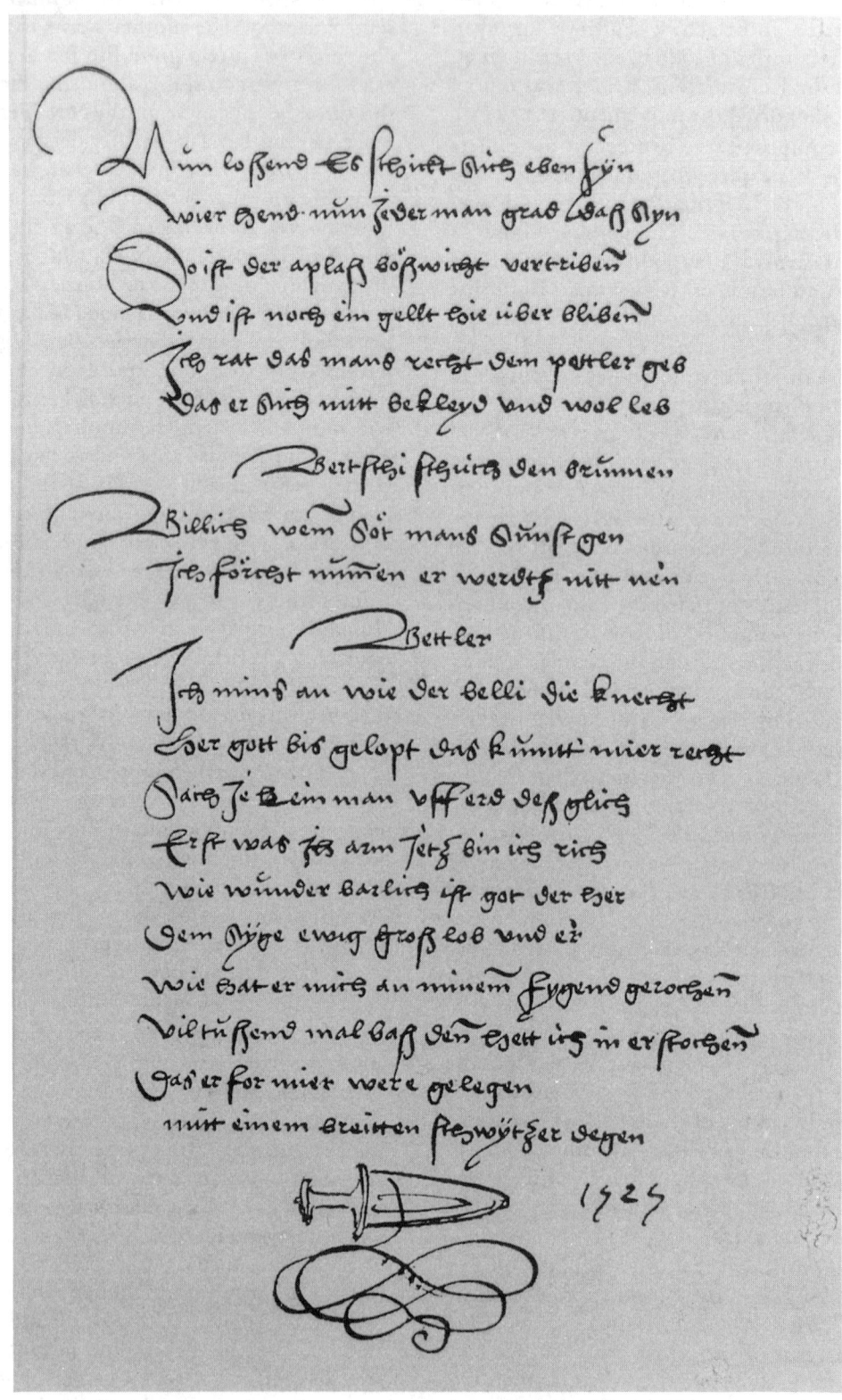

Page from the manuscript for Manuel's carnival play Der Ablaßkrämer. His Swiss-dagger device appears at the bottom (Bürgerbibliothek Bern).

tin Luther's opponent during the Leipzig debate of 1519; Johann Faber, the vicar of Constance; and Murner, the author of *Von dem großen Lutherischen Narren* (The Great Lutheran Fool, 1522) and, since late 1525, a lay priest in Lucerne. Despite assurances of safe conduct Zwingli did not appear, and without their champion, Johannes Oekolampadius of Basel and Bertold Haller of Bern could do little to prevent a Catholic majority from declaring the old faith to be the only true religion.

Manuel was among the Swiss Protestants who refused to recognize the disputation's decision. Before the year was out he had written the song *Ein hüpsch lied in schilers hoff thon, Meyster gsang, innhaltende ein gespräch, des Fabers und Eggen Badenfart betreffende* (A Pleasant Song, Set to Schilher's Court Melody, Containing a Dialogue on Eck's and Faber's Trip to Baden). The two extant printings are anonymous; even the Schwytzerdegen of Manuel's earlier works is missing. In those works, however, Manuel had attacked his opponents, such as Cardinal Schiner or the Franciscan monk Sanson, indirectly; now he was assailing Catholic theologians by name. But Bullinger's Reformation chronicle attributes the song to Manuel; among Protestants, apparently, his authorship was no secret. In nineteen fourteen-line strophes two peasants summarize the course of the disputation from a Protestant perspective. As in Manuel's other writings, there is little earnest theological discussion. Though the participants debated a total of seven theses, all of them formulated by Eck, Manuel recounts only the second exchange, concerning the sacrificial nature of the Mass. In general, he lauds Oekolampadius and Haller as defenders of God's Word while constructing elaborate swine metaphors for Eck and Faber. In the closing two strophes he claims that if the Catholics had truly won the disputation Murner would not hesitate to print the proceedings at his newly founded Lucerne press. Murner did not publish them until 18 May 1527.

Despite the Whitmonday oath, Bern grew exceedingly estranged from its Catholic confederates following the Baden Disputation. In the absence of published proceedings, the local councils requested a handwritten copy of the debate from the inner cantons. Not only did they refuse to provide it, but they also threatened to establish direct contact with Bernese territories if the council did not comply with the Baden resolutions. The latter act would have been a clear violation of the city's sovereignty, and the threat alienated Bern's Protestants and Catholics alike. After the Easter elections of 1527 established a Protestant majority on the council, it was only a matter of time before the city adopted the Reformation. On 17 November 1527 Bern announced its own disputation, threatening the bishops of Basel, Constance, Sitten, and Lausanne with the loss of their rights in the Bernese territories if they did not attend. They did not, nor did Eck, Murner, Faber, or delegates from the Catholic cantons. Protestant theologians from Switzerland and southern Germany, however, were well represented. Held from 6 to 26 January 1528, the disputation included Haller, Oekolampadius, Zwingli, Joachim Vadianus, Martin Bucer, Wolfgang Capito, and sixty-nine councilmen, pastors, and burghers from Zurich; clerics from the city of Bern and from the surrounding countryside were also required to attend, regardless of their disposition toward the new faith. Manuel served as moderator. According to contemporary accounts he remained impartial, encouraging Catholic participants to defend their cause. A Protestant victory was, nonetheless, guaranteed.

As an author, Manuel remained partisan. He composed his last two pamphlets during the disputation: *Ein klegliche Botschafft dem Bapst zuo komen, antreffend des gantzen Bapsthuombs weydung, nit des viechs, sonder des zartten völcklins, und was syn heydischeyt darzuo geantwurt und than hatt* (Lamentable Tidings Received by the Pope Concerning the Papacy's Grazing, Not of Sheep but of Tender People, and What His Heathenness Answered and Did in Response, 1528), generally known as *Krankheit der Messe* (The Mass's Illness), and *Die ordnung und letster will der Messz, so da die gantz Pfaffheyt, gesöygt, erneert, und beschirmet hat wie ein muoter ein kind* (The Last Will and Testament of the Mass, Which Has Nursed, Nourished, and Protected the Clergy as a Mother Her Child, 1528) during the disputation. Again the works appeared anonymously, but again Bullinger verifies Manuel's authorship. In addition, a letter from Heinrich Utinger in Zurich to Zwingli, written during the Bernese disputation, allows for a fairly precise dating of Manuel's work. On 15 January 1528 Utinger wrote: "Emanuelis operam cuperem habere de infirmitate misse, et depost planctum ad funus, quem eum quoque decet poetare" (I would like to have Manuel's work on the sickness of the Mass and its dirge, which it would befit him to write as well). On 15 January *Krankheit der Messe* was, therefore, composed but not yet published, and Utinger's comments might have inspired Manuel to write *Die ordnung und letster will der Messz*. The two satires were published in 1528; most printings include both together, though five from early 1528 contain *Krankheit der Messe* alone.

The pamphlets' prose form is new, but they continue Manuel's earlier attacks on Eck, Faber,

Drawing by Manuel in his manuscript for Der Ablaßkrämer, *showing the torture of the monk Richardus Hinderlist by Protestant peasants who wanted their money back for indulgences he had sold them (Bürgerbibliothek Bern)*

and Murner. *Krankheit der Messe* gives the three the satiric names "Rundegk" (Round-Corner), "Heioho" (roughly, "Ho-ho," based on Faber's real name, Heigerlin), and "Katzenlied" (Cat Song–a variation on "Murr-Narr" [Meow-Fool], a name with which other Protestant pamphleteers frequently mocked Murner), respectively. Now, however, prominent Swiss Catholics are ridiculed, as well, including the Augustinian Konrad Träger of Fribourg and Mayor Hans Hug of Lucerne. All try to nurse the Mass back to health after the Pope has discovered that it is deathly ill. Eck and Faber prescribe a thermal bath, which is unsuccessful; then they literally yell to wake the dead, in accordance with the medieval belief that lions give birth to stillborn cubs and then bring them to life by roaring. They contemplate other remedies–the warming fires of purgatory, saints, oblates, holy oil, and consecrated palm leaves–but the Reformation, as revealed by the "Früemesser" ("Early Measure Taker," i.e., Haller), "Pauli Wattimtauw" (Vadianus), "Niklaus Welenman" (Manuel), and others, has done away with them. The doctors, seeing no hope, steal away, lest the patient die under their care–a swipe at the Catholic theologians for avoiding the Bernese disputation.

In *Die ordnung und letster will der Messz* the Mass states that its hour has come, especially since the doctors of Baden have abandoned it, and that its survivors should carry out its wishes: Faber, whose father was a blacksmith, is to be given a leather apron cut from an altar covering; Eck is to receive lamp oil to soothe his throat, which is sore from all his shouting; Murner is to get the white altar cloth as a picnic blanket for the mowers of the *Geuchmat* (Fools' Meadow), the title of his popular pre-Reformation satire (1519). In other satiric references, some of them now indecipherable, prominent Swiss Catholics are bequeathed further instruments of the mass. Altars, chalices, monstrances, and crucifixes are to be given to the secular authorities, who will melt them down and mint coins from the precious metals they contain.

Two further Swiss pamphlets appear in Baechtold's edition of Manuel's writings. In tone and form they are similar to his earlier works, but they are generally no longer attributed to him. *Klagred der armen Götzen* (Plaint of the Poor Idols, 1528) treats the demise of religious art at the hands of Zwinglian iconoclasts. The "heathen" images themselves confess their misdeeds but point out that humankind is to blame for creating and venerating them. Given Manuel's profession as a painter, it seems natural that he would sympathize with artistic creations; *Testament der Messe,* however, demonstrates that he had no qualms about melting down religious objects for the perceived good of the community, and surviving documents reveal that Manuel, together with the goldsmith Bernhard Tillmann, oversaw the collection of religious instruments and art for new Bernese coins in 1529. Above all, the criticism of secular government in *Klagred der armen Götzen* is found in no other Manuelian work, making it highly unlikely that he is its author.

The anonymous carnival play *Elsli Tragdenknaben* (Elizabeth Carry-the-Boy), performed in Bern on 27 February 1530, begins as a traditional courtroom farce. Elsli, a young peasant woman, appears in court with her mother to charge Uli Rechenzan (Ulrich Rake-tooth) with breaking his promise of marriage. Uli denies everything and, noting Elsli's sordid past, refuses to marry her. But when Küni Süwtrog (Küni Sow-trough), a Protestant, reminds him that Christ defended an adulteress against the charges of the Pharisees, Uli agrees to take Christ as his example and Elsli as his wife. Uli's father then asks for Elsli's mother's hand, and the play ends with the complaints of the judges and lawyers who have lost money because of the parties' sudden concord. Nineteenth-century scholars saw in the courtroom satire a parody of the Reformation *Chorgericht* (Morality Court), which was created in Bern on 29 May 1528 to watch over local mores and replaced the previous episcopal jurisdiction based on canon law. Manuel served on the court's board from its inception until 12 April 1529, and it was assumed that *Elsli Tragdenknaben* was taken from his experiences there and was identical with the pamphlet *ein korgricht* that Manuel had lent Zwingli along with *ein troumm* and other writings. Adolf Kaiser, however, demonstrated in 1899 that the work is a hasty redaction of Tirolean "Rumpolt and Mareth" plays, traditional carnival farces in which a pregnant young woman (Mareth) takes the reluctant father (Rumpolt) to court to force him to marry her, inserting a Protestant conversion into an otherwise nonpolemical farce. Afterward, scholars were eager to deny Manuel's authorship of such an "inferior" play, though the suggestion still circulates that he may have advised a younger playwright in composing the work.

Considering Manuel's stellar political career following the success of the Reformation in Bern, it is likely that he no longer had time to write at all. As steward in Erlach he had proven himself a capable administrator, and his writings left no doubt as to his determination to defend the new faith. He entered the Small Council during the Easter elections (14 April) of 1528 and assumed the influential office of *Venner* on 7 October of the same year. Each of the four Venner was originally responsible for the military and financial administration of one of the city quarters; but by the sixteenth century they had assumed a key position in the city administration, forming the *Geheimer Rat* (Secret Council) with the mayor and the treasurer. After 1528 the Venner were responsible for the secularization of monasteries and the revision of tithes and benefices. Manuel, however, had many additional responsibilities. Beyond his activities as military officer and member of the Chorgericht he oversaw the city's *Mushafen* (food rations for poor inhabitants and students) from 20 November 1528 to 20 May 1529. Above all, he was indispensable as a diplomat during the growing confessional tensions in the confederacy, traveling at least once a month to other Swiss cities. He helped conduct the entry of Schaffhausen and Strasbourg into the Christliches Burgrecht, the alliance of Swiss Protestant cities, and he mediated between Catholics and Protestants in Basel during the unrest of December 1528 and carnival 1529. Moreover, he often represented Bern on the Tagsatzung, the body that decided matters concerning the whole confederacy. On 3 June 1529, immediately before the outbreak of the First War of Kappel between the two confessions, he made a speech before the Zurich council, which was intent on battle. In contrast to Zwingli, who was willing to spread the Reformation by force, Manuel pleaded for tolerance: "Warlich man mag mit spies und halbarten den glouben nit ingeben" (Truly, one cannot sow faith with pike and halberd). Though he temporarily persuaded the Zurich council to withhold its troops, a delegation from Zurich simultaneously convinced the Bernese magistrates of the necessity of armed conflict. Zurich declared war on 8 June, but no blood was spilled. Manuel subsequently headed the Bernese delegation during peace negotiations, which favored the Protestant cities.

Manuel did not experience the humiliating Protestant defeat in the Second War of Kappel in October 1531, which left Zwingli and most of the Zurich council dead. A letter from the Bernese schoolmaster Albrecht Burer to Vadianus in Saint Gall indicates that Manuel died on 28 April 1530 but does not give a cause. As he had been reelected Venner on 18 April, his death seems to have been unexpected. The common assumption is that he literally worked himself to death in the service of the Reformation, although a long rest at the baths of Baden from July to September 1529 suggests that he may have been suffering from poor health for some time. Though it is questionable whether one man could have determined the course of Swiss history, there are those who believe that if Manuel had lived Bern would have pursued a less confrontational policy toward the inner cantons than Zurich and would have avoided the Second War of Kappel. It is certain, however, that as a politician Manuel adopted a more tolerant tone than he did as a polemical author. In his 1529 Zurich speech he said: "Ich retz tür und alß hoch ichs reden kan, das ich im ersten mich letz und fiendselig gnuog geßellt hab, bin aber ouch bericht worden" (I swear dearly and as solemnly as I can that, though I at first was unjust and hostile, I have now changed).

Much of the scholarship on Manuel comes from Bern, because of his prominent role in local history. Among earlier investigations, the work of Vetter, Adolf Fluri, and Samuel Singer stands out, though Vetter occasionally glorifies the artist and the Bernese past. More recently, the Genevan Beerli's *Le peintre poète Nicolas Manuel et l'evolution sociale de son temps* (The Painter Poet Niklaus Manuel and the Social Evolution of His Time, 1953) was the first work to place Manuel's artistic and poetic works in their sociohistorical context. In 1967 Tardent provided a detailed analysis of Manuel's activities as a "statesman," which had been previously neglected. Two recent Bernese contributions are essential for any examination of Manuel's works: *Niklaus Manuel Deutsch: Maler, Dichter, Staatsmann* (Niklaus Manuel Deutsch: Painter, Poet, Statesman), the catalogue of the Kunstmuseum Bern's 1979 exhibition, edited by Cäsar Menz and Hugo Wagner; and *450 Jahre Berner Reformation: Beiträge zur Geschichte der Bernischen Reformation und zu Niklaus Manuel* (450 Years of the Bernese Reformation: Contributions on the History of the Bernese Reformation and on Niklaus Manuel, 1980), comprising the papers presented at a 1978 Manuel colloquium. The catalogue, especially, is an indispensable compendium of scholarship and documentary evidence on the artist and his works. In 1989 new anthropological theories of carnival led Peter Pfrunder to examine the plays in the context of carnivalesque phenomena. In 1995 Glenn Ehrstine investigated Manuel's role in the development of Bernese Reformation dramaturgy and the unique juncture of art and literature in his plays. Beerli's monograph remains the only recent work to treat Manuel's nondramatic writings in detail. A new edition of Manuel's works by Zinsli is nearing completion, however, and will provide new impetus for a closer investigation of the author's dialogues and songs.

Biography:
Carl von Grüneisen, *Niclaus Manuel: Leben und Werke eines Malers und Dichters, Kriegers, Staatsmannes und Reformators im sechzehnten Jahrhundert* (Stuttgart: Cotta, 1837).

References:
Derek van Abbé, "Change and Tradition in the Work of Niklaus Manuel of Berne," *Modern Language Review*, 47 (1952): 181-198;

Valerius Anshelm, *Die Berner Chronik des Valerius Anshelm*, 6 volumes, edited by the Historischer Verein des Kantons Bern (Bern: Wyss, 1884-1901), IV: 475;

Jakob Baechtold, *Geschichte der deutschen Literatur in der Schweiz*, second edition (Frauenfeld: Huber, 1919);

Conrad-André Beerli, *Le peintre poète Nicolas Manuel et l'evolution sociale de son temps* (Geneva: Librairie Droz, 1953);

Heinrich Bullinger, *Reformationsgeschichte*, 3 volumes, edited by J. J. Hottinger and H. H. Vögeli (1838-1840), I: 72-75;

Glenn Ehrstine, "From Iconoclasm to Iconography: Reformation Drama in Sixteenth-Century Bern," dissertation, University of Texas at Austin, 1995;

Emil Ermatinger, *Dichtung und Geistesleben der deutschen Schweiz* (Munich: Beck, 1933), pp. 146-159;

Adolf Fluri, "Dramatische Aufführungen in Bern im 16. Jahrhundert," in *Neues Berner Taschenbuch auf das Jahr 1909*, edited by Heinrich Türler (Bern: Wyss, 1908), pp. 133-159;

Fluri, "Niklaus Manuels Totentanz in Bild und Wort," in *Neues Berner Taschenbuch auf das Jahr 1901*, edited by Türler (Bern: Wyss, 1900), pp. 119-266;

Max Herrmann, *Forschungen zur deutschen Theatergeschichte des Mittelalters und der Renaissance* (Berlin: Weidmann, 1914), pp. 446-454;

Historischer Verein des Kantons Bern, ed., 450 Jahre Berner Reformation: Beiträge zur Geschichte der Bernischen Reformation und zu Niklaus Manuel (Bern: Historischer Verein des Kantons Bern, 1980);

Hugo Holstein, *Die Reformation im Spiegelbilde der dramatischen Literatur des sechzehnten Jahrhunderts* (Halle: Verein für Reformationsgeschichte, 1886), pp. 171-174;

Frida Humbel, *Ulrich Zwingli und seine Reformation im Spiegel der gleichzeitigen, schweizerischen Literatur*, Quellen und Abhandlungen zur schweizerischen Reformationsgeschichte, no. 2, part 1 (Leipzig: Heinsius, 1912);

Adolf Kaiser, *Die Fastnachtspiele von der Actio de sponsu: Ein Beitrag zur Geschichte des deutschen Fastnachtspieles* (Göttingen: Vandenhoeck & Ruprecht, 1899), pp. 51-120;

Barbara Könneker, *Die deutsche Literatur der Reformationszeit: Kommentar zu einer Epoche* (Munich: Winkler, 1975), pp. 124-131;

Könneker, *Satire im 16. Jahrhundert: Epoche–Werk–Wirkung* (Munich: Beck, 1991), pp. 169-186;

Conrad von Mandach and Hans Koegler, *Niklaus Manuel Deutsch* (Leipzig: Asmus, 1940);

Cäsar Menz and Hugo Wagner, eds., *Niklaus Manuel Deutsch: Maler, Dichter, Staatsmann* (Bern: Kunstmuseum Bern, 1979);

Wolfgang F. Michael, *Das deutsche Drama der Reformationszeit* (Bern: Peter Lang, 1984);

Eugen Müller, *Schweizer Theatergeschichte: Ein Beitrag zur Schweizer Kulturgeschichte*, Schriftenreihe des Schauspielhauses Zürich, no. 2 (Zurich: Oprecht, 1944), pp. 47-52;

Josef Nadler, *Literaturgeschichte der deutschen Schweiz* (Leipzig: Grethlein, 1932), pp. 180-184;

Peter Pfrunder, *Pfaffen, Ketzer, Totenfresser: Fastnachtskultur der Reformationszeit–Die Berner Spiele von Niklaus Manuel* (Zurich: Chronos, 1989);

Stephan Schmidlin, *Frumm byderb lüt: Ästhetische Form und politische Perspektive im Schweizer Schauspiel der Reformationszeit,* Europäische Hochschulschriften, no. 747 (Bern: Peter Lang, 1983), pp. 125-151;

Samuel Singer, "Niklaus Manuels Ablasskrämer," *Blätter für bernische Geschichte, Kunst und Altertumskunde,* 24 (1928): 54-60;

Wolfgang Stammler, *Von der Mystik zum Barock 1400-1600,* second edition (Stuttgart: Metzler, 1950), pp. 362-363;

Lucie Stumm, *Niklaus Manuel Deutsch von Bern als bildender Künstler* (Bern: Stämpfli, 1925);

Jean-Paul Tardent, *Niklaus Manuel als Staatsmann,* Archiv des Historischen Vereins des Kantons Bern, no. 51 (Bern: Historischer Verein des Kantons Bern, 1967);

Hans Christoph von Tavel, *Niklaus Manuel: Zur Kunst eines Eidgenossen der Dürerzeit* (Bern: Wyss, 1979);

Ferdinand Vetter, "Über die zwei angeblich 1522 aufgeführten Fastnachtsspiele Niklaus Manuels," *Beiträge zur Geschichte der deutschen Sprache und Literatur,* 29 (1904): 80-117;

Paul Zinsli, *Der Berner Totentanz des Niklaus Manuel* (Bern: Haupt, 1979);

Zinsli, "Manuel und Murner: Die Begegnung zweier doppelt begabter Glaubensstreiter in der Reformationszeit," *Berner Zeitschrift für Geschichte und Heimatkunde,* 50 (1988): 165-196;

Zinsli, "Zu den Versen auf der Rückseite der Zeichnung Niklaus Manuels vom 'Krieger, der zum Bettler wird,' " *Zeitschrift für Schweizerische Archäologie und Kunstgeschichte,* 37 (1980): 260-263.

Philipp Melanchthon
(16 February 1497 – 19 April 1560)

Derk Visser
Ursinus College

SELECTED BOOKS: *De artibus liberalis* (Tübingen: Thomas Anshelm, 1517);

De corrigendis adulescentiae studiis (Wittenberg: Joh. Grunenberg, 1518);

Integra graeca grammatica institutiones (Hagenau: Johann Lauchenius, 1518);

De rhetorica libri tres (Basel: Johann Froben, 1519);

Loci Communes rerum theologicarum seu Hypotyposes theologicae (Wittenberg: Melchior Lotter, 1521; revised edition, Wittenberg: Peter Seitz, 1535; revised, 1544; revised edition, Leipzig: Ernst Vögelin, 1559); translated by Charles Leander Hill as *The Loci Communes of Philip Melanchthon* (Boston: Meador, 1944); Latin edition of 1544 translated into German and revised by Melanchthon as *Heubtartikel Christlicher Lere im latin genannt Loci Theologici* (Wittenberg: Veit Creutzer, 1553); translated by Clyde Manschreck as *Melanchthon on Christian Doctrine* (New York: Oxford University Press, 1965);

Institutiones rhetoricae (Wittenberg: Melchior Lotter, 1521); adapted and translated by Leonard Cox as *The arte or crafte of rhetoryke* (London: Robert Redman, 1535?; edited by Frederic Ives Carpenter, Chicago: University of Chicago Press, 1899);

Annotationes in Evangelium Matthaei iam recens in gratiam studiosorum editae (Basel: Valentin Curio or Thomas Wolff, 1523);

Epitome Renovatae ecclesiasticae doctrinae ad illustrissimum Principium Hessorum (Wittenberg: Joseph Klug, 1524);

Adversus anabaptistas iudicium (Wittenberg: Nicolaus Schirlentz, 1528);

Unterricht der Visitatoren (Wittenberg: Nicolaus Schirlentz, 1528); translated by Richard Lawrence as *The Visitation of the Saxon Reformed Church in the Years 1527 and 1528* (Dublin: Milliken, 1839);

Confessio fidei exhibita invictissimo Imperatori Carolo V. (Wittenberg: Georg Rhau, 1531); translated by Richard Taverner as *The confessyon of the fayth of the Germaynes exhibited to ... Emperour*

Philipp Melanchthon in 1543; painting by Lucas Cranach the Elder (Uffizi Gallery, Florence)

Charles the v in the councell ... holden at Augusta 1530 (London: Robert Redman, 1536); revised as *Confessio Augustana Variata* (Wittenberg: Joseph Klug, 1540); excerpt translated by Nicholas Lesse as *The ivstification of man by faith only: made and written by Phylyp Melanchton, and translated out of the Latyn into this oure mother tonge* (London, 1548);

Apologia Confessionis (Wittenberg: Georg Rhau, 1531); translated anonymously as *The Apologie that is to say the defense of the Confessyon* (London: Robert Redman, 1536);

Elementorum rhetorices libri duo (Wittenberg: Georg Rhau, 1531); edited and translated by Mary

Joan LaFontaine as "A Critical Translation of Philip Melanchthon's Elementorum rhetorices libri duo," dissertation, University of Michigan, 1979;

Grammatica latina (Frankfurt am Main: Christian Egenolff, 1532);

Commentarii in Epistolam Pauli ad Romanos (Wittenberg: Joseph Klug, 1532); translated by Fred Kramer as *Commentary on Romans* (Saint Louis: Concordia, 1992);

Philosophiae moralis epitome (Strasbourg: Crato Mylius, 1538); translated by John Goodale as *A civile nosgay wherin is contayned not onely the offyce and dewty of all magestrates and judges but also of all subiectes* (London, 1550?);

De ecclesia et de autoritate verbi Dei (Wittenberg: Hans Lufft, 1539); translated anonymously as *On the true auctorities of the churche* (Ipswych: John Owen, 1548);

Arbor Consanguinitatis (Wittenberg: Joseph Klug, 1540);

Defensio coniugii sacerdotum pia (Strasbourg: Crato Mylius, 1540); translated anonymously as *The epistle of the famous and great clerke Philip Melancton made vnto oure late Souereygne Lorde Kynge Henry the eight, for the reuokinge and abolishing of the six articles set forth and enacted by the craftie meanes and procurement of certeyne of our prelates of the clergie* (London?: John Day?, 1547);

Operum Phil. Melanthonis Tomi quinque, 5 volumes (Basel: Johann Herwagen, 1541);

Von des Bapsts Gewalt und der ersten Kirchen Brauch (Wittenberg: Joseph Klug, 1541);

Ursach, Warumb die Stende, so der Augspurgischen Confession anhangen, Christliche Leer erstlich angenommen und endlich auch dabei zuverharren gedencken (Wittenberg: Joseph Klug, 1546);

Erotemata Dialectices (Wittenberg: Hans Lufft, 1547);

Bedencken auffs interim (Magdeburg: Michel Lotter, 1548); translated by John Rogers as *A waying and considering of the interim by the honourworthy and highly learned Philip Melancthon* (London: Edward Whitchurche, 1548);

Historia de vita et actis reverendiss. viri d. Martini Lutheri (Wittenberg: Hans Lufft, 1548); translated by Henry Bennet as "The history of the life and actes of Martine Luther," in his *A famous and godly history contayning the lyves and actes of three renowned reformers . . . Martine Luther, John Ecolampadius and Huldericke Zwinglius* (London: John Awdeley, 1561);

Initia doctrinae physicae, by Melanchthon and Paul Eber (Wittenberg: Peter Seitz, 1549);

Kirchenordnung: wie es mit christlicher Lere, reichung der Sacrament, Ordination der Diener des Evangelii im Herzogthumb zu Meckelnburg etc. gehalten wird (Wittenberg: Hans Lufft, 1552);

Liber de anima (Wittenberg: Peter Seitz, 1553);

Chronicon Carionis latinum expositum et auctum multis Historiis a Philippo Melanch., 2 volumes (Wittenberg: Georg Rhau, 1558, 1560);

Corpus doctrinae (Leipzig: Voegelin, 1560).

Collections: *Philippi Melanchthonis opera quae supersunt omnia,* 28 volumes, edited by Carl G. Bretschneider and Heinrich E. Bindseil (Halle & Brunswick: Schwetschke, 1834–1860);

Supplementa Melanchthoniana, 5 volumes, edited by Otto Clemens and others (Leipzig: Haupt, 1910–1929);

Melanchthons Werke in Auswahl: Studien Ausgabe, 7 volumes, edited by Robert Stupperich and others (Gütersloh: Bertelsmann, 1951–1975).

Editions in English: *A godly and learned assertion in defence of the true church of God and of His Woorde,* translated by Richard Robinson (London: Thomas Dawson, 1580);

Melanchthon: Selected Writings, translated by Charles Leander Hill (Saint Louis: Augsburg, 1962);

A Melanchthon Reader, translated by Ralph Keen (New York: Peter Lang, 1988).

OTHER: Terence, *Commoedia sex,* edited by Melanchthon (Tübingen: Thomas Anshelm, 1516);

Passional Christi und Antichristi, text by Melanchthon, woodcuts by Lucas Cranach the Elder (Wittenberg: Georg Rhau, 1521); adapted anonymously as *A pistle to the christen reader. The revelation of Antichrist* (Marburg: Hans Lufft, 1529);

Johann Carion, *Chronica,* edited by Melanchthon (Wittenberg: Georg Rhau, 1532);

"De consideratione humani corporis," on the flyleaf of the first edition of Andreas Vesalius's *De humanis corporis fabrica* (Basel: Johann Herwagen, 1543); translated by Dorothy M. Schullian as *Observations on the Human Body* (Los Angeles: Ward Ritchie, 1949);

Martin Bucer, *Von Gottes genaden unser Hermanns Ertzbisschoffs zu Coln einfaltigs bedencken,* edited by Melanchton (Bonn: Laurentius von der Müllen, 1543); translated as *The Consultation of Hermann of Cologne* (London, 1548);

Justus Mennius, *Von der Notwehr Unterricht,* edited and revised by Melanchthon (Wittenberg: Veit Creutzer, 1547);

Ptolemy, *De predictionibus astronomicis,* translated by Melanchthon and Johann Camerarius (Basel: Oporinus, 1553).

Philipp Melanchthon, who received his Greek last name–a translation of his real name, Schwartz-

Melanchthon in 1526; engraving by Albrecht Dürer

erd (Black Earth)—from his early mentor and distant relative Johann Reuchlin, is now chiefly known as one of the German Reformers, a close associate of Martin Luther. He was honored during Luther's lifetime, but after Luther's death he was attacked for allegedly altering some of Luther's theological doctrines. In the nineteenth century his reputation as a humanist teacher was established by Karl Hartfelder, who called him "Praeceptor Germaniae" (the Teacher of Germany). Modern church historians have called Melanchthon "the man who helped Luther discover the gospel."

Unlike Luther, Melanchthon published little in German—he wrote mostly for students and scholars, whose universal language was Latin—but many of his works were translated into German by others (not always with his knowledge). Although he is now best known as a Reformer, from the beginning of his career he served the great enterprise of Renaissance humanism, that of "restoring" ancient literature by editing original texts and translating them into Latin. His collected works, edited between 1834 and 1860, comprise twenty-eight volumes, with five supplementary volumes appearing from 1910 to 1929; but more items have been discovered since then, especially in regard to his extensive correspondence. A new edition of the letters that is being prepared under the leadership of Heinz Scheible (1977-) includes some three hundred previously unpublished items, as well as many corrections of earlier ones. Melanchthon's importance in German intellectual history is indicated by the fact that some 2.5 million copies of his more than seven hundred works may have existed by 1600—a time when the Germanies had a population of perhaps twenty million, many of whom were literate in neither German nor Latin.

Melanchthon was born on 16 February 1497 in Bretten to George Schwartzerd, an armorer of the elector palatine in Heidelberg, and Barbara Schwartzerd, née Reuter, the daughter of a well-to-do merchant. After receiving his primary education from a tutor in Bretten he went to Reuchlin's Latin School in Pforzheim, where he lived in Reuchlin's sister's house. The Pforzheim school had an excellent reputation because of Reuchlin's humanist scholarship, and Melanchthon became acquainted with several future humanists there.

In October 1509 Melanchthon enrolled at the University of Heidelberg, which, in spite of a brief association with Rudolph Agricola and the circle of literati around Johann von Dahlberg, bishop of Worms, was still rather medieval in its teaching. Thus, it was in the Scholastic method, or *via antiqua,* that he obtained his baccalaureate in 1511. At Heidelberg, too, he met important future leaders, among them the Reformer Johann Brenz. Considered too young to receive a master's degree at Heidelberg, he moved to Tübingen University. There he received the degree, this time in the *via moderna,* or nominalism, in 1514. When, in the manner of Renaissance scholars, Melanchthon criticized the sterile speculations of the late-medieval Scholastics, or "schoolmen," he knew whereof he spoke.

While teaching at Tübingen, Melanchthon continued his linguistic studies. He acquired a solid grounding in Hebrew, and he considered producing an edition of the works of Aristotle. Like many of his colleagues, he worked as a proofreader for a printer. In 1516 he published a modern edition of the works of the Roman playwright Terence, for which he wrote a historical introduction. As would be the case with nearly all of Melanchthon's works, the Terence volume was republished repeatedly, with emendations, during his lifetime. Ralph Keen's checklist (1988) gives thirty-four editions, some of which were printed in Antwerp, Hagenau, Lyons, Venice, and Paris. Desiderius Erasmus, the "Prince of Humanists," praised the young scholar handsomely and received a poem, written in classical Greek, in return. Melanchthon's Greek grammar appeared in 1518; it would go through thirty-six editions by 1560. In his first academic oration, *De artibus liberalis* (On the Liberal Arts, 1517), he advocated the study of dialectics and mathematics; but he also considered poetry and history useful disciplines, because they illustrated the subjects encountered in the seven liberal arts. Such orations, which he often wrote for others to deliver, were an important educational tool for Melanchthon; some 180 of them are known. They praise famous men, encourage liberal studies as a work pleasing to God, foster correct (Lutheran) doctrine, and generally serve to inculcate Christian morality. He also wrote poems in Latin and Greek, including epitaphs; epigrams announcing or canceling lectures or inviting or thanking friends for dinner; and paraphrases of biblical texts.

On Reuchlin's recommendation Friedrich III, Elector of Saxony, named Melanchthon in 1518 to the chair of Greek at the recently established University of Wittenberg. His inaugural address, *De corrigendis adulescentiae studiis* (On Improving the Undergraduate Curriculum, 1518), ending with Horace's *Sapere aude* (dare to know), sketches the decline of the liberal arts after the barbarian invasions of Rome and calls for their restoration. In his lectures Melanchthon treated the original Greek text of the New Testament, thus demonstrating the humanist thesis that the knowledge of ancient languages, like all other knowledge, is essential for the correct understanding of God's Word; he lectured on the Hebrew text of the Psalms, as well. At the same time he was studying for his bachelor of theology degree, which he obtained in September 1519. He also wrote a Latin grammar (1532) that went through ninety-four editions by 1560.

Prodded by Luther, who believed that his physically weak younger colleague needed a helpmate, Melanchthon somewhat unwillingly married Catharine Krapp on 25 November 1520. During their long marriage, however, he developed a great affection for her. Catharine's rejection of his idea of setting up house together with his friend Johann Agricola and Agricola's young wife was, in view of Agricola's later vehement disagreements with Melanchthon, probably fortunate. Their first child, Anna, was born in 1522; Philipp, born in 1525, would be in poor health all his life, though he would live to the age of eighty; George, born in 1527, died before his second birthday; and Magdalen, born in 1553, would be her widowed father's main support in his old age.

As was customary, Melanchthon took in boarding students, including young ones for whom he organized a *Hausschule* (house school). To encourage these students Melanchthon set up competitions, crowning the winners "poets laureate." In this teaching he was assisted by Johannes Koch, who, with a master's degree, was much more than the typical famulus. Koch lived with the Melanchthons for more than thirty years and became a trusted associate. It is clear from Melanchthon's letters during Koch's last days in 1553 that Melanchthon held him in high and warm regard.

During Luther's absences from Wittenberg, Melanchthon assumed Luther's lectures on books of the Bible. From 1518 through 1529 he delivered twenty-six lectures on seventeen books or parts of books. Paul's Epistle to the Romans served as an important preparation for Melanchthon's *Loci Communes rerum theologicarum seu Hypotyposes theologicae* (The Common Places of Christian Doctrine, 1521;

translated as *The Loci Communes of Philip Melanchthon,* 1944), which was first printed in installments. Although Melanchthon would compose the Augsburg Confession in 1530, he would do so in consultation with others; therefore, the *Loci Communes* may well be his most important independent contribution to the Reformation. The work uses the method of excerpting the main concepts of one's studies that was practiced by the ancients and revived by Agricola and others; Melanchthon had developed it in his *De rhetorica libri tres* (Three Books on Rhetoric, 1519). But where others used the commonplaces as glosses on the text, Melanchthon used them to compose a guide to the meaning of Christianity.

The bibliographical history of the *Loci Communes* is typical of that of many of Melanchthon's works. He continued to revise his writings, even after they had been published in ostensibly complete form, as he lectured on the same subjects in subsequent years. Frequently, the later editions virtually constitute new works. In some cases, including the *Loci Communes,* the later versions have a different organization and present the material in a more precise fashion and in a wider context than the original one. In other cases, such as his books on ethics, the content also changes. He improved the *Loci Communes* constantly, on the basis both of his studies of the Bible in preparation for his lectures and of the deeper understanding that resulted from the polemics and colloquies that occupied much of his time. In 1535 he published a totally revised version, dedicated to King Henry VIII of England; it was followed in 1544 by another revision, and in 1559 by yet another. The influence of the *Loci Communes* was increased by its translations into German: Georg Spalatin translated the 1521 edition, and Justus Jonas translated the other editions. In 1553 Melanchthon published his own German translation of the 1544 edition; he called this translation his favorite version of the work, and it became quite popular. This version of the work was reprinted annually, often in several cities, and many copies survive. As its author often wrote dedications on the flyleaves, and students used their copies as autograph books, these copies (as well as those of Melanchthon's other works) provide a marvelous insight into the academic and spiritual life of the time. The impact of the *Loci Communes* outside the German-speaking world was also great: the Latin versions of the work were required reading in Latin at the University of Cambridge, and Queen Elizabeth memorized large portions of it.

While serving as rector of the university in 1523-1524 Melanchthon established new regulations. For example, he insisted that each student be registered and assigned a preceptor who was to formulate an ordered sequence of studies, depending on the student's prior preparation. He also issued prohibitions against such acts as breaking down doors, destroying gardens, whoring, and drinking. (The elector had forbidden the bearing of arms, though this prohibition apparently did not apply to aristocratic students: in the 1550s the elderly Melanchthon, in his nightshirt, would have to separate two Polish noble youths who engaged in a sword fight in front of his house late at night.)

In 1525 Melanchthon was promoted to the rank of university professor, which allowed him to lecture on subjects of his choice; his Greek chair was taken over by a colleague. At this time he also became involved in the reform of school systems in various cities, in response to requests from local authorities; the call to establish schools had been issued by Luther in 1524. Melanchthon accomplished some of these reforms through placing his students as teachers in the schools; in other cases, such as that of the Latin School in Nuremberg, he became personally involved. In that city his work was helped along by his dearest friend and first biographer, Johann Camerarius, who was appointed one of the first four teachers at the school.

Like all of Melanchthon's lectures, his expositions of the Gospel of Matthew and of Paul's Epistles led to publications. His extensive commentary on Paul's Epistle to the Romans of 1532 was dedicated to Elector Albrecht of Brandenburg, the archbishop of Mainz. Because he believed that it contained the central doctrines of Christianity—justification and grace—Melanchthon returned again and again to Romans for inspiration and for supporting texts for his own writings.

In addition to composing his own works, Melanchthon also sponsored the publication of works by others—either because he considered the works important, or to advance the careers of the authors. Often, this activity involved writing to some Maecenas or composing prefaces and letters of dedication. One work that he edited was the *Chronicon* (1532), a world history by Johann Carion. Melanchthon's interest in history also emerged in his academic orations, and he was instrumental in raising history to an autonomous discipline.

In these early years he lectured on Aristotle's *Nicomachean Ethics* and *Politics.* From these lectures he gradually developed his own system of Christian ethics that was first published in 1538 as *Philosophiae moralis epitome* (Summary of Moral Philosophy; translated as *A civile nosgay wherin is contayned not onely the offyce and dewty of all magestrates and judges but also of all subiectes,* 1550?). Among the practical questions discussed is whether young people should become engaged without their parents' knowledge and permission.

Melanchthon's services were also demanded in the reform of the parishes in electoral Saxony. This project not only involved traveling as part of a team of inspectors but also often led to polemics about doctrine—for example, against the Anabaptists on child baptism (1528). His observations of the problems in the parishes led to his *Unterricht der Visitatoren* (Instructions for the Church Visitors; translated as *The Visitation of the Saxon Reformed Church in the Years 1527 and 1528*, 1839). Published in 1528 with a foreword by Luther, it was frequently reprinted and served as a model for many other German states. More than a manual for the organization of parishes, the tasks of pastors and the liturgy, and the establishment of school systems, it is a summary of Reformed doctrine in which Melanchthon stresses the need for contrition and penance but rejects good works as a means to salvation. Among those who criticized the work's emphasis on penance was Johann Agricola—a first indication of the rift that would develop between the two friends.

The system of Latin schools described in *Unterricht der Visitatoren* was meant for smaller parishes; large cities, such as Nuremberg and Strasbourg, established full-fledged Latin schools, or gymnasia. The smaller Latin school was to comprise three levels, to avoid overburdening the beginner or boring the advanced student. The beginner was to study grammar by analyzing the texts of the catechism and of the medieval collection of moral teachings known as the *Dicta Catonis* (Cato's Aphorisms). Those who already had a rudimentary education were to begin at the second level, where the readings would be taken from the works of Aesop and Terence and the emphasis would be on etymology and syntax; plays by Plautus and the colloquies of Erasmus could also be used, as long as the teacher picked the unobjectionable ones. In a letter of 1540 elaborating on this program, Melanchthon recommends Erasmus's *Christiani matrionii institutio* (On Marriage, 1526) by name. Students on the highest level were to study the works of the great Roman authors and receive training in rhetoric, dialectics, and the rules of poetry. Throughout, Melanchthon is concerned to maintain simplicity: teachers should not show off by teaching material that is too difficult for their students.

In 1529 Melanchthon was sent by the elector of Saxony to Speyer to attend his first *Reichstag* (a meeting called by emperors to settle disputes and discuss the affairs of the empire). These missions fell to Melanchthon because Luther, who had been

Melanchthon in 1532; portrait by Lukas Cranach (Gemäldegalerie, Dresden)

placed under an imperial ban in 1521, could not travel freely outside Protestant areas. At the Reichstag, Melanchthon learned firsthand about the political ramifications of Reform; gradually he became critical of the princes, including his own elector, Johann Friedrich, whose dynastic and political ambitions threatened the achievements of the Reformation. Later that year he took part in the Colloquy of Marburg. Landgrave Philipp of Hesse, for whom Melanchthon had composed a program for religious reform in 1524, called the meeting, which included Luther and the Zurich Reformer Huldrych Zwingli, to try to produce a consensus on the doctrine of the Lord's Supper. No agreement was reached, as Luther insisted on the real presence of Christ's body and blood in the sacrament against the symbolic interpretation favored by Zwingli. The doctrine of the "real presence" would remain the most significant point separating Luther and his followers from the other Reformers.

Their understanding of the Lord's Supper, as well as other doctrines, also separated the Wittenbergers from the Roman Catholic Church. In 1530 Emperor Charles V, who needed peace in the German lands if he was to pursue his international political goals, called a Reichstag in Augsburg to try to reunify the church. Melanchthon was, once again, the major spokesman; Luther stayed in Torgau, the nearest place where he would be safe. Communication between him and Melanchthon was not smooth, and Luther fretted that Melanchthon might give too much away under the pressure of the princes. Yet it was on this occasion that Melanchthon composed *Confessio fidei exhibita invictissimo Imperatori Carolo V.* (1531; translated as *The confessyon of the fayth of the Germaynes exhibited to . . . Emperour Charles the v in the councell . . . holden at Augusta 1530*, 1536)–the Augsburg Confession–which remains the basis of Lutheran doctrine.

As in Marburg, no agreement was reached in Augsburg. The imperial theologians issued a confutation of the Augsburg Confession, to which Melanchthon wrote a rebuttal that was revised and published in 1531 as *Apologia Confessionis* (translated as *The Apologie that is to say the defense of the Confessyon,* 1536). The result of Marburg and Augsburg was that the Lutherans clearly established themselves as separate from Rome, on the one hand, and from the rest of the Protestants, on the other hand. During the next ten years Melanchthon would continue to participate in colloquies and discussions aiming at accommodation, first with other evangelicals–a name Luther preferred to "Lutherans"–and then, if they could be united, with Rome.

The need for a united evangelical position was accentuated by the establishment in 1530 of the Smalkaldic League, a defensive agreement among Protestant princes and cities who feared that the emperor might use religion as a pretext to attack them so as to increase his power. Martin Bucer, the Reformer of Strasbourg, was most active in bringing about a common confession. After lengthy consultations Melanchthon, Bucer, and representatives of several south German cities agreed in 1536 on the Wittenberg Doctrine, a formula that permitted the non-Lutherans to interpret the language pertaining to the Lord's Supper to their satisfaction. In 1537 the common position was laid down in the Smalkaldic Articles, in which the Augsburg Confession was the accepted confession. As an addendum to the articles Melanchthon wrote a treatise denying the primacy of the Pope. On the jurisdictional powers of bishops he adopted the view that bishops who taught "correctly" could be tolerated.

In 1536 Melanchthon's favorite daughter, Anna, who was then only fourteen, married Georg Sabinus, one of Melanchthon's students and a gifted Neo-Latin poet. The marriage was an unhappy one. Melanchthon blamed himself for having been blinded by the ambitious Sabinus, who may have wanted to marry Anna only to become Melanchthon's son-in-law. Melanchthon even proposed that the couple separate, an unheard-of solution at that time. Anna died in 1547, having borne six children. After her death several of the children were cared for in Melanchthon's home by their grandmother; Magdalen remained with them, while the others were brought up in Königsberg after Sabinus remarried.

The effect his daughter's marriage had on Melanchthon can be seen in the many opinions he was asked to give on problems of marriage law. One of the consequences of the Reformation was the raising of the question of whether the canon law of the Roman Catholic Church, which governed such matters as usury and marriage, still applied. Much of it was based on the laws of Moses and was, therefore, still considered valid; but pastors and city magistrates–many of them, increasingly, Melanchthon's former students–solicited his advice on complicated cases. Beginning in the 1540s, Melanchthon's opinions showed more concern than was then the norm for the plight of women who were clearly victimized in their marriages. The relationship between husband and wife is frequently addressed in Melanchthon's occasional writings and in the Latin sermons he wrote for foreign students who had difficulty following the service in German, and the image he paints is that of an equal partnership with separate spheres. In 1540 he published a short treatise, *Arbor Consanguinitatis* (Tree of Consanguinity), in which he uses the family trees of German noble families to illustrate the degrees of kinship for which marriage is allowed.

In the 1530s the Wittenberg reformers, including Melanchthon, became increasingly involved in the politics of the Smalkaldic League. Its leaders, Landgrave Philipp of Hesse and Elector Johann Friedrich of Saxony, asked repeatedly for advice on whether it was legitimate to offer military resistance to the emperor for the sake of protecting the religion of their states, and even whether it was legitimate to begin a preventive war. The documents edited by Scheible demonstrate that before the founding of the league, Luther and Melanchthon had always answered such questions in the negative; but by 1540 they were arguing that resistance was permissible, although a preventive war could be waged only if the emperor's intentions were made clear–for example, by his placing a league member under the imperial ban.

During the colloquies of 1539 to 1542 Melanchthon was the chief spokesman for the evangelical side. Among his opponents was Johann Eck, a theologian who had debated Luther at Leipzig and had ridiculed Melanchthon for his defense of Luther. In Hagenau and Frankfurt am Main Melanchthon be-

Page from Melanchthon's letter to Friedrich Staphylus, theology professor at the University of Königsberg, dated 1 January; the year is thought to be 1551 (Königliches Geheimes Staatsarchiv, Berlin)

came acquainted with John Calvin, and he also worked with Bucer and others he had met previously. On the basis of the Wittenberg Concord and the Smalkaldic Articles, Melanchthon wrote a revision of the Augsburg Confession titled *Confessio Augustana Variata* (Variations on the Augsburg Confession, 1540) to present the unified position of the Protestants. Melanchthon's skill at formulating evangelical positions annoyed Eck to such an extent that, according to Melanchthon, he died of apoplexy in 1543. But, as Melanchthon also intimated in some nasty distichs, Eck might have killed himself through his drinking and whoring. In part because it was signed by Calvin, the *Confessio Augustana Variata* was used by Melanchthon's critics to argue that he had departed from Luther's views. Although Luther had not condemned it, after 1561 the *Confessio Augustana Variata* was no longer cited among the confessional texts of the Lutheran Church.

When the Smalkaldic War broke out in 1546, Melanchthon edited and softened Justus Mennius's *Von der Notwehr Unterricht* (Instruction on the Right of Self Defense, 1547), a work that extended the natural right of self-defense to the right to resist rulers. These ideas, sharpened by the pastors of Magdeburg in the *Magdeburg Bekänntniss* (Confession of Magdeburg, 1550), formed part of the basis for the political theory of resistance to tyrants.

The Smalkaldic War was caused by the emperor's attempt to force the issue of reunification of the German Church after the colloquies of 1539 to 1542, ending in Regensburg, and the ensuing polemics showed that reconciliation was not only impossible but also opposed by the papacy. The stumbling blocks, as always, were the divergent positions on justification, with Rome insisting on the importance of good works, and the doctrine of the Eucharist, with Rome insisting on transsubstantiation. One of the reasons the emperor decided on armed intervention was the Reform instituted by the archbishop of Cologne, Hermann von Wied, who was also an elector and, as such, could help swing the election of a future emperor away from the Hapsburgs: of the seven electors, those of Saxony and Brandenburg were already Lutherans, while the likely heir to the electorship of the Palatinate, Otto Henrich, was leaning toward the Reformation. For the Reformation of Cologne the archbishop called on Bucer and Melanchthon. The archbishop's Reform program, published in 1543 and variously known as the *Consultatio, Hermanns Buch* (Hermann's Book), or *Einfältigs Bedencken* (A Simple Consultation), was written by Bucer and edited by Melanchthon. Bucer was seen by many Lutherans as favoring the Zwinglian, or Swiss, doctrine of the Lord's Supper, and one of them, Nicholas Amsdorf, sent a copy of the work to Luther along with his own negative comments on it. Luther was informed of certain doubtful phrases in the document. Luther went into a rage, and Melanchthon feared that he would be forced to leave Wittenberg. But although Luther wrote a scathing indictment of the Swiss position, he did not condemn Melanchthon.

When Luther died on 18 February 1546, Melanchthon inherited the leadership of the evangelical movement. In his funeral oration he called Luther the driver of the evangelical wagon, a third Elias who had pointed the way to Christ just as the prophet and John the Baptist had done in their times. He warned against those who would be ready to pounce now that they no longer needed to fear Luther's anger. He knew that he was emotionally ill-equipped to assume Luther's mantle and was fully aware that his critics, previously silenced by Luther, would no longer feel restrained.

Under the threat of war the university was closed. Melanchthon, who had publicly advocated armed resistance to authority, became a target of imperial revenge. He sent his family away to safety, planning to follow after he had seen his *Erotemata Dialectices* (Principles of Dialectics, 1547) through revision and printing. The *Erotemata Dialectices,* dealing with the organization of materials in exposition, was the crowning work of Melanchthon's long years of teaching the correct use of language. Like many of his other textbooks, it would remain in use long after his death.

The war ended badly for the Smalkaldic League. The emperor took Philipp of Hesse and Johann Friedrich prisoner, and Johann Friedrich's electoral title and lands, including Wittenberg, were given to Duke Moritz, who, though a Protestant, had sided with the emperor to reacquire the electorship that he believed had been unfairly taken away from his branch of the family by an earlier emperor. Moritz reopened the university and invited Melanchthon to return. Consequently, Melanchthon was regarded as a traitor to Johann Friedrich, from whom he had received many favors. Some modern scholars believe that Moritz was truly committed to preserving the Reformation, which had been adopted by his father against the vehement opposition of the head of their branch, the Roman Catholic Duke Georg. In this light Melanchthon's declaration that he took Moritz at his word and that Wittenberg, where the Reformation had begun, was the only place to continue Luther's work becomes plausible. But many of his former colleagues, who had been students of Luther and of Melanchthon himself, turned against him—particularly when the emperor used his new dominance to issue the Interim, a temporary measure whereby ceremonies were reformed and doctrinal language that had been formulated at Regensburg was imposed. But when the Interim was declared binding only on the Protestants, they balked. Asked to give his theological opinion, Melanchthon wrote a memorandum in which he questioned the doctrinal language of the Interim, especially on "justification." He sent it to some of his friends as a private communication, but it was promptly published as *Bedencken auffs interim* (An Examination of the Interim, 1548; translated as *A waying and considering of the interim,* 1548), probably to force him to take a public stand against the Interim.

In the ensuing negotiations between the Saxon theologians and political counselors, however, Moritz sacrificed too much for political reasons, and Melanchthon's opponents blamed Melanchton for that outcome. Melanchthon acted in the spirit that had guided Luther and himself at the beginning of the Reformation, when, in *Unterricht der Visitatoren,* he had advised going slowly to avoid upheaval in the parishes. It seemed imperative to do whatever was needed to keep the imperial troops out of Saxony, since wherever they held sway, evangelical pastors were removed. As it turned out, Moritz organized a league of German princes in 1552 and made an agreement with Henry II of France against Charles V; with the Treaty of Passau, which ended the hostilities, the results of the Smalkaldic War were undone. Still, Melanchthon's reputation with his former students and colleagues remained tarnished.

In trying to save whatever he could of the Reformation in those dangerous times, Melanchthon used his academic orations in praise of famous men to show how God fulfilled his promise to preserve his church by sending extraordinary figures to restore learning in general and theology in particular. In 1548 Melanchthon composed an oration on Luther and the five ages of the church in which he returned to the image of Luther as evidence of God's care for the church that he had sketched in the funeral oration of 1546.

In the last decade of his life Melanchthon remained active in defense of the achievements for which he and Luther had worked so arduously. He hoped for continued cooperation among all Protestants so that evangelical theology could be clearly defined. But the Swiss thought him too Lutheran, and by 1560 his Lutheran antagonists considered him too accommodating to the Swiss. Some of these antagonists also accused him, on the basis of the phrase "Deus trahit, sed volentes trahit" (God draws the willing), of holding that human beings can decide, of their own free will, to turn to God—a position that had been rejected by Luther and Calvin alike. What Melanchthon actually taught is that one must not resist God's drawing.

In spite of the interminable theological disputes, Melanchthon continued to lecture on his customary topics in the arts and sciences. With Eber he brought out *Initia doctrinae physicae* (Introduction to Physics) in 1549. Although followers of Nicolaus Copernicus were among his colleagues and friends, he rejected the Copernican heliocentric theory. His interest in the natural sciences, including astrology—then still considered a science—derived from his desire to know all aspects of creation and, thereby, to attain better knowledge of the Creator.

Woodcut of Melanchthon, executed by Dürer after Melanchthon's death

He also developed a Christian anthropology out of his lectures on Aristotle; after consultations over many years with colleagues, this doctrine took its final form in his *Liber de anima* (On the Soul, 1553). In its dedicatory letter he said that in these times of great unrest one should study how the church is maintained, as promised, by God and that to gain insight into the actions of people one must study psychology. Undoubtedly, he was moved to this advice by the Socratic maxim "Know thyself"; but he also wanted to understand the motivations of his antagonists, who were accusing him of self-serving actions, as when he accepted compromises that would allow him to stay in Wittenberg. As he saw it, they were creating a schism in evangelical ranks. In the book he worked out concepts he had already established in his other works, such as the infirmity of the human will—that is, its inability to obey God's law—as a result of the Fall. With Camerarius he produced a Latin version of Ptolemy's *De predictionibus astronomicis* (On Astronomical Predictions, 1553). In its preface he reiterated his belief that science can help one to understand God; the influence of the celestial bodies on the earth furnishes physical evidence of divine providence, and natural disasters may bring people to their senses where calamities such as war have failed.

Understanding God through his work is also

the theme of Melanchthon's preface to his German version of the *Loci Communes,* which he dedicated to Anna Camerarius, the wife of his closest friend: God reveals himself through signs and gives testimony through his Word because he does not want to be unknown. The books of the prophets and the apostles constitute a story that is an excellent means of teaching the doctrine of salvation, the infirmity of the human will, and the remedies for that infirmity. The best of these remedies is the consolation one receives from the evidence that God will at all times preserve his church.

Melanchthon's friend and assistant, Koch, died in 1553, and some of the great men he had worked with in colloquies and elsewhere died in the same year. Gradually he reconciled himself with his son-in-law, Sabinus, the professor, diplomat, and Neo-Latin poet. Sabinus was one of many among Melanchthon's students who excelled in poetry. One of them, whose career Melanchthon promoted, was Johann Stigel, who became a professor at Jena University; though the atmosphere there became anti-Melanchthonian as a result of the polemics after the Interim, Stigel remained a friend. He was also the nucleus of a circle of late-humanist poets who had ties to Wittenberg and Melanchthon and who, as Manfred P. Fleischer has shown, were important in developing the literary taste of the German provinces.

Poetry was also used as a weapon. In the late 1550s, when the polemics over Lutheran doctrine divided Wittenberg graduates, bitter satires were produced by Melanchthon's partisans. In one of these, *Synodus avium* (The Convention of Birds, 1557), Melanchthon's opponents are depicted as chattering birds; some are recognizable by plays on their names, others by character traits exhibited by particular birds. Melanchthon is Philomel, the sweet-singing nightingale. Not all of this was in the spirit of the regulations Melanchthon had issued during his rectorate in 1524, one of which prohibited slandering persons in verse. But he himself had sinned against that rule, for example, in his distichs on the death of Eck.

These literary exchanges were written in 1557, when it had become clear that the rift among the Lutherans could not be healed. At the Colloquy of Worms later that year some of Melanchthon's Lutheran antagonists produced a list of points to be condemned before they would sit together with their colleagues and negotiate with the Roman Catholics. Among these points were the Swiss doctrine of the Lord's Supper; Melanchthon's alleged errors on free will; his compromises on the Interim; and his rejection of the doctrine of ubiquity (the claim that, because Christ was God and God was everywhere, Christ's body and blood were present in the Eucharist). Melanchthon and his adherents refused this demand, and the imperial theologians declared that without evangelical unity the colloquy could not proceed.

While Melanchthon was in Worms his wife died, and Camerarius traveled from Saxony in the inclement November weather to be with his friend. References in Melanchthon's letters, especially those of consolation to others, show that her death left a large void in Melanchthon's life. His letters also show that this void was filled to a large extent by his daughter Magdalen–who had married Caspar Peucer, a student and colleague of Melanchthon's–and his grandchildren.

Melanchthon also filled the void with the composition of a history of the world that took his editions of Carion's chronicle as its starting point. He retained the title *Chronicon Carionis* to memorialize the merits of the original author. Two volumes (1558, 1560) brought the history up to Charlemagne; after Melanchthon's death on 19 April 1560, Peucer completed the work in two additional volumes, published in 1572. According to Melanchthon, history is not merely a handbook in which politicians and military strategists can study the successes and failures of past leaders; it also reveals the psychology of people who engage in unnecessary actions because of their *inquietis ingeniis* (restless minds); Alcibiades, the Athenian military leader who switched allegiances between Athens and Sparta during the Peloponnesian War, is his leading example. History shows the wisdom of common sayings: evil punishes itself (atrocity provokes atrocity); he who takes up the sword perishes by the sword. But, first and foremost, the teaching of history, to show God's goodness through the evidence that he keeps his promises, is the most important task of the church. The *Chronicon Carionis* was translated into German and remained an academic textbook for two centuries.

Any assessment of Melanchthon's importance as a Reformer requires one to deal with questions concerning his role in formulating evangelical doctrine during Luther's lifetime and whether he departed from these doctrines after Luther's death. These issues, which remain controversial, have been addressed by Clyde Manschreck and Lowell C. Green. Melanchthon's importance as *Praeceptor Germaniae,* on the other hand, is firmly established. In addition to the essays by Scheible, Robert Kolb's research has highlighted the careers of several of the younger among Melanchthon's antagonists. Although they parted with Melanchthon over theology, they used his rhetorical and dialectical methods in their own works and so helped to expand Melanchthon's influence. At a colloquium held in Wolfenbüttel in June 1995, "Melanchthon in seinen Schülern" (Melanchthon in His Students), several scholars examined Melanchthon's impact on the formulation of doctrines of the German Reformed Church in Bremen and the Palatinate and, thus, of the German Reformed Church in the United States. It was pointed out that, as Melanchthon's *Loci Communes* continued to be used even by his critics, his role as a theologian was significant. Other participants showed that the methodology of the *Loci Communes* influenced the development of the disciplines of jurisprudence and medicine.

Letters:

Melanchthons Briefwechsel: Kritische und kommentierte Gesamtausgabe, 10 volumes published, edited by Heinz Scheible, Walther Thüringer, and Richard Wetzel (Stuttgart-Bad Cannstatt: Fromann-Holzboog, 1977-).

Bibliographies:

Wilhelm Hammer, *Die Melanchthonforshung im Wandel der Jahrhunderte: Ein beschreibendes Verzeichnis,* 3 volumes (Gütersloh: Mohn, 1967-1981);

Ralph Keen, *A Checklist of Melanchthon Imprints through 1560* (Saint Louis: Center for Reformation Research, 1988).

Biographies:

Joachim Camerarius, *De vita Philippi Melanchthonis narratio* (Leipzig: Ernst Voegelin, 1565); edited, with annotations, by Georg Theodorus Strobelius (Halle: Gebauer, 1777);

Karl Hartfelder, *Philipp Melanchthon als Praeceptor Germaniae* (Berlin: Hofmann, 1889);

Werner Hehl, *Philipp Melanchthon: Der Freund Martin Luthers* (Stuttgart: Quell, 1982);

Clyde Manschreck, *Melanchthon: The Quiet Reformer* (New York & Nashville: Abingdon, 1958);

Heinz Scheible, "Melanchthon, Philipp (1497-1560)," in *Theologische Realenzyklopädie,* volume 23, edited by Gerhard Müller (Berlin & New York: De Gruyter, 1992), pp. 371-410.

References:

Manfred P. Fleischer, "Melanchthon as Praeceptor of Late-Humanist Poetry," *Sixteenth Century Journal,* 20 (1989): 559-580;

Lowell C. Green, *How Melanchthon Helped Luther Discover the Gospel* (Fallbrook, Cal.: Verdict, 1980);

Robert Kolb, "Philip's Foes, but Followers Nonetheless: Late Humanism among the Gnesio-Lutherans," in *The Harvest of Humanism in Central Europe,* edited by Manfred P. Fleischer (Saint Louis: Concordia, 1992), pp. 159-178;

Wilhelm Maurer, "Confessio Augustana Variata," *Archiv für Reformationsgeschichte,* 53 (1962): 97-151;

E. P. Meijering, *Melanchthon and Patristic Thought* (Leiden: Brill, 1983);

Philipp Melanchthon: Humanist, Reformator, Praeceptor Germaniae (Berlin: Melanchthon-Komittee der DDR, 1963);

Heinz Scheible, "Melanchthon zwischen Luther und Erasmus," in *Renaissance Reformation: Gegensätze und Gemeinsamkeiten,* edited by August Buck (Wiesbaden: Harrassowitz, 1984), pp. 155-180;

Scheible, "Melanchthons Bildungsprogramm," in *Lebenslehren und Weltentwürfe im Übergang vom Mittelalter zur Neuzeit,* edited by Hartmut Boockmann and others (Göttingen: Vandenhoeck & Ruprecht, 1989), pp. 233-248;

Scheible, *Philipp Melanchthon–ein Lehrer Deutschlands* (Stuttgart: Landeszentrale für politische Bildung Baden-Württemberg, 1989);

Scheible, *Das Widerstandsrecht als Problem der deutschen Protestanten, 1523-1546* (Gütersloh: Mohn, 1968);

Scheible, ed., *Melanchthon in seinen Schülern* (Wolfenbüttel: Herzog August Bibliothek, 1997);

Wolfgang Trilhaas, "Philipp Melanchthon, der Ethiker der Reformation," *Evangelische Theologie,* 6 (1946/1947): 389-404;

Derk Visser, "Among the Good Teachers: Melanchthon on Wessel Gansfort," in *Wessel Gansfort (1419-1489) and Northern Humanism,* edited by Fokke Akkerman and others (Leiden: Brill, 1993), pp. 142-156;

Günther Wartenberg, "Philipp Melanchthon und die sächsisch-albertinische Interimspolitik," *Lutherjahrbuch,* 55 (1988): 60-82.

Olympia Fulvia Morata
(1526 – 26 October 1555)

John L. Flood
University of London Institute of Germanic Studies

BOOKS: *Olympiae Fulviae Moratae mulieris omnium eruditissimae Latina et Graeca, quae haberi potuerunt, monumenta, eaque plane divina, cum eruditorum de ipsa iudiciis et laudibus. Hippolytae Taurellae elegia elegantissima. Ad ill. Isabellam Bresegnam,* edited by Celio Secondo Curione (Basel: P. Perna, 1558); enlarged as *Olympiae Fulviae Moratae foeminae doctissimae ac plane diuinae Orationes, Dialogi, Epistolae, Carmina, tam Latina quam Graeca: cum eruditorum de ea testimonijs & laudibus. Hippolytae Taurellae elegia elegantissima. Ad sereniss. Angliae Reginam D. Elisabetam,* edited by Curione (Basel: P. Perna, 1562); enlarged as *Olympiae Fulviae Moratae foeminae doctissimae ac plane divinae opera omnia quae hactenus inueniri potuerunt: cum eruditorum testimonijs & laudibus. Hyppolitae Taurellae Elegia elegantissima. Quibus Caelii S. C. selectae Epistolae ac orationes accesserunt,* edited by Curione (Basel: P. Perna, 1570); enlarged as *Olympiae Fulviae Moratae, Foeminae doctissimae, ac plane diuinae, Opera omnia cum eruditorum testimonijs. Quibus, praeter C. S. C. Epistolas selectas & orationes: Nunc demum accesserunt M. Antonij Paganutij fabulae ex Aesopo Latine factae, et Ioannis Boccacii quaedam ex Italico,* edited by Curione (Basel: P. Perna, 1580);
Olimpia Morata: Opere, edited by Lanfranco Caretti (Ferrara, 1954).

Olympia Fulvia Morata

Olympia Fulvia Morata was a woman whose erudition and religious fervor earned her the admiration of her Italian and German friends in a male-dominated world torn apart by ideological strife and war. Though she spent only the last five years of her life in Germany, she played an important role in promoting humanist interests in Schweinfurt and corresponded extensively with German humanists.

Born in Ferrara in 1526, Morata was the eldest child of Fulvio Pellegrino Morato and Lucrezia Morata. Her father, who came from Mantua, had been appointed tutor to the younger sons of Alfonso I, duke of Ferrara, in 1522. In 1532 he was banished from court because of his Reformist inclinations. In 1539, under Duke Ercole II, he was permitted to return to Ferrara. Ercole was probably influenced in this matter by his wife, Renée; the daughter of King Louis XII of France, she had strong Calvinist sympathies.

Morata received her initial instruction in Latin grammar, rhetoric, moral philosophy, and history from her father. In 1540 Duchess Renée summoned Morata to court to be a pacemaker for her daughters, who were to be taught Greek and Latin by two Germans: Johannes Sinapius, the duchess's personal physician, who had previously held the chair of Greek at Heidelberg University; and his brother Kilian, a lawyer. Under their guidance the girls made excellent progress—especially Morata, whose command of Greek and Latin astonished everyone. She and the duchess's daughter Anna d'Este were not only able to translate works by Latin and Greek authors but also once held a disputation in Latin, before the assembled court and a glittering company of scholars, on the *Paradoxa Stoicorum* (Paradoxes of the Stoics) of Cicero. As the Ferrara humanist Celio Secondo Curione wrote to Sixtus Birk (Xystus Betuleius), rector of the grammar school at Augsburg, on 25 December 1550: "Ibi audivimus nos eam ita Latinè declamantem Graecè loquentem, Ciceroni Paradoxa explicantem, ad quaestiones respondentem, ut cum veterum puellorum quavis, quae quidem ingenii laude excelluerit, conferre posse videretur" (We have heard her here so declaiming Latin, speaking Greek, expounding Cicero's *Paradoxa,* answering questions, that it was as if one could compare her to any young woman whatever among the ancients who excelled in the praise she received for her intellect.) Morata's three introductions to the interpretation of the *Paradoxa Stoicorum* appear in the 1580 edition of her collected writings, edited by Curione; her *Defensio Ciceronis* (Defense of Cicero) has been lost. In *De poetis nostrorum temporum* (On the Poets of Our Times, 1551) Lilio Gregorio Giraldi says of her: "Quos inter est Olympia Morata, puella super sexum ingeniosa; nam non contenta vernaculo sermone latinas et Graeras litteras apprime erudita miraculum fere omnibus, qui eam audiunt, esse videtur" (The girl is gifted beyond her sex, for not content with her own language, she is extremely learned in Latin and Greek letters, as to appear almost miraculous to everyone who hears her.)

Deserving of notice, as throwing light on the atmosphere in Ferrara, is Morata's translation into Latin, ostensibly as a school exercise, of the first two stories from Giovanni Boccaccio's *Decameron* (1348-1353); the translations are included in the 1580 edition of her works. In the first story a Jewish merchant, urged by a Christian friend to change his religion, decides to visit the metropolis of Christianity before making a decision. In Rome he observes the corruption of the churchmen and, convinced of the divinity of a religion that subsists despite so many abuses, gets himself baptized immediately on his return home. The second story tells of a hypocrite who resolves, after a profligate life, to die as a holy man. He deceives his confessor, lies with his last breath, and, as Boccaccio says in Morata's translation, works just as many miracles as another saint. Such were the pungent satires that found an echo in the school at the palace at Ferrara. Beneath the veil of Ciceronian expression one may perhaps discern an intimation of Morata's inner separation from Roman Catholicism.

Another instance of Morata's talent is found in the Greek tribute she composed on the death of Pietro Bembo on 18 February 1547. In praising one of the men who had done so much for the revival of the ancients, she encapsulated the sorrow of the literary world: it was, she wrote, as though eloquence and Cicero himself had again descended into the gloomy shades. In addition to various Greek poems and epigrams, she composed a speech in Attic prose on the Roman hero Caius Mucius Scaevola.

Most of what is known about Morata's life and thought has been gleaned from her correspondence and that of others. In addition to the fifty-three letters from her own hand (one in Greek, three in Italian, forty-nine in Latin), not all of which can be securely dated, fifteen letters written to her survive; she is also the subject of seventeen letters by and to others. In total, this body of correspondence tells of her contacts with forty-one persons. Her letters breathe the spirit of Christian humanism and convey a vivid impression of the terrors life held during the Reformation period. Among Morata's surviving letters is one to Kilian Sinapius, in both a Greek and a Latin version, written in 1542 or 1543. In the Latin version she writes: "Neque enim in scientia, sed in exercitatione atque actione et initium virtutis est et finis. Ac quemadmodum ludis Olympicis non formosissimi et valentissimi quique sed qui certant coronantur, quippe quorum aliqui vincant, sic et bonorum huius vitae compotes fiunt, qui recte vivunt" (The prize of life is not to be won by learning, but by conflict and trial: as in the Olympic games, it was not the wrestler of finest form and manner who received the crown, but he who fought and left the arena the conqueror).

After Morata's father died in 1548, "conflict and trial" were to be her lot. Around this time some of her friends left Ferrara: Anna d'Este married François of Lorraine, the later duc de Guise and one of the firmest opponents of the Reformation, and went to France; Kilian Sinapius had left in 1545 to take up an appointment as jurisconsult in Speyer, and his brother, Johannes, left in 1548 to become physician to Melchior Zobel, prince-bishop of Würzburg. Bereft of the close support of her friends, Morata soon fell victim to court intrigues. A letter from Johannes Sinapius to John Calvin (5 December 1553) explains that the machinations of the duchess's almoner, Hieronymus Bolsec, were responsible for Morata's fall from favor. Duke Ercole, who had long been urged to give proofs of his fidelity to Rome, believed whatever Bolsec told him, and Morata was the first victim of Bolsec's machinations. As she wrote to Curione on 7 October 1550:

Me vero post mortem illius (ut sapientius a Graecis συμφοράν, quam a Latinis calamitatem, appellari iudices) statim mea desertam indignisque acceptam modis fuisse. Neque mihi hoc separatim a meis sororibus accidit sed hos fructus omnes a nostris Principibus retulimus, nimirum pro labore tulimus odium. Quanto vero fuerim dolore affecta, tu existimare potes. Nullus erat qui nos respiceret et tot nos res eodem tempore circumvallabant, unde emergi nunquam posse videbatur.

(After the death of my father [which you may consider the Greeks are wiser to call συμφοράν (catastrophe) while the Romans speak of a calamity], I remained alone, betrayed, abandoned by those who ought to have befriended me, and exposed to the most unjust treatment. My sisters shared my lot, and we all received nothing for our pains but ingratitude from our patrons. You can guess how much this affected me. None of those whom we were formerly accustomed to call our friends could venture to show any interest in us; and we were plunged into an abyss so profound that it seemed impossible for us ever to be rescued from it.)

Fortunately for Morata, rescue was at hand. Andreas Grundler (also spelled *Grunthler* and *Gründler*), the son of a Schweinfurt city councillor and a friend and possibly a relative of the Sinapius brothers, had studied at the Universities of Leipzig, Heidelberg, and Paris and had taken his doctorate in medicine at Ferrara on 9 May 1549. The couple were well matched, for Grundler, too, was skilled in Greek and Latin. They were married in late 1549 or early 1550 according to the practices of the Reformed Church, and Morata marked the occasion by composing an elegant Greek nuptial hymn that has been preserved in the 1580 edition of her works. Morata's remarkable learning and her marriage to Grundler are mentioned in a letter from Jakob Baldenberger, then a medical student, to Joachim Vadianus, written from Basel on 20 November 1550:

Finally (and it has got to be said even if it sounds ridiculous), I am much moved by the erudition of Olympia Morata, a most learned lady, and am spurred on to the study of literature myself; for it piques me to be surpassed by a woman, and a young one at that. However, this lady comes from a greatly distinguished family; she lived at the ducal court of Ferrara, has from an early age been well schooled in the liberal arts and in religious studies, and when the courtiers would not allow her to devote herself to these, the young lady married a German doctor, Andreas Grundler, in order to devote herself more easily to the study of theology; I cannot admire her learning enough. And since there is nothing in this letter worthy to be read by a most learned man [such as you], I add below some Greek verses composed by this time woman.... From these verses you will see how devoutly she practices our religion, with how much piety she has been endowed, finally, with how much learning she is imbued.

In 1550 the Grundlers moved to Andreas's native Schweinfurt, where he had been appointed municipal physician. On the way they visited the Kaufbeuren patrician Georg Hörmann. A patron of the arts and a man who enjoyed contacts with such humanists as Johannes Oecolampadius, Philipp Melanchton, and Viglius Zuichemus, Hörmann allowed Morata to use his library and expressed the wish that she remain longer. In Schweinfurt the couple remained in close touch with Johannes Sinapius and his wife, who were living nearby in Würzburg. In a letter to Curione, Morata expresses her relief that God has removed her from Ferrara: "Ego enim si diutius in aula haesissem, actum de me et de mea salute fuisset. Nunquam enim, dum ibi fui, quicquam altum aut divinum sapere potui neque libros utriusque testamenti legere.... Deus cupiditatem meam incendit habitandi in illa coelesti domo, in qua iucundius est dieculum vnam commorari, quam annis mille in istis principium aulis" (As for myself, if I had stayed any longer at the court, it would have been the end of me and of my well-being. For in all the time I was there, I was never able to learn anything sublime or sacred or to read any books of either the Old or the New Testament.... God has kindled in me a desire to dwell in that heavenly mansion, where it is more pleasant to live for one short day than for a thousand years in those foul princely courts).

In Schweinfurt the Grundlers and Morata's young brother Emilio lived in Grundler's parents' home (the house, at Brückenstraße 12, was damaged during World War II and demolished in the 1950s). Small as it was, Schweinfurt nevertheless provided some intellectual stimulation. Among the congenial spirits the Grundlers found there was Johannes Cremer, rector of the Latin school, whom Morata had met in Ferrara; others with humanist interests included the Rosarius brothers—one of whom was an astronomer, the other a cantor—and Andreas Campanus (Glock), who later took charge of the Latin school at Mosbach. It is presumably with these people—"the good men who are here"—that she proposed to read the *Pasqillus ecstaticus* (Ecstatic Satire) of Curione. Morata also occupied herself with teaching Greek and Latin to her brother and to Johannes Sinapius's daughter Theodora, and with translating Psalms 1, 2, 23, 34, 46, 70, and 125 into Greek hexameters. Above all, Morata spent her time studying the Bible and the writings of the German Reformers. "La parola del Signore sia la lucerna a piedi vostri" (Let the Word

Title page for the first edition of Morata's posthumously published collected writings (courtesy of the Lilly Library, Indiana University)

of the Lord be a lamp for your feet), she wrote to Cherubina Orsini on 8 August 1554. Homesick for Italy, she followed events there with interest, and she was so horrified by the progress of the Counter-Reformation that on 26 May 1553 she wrote to urge Matthias Flacius Illyricus, a pupil of Luther's, to translate Luther's works into Italian so that they might become known to her compatriots. She would later propose to Pietro Paolo Vergerio, one of the Italian Reformers who had fled from Italy in 1549, that he translate Luther's *Großer Katechismus* (Large Catechism, 1529) into Italian.

In 1552 Andreas Grundler had turned down a professorship in Linz, offered to him in the name of

Ferdinand, king of the Romans by Hörmann—Morata feared, as she said in a letter of 1 October 1551, that "ubi potestatem habet tantam Antichristus" (the Antichrist might be raging there) and that their free exercise of religion might be impeded. By the spring of 1553, however, they must have regretted their decision to stay in Franconia. Schweinfurt was occupied by the forces of Albrecht Alcibiades, margrave of Brandenburg-Kulmbach; it was then besieged and finally destroyed by Albrecht's enemies, the allied cities of Bamberg, Würzburg, and Nuremberg, in the so-called *Margräflerkrieg* (War of the Margraves) of 1553–1554. The horrors of this experience are vividly described by Morata in a letter to Curione (25 July 1555) that reveals her humanity, her piety, and her acceptance of the rigors of life as God's will. The Grundlers fled the town, but even then Andreas only narrowly escaped execution. They eventually found refuge in the Odenwald with Counts Georg and Eberhard von Erbach, supporters of the Reformation.

Grundler was offered a chair of medicine at Heidelberg University—probably through the influence of Jacob Micyllus, who was teaching Greek there and who was a friend of Johannes Sinapius and also of Georg von Erbach and his wife, Elisabeth, a sister of Frederick II, elector palatine. When they reached Heidelberg they were practically destitute, having lost everything—including her writings—in the disaster of Schweinfurt; it must have been some small consolation when Johannes Sinapius sent Morata her own copy of Plutarch's *Lives,* with her name written in it, which he had salvaged from the town. There is evidence that Morata taught Greek in Heidelberg, no doubt privately; had she lived longer, she might have become the first woman university teacher in Germany, and Heidelberg would have played a pioneering role in the history of the emancipation of women. But she died of tuberculosis on 26 October 1555; her husband and brother both died on 22 December, apparently of the plague. The three were buried in the churchyard of Saint Peter's in Heidelberg. Their tomb, erected by Wilhelm Rascalon, a physician and apothecary, bears an inscription that testifies to the great esteem in which Morata was held:

> Et virtuti ac memoriæ Olympiae Moratae, Fulvii Morati Ferrariensis Philosophi filia, Andreæ Grundleri Medici conjugis, lectissimae foeminae cujus ingenium ac singularis utriusque linguae cognitio, in moribus autem probitas summumque pietatis studium, supra communem modum semper existimata sunt. Quod de eius vita hominum judicium, beata mors, sanctissime ac pacatissime ab ea obita divino quoque confirmavit testimonio. Obiit mutato solo A. salut. D.LV. super milles. s. Aetat. XXIX. hic cum marito & Aemilio fratre sepulta.

(To the virtue and memory of Olympia Morata, daughter of Fulvio Morato, the philosopher, the wife of the physician Andreas Grundler, a woman in a class by herself, whose intelligence and singular knowledge of both of the ancient languages, allied to the probity of her conduct and intense study of religion, have always been esteemed beyond the common measure. How her life has been judged by men, her happy death, which she underwent in the most holy and peaceful fashion, has also confirmed with divine testimony. She died in the Year of Our Salvation 1555, aged 29 years, and is buried here with her husband and her brother Emilio.)

Kilian Sinapius also supplied an epitaph and an elegy on Morata.

Morata's surviving writings, collected and edited by Curione, are not extensive, but one can recognize in them her devotion to Cicero, her command of Greek poetic language and metrical models, her espousal of humanist ideals, and, above all, her pious zeal. She employed the dialogue, popular since Plato but particularly favored by the humanists, as a form in which she could give literary expression to the intensity of her religious feeling. The characters in her dialogue between Theophila (One Who Loves God) and Philotima represent, respectively, Morata and her friend Lavinia Orsini. In the dialogue she strives to understand suffering as something God imposed on her to test her. For the modern reader, however, it is her letters that hold the chief interest: while they are, in humanist style, richly adorned with learned quotation and classical allusion, they afford a vivid picture of the life and thoughts of this remarkable woman.

Curione's editions of Morata's letters and other writings enjoyed considerable popularity in the sixteenth century (the 1562 edition was dedicated to another learned woman, Queen Elizabeth I of England). Thereafter, it was not until the eighteenth century that they again attracted attention. Georg Ludwig Nolten presented a Latin dissertation on Morata's life and writings at the University of Frankfurt an der Oder in 1731; later, Johann Wolfgang von Goethe discovered and read her letters while he was working on the background for his play *Torquato Tasso* (1790), which is set in Ferrara. Goethe was particularly impressed by the seriousness of purpose and the strength of character they revealed. In the nineteenth century Morata became the subject of devotional biographical literature, which depicted her as a kind of Protestant saint. In 1965 Florence Whitfield Barton published a biographical novel about her. There is a need for an

English edition of her works and a full commentary on them. The best recent edition of her correspondence is that by Rainer Kössling (1990), which, however, provides only a German translation and commentary, without the original text.

Letters:

Oposcoli e lettere di riformatori italiani del cinquecento, volume 2, edited by Giuseppe Paladino (Bari: Laterza, 1927), pp. 171–227, 265–279;

Olimpia Fulvia Morata: Epistolario (1540–1555) con uno studio introduttivo, edited by Lanfranco Caretti, R. Deputazione di storia patria per l'Emilia e la Romagna. Sezione di Ferrara (Ferrara: Tipografia sociale, 1940);

Olympia Fulvia Morata: Briefe, edited by Rainer Kössling (Leipzig: Reclam, 1990).

Biographies:

Amanda Gillespie Smythe, *Olympia Morata: Her Times, Life and Writings,* third edition (London: Smith, Elder, 1836);

R. Turnbull, *Olympia Morata: Her Life and Times* (Boston: Sabbath School Society, 1846);

Jules Bonnet, *Vie d'Olympia Morata: Episode de la renaissance et de la réforme en Italie* (Paris: Ducloux, 1850); translated as *The Life of Olympia Morata: An Episode of the Revival of Letters and of the Reformation in Italy: A New Translation* (Edinburgh: Johnstone & Hunter, 1854);

Uwe Müller, "Olympia Fulvia Morata," in *Lebensbilder Schweinfurter Frauen,* edited by Barbara Vogel-Fuchs (Schweinfurt: Stadtarchiv Schweinfurt, 1991), pp. 158–168.

References:

Roland H. Bainton, *Women of the Reformation in Germany and Italy* (Minneapolis: Augsburg, 1971);

Florence Whitfield Barton, *Olympia: A Novel of the Reformation* (Philadelphia: Fortress, 1965);

John L. Flood and David J. Shaw, *Johannes Sinapius (1505–1560): Hellenist and Physician in Germany and Italy* (Geneva: Droz, forthcoming 1997);

Lilius Gregerius Gyraldus, *De peotis nostrorum temperum,* edited by Karl Wotke, Lateinische Litteraturdenkmäler des XV. und XVI. Jahrhunderts, no. 10 (Berlin: Weidmann, 1894), p. 94;

Maria Heinsius, *Das unüberwindliche Wort: Frauen der Reformationszeit* (Munich: Kaiser, 1951), pp. 96–133;

Ursula Hess, "Olympia Morata (1526–1555): Die poeta docta als Verwirklichung eines humanistischen Ideals," in *Deutsche Literatur von Frauen,* volume 1, edited by Gisela Brinker-Gabler (Munich: Beck, 1988), pp. 138–148;

Niklas Holzberg, "Olympia Morata," in *Fränkische Lebensbilder,* volume 10, edited by Alfred Wendehorst and Gerhard Pfeiffer (Neustadt an der Aisch: Degener, 1982), pp. 141–156;

Holzberg, "Olympia Morata und die Anfänge des Griechischen an der Universität Heidelberg," *Heidelberger Jahrbücher,* 31 (1987): 77–93;

Markus Kutter, *Celio Secundo Curione: Sein Leben und sein Werk (1503–1569)* (Basel & Stuttgart: Helbing & Lichtenhahn, 1955);

Georgius Ludovicus Noltenius, *Dissertatio historica de Olympiae Moratae vita, scriptis, fatis et virtutibus* (Frankfurt an der Oder, 1731);

Silvio Pellini, *Una novella del Decamerone: Saggio di un testo e comento nuovo col raffronto delle migliori edizioni* (Turin: Paravia, 1887), pp. 467–482;

R. de Rosa, "Olympia Morata," in *Ruperto-Carola: Mitteilungen der Vereinigung der Freunde der Studentenschaft der Universität Heidelberg e.V.,* 8. Jahrgang, 19 (1956): 47–53;

Dorothea Vorländer, "Olympia Fulvia Morata, eine evangelische Humanistin in Schweinfurt," *Zeitschrift für bayerische Kirchengeschichte,* 39 (1970): 95–113;

Vorländer, "Olympia Fulvia Morata, eine italienische Humanistin und evangelische Christin in Schweinfurt," in *Streiflichter auf die Kirchengemeinde in Schweinfurt: Schriften zum 450jährigen Jubiläum der Reformation in Schweinfurt,* edited by Johannes Strauss and Kathi Petersen (Schweinfurt: Weppert, 1992), pp. 65–76;

Gertrud Weiss-Stählin, "Die Briefe der Olympia Fulvia Morata: Goethes letzte Auseinandersetzung mit der Reformation," in *Goethe: Neue Folge des Jahrbuchs der Goethe-Gesellschaft,* 25 (1963): 220–249;

Weiss-Stählin, "Dr. Andreas Grundler (ca. 1506–1555)," *Mainfränkisches Jahrbuch für Geschichte und Kunst,* 34 (1982): 1–32;

Weiss-Stählin, "Olympia Fulvia Morata und Schweinfurt: Wechselbeziehungen zwischen italienischer und deutscher Frömmigkeit im Zeitalter der Reformation," *Zeitschrift für bayerische Kirchengeschichte,* 30 (1961): 175–183;

Weiss-Stählin, "Per una biografia di Olympia Morata," in *Miscellanea di studi in memoria di Cesare Bolognesi,* edited by Lucio Puttin (Schio: Menin, 1976), pp. 79–99.

Papers:

The handsomely written manuscript for Olympia Fulvia Morata's translation of Psalm 46 survives among Joachim Camerarius's papers in the Bayerische Staatsbibliothek, Munich, Clm 10363, fol. 103^{r-v}.

Thomas Murner
(24 December 1475 – before 23 August 1537)

Linda L. Gaus
University of California, Berkeley

Invectiva contra astrologos, Serenissimo Romanor Regi Maximiliano piissimo predicentes fris Thome Murner Liberalium artium magistri felice exorditur sidere (Strasbourg: Matthias Hupfuff, 1499);

Tractatus perutilis de phitonico contractu fratris Thome murner liberalium artium magistri ordinis minorum, Ad instantiam Generosi domini Johannis Woernher de Moersperg compilatus (Strasbourg: Matthias Hupfuff, 1499);

Germania nova (Strasbourg: Matthias Hupfuff, 1502);

Oratio eiusdem ad capitulum provincie superioris Alemanie in Ecclesia maiori civitatis Solodorensis perorata (Strasbourg, 1502);

Honestorum poematum condigna laudatio Impudicorum vero miranda Castigatio (N.p., 1503);

Chartiludium logicae seu Logica poetica vel memorativa, cum iocundo pictasmatis excitamento pro communi omnium studentum utilitate (Kraków, 1507);

Scacus infallibilis quantitatis syllabarum hoc tam utili, quam iucundo pictasmate memoratus (Basel, 1508);

De sillabarum quantitatibus et arte carminandi facilima praxis (Frankfurt am Main, 1508);

De augustiniana hieronymianaque reformatione poetarum (Strasbourg: Johann Schott, 1509);

Logica memorativa. Chartiludium logice, sive totius dialectice memoria: & nonus Petri hyspani textus emendatus: Cum iucundo pictasmatis exercitio, etc. (Strasbourg: Johann Grüninger, 1509);

De quattuor heresiarchis ordinis praedicatorum de Observantia nuncupatorum (Basel: Pamphilus Gengenbach, 1509);

Historia mirabilis quattuor heresiarcharum ordinis Praedicatorum de Observantia apud Bernenses combustorum Anno MDIX (N.p., 1509);

Die war History von den vier ketzeren prediger ordens zuo Bern in der Eydgnosschafft verbrant (Strasbourg: Johann Prüss the Younger, 1509);

Von den vier ketzeren Prediger ordens der observantz zu Bern im Schwytzer land verbrannt (Strasbourg: Johann Prüss the Younger, 1509);

Ludus studentum Friburgensium (N.p., 1511);

Arma patientiae contra omnes saeculi vanitates (Frankfurt am Main: Beat Murner, 1511);

Der schelmen zunfft. Anzeigüng alles Weltleuffigen mütwils, Schalckheiten und bieberyen diser zeyt. Durch den hochgelerten herren doctor Thomas mürner von Straßburg schimpfflichen erdichtet und zuo Franckfurt an dem meyn mit ernstlichem fürnemen geprediget (Frankfurt am Main: Beat Murner, 1512);

Doctor murners narren bschwerung (Strasbourg: Matthias Hupfuff, 1512);

Ein andechtig geistliche Badenfart des hochgelerten Herren Thomas mürner der heiligen geschrifft doctor barfuoser orden zuo Straß burg in dem bad erdicht gelert und ungelerten nutzlich zuo bredigen und zuo lesen

(Strasbourg: Johann Grüninger, 1514);

Die Mülle von Schwyndelszheym und Gredt Müllerin Jarzit (Strasbourg: Matthias Hupfuff, 1515);

Allen und yeglichen geistlichen oder weltlichen wes stadts würden oder wesen (Strasbourg, 1515);

Chartiludium institutae summarie doctore Thoma Murner memorante et ludente. Justinianus Cesar in prohemio digestorum (Strasbourg: Johann Knobloch, 1518);

Utriusque iuris tituli et regule a doctore Thoma Murner Argentinensi or. Minorum in Alemanicum traducti eloquium ad utilitatem eorum qui in inclyta Basiliensi universitate Jura suis studiis profitebantur (Basel: Adam Petri von Langendorff, 1518);

Die geuchmat zuo straff alle[n] wybsche[n] mannen durch den hochgelerten herren Thoman Murner der heyligen geschrifft doctor beyder rechten Licentiaten und der hohen schuol Basel des Keyserlichen rechtens ordenlichen lerer erdichtet unnd eyner frummen gemeyn der löblichem statt Basel in freyden zuo eyner letz beschriben und verlassen (Basel: Adam Petri von Langendorff, 1519);

Der keiserlichen stat vechten ein ingang und wares fundament. Meister und Rädten tütscher nation (Basel, 1519);

Eine christliche und briederliche ermanung zuo dem hochgelerten doctor Martino luter Augustiner orde[n] zu Wittemburg (Daz er etlichen reden von dem newen testament der heilligen messen gethon) abstande und wider mit gemeiner christenheit sich vereinige (Strasbourg: Johann Grüninger, 1520);

Von Dr. Martinus luters leren und predigen. Das sie argwenig seint, und nit gantzlich glaubwirdig zu halten (Strasbourg: Johann Grüninger, 1520);

Von dem babstenthum das ist von der höchsten oberkeyt Christlichs glauben wyder doctor Martinum Luther (Strasbourg: Johann Grüninger, 1520);

An den Groszmechtigsten und Durchlüchtigsten adel tütscher nation das sye den christlichen glauben beschirmen wyder den zerstörer des glaubens christi Martinum luther einen verfierer der einfeltigen christen (Strasbourg: Johann Grüninger, 1520);

Wie Dr. M. Luter usz falschen ursachen bewegt Daz geistlich recht verbrennet hat (Strasbourg: Johann Grüninger, 1521);

Defension und Protestation D. Thome Murner das er wider Doc. Mar. Luther nichtsz unrechts gehandlet hab (Strasbourg: Johann Grüninger, 1521);

Ain new Lied von dem undergang des Christlichen glaubens Doct. Murner. inn Bruoder Veiten thon (Strasbourg, 1522);

Antwurt und klag mit entschuldigung doctor Murners wider bruoder Michel stifel weyt von eß lingen daheim uff das stüfelbuch, so er wider meyn lied gemachet hat daruß er des lieds den rechten thon erlernen mag (Strasbourg: Johann Grüninger, 1522);

Ob der künig uss engelland ein lügner sey oder der Luther (Strasbourg: Johann Grüninger, 1522);

Von dem großen Lutherischen Narren wie in doctor Murner beschworen hat (Strasbourg: Johann Grüninger, 1522); excerpts translated by Erika Rummel as "The Great Lutheran Fool," in *Scheming Papists and Lutheran Fools: Five Reformation Satires* (New York: Fordham University Press, 1993);

Purgatio vulgaris (N.p., 1524);

Mendatia Lutheri in Serenissimum Anglorum et Frantiae Regem Henricum Octavum Fidei Defensorum. Literis et Armis Triumphatorem Magnificum (N.p., 1524);

Instituta Helvetiorum (N.p., 1525);

Murneri responsio libello cuidam insigniter et egregie stulto Ulrici Zvuyngel apostate heresiarche, ostendens Lutheranam doctrinam infamiam irrogare et verbum dei humanam iudicem pati posse (Lucerne, 1526); translated by Murner as *Doctor Murners Antwurt uff die Anklag eines Eersamen Wysen Radtes der Statt Zürich gemeinen Eidgnossen über ihn gethan* (Lucerne, 1526);

Ein brieff den Strengen eren not festen Fursuhtigen Ersamen wysen der xij örter einer löblichen eydtgnoschafft gesandten botten. Thome Murner der heiligen geschrifften und beider rechten Doctor barfuosser orden, uff dem tag zuo Einsidlen ... wider die lesterlich flucht, und das verzwifflet abschreiben Ulrich Zwinglins, worum er uff der disputation zuo Baden von den xij örteren ersetzet nit wil erschinen, so er doch frey geleit hat dar und dannen zuo reiten (Lucerne, 1526);

Ein worhafftigs verantworten der hochgelorten doctores und herren, die zuo Baden uff der disputation gewesen sint vor den xij. orten einer loblichen eidtgnoschafft wider das schentlich, erstuncken, und erlogen anklagen Ulrich Zwinglyns, das der fierzig mal erloß diebsch böszwicht uff die frummen herren geredt hat und in den druck het lassen kummen. Von doctor Thoma. Murner gemacht, ob der Zwingly lüstig wurde das er im das überig ouch hin uß geben noch dem rechten winckel meß. Mit ufflösung der Argument die Ulrich Zwingly noch der disputation hinder dem offen für har gebollen hat mit guot schenckel von Bern (Lucerne, 1526);

Der Lutherischen Evangelischen Kirchen dieb- und Ketzer Kalender. Getruckt und bsehen durch mich Thomas Murner Barfüßer Ordens Doctor der Heil. Gschrifft und beyder Rechten, Pfarrer in der christlichen Stat Lucern (Lucerne, 1527);

An die Fürsuchtigen ersamen vuysenn und frommen standhafftigen christen des alten woren und ungezwiffleten glaubens der gemeinen christenheit alle underthon und verwanten der löblichen herschafft von Lutzern ein entschuldigung Doctor Murners (Lucerne, 1527);

Die disputacion vor den xij orten einer loblichen eidtgnoschafft namlich Bern Lutzern Vry Schvuytz Vndervualden ob vnnd nidt dem kernwalt Zug mitt dem sampt vsseren ampt Glaris Basel Friburg Solathorn Schaffhusen vnd Appenzell, von wegen der einigkeit in christlichem glauben in iren landen vnd vndterthonen der fier bistumb Costentz, Basel, Losanen vnd Chur beschehen (Lucerne: Thomas Murner, 1527);

Ursach und verantwurtung worumm doctor Thomas Murner kilchherr zuo Lutzern nit ist uff der disputation zuo Baden gehalten erschinen (Lucerne, 1527);

Appellation und beruoff der hochgelörten doctores Johannis Ecken Johannis Fabri und Thome Murner für die xij. ort einer loblichen Eydtgnoschafft wider die vermeinte disputation zuo Bern gehalten beschehen vor den kleinen rädten und hunderten einer loblichen stadt Lutzern und durch doctor Thomas Murner exequiert (Lucerne, 1527);

Caussa Helvetica orthodoxae fidei. Disputatio Heluetiorum in Baden Superiori, coram duodecim cantonum oratoribus & nuntijs, pro sanctae fidei catholicae ueritate, & diuinarum literarum defensione, habita contra Martini Lutheri, Vlrichi Zwinglij, & Oecolampadij peruersa & famosa dogmata (Lucerne, 1528);

Hie würt angezeigt das unchristlich frevel, ungelört und unrechtlich ußrieffen und fürnemmen einer loblichen herschafft von Bern ein disputation zuo halten in irer gnaden statt, wider die gemein Christenheit, wider das heylig gots wort, wider das Evangelion Christi Jhesu, wider die heyligen geschrifften des alten und nuwen testaments, wider den alten woren und ungezwifleten Christlichen glauben, und wider alle menschliche fromkeit und erberkeit (Lucerne, 1528);

Des alten christlichen beeren Testament (Lucerne, 1528);

Von des jungen Beren zenvue im mundt (Lucerne, 1528);

Die gots heylige meß von gott allein erstifft ein städt und lebendigs opffer für die lebendigen und die dodten die höchste frucht der Christenheit wider die fünffte schlußred zuo Bern disputiert in der Eidtgnoschafft den frommen alten Christlichen Bernern zuo trost und behilff gemacht und zuo Lutzern offentlich durch doctor Thomas Murner geprediget und mit dem woren gots wort befestiget (Lucerne: Thomas Murner, 1528);

Ein sendbrieff der acht Christlichen ort einer loblichen Eidtgnoschafft mit namen Lutzern, Ury, Schwytz, Underwalden, Zug, Friburg, Solathorn, Glariß, an ein lobliche herschafft von Bern flehelich, und uff das höchst bittend und ermanendt, by dem alten waren Christlichen glauben zuo beliben, und sich der evangelischen und Lutherischen ketzerien nit belanden noch enteren sollen. Ein spötliche und unfrüntliche antwort der loblichen herschafft von Bern den obgenannten acht Christlichen örtern gethon: und durch den druck uß gespreitet (Lucerne, 1529);

Ein ußlegung und ercleren des selbigen spötlichen, unchristlichen und ungesaltzenen brieffs der herschafft von Bern durch doctor Thomas Murner uß gelegt und zuo verston geben (Lucerne, 1529).

Editions and collections: *Zwei Kalender vom Jahre 1527. D. Joannes Copp evangelischer Kalender und D. Thomas Murner Kirchendieb- und Ketzerkalender,* edited by Ernst Götzinger (Schaffhausen, 1865);

Thomas Murners Deutsche Schriften mit den Holzschnitten der Erstdrucke, 9 volumes, edited by Gustav Bebermeyer, Eduard Fuchs, Paul Merker, and others (Berlin: De Gruyter, 1918–1931);

"Des alten christlichen Bären Testament: Eine Kampfschrift Thomas Murners," edited by Max Scherrer, *Anzeiger der schweizerische Geschichte,* 50 (1919): 6–38;

"Des jungen Bären Zahnweh," edited by Joseph Lefftz, *Archiv für Elsässische Kirchengeschichte,* 1 (1926): 141–167;

"Germania nova," edited by Emil von Borries, in his *Wimpfeling und Murner im Kampf um die ältere Geschichte des Elsasses: Ein Beitrag zur Charakteristik des deutschen Frühhumanismus* (Heidelberg: Winter, 1926), pp. 198–272;

Die gottesheilige Messe von Gott allein erstiftet, edited by Wolfgang Pfeiffer-Belli, Flugschriften aus der Reformationszeit XIX, Neudrucke deutscher Literaturwerke des XVI und XVII Jahrhunderts, no. 257 (Halle: Niemeyer, 1928);

Thomas Murner als Astrolog, edited by Moriz Sondheim, Schriften der Elsass-Lothringischen Wissenschaftlichen Gesellschaft zu Strasbourg. Reihe A. Alsatica and Lotharingica XX (Strasbourg: Elsass-Lothringische Wissenschaftliche Gesellschaft, 1938)—facsimile and translation of Murner's *Tractatus perutilis de phitonico contractu*;

Thomas Murner im Schweizer Glaubenskampf: "Ein brieff den Strengen eren not festen Fursuhtigen Ersamen wysen der XII örter einer löblichen eydtgnoschafft" (1526). "Hie würt angezeigt das vnchristlich freuel, vngelört vnd vnrechtlich vßrieffen vnd fürnemen einer loblichen herschafft von Bern" (1528), edited by Wolfgang Pfeiffer-Belli, Corpus Catholicorum: Werke Katholischer Schriftsteller im Zeitalter der Glaubensspaltung, volume 22 (Münster: Aschendorff, 1939).

OTHER: *Ritus et celebratio phase iudaeorum cum orationibus eorum et benedictionibus mense ad litteram interpretatis cum omni observatione uti soliti sunt suum* *pasca extra terram promissionis sine esu agni pascalis celebrare per egregium doctorem,* translated by Murner (Frankfurt am Main: Beat Murner, 1512);

Benedicite iudaeorum uti soliti sunt ante et post cibi sumptionem benedicere et gratias agere deo Egregio, translated by Murner (Frankfurt am Main: Beat Murner, 1512);

Der iuden Benedicite wie sy gott den herren loben, und im umb die speyß dancken. Durch den hochgelerten herren doctor Thomas murner barfüsser orden von hebrayscher sprach in deutsch verdalmetschett, und wie sy iren dodten begraben, translated by Murner (Frankfurt am Main: Beat Murner, 1512);

Virgil, *Vergilij maronis dreyzehen Aeneadischen Bücher von Trojanischer Zerstörung und uffgang des Römischen Reichs,* translated by Murner (Strasbourg: Johann Grüninger, 1515);

Instituten ein warer ursprung unnd fundament des Keyserlichen rechtens, von dem hochgelerten herren Thoman Murner der heiligen geschrifft Doctor, beyder rechten Licentiaten, verdütschet Und uff der hohen schuol Basel in syner ordenlichen lectur offenlich mit dem latin verglichet, translated by Murner (Basel: Adam Petri von Langendorff, 1519);

Ulrich von Hutten, *Ulrichen von Hutten eins teutschen Ritters von der wunderbarlichen artzney des holtz Guaiacum genant, und wie man die Frantzosen oder blatteren heilen sol, zuo herrn Albrechten dem Churfürsten, Cardinalen, und Ertzbischoff von Mentz ein buoch beschriben,* translated by Murner (Strasbourg: Johann Grüninger, 1519);

Martin Luther, *Von der Babylonischen gefengknuß der kirchen,* translated by Murner (Strasbourg, 1520);

King Henry VIII of England, *Bekennung der süben Sacramenten wider Martinum Lutherum gemacht von dem unüberwintlichen künig zuo Engelland und in Frankreich einem Herren zu Hibernien, Henrico des namens dem achtesten,* translated by Murner (Strasbourg, 1522);

Marcus Antonius Sabellicus, *Hystory von anbeschaffener Welt,* 3 volumes, translated by Murner (Karlsruhe: Badenia, 1987).

The life and works of Thomas Murner, Franciscan, humanist, educator, author of vernacular satire, and vociferous opponent of the Protestant Reformation, reflect the tumultuous changes that were taking place all around him. Murner was in many ways a man stranded between two eras. A representative of a thoroughly medieval institution, he was nonetheless an innovative educator and a humanist who took full advantage of a new technology—the printing press—to make his opinions

Title page for Murner's first German verse satire

known. An author of learned Latin texts on esoteric subjects, he was also a preacher and author of popular literature who insisted on speaking to the common people in the language they knew best: German. Murner's works present a veritable panorama of early modern life; as the eighteenth-century German author and critic Gotthold Ephraim Lessing said of the Strasbourg Franciscan, anyone who wishes to understand early modern German culture and language should become acquainted with Murner's oeuvre.

Murner was born on 24 December 1475 in Obernai, Alsace, to Matthäus Murner, a lawyer, and Ursula Murner, née Studeler. Shortly after his birth he contracted a spinal illness that would leave him with a lifelong limp. He had six siblings: Johannes, Beat, Sixt, Gertrud, Richard, and Barbara. Johannes would follow in their father's footsteps by becoming a prominent Strasbourg lawyer and serving on the city council; Beat would become a printer in Frankfurt am Main and would publish some of Thomas's works. In 1481 the Murners moved to Strasbourg, where Matthäus and his brother Jakob were granted citizenship in 1482 and Matthäus entered into the service of the city council. Thomas attended the Franciscans' cloister school in Strasbourg; he was

Title page for Murner's second satire, written in response to Sebastian Brant's Das Narrenschiff

admitted into the Franciscan monastery as a novice in 1490 and ordained as a priest in 1494.

Murner began his university studies, which took him on a tour of Europe, after his ordination to the priesthood. In a span of seven years he attended the Universities of Freiburg, Cologne, Paris, Rostock, Kraków, Prague, and Vienna, coming into contact with some of the most influential humanist educators of his day. He earned his *Baccalaureus artium* in Paris in 1498, his *Magister artium* in Freiburg in 1499, and his *Baccalaureus theologiae* in Kraków in 1500. He would earn a doctorate in theology at the University of Freiburg in 1506 and a doctorate in law at the University of Basel in 1519. Such an education was considered a great extravagance; Matthäus Murner financed the lion's share of his son's studies and is said to have boasted that they cost him six hundred florins, a small fortune. The peripatetic nature of Murner's university years was highly unusual for the late fifteenth century and reflects the restlessness that characterized his entire life.

Murner's first two published works appeared during the latter years of his university education. In *Invectiva contra astrologos* (Invective against Astrologers, 1499) Murner derides the astrologers who had predicted Emperor Maximilian I's victory over the Swiss Confederation and ridicules the notion that the stars influence human affairs. *Tractatus perutilis de phitonico contractu* (A Very Useful Treatise about Consorting with Witches, 1499) was inspired by the antiwitchcraft polemics of Ulrich Molitor of Constance. Murner seeks to prove that belief in witches is justified, and he recommends the means by which one can combat the forces of evil and black magic. The topic of witchcraft, although popular at the time *Tractatus perutilis de phitonico contractu* appeared, may have been particularly dear to his heart since he apparently believed that his physical disability was the result of a curse placed on him by a spiteful neighbor.

In 1501 Murner returned to Strasbourg, where he taught philosophy at the Franciscans' cloister school and began an active preaching career. Within months of his return he became embroiled in the first of the bitter disputes that would become a defining characteristic of his life. In December 1501 his friend and fellow priest Jakob Wimpfeling published *Germania,* a treatise that aspired to establish a tradition of German national history by arguing that the Germans had always ruled the western Rhineland. Murner's *Germania nova* (New Germania, 1502) attempts to correct Wimpfeling's history. Murner attributes both the Christianization of Germany and the founding of many of its important institutions to the French. Wimpfeling took offense at Murner's attack and petitioned the Strasbourg City Council to forbid distribution of *Germania nova*. The request was granted, beginning a long and bitter feud between the two men that would ultimately result in Murner's expulsion from the circle of Strasbourg humanists. Murner's banishment from this rarefied intellectual milieu had no perceptible effect on his position within the Franciscan order, where his climb through the ranks was swift, if not always smooth.

Honestorum poematum condigna laudatio (In Praise of Proper Poetry, 1503) constituted Murner's second polemical contribution to the feud with Wimpfeling. In the pamphlet he defends himself against his enemies and ridicules their reliance on the works of non-German authors to support their pro-German arguments. The biting tone of *Honestorum poematum condigna laudatio* led to another censorship order from the Strasbourg City Council, and this one was approved by the emperor himself. Even so, Maximilian bestowed the honor of poet laureate on him at court in Vienna in 1505.

In 1506 Murner attended the general council of the Franciscan order in Rome. On his return to Strasbourg his order dispatched him to Freiburg to serve as reading master in the Franciscan monastery and to lecture at the university. While in Freiburg, Murner experimented with innovative pedagogical methods; his *Chartiludium logicae* (Chart of Logic, 1507) is an illustrated card game designed to help students memorize the principles of logic. Although Murner's methods were apparently well received by his students, they were ridiculed by other humanists and caused Murner to come under suspicion of witchcraft when his students mastered the difficult material far more quickly than was typical. Two works that appeared in 1508, *Scacus infallibilis quantitatis syllabarum* (An Infallible Scheme for the Quantity of Syllables) and *De sillabarum quantitatibus* (Of Counting Syllables), document Murner's attempts to teach prosody and metrics using the analogy of a chess game and the five fingers of a hand. Both texts are richly illustrated, providing fascinating examples of early modern pedagogy and the state of the art of printing around the turn of the sixteenth century.

Another product of Murner's Freiburg years, *De augustiniana hieronymianaque reformatione poetarum* (About the Reform of Poetry according to Augustine and Jerome, 1509), is a Christian theory of aesthetics derived from the works of Saint Augustine and Saint Jerome. Dedicated to Murner's own beloved teacher Jakob Locher, the treatise discusses the nature of poetry, the role of poetry in education, and the dangers of reading poetry by pagan authors. Although Murner was a popular teacher at the university, his sojourn in Freiburg was cut short when he attacked two people from the pulpit: a recently deceased relative of the city secretary and a local law professor. The university administration complained to Murner's superiors, and the Franciscan order transferred Murner to Bern in 1509. It was but the first time that Murner's tendency to speak his mind would force him to relocate.

In Bern, Murner served as the reading master of the Franciscan monastery. He arrived in the city just in time to witness the fiery execution of four Dominicans for allegedly promulgating lies. The event inspired Murner to write two Latin and two German pamphlets, all of which appeared in 1509. *De quattuor heresiarchis* (Of the Four Heretics) and *Historia mirabilis quattuor heresiarcharum* (An Amazing History of the Four Heretics) relate what happened in Bern and discuss the dispute between the Franciscans and Dominicans about the doctrine of the Immaculate Conception, the issue over which the four Dominicans were burned. *Die war History von den vier ketzeren prediger* (The True Story of the Four Heretical Preachers) is a folksy German prose version of what had occurred in Bern, while *Von den vier ketzeren Prediger* (Of the Four Heretical Preachers) presents the same events in rhymed German couplets—Murner's first foray into vernacular verse. In 1510 Murner was transferred from Bern to Speyer, where he served as guardian of the Franciscan monastery. He then moved to the Franciscan monastery in Frankfurt am Main, where he was installed as preacher and reading master in 1511.

Woodcut from Murner's Die geuchmat. *According to Murner's explanation on the same page, the picture is to be considered a portrait of the author.*

Murner's time in Frankfurt was one of his most prolific periods. In his first two years there he published a series of short works. *Ludus studentum Friburgensium* (A Game for the Freiburg Students, 1511) is another treatise about how to teach prosody and poetics; Murner had begun, and may have completed, it during his stay in Freiburg. *Arma patientiae contra omnes saeculi vanitates* (Arms of Patience against All Secular Vanities, 1511) describes the duties of a preacher and details Murner's objections to the decadence of life in Frankfurt. By publishing this sermon Murner claimed to be doing nothing more than following the example of Johannes Geiler von Kaisersberg; the work, however, which was printed

Caricature of some of Luther's opponents, circa 1520: Murner, Jerome Emser, Pope Leo X, Johann Eck, and Jacob Lemp. Murner's depiction as a cat derives from a pun on his name: "Mur-narr" (Feline Fool).

by his brother Beat, seems to have been calculated to enhance Murner's reputation.

Murner also involved himself in the controversy over Hebrew books. Johannes Pfefferkorn, the leader of the Cologne Dominicans and a convert from Judaism, had called in 1510 for the destruction of all nonbiblical Hebrew books; in 1510 Johannes Reuchlin, an eminent Hebraist and humanist, issued a statement condemning Pfefferkorn's proposal. Reuchlin's statement and his ensuing public feud with Pfefferkorn attracted the attention of many scholars, including Murner and some of his fellow Franciscans. Apparently inspired by his colleagues' desire to inform themselves about the intellectual controversy of the day, Murner published three translations of Jewish prayers: *Ritus et celebratio phase iudaeorum* (The Jews' Rights and Celebrations, 1512), *Benedicite iudaeorum* (The Jews' Prayers, 1512), and *Der iuden Benedicite* (The Jews' Prayers, 1512). Modern scholarly opinion as to Murner's knowledge of Hebrew and, thus, as to the accuracy of the translations varies. Some of his contemporaries cast doubt on his linguistic abilities, but the renowned humanist Willibald Pirckheimer reportedly esteemed Murner's efforts.

The year 1512 marks the beginning of Murner's literary career. *Der schelmen zunfft* (The Fools' Guild), his first German verse satire, was printed in Frankfurt by his brother Beat. With a character resembling the author serving as the recording secretary of the fools' guild, each chapter of this richly illustrated work begins with a proverb or proverbial expression and depicts the misdeeds of a fool or fools. *Der schelmen zunfft* proved extremely popular, as did *Doctor murners narren bschwerung* (Doctor Murner's Exorcism of Fools, 1512), his second German verse satire. According to its introduction, the *Narren bschwerung* aims to pick up where Sebastian Brant's *Das Narrenschiff* (The Ship of Fools, 1494), one of the runaway best-sellers of the early modern period, left off. In *Das Narrenschiff* a narrator resembling Brant serves as marshal for a parade of more than a hundred kinds of fools, chiding them and urging them to mend the error of their ways. The tone of *Das Narrenschiff* is gently pedantic; Brant's narrator seems optimistic that the world can yet be saved from the "dark night" of ignorance. By contrast, in *Narren bschwerung* a Murner-like figure tries in vain to drive the foolish demons from men and women. Murner's narrator despairs of accomplishing the task he has set for himself; he, unlike Brant's narrator, regards foolishness as sin and doubts that human beings will ever change for the better. By using and reinterpreting the familiar *Narrenschiff* woodcuts Murner both critiques what he perceives as Brant's ineffective method and advances his own, more-radical notions about how best to cure the world of its evils. Both *Der schelmen zunfft* and the *Narren bschwerung* must be seen in the context of Murner's preaching activities; the satires convey a reformist message in a medium designed to attract and hold the attention of a general audience. In this sense Murner's literary efforts were consistent with the Franciscan directive to go forth and preach to the people.

In 1513 Murner was named guardian of the Franciscan monastery in Strasbourg; he was removed from the guardianship the following year, after his fellow monks accused him of mismanaging the monastery's affairs. Murner defends himself against these accusations in a pamphlet, *Allen und yeglichen geistlichen oder weltlichen wes stadts würden oder wesen* (To Any- and Everyone, Whether Secular or of the Clergy, Regardless of Estate, 1515). During this stay in Strasbourg, Murner continued his literary activities, producing three more German works. A trip to the baths on his way from Frankfurt to Strasbourg inspired *Ein andechtig geistliche Badenfart* (A Devout Spiritual Journey to the Baths, 1514). God is the master of the baths; he invites Murner to partake of his healing treatments. At the end of this allegorical verse text the patient leaves the baths spiritually and physically rejuvenated.

Although *Die Mülle von Schwyndelszheym und Gredt Müllerin Jarzit* (The Mill of Swindletown and the Memorial Mass for the Miller's Wife, 1515) and *Die geuchmat* (The Fools' Meadow, 1519) appeared four years apart, Murner composed both accounts of the exploits of love-fools in 1514–1515. *Die Mülle von Schwyndelszheym und Gredt Müllerin Jarzit*, written after, and borrowing liberally from, *Die geuchmat*, plays off the name of Schwindratzheim, a town near Strasbourg to which Murner alludes in the introduction, and *Gredt Müllerin*, a local term for a woman of questionable morals. Murner appears in the guise of a miller who assembles an astonishing company of lechers, drunks, and fools on the anniversary of his late wife's death. *Die geuchmat* parodies the medieval ideal of courtly love by painting a picture of a society where men behave like women and women behave like men. *Die geuchmat* is rife with the most extreme examples of love foolishness drawn from the corpus of *Minnesang* (medieval courtly love poetry), the Bible, and classical literature. Through examples Murner strives to stigmatize the behavior of love-fools so that his readers will not be tempted to emulate it. Because of the furor surrounding Murner's departure from Strasbourg in 1514, the Strasbourg censor, Brant–the author of *Das Narrenschiff*–ordered *Die geuchmat* withheld from publication. Murner protested to the city council; eventually Brant approved the return of the manuscript to Murner, who arranged for its publication in Basel in 1519.

Murner spent 1515 in Trier, where he produced the first German translation of Virgil's *Aeneid*, titled *Vergilij maronis dreyzehen Aeneadischen Bücher von Trojanischer Zerstürung und uffgang des Römischen Reichs* (Vergil Maro's Thirteen Books of the Aeneid about the Trojan War and the Fall of the Roman Empire, 1515), and lectured on Justinian's *Institutions* at the university. Four works published in the next few years reflect his pedagogical efforts in Trier and his continuing preoccupation with the law after he moved to Strasbourg in 1516, then to Basel in 1518, with a brief detour to Rome in 1517 on business for the Franciscans. *Chartiludium institutae* (Chart of the Institutions, 1518), like the earlier *Chartiludium logicae*, is a card game designed to help students master the difficult Justinian Code. *Utriusque iuris tituli et regule* (The Titles and Rules of Both Laws, 1518) comprises a bilingual (Latin and German) legal practice guide that includes, among much else, terms and texts used frequently by lawyers practicing before civil and ecclesiastical courts. *Instituten ein warer ursprung unnd fundament des Keyserlichen rechtens* (The Institutes, a True Source and Foundation of Imperial Law, 1519) provides the first German translation of the Justinian Code. This text, like *Utriusque iuris tituli et regule*, was intended for students seeking to familiarize themselves with the code, which was a vital part of the legal curriculum. Finally, *Der keiserlichen stat rechten ein ingang und wares fundament* (An Introduction to and True Foundation of the Laws of the Imperial State, 1519) is a freer translation of the Justinian Code in the form of a textbook on Roman civil law. The year 1519 also brought Murner's promotion to *Doktor beider rechte* (doctor of both laws) in Basel, signifying that he had attained doctorates in theology and law. That same year Murner undertook a journey to Italy at the behest of his order and published a translation of a Latin text by Ulrich von Hutten: *Ulrichen von Hutten eins teutschen Ritters von der wunderbarlichen artzney des holtz Guaiacum genant* (About the Marvelous Remedy Guava Wood, by Ulrich von Hutten, a German Knight). This treatise on the history of syphilis in Europe describes an experimental cure that Hutten himself had undergone. The work was reprinted several times during Murner's lifetime.

In 1520 Murner spent brief periods as the reading master in the Franciscan houses in Strasbourg and Augsburg before taking up residence in Strasbourg once again. That year also marked the beginning of the steady stream of anti-Reformation propaganda that Murner would produce until 1529, when he withdrew from public life. Every pamphlet, sermon, and literary work Murner produced for the rest of his career endeavored to further the cause he so ardently supported.

Although Murner is known as a vociferous, often bitterly sarcastic opponent of the Protestant Reformation, the tone of his first four pamphlets is relatively moderate. *Eine christliche und briederliche ermanung* (A Christian and Brotherly Warning, 1520) is a friendly criticism of Martin Luther's *Eyn Sermon von dem newen Testament* (A Sermon on the New Testament, 1520). While Murner freely admits that there are many aspects of the church that require re-

Title page for Murner's last, and most important, German verse satire; the cat-headed monk represents the author

form, he takes Luther to task for the latter's stand on such important doctrinal questions as the sacramental character of holy mass. *Von Dr. Martinus luters leren und predigen* (Of Dr. Martin Luther's Teaching and Preaching, 1520) challenges Luther's claim to have found the truth but expresses no particular hostility toward him. In *Von dem babstenthum* (On the Papacy, 1520) Murner uses the Bible in an attempt to prove that the papacy was founded by Christ himself and is the highest authority in spiritual matters. Finally, in *An den Groszmechtigsten und Durchlüchtigsten adel tütscher nation* (To the Most Powerful and Illustrious Nobility of the German Nation, 1520) Murner responds to Luther's pamphlet *An den christlichen Adel deutscher Nation* (To the Christian Nobility of the German Nation, 1520). The last is perhaps the most revealing of the four initial pamphlets, since it delineates the doctrinal disagreements between Murner and Luther. One other product of the earliest stage of Murner's anti-Reformation agitation is *Von der Babylonischen gefengknuß der kirchen* (On the Babylonian Captivity of the Church, 1520). Although little more than a loose translation of Luther's *De captivitate babylonica ecclesiae* (1520), it aroused suspicion against Murner in Strasbourg, where he was already known as a troublemaker. In the introduction Murner claims that his motive in translating Luther is to help Catholics know their enemy. This explanation, however, did not satisfy his detractors, who sought to have *Von der Babylonischen gefengknuß* suppressed.

In 1521 the tone of Murner's writings changed dramatically. From this point on Murner regarded Luther not as a kindred spirit trying to bring about much-needed reform in the church but as something akin to the Antichrist. This change in attitude was produced by Luther's first published attack on Murner and his burning of the papal bull *Exsurge Domine*. Murner's *Wie Dr. M. Luter usz falschen ursachen bewegt Daz geistlich recht verbrennet hat* (How Dr. Martin Luther, Motivated by False Reasons, Burned the Godly Law) is an article-by-article refutation of Luther's ninety-five theses. In a second pamphlet of 1521, *Defension und Protestation D. Thome Murner das er wider Doc. Mar. Luther nichtsz unrechts gehandlet hab* (Defense and Protestation of Dr. Thomas Murner That He Did Not Act Wrongly against Dr. Martin Luther), Murner defends himself against accusations that his attack on Luther in *Wie Dr. M. Luter usz falschen ursachen bewegt Daz geistlich recht verbrennet hat* was unprovoked and immoderate.

In 1522 Murner published a satiric song, two pamphlets, a translation, and his final German verse satire. The song, *Ain new Lied von dem undergang des Christlichen glaubens* (A New Song about the Destruction of Christian Faith), warns against the decline and fall of the church. Murner communicates his concern about the unity of Christians; he asserts that the common folk are often excluded from discussions about what the church should be and that his "folk songs" are an attempt to reach out to all Christians willing to listen. Shortly after the publication of *Ain new Lied* Michael Stifel, a former Augustinian who had defected to the Protestant camp, composed his own "folk song," ridiculing Murner's. As he so often did, Murner expressed his outrage in the form of a pamphlet, the polemical *Antwurt und klag mit entschuldigung doctor Murners wider bruoder Michel stifel* (Answer and Lament with Apologies by Dr. Murner against Brother Michael Stifel).

The translation, *Bekennung der süben Sacramenten,* is a German rendering of King Henry VIII of England's *Defense of the Seven Sacraments,* which was a response to Luther's *De captivitate Babylonica ecclesiae*. Henry's work seems to have inspired Murner to publish his own pamphlet, provocatively titled *Ob der künig uss engelland ein lügner sey oder der Luther* (Whether the King of England or Luther Is a Liar).

This ardent defense of Henry's position on the seven sacraments explains in large part the warm reception Murner received when he visited England in 1523 at the king's invitation.

Some critics consider Murner's last German verse satire, *Von dem großen Lutherischen Narren wie in doctor Murner beschworen hat* (The Great Lutheran Fool, How He Was Exorcised by Dr. Murner, 1522; excerpts translated as "The Great Lutheran Fool," 1993), the most important of his anti-Reformation writings. This satire of epic proportions pits the Great Lutheran Fool, an embodiment of the evils set free by Luther and the Reformers, against a Murner-like character who is, in part, the invention of Murner's enemies. In a self-effacing gesture seldom matched by any pro- or anti-Reformation agitator Murner adopts the humorous nickname and representation his enemies assigned to him, the "Mur-narr" (Feline Fool). Throughout *Von dem großen Lutherischen Narren* Murner portrays himself as a cat in a monk's cowl and proceeds to take revenge against those who have attacked him. The climax of the satire is a grotesque scene in which the feline monk marries Luther's daughter, only to discover on their wedding night that she has been disfigured by mange. The explosive potential of *Von dem großen Lutherischen Narren* was not lost on the Strasbourg City Council: almost as soon as the first edition came off the press the council banned it, and many copies of the work were destroyed.

By 1523 Murner had caused so much trouble in Strasbourg that the city council warned him that he would be punished if he published any more inflammatory works. With the victory of the Reform in Strasbourg in 1524 he officially became persona non grata, but, true to form, this status did not stanch the flow of his anti-Protestant propaganda. He produced two pamphlets that year: in *Purgatio vulgaris* (I Defend [Myself] against the Usual Things) he claims that five charges leveled against him by his enemies are all vicious lies, and in *Mendatia Lutheri* (Of Luther's Lies) he again defends Henry VIII's objections to Luther's teachings. Finally, in September 1524, the people of Strasbourg accomplished by force of arms what the city council could not achieve by force of law: a mob raided Murner's cell in the Franciscan monastery, destroying his printing equipment and several works in progress.

When the Franciscan monastery in Strasbourg was dissolved in 1525 Murner returned briefly to Obernai, but he was soon forced to flee Alsace. The outbreak of the Peasants' War, which pitted the common people against the nobility and clergy in many areas of southwest Germany, forced Murner, like many of his fellow clergymen, to seek safe haven. He settled in Lucerne, a city not yet wracked by religious conflict.

Murner's first publication after moving to Lucerne, *Instituta Helvetiorum* (Swiss "Institutions," 1525), is a more elaborate version of the legal-education card game he had published in Basel in 1518. Why he chose to republish the game at this time is unclear; it seems likely that it was done at the request of a friend or colleague, for virtually all of Murner's publications during his sojourn in Lucerne concern the Swiss religious wars. That is, with his change of venue Murner did not cease his campaign against the Reform; he merely altered the primary target of his hostility, shifting his focus from Luther to Huldrych Zwingli, the leader of the Reform in the Swiss Confederation.

Murner initiated his series of anti-Zwingli publications in 1526 with *Murneri responsio libello* (Murner's Response to the Little Book), which he translated into German the same year as *Doctor Murners Antwurt uff die Anklag eines Eersamen Wysen Radtes der Statt Zürich* (Dr. Murner's Response to the Accusation of an Honorable, Wise Councilman of the City of Zurich). Murner accuses Zwingli of having seduced the people of Zurich with his evil lies. The bitter tone of Murner's polemic reflects his anger at being driven out of Strasbourg and the consequent deepening of his stubborn commitment to the Catholic cause.

Another weapon Murner employed was satire. *Der Lutherischen Evangelischen Kirchen dieb- und Ketzer Kalender* (The Lutheran Evangelical Church's Calendar of Thieves and Heretics, 1527) comprises satiric jibes at the enemies of the Catholic Church. With this grotesque parade of the most hated Protestants, Murner aims to warn his readers about the dangers that followers of the new faith represent. Murner's serious and satiric attacks on Zwingli and the Swiss Protestants obviously caused some consternation, for he felt it necessary to defend his actions before the people of Lucerne in the pamphlet *An die Fürsuchtigen ersamen vuysenn und frommen standhafftigen christen des alten woren und ungezwiffleten glaubens* (To the Prudent, Honorable Neighbors and the Pious, Loyal Christians of the Old, True, and Undoubted Faith, 1527). Here, as elsewhere, Murner reminds his readers that his aim has not been to start wars but to preserve peace–a rather incredible assertion, given the warlike tone of many of his pamphlets.

The climax of Murner's involvement in the Swiss religious wars came in 1526, when he, Johannes Eck, and Johannes Fabri took part in a disputation held in Baden. The disputation represented a last-ditch attempt by Swiss Catholics to maintain re-

Woodcut from Von dem großen Lutherischen Narren: *on their wedding night, Murner drives Martin Luther's daughter from his house after discovering that she has mange*

ligious unity in the face of the challenge presented by Zwingli and his followers. Zwingli was also scheduled to participate and had been granted the right of free passage for that purpose, but he never arrived. Two of Murner's works from 1526 castigate Zwingli for his failure to appear. In *Ein brieff den Strengen eren not* (A Truly Necessary Letter) he accuses Zwingli of cowardice and intellectual dishonesty. Zwingli replied in a similarly polemical manner, which prompted Murner to publish *Ein worhafftigs verantworten der hochgelorten doctores und herren* (A True Answer to the Learned Doctors and Gentlemen), in which he showers Zwingli and his followers with the insults that they have earned by committing crimes against the one and only church. As one of the principals in the Baden disputation, Murner was charged with the duty of preparing the record of the disputation, a task he took quite seriously. He published two versions of his protocol, one in German, the other in Latin: *Die disputacion vor den xij orten einer loblichen eidtgnoschafft* (The Disputation of the Twelve Cantons of the Praiseworthy Confederation, 1527) and *Caussa Helvetica orthodoxae fidei* (For the Cause of Swiss Orthodoxy to the Faith, 1528).

Murner's meticulous preparation of the protocol did not mean that he judged the Baden disputation a success, however. When a proposal was advanced for a second disputation in Bern, he protested strenuously on the grounds that such a disputation would be both hypocritical and useless since Bern had already all but declared itself reformed. Two pamphlets that appeared in 1527 attest to Murner's opposition to the Bern disputation: *Ursach und verantwurtung worumm doctor Thomas Murner kilchherr zuo Lutzern nit ist uff der disputation zuo Baden gehalten erschinen* (Cause and Answer Why Dr. Thomas Murner, Pastor in Lucerne, Did Not Appear at the Disputation in Bern) and *Appellation und beruoff der hochgelörten doctores* (A Plea and Calling Out from the Highly Learned Doctors). In the pamphlet *Hie würt angezeigt das unchristlich frevel, ungelört und unrechtlich uß rieffen und fürnemmen einer loblichen herschafft von Bern ein disputation zuo halten in irer gnaden statt* (Herewith Is Noted the Unchristian Crime, without Learning and Illegally, of Calling and Holding a Disputation in Their Honorable City, 1528) he rebukes the Bern City Council for sponsoring the second disputation.

Murner's stinging rebuke had no perceptible effect on the choice of religion in Bern: the city officially adopted the new faith in 1528. This turn of events inspired his two final poetic efforts, *Des alten christlichen beeren Testament* (The Old Christian Bear's Last Testament) and *Von des jungen Beren zenvue im mundt* (Of the Young Bear's Toothache in His Mouth), both published in 1528. In these poems the figures of the old bear and the young bear represent Catholicism and Protestantism, respectively. Murner's choice of animal is no coincidence; the words *bear* and *Bern* sound as much alike in Swiss German as they do in English. In *Des alten christlichen beeren Testament* Murner accuses those who have defected to the Protestant camp of ingratitude and disloyalty. At the end of the poem the dying old bear wishes those who have remained loyal to the Catholic Church good luck, for they will certainly need it. *Von des jungen Beren zenvue im mundt* warns of the "toothaches" to come and predicts the ultimate failure of the Reformers' plans.

Three other products of Murner's anti-Reformation agitation are a sermon he published in 1528 and two final pamphlets he wrote in the service of the Catholic cause. The sermon, *Die gots heylige meß von gott allein erstifft* (God's Holy Mass, Sponsored by God Alone), examines some of the same doctrinal questions Murner treated in *Eine christliche und briederliche ermanung*. In *Die gots heylige meß von gott allein erstifft*, however, Murner demonstrates that he has done his homework in the intervening years, for he advances many more biblical citations to support the points he makes. The first of the two pamphlets, *Ein sendbrieff der acht Christlichen ort einer loblichen Eidtgnoschafft* (An Open Letter to the Eight Christian Cantons of the Praiseworthy Confederation, 1529), written in the form of a dialogue, is a heartfelt plea to the members of the Swiss Confederation to remain Catholic. That the Bern City Council rejected Murner's plea is evidenced by what Murner calls in the second pamphlet, *Einußlegung und ercleren des selbigen spötlichen, unchristlichen und ungesaltzenen brieffs der herschafft von Bern* (An Interpretation and Explanation of the Very Same Mocking, Unchristian, and Unwise Letter of the Gentlemen of Bern, 1529), "ein spotlich und unfreundlich antwort" (a mocking and unfriendly reply). This work is Murner's last salvo in his campaign against the Reformation.

Murner left Lucerne voluntarily in 1529 instead of waiting to be thrown out. After a brief stay at the court of Ludwig V in Heidelberg he returned to Obernai, where he served as the preacher at Saint John's Church. The years between 1529 and his death in 1537 seem to have been sedate in comparison to the frenetic pace of Murner's activities in Strasbourg and Lucerne. The only known work that dates from the last years of his life is his translation of parts of Marcus Antonius Sabellicus's *Enneades* as *Hystory von anbeschaffener Welt* (History of the World Order, 1987). The translation was not published during Murner's lifetime; the manuscript, which contains pen-and-ink drawings that Murner himself may have executed, was published in a facsimile edition in 1987. No other details about the end of Murner's life are known. He died in Obernai in 1537, at some time before 23 August, and is presumably buried there.

Reviled by Protestants because he attacked Luther and Zwingli so relentlessly, distrusted by Catholics because his works sometimes offended critics' sensibilities, Murner remains one of the most prolific yet underresearched figures of the early modern period. His legacy has never been objectively evaluated. The liberal use in his vernacular works of proverbs and vocabulary specific to sixteenth-century Strasbourg, in addition to his bilingualism and the diverse nature of his oeuvre, have also impeded an assessment of Murner's contribution to early modern German culture. In the past thirty years German-speaking scholars have examined a few of Murner's works, but they have done so within the strictures of modern disciplinary boundaries: legal historians have considered his contribution to early modern legal education; linguists and literary critics have studied his vernacular satires; and historians of the Reformation have investigated his anti-Protestant propaganda. No one has tried to evaluate all aspects of the man and his works. Murner has been all but ignored by the English-speaking world because his works had not been translated into English until Erika Rummel's rendition of a portion of *Von dem großen Lutherischen Narren* in 1993. Although it is the opinion of many that Murner will never rank among the greatest sixteenth-century educators, authors of vernacular literature, or propagandists, his efforts in all these areas furnish the modern reader with a rich picture of early modern life, providing details that would otherwise remain inaccessible.

Biography:

Theodor von Liebenau, *Der Franziskaner Dr. Thomas Murner*, Erläuterungen und Ergänzungen zu Janssens Geschichte des deutschen Volkes IX, 4–5, edited by Ludwig von Pastor (Freiburg: Herdersche Verlagshandlung, 1913).

References:

Gustav Bebermeyer, "Zu Murners Gäuchmatt und Mühle von Schwindelsheim," *Beiträge zur Geschichte der Deutschen Sprache und Literatur*, 44, no. 1 (1919): 53–77;

Eckhard Bernstein, *Die erste deutsche Aneis: Eine Untersuchung von Thomas Murners Aneis-Übersetzung aus dem Jahre 1515*, Deutsche Studien, no. 23 (Meisenheim am Glan: Hain, 1974);

Emil von Borries, *Wimpfeling und Murner im Kampf um die ältere Geschichte des Elsasses: Ein Beitrag zur Charakteristik des deutschen Frühhumanismus* (Heidelberg: Winter, 1926);

Frauke Büchner, "Thomas Murner: Sein Kampf um die Kontinuität der kirchlichen Lehre und die Identität des Christenmenschen in den Jahren 1511–22," dissertation, University of Berlin, 1974;

Friedrich Eckel, *Der Fremdwortschatz Thomas Murners: Ein Beitrag zur Wortgeschichte des frühen 16. Jahrhunderts*, edited by Ulrich Müller, Franz Hundsnurscher, and Cornelius Sommer, Göppinger Arbeiten zur Germanistik, no. 210 (Göppingen: Kümmerle, 1978);

Adalbert Erler, *Thomas Murner als Jurist,* Frankfurter Wissenschaftliche Beiträge, Rechts- und Wirtschaftswissenschaftliche Reihe, no. 13 (Frankfurt am Main: Klostermann, 1956);

Eduard Fuchs, "Neuerscheinungen auf dem Gebiete der Murner-Forschung 1923–26," *Zeitschrift für deutsche Philologie*, 52 (1927): 183–195;

Fuchs, "Thomas Murners Belesenheit, Bildungsgang und Wissen," *Franziskanische Studien*, 9 (1922): 70–79;

Linda L. Gaus, " 'Zuo nutz und heylsamer ler': Representations of Women in Early Modern German Satire," dissertation, University of California, Berkeley, 1995;

Joan Gibson, "The Picture of Rationality: Visual Evidence for Gender Relations in Late Medieval and Renaissance Logic," in *Against Patriarchal Thinking: A Future without Discrimination: Proceedings of the Sixth Annual Symposium of the International Association of Women Philosophers 1992*, edited by Maja Pellikaan-Engel (Amsterdam: VU University Press, 1992), pp. 29–33;

Lily Greiner, "Thomas Murner (1475–1537), humaniste et théologien alsacien," in *Actes du 113e Congrès national des Sociétés savantes (Strasbourg 1988)* (Paris, 1990), pp. 279–288;

Rainer Gruenter, "Thomas Murners Satirischer Wortschatz," *Euphorion*, 53 (1959): 24–40;

Amelia J. Harris, "The Functions and Applications of the Proverb and Proverbial Expression in the German Poetry of Thomas Murner," dissertation, University of North Carolina at Chapel Hill, 1991;

Hedwig Heger, "Ideologisch vereinnahmt: Beobachtungen zu Murner-Illustrationen," in *Vänbok: Festgabe für Otto Gschwantler zum 60. Geburtstag*, edited by Imbi Sooman (Vienna: VWGO, 1990), pp. 127–162;

Heger, "Thomas Murner," in *Deutsche Dichter der frühen Neuzeit (1450–1600): Ihr Leben und Werk*, edited by Stephan Füssel (Berlin: Erich Schmidt, 1993), pp. 296–310;

Sabine Heimann, *Begriff und Wertschätzung der menschlichen Arbeit bei Sebastian Brant und Thomas Murner*, edited by Ulrich Müller, Franz Hundsnurscher, and others, Stuttgarter Arbeiten zur Germanistik, no. 225 (Stuttgart: Heinz, 1990);

Günter Hess, *Deutsch-Lateinische Narrenzunft: Studien zum Verhältnis von Volkssprache und Latinität in der satirischen Literatur des 16. Jahrhunderts*, Münchener Texte und Untersuchungen zur Deutschen Literatur des Mittelalters, no. 41 (Munich: Beck, 1971);

Anita Homolka, "Die Tischzuchten von Sebastian Brant, Thomas Murner und Hans Sachs und ihr realer Hintergrund in Basel, Strassburg und Nürnberg," dissertation, University of Munich, 1983;

Waldemar Kawerau, *Thomas Murner und die deutsche Reformation* (Halle: Verein für Reformationsgeschichte, 1891);

Kawerau, *Thomas Murner und die Kirche des Mittelalters* (Halle: Verein für Reformationsgeschichte, 1890);

H. Koegler, "Druck und Illustration der Murner'schen Geuchmatt," *Basler Bücherfreund*, 2 (1926): 131–140;

Barbara Könneker, "Thomas Murner," in *Reformation, Renaissance und Barock*, volume 2 of *Deutsche Dichter: Leben und Werk deutschsprachiger Autoren*, edited by Gunter E. Grimm and Frank Rainer Max (Stuttgart: Reclam, 1988), pp. 21–32;

Könneker, *Wesen und Wandlung der Narrenidee im Zeitalter des Humanismus* (Wiesbaden: Steiner, 1966);

Florenz Landmann, "Thomas Murner als Prediger: Eine kritische Nachprüfung," *Archiv für Elsässische Kirchengeschichte*, 10 (1935): 295–368;

Landmann, "Zur Charakteristik Thomas Murners," *Archiv für Elsässische Kirchengeschichte*, 15 (1941–1942): 199–210;

Joseph Lefftz, *Die volkstümlichen Stilelemente in Murners Satiren*, Einzelschriften zur Elsässischen Geistes- und Kulturgeschichte, no. 1, edited by the Gesellschaft für elsässische Literatur (Strasbourg: Trübner, 1915);

Klaus Manger, *Literarisches Leben in Strassburg während der Prädikatur Johann Geilers von Kaysersberg (1478–1510)*, edited by Albrecht Dihle, Peter Michelsen, and others, Heidelberger Forschungen, no. 24 (Heidelberg: Winter, 1983);

Richard Newald, *Elsässische Charakterköpfe aus dem Zeitalter des Humanismus* (Colmar: Alsatia, 1944);

Newald, "Wandlungen des Murnerbildes," in *Beiträge zur Geistes- und Kulturgeschichte der Oberrheinlande, Franz Schultz zum 60. Geburtstag gewidmet*, edited by Hermann Gumbel, Schriften des wissenschaftlichen Instituts der Elsass-Lothringer im Reich an der Universität Frankfurt, new series 18 (Frankfurt am Main: Diesterweg, 1938), pp. 40–78;

Karl Ott, *Über Murners Verhältnis zu Geiler* (Bonn: Hanstein, 1896);

Jürgen Pelzer, " 'Alle Ding Sindt Koeuflich Worden': Geldklage und satirische Gesellschaftskritik in Thomas Murners *Narrenbeschwörung*," *Germanisch-Romanische Monatsschrift*, 29, no. 2 (1979): 146–158;

Wolfgang Pfeiffer-Belli, *Thomas Murner im Schweizer Glaubenskampf*, Corpus Catholicorum: Werke Katholischer Schriftsteller im Zeitalter der Glaubensspaltung, no. 22 (Münster: Aschendorff, 1939);

Marthe Philipp, "Moderne Sprachwissenschaftliche Methoden am Beispiel des Werks Thomas Murners," *Zeitschrift für deutsche Philologie*, 88 (1969): 436–448;

Philipp, *Phonologie des Graphie et des Rimes: Recherches structurales sur l'alsacien de Thomas Murner (XVIe siècle)* (Paris: Editions du Centre National de la Recherche Scientifique, 1968);

Henri Plard, "Folie, subversion, hérésie: La polémique de Thomas Murner contre Luther," in *Folie et Déraison à la Renaissance: Colloque international tenu en novembre 1973 sous les auspices de la Fédération Internationale des Instituts et Sociétés pour l'Etude de la Renaissance,* Travaux de l'Institut pour l'étude de la Renaissance et de l'Humanisme, no. 5 (Brussels: Editions de l'Université de Bruxelles, 1976), pp. 197-208;

Susanne M. Raabe, *Der Wortschatz in den deutschen Schriften Thomas Murners,* 2 volumes, edited by Stefan Sonderegger, Studia Linguistica Germanica, no. 29 (Berlin: De Gruyter, 1990);

Francis Rapp, "Les Franciscains et la Réformation en Alsace: deux religieux humanistes dans la tourmente, Murner et Pellican," *Annales de l'Est* (1985): 151-165;

Rapp, "Die Mendikanten und die Strassburger Gesellschaft am Ende des Mittelalters," in *Stellung und Wirksamkeit der Bettelorden in der städtischen Gesellschaft,* edited by Kaspar Elm, Berliner Historische Studien, Ordensstudien, no. 3 (Berlin: Duncker & Humblot, 1981), pp. 85-102;

Anna Risse, "Sprichwörter und Redensarten bei Thomas Murner," *Zeitschrift für den deutschen Unterricht,* 31 (1917): 215-227;

Charles Schmidt, *Histoire Litteraire de l'Alsace a la fin du XVe et au commencement du XVIe siecle,* 2 volumes (Paris: Librarie Sandoz et Fischbacher, 1879), p. 211-315;

Georg Schuhmann, *Thomas Murner und seine Dichtungen* (Rome & Regensburg: Pustet, 1915);

Schuhmann, "Wetterzeichen der Reformation nach Murner Satiren aus der vorlutherischen Zeit," *Römische Quartalschrift,* 25 (1911): 162-184;

Jürgen Schutte, *"Schympf red": Frühformen bürgerlicher Agitation in Thomas Murners "Grossem Lutherischen Narren,"* Germanistische Abhandlungen, no. 41 (Stuttgart: Metzler, 1973);

Schutte, *"schympff und ernst vermischet schon:* Die Rechtfertigung der Satire bei Thomas Murner," *Jahrbuch für Internationale Germanistik,* 3, no. 1 (1971): 42-62;

Moriz Sondheim, "Die Illustrationen zu Thomas Murners Werken," *Elsass-Lothringisches Jahrbuch,* 12 (1933): 5-82;

Sondheim, "Thomas Murner als Illustrator," in his *Gesammelte Schriften* (Frankfurt am Main, 1927), pp. 5-82;

Thomas Murner: Elsässischer Theologe und Humanist 1475-1537: Eine Ausstellung der Badischen Landesbibliothek Karlsruhe und der Bibliothèque Nationale et Universitaire de Strasbourg (Karlsruhe: Badische Landesbibliothek Karlsruhe in Zusammenarbeit mit der Bibliothèque Nationale et Universitaire de Strasbourg, 1987);

Paul Zinsli, "Manuel und Murner: Die Begegnung zweier begabter Glaubensstreiter in der Reformationszeit," *Berner Zeitschrift für Geschichte und Heimatkunde,* 50 (1988): 165-196.

Oswald von Wolkenstein
(1376 or 1377 – 1445)

Albrecht Classen
University of Arizona

WORKS: *Songs* (circa 1400–1441)

Manuscripts: Oswald von Wolkenstein twice had collections made of his songs, and he personally supervised the arrangement of his works in these manuscripts. The first of the two, known as Manuscript A, is in the Österreichische Nationalbibliothek, Vienna, cod. Vind. 2777. It consists of sixty-one parchment leaves and was copied between 1423 and 1441. Manuscript A includes 108 songs with their melodies. Manuscript B, in the Universitätsbibliothek Innsbruck (no call number), consists of forty-eight parchment leaves; most of the songs in it were copied by 30 August 1432, according to a note by a scribe at the top of the table of contents on folio 1; the other songs were copied by other scribes until 1438. Manuscript B contains 118 songs, 18 of which are not included in Manuscript A; 8 songs in Manuscript A are missing from Manuscript B. Like Manuscript A, Manuscript B includes musical notations. Manuscript C, in the Tiroler Landesmuseum Ferdinandeum, Innsbruck, FB 1950, is a paper manuscript of 115 pages copied after 1450 by one hand. This manuscript also includes songs not by Oswald on folios 103ʳ–104ʳ. Except for those songs, and songs Kl. 108 (the numbering of the songs is based on the edition by Walter Weiß, Notburga Wolf, and Karl Kurt Klein, 1987; the designation *Kl.* is taken from Klein's name) and Kl. 109 by Oswald, Manuscript C is a close copy of Manuscript B; a few songs at the end of the manuscript are arranged in a slightly different order than in Manuscript B. Manuscript C does not include musical notations. Song Kl. 112 is included in Manuscript D, in the British Museum, Manuscript Add. 24946. Songs Kl. 20, Kl. 43, Kl. 88, and Kl. 91 are in Manuscript E, in the Knihovna Národního Musea, Prague, Manuscript x A 12. Song Kl. 67 is in Manuscript H, in the Bayerische Staatsbibliothek, Munich, Cgm 3897,

Oswald von Wolkenstein in 1432; portrait by Antonio Pisanello or one of his students. Oswald is the earliest German writer whose likeness has been preserved (Universitätsbibliothek Innsbruck, Manuscript B).

from the first half of the fifteenth century. Fragments of song Kl. 70 are in Manuscript L, in the Bayerische Staatsbibliothek, Munich, Cgm 715, from the middle of the fifteenth century. Songs Kl. 84 and Kl. 84 are in Manuscript G, in the Bayerische Staatsbibliothek, Cgm 379, circa 1454. Verses 57 through 62 and 77 of Song Kl. 91 are in Manuscript K, in the Stadtarchiv of Freiberg in Saxony, Reg.-Nr. I Bf 39, from the first half of the fifteenth century. Song Kl. 84, verse 25, is in paper manuscript ß in the Sächsische Landesbibliothek, Dresden, Msc. Dresd. M 65. copied between 1428 and 1430. Kl. 88 and Kl. 91 are in paper manuscript o, in the Staatsbibliothek, Preußischer Kulturbesitz, Berlin, Mgf 488, from 1530. Song Kl. 101 is in Manuscript J, in the Staatsbibliothek, Preußischer Kulturbesitz, Berlin, Manuscript mus. 40. 613, from the second half of the fifteenth century. Song Kl. 101 is in Manuscript N, in the Universitätsbibliothek, Rostock, Manuscript phil. 100/2, circa 1465. Song Kl. 131 is in paper manuscript p, in the Bayerische Staatsbibliothek, Cgm 4871, from the fifteenth century. Song Kl. 132 is in paper manuscript q, in the Germanisches Nationalmuseum, Nuremberg, Wolkensteinarchiv. Song Kl. 133 is in paper manuscript r, in the British Museum, Manuscript Add. 16581, from the fifteenth century. Song Kl. 134 in paper manuscript s, in the Stadtmuseum, Regensburg, Nr. R 58, dated after 1432. Song Kl. 128 is in paper manuscript t, in the Universitätsbibliothek, Heidelberg, Cpg 343, from the middle of the sixteenth century and in paper manuscript u, in the Berlin Staatsbibliothek, Preußischer Kulturbesitz, Mgf 753, dated 1575. Songs Kl. 130 and Kl. 129, in reversed order, are in paper manuscript w, in the Bayerische Staatsbibliothek, Cgm 1115, from the fifteenth century. Songs Kl. 130 and Kl. 129 are in paper manuscript x, in the Österreichische Nationalbibliothek, Vienna, Cod. Vind. 4696, from the late fifteenth century. Songs Kl. 130 and Kl. 129 are in paper manuscript y, in the Österreichische Nationalbibliothek, Cod. Vind. 2975, dating from 1465.

Standard editions: *Die Gedichte Oswalds von Wolkenstein: Mit Einleitung, Wortbuch and Varianten,* edited by Beda Weber (Innsbruck: Wagner, 1847); *Gedichte Oswalds von Wolkenstein, des letzten Minnesängers,* edited by Johannes Schrott (Stuttgart: Cotta, 1886); *Oswald von Wolkenstein: Geistliche und weltliche Lieder, ein- und mehrstimmig,* edited by Josef Schatz, music by Oswald Koller (Vienna: Artaria, 1902); revised and enlarged as *Die Gedichte Oswalds von Wolkenstein* (Göttingen: Vandenhoeck & Ruprecht, 1904); *Die Lieder Oswalds von Wolkenstein,* edited by Walter Weiß, Notburga Wolf, and Karl Kurt Klein, musical notation edited by Walter Salmen, third revised and enlarged edition, edited by Hans Moser, Norbert Richard Wolf, and Notburga Wolf, Altdeutsche Textbibliothek, no. 55 (Tübingen: Niemeyer, 1987).

Edition in modern German: *Oswald von Wolkenstein: Sämtliche Lieder und Gedichte. Ins Neuhochdeutsche übersetzt,* translated and edited by Wernfried Hofmeister (Göppingen: Kümmerle, 1989).

Editions in English: A few songs translated by J. W. Thomas, in his *Medieval German Lyric Verse* (Chapel Hill: University of North Carolina Press, 1968); many stanzas translated by George F. Jones, in his *Oswald von Wolkenstein* (New York: Twayne, 1973); two songs in *McGraw-Hill Anthology of German Literature,* volume 1: *Early Middle Ages to Storm and Stress,* edited by Kim Vivian and others (New York: McGraw-Hill, 1994); several songs translated by Albrecht Classen, in *Eroticism and Love in the Middle Ages,* edited by Classen, third edition (New York: American Heritage Custom Publishing, 1995).

The South Tirolean poet Oswald von Wolkenstein produced one of the most sophisticated and exciting bodies of lyric poetry in the Middle Ages. His songs, somewhat influenced by early modern thought, seem to have much more in common with twentieth-century postmodern lyrical poems than with anything else written during the medieval period. Nevertheless, Oswald was in full command of the lyrical traditions of the Middle Ages. He freely used genres and themes from a wide range of literary sources, although he transformed them considerably. He composed his works for his own enjoyment, ignoring public expectations. Many of his songs are autobiographical. Never in the history of German literature had a poet detailed his life as meticulously as Oswald, not even the so-called Archpoet or Walther von der Vogelweide in the High Middle Ages. In this respect he has been compared to his French contemporaries François Villon and Charles d'Orléans and the Italian poets Antonio Pucci, Giannozzo Sacchetti, Franco Sacchetti, and Cecco Angiolieri. In his songs Kl. 18, Kl. 19, Kl. 23, Kl. 26, Kl. 41, and Kl. 44 he relates his extensive travels, describing his meetings with dignitaries of many countries. He also contrasts the splendor of the life of a royal diplomat with the boredom, discomfort, and financial distress that he experienced at home in South Tirol.

Born in 1376 or 1377, Oswald was the second son of Friedrich von Wolkenstein. He may have attended the Brixen Cathedral school or the nearby convent school at Neustift. While Oswald seems to have been largely an autodidact, he would later send his sons to the University of Bologna; and he himself would gain respect as a legal adviser because

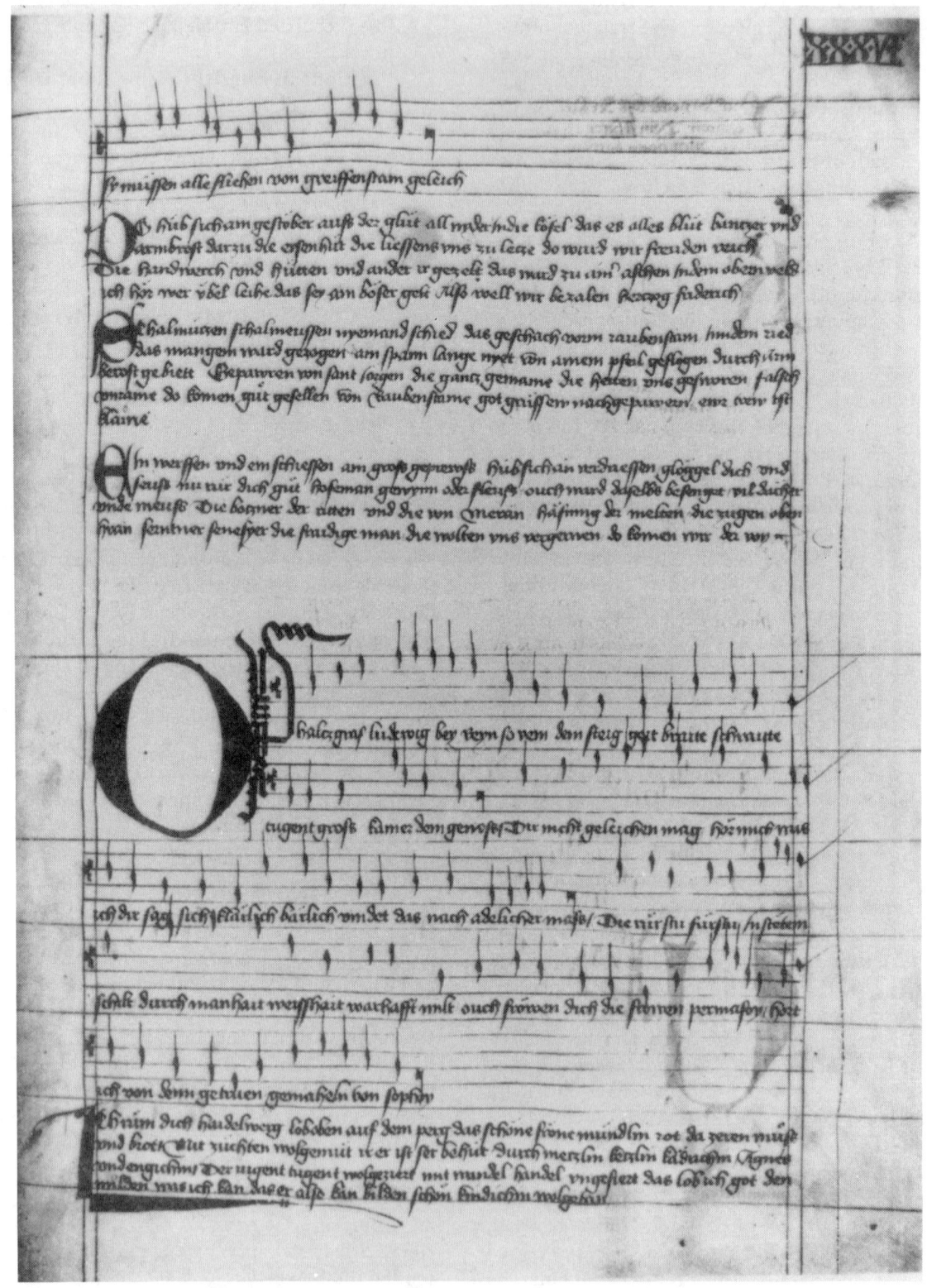

Page from the manuscript for Oswald's second collection of his songs (Universitätsbibliothek Innsbruck, Manuscript B, folio 36ʳ)

of his practical experience and political skills. He left home at ten, probably in the service of a knight. In his songs he mentions meeting *Kriechen* (Christians) and heathens; serving as a messenger, cook, horse groom, and rower on a ship; and suffering hunger and other hardships. He claims the ability to speak French, Arabic, Catalan, Spanish, German, Latin, Slovak, Greek, and Russian–along with Italian, which was natural because of the many language contacts between Italy and his home region; Oswald's grandmother was also of Italian descent, and he often traveled to Lombardy. Although he may have exaggerated his linguistic skills, the display of foreign languages in his songs and his later role as translator for Emperor Sigismund indicate that he was indeed multilingual. His travels took him to Prussia and Lithuania, where he participated in crusades. He also made his way to eastern and southern Europe, and probably to the Crimea, where he seems to have tried his luck as a merchant–a venture that ended in a shipwreck that he survived by clinging to a barrel of wine. He may also have seen parts of Armenia and Persia.

With his father's death in 1400 Oswald's financial situation became precarious, since his older brother, Michael, inherited the bulk of the estate. Oswald was forced to assume various administrative positions in the Brixen area. In 1401-1402 he participated in the campaign of King Ruprecht of the Palatinate to subdue the Visconti family of Milan and be crowned by the Pope. These efforts were quickly thwarted by the Italians. Back home in 1404-1405, Oswald desperately tried to gain financial security. At one point he stole a chest of jewels from his sister-in-law, accusing her of having spent the treasure on a lover. But his brother Michael saw through the ruse and, after inflicting a nearly mortal wound on him, forced him to apologize to his sister-in-law.

In 1409 Oswald entered the service of Bishop Ulrich II of Putsch in Brixen, acting as the bishop's legal proxy during his absence. At the end of the year he joined a pilgrimage to Palestine and seems to have visited various parts of the eastern Mediterranean. In song Kl. 17 he describes the trip, especially his impressions on shipboard. Exclamations and commands uttered by the sailors in their Venetian dialect combine with other elements to form a highly complex poem that must have been as difficult to understand for Oswald's contemporary audience as it is for the modern philologist. Oswald seems to have composed the song for his fellow travelers, with little regard for posterity's ability to decipher it. On his return to Germany late in 1410 he began to work full time for the bishop, probably as legal and military adviser, positions that required him to travel widely in northern Italy and Tirol. Apparently, he was paid only sporadically, which led to many quarrels with the bishop. In 1415, while attending the Council of Constance, Oswald entered the service of Emperor Sigismund. He was immediately dispatched to represent the emperor as translator or legal counselor in negotiations in Italy, Spain, and France.

Oswald also seems to have traveled to Ireland and Scotland in 1415 and 1416 on an imperial mission. He returned to Portugal and then went to Spain, where Sigismund was attempting to persuade the Castilian, Catalan, and Aragonese courts to drop their candidate for Pope. Oswald joined the imperial troops in defeating the Arabian Sea fortress of Ceuta on 21 August, then met the emperor in Perpignan. Queen Margarethe of Prades honored him by attaching rings to his beard, probably because he had brought the good news from Ceuta. Oswald entertained the court by masquerading as the eleventh-century Spanish national hero El Cid at a celebration of the victory over the Moors, and Queen Eleonore of Aragon inducted him into the Order of the Griffin, a knightly order recently founded by her husband. He repeated his performance as El Cid at the French court in Paris.

In the summer of 1417 Oswald married Margaretha of Schwangau, through whom he gained the rank of imperial knight. He uninhibitedly describes Margaretha's body in Kl. 110, and in the erotic marriage songs Kl. 75 and Kl. 77 the newlyweds exchange sexual favors in a bathtub in a meadow. Some of Margaretha's letters to her husband from late in their lives have been preserved; they confirm that Oswald's love poems were based on real-life experiences, even if the poet couched them in traditional topoi and used typical medieval metaphors. Over the following years Oswald established himself more firmly at the family castle of Hauenstein and came into conflict with the Tirolean duke Friedrich IV's efforts to subdue the local nobility. The duke's siege of Castle Greifenstein in 1418, which was resisted by the Starkenberg family along with Oswald and his brothers, Michael and Lienhard, was militarily insignificant; but in song Kl. 85, one of the best German military ballads from the Middle Ages, Oswald jubilantly describes a successful sortie leading to the defeat of the ducal forces and their allies.

Oswald's conflicts with Friedrich IV aroused anger, frustration, and fear in him, and he confesses in song Kl. 44 that at times he ventilated his feelings by beating his children:

Vor angst slach ich mein kinder
offt hin hinder.
So kompt ir mütter zü gebraust,
zwar die beginnt zu schelten;
gäb si mir aines mit der fawsst,
des müsst ich ser engelten.

(Out of frustration I hit my children,
chasing them away from me.
Then their mother comes rushing out
and begins to scold me;
if she were to hit me with her fist,
I would have to suffer for it dearly.)

Oswald participated in the war against the Hussites in 1420–1421; he mocks the Czech soldiers in song Kl. 27, although the Hussites were never defeated by a German army. In 1421 the burgher Martin Jäger, the co-owner of Castle Hauenstein, whom Oswald had violently evicted from the property, ambushed and imprisoned Oswald by tricking him into thinking that he was going to meet a former girlfriend, Anna Hausmannin, with whom he had had a thirteen-year liaison. In Kl. 3, composed shortly after his imprisonment, Oswald severely chastises his former girlfriend and criticizes women in general, referring to their evil influence on men throughout history. He casts himself in the role of Adam, Samson, David, Solomon, Aristotle, Alexander the Great, Absalom, and John the Baptist. Women are like a beautifully decorated rope that binds one, or like a lance pointing toward the heart. Oswald does not, however, reject love service altogether, as long as the wooed ladies are virtuous and chaste. Oswald was tortured but seems to have resisted signing over Castle Hauenstein to Jäger. In song Kl. 60 he claims that his mistreatment forced him to use crutches. Late in 1421 Duke Friedrich applied legal means to extort from Oswald an enormous pawn of six thousand gulden. Oswald's friends and relatives, especially his brother Michael and Hans von Villanders, bailed him out by guaranteeing a loan in March 1422, but only on his promise to repay them at a high rate of interest. This debt would be a lifelong burden for the poet.

During the 1420s Oswald was deeply involved in the battles of the landed gentry against Duke Friedrich. Forced to spend much of his time in his mountain castle to avoid capture by the duke's forces, he complains in his songs about the noisy rushing of the nearby creek and about the donkeys and peacocks that disturb his peace. He laments that the duke is hostile to him and that his neighbors are fighting with him. He casts himself as "arme Wolkenstein" (poor Wolkenstein), who is in danger of being torn to pieces by his enemies. In 1423 he began to collect his songs in a manuscript, a process that would involve as many as nine scribes. The main part was completed by 1425, but later entries date from 1436 and 1441.

During the 1420s the estates buckled under Friedrich's efforts to consolidate his control over the country. Oswald was one of the last aristocrats fighting a losing battle, and in 1427 he was captured and imprisoned at Castle Vellenberg. Friedrich used the still-unsettled dispute over the ownership of Castle Hauenstein to force Oswald into submission. In return for helping Oswald gain control of the entire castle, Friedrich forced the poet to sign a document making him the duke's obedient subject. Oswald was released from prison on 1 May 1427. Although from this point onward Oswald's works portray Duke Friedrich as a song-loving lord, the poet's friend, and a true leader of his people, the excessive use of laudatory images suggests parody and sarcasm.

Oswald resumed his travels and political activities, directing his energies toward Germany and the Rhine and establishing a closer relationship with Count Ludwig of the Palatinate. His real purpose seems to have been to join the *Feme,* an underground court of justice with considerable influence over northern and central Europe. As a magistrate of the Feme, Oswald gained new powers to deal with local administrators and dignitaries; in 1428 he returned home and freely played this card against his old enemies. In the following years Oswald reentered Emperor Sigismund's service as a diplomat, political negotiator, and adviser. Internationally he was increasingly recognized as an important voice and expert in legal matters. In recognition of his achievements he was inducted into the prestigious chivalric Order of the Dragon in 1431. His membership in the order obliged him to participate that same year in the fifth war against the Hussites, which turned into an debacle. Although he had no particular function to perform at the Council of Basel in 1432, it was not unusual for him to make an appearance at such an international gathering.

In 1432 Oswald commissioned the production of his second collection of songs; the manuscript's frontispiece is a remarkably realistic portrait of Oswald painted by Antonio Pisanello or one of his students when the poet was in Piacenza, Italy, that year in the entourage of Emperor Sigismund. Oswald's facial features, including his unshaven cheeks and his empty eye socket (he probably lost the eye when he was a child), as well as his full regalia as a knight, are depicted in vivid colors. Entries continued to be made to this manuscript until 1438. Both manuscripts were probably produced at the

Augustinian convent of Neustift, near Brixen. Many of the songs in the two manuscripts are accompanied by musical notations, showing that Oswald was familiar with the full spectrum of melodies and musical genres. He introduced into Germany the most advanced types of tunes with several voices—the *ars nova*—as they had been developed in northern Italy and France.

In 1434 Oswald went to Ulm for an imperial diet, but after 1435 he seems not to have left Tirol again. Duke Friedrich died in 1439; his successor, his son Sigmund, was not yet of age and had to rely on the help of the landed gentry. Sigmund's guardian, Friedrich V, granted Wolkenstein release from the pawn that had burdened him since 1427. Oswald died in 1445. Although he was unsuccessful in preventing the rise of centralized government in the southern Tirol, he is remembered as a skillful politician who rose from modest origins to become one of the most highly esteemed leaders in the country. His sons and grandsons continued this tradition, albeit in a more subdued manner. For instance, at the end of the fifteenth century Oswald's grandson Veit von Wolkenstein became an influential advisor to Emperor Maximilian I, and later generations secured similar connections.

In his songs Oswald freely combined elements from the major European languages, copying liberally from contemporary French, Flemish, and Italian poetry and borrowing melodies from various sources and remodeling them to suit his own purposes. He brought many important themes and topics from the Middle High German *Minnesang* (love poetry) to perfection, sometimes parodying them, sometimes injecting them with new realistic features, sometimes reworking them thematically and conceptually. Among the many lyric genres that Oswald used are the repentance song, the religious admonition song, the good-bye-world song, the Marian song, the dawn song, the crusade song, the autobiographical song, the spring song (in the tradition of Neidhart von Reuental), the astronomical song, the political song, the travel song, the war song, the calendar song or *Cisiojanus*, the warning-against-hell song, the pilgrimage song, the city encomium (both positive and negative), the farm song, the chase song, the Shrovetide song, the polyglot song, the marriage song, the pastourella, and the didactic song.

Oswald's willingness to experiment with old and new types of songs, his open-mindedness toward other cultures, his tentative exploration of the philosophy of the Italian Renaissance, and his adoption of the ars nova reveal a progressive attitude. Politically, however, Oswald looked backward, rejecting the urban world with its rich and independent burghers. At the same time, he was sarcastic toward courts and courtiers. In song Kl. 25 a rich burgher and a poor but arrogant nobleman are vying for the favors of a prostitute; in the end the merchant is victorious because of his money, but both men emerge as dubious characters. Although Oswald also strongly criticized the peasants, he repeatedly expressed a subtle but noticeable envy of their harmony with nature and enjoyment of physical love.

Oswald's poetry is often strikingly erotic. In song Kl. 33 the singer is lying in bed alone, without his beloved. In a reversal of the traditional dawn song, night is falling. Loneliness tortures the poet, and he describes in erotic detail the desires that take control of him. The image of a "ratz mit grossem tratz" (rat full of animosity) is clearly a phallic metaphor. The rat disturbs the narrator's sleep, and he appeals to his beloved to help him make the bed shake and creak in lovemaking.

Some of Oswald's songs are immensely onomatopoetic. In song Kl. 50, for example, he imitates a chorus of birdsongs:

oci oci oci oci oci oci,
fi fideli fideli fideli fi,
ci cieriri ci ci cieriri,
ci ri ciwigk cidiwigk fici fici.
so sang der gauch neur [thus sang the cuckoo]: "kawa wa cu cu."

Song Kl. 21 ends in a thunderous sequence of onomatopoetic expressions based on nursery rhymes and erotic games; it is virtually untranslatable:

Da zissli müssli
fissli füssli
henne klüssli
kompt ins hüssli
werfen ain tüssli,
sussa süssli,
niena grüssli
....
vacht das rëtzli!
tula hëtzli,
trutza trätzli,
der uns freud vergan.

Oswald also created calendar songs in which names of saints make up the entire text, with few syntactical connections.

Although about 22 of Oswald's 133 songs found their way into a handful of manuscripts and printings in the fifteenth and sixteenth centuries, his work was forgotten rather quickly after his death. The two manuscripts he had commissioned were rediscovered in 1799 and 1803, respectively, but only a few enthusiastic scholars paid attention to them. Beda Weber edited his songs in 1847 and published a brilliant but perhaps too imaginative biographical sketch in 1850 based on alleged travel notes by the poet. Josef Schatz made another attempt at a critical edition in 1902. In 1930 Arthur Graf von Wolkenstein-Rodenegg's biography appeared, and several philologists wrote important articles on Oswald in the 1930s. But it was not until 1961 that Norbert Mayr's groundbreaking and influential study radically changed the scholarly perception of Oswald's work. Since then his outstanding role as a late-medieval poet has been fully recognized. He has been the subject of a multitude of monographs, dissertations, and articles, and an international Oswald von Wolkenstein Gesellschaft (Society) has published a yearbook since 1980 and sponsors yearly conferences dedicated to the Late Middle Ages. Musicologists argue that Oswald's songs represent the most sophisticated contributions to late-medieval music, a claim corroborated by the ever-growing number of recordings and performances of his songs. There is, however, still no comprehensive translation of Oswald's oeuvre in English. In summary, this South Tirolean singer was a master poet and composer, greatly misunderstood in his time and perhaps a more kindred spirit to the late twentieth century than to the Middle Ages.

Biographies:

Beda Weber, *Oswald von Wolkenstein und Friedrich mit der leeren Tasche* (Innsbruck: Wagner, 1850);

Arthur Graf von Wolkenstein-Rodenegg, *Oswald von Wolkenstein* (Innsbruck: Wagner, 1930);

George F. Jones, *Oswald von Wolkenstein* (New York: Twayne, 1973);

Dieter Kühn, *Ich Wolkenstein: Eine Biographie,* second edition (Frankfurt am Main: Insel, 1981);

Anton Schwob, *Oswald von Wolkenstein: Eine Biographie,* third edition (Bozen: Athesia, 1989).

References:

Frank G. Banta, "Dimensions and Reflections: An Analysis of Oswald von Wolkenstein's *Frölich, zärtlich,*" *Journal of English and Germanic Philology,* 66 (1967): 59–75;

Siegfried Beyschlag, "Zu den mehrstimmigen Liedern Oswalds von Wolkenstein: Fuga und Duett," in *Literatur und Geistesgeschichte: Festgabe für Heinz Otto Burger,* edited by R. Grimm and C. Wiedemann (Berlin: Schmidt, 1968), pp. 50–69;

Albrecht Classen, *Autobiographische Lyrik des europäischen Spätmittelalters* (Amsterdam & Atlanta: Rodopi, 1991);

Classen, "Der Bauer in der Lyrik Oswalds von Wolkenstein," *Euphorion,* 82, no. 2 (1988): 150–167;

Classen, "French and Italian Sources for Oswald von Wolkenstein's Onomatopoetic Lyric Poetry," *Fifteenth-Century Studies,* 15 (1989): 93–105;

Classen, "Giannozzo Sacchetti's *Mentr' io d' amor pensava* as a Source for Oswald von Wolkenstein's Song-Poetry," *Monatshefte,* 80, no. 4 (1988): 459–468;

Classen, "Liebesehe und Ehelieder in der Dichtung Oswalds von Wolkenstein," *Jahrbuch der Oswald von Wolkenstein Gesellschaft,* 5 (1988–1989): 445–464;

Classen, "Love and Marriage in Late Medieval Verse: Oswald von Wolkenstein, Thomas Hoccleve, and Michel Beheim," *Studia Neophilologica,* 62 (1990): 163–188;

Classen, "Oswald von Wolkenstein–a Fifteenth-Century Reader of Medieval Courtly Criticism," *Mediaevistik,* 3 (1990): 27–53;

Classen, "Oswald von Wolkenstein und Leonardo Giustiniani: Zwei Zeitgenossen des frühen 15. Jahrhunderts," *Literaturwissenschaftliches Jahrbuch,* 35 (1994): 33–62;

Classen, "Peasant Satire in Oswald von Wolkenstein's Lyric Poetry: Reception and Adaptation of a Poem by Raimbaut de Vaqueiras," *Seminar,* 24, no. 4 (1988): 287–309;

Classen, *Zur Rezeption norditalienischer Kultur des Trecento im Werk Oswalds von Wolkenstein (1376/77–1445)* (Göppingen: Kümmerle, 1987);

Sieglinde Hartmann, *Altersdichtung und Selbstdarstellung bei Oswald von Wolkenstein: Die Lieder Kl. 1 bis Kl. 7 im spätmittelalterlichen Kontext* (Göppingen: Kümmerle, 1980);

Dagmar Hirschberg, "Zur Funktion der biographischen Konkretisierung in Oswalds von Wolkenstein Tagelied-Experiment *Ain tunckle farb von occident* Kl. 33," *Beiträge zur Geschichte der deutschen Sprache und Literatur,* 107 (1985): 376–388;

Dirk Joschko, *Oswald von Wolkenstein: Eine Monographie zu Person, Werk und Forschungsgeschichte* (Göppingen: Kümmerle, 1985);

Wolfgang Kersken, *Genner beschnaid: Die Kalendergedichte und der Neumondkalender des Oswald von Wolkenstein. Überlieferung–Text–Deutung* (Göppingen: Kümmerle, 1975);

Eugen Kühebacher, ed., *Oswald von Wolkenstein: Beiträge der philologisch-musikwissenschaftlichen Tagung in Neustift bei Brixen 1973* (Innsbruck: Institut für Deutsche Philologie der Universität Innsbruck, 1974);

Werner Marold, *Kommentar zu den Liedern Oswalds von Wolkenstein,* revised and edited by Alan Robertshaw (Innsbruck: Institut für Germanistik, 1995);

Norbert Mayr, *Die Reiselieder und Reisen Oswalds von Wolkenstein* (Innsbruck: Wagner, 1961);

Hans-Dieter Mück, *Untersuchungen zur Überlieferung und Rezeption spätmittelalterlicher Lieder und Spruchgedichte im 15. und 16. Jahrhundert: Die "Streuüberlieferung" von Liedern und Reimpaarreden Oswalds von Wolkenstein,* 2 volumes (Göppingen: Kümmerle, 1980);

Mück and Ulrich Müller, eds., *Gesammelte Vorträge der 600-Jahrfeier Oswalds von Wolkenstein, Seis am Schlern 1977* (Göppingen: Kümmerle, 1978);

Müller, *"Dichtung" und "Wahrheit" in den Liedern Oswalds von Wolkenstein: Die autobiographischen Lieder von der Reise* (Göppingen: Kümmerle, 1968);

Müller, "Exemplarische Überlieferung und Edition: Mehrfassungen in authentischen Lyrik-Handschriften," *editio,* 6 (1992): 112–122;

Müller, " 'Wie wol ich suns tichten chann': Veracity in German 'Spruchdichtung' from Walther von der Vogelweide to Michel Beheim," *Fifteenth-Century Studies,* 12 (1987): 115–130;

Müller, ed., *Oswald von Wolkenstein* (Darmstadt: Wissenschaftliche Buchgesellschaft, 1980);

Petra-Marion Niethammer, *Urkundenfindbuch zu Oswald von Wolkenstein: Verzeichnis der veröffentlichten Dokumente (1400–1445)* (Göppingen: Kümmerle, 1984);

Lambertus Okken and Mück, *Die satirischen Lieder Oswalds von Wolkenstein wider die Bauern: Untersuchungen zum Wortschatz und zur literarischen Einordnung* (Göppingen: Kümmerle, 1981);

Christoph Petzsch, "Die Bergwaldpastourelle Oswalds von Wolkenstein," *Zeitschrift für deutsche Philologie,* 87 (1968): 195–222;

Petzsch, "Text- und Melodietypenveränderung bei Oswald von Wolkenstein," *Deutsche Vierteljahrsschrift für Literaturwissenschaft und Geistesgeschichte,* 38 (1964): 491–512;

Hans Pörnbacher, *Margareta von Schwangau, Herrn Oswalds von Wolkenstein Gemahlin* (Weißenhorn: Konrad, 1983);

Alan Robertshaw, *Oswald von Wolkenstein: The Myth and the Man* (Göppingen: Kümmerle, 1977);

Walter Röll, *Oswald von Wolkenstein* (Darmstadt: Wissenschaftliche Buchgesellschaft, 1981);

Anton Schwob, *Historische Realität und literarische Umsetzung: Beobachtungen zur Stilisierung der Gefangenschaft in den Liedern Oswalds von Wolkenstein* (Innsbruck: Institut für Germanistik, 1979);

Johannes Spicker, *Literarische Stilisierung und artistische Kompetenz bei Oswald von Wolkenstein* (Stuttgart & Leipzig: Hirzel, 1993);

Burghart Wachinger, "Sprachmischung bei Oswald von Wolkenstein," *Zeitschrift für deutsches Altertum und deutsche Literatur,* 106 (1977): 277–296;

Stephen L. Wailes, "Oswald von Wolkenstein and the Alterslied," *Germanic Review,* 50 (1975): 5–18.

Paracelsus
(Philippus Aureolus Theophrastus Bombastus von Hohenheim)
(10 November? 1493 – 24 September 1541)

Gerhild Scholz Williams
Washington University, Saint Louis

SELECTED BOOKS: *Von der Frantzösischen Krankheit. Drey Bücher* (Nuremberg: Friedrich Peypus, 1530);

Usslegung des Commeten erschynen im hochgebirg, zu mitlem Augsten/Anno 1531 (Zurich, 1531);

Prognostication auff XXIIII jar zukünfftig (Augsburg: Heinrich Steiner, 1536);

Der grossenn Wundartzney, 2 volumes (Augsburg: Heinrich Steiner, 1536, 1537);

Von der Frantzösischen kranckheit drey Bücher (Frankfurt am Main: Herman Gülfferich, 1553);

Labyrinthus medicorum errantium (Nuremberg: Valentinum Neuberum, 1553);

Liber quatuor De vita longa (Basel, 1560);

Das Buch Paramirum (Mühlhausen: Peter Schmid, 1562);

Von Ursprung und Herkommen der tartarischen kranckheiten (Cologne: Arnold Byrckmann's heirs, 1564);

Die elf Traktat von Ursprung, Ursachen, Zeichen und Kur einzelner Krankheiten (Cologne: Arnold Birckmann's heirs, 1564);

Labyrinthus medicorum errantius: Von Irrgang und Labyrinth der Artzten (Cologne: Arnold Birckmann's heirs, 1564);

Die Verantwortung über ertzliche Verunglimpfung (Cologne: Arnold Birckmann's heirs, 1564);

Das Buch Paragranum (Frankfurt am Main: Christian Egenolff's heirs, 1565);

De morbis invisibilibus, das ist: Von den unsichtbaren Krankheiten (Cologne: Arnold Birckmann's heirs, 1565);

Ex libro de nymphis, sylphis, pygmaeus et salamandris et caeteris spiritibus (Neisse: Johann Cruciger, 1566);

Libri Duo. Defensiones septem. II. De Tartaro, sive morbis Tartareis (Argentorati: Christan Mylius, 1566);

Von der Bergsucht oder Bergkranckheiten drey Bücher (Dilingen: Sebaldum Meyer, 1567);

Paracelsus in 1538; engraving by Augustin Hirschvogel

Archidoxae Libri X (Kraków: Mathias Wirzbieta, 1569); translated by James Howell as *Paracelsus His Archidoxes . . . in Ten Books. Disclosing the Genuine Way of Making Quintessences, Arcanums, Magisteries, Elixirs, etc.* (Oxford & London: Printed for Giles Calvert, 1659);

Astronomia magna; oder, Die gantze Philosophia sagax der großen und der kleinen Welt, edited by Michael Toxites (Frankfurt am Main: Printed by Martin Lechler for Hieronymus Feyerabend, 1571).

Editions and collections: *Bücher vnd Schrifften des edlen . . . Philippi Theophrasti Bombast von Hohenheim . . . jetzt auffs new auss den Originalien vnd Theophrasti eigner Handschrifft . . . an Tag geben,* 10 volumes, edited by Johann Huser (Basel: Waldkirch, 1589–1591);

Paracelsus: Sämtliche Werke. I. Abteilung: Medizinische, naturwissenschaftliche und philosophische Schriften, 14 volumes, edited by Karl Sudhoff (Munich &

Berlin: Oldenbourg, 1922-1933);

Paracelsus: Sämtliche Werke. II. Abteilung: Theologische und religionsphilosophische Schriften, volume 1, *Philosophia magna,* edited by Wilhelm Matthießen (Munich: Barth, 1923);

Sämtliche Werke, 4 volumes, translated and edited by Bernhard Aschner (Jena: G. Fischer, 1932);

Paracelsus: Sozialethische und sozialpolitische Schriften, edited by Goldammer (Tübingen: Niemeyer, 1952);

Paracelsus: Sämtliche Werke. II. Abteilung: Theologische und religionsphilosophische Schriften, 8 volumes published, edited by Kurt Goldammer (Wiesbaden: Steiner, 1955-);

Paracelsus: Werke, 5 volumes, edited by Will-Erich Peuckert (Darmstadt: Wissenschaftliche Buchgesellschaft, 1965-1976).

Editions in English: *Paracelsus of the Supreme Mysteries of Nature, of the Spirits of the Planets, Occult, Philosophy, the Magical, Sympathetical and Antipathetical Cure of Wounds and Diseases. The Mysteries of the 12 Signs of the Zodiac,* translated by Robert Turner (London: Printed by J. C. for N. Brook and J. Harrison, 1656; New York: Weiser, 1975);

Paracelsus of the Chymical Transmutation, Genealogy, and Generation of Metals & Minerals. Also, of the Urim and Thumim of the Jews, translated by Turner (London: Printed for Richard Moon & Henry Fletcher, 1657);

The Hermetic and Alchemical Writings of Aureolus Philippus Theophrastus Bombast, 2 volumes, edited by Arthur Edward Waite (London: Elliott, 1894; Chicago: De Laurence, Scott, 1910);

Paracelsus: Selected Writings, edited by Jolande Jacobi, translated by Norbert Guterman (New York: Pantheon, 1958).

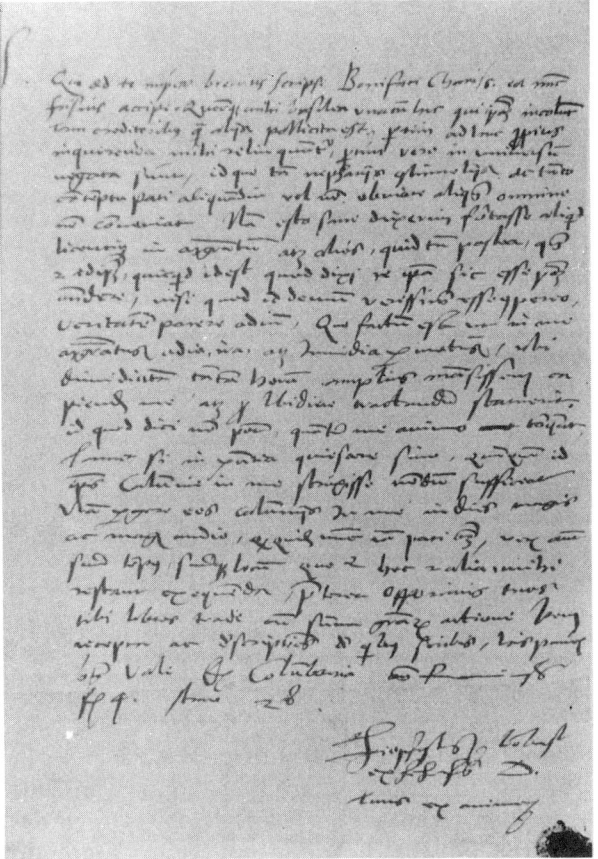

Letter from Paracelsus to the Basel City Council, 1527 (Staatsarchiv, Basel, Stadt)

As a physician, natural philosopher, alchemist, magus, astronomer, astrologer, lay theologian, religious philosopher, and social thinker, Paracelsus influenced the thinking of sixteenth-century intellectuals in significant ways. His concept of magic as a universal system of scientific and theoretical inquiry into the relationship of God, nature, and humanity had a profound impact on the way the European scientific and religious communities would think about the cosmos and humanity's place in it. His insistence on lecturing and writing in German—a gesture of defiance against the university establishment—was a forecast of the ultimate fate of Latin as the universal scholarly language. His vast learning, his extended wanderings across Europe, and his ability to think synchretistically enabled him to blend his critical analysis of the revered authorities of antiquity and the Middle Ages with the knowledge of contemporary scholars, as well as of common folk. The result was a cosmology that was as original as it was arcane. It is the arcana that make Paracelsus the darling of New Age followers of the twentieth century; for more mainstream scholars and students, Paracelsus's writings remain important for understanding early modern science and theosophical thinking.

Philippus Aureolus Theophrastus Bombastus von Hohenheim was born on 10 November (the date is sometimes given as 17 December) 1493 in Einsiedeln, Canton Schwyz, Switzerland. His father, the physician Wilhelm von Hohenheim, came from a family of the Swabian petit nobility from around Stuttgart in southwestern Germany; the family of his mother, Elsa, née Ochsner, had service ties to the monastery of Einsiedeln. The young Hohenheim went to school in Villach, Carinthia, where his father worked as the town physician and as a teacher in the local mining school.

It is now believed that Hohenheim left Villach in 1509, possibly bound for Vienna. His whereabouts are unknown prior to 1512, when records show him at the University of Ferrara. In 1516 he

Title page for Paracelsus's book on a comet that appeared in August 1531

may have passed examinations in *Leib- und Wundarznei* (academic and surgical medicine), the two arts of healing. During his sojourn in Italy, Paracelsus seems to have first come into contact with the thought of the fifteenth-century Florentine Neo-Platonists Marsilio Ficino and Giovanni Pico della Mirandola. From this period date his seminal studies of the "French disease," syphilis. The years 1516 to 1524 seem to have been spent traveling throughout Europe, collecting information on folk medicine. During these travels he may have come into contact with the ideas of the radical Reformers whose opposition to the Protestant orthodoxy of Martin Luther, Huldrych Zwingli, and John Calvin were leading to increasing religious, political, and social tensions. He may have visited the centers of traditional Galenic medicine at Salamanca, Valladolid, Paris, Montpellier, and Salerno, against whose teaching practices he would polemicize vigorously in his later years. He may also have participated in several military campaigns as field physician.

By 1524 he was practicing medicine in Salzburg, but his support for the rebellious peasants soon forced him to flee the city. Two years later, in 1526, he applied for citizenship in Strasbourg as a *Wundarzt* (physician). In 1527, after having successfully treated Basel's best-known publisher, Johann Froben, he accepted a call to that city as *Stadtarzt* (city physician). An appointment to the faculty of the University of Basel established him as a member of the scholarly community; correspondence with Desiderius Erasmus of Rotterdam dates from this period. During this time he developed the theory that was published as *Von Ursprung und Herkommen der tartarischen kranckheiten* (On the Source and Origin of Stone-forming Illnesses, 1563). Acrimony arose between Hohenheim and the medical establishment, however, over his unorthodox healing methods, his use of German in his lectures, and his irreverent comments about book learning and traditional academic medicine. The resentment became open censure when, at the summer solstice of 1527, he burned several orthodox medical treatises in a public gesture of contempt for his physician colleagues at the university. He was forced to flee to Colmar, where he undertook his first experiments using mercury in an attempt to find a cure for syphilis. During this period he wrote commentaries on the Psalms and the Gospel of Matthew. In 1529 he was in Nuremberg, polemicizing against the use of Guajar wood as a remedy for syphilis. This activity brought him into conflict with the wealthy and powerful Fuggers, an Augsburg merchant family who held the monopoly in the Guajar trade. It was at this time that he began to use the name Paracelsus, indicating that he considered himself equal or superior to Celsus, the first-century Roman writer on medicine.

In 1530 he worked on *Das Buch Paragranum* (1565), the first comprehensive exposition of his theory of medicine. According to this theory, medicine rests on four supports or *Säulen* (columns): philosophy, astronomy, alchemy, and the less clearly defined notion of *virtus,* the moral and religious purity of the medical practitioner. *Das Buch Paragranum* takes philosophy to be the understanding of the two most active elements in nature: earth and water. Astronomy and astrology have to do with the unseen influence of the heavens on the human condition. Alchemy is the art of manipulating the four elements—earth, water, air, and fire—and all plants and minerals in order to understand and set free their hidden forces in the service of healing human ailments. Virtus imbues medicine with high moral and religious standing, making medicine the most noble of scientific enterprises.

Toward the end of 1530 and in the early months of 1531, in Nuremberg and Saint Gall, Paracelsus worked on *Das Buch Paramirum* (1562), elaborating his *Entientheorie* (theory of essences), which holds that each disease has its own *archeus* (essence) that is identifiable by the physician. Sickness is caused by the archeus of a disease fighting against the archeus of the healthy body; divine wisdom has established that somewhere in nature a plant or mineral can be found with the right properties to fight the archeus of any illness, and it is the physician's task to discover and administer these agents.

At this time Paracelsus wrote *De morbis invisi-*

bilibus, das ist: Von den unsichtbaren Krankheiten (Of Invisible Illnesses, 1565), an influential study of diseases of the mind, such as visions, melancholy, delusions, and madness. In this book, contrary to the received opinion of the time, Paracelsus sees mental illness as a natural phenomenon, even though its symptoms may not be as easily identified as those of obviously physical ailments such as the plague or syphilis. Healing must include balancing the elemental and spiritual forces of body and soul through the use of appropriate distillations and the application of spiritual healing—the latter not to be confused with exorcism, a practice he condemns as superstitious and ineffectual. He also produced a tract on the appearance of what would later become known as Halley's Comet, which he observed in Saint Gall on 17 August 1531. His *Usslegung des Commeten erschynen im hochgebirg, zu mitlem Augsten/Anno 1531* (Interpretation of the Comet That Appeared in the Mountains, during the Middle of August in the Year 1531) appeared in print in Zurich shortly after the event.

In 1536 Paracelsus completed what was to be his most successful and widely read work, *Der grossenn Wundartzney* (The Great Book of Medical Practice). Printed in Augsburg in 1536 and 1537, this first compendium of what was to become known as the bedrock of Paracelsian medicine was dedicated to Ferdinand I of Austria. It brings together much of what he had written previously on the treatment of wounds, syphilis, and mental illness and on the relationship between a virtuous life and the practice of medicine.

Paracelsus believed, as did many of his contemporaries, that the end of the world was near; horoscopes and prognostications of the Last Days circulated widely. Shortly after completing *Der grossen Wundartzney* he published *Prognostication auff XXIIII jar zukünfftig* (Prognostications about the Next Twenty-Four Years, 1536), a popular and often reprinted work. Paracelsus's prophetic writings, which combined interpretations of the book of Daniel and of Revelation and applied them to contemporary fears of the Last Judgment, bad harvests, pestilence, and political and religious upheavals, were highly valued by his contemporaries.

In 1537 Paracelsus completed the major exposition of his natural philosophy and cosmology, *Astronomia magna; oder, Die gantze Philosophia sagax der großen und der kleinen Welt* (Astronomia Magna; or, The Complete Discerning Philosophy of the Greater and the Smaller World, 1571), in which he establishes magic as the universal science of humanity's place in the universe, the science of all that is, both seen and unseen. The microcosm, hu-

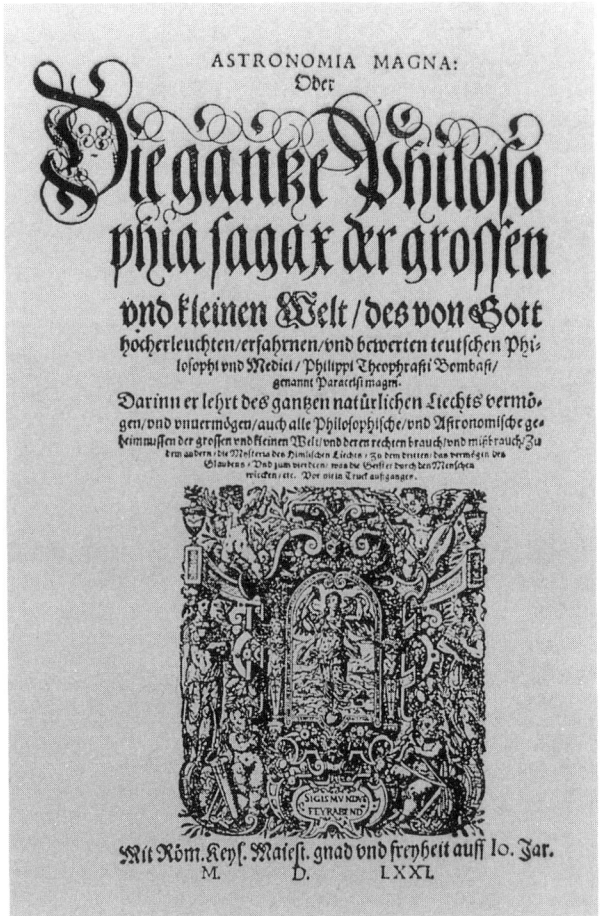

Title page for Paracelsus's major exposition of his natural philosophy and cosmology

mankind, is constituted in direct analogy to the macrocosm, the universe. Humanity, as a microcosm, holds within its essence three natures—the elemental (earthly), the astral (of the stars), and the divine—and lives and learns in the light of nature and the light of the heavens. Created after God had brought everything else into being, humankind contains all the constituent matter of the universe; for this reason human beings can comprehend and, ultimately, manipulate the forces of the universe. Humankind's mission on earth is to strive for an ever more profound understanding by studying the two books that contain all knowledge, the Book of Nature and the Book of God (the Bible). All of creation is united in a vast cosmos that will be known to the inquiring mind of the devout and virtuous magus, because God has destined humanity to know. The *Astronomia magna* is Paracelsus's attempt to create a system that combines theology, astronomy, and physical science. It has been called a work of Protestant mysticism, and it remains the most arcane and challenging of his writings. Other works written in the 1530s but not published until much later include

Paracelsus the year before his death; engraving by Hirschvogel

Ex libro de nymphis, sylphis, pygmaeus et salamandris et caeteris spiritibus (Book of Nymphs, Sylphs, Pigmies, and Salamanders and Other Spirits, 1566) and "De sagis" (On Witches), which appeared in his *Archidoxae Libri X* (1569; translated as *Paracelsus His Archidoxes . . . In Ten Books,* 1659). In the former work he affirms the reality of elemental spirits and their ability to acquire souls if wedded to humans until death. In the latter fragment he offers tantalizing observations on the nature and reality of witches.

In 1538 Paracelsus returned to Villach. He soon moved on to Saint Veit, where he produced a chronicle of Kärnten; a polemical tract, *Labyrinthus medicorum errantius: Vom Irrgang der Ärzte* (Of the Confusion of Physicians); and *Die Verantwortung über ertzliche Verunglimpfung* (1564), an apologia of his life and work. In 1540 he received an offer to become physician to Archbishop Ernst of Wittelsbach in Salzburg. He died on 24 September 1541 and was buried in Saint Sebastian, the cemetery for the poor in Salzburg.

Paracelsus wrote most of his works in German, liberally mixing in Latin terms and phrases. Seeking a language that would adequately express his new philosophical, theological, social, and medical speculations, he invented many new words and categories, earning the honorific "the Luther of Medicine" during his lifetime.

Now and again Paracelsus's writings afford the reader a glimpse of radical Protestant ideas. In spite of his obvious sympathies for the radical reform movements of the 1520s and 1530s, however, Paracelsus never officially left the Catholic faith. But he did reject what he called the *Mauerkirche* (walled church)—the ecclesiastical establishment—in favor of a more direct, evangelical relationship with God. He thought that the Catholic Church had fallen from its erstwhile state of purity and that the Protestant Reformation had become petrified in a deplorable state of orthodoxy. The "True Church" could be found in the writings and actions of those who were called heretics, among whom were many radical Reformers. Paracelsus's commentaries on biblical and patristic texts include much acerbic criticism of the church and an intense concern for the poor.

While he shared many of the misogynist tenets of his time, Paracelsus said repeatedly that women were created with the same nature as men and were their equals. He followed the Reformers in his praise of marriage as a divinely ordained state, the cornerstone of civil and familial order and harmony; he rejected adult virginity and celibacy as contrary to nature and to men's and women's duty to live in harmony and to raise children to become responsible adults. He repeatedly stressed the importance of education for men and women as a defense against satanic temptations.

Paracelsus's restless wanderings and his tireless search for knowledge found expression in his positive valuation of *experientia* (experience) and *curiositas* (curiosity). He believed that only those who saw and heard for themselves what was visible as well as what was hidden in nature and in the heavens could gain true understanding. He had contempt for the scholars who remained in their studies and ignored the world of experience.

Bibliographies:

Adam von Bodenstein, *Onomasticon Theophrasti Paracelsi* (Basel: Peter Perna, 1575);

Karl Sudhoff, *Bibliographia Paracelsica* (Berlin: Reimer, 1894);

Sudhoff, *Nachweise zur Paracelsusliteratur (1589–1932)* (Munich: Beilage zu Acta Paracelsica, 1932);

Karl-Heinz Weimann, *Paracelsus-Bibliographie 1932–1960* (Wiesbaden: Steiner, 1963).

Biographies:

Henry M. Pachter, *Paracelsus: Magic into Science* (New York: Schuman, 1951);

Ernst Kaiser, *Paracelsus in Selbstzeugnissen und Bilddokumenten* (Reinbeck: Rowohlt, 1969);

Frank Geerk, *Paracelsus: Arzt unserer Zeit. Leben, Werk und Wirkungsgeschichte des Theophrastus von Hohenheim* (Zurich: Benzinger, 1992);

Pirmin Meier, *Paracelsus: Arzt und Prophet. Annäherung an Theophrastus von Hohenheim,* third edition (Zurich: Amman, 1993).

References:

Kilian Blümlein, *Naturerfahrung und Welterkenntnis: Der Beitrag des Paracelsus zur Entwicklung des neuzeitlichen naturwissenschaftlichen Denkens* (Frankfurt am Main: Peter Lang, 1992);

Allen Debus, *The Chemical Philosophy: Paracelsian Science and Medicine in the 16th and 17th Centuries* (New York: Science History Publications, 1977);

Debus, *The French Paracelsians: The Chemical Challenge to Medical and Scientific Tradition in Early Modern France* (Cambridge: Cambridge University Press, 1991);

Debus, *Science, Medicine, and Society in the Renaissance* (New York: Science History Publications, 1972);

Peter Dilg and Hartmut Rudolph, eds., *Neue Beiträge zur Paracelsus-Forschung,* Hohenheimer Protokolle, no. 47 (Stuttgart: Adademie der Diözese Rottenburg-Stuttgart, 1995);

Sepp Domandl, *Erziehung und Menschenbild bei Paracelsus: Anfänge einer verantwortungsvollen Pädagogik* (Vienna: Nohring, 1970);

Heinz Dopsch, Kurt Goldammer, and Peter F. Kramml, eds., *Paracelsus (1493–1541): "Keines andern Knecht..."* (Salzburg: Pustet, 1993);

Kurt Goldammer, *Der göttliche Magier und die Magierin Natur: Religion, Naturmagie und die Anfänge der Naturwissenschaft vom Spätmittelalter bis zur Renaissance. Mit Beiträgen zum Magie-Verständnis des Paracelsus* (Stuttgart: Steiner, 1991);

Alexandre Koyré, *Mystiques, spiritualistes, alchemistes: Schwenckfeldt, Sebastian Franck, Weigel, Paracelsus* (Paris: Colin, 1955);

Erwin Metzke, *Coincidentia oppositorum* (Witten: Luther Verlag, 1961);

Walter Pagel, *Das medizinische Weltbild des Paracelsus: Seine Zusammenhänge mit dem Neoplatonismus und der Gnosis* (Wiesbaden: Steiner, 1962);

Will-Erich Peuckert, *Gabalia: Ein Versuch zur Geschichte der Magia naturalis im 16. bis 18. Jahrhundert* (Berlin: Schmidt, 1967);

Heinrich Schipperges, *Paracelsus: Der Mensch im Licht der Natur* (Stuttgart: Klett, 1974);

Joachim Telle, ed., *Pererga Paracelsica: Paracelsus in Vergangenheit und Gegenwart* (Stuttgart: Steiner, 1991);

Charles Webster, *From Paracelsus to Newton: Magic and the Making of Modern Science* (Cambridge: Cambridge University Press, 1982);

Gerhild Scholz Williams, *Defining Dominion: The Discourses of Magic and Witchcraft in Early Modern France and Germany* (Ann Arbor: University of Michigan Press, 1995), pp. 45–65.

Papers:

Among the repositories of Paracelsus's papers are the Herzog-August-Bibliothek Wolfenbüttel, the Universitätsbibliothek Munich, the Universitätsbibliothek Zurich, and the Medical School Library of Washington University in Saint Louis.

Caritas Pirckheimer
(21 March 1467 – 19 August 1532)

Paula Datsko Barker
Seabury-Western Theological Seminary

MAJOR WORKS: *Deutsche Chronik des Klaraklosters / Lateinische Chronik des Klaraklosters* (circa 1500)
Manuscripts: Pirckheimer was instrumental in the creation by nuns in her convent of two unbound manuscript chronicles recounting the history of their Nuremberg convent in connection with the histories of the Franciscan and Poor Clare religious orders. Her handwriting appears in corrections and editorial instructions in the *Deutsche Chronik* and the *Lateinische Chronik,* held in the Nuremberg Staatsarchiv (Reichsstadt Nürnberg, Kloster Saint Klara, Akten und Bände, Rep. 5a, nos. 1 and 2, respectively). A fragmentary rough draft in German also can be found in the same collection (no. 3). A clean copy on parchment of the *Deutsche Chronik* is held by the Bayerisches Nationalmuseum in Munich (Ms. 1191);

Denkwürdigkeiten (1528)
Manuscripts: This text, compiled under Pirckheimer's editorial supervision, includes many documents written by Pirckheimer during the Reformation crisis. Four manuscript copies exist in the Nuremberg Staatsarchiv (Reichsstadt Nürnberg, Kloster Saint Klara, Akten und Bände, Rep. 5, codices A, B, C, D). Codex D is the earliest: five hands contributed to it, and Pirckheimer's handwriting is evident in the editorial comments and directions. Codex A is a clean copy based on D, as are codices B and C. The latter two were completed at the Poor Clare convent of Bamberg in the early seventeenth century. The original is untitled; the commonly used name *Denkwürdigkeiten* derives from the first publication.
First publication: *Der hochberühmten Charitas Pirkheimer, Äbtissin von S. Clara zu Nürnberg, Denkwürdigkeiten aus dem Reformationszeitalter,* edited by Constantin Höfler, in *Bericht über das Wirken des historischen Vereins zu Bamberg,* volume 15 (Bamberg: Reindl, 1852).
Standard edition: "Die 'Denkwürdigkeiten' der Caritas Pirckheimer," edited by Josef Pfan-

Caritas Pirckheimer

ner, in *Caritas Pirckheimer–Quellensammlung,* volume 2, edited by the Caritas Pirckheimer-Forschung (Landshut: Solanus-Druck, 1962).
An Heroic Abbess of Reformation Days: The Memoirs of Mother Charitas Pirkheimer, Poor Clare, of Nuremberg, excerpted and translated by Francis Mannhardt (Saint Louis: Central Bureau Catholic Verein of America, 1930).

Caritas Pirckheimer was born into a family that valued humanist scholarship and monastic life. She pursued both in exemplary fashion, employing her learning to cultivate devotion. When the Lutheran reformers of Nuremberg began to attack monastic life and attempted to force the nuns to leave their convents, she vigorously defended her way of life. Her efforts enabled her convent and others in the Nuremberg territory to survive, at least temporarily. Whereas other women facing similar circumstances during the Reformation quietly capitulated or went into hiding, Pirckheimer argued with the authorities. The status and the skills that she had developed through her engagement with humanist scholarship made this unusual response to the Reformation possible.

Barbara Pirckheimer was born in the Bavarian city of Eichstätt on 21 March 1467. She was the first child of Johann Pirckheimer, a jurist and diplomat from a patrician family of Nuremberg, and Barbara Löffelholz Pirckheimer. Aside from a sister and two brothers who died young, she had eight sisters, all but one of whom would enter convents, and a brother, Willibald, who would become notable among the humanists of Germany. Her family had a tradition of achievement in education and of special interest in humanist scholarship. These activities were not limited to the male members of the family: her great-aunt Katharina was a learned woman, as were her sister Clara and her niece Katharina.

At the age of twelve Pirckheimer entered the convent of Saint Clare in Nuremberg. The convent had a substantial library, a community of literate nuns, and a series of preachers and confessors assigned from the nearby Franciscan friary. After two years she won permission to make her vows, even though she had not yet reached the required age, by impressing the Franciscan vicar general with her knowledge of Latin. By 1485 she had adopted the name Caritas (Charity).

The first manuscripts connected with her are transcriptions of sermons by the Franciscans Stephan Fridolin and Heinrich Vigilis, both of whom served as preachers in the convent of Saint Clare. These transcriptions exist in copies made by other nuns during Pirckheimer's lifetime and conclude with notations, added after her death, that the texts were based on transcripts Pirckheimer had made "von Wort zu Wort" (word for word) from the sermons as they were preached.

Another Franciscan who engaged Pirckheimer's attention was the historian Nicholas Glassberger. As confessor for the convent from 1483 until his death in 1508, he encouraged the nuns' creation, under Pirckheimer's editorial supervision, of Latin and German versions of a chronicle of the early history of the Order of Saint Clare and of the Nuremberg convent. Tales about Saints Francis, Clare, and Agnes, along with testimonies about the wholeheartedness with which the Nuremberg sisters embraced reform and about their efforts to lead other convents into "holy observance," evoke admiration for those who will not settle for less than a rigorous form of religious life. The narrative is reinforced at crucial points with texts of relevant documents that have been copied into the manuscripts. The chronicles reflect the humanist interest in original source materials and in drawing from the past lessons that will inspire virtuous action in the present.

While engaged in this historical work Pirckheimer began exchanging letters in Latin with several leading figures of German humanism. One of these correspondents was Sixtus Tucher; his letters to her survive in a German translation published in 1515 by his nephew Christoph Scheurl, who was also an enthusiast for humanist studies and an admirer of Pirckheimer. The letters reveal a relationship characterized by mutual personal affection, a theme that echoes repeatedly in discussions of Pirckheimer by her male humanist contemporaries. These men legitimized Pirckheimer's scholarly activity, and their own role in encouraging it, by referring to the example of the learned virgins who were instructed by Saint Jerome. Pirckheimer used this analogy herself when she wrote to thank her brother Willibald for dedicating his Latin translation of the works of Plutarch (1513) to her.

Willibald actively promoted her learning: he refined her use of Latin and encouraged her exploration of classical and patristic texts by lending her volumes from his extensive library and by sending her copies of new publications. He dedicated three books to her, each with a preface acclaiming her learning. Through his efforts Pirckheimer became known to the humanists Johannes Reuchlin, Desiderius Erasmus, and Conrad Celtis, as well as to many lesser figures. Reuchlin sent her a copy of his translation of Athanasius's treatise on virgins; Erasmus sent her greetings and compared her, along with her sister Clara, to the learned daughters of Thomas More; and Celtis composed for her an epistle and an ode that attempted to elevate her to the level of a national symbol.

Celtis's epistle and ode for Pirckheimer were dedicatory pieces attached, respectively, to his description of Nuremberg (1502) and his edition of the works of Hrotsvit of Gandersheim (1501), the tenth-century canoness whose Latin dramas he had recently discovered in a monastery library. Celtis was waging a cultural battle, attempting to establish the ascendancy of German over Italian culture, and he drafted Hrotsvit for service in this battle by portraying her as a German counterpart to the great women of classical antiquity. Pirckheimer received the same treatment at his hands: she became the contemporary manifestation of Hrotsvit. Pirckheimer wrote two letters in response to Celtis. They were published in 1515 by Friedrich Pepys, the noted Nuremberg printer of humanist works, along with three letters she had written to Willibald. Pepys included a preface in which he praised Pirckheimer as a special ornament of the feminine sex and of their city.

In writing to her brother and to Celtis, Pirckheimer, using a familiar rhetorical device, describes herself as unworthy for the task. To her brother she writes: "Non enim, ut ipse scis, docta sum, tametsi amatrix doctorum" (You know that I am not learned but merely a friend of learned men). Yet she continues, with a flourish of rhetorical eloquence that plays on the meaning of her name, to commend him for dedicating his book to Caritas, or Charity, since charity makes good things available for everyone. Similarly, her first letter to Celtis, thanking him for the dedication of his edition of the writings of Hrotsvit, rehearses the theme of the humble female while making a claim for the legitimacy of female scholarship on religious grounds:

> Ceterum superioribus diebus accepi etiam scripta amabilia Rosuitae virginis doctissimae, a vestra dominatione mihi exiguae, nullis meis meritis exigentibus, destinata, unde immortales gratias ago et habeo, gaudeo autem quod largitor ingenii, non solum iuris sapientibus et doctis profundam sapientiam impartiri solet, sed et fragili sexui abiectisque personis, aliquando non denegat micas de mensa divitum doctorum cadentes. Verificatum est in illa prudentissima virgine illud apostoli: Infirma mundi elegit Deus, ut fortia quaeque confundat.
>
> (A few days ago I received the lovely writings of the learned virgin Hrotsvit, which your lordship sent to me for no merits of my own, for which I have eternal thanks. I rejoice that he who bestows powers of mind grants deep wisdom not only to right-thinking and learned men, but also does not deny to the weak and humbler sex a few crumbs that fall from the tables of the richly learned. In this wise virgin is fulfilled the apostle's statement: "God chooses the weak of the world to confound the strong.")

In her second letter to Celtis, Pirckheimer proceeds again from an assertion of her unworthiness. Then, with expressions of religious concern for him, she exhorts him not to abandon the pursuit of worldly wisdom but to direct his scholarship toward higher purposes: "Enimvero non est culpanda scientia aut quaevis rei notitia, quae bona est, etsi considerata et a Deo ordinata, sed praeferenda est semper mystica theologia ac bona et virtuosa vita" (Indeed, neither knowledge nor any subject of investigation that is considered good and is ordained by God is to be condemned, but mystical theology and a good virtuous life must be preferred).

Pirckheimer clearly did not view her involvement in humanist studies as posing a danger to her religious life; yet when she was elected abbess of her convent in 1503, one of her Franciscan superiors ordered her to terminate her Latin correspondence. The injunction illustrates the ambiguous conditions in which female humanists functioned: women's learning could be applied only in the private sphere of cloistered religious life. Pirckheimer adhered to the monastic humanist tradition, which had been endowed with new strength through the monastic reform movements of the late Middle Ages. Learning was viewed as a means of improving religious life within the cloister; it was a spiritual discipline that purified the affections and directed them toward their proper end, God. Thus, for Pirckheimer, commitment to religious life was the reference point for her studies. Her circumstances as a woman gave this correlation additional significance: it was only because humanist studies had value for religious life that she, a woman, could engage in them at all. Monastic life offered her both the opportunity and the rationale for scholarship.

The principal threat that the Lutheran Reformation posed for Pirckheimer was its attack on monastic life. Martin Luther taught that each person's hope for salvation must rest on faith in Christ's righteousness, not on personal attempts to become righteous through asceticism or good deeds. Consequently, some monks and nuns left their religious communities and married. Political authorities who supported Luther attempted to exert control over, and ultimately to close, the monasteries and convents.

Initially, Pirckheimer's activity against the Reformation consisted of defending traditional beliefs against what she perceived as the Lutheran heresy. In the first of her letters that mention the Reformation, written in December 1521, she urges her cousin in Augsburg to hold to the old, true faith of her childhood rather than suffer injury to her soul, as so many others had done, through the seduction of the new teaching. Six months later she wrote a letter of appreciation to the theologian Hieronymus Emser for his efforts in refuting Luther. She describes the joy exhibited by the sisters when his book was read in the refectory, reveals that she sent the book far and wide to many convents, and urges him not to allow himself to be silenced, so that their descendants may see "daz nich alle menschen yn deutscher nation dyßer verfluchten ketzerey haben nachgefolget" (that not everyone in the German nation followed after this cursed heresy). The letter was intercepted by Lutheran sympathizers, who published it in 1523 with a satiric commentary in an attempt to discredit Pirckheimer.

After Nuremberg's governing council began to move against the monasteries and convents in the city at the end of 1524, Pirckheimer's focus shifted to defending her convent and its way of life. This focus is evident from the way she structured her *Denkwürdigkeiten* (Memoirs, 1528) on the Reformation and from the material she included.

The *Denkwürdigkeiten* consists of a series of letters and reports by Pirckheimer and by her principal antagonists. She selected, organized, annotated, and supervised the copying of the documents to create a permanent account of her view of what had transpired. Judging from the sections that reproduce letters that still exist independently, the documents were copied without significant alteration. Caspar Bruschius, a mid-sixteenth-century historian, consulted the work in composing his history of German monasteries.

The story Pirckheimer tells begins with the council expelling the Franciscan preachers and confessors from the convent and replacing them with Lutheran pastors who harangued the nuns in chapel. Four months later the council prohibited Pirckheimer from enforcing among the nuns the traditional monastic practices of regular prayer, fasts, vows, the wearing of habits, and enclosure. The council also determined that parents should be allowed to remove their daughters from the convents, even against the daughters' will. Consequently, three nuns were attacked and removed forcibly from the convent of Saint Clare by their parents in a violent scene that Pirckheimer describes passionately and in apocalyptic terms.

Pirckheimer employed her considerable skills and prestige to argue with the authorities and cultivate support for her cause. The authorities were well aware of the esteem with which her opinions were regarded by others; one who had been acclaimed as a special ornament to her city could not be brushed aside easily. Her elevated status is evident in her report of a conversation with an emissary from the council:

> Es hetten sich doch all prelatten in seiner herrn clostern gutwillig erzaigt, wollten all volgen, dann allein ich wer so halßstreytig und machet auch den c[onvent] widerspenig wider sein herrn; wenn ich woll wollt und den c[onvent] darzu hilt, so het er keinen zwiffel, dy swester wurden all gern volgen, es wer aber daz geschrey uber mich, daz ich nit alleyn meinen convent gegen den herrn verweißet, sunder auch alle umbligente frawencloster, dy all rat pey mir suchenten und sagten, wy ich mich hyelt, wollten sy sich auch hallten. Darumb wen ich mich bekeret, so wurd sich daz ganz lant bekern.

(All the prelates in the monasteries had shown themselves willing; all wished to follow; I alone was stubborn and turned the convent against [the council]. If I truly wanted and helped the convent in it, he was sure the sisters would all gladly follow. There was, however, the outcry about me that I did not just lead my convent against [the council] but also all the surrounding convents, which all sought my advice and said whatever stance I took they would also take. Therefore, if I converted, the entire land would convert.)

At the end of this year of tribulation Luther's colleague Melanchthon agreed to meet with Pirckheimer. She reported on their meeting in glowing terms. He had spoken at length about the new teaching, she says, until he was persuaded by Pirckheimer that the foundation of the nuns' lives was trust in the grace of God rather than in their own works. He conceded that they could live in the convent, as well as in the world, if only they would not hold themselves bound by their vows. But she could not agree to nullify vows. Threatened with the dismantling of the institutional structure that made her way of life possible, she was struggling to maintain its defining features as best she could. Melanchthon parted with her on friendly terms, and he advised the council to leave the nuns in peace. As a result, not only Pirckheimer's convent but all the convents in the Nuremberg territory were permitted to remain, though novices could no longer be admitted.

In 1529 Willibald Pirckheimer delivered an eloquent Latin *Oratio apologetica* to the council on behalf of the nuns. The text of the speech is written in a plural feminine voice and repeats Caritas's arguments throughout; it was probably the product of a collaboration between her and Willibald. The oration responds to the three principal complaints that continued to be raised against the nuns: that they spurned the gospel by trusting in their own works for salvation, that they stubbornly relied on human traditions and remained loyal to the Pope, and that they refused to leave their convent to marry. It concludes with a recitation of the adversities that the nuns had endured. A notation at the end of the manuscript reports that the speech had no effect.

Having avoided the immediate threat of liquidation of the convent, Pirckheimer was left with the long-term struggle of sustaining religious life without sacramental support: since her refusal to accept the services of the Lutheran pastors was, at last, being honored, she had no sacraments at all. The loss was bitterly lamented. It appears, however, that the nuns did, at least on special occasions, go through the motions of receiving the Eucharist under Pirckheimer's leadership. A ceremony of spiritual communion was described to Willibald by his daughter Katharina in a letter reporting the convent's celebration of Caritas's twenty-fifth anniversary as abbess in 1529.

A book of prayers found in the Saint Clare convent has the name Caritas Pirckheimer written inside its front cover; until recently, scholars assumed that it was Pirckheimer's prayer book, perhaps one that was given to her on the occasion of her anniversary as abbess. It has been established, however, that the handwriting is that of a niece of Pirckheimer's, who had the same name and lived in the convent after the older Caritas Pirckheimer died. Since the book appears to have been created cumulatively, with various entries copied by diverse hands, and since some of the earlier handwriting samples match those in other works dating from Pirckheimer's period of residence in the convent, one may conclude that the book was at least begun during the elder Caritas's lifetime and eventually found its way into the younger Caritas's possession.

Pirckheimer died on 19 August 1532. In the death records of her convent she is memorialized with tender words of devotion for her piety and learning and with gratitude for her leadership during the Reformation crisis.

Pirckheimer's literary accomplishments did not approach those of the luminaries with whom she associated. Yet from her case one can observe how humanist studies were appropriated by a woman, how the male leaders of humanism viewed such a woman, and how such a woman viewed herself in relation to them. Similarly, Pirckheimer was not a significant force in the struggle of the Reformation, and her resistance had limited success. Yet her memoirs offer a gripping account of how the practical consequences of the Reformation were experienced by one who remained committed to late-medieval ideals of reformed religious life. Yet as scholarly inquiry probes beyond the great names, her bold testimony increasingly attracts fascinated scrutiny.

Letters:

Epistola Doctorus Scheurli ad Charitatem Abbatissam Sanctae Clarae de laudibus familiale Pyrckheymer . . . Epistole Reverende matris Charitatis Pirckheymerin Abbatisse Sancta Clarae (Nuremberg: Friedrich Peypus, 1515);

Eyn missyue oder Sendbrieff so die Aebtissche von Nuernberg und den hoch beruemptenn Bock Emser geschrieben hatt (Nuremberg: Hieronymus Höltzel, 1523);

Briefe der Äbtissin Caritas Pirckheimer des St. Klara-Klosters zu Nürnberg nach der Erstveröffentlichung von Dr. Josef Pfanner, translated into modern German by Benedicta Schrott, edited by Georg Deichstetter (Saint Ottilie: EOS, 1984).

Biographies:

Wilhelm Loose, *Aus dem Leben der Charitas Pirchkheimer, Abtissin zu St. Clara in Nürnberg: Nach Briefen* (Dresden: Heinrich, 1870);

Johannes Kist, *Charitas Pirckheimer: Ein Frauenleben im Zeitalter des Humanismus und der Reformation* (Bamberg: Meisenback, 1948);

Gerta Krabbel, *Caritas Pirckheimer: Ein Lebensbild aus der Zeit der Reformation* (Munster: Aschendorff, 1982).

References:

Paula Datsko Barker, "Caritas Pirckheimer: A Female Humanist Confronts the Reformation," *Sixteenth Century Journal,* 26 (1995): 259-272;

Barker, "A Mirror of Piety and Learning": Caritas Pirckheimer against the Reformation," dissertation, University of Chicago, 1990;

Gwendolyn Bryant, "Caritas Pirckheimer: The Nuremberg Abbess," in *Women Writers of the Renaissance and Reformation,* edited by Katharina Wilson (Athens: University of Georgia Press, 1987), pp. 287-303;

Georg Deichstetter, ed., *Caritas Pirckheimer: Ordensfrau und Humanistin–ein Vorbild für Okumene. Festschrift zum 450. Todestag* (Cologne: Wienand, 1982);

Deichstetter, ed., *Gebetbuch aus dem St. Klara-Kloster zu Nürnberg zur Zeit der Äbtissin Caritas Pirckheimer, 1467-1532, nach der Erstveröffentlichung von Dr. Josep Pfanner,* translated into modern German by Benedicta Schrott (Saint Ottilie: EOS, 1984);

Lina Eckenstein, *Woman under Monasticism* (New York: Russell & Russell, 1963);

Ursula Hess, "Oratrix Humilis: Die Frau als Briefpartnerin von Humanisten am Beispiel der Caritas Pirckheimer," *Mitteilungen der Kommission für Humanismusforschung,* 9 (1983): 173-203;

Christoph von Imhoff and Georg Deichstetter, *Caritas Pirckheimer und die Reformation in Nürnberg* (Nuremberg: Hofmann, 1982);

Margaret King, *Women of the Renaissance* (Chicago: University of Chicago Press, 1991);

Johannes Kist, *Das Klarissenkloster in Nürnberg bis zum Beginn des 16. Jahrhunderts* (Nuremberg: Sebaldus, 1929);

Lotte Kurras and Franz Machilek, eds., *Caritas Pirckheimer, 1467-1532: Eine Ausstellung der Katholischen Stadtkirche Nürnberg* (Munich: Prestel, 1982);

Walther von Loewenich, "Charitas Pirckheimer," *Jahrbuch für fränkische Landesforschung,* 31 (1971): 35-51;

Ernst Munch, *Charitas Pirckheimer, ihre Schwestern und Nichten* (Nuremberg: Campe, 1826);

Gerald O'Collins, "A Woman for All Seasons," *America*, 147 (1982): 212–213;

Catherine Bernardi Ryan, "Charitas Prickheimer: A Study of the Impact of the Clarine Tradition in the Process of Reformation in Nuremburg, 1525," dissertation, Ohio State University, 1976;

Karl Schlemmer, *Die frommen Nürnberger und die Äbtissin von St. Klara: Nürnberg als religiöse Stadt in der Lebenszeit der Caritas Pirckheimer* (Nuremburg: Vier-Türme, 1982);

Lewis Spitz, *Conrad Celtis: The German Arch-Humanist* (Cambridge, Mass.: Harvard University Press, 1957), pp. 85–87;

Spitz, *The Religious Renaissance of the German Humanists* (Cambridge, Mass.: Harvard University Press, 1963);

Gerald Strauss, *Nuremberg in the Sixteenth Century* (Bloomington: Indiana University Press, 1976);

August Syndikus, *Das Grab der Caritas Pirckheimer* (Landshut: Solanus-Druck, 1966);

Sixtus Tucher, *Vierzig Sendbriefe aus dem Latein in das Teutsch gezogen,* translated by Christoph Scheurl (Nuremberg: Friedrich Pepys, 1515);

Stephen L. Wailes, "The Literary Relationship of Conrad Celtis and Caritas Pirckheimer," *Daphnis,* 17 (1988): 423–440;

Adam Wienand, "Caritas Pirckheimer, Ordensfrau und Humanistin," in *Willibald Pirckheimer: Dürers Freund,* edited by Willihad Paul Eckert and Christoph von Imhoff (Cologne: Wienand, 1971);

Merry Wiesner, "Ideology Meets the Empire: Reformed Convents and the Reformation," in *Germania Illustrata: Essays on Early Modern Germany Presented to Gerald Strauss,* edited by Andrew Fix and Susan Karant-Nunn, Sixteenth Century Essays & Studies, no. 18 (Kirksville, Mo.: Sixteenth Century Journal, 1992), pp. 181–195;

E. Zeydel, "The Reception of Hrotsvitha by the German Humanists after 1493," *Journal of English and Germanic Philology,* 44 (1945): 239–259.

Papers:

Principal repositories of Caritas Pirckheimer's letters are the Germanisches National Museum, the Staatsarchiv, the Stadtarchiv, and the Stadtbibliothek, all in Nuremberg. The Bibliothek des Metropolitankapitels, Bamberg, holds a manuscript (Ms. 29) made by a nun in Pirckheimer's religious community, Barbara Stromer, based on Pirckheimer's verbatim transcription of sermons preached in the convent. Margaretha Kress, another nun in the convent, also created from Pirckheimer's transcriptions of sermons preached in the convent a manuscript (Ms. 3801) that is now held by the Bayerisches Nationalmuseum in Munich; corrections in Pirckheimer's handwriting occur on many pages.

Willibald Pirckheimer

(5 December 1470 – 22 December 1530)

Eckhard Bernstein
College of the Holy Cross

MAJOR WORKS: *Eccius dedolatus authore Joannefrancisco cotta Lembergio Poeta laureato* (Erfurt?: Matthäus Maler?, 1520?);

Apologia seu podagrae laus (Nuremberg: Friedrich Peypus, 1522); translated by William Est as *The Praise of the Govt, or, The Govts Apologie. A paradox, both pleasant and profitable* (London: Printed by G. Purslow for John Budge, 1617);

De vera Christi carne et vero eius sanguine, ad Ioan. Oecolampadius responsio (Nuremberg: Johann Petreius, 1526);

De uera Christi carne et uero eius sanguine, aduersus conuicia Ioannis, qui sibi Oecolampedij nomen indidit, responsio secunda (Nuremberg: Johann Petreius, 1527);

De convitiis monachi illius, qui graecolatine Caecolampadius, germanice vero Ausschin nuncupatur (Nuremberg: Johann Petreius, 1527);

Germaniae ex variis scriptoribus perbrevis explicatio (Nuremberg: Johann Petreius, 1530);

Priscorum Numismatum ad Nurembergensis Monetae valorem facta aestimatio (Tübingen: Ulrich Morhart, 1533);

Theatrvm Virtvtis et Honoris; oder, Tugend Büchlein, edited by Johann Im Hof (Nuremberg: P. Kaufmann, 1606);

Opera politica, historica, philologica et epistolica, edited by Melchior Goldast (Frankfurt am Main: Printed by Johann Bringer for Jacob Fischer, 1610).

Editions: "Eckius Dedolatus," in *Lateinische Literaturdenkmäler des 15. und 16. Jahrhunderts*, edited by Siegfried Szamatolski (Berlin: Speyer & Peters, 1891);

Willibald Pirckheimers Schweizerkrieg, edited by Karl Rück (Munich: Verlag der K. Akademie, 1895);

Opera politica, historica, philologica et epistolica, edited by Melchior Goldast (Hildesheim & New York: Olms, 1969);

Eckius dedolatus–Der entechte Eck, Lateinisch/Deutsch, edited and translated by Niklas Holzberg (Stuttgart: Reclam, 1983); translated by Thomas W. Best as *Eccius dedolatus: A Reformation Satire* (Lexington: University Press of Kentucky,

Willibald Pirckheimer in 1503; charcoal drawing by Albrecht Dürer (Kupferstichkabinett SMPK, Berlin)

1971);

Der Schweizerkrieg, edited by Wolfgang Schiel, translated by Ernst Münch (Berlin: Militärverlag der DDR, 1988).

OTHER: "Elegia Bilibaldi Pirckheymeri in obitum Alberti Düreri," in *Hierinn sind begriffen vier Bücher menschlicher Proportion*, by Albrecht Dürer (Nuremberg: Hieronymus Andreae, 1528);

"18 Propositiones contra digamiam episcoporum," in *De Digamia episcoporum propositiones Martini Lutheri* (Wittenberg: Hans Lufft, 1528).

TRANSLATIONS: Plutarch, *De his qui tarde a*

numine corripiuntur (Nuremberg: Friedrich Peypus, 1513);

Plutarch, *De vitanda usura ex greco in latinum traductus* (Nuremberg: Friedrich Peypus, 1515);

Lucian, *De ratione conscribendae historiae ex graeco in latinum traductus* (Nuremberg: Friedrich Peypus, 1515);

Saint Nilus Ancyranus, *Sententiae morales* (Nuremberg: Friedrich Peypus, 1516);

Lucian, *Piscator seu reviviscentes* (Nuremberg: Friedrich Peypus, 1517)—includes Pirckheimer's "Epistola apologetica";

Isocrates, *Ein nutzbar underweysung des hochberumbten redners Isokratis zu einem jugenn Demonicus genant* (Augsburg, 1519);

Lucian, *Luciani Rhetor a Bilibaldo Pirckhaimero in Latinum versus* (Hagenau: Thomas Anshelm, 1520);

Lucian, *Luciani Fugitivi a Bilibaldo Pirckaimero in Latinum versus* (Hagenau: Thomas Anshelm, 1520);

Gregory of Nazianzus, *Theologi orationes sex* (Nuremberg: Friedrich Peypus, 1521);

Lucian, *Navis seu vota* (Nuremberg: Friedrich Peypus, 1522);

Dialogi Platonis, Axiochus, vel de morte. Eryxias, vel de diuicijs. De Iusto Num virtus doceri possit (Nuremberg: Friedrich Peypus, 1523);

Plutarch, *De compescenda ira. De Garrulitate. De Curiositate. De iis qui sero a numine corripiuntur. De vitanda usura* (Nuremberg: Friedrich Peypus, 1523);

Ptolemy, *Claudii Ptolomaei Geographicae enarrationis libri octo,* 2 volumes (Strasbourg: Johann Grüninger, 1525);

Theophrastus, *Characteres. Cum interpretatione Latina per Bilibaldum Pirckheymerum, iam recens aedita* (Nuremberg: Johannes Petreius, 1527);

Gregory of Nazianzus, *Orationes duae Julianum Caesarem infamia notantes* (Nuremberg: Friedrich Peypus, 1528);

Gregory of Nazianzus, *Orationes XXX, Bilibaldo Pirckheimero interprete nunc primum editae* (Basel: Froben, 1531);

Saint Nilus Ancyrabus, *Vil schöner sprüch des heyligen Bischoves vnd Marterers S. Nili, zu Gottes furcht vnd zucht der jugent seer nutzlich* (Augsburg, 1536);

Xenophon, "Rerum graecarum liber primus, Bilibaldo Pirckemhero interp.," in *Xenophontis philosophi et historici clarissimi opera, partim Graecorum exemplarium collatione recognita, partim a uiris doctissimis iam pridem latinitate donata* (Basel: Andreas Cratander, 1543).

Willibald Pirckheimer was one of the most important representatives of German Renaissance humanism. A scholar who worked in philosophy, history, geography, theology, philology, ethics, astronomy, and astrology—Emperor Maximilian praised

Pirckheimer's bookplate

him as the most learned doctor in the empire—he was, at the same time, not a man of the ivory tower. For almost twenty-five years he served the imperial city of Nuremberg as city councillor, diplomat, and military leader. He had an excellent command of Latin, knew Hebrew, and was responsible, together with Rudolf Agricola, Conrad Celtis, Desiderius Erasmus of Rotterdam, and Philipp Melanchthon, for introducing Greek studies into Germany. A pioneer of classical archaeology and philology, he was also keenly interested in the visual arts. He corresponded with all of the major figures of the European Renaissance, so that, as Lewis W. Spitz observes, "a list of his correspondents reads like a dictionary of Renaissance scholars." His library, inherited from his father and expanded throughout his life, was one of the most extensive north of the Alps. With his many interests and skills he came closest to what the Italians called "uomo universale" (a universal man).

Pirckheimer was descended from a well-known patrician Nuremberg family. He was born on 5 December 1470 in Eichstätt to Barbara Pirckheimer, née Löffelholz, and Johann Pirckheimer, legal counselor to the bishop of Eichstätt. In 1478 his father moved to Munich, where for the next ten years he served Duke Albrecht IV of Bavaria and Duke Siegmund of Tirol in a variety of functions. Johann Pirckheimer introduced his son to literature and art, even taking the boy along on a diplomatic mission to Italy, Switzerland, and the Netherlands so as not to interrupt his instruction. In 1488-1489 Willibald Pirckheimer received a basic military and courtly training at the court of the bishop of Eichstätt. His wish, however, to embark on a career in the service of Emperor Maximilian I was thwarted by his father, who had other plans for him. Following a family tradition—both his grandfather and father had studied in Italy—Pirckheimer enrolled for the winter semester of 1489-1490 at the University of Padua, studying law but also the *studia humanitatis,* which included rhetoric, poetry, moral philosophy, and history. He was also introduced by Laurentius Camers to the fundamentals of Greek.

At the insistence of his father, who was afraid that his son was too distracted by humanist studies, Pirckheimer transferred to the University of Pavia in the fall of 1492. He returned to Germany in 1495 without an academic degree; his father had opposed his intention of obtaining a doctorate of law, which would have automatically excluded him from serving on the Nuremberg City Council. On 13 October 1495 Pirckheimer married the daughter of an impeccably patrician family, Crescentia Rieter, who had been selected by his father. Crescentia would die in 1504, following the birth of their sixth child, and Pirckheimer would never remarry. In 1496 Pirckheimer was elected to the city council, on which he would serve, with an interruption from 1502 to 1505, until 1523. Because of his legal training and his diplomatic skills, but also because of his phenomenal memory and superb command of Latin, he was on many occasions entrusted with undertaking missions within and outside the Holy Roman Empire, and, at least once, with leading the Nuremberg military contingent in the so-called Swiss War. A clash between the Hapsburg dynasty and the Swiss Confederation, this conflict was caused by several factors, including the refusal of the Swiss to pay the newly instituted imperial tax, the so-called common penny, and to recognize the *Reichskammergericht* (Imperial Court). Without much enthusiasm, for fear of endangering their excellent trade relations, the Nurembergers contributed to the imperial army four hundred foot soldiers and sixty horsemen. The hostilities began in February 1499 and ended in August of the same year with the Peace of Basel, in which the Swiss were granted virtual independence—although de jure they would belong to the German Empire until 1648, when the Treaty of Westphalia was concluded.

The war was the inspiration for Pirckheimer's "Bellum Helveticum" (The Swiss War), a work that was finished only in the last years of his life and not printed until 1610, eighty years after his death, when it was included in his *Opera politica, historica, philologica et epistolica*. In the first of its two books he sketches Swiss history prior to the outbreak of the war, relying mainly on *Kronika von der löblichen Eidgenossenschaft* (Chronicle of the Praiseworthy Swiss Confederacy, 1509), by Petermann Etterlin. The second book deals with the immediate causes of the war and its course. Since Pirckheimer entered the war in the middle of the conflict, and then only in a subordinate function, he had to rely heavily on hearsay in addition to Etterlin's chronicle.

"Bellum Helveticum" has all the characteristics of a humanist work: it is written in Latin and is not only filled with appropriate quotes from Cicero and Sallust on the value of historiography but is also imbued with the patriotic spirit so characteristic of the historical writings of the German humanists. What makes it worthwhile reading even today, besides its value as a historical source, are the vivid eyewitness accounts that reveal Pirckheimer's sensitivity and his personal involvement in the events he describes. Although not blind to the bravery of the soldiers, including the Swiss, he also describes with great sympathy the suffering of the civilian population.

After Pirckheimer resigned from the city council in 1502, he found time to devote himself to Greek studies, an interest that would make him one of the pioneers of such studies in Germany. In contrast to Italy, where Greek was flourishing and where Aldus Manutius had established a Greek press in 1490, in Germany the study of Greek literature was in its infancy at the beginning of the sixteenth century. Since the late-medieval clergy regarded the Greeks as apostates and the study of Greek as an attack on the sacrosanct authority of Latin, Greek had to fight for legitimacy. Although Pirckheimer had been introduced to Greek in Italy, he was far from proficient, as his first translations into Latin show. Never published, they are linguistic exercises of a self-taught scholar: awkward, full of errors, and comparable to medieval interlinear translations. But, encouraged by Celtis, the German "arch-humanist," he persisted.

Only in 1513, when he had become fairly proficient in the language, did Pirckheimer begin to publish his Latin translations of Greek texts. In the selection of works for translation he was guided not by antiquarian considerations but by his interest in ethical questions. He used his translations to speak out on topical issues: for instance, his translation of Plutarch's *De his qui tarde a numine corripiuntur* (On the Late Revenge of the Divinity, 1513) must be seen in the context of the tensions between the strong-willed and cantankerous humanist and individual members of the conservative city council, especially the second "Losinger" (mayor) Anton Tetzel. In his dedicatory preface to his sister Charitas, Pirckheimer alludes to Plutarch's work by saying that God will eventually punish those who oppose him, even though, for the time being, he seems to spare them. With his rendering of Plutarch's *De vitanda usura* (On the Avoidance of Interest-Taking, 1515) Pirckheimer spoke out against Johann Eck, a theology professor at the University of Ingolstadt and a protégé of the wealthy Fugger family of Augsburg who, with great erudition, had argued for loosening the biblical prohibition against charging interest.

It was also with an appropriate translation, Lucian's *Piscator seu reviviscentes* (The Fisherman; or, The Philosophers Returned to Life, 1517), that Pirckheimer interjected himself into the so-called Reuchlin affair–a heated pre-Reformation controversy, conducted in a flood of pamphlets, that dominated Germany's intellectual life in the second decade of the sixteenth century. Initially a dispute about the confiscation of Hebrew books, it erupted into a full-fledged polemic between the converted Jew Johann Pfefferkorn and the Cologne theologians, on one side, and the eminent Hebraist Johannes Reuchlin and most of the German humanists, on the other. Humanists such as Ulrich von Hutten saw the controversy as a historical struggle that pitched the reactionary forces of Scholasticism against the progressive forces of humanism. Reuchlin became the champion of the humanists, who wore the epithet "Reuchlinist" as a badge of honor. The main literary fruit of the affair was the biting satire *Epistolae obscurorum virorum* (Letters of Obscure Men, 1516; revised, 1517) in which the anonymous authors– who probably included Hutten, Crotus Rubeanus, and Hermannus Buschius–ridiculed the "obscure men," the Scholastic theologians.

Possibly stung by the Cologne theologians' unflattering reference to him as a "Bilibaldus nescio quis" (certain unknown Willibald) and convinced that their narrow-minded attack on Hebrew books was a threat to humanist scholarship, Pirckheimer prefaced his translation of *Piscator* with a lengthy "Epistola apologetica" (Letter of Defense) that combines praise for Reuchlin with a denunciation of Scholastic theologians. Pirckheimer sketches, as an alternative to the Scholastics, the ideal of a modern theologian as a scholar who should not only be proficient in the three sacred languages of Hebrew, Greek, and Latin but should also be familiar with the church fathers and ancient philosophy, especially the writings of Plato. The catalogue of con-

Pirckheimer in 1624; engraving by Dürer

temporary "theologians" that follows, however, includes men who were not professional theologians but Christian humanists with theological interests. Thus, the preface is an important document of the self-conception of German humanism. The translation itself provided many parallels with current problems: Lucian stages a mock trial in which dead philosophers, furloughed from Hades, accuse the author of ridiculing them in a previous work. Lucian turns his defense into an attack by pointing out the contradictions between the philosophers' teaching and their conduct.

Like most German humanists, Pirckheimer initially welcomed Martin Luther's ninety-five theses, mistakenly viewing Luther's fight against the old church as a continuation of the Reuchlin affair. Consequently, almost against his will, he became embroiled in a bitter controversy. In July 1519 Luther had engaged in a heated theological disputation at the University of Leipzig with Eck, a staunch defender of the old faith and of the papacy. Each side had claimed victory: in the eyes of Eck and his followers Luther had been unmasked as a radical who recognized the Bible as the sole authority in matters of faith, while Luther's supporters saw in Eck the prototype of the old Scholastic, a typical "obscure man." In the aftermath of the debate there appeared a satire on Eck titled *Eccius dedolatus* (Eck Planed Down, 1520?). Brilliantly written and full of witty allusions to Greek and Latin authors, it is one of the best Reformation satires produced in Germany.

The work is set in Eck's house in Ingolstadt. Suffering from a feverish thirst that can be quenched only by huge quantities of wine, Eck dispatches the witch Canidia to Leipzig to fetch medical help. Riding on a smelly goat, she returns to Ingolstadt with Eck's faithful student Rubeus, an allusion to the theology student Johannes Rubeus Longopolitanus, and a surgeon in tow. Before Eck submits to the painful and potentially lethal operation, he admits to his confessor that his motives in opposing Luther were entirely selfish. As punishment, he is beaten until his rough edges are removed: he is "ent-eckt" (planed down). Then his hair is shaved off, revealing a swarm of syllogisms, sophisms, and propositions. After half of his split tongue (hypocrisy) has been removed and a canine tooth (denunciation) extracted, Eck is bound to the four posts of his bed and given an anesthetic that does little to deaden his pain but that functions both as a laxative and as an emetic. He is then skinned and opened up. Half-digested Scholastic commentaries shoot from his mouth, while from the lower regions smelly indulgences pour forth. His carbuncles represent the vice of boasting, carcinomas that of scheming, stinking glands that of egotism, and swollen lymph nodes that of flattery. Finally, Eck is castrated, and his wounds are dressed with scalding pitch.

Drawing on the old carnival-play tradition of the *Narrenschneiden* (foolectomy) and on the late-medieval university ritual of the *depositio beani* (hazing of freshmen), the work is a satiric comedy in the Aristophanean spirit that adapted well to the stage. That Pirckheimer viewed the Eck-Luther dispute as a continuation of the Reuchlin affair emerges clearly from the text. As in the *Epistolae obscurorum virorum*, the principal opponents of humanist learning are three men from Cologne: Arnold von Tungern, Jakob von Hochstraten, and Pfefferkorn. The magic formula "SUREGNUT, TARTSHCOH, NEROKREFFEFP," which allows the witch's goat to fly, is based on their names read backward. Eck ridicules Luther's Wittenberg supporters as *poetae,* the usual term for humanists in the sixteenth century, and Eck and Rubeus denounce the *bonae litterae* (humanist studies) as nonsense.

Though the satire appeared under the pseudonym "Joanne-Franciscus Cotta Lembergius," most contemporaries, including Eck, suspected Pirckheimer of having written it. A month after its publication Eck went to Rome to press his case against Luther and his followers; there he drafted the papal bull *Exsurge Domine* (Rise, O Lord), which threatened Luther with excommunication unless he retracted the forty-one articles listed in it. Authorized to include in the bull the names of others who allegedly favored the Lutheran cause, Eck seized the opportunity to revenge himself on his hated opponent by adding Pirckheimer along with six other followers of Luther. Though Pirckheimer recanted within the grace period, Eck—whether intentionally or inadvertently—failed to forward the information to Rome, and Pirckheimer was excommunicated. Though Pirckheimer would be absolved in August 1521, Eck had achieved his goal of humiliating his opponent.

A great deal of scholarly acumen has been devoted to the question of the authorship of *Eccius dedolatus*. Formerly, various humanists were credited with having written the satire; more-recent scholars, however—including Niklas Holzberg, who published an edition of it in 1983—have agreed with Pirckheimer's contemporaries in identifying him as the author. The writer's familiarity with Latin and Greek literature, especially the works of Lucian and Aristophanes; his intimate knowledge of events in Nuremberg; as well as confidential letters he exchanged with Bernhard Adelmann all point to the Nuremberg humanist as the person responsible for this gem of Neo-Latin satire.

As Pirckheimer grew older, however, he regarded the Reformation with more and more misgivings. Caught between Luther's theological positions, which he generally supported, and what he viewed as the disastrous social repercussions—manifested, for instance, in the Peasants' War—he could not decide unequivocally between the Lutheran cause and the old faith. This persistent ambivalence comes through in the three controversies into which he was drawn in the mid 1520s: his defense of monastic life, his dispute with the Protestant theologian Johannes Oecolampadius, and the question of the remarriage of priests.

Pirckheimer was torn between his rejection of the monastic life as a way to God's grace—a view he shared with the Lutherans—and the involvement of his family in that life: seven of his sisters and three of his daughters lived in convents. Therefore, in 1525, when the Nuremberg City Council ordered the dissolution of the convents and monasteries, Pirckheimer persuaded it to accept an arrangement by which the nuns were allowed to stay in the convents but novices were not to be admitted. A similar inner conflict can be observed in Pirckheimer's dispute with Oecolampadius in 1526-1527. Beginning as a theological controversy over the presence of Christ in the Eucharist–Luther saw it as real, whereas the Swiss Reformer Huldrych Zwingli regarded it as symbolic–the dispute degenerated into a vicious debate, conducted on Pirckheimer's part with three increasingly violent invectives: *De vera Christi carne et vero eius sanguine, ad Ioan. Oecolampadius responsio* (An Answer to Johannes Oecolampadius on the True Flesh of Christ and His True Blood, 1526), *De vera Christi carne et vero eius sanguine, adversus convicia Ioannis, qui sibi Oecolampedii nomen indidit, responsio secunda* (The Second Answer to Johannes Oecolampadius on the True Flesh of Christ and His True Blood, 1527), and *De convitiis monachi illius, qui graecolatine Caecolampadius, germanice vero Ausschin nuncupatur* (The Insults of That Monk Who in Greek-Latin Is Called Caecolampadius, but in German Ausschin, 1527). For Pirckheimer, the theological issues were soon overshadowed by the suspicion that Zwingli was a radical extremist who was not to be trusted. The same pattern of halfhearted support for Luther and retreat showed itself, finally, in his supporting the marriage of priests but opposing their remarriage.

In addition to the mental anguish caused by his inclusion in the papal bull and his being torn between the confessional fronts, Pirckheimer also endured considerable physical pain, for since 1512 he had suffered periodically from gout. The illness became more severe as he grew older, forcing the once-athletic man to cover the short distance between his house and the city council chambers on horseback. The affliction prompted Pirckheimer in 1522 to write *Apologia seu podagrae laus* (translated as *The Praise of the Gout, or, The Gouts Apologie,* 1617), his single major original literary composition.

The work was inspired by Lucian's dramatic joke *Tragipodagra,* in which a chorus of podagrists, or gout sufferers, sing the praises of their powerful mistress, as well as by Erasmus's *Moriae encomium seu laus stultitiae* (Praise of Folly, 1509). Podagra, or Gout, is summoned to an imaginary court by the many persons who are subjected to her cruel domination. She defends herself by saying that it is really the lifestyle of the people themselves that brings about the disease. Having shifted the blame to her victims, Podagra points out that the evils of which she is accused are not as bad as alleged, and that she in fact provides many benefits. For instance, if you are stricken with gout, you cannot go to sea, and so–she argues with impeccable logic–you escape the threat of drowning. Nor need you fear, if you are bedridden, the dangers of hunting, or walking, or of falling roof tiles. If you cannot exercise your body, Podagra continues, you exercise your mind. She therefore takes credit for the study of languages, music, rhetoric, astronomy, and so on, as well as of medicine–which shows how unselfish she is, for medical research might reveal a way to get rid of her. Her speech culminates in the claim that gout directs attention away from the physical toward the spiritual and eternal.

None of the other ironic encomiums so popular during the Renaissance, with the exception of Erasmus's *Moriae encomium,* had as lasting an impact as *Apologia seu podagrae laus*. It was reprinted until the end of the seventeenth century; it was translated into German, English, French, and Czech; and it was adapted by Johann Fischart, Hans Sachs, and Jacob Ayrer. Through this work alone Pirckheimer assured himself a place in the history of German literature.

As if to confirm its redeeming qualities, the gout forced Pirckheimer to resign permanently from the city council, giving him the leisure he had longed for during his busy years in city politics. He reimmersed himself in the translation of Greek texts, including the works of Plutarch, Theophrastus, and the church father Gregory of Nazianzus, and in Ptolemy's *Geography* (1525). In addition, he wrote two original scholarly works: *Germaniae ex variis scriptoribus perbrevis explicatio* (Short Explanation of Germany Drawn from Various Authors, 1530), in which he tries to establish correspondences between places, mountains, and rivers mentioned by ancient authors and their modern equivalents; and *Priscorum Numismatum ad Nurembergensis Monetae valorem facta aestimatio* (An Appraising of Ancient Coins According to the Value of the Nuremberg Currency, 1533), which includes a description of his collection of ancient coins as well as a conversion table, informing the reader, for instance, how much Cleopatra's pearls would have cost in Nuremberg currency.

The last years of Pirckheimer's life were clouded not only by his disease but also by the death in 1528 of his closest friend, Albrecht Dürer. Although from entirely different social backgrounds, the two had formed a friendship as young men–their earliest documented contacts occurred in 1494–and remained lifelong friends, meeting almost daily in their later years. Apart from receiving financial assistance from Pirckheimer during a difficult period, Dürer became acquainted through him with descriptions of ancient works of art and could draw on Pirckheimer's vast knowledge of Greek and Roman literature, philosophy, and mythology. Through Pirckheimer, Dürer also came into the orbit of Emperor Maximilian, who employed a team of scholars

Title page for Pirckheimer's first polemic directed against the Protestant theologian Johannes Oecolampadius (courtesy of the Lilly Library, Indiana University)

and artists to preserve the memory of his achievements.

Pirckheimer and Dürer cooperated on two works sponsored by the emperor. The first was *Hieroglyphica,* ascribed to the Egyptian Horos Apollon, who, fifteen hundred years before the discovery of the Rosetta Stone, had attemped an interpretation of the hieroglyphs. The emperor had been drawn to this work because of his interest in emblems. Dürer provided some of the illustrations, while Pirckheimer translated the work from Greek into Latin and presented the manuscript, which was never printed, in 1514 to Maximilian in Linz. Though of limited value to the modern Egyptologist because of its many misconceptions and fanciful explanations, the work is interesting to the student of humanism and the baroque because of its influence on the emblem literature of the sixteenth and seventeenth centuries. Allegories and emblematics were also dominant concepts in the next two works by the friends, the *Triumphzug* (Triumphal Procession), a sequence of large woodcuts representing the genealogy of the Hapsburg dynasty, and the *Ehrenpforte* (Triumphal Gate), glorifying Maximilian's family and his military exploits. Whereas Pirckheimer suggested the iconographical program, Dürer was one of the artists involved in its execution.

The loss of his friend occasioned "Elegia Bilibaldi Pirckheymeri in obitum Alberti Düreri" (Willibald Pirckheimer's Elegy on the Death of Albrecht Dürer, 1528), one of the most moving and remarkable poems of German Renaissance humanism. Although he had written some poems of undistinguished quality in his youth, Pirckheimer later gratified his lyrical muse only rarely. But near the end of his life, driven by the intensity of his grief, he crafted a work that stood head and shoulders above many of those written by professional poets of his time. The mood is one of profound anguish over the loss of a close friend and an outstanding artist, and it expresses the conviction that Dürer's art will live forever.

The same can be said of Willibald Pirckheimer's scholarly and literary works. Under his copper engraving of his friend, Dürer wrote in Latin: "Vivitur ingenio–caetera mortis erunt" (Man lives through his creative spirit–the rest will be gone with death). The great Renaissance artist could not have chosen a more fitting motto. Pirckheimer died on 22 December 1530 and is buried in Saint John's Cemetery in his native city.

Letters:

Willibald Pirckheimers Briefwechsel I, edited by Emil Reicke and Arnold Reimann (Munich: Beck, 1940);

Willibald Pirckheimers Briefwechsel II, edited by Reicke and Reimann (Munich: Beck, 1956);

Willibald Pirckheimers Briefwechsel III, edited by Dieter Wuttke, revised by Helga Scheible (Munich: Beck, 1989).

Bibliographies:

Karl Borromäus Glock, "Willibald Pirckheimer– eine Bibliographie," in *Willibald Pirckheimer, 1470–1970: Dokumente–Studien–Perspektiven,* edited by the Willibald-Pirckheimer-Kuratorium (Nuremberg: Glock & Lutz, 1970), pp. 111–124;

Niklas Holzberg, *Willibald Pirckheimer: Griechischer Humanismus in Deutschland* (Munich: Fink, 1981).

Biography:

Willehad Paul Eckert and Christopher von Imhoff, *Willibald Pirckheimer: Dürers Freund im Spiegel seines Lebens, seiner Werke und seiner Umwelt* (Cologne: Wienand, 1971).

References:

Paula S. Datsko Barker, "Caritas Pirckheimer: A Female Humanist Confronts the Reformation," *Sixteenth Century Journal*, 26 (1995): 259-272;

Eckhard Bernstein, *German Humanism* (Boston: Twayne, 1983), pp. 95-105;

Bernstein, "Willibald Pirckheimer und Ulrich von Hutten: Stationen einer humanistischen Freundschaft," *Pirckheimer Jahrbuch*, 4 (1988): 11-36;

George Boas, *The Hieroglyphics of Horapollo* (New York: Pantheon, 1950);

Paul Drews, *Willibald Pirckheimers Stellung zur Reformation* (Leipzig: Grunow, 1887);

Walther Peter Fuchs, "Willibald Pirckheimer," *Jahrbuch für fränkische Landesforschung*, 31 (1971): 1-18;

Harald Grimm, *Lazarus Spengler: A Lay Leader of the Reformation* (Columbus: Ohio State University Press, 1978), pp. 38-45;

Karl Hagen, *Deutschlands literarische und religiöse Verhältnisse im Reformationszeitalter mit besonderer Rücksicht auf Willibald Pirckheimer* (Frankfurt am Main: Völcker, 1868);

Niklas Holzberg, "Willibald Pirckheimer," in *Deutsche Dichter der frühen Neuzeit 1450-1600*, edited by Stephan Füssel (Berlin: Erich Schmidt, 1993), pp. 258-269;

Holzberg, *Willibald Pirckheimer: Griechischer Humanismus in Deutschland* (Munich: Fink, 1981);

Holzberg, "Zum Problem der Verfasseridentifizierung: Der 'Eckius dedolatus'-ein Werk Willibald Pirckheimers," in *Germanistik in Erlangen*, edited by Dietmar Peschel (Erlangen: Universitätsbund Erlangen-Nürnberg, 1983), pp. 127-141;

Barbara Könneker, *Satire im 16. Jahrhundert: Epoche-Werke-Wirkung* (Munich: Beck, 1991), pp. 155-168;

Könneker, "Willibald Pirckheimer," in *Contemporaries of Erasmus: A Biographical Register of the Renaissance and Reformation*, volume 3, edited by Peter C. Bietenholz and Thomas B. Deutscher (Toronto: University of Toronto Press, 1987), pp. 90-97;

Otto Markwart, *Willibald Pirckheimer als Geschichtsschreiber* (Zurich: Meyer & Zeller, 1886);

Wilhelm Maurer, "Humanismus und Reformation in Nürnberg Pirckheimers und Dürers," *Jahrbuch für fränkische Landesforschung*, 31 (1971): 19-34;

Émile Offenbacher, "La Bibliothèque de Willibald Pirckheimer," *La Bibliofilia*, 40 (1938): 241-263;

Arnold Reimann, *Die älteren Pirckheimer: Geschichte eines Nürnberg Patriziergeschlechtes im Zeitalter des Frühhumanismus* (Leipzig: Koehler & Amelung, 1944);

Hans Rupprich, "Dürer und Pirckheimer: Geschichte einer Freundschaft," in *Albrecht Dürers Umwelt: Festschrift zum 500. Geburtstag Albrecht Dürers am 21. Mai 1971*, edited by the Verein für Geschichte der Stadt Nürnberg und Senatskommission für Humanismus-Forschung der Deutschen Forschungsgemeinschaft (Nuremberg: Selbstsverlag des Vereins für Geschichte der Stadt Nürnberg, 1971), pp. 78-100;

Rupprich, "Willibald Pirckheimer: A Study of His Personality as a Scholar," in *Pre-Reformation Germany*, edited by Gerald Strauss (New York: Harper & Row, 1972), pp. 380-435;

Rupprich, *Willibald Pirckheimer und die erste Reise Dürers nach Italien* (Vienna: Schroll, 1930);

J. J. Spielvogel, "Willibald Pirckheimer and the Nuernberg City Council," dissertation, Ohio State University, 1967;

Lewis W. Spitz, *The Religious Renaissance of the German Humanists* (Cambridge, Mass.: Harvard University Press, 1963), pp. 155-196;

F. J. Stopp, "Reformation Satire in Germany: Nature, Conditions, and Form," *Oxford German Studies*, 3 (1968): 53-68;

Gerald Strauss, *Nuremberg in the Sixteenth Century: City Politics and Life between Middle Ages and Modern Times* (Bloomington & London: Indiana University Press, 1976);

Willibald Pirckheimer 1470-1970: Eine Dokumentation in der Stadtbibliothek Nürnberg (Nuremberg: Selbstsverlag der Stadtbibliothek Nürnberg, 1970);

Willibald-Pirckheimer-Kuratorium, ed., *Willibald Pirkheimer 1470-1970: Dokumente-Studien-Perspektiven* (Nuremberg: Glock & Lutz, 1970).

Papers:

The Arundel Collection in the British Library includes papers of Willibald Pirckheimer.

Paul Rebhun
(circa 1500 – May 1546)

Paul F. Casey
University of Missouri

WORKS: *Ein Geistlich spiel von der Gotfurchtigen vnd keuschen Frawen Susannen, gantz lustig vnd fruchtbarlich zu lesen* (Zwickau: Wolfgang Meyerpeck, 1536; revised, 1544); translated by M. John Hanak as *A Miracle Play about the God-fearing and Chaste Lady Susanna, for Entertaining and Profitable Reading,* in *German Theater before 1750,* edited by Gerald Gillespie (New York: Continuum, 1992);

Ein hochzeit spiel auff die Hochzeit zu Cana Galileae gestellet dem Gottgeordneten Ehestand zu ehren vnd allen gottfürchtigen Eheleuten, Gesellen, vnd Junckfrawen zu trost vnd vnterricht (Zwickau: Wolfgang Meyerpeck, 1538; revised, 1546);

Klag des armen Manns vnd Sorgenuol yn theurung vnd hungers not Vnd warmit er sich darin zu trösten aus schönen Historien der heyligen schrifft der lieben Armut inn dieser theurung zu trost reymweis gestellet (Zwickau: Wolfgang Meyerpeck, 1540);

Latine Dicendi Formvlae, ad informandam puerilem linguam, ex Terentio collectae, as Paulus Perdix (Leipzig: Nicolaus Wolrab, 1545);

Hausfried. Was fur vrsachen den Christlichen Eheleuten zubedencken, den lieben Hausfried in der Ehe zuerhalten. In kurtzer Summa gepredigt vnd schrifftlich weiter erkleret (Wittenberg: Veit Creutzer, 1546);

Ein Christlich vnnd nötig Gesprech. Von der Summa des Christlichen glaubens vnd wesens. Allen jungen vnnd einfeltigen Christen zu lernen nützlich (Leipzig: Jacob Berwaldt, n.d.).

Collection: *Paul Rebhuns Dramen,* edited by Hermann Palm (Stuttgart: Litterarischer Verein, 1859).

OTHER: Thomas Naogeorgus, *Pammachius,* translated by Hans Tirolf, preface by Rebhun (Wittenberg?, 1538?).

Since the end of the nineteenth century literary critics have generally acknowledged Paul Rebhun as one of the best dramatists—perhaps *the* best—who wrote in German during the sixteenth century. They see him as the first German dramatic artist in an era when theology was more important than dramatic structure in the production of theatrical experiences. Astonishingly, his exalted reputation rests solely on his *Ein Geistlich spiel von der Gotfurchtigen und keuschen Frawen Susannen, gantz lustig und fruchtbarlich zu lesen* (1536; translated as *A Miracle Play about the God-fearing and Chaste Lady Susanna, for Entertaining and Profitable Reading,* 1992), his first published work and one of only two plays he wrote during his lifetime. His second drama, *Ein hochzeit spiel auff die Hochzeit zu Cana Galileae* (A Wedding Play about the Marriage at Cana in Galilee, 1538), is not as accomplished dramatically as its predecessor: the wine miracle does not lend itself to dramatization as well as does the story of Susanna. In addition to the two plays, Rebhun also published a dialogue on poverty; a sermon; and a textbook of useful Latin phrases from the comedies of Terence, with their German equivalents, for school use.

Rebhun was born around 1500 in Waidhofen an der Ybbs in Lower Austria; he is presumed to have been the son of Hans Rebhun, a tanner, though conclusive evidence of his parentage is lacking. Contemporary documents spell his name *Rebhun* or *Rephun,* as he did himself, not *Rebhuhn* (partridge), as is frequently encountered in modern critical works; in his Latin texts and letters he identifies himself as Paulus Perdix. He attended school in Saxony and probably matriculated at Wittenberg University, but the university's matriculation records for 1525 to 1532 are missing. There is no substantiation for the frequent assertion that he lived in Martin Luther's house while studying in Wittenberg.

Rebhun began his career in 1526 or 1527, with a position as cantor and part-time teacher in Zwickau, a flourishing Saxon city that as recently as 1469 had been considerably larger than Dresden: a "cantor Paulus" is mentioned in contemporary city council records and receipts. In 1525 the Proclamation Book of the Saint Maria Church in Zwickau announced the marriage of Rebhun and Anna Thiel, daughter of the deceased Hans Thiel and stepdaughter of Hans Widmann.

Title page for Paul Rebhun's first published work

In 1529 Rebhun took a teaching position in Kahla, a small town in Thuringia not far from Jena. During his residence there he apparently attracted admirers and patrons, for he dedicated *Susanna* to Stephan Reich of Kahla, whom he calls his special patron and friend. During this period he became acquainted with the playwright Hans Tirolf, another Kahla resident, whose translation of Thomas Naogeorgus's *Pammachius* (1538?) Rebhun would later provide with a preface.

The first performance of *Susanna* was held in Kahla on 14 February 1535, with its citizens playing the roles of the biblical characters from Daniel 13 in the Apocrypha. (The play is based on the Book of Susanna in the Apocrypha.) Rebhun's achievements in this drama are substantial, although perhaps not as overwhelming as some critics claim. The play is theatrically effective, with the action evenly divided over its five acts—the first known use in German drama of the five-act structure and a reflection of the author's acquaintance with the models of antiquity so admired by the humanists. Despite some lapses in the organization of the last act, the work is on a higher level literarily, as well as dramatically, than virtually all other contemporary works. The choruses concluding the first four acts, for which Rebhun himself composed the music, are unique creations and are integrated skillfully into the dramatic events. The characterization of the title figure has proven susceptible to criticism: some scholars find her too passive, wooden, and one-dimensional in her exemplification of virtue triumphant. But if Rebhun does not achieve in her characterization the color that he does in some of the minor figures, she is still a considerable improvement on previous and subsequent renderings of the figure by other early modern German dramatists. The scenes of Susanna with her husband, children, and servants are particularly well executed and moving. Metaphorically, *Susanna* exemplifies contemporary theological tensions: Susanna's youth and innocence symbolize the embryonic Lutheran Church set upon by the older, venal, and corrupt Catholic Church embodied by the Elders. A firm Lutheran adherent, Rebhun wrote his drama to illustrate reliance on God and virtue rewarded.

The aspect of the play to which the author devoted most care, and the one that has compelled the most praise from critics, is the innovative use of verse and meter. Rebhun saw his task as that of regulating the meter, insuring that stressed and unstressed syllables alternated in a smooth pattern, and, thereby, bringing order to the metrical confusion that reigned in German drama of the period. Although the cadence of the iambic and trochaic lines is not flawless, the variety and quality of Rebhun's metrical innovations contribute to the drama's effectiveness.

In 1535 Rebhun took up the post of *Tertius* at the Latin school in Zwickau, where *Susanna* was printed by his brother-in-law Wolfgang Meyerpeck in 1536. The publication of the drama in Zwickau has traditionally confused Rebhun specialists, who erroneously placed Rebhun in Zwickau from 1531 onward and assumed that since the drama was published there, Rebhun also wrote it there, even though the printed version says that it was first performed by citizens of Kahla.

The Zwickau Latin school was warmly regarded by Reformation leaders: Luther called it and the school at Torgau "zwei . . . edle Kleinode in Lande" (two precious jewels of the country). In 1536 Rebhun became corector of the school. It is curious that Rebhun's name is never preceded by an academic title—the usual procedure—in contemporary documents; but it is unlikely that he would have attained the rank of corector of a distinguished school, one that exercised great care in the selection of its teachers, without adequate academic qualifications and preparation.

At Easter 1538 Rebhun took up a teaching post at the only Latin school in the small Saxon city of Plauen, about eighteen miles southwest of Zwickau. A few weeks later he succeeded Georg Raudt (or Raute) as preacher in Plauen, and Luther ordained him to the clergy in Wittenberg on 30 May. *Ein hochzeit spiel auff die Hochzeit zu Cana Galileae* was printed by Meyerpeck in Zwickau in 1538, when Rebhun was already in Plauen: its dedication identifies him as the schoolmaster there, and in a postscript he expresses regret for his absence during the proofreading stages of the printing. Rebhun dedicated the play to Christoff von der Planitz, the administrator of the Vogtsberg district. With its inclusion of a marriage devil and the Archangel Raphael, this play lacks the verisimilitude of the earlier drama. The story of Jesus' first miracle is quite compact in the Bible; here it is drawn out over five acts, vitiating the work's effectiveness as drama. Most of the characters hold lengthy, didactic discourses more characteristic of sermons than of drama, setting up in pedantic fashion a canon of Lutheran principles regarding the obligations of matrimony. The play elaborates the function of the husband as protector and provider and the wife's duty to respect, obey, and serve her master. The relationship between husband and wife becomes a reflection of the authoritarian state, exemplary of the God-ordained world order elucidated by Luther in his Pauline sermons and pamphlets. In *Susanna* Rebhun had proved himself a consummate dramatic artist, producing from the biblical material a balanced theatrical work that retains elements of folk humor. In *Ein hochzeit spiel auff die Hochzeit zu Cana Galileae,* with its heavily didactic preaching that stalls the action from the inception, Rebhun evidently intended to create a different type of drama, one meant for recitation or reading rather than for performance. There is no evidence that the play was ever performed, substantiating this contention.

Rebhun made many metrical innovations in both plays, but few of them influenced other German dramas of the period. This failure can be attributed to several factors. First, Rebhun wrote only two plays. Second, it was in a truncated edition published by Sebastian Wagner in Worms in 1538, which removed every vestige of metrical innovation, that *Susanna* enjoyed much of its popularity. Third, Rebhun presented his dramas as examples of his innovations but never published a proposed German grammar that would have codified his ideas in theoretical form.

In addition to the two dramas, Rebhun's oeuvre consists of works related to his professional activities. The dialogue *Klag des armen Manns* (Lament of the Poor Man) was published in 1540 by Meyerpeck. In the preface Rebhun thanks his stepfather-in-law for urging him to complete the dialogue, which was begun many years ago when the author was living in Zwickau but had been interrupted by more pressing business. The dialogue itself reflects the hunger and inflation that had been prevalent in Zwickau in the 1520s, and Rebhun intended the work to provide consolation to the suffering populace. In the dialogue the Poor Man engages successively in discussions with Adam, Isaac, Jacob, Moses, Elias, a widow, and Christ on means of combating the hardships of poverty. That the work predates *Susanna* in conception, if not in execution, would help to explain Rebhun's achievements in his first drama: he had acquired preliminary experience in the genre of the dramatic dialogue before he wrote the play, which was, thus, not the work of a total neophyte.

On 1 May 1542 the elector Johann Friedrich, on the recommendation of Luther and Philipp Melanchthon, promoted Rebhun to the posts of pastor in Oelsnitz, a small town about six miles south of Plauen, and Lutheran superintendent of the district of Vogtsberg. Of the two titles, the pastorship was the more important to Rebhun, for from this point on he signed himself "Pastor Oelssnicensis" (Pastor at Oelsnitz) both in his published works and in his letters. During his tenure in Oelsnitz he wrote a revised version of *Susanna*, which was published by Meyerpeck in 1544. In 1546 he revised *Ein hochzeit spiel auff die Hochzeit zu Cana Galileae*, dedicating the new version to his brother-in-law Wolf Prager; the revision does not remedy the play's defects, and the new version, like the original one, seems never to have been performed.

In 1545 Rebhun published *Latine Dicendi Formulae, ad informandam puerilem linguam, ex Terentio collectae*, a collection of more than forty-five hundred Latin phrases, with German translations, from Terence's plays *Andria, Eunuchus, Heauton Timorumenos, Adelphi, Hecyra*, and *Phormio*. The work was intended for use in the Latin schools, but to what extent it was so used is unknown. It gives proof of Rebhun's extensive knowledge of the plays of Terence, which were an important influence on his own dramas. In addition, it may indicate that one of his responsibilities as a teacher in Kahla and Zwickau had been the production of Terence's plays, which found many enthusiasts among humanist schoolmasters.

In 1546 Rebhun's last published work, *Hausfried* (Peace of the Hearth), a revised and expanded edition of a sermon on marriage he had preached some years earlier, was published by Veit Creutzer in Wittenberg. Printed sermons enjoyed a wide readership during the sixteenth century; Lutheran preachers and pastors, especially in the decades following Luther's death in 1546, were in need of edifying texts—not only to inspire them in their sometimes dismal and penurious lives in the provinces and to keep them on the orthodox path but also to serve as models for their own preaching and teaching. Official visitations discouraged perfunctory preaching and aimed at raising the level of pastoral performance, and in this context expanded sermons such as *Hausfried* performed a distinct service. The many editions of the work—more than twenty in the sixteenth century—attest to Rebhun's adherence to Lutheran orthodoxy and his talent as a preacher. Innovatively, he suggests in the work that women contribute to the family income by seeking employment outside the home.

In addition to his other works, Rebhun composed songs that demonstrate his considerable talent as a musician. Song collections of the period reproduced some of his pieces repeatedly, testimony to their popularity.

Rebhun died in Oelsnitz in May 1546. Wolfgang Michel, the town clerk, recording his death in the minutes of the city council, praised him as orderly, loyal, reliable, dedicated, and hardworking and stressed the care he took of his parishioners, the orthodoxy of his teaching, his aversion to self-indulgence, and his respect for the value of time. According to Michel, Rebhun's death resulted from the performance of his pastoral duties: the inattention of the congregation at a Friday sermon so sickened him that he took to his bed and was unable to recover. The medical cause of his death is unknown; Rebhun had been in poor health for some time, and, as Michel related, he was an industrious man who did not spare himself in the exercise of his duties.

As Rebhun left behind no theoretical work outlining his thoughts on dramatic structure and metrical innovation, his contemporaries and successors often failed to note the subtleties of his achievements. Some critics misleadingly paint Rebhun as having had no substantive effect on contemporary drama, but while it is true that no Rebhun school developed in his wake, at least in Saxony his direct influence is detectable in the work of Hans Ackermann, Hans Tirolf, Johannes Chryseus, and Johann Criginger (or Krüginger), while the plays of Lucas Maius, Martin Hayneccius, Andreas Calagius, and Ludwig Hollonius show evidence of at least an indirect influence.

Paul Rebhun exemplifies the Lutheran pastor and schoolmaster of the Reformation period who illustrated for his flock the often confusing new theological teachings with concrete examples. In his plays he correctly diagnosed the malady that beset sixteenth-century verse; that other practitioners of the genre did not immediately perceive his innovations as a remedy in no way detracts from their value, nor does it diminish Rebhun's secure position in the history of German drama.

Biography:

Paul F. Casey, *Paul Rebhun: A Biographical Study* (Wiesbaden: Steiner, 1986).

References:

Georg Buchwald, "Ein ungedruckter Brief Paul Rebhuns vom Jahre 1542," *Mitteilungen des Altertumsvereins zu Plauen,* 13 (1900): 45–47;

Paul F. Casey, "Paul Rebhun: A Biographical Sketch," in *The Transmission of Ideas in the Lutheran Reformation,* edited by Helga Robinson-Hammerstein (Dublin: Irish Academic Press, 1989), pp. 133–139;

Casey, "Paul Rebhun als Komponist," *Daphnis,* 19 (1990): 379–421;

Casey, "The Power of a Preface," *Daphnis,* 16 (1987): 33–45;

Casey, "Serious Humor: An Extended Word-Play in Paul Rebhun's *Hochzeit zu Cana,*" in *"Der Buchstab tödt–Der Geist macht Lebendig": Festschrift zum 60. Geburtstag von Hans-Gert Roloff,* edited by James Hardin and Jörg Jungmayr (Bern: Peter Lang, 1992), pp. 597–604;

S. L. Clark and David Duewell, "Give and Take: Good, Evil and Language in Rebhun's *Susanna,*" *Euphorion,* 75 (1981): 325–341;

Joe Delap, "Early Modern German Dialogs of Poverty and Paul Rebhun's *Klag des armen Manns,*" *Daphnis,* 22 (1993): 603–620;

G. E. Frieß, "War Paul Rebhun, der erste deutsche Kunstdramatiker, aus Waidhofen an der Ips gebürtig?," *Blätter des Vereins für Landeskunde von Niederösterreich,* 28 (1894): 311–332;

Karl Hahn, "Biographisches von Paul Rebhun und Hans Ackermann," *Neues Archiv für sächsische Geschichte und Altertumskunde,* 43 (1922): 80–97;

Rudolf Kreczy, "Paul Rebhuns Reform der deutschen Verskunst," dissertation, University of Vienna, 1938;

Johannes Müller, "Eine Predigt Paul Rebhun's nebst Bemerkungen über seine Schriften," *Mitteilungen des Altertumsvereins zu Plauen,* 6 (1887): 65–72;

David Price, "'Schweyg liebe tochter': A Reevaluation of Paul Rebhun's *Susanna* (1536)," in *Studies in German and Scandinavian Literature after 1500: A Festschrift for George C. Schoolfield,* edited by James A. Parente and Richard Schade (Columbia, S.C.: Camden House, 1993), pp. 39–49;

Hans-Gert Roloff, *Susanna* (Stuttgart: Reclam, 1980), pp. 121–142;

Waltraud Timmermann, "Theaterspiel als Medium evangelischer Verkündigung: Zu Aussage und Funktion der Dramen Paul Rebhuns," *Archiv für Kulturgeschichte,* 66 (1984): 117–158.

Johannes Reuchlin
(29 January 1455 – 30 June 1522)

David Price
University of Texas at Austin

BOOKS: *Vocabularius breviloquus* (Basel: Johann Amerbach, 1478);

De verbo mirifico (Basel: Johann Amerbach, 1494);

Ad Alexandrum Sextum pontificem maximum (Venice: Aldus Manutius, 1498);

Scaenica progymnasmata (Basel: Johann Bergmann von Olpe, 1498);

Sergius, sive caput capitis (Erfurt: Wolfgang Schenk, circa 1504);

Liber congestorum de arte praedicandi (Pforzheim: Thomas Anshelm, 1504);

Tütsch missiue. warumb die Juden so lang im ellend sind (Pforzheim: Thomas Anshelm, 1505);

De rudimentis hebraicis (Pforzheim: Thomas Anshelm, 1506);

Augenspiegel (Tübingen: Thomas Anshelm, 1511);

Ain clare verstentnus in tütsch (Tübingen: Thomas Anshelm, 1512);

Defensio Joannis Reuchlin . . . contra calumniatores suos Colonienses (Tübingen: Thomas Anshelm, 1513);

De arte cabalistica (Hagenau: Thomas Anshelm, 1517);

De accentibus et orthographia linguae hebraicae (Hagenau: Thomas Anshelm, 1518);

Johann Reuchlins Komödien, edited by Hugo Holstein (Halle: Waisenhaus, 1888);

Gutachten über das jüdische Schrifttum, edited by Antonie Leinz-von Dessauer (Constance: Thorbecke, 1965).

Edition in English: *De arte cabalistica,* edited and translated by Martin Goodman and Sarah Goodman, introduction by G. Lloyd Jones (New York: Abaris, 1983).

OTHER: Pseudo-Homer, *Batrachomiomachia* (Vienna: Johann Winterburger, circa 1510);

In septem psalmos poenitentiales hebraicos interpretatio, edited and translated by Reuchlin (Tübingen: Thomas Anshelm, 1512);

Clarorum virorum epistolae, edited by Reuchlin (Tübingen: Thomas Anshelm, 1514); enlarged as *Il-*

Johannes Reuchlin; woodcut attributed to Hans Holbein the Younger

lustrium virorum epistolae (Hagenau: Thomas Anshelm, 1519);

Athanasius, *In librum Psalmorum,* translated by Reuchlin (Tübingen: Thomas Anshelm, 1515);

Athanasius, *De variis quaestionibus* (Hagenau: Thomas Anshelm, 1519).

Scholars have celebrated Johannes Reuchlin as the first Renaissance humanist to master the three sacred languages, Latin, Greek, and Hebrew; as the initiator of humanist drama in Germany; and as the defender of Jewish writing. Although all of these

Inscription by Reuchlin in the manuscript for Rabbi David Kimchi's Hebrew commentary on Ezekiel (Baden State Library, Karlsruhe)

claims have been qualified somewhat, Reuchlin's stature in the first rank of the history of philology and of German literature remains secure.

Reuchlin was born in Pforzheim, Baden, on 29 January 1455. (Older works often erroneously cite 22 February as his birthday.) His father, Georg, was an administrator for the Dominican monastery at Pforzheim. Nothing is known of his mother except her name, Elisabeth Eck. Proud of his hometown, he would often refer to himself as *Phorcensis,* the Latin designation for Pforzheim; he would also bequeath his precious library to the Michaelsstift there. No detailed portraits of Reuchlin survive from his lifetime, although, owing to his renown, several fanciful ones have been made over the centuries. The only representation of him from his lifetime is a sketchy woodcut on the title page of a polemical tract of 1521 that associates him, inappropriately, with Martin Luther's cause. He is known to have married twice, although the name of neither wife is explicitly attested in the documents. Hansmartin Decker-Hauff has plausibly argued (in *Johannes Reuchlin 1455–1522,* edited by Manfred Krebs, second edition, edited by Hermann Kling and Stefan Rhein, 1994) that Rebhun's first wife was surnamed Müller and was from a prominent family of Ditzingen; the second wife appears to have been from the Decker family of Cannstadt.

After studying at the Pforzheim Latin school, Reuchlin enrolled at the University of Freiburg, then the only university in Baden, on 19 May 1470. According to the account of his grandnephew Philipp Melanchthon, Reuchlin left the university because of the absence of humanist studies there. Already recognized as a gifted Latinist, Reuchlin was asked to accompany a son of Margrave Karl I of Baden to the University of Paris. There Reuchlin began the study of Greek, initiated friendships with Rudolf Agricola and Johann Amerbach, and became a student of Johannes Heynlein von Stein. He followed Heynlein von Stein to the University of Basel at the beginning of the summer semester of 1474; he received his B.A. there in 1475 and his M.A. in 1477. In Basel he became friends with Sebastian Brant, who would contribute a congratulatory poem to the first edition of Reuchlin's *Scaenica progymnasmata* (Theatrical Exercises, 1498); and, like Brant, he seems to have worked for humanistically minded printers. His first publication was a Latin dictionary, *Vocabularius breviloquus* (Concise Dictionary, 1478), which went through twenty-two editions. Although it appeared without any indication of authorship, Reuchlin took credit for the work in a letter of 7 March 1507 to his brother Dionysius. A handwritten note in a copy of the dictionary, however, suggests that it might have been a collaborative project.

By the autumn of 1477 Reuchlin had left Basel for Paris, with the intention of continuing his legal studies. By January 1479 he was a student at the University of Orléans, specializing in civil law. He enrolled at the University of Poitiers in the winter semester of 1480–1481 and received the licentiate degree in civil law there on 14 June 1481. On his return to Germany he apparently went to the University of Tübingen. The chronology and precise nature of his activities there are not known, although evidence suggests that he taught some humanist courses in 1482. In 1485 he received the doctorate in civil law from Tübingen.

From 1482 to 1496 Reuchlin was primarily engaged in government service in Stuttgart. He was an adviser to Count–later Duke–Eberhard the Bearded of Württemberg, whom he served on several diplomatic missions; he was also assessor at Eberhard's court in Stuttgart, starting in 1484. A trip to Rome with Eberhard in 1482 was Reuchlin's first opportunity to meet Italian humanists and the Greek émigré and scholar Joannes Argyropulos. In 1486 he represented Eberhard at the Diet of Frankfurt, and in 1490 he escorted Eberhard's son on a study trip to Italy. There he met Giovanni Pico della

Pages XI'' – XII' of Reuchlin's De accentibus et orthographia linguae hebraicae, *the first example of Hebrew printed with musical notation*

Mirandola, who inspired Reuchlin's interest in the Cabala, and another Greek émigré scholar, Demetrios Chalcondyles, who in 1488 had finished the editio princeps of Homer's works—a landmark in the history of Greek philology. During this trip Ermolao Barbaro honored Reuchlin by coining a Greek version of his name: *Capnion* (little smoke—*Rauch* means smoke, and *lin* is a diminutive ending). Reuchlin later adopted a coat of arms that depicted an altar labeled *Ara Capnionis* (Altar of Capnion) with smoke rising from it. In 1492 he was dispatched to the imperial court at Linz to secure approval of the Esslingen Treaty, which reunited Württemberg. At this time Emperor Friedrich III raised him to the lower nobility as a *comes palatinus* (count palatine).

In the introductory letter to *De rudimentis hebraicis* (The Rudiments of the Hebrew Language, 1506) Reuchlin records that he began his serious study of Hebrew in Linz on 25 September 1492 under Jacob ben Jehiel Loans, a learned Jewish physician at the court. He had already dabbled in Hebrew, starting, perhaps, as early as 1486, but it was only with Loans, according to Reuchlin, that he made meaningful progress. After concluding his mission for Eberhard, Reuchlin returned briefly to Stuttgart; he then went back to Linz and spent most of 1493 immersed in the study of Hebrew. The first result of his studies was *De verbo mirifico* (The Miracle-Making Word, 1494), a dialogue on Jewish, Greco-Roman, and Christian philosophy among Baruchias, a Jew; Sidonius, a philosopher; and Capnion (Reuchlin), a Christian. Notions taken from Pythagoreanism and the Cabala are used to posit a unity of learning and of faith between them and Christianity. The most significant unity, however, is between humanity and God, which is achieved in the "miracle-working word," a philologically indefensible construction of *Jesus* as a pentagrammaton (*Jhsvh*) arising from the effort to make the tetragrammaton (*Jhvh*) utterable through the insertion of a *shin* (Hebrew *s*). Tetragrammaton, pentagrammaton, and much besides are interpreted numerologically, in reliance both on the mysticism of numerology and the fact that Hebrew letters have conventional numerical values.

Eberhard the Bearded died in 1496 and was succeeded by the corrupt and ineffective Eberhard the Younger. Reuchlin left Württemberg not only because of the unpleasant prospect of working with such a man but also because his bitter enemy Conrad Holzinger, an Augustinian monk, was a close adviser to the new duke. Reuchlin may have been involved in earlier efforts, under Eberhard the Bearded, to imprison Holzinger.

Reuchlin accepted an invitation to live in Hei-

Title page for Reuchlin's study of the cabala, showing his coat of arms

delberg with Johann von Dalberg, bishop of Worms, and to participate in the activities of the Sodalitas Rhenana (Rhenish Sodality), an active group of humanists formed by Conrad Celtis. Reuchlin also held a minor position as librarian for Dalberg. Although he had already tried his hand at translation (he had translated Cicero's *Tusculan Dialogues* and two of Demosthenes' *Philippics* into German for Eberhard), this was the period of his greatest activity as a translator of Greek texts. Eventually his translations would include the pseudo-Homeric *Batrachomiomachia* (The Battle of Frogs and Mice, 1510); Athanasius's *In librum Psalmorum* (On the Book of Psalms, 1515) and *De variis quaestionibus* (Concerning Various Questions, 1519); and, probably, several books of the *Iliad*, although this last effort does not survive.

Reuchlin's greatest accomplishment in Heidelberg was the composition of two plays: *Sergius, sive caput capitis* (Sergius; or, The Head of the Head, 1504) and *Scaenica progymnasmata*—the latter known, since Hans Sachs's translation of 1531 (published in 1560), as *Henno*. *Sergius* was written in the summer of 1496 but was neither performed nor published until around 1504. According to a biographical speech about Reuchlin given by Melanchthon after Reuchlin's death (which, however, is not always reliable), Dalberg advised Reuchlin not to have the play performed because it had the potential of offending a Franciscan friar at the court of Elector Philipp of the Palatinate. The play has three acts and a minimalist plot concerning a scheme to make money by presenting a human skull, which must first be cleaned up, as a holy relic; the skull, however, turns out to be that of Sergius, an apostate monk who embraced Islam. The thought of worshiping such a relic proves too offensive even to the wastrels who proposed the deceit. As clumsy as the plot is, such a satire of the cult of the saints might well have offended clerics anywhere. Moreover, *Sergius* includes a long, irrelevant passage that inveighs against the control of a ruler by a corrupt adviser. The apparent reference to Holzinger and Eberhard the Younger may also be reflected in the title of the play—"the head of the head" might allude to the adviser of the head of state. The play was printed at least twenty-one times during the sixteenth century (six times in combination with *Henno*); the Pforzheim schoolmaster Georg Simler wrote a commentary on it for use in the schools (1507); and Luther is said to have attended Hieronymus Emser's lectures on the play at the University of Erfurt in 1504. A German translation of *Sergius* by Martin Roet was published in Augsburg in 1538.

Henno was first performed by students of the University of Heidelberg on 31 January 1497, in the presence of the rector of the university, Adam Werner von Themar, and under the auspices of Dalberg. It has achieved canonical status as the first successful humanist comedy in Germany. The play had predecessors, including Reuchlin's own *Sergius*, Jacob Wimpfeling's *Stylpho* (1480), and the early plays of Jacob Locher. *Henno*, however, gained recognition as the first to conform to the style and language of Roman New Comedy, the principal model for Renaissance comedy, even though it was probably based on a late-medieval French farce, *Maître Pathelin*. The plot concerns the craftiness of the servant Dromo, who swindles his master, Henno, out of money that Henno has stolen from his wife; Dromo

Title page for Reuchlin's response to the *Handspiegel* of Johannes Pfefferkorn; the work resulted in heresy charges against Reuchlin

also swindles a cloth merchant and a lawyer. He is reconciled with Henno at the end, when he reveals that the money is intended as a dowry for Henno's daughter, whom Dromo wishes to marry. Like New Comedy, the play has a five-act plot culminating in matrimony, a Roman-like *didascalia* at the end, Terentian-Plautine language, dialogue written in meter, and, most striking, stereotypical characters similar to those found in Roman comedy. Nonetheless, the play diverges significantly from New Comedy: marriage is a blind motif appearing out of nowhere at the conclusion; the meter is uniformly iambic trimeter, whereas Terence and Titus Maccius Plautus use many meters in their plays; and it includes four choral interludes, while Roman comedy never has choruses. The most peculiar feature is that the choral entr'acte songs, which were set to music by the otherwise unknown Daniel Megel, are written in medieval rhythmic verse with rhyme, a style of writing deplored by humanists. The choral interludes may express Reuchlin's dissatisfaction with his legal-governmental career, which at that time appeared to have ended ingloriously and unjustly: the songs after acts 2 and 3 praise the cultivation of poetry, and the song after act 4, with striking enthusiasm, elevates the pursuit of a poet's life over a legal vocation.

Henno is an example of Latin school drama, the immense corpus of sixteenth- and seventeenth-century Latin drama written for production at schools and universities. The original title, *Scaenica progymnasmata*, suggests that it was intended as a pedagogical exercise, as does a commentary on it by Jacob Spiegel (1513). It was printed some thirty-eight times between 1498 and 1615 and was translated into German by Sachs, by Johann Betz (1546), and by Gregor Wagner (1547); it probably also served as the source text for the anonymous *Der getreue Knecht* (The Faithful Servant, circa 1560; generally referred to as New Year's Play of Lucerne) and for Christian Weise's *Der betrogene Betrug* (The Deceived Deceit, 1690).

During this time Reuchlin was employed by Elector Philipp of the Palatinate, first as supervisor of his children's education and then on a diplomatic mission: in June 1498 Reuchlin went to Rome to request a dispensation for the marriage of Philipp's son Ruprecht to Ruprecht's cousin Elisabeth of Bavaria and, what is more significant, the removal of

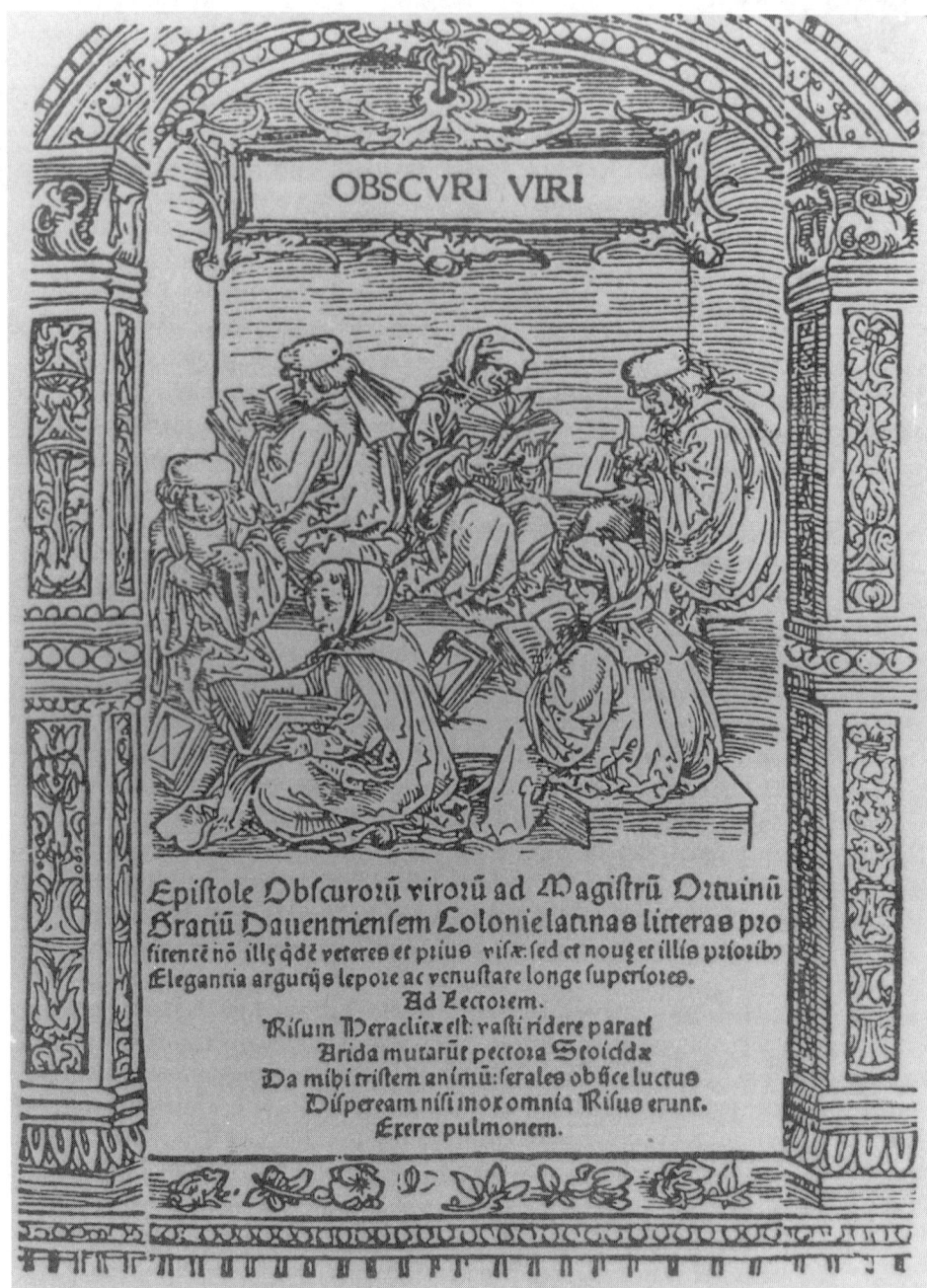

Title page for the enlarged edition of the satiric defense of Reuchlin by a group of humanist authors, including Ulrich von Hutten and Crotus Rubeanus

Philipp's excommunication. Reuchlin was successful in both matters; a speech he delivered before Pope Alexander VI in defense of the elector was published in 1498 and is one of the few remnants of his legal-diplomatic career. While in Rome he continued his Hebrew studies with Obadja Sforno and purchased several Hebrew manuscripts and books. A manuscript for Rabbi David Kimchi's Hebrew commentary on Ezekiel survives in the Baden State Library in Karlsruhe with the inscription "Ego Joannes Reuchlin . . . emi hunc librum David Kimhei . . . Romae VII. Idibus Sextiles Anno MCCCCXCVIII" (I, Johannes Reuchlin . . . bought this book of David Kimchi at Rome on 7 August 1498).

After 1498 Reuchlin returned to government service in Württemberg. Eberhard the Younger had been deposed in the spring of 1498, and Duke Ulrich, then a minor, had been declared his successor; the duchy was to be ruled by a group of regents. Reuchlin functioned as an adviser to Ulrich, although he would later join the many voices critical of Ulrich's serious failings. Reuchlin was one of three judges appointed by the Swabian League to adjudicate disagreements among its members; he held that office at least from 1502 until his resignation in 1512.

Although he experienced many legal and financial difficulties, Reuchlin was an unusually productive scholar from 1498 to 1519. Among his minor works was the humanist *Liber congestorum de arte praedicandi* (Handbook on the Art of Preaching, 1504); he composed it as a present for the monks at the monastery of Denkendorf, where he found refuge during an outbreak of plague in Stuttgart in 1502. In 1505 he published a somewhat mysterious tract, *Tütsch missiue. warumb die Juden so lang im ellend sind* (A Letter in German, Explaining Why the Jews Have Been in Misery So Long); it is addressed to an unnamed nobleman who, Reuchlin claims, had many Jews in his territory and wanted to improve their condition. Scholars are uncertain what to make of this work, since in it Reuchlin–who since the Enlightenment has enjoyed a reputation for tolerance–espouses the harsh view, ubiquitous among Christians during the Renaissance, that the Jews are being punished for having crucified Jesus and for their continued spite toward Christians; he even repeats the erroneous belief, always cited by rabid anti-Jewish propagandists of the period, that Jews pray for the destruction of Christianity (this charge refers to the prayer beginning "Welameschumodim," which is an imprecation against heretics and has nothing to do with Christians). Nonetheless, in the tract Reuchlin strongly opposes persecution and expulsion of Jews, advocating instead efforts to convert them without resorting to force or compulsion.

In 1506 Thomas Anshelm published *De rudimentis hebraicis,* the crowning achievement of Reuchlin's Hebrew scholarship. Konrad Pellikan had published a study of Hebrew in 1504, but it was incomplete and marred by errors; Reuchlin's work is considered the modern foundation of Hebrew scholarship by Christians. Based on several works by David Kimchi and, according to Hermann Greive, also on a work by Moses Kimchi, *De rudimentis hebraicis* includes both a comprehensive grammar (book 3) and a Hebrew lexicon (books 1 and 2). Reuchlin understood the incompatibilities of the grammatical systems of Hebrew, Latin, and Greek but used Latin paradigms to describe Hebrew, showing, for example, Hebrew equivalents for the five noun cases of Latin. Even though the work is in Latin, it is printed, like Hebrew books, from back to front.

The work's impact on biblical studies, although mostly indirect, was profound enough to justify Reuchlin's boastful words, taken from Horace, in the colophon: "Exegi monumentum aere peren-

Bust of Reuchlin by Emil Salm (Stadtarchiv, Pforzheim)

nius" (I have built a monument more lasting than bronze). For one thing, *De rudimentis hebraicis* offered several hundred corrections of Vulgate renderings, by virtue of which the work immediately joined those of Nicholas of Lyra and of Saint Jerome as an important source for all Christian exegetes who did not know Hebrew. Reuchlin's goal, however, extended significantly beyond the task of correcting Jerome: he advocates in the work that Christian expositors have direct access to Hebrew Scripture, which he, like many others since Jerome, called "veritas Hebraica" (Hebrew truth). He eloquently expresses the need for direct access, in addition to continued use of the old authorities, in the introductory letter to book 3: "Quamquam enim Hieronymum sanctum veneror ut angelum et Lyram colo ut magistrum, tamen adoro veritatem ut deum" (For although I venerate Saint Jerome as an angel and I revere Lyra as a master, I nonetheless worship the [Hebrew] truth as God). Even though the book apparently did not have brisk sales, it inspired others–the most important being Sebastian Münster—to write Hebrew grammars and promote the study of Hebrew at universities. Luther is known to have had a copy of the *De rudimentis hebraicis* in hand when he translated Hebrew Scripture.

Reuchlin prepared a Hebrew edition, with Latin translation and commentary, of the seven penitential psalms, titled *In septem psalmos poenitentiales hebraicos interpretatio* (1512), as an exercise book to accompany *De rudimentis hebraicis*. His translation of Athanasius's commentary on the Psalms appeared in 1515. He subsequently published a complementary study of Hebrew, *De accentibus et orthographia linguae hebraicae* (1518), which offers several corrections of *De rudimentis hebraicis* but also explains word accent, prosody, and musical notation for Hebrew. It has the distinction of being the first example of Hebrew ever printed with musical notations.

Reuchlin's study of the Cabala, *De arte cabalistica* (1517), is a fundamental work for Christian cabalism. The work, which is dedicated to Pope Leo X, who was then adjudicating Reuchlin's controversy with the Cologne Dominicans, is a Socratic-style dialogue set in Frankfurt am Main. The interlocutors are Philolaus, a Pythagorean; Marranus, a Muslim; and Simon, a Jew. Simon, an exile of the 1492 Spanish expulsion, teaches the others at great length about the Cabala, with particular emphasis on its compatibility with Pythagorean numerology and on the hidden meanings of Hebrew characters. Reuchlin, however, appropriates the Cabala as a source of Christian revelation. At a high point in the work Philolaus concludes that "Omnia nanque studia nostra utrique reducunt ad humani generis salutem" (all our studies in both [Pythagoreanism and cabala] lead back to the salvation of humankind). Though influential, the study was not well received in all quarters; John Colet and Desiderius Erasmus were unimpressed, and Reuchlin's archenemy Jacob von Hochstraten published a polemical refutation, *Destructio cabale* (Destruction of the Cabala, 1519).

Because of his command of Hebrew, at the time an extremely rare accomplishment for a Christian, Reuchlin was drawn into the greatest controversy of the period: the attempt to destroy Hebrew writings in the possession of Jews. The affair began when Johannes Pfefferkorn, a recent convert from Judaism, received an imperial mandate, dated 19 August 1509, from Maximilian I, authorizing Pfefferkorn to confiscate and destroy books belonging to Jews that were injurious to Christianity. Pfefferkorn first confiscated books in Frankfurt am Main; later confiscations took place in other cities. Complicated legal maneuvers ensued. After having initially stopped Pfefferkorn, Uriel von Gemmingen, archbishop of Mainz, was authorized in a third imperial mandate (6 July 1510) to adjudicate the issue, although only after consulting theologians at the Universities of Cologne, Erfurt, Mainz, and Heidelberg, as well as Reuchlin, Hochstraten, and Victor von Karben.

Reuchlin, who completed his assessment on 6 October 1510, was the only authority to conclude that there was no legal or religious justification for the confiscations. He claimed that Jews enjoyed rights as *concives* (citizens) of the Holy Roman Empire and that Jewish writings, with few exceptions (which he himself had misunderstood), were not injurious to Christianity. Moreover, he argued that Jewish writings, especially the Cabala and the Talmud, were important for the Christian study of Scripture. He further noted that the New Testament forbade Christians from such action, citing Rom. 14:4 and Luke 9:53 among his authorities for this view and quoting John 5:39 in support of the need of Scriptures for Jews. This last passage would incite Reuchlin's opponents, who claimed that it was blasphemous to suggest that the Talmud might contain God's revelation.

On 29 October 1510 Gemmingen sent the opinions he had received to Maximilian, along with his own recommendation that the legality of the confiscations be endorsed. An imperial commission approved Gemmingen's recommendation, with a few alterations regarding procedure. The threat to Hebrew books ended, however, when Maximilian, in an action that has never been fully understood, issued a mandate on 11 January 1511 that no further confiscations be permitted until the matter had been decided by a diet of the imperial estates; the issue was never raised at an imperial diet. It appears that most of the books—as many as fifteen hundred, according to Pfefferkorn—were returned to the Jews of Frankfurt am Main by another imperial mandate.

In the meantime, Reuchlin published his opinion, "Ratschlag ob man den Juden alle ire bücher nemmen abthun unnd verbrennen soll" (Opinion as to Whether One Should Take, Remove, and Burn All the Books of the Jews) in August or September of 1511 as part of his *Augenspiegel* (Eye Mirror, 1511), an aggressive self-defense in answer to the polemical *Handspiegel* (Hand Mirror, 1511) published by Pfefferkorn. Reuchlin was soon embroiled in a lengthy public dispute and legal case over the orthodoxy of his *Augenspiegel*.

With the support of professors at the University of Cologne, especially Arnold von Tongern and Ortwin Gratius, and at the University of Paris and the University of Louvain, Hochstraten brought heresy charges against the *Augenspiegel* on the grounds that it was impermissibly favorable to the Jews and injurious to Christianity. The case was decided in Reuchlin's favor by an ecclesiastical court in Speyer on 19 March 1514, but Hochstraten appealed the case to Rome. The proceedings in Rome were lengthy and complex.

In an attempt to solidify public support for his case Reuchlin published a large collection of letters by eminent scholars who had written favorably to him. *Clarorum virorum epistolae* (Letters of Famous Men, 1514), with an introduction by the young Melanchthon, is something of a who's who of humanism. Reuchlin's case had become a defining issue for those who pressed for a humanist reform of university curricula and, in particular, for a stronger philological basis for the study of theology. These letters inspired one of the most successful satires of the Renaissance, *Epistolae obscurorum virorum* (The Letters of Obscure Men, 1515). These letters are addressed to Gratius by the "obscurantists," a fictional group of academic quacks, in support of the efforts against Reuchlin. The letters implicate all the Cologne figures in various kinds of immorality (drinking, sexual improprieties, profiteering, hypocrisy in the Reuchlin case) and, more important, satirize Scholasticism and the inability of Reuchlin's opponents to grasp the importance of humanism. Of the authors who contributed to the work, the most prominent were Crotus Rubeanus and Ulrich von Hutten; Hutten had primary responsibility, it seems, for the enlarged edition of 1517, which includes a second book of letters. Hutten also published *Triumphus Capnionis* (The Triumph of Reuchlin), a polemical glorification of the cause, in 1518.

After many indications to the contrary, including the eclipse of Hochstraten's prestige in Cologne, an initial finding on 2 July 1516 in Reuchlin's favor, and letters of support from such luminaries as Maximilian I, Pope Leo X issued a papal directive on 23 June 1520 pronouncing Reuchlin's *Augenspiegel* heretical and worthy of being suppressed and burned. Reuchlin, furthermore, was to bear the costs of the proceedings. It is generally thought that the onset of the Reformation in Germany made it impossible for Leo to take a decision that would have diminished the authority of any group, such as the Cologne Dominicans, that was loyal to Rome. Reuchlin accepted the papal directive and remained an obedient member of the church.

War between Ulrich and the Swabian League, which resulted in Ulrich's exile, brought military occupations of Stuttgart in 1519. The political turmoil and his own loss of property made Reuchlin eager to leave Swabia. He was a member of the faculty of the University of Ingolstadt by 21 November 1519, and on 29 February 1520 he was appointed professor of Greek and Hebrew. He is known to have lectured

Reuchlin's grave marker in the Saint Leonhard Church in Stuttgart

on the Hebrew grammar of Moses Kimchi and on Aristophanes' *Ploutos*. By the winter semester of 1521 he was professor of Greek and Hebrew at the University of Tübingen, where he taught courses on Demosthenes, Aeschines, and Ecclesiastes. A 23 September 1521 letter from Reuchlin to Daniel Bomberg in Venice–the greatest printer of Hebrew texts during the Renaissance–indicates that Reuchlin had requested some Hebrew books for his courses.

Reuchlin's health was failing, and, apparently after taking a cure in Bad Liebenzell, he died in Stuttgart on 30 June 1522. He was buried in the Saint Leonhard Church, where a marker from the period, with an inscription in Latin, Greek, and Hebrew, still commemorates him.

Among the many tributes to Reuchlin is Erasmus's celebratory *Apotheosis Capnionis* (Apotheosis of Reuchlin, 1522) in which Saint Jerome, the patristic *vir trilinguis* (trilingual man), welcomes the first Renaissance trilingual scholar to heaven: "Salue, collega sanctissime. Datum est hoc mihi negotium, ut te exceptum deducam in consortium coelitum, quod tuis sanctissimis laboribus destinauit divina benignitas" (Greetings, most holy colleague. I have been given the task of leading you into the society of heavenly people, which the divine graciousness has destined for you in return for your most holy labors). Reuchlin has, ever since, enjoyed a charmed reception, attracting many studies by scholars interested in Cabala, sacred philology of the Renaissance, and, above all, the history of Christian-Jewish relations. Occasionally his philosophical-religious dialogues have found admirers of their literary qualities. Nonetheless, it is as the author of *Henno* that he continues to claim pride of place in literary histories as the originator of humanist drama in Germany.

Letters:

Johann Reuchlins Briefwechsel, edited by Ludwig Geiger (Stuttgart: Litterarischer Verein, 1875).

Bibliographies:

Josef Benzing, *Bibliographie der Schriften Johannes Reuchlins im 15. und 16. Jahrhundert* (Bad Bocklet: Krieg, 1955);

Bavarian State Library in Munich, ed., *Verzeichnis der im deutschen Sprachbereich erschienenen Drucke des XVI. Jahrhunderts,* volume 17 (Stuttgart: Hiersemann, 1991), entries R1234-R1307.

Biographies:

Ludwig Geiger, *Johann Reuchlin: Sein Leben und seine Werke* (Leipzig: Dunker & Humblot, 1871);

Max Brod, *Johannes Reuchlin und sein Kampf* (Stuttgart: Kohlhammer, 1965);

Stefan Rhein, "Johannes Reuchlin," in *Deutsche Dichter der frühen Neuzeit,* edited by Stephan Füssel (Berlin: Erich Schmidt, 1993), pp. 138-155.

References:

Eckehard Catholy, *Das deutsche Lustspiel* (Stuttgart: Kohlhammer, 1969), pp. 94-112;

Hermann Greive, "Die hebräische Grammatik Johannes Reuchlins," *Zeitschrift für die alttestamentliche Wissenschaft,* 90 (1978): 395-409;

Arno Herzig and Julius Schoeps, eds., *Reuchlin und die Juden* (Sigmaringen: Thorbecke, 1993);

Adalbert Horowitz, "Zur Biographie und Correspondenz Johannes Reuchlins," *Sitzungsberichte der Akademie der Wissenschaften zu Wien,* 85 (1877): 117-190;

Guido Kisch, *Zasius und Reuchlin* (Constance: Thorbecke, 1961);

Manfred Krebs, ed., *Johannes Reuchlin 1455-1522,* second edition, edited by Hermann Kling and Stefan Rhein (Sigmaringen: Thorbecke, 1994);

Ellen Martin, *Die deutschen Schriften des Johannes Pfefferkorn: Zum Problem des Judenhasses und der Intoleranz in der Zeit der Vorreformation* (Göppingen: Kümmerle, 1994);

Jane O. Newman, "Textuality versus Performativity in Neo-Latin Drama: Johannes Reuchlin's *Henno,*" *Theatre Journal,* 38 (1986): 259-274;

Heiko Oberman, *Roots of Antisemitism in the Age of the Renaissance and Reformation* (Philadelphia: Fortress, 1984);

James A. Parente Jr., "Empowering Readers: Humanism, Politics, and Money in Early Modern German Drama," in *The Harvest of Humanism in Central Europe: Essays in Honor of Lewis W. Spitz,* edited by Manfred P. Fleischer (Saint Louis: Concordia, 1992), pp. 263-280;

Hans Peterse, *Jacobus Hoogstraeten gegen Johannes Reuchlin: Ein Beitrag zur Geschichte des Antijudaismus im 16. Jahrhundert* (Mainz: Zabern, 1995);

Gershom Scholem, "Die Erforschung der Kabbala von Reuchlin bis zur Gegenwart," in his *Judaica,* volume 3 (Frankfurt am Main: Suhrkamp, 1987), pp. 247-263;

Martin Sicherl, *Zwei Reuchlin-Funde aus der Pariser Nationalbibliothek* (Mainz: Verlag der Akademie der Wissenschaften und der Literatur, 1963);

Lewis W. Spitz, "Reuchlin: Pythagoras Reborn," in his *The Religious Renaissance of the German Humanists* (Cambridge, Mass.: Harvard University Press, 1963), pp. 61-80;

Edwin H. Zeydel, "Johann Reuchlin and Sebastian Brant: A Study in Early German Humanism," *Studies in Philology,* 67 (April 1970): 117-138;

Charles Zika, "Reuchlin and Erasmus: Humanism and Occult Philosophy," *Journal of Religious History,* 9 (1977): 223-246;

Zika, "Reuchlin's 'De verbo mirifico' and the Magic Debate of the Late Fifteenth Century," *Journal of the Warburg and Courtauld Institutes,* 39 (1979): 104-138.

Hans Sachs

(5 November 1494 - 19 January 1576)

Eckhard Bernstein
College of the Holy Cross

SELECTED BOOKS: *Von der Lieb. Ich bin genant der liebe streit. Sag von der liebe wunn vnd freyt. Darzu von schmertz vnd trawrickeit. So in der lieb verporgen leit* (Nuremberg: Wolfgang Formschneider, 1515?);

Ein kleglich lied von eines Fürsten tochter vnd einem Jüngling die von lieb wegen beyde jr leben haben verloren. Vnd ist in Fraw Eren thon zu singen (Nuremberg: Hans Guldenmundt, 1515?);

Die Wittenbergisch Nachtigall Die man yetz höret vberall. Ich sage euch wa diese schweygen so werden die stein schreyen Luce 19 (Nuremberg, 1523);

Disputation zwischen einem Chorherren vnd Schuchmacher darin das wort gottes vnnd ein recht Christlich wesen verfochten würdt (N.p., 1524);

Ein gesprech von den Scheinwercken der Gaystlichen, vnd jren gelübdten, damit sy zuverlesterung des bluts Christi vermaynen selig zu werden (N.p., 1524);

Ein Dialogus des inhalt: ein argument der Römischen wider das Christlich heüflein den Geytz auch ander offenlich laster betreffend (N.p., 1524);

Ain gesprech eins Ewangelischen Christen mit einem Lutherischen Darinn der ergerlich wandel etzlicher die sich Lutherisch nennen angezaigt vnd bruderlich gestrafft wirdt (N.p., 1524);

Eyn wunderliche Weyssagung von dem Babstumb wie es yhm biß an das endt der welt gehen sol, jn figuren oder gemäl begriffen, gefunden zu Nürnberg ym Cartheuser Closter vnd ist seher alt. Eyn vorred Andreas Osianders. Mit gutter verstendtlicher auß legung durch gelerte leut verklert. Welche Hans Sachs yn teutsche reymen gefast vnd darzu gesetzt hat (Nuremberg: Hans Goldenmund, 1527);

All Römisch Kaiser nach ordnung vnd wie lang yeder geregiert hat zu welcher zeit was sitten der gehabt vnd was todes er gestorben sey von dem ersten an biß auff den yetzigen großmechtigsten Kaiser Carl (Nuremberg, 1530);

Ein lobspruch der statt Nürmberg. Der Stadt Nürmberg ordnung vnd wesen Findstu du in disem gdicht zulesen (Nuremberg: Kunegund Hergotin, 1530);

Hans Sachs; portrait by Andreas Herneisen (Germanisches Museum, Nuremberg)

Ein kurtzweilig Faßnacht Spiell Vonn einem bösen Weib durch Hans Sachs (Nuremberg: Valentin Newber, 1530);

Ein vermanung Kayserlicher Mayestat sampt aller Stend des Römischen Reychs Eynes heerzugs wider den blutdurstigen Türcken (Nuremberg: Georg Wachter, 1532);

Clagred der Neün Muse oder künst vber Teütschlandt (Nuremberg, 1535);

Ein Gesprech mit dem schnöden Müssiggang vnd seynen acht schendtlichen Eygenschafften (Nuremberg: Jörg Merckel, 1535?);

Ein spruch von dem freüden fewer zu Nürnberg verbrent am xiij tag Septembris ob dem Keyserlichen erlangetn syg in Affrica am Königreich Thunis (Nuremberg: Hans Guldenmund, 1535);

Das Narren schneiden. Ein schön Faßnacht Spiel mit dreyen Personen (Nuremberg: Friedrich Gutknecht, 1536);

Anzeigung wider das schnöd laster der Hurerey (Nuremberg: Hanns Wandereisen, 1540);

Kaiserlicher Mayestat Karoli der 5. einreyten zu Nürnberg in des heyligen Reychs Stat, Den 16. tag des 1541 jars (Nuremberg: Georg Wachter, 1541);

Ein war Contrafactur oder verzeychnuß der Königlichen stat Ofen in Vngern jr belagerung sampt dem vnglückhafftigen Scharmuetzel des pluturstigen Tüercken mit dem Königklichen heerleger im September des 1541 jars (Nuremberg: Steffan Hamer, 1541);

Das pitter süß Eelich leben (Nuremberg: Georg Wachter, 1541);

Der Todt ein Endt aller Yrdischen ding (Nuremberg: Georg Merckel, 1542);

Der gantz haußrat (Nuremberg: Hans Guldenmund, 1545);

Ein Epitaphium oder klagred ob der leich D. Martini Luthers (Nuremberg: Georg Wachter, 1546);

Ein Klagred Teutschen landts mit dem treuwen Eckhart (Nuremberg: Merckel, 1546);

Ein New Lied Wie Hertzog Johan Friderich vonn der Römi. Kaiserlichen Mayestät den 24.tag Aprils erlegt vnd gefangen worden ist (N.p., 1547);

Ein nutzlicher rath den jungen gsellen. So sich verheyraten wollen (Nuremberg: Hans Guldenmund, 1549);

Ein Faßnachtspiel der böß rauch im Hauß mit dreyen personen kurtzweylig zu hören (Nuremberg: Georg Merckel, 1551);

Ein Faßnacht Spil Die fünff Elenden wandrer mit sechs personen kurtzweylig zu hören (Nuremberg: Georg Merckel, circa 1551);

Ein schöne Comedi, mit xvj Personen zu recitieren, Die Judith, wie sie dem Holoferni das haupt, in seinem Zelt abschlegt, vnd hat Fünff Actus (Nuremberg: Friedrich Gutknecht, circa 1551);

Die Gemarthert Theologia. Mer das Klagent Ewangelium (Nuremberg: Georg Merckel, 1552);

Warhafftige Contrafactur der andern Schlacht so Margraff Albrecht der Jünger von Brandenburg verloren hat durch Hertzog Heynrich zu Braunschweig den XI tag Septembris Anno M.D.Iiij. Jar (Nuremberg: Steffan Hamer, 1553);

Ein ardlich gesprech der Götter die zwitracht des Römischen Reychs betreffende (Nuremberg: Georg Merckel, 1553);

Der Ehren spiegel der Zwölff Durchleuchtigenn Frawen des Alten Testaments (Nuremberg: Hermann Hamsing, 1553);

Die vier wunderbarlichen Eygenschafft und würckung des Weins, ein kurtzweylicher Spruch. Mehr ein Newer spruch von der Insel Bachi und jrer Eygenschafft (Nuremberg: Georg Merckel, 1553);

Der klagent Waldtbruder vber alle Stendt auff erden (Nuremberg: Georg Merckel, 1553);

Ein gesprech mit der Faßnacht von jrer eygenschafft (Nuremberg: Georg Merckel, 1554);

Ein gesprech der Götter ob der Edlen und Burgerlichen Kranckheit des Podagram oder Zipperlein (Nuremberg: Georg Merckel, 1554);

Der Teuffel lest kein Landtknecht mehr in die Helle faren (Nuremberg: Georg Merckel, 1555);

Ein Gesprech vnd klagred Fraw Arbeit vber den grossen müssigen hauffen (Nuremberg: Friedrich Gutknecht, 1556);

Ein klaggesprech vber das schwere Alter (Nuremberg: Valentin Neuber, 1558);

Sehr Herrliche Schöne vnd warhaffte Gedicht. Geistlich vnd Weltlich, allerley art, als ernstliche Tragedien, liebliche Comedien, seltzsame Spil, kurtzweilige Gesprech, sehnliche Klagreden, wunderbarliche Fabel, sampt andern lecherlichen schwencken vnd bossen [Folio I] (Nuremberg: Christoph Heußler, 1558);

Das ander Buch. Sehr Herrliche Schöne Artliche vnd gebundene Gedicht macherley art. Als Tragedi, Comedi, Spiel, Gesprech, Sprüch vnd Fabel, darinn auff das kürtzt vnd deutlichst an Tag gegeben werden, viel guter Christlicher vnd sittlicher Lehr, auch viel warhaffter vnd seltzamer Histori, sampt etlichen kurtzweyligen Schwencken, doch niemandt ergerlich, sondern jedermann nützlich vnnd gut zu lesen [Folio II] (Nuremberg: Christoph Heußler, 1560;

Ein Fasnacht Spiel. Der farend Schuler mit der Beurerin mit dreyen personen kurtzweylich zu hören (Nuremberg: Georg Merckel, 1560);

Tragedia des Jüngsten Geriechts vnnd Sterbenden Menschen einen Erbarn Raht der Churfürstlichen Statt Amberg zu gefallen gemacht durch Hanns Sachsen zu Nürnberg (Amberg: Wolff Guldenmund, 1560);

Zwey schöne Newe Geystliche Lieder, Das Erste, warumb betrübst du dich mein hertz. Ein Ander Geistlich Lied, Biß mir gnedig O Herre Gott (Nuremberg: Valentin Newber, circa 1560);

Das dritt vnd letzt Buch. Sehr Herrliche Schöne Tragedi, Comedi vnd schimpf Spil, Geistlich vnd Weltlich, viel schöner alter warhafftiger Histori, auch kurtzweyliger geschicht auff das deutlichst an tag geben. Welche Spil auch nit allein gut, nutzlich vnd kurtzweilig zu lesen sindt, sonder auch leichtlich aus disem Buch spilweis anzurichten, weil es so ordenlich alle Person, gebärden, wort vnd werck, außgeng vnd eingeng auffs verstendigst anzeiget, durch alle Spil, der vormal keins im Truck ist außgangen, noch gesehen worden [Folio III] (Nuremberg: Christoph Heußler, 1561);

Eygentliche Beschreibung Aller Stände auff Erden Hoher vnd Nidriger, Geistlicher vnd Weltlicher, Aller Künsten, Handwercken vnd Händeln, vom grösten biß zum kleinesten. Auch von jrem Vrsprung, Erfindung vnd gebreuchen. Durch den weitberümptern Hans Sachsen Gantz fleissig beschrieben vnd in Teutsche Reimen gefasset. Sehr nutzbarlich vnd lustig zu lesen vnd auch mit kunstreichen Figuren deren gleichen zuvor niemands gesehen allen Ständen so in diesem Buch begriffen zu ehren vnd wolgefallen Allen Künstlern aber als Malern, Goldschmieden zu sonderlichen dienst in Druck verfertigt (Frankfurt am Main: Sigmund Feyerabend, 1568); translated as *The Book of Trades: Jost Amman and Hans Sachs*, introduction by Benjamin A. Rifkin (New York & London: Dover, 1973);

Zwey schöne newe kurtzweylige Faßnacht Spil. Das erste mit vier Personen Von eines Bawrn Son der zwey Weyber wolt haben. Das ander mit fünff Personen von dem Schwangern Bawrn (Nuremberg: Valentin Newer, circa 1570);

Drey kurtzweylicher Faßnacht Spiel. Das erste mit vier Personen Nemlich ein Richter ein Buler ein Spieler vnd ein Trincker. Das ander mit dreien personen Nemlich ein Kelner vnd zwen Bawrn die holen den Bachen im Teutschen Hoff. Das dritte auch mit dreien Personen Nemlich ein Burger vnd ein Bawer vnd ein Edelman die holen Krapffn (Nuremberg: Valentin Newber, 1570);

Valete, Des Weitberhümbten Teutschen Poeten Hans Sachsen zu NürnbergDarinn er selbs im 71. Jar seines alters sein leben vnd inhalt, anzal vnd ordnung aller seiner Gedicht reimenweiz verfaßt, gestelt vnd beschriben, im Jar nach Christi geburt 1567. Vorhin nie im Truck außgangen (Nuremberg: Katharina Gerlach & Johann vom Berg's heirs, 1576);

Hans Sachsen spruch damit er dem Maler sein Valete dediciert (Nuremberg: Katharina Gerlach & Johann vom Berg's heirs, 1576);

Ein new Lied Von eines Ritters Tochter der jr Bul an jren armen starb nach laut eines wunderlichen Traums (Nuremberg: Hans Guldenmundt, n.d.);

Das heyß Eysen und Der böse Rauch (Nuremberg: Valentin Neuber, 1576);

Das vierdt Poetisch Buch. Mancherley artliche Newe Stück, Schöner gebundener Reimen, in drey unterschiedliche Bücher getheylt [Folio IV] (Nuremberg: Leonhard Heußler, 1578);

Das fünfft vnd letzt Buch. Sehr Herrliche Schöne newe Stück artlicher, gebundener, Künstlicher Reimen, in drey unterschiedliche Bücher verfaßt [Folio V] (Nuremberg: Leonhard Heußler, 1579);

Editions and Collections: *Dichtungen von Hans Sachs*, 3 volumes, edited by Karl Goedeke and Julius Tittmann (Leipzig: Brockhaus, 1870–1871);

Hans Sachs Werke, 26 volumes, edited by Adelbert von Keller and Edmund Goetze (Stuttgart: Hiersemann, 1870–1908);

Sämtliche Fastnachtspiele von Hans Sachs, 7 volumes, edited by Goetze (Halle: Niemeyer, 1880–1887);

Sämtliche Fabeln und Schwänke von Hans Sachs, 6 volumes, edited by Goetze and Carl Drescher (Halle: Niemeyer, 1893–1913);

Die Prosadialoge von Hans Sachs, edited by Ingeborg Spriewald (Leipzig: VEB Bibliographisches Institut, 1970);

Hans Sachs: Werke in zwei Bänden, 2 volumes, edited by Reinhard Hahn (Berlin & Weimar: Aufbau, 1992).

Editions in English: *A Goodly dysputacion betwene a Christen Shomaker and a Popysshe Parson with two other parsones more, done within the famous citie of Noremborough*, translated by Anthony Scoloker (London: Anthony Scoloker & W. Seres, 1548);

Merry Tales and Three Shrovetide Plays, translated by William Leighton (London: Nutt, 1910)—includes *The Horse Thief, The Hot Iron, The Travelling Scholar*;

The Wandering Scholar from Paradise: A Fastnachtspiel with 3 Persons, edited by Samuel A. Eliot Jr., in *Little Theatre Classics*, volume 4 (Boston: Little, Brown, 1922), pp. 115–137;

Seven Shrovetide Plays, translated and annotated by E. U. Ouless (London: Deane, 1930)—comprises *The Children of Eve, Dame Truth, The Wandering Scholar, The Old Game, The Horse Thief, Five Poor Travellers, Death in the Tree*;

Away with Surly Husbands, translated and annotated by Ouless (London: Deane, 1934; Boston: Baker, 1934);

The Glutton's Paradise, translated by Hans Hinrichs (Mount Vernon, N.Y.: Peter Pauper, 1955);

Nine Carnival Plays by Hans Sachs, translated, with an introduction and notes, by Randall W. Listerman (Ottawa: Dovehouse, 1990)—comprises *The Nose Dance, The Stolen Bacon, The Calf-Hatching, The Wife in the Well, The Farmer with the Blur, The Evil Woman, The Grand Inquisitor in the Soup, The Dead Man, The Pregnant Farmer*.

Although chiefly remembered today as the genial shoemaker-poet and leader of Nuremberg's Meistersinger Guild in Richard Wagner's opera *Die Meistersinger von Nürnberg* (1862; translated as *The Master-Singers of Nuremberg*, 1892), Hans Sachs was, in his time, one of Germany's best-known poets. A

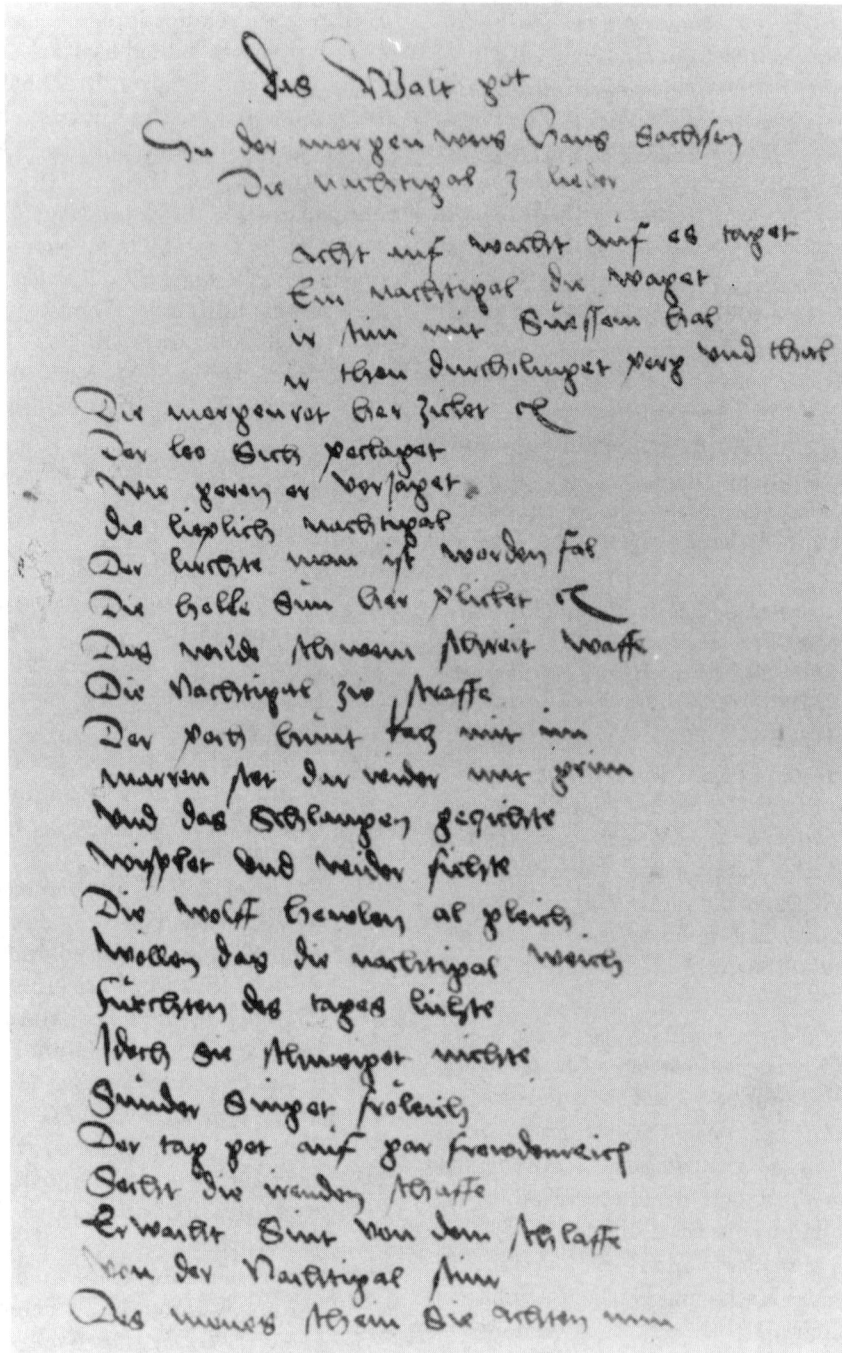

Page from the manuscript for Sachs's Meisterlied *"Das Walt got," thought to be the nucleus for* Die Wittembergisch Nachtigall *(Municipal Archives, Zwickau)*

man of unparalleled literary productivity, he wrote more than 4,000 *Meisterlieder* (master songs), almost 2,000 *Spruchgedichte* (poems), 85 *Fastnachtspiele* (carnival, or Shrovetide, plays), 128 other dramas, and 6 prose dialogues. A loyal champion of the Lutheran cause, he was, at the same, time, a critical and keen observer and chronicler of his times. Today only a small fraction of his enormous oeuvre is familiar to the general public. For anyone who is interested in the social history and mentality of early modern Germany, Sachs provides an inexhaustible source.

Sachs was born in Nuremberg on 5 November 1494 to the tailor Jörg Sachs, who had emigrated from Zwickau, and Christina Sachs, née Prunner. His relatively prosperous artisan family could afford to send its only son to one of the four Latin schools in the city, a school that awakened his lifelong passion for books. From 1509 to 1511 he was apprenticed to a shoemaker, and in the spring of 1512 he began his travels as a journeyman to Regensburg, Passau, Braunau, Otting, Burghausen, Wels, Salzburg, Munich, Frankfurt am Main, Koblenz, Cologne, and Aachen, and possibly also to Lübeck and cities in Saxony. In addition to getting to know large parts of Germany and becoming acquainted with the latest production techniques, he also made contacts with the Meistersinger, guild craftsmen who practiced the art of the *Meistergesang*, to which Sachs had been introduced as an apprentice by the Nuremberg linen weaver Lienhart Nunnenbeck. There is some evidence that he arranged his travels to take him to places where Meistersinger guilds existed. His earliest dated and preserved literary attempts come from this period: prompted by a love affair in Munich, Sachs wrote several texts, among them the moving *Buhlscheidlied Ach ungelück* (Song about the Pangs of Separation from a Loved One, 1513; printed in *Dichtungen von Hans Sachs*, 1870) and *Historia. Ein kleglich geschichte von zweyen liebhabenden. Der ermört Lorenz* (The Pitiful Story of Two Lovers. The Murdered Lorenz, 1515; printed in Folio I, 1558); and two carnival plays, *Das hoffgsindt Veneris* (Venus's Servants at the Court, 1517; printed in Folio III, 1561) and *Von der eygenschafft der lieb* (Love's Character, 1518; printed in Folio III). On 19 September 1519 Sachs married Kunigunde Kreutzer; the marriage would produce seven children and would last until Kunigunde's death forty-one years later. As a wedding gift his parents signed over their house in the Kotgasse, now Brunnengasse, to the young couple. In January 1520 Sachs became a master shoemaker.

Aside from a few trips to the trade fair in Frankfurt am Main, Sachs spent the remaining five and one-half decades of his life in Nuremberg, which at the beginning of the sixteenth century was one of the largest and most important of the free imperial cities in Germany. All political power lay in the hands of the forty patrician families who, through the *Rat* (council), regulated the lives of Nuremberg's citizens; Sachs, along with the vast majority of the population, was excluded from the political decision-making process. Since a failed revolt in 1348, the craftsmen were banned from organizing themselves into guilds. Nuremberg's wealth was based on commerce and manufacturing, and its products enjoyed an excellent reputation throughout Europe. Men such as Willibald Pirckheimer, Veit Stoß, Adam Krafft, and Albrecht Dürer made Nuremberg one of the centers of intellectual and artistic life in Germany.

Title page for Sachs's allegorical poem that helped to spread Martin Luther's teachings to the common people of Germany

Martin Luther's Ninety-five Theses, published in Latin in October 1517 and translated into German shortly thereafter by the Nuremberg patrician Kaspar Nützel, were well received in Nuremberg. Sachs, who had in his personal possession some forty Lutheran pamphlets, did not speak out on behalf of the Reformer until 1523, when he published the seven-hundred-verse poem *Die Wittenbergisch Nachtigall* (The Wittenberg Nightingale). An allegory in which the nightingale represents Luther, the lion Pope Leo X, and other animals bishops and prelates, the poem denounces the church, its institutions and representatives, its fiscal exploitation, the cults of relics, and the veneration of saints and expounds in simplified form Luther's teachings of justification through faith alone. Its catchy doggerels contributed to the poem's immediate success; it went through seven editions in short order and made the author famous throughout Germany.

In 1524, a year before the official introduction of the Reformation in Nuremberg, Sachs attempted to influence public opinion with four prose dialogues. Dealing with a wide spectrum of religious and social topics, these texts, with their lively discussions, vivid depiction of characters, and dra-

Title page for the first of the four pro-Reformation dialogues Sachs published in 1524 (courtesy of the Lilly Library, Indiana University)

matic structure, represent some of the best prose of the sixteenth century. *Disputation zwischen einem Chorherren und Schuchmacher* (Disputation between a Canon and a Shoemaker), featuring an indolent canon and a Bible-quoting cobbler, clearly takes sides with the Lutheran cause. *Ein gesprech eins Ewangelischen Christen mit einem Lutherischen* (A Conversation of an Evangelical Christian with a Lutheran) articulates Sachs's uneasiness with some of the radical changes taking place. In this conversation between two friends, Hans attacks those whose new faith amounts to nothing more than a provocative rejection of centuries-old customs and rituals; and whereas Peter seeks confrontation with the Catholics, Hans pleads for a slow and deliberate process based on understanding, love, and patient persuasion. Social and economic problems posed by monasticism are the topics of *Ein gesprech von den Scheinwercken der Gaystlichen, und iren gelübdten* (A Conversation about the Phony Works of the Clergy and Their Vows), in which Sachs contrasts the productive lives of the craftsmen with the parasitic existence of the monks. Although Sachs never wavered in his commitment to the Lutheran cause, his initial hope that the acceptance of the Reformer's teachings would inaugurate a more just social order had been replaced with disillusionment. Nowhere is this attitude clearer than in his fourth dialogue, *Ein Dialogus des inhalt: ein argument der Römischen wider das Christlich heüflein den Geytzn . . . betreffend* (A Dialogue to the Effect: An Argument of the Romans against the Christian Crowd Concerning Excessive Profit Seeking and Other Public Vices), a criticism of the early capitalist economic system. Having the Catholic Romanus articulate these views against the Evangelical merchant Reichenburger may have been Sachs's way of distancing himself from this critique, thus circumventing Nuremberg's harsh censorship practices.

In 1527 Sachs experienced the narrow limits the patrician council set for its citizens when he collaborated with Andreas Osiander, the fiery preacher of Saint Lorenz Church, and the well-known woodcutter Erhard Schön on *Eyn wunderliche Weyssagung von dem Babstumb* (A Strange Prophecy of the Papacy). Although the pamphlet, in its antipapal thrust and skillful combination of illustration and text, did not differ markedly from other broadsheets flooding the German market, the Nuremberg censor banned the work, had all printed copies confiscated, censured Osiander and Hans Guldenmund (the printer), and ordered Sachs—literally—to stick to his trade of shoemaker and desist from further publishing. Such an action against a pro-Lutheran work by a Lutheran city council seems odd, but Nuremberg was dependent on trade with its Catholic neighbors and good relations with the Catholic emperor. Although Sachs observed the ban for the next three years, in the long run the perceptive and critical shoemaker-poet could not be prevented from interpreting critically the religious, social, and political issues of the day. He did so primarily in the form of Spruchgedichte of varying lengths, consisting of rhymed couplets commenting on topics from the Turkish threat to his increasing concern with the dissensions within the Protestant camp. Having experienced censorship at first hand, however, he couched his criticism increasingly in the form of allegories, dreams, and mythological stories. In *Die Gemarthert Theologia* (Tortured Theology), which was not published until 1552, it is the allegorical figure Theology who diagnoses *Eygennutz* (egotism), especially that of the territorial princes, as the root of all evil. In the poem "Der Interim" (The Interim), written in 1548, Sachs turned against the city council, which reluctantly favored adoption of the imperial mandate reintroducing Catholic holidays, aural confession, and fasting. But he disguises his criticism by presenting the emperor as Jupiter, the Pope as Saturn, and the Reformer Philipp Melanchthon as Minerva. In addition, he pretends to have dreamed the whole episode, thus distancing himself twice from his criticism. Even in this encoded form, the poem was never published.

In the 1550s it was not the Catholic emperor but the Protestant margrave Albrecht Alcibiades of Brandenburg-Kulmbach who was a source of pain and suffering for Nuremberg. In 1552, in an attempt to annex parts of the extensive Nuremberg territory, Albrecht put the torch to castles, villages, and mills, terrorized the rural population with murder and lootings, and laid siege to the city itself. Only by paying the enormous sum of 200,000 gulden could the Nurembergers relieve themselves of the siege. But the threat continued to force the imperial city into costly war preparations and payments of tribute. Peace returned only with Albrecht's death in 1557, an event that prompted Sachs to one of his sharpest attacks. Presented as a dream vision, "Gesprech von der himelfart margraff Albrechts anno 1557" (The Conversation of the Ascension of Margrave Albrecht in the Year 1557) is by no means an apotheosis of the former enemy, as the title suggests, but a grim description of his descent into hell. In this poem Sachs creates scenes of oppressive gruesomeness. As the lonely figure walks silently through the valley of death, he is surrounded by a throng of burghers, women, and children whose demise he has caused. The contrast between the wailing victims and the solitary tyrant, as well as that between the ghostly darkness of purgatory and the blinding light of hell, is described in vivid detail. Like all of Sachs's poems having to do with Albrecht, however, this one was never printed. One day after the poet's death the ever-cautious city council would have the manuscripts for some of Sachs's unpublished works, including this poem, confiscated out of fear that they would bring harm to the city.

Sachs was not a revolutionary, as some Marxist critics have maintained; on the other hand, he was not the apolitical moralist portrayed by nineteenth-century critics. He was an independent, at times courageous man who did not hesitate to express his views on controversial and religious topics, albeit in masked fashion. Although these works did not appear in print, they were not written for the drawer but were circulated among friends. Even in manuscript form, however, some of them were considered too dangerous by the city authorities.

Today, thanks to Wagner, Sachs is primarily known as the Meistersinger of Nuremberg; and

Title page for the fourth dialogue in which Sachs tried to persuade the citizens of Nuremberg to accept the Reformation

there is some historical justification for that image. For decades the composition and performance of Meisterlieder were at the center of Sachs's creative work, even during the years 1527 to 1530, when he was not allowed to publish: Meisterlieder, by statute, could not appear in print and, thus, were not subject to censorship. Sachs collected his more than four thousand Meisterlieder—two-thirds of his literary production—in sixteen handwritten volumes.

The Meistersinger were literary-musical artisans in Nuremberg and other southern German cities who organized themselves into associations. In their *Singschulen* (concerts), held on Sundays after the main church service, they competitively performed their songs, solo and unaccompanied, following, like every other trade, strict rules and conventions. The competitions were judged by four *Merker* (markers) on the basis not of originality and artistic merit but of strict conformance with the *Tabulatur* (the tablet on which the rules were written). Initiated into the art by Nunnenbeck, Sachs practiced it during his travels as a journeyman and joined the Nuremberg Meistersinger guild on his re-

Sachs in 1545; woodcut by Hans Brosamer

turn. From 1524 to 1560 he was the guild's undisputed leader; by 1560 his interest in the genre had waned, but he remained the venerated master up to his death.

While in the *Hauptsingen* (Main Singing) part of the competition the Meistersinger concentrated on versifying Luther's translation of the Bible, in the *Freisingen* (Free Singing) part they treated a wide range of topics, from the sober and serious to the humorous and farcical, from ancient to modern, and from literary to anecdotal. All creation became the stuff of Sachs's songs. His curiosity was insatiable and his reading enormous, as is evidenced both by his sizable library and by the list of ancient, medieval, and contemporary sources on which he drew: Pliny, Plutarch, Ovid, Giovanni Boccaccio's *The Decameron* (1351–1353), the *Gesta Romanorum* (1472), Heinrich Steinhöwel's *Aesop* (1477), Herman Bote's *Dil Ulenspiegel* (1510 or 1511; translated, 1518), Johannes Pauli's *Schimpf und Ernst* (Jest and Seriousness, 1522), farces, histories, and chronicles. In reworking the themes found in these works Sachs skillfully sharpened points and condensed or expanded the stories. In the force of his personality, his indefatigable energy, his tuneful melodies, and his adroit handling of hundreds of meters he stood head and shoulders above his colleagues. His thousands of unprinted Meisterlieder still await analysis.

Although Sachs is known as the outstanding Meistersinger of Nuremberg, it is doubtful whether any of his Meisterlieder are actually read or sung today. His Fastnachtspiele, on the other hand, are still read and performed. The plays were an integral part of the pre-Lenten carnival celebrations, a time of ribaldry and boisterousness in which the world was turned upside down. Costumed journeymen went from street to street and from pub to pub performing skits that poked fun at social conventions. Among pre-Reformation Nuremberg carnival playwrights, the best known are Hans Rosenplüt and Hans Folz. Sachs surpassed his predecessors and contemporaries not only in the quantity but also in the quality of his plays. He wrote more than eighty Fastnachtspiele between 1517 and 1566 – three-quarters of them between 1550 and 1560, a decade of unparalleled productivity during which he also wrote ninety-four comedies and tragedies, remained an active Meistersinger, commented on current events in Spruchgedichte, and practiced his trade as a shoemaker.

Though he wrote two carnival plays before the Reformation, Sachs did not really begin his career as an author of such plays until the mid 1530s. With the official introduction of the Reformation in 1525 the council abolished Lent, the season of penitence and fasting; thus, the pre-Lenten carnival, a time of officially sanctioned ribaldry, lost its meaning and came to be considered an undesirable interruption of work and a threat to morality, health, and the economy. For Sachs, the carnival plays assumed a didactic as well as an entertaining function; each of his plays ends with a moral.

Reliance on reason and the power of the mind, as well as belief in the improvability of humanity, lie at the core of Sachs's anthropology and of his self-concept as a poet: the poet's function is to help the individual to see his or her own foolishness. Whether Sachs used literary sources or drew on his own observations, he created a colorful crowd of figures: greedy merchants, simple-minded peasants, pathologically jealous husbands, wives who cheat on their husbands with the help of cunning matchmakers, young widows who console themselves with young lovers, and sexually deprived priests. There are cases of mistaken identity, intrigues, and, again and again, the theme of the deceived deceiver. Marriage, with its daily frictions, jealousies, and large and small deceptions, is an inexhaustible topic. Among Sachs's best-known carnival plays are *Das Narren schneiden* (The Foolectomy, 1536), *Der farendt Schuler im Paradeiss* (The Traveling Scholar in Paradise, 1550; translated as *The Travelling Scholar*, 1910), *Das Kelberbrüten* (1551; translated as *The Calf-Hatching*, 1990), *Das heyß eysen* (1551; translated as *The Hot Iron*, 1910), *Der bös rauch* (The

Evil Smoke, 1551), *Der roß dieb zw Fünsing* (The Horse Thief of Fünsing, 1553; translated as *The Horse Thief,* 1910), and *Der Kremer Korb* (The Merchant's Basket, 1554). Of the thousands of works by Sachs, only his carnival plays have been translated into English.

Sachs also achieved undisputed mastery in the genre of the *Schwank* (farce). As in the carnival plays, with which the farces share many thematic and functional similarities, Sachs's message is a plea for tolerance and forgiveness. His laughter at the many foibles of his fellow human beings is mostly good-natured, rarely ironic, never sarcastic. Unlike the pessimist Sebastian Brant, whose *Das Narrenschiff* (The Ship of Fools, 1494; translated, 1509) held up a merciless mirror to his contemporaries, and Thomas Murner, whose *Narren bschwerung* (Exorcism of Fools, 1512) and *Der schelmen zunfft* (The Rogues' Guild, 1512) castigate his time in sharp words, Sachs tries to bring his contemporaries to a recognition of their mistakes and shortcomings through laughter.

Less well known today are Sachs's 128 tragedies and comedies, written to provide moral guidance and to contribute, as Sachs himself said, "zu anraitzung der guten tugendt unnd zu abschneidung der schendlichen laster" (to encourage good virtue and to cut out the bad vices). Drawing on the Bible and on ancient and medieval literature, each play follows the same pattern: a *Herolt* (announcer) greets the audience, names the literary source, briefly sums up the plot, and points to the moral. As in Bertolt Brecht's epic theater, the spectator is not allowed to be caught up in the action. The plot jumps boldly from place to place, occasionally from country to country, and extends over weeks, months, and sometimes decades. Unlike the carnival plays, the tragedies and comedies consist of acts, ranging from one to ten. After the actors exit, the Herolt reappears and establishes links between the play and the situation of contemporary Nuremberg. Since Sachs's primary intention was moral guidance, his characters are not unique individuals with all their contradictions and inner conflicts but paradigms for right and wrong behavior: a person is either good or bad. To get the audience to identify with the characters, Sachs gives them the features of burghers of sixteenth-century Nuremberg. This *Vernürnbergern* (Nurembergizing), as the nineteenth-century philosopher Georg Wilhelm Friedrich Hegel mockingly termed it, makes good, industrious, honest Nurembergers, or their opposites, out of Adam and Eve, Cain and Abel, the Old Testament prophets and patriarchs, the Homeric heroes, the half-mythical and historical figures of Livy, and the

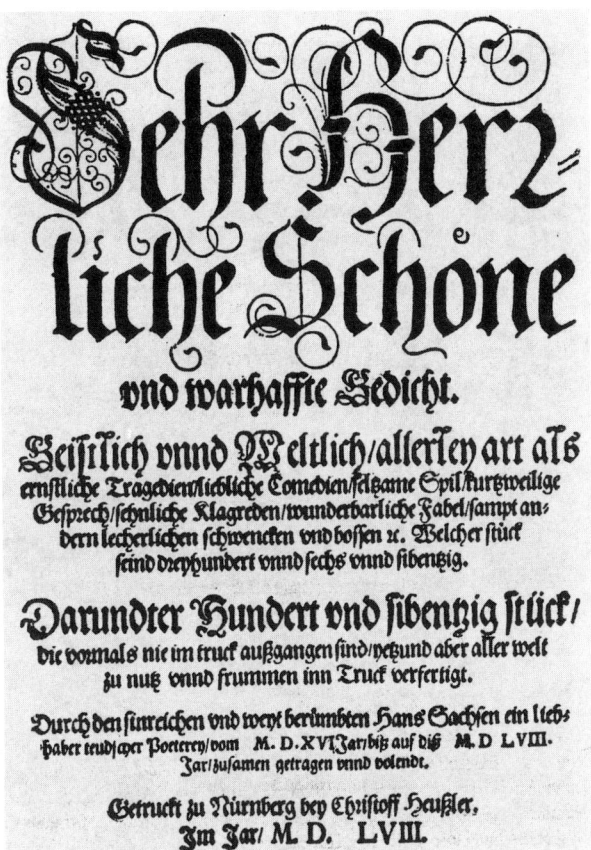

Title page for the first volume of Sachs's edition of his collected works

heroes of the chapbooks. The tragedies and comedies include *Tragedia von schöpfung, fal und auß treibung Ade auß dem paradeyß* (Tragedy of the Creation, Fall and Expulsion of Adam from Paradise, 1548), *Der wütrich könig Herodes* (The Tyrant King Herod, 1552), *Die mördisch königin Clitimestra* (The Murderous Queen Clytemnestra, 1554), *Tragedia könig Sauls* (The Tragedy of King Saul, 1557), *Von Alexander Magno* (Of Alexander the Great, 1558), *Die gedultig und gehorsam margräfin Griselda* (The Patient and Obedient Margravine Griselda, 1546), *Die ungeleichen kinder Eve* (The Unequal Children of Eve, 1553), *Tragedia des Jüngsten Geriechts* (The Tragedy of the Last Judgment, 1560), and *Die jung witfraw Francisca* (The Young Widow Francisca, 1560); with the exception of *Tragedia des Jüngsten Geriechts,* they were all first printed in the Nuremberg Folio editions.

All of Sachs's works, except the Meisterlieder and, of course, the prose dialogues, are written in *Knittelvers,* a rhymed couplet consisting of four stressed syllables and four to eleven unstressed syllables. That not every line is a masterpiece is not surprising, considering the enormous scope of Sachs's oeuvre: it is estimated that he wrote about half a million lines. But his mastery of this confining

Page from Eygentliche Beschreibung Aller Stände auff Erden, *with woodcut by Jost Amman and poem by Sachs describing the printing trade*

midst of this undertaking he lost his wife; he paid her a moving tribute in *Der wunderliche traum von meiner abgeschiden lieben gemahel Künigundt Sächsin* (The Strange Dream of My Dear Departed Wife Kunigunde Sachs, 1560; printed in Folio III). A year and a half later Sachs married Barbara Endres, née Harscher, a twenty-seven-year-old widow. Practical considerations may have been the primary reason for this alliance: she had six children and a small inheritance; he needed an efficient manager for his household, with its apprentices and journeymen. Barbara restored his optimism, revitalized his creativity, and turned the sixty-seven-year-old Sachs into a love poet. *Das künstlich frawen-lob* (The Artistic Praise of Women, 1562; printed in Folio V, 1579), a poetic homage to his young wife, is one of the most beautiful lyrical poems to come from his pen. After a description of her anatomical charms that approaches indiscretion, he hastens to add her chastity, humility, fidelity, and modesty to his portrayal.

In 1568 Sachs, at the request of the Frankfurt publisher Sigmund Feyerabend, collaborated on a book describing contemporary professions, trades, and crafts in word and picture. For each of the 117 woodcuts by Jost Amman, Sachs contributed four rhymed couplets sketching the artisan's work process and products or the human or mythological inventors of the craft. Published under the title *Eygentliche Beschreibung Aller Stände auff Erden* (Exact Description of All Ranks on Earth, 1568; translated as *The Book of Trades,* 1973), it allows Sachs, once again, to condemn egotism and *Müssiggang* (indolent leisure) and to emphasize a community-oriented work ethic. Today the work is a valuable document for the social history of sixteenth-century Germany.

Sachs died on 19 January 1576. He was buried outside the city gates in the Cemetery of Saint John. His grave site is not known.

Although Hans Sachs was never totally forgotten, the literary climate of the two centuries after his death did not favor artisan-poets. The ideal had become the *poeta doctus* (learned poet), who had studied the literary traditions of the Romans and Greeks at a university and composed poems after Latin and French models. A new appreciation of the Nuremberg poet began in Weimar on the two-hundredth anniversary of his death, when Christoph Martin Wieland dedicated a special issue of his *Teutscher Merkur* to Sachs; it featured an essay by Wieland and a poem by Johann Wolfgang von Goethe, "Hans Sachsens poetische Sendung" (Hans Sachs's Poetic Mission). For the Romantics, the image of the upright cobbler-poet merged with that of an idealized Nuremberg with its maze of medieval streets. In the nineteenth century Sachs became the subject of poems, dramas,

meter is superior to that of any other poet of the sixteenth century.

His awareness of his advancing age, along with a sense that his inspiration was drying up and the fear that his works might be dispersed and forgotten, prompted Sachs to edit and collect his works. The first volume appeared in 1558, volumes two and three in 1560 and 1561, and volumes four and five posthumously in 1578 and 1579. His *Generalregister,* a list of the fifty-four hundred works he had written to that time, also belongs to this period of personal and poetic stocktaking. The process was simplified by the fact that Sachs had, over the decades, faithfully copied all of his texts in thirty-three volumes. In the

and operas, of which Wagner's is the best and the one that has shaped the modern image of Sachs. The Sachs renaissance reached its high point in 1894 when Nuremberg celebrated the four-hundredth birthday of its native son with pageantry, essays, books, and speeches. Glorified as the pious, hardworking, patriotic, and loyal German, he became a model for the good citizen of Wilhelminian Germany.

Bibliographies:

Emil Weller, *Der Volksdichter Hans Sachs und seine Dichtungen: Eine Bibliographie* (Nuremberg: Sichling, 1868); republished, with a supplement, "Die Bibliothek Hans Sachs," by Erich Carlsohn (Wiesbaden: Martin Sändig, 1966);

Niklas Holzberg, *Hans-Sachs-Bibliographie: Schriftenverzeichnis zum 400-jährigen Todestag im Jahr 1976* (Nuremberg: Selbstverlag der Stadtbibliothek Nürnberg, 1976);

Holzberg, "Nachtrag zur Hans-Sachs-Bibliographie," *Mitteilungen des Vereins für Geschichte der Stadt Nürnberg*, 64 (1977): 333-343.

Biographies:

Salomon Ranisch, *Historisch-kritische Lebensbeschreibung Hanns Sachsens, ehemals berühmten Meistersängers zu Nürnberg* (Altenburg, 1765);

Charles Schweitzer, *Un poète allemand au XVI siècle: Étude sur la vie et les oeuvres de Hans Sachs* (Paris: Berger-Levrault, 1887);

Rudolph Genée, *Hans Sachs und seine Zeit* (Leipzig: Weber, 1894);

Klaus Wedler, *Hans Sachs* (Leipzig: Reclam, 1976);

Eckhard Bernstein, *Hans Sachs: Mit Selbstzeugnissen und Bilddokumenten* (Reinbek: Rowohlt, 1993).

References:

Roland Bainton, "Eyn wunderliche Weyssagung: Osiander-Sachs-Luther," *Germanic Review*, 21 (1946): 161-164;

Bernd Balzer, *Bürgerliche Reformationspropaganda: Die Flugschriften des Hans Sachs in den Jahren 1523-1525* (Stuttgart: Metzler, 1973);

Anne-Kathrin Brandt, *Die "tugentreich fraw Armut": Besitz und Armut in der Tugendlehre des Hans Sachs* (Göttingen: Gratia, 1979);

Neil C. Brooks, "The Artisan and Mastersinger Drama in Nürnberg," *Journal of English and Germanic Philology*, 17 (1918): 565-584;

Horst Brunner, Gerhard Hirschmann, and Fritz Schnelbögl, eds., *Hans Sachs und Nürnberg* (Nuremberg: Selbstverlag des Vereins für Geschichte der Stadt Nürnberg, 1976);

Eckehard Catholy, *Das deutsche Lustspiel* (Stuttgart: Kohlhammer, 1969), pp. 49-75;

Catholy, *Fastnachtspiel* (Stuttgart: Metzler, 1966);

Thomas Cramer and Erika Kartschoke, eds., *Hans Sachs: Studien zur frühbürgerlichen Literatur im 16. Jahrhundert* (Bern, Frankfurt am Main & Las Vegas: Peter Lang, 1978);

Ferdinand Eichler, *Das Nachleben des Hans Sachs vom XVI. bis ins XIX. Jahrhundert* (Leipzig: Harrassowitz, 1904);

Stephan Füssel and others, eds., *Hans Sachs: Katalog zur Ausstellung*, second edition (Göttingen: Gratia, 1979);

Eugen Geiger, *Der Meistergesang des Hans Sachs: Literarhistorische Untersuchung* (Bern: Francke, 1956);

Germanisches Nationalmuseum, ed., *Hans Sachs und die Meistersinger in ihrer Zeit* (Nuremberg: Germanisches Nationalmuseum, 1981);

Joseph E. Gillert, "The German Dramatist of the Sixteenth Century and the Bible," *PMLA*, 34 (1919): 465-493;

Reinhard Hahn, "Hans Sachs," in *Deutsche Dichter der frühen Neuzeit 1450-1600*, edited by Füssel (Berlin: Erich Schmidt, 1993), pp. 406-427;

Samuel Kinser, "Presentation and Representation: Carnival at Nuremberg 1450-1550," *Representations*, 13 (1986): 1-41;

Barbara Könneker, *Hans Sachs* (Stuttgart: Metzler, 1971);

Könneker, "Hans Sachs: Die Wittembergisch Nachtigall und die Reformationsdialoge," in her *Die deutsche Literatur der Reformationszeit: Kommentar zu einer Epoche* (Munich: Beck, 1975), pp. 148-157;

Helmut Krause, *Die Dramen des Hans Sachs: Untersuchungen zur Lehre und Technik* (Berlin: Hofgarten, 1979);

Georg F. Lussky, "The Structure of Hans Sachs' Fastnachtspiele in Relation to Their Place of Performance," *Journal of English and Germanic Philology*, 26 (1927): 521-565;

George R. Marek, "Nuremberg's Cobbler Poet," *Opera News*, 41 (18 December 1976): 19-20;

Wolfgang F. Michael, *Das deutsche Drama der Reformationszeit* (Bern, Frankfurt am Main & Las Vegas: Peter Lang, 1984), pp. 323-356;

Bert Nagel, *Meistersang*, second edition (Stuttgart: Metzler, 1971);

Franz Otten, *Mit hilff gottes zw tichten . . . got zw lob und zw auspreittung seines heilsamen wort: Untersuchungen zur Reformationsdichtung des Hans Sachs* (Göppingen: Kümmerle, 1993);

Gerhard Pfeiffer, ed., *Nürnberg-Geschichte einer europäischen Stadt* (Munich: Beck, 1971), pp. 199-211;

Ralf Erik Remshardt, "The Birth of Reason from the Spirit of Carnival: Hans Sachs und Das Narrenschneyden," *Comparative Drama,* 23 (1989): 70–94;

Maximilian J. Rudwin, "The Origin of the German Carnival Comedy," *Journal of English and Germanic Philology,* 18 (1919): 402–454;

Richard Erich Schade, *Studies in Early German Comedy: 1500–1650* (Columbia, S.C.: Camden House, 1988);

Gottfried Seebass, "The Reformation in Nürnberg," in *The Social History of the Reformation,* edited by Lawrence P. Buck and Jonathan W. Zophy (Columbus: Ohio State University Press, 1972), pp. 17–40;

Eli Sobel, "Martin Luther and Hans Sachs," *Michigan Germanic Studies,* 10 (1984): 129–141;

Ingeborg Spriewald, "Der Bürger ergreift das Wort: Luther und die Reformation im Werk von Hans Sachs," *Weimarer Beiträge,* 29 (1983): 1908–1927;

Spriewald, *Literatur zwischen Hören und Lesen: Wandel von Funktion und Rezeption im späten Mittelalter: Fallstudien zu Behaim, Folz und Sachs* (Berlin & Weimar: Aufbau, 1990);

Gerald Strauss, *Nuremberg in the Sixteenth Century: City Politics and Life Between Middle Ages and Modern Times* (Bloomington & London: Indiana University Press, 1976);

Archer Taylor, *The Literary History of Meistergesang* (New York & London: Oxford University Press, 1937);

Martin W. Walsh, "Quacks, Empirics, Spiritual Physicians: The Dramatic Function of the Medicus in the 15th and 16th Century Fastnachtspiele," *Fifteenth Century Studies,* 8 (1983): 239–274;

Friedrich Windolph, *Der Reiseweg Hans Sachsens in seiner Handwerksburschenzeit nach seinen eigenen Dichtungen* (Greifswald: Adler, 1911);

Dieter Wuttke, *Nuremberg: Focal Point of German Culture and History,* second edition (Bamberg: Wendel, 1988).

Papers:

Hans Sachs copied all of his *Meisterlieder* in sixteen volumes, of which seven have been lost; eight (numbers 2, 3, 4, 5, 8, 12, 13, and 15) are in the Ratsarchiv Zwickau, and one is in the Stadtbibliothek Nürnberg (Amb. 2° 784). Sachs also copied his *Spruchgedichte* in eighteen volumes; seven of these volumes have been lost, six (numbers 4, 11, 12, 13, and 16) are in the Ratsarchiv Zwickau, one is in the Staatsbibliothek Preußischer Kulturbesitz Berlin (Ms germ. 2° 591), one is in the Sächsische Landesbibliothek Dresden (M10°), two are in the Museum of German History Berlin (RA 52/3470), and one is in the Stadtbibliothek Nürnberg (Am 2° 784). The Ratsarchiv Zwickau also has, in Sachs's hand, a list of all of his works (the *Generalregister*), a list of the books he owned, and the *Singschulordnung* (statutes of the Nuremberg Meistersinger Guild) of 1540.

Joannes Sapidus (Hans Witz)
(1490 – 8 June 1561)

Peter Schaeffer
University of California, Davis

BOOKS: *Epigrammata* (Schlettstadt: Lazarus Schürer, 1520);

Ursach, warumb der vermeint geystlich huff mit yren patronen, das Evangelion Jesu Christ nit annimpt, sunder schendet, lestert, und verfolget, mit kurtzer Contrafactur der Pfafferey, Müncherey, Nonnerey, Allen liebhabern der warheyt nützlich zu lesen, as Johan Sonnentaller (N.p., 1524);

Sylva epistolaris seu Barba (Strasbourg: Johann Albrecht, 1534);

Anabion sive Lazarus Redivivus (Strasbourg: Crato Mylius, 1539);

Epitaphia sive Gymnasii Argentoratensis luctus (Strasbourg: Wendelin Richel, 1542);

Paraclesis sive Consolatio de Morte Illustrissimi Principis Alberti Marchionis Badensis (Strasbourg: Crato Mylius, 1543).

Edition: *Anabion sive Lazarus Redivivus,* edited by Wolfgang Michael and Douglass Parker (Bern: Peter Lang, 1991).

OTHER: "Apotheosis Erasmi," in *Epitaphiorum ac Tumulorum Libellus, quibus Des. Erasmi Roterodami Mors defletur* (Basel: Hieronymus Froben, 1536), pp. 96-108;

"Romulus," as Eucharius Synesius, in *Bucolicae Querelae* (Strasbourg: Jacobus Jucundus, 1540) – also includes "Thyrsis," by Johann Sturm, as Baptista Persius;

Conradus Hubertus, *Historia vera de Vita, Obitu, Sepultura . . . D. Martini Buceri,* contributions by Sapidus (Strasbourg: Johann Oporinus, 1561) – includes Sapidus's "Colloquuntur Viator et Religio" and "Eiusdem in eundem exhumatum et crematum."

Joannes Sapidus, as Hans Witz was known during his lifetime and has been known since, was a highly esteemed scholar in the close-knit republic of letters of northern humanism in the first half of the sixteenth century. He was headmaster of the Latin School at Schlettstadt (Sélestat) in Alsace at the zenith of its reputation and later a tirelessly dedicated teacher in Strasbourg; a friend and correspondent of some of the most distinguished personages of the Reformation period – Desiderius Erasmus, Beatus Rhenanus, Martin Bucer, Huldrych Zwingli, Johannes Oecolampadius, and Wolfgang Capito; and a Neo-Latin author in the genres of drama, poetry, and prose. Although Paul Volz described Sapidus in a letter to Rhenanus (1 December 1536) as "gloriae propriae negligens" (indifferent to his own fame), and although the body of Sapidus's publications was not extensive, what did see the light of day is of the first quality of Renaissance Latinity. For the most part it is still awaiting full critical appreciation, but it is of particular interest for its intrinsic literary excellence; its intimate connection with luminaries of the Reformation, particularly in Alsace; and its documentation of humanism during the turbulent period of confessional conflict.

Little is known of the family into which Sapidus was born in 1490; the name Witz was a common one, and Heinrich Pantaleon's description of Sapidus in the *Prosopographiae heroum atque illustrium virorum totius Germaniae* (Biographies of Distinguished and Illustrious Men throughout All of Germany, 1565) as "natus honestis parentibus" (born of upright parents) is clearly formulaic. Sapidus attended the Latin School of his native Schlettstadt under its headmasters Crato Hofmann and Hieronymus Gebwiler, then continued his studies in Paris with Jacques Le Fèvre d'Étaples in philosophy and Fausto Andrelino in rhetoric and poetics. In addition to a compendious mastery of classical Roman literature, he acquired at least a good fundamental knowledge of Greek – an uncommon specialty north of the Alps at that time and one that he would introduce into the curriculum at Schlettstadt. Returning there, he was named, at the age of twenty, rector of the school – first on a one-year provisional basis, then permanently.

Title page for Joannes Sapidus's poetic defense of bearded clergy (Houghton Library, Harvard University)

It was in this capacity, as well as in that of a member of the flourishing literary society of Schlettstadt, that Sapidus came to the attention of Erasmus, who commemorated his visit there in 1515 with an elegy, *Encomium Selestadii* (The Praise of Schlettstadt, 1515), in which he exalts the small but distinguished imperial city as containing as many renowned scholars as the Trojan horse could hardly have concealed warriors; among them is Sapidus, who is apostrophized as "doctis quoque dignus Athenis" (worthy of learned Athens). In the same year, 1520, that Sapidus's first publication, *Epigrammata* (Epigrams), appeared as the inaugural imprint at Lazarus Schürer's press in Schlettstadt, Erasmus dedicated his *Antibarbari* (The Antibarbarians) to him. The tribute was all the more distinctive as Erasmus, who had all the lords spiritual and temporal in Europe available as recipients of his dedications, singled out the Alsatian headmaster to receive this major manifesto on behalf of humanistic studies.

Epigrammata is a poetic miscellany; only part of it consists of epigrams in the strict sense. Thematically the pieces range from tributes to famous persons, including epitaphs—a form Sapidus was to favor throughout his life—to animal fables, riddles, ribald anecdotes, and local backstairs gossip; the work concludes with twenty distichs on a series of pictures depicting the life and miracles of Saint Nicholas at an Alsatian monastery. In all, *Epigrammata* consists of nearly 150 items in a glittering array of poetic virtuosity. Shortly after the appearance of the work the renowned Schlettstadt educator Jakob Wimpfeling, in a letter appended to Jacob Spiegel's *In Aurelii Prudentii Clementis Caesaraugustani* (Commentary on Prudentius's Hymn for All Seasons, 1520), recommended it in the context of promoting Christian rather than pagan poetry for use in the schools.

The epigram "De se celebrato ab Erasmo Roterodamo" (Of Himself as Celebrated by Erasmus of Rotterdam) may serve as an example of Sapidus's art:

> Mortalem me mortales genuere parentes,
>   Idaliae functi munere militiae.
> Immortalem immortalis me fecit Ersamus,
>   Palladiae functus munere militiae.
> Heus dea quae Phrygio sub iudice digna fuisti,
>   Tollere non meritis aurea poma tuis,
> Me censore, manu vacua & despecta recedes,
>   Nam Pallas Sapido, quod Venus est Paridi,
> Rebus enim quantum praestant aeterna caducis,
>   Tantundem Paphiae diva Minerva tibi.

> (My mortal parents brought me forth a mortal,
>   Having performed the service of Venus.
> Immortal Erasmus has made me immortal,
>   Having performed the service of Pallas.
> Hearken, you goddess, found worthy by the Trojan judge,
>   To take the golden apples without merit of your own,
> Were I to judge, you would withdraw empty-handed and spurned,
>   For Pallas is to Sapidus what Venus to Paris,
> As much as eternal surpasses temporal,
>   So much is Minerva superior, O Cyprian goddess, to you.)

This piece contains several recurrent themes found in the epigrammatic art of the period: the expression of friendship and mutual admiration among humanists; a belief in the immortality of reputation that is not opposed to but consonant with a belief in Christian immortality; and the resourceful use of ancient mythology, not merely for decoration but to express the consciousness of being an heir to classical culture, both as recipient and as emulator. Although the satiric thrust in *Epigrammata* against certain Roman Catholic doctrines, practices, and corruptions does not exceed what many such polemics had expressed in the century after the Council of Constance, and although the open admiration for Luther in 1520–the year of his great programmatic pamphlets–but before the Diet of Worms–did not yet represent a breach with Catholicism, Sapidus was tending more and more in that direction. Meanwhile, the patriciate of Schlettstadt remained faithful to the old religion.

That by 1524 Sapidus had broken with the Catholic Church seems to be documented by the pamphlet *Ursach, warumb der vermeint geystlich huff mit yren patronen, das Evangelion Jesu Christ nit annimpt, sunder schendet, lestert, und verfolget, mit kurtzer Contrafactur der Pfafferey, Müncherey, Nonnerey, Allen liebhabern der warheyt nützlich zu lesen* (Reasons Why the Supposedly Spiritual Hordes along with Their Patrons Do Not Accept the Gospel of Jesus Christ, but Dishonor, Scorn and Persecute It, Together with a Brief Depiction of Priestcraft, Monkery, and Nunnery, Useful to Read for All Lovers of the Truth). Although the attribution of this pseudonymous publication to Sapidus is probable in view of his handwritten dedication to Count Ulrich von Rappolstein on the only extant copy (now in the municipal library of Colmar), it is not absolutely certain. If he did write it, it is his only published work in the vernacular. In vitriolic diatribe it matches anything that came out of Reformation polemics.

In 1525 the breach became complete when Sapidus refused to take part, as headmaster, in a commonplace ecclesiastical procession. At his request he was dismissed. The following year he moved to Strasbourg, where, under the guidance of his erstwhile townsman Bucer and Wolfgang Capito, the Reformation had built a solid foundation. The Latin School of Schlettstadt never again attained as brilliant a reputation as it had enjoyed under Sapidus; its rapid decline from nine hundred pupils—an enormous number for the time—and also in quality was owing chiefly to the turbulence of the Reformation, as well as the Peasants' War and its aftermath, but the departure of Sapidus could only have served to accelerate it.

In Strasbourg Sapidus was installed as headmaster of one of the three municipal Latin schools that the educational reform had created out of the previous religious foundations; he attained a permanent appointment in 1528. Little is known of his life in the following decades beyond a few references in humanistic or official correspondence and what his own works, at least obliquely, reveal about him.

Following a poetic contribution to a slender memorial volume for two Reformers—Zwingli, who had fallen in battle in October 1531, and Oecolampadius, who had died the following month—Sapidus's curious verse epistle *Sylva epistolaris seu Barba* (Epistolary Collections or The Beard) appeared in 1534, though, as the preface recounts, it had been written eight years earlier. It treats in a humorous manner the currently questioned propriety of ecclesiastics wearing beards; drawing on copious examples from nature, mythology, and history, Sapidus vigorously defends the practice. The book is a showpiece of the stylistic and dia-

Title page for the volume of satiric eclogues Sapidus co-authored with his son-in-law, Johann Sturm

lectic skill of a poet who here, as he did so often, dismisses his own work as a mere trifle.

When Erasmus died in July 1536, Sapidus contributed to the extensive collection of literary tributes to the Sage of Rotterdam. Sapidus's contribution is by far the longest and is also the most ambitious of the encomiums. With its 388 hexameters—about the length of a Homeric canto—in the epic genre, Sapidus creates a poignantly dramatic situation, portraying himself as consumed by grief over the death of Erasmus and unable to summon up words to express it. In a dream vision he is visited by Erasmus, who is flanked by Saints Paul and Jerome; they have welcomed Erasmus into heaven and accorded him the place of honor between them, since it was by his tireless endeavors that the New Testament and the Fathers, whom they represent, are again to be read in pristine splendor. With a prayer for Sapidus—in which Sapidus, without leaving the hexametric flow, follows the schema of the liturgical collect—they dismiss him, consoled and eager to take up his mission of propagating the works of Erasmus. In an allusion to the eucharistic Real Presence, Erasmus is depicted as present, living and speaking, in his works, nourishing his readers with the food and drink of knowledge. Finally, in a bold flight of fancy Sapidus presents a triune Erasmus, one buried in the ground, one exalted to the stars, and one abiding as the sovereign teacher of all that humanity has to learn. Seizing on the dream vision, a technique that goes back at least to Cicero's *Dream of Scipio,* but also drawing on the celestial visions of Christian hagiography, Sapidus, in this final monument to his friendship with and his supreme admiration for Erasmus, has created a literary gem. It is, moreover, a document of the spirit that bound Erasmus's loyal followers together, even across the deepening chasms of the advancing Reformation.

On the basis of a few observations in the correspondence of other humanists, it is known that Sapidus was married three times; the last time was in 1542. In 1537 a daughter from his first marriage became the wife of the genial young educator Johann Sturm, whom Bucer had just brought to Strasbourg; until 1581 Sturm directed the newly consolidated school that was to burgeon into the University of Strasbourg. The consolidation reduced Sapidus from headmaster to an ordinary master of the third form; but he apparently took the demotion in stride, since the new headmaster was his son-in-law. Sapidus contributed a commendatory poem to the publication of Sturm's educational program in 1538.

Meanwhile, Sapidus had been commissioned to write the festive drama for the inauguration of the new school; the result was his greatest work, *Anabion sive Lazarus Redivivus* (Anavion; or, Lazarus Revived, 1539). Dedicated to Erasmus of Limburg, the archdeacon of the cathedral chapter (and, two years later, elected bishop of Strasbourg for his conciliatory disposition toward the Reformation), this elaborate dramatization of John 11:1-44 on the death and resurrection of Lazarus was a resounding success. It received several performances and went through at least six printed editions and a few German translations—or, more properly speaking, adaptations. In the prologue Sapidus develops a brief general theory of the drama. Though his own art is founded in the language, meters, and techniques of antiquity, he stresses that these times are marked by a different way of life, religion, and relationships among people both in public and in private, and, accordingly, call for a decidedly different style of writing. Throughout there are allusions to contemporary customs and proverbial and idiomatic expressions, elegantly veiled in the choicest neoclassical Latin. A verse paraphrase of the Lord's Prayer at Lazarus's funeral graphically sets forth the seamless symbiosis of antiquity and modernity, of classical civilization and Christian piety, as the ideal of the Alsatian humanists.

To transform the biblical episode into a full-fledged drama, the playwright adds to the household of Lazarus, Mary, and Martha servants whose conversation reflects the individuality of the principals and adds humor to interludes amid the serious events of the illness, death, burial, and miraculous raising of Lazarus. Similarly, the entrance of Jesus in the fifth act is amply prepared by the anticipatory reflection of those who, in part mournfully, in part hopefully—and, among the outsiders, skeptically—await his coming. Innumerable small details are stressed: for example, the apothecary's ultimately futile medication for Lazarus; the interaction among the Apostles, contrasted with that among the Pharisees; and the rites surrounding the death and burial of Lazarus. This emphasis on details makes the persons in the play genuinely plausible individuals, far beyond the mere functional types usually met with in contemporary drama. Wolfgang Michael and Douglass Parker call *Anabion* the most subtly characterized modern European character drama prior to the plays of William Shakespeare. It remained unique both in the oeuvre of Sapidus and in the otherwise abundant dramatic production of the time; to this towering creative achievement his remaining literary work seems rather like an elaborate postlude.

By 1540 Sapidus had been relieved of his general teaching obligations and given a new assignment, probably more in accord both with his preference and affinities, of *lectio poetices* (teaching of literature). The position included the interpretation of classical and contemporary authors, as well as poetics—not merely literary theory but also creative writing, since Latin prose and verse composition were an integral part of the humanistic curriculum.

From 1540 dates the satiric jeu d'esprit *Bucolicae querelae,* which Sapidus brought out pseudonymously with his son-in-law, Sturm. To the inner circle the pen name Eucharius Synesius was easily decipherable as a Greek rendering of the Latin Joannes Sapidus, just as Baptista Persius conceals Johann Sturm. Sapidus contributes the first of the two eclogues, "Romulus." The title character is a shepherd on the banks of the Tiber; he stands for the Pope—not necessarily the incumbent Paul III but a generic sort of post-Reformation pope. In colorful detail he laments the loss of his flocks of cattle, sheep, and

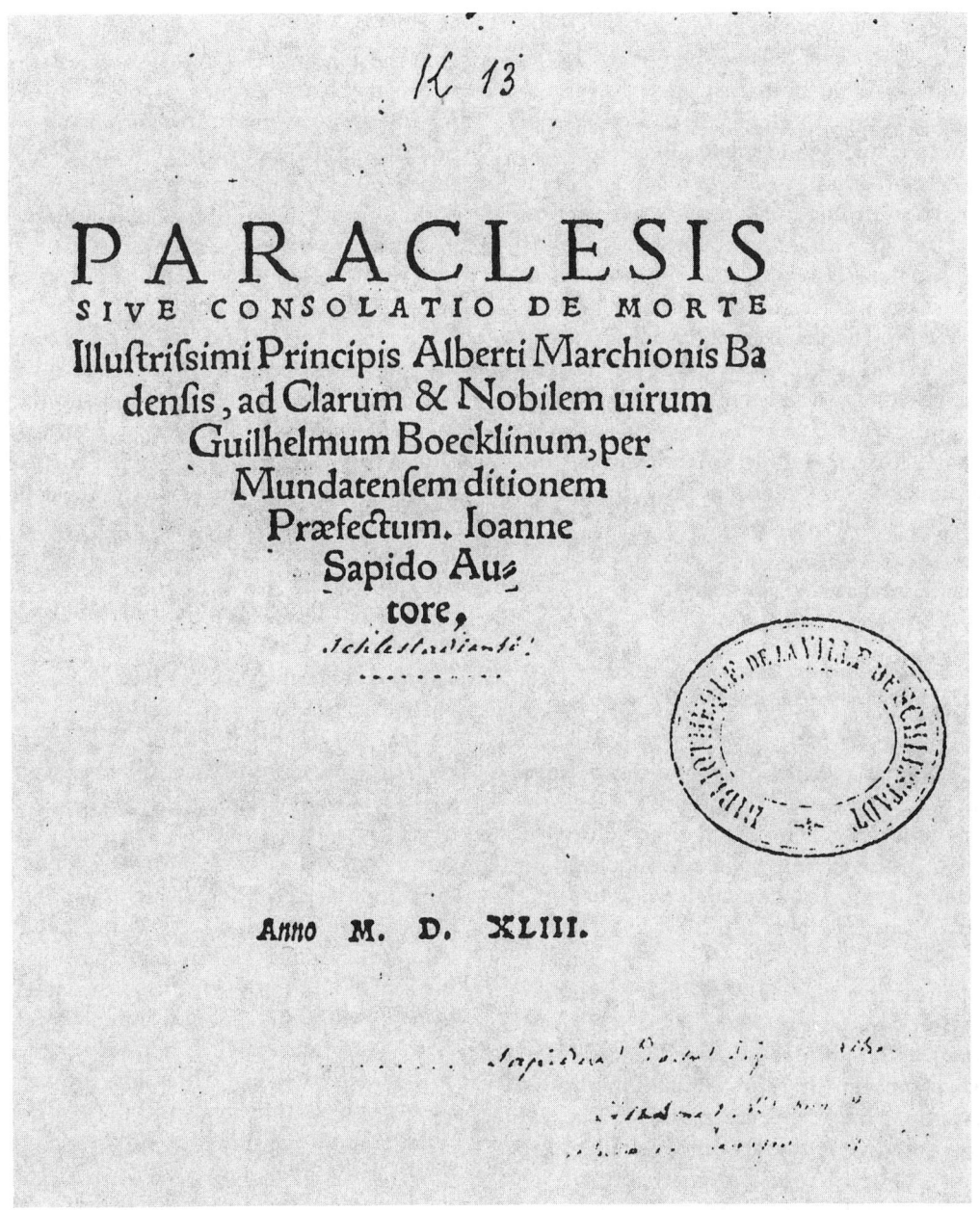

Title page for Sapidus's only lengthy prose work (Bibliothèque Humaniste, Sélestat)

swine, revenues from the shepherds once subservient to him, and the gastronomic delights they had provided, all because a certain German sheepherder, clearly identifiable as Luther, has fomented rebellion throughout his domain. In utter despair he decides to end his own life. In pondering the most expedient way to die he falls asleep and thus escapes becoming fodder for wild game, birds, and fishes. In its 171 hexameters this little gem traces the origins and principal events of the Reformation up to Sapidus's time without leaving the idiom and imagery proper to pastoral poetry. In 1546 it was anthologized by Gilbert Cousin in a collection of more than 150 items of this immensely popular genre.

Death had occupied Sapidus in some of the epigrams of the 1520 collection and in *Anabion,* whose epilogue generalizes from the extraordinary fate of Lazarus to the common experience of humanity. The theme dominates his literary endeavors after 1540, not merely from the personal inclination in advancing years of a poet otherwise known for his polished sense of humor but also, and just as much, from the course of external events.

Epitaphia sive Gymnasii Argentoratensis luctus (Epitaphs or Mourning of the Strasbourg School) appeared in June 1542 in the wake of the pestilence that had ravaged the city in 1541. Most of the thirty-seven poetic epitaphs comprising the book's thirty-two pages, following an elaborate elegiac eclogue on the distinguished Strasbourg jurist Franz Frosch and the eminent humanist poet Helius Eobanus Hessus, are quite brief. The names of most of those commemorated would hardly be recognized today, but there do occur those of Wolfgang Capito, one of the earliest protagonists of the Reformation in Strasbourg, along with that of an infant son of the same name, and the relatives of other Reformers, often children, such as those of Oecolampadius, Zwingli, Caspar Hedio, Nicolas Gerbel, and Bucer, who during the year had lost his wife and four children in rapid succession. Even in the fulfillment of this melancholy task a certain wistful humor does not desert Sapidus, as, for example, when he begins the epitaph on one of Bucer's children, Felicity:

Felicitas, ut cito foret, quod dicitur,
Cito moritur, nam cito mori felicium est.

(Felicity, that quickly might occur what she is called,
Dies quickly, for quickly to die befits the felicitous.)

With such subtleties Sapidus individualizes the commemorations of young and old, famous and obscure, noble and lowly, who are all alike before the Grim Reaper. In the chilling concluding epitaph on all the dead of that single year Sapidus numbers the victims buried in Strasbourg's three cemeteries at 3,208.

Paraclesis sive Consolatio de Morte Illustrissimi Principis Alberti Marchionis Badensis (Paraclesis; or, Consolation on the Death of Prince Albert of Baden, 1543) is Sapidus's last major literary publication and his only extensive work in prose. *Epitaphia* had expressed his thoughts on the deaths of diverse individuals in brief poetic form; *Paraclesis* pursues the phenomenon of the death of one highly placed person by illuminating it from every possible perspective. It is addressed to Wilhelm Böcklin, who came from a distinguished Strasbourg family, was in the administrative service of Margrave Ernst of Baden, and, evidently, was closely connected with Ernst's son, the lamented Albert, who had succumbed to illness on his return from a campaign against the Turks. Ever the dramatist, Sapidus begins with a scenic account of the occasion of his treatise: at a dinner Sapidus had given, Böcklin had seemed quite unlike his usual jovial self; asked the cause of his dejection, he had revealed to Sapidus that he had just received word of Prince Albert's demise and was overwhelmed by grief. Thereupon Sapidus seizes the opportunity to perform the office of true friendship by consoling Böcklin for his loss.

In the nearly fifty pages of this treatise Sapidus runs the gamut of the traditional classical arguments for death's being as integral to the life cycle as birth, for its power of liberation from countless physical and moral afflictions, for constancy in the face of death and even the embracing of it when it cannot be honorably averted; he rejects suicide, however, as opposed not only to Christian belief but also to that of the best of the ancients, especially Socrates. Again Sapidus's flair for the dramatic comes to the fore when Death refutes, in his own defense, the calumnies leveled against him and extols all the benefits he confers on an ungrateful humanity. Every turn of the astoundingly variegated argumentation is illustrated by examples taken for the most part from Valerius Maximus, the immense popularity of whose *Facta et Dicta Mirabilia* (An Anthology of Admirable Deeds and Words of Antiquity) is confirmed by more than a hundred separate imprints in the fifteenth and sixteenth centuries. Indeed, the whole treatise seems to derive much more from a Greco-Roman than a Christian position, though the Christian hope of resurrection and eternal life is mentioned—especially where Sapidus seeks to correct the impression that all admirable deeds occurred long ago, among the pagans, as if the pages of sacred Scripture were not equally filled with instances of loftiness of spirit or that heroism no longer abounded right in our midst. This reflection presents the occasion for another tribute to Bucer, who unflinchingly continued to perform his office in the face of ubiquitous death. In the elaborate conclusion Sapidus exhorts his recipient to retain in mind all that is immortal, even in this life, from the legacy of his beloved prince. He points to Margrave Ernst, the prince's father, as a singular example of fortitude, embodying the same noble traits of character that Böcklin had admired in the son. Having acquitted himself of his lofty task, Sapidus pragmatically asks Böcklin to put in a good word for him with the bishop of Strasbourg, whom Böcklin frequently sees on official business.

Of the few occasional verses remaining from Sapidus's final years, two closely connected poetic epitaphs are noteworthy because of their link with the gruesome posthumous fate of Bucer. They represent the final tribute to a lifelong friendship, and they may well be Sapidus's last published work in a form he particularly favored, the miniature dramatic dialogue. When, in consequence of his refusal of the Interim of 1548—a temporary compromise between Reformation and Catholicism—Bucer was virtually exiled from Strasbourg, he fled to England, where he received a chair of theology at Cambridge and died early in 1551. He was given a magnificent funeral, with the principal oration delivered by the future archbishop of Canterbury, Matthew Parker. Three years later he was ordered exhumed by Queen Mary and convicted of heresy, and his remains, along with those of his associate, Paul Fagius, and their writings were burned in the market square of Cambridge. In July 1560, under Queen Elizabeth I, the two were officially rehabilitated. The following year a sizable memorial volume in Latin, relating these events and including full documentation of them, including a vast quantity of encomiastic or commemorative poems in Latin and Greek, appeared in Strasbourg, followed by abridged German and English versions without the poetry. To this monument to Bucer's stature throughout Europe Sapidus contributed two brief but telling poetic dialogues between a *Viator* (Wayfarer) at the grave and personified Religion, the former outspokenly addressing Bucer's exile and Germany's loss as Britain's gain, the latter his horrendous exhumation and cremation. A third poem in the sequence, on Bucer's rehabilitation, comes from the pen of the otherwise unknown Matthias Hübner; since it resumes the dialogue between the Wayfarer and Religion, its author may have been one of Sapidus's students.

What little is known of Sapidus's final years is impressively summed up in the stylized phrases of the funeral oration delivered by the president of the Strasbourg Consistory, Johannes Marbach, on the day following Sapidus's death on 8 June 1561. He eulogizes Sapidus as "collega noster, ac tanquam pater nostrum omnium" (our colleague and, as it were, a father to us all), one who, for his profound learning, exemplary character, and meritorious service to the schools, is worthy of immortality. He recalls Sapidus's earlier years in Schlettstadt, borrowing the felicitous phrase from the encomium of Erasmus that under his headmastership men of learning issued from that school like warriors from the Trojan horse, some to go on to the civil service and others to direct the schools, where they continue to form the people of Christ in the pure religion and instruct the younger generation. The published version of this oration concludes with an elaborate Greek elegy by Sapidus's student Caspar Grasberger, which the eminent Graecist Thomas Chance has established to be no mere pastiche of standard elegiac phrases but a work of notable polish and originality, a fitting final tribute to the man who had introduced the study of Greek in Schlettstadt and ardently promoted it in Strasbourg for more than half a century.

Articles on Sapidus appeared regularly in standard collective biographies and other reference works in the centuries following his death. There is as yet neither an independent full-length biography nor a monograph devoted to his work; a modern edition, translation, and critical analysis of his writings is still in the beginning stages.

Biographies:

Heinrich Pantaleon, "Sapidus," in his *Prosopographiae heroum atque illustrium virorum totius Germaniae,* volume 3 (Basel: Niolas Brylinger, 1565), p. 233;

Melchior Adam, "Sapidus," in *Dignorum Laude Virorum . . . Immortalitas* (Frankfurt am Main: J. M. à Sande, 1706), pp. 205–206;

Paul Merker, "Der elsässische Humanist Johannes Sapidus," in *Beiträge zur Geistes- und Kulturgeschichte der Oberrheinlande Franz Schultz zum 60. Geburtstag gewidmet* (Frankfurt am Main: Moritz Diesterweg, 1938), pp. 79–111;

Miriam Usher Chrisman, "Sapidus," in *Contemporaries of Erasmus,* volume 3, edited by Peter G. Bietenholz (Toronto: University of Toronto Press, 1987), pp. 195–196.

References:

Epitaphia Ioan. Oecolampadii et Huldrychi Zvinglii per eruditos quosdam conscripta (Basel: Oporinus, 1531);

Desiderius Erasmus, *Antibarbarorum liber unus* (Basel: Froben, 1520);

Erasmus, *Encomium Selestadii* (Basel: Froben, 1515);

Conrad Gesner, "Ioan. Sapidus," in *Bibliotheca universalis sive Catalogus omnium scriptorum,* volume 1 (Zurich: Christoph Froschauer, 1545), p. 452;

Caspar Grasberger, "Elegion," in *Consolatio funebris,* by Joannes Marbach (Strasbourg, 1561), fol. A5^r–A6^r;

Peter Schäffer, "Zur Erasmus-Apotheose des Joannes Sapidus," *Annuaire des Amis de la Bibliothèque Humaniste de Sélestat,* 40 (1990): 17–24;

Schäffer, "Joannes Sapidus im Hirtenkleid: die *Bucolicae Querelae* des Eucharius Synesius," *Annuaire des Amis de la Bibliothèque Humaniste de Sélestat,* 42 (1992): 27–35;

Schäffer, "Sapidus Consolator," *Annuaire des Amis de la Bibliothèque Humaniste de Sélestat,* 46 (1996): 81–98;

Johann Sturm, *De literarum ludis recte aperiendis liber* (Strasbourg: Wendelin Richel, 1538);

Jakob Wimpfeling, "Candido Lectori," in *In Aurelii Prudentii Clementis Caesaraugustani. V. C. De miraculis Christi Hymnum ad omnes horas, Iacobi Spiegel Selestradiensis interpretatio,* by Jacob Spiegel (Schlettstadt: L. Schürer, 1520), fol. Miiij^v.

Paul Melissus Schede
(20 December 1539 – 3 February 1602)

David Price
University of Texas at Austin

BOOKS: *Cantionum musicarum, quatuor et quinque vocum liber unus* (N.p., 1566);

Schediasmata Poetica. Item Fidleri Flumina (Frankfurt am Main: Corvinus, 1574); enlarged as *Schediasmata poetica. Secundo edita multo auctiora* (Paris: Arnold Sittard, 1586);

Schediasmatum reliquiae (Frankfurt am Main: G. Corvinus, 1575);

Mele sive odae ad Noribergam et septemviros reipub. norib. (Nuremberg: Heirs of Montanus, 1580);

Odae palatinae . . . Epigrammata (Heidelberg, 1588);

Meletematum piorum libri VIII. Paraeneticorum II. Parodiarum II. Psalmi aliquot (Frankfurt am Main: Hieronymus Commelinus, 1595).

OTHER: *Di Psalmen Davids in Teutische gesangreymen nach französischer melodeien und sylben art,* translated by Schede (Heidelberg: Schirat, 1572);

"Epigrammata in urbes Italiae," in *De Italia, regione Europae nobilissima libri duo,* by Nicolaus Reusner (Strasbourg: Jobin, 1585);

Delitiae poetarum germanorum, volume 4, edited by Janus Gruterus, contributions by Schede (Frankfurt am Main: Nicolaus Hoffmann, 1612), pp. 342-493;

Clariss. v. Jani Dousae et Pauli Melissi musae errantes, edited by Justus Grisius (Frankfurt an der Oder: Nicolaus Voltz, 1616)—includes contributions by Schede;

Martin Opitz, *Teutsche Poemata und Aristarchus,* edited by Julius Zincgref, contributions by Schede (Strasbourg: Eberhard Zetzner, 1624), pp. 162-166, 169-172;

Die Psalmenübersetzungen des Paul Schede Melissus (1572), edited by Max Hermann Jellinek (Halle: Niemeyer, 1896)—includes a previously unpublished translation of Psalm 128.

Paul Melissus Schede, now considered a transitional figure from the classical humanist to the manneristic baroque style of poetry, was perhaps the most significant poet in Germany during the second half of the sixteenth century. He prefigured the poetic orientation, although not the metrical reforms, of Martin Opitz, as well as the style of several later baroque poets. The first to draw the attention of his countrymen to the vernacular poetry of other European countries, Schede was, perhaps, more internationally minded than any other German poet of his age. Despite his internationalism, however, he repeatedly expressed pride in his Franconian origins. On several occasions he compared himself to three other Franconian neo-Latin poets who were among the best-known German authors of the sixteenth century: Conrad Celtis, Ulrich von Hutten, and Petrus Lotichius Secundus. He published poems not only in German, Latin, and Greek but also in French.

Schede was born on 20 December 1539 in Mellrichstadt, Franconia, to Balthasar Schede, who was, evidently, a government bureaucrat, and Ottilie Schede, née Melisse. Paul Schede adopted a Latinized form of his mother's maiden name as a nom de plume, publishing under the names Paulus Melissus, Paul Melissus, Paul de Melisse, and, occasionally, Paulus Melissus Schedius and Paulus Schedius. *Melissus* suggests both *mel* (honey) and *melos* (song or lyric poem), associations that he and his literary friends exploited repeatedly.

Schede attended school in Mellrichstadt, Erfurt, and Zwickau before matriculating in 1557 at the University of Jena, where he studied with the neo-Latin poet Johannes Stigel. These studies were interrupted in 1559 when he became cantor (music teacher or assistant schoolteacher) in Königsberg in Franconia. By 1561 he had resumed his studies, this time at the University of Vienna, where he concentrated on Greek. In 1564 Emperor Ferdinand I conferred on him the title *poeta laureatus*.

After Ferdinand's death in 1564 Schede left Vienna for Wittenberg University, where he studied under Paul Eber. There is some evidence that he wanted to marry Eber's daughter but was spurned by the father. In any case, it was Eber who encouraged him to publish his first musical composition, a motet in five voices for a Greek text about Jesus' calming of the storm. (The only attested copy of the book was once held by the State Library in Berlin but is apparently no longer extant.) By the autumn of 1565 Schede had gone to Leipzig; he then served briefly at the court of the archbishop of Würzburg before returning to Vienna, at the request of Emperor Maximilian II, to become a tutor to aristocratic boys. During his two years in Maximilian's service he participated in a military campaign in Hungary; met Orlando di Lasso, then court composer at Munich, whom Schede considered the greatest musician of all time; and published a modest set of motets, *Cantionum musicarum, quatuor et quinque vocum liber unus* (One Book of Songs for Four or Five Voices, 1566).

In 1567 Schede went to Paris to study under Jean Dorat and Pierre Rameau and, most significantly, to meet the humanist poets in France who had begun using the vernacular—especially the poets of the Pléiade, the circle around Pierre de Ronsard. This brief but productive period holds enormous importance in the history of German literature, because Schede, on his return, would introduce into Germany a humanist-Petrarchistic style that was to become a significant impetus for seventeenth-century German poetry. In a poem addressed to Ronsard, published in the enlarged 1586 edition of his *Schediasmata poetica* (Caprices), Schede acknowledged his role as a conduit of literary innovation to his native country: "Germanos docere / Callidus insolitum canorem" (I am eager to teach the Germans unaccustomed song). He eventually published Latin translations of Pléiade poets, as well as many poetic tributes to them. The French authors inspired him to write love sonnets in Latin, French, and German. He also enthusiastically embraced the Pléiadean association of poetry with music, an orientation encouraged by Ronsard and realized, in particular, by Antoine de Baïf.

Schede's exposure to the French language and culture continued during a residence from 1568 to 1571 in Geneva, which, in the wake of the French civil wars, was crowded with refugees. It seems almost certain that he had converted to Calvinism during his time in France, which would account for his connections with Louis Desmazures, a Calvinist poet then celebrated for his translation of Virgil's *Aeneid,* and the composer Claude Goudimel, whom Schede met in 1568 in Besançon. In later years he would publish poems on the murder of Goudimel in 1572, in the aftermath of the Saint Bartholomew's Day Massacre, as well as several epistolary exchanges with Goudimel from shortly before the latter's murder. In Geneva he associated with Théodore de Bèze, Calvin's successor and a humanist poet of distinction, as well as the brilliant scholars Henri Estienne II, through whom he became familiar with the *Anacreontica,* and Joseph Scaliger, to whom he dedicated the first edition of his *Sche-*

Title page for Paul Melissus Schede's collection of brief epigrammatic poems, with the author depicted in classical attire

diasmata Poetica (1574) and his *Schediasmatum reliquiae* (Remnants of the Caprices, 1575).

Schede's first major publication, in 1572, was a German translation of Psalms 1 through 50 of the Huguenot Psalter (1562). Elector Friedrich III of the Palatinate invited Schede to Heidelberg to translate the texts by Clément Marot and Théodore de Bèze so that they could be sung in German to the extraordinarily successful melodies of the French version by Goudimel, Louis Bourgeois, and others. His effort must be accounted a failure, despite spirited defenses by later scholars: his German versions are unnecessarily odd, in part because he attempted an idiosyncratic reform of German orthography (in the seventeenth century, though, Georg Philipp Harsdörffer would admire Schede's orthographic efforts); he generally observed French versification rather than a patterned alternation of stressed and unstressed syllables; and, as he admitted in an apologetic Latin poem, he aimed for an elevated style, which frequently results in a wearisome stiltedness. Literal translations and prayers accompany the poetic-musical renderings. For the literal translations he consulted the Hebrew original with the assistance of Immanuel Tremellius, a noted Hebraist of the University of Heidelberg. His translations were, however, almost immediately superseded by the fluent renderings of Ambrosius Lobwasser (1573); Friedrich III authorized use of Lobwasser's versions.

During his stay in Heidelberg, Schede and the physician-poet Johannes Posthius formed a "sobriety society" to compose moralistic or satiric poetry against alcoholism. The group became an object of derision for several other writers, most notably Johann Fischart. For Fischart, the German adapter of the works of François Rabelais, Posthius and Schede had formed a literary heresy, "die unpoetisch Postimeliseische Ketzerey" (the unpoetic Posti-Melissean heresy). Fischart was, obviously, referring to their Calvinism, as well.

In 1574 Schede published the *Schediasmata Poetica,* whose title is a pun on the poet's name. His first important collection of Latin poetry, the work is divided into four parts: "Melica" (Lyric Poems); "Earina" (Licensed Poems), a collection of mostly hendecasyllabic poems; "Elegiae" (Elegies); and "Miscella" (Miscellaneous Poems). Noteworthy for their inventiveness and metrical virtuosity, the poems are casually formulated reflections on literature, politics, friendship, and humanist education, most of which are addressed to fellow Latin poets. The "Miscella" include exchanges of verse letters, mostly panegyrics with replies. Among them is Schede's first published French sonnet, a reply to a sonnet by Pierre Enoch.

The *Schedasmatum reliquiae* of 1575 shows the young Schede at his best, the master of the brief epigrammatic poem. The work's organization into books is somewhat whimsical. It begins with nine books of "Musae" (Muses), epigrams in various meters to the nine Muses, followed by "Epigrammata aliquot musis adiicienda" (Several Epigrams Appended to the Muses); "Epigrammata Greco translata" (Epigrams Translated from Greek); "Lilietum Cygneum" (Swan's Bed of Lilies), poems by friends on Schede's impresa, which included a swan and three fleurs-delis; "Miscellorum appendix" (Appendix of Miscellaneous Poems), more celebratory poems addressed to Schede; and "Spinae" (Thorns), a collection of brief poems). The "Musae" include Latin translations of works by Ronsard and other Pléiade poets, as well as several tributes to Camille Morel, the poetic prodigy of France, and one tribute–the first of many–to Elizabeth I of England. The "Spinae" and the "Musae" (especially book 6) have several love poems addressed to "Rosina"; the "Spinae" also contain a Latin translation of Petrarch's *Rime sparse* 133. Though steeped in Petrarchan paradoxes and antitheses, Schede's love poetry is distinctive for its admissions of fictionality and for the chasteness of its persona. The "I" of Schedian love poetry desires, explicitly and repeatedly, matrimony with Rosina but also concedes that an actual Rosina has not yet been found.

The succession of Elector Ludwig VI in 1577 on the death of Friedrich III meant suppression of Calvinism in the Palatinate. Schede found Ludwig's reign to be a good time for travel abroad, including a grand tour of Italy from 1577 to 1580; he recorded the journey in his "Epigrammata in urbes Italiae" (Epigrams on the Cities of Italy, 1585). By 1577 he enjoyed a measure of fame in humanist circles all over Europe, and the humanists he met in Italy, even the great Marc-Antoine Muret, lavished tributes and honors on him. During this time he was made *comes palatinus, civis romanus,* and *eques auratus.* He was back in Germany between 1580 and 1584, staying briefly in Augsburg but principally in Nuremberg, where he published a slender celebratory volume, *Mele sive odae ad Noribergam* (Lyric Poems or Odes to Nuremberg, 1580). The most astonishing poem in this collection is "Reginae Responsum" (Response of the Queen), which has been–probably wrongly–considered a genuine work by Elizabeth I. It is more likely that Schede wrote the reply to his poem in Elizabeth's voice, just as he occasionally wrote fictitious replies from Rosina. Whether authentic or not, the Elizabeth of the poem pronounces Schede "vatum . . . princeps" (prince of the poets).

During his second residency in Paris, in 1584–1585, Schede finished his most important book: a massive expansion of his *Schediasmata Poetica.* While the title page gives the date of publication as 1586, it is possible that Schede took a printed copy with him when he departed for England at the end of 1585: he evidently presented such a copy to Elizabeth during the winter of 1585–1586. According to Schede's earliest biographer, Jean-Jacques Boissard, the queen tried to keep him in London; but he declined her invitation in favor of becoming librarian of the Palatine Library in Heidelberg, a position offered to him after Johann Casimir, a Calvinist, became regent for Elector Friedrich IV on Ludwig's death. The Palatine Library was one of the greatest libraries in the world prior to Johann Tserklaes, Graf von Tilly's infamous sack of Heidelberg in 1622 and the eventual conveyance of the books to the Vatican Library. Schede's position there was the crowning distinction of his life.

The second edition of the *Schediasmata Poetica*

marks a shift from the nugatory style of the epigram to the elevated style of the Augustan Latin ode. The work is divided into three parts. The first contains a collection of "Emmetra" (Pindaric odes in Latin) and "Melica" (odes). Schede's imitations of the Pindaric and Horatian odes–inspired both by the ancient sources and by French imitations–prefigure the German odes of the seventeenth century. The second part comprises a set of "Epica," mostly occasional poetry in dactylic hexameter, and four books (inexplicably labeled 1, 3, 4, and 5) of elegies. The third part is a significantly expanded version of the "Musae," comprising nine books of epigrams.

Besides experimentation with many odic meters and stanzas, the most striking quality of the *Schediasmata poetica* is the preoccupation with Elizabeth I and her court. Each of the three parts has a dedicatory prose letter to Elizabeth, and each book begins with a poem addressed to her. This feature, as well as the many other poems addressed to her and members of her court (for example, Robert Dudley, First Earl of Leicester; William Cecil, First Baron Burghley; Sir Philip Sidney; and Daniel Rogers) make the *Schediasmata poetica* a sizable corpus of Elizabethan poetry, none of which has been translated into English. In the dedicatory epigram he says that he places himself under the queen's regal yoke, even though he is a German of Franconian stock. Nonetheless, he also associates his praise for "Elisa" (his Latin equivalent for *Elizabeth*) with his love poetry for "Rosina," usually by pairing poems to Elisa and Rosina. In one case he combines the two names with an acrostic to Elisa and a telestich to Rosina:

> E Lisa claro tota fulgis au RO
> LI mbos et oras. proximet tuo SI
> SA ltim nitori, en aurea est Rosi NA.

(Elizabeth, you are resplendent with bright gold all over, on your arms and face. If, at the least, she should come near your brightness, behold, Rosina is golden.)

Schede's final years were, it seems, personally fulfilling, though several late poems complain of failing health. He worked on a large collection of German poetry, which disappeared, along with the rest of his literary papers, during the first half of the seventeenth century. He also never completed the German dictionary and introduction to the German language he had mentioned in earlier years. In 1593 he married Emilie Jordan, daughter of a deceased councillor at the Heidelberg court. He recorded his joy over his marriage in a Sapphic poem in which he implies that the bride's beauty and virtue compensate for a small dowry. Emilie gave birth to a son, who died in infancy, and a daughter, who was named Rosina. Schede's final published collection of poetry was *Meletematum piorum libri VIII. Paraeneticorum II. Parodiarum II. Psalmi aliquot* (Eight Books of Pious Odes, Two of Hortatory Poetry, Two of Parodies and Several Psalms, 1595). These poems continue in the vein of the earlier reflections on politics, literature, and personal happenstance, though with a new focus on Christian piety. The two books of parodies are based on Horace and Catullus, respectively, with several instances, especially in the first book, of Christian parody. The "Paraenetica" (Hortatory Poems) document Schede's close affiliation with the court of Friedrich IV, an association he had already celebrated in 1588 in *Odae palatinae* (Palatine Odes), six odes honoring Friedrich and Johann Casimir. Schede died on 3 February 1602.

Schede is most often remembered for five modest German-language poems that Julius Zincgref, an-

Title page for the enlarged edition of Schede's first collection of original poetry

other Heidelberg poet, published in the "Anhang" (appendix) to his edition of Opitz's *Teutsche Poemata und Aristarchus* (German Poems and Aristarchus, 1624). Of these, "Rot Röslein wolt ich brechen" (A Red Rose I Wanted To Break) is often discussed as a balladesque poem with a Petrarchan cast and often in conjunction with Johann Wolfgang von Goethe's "Röslein auf der Heide" (Little Rose on the Heath). Schede's wedding sonnet for Jörg von Averli (Georges d'Averly) was long considered the first German sonnet in Alexandrines (an honor now assigned to a 1572 poem by Jan van der Noot).

Schede had a thoroughly Calvinist motto: *Manet immutabile fatum* (Fate remains immutable). The fate of his reception, however, has been far from immutable. From the beginning his poetry found strong advocates in Scaliger, the poets of the Pléiade, Johann Rist, and Harsdörffer, as well as strident detractors in Opitz and Fischart. Opitz even singled out Schede as the embodiment of the bad poet in his landmark *Buch von der deutschen Poeterey* (Book of German Poetry, 1624), especially in chapter 7. Disagreement also characterizes modern critical opinion of Schede's work: literary historians have never questioned Schede's importance in his own day, but for several of them he represents the sterility of late humanist poetry, whereas, at the other extreme, Pierre de Nolhac considered him "le plus intéressant des poètes humanistes de l'Allemagne" (the most interesting of the German humanist poets). Modern scholarship on Schede has been severely hampered, however, by the lack of a critical edition of his Latin poetry or a vernacular translation of his oeuvre.

Letters:

Virorum clarorum saeculi xvi et xvii epistolae selectae, edited by Ernst Weber (Leipzig: Teubner, 1894), pp. 25–30.

Bibliography:

Bavarian State Library in Munich, ed., *Verzeichnis der im deutschen Sprachgebiet erschienenen Drucke des XVI. Jahrhunderts*, volume 18 (Stuttgart: Hiersemann, 1992), pp. 210–215.

Biographies:

Jean-Jacques Boissard, *Icones quinquaginta virorum illustrium*, volume 2 (Frankfurt am Main, 1598), pp. 86–94;

Otto Taubert, *De vita et scriptis Pauli Schedii Melissi* (Bonn: Typis Carthausii, 1859);

Taubert, *Paul Schede (Melissus): Leben und Schriften* (Torgau: Jakob, 1864);

E. Hoepfner, "Paul Schede," *Zeitschrift für deutsches Gymnasialwesen,* 19 (1865): 337–352;

Ludwig Krauß, "Paul Schede-Melissus: Sein Leben nach den vorhandenen Quellen und nach seinen lateinischen Dichtungen als ein Leitweg zur Gelehrtengeschichte jener Zeit," 2 volumes, unpublished manuscript, 1918, Erlangen University Library, Ms. 2254;

Pierre de Nolhac, *Un poète rhénan ami de la Pléiade* (Paris: Champion, 1923).

References:

Karl Otto Conrady, *Lateinische Dichtungstradition und deutsche Lyrik des 17. Jahrhunderts* (Bonn: Bouvier, 1962);

A. M. M. Dekker, "Ein unbekanntes Gedicht aus den *Acanthae* des Paulus Melissus," *Humanistica Lovaniensia,* 30 (1981): 194–196;

Leonard Forster, "Fremdsprache und Muttersprache: zur Frage der polyglotten Dichtung in Renaissance und Barock," *Neophilologus,* 45 (1961): 177–195;

Forster and J.-U. Fechner, "Das deutsche Sonett des Melissus," in *Rezeption und Produktion zwischen 1570 und 1730: Festschrift für Günther Weydt,* edited by Wolfdietrich Rasch, Hans Geulen, and Klaus Haberkamm (Bern: Franke, 1972), pp. 33–51;

Dieter Mertens, "Zu Heidelberger Dichtern von Schede bis Zincgref," *Zeitschrift für deutsches Altertum,* 103 (1974): 200–241;

James E. Phillips, "Elizabeth I as a Latin Poet: An Epigram on Paul Melissus," *Renaissance News,* 16 (1963): 289–298;

Eckart Schäfer, *Deutscher Horaz: Conrad Celtis, Georg Fabricius, Paul Melissus, Jacob Balde* (Wiesbaden: Steiner, 1976);

Schäfer, "Die 'Dornen' des Paul Melissus," *Humanistica Lovaniensia,* 22 (1973): 217–255;

Remigius Stölzle, "Ein unbekanntes deutsches Lied des Paul Schede Melissus," *Archiv für Reformationsgeschichte,* 17 (1920): 41–46;

Erich Trunz, "Die deutschen Übersetzungen des Hugenottenpsalters," *Euphorion,* 29 (1928): 578–617; 39 (1938): 431–433.

Papers:

The Newberry Library, Chicago; University Library, Leiden; Bayerische Staatsbibliothek, Munich; University Library, Utrecht; Biblioteca Apostolica Vaticana; and Herzog August Bibliothek Wolfenbüttel have unpublished material, mainly letters, by or about Paul Melissus Schede, although none of them has an archive devoted to him.

Heinrich Seuse (Henry Suso)
(21 March 1295? - 25 January 1366)

Debra L. Stoudt
University of Toledo

WORKS: *Büchlein der Wahrheit* (circa 1326-1328)
    Manuscripts: Included in most manuscripts of the *Exemplar* and in an additional ten manuscripts, including Berlin, Ms. germ. quarto 191 (fourteenth-fifteenth century), and Colmar, Stadtbibliothek Nr. 266 (fifteenth century).
    First publication: In *Das Buch genannt der Seusse*, edited by Felix Fabri (Augsburg: Anton Sorg, 1482).
    Edition in English: "Little Book of Truth," in *Little Book of Eternal Wisdom and Little Book of Truth*, translated by James M. Clark (London: Faber & Faber, 1953), pp. 173-208;

Büchlein der ewigen Weisheit (circa 1327-1334)
    Manuscripts: Included in more than half of the extant manuscripts of the *Exemplar,* and in full or in fragment form in more than three hundred manuscripts. The oldest surviving Seuse manuscript, Engelberg, Nr. 141, contains an incomplete version of the work; the first chapter of part 2, the *Sterbebüchlein*, and part 3, the *100 Betrachtungen,* were often transcribed separately.
    First publication: In *Das Buch genannt der Seusse*, edited by Anton Sorg (Augsburg, 1482).
    Editions in English: *The Little Book of Eternal Wisdom*, translated by Richard Raby (London: Richardson, 1852); republished as *Blessed Henry Suso's Little Book of Eternal Wisdom* (Boston: Noonan, 1887); *Little Book of Eternal Wisdom and Little Book of Truth,* translated by James M. Clark (London: Faber & Faber, 1953), pp. 43-169;

Horologium sapientiae (circa 1332-1334)
    Manuscripts: An expanded Latin version of the *Büchlein der ewigen Weisheit,* the work survives in more than four hundred complete or fragmentary transcriptions.
    First publication: *Horologium sapientiae* (Paris, circa 1480).
    Standard edition: *Heinrich Seuses Horologium sapientiae. Erste kritische Ausgabe unter Benutzung der Vorarbeiten von Dominikus Planzer OP,* edited by Pius Künzle, Spicilegium Friburgense, volume 23 (Freiburg, Switzerland: Universitätsverlag, 1977).
    Editions in English: "A Chapter from the Orologium Sapientiae by Henry Suso," in *Ars moriendi. The book of the craft of dying, and other early English tracts concerning death taken from manuscripts and printed books in the British museum and Bodleian libraries,* edited by William Caxton (London, 1491); "Thes ben the chapitres of thys tretyse of ye seuen poyntes of trewe loue and euerlastyng wysdom drawen oute of y^t booke y^t is writen in latyn an cleped Orologium sapiencie," in *The Book of divers ghostly matters* (Westminster, 1491); *Wisdom's Watch upon the Hours,* translated by Edmund Colledge (Washington, D.C.: Catholic University of America Press, 1994);

Cursus de aeterna Sapientia, attributed to Seuse (circa 1332-1334)
    Manuscripts: Appended to slightly fewer than half of the manuscripts containing the complete *Horologium sapientiae.*
    First publication: In *Heinrich Seuses Horologium sapientiae. Erste kritische Ausgabe unter Benutzung der Vorarbeiten von Dominikus Planzer OP,* edited by Pius Künzle, Spicilegium Friburgense, volume 23 (Freiburg, Switzerland: Universitätsverlag, 1977), pp. 606-618.
    Edition in English: "Certayne sweete prayers of the glorious name of Iesus, commonly called Iesus mattens, with the howers thereto belonging, written in Latin aboue two hundred yeres agoe, by H. Susonne," translated anonymously, in *A breefe Directory, and playne way how to say the Rosary of our blessed Lady: With Meditations for such as are not exercised therein* (Bruges: Holost, 1576);

Bruderschaft der ewigen Weisheit, attributed to Seuse (circa 1332-1334)

Manuscripts: A free German translation of part 2, chapter 7, of *Horologium sapientiae*, the treatise appears in many manuscripts of *Horologium sapientiae*.

First publication: In the two earliest printed editions (1482 and 1512) of Seuse's works;

Exemplar (circa 1362–1366)

Manuscripts: Consisting of Seuse's *Vita*, the *Büchlein der ewigen Weisheit*, the *Büchlein der Wahrheit*, and the *Briefbüchlein*, the work appears in fourteen extant manuscripts; the oldest and most important is Strasbourg, Ms. 2929 (fourteenth century; previously catalogued as Strasbourg, Stadtbibliothek B 139, and by Karl Bihlmeyer as Berlin, Ms. germ. quarto 840); others include Einsiedeln, Ms. Nr. 710; Breslau, no signature; Wolfenbüttel, Cod. Guelf 78. 5. Aug. fol.; and Freiburg, Universitätsbibliothek, Nr. 453 (fifteenth century). The *Vita* is found in an additional forty manuscripts, many of which derive from the Strasbourg version and most of which are fragmentary versions, among them Strasbourg, L germ. 75, and Munich, Cgm. 362 (fifteenth century). The *Briefbüchlein* has no separate manuscript tradition, although several manuscripts contain transcriptions of individual letters. The *Vita* and the *Briefbüchlein* were first published as part of the *Exemplar*.

First publication: *Das Buch genannt der Seusse*, edited by Fabri (Augsburg: Anton Sorg, 1482).

Edition in modern German: *Heinrich Suso's, genannt Amandus, Leben und Schriften, nach den ältesten Handschriften und Drucken mit unverändertem Texte in jetziger Schriftsprache herausgegeben*, edited by Melchior Diepenbrock, introduction by Joseph von Görres (Regensburg: Pustet, 1829).

Standard edition: *Heinrich Seuse: Deutsche Schriften*, edited by Karl Bihlmeyer (Stuttgart: Kohlhammer, 1907).

Editions in English: *The Life of Blessed Henry Suso*, translated by Thomas Francis Knox (London: Burns, Lambert & Oates, 1865); *Three Friends of God: Records from the Lives of John Tauler, Nicholas of Basle, Henry Suso*, translated by Emma F. Bevan (London: Nisbet, 1887); *Hymns of Tersteegen, Suso, and Others*, translated by Bevan (London: Nisbet, 1894); *The Life of the Servant*, translated by James M. Clark (London: James Clarke, 1952); *The Exemplar. The Life and Writings of Blessed Henry Suso, O.P. Complete Edition Based on Manuscripts with a Critical Introduction and Explanatory Notes by Nicholas Heller*, 2 volumes, translated by Sister M. Ann Edward (Dubuque, Iowa: Priory Press, 1962); *The Exemplar, with Two German Sermons*, translated by Frank Tobin (Mahwah, N.J.: Paulist Press, 1989);

Großes Briefbuch (N.d.)

Manuscripts: More than half of the twenty-seven letters of the *Großes Briefbuch* are extant in eleven manuscripts; another fifty manuscripts contain individual letters. The most complete collections are found in Cues, Ms. 115; Darmstadt, Cod. 1847; Heidelberg, Cod. 358.38 (now Ms. 33); and Stuttgart, Cod. theol. et phil. quarto 67.

First publication: In *Güldene sendtbrieff vieler Alten Gottseeligen Kirchen Lehrer: Als Johann Thaulers, Heinrich Seüssen, Johan Creützers vnd mehr Anderer: In etliche Theil abgeteilt vnd den vhralten Schrifften durchausz gemäsz gantz vnverfälscht an dasz Liecht gegeben*, edited by Daniel Sudermann (N.p., 1622).

Standard edition: *Die Briefe Heinrich Suso's nach einer Handschrift des XV. Jahrhunderts*, edited by Wilhelm Preger (Leipzig: Dörffling & Franke, 1867).

Edition in English: *The Letters of Henry Suso to his Spiritual Daughters*, translated by Kathleen Goldmann (London: Blackfriars, 1955);

Testament der Minne oder Minneregel (N.d.)

Manuscript: A twenty-eighth letter not found in the *Großes Briefbuch*, the work exists in only one manuscript, Berlin, Ms. germ. octavo 69 (fourteenth-fifteenth century).

First publication: In *Heinrich Seuse: Deutsche Schriften*, edited by Karl Bihlmeyer (Stuttgart: Kohlhammer, 1907), pp. 486–494;

Minnebüchlein, attributed to Seuse (N.d.)

Manuscript: The *Minnebüchlein* survives in only one manuscript: Zurich, Stadtbibliothek C 96 (fourteenth-fifteenth century).

First publication: "Eine noch unbekannte Schrift Susos," edited by Wilhelm Preger, *Königliche-bayerische Akademie der Wissenschaften, Historische Classe, Abhandlungen*, 2. Abteilung, 21 (1898): 425–472.

Editions in English: "The Soul's Love-Book," in *The Exemplar: The Life and Writings of Blessed Henry Suso, O.P. Complete Edition Based on Manuscripts with a Critical Introduction and Explanatory Notes by Nicholas Heller*, volume 2, translated by Sister M. Ann Edward (Dubuque, Iowa: Priory Press, 1962), pp. 335–349; *The Little Book of Love*, translated by Peter Meister (Toronto: Peregrina, 1987);

Sermons (N.d.)

Manuscripts: No manuscript corpus of

Seuse's sermons exists; only sermon 1, "Lectulus noster floridus," appears with any frequency.

First publication: Sermon 1, in *Güldene sendtbrieff vieler Alten Gottseeligen Kirchen Lehrer: Als Johann Thaulers, Heinrich Seüssen, Johan Creützers vnd mehr Anderer: In etliche Theil abgeteilt und den vhralten Schrifften durchausz gemäsz gantz vnverfälscht an dasz Liecht gegeben,* edited by Daniel Sudermann (N.p., 1622); sermons 2, 3, and 4, in *Des erleuchten D. Joannis Tauleri, Von eym waren euangelischen Leben, götliche Predig, Leren, Epistolen, Cantilenen, Prophetien, Alles eyn kostpar Sellen Schatz, in alten geschreyben Büchern fuonden, vnd nuo erstmals ins Liecht kommen,* edited by Petrus Canisius (Cologne: Casper von Gennep, 1543);

Edition in modern German: In *Altdeutsche Predigten und Gebete aus Handschriften,* edited by Wilhelm Wackernagel (Basel: Schweighauserische Verlagsbuchhandlung, 1876), pp. 552–561.

Collection: *Diss buch das da gedicht hat der erleücht vater Amandus, genannt Seüss. begreift in jm vil guter gaistlicher leeren* (Augsburg: Printed by Hans Othmar for Johann Rynmann, 1512).

Late-medieval representation of Heinrich Seuse by an unknown artist (Maria Medingen monastery, near Augsburg, Germany)

Heinrich Seuse—also known as Suso, the Latin form of his chosen surname—was one of the most renowned religious figures of late medieval Europe. His devotional works, remarkable for their poetic eloquence, were translated into many vernaculars, and the *Büchlein der ewigen Weisheit* (circa 1327–1334; first published, 1482; translated as *The Little Book of Eternal Wisdom,* 1852) was the most popular work of its kind in the second half of the fourteenth century and in the fifteenth century. Through his life story and didactic dialogues with the allegorical figures of Truth and Eternal Wisdom, the Dominican preacher and teacher provided spiritual inspiration and guidance to many religious men and women, particularly in his native southern Germany. Along with his fellow Dominicans Meister Eckhart and Johannes Tauler, Seuse was a major proponent of the mystical tradition in late-medieval Germany. Whereas Eckhart's fame stems from his interpretation of aspects of speculative mysticism and Tauler's renown derives from his homiletic influence, Seuse's contribution to late-medieval spirituality is his lyrical writing style, which he uses to evoke powerful and poetic images of the suffering Christ and of humanity suffering for Christ's sake.

Seuse's *Vita* (Life, circa 1362–1366; first published, 1482) provides much of what is known about his life, especially his early years; there are, however, questions as to the authenticity of the autobiography, parts of which are modeled after contemporaneous and earlier hagiographic literature. Seuse was born Heinrich von Berg in the southern German town of Constance or in nearby Überlingen on 21 March, probably in 1295, although the year of his birth could be as late as 1300. The patrician von Berg family had offered ministerial service to the bishops of Constance for several generations. Around the middle of the thirteenth century the von Bergs had moved into Constance and become involved in trade, probably of textiles. Whereas Seuse's father is described as a worldly individual, his mother, from the Sus or Süs family of Überlingen, was a devout woman whose asceticism and piety deeply influenced her son.

Weak and sickly as a child, Heinrich was not suited for a life of public service or trade; instead, he modeled himself on his mother, whose maiden name he chose to use. The Alemannic form *Süs* is related linguistically to the Middle High German *sueze* (sweet) and *suoze* (pleasant), terms that describe Seuse's sensitive nature and lyrical writing style;

Sûs, another Alemannic variant, is related to the Middle High German *sûsen* (roar) and *siusen* (shout). The latter etymology is played on in an anecdote in the prologue to the 1512 edition of Seuse's works that describes how Seuse felt compelled to preach with vigor: "Da müsz der seüss seüsen" (So must the fervent one roar). The Swabian-Bavarian version *Súse* is rendered in New High German as Seuse, and it is this form, first used by the Dominican scholar Heinrich Suso Denifle in 1876, that has gained acceptance alongside the Latin form Suso.

At thirteen Seuse entered the Saint Nicholas monastery in Constance; a contribution by his parents to the Dominican order enabled him to join the community two years earlier than usually permitted by church law, a circumstance that distressed him greatly during the initial phase of his religious life. After his year as a novice he professed his vows; around this time he also embarked on the general course of study. Following two to three years of basic instruction in Latin and in the practices and precepts of the Dominican order, Seuse devoted comparable periods of time to study in the *philosophia rationalis* (matters pertaining or related to reason), which focused on Aristotelian logic, and the *philosophia realis* (matters based on reality and existing in fact, not merely in thought or language). At eighteen, before he embarked on the final course of required study–theology–Seuse experienced a dramatic spiritual conversion that caused him to regard his religious vocation, and perhaps his studies as well, with more seriousness. Seuse completed his basic education between 1319 and 1322, either in Constance or in Strasbourg.

Because of his intellectual potential Seuse was selected to continue his education, and around 1324 he moved to Cologne to attend the *studium generale*, the institution that provided an advanced education to scholars in the entire Dominican province and not just to those in one region; this course of study generally lasted three years. There Seuse was instructed by Meister Eckhart, and he probably remained in Cologne until Eckhart's death in 1327. That year he returned to Constance and became lector at the friary, guiding the education of the younger brothers, lecturing on the Holy Scriptures, and supervising disputations. Possibly during his last year in Cologne and his earliest years as lector Seuse wrote his first works, *Büchlein der Wahrheit* (first published, 1482; translated as "Little Book of Truth," 1953) and *Büchlein der ewigen Weisheit*.

The prologue and first chapter of the *Büchlein der Wahrheit* introduce the man in Christ, Seuse, whose external life exemplifies his religious calling but whose inner life seems inadequate because he has not yet been able to achieve the inner goal of self-detachment. Struggling through the years, he finally experiences divine Truth within himself; as her disciple he entreats the allegorical figure to teach him about *gelassenheit* (true detachment). She does so in a series of dialogues. The subsequent six chapters consist of questions and answers that examine the nature of true detachment and how it manifests itself in the behavior and actions of an individual. The dialogues also describe the relationship between the oneness of the Godhead and its triune nature. Just as there is such a differentiation within the divine, so, too, there is still a distinctness between human beings and God even when individuals who experience union with the divine are no longer cognizant of it. This Eckhartian concept is the basis of the argument in the final two chapters between the disciple and the nameless wild one, whose unrestrained liberty leads him astray from the Truth. The emphasis on theology and speculative mysticism characterizes the *Büchlein der Wahrheit* as a work written to educate Seuse's fellow Dominicans against the heresies of the Beghards and the Brethren of the Free Spirit, who were especially active in Cologne at the time. The polemical style of the tract contrasts with the poetic and anecdotal style of his later works. Throughout the work, but most prominently in chapter 6, Seuse defends Eckhart's mystical teachings on the union of the soul with God. An allusion to the master in the past tense indicates that at least some sections of the *Büchlein der Wahrheit* were written after Eckhart's death. Because the orthodoxy of his teacher's writings was still under scrutiny, Seuse's support of Eckhartian ideas may have been one reason he was forced to relinquish the lectorship in Constance around 1330; in chapter 23 of the *Vita* he relates how he suffered at the hands of fellow Dominicans who had him summoned to the Netherlands, probably to Maastricht, on charges that his works contained heretical ideas. Although Seuse was dismissed from the position of lector, only four years later he was appointed prior of the same community in Constance.

The *Büchlein der ewigen Weisheit* dates from about the same period as the *Büchlein der Wahrheit*. Its form and content, however, reveal a different purpose and intended readership. Substantially longer than its predecessor, the *Büchlein der ewigen Weisheit* consists of three parts. In the first part, as Seuse meditates before a crucifix one morning after matins, God illumines him and bestows upon him one hundred meditations on Christ's Passion. As a result of performing the meditations, Seuse experiences interior conversations with Christ, personified as Eternal Wisdom. The dialogues consider the misfortune that results from sin, the deceitfulness of worldly love and the nobility of divine love, and the merits of earthly suffering. As Seuse, who characterizes himself as the Servant, meditates on the Passion, he describes not only Christ's experiences but Mary's, as well. The second part of the work offers instructions for souls at various points on the mystical journey toward union with God: how one should live inwardly, how one should receive God lovingly, how one should learn to die. (The chapter on learning to die was copied separately in manuscripts as the *Sterbebüchlein* [How to Die Well]; it appeared in print in German and English translations in the fifteenth century.) The meditations, along with Seuse's own prayers, comprise the third part of the work, the "Hundert Betrachtungen" (One Hundred Meditations). Seuse recorded the prayers and petitions separately and distributed them to other devout individuals; they were exceedingly popular for use in personal meditation among the religious and the laity, especially women. This section of the *Büchlein der ewigen Weisheit* was translated into Latin as *Centum Meditationes;* early in the fifteenth century the Latin version was translated into Low German as *100 Betrachtungen,* in which form it survives in more than one hundred manuscripts.

The *Büchlein der ewigen Weisheit* is replete with nature imagery and allusions to the *Brautmystik* (bridal mysticism) based on the Song of Songs. The content and style of the tract, which draw on the tradition of Bernard of Clairvaux, contrast starkly with the speculative mystical theology and straightforward prose of the *Büchlein der Wahrheit*. Because of Seuse's poetic language, use of love imagery and other images easily visualized by the reader, and allusions to knighthood—all of which manifest themselves in this work—he has often been described as the *Minnesinger* (courtly love poet) among the medieval German mystics. The easily comprehensible spiritual message and the engaging style in which it is communicated made the *Büchlein der ewigen Weisheit* the most popular devotional work of the second half of the fourteenth century and the fifteenth century.

Perhaps while completing the *Büchlein der ewigen Weisheit* Seuse began his sole work in Latin, *Horologium sapientiae* (Clock of Wisdom, circa 1332–1334; first published, 1480; translated, 1491). Based on the *Büchlein der ewigen Weisheit,* it is divided into twenty-four chapters corresponding to the number of hours in the day. The Latin work is not a translation of the German but an expanded version of the first two parts. The supplements include autobiographical references, allusions to contemporaneous political events, and, especially, ideas on reforming various aspects of monastic life. The hundred meditations are omitted from the *Horologium sapientiae;* in their stead are a chapter describing the betrothal of the devout with Eternal Wisdom, which was subsequently translated into German as *Bruderschaft der ewigen Weisheit* (Brotherhood of Eternal Wisdom, circa 1332–1334), and a prayer for the followers of Eternal Wisdom. *Cursus de aeterna Sapientia* (Liturgical Prayers for Eternal Wisdom, circa 1332–1334), referred to in book 2, chapter 7 of *Horologium sapientiae,* follows in many manuscripts and printed editions; these prayers are to be recited by the faithful according to the canonical hours. Of less certain authenticity is the *Officium Missae de aeterna Sapientia* (Office of the Mass of Eternal Wisdom), which is also often appended to manuscripts of Seuse's Latin work. In the *Horologium sapientiae* Eternal Wisdom bestows upon the Servant the name Amandus (good, kind), a pseudonym for Seuse that appears only in this work. Seuse may have composed the work in Latin because he deemed classical terminology less susceptible to misunderstandings that could elicit new accusations of heresy; or he may have considered Latin more appropriate for his intended audience, his Dominican brothers and superiors—the work is dedicated to the general of the order, Hugo of Vaucemain. By writing in Latin Seuse was, in any case, able to address a broader European public. Perhaps the choice of language had an effect on the popularity of the work: during the next two centuries many manuscripts and incunabula of the *Horologium sapientiae* were produced, not only of the original Latin version but also of translations into various European vernaculars. In the fifteenth century the *Horologium sapientiae* was particularly influential in the Netherlands among the followers of the Devotio moderna, the Brothers and Sisters of the Common Life, whose religious reform movement based on inner devotion was founded by Gerhard Groote and shaped by *De Imitatio Christi* (The Imitation of Christ, 1426), attributed to Thomas à Kempis.

Related in content to the *Büchlein der ewigen Weisheit* and the *Horologium sapientiae* is the *Minnebüchlein* (first published, 1898; translated as "The Soul's Love-Book," 1962). References in the two genuine works also support the authenticity of the *Minnebüchlein,* or at least some connection between Seuse and the work. The three chapters of the *Minnebüchlein* contain prayers and meditations on the Passion of Christ and the suffering of Mary. Stylistically the work reveals rhetorical devices that are common in Seuse's other writings, but it also includes terms that are not found in any of those works.

Page from the earliest extant manuscript for Seuse's Exemplar, *dating from the second half of the fourteenth century (Strasbourg, Bibliothèque Nationale et Universitaire, L. Germ. 721, folio 8^v)*

Since the conversion experience in his eighteenth year Seuse had followed ascetic practices that he describes in the *Vita:* he fasted regularly, bathed infrequently, and observed the vow of silence at meals. More harsh and unusual were his self-mortifications: for sixteen years he slept on top of an old door or in a chair; he hung a nail-studded cross on his back; he wore a hair shirt and fastened an iron chain around his body; and he inscribed the name of Christ on his chest with an iron stylus. Although illnesses resulted from the practices, he was comforted by visionary experiences that gave him courage to pursue this path toward his spiritual goal. Seuse continued the disciplines until around 1335, when he believed God told him to abandon them and turn his attention in new directions. At this time Seuse began his career as an itinerant preacher and spiritual adviser in Switzerland and Alsace and along the Upper Rhine, although his responsibilities led him as far northwest as Aachen and the Netherlands.

Even though he was charged occasionally to preach and minister to the laity, Seuse frequented primarily religious communities for women, whom he served as *Beichtvater* (confessor) and as friend. Most of these were Dominican convents in the vicinity of his friary, such as Saint Peter and Zofingen in Constance and Katharinental near Dießenhofen;

others were located farther away: Ötenbach near Zurich, Unterlinden at Colmar, Saint Nicholas in Undis in Strasbourg, and, especially, Töß near Winterthur, where Elsbeth Stagel resided. Stagel, a well-educated woman with a probing mind, wished to learn more about the teachings of Meister Eckhart and wrote to Seuse for guidance; what began as a professional correspondence developed into a friendship. Although no other such relationships with women of religious communities are documented, Seuse's influence is apparent in the popularity of his writings among them. Letters of the secular priest Heinrich of Nördlingen to the Medingen mystic Margaretha Ebner confirm that Seuse's works were circulated among the communities. The impact of the devotional literature and the spiritual care provided by Seuse and other male religious is reflected in the wealth of revelations and vitae composed and transcribed by Dominican nuns in the province of Teutonia at this time. Seuse was acquainted with the other religious men dedicated to the care of the nuns—Heinrich of Nördlingen and Tauler—as well as others among the *Gottesfreunde* (Friends of God), a loosely knit group of religious and laymen and laywomen devoted to prayer, meditation, and the *vita apostolica* (apostolic life).

Along with most of his Dominican brothers, Seuse supported Pope John XXII and, after 1334, Pope Benedict XII in their struggle against Emperor Ludwig of Bavaria. The Dominicans were forced into exile from Constance in 1338 or 1339, and Seuse sought refuge either at the Schottenkloster—the Scots monastery outside the city gates—or at the Dominican convent of Katharinental. Whether he served as prior beginning around 1343 or 1344, as related in the *Vita,* is uncorroborated. When the Dominicans returned to Constance in 1346, Seuse probably was among them. Shortly thereafter, his reputation suffered a tremendous blow: chapter 38 of the autobiography recounts how he was accused by "ein bös wib" (a vicious woman) of fathering her child. Although he was eventually exonerated, Seuse lost many friends and supporters—among them Heinrich of Nördlingen, who made an oblique reference to the incident in one of his letters to Ebner. Even before the general of the order and the provincial of Teutonia, the southern Dominican province in German-speaking territory, arrived in Constance to consider the matter, Seuse presumably had been relocated to another community. By the time his innocence was confirmed, he had established himself at the Dominican monastery in Ulm. Even though Seuse had forsworn self-mortification years earlier, the interdict and the personal slander challenged him to lead a humble and ascetic life in his later days.

In his final years, between 1363 and 1366, Seuse undertook the editing of his works for publication. According to the prologue, the collection, the *Exemplar* (Book of Examples, circa 1362-1366; first published, 1482; translated as *The Life of Blessed Henry Suso,* 1865), is a sort of *Ausgabe letzter Hand* (final authorized edition); the extent to which the final product is the work of Seuse's own hand is, however, greatly disputed. Because of Seuse's popularity, many unauthentic works bearing his name, as well as error-ridden manuscript copies of his actual works, appeared during his lifetime; the prologue to the *Exemplar* says that it is because of these productions that Seuse decided to gather and edit his works. The *Exemplar* includes many models of piety and devotion to God from which others can learn. It consists of the *Vita,* the *Büchlein der ewigen Weisheit,* the *Büchlein der Wahrheit,* and the *Briefbüchlein* (Little Book of Letters).

The *Vita* is a third-person narrative of the life of Seuse, the Servant of Eternal Wisdom. Like contemporary courtly epics and many written a century earlier, the *Vita* depicts the protagonist as a hero who, despite setbacks, rises to the status of a paradigm of religious virtue. Some incidents recounted are analogous to events from saints' lives, and some parallel occurrences in the lives of the desert fathers. Others are more unusual: for example, Seuse is shunned by his companions because his sister, a Dominican nun at Saint Gall, has fallen into sin (chapter 24); he is accused of poisoning the wells in a village (chapter 25); and he encounters a murderer along the banks of the Rhine (chapter 26). Although it has been argued that the *Vita* is the first autobiography in German, one must be aware of the hagiographic elements and the expressed purpose of the writing of the life: to record the Servant's spiritual journey as an example for others. The chronology of events in Seuse's life and their accuracy are secondary to the portrayal of his spiritual development.

In addition to the problem of genre, the question of authorship remains unanswered. Whether Seuse was the sole author or the sole editor or whether he merely authorized the *Vita* is unclear. In addition to Seuse himself, those involved included the provincial of the German province of Teutonia, Master Bartholomew of Bolsenheim, who approved the final section (chapters 46 to 53) before his death in 1362, and Stagel. The death of Stagel around 1360 precluded any contribution by her to the final redaction of the *Exemplar*. The prologue to the first part of the *Vita* chronicles Stagel's role, which began many years earlier: she secretly recorded Seuse's responses to her queries about his personal life during his visits to the community; when Seuse discovered what he calls the "geischlichen dúpstal" (spiritual theft), he confiscated her writings and burned a portion of them—only to be warned from heaven not to destroy the rest. Those that remained served as the basis for the first part of the *Vita*.

Part 1 (chapters 1 to 32) documents Seuse's early years of asceticism, his visionary experiences, and the personal and professional trials he endured before he devoted himself to pastoral care. Among the most memorable and best-known accounts in the first part is the narrative in chapter 20 relating Seuse's progress beyond the life of a spiritual beginner. The Servant rejoices that God has forbidden him to continue the outward ascetic practices he engaged in for so many years; but his struggle is not over. God calls on him to put on the boots and clothes of a knight and become a spiritual knight of God. Whereas the beginner had inflicted suffering on himself for God's sake, the spiritually superior knight will suffer at the hands of others; his reputation will be destroyed, and he will be publicly persecuted by friends and enemies alike. The suffering portended here is symbolized by the dog Seuse sees running about the cloisters with a doormat in his mouth. Seuse reconciles himself to be as ill-treated as the doormat, which he retrieves and keeps as a reminder to endure suffering patiently. He now must leave the solitude of his cell in the island friary and adopt the itinerant lifestyle of a preacher.

The second part (chapters 33 to 53) introduces Stagel, who requests from Seuse the discernment necessary to understand Eckhart's teachings. Seuse offers Stagel direction in the initial steps of the holy life. He also provides her with the teachings of the desert fathers for meditation; her self-mortifications in imitation of the desert fathers, however, evoke remonstrances from Seuse, who tells her to put aside such austere practices. Seuse's advice in these chapters centers on examples of exterior and interior suffering: his own, his mother's, and that of other holy persons and of Christ. These provide Stagel with the model for the spiritual life. Many of the discussions between Seuse and Stagel recorded in the *Vita* are taken from letters that are no longer extant.

The final seven chapters of the work were added by Seuse after Stagel's death and constitute the mystical teaching inherent in the autobiography. Now that she has been initiated, Stagel is prepared to contemplate more fully the blessed life of perfection. She inquires about the distinction between true and false reasoning and between true and false detachment. In characterizing the differences Seuse provides her with sayings and teachings to direct the outer person toward inwardness. He then offers instruction as to what, where, and how God is, admonishing her to open her inward ears and eyes to hear and see him. In response to Stagel's questions concerning the achievement of the sublime goal in the abyss of the Godhead, Seuse characterizes the unity in nature of the threeness of persons of the Godhead. At his spiritual daughter's request, he concludes with a brief summary of the nature of the Godhead and the progression of the human being into the abyss.

The *Exemplar* concludes with the *Briefbüchlein*, a selection of eleven letters from Seuse to the Dominican women in his charge, primarily those at the convent of Töß. The pieces were chosen from a twenty-seven-letter collection, the *Großes Briefbuch* (Great Book of Letters; first published, 1622; translated as *The Letters of Henry Suso to his Spiritual Daughters*, 1955). In his edition of the *Exemplar*, titled *Heinrich Seuse: Deutsche Schriften* (Heinrich Seuse: German Writings, 1907), Karl Bihlmeyer added a twenty-eighth letter, the *Testament der Minne oder Minneregel* (Testament or Rule of Love), which is extant in only one manuscript. Bihlmeyer also appended several supplements: the *Erzählung von der Verehrung des Namens Jesu* (Story of the Devotion to the Name of Jesus), the *Morgengruß* (Morning Prayer), and some *Sprüche* (Sayings). The additions are not part of the original collection but are found in later manuscripts of the *Exemplar*.

The correspondence in both the *Großes Briefbuch* and the *Briefbüchlein* is addressed either to Stagel specifically or to several sisters in the community; no responses from the religious women are extant in letter form, although excerpts from letters are incorporated into the second half of the *Vita*. The letters of the *Briefbüchlein* are substantially shorter than their *Großes Briefbuch* counterparts and are frequently so drastically edited as to be comprehensible only in light of the larger collection. The principle behind the editing of the *Briefbüchlein* is the development of the mystical experience from conversion to the highest level of the spiritual union. The first five letters survey the foundation and progression of religious life, beginning with withdrawal from the world and concluding with preparation for death. Following instructions for the conventual superior, the collection turns to commentary on spiritual behavior during mystical experiences; it concludes with recommendations regarding the veneration of the name of Jesus and for fervent prayer as the crowning exercise.

The authorship and editorship of the two versions of the *Großes Briefbuch* have sparked almost as much controversy as the same questions regarding the *Vita*. Between 1867 and 1878 the Protestant historian Wilhelm Preger and the Dominican Denifle debated the relationship between the two letter collections. Preger contended that the two collections represented different redactions by Seuse himself, and that the original collection had been lost; Denifle's thesis, bolstered by Bihlmeyer's research, identified the *Großes Briefbuch* as the original collection, probably transcribed by Stagel.

Differences in style and content between the two collections can be explained in light of the respective purpose of each collection. The style of the letters of the *Großes Briefbuch* is more personal and the content more descriptive; if they are not the originals, they reflect the prototypes closely. Seuse claimed to have destroyed the collection from which he excerpted the *Briefbüchlein;* but considering the circumstances surrounding the production of the *Vita* and the popularity and extensive manuscript tradition of some of Seuse's other works, it is not surprising that the *Großes Briefbuch* has survived.

None of Seuse's letters contains biographical or historical references and, hence, they cannot be considered personal letters in the modern sense. The common feature of the letters in both collections is their homiletic nature. The emphasis on mystical teaching and the form the teaching often takes—for example, numbered points, anecdotes, and examples—suggest a close relationship between Seuse's letters and the medieval sermon. Indeed, sermon 1, "Lectulus noster floridus" (Our bed is covered with blossoms), appears among the letters of the *Großes Briefbuch* in half of its extant manuscripts. Additional support for the thesis is found in the rubric *bredie* or *bredige* (sermon) preceding several of the letters in a Berlin manuscript of the *Großes Briefbuch*. If the letters are edited homiletic works, this could explain why so few sermons by Seuse are extant.

Seuse's lack of interest in his homiletic works is apparent in the meager number of extant sermons. Only sermon 1 appears consistently in manuscripts that include Seuse's other works. Sermons 2, 3, and 4 survive almost exclusively in Middle and Low German manuscripts, often intermingled with the homiletic works of Tauler. As in Seuse's other works, the focus in the sermons is on detachment from the world and abandonment of the self to God; the homiletic works are intended for a religious, not a lay, audience.

The oldest manuscript containing the entire *Exemplar* dates from the last two decades of the fourteenth century and originated at the Johanniterhaus zum Grünen Wörth in Strasbourg, where the mystic Rulman Merswin had established his spiritual community and from which the writings of the fictional "Gottesfreund vom Oberland" (Friend of God in the Oberland) originate. The manuscript was presumed lost when the Strasbourg municipal library burned in 1870. Shortly after the turn of the century, however, Bihlmeyer discovered the manuscript in Berlin. In 1907 the manuscript was returned to Strasbourg. The thirteen additional extant manuscripts of the *Exemplar* or portions of it date mostly from the fifteenth century and were produced, by and large, in Dominican female communities in southern Germany and Switzerland. Only one extant manuscript of an individual work predates the Strasbourg manuscript of the *Exemplar:* the Engelberg manuscript number 141, which contains an incomplete version of the *Büchlein der ewigen Weisheit,* is dated 1378 and, hence, is the oldest extant Seuse manuscript. Several entries on the final page concerning its provenance trace the manuscript to the Töß community and suggest that Stagel either wrote or edited the copy.

Included in five of the *Exemplar* manuscripts and in the 1482 and 1512 printed editions of the collection are a series of twelve pictures that allowed Seuse to provide guidance through both image and word. Whether Seuse himself sketched the prototypes has been debated; in any case, because of the detail included he undoubtedly closely supervised the work. Most of the images depict Seuse as Servant, often kneeling at the feet of the regally adorned Eternal Wisdom or enfolded in her arms. Seuse's interest in art is attested in chapters 20 and 35 of the *Vita,* which describe how he had a painter decorate the walls of his cell in Constance with sketches of and sayings from the desert fathers.

Seuse remained in Ulm until his death, preaching and attending to other duties associated with pastoral care and actively engaged in or supervising the preparation of the *Exemplar*. He died on 25 January 1366 and was buried in the monastery church; when the church was rebuilt in the seventeenth century, his grave was lost. Seuse was canonized in 1831.

Seuse's legacy consists of the examples of devotion that he established with the model of his own life and through the meditations and prayers that he formulated and shared with others. Ever conscious of his responsibilities as adviser and spiritual guide, he adopted literary forms and a writing style best suited to his didactic purpose. Seuse frequently used the dialogue form to make his works more accessible and comprehensible to his readers. Likewise, his frequent insertion of exclamations such as *wafen* (oh, help, alas) to express joy, surprise, or encouragement and *ach* (alas) or *owe* (oh) to signify suffering add immediacy to his writing. The Dominican's masterful borrowing from the Bernhardian tradition, the poetic style and skillful use of rhetoric in the devotional works, and the engaging, anecdotal style of the *Vita* achieved for his writings popularity unparalleled at the time and touched the hearts and captivated the spirits of several generations of devout religious and laypersons in medieval Europe.

In his works Seuse focuses on the spiritual growth and ultimate transformation of individuals seeking mystical union; he does not expound on the theological or philosophical underpinnings of the religious experience, eschewing the speculative, rational mysticism of his mentor Eckhart. By presenting himself as the example, the Exemplar, of the fallible human who, through inner searching and suffering, is able to attain unity with God, Seuse offers a credible and inspiring witness to the mystical experience that his readers can learn from and emulate. Because of the humanity depicted in his works, Seuse is an eloquent and influential representative of the religious reform movements of the later Middle Ages.

Bibliography:
Angelus Walz, "Bibliographiae susonianae conatus," *Angelicum*, 46 (1969): 430-491.

Biographies:
Ferdinand Vetter, *Ein Mystikerpaar des 14. Jahrhunderts: Schwester Elsbeth Stagel in Töss und Vater Amandus (Suso) in Konstanz* (Basel: Schweighauser, 1882);

Friedrich Zoepfl, *Heinrich Seuse*, Lebensschule der Gottesfreunde, no. 48 (Meitingen: Kyrios, 1947).

References:
Jeanne Ancelet-Hustache, "Le problème de l'authenticité de la vie de Suso," in *La mystique rhénane: Colloque de Strasbourg 16-19 mai 1961*, edited by Jean Dagens (Paris: Presses Universitaires de France, 1963), pp. 193-205;

Karl Bihlmeyer, "Kleine Beiträge zur Geschichte der deutschen Mystik," in *Beiträge zur Geschichte der Renaissance und Reformation: Joseph Schlecht zum sechzigsten Geburtstag*, edited by Ludwig Fischer (Munich: Datterer, 1917), pp. 45-62;

Bihlmeyer, "Zur Chronologie einiger Schriften Seuses," *Historisches Jahrbuch der Görres-Gesellschaft*, 25 (1904): 176-190;

Maria Bindschedler, "Heinrich Seuses Auffassung von der deutschen Sprache," in *Philologia Deutsch: Festschrift zum 70. Geburtstag von Walter Henzen*, edited by Werner Kohlschmidt and Paul Zinsli (Bern: Francke, 1965), pp. 57-61;

Jules-Augustin Bizet, *Suso et le Minnesang ou La Morale de l'amour courtois* (Paris: Aubier, 1944);

Bruno Boesch, "Seuses religiöse Sprache," in *Festgabe für Friedrich Maurer: Zum 70. Geburtstag am 5. Januar 1968*, edited by Werner Besch, Siegfried Grosse, and Heinz Rupp (Düsseldorf: Schwann, 1968), pp. 223-245;

Boesch, "Zur Minneauffassung Seuses," in *Festschrift Josef Quint anläßlich seines 65. Geburtstages überreicht*, edited by Hugo Moser, Rudolf Schützeichel, and Karl Stackmann (Bonn: Semmel, 1964), pp. 61-68;

Adelheid Bohnet-von der Thüsen, *Der Begriff des Lichts bei Heinrich Seuse* (Munich: Dissertationsdruck Schön, 1972);

Dieter Breuer, "Zur Druckgeschichte und Rezeption der Schriften Heinrich Seuse," in *Frömmigkeit in der frühen Neuzeit: Studien zur religiösen Literatur des 17. Jahrhunderts in Deutschland*, edited by Breuer (Amsterdam: Rodopi, 1984), pp. 29-49;

James M. Clark, *The Great German Mystics: Eckhart, Tauler and Suso* (Oxford: Blackwell, 1949);

Edmund Colledge and J. C. Marler, " 'Mystical' Pictures in the Suso 'Exemplar' Ms Strasbourg 2929," *Archivum Fratrum Praedicatorum*, 54 (1984): 293-354;

Heinrich Suso Denifle, "Ein letztes Wort über Seuses Briefbücher," *Zeitschrift für deutsches Altertum*, 21 (1877): 89-142;

Denifle, "Zu Seuses ursprünglichem Briefbuch," *Zeitschrift für deutsches Altertum*, 19 (1876): 346-371;

Ephrem M. Filthaut, ed., *Heinrich Seuse: Studien zum 600. Todestag, 1366-1966* (Cologne: Albertus Magnus, 1966);

Adam Gebhard, *Die Briefe und Predigten des Mystikers Heinrich Seuse, gen. Suso, nach ihren weltlichen Motiven und dichterischen Formen betrachtet: Ein Beitrag zur deutschen Literatur- und Kulturgeschichte des 14. Jahrhunderts* (Berlin & Leipzig: De Gruyter, 1920);

Carl Greith, "Heinrich Suso und seine Schule unter der Ordensschwestern von Töß, bei Winterthur, im vierzehnten Jahrhundert," *Katholische Schweizer-Blätter für Wissenschaft und Kunst*, 2 (1860): 65-77, 137-151, 399-416;

Conrad Gröber, *Der Mystiker Heinrich Seuse: Die Geschichte seines Lebens. Die Entstehung und Echtheit seiner Werke* (Freiburg in Breisgau: Herder, 1941);

Alois M. Haas, "Deutsche Mystik," in *Die deutsche Literatur im späten Mittelalter 1250-1370*, edited by Ingeborg Glier, volume 3/ii of *Geschichte der deutschen Literatur* (Munich: Beck, 1987), pp. 275-291;

Haas and Kurt Ruh, "Seuse, Heinrich OP," in *Die deutsche Literatur des Mittelalters–Verfasserlexikon*, volume 8, second edition, edited by Ruh (Berlin: De Gruyter, 1992), pp. 1109-1129;

Jeffrey E. Hamburger, "The Use of Images in the Pastoral Care of Nuns: The Case of Heinrich Suso and the Dominicans," *Art Bulletin*, 71 (March 1989): 20-46;

Paul Heitz, *Zur mystischen Stilkunst Heinrich Seuses in seinen deutschen Schriften: Teildruck* (Halle: Karras, 1914);

Curt Heyer, "Stilgeschichtliche Studien über Heinrich Seuses Büchlein der ewigen Weisheit," *Zeitschrift für deutsche Philologie*, 46 (1915): 175-228, 393-443;

Georg Hofmann, "Seuses Werke in deutschsprachigen Handschriften des späten Mittelalters," *Fuldaer Geschichtsblätter*, 45 (1969): 113-206;

Anne-Marie Holenstein-Hasler, *Studien zur Vita Heinrich Seuses* (Freiburg, Switzerland: Paulusdruckerei, 1968);

Rufus M. Jones, *The Flowering of Mysticism: The Friends of God in the Fourteenth Century* (New York: Macmillan, 1939), pp. 139-157;

Paul Michel, "Stilwandel bei Heinrich Seuse," in *Verborum amor: Studien zur Geschichte und Kunst der deutschen Sprache. Festschrift für Stefan Sonderegger zum 65. Geburtstag*, edited by Harald Burger, Haas, and Peter von Matt (Berlin & New York: De Gruyter, 1992), pp. 297-341;

Barbara Molinelli-Stein, "Ein Beitrag zur Echtheitsfrage des 'Minnebüchleins' (Heinrich Seuse?)," in *"Getempert vnd gemischet": für Wolfgang Mohr zum 65. Geburtstag von seinen Tübinger Schülern*, edited by Franz Hundsnurscher and Ulrich Müller, Göppinger Arbeiten zur Germanistik, no. 65 (Göppingen: Kümmerle, 1972), pp. 313-354;

Anna Nicklas, *Die Terminologie des Mystikers Heinrich Seuse unter besonderer Berücksichtigung der psychologischen, logischen, metaphysischen und mystischen Ausdrücke* (Königsberg: Lankeit, 1914);

Susan R. Norris, "The Diffusion of Seuse's *Büchlein der ewigen Weisheit* in Middle Low German Manuscripts," *Manuscripta*, 25 (1981): 164-171;

Dominikus Planzer, "Das Horologium Sapientiae und die Echtheit der Vita des seligen Heinrich Seuse O.P.," *Archivum Fratrum Praedicatorum*, 1 (1931): 181-221;

Wilhelm Preger, "Die Briefbücher Susos," *Zeitschrift für deutsches Altertum*, 20 (1876): 373-415;

Preger, *Geschichte der deutschen Mystik im Mittelalter: Nach den Quellen untersucht und dargestellt*, volume 2 (Leipzig: Dörffling & Franke, 1881), pp. 309-415;

Anna Groh Seesholtz, *Friends of God: Practical Mystics of the Fourteenth Century* (New York: Columbia University Press, 1934);

Reinhard Senn, *Die Echtheit der Vita Heinrich Seuses*, Sprache und Dichtung, no. 45 (Bern: Haupt, 1930);

Heinrich Stirnimann, "Mystik und Metaphorik: Zu Seuses Dialog," in *Das "einig Ein": Studien zu Theorie und Sprache der deutschen Mystik*, edited by Haas and Stirnimann (Freiburg, Switzerland: Universitätsverlag, 1980), pp. 209-280;

Debra L. Stoudt, "The Structure and Style of the Letters of Seuse's *Großes Briefbuch*," *Neuphilologische Mitteilungen*, 90 (1989): 359-367;

Frank Tobin, "Coming to Terms with Meister Eckhart: Suso's *Büchlein der Wahrheit*," in *"Semper idem et novus": Festschrift für Frank Banta*, edited by Francis G. Gentry, Göppinger Arbeiten zur Germanistik, no. 481 (Göppingen: Kümmerle, 1988), pp. 321-344;

Ursula Weymann, *Die Seusesche Mystik und ihre Wirkung auf die bildende Kunst* (Berlin: Pfau, 1938).

Heinrich Steinhöwel
(1411/1412 – 1 March 1479)

Albrecht Classen
University of Arizona

BOOKS: *Buochlin der ordnung, wie sich der mensch halten sol, zu den zyten diser grúsenlichen kranckheit* (Ulm: Johann Zainer, 1473);

Ein tütsche Cronica von anfang der welt uncz uff keiser fridrich (Ulm: Johann Zainer, 1473).

Edition: "Pestbüchlein," in *Die ersten gedruckten Pestschriften: Geschichte und bibliographische Untersuchungen,* edited by Arnold Klebs and Karl Sudhoff (Munich: Münchner Drucke, 1926).

TRANSLATIONS: *Die hystory des Küniges Appolonij von Latin zu teutsch gemachet,* (Augsburg: Günther Zainer, 1471);

Petrarch, *Diß is eyn epistel francisci petrarche, von grosser stetigkait eyner frawen Grysel gehaissen* (Augsburg: Günther Zainer, 1471); republished, with introduction by Steinhöwel (Ulm: Johann Zainer, 1473);

Giovanni Boccaccio, *Von den erlauchten Frauen* (Augsburg: Günther Zainer, 1475);

Rodrigo Sánchéz de Arevalo, *Spiegel des menschlichen Lebens* (Augsburg: Günther Zainer, circa 1475);

Das selb leben Esopi (Augsburg: Günther Zainer, 1476/1477);

Maister Constantini Buch: Der Entwurf des Ulmer Stadtarztes Heinrich Steinhöwel zu einem Arzneibuch, edited by Anneliese Seiz-Hauser (Weissenhorn: Konrad, 1989).

The Swabian author Heinrich Steinhöwel was one of the few German writers of his time who was strongly influenced by the Italian Renaissance. His translations from Latin into German opened an important window onto European literature for Germans and paved the way for the intellectual transformation from the late Middle Ages to the early modern age. His medical treatises and translations of fiction became the most influential reading material of his time.

Steinhöwel was born in 1411 or 1412 in Weil. He probably attended the Latin school there, but his parents may have sent him to nearby Esslingen. By the summer semester of 1429 he was enrolled at the University of Vienna, where he earned his bachelor of arts on 13 July 1432 and his master of arts on 12 February 1436. The latter degree obliged him to teach until the winter semester of 1437–1438. Around 1439 he moved to Padua, Italy, to study canon law but soon switched to medicine. In 1442 he assumed the post of *rector artistarum* (dean of the liberal arts) at the University of Padua. He earned his doctorate in medicine on 5 January 1443. According to a document dated 19 December 1444, Steinhöwel taught, or at least studied, medicine at the University of Heidelberg for a brief period. In 1446 he held a temporary position as a doctor in his hometown, Weil; in 1449 he spent some time in Esslingen, where he cosigned with the city's representatives a declaration of war against Count Ulrich V of Württemberg on 3 September. On 18 July 1450 the City of Ulm appointed him doctor for the city council at a salary that was more than twice that of the mayor. At the same time, he served as the private doctor of Count Eberhard the Bearded of Württemberg. This connection seems to have been made through Steinhöwel's friendship with the court counselor Georg Ehingen, whom he knew from the University of Padua. He gained many privileges from the count and rose to a social position similar to that of a nobleman.

Steinhöwel began his literary career with a medical treatise, *Buochlin der ordnung, wie sich der mensch halten sol, zu den zyten diser grúsenlichen kranckheit,* (Little Book on How a Person Should Lead His Life during These Times of Horrible Sickness), commonly known as the *Pestbüchlein* (Little Book on the Plague), which he composed shortly after he began his practice in Weil. The work was not printed until 1473, the year after Steinhöwel's friend Johann Zainer opened a print shop in Ulm; the book about the plague became one of Zainer's first publications. In the prologue to the printed edition the author expresses his thanks to the mayor, city council, and community of Ulm for their support since 1450. Steinhöwel's coat of arms and that of the city of Ulm are combined on the decorative margin of the first page. The first part of the treatise deals with the weather conditions that influence the course of the disease, describes its early signs and sources of infection, and recommends preventive measures. The second part discusses measures to be taken once the sickness has struck, such as bleeding and the application of bandages, and suggests medication.

In 1454 Steinhöwel served as personal physician to Duke Philipp of Burgundy, whom he accompanied on the duke's journeys through southwestern Germany. In Freiburg im Breisgau he came into contact with important literary patrons, such as Archduchess Mechthild of Austria and Countess Mechthild of the Palatinate. In 1454 or 1455 Steinhöwel married Anastasia Egen, of a wealthy Augsburg family. He owned a pharmacy, the Mohrenapotheke, from 1455 until 1458, and became a wealthy and influential citizen of Ulm.

Steinhöwel's translation of the *Apollonius* from Latin into German in 1461 made one of the most popular medieval texts available to a wide audience; the translation circulated in manuscript form and was first printed in 1471. The narrative consists of a succession of events that are sometimes only loosely linked and include many dialogues. King Antiochus of Antiocha commits incest with his daughter and tries to hide his crime by posing to her suitors a riddle in which he has woven clues to the act; anyone who fails to solve the riddle is beheaded. Apollonius of Tyrus finds the answer; but the king denies that it is true, orders his beheading, but gives him a reprieve of thirty days. Apollonius returns to Tyrus, then escapes to Tarsus, where he saves the city from famine with the provisions he has brought with him. Leaving Tarsus, he is shipwrecked near Cyrene; rescued, he meets and subsequently marries the daughter of King Archestrates. Receiving the news that Antiochus and his daughter were killed by lightning and that he has been chosen as the successor to the throne, he travels to Antiocha with his wife. During the voyage she bears a daughter but apparently dies during labor. She is placed in a coffin and buried at sea. In Tarsus, Apollonius entrusts his daughter, Tarsia, to the care of a lady and resumes his travels. In the meantime, his wife, who had not in fact died, is rescued by two doctors and becomes a priestess in the temple of Diana at Ephesus. In a long digression the author follows the daughter's struggle to maintain her virginity and to survive her foster mother's attempts to murder her so that her own daughter's beauty will not pale in Tarsia's presence. At the end Apollonius is reunited with his daughter and his wife and adds the crown of Cyrene to that of Antiocha.

Page from Von den erlauchten Frauen, *Heinrich Steinhöwel's translation of Giovanni Boccaccio's* De claribus mulieribus

Apollonius is based on a tale that dates back to antiquity and was included in the twelfth-century *Gesta Romanorum*, but it incorporates many elements from other narrative traditions, such as Gottfried of Viterbo's *Pantheon* (1125–after 1202). Steinhöwel explains in his introduction why he was motivated to do the translation: "Eigen gedicht wer mir zeschwer, Latin zetútschen ist min ger" (To compose my own poetry is too hard for me; I prefer to translate from the Latin).

At the end of 1461 or in early 1462 Steinhöwel translated the Italian tale *Griseldis* into German. Giovanni Boccaccio had produced the first written version of the story in his *Decameron* (1348), but he claimed to have heard an oral version of it. Petrarch's translation of the story into Latin in epistolary form in 1373 became the source for many adaptations, including Steinhöwel's and Geoffrey Chaucer's "The Clerk's Tale" in *The Canterbury Tales*

Frontispiece for Steinhöwel's collection of fables

(circa 1375–1400). In Germany alone many authors tried their hand at translating the novella, including Erhard Grosz, Niklas von Wyle, Arigo (Heinrich Schlüsselfelder), and some Franconian and Middle German authors; the female protagonist is variously called Grisel, Grisardis, Griseida, or Grisildis. Steinhöwel's version, however, first printed by Günther Zainer in Augsburg in 1471, quickly proved to be the most popular one.

Griseldis is a poor farm girl who marries the young margrave of Saluzzo. The latter tests her submission and loyalty by taking away her children and pretending that he has killed them. Finally, he threatens to expel her and marry another woman. Griseldis accepts everything with the greatest humility, and her husband finally rewards her with the greatest honors because she has demonstrated absolute constancy and respect for him. The "other woman" turns out to be her own daughter, by now an adult.

Boccaccio had formulated his version of the tale as a criticism of male brutality to women; Petrarch restructured it as an allegory in which the husband represents God and Griseldis symbolizes the humble Christian who unquestioningly follows God's will. Steinhöwel purges the narrative of the religious dimension; in the introduction to the 1473 edition, printed in Ulm by Johann Zainer and personally corrected by Steinhöwel, he explains the literary and historical background of the tale and says that *Griseldis* serves "umb ander frowen manung zuo gedult geseczet werden" (for other women as an exhortation to learn patience). This conservative reorientation of the tale appealed to a wide audience in patriarchal Germany; the work was an early "best-seller," with fifteen manuscripts and fourteen incunabula from the fifteenth century and at least ten editions from the sixteenth. In the middle of the sixteenth century Cyriacus Spangenberg identified Steinhöwel's *Griseldis* as one of the best-known and most-loved tales in Germany.

In 1472 Steinhöwel was away from Ulm for an extended period, perhaps staying at the court of Duke Sigmund of Tyrol. There is good reason to believe that around that time he translated *Maister Constantini, so ein Münch war von Ainem berg, genannt Casin, Buch, gemacht auß allen andern guten Artzet Büchern, die er in Latin je erfuhr* (A Book by Master Constantini, a Monk on a Mountain Called Casin: Based on All Good Medical Books He Ever Found in Latin), which would not be published until 1989. Steinhöwel's name does not appear in the text, but the circumstances point to him as the translator: the work is dedicated to Duke Sigmund and his wife, Eleonore of Scotland, and the most important areas treated in it are gynecology and sexual hygiene—topics of great concern to the duke and his wife, who were childless. Steinhöwel's sources were a book of remedies by Bartholomaeus Anglicus (after 1235) and the *Arzneibuch* (Medicine Book, circa 1300), by Ortolf of Bavaria.

A month after the publication of *Pestbüchlein* Steinhöwel's *Ein tütsche Cronica von anfang der welt uncz uff keiser fridrich* (A German Chronicle from the Beginning of the World to Emperor Friedrich), commonly known as the *Deutsche Chronik* (German Chronicle), appeared; it can be attributed to him by his coat of arms, which is depicted in the border of the first page. The *Deutsche Chronik,* based on the anonymous *Flores temporum* (Flowers of Time, circa 1290), is only thirty-six pages in length. Steinhöwel did not simply translate the *Flores temporum* but expanded it, adding references to local events and customs. The work's popularity seems to have been rather limited, although it was reprinted in 1531 and 1535. Steinhöwel claimed to have translated another chronicle, by a "doctor gwido"—possibly

Guibert of Nogent, who died in 1124—but this work does not seem to have been preserved.

In 1475 Steinhöwel published his translation and adaptation of Boccaccio's *De claribus mulieribus* (On Famous Women), a collection of lives of exemplary women from antiquity, as *Von den erlauchten Frauen.* Instead of the 104 *Vitae* in Boccaccio's version, Steinhöwel has only 99; among them is a translation of Livy's tale of Tullia, which is not found in Boccaccio's text. Steinhöwel promoted, and possibly even edited, Arigo's German translation of Boccaccio's *Decameron,* which was printed by Johann Zainer in 1476 or 1477.

Rodrigo Sánchéz de Arevalo, bishop of Zamora, published his *Speculum vitae humanae* (Mirror of Human Life) in 1467; Steinhöwel rendered the work into German as *Spiegel des menschlichen Lebens* and had it printed by Günter Zainer in Augsburg around 1475. The dedication thanks Duke Sigmund of Tyrol for his generous contributions to Steinhöwel's translation of Boccaccio's treatise on famous women. *Spiegel des menschlichen Lebens* deals with the strengths and weaknesses of the various social classes; the first part focuses on civil administrators, the second on those who hold clerical ranks.

The most important work from Steinhöwel's pen proved to be his collection and prose translation of fables and exemplary tales under the title *Das selb leben Esopi* (The Life of Aesop), which appeared in 1476/1477. The sources, from the late classical period, the High Middle Ages, and the Italian Renaissance, include the *Romulus* collection, Adolf of Vienna's *Dogliamus,* Anonymus Neveleti, Rinuccio da Castiglione, Avianus, Petrus Alfonsi, and Gian Francesco Poggio Bracciolini; none of the fables are actually taken from Aesop. Steinhöwel apologizes to his female readers for the obscenity of Poggio Bracciolini's *fascetiae* (jocular tales) and points out that many other tales by Poggio Bracciolini that he has not included are much more obscene; to prove the point he summarizes those stories in some detail. *Das selb leben Esopi* has more than two hundred woodcuts of the highest quality and is one of the most attractive incunabula from the period between 1455 and 1500. In his dedication to Duke Sigmund, Steinhöwel says that his purpose is to offer moral lessons with the help of literary examples presented in "ruigem verstentlichem tütsch" (clear, understandable German). The work was a huge success; between 1477 and 1545 at least twenty-four editions appeared. Martin Luther criticized Steinhöwel for composing the anthology for the sole purpose of entertaining his audience, but this observation, which was untrue in any case, had no effect on the popularity of the work.

On 15 June 1478 Steinhöwel was inducted into the Roman Catholic *Heiliggeistbruderschaft* (Brotherhood of the Holy Spirit). He died on 1 March 1479.

It would be incorrect to label Steinhöwel a humanist; he had learned much from the Italian humanists, but he was still steeped in the medieval tradition. Unlike those of the humanists, his works include neither texts nor literary correspondences written in Latin. Steinhöwel did not belong to any of the learned societies that were common during the Renaissance, and he had virtually no contact with humanists such as Sigmund Gossembrot, Hartmann Schedel, and Sigismund Meisterlin, who lived in nearby Augsburg. Nevertheless, his work represents an important bridge between the late Middle Ages and the Renaissance.

References:

Peter Amelung, *Der Frühdruck im deutschen Südwesten, 1473–1500: Eine Ausstellung der Württembergischen Landesbibliothek Stuttgart,* volume 1 (Ulm & Stuttgart: Württembergische Landesbibliothek, 1979);

Eckhard Bernstein, *Die Literatur des deutschen Frühhumanismus* (Stuttgart: Metzler, 1978), pp. 75–90;

Christa Bertelsmeier-Kierst, "Griseldis" in Deutschland: Studien zu Steinhöwel und Arigo (Heidelberg: Winter, 1988);

Volker Borvitz, *Die Übersetzungstechnik Heinrich Steinhöwels dargestellt auf Grund seiner Verdeutschung des "Speculum Vitae Humanae" von Rodericus Zamorensis* (Halle: Karras, 1914);

Curt Bühler, "The Fifteenth-Century Editions of Petrarch's *Historia Griseldis* in Steinhöwel's German Translation," *Library Quarterly,* 15 (1945): 231–236;

Pack Carnes, *Fable Scholarship: An Annotated Bibliography* (New York & London: Garland, 1985);

Carnes, "Heinrich Steinhöwel's *Esopus* and the Corpus of Aesopica in Sixteenth-Century Germany," dissertation, UCLA, 1979;

Gerd Dicke, "Neue und alte biographische Bezeugungen Heinrich Steinhöwels: Befunde und Kritik," *Zeitschrift für deutsches Altertum und deutsche Literatur,* 120, no. 2 (1991): 156–184;

Dicke, *Steinhöwels "Esopus" und seine Fortsetzer: Untersuchungen zu einem Bucherfolg der Frühdruckzeit* (Tübingen: Niemeyer, 1994);

Xenia von Ertzdorff, *Romane und Novellen des 15. und 16. Jahrhunderts in Deutschland* (Darmstadt: Wissenschaftliche Buchgesellschaft, 1989), pp. 9, 34–37, 45, 55–58, 218, 239;

Bodo Gotzkowsky, *"Volksbücher": Prosaromane, Renaissancenovellen, Versdichtungen und Schwankbücher,* volume 1: *Drucke des 15. und 16. Jahr-*

hunderts (Baden-Baden: Koerner, 1991), pp. 184-191, 204-221;

Irene Hänsch, *Heinrich Steinhöwels "Griseldis": Studien zur Text- und Überlieferungsgeschichte einer frühhumanistischen Prosanovelle* (Munich: Beck, 1975);

Nikolaus Henkel, "Heinrich Steinhöwel," in *Deutsche Dichter der frühen Neuzeit (1450-1600): Ihr Leben und Werk,* edited by Stephan Füssel (Berlin: Erich Schmidt, 1993), pp. 51-70;

Ursula Hess, *Heinrich Steinhöwels "Griseldis": Studien zur Text- und Überlieferungsgeschichte einer frühhumanistischen Prosanovelle* (Munich: Beck, 1975);

Joachim Knape, *De oboedientia et fide uxoris: Petrarcas humanistisch-moralisches Exempel "Griseldis" und seine frühe deutsche Rezeption* (Göttingen: Gratia, 1978);

Robert T. Lenaghan, "Steinhöwel's 'Esopus' and Early Humanism," *Monatshefte,* 60 (1968): 1-8;

Leander Petzold, "Die unschuldig verstoßene Ehefrau": Zur Stoff- und Überlieferungsgeschichte des Volksbuchs von 'Griseldis' in der mündlichen Tradition," in *Festschrift für Hans Engels zum 65. Geburtstag,* edited by Gerhard Augst (Göppingen: Kümmerle, 1991), pp. 64-82;

Werner Schwarz, "Translation into German in the Fifteenth Century," *Modern Language Review,* 39 (1944): 368-373;

Rolf Schwenk, *Vorarbeiten zu einer Biographie des Niklas von Wyle und zu einer kritischen Ausgabe seiner ersten Translatze* (Göppingen: Kümmerle, 1978);

Barbara Weinmayer, *Studien zur Gebrauchssituation früher deutscher Druckprosa* (Munich: Beck, 1982);

Franz Josef Worstbrock, "Zur Einbürgerung der Übersetzung antiker Autoren im deutschen Humanismus," *Zeitschrift für deutsches Altertum und deutsche Literatur,* 99 (1970): 45-81.

Papers:

The autograph manuscript of Heinrich Steinhöwel's translation of Rodrigo Sánchéz de Arevalo's *Speculum vitae humanae* is in the Munich Staatsbibliothek (Cgm 1137). A paper manuscript for the *Maister Constantini Buch* is in the Stadtbibliothek Ulm. *Die hystory des Küniges Appollonii* exists as Ms. D, Donaueschingen, Fürstlich-Fürstenbergische Hofbibliothek cod. 150, 1461. *Diß ist eyn epistel francisci petrarche, von grosser stetigkait eyner frawen Grysel gehaissen* exists as Ms. M 3, Munich, Bayerische Staatsbibliothek, Cgm 311, from 1474, and as Ms. 727 (F), paper, Fribourg, Bibliothèque de la Société économique, after 1480.

Johannes Tauler
(circa 1300 – 1361)

David Blamires
University of Manchester

WORKS: *Sermons*

Manuscripts: The approximately eighty sermons or homilies that Tauler wrote in German have come down in more than ninety manuscripts dating chiefly from the fourteenth to the sixteenth centuries. Eight of these manuscripts are from the fourteenth century: Basel, Universitätsbibliothek, Cod. B XI, 23; Berlin, Deutsche Staatsbibliothek Preussischer Kulturbesitz, Ms. germ. 8° 68; Engelberg, Stiftsbibliothek, Nr. 124; Freiburg im Breisgau, Universitätsbibliothek, Nr. 41; Strasbourg, Bibliothèque Nationale et Universitaire, Cod. A 89 and Cod. A 91 (both destroyed in 1870; transcripts by Karl Schmidt are extant); Vienna, Österreichische Nationalbibliothek, Cod. 2739 and Cod. 2744. The Engelberg manuscript, dated 1359, was written during Tauler's lifetime and, with forty-four sermons, contains slightly more than half the authentic corpus. The Strasbourg Cod. A 89 contained eighty-three items attributed to Tauler, while Vienna 2744 has a mere dozen. All the German manuscripts except one present texts written in some dialect or other of High German; the exception, a Hildesheim manuscript, is in Low German. As is common with religious literature of this period, however, there is a continuity of transmission between Germany and the Netherlands, so there are, in addition, nearly forty manuscripts providing Middle Dutch or Flemish versions of Tauler's works.

First publication: *Sermon des groß gelarten in gnaden erlauchten doctoris Johannis Thauleri predigerr ordens* (Leipzig: Conrad Kachelofen, 1498); enlarged as *Joannis Tauleri des seligen lerers Predig, fast fruchtbar zuo eim recht christlichen Leben* (Basel: Printed by Adam Petri for Johann Rynmann, 1521; reprinted, Frankfurt am Main: Minerva, 1996); enlarged as *Des erleuchten D. Joannis Tauleri, Von eym waren euangelischen Leben, götliche Predig, Leren, Epistolen, Cantilenen, Prophetien, Alles eyn kostpar Sellen Schatz, in alten geschreyben Büchern fuonden, vnd nuo erstmals ins Liecht kommen*, edited by Peter Canisius (Cologne: Casper von Gennep, 1543).

Edition in Low German: *Joannis Tauleri des hilligen lerers Predige faste fruchtbar vnd nutlick to einen rechten Christlycken leuende* (Halberstadt, 1523).

Edition in Latin: *D. Ioannis Thavleri . . . tam de tempore qvam de Sanctis Conciones plane pijssimae, caeteraque . . . opera omnia*, edited by Laurentius Surius (Cologne: Johannes Quentel, 1548; reprinted, Hildesheim, Zurich & New York: Olms, 1985).

Standard editions: *Die Predigten Taulers*, edited by Ferdinand Vetter (Berlin: Weidmann, 1910); *Ausgewählte Predigten Johann Taulers*, edited by Leopold Naumann (Berlin: De Gruyter, 1914); *Sermons de Tauler et autres écrits mystiques*, 2 volumes, edited by A. L. Corin, (Paris: Champion, 1924, 1929).

Editions in modern German: *Johannes Tauler: Predigten*, translated by Georg Hofmann (Freiburg, Basel & Vienna: Herder, 1961); *Johannes Tauler: Predigten*, translated by Louise Gnädinger (Olten: Walter, 1983).

Editions in English: *The History and Life of the Reverend Doctor John Tauler of Strasbourg*, translated by Susanna Winkworth (London: Smith, Elder, 1857); *The Inner Way, Being Thirty-six Sermons for Festivals by John Tauler, Friar-Preacher of Strasburg*, translated by Arthur Wollaston Hutton (London: Methuen, 1901); *The Sermons and Conferences of J. Tauler*, translated by W. Elliot (Washington, D.C.: Apostolic Mission House, 1910); *Signposts to Perfection: A Selection from the Sermons of Johann Tauler*, translated by Elizabeth Strakosch (London: Blackfriars, 1958); *Johannes Tauler: Sermons*, translated by Maria Shrady (New York: Mahwah / Toronto: Paulist Press, 1985); *The Rhineland Mystics*, translated by Ol-

Page from the Engelberg manuscript of Johannes Tauler's sermons (Engelberg, Stiftsbibliothek, Nr. 124, folio 197ᵛ)

iver Davies (London: Society for the Propagation of Christian Knowledge, 1989).

Johannes Tauler is one of the four outstanding figures in the amazing flowering of mystical experience and writing that took place in late-medieval Germany. This phenomenon included the unlettered Beguine Mechthild of Magdeburg and Tauler's fellow Dominicans Meister Eckhart and Heinrich Seuse. Tauler's sermons, written only in German, circulated widely in the Middle Ages in Germany and the Low Countries. Since Martin Luther made marginal notes on his copy of the 1508 Augsburg edition of Tauler's sermons and obviously valued him highly, Tauler's works were later read by Protestants as well as by Catholics. Tauler was less erudite and more practical than Eckhart, and his teaching was built on the devotional habits of his day. As a result he was able to transmit much of Eckhart's basic teachings when

Eckhart himself was branded as heretical. Some of Eckhart's sermons were preserved under Tauler's name and found their way into print in the 1521 Basel edition of Tauler's works.

About Tauler's life only scanty information is available, derived from his sermons, occasional references elsewhere, and conjectures based on known events and practices of the time. The "Historie des erwirdigen Docters Johannis Thauleri" (History of the Venerable Doctor Johannes Tauler," first printed in the 1498 edition of his sermons and reprinted in most later editions, was shown to be fictional in 1879 by Heinrich Denifle. Tauler was born around 1300 into a well-to-do burgher family in Strasbourg and entered a Dominican friary there not earlier than his fourteenth year. His training would have included the study of logic, natural and moral philosophy, and theology based on the *Sententiarum libri quatuor* (Four Books of Sentences, circa 1160) of Peter Lombard. This course of study would have occupied six to eight years; he could not have become a priest before the age of twenty-five. In the manuscripts of his works Tauler is referred to as "brother," so it is unlikely that he gained the academic title of master, still less that of doctor, with which he is credited in the early printed editions.

It is not known whether Tauler was personally acquainted with Eckhart; but he must have heard Eckhart preach, and he was a disciple of Eckhart's mystical teaching. More certain is Tauler's contact with the Friends of God, a group of mystics in the Upper Rhine area. Among them was the nun Margaretha Ebner in Medingen, near Dillingen, whom Tauler visited sometime before 1339 and again in 1347 or 1348. A letter is preserved from Tauler to Ebner and the prioress of Medingen, Elsbeth Scheppach, accompanying a gift of four cheeses to the nunnery. Another letter, from the secular priest Heinrich von Nördlingen, who belonged to the same circle of mystics, attests to Tauler's presence in Basel in 1339. It is generally assumed that Tauler spent the period from 1339 to 1343 there on account of the interdict placed on Strasbourg by Pope John XXII because the city took the side of the Emperor Ludwig the Bavarian in his quarrel with the papacy: the Dominicans took the papal side and were, therefore, expelled from the city. Sometime during 1339 Tauler also traveled to Cologne; another visit there took place in 1346, when he preached several sermons in the convent of Saint Gertrude. In 1347 Rulman Merswin, one of the leading Friends of God, documented that he took Tauler as his confessor in Strasbourg. Two other journeys have been suggested, but neither can be accepted as certain: a visit to the Flemish mystic Jan van Ruusbroec in Groenendael, near Waterloo, and a possible journey to Paris as the companion of another Strasbourg Dominican, Johannes von Dambach. Tauler died in 1361.

Tauler's sermons owe their origin to the fact that the Dominicans were entrusted with the pastoral care of nuns and Beguines. There were seven Dominican nunneries and many Beguinages in Strasbourg, where Tauler spent the major part of his life. Several of his sermons point to such an audience because of the terms of address that are used in them. Others were directed to fellow Dominican friars. Whether, in addition, some sermons were preached to lay congregations cannot be proved.

As is generally the case with medieval sermons, Tauler's were based on the biblical texts used for Sundays and feast days within the liturgical year. These he expounded almost exclusively in relation to the inward spiritual life and sacramental practices of his hearers, submitting the texts to spiritual rather than literal or historical exegesis. The spiritual senses in which the texts could be interpreted were threefold: the allegorical or typological sense, focusing on human redemption through the sacrifice of Christ on the cross and viewing the Old Testament in terms of a systematic prefiguration of the New; the tropological or moral sense, concerned with the progress of the individual soul from sin to grace; and the anagogical sense, relating to the hope of eternal life. Tauler's sermons are practical rather than speculative in approach. He allowed for differences in the experiences of his flocks—for example, in their use of ascetic practices (he discouraged excessive asceticism)—and in the stages of their spiritual development. His preaching style is vivid, direct, and straightforward, though he is fond of repetition, double formulas, and cumulative sequences of adjectives. He refers in moderation to other authorities—the Bible, the church fathers, and other spiritual writers—not making a show of his knowledge but using it to reinforce a point. From time to time he brings in details of ordinary life, mentioning, for example, the Rhine in flood or aspects of viticulture, to illustrate a specific point in his teaching. Everywhere he displays a deep concern for the pastoral care of the souls entrusted to him.

Tauler's sermons are remarkably consistent in their tone and message. While a few focus strongly on sacramental mysticism and devotion to the Passion of Christ—a feature of late-medieval Christianity that is reflected in much of the painting and sculpture of the period, as well as in other religious prose and poetry—the majority of the sermons concentrate on the development of an inward spirituality that can be achieved only through overcoming or transcending outward practices—prayer, singing, fasting, and vigils—and attachment to outward things. The goal is "ein inwendige gantz gelossen stilles swigen in einem in gekerten gemuete" (an inward, completely detached, still silence in an inwardly turned spirit), a spirit that has experienced the *ker* (turning) from everything outward. Tauler insists constantly on the antithesis of outward and inward. The total concentration on the inward is not achieved with ease, nor does it produce unalloyed joy. The path toward it is fraught with difficulties and pain.

By far the greater part of Tauler's mystical teaching centers on the *via purgativa* (purgative way) rather than on the other two paths—the *via illuminativa* (way of enlightenment) or the *via unitiva* (unitive way). He is concerned with the *grunt* (ground, basis) of the soul, which must be made bare and empty and ready for God to fill and occupy. The notion of the grunt also appears in Eckhart's writings, but Tauler uses it even more extensively, especially in connection with the *abgrunt* (abyss) that is God. The metaphor of the emptying of the soul links up with the idea that God, like nature, abhors a vacuum, so that when the soul is empty of self and attachment to outward things, God will of necessity take their place. As well as rooting out all sinful desires, such as spiritual pride, unchastity, and malice, the individual must learn to accept all pain and suffering as coming from God and be willing to endure even hell for God's sake; then the soul will be taken into eternity and into the abyss where God is enjoyed without any mediation.

This willingness to accept suffering is linked by Tauler with the virtues of humility and obedience to authority. He illustrates these virtues by reference to himself: since it is through God's grace that he has received his priesthood, membership in the Dominican order, and the ability to teach and to hear confession, he should, if the Pope wished to remove these things from him, accept their loss without question. Like the physical reception of the Eucharist, they are outward; what is inward, like the spiritual reception of the Eucharist, cannot be taken away. What is possessed inwardly is the only true possession.

Tauler declares six things to be essential for following God: the three higher powers of faith, hope, and love and the three lower ones of humility, gentleness, and patience. Faith shows mere reason to be blind and thereby deprives it of its power; hope displaces outward security and possessions; love supersedes the will. The three lower powers bring the soul to a recognition and acceptance of its own nullity, the state in which God can unite with it: "wan die über namlos gotheit die enhat niergen eigenlichen stat ze würkende denne in dem grunde der aller tiefster vernútheit" (for the deity that is beyond name has nowhere its proper place to work than in the ground of the deepest annihilation). The death of the creature is necessary for the birth of God in the soul.

The stages of the mystical life are threefold. The first stage, an inward virtuous life in which the individual is filled with wonder at the ineffable gifts of God, is *jubilacio* (jubilation). The second is a poverty of the spirit, a way of suffering known as the dark night of the soul. The third is "ein übervart in ein gotformig wesen in einikeit des geschaffenen geistes in den istigen geist Gotz, daz man einen weselichen ker mag heissen. Und die her in recht geratent, das enist nút glöiplich das si iemer von Gotte múgen gevallen" (a transition into a God-formed being in a union of the created spirit into the absolute essence of God. This one can term a true transformation. And those who properly attain this, it is inconceivable that they should ever fall away from God).

Tauler's teaching is firmly embedded in the devotional practice of his time. In interpreting the psalmist's image of the stag thirsting for the brooks, he describes the hounds hunting the stag as the seven deadly sins, which the stag can only get rid of by dragging them to a tree and breaking their heads on it. Similarly, individuals must betake themselves to the tree of the cross and the suffering of Christ to rid themselves of mortal sins. Tauler uses many other contemporary images and analogies in his depiction of the stages of the mystical life, but he does not deprecate the active life. There are outward tasks, such as caring for the sick, that God may require the individual to undertake and abandon the inward. About himself Tauler says: "Und ob ich der menschen einer were und solte das denne lossen und solte her us keren ze brediende oder des gelich tun, es mochte wol geschehen das mir Got gegenwúrtiger were und me gutz tete in dem usserlichen werke denne lichte in vil grosser schouwelicheit" (If I were one of those people and had to abandon the inward and go out to preach or the like, it might be that God was more present to me and did more good to me in the outward task than perhaps in a state of great illumination).

Luther's high regard for Tauler meant that Tauler's sermons, and other writings wrongly attributed to him, were not rejected by Protestants along with much of the late-medieval Catholic tradition. Luther was also devoted to the *Theologia deutsch,* a late-medieval mystical treatise known in the English-speaking world under its Latin title, as the *Theologia germanica,* and into one copy of this work, which Luther edited in 1516, a sixteenth-century writer copied extensive passages from Tauler's and Eckhart's sermons that form parallels to that text. In this way, and through other authors, it is known that Tauler was much valued as a spiritual writer up to the early eighteenth century. He was appreciated by Johannes Arndt, Daniel Spener, Johann Wilhelm Ueberfeld, Johann Baptista Helmont, Peter Poiret, Caspar Schwenckfeld, Valentin Weigel, and Johann Schemer.

A translation of Tauler's writings into French was made as early as 1614, but no further one appeared until 1855. Meanwhile, in the English-speaking world Tauler was known largely through the Latin translation of his works and Latin works wrongly ascribed to him. Of English cathedral libraries, only Chichester has a copy of the German sermons published in Basel in 1521, while Peterborough, Chester, Durham, Norwich, and Salisbury possess a variety of sixteenth- and seventeenth-century Latin editions. Several other secular libraries also have Latin versions of Tauler's writings, but it was not until the middle of the nineteenth century that Tauler became more widely known through Susanna Winkworth's 1857 translation of a selection of his German sermons, together with the spurious "life." A sizable preface by Charles Kingsley gave this translation the seal of approval for Victorian Protestants, and since that time a variety of translations, mainly selections, have made Tauler accessible to English readers.

Tauler is possibly the only writer in German from the fourteenth century who has not suffered an eclipse at some time in the passing of the centuries. Even at the low point of the eighteenth century his work was noted in encyclopedias. As a living part of German spirituality, his work has been known, read, and valued from his own day to the present, though it was not until the late nineteenth century that its dimensions were pared down and properly understood. Since the mid nineteenth century, however, Tauler has stood in Eckhart's shadow, as the full extent of the latter's challenging thought and spirit has been explored. Nonetheless, Tauler's sermons remain a clear, comprehensive, and moving expression of late-medieval German mystical experience in its "classical" form, centered in traditional Christian faith, worship, and practice. They have not been affected by the contentiousness surrounding Eckhart but have consistently fed the devotional lives of both Catholics and Protestants, and they still do so today.

Biography:

Louise Gnädinger, *Johannes Tauler: Lebenswelt und mystische Lehre* (Munich: Beck, 1993).

References:

Raymond Alexis, "Die Bibelzitate in Werken des Straßburger Predigers Johannes Tauler: Ein Beitrag zum Problem der vorlutherischen Bibelverdeutschung," *Revue des Langues Vivantes,* 20 (1954): 397-411;

David Blamires, "Eckhart and Tauler: A Comparison of Their Sermons on 'Homo quidam fecit cenam magnam' (Luke xiv. 16)," *Modern Language Review,* 66 (1971): 608-627;

Blamires, "Tauler and Eckhart Marginalia in a Copy of *Theologia Teutsch* (1518)," *Bulletin of the John Rylands University Library of Manchester,* 73, no. 1 (1991): 91-103;

James M. Clark, *The Great German Mystics: Eckhart, Tauler and Suso* (Oxford: Blackwell, 1949);

Oliver Davies, *God Within: The Mystical Tradition of Northern Europe* (London: Darton, Longman & Todd, 1988);

Suzanne Debèfre, "Tauler oder Eckhart als Verfasser der Weihnachtspredigt von dreierlei Geburten," *Revue des Langues Vivantes,* 8 (1942): 105-114, 150-158, 186-196;

Heinrich Denifle, *Taulers Bekehrung kritisch untersucht* (Strasbourg: Trübner, 1879);

Ephrem Filthaut, ed., *Johannes Tauler, ein deutscher Mystiker: Gedenkschrift zum 600. Todestag* (Essen: Driewer, 1961);

Louise Gnädinger, "Der Abgrund ruft dem Abgrund: Taulers Predigt *Beati oculi* (V 45)," in *Das "einig Ein": Studien zu Theorie und Sprache der deutschen Mystik,* edited by Alois M. Haas and Heinrich Stirnimann (Freiburg, Switzerland: Universitätsverlag, 1980), pp. 167-207;

Gnädinger, *Johannes Tauler: Lebenswelt und mystische Lehre* (Munich: Beck, 1993);

Alois M. Haas, "'Die Arbeit der Nacht': Mystische Leiderfahrung nach Johannes Tauler," in *Die dunkle Nacht der Sinne: Leiderfahrung und christliche Mystik,* edited by Gotthard Fuchs (Düsseldorf: Patmos, 1989), pp. 9-40;

Haas, *Nim din selbes war: Studien zur Lehre von der Selbsterkenntnis bei Meister Eckhart, Johannes Tauler und Heinrich Seuse* (Freiburg, Switzerland: Universitätsverlag, 1971);

Haas, *Sermo mysticus: Studien zu Theologie und Sprache der deutschen Mystik* (Freiburg, Switzerland: Universitätsverlag, 1979);

Dick Helander, *Johann Tauler als Prediger* (Uppsala: Almqvist & Wiksell, 1923);

Etienne Hugueny, "La doctrine mystique de Tauler," *Revue des Sciences Philosophiques et Théologiques,* 10 (1921): 194-221;

Rufus M. Jones, *The Flowering of Mysticism* (New York: Macmillan, 1939), pp. 86-103;

G. I. Lieftinck, *De middelnederlandsche Tauler-Handschriften* (Groningen: Wolters, 1936);

Dietmar Mieth, *Die Einheit von* vita activa *und* vita contemplativa *in den deutschen Predigten und Traktaten Meister Eckharts und bei Johannes Tauler* (Regensburg: Pustet, 1969);

Gunther Müller, "Scholastikerzitate bei Tauler," *Deutsche Vierteljahrsschrift für Literaturwissenschaft und Geistesgeschichte,* 1 (1923): 400-418;

Steven E. Ozment, *Homo spiritualis: A Comparative Study of the Anthropology of Johannes Tauler, Jean Gerson and Martin Luther (1509-16) in the Context of their Theological Thought* (Leiden: Brill, 1969);

A. de Pelsemaeker, "Canisius éditeur de Tauler," *Revue d'Ascétique et de Mystique,* 36 (1960): 101-108;

Christine Pleuser, *Die Benennungen und der Begriff des Leides bei J. Tauler* (Berlin: Schmidt, 1967);

Jutta Prieur, *Das Kölner Dominikanerinnenkloster St. Gertrud am Neumarkt* (Cologne: dme, 1983);

Bernd Ulrich Rehe, *Der Reifungsweg des inneren Menschen in der Liebe zu Gott: Zum Gespräch bereit: Johannes Tauler* (Bern: Peter Lang, 1989);

Carl Schmidt, *Johannes Tauler von Straßburg: Beitrag zur Geschichte der Mystik und des religiösen Lebens im 14. Jahrhundert* (Aalen: Scientia, 1972);

Loris Sturlese, "Tauler im Kontext: Die philosophischen Voraussetzungen des 'Seelengrundes' in der Lehre des deutschen Neuplatonikers Berthold von Moosburg," *Beiträge zur Geschichte der deutschen Sprache und Literatur,* 109 (1987): 390-426;

Ignaz Weilner, *Johannes Taulers Bekehrungsweg: Die Erfahrungsgrundlagen seiner Mystik* (Regensburg: Pustet, 1961);

Irmgard Weithase, "Die Pflege der gesprochenen Sprache durch Berthold von Regensburg, Meister Eckhart und Johannes Tauler," in *Gestaltung, Umgestaltung: Festschrift H. A. Korff,* edited by Joachim Müller (Leipzig: Koehler & Amelang, 1957), pp. 46-75;

Paul Wyser, "Der Seelengrund in Taulers Predigten," in *Altdeutsche und altniederländische Mystik,* edited by Kurt Ruh (Darmstadt: Wissenschaftliche Buchgesellschaft, 1964), pp. 324-352;

Stefan Zekorn, *Gelassenheit und Einkehr: Zu Grundlage und Gestalt geistlichen Lebens bei Johannes Tauler* (Würzburg: Echter, 1993).

Johannes von Tepl (Johannes von Saaz)
(circa 1350 – 1414/1415)

Anne Winston-Allen
Southern Illinois University

MAJOR WORKS: *Der Ackermann aus Böhmen* (circa 1400/1401)

Manuscripts: None of the surviving manuscripts of *Der Ackermann aus Böhmen* is considered an accurate copy of Johannes von Tepl's text. Arranged according to Willy Krogmann's classification of the variants, the manuscripts fall into four families. The first group comprises H (cgm. 579) and the fragment E (clm. 27063), both in the Bayerische Staatsbibliothek, Munich. The second group comprises A (Cod. H.B.X 23), in the Württembergische Landesbibliothek, Stuttgart, and B (Cod. pal. germ. 76), in the Universitätsbibliothek, Heidelberg. The third group comprises C (Cod. H.B.X 22), in the Württembergische Landesbibliothek; F (clm. 17662) and G (clm. 8445), both in the Bayerische Staatsbibliothek; N (Ms. germ. 4° 763), in the Berlin Staatsbibliothek; O (Mscr. B 325), in the Stadtbibliothek Zurich; P (Sag. f. 13), in the Universitätsbibliothek, Jena; and Q (Hs. 60), in the Universitätsbibliothek, Innsbruck. Group 4 comprises D (MS 75. 10. Aug.), in the Herzog-August-Bibliothek, Wolfenbüttel; I (St. Georgen 70) and K (St. Blasien 11), both in the Badische Landesbibliothek, Karlsruhe; M (Ms. germ. 4° 581), in the Berlin Staatsbibliothek; and L, which is preserved in two parts, one privately held by the Bernt family and the other by the Bibliothèque Royale, Brussels (Inv. No. 1634–1635).

First publication: *[I]Nn dem buchlein ist beschriben ein krig wann einer dem sein libes weib gestorben ist schildtet den todt* (Bamberg: Pseudo-Pfister, circa 1460?).

Standard editions: *"Der Ackermann aus Böhmen": Herausgegeben und mit dem tschechischen Gegenstück "Tkadleček" verglichen,* edited by Johann Knieschek (Prague: Verlag des Vereins, 1877); *Der Ackermann aus Böhmen,* edited by Alois Bernt and Konrad Burdach, volume 3, part 1 of *Vom Mittelalter zur Reformation* (Berlin: Weidmann, 1917); *"Der Ackermann aus Böhmen" des Johannes von Saaz,* edited by Bernt (Heidelberg: Winter, 1929); *Der Ackermann aus Böhmen: Textausgabe,* edited by Arthur Hübner (Leipzig: Hirzel, 1937); *Der Ackermann aus Böhmen,* edited by Keith Spalding (Oxford: Blackwell, 1950); *Der Ackermann aus Böhmen: Textausgabe,* edited by L. L. Hammerich and Günther Jungbluth (Heidelberg: Winter, 1951); *Der Ackermann aus Böhmen,* edited by Maurice O'C. Walshe (London: Duckworth, 1951); *"Der ackerman," auf Grund der deutschen Überlieferung und der tschechischen Bearbeitung,* edited by Willy Krogmann (Wiesbaden: Brockhaus, 1954); *Johannes von Saaz, "Der Ackermann aus Böhmen,"* 2 volumes, edited by Günther Jungbluth and Rainer Zäck (Heidelberg: Winter, 1969, 1983); *Der Ackermann aus Böhmen: A Working Edition with Introduction, Notes and Glossary and the Full Text of Mss. E and H,* edited by Walshe (Hull, U.K.: German Department, Hull University, 1982); *Die "Ackermann"-Handschriften E (clm 27063) und H (cgm 579). Faksimiles, Transkriptionen und bereinigte Texte mit kritischem Apparat,* 2 volumes, edited by Werner Schröder (Wiesbaden: Reichert, 1987); *Der Ackermann aus Böhmen: Eine Faksimileausgabe der Handschriften und Drucke a und b,* 2 volumes projected, 1 volume published, edited by James C. Thomas (Bern: Peter Lang, 1990–); *Johannes de Tepla, Civis Zacensis, Epistola cum libello Ackermann und das Büchlein Ackermann: Nach der Freiburger Hs. 163 und nach der Stuttgarter Hs. HB x 23,* 2 volumes, edited by Karl Bertau (Berlin: De Gruyter, 1994).

Editions in English: *Death and the Ploughman: An Argument and a Consolation from the Year 1400,* translated and edited by K. W. Maurer (London: Langley, 1947); *Death and the Plowman or*

Illumination from the first page of the manuscript for Johannes von Tepl's votive Office of Saint Jerome for the altar of the church of Saint Nicholas at Eger. The figure on the right is presumably Tepl (National Museum, Prague, Latin MS 3157 sig. XII A 18).

The Bohemian Plowman, translated by Ernest N. Kirrmann (Chapel Hill: University of North Carolina Press, 1958); *The Plowman from Bohemia,* translated by Alexander Henderson and Elizabeth Henderson (New York: Ungar, 1966);

St. Hieronymus-Offizium, attributed to Tepl (circa 1404)
Manuscript: Latin MS 3157 Sig. XII A 18, National Museum, Prague;

Tkadleček, sometimes attributed to Tepl, edited by Hynek Hrubý and František Šimek (Prague: České akademie věd, a umění, 1923).

Johannes von Tepl is the author of what has been called "the best and most noteworthy example of poetic prose before Goethe's *Werther.*" His *Der Ackermann aus Böhmen* (The Plowman from Bohemia, circa 1400/1401; translated as *Death and the Ploughman,* 1947) was one of the earliest books to be printed in German (between 1460 and 1473). By 1547 it had been republished in seventeen editions. A work that marks a turning point in German literary history, Tepl's *Der Ackermann aus Böhmen* is both a profound treatment of the problem of mortality and a stylistic tour de force that successfully assimilates the rhetorical forms of the Italian humanists to early New High German prose.

Born around 1350 in either Schüttwa (Sitbor) or Tepl (Teplá) in western Bohemia, Tepl was the son of Henslinus (Hänslein) of Sitbor, a priest. It is not known whether Tepl and his brother were illegitimate, or whether their father entered the priesthood after their mother's death. By 1378 records show Tepl living in the city of Saaz, where he had received an appointment as city notary and later as rector of the Latin school. In 1386 he was made an imperial notary, a distinction that entitled him to prepare documents under his own seal. As the holder of three such responsible positions, Tepl was a respected citizen of Saaz and a prosperous man. In 1401 King Wenceslas granted Tepl and his heirs the privilege of collecting one groschen from each butcher doing business in the city marketplace. Such an award may lend support to the thesis that Tepl could have been the translator of the magnificent German Bible, now in the Austrian National Library, that was presented to King Wenceslas by a citizen of Prague, Martin Rotlöw, with whom Tepl can be distantly connected.

In legal documents Tepl is referred to several times as "magister," indicating that he had earned a degree of master of arts. Just where he might have received such a degree is unclear, however, since Tepl is not listed in the records of the University of Prague, which, founded in 1348, was the first university north of the Alps. Other locations where Tepl might have studied would have been Bologna, Padua, or, more likely, Paris.

Tepl's chief work, *Der Ackermann aus Böhmen,* is an audacious debate between a grief-stricken widower, a plowman of the pen—that is, a scribe—and the personified figure of Death. It is framed as a legal proceeding that erupts in a show of rhetorical fireworks. In sixteen rounds of spirited debate the enraged plowman, unable to come to terms with the loss of his virtuous young wife, Margaretha, attacks death and its justification in God's world order. Death responds with an equally animated attack on the plowman's inflated sense of the value of human life. Forced to the defense, the former plaintiff becomes the advocate for life, love, and humankind's place in God's creation.

The emotional character of the plowman's arguments and the correspondence of certain biographical details in the text to facts of Tepl's life led many scholars to conclude that the work must have been precipitated by an actual bereavement experienced by the author. The work cites, for example, the date and year (1 August 1400), as well as the name of the city (Saaz), where Margaretha, the mother of two children, died. Besides revealing the speaker's occupation as scribe, the text discloses his first name in an acrostic: IOHANNES MA. The last two letters may be the first two letters of Margaretha or the initials of the author's academic degree, *magister artium*. While these details fit with what is known about Tepl's biography, scholars have not been able to establish whether he was actually widowed before wedding Clara, the wife who survived him.

In 1411 Tepl moved to Prague, where he had received an appointment as notary of the Neustadt district. That Tepl was held in high esteem by the citizens of Saaz is attested by a letter of commendation, issued by the city council shortly before his departure, praising his character and honesty throughout many years of distinguished service. In Prague, Tepl bought a house at 100 Brennte-Gasse. By 1413 he had fallen ill and was no longer able to perform his duties as notary. Although his appointment was guaranteed for life, Tepl was forced to engage a substitute to carry out his responsibilities. Sometime between 1414 and the spring of 1415 Tepl died. Records show that in April 1415 his widow, Clara, sold the house in the Brennte-Gasse and paid a son, Georg, then living at home, his inheritance. Besides Georg, Tepl had three other sons—Paul, Jerome, and John—who are mentioned in an undated letter asking a nephew in Rome to seek benefices for them. A daughter, Christinella, was married twice, each time to a member of the Saaz city council. By 1413 she, too, had moved to Prague-Neustadt.

In 1933 the historian Konrad Heilig happened on a letter written to accompany a copy of *Der Ackermann aus Böhmen* sent to Peter Rothers of Prague, in which Tepl introduces and comments on his work. After Heilig's find, questions began to be raised as to whether *Der Ackermann aus Böhmen,* which previously had been regarded as autobiographical, was not rather a rhetorical fiction, a demonstration of the forms and stylistic devices that Tepl describes in the letter. Indeed, the tone of the letter itself seemed to be at odds with the theory of a personal bereavement. But, regardless of whether the work might have been precipitated by the loss of a spouse or whether it began as an exercise in rhetorical stylistics, Tepl's profound treatment of the subject of coming to terms with death propelled *Der Ackermann aus Böhmen* into what Maurice O'C. Walshe has called the realm of the "existential."

As a work of consolation, it strives to reconcile the protagonist's personal rage and anguish with traditional explanations of God's justice. Underlying the debate is the problem of theodicy: how to explain the coexistence of evil and a God who is both all-powerful and all-good. The plowman condemns death while defending life, love, and humanity—God's finest creation. Death denies that humankind has any dignity or any right of life, vaunting, instead, his own power and arbitrariness. In chapter 33 God is called on to deliver a verdict in the case. Because the plaintiff has fought well, God awards him honor but gives the victory to Death by affirming the status quo. The epilogue praises God's mystery and majesty in a moving prayer for the soul of Margaretha.

Der Ackermann aus Böhmen was rediscovered in the eighteenth century; interest in it was revived by the publication of Johann Kniescheck's critical edition in 1877 and, subsequently, by the 1917 edition by Alois Bernt and Konrad Burdach and Burdach's extensive commentaries on it. Many heralded the work as a landmark of early Renaissance humanism, interpreting it as an affirmation of the freedom, beauty, rationality, and essential goodness of humankind. This interpretation was questioned by others, who denied any humanist influence in the work and argued that it reflected strictly medieval (particularly Thomist) doctrines and attitudes. Thus, *Der Ackermann aus Böhmen* became the center of a controversy over whether it should be considered more characteristic of medieval or of early-Renaissance thinking. Other scholars took up a position between the two extremes, on the one hand pointing to the close connections between Tepl's work and earlier German literary forms while, on the other hand, acknowledging the form of the work to be something new in the German literary tradition.

The language of *Der Ackermann aus Böhmen* echoes that of Johann von Neumarkt's chancery German, showing the influence of the Latin rhetorical forms of Italian humanists. Characteristic of the work's rhythmical, periodic sentences with two- and three-part repetitions, variations, and rhetorical formulas is the well-known opening sentence, the widower's outraged denunciation of death, which begins, "Grimmiger tilger aller leute, schedlicher echter aller werlte, freissamer morder aller menschen ir Tot, euch sei verflucht!" (Grim destroyer of all people, shameful sunderer of all beings, terrible murderer of all mankind, thou, Death, be cursed!). Tepl's admiration for the new Latinate chancery style is evidenced by his inclusion of passages from Neumarkt's German translation of the pseudo-Augustinian *Soliloquia animae ad deum* (The Soul's Soliloquy to God) in the epilogue to *Der Ackermann aus Böhmen*.

Death holding court, illustration from the first edition of Tepl's
Der Ackermann aus Böhmen

Other works attributed to Tepl include a Latin votive Office of Saint Jerome for the new altar of the church of Saint Nicholas at Eger. On its first page the illuminated manuscript contains an illustration showing Saint Jerome and the donor, a man of approximately fifty–presumably Tepl. While the ten lines of German verse and the accompanying Latin dedication are in Tepl's hand, it is unclear whether he made the selections for the Office, which is copied in another hand. City records in Latin from Saaz and Prague-Neustadt, as well as collections of sample letters and forms, in Latin are also attributed to Tepl. More important is the *Tkadleček* (Little Weaver), a work composed in old Czech about 1407 that is highly similar in form and content to *Der Ackermann aus Böhmen*. In this work a weaver debates with Misfortune over the loss of his unfaithful sweetheart. While some scholars assert that Tepl was the author of both works, others maintain that the *Tkadleček,* a work of substantial literary merit but not of the same quality as *Der Ackermann aus Böhmen,* was adapted by someone else from Tepl's work. Antonín Hrubý has argued that both *Der Ackermann aus Böhmen* and the *Tkadleček* are based on an earlier source that has been lost. Other scholars, however, question why, if that is the case, no copies or even allusions to a work of such exceptional character remain. In comparison, the many manuscripts and early editions of *Der Ackermann aus Böhmen* show how widely known it already was within thirty-five years of Tepl's death: copies were circulated as far away as Basel and Strasbourg, where it was eagerly read in religious communities.

Because of its significance as a pivotal work in German literary history, *Der Ackermann aus Böhmen* continues to be a subject of debate and to attract interest in new critical editions. While the controversy over Tepl's relationship to the beginnings of Renaissance Humanism in Germany remains unresolved, scholars are united in their assessment of his work as a literary achievement of the first rank.

References:

Robert Anderson and James C. Thomas, *Index verborum zum "Ackermann aus Böhmen": Ein alphabetisch angeordnetes Wortregister zu Textgestaltungen des "Ackermann aus Böhmen" von Knieschek bis Jungbluth,* 2 volumes (Amsterdam: Rodopi, 1973);

Isaac Bacon, "A Survey of Changes in the Interpretation of the 'Ackermann aus Böhmen': With Special Emphasis on the post-1940 Developments," *Studies in Philology,* 53, no. 2 (1956): 101-113;

Franz Bäuml, "Der Ackermann aus Böhmen and the Destiny of Man," *Germanic Review,* 33 (1958): 223-232;

Bäuml, *Rhetorical Devices and Structure in the Ackermann aus Böhmen* (Berkeley: University of California Press, 1960);

Anton Blaschka, "Der topos scribendo solari—Briefschreiben als Trost," *Wissenschaftliche Zeitschrift der Universität Halle,* 5 (1956): 637-638;

Václav Bok, "Zwei Beiträge zu Johannes von Tepl," *Zeitschrift für deutsches Altertum,* 118 (1989): 180-189;

Renée Brand, "Zur Interpretation des 'Ackermann aus Böhmen,'" *Monatshefte für deutschen Unterricht,* 32 (1940): 387-397;

Konrad Burdach, *Der Dichter des Ackermann aus Böhmen und seine Zeit,* volume 3, part 2 of *Vom Mittelalter zur Reformation* (Berlin: Weidmann, 1932);

Albrecht Classen, "Der 'Ackermann aus Böhmen'—Ein literarisches Zeugnis aus der Schwellenzeit: Mittelalterliches Streitgespräch oder Dokument des deutschen Frühhumanismus?," *Zeitschrift für deutsche Philologie,* 110 (1991): 348-373;

Evelyn Scherabon Firchow, "Was wissen wir über den Dichter des 'Ackermann aus Böhmen'?," in *Dialectology, Linguistics, Literature: Festschrift für Carroll E. Reed,* edited by Wolfgang W. Moelleken (Göppingen: Kümmerle, 1984), pp. 72-92;

Firchow, "Wege und Irrwege der Textkritik zum 'Ackermann aus Böhmen': Ein Forschungsbericht," in *"In hôhem prîse": A Festschrift in Honor of Ernst S. Dick,* edited by Winder McConnell (Göppingen: Kümmerle, 1989), pp. 45-60;

Francis Gentry, "Silent That Others Might Speak: Notes on the 'Ackermann aus Böhmen,'" *German Quarterly,* 67 (1994): 484-492;

George T. Gillespie, "'Der Ackermann aus Böhmen': Style and Sincerity," *Trivium,* 16 (1981): 29-43;

Gerhard Hahn, *Der Ackermann aus Böhmen des Johannes von Tepl* (Darmstadt: Wissenschaftliche Buchgesellschaft, 1984);

Hahn, *Die Einheit des Ackermann aus Böhmen: Studien zur Komposition* (Munich: Beck, 1963);

W. Hammer, "Johann von Tepl, 'Death and the Ploughman': An Argument and a Consolation from the Year 1400," *Journal of English and German Philology,* 48 (1949): 152-154;

Antonín Hrubý, *Der Ackermann und seine Vorlage* (Munich: Beck, 1971);

Samuel Jaffee, "Die Konzipierung der Ackermanndichtung im Prager Metropolitankapitel Codex O.LXX," in *Virtus et Fortuna: Zur deutschen Literatur zwischen 1400 und 1720. Festschrift für Hans-Gert Roloff zu seinem 50. Geburtstag,* edited by Joseph P. Strelka and Jörg Jungmayr (Frankfurt am Main: Peter Lang, 1983), pp. 46-63;

Jaffee, "Des Witwers Verlangen nach Rat: Ironie und Struktureinheit im 'Ackermann aus Böhmen,' " *Daphnis*, 7 (1978): 1-53;

Günther Jungbluth, "Probleme der 'Ackermann'-Dichtung," *Wirkendes Wort*, 18 (1968): 145-155;

Wenzel Katzerowsky, "Ein Formelbuch aus dem 14. Jahrhundert," *Mitteilungen des Vereins für Geschichte der Deutschen in Böhmen*, 29 (1891): 1-30;

Johann Knieschek, "Das Verhältnis des Ackermann zum Tkadleček und die Hypothese einer gemeinsamen Vorlage," *Mitteilungen des Vereins für Geschichte der Deutschen in Böhmen*, 16 (1878): 302-310;

Willy Krogmann, "Neue Funde der Ackermannforschung," *Deutsche Vierteljahresschrift für Literaturwissenschaft und Geistesgeschichte*, 37 (1963): 254-265;

Rosemarie Natt, *Der 'Ackermann aus Böhmen' des Johannes von Tepl: Ein Beitrag zur Interpretation* (Göppingen: Kümmerle, 1978);

G. Orton, "A Note on 'Der Ackermann aus Böhmen XXIX,' " *Modern Language Review*, 48 (1953): 56-57;

E. A. Philippson, "Der Ackermann aus Böhmen: A Summary of Recent Research and an Appreciation," *Modern Language Quarterly*, 2 (1941): 263-278;

Ella Schafferus, "Der Ackermann aus Böhmen und die Weltanschauung des Mittelalters," *Zeitschrift für deutsches Altertum*, 72 (1935): 209-239;

Arno Schirokauer, "Der Ackermann aus Böhmen und das Renaissanceproblem," *Monatshefte*, 41 (1949): 213-217;

Ludwig Schlesinger, ed., *Das Urkundenbuch der Stadt Saaz bis zum Jahre 1526* (Prague: Verein für Geschichte der Deutschen in Böhmen, 1892);

Werner Schröder, *Der Ackermann aus Böhmen: Das Werk und sein Autor* (Munich: Fink, 1985);

Ernst Schwarz, ed., *Der Ackermann aus Böhmen des Johannes von Tepl und seine Zeit* (Darmstadt: Wissenschaftliche Buchgesellschaft, 1968);

Hilda Swinburn, "Chapter XVIII of the 'Ackermann aus Böhmen,' " *Modern Language Review*, 48 (1953): 159-166;

Swinburn, "Echoes of the 'De consolatione philosophiae' in the 'Ackermann aus Böhmen,' " *Modern Language Review*, 52 (1957): 88-91;

Swinburn, "Word-order and Rhythm in the 'Ackermann aus Böhmen,' " *Modern Language Review*, 48 (1953): 413-420;

James C. Thomas, "Die Umdatierung eines Wolfenbütteler Frühdruckes des 'Ackermann aus Böhmen' (GW 193) aufgrund beta- und elektronenradiographischer Untersuchungen seiner Papierwasserzeichen," *Wolfenbütteler Notizen zur Buchgeschichte*, 13, no. 2 (1988): 106-111;

Maurice O'C. Walshe, " 'Der Ackermann aus Böhmen': A Structural Interpretation," *Classica et Mediaevalia*, 15 (1954): 130-145;

Walshe, "'Der Ackermann aus Böhmen' and its Latin Dedication," *Modern Language Review*, 47 (1952): 211-212;

Walshe, "'Der Ackermann aus Böhmen': Quellenfrage und Textgestaltung," in *Deutsche Literatur des späten Mittelalters*, edited by Wolfgang Harms and L. Peter Johnson (Berlin: Schmidt, 1975), pp. 282-292;

Anne Winston, "Using the 'Tractatus' to Interpret the 'Ackermann,' " *Daphnis*, 18 (1989): 369-390;

Wilhelm Wostry, *Saaz zur Zeit des Ackermann-Dichters* (Munich: Lerche, 1951);

Leopold Zatočil, "Lateinische Texte und Quellen zum 'Ackermann aus Böhmen,' " *Brünner Beiträge zur Germanisik und Nordistik*, 3 (1982): 7-19;

Zatočil, "Quellenkundliches und Textkritisches zum 'Ackermann aus Böhmen,' " *Brünner Beiträge zur Germanistik und Nordistik*, 6 (1988): 83-91;

Zatočil, "Textkritisches und Texte zum 'Ackermann aus Böhmen,' " *Brünner Beiträge zur Germanistik und Nordistik*, 5 (1986): 7-26.

Papers:

A formula book of letters and documents from the city of Saaz, Latin MS 163, is in the Universitätsbibliothek, Freiburg im Breisgau.

Joachim Vadianus (Joachim von Watt)
(29 November 1484 – 6 April 1551)

Peter Schaeffer
University of California, Davis

BOOKS: *De undecim milibus virginum oratio* (Vienna: Hieronymus Vietor, 1510);

Oratio de Iesu Christi die natali (N.p., 1511);

Mythicum syntagma, cui titulus Gallus pugnans (Vienna: Hieronymus Vietor, 1514);

Carmen maximorum caesarum Friderici tertii patris et Maximiliani filii laudes continens (Vienna: Lucas Alantsee, 1514);

Habes lector hoc libello Rudolphi Agricolae . . . ad Ioachimum Vadianum . . . epistolam, qua de locorum nonnullorum obscuritate quaestio sit . . . Ioachimi Vadiani ad eundem epistolam . . . ratio explicatur (Vienna: Joannes Singrenius, 1515);

Divo Maximiliano Caes. Augusto . . . oratio (Vienna: Joannes Singrenius, 1515);

Oratio coram . . . Sigismundo Rege Poloniae . . . habita (Vienna: Hieronymus Vietor, 1515);

Aegloga cui titulus Faustus; De Vadianorum insignibus (Vienna: J. Metzker, 1517);

De nuptiis . . . Poloniae regis, D. Sigismundi, et . . . D. Bonae Sfortiae . . . carmen elegiacum (Vienna: Joannes Singrenius, 1518);

Pomponii Melae Hispani libri de situ orbis tres, adiectis Ioachimi Vadiani . . . in eosdem scholiis, addita quoque in geographiam catechesi et epistola Vadiani ad Agricolam (Vienna: Lucas Alantsee, 1518; revised and enlarged edition, Basel: Cratander, 1522);

De poetica et carminis ratione liber ad Melchiorem Vadianum fratrem (Vienna: Lucas Alantsee, 1518);

Unterricht wider die sorglich Krankheit der Pestilenz (Basel: Adam Petri, 1519);

Epitome trium terrae partium, Asiae, Africae et Europae compendiariam locorum descriptionem continens, praecipue autem quorum in Actis Lucas, passim autem Evangelistae et Apostoli meminere (Zurich: Christoph Froschauer, 1534);

Aphorismorum libri sex de consideratione Eucharistiae, de sententiis videlicet super hac re controversis, de Sacramentis antiquis et novis . . . de Transubstantiationis dogmate (Zurich: Christoph Froschauer, 1536);

Orthodoxa et erudita . . . Epistola (Zurich: Christoph Froschauer, 1539);

Epistola in qua . . . Iesum servatorem nostrum, vel in gloria veram esse creaturam, tum oraculis scripturarum sacrosanctis, tum interpretum orthodoxorum authoritate docetur et demonstratur; Antilogia ad . . . Schvenckfeldii argumenta (Zurich: Christoph Froschauer, 1540);

Pro veritate carnis triumphantis Christi (Zurich: Christoph Froschauer, 1542);

Alamannicarum rerum scriptores aliquot recentiores cumprimis Ioachimi Vadiani antiquitates, ex bibliotheca Melchioris Haiminsfeldii Goldasti (Frankfurt am Main: J. M. Porssius, 1606);

Deutsche Historische Schriften, 3 volumes, edited by Ernst Götzinger (Sankt Gallen: Zollikofer, 1875–1879);

Brevis Indicatura Symbolorum (1522), edited by Conradin Bonorand, with German translation by Konrad Müller, Vadian-Studien, no. 4 (Sankt Gallen: Fehr, 1954).

Editions: *Lateinische Reden,* edited, with translations into German and annotations, by Matthäus Gabathuler, Vadian-Studien, no. 3 (Sankt Gallen: Fehr, 1953);

"Oratio de Iesu Christi die natali," in *Arbogast Strub,* by Elisabeth Brandstätter and Hans Trümpy, Vadian-Studien, no. 5 (Sankt Gallen: Fehr, 1955), pp. 154–167;

De poetica et carminis ratione liber ad Melchiorem Vadianum fratrem, 3 volumes, edited, with German translation and commentary, by Peter Schäffer (Munich: Fink, 1973–1977);

Vom Mönchs- und Nonnenstand und seiner Reformation, (1548), edited by Ernst Gerhard Rusch, Vadian-Studien, no. 14 (Sankt Gallen: Verlagsgemeinschaft, 1988).

OTHER: Pseudo-Homer, *Homeri Batrachomyomachia Ioanne Capnione Phorcensi metaphraste,* edited by Vadianus (Vienna: Hieronymus Vietor, 1510);

Walahfrid Strabo, *Strabi Galli poetae et theologgi . . . Hortulus,* edited by Vadianus (Vienna: Hieronymus Vietor, 1510);

"Carmen de morte," in *Orationes duae,* by Arbogast Strub (Vienna: Hieronymus Vietor, 1511), fol. E4^r–F3^v;

Sallust, *C. Crispi Sallustii de coniuratione Catilinae et bello Iugurthino historiae,* edited by Vadianus (Vienna: Lucas Alantsee, 1511);

Cicero, *M. T. Ciceronis de officiis libri tres, dein Laelius et Cato maior et Somnium Scipionis cum Paradoxis,* edited by Vadianus (Vienna: Lucas Alantsee, 1512);

Ovid, *P. Ovidii Nasonis artis amandi libri tres, remedii amoris duo,* edited by Vadianus (Vienna: Lucas Alantsee, 1512);

Donatus, *Donati grammatici . . . argumenta compendiaria in fabulas potiores Ovidianae metamorphosis,* edited by Vadianus (Vienna: Lucas Alantsee, 1513);

Dionisius Afer, *Dionisii Afri ambitus orbis,* edited by Vadianus (Vienna: Joannes Singrenius, 1515);

Pliny the Elder, *C. Plinii Secundi liber septimus naturalis historiae,* edited by Vadianus (Vienna: Joannes Singrenius, 1515);

Lorenzo Valla, *Laurentii Vallae dialogus de libero arbitrio . . . Apologia pro se . . . Ad Candidum contra Bartoli libellum, quem de insigniis et armis scripsit,* edited by Vadianus (Vienna: Lucas Alantsee, 1516);

Giovanni Pontano, *Ioannis Ioviani Pontani . . . meteororum liber cum epistolio Vadiani, quo docetur quam pulchrum sit bonis literis bonas artes coniungere,* edited by Vadianus (Vienna: Joannes Singrenius, 1517).

That two names, of which neither can be given preference, designate the same individual–Joachim von Watt, the name he was given at his birth in the Swiss Sankt Gallen, and Joachim Vadianus, often shortened to Vadian, his humanist appellation at the University of Vienna–reflects the manifold genius of a man who was at once a distinguished citizen of his native canton and of the universal Republic of Letters. He represents not only an extraordinarily wide range of scholarly interests–classical, medieval, and contemporary literature; law; civil and ecclesiastical history; geography; music; medicine; and theology, so that, despite his own modest disclaimer he illustrates in himself the universal education, the "encyclopedia" for which he calls in the penultimate chapter of his *De poetica et carminis ratione* (Of Poetics and the Structure of Poetry, 1518)–but also the application of learning and scholarship to the administration, medical care, and transition to the Reformation of his native city. Humanism was for him far more than merely the mastery of disciplines; it was a guiding principle in the public as well as the private sphere, not simply an academic career but a way of life. By this integration of the mind inseparably joined with integrity of character his life and work stand as a singular example of all that is finest and enduring in the age of humanism.

Vadianus was born on 29 November 1484, the eldest son of Lienhard von Watt and Magdalena von Watt, née Talmann. His family was moderately prosperous and for several generations had been distinguished in the service of the town of Sankt Gallen. After attending the local Latin school he was sent in 1502 to the University of Vienna, where his father had business connections through the family linen trade. He was the first in his family to attend a university.

In 1508 Vadianus obtained the licentiate and the promotion to master of arts. During the following ten years his activities included lectures on classical and modern authors; the vice chancellorship of

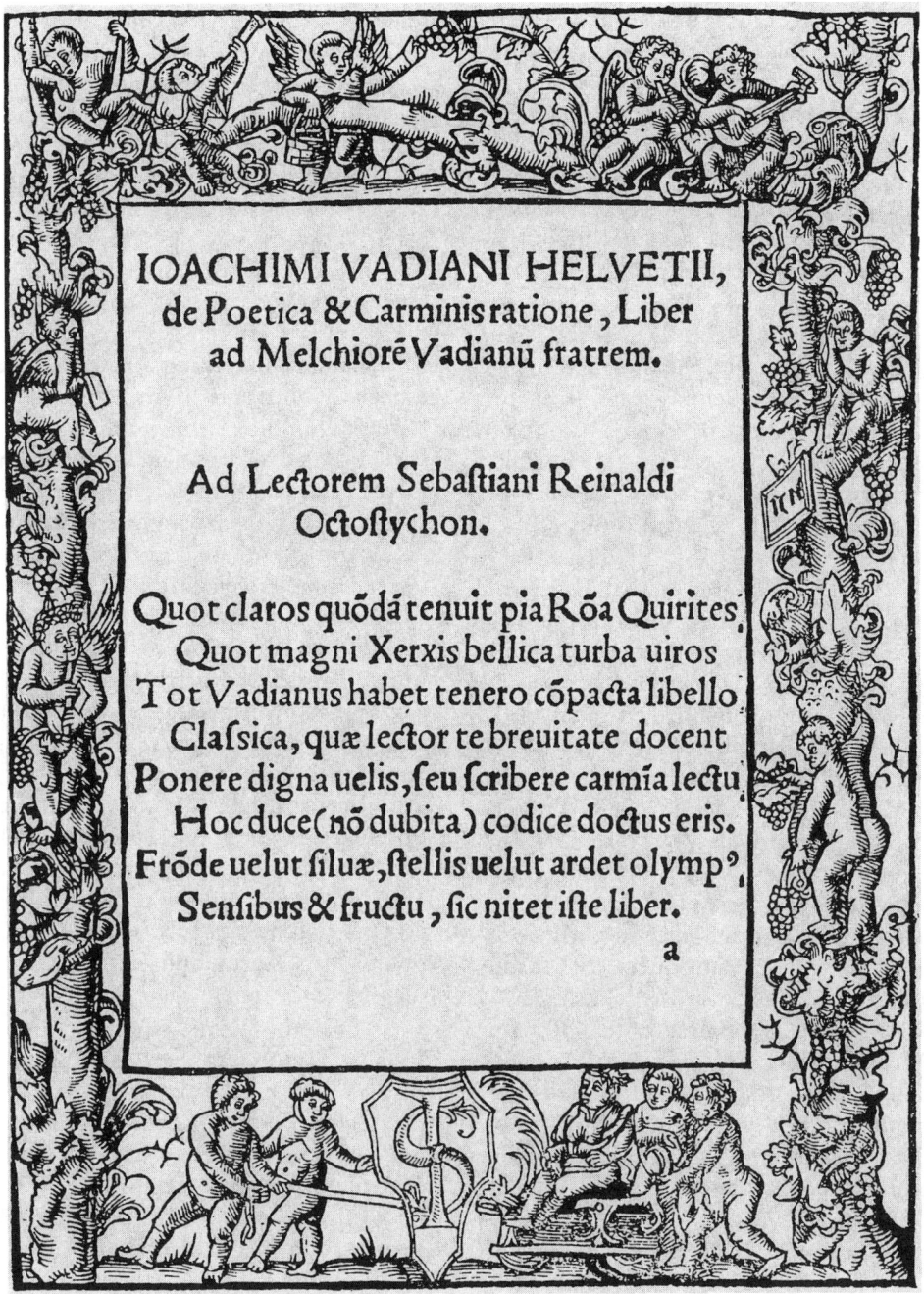

Title page for Vadianus's treatise on literature

the university in 1514 and the rectorship in 1516-1517; the completion of a course of study in medicine; and the composition of original verses sufficient to win him crowning as poet by Emperor Maximilian in 1514. The coronation of poets—a practice revived from antiquity by the crowning of Petrarch in Rome in 1341—became an essential ritual among the humanists and, though losing much of its original splendor, was continued until the Holy Roman Empire ended in the early nineteenth century (a vestige remains today in the appointment of poets laureate). In chapter 23 of *De poetica,* where he discusses why poets are believed to be under the protection of Apollo and Bacchus, Vadianus recounts this event in the engaging manner in which he often includes personal reflections or experiences as asides in his scholarly works. He says that the emperor's serene countenance and rapt attention to Vadianus's festive oration moved him to the point where he felt himself directly under the tutelage of

Apollo and the Muses. Yet he adds that he realized that honors add little to the stature of a man, making him neither more learned nor a better man, since distinctions merely point to, but do not bring about, achievements. Still, he recalls with awe how, in a close parallel to a sacramental rite, the hallowed hands of the emperor touched his temples, put a ring on his finger, and, with the acclamation of the distinguished company present, proclaimed him a poet.

But it is not in his craftsmanlike, if not especially distinguished, poetry that the most enduring monument to Vadianus's Vienna years is to be found, but rather in the *scholia* to the geography of Pomponius Mela and in his most distinctive humanistic achievement, the treatise *De poetica et carminis ratione,* both published in 1518, the year of his return to Sankt Gallen.

Geography had been among Vadianus's earliest predilections; his interest in the subject was probably encouraged by his revered teacher Conrad Celtis, whose early death in 1508 left the *Germania illustrata* among his many unfinished projects, and certainly by Vadianus's slightly older colleague in Vienna, the mathematician and astronomer Georg Tanstetter (Collimitius). In a lengthy letter dated 16 October 1514 replying to questions raised by Rudolf Agricola, in which he sets forth the geographical methodology he later incorporated into the Mela *Scholia,* Vadianus had been among the earliest to adopt the neologism *America,* introduced by Martin Waldseemüller in his *Cosmographiae Introductio* (1507). The *Chorographia* of the first-century Roman Pomponius Mela, of which Ermolao Barbaro's corrected edition had been printed around 1498 and reprinted in Vienna in 1512, was the earliest work of cultural geography and ethnography extant from antiquity and had been the subject of Vadianus's lectures in 1514 and in 1517.

In Vadianus's hands Mela's slender volume of seventy-six octavo pages grew by tenfold into a sizable folio, with the text surrounded and—often for pages—interrupted by his scholia. A form frequently employed by humanists, scholia are far more than mere commentaries or explanations; rather, they are annotations, elaborations, and often loosely associative excursuses providing the scholiast with a vehicle for the expression of his own ideas and—hardly less important in humanist circles—the display of his own erudition.

Beginning with an introduction to the terminology and methodology of geography, Vadianus immediately establishes its connection with other disciplines: the historian must know where Actium is situated, the reader of Scripture must be aware that incense and myrrh come from Arabia; the theologian must be acquainted with the terrain of the Holy Land. From the polar regions to the antipodes, from folklore and legends surrounding exotic as well as more-familiar regions to flora and fauna, celebrated landmarks, and cultural practices found all over the world, Vadianus's store of knowledge, his driving curiosity, and especially his tireless pedagogical motivation seem inexhaustible. He does not hesitate to inject personal comments, such as that the pyramids are mindless memorials to profligate rulers and avail nothing, or autobiographical asides, especially in tribute to his native land, or, in an observation on the griffins in distant Scythia, that this fabled beast also appears on his family crest. A methodological principle that finds repeated application is that even venerated authors must be updated and, where necessary, corrected by empirical observation. Accordingly, Vadianus undertook in August 1518 to climb Mount Pilatus to test the legend that its lake, when willfully disturbed, churns up to punish the intruder. This early scientific climbing expedition is mentioned in the second edition of the *Scholia* (1522), which also addresses new questions, such as the constellations visible at the founding of Rome, the sources of the Danube, the flooding of the Euphrates and the Nile, and the exact location of Ceylon. Reprints in 1530, 1540, 1557, and 1564 and the subsequent inclusion of excerpts from the *Scholia* in variorum editions of Pomponius Mela's geography attest to the success of Vadianus's endeavor.

The most original and profound monument of Vadianus's Vienna years, the treatise *De poetica et carminis ratione,* takes its origin from lectures given, most likely, in the winter semester of 1513–1514. In his dedicatory letter to a Swiss student, Johannes Hinwiler, Vadianus sets forth the distinctive character of this treatise and the goals it seeks to attain. Leaving behind the many handbooks of metrics and versification, anthologies of quotations, and annalistic catalogues of authors and works, Vadianus proposes to proceed along entirely different paths to encompass nothing less than literature itself: its concept, origins, and history; the genesis and maturation of the poet; auxiliary and related disciplines; and the defense of literature against charges of impiety and frivolity.

The first section of the book's two hundred octavo pages is concerned with the history of literature, from its earliest traces to the present. According to the definition of Diomedes, poetry is a metric structure of true or fictitious narrative, destined to provide utility or pleasure. The origins of poetry are as old as humanity and are founded in humanity's kinship with its creator: as God called the universe into being by his word, so the poet, in imitation of God, calls the world of literary imagination into being through the human word. The individual mark of poetry is the *numerus* that underlies metric structure, analogous to the number that underlies the harmony of Creation. Significantly, Vadianus points out, the first institute of humanities in Vienna had been called the *Collegium poetarum et mathematicorum*. With the Hebrews—the oldest known people—and their poetic prophets Moses and David, literature takes its beginning; it comes, by way of Eusebius's hypothesis that the Pentateuch was known to the Greeks before the Persian Wars, to Greece and thence to Rome, to Ennius as the first and Virgil as the greatest of the Roman poets. Latin literature grows from childhood to maturity and, at the end of antiquity, to old age; its fate is like that of the harvest under different skies, flourishing in benign cultural climates and withering in adverse ones. After a marginal existence in the age of barbarism, the new rebirth of letters occurred first in Italy, then in Germany, whither the elder Rudolf Agricola had led the Muses across the Alps just as Horace had imported them from Greece.

In an essay on the contribution of Vadianus's contemporary Beatus Rhenanus to the renewal of classical studies, Ulrich Muhlack has shown how philology, in its reception and criticism of texts, developed its own historical method long before one can speak even of the beginnings of historicism in general historiography. At about the same time, and apparently independently, Beatus Rhenanus and Vadianus developed the category of the "Middle Ages" to describe the period between the decline and fall of classical literature at the end of antiquity and its *renascentia* (rebirth) in what later became known as the Renaissance.

Following his historical panorama, in which Vadianus even includes some vernacular literature because it, too, meets the classical aesthetic and formal criteria, the second section deals with the poet's formation and growth to maturity along organic lines analogous to those suggested by literary history. On the perennial question whether natural talent or study makes one a poet, the authorities are cited to substantiate the necessity of both; but both are fulfilled only by practice: the constant conversance with the great models by reading and reflection and the unflagging endeavor to follow their example by *imitatio*. The crown of practice is the ability to extemporize, to express oneself in polished verse instantly and without effort. Nature, study, and practice are superseded, however, by the Platonic *furor poeticus*. Vadianus here ventures an opinion that has rarely been so clearly expressed: that the furor poeticus is the work of the Holy Spirit, that scriptural or prophetic inspiration and poetic inspiration derive ultimately from the same source. This view could only have been expressed at this time, when Neoplatonism had attained something of a synthesis with Christian doctrine and before the Reformation, when the question of inspiration became a dogmatic and sectarian issue.

The apologetic mode present throughout the book comes to the foreground in its latter half. There is no opposition, Vadianus contends, between literature and Christianity. In the earliest times poets and theologians, seers and seekers after God, were all the same, whether one looks at the Bible or at the poets of early antiquity such as Orpheus, Hesiod, and Parmenides, while in the first Christian centuries poets such as Prudentius, Arator, Venantius Fortunatus, and Sedulius were incorporated into the liturgy. The contention that the poetry of the ancients is primarily concerned with the pagan gods and, for that reason, is incompatible with Christianity leads Vadianus into his longest single chapter, on the pagan gods and how the ancients presumably viewed them. Magnanimously, the Christian must look upon what the ancients, before the dispensation of grace, were trying to express, with admiration for what they accomplished rather than censure for where they fell short. Often the tales of the gods are ciphers for recognized truths of history or natural philosophy, and deeper meaning vindicates the manner of expression—just as, in Christian art, no one takes offense at God portrayed as a bearded old man or Christ and the apostles in robes studded with gold and jewels. The same holds good for Apollo and the Muses, understood as personifications of natural phenomena or spiritual powers. A little common sense shows where the ancients patently erred, for who seriously believes that girls of flesh and blood or goddesses appeared to Hesiod? This almost Feuerbachian reduction of the antique cosmos of divinities to data of cosmology or psychology is carried out with meticulous care; Vadianus stops short, of course, of applying this method to the Christian view of the cosmos.

In the last section of his book Vadianus describes the process whereby the student of literature is integrated into the tradition. Again, his method is both didactic and apologetic; the former aspect is explicit, while the latter is implied in his concern for the rightful place of literature in the system of the arts and sciences—for its recognition as a legitimate area of scholarly enterprise, not merely as a pursuit of pleasant but inconsequential diversion. The whole system of the liberal arts, the trivium and the

Title page for Vadianus's historical and geographical companion to the New Testament (courtesy of the Lilly Library, Indiana University)

quadrivium, comprising the Encyclopedia, underlies any education worthy of the name, but in particular that of the poet. The study of grammar is considered under the two aspects described by Quintilian: first the study of language as such, and then its application to the interpretation of authors. One may note the irony of this chapter's—or, indeed, the whole book's—composition in a style of Latin that challenges even an expert present-day reader; the young men in their early teens who heard Vadianus in Vienna must have been thoroughly versed in grammar to understand his insistent commendation of it. Rhetoric is no less important, and perhaps even more so, for the poet than for the orator, since the poet is called upon to portray all manner of people speaking appropriately according to their character, their stations, and their purpose. A comparison of the orator's and the poet's craft sets forth the traits of poetic language, which is freer than prose in imagery but more limited by metric constraints.

Toward the body of tradition the young poet is to acquire and assimilate, he will require sound judgment. The catalogue of Latin authors, classical and contemporary, is presented a second time, with remarks on their serviceability as models and on the possible obscenity of the contents of their works, which may suggest postponement of their study to more-mature years. The characteristic humanistic turn of mind is in evidence here: even the most flagrant example, Martial, is not rejected, as he is so good a Latinist that one would profit by his study; conversely, the Christian poets are assigned no special place for the content of their works but are esteemed according to how closely they attain to the classical models.

The final three chapters sum up or elaborate several points made before. There is another defense of the dignity of the literary profession; advocacy of the further education of the poet in the quadrivium, since he must be conversant with all the highways and byways of gods and humans of whom he is to sing; and, in conclusion, some remarks about the practical tasks of composition. These last remarks are extremely brief, since good handbooks are available for questions of metrics and versification, syntax and usage.

Unlike the *Scholia* to Pomponius Mela, the *De poetica et carminis ratione,* though a monument to the erudition of its author, who was barely thirty when the lectures were first delivered, and a memorial to his distinguished associates at the Viennese court and university, who are stylized as the pillars of the Republic of Letters, was, at best, a qualified success within a small circle of enthusiasts. By 1522 the publisher, Lucas Alantsee, was complaining in a letter to Vadianus that he put copies on the market in Frankfurt am Main, Krakow, Venice, and elsewhere but it simply would not sell. In his *Bibliotheca Universalis* (1545) Conrad Gesner accords it the unusual tribute of quoting at length from the dedicatory letter and listing all thirty-two chapter headings, but subsequent editions of his encyclopedic work mention only the title, and in his *History of Publishing in Vienna to 1560* (1782) Michael Denis regrets that he cannot say anything further about it. Only its rediscovery by Josef Nadler in 1924 and its more recent critical edition (1973-1977) have brought it into focus again—not, of course, as an influential work but as an expression of a summit attained in literary historiography and criticism in central European humanism.

After his departure from Vienna, for reasons that are not entirely clear, in 1518 Vadianus undertook the longest journey of his life, which took him to Leipzig, Posen, Breslau, Krakow, once again to Vienna, and finally, by May 1519, back to Sankt Gallen. Notably absent from his itinerary is Wittenberg; while his correspondence, which included Martin Luther, indicates a lively interest in the beginnings of what was to become the Reformation, it would not be until 1522 that he would be ready to declare his commitment to it. Meanwhile, he received an appointment as town physician, and on 11 July 1519 he married Martha Grebel, sister of the future Anabaptist leader Conrad Grebel. An outbreak of the plague gave rise that same year to a short book in the ominous genre of *Pestbüchlein* (plague booklets), containing advice on avoiding and coping with the dreaded disease.

Vadianus's *Brevis Indicatura Symbolorum* (Short Treatise on the Creeds), written in 1522 but not published until 1954, establishes the biblical foundation of the early creeds and, thereby, Sacred Scripture as the sole criterion of faith. At this time Vadianus was elected to the city council of Sankt Gallen, on which he would serve several times; he would also serve as mayor. In this threefold capacity—the practice of medicine; public service, including diplomatic missions in the complex arbitrations among the Swiss cantons, as well as in the city's traditionally uneasy relationship with the Abbey of Sankt Gallen, which held extensive possessions in the outlying districts of the canton; and, finally, as a guiding light of the Reformation until it was firmly established in Sankt Gallen in 1532—Vadianus spent the remainder of his years and was, even during his lifetime, honored as *pater patriae* (father of his country). Though he produced no further specifically literary writings, the geographical, historical, and theological works of these later years continue to show the humanistic concerns of the Vienna period.

In January 1523 Vadianus lectured on the Acts of the Apostles, presumably to a small group of scholars. The manuscript of these lectures, which extends to nearly five hundred pages, has never been published in full. Conradin Bonorand has, however, shown the work's key position on Vadianus's path to the Reformation, to which the Acts were of singular significance as documenting the life of the Apostolic Church and providing the Reformers with a model for the restoration of what centuries of Roman aberration had disfigured and obscured.

In 1534 Vadianus expanded the geographical excursus that introduced Paul's travels in the lectures to become an independent publication, the *Epitome trium terrae partium* (A Brief Description of the Three Continents) a historical and geographical companion to the whole New Testament. This guide places the biblical past and the historic present in conjunction, so that many modern European cities—not least Sankt Gallen, "Sangallum, patria mea, oppidum Linificio nobile" (my home, a town noted for its linen manufacture)—also find mention in it. In his dedicatory letter to Heinrich Bullinger, who had succeeded Huldrych Zwingli as head of the church at Zurich after Zwingli's untimely end in battle at Cappel in 1531, Vadianus echoes the Erasmian idea that a proper understanding of Scripture and theology requires not only a command of the sacred languages and their secular literature but also of history and geography. The *Epitome trium terrae partium* was a resounding success, as shown by the publisher Christoph Froschauer's report that he had sold a thousand copies at the Frankfurt Book Fair—an astonishing number, particularly for a book in Latin and an expensive one, at that.

Stimulated by a visit of the Strasbourg Reformer Martin Bucer in 1533 to a renewed interest in overcoming the disharmony among the various Protestant communities, particularly the acrimonious controversies about the Lord's Supper, Vadianus contributed his elaborate treatise in six books on the Eucharist, published in 1536, the year of the death of Desiderius Erasmus and the execution of William Tyndale. His name on the title page, followed by his title *Consul Sangallensis,* underscores that he is writing not as a theologian but as an erudite public official, the head of a Protestant city. Averse by innate temperament as well as humanistic refinement to all polemicism, Vadianus endeavors to derive the doctrine of the Lord's Supper from the New Testament, the church fathers, and the practice of the early church and to formulate his findings in a conciliatory idiom acceptable to all the quarreling parties—though he categorically rejects the concept of transubstantiation, which he saw as an unacceptable deviation from sound doctrine and an innovation of the Church of Rome. Again, his sovereign historical and philological command is in evidence, along with the recurring theme that the Reformation seeks not to overthrow but to restore sound and scripturally approved doctrinal and liturgical traditions: in a word, to apply to the lofty matter in hand that return *ad fontes* (to the sources) that motivated all Renaissance humanism.

Vadianus's three remaining publications during his lifetime address the theology, in particular the Christological positions, of Caspar Schwenkfeld, whose sect continued to exist in his native Silesia into the early nineteenth century and figures in American church history through the settlement of the Schwenkfeldians in the vicinity of Philadelphia. As is indicated by the titles of Vadianus's works—*Orthodoxa et erudita . . . Epistola* (An Orthodox and Erudite Letter, 1539), *Epistola in qua . . . Iesum servatorem nostrum, vel in gloria veram esse creaturam, tum oraculis scripturarum sacrosanctis, tum interpretum orthodoxorum authoritate docetur et demonstratur; Antilogia ad . . . Schvenckfeldii argumenta* (A Letter in Which By Both the Sacred Pronouncements of the Holy Scriptures and the Authority of Orthodox Interpreters It Is Taught and Shown that Jesus Our Savior Even in Glory Is a Creature; Responses to Schwenkfeld's Arguments, 1540), and *Pro veritate carnis triumphantis Christi* (On Behalf of the True Flesh of the Triumphant Christ, 1542)—Schwenkfeld considered the Incarnation of Christ as merely a transitional stage that was followed by his complete spiritualization in heaven. This doctrine touches the substance of the belief not only in Christ's Ascension but also in the possibility of his Presence in the Eucharist and of the Second Coming. Vadianus was presumably, as in all his theological writing, responding to a request, though in this instance it is not known from whom. Subsequent vernacular publications of excerpts from the works attest to the esteem in which they were held.

Vadianus's most profound interest from about 1532, following the conclusion of the earlier controversies of the Reformation, to his death in 1551 was the history of Sankt Gallen, to the investigation of which he devoted himself continuously, even amid the demands his civic obligations placed on him. This history had to be founded in that of the Abbey of Sankt Gallen, to which he understood his city to be the legitimate cultural heir, but beyond that in the history of the Roman Empire and the Frankish empire. His compendious mastery of the sources—Patristic literature, the sources of Civil and Canon Law, medieval historiography, Scholasticism, and particularly the abundant documentation at hand in the Abbey of Sankt Gallen—remains astounding. None of this work appeared during his lifetime. The major Latin works—in particular, the "De Collegiis Monasteriisque Germaniae veteribus libri duo" (Two Books on the Ancient Religious Foundations and Monasteries in Germany), written in 1537, and the incomplete "De primitivae ecclesiae statu sive Christianismi aetatibus" (On the Condition of the Early Church or the Ages of Christianity), written in 1544—were published in part by the renowned polyhistor Melchior Goldast in 1606 in his collection of ancient and recent writings on Alemannic history. The most important German works—"Chronik der Äbte von St. Gallen" (Chronicle of the Abbots of Sankt Gallen), written between 1525 and 1533); "Kleinere Chronik der Äbte von St. Gallen" (Shorter Chronicle of the Abbots of Sankt Gallen, written in 1545-1546; "Geschichte der fränkischen Könige" (History of the Frankish Kings), written in 1545; and "Vom Mönchs- und Nonnenstand und seiner Reformation" (On the State of Monks and Nuns and their Reformation), written between 1545 and 1548, which, far beyond the immediate subject expressed in the title, touches on all of the fundamental concerns of the Reformation, including the nature of faith, the process of justification, and the practice of Christian piety—did not appear until they were published in the collection *Deutsche Historische Schriften* (German Historical Writings, 1875-1879).

For Vadianus the historiographical process is never merely a recounting of sequences of events; it involves tracing lines of development and evaluating the forces underlying continuity, progress, and diversion. For the Protestant investigator of ecclesiastical and monastic history, the underlying theme is always the distortion of the message and mission of salvation in a church turned into an apparatus of power, the transmutation of popes, bishops, and abbots into secular princes.

In a letter to Bullinger of November 1550, which had to be dictated, Vadianus mentions a painful inflammation in his right shoulder and expresses the fear that it would spread to the other joints of his body. By the end of January 1551 he had made a formal bequest of his valuable library to the city of Sankt Gallen as the foundation of a public library, which, to the present day, retains the name Vadiana. He died after this painful but brief illness on 6 April 1551, holding the hand of his oldest and most trusted friend, Johannes Kessler, who also became his first biographer. While interest of a local and patriotic nature in the father of his country, distinguished city councilor, mayor, and Reformer of Sankt Gallen was never dormant—as is attested by his imposing statue in the city's marketplace—it was the monumental definitive biography by Werner Näf (1944, 1957), presenting "die harmonische persönlichkeit, in der humanistische bildung als humane Gesinnung Segensreich Wirksam worde" (the harmonious personality in which humanistic erudition became felicitously active as humane conviction), as well as the series of monographs, including textual editions, titled *Vadian-Studien* initiated by him, that gave a decisive impetus to further research into the manifold work of Vadianus the humanist.

Letters:

Die Vadianische Briefsammlung der Stadtbibliothek St. Gallen, 7 volumes, edited by E. Arbenz (Sankt Gallen: Huber, 1890-1913).

Biographies:

Werner Näf, *Vadian und seine Stadt St. Gallen,* 2 volumes (Sankt Gallen: Fehr, 1944, 1957);

Gordon Rupp, "A Sixteenth-Century Dr. Johnson and his Boswell, Vadianus and Johannes Kessler of St. Gall," in his *Patterns of Reformation* (Philadelphia: Fortress Press, 1969), pp. 357-378.

References:

Conradin Bonorand, *Aus Vadians Freundes- und Schülerkreis in Wien,* Vadian-Studien, no. 8 (Sankt Gallen: Fehr, 1965);

Bonorand, *Joachim Vadian und der Humanismus im Bereich des Erzbistums Salzburg; Personenkommentar zum Vadianischen Briefwerk,* Vadian-Studien, no. 10 (Sankt Gallen: Fehr, 1980);

Bonorand, *Vadians Humanistenkorrespondenz mit Schülern und Freunden aus seiner Wiener Zeit; Personenkommentar IV zum Vadianischen Briefwerk,* Vadian-Studien, no. 15 (Sankt Gallen: Verlagsgemeinschaft, 1988);

Bonorand, *Vadians Weg vom Humanismus zur Reformation und seine Vorträge über die Apostelgeschichte (1523),* Vadian-Studien, no. 7 (Sankt Gallen: Fehr, 1962);

Bonorand, *Vadian und die Ereignisse in Italien im ersten Drittel des 16. Jahrhunderts; Personenkommentar III zum Vadianischen Briefwerk,* Vadian-Studien, no. 13 (Sankt Gallen: Verlagsgemeinschaft, 1985);

Bonorand and Heinz Haffter, eds., *Die Dedikationsepisteln von und an Vadian: Personenkommentar II zum Vadianischen Briefwerk,* Vadian-Studien, no. 11 (Sankt Gallen: Verlagsgemeinschaft, 1983);

Conrad Gesner, *Bibliotheca universalis,* volume 1 (Zurich: Christoph Froschauer, 1545), pp. 377^r-379^v;

Bernhard Hertenstein, *Joachim von Watt (Vadianus), Bartholomäus Schobinger, Melchior Goldast: Die Beschäftigung mit dem Althochdeutschen von St. Gallen im Humanismus und Frühbarock* (Berlin & New York: De Gruyter, 1975);

Johannes Kessler, "Vita Vadiani," in his *Sabbata, mit kleineren Schriften und Briefen* (Sankt Gallen: Historischer Verein, 1902), pp. 601-609;

Guido Kisch, *Vadians Valla-Ausgaben,* Vadian-Studien, no. 8 (Sankt Gallen: Fehr, 1965);

Bernhard Milt, *Vadian als Arzt,* Vadian-Studien, no. 6 (Sankt Gallen: Fehr, 1959);

Ulrich Muhlack, "Beatus Rhenanus," in *Einführung in die Geschichte der klassischen Philologie,* by Muhlack and Ada Hentschke (Darmstadt: Wissenschaftliche Buchgesellschaft, 1972), pp. 14-59;

Werner Näf, *Die Familie von Watt* (Sankt Gallen: Mitteilungen zur vaterländischen Geschichte 37, 2, 1936);

Näf, *Vadianische Analekten,* Vadian-Studien, no. 1 (Sankt Gallen: Fehr, 1945);

Dora Fanny Rittmeyer, *Vadian-Bildnisse,* Vadian-Studien, no. 2 (Sankt Gallen: Fehr, 1948);

Ernst Gerhard Rüsch, *Vadian 1484-1984: Drei Beiträge,* Vadian-Studien, no. 12 (Sankt Gallen: Verlagsgemeinschaft, 1985);

Peter Schaeffer, "The Emergence of the Concept 'Medieval' in Central European Humanism," *Sixteenth Century Journal,* 8 (1976): 21-30;

Verena Schenker-Frei, *Bibliotheca Vadiani: Die Bibliothek des Humanisten Joachim von Watt nach dem Katalog des Josua Kessler von 1553,* Vadian-Studien, no. 9 (Sankt Gallen: Fehr, 1973);

Gustav Scherer, ed., *Verzeichnis der Manuscripte und Incunabeln der Vadianischen Bibliothek in St. Gallen* (Sankt Gallen: Historischer Verein, 1864).

Papers:

Joachim Vadianus's manuscripts and other papers are in the Vadianische Bibliothek in Sankt Gallen.

Burkhard Waldis
(circa 1490 - 1556?)

Joe Delap
Kansas Wesleyan University

BOOKS: *De Parabell vam vorlorn Szohn. Luce am XV. gespelet vnnd Christlick gehandelt nha ynnholt des Texts ordentlick na dem geystlichen vorstande sambt aller vmstendicheit vthegelacht* (Riga, 1527);

Ein wunderliche Geburt eines zweyköpffigen Kindes, zu Witzenhausen in Hessen geschehen (N.p., 1542);

Warhaffte beschreibung der belegerung und schantzens vor dem haus Wolffenbuettel (N.p., 1542);

Der Wilde Man von Wolfenbuttel (N.p., 1542);

Hertzog Heinrichs vonn Braunschweig Klage Lied (N.p., 1542);

Wie der Lycaon von Wolfenbuttel, jcz newlich in einen Münch vorwandelt ist (N.p., 1542);

Ein warhafftige Historien von Zweyen Mewsen. So die pfaffen im Hüttenberge bey Wetzfalar haben verbrennen lassen. Darumb das sie ein Monstrantzen Sacrament gefressen hatten. Item. Drey schonen newer Fabeln (N.p., 1543);

Vrsprung vnd Herkummen der zwölff ersten alten König vnd Fürsten deutscher Nation, wie vnd zu welchen zeytten jr yeder Regiert hat (Nuremberg: Hans Guldenmundt the Elder, 1543);

Esopus, Gantz New gemacht, vnd in Reimen gefaßt. Mit sampt Hundert Newer Fabeln, vormals im Druck nicht gesehen, noch außgangen, 4 volumes (Frankfurt am Main: Hermann Gülfferichen, 1548);

Eyne warhafftige vnd gantz erschreckliche historien, Wie ein weyb jre vier Kinder tyrannigklichen ermordet vnd sich selust auch vmbbracht hat, Geschehen zu Weidenhausen bei Eschweh in Hessen (Erfurt, 1551).

Editions: *Burkard Waldis parabel vom verlornen sohn, ein niederdeutsches fastnachtspiel*, edited by Albert Hoefer (Greifswald: Koch, 1851);

Esopus, edited by Heinrich Kurtz (Leipzig, 1862);

Der Verlorene Sohn, ein Fastnachtspiel, edited by Gustav Milchsack (Halle: Niedermeyer, 1881);

Esopus, 2 volumes, edited by Julius Tittmann (Leipzig: Brockhaus, 1882);

Streitgedichte gegen Herzog Heinrich den Jüngern von Braunschweig von Burkard Waldis, edited by Friedrich Koldewey (Halle: Niemeyer, 1883).

OTHER: *Der Psalter, In Newe Gesangs weise, vnd künstliche Reimen gebracht*, translated by Waldis (Frankfurt am Main: Christian Egenolff, 1553);

Melchior Pfintzing and Emperor Maximilian I, *Die ehr vnd mannlich Thaten, Geschichten vnnd Gefehrlichaitenn des Streitbaren Ritters, vnnd Edlen Helden Tewerdanck . . . New zugericht. Mit schönen Figuren vnnd lustigen Reimen volendet*, revised by Waldis (Frankfurt am Main: Christian Egenolff, 1553); republished as *Tewerdanck Des Edlen, Streitbaren Helden vnd Ritters, Ehr vnd mannliche Thaten, Geschichten vnd Gefehrlicheiten* (Frankfurt am Main: Christian Egenolff, 1563);

Thomas Naogeorgus, *Das Päpstlich Reych. Ist ein Buch lüstig zu lesen allen so die warheit lieb haben, Darin der Babst mit seinen geliedern, leben, glauben, Gottesdienst, gebreüchen vnd Cerimonien, so vil müglich, warhafftig vnd auffs kürtzeste beschrieben, getheilt in vier Bücher*, translated by Waldis (N.p., 1555);

Rudolph Gualtherus, *Argumentorum in sacra Biblia, a Rudolpho Gualthero carminibus comprehensorum Tomus prior (et posterior) in uetus (et nouum) uidelicet Testamentum. Erste (vnd Ander) Theil der Summarien vber die gantz Bibel, Nemlich vber das alte (vnd newe) Testament, Mit schönen Figuren geziert, vnd in Reimen verfaszt*, 2 volumes, translated by Waldis (Frankfurt am Main: Weygandt Han, 1556).

Burkhard Waldis (also known as Burchard, and referred to as Burchardus Vualdis Hessus in Wittenberg records) was one of the principal sixteenth-century playwrights who helped to transform the medieval *Fastnachtspiel* (Shrovetide play) into a new dramatic form, one that began a new chapter in the history of German literature. But Waldis was far more than a dramatist. His influential collection of fables (part Aesop's, part his own), his translation of the Psalms, his polemics against the duke of Brunswick, and his revival of the Teuerdank legend attest to his skill and flexibility and to the turbulent life that affected his many writings.

Waldis was born around 1490 into a wealthy

Title page for Burkhard Waldis's play about the Prodigal Son

and respected family in the Hessian town of Allendorf an der Werra. His father was probably Hermann Waldis, who enjoyed the prestigious positions of alderman and chamberlain in Allendorf. The earliest available records of Burkhard Waldis's life place him in Riga as a member of the Franciscan order in 1522. Late that year Waldis, along with three other Franciscans—Antonius Boemhover, Augustin Ulfeld, and Theodoricus Ulfeld—was dispatched by Archbishop Jasper van Linden to seek support, in the form of an edict from both the Pope and the Holy Roman Emperor, against growing Livonian Protestantism and iconoclasm. In Rome, Waldis experienced disturbing revelations about the Catholic Church's corrupt practices and careless attitude in regard to Germany that permanently altered his attitude toward the church. On returning to Riga with the edict, Waldis was imprisoned for a few weeks on the order of the predominantly Protestant city council for his dealings on behalf of the unrelenting archbishop. During his imprisonment Waldis renounced Rome and converted to the Evangelical faith.

Waldis remained in Riga, where he became a pewterer, bought a home, and married (with unhappy results). His craft and trade led him to undertake extensive travels across Germany and the Netherlands, whereby he acquired a rich store of materials that he would incorporate into his writings. It was during his early years as *Kangeter tho Ryga* (pewterer in Riga) that Waldis wrote, and probably directed, his Prodigal Son play, which was published in 1527 in Low German under the title *De Parabell vam vorlorn Szohn* (The Parable of the Prodigal Son). It is the only known dramatic rendering at the time of the parable from Luke 15:11–32 in German, though the subject was soon to become popular among sixteenth-century German dramatists. It follows the biblical story closely, except for certain literary embellishments: for example, in keeping with other, Latin dramatizations of the story, in the first of the two acts Waldis provides a realistic depiction of the prodigal son's downfall, complete with scheming rogues and prostitutes who help him squander his inheritance. The second act is unique not so much for its rendering of the subject matter—the son's return—as for its interpretation of the parable's ending: the forgiven prodigal son as the embodiment of salvation through faith alone. Thus, it appears that Waldis's conversion to the Evangelical faith was, by this point, complete and sincere. His primary motive for creating the drama was less to entertain, which was the purpose of the Shrovetide plays of his contemporaries, than to impart and further the Reformers' program. Waldis's play stands at the forefront of a movement to create plays for the purpose of propagating Reformation ideas.

Waldis's Prodigal Son play has frequently, but inappropriately, been labeled a Fastnachtspiel. In fact, certain passages in the play seem to belittle the tradition of the Fastnachtspiel, but it is not clear that Waldis intended the play as a reaction against the tradition. What is clear is that the play is by far his most significant work; indeed, it is considered one of the most important German dramas of the sixteenth century in that it serves as a transitional work from the medieval Fastnachtspiel to the modern German biblical drama. In terms of dramatic style, Waldis is less whimsical than his immediate forerunners and contemporaries, showing a preference for serious interpretation and dissemination of biblical content and meaning. This tendency toward exegesis and religious fervor, a trait often found in biblical and school dramas, does not diminish the artistic value of the play, which is a thoroughly entertaining piece with well-drawn characters and lively exchanges. A minor obstacle to the play's popularity was the Low German dialect in which it was composed; but this feature apparently posed little problem, since dramatists such as Hans Sachs and Hans Salat borrowed from or otherwise responded to Waldis's version of the Prodigal Son story. The work still stands as one of the oldest and best representations of Low German literature from the early modern period.

As a frequent business traveler Waldis sometimes acted as an agent and courier for a group of Protestants led by Johann Lohmüller, a radical Reformer who sought to convert the region around Riga from a Roman Catholic archdiocese under the jurisdiction of the Teutonic Order into a secular duchy of Evangelical persuasion. Arrested while visiting relatives in Bauske, Latvia, around Christmas 1536 on his return from a business trip in the German lands, Waldis suffered three and a half years of imprisonment and torture at the hands of the Teutonic Order under the command of Hermann von Brüggenei. While imprisoned, Waldis began his musical rendering of the Psalms, primarily, by his own admission, as a means of escape from the mental anguish and physical torment. The resulting work, published in Frankfurt am Main in 1553 as *Der Psalter, In Newe Gesangs weise* (The Psalter in New Songful Melody) is, according to Ute Mennecke-Haustein, the most well-crafted and significant rendition of the Psalms in German of the first half of the sixteenth century because of its abundance of verse forms—some eighty-six different strophic forms are found among the 155 songs—and power of expression. Whereas most modern critics find an uplighting feeling in these Psalms, some commentators note their occasional mechanical, near-doggerel quality.

Four of Waldis's brothers, with the support of Landgrave Philip of Hesse, leader of the Schmalkaldic League, traveled to Riga in 1538 and tried unsuccessfully to win his freedom. In July 1540 two of his brothers, Hans and Bernhard, with the help of one of Waldis's journeymen, Cyriacus Klinth, procured his release—an act for which Waldis gratefully dedicated his Psalter to them. In the dedication Waldis mentions the consolation he received from working on the text while under extreme personal duress and notes that the Psalms reflect both the joys and the sorrows of the human condition.

In the winter of 1541 Waldis enrolled at Wittenberg University, where he studied theology under Martin Luther in preparation for becoming an Evangelical minister. A clerical assignment was not immediately available for him on his return to Hesse, but Waldis kept himself occupied by composing a series of invectives against Archduke Heinrich the Younger of Brunswick-Wolfenbüttel, a boyhood friend of Landgrave Philip of Hesse who had become Philip's enemy in the Schmalkaldic War. Appearing in 1542, the four political pamphlets bear the titles *Warhaffte beschreibung der belegerung und schantzens vor dem haus Wolffenbuettel* (True Description of the Siege and Entrenchment before the House of Wolfenbüttel), *Der Wilde Man von Wolfenbuttel* (The Wild Man of Wolfenbüttel), *Hertzog Heinrichs vonn Braunschweig Klage Lied* (Duke Heinrich of Brunswick's Plaintive Song), and *Wie der Lycaon von Wolfenbuttel, jcz newlich in einen Münch vorwandelt ist* (How the Lycaon of Wolfenbüttel Recently Converted to a Monk). Of the many published denunciations of Archduke Heinrich, Waldis's were not only the most popular—each went through multiple printings—but also, despite their sometimes coarse polemics, the most eloquent.

Warhaffte beschreibung der belegerung und schantzens vor dem haus Wolffenbuettel gives a detailed description of Landgrave Philip's siege of Heinrich's stronghold and residence at Wolfenbüttel from 9 to 12 August 1542. Whether Waldis experienced the events firsthand or depended on eyewitness accounts of others is not known. At the time of the siege and fall of his palace to Protestant forces Heinrich was abroad, mainly in Bavaria, seeking assistance from allies sympathetic to the anti-Reformation cause. Waldis depicts the absent ruler as an evil tyrant and instigator of arson and murder, charges often brought against him for his relentless plottings against cities tied to the Schmalkaldic League. The Protestant seizure of the archduke's palace is presented as a victory over those who despise the Word of God—that is, the Catholic rulers who would suppress the progress of the Reformation in Brunswick and Wolfenbüttel. The facts of the siege as Waldis gives them are intended to verify his opening claim that Heinrich and his supporters are *Gottlos* (godless, or out of God's favor) and that Philip and his supporters are *Goettlich* (godly, or in God's favor). For example, some of the Protestant forces had established their positions early, making them vulnerable to a surprise attack on their trenches by Heinrich's soldiers; after only two days of battle, however, Philip's forces had driven Heinrich's surviving men into the cellars and frightened the inhabitants of the palace into surrender, thus winning a seemingly miraculous early victory.

Der Wilde Man von Wolfenbuttel depicts the misdeeds of Archduke Heinrich and his subsequent punishment in greater detail. To the accusations against the archduke mentioned in his previous pamphlet Waldis adds blasphemy, heresy, adultery, and molestation of women. He further characterizes Heinrich as an Antichrist and archenemy of all pious rulers, one who has been banned not only from his own palace but from earth as well: Heinrich and all of his retinue will soon be eternally banished to hell. Waldis warns his readers against trusting in

Title page for Waldis's collection of fables

their own righteousness and admonishes them to avoid the ungodly practice of hoarding power and goods, as the archduke has done. It is curious and indicative of the superstition of his day that, in the end, Waldis turns to a "gmeyn Sprichwort . . . bei den alten" (common proverb . . . of the ancients) to explain the archduke's fate: change is in the nature of things. With this dictum Waldis implies that Archduke Heinrich should have accepted the changes that came with the introduction of the Protestant faith into his duchy, rather than resisting the Reformation with all his might. It would, of course, Waldis admits, be unreasonable to expect such flexibility from a liar, slanderer, and "wild man." An anonymous revision of *Der Wilde Mann von Wolfenbuttel,* produced around 1560 and titled *Ein spruch von ainem hungerigen wolffen* (A Proverb of a Hungry Wolf), is one of several later rewritings that show the continued popularity of Waldis's polemical works in the second half of the sixteenth century.

Hertzog Heinrichs vonn Braunschweig Klage Lied purports to tell of Heinrich's woes in his own voice. The song has a frame in which a narrator recounts that, while lurking nearby one morning, he overheard a wolf complaining that his lair has been destroyed and his pouch torn. The imagery of the torn money pouch, symbolic of Philip's plundering of Heinrich's treasury, is also found in the description of the siege of Wolfenbüttel. Other imagery in the work includes Heinrich's frequent references to his white horse, the heraldic animal of the Brunswick dukes that still appears on Wolfenbüttel's city emblem, and to other animals representing cities and states that have failed or refused to come to his aid. Whereas in the beginning of the song the reader is likely to feel some sympathy for the fallen ruler, by the end all doubt as to his wickedness has been removed by his own admission: his heroes include such villains as Cain, Pharaoh, Nero, and Caligula.

In *Wie der Lycaon von Wolfenbuttel, jcz newlich in einen Münch vorwandelt ist* Heinrich is portrayed as the Arcadian king Lycaon, who offered Jupiter human flesh for food and was transformed into a wolf by the angry god. The story jumps without explanation to the sixteenth century and continues with Heinrich, the wolf, persecuting the innocent Protestant sheep with arson, murder, and theft. Two shepherds, representing Landgrave Philip and Elector Johann Friedrich of Saxony, rescue the sheep by destroying the wolf's lair and keeping him at bay. Heinrich decides to reform his life and has the devil transform him into a monk; he then hides out among the clergy as a "Wolff in Lemmer vell" (wolf in sheep's skin). Waldis reminds his readers in the concluding lines that Heinrich is fooling no one by taking on the monk's cowl, for evildoers can never belie their foul nature. When he claims that the wolf cannot be trusted any more than the Jew cannot be taken at his word or the papist trusted to have a conscience, Waldis reveals the intolerance that characterized many Reformation publications.

In 1543 Waldis published a rhymed pamphlet attacking the Catholic clergy, *Ein warhafftige Historien von Zweyen Mewsen* (A True Story of Two Mice), in which two mice eat sacramental wafers and are burned by priests. The following year Landgrave Philip appointed Waldis a Lutheran minister and gave him jurisdiction over the wealthy priory at Abterode, near Waldis's birthplace. Meanwhile, either through divorce or death, Waldis had become separated from his wife, with whom he had always quarreled bitterly. Shortly after his appointment as prior of Abterode he married the widow of Pastor Heistermann of Hofgeismar.

Begun in Riga, probably before 1533, and completed in Abterode, Waldis's *Esopus* (Aesop's Fables) was published in four volumes in Frankfurt am Main in 1548. Waldis translated and adapted the first 283 of the 397 fables from Martin Dorpius's Latin collection of 1530, with the remaining 114 either of Waldis's own invention or from unknown sources. What distinguishes Waldis's collection from earlier such works is its local color, its backdrops of various German cities and social settings with which he had become acquainted during his travels. Some of the stories, especially those in the fourth volume, are, thus, part fable and part autobiography. Waldis exhibits particular concern for the injustices he has witnessed in his eventful life, injuries done not only to himself but also to the poor, the old, and the otherwise underprivileged. Many of his fables deal with relationships between opposites—master and servant, rich man and poor man, wolf and lamb—all of which point to more-general problems in the social order.

Waldis's criticism in his fables is not, however, limited to the social sphere. He shows a blatant disdain for Rome, the Pope, and the Catholic Church, directing crude humor and insults at them in dozens of his fables. The fables leave no aspect of the Catholic Church unscathed, from the preachings of the lowly barefoot monk to the enunciations of the Pope himself, from the common practice of confession to the less common practice of dealing in relics. Waldis's fables reveal him as not only a translator of ancient fables but also as a contemporary social critic and staunchly anti-Catholic Lutheran minister.

Also worth noting is Waldis's thoroughly revised version of the popular but outmoded romance *Teuerdank* (1553). Waldis set aside his normally polemical inclination and his good taste in literature to re-create for a mid-sixteenth-century audience the allegorical poem that had been written by Emperor Maximilian I's chaplain, Melchior Pfintzing, according to the emperor's instructions and published in 1517. Waldis adds an original chapter allegorizing Maximilian's war against France. Though his *Die ehr und mannlich Thaten, Geschichten unnd Gefehrlichaitenn des Streitbaren Ritters, unnd Edlen Helden Tewerdanck* (The Honorable and Manly Deeds, Stories, and Dangers of the Valiant and Noble Hero Teuerdank) is not his greatest creative effort, his revision gave the reading public what it desired: the old version of the legend ceased to be printed, while Waldis's saw no fewer than four reprintings by the end of the sixteenth century.

Waldis dedicated his translation of Thomas Naogeorgus's *Regnum papisticum* (1553) as *Das Päpstlich Reich* (The Papal Realm) to Philip of Hesse's second wife, Margarete von der Saal. This papal caricature and moral commentary on the times was completed and presented to Margarete in July 1554 and published the next year. It served as a resource for later satiric writers, such as Johann Fischart. Waldis's final work was his translation from the Latin of Rudolph Gualtherus's *Argumentorum in sacra Biblia* (Summary of the Holy Bible, 1556).

According to accounts by his parishioners, Waldis was a diligent clergyman who served his congregation well until his final days, when his health began to fail. Pastor Balthasar Hiltbrandt, the husband of Waldis's stepdaughter by his second wife, proved to be a valuable assistant toward the end of the elder minister's life. The faithful son-in-law took over the ailing pastor's duties in August 1556 and was appointed minister in Abterode in 1557, by which time Waldis must have died.

While Waldis's Prodigal Son play was probably of some significance to Sachs and other sixteenth-century playwrights, the innovations in strophic form found in his Psalms were too far ahead of their time to be comprehended, let alone appreciated, by his contemporaries. It is unfortunate that Waldis should be remembered more for his short-lived influence on the biblical or school drama than for his songwriting abilities. His Psalms, had they been popular, would have had more far-reaching implications, as the *Kirchenlied* (hymn) was one of the most widely used literary vehicles of the Reformation. In the end, Waldis must be recognized for his positive impact on eighteenth- and nineteenth-century editors of German fables and for the rich sources of cultural and historical information his works provide.

References:

Karl Goedeke, "Burkard Waldis," in his *Grundriß zur Geschichte der deutschen Dichtung aus den Quellen,* second edition, volume 2 (Dresden: Ehlermann, 1886), pp. 447–453;

Barbara Könneker, "Burkard Waldis: De Parabell vam vorlorn Szohn," in her *Die deutsche Literatur der Reformationszeit: Kommentar zu einer Epoche* (Munich: Winkler, 1975), pp. 157–164;

Wilhelm Kosch, "Waldis, Burkard," in *Deutsches Literatur-Lexikon,* edited by Kosch, second edition (Bern: Francke, 1958), p. 3198;

Ute Mennecke-Haustein, "Waldis, Burkhard," in *Literaturlexikon: Autoren und Werke deutscher Sprache,* volume 12, edited by Walter Killy (Gütersloh: Bertelsmann, 1989), pp. 113–114;

Wolfgang F. Michael, "Burkard Waldis," in *Das deutsche Drama der Reformationszeit* (Bern: Peter Lang, 1984), pp. 46–49;

Ernst Heinrich Rehermann and Ines Köhler-Zülch, "Aspekte der Gesellschafts- und Kirchenkritik in den Fabeln von Martin Luther, Nathanael Chytraeus und Burkhard Waldis," in *Die Fabel: Theorie, Geschichte und Rezeption einer Gattung,* edited by Peter Hasubek (Berlin: Schmidt, 1982), pp. 27–42;

Angelika Reich, "Burkhard Waldis," in *Deutsche Dichter der frühen Neuzeit (1450–1600): Ihr Leben und Werk,* edited by Stephan Füssel (Berlin: Schmidt, 1993), pp. 377–388;

John Lancaster Riordan, "The Status of the Burkhard Waldis Studies," *Modern Language Quarterly,* 2 (1941): 279–292;

Rolf Tarot, "Schuldrama und Jesuitentheater," in *Handbuch des deutschen Dramas,* edited by Walter Hinck (Düsseldorf: Bagel, 1980), pp. 38–39.

Georg Wickram
(circa 1505 – circa 1561)

Elisabeth Wåghäll
Växjö University

BOOKS: *Die Zehen alter* (Strasbourg: Jacob Frölich, 1531);

Das Narren gießen (Strasbourg: Jacob Frölich, 1538);

Der trew Eckart (Strasbourg: Jacob Frölich, 1538);

Ritter Galmy vß Schottland (Strasbourg: Jacob Frölich, 1539);

Eine Schöne und fast schimpfliche kurtzweil (Strasbourg, 1539);

Ein schönes vnd euangelisches Spil von dem verlornen Sun (Colmar: Bartolomeus Grüninger, 1540);

Ein new Faßnacht Spil, darin angezogen werden etliche fürneme menner (N.p., 1543);

Ein schön vnd nützliches Biblisches Spiel von . . . Tobia (Frankfurt am Main: Hermann Gülfferichen, 1550); republished as *Ein recht schön christlich Burger Spiel, Tobias genannt* (Strasbourg: Thiebolt Berger, 1562);

Eine schöne und doch klägliche History (Strasbourg: Jacob Frölich, 1551);

Ein schönes . . . Spyl auß den geschichten der Aposteln gezogen (Strasbourg: Jacob Frölich, 1552);

Knaben Spiegel (Strasbourg: Jacob Frölich, 1554);

Eine Wahrhafftige History von einem ungerathenen Son in ein Dialogum gestellet (Strasbourg: Jacob Frölich, 1554 or 1555);

Der Jungen Knaben Spiegel (Strasbourg: Jacob Frölich, 1555);

Rollwagenbüchlein (Strasbourg: Johann Knobloch the Younger, 1555);

Dialogus, in welchem angezogen wirt das mechtig hauptlaster von der trunckenheit (Strasbourg: Köpfflein, 1555);

Von guten und bösen Nachbaurn (Strasbourg: Johann Knobloch the Younger, 1556);

Der Irr Reitend Bilger (Strasbourg: Johann Knobloch the Younger, 1556);

Die Siben Hauptlaster (Strasbourg: Johann Knobloch the Younger, 1556);

Der Goldtfaden (Strasbourg: Jacob Frölich, 1557); translated by Pierre Kaufke as *The Golden Thread* (Gainesville: University of Florida Press, 1991).

Editions and collections: *Der Goldfaden: Eine schöne alte Geschichte wieder herausgegeben,* edited by Clemens Brentano (Heidelberg: Mohr & Zimmer, 1809);

Werke, 8 volumes, edited by Johannes Bolte and Willy Scheel (Tübingen: Bibliothek des Stuttgarter Literarischen Vereins, 1901–1906);

Sämtliche Werke, 11 volumes, edited by Hans-Gert Roloff (Berlin: De Gruyter, 1967–1992).

OTHER: Ovid, *P. Ovidii Nasonis des aller sinnreichsten Poeten Metamorphosis,* translated by Albrecht von Halberstadt, adapted by Wickram (Mainz: Iwo Schöffer, 1545);

Thomas Murner, *Die Narrenbeschwerung,* revised by Wickram (Strasbourg: Jacob Frölich, 1557).

The nineteenth-century literary critic and historian Karl Goedeke called Georg (also known as Jörg) Wickram the founder of the German novel. This claim has often been challenged, but Wickram's position as one of the more important authors of sixteenth-century popular, as opposed to learned, literature is no longer questioned. Wickram's works were rarely mentioned for more than two hundred years after his death, but in 1806 Friedrich de la Motte Fouqué published *Historie vom edlen Ritter Galmy und einer schönen Herzogin aus Bretagne* (Story of the Noble Knight Galmy and a Beautiful Duchess from Brittany), a novel based on Wickram's *Ritter Galmy uß Schottland* (The Knight Galmy from Scotland, 1539); in 1808 Jakob Grimm expressed interest in Wickram in a letter to G. F. Bencke; and in 1809 Wickram's *Der Goldtfaden* (1557; translated as *The Golden Thread,* 1991) was republished by Clemens Brentano. Despite the interest the Romantics showed in Wickram, little research was done on his life and work until Goedeke compiled the first extensive bibliography of Wickram's works in his *Grundriß zur Geschichte der deutschen Dichtung* (Outline of the History of German Writing, 1859). Important biographical and bibliographical research on Wickram was published later in the century

Title page for Georg Wickram's play about the Prodigal Son

by August Stöber, Wilhelm Scherer, and Erich Schmidt.

In the nineteenth century Wickram was criticized for using old topics and themes without adding anything new or interesting, and it was argued that his texts were of poor stylistic quality. Twentieth-century critics have reevaluated his work in the light of a more differentiated picture of sixteenth-century society and literature. There is, however, complete agreement on one matter: Wickram had no successors. His novels about the everyday lives of bourgeois protagonists are unique for their time. The rise of absolutism made the court the center of cultural life; by the end of the sixteenth century interest in courtly literature grew with the introduction of the *Amadís de Gaula* (Amadís of Gaul) series of novels into Germany, and Wickram's works lost their importance.

Wickram spent most of his life in the area around Strasbourg, working as a city clerk and writing novels, plays, and didactic texts. All of his writings are in the vernacular, and the themes are simple and straightforward. Love, friendship, education, and family life were topics of interest to the humanists as well as to the German Reformers; Wickram discusses these topics in all his works, but without making overt comments on the political, economic, or religious developments of his time. At first sight he seems neither to approve nor to disapprove of phenomena such as the Reformation or the peasants' war; he simply describes interpersonal relationships.

Born around 1505, Wickram was the illegitimate son of Konrad Wickram, who was a member of the Colmar city council and at one point served as its chairman. Wickram's mother's name is not known. His illegitimacy meant that he was excluded from many of the privileges he otherwise would have enjoyed as the son of a patrician; he received no higher education and probably only learned elementary reading, writing, and mathematics at a city school.

Wickram does not appear in the records until the 1530s, when he was working as a lower clerk for the city council. At the same time he was in charge of the theater in Colmar, writing, directing, and performing in plays in which the town's citizens also acted. Wickram's first Shrove Tuesday play, *Die Zehen alter* (The Ten Ages), a moralistic piece about the different stages of life based on a work by Pamphilus Gengenbach of Basel, was performed and published in 1531. His next published work appears to have been *Das Narren gießen* (Casting Fools, 1538), a play influenced by Sebastian Brant's *Das Narrenschiff* (The Ship of Fools, 1494) that uses humor to show the absurdity of a world populated by fools. That same year the play *Der trew Eckart* (Faithful Eckart) was published; in it Eckart, a well-known figure from Germanic heroic epics, seeing nothing but foolishness in the world around him, warns his fellowmen not to drink and gamble but to turn their hearts to God. Although his warnings are not heeded, Eckart continues his mission faithfully and indefatigably.

In 1539 Wickram published his first novel, *Ritter Galmy uß Schottland*. In general, Wickram's novels are more original than his plays, which are strongly influenced by such authors as Brant, Gengenbach, Hans Sachs, and Thomas Murner. The plot of *Ritter Galmy uß Schottland,* however, is familiar from other texts. Galmy, a young knight serving the duke of Brittany at his court in Vannes, falls in love with the duchess. He suffers from lovesickness until the duchess, who is unaware of his feelings, agrees to see him. She is immediately touched by the young knight. In the courtly literature of the Middle Ages the love of a socially superior married lady for a knight was a common theme, but to Wickram love relationships are impossible if they cannot be legitimized through marriage. In *Ritter Galmy uß Schottland* he defends the relationship between Galmy and the duchess by comparing their love to that between siblings: the duchess claims to feel only sisterly love for Galmy, though her behavior suggests otherwise.

The evil knight Wernhard, who is envious of Galmy's success in tournaments and of his status as

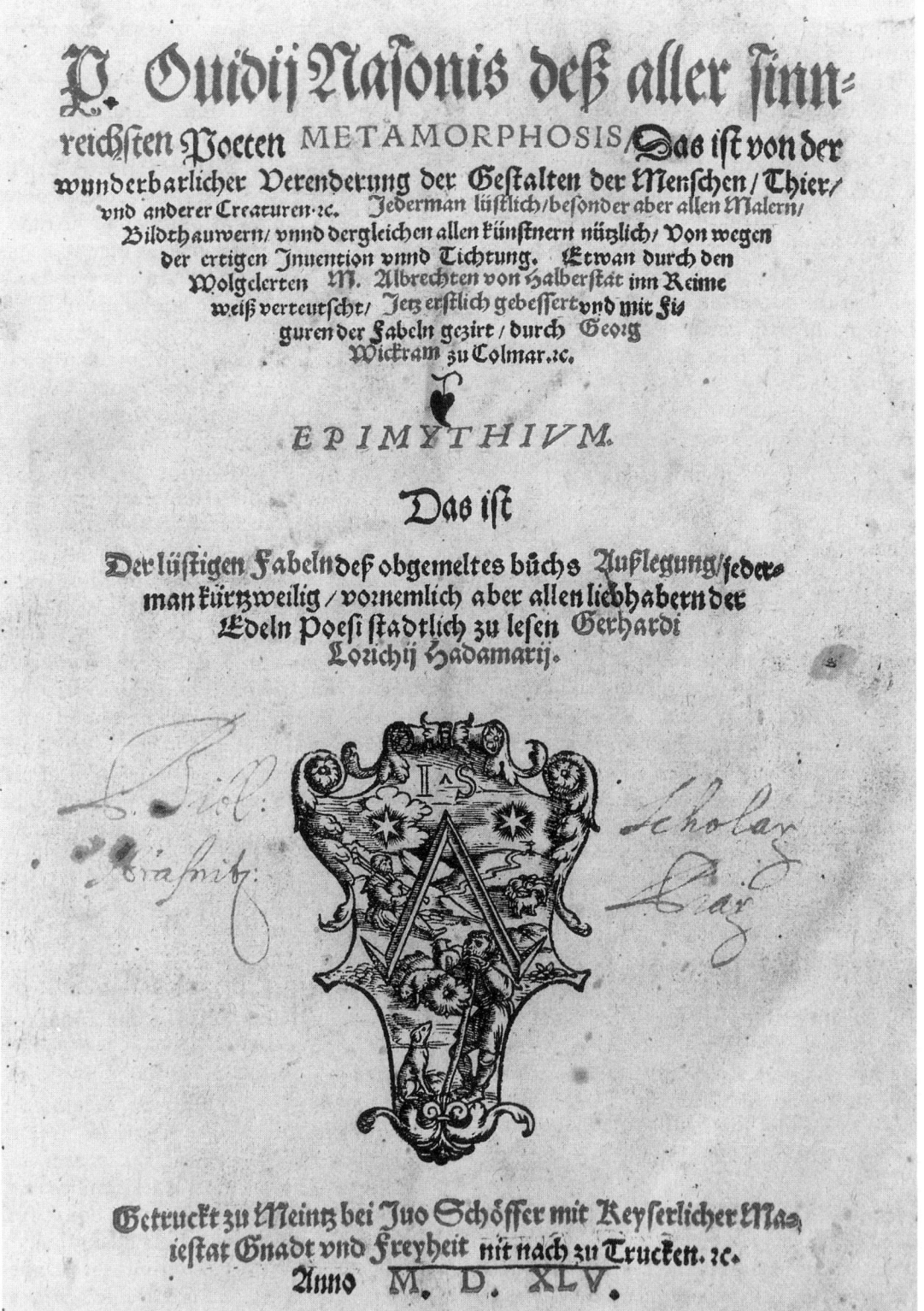

Title page for Wickram's revision of an earlier translation of Ovid's Metamorphoses (courtesy of the Lilly Library, Indiana University)

one of the duke's favorites, finds out about the growing love between Galmy and the duchess and conspires to take advantage of the situation. Like most evil characters in Wickram's works, he will only hurt himself and his own reputation in the end, but first Galmy is forced to flee to his parents in Scotland. Shortly thereafter the duke embarks on a journey to the Holy Land, leaving his marshal in charge at home. It soon becomes clear that the marshal is secretly in love with the duchess, but she has no interest in him. Out of spite, the marshal spreads the rumor that the duchess has committed adultery. She is held prisoner in her own home, with only Galmy's friend Friedrich to talk to, and dreams of being rescued by Galmy. On his return the duke is greeted with the lies about his wife and condemns her to be burned at the stake. Galmy arrives, disguised as a monk; the duchess is saved, without knowing by whom, and is forgiven by her husband. The marshal is punished for his sins, and the duke and duchess live happily for some time. But the brave knight Galmy has to be rewarded for his splendid deeds: after the duke dies in an accident, Galmy is allowed to return to Brittany and marry his beloved duchess. Having saved her life, he has proven himself a worthy successor to the duke.

As he does in his later novels, Wickram makes clear transitions between chapters and events, and the narrative proceeds with few interruptions. Almost all of the incidents occur in succession; only rarely does the reader encounter simultaneous happenings. Wickram indicates most breaks in the narrative by using phrases equivalent to: "I will now turn to . . ." or "enough of this," but the reader does not encounter phrases such as "while X was asleep, Y was reading a book." This feature is not unique to Wickram's works: in the popular literature of the sixteenth century simultaneity had not yet been developed. The duke's travels to the Holy Land must have lasted for years, but what happens at the court while he is away could have taken place within months. The characters do not seem to age; the long journey does not change the duke, nor does her imprisonment change the duchess.

Wickram's fear of controversy, especially religious controversy, is also characteristic of all of his novels. He rarely mentions the religious changes that were occurring in the sixteenth century. Martin Luther and the humanist Desiderius Erasmus of Rotterdam are the only historical figures of the time whom Wickram mentions: Erasmus is praised as a very learned man whose name will never be forgotten, while Luther is mentioned incidentally and in a surprisingly negative tone. The fact that the Reformation was not accepted in Colmar until 1575 might be the reason for Wickram's hesitation to show openly where he stood on issues regarding the Reformation. Only indirectly, in his descriptions of everyday life, is it possible to see Wickram's approval of many of the ideas of the Reformers.

In 1540 Wickram's play *Ein schönes und evangelisches Spil von dem verlornen Sun* (A Beautiful and Evangelical Play about the Prodigal Son) was published. The topic was popular at the time and was commonly used in dramas written to be performed in schools. In 1542 Wickram was sent as a representative of Colmar to the book fairs in Frankfurt am Main and Speyer, the longest journey he would make in his life. The purpose of the trip was to sell a translation of the works of Plutarch that had been made by the mayor, Hieronymus Boner, and published by the city council. Wickram used his journeys as an inspiration for his writing: his works show that wild animals and robbers were constant threats to the traveler in the sixteenth century.

In 1545 a "translation" by Wickram of Ovid's *Metamorphoses* was published, but the book is really a slightly altered version of Albrecht von Halberstadt's translation (1190 or 1210). Wickram on several occasions admitted that he did not know Latin; thus, a complete translation by Wickram is inconceivable. The book has been used by critics as evidence of the lack of originality in Wickram's works in general; some have accused him of plagiarism. The woodcuts in the 1545 edition, at least, are Wickram's own, but it is doubtful that he worked professionally as an artist. It is not known how Wickram acquired a copy of Albrecht's manuscript, which exists today only in fragmentary form. Wickram's adaptation of the text was accompanied by a critical commentary by the Catholic cleric Gerhard Lorichius. Three later editions of Albrecht's translation, printed between 1581 and 1609, used Wickram's adaptation as a model but completely reworked it.

In 1546, in Schlettstadt, Wickram bought a manuscript of *Meistersingerlieder* (Meistersinger songs) by the Nuremberg shoemaker and author Sachs. In the same year Wickram became a citizen of Colmar when he inherited a house from his father; citizenship made it possible for him to join one of the guilds, the organizations that carried out the strictly organized and hierarchic *Meistersang*. That same year a Meistersinger group was formed in Colmar, modeled after those in Freiburg, Nuremberg, and Augsburg. Some of Wickram's narratives include short songs in the tradition of the Meistersinger. In 1549 the *Meistersingerschule* (Meistersinger school) was approved by the city council. Around this time Wickram married a woman named Anna; no other information is available about the marriage.

The last decade of Wickram's life was his most productive period. The year 1550 brought the publication of his *Ein schön und nützliches Biblisches Spiel von . . . Tobia* (A Beautiful and Useful Biblical Play about . . . Tobias), and the following year his novel *Eine schöne und doch klägliche History* (A Beautiful and Lamentable Story), generally known as *Gabriotto und Reinhart,* appeared. Based on a novella in Giovanni Boccaccio's *Decameron* (1351-1353), *Gabriotto und Reinhart* is the story of two virtuous young men of the lower nobility who fall in love with women of a higher social class; it ends with the deaths of the four young people, who are unable to comply with the rules set by society. Gabriotto and Reinhart leave the royal court in Paris with Gabriotto's father after a disagreement with the king. The two young men decide to move to the royal court of England but want to see some other countries on their way; their rather peculiar journey shows that the sixteenth-century burgher had a somewhat vague idea of European geography. Arriving in London, Gabriotto and Reinhart are welcomed and shown great respect, which grows as their talents and skills prove to be outstanding. The young men are knighted, less because of their success in tournaments than because of their virtue; Wickram's knights have much more in common with the rising city dwellers than with the heroes of medieval epics. Gabriotto and Reinhart fall in love with Philomena, the king's sister, and Rosamunda, the daughter of a wealthy count, respectively; their love is immediately reciprocated. As in *Ritter Galmy uß Schottland,* love has to be kept secret, and the relationships are betrayed by envious rivals. Gabriotto and Reinhart have to leave the court, but they do so only after secretly marrying the young women. The marriages are never consummated; sexual love does not exist in Wickram's works unless it is used to show the immorality of humankind. His characters never go beyond friendly hugs and longing looks. Gabriotto and Reinhart are allowed to return after a while, but Gabriotto has to flee again after the king finds out—apparently for the first time— about his relationship with Philomena. Gabriotto dies of a broken heart; after Philomena learns of his death, she, too, dies. Reinhart and Rosamunda soon follow them. Not until they are all dead does the king regret his harshness.

One can interpret the ending of *Gabriotto und Reinhart* in two ways. On the one hand, Wickram may want to show that young people must accept the rules of society; if they act secretly, marrying clandestinely to get around the law, they must be punished. On the other hand, he may want to show that the existing rules are cruel: virtuous people should be rewarded for their virtue; if they truly love each other they

Title page for Wickram's play that presents a modernized version of the Prodigal Son story

should be allowed to marry, regardless of their social status. The two interpretations are not mutually exclusive. Wickram believed in an orderly society; he was opposed to clandestine marriages. But he regarded nobility of the heart and soul as equal to that of blood. The main characters in *Gabriotto und Reinhart* are punished for acting without parental consent; but they are all buried together, and the king regrets having caused them so much pain. *Gabriotto und Reinhart* appeared in nine editions before 1650. As in *Ritter Galmy uß Schottland,* Wickram here reworked an old plot for his own purposes. The use of well-known themes and topics was common in this precopyright era, but the sixteenth century witnessed a change in this situation as authors started to regard their texts as their own: Erasmus, for example, often complained about his works being published without his permission. *Ritter Galmy uß Schottland* had originally been published anonymously, but Wickram's later works all carried his name.

Gabriotto und Reinhart was followed in 1552 by *Ein schönes . . . Spyl auß den geschichten der Aposteln gezogen* (A Beautiful . . . Play Drawn from the Stories of

Title page for the second edition of Wickram's collection of anecdotes for travelers

the Apostles), better known as the *Apostelspiel* (Drama of the Apostels)—the first known independently published German drama of its kind in the sixteenth century. In 1555 Wickram returned to the theme of the Prodigal Son for one of his more popular prose narratives, *Der Jungen Knaben Spiegel* (Manual for Young Boys), in which an old knight and his wife raise Friedbert, a farmer's son, as their own, believing themselves unable to produce children. After a year the wife gives birth to a son, Wilbald, and the two boys are brought up together. While Friedbert becomes a virtuous adolescent, Wilbald comes under the influence of the butcher's son, the evil Lothar. Wilbald and Lothar gamble, drink, and steal and are forced to leave town. For a time they travel together through central Europe as outlaws, but after a disagreement they separate. Wilbald is finally forgiven by his parents after falling to the bottom rung of the social ladder and repenting for his behavior, while Lothar is convicted of theft and hanged. In the preface Wickram says that the work is meant to teach young boys to obey their parents and avoid bad company. A dramatic version of *Der Jungen Knaben Spiegel* had been published the previous year under the title *Knaben Spiegel*.

Shortly thereafter followed the chapbook *Rollwagenbüchlein* (Carriage Booklet, 1555), which was printed in at least seventeen editions between 1555 and 1613. The book was intended as educational entertainment for people traveling long distances in carriages. None of the stories is more than a few pages long; they are anecdotes, using humor and satire to describe the foolishness of humankind in a manner similar to that of Johannes Pauli's *Schimpf und Ernst* (Mischief and Morality, 1522).

Von guten und bösen Nachbaurn (Of Good and Bad Neighbors, 1556) was Wickram's last, and least successful, prose narrative. In this novel Wickram portrays, for the only time in his career, the lives of city dwellers; this feature has made the work an important text for twentieth-century researchers. Here there are no more social conflicts. The story follows a family and their friends and neighbors through three generations. The merchant Robertus and his family live in Antwerp. An evil neighbor causes Robertus constant trouble, and when nine of his ten children die of a terrible disease, Robertus decides to leave Antwerp and take over a relative's business in Lisbon. The transition is made without difficulty; there are no language barriers or culture shocks. Having traveled away from his native Alsace only a few times, and never to a foreign country, Wickram was probably not aware of differences in culture or geography; in his works Europe looks the same everywhere, and his characters never have a problem communicating with each other. Only once in *Von guten und bösen Nachbaurn* does a character have to leave home to learn a different language.

On a business trip Robertus meets a Spanish merchant, Richard, who becomes his best friend and marries his only daughter. The newlywed couple stays with her parents—the beginning of an extended family. Soon a third friend, the goldsmith Lasarus, is introduced. He and his wife move into the house next to Robertus's. Lasarus's wife and Robertus's daughter become pregnant at the same time and give birth, respectively, to Lasarus Jr. and Amelia. The youngsters grow up as friends and fall in love in their teens. Their marriage is desired by all members of both families; the only problem is that Lasarus Jr. and Amelia have fallen in love too young. Though it is difficult to determine Wickram's confessional standing, he was clearly opposed to the Catholic custom—especially practiced by the upper classes—of child marriage. Before the marriage Lasarus Jr. is sent away to finish his education so that he will be able to support a family. At the end all the couples are living happy and peaceful Christian lives, with God as the head of the "family." *Von guten und bösen Nachbaurn* is clearly a didactic work, presenting models of good behavior. Sexual love is assumed to exist only within marriage; anything that might give the rising urban middle class a bad reputation is left out.

The novel *Der Goldtfaden,* published in 1557, was already completed when Wickram published *Eine Wahrhafftige History von einem ungeratenen Son in ein Dialogum gestellet* (A True Story of a Prodigal Son Presented in a Dialogue), in which he defends his right to write fiction, in late 1554 or early 1555. In the dialogue Wickram mentions that *Der Goldtfaden* is soon to appear in print. It is unknown why it took so long for the book to be published, but in late 1554 or early 1555 Wickram became town clerk in Burgheim on the Rhine, and at this time there was a change of publishers: with few exceptions, Wickram used the Strasbourg printery of Jacob Frölich until 1554; after that year all but two of his works were printed by Johann Knobloch the Younger, also in Strasbourg. *Der Goldtfaden* was printed by Frölich; possibly an agreement to publish the book had been made with Frölich before Wickram moved to Burgheim. In *Der Goldtfaden,* the most popular of Wickram's works, Lionel, the son of a poor shepherd, rises to the nobility through virtuous conduct and diligence. Once again, Wickram is showing that nobility derives not from the bloodline but from the heart.

According to his own statements in *Der Irr Reitend Bilger* (The Lost Pilgrim, 1556), in 1555 Wickram suffered severe health problems and was bedridden for various periods. His poor health is evident in his choice of topics: while *Rollwagenbüchlein* shows Wickram's humorous side, his three last works—*Dialogus, in welchem angezogen wirt das mechtig hauptlaster von der trunckenheit* (Dialogue, in Which the Powerful Major Sin of Drunkenness Is Pointed Out, 1555), *Der Irr Reitend Bilger,* and *Die Siben Hauptlaster* (The Seven Major Sins, 1556)—present the thoughts of an old person facing death.

After January 1556 Wickram is unheard of until he is claimed to be dead in the preface to the 1562 edition of *Tobias.* Scholars of the twentieth century have come to the conclusion that Wickram's weakness is also his strength: the lack of a formal education cut him off from much humanist thinking and theorizing, and that, in addition to his life away from the cultural centers of Europe, enabled him to develop an original style.

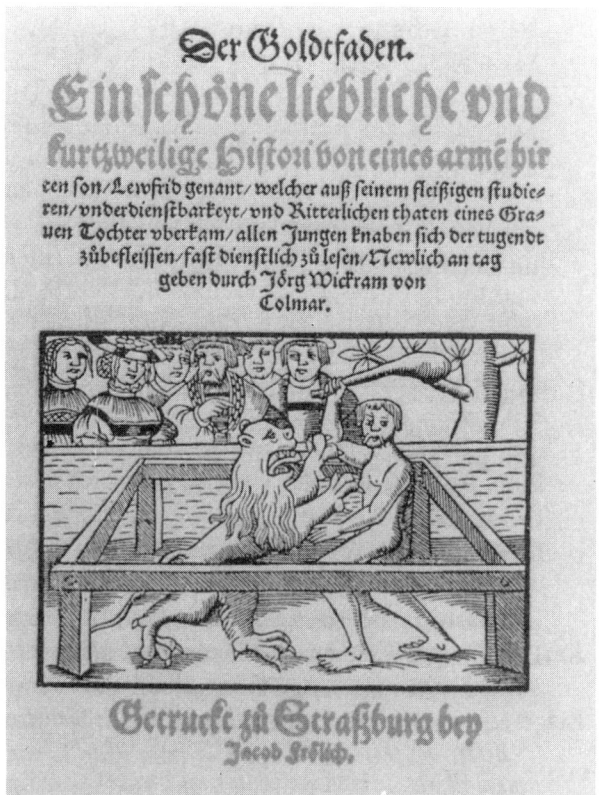

Title page for Wickram's most popular work, a novel about a poor shepherd's son who rises to the aristocracy because of his virtue

References:

Eleanor Margaret Barnes, "Georg Wickram's Meisterlied Anthology from Colmar: Ms cgm 4998," dissertation, University of California at Los Angeles, 1969;

Wolfgang Beutin, "Jörg Wickram," in *Deutsche Dichter: Leben und Werk deutschsprachiger Autoren,* volume 2: *Reformation, Renaissance und Barock,* edited by Gunter E. Grimm and Frank Rainer Max (Stuttgart: Reclam, 1988), pp. 78–88;

Miriam Usher Chrisman, *Lay Culture, Learned Culture: Books and Social Change in Strasbourg, 1480–1599* (New Haven: Yale University Press, 1982), pp. 209–222;

Hannelore Christ, *Literarischer Text und historische Realität: Versuch einer historisch-materialistischen Analyse von Jörg Wickrams Knabenspiegel- und Nachbarn- Roman,* Literatur in der Gesellschaft, volume 22 (Düsseldorf: Bertelsmann, 1974);

Karl Goedeke, *Grundriß zur Geschichte der deutschen Dichtung* (Hannover: Ehlermann, 1859);

Bodo Gotzkowsky, *'Volksbücher': Prosaroman, Renaissancenovellen, Versdichtungen und Schwankbücher. Bibliographie der Deutschen Drucke,* 2 volumes

(Baden-Baden: Koermer, 1991, 1994), I: 442-453, 574-583; II: 120-125, 180-181;

Walter Haug, "Jörg Wickrams *Ritter Galmy:* Die Zähmung des Romans als Ursprung seiner Möglichkeit," in *Traditionswandel und Traditionsverhalten,* edited by Haug and Burckhart Wachinger (Tübingen: Niemeyer, 1991);

Reinhold Jacobi, "Jörg Wickrams Romane: Interpretation unter besonderer Berücksichtigung der zeitgenössischen Erzählprosa," dissertation, Bonn University, 1970;

Hannes Kästner, "Der irr reitende Pilger: Jörg Wickrams Reisephantasien und das Ende der Pilgerfahrt," *Germanisch-Romanische Monatsschrift,* new series 36 (1986): 380-398;

Dieter Kartschoke, " 'Bald bracht Phebus seinen Wagen . . . ': Gattungsgeschichtliche Überlegungen zu Jörg Wickrams Nachbarn-Roman," *Daphnis,* 11 (1982): 717-741;

Kartschoke, "Jörg Wickrams Dialog vom ungeratenen Sohn," *Daphnis,* 7 (1978): 377-401;

Erich Kleinschmidt, "Jörg Wickram," in *Deutsche Dichter der frühen Neuzeit (1450-1600): Ihr Leben und Werk,* edited by Stephan Füssel (Berlin: Erich Schmidt, 1993), pp. 494-511;

Kleinschmidt, *Stadt und Literatur in der frühen Neuzeit: Voraussetzungen und Entfaltung im südwestdeutschen, elsässischen und schweizerischen Städteraum* (Cologne & Vienna: Böhlau, 1982), pp. 238-261;

Jan Knopf, *Frühzeit des Bürgers: Erfahrene und verleugnete Realität in den Romanen Wickrams, Grimmelshausens, Schnabels* (Stuttgart: Metzler, 1978);

Clemens Lugowski, *Die Form der Individualität im Roman* (Frankfurt am Main: Suhrkamp, 1976);

Irmela von der Lühe, "Jörg Wickram: Von guten und bösen Nachbarn," in *Einführung in die deutsche Literatur III,* edited by Winfried Frey, Walter Raitz, and Dieter Seitz (Opladen: Westdeutscher Verlag, 1981), pp. 190-210;

Ulrich Maché, "Soziale Mobilität in den Romanen Jörg Wickrams," in *Virtus et Fortuna: Festschrift für Hans-Gert Roloff,* edited by Joseph P. Strelka and Jörg Jungmayr (Bern: Peter Lang, 1983), pp. 184-197;

G. J. Martin-ten Wolthuis, "Der Goldfaden des Jörg Wickram von Colmar," *Zeitschrift für deutsche Philologie,* 87 (1968): 46-85;

Jan-Dirk Müller, "Frühbürgerliche Privatheit und altständische Gemeinschaft: Zu Jörg Wickrams Historie von Guten und Bösen Nachbarn," *Internationales Archiv für Sozialgeschichte der Deutschen Literatur,* 5 (1980): 1-32;

Müller, "Jörg Wickram zu Liebe und Ehe," in *Wandel der Geschlechterbeziehungen zu Beginn der Neuzeit,* edited by Heide Wunder and Christina Vanja (Frankfurt am Main: Suhrkamp, 1991), pp. 27-42;

Müller, "Vertauschte Väter und verlorene Söhne: Versuch der sozialhistorischen Entzifferung eines literarischen Motivs bei Jörg Wickram," in *Akten des VI. Germanisten-Kongreßes Basel 1980: Jahrbuch für Internationale Germanistik,* series A, volume 8 (IV), edited by Heinz Rupp and Hans-Gert Roloff (Bern: Peter Lang, 1980), pp. 247-255;

Christoph Petzsch, "Jörg Wickrams Singergesellschaft und ihre große Liederhandschrift," *Annuaire de Colmar,* 25 (1975-1976): 91-119;

Hans-Gert Roloff, "Gabriotto und Reinhardt," "Der Jungen Knaben Spiegel," "Der Goldtfaden," in *Lexikon der Weltliteratur: Hauptwerke der Weltliteratur,* volume 2, edited by Gero von Wilpert (Stuttgart: Kroner, 1968), pp. 337, 396, 540;

Roloff, "Überredung–Unterricht–Ergetzung der Leute: Zur Funktion der Romane Georg Wickrams," *Rechèrches Germaniques,* 9 (1979): 263-277;

Wilhelm Scherer, *Die Anfänge des deutschen Prosaromans und Jörg Wickram von Colmar* (Strasbourg: Trübner, 1877);

Erich Schmidt, "Beiträge zur Geschichte der Deutschen Literatur im Elsaß: Jörg Wickram," *Archiv für Literaturgeschichte,* 8 (1879): 317-357;

Eli Sobel, "Jörg Wickram, Hans Sachs und Meistergesang in Colmar," in *Virtus et Fortuna: Festschrift für Hans-Gert Roloff,* edited by Joseph P. Strelka and Jörg Jungmayr (Bern: Peter Lang, 1983), pp. 198-207;

Ingeborg Spriewald, "Jörg Wickram und die Anfänge der realistischen Prosaerzählung in Deutschland," dissertation, University of Potsdam, 1971;

Karl Stackmann, "Auslegungen des Gerhard Lorichius zur Metamorphosen-Nachdichtung Jörg Wickrams," *Zeitschrift für deutsche Philologie,* Sonderheft, 86 (1967): 120-160;

Marga Stede, " 'Ein grausame unnd erschrockenliche History . . . ': Bemerkungen zum Ursprung und zur Erzählweise von Georg Wickrams Rollwagenbüchlein-Geschichte über einen Mord im Elsaß," *Daphnis,* 15 (1986): 124-134;

August Stöber, *Jörg Wickram* (Mühlhausen: Rißler, 1866).

Jakob Wimpfeling

(25 June 1450 – 15 November 1528)

James H. Overfield
University of Vermont

BOOKS: *De arte metrificandi libellus* (Memmingen, 1484);

Laudes ecclesiae Spirensis (Basel: Michael Wenssler, 1486);

Epistole et carmina quibus elegantissime in medium datur repudiatio filie Regis Romanorum Maximiliani per Regem Francorum Carolum facta et superductio filie ducis Britonum, prefati Romanorum Regis sponse (N.p., 1492);

Immunitatis et libertatis ecclesiasticae statusque sacerdotalis defensio (N.p., 1493);

Oratio querulosa contra Invasores Sacerdotum (N.p., 1493);

De triplici candore Mariae ad reverendissimum D. Bertholdum Hennenbergensem Archiepiscopum Maguntinum et principem sacrosancti Ro. imperii electorem (N.p., 1493);

Elegantiarum Medulla: oratoriaque precepta. in ordinem inventu facilem copiose: clare: breviterque reducta (N.p., 1493);

Elegantiae majores. Rhetorica pueris utilissima (N.p., 1493);

De nuntio angelico ad Philippum Comitem palatinum Heroicum ad Ludovicum eius primogentium, Elegiacum (Basel: Johann Bergmann von Olpe, 1494);

Ad illustrissimum Principem Eberardum Wyrtenbergensem Theccensemque ducem Carmen Heroicum, Hecatostichon (Strasbourg: Johann Prüss, 1495);

Stylpho (N.p., 1496);

Isidoneus germanicus ad R. D. Georgium de Gemmingen Spirensem prepositum (Strasbourg: Johann Grüninger, 1497);

Philippica Jacobi Wimpflingi Sletstatini. In laudem et defensionem Philippi Comitis Rheni Palatini Bavariae Ducis (Strasbourg: Martin Schott, 1498);

Agatharchia. Id est bonus Principatus: vel Epithoma condicionum boni Principis (Strasbourg: Martin Schott, 1498);

Pro concordia dialecticorum et oratorum inque philosophia diversas opiniones sectantium quos modernos et antiquos vocant (N.p., 1499);

De Himnorum et Sequentiarum auctoribus. Generibusque Carminum que in Hymnis inveniuntur (Speyer: Conrad Hist, 1499);

Adolescentia (Strasbourg: Martin Flach, 1500);

Germania Jacobi Wimpffelingi ad Rembublicam Argentinensem (Strasbourg: Johann Prüss, 1501)–includes "Declamatio Philippi beroaldi de tribus fratribus ebrioso, scortatore et lusore" and "Oratio de annuntiatione angelica";

Declaratio Jacobi Wimpfelingii ad mitigandum adversarium (N.p., 1502);

Epistola Ia. Wymphelingi de inepta et superflua verborum resolucione in cancellis: et de abusu exempcionis in favorem omnium episcoporum et archiepiscoporum (Basel: J. Wolff, 1503);

De integritate libellus (Strasbourg: Johann Knobloch the Elder, 1505);

Epithoma rerum Germanicarum usque ad nostra tempora (Strasbourg: Johann Prüss, 1505);

Soliloquium Wimphelingii Pro pace Christianorum et pro Helvetiis ut resipiscant (N.p., 1505);

Appologetica [sic] declaratio Wimphelingij in libellum suum de integritate (Strasbourg: Johann Knobloch the Elder, 1505);

Apologia pro Republica Christiana (Pforzheim: Thomas Anshelm, 1506);

Contra quendam qui se Franciscum Schatzer appellat: complicesque suos: Expurgatio Ja. wimphelingi (Strasbourg: Johann Prüss, 1506);

Epistola excusatoria ad Suevos (Strasbourg: Matthias Hupfuff, 1506);

De vita et miraculis Joannis Gerson. Defensio Wimphelingii pro divo Joanne Gerson: et clero seculari: qui in libro (cui titulus supplementum celifodine) graviter taxati sunt et reprehensi (Strasbourg: Johann Knobloch the Elder, 1506);

Jacobi Vimpfelingii Schletstattensis Theosophi Oratio de sancto spiritu (Pforzheim: Thomas Anshelm, 1507);

Ad Julium II. Pontificem max. Querulosa excusatio Iacobi Wimphelingii ad instantiam Fratrum Augustinensium ad curiam Romanam citati: ut propria in persona ibidem compareat: propterea quod scripsit divum

Augustinum non fuisse monachum vel fratrem mendicantem (Strasbourg: Johann Prüss, 1507);

Avisamentum de concubinariis non absolvendis quibuscunque: ac eorum periculis quamplurimis. A theologis coloniensibus approbatum cum additionibus sacratissimorum canonum (Nuremberg: Hieronymus Höltzel, 1507);

Argentinensium Episcoporum Cathalogus: cum eorundem vita atque certis historiis: rebusque gestis: et illustratione totius fere Episcopatus Argentinensis (Strasbourg, 1507);

In Johannis Keiserspergii theologi: doctrina: vitaque probatissimi: primi Argentinensis Ecclesie predicatoris mortem: Planctus et Lamentatio cum aliquali vite sue descriptione et quorundam Epitaphiis (Oppenheim, 1510);

Contra turpem libellum Philomusi. Defensio theologiae scholasticae et neotericorum. Continentur in hoc opusculo, a Jacobo Vuim. licen. extemporali et tumultuaria syntaxi concinnato: Virtuosa sterilis musae ad nobilem et subtilem philosophiam comparatio. Subtilis dialecticae theologiaeque scholasticae quae per questiones procedit defensio. Theologorum de duobus vitiis quae mulopoeta ipsis asscripsit excusatio (N.p., 1510);

Soliloquium ad divum Augustinum (N.p., 1512);

Orationis Angeli Anachoritae vallis Umbrosae ad Julium II super concilio Lateranensi confirmatio cum exaggeratione Jac. Wimph. heremitae sylvae hercinae (N.p., 1512);

Oratio vulgi ad deum Op. Max. Pro ecclesia catholica et romana (N.p., 1512);

Casigationes locorum in canticis ecclesiasticis et divinis officiis depravatorum Iacobi Wimpfelingii Sletstattensis (Strasbourg: Johannes Schott, 1513);

Hymni de tempore et de sanctis: in eam formam qua a suis autoribus scripti sunt denuo redacti: et secundum legem carminis diligenter emendati atque interpretati (Strasbourg: Johann Knobloch the Elder, 1513);

Ad Leonem decimum pontificem maximum carmen Jacob Wimphelingii contra prodigos in scorta in tanta pauperum, pustulatorum et puerorum expositorum multitudine (N.p., 1514);

Diatriba jacobi wimphelingii Seletstattini: sacre pagine licentiati De proba institutione puerorum in trivialibus: et adolescentum in unversalibus gymnasiis. De interpretandis ecclesiae collectis Regulae XVI. De ordine vite sacerdotalis (Hagenau, 1514);

Germania Aeneae Sylvii. In qua candide lector continentur. Gravamina Germanicae nationis. Confutatio eorundum cum replicis, Etc. (Strasbourg: Reinhard Beck, 1515);

Gravamina germanicae nationis cum remediis et avisamentis ad Caesarem Maiestatem (Sélestat: Lazarus Schürer, 1518);

Divo Maximiliano iubente Pragmticae sanctionis Medulla excerpta (Sélestat: Lazarus Schürer, 1520).

Editions: *Germania,* edited by Charles Schmidt Straßburger Studien, no. 3 (Geneva: Flick, 1875)—also includes "Nova Germania," by Thomas Murner;

Jacob Wimpfelings Germania, edited by Ernst Martin (Strasbourg: Schultz, 1884);

Stylpho, edited by Martin (Strasbourg: Schultz, 1888);

Jacobus Wimpfelingius Stylpho in der ursprünglichen Fassung, Lateinische Literaturdenkmäler des XV. und XVI. Jahrhunderts, no. 6 (Berlin: Weidmann, 1892);

Pädagogische Schriften, edited and translated into German by Joseph Freundgen (Paderborn: Schöningh, 1898)—comprises "Isidoneus Germanicus" and "Adolescentia";

Responsa et replicae ad Eneam Silvium, und Aeneas Sylvius, Germania, edited by Adolf Schmidt (Cologne & Graz: Böhlau, 1962);

Adolescentia, edited by Otto Herding, Jacobi Wimpfelingi opera selecta, volume 1 (Munich: Fink, 1965);

Das Leben des Johannes Geiler von Kaysersberg, by Wimpfeling and Beatus Rhenanus, edited by Herding, Jacobi Wimpfelingi opera selecta, volume 2 (Munich: Fink, 1970);

Stylpho. Lateinisch und deutsch, edited and translated by Harry S. Schnur (Stuttgart: Reclam, 1971);

"Agatharchia," edited by Bruno Singer, in his *Die Fürstenspiegel in Deutschland im Zeitalter des Humanismus und der Reformation* (Munich: Fink, 1981).

OTHER: *Tractatus resitutionum usuarum et excommunicationum,* edited by Wimpfeling (Speyer, 1489);

Ludolf of Saxony, *Ludolfi Carthusiensis qui et autor fuit vite Christi: in Psalterium expositio,* edited by Wimpfeling (N.p., 1491);

Theodore Gresemund the Younger, *Theoderici Gresemundi junioris Moguntini lucubratiunculae, bonarum septem artium liberalium Apologiam eiusdemque cum philosophia dialogum et orationem ad rerum publicarum rectores in se complectentes,* edited by Wimpfeling (Mainz: Peter Friedberg, 1495);

Conrad Schellig, *In pustulas malas, morbum, quem malum de Francia vulgus appellat, quae sunt de genere formicarum: salubre consilium doctoris Conradi Schellig Heidelberg,* edited by Wimpfeling (N.p., 1500);

Marsilus of Inghen, *Questiones Marsilii super quattuor libros sententiorum,* edited by Wimpfeling (Strasbourg: Martin Flach, 1501);

Hrabanus Maurus, *Magnencii Rabani Mauri de laudibus sancte crucis opus eruditione versu prosaque mirificum,* edited by Wimpfeling (Pforzheim: Thomas Anshelm, 1501);

Battista Mantovano, *Baptistae Mantuani duarum Parthenicum libri,* edited by Wimpfeling (N.p. 1502);

John Gerson, *Quarta pars operum Johannis Gerson prius non impressa,* edited by Wimpfeling (Strasbourg: Johann Prüss, 1502);

Mantuanus, *F. Baptiste Mantuani Bucolica seu adolescentia in decem aeglogas [sic] divisa,* edited by Wimpfeling (Strasbourg: Johann Prüss, 1503);

Statuta synodalia episcopatus Basiliensis, edited by Wimpfeling (N.p., 1503);

Giovanni Pico della Mirandola, *Opera Joannis Pici Mirandule Comitis Concordie: litterarum principis novissime accurate revisa . . . quarumcunque facultatum professoribus tam iucunda quam proficua,* edited by Wimpfeling (Strasbourg: Johann Prüss, 1504);

Biblia latina cum postillis Hugonis a S. Caro tituli Sabinae cardinalis primi de ordine divi Dominici, edited by Wimpfeling (Basel: Johannes Amerbach, 1504);

Johann Eck, *Logicae exercitamenta, appellata parva logicalia,* edited by Wimpfeling (N.p., 1506);

Konrad Summenhart, *Conradi Summenhard Commentaria in summam physicae Alberti magni,* edited by Wimpfeling (Hagenau, 1507);

Henry of Langenstein, *Speculum anime seu soliloquium Heinrici de Hassia maximi theologi secularis,* edited by Wimpfeling (Strasbourg: Johann Knobloch the Elder, 1507);

Lupold of Bebenburg, *De juribus et translatione imperii,* edited by Wimpfeling (Strasbourg: Matthias Schürer, 1508);

Johannes Altenstag, *Vocabularius Joh. Altenstaig,* edited by Wimpfeling (Pforzheim: Thomas Anshelm, 1511);

Desiderius Erasmus, *Moria encomium. Erasmi Rhoterodami declamatio,* edited by Wimpfeling (Strasbourg: Matthias Schürer, 1511);

Johannes Oecolampadius, *Declamationes Jo. Icolampadii De passione et ultimo sermone, Hoc est sacrosanctis septem dictis domini nostri Jesu Christi in cruce,* edited by Wimpfeling (Strasbourg: Matthias Schürer, 1512);

Stephan Hoest, *Modus predicandi subtilis et compendiosus Stephani Hoest theologi viae modernae Heidelbergensis. Oratio eiusdem ad synodum Spirensem. . . . Tetrastichum eiusdem in ambitionem cuisdam fraterculi,* edited by Wimpfeling (Strasbourg: Johann Prüss, 1513);

Jodocus Clichtoveus, *Dogma moralium philosophorum, compendiose et studiose collectum a Jodoco Clichtoveo,* edited by Wimpfeling (Strasbourg: Matthias Schürer, 1513);

Erasmus, *Desiderii Erasmi Roterodami de duplici copia verborum et rerum commentarii duo,* edited by Wimpfeling (Strasbourg: Matthias Schürer, 1514);

Petrus Aureolus, *Breviarium bibliorum seu epitome universe s. Scripturae juxta literalem sensum,* edited by Wimpfeling (Strasbourg: Johannes Schott, 1514);

Henry of Langenstein, *Henricus de Hassia plantator Gymnasii Viennensis in Austria contra disceptationes et contrarias praedicationes fratrum mendicantium super conceptione beatissime Virginis Mariae et contra maculam S. Bernhardo mendicatium impositam,* edited by Wimpfeling (Strasbourg: Reinhard Beck, 1516);

Nicholas of Dinkelsbühl, *Tractatus hoc volumine contenti. I De dilectione dei et proximi. II De preceptis decalogi. III De Oratione dominica. IIII De tribus partibus penitentie. V De octo beatitudinibus. VI De septem peccatis mortalibus et septem virtutibus illis oppositis. VII Confessionale. VIII De quinque sensibus,* edited by Wimpfeling (Strasbourg: Johannes Schott, 1516);

Johannes Nider, *Formicarius Joannis Nyder theologi profundissimi, pulcherrimus Dialogus ad vitam christianam exemplo conditionum Formice incitativus historiisque Germanie refertissimus,* edited by Wimpfeling (Strasbourg: Johannes Knobloch the Elder, 1517);

Egidius of Rome, *Lamentatio Petri Aegidii in obitum Caesaris Maximiliani. Et in hanc Scholia pauca in gratiam amici a Jacobo Spiegel Schlestadiensis adiecta,* edited by Wimpfeling (Strasbourg: Matthias Hupfuff, 1519);

Mantovano, *F. Baptistae Mantuani Carmelitae theologi fastorum libri XII quibus praemittitur Carmen ad Julium II pontificem maximum. Carmen ad Leonem X pontificem maximum. Vita auctoris a se ipso descripta carmine elegiaco,* edited by Wimpfeling (Sélestat: Lazarus Schürer, 1520);

Ersamus, *D. Erasmi Roterodami epistola ad reverendissimum archiepiscopum ac Cardinalem Moguntinum, qua commonefacit illius celsitudienem de causa Martini Lutheri,* edited by Wimpfeling (Sélestat: Matthias Schürer, 1520);

Hieronymus Emser, *Canonis missae contra Huldricum Zwinglium defensio,* edited by Wimpfeling (N.p., 1524).

In the twenty-second chapter of his *De integritate* (On Uprightness, 1505), a fervent plea for priests to lead blameless lives and serve as moral beacons for their parishioners, the fifty-five-year-old

Jakob Wimpfeling recalled an event from his youth that changed his life. As a new student at the University of Erfurt the nineteen-year-old Wimpfeling was sitting in a church when his eyes were drawn to a motto written on the wall: "Sin not, God sees it." Wimpfeling, perhaps uneasy over his adolescent romances and the sensuous, Ovid-inspired love poems he had recently composed, was struck to the core. So searing was the message, Wimpfeling recalled, that from that time onward he dedicated himself to the pursuit of modesty, chastity, and holiness. In this pursuit he was, to a great degree, successful. He became a deeply pious, earnest, and industrious man, who, through scholarship, example, and exhortation, worked tirelessly for educational and religious reform and the betterment of German society.

Wimpfeling's contemporaries and later historians have included him in the ranks of the German humanists, but he represented the most conservative and tentative wing of the movement. Trained in Scholastic theology and philosophy, he knew no Greek, never traveled to Italy, and, although a vehement critic of clerical abuses, never questioned the rites and teachings of the Catholic Church. He shared the humanists' conviction that classical literature provided the best models for speaking and writing Latin, but he was equally convinced that classical literature was filled with moral perils and had to be read with great circumspection. He also shared the humanists' goal of achieving the moral regeneration of society through improved education; but for Wimpfeling, morality was narrowly and exclusively defined by traditional Catholic doctrine and practice.

Wimpfeling's ancestors had been peasants, but his father, Nikolaus, had moved to the Alsatian imperial city of Sélestat (Schlettstadt), where he was a saddler and harness maker. Nikolaus married a local woman, Katarina Bleger, and they had three children: Ulrich, who would take over his father's business; Magdalena, who would marry a local baker; and, on 25 June 1450, Jakob, who was groomed for the priesthood from an early age. He was sent to the local Latin school, whose director, Louis Dringenberg, stressed traditional methods of Latin instruction and sought to inculcate in his students self-discipline and reverence for the ceremonies and rites of the church.

Nikolaus Wimpfeling died in 1463, and Jakob was placed under the guardianship of his paternal uncle Ulrich, a parish priest in the Alsatian town of Sulz. In 1464 he was sent to the University of Freiburg im Breisgau, where he continued his studies of Latin grammar and learned the rudiments of Scholastic logic and philosophy. Humanism was not yet a major force at the university, but while there Wimpfeling developed a mild interest in classical poetry. As a student he wrote his first Latin verse, modeled on the *carmina amatoria* (love songs) of Ovid. The most significant event in his two years at Freiburg was the beginning of his acquaintance with Johannes Geiler von Kaysersberg, then a student of theology and an instructor in the arts faculty. Geiler von Kaysersberg, who would later have a distinguished career as the Strasbourg cathedral preacher, became Wimpfeling's model and lifelong friend. Wimpfeling received his bachelor of arts degree in 1466. In 1469 he briefly attended the University of Erfurt, then matriculated at the University of Heidelberg, where he received his master of arts degree in 1471.

After trying and quickly abandoning the study of canon law, Wimpfeling began to study theology at Heidelberg. He became a bachelor of theology in 1479 and a bachelor of the sacred page in 1481. While studying theology he taught in the faculty of arts and was chosen to fill several university offices: member of the university council, dean of the arts faculty, and, in 1481–1482, rector of the university. He supported himself through livings provided by local Heidelberg churches and in 1478 succeeded his uncle as priest in the parish church in Sulz. Naming a vicar to carry out the actual priestly duties, Wimpfeling remained in Heidelberg but received income from the benefice until he relinquished it in 1500.

As a prominent Heidelberg academic, Wimpfeling was called upon to address university audiences and gatherings of local clergy. In these speeches he introduced themes that he would emphasize throughout his life. In 1477, for example, he exhorted the clergy of Mainz to maintain high moral standards, administer the sacraments with reverence, and seek individual and societal reform through education. In 1482, in a speech to an academic audience in the Church of the Holy Ghost in Heidelberg, he censured students for their debaucheries and depravities—most notably, brawling, drunkenness, gambling, whoring, and vandalism but also for wearing their hair too long. He also condemned monks for their ignorance and their failure to live up to the standards of Saint Bernard.

While at Heidelberg, Wimpfeling continued to write Latin poetry, much of it in praise of the university's patrons, the Palatine Wittelsbachs, and their ancestors. He also composed his *De arte metrificandi* (The Art of Metrifying), a thin volume on versification that became his first published work in 1484. It went through many editions and for a quarter of a century was Germany's most popular textbook on how to write poetry. His best-known literary work from his Heidelberg years was *Stylpho*, a student drama performed in 1480 under his direction as part of the faculty of arts graduation ceremonies; it was published in 1496. Supposedly inspired by Terence, the play traces the lives of two churchmen. The hero, Vincentius, studies hard, becomes an exemplary priest, and ascends through the ecclesiastical hierarchy until he becomes a bishop. Stylpho drops out of school and heads for Rome, where he seeks ecclesiastical preferment by ingratiating himself with a cardinal. His strategy seems to pay off when he is nominated to a prime ecclesiastical office in Germany, but a worthy bishop blocks his path by demanding that Stylpho first pass a Latin examination. Stylpho fails and becomes a pig-keeper. *Stylpho* is credited with being Germany's first Latin school drama, a genre that was to become a staple of German schools during the Reformation era.

In 1484 Wimpfeling abandoned academic life to become a canon in the Speyer cathedral chapter with special responsibilities for preaching. He did relatively little preaching—according to some biographers, because of his weak voice and lack of stamina—but he participated fully in the liturgical life of the cathedral while continuing to write and publish. He made occasional trips to Heidelberg, where he worked toward his licentiate in theology—he would receive it in 1496—and to Worms, where he maintained contacts with the humanist circle around Bishop Johann von Dalberg.

Wimpfeling's writings during his years in Speyer attest to his broad intellectual interests. His devotion to the rich heritage of medieval Catholic rituals and beliefs is revealed in his poems dedicated to the Virgin Mary (in which he staunchly defends Mary's Immaculate Conception); his long and detailed poetic description and history of the Speyer cathedral, *Laudes ecclesiae Spirensis* (1486); and his efforts to collate and correct liturgical texts used in the local churches. His zeal as a reformer is shown in writings such as *Immunitatis et libertatis ecclesiasticae statusque sacerdotalis defensio* (Defense of Ecclesiastical Immunity and Liberty, 1493) and *Oratio querulosa contra Invasores Sacerdotum* (Plaintive Oration against Attackers of the Clergy, 1493), in which he defends the privileges of the clergy and demands that they lead exemplary lives. His German patriotism and pugnaciousness are revealed in the attack he published in 1492 on the French people, their king, Charles VIII, and the king's minister Robert Gaguin after Charles broke off his engagement to Emperor Maximilian I's daughter, Margarita, and married Anne of Brittany, who had been the emperor's fiancée. Finally, his conviction that Germany's future rested on its schools is shown in his *Elegantiarum Medulla* (Kernel of Elegancies, 1493), a Latin textbook, and his *Isidoneus germanicus* (German Guide, 1497), a long and rambling "how to" book for teachers. In these last two works Wimpfeling reveals his humanistic leanings in his interest in promoting good Latin style and his belief that education should teach morality, not just impart information. But he also shows his conservatism by warning teachers to avoid many ancient authors who would incite young readers to immorality.

By the end of the 1490s Wimpfeling seems to have become dissatisfied with his life at Speyer and to have considered withdrawing to monastic solitude in the Black Forest. Instead, in 1498 he rejoined the faculty of the University of Heidelberg in response to a call from Elector Philip, who sought Wimpfeling's assistance in implementing a reform of the university's curriculum along humanist lines. At Heidelberg he lectured on the letters of the church father Saint Jerome and the works of the fourth-century Christian poet Prudentius. He delivered several speeches before university audiences in which he reiterated his favorite themes: faculty members should suppress their bickering and open their minds to the introduction of literary studies into the curriculum; students should stay sober, put away their cards and dice, stay out of the brothels, and try harder to get along with the Heidelberg burghers. No major curriculum revisions, however, were accomplished while Wimpfeling was in residence.

Wimpfeling continued to publish prolifically during this second Heidelberg period. In 1498 he joined the ranks of the many medieval and early modern authors of "mirrors of princes." Wimpfeling's contribution to the genre, *Agatharchia* (Rule of the Good), written for the edification of Elector Philip's eldest son, Ludwig, said what literally hundreds of previous such works had said: a good prince should love his people, put his subjects' interests before his own, honor the church, and be honest, gracious, benevolent, just, and generous. Such a prince would be rewarded by a peaceful and prosperous reign on earth and heavenly bliss in the afterlife. In 1500 Wimpfeling published his second major treatise on education, *Adolescentia* (Youth). It is quintessential Wimpfeling—lengthy, rambling, and filled with quotes from the Bible, classical authors, medieval Scholastics, the church fathers, and Italian humanists. Through it all there is no missing the intensity of the author's message: education should teach self-discipline, moral earnestness, and respect for the church; it is the key to Germany's future.

In 1501, for reasons that are unclear, Wimpfeling left Heidelberg; for the next decade and a half he lived mainly in Strasbourg, close to his friends Geiler von Kaysersberg and Sebastian Brant. He also spent short periods in Basel, Speyer, Freiburg, and Solden, a small town near Freiburg. These were stormy, difficult years. After resigning from his parish in Sulz in 1500 and surrendering his prebend from the Church of the Holy Spirit in Heidelberg in 1501 in expectation of receiving a canonry in the Strasbourg cathedral, he was outraged when one of the bishop's favorites was named to the position instead. He struggled to make ends meet by piecing together several meager church offices, publishing voluminously, and tutoring sons of the Strasbourg patriciate—most notably, Jakob Sturm. Embittered by his circumstances, he became even more disillusioned with an ecclesiastical system that awarded men with connections and social standing but not learned and earnest priests like himself.

Yet his approach to church reform remained conservative and, in some respects, naive. In 1510 Emperor Maximilian I, angry because Pope Julius II had abandoned their alliance in the Italian Wars, announced his intention to reform the German Church along the lines of the French Pragmatic Sanction, and he called on Wimpfeling to come up with a plan of action. In his response, which was written in 1511 and published in 1518 as *Gravamina germanicae nationis* (Grievances of the German Nation) Wimpfeling compiled a long list of German complaints about corruption, financial exploitation, and favoritism in church appointments. But he cautioned Maximilian to move carefully: to limit papal power in Germany severely, as was done in the Pragmatic Sanction, would be a political and diplomatic disaster for the emperor. Rather than attack papal power, the emperor should attempt to persuade the Pope that everyone's best interest would be served if the Holy Father did something to respond to the Germans' complaints. Wimpfeling's strong propapal sentiments were confirmed when he published a speech, *Orationis Angeli Anachoritae . . . ad Julium II super concilio Lateranensi confirmatio cum exaggeratione* (An Affirmation with Added Material of the Speech of the Hermit Angelus to Julius II Concerning the Lateran Council, 1512), in which he supports the views of a monk named Angelus that the Pope, not secular princes, should shoulder the task of reforming the church.

Wimpfeling remained an active scholar during his years in Strasbourg. Around 1508 he organized the Strasbourg Literary Sodality, a loose association of friends of the classics modeled on the Rhenish and Danubian sodalities founded by the humanist poet Conrad Celtis. The high point in the organization's history took place in August 1514, when it hosted Desiderius Erasmus at the end of his trip from England to Basel. Wimpfeling toasted Erasmus as the "prince of all belles lettres," and Erasmus responded by praising his hosts' learning and morality.

Wimpfeling also kept dozens of publishers busy in Deventer, Basel, Pforzheim, and Strasbourg. Aside from the many pamphlets he wrote in the heat of battle against ecclesiastical and literary opponents, he edited, provided introductions for, and published works of such writers as Brant, Geiler von Kaysersberg, Erasmus, Egidius of Rome, Battista Mantovano, Hrabanus Maurus, Theodore Gresemund the Younger, John Gerson, Giovanni Pico della Mirandola, Ludolf of Saxony, Henry of Langenstein, Bernard of Clairvaux, Saint Bonaventura, Lupold of Bebenburg, Stephan Hoest, and Saint John Chrysostom.

Perhaps the most notable feature of Wimpfeling's intellectual development in the decade following his departure from Heidelberg was the intensification of his German patriotism, hints of which had been evident in 1492 when he castigated Charles VIII for breaking his engagement to Maximilian's daughter. Two factors deepened his devotion to Germany and its imperial tradition in the early 1500s. First, he was becoming disillusioned with the Palatine Wittelsbachs under Elector Philip, who, Wimpfeling feared, was tilting diplomatically toward France and showing territorial ambitions in Alsace. Second, Wimpfeling was becoming increasingly hostile toward the Swiss, whose free cities were political and military threats to south Germany and whose rural cantons were an inspiration for peasant rebellion. The Swabian War of 1499, which pitted the Swiss Confederates against the emperor and his allies in the Swabian League, and the defection of the imperial city of Basel to the Swiss Confederation confirmed his fears.

The first fruit of Wimpfeling's stronger pro-German, proimperial sentiment was his *Germania*, published in 1501 and dedicated to the Strasbourg City Council. The first part of this slim volume draws on history to counter French claims that Alsace belongs to France rather than to the empire. Going back to the late Roman Empire and the era of Charlemagne, Wimpfeling argues that the Rhine had never been a boundary between Alsace and Germany and that the French had no valid claim to a region that was legally and culturally German. The second part of *Germania* outlines Wimpfeling's ideas about what policies and qualities are necessary for Strasbourg and other similar cities to maintain their independence, cohesiveness, prosperity, and political well-being: they include peace with neighbors; harmony among the burghers; a dedication to justice, prudence, and careful fiscal management; support for the clergy; loyalty to the emperor; and a public-spirited citizenry. Wimpfeling especially emphasizes the importance of good schools. He proposes that Strasbourg establish a gymnasium where young men in their midteens can polish their Latin, become acquainted with acceptable classical authors, learn discipline, and build character before they leave for the university.

Wimpfeling's effort to enlist history on behalf of German patriotism embroiled him in several controversies in the early 1500s. Thomas Murner, a young Franciscan and a native of the Alsatian town of Oberehnheim, attacked Wimpfeling's view of Alsatian history in 1502 in his *Germania nova* (New Germany). This work led to a brief but bitter exchange of pamphlets between the two men more noteworthy for its colorful invective than for its discussion of historical issues. In 1505 Wimpfeling published *Epithoma rerum Germanicarum* (A Short Summary of German Affairs), which is credited with being the first historical work dedicated exclusively to Germany's past. Most of the work is a celebration of the lives and deeds of the German emperors and a denunciation of villains—the French, the Swiss Confederation, the Hussites, certain popes—who have made trouble for Germany. Wimpfeling's history is not narrowly political, however; it also praises the Germans' artistic, literary, and intellectual achievements. Later in 1505 Wimpfeling angered the Swiss with his pamphlet *Soliloquium Wimphelingii Pro pace christianorum et pro Helvetiis ut resipiscant* (Wimpfeling's Soliloquy for the Peace of Christians and for the Swiss, That They May Come to Their Senses). He dismisses the Swiss as "rudes rustici" (half-civilized peasants) and castigates them for their lawlessness, belligerence, and disobedience to the emperor. He wonders if the Swiss are not a greater threat to Christendom than the Bohemians and the Muslims. After this work was published, his Swiss friends in Basel warned Wimpfeling it would be dangerous for him to visit the city.

But politics was only one source of controversy for Wimpfeling. In 1505 he entered the lists against Jacob Locher, a young humanist professor at Freiburg im Breisgau who had been drawing large crowds of eager students to his lectures on the poets. The rakish Locher, with his flamboyant lectures, ridicule of Scholastic philosophy, and passion for "unacceptable" poets, was Wimpfeling's worst nightmare. Wimpfeling urged his friends on the Freiburg faculty to dismiss or at least silence Locher, especially after Locher attacked a venerable member of the theology faculty, Georg Zingel. The feud dragged on until 1510, several years after Locher had left Freiburg to assume a new position at the University of Ingolstadt, when Wimpfeling published his *Contra turpem libellum Philomusi* (Against the Sordid Pamphlet of Philomusus). Although Wimpfeling's broadside contains its share of slanders against Locher, it is more than just a personal attack. Wimpfeling dismisses poetry as worthless and goes out of his way to lavish praise on the Scholastic doctors of the Middle Ages. Wimpfeling's loathing of Locher had pushed him into an awkward position for one identified with Germany's humanists.

Wimpfeling's most dangerous feud grew out of *De integritate*. Like most of Wimpfeling's works, this treatise has several themes. It is, first of all, his most vehement attack to that time on clerical abuses, especially unchastity and favoritism in the doling out of benefices. In addition, toward the end of the book he advances the argument that the parish clergy are more important than the monks and friars in maintaining the spiritual health and well-being of the church. He also denies that Saint Augustine had ever been a monk and asserts that he had had little use for monasticism. The Augustinians responded predictably, and their denunciations forced Wimpfeling to leave Freiburg soon after his book appeared. In subsequent works Wimpfeling admitted that there was room for disagreement about whether Augustine had been a monk; but, if anything, he stepped up his attacks on the monks of his own day. In his *Apologia pro Republica Christiana* (Apology for the Christian Commonwealth, 1506) he depicts monks as ignorant, greedy, arrogant, and immoral and blames them for opposing reform and undermining the religious life in parish churches by drawing worshipers to monastery chapels. The German Augustinians demanded Wimpfeling's citation to Rome to answer to the Pope. The case was dropped, but only after Wimpfeling appealed to Julius II to exempt him from the citation, pleading old age and poor health, and after many of his friends spoke up in his favor.

In 1515 Wimpfeling returned to Sélestat to live with his sister, Magdalena, who had been widowed and had married another Sélestat baker. There he lived out the rest of his days, except for brief visits to Strasbourg and Sulz in 1517. Wimpfeling's health, never robust, deteriorated further, and he suffered especially from gout. His publishing activity slowed, and at times he became despondent, especially after the onset of the Protestant Reformation. Wimpfeling at first had high hopes for Martin

Luther, whom he believed to be sympathetic to the new learning and capable of striking a blow at corrupt religion. He warned against a premature condemnation of Luther and urged that the Reformer be given a fair hearing. In 1520 he had the Schürer firm in Sélestat publish Erasmus's letter to the archbishop of Mainz, in which Erasmus expressed guarded support for Luther and blamed monkish ceremonialism and Scholastic obscurantism for the ills of the church. By 1521, however, when it became clear that the Lutheran movement was leading to a schism within the church, and when pro-Lutheran preachers in Sélestat began attacking the Mass and the veneration of the saints and of Mary, Wimpfeling rejected the Lutheran cause. Nonetheless, Wimpfeling's reputation as a fiery critic of clerical abuses caused many to suspect him of favoring Protestantism. In 1522, under threats from Jerome Aleander, the papal legate to Germany, he was pressured into writing a meek letter in which he affirmed his loyalty to the papacy, his devotion to Scholastic theology, and his opposition to conciliarism and the Lutheran cause. Even this was not enough, and in 1523 there was again talk of citing him to Rome because of his supposedly Lutheran sympathies. In 1524, in his last published work, an edition of Hieronymus Emser's *Canonis missae contra Huldricum Zwinglium defensio* (Defense of the Canon of the Mass against Huldrych Zwingli), he addressed a letter to both Luther and the Zurich Reformer Zwingli, urging them to reconsider their rejection of the Mass and not dismiss venerable religious practices simply because they were sanctioned by the papacy.

In his correspondence during the 1520s the ill and beleaguered Wimpfeling occasionally expressed the wish that God would release him from his stormy life and grant him peace in death. His wish was granted on 15 November 1528.

Many historians and biographers have been dismissive of Wimpfeling. He has been depicted as puritanical, overbearing, cantankerous, rigid, shallow, and unoriginal. Certainly his scholarship, although impressive in volume, was largely derivative. And in comparison with colorful figures such as Conrad Celtis and Ulrich von Hutten, Wimpfeling can be described as dull. Yet in many ways the future of Germany belonged to conservative humanists like Wimpfeling rather than to some of his more "interesting" humanist contemporaries. As confessional lines hardened in the sixteenth century, and Protestant and Catholic leaders considered how youth could best be trained to become obedient subjects and pious Christians, the schools they sponsored emphasized the mastery of Latin, modest and selective study of classical literature, strict discipline, and respect for religious and political leaders. In schools such as these there was no hint of Hutten's fiery assaults on authority, Celtis's sensuous lyrics, Johannes Reuchlin's esoteric cabalist studies, or even Erasmus's light-handed satire. Humanism in the sixteenth century was tamed and harnessed in the service of conservative social and religious values. Wimpfeling would have been pleased.

Letters:

"Neun Briefe von und an Jakob Wimpfeling, edited by Gustav Knod, *Vierteljahrsschrift für Kultur und Literatur der Renaissance,* 1 (1896): 229-243;

Briefwechsel, 2 volumes, edited by Otto Herding and Dieter Mertens, Jacobi Wimpfelingi opera selecta, volume 3 (Munich: Fink, 1990).

Biographies:

Paul Wiskowatoff, *Jakob Wimpfeling, sein Leben und seine Schriften* (Berlin: Mitscher & Rostell, 1867);

Bernard Schwarz, *Jacob Wimpfeling, der Altvater des deutschen Schulwesens* (Gotha: Perthes, 1875);

Charles Schmidt, "Jacques Wimpfeling," in his *Histoire Littéraire de L'Alsace,* 2 volumes (Paris: Sandoz & Fischbacher, 1879), I: 1-188; II: 317-340;

Hugo Holstein, "Zum Biographie Jakob Wimpfeling," *Zeitschrift für vergleichende Litteraturgeschichte und Renaissance-Literatur,* new series 4 (1891): 227-252;

Joseph Knepper, *Jakob Wimpfeling (1450-1528): Sein Leben und seine Werke* (Freiburg im Breisgau: Herder, 1902).

References:

Emil von Borries, *Wimpfeling und Murner im Kampf um die ältere Geschichte des Elsasses: Ein Beitrag zur Charakteristik des deutschen Frühhumanismus* (Heidelberg: Winter, 1926);

Rainer Donner, *Jakob Wimpfelings Bemühungen um die Verbesserung der liturgischen Texte,* Quellen und Abhandlungen zur mittelrheinischen Kirchengeschichte, no. 26 (Mainz: Gesellschaft für mittelrheinischen Kirchengeschichte, 1976);

Otto Herding, "Pädagogik, Politik, Geschichte bei Jakob Wimpfeling," in *L'Humanisme allemand (1480-1540): 18th International Colloquium on Humanist Studies, Tours, 1975* (Munich: Fink, 1979), pp. 113-130;

Herding, "Wimpfelings Begegnung mit Erasmus," in *Studien zum Nachleben der Antike und zur europäischen Renaissance: August Buck zum 60. Geburt-*

stag, edited by Klaus Heitmann and Eckhart Schroeder (Frankfurt am Main: Athenaeum, 1973), pp. 131-155;

Paul Kalkoff, "Jakob Wimpfeling und die Erhaltung der Katholischen Kirche in Schlettstadt," *Zeitschrift für die Geschichte des Oberrheins,* new series 12 (1897): 577-619; 13 (1898): 84-123, 264-301;

Kalkoff, "Wimpfelings kirchliche Unterwerfung," *Zeitschrift für die Geschichte des Oberrheins,* new series 21 (1906): 262-270;

Gustav Knod, "Wimpfeling und die Universität Heidelberg," *Zeitschrift für die Geschichte des Oberrheins,* new series 1 (1886): 317-335;

Dieter Mertens, "Jakob Wimpfeling, Pädagogischer Humanismus," in *Humanismus im deutschen Südwesten: Biographische Profile,* edited by Paul Gerhard Schmidt (Sigmaringen: Thorbecke, 1993), pp. 35-57;

Richard Newald, "Jakob Wimpfeling," in his *Elsässische Charakterköpfe aus dem Zeitalter des Humanismus* (Colmar: Alsatia, 1944), pp. 55-84;

Peter Oschenbein, "Jakob Wimpfelings Fehde mit den Baselern und Eidgenossen," *Baseler Zeitschrift für Geschichte und Altertumskunde,* 79 (1979): 37-65;

Francis Rapp, *Réformes et Réformation à Strasbourg: Eglise et société dans le Diocèse de Strasbourg, 1450-1525* (Paris: Ophrys, 1974);

Joseph Schlecht, "Zu Jakob Wimpfelings Fehden mit Jakob Locher und Paul Lang, in *Festgabe Karl Theodor von Heigel,* edited by Theodor Bitterauf (Munich: Haushalter, 1903), pp. 236-265;

Bruno Singer, *Die Fürstenspiegel in Deutschland im Zeitalter des Humanismus und der Reformation: Bibliographische Grundlagen und ausgewählte Interpretationen. Jakob Wimpfeling, Wolfgang Seidel, Johann Sturm, Urban Rieger* (Munich: Fink, 1981), pp. 173-249;

Lewis Spitz, "Jakob Wimpfeling—Sacerdotal Humanist," in his *Religious Renaissance of the German Humanists* (Cambridge, Mass.: Harvard University Press, 1963), pp. 41-60.

Papers:

Letters of Jakob Wimpfeling are in the Uppsala Universitätsbibliothek; the Bibliothèque Nationale et Universitaire, Strasbourg; and the Newberry Library, Chicago.

Heinrich Wittenwiler
(before 1387 – circa 1414?)

Albrecht Classen
University of Arizona

WORK: *Der Ring* (circa 1410)

Manuscript: The text is known to survive in only one manuscript, today located in the Staatsarchiv, Meiningen, Nr. 502, Hs. 29 (Saxony). It was copied by the author himself or by a scribe around 1410 or 1420. The manuscript is on parchment and consists of fifty-seven leaves measuring 25.9 centimeters by 18.8 centimeters; the text is written in two columns on each page. The text begins with an almost round initial *D*, in which a man is depicted holding a ring with a stone. Below the initial is a coat of arms showing a ram. Below the second column on the first page is the notorious ink drawing of a peasant couple: as they embrace each other, he puts two fingers of his right hand into her vagina. Red lines in the margins indicate serious discussions or truth; green lines stand for foolishness or lies.

First publication: *Der Ring, von Heinrich Wittenweiler* [sic], edited by Ludwig Bechstein, introduction by Adelbert Keller (Stuttgart: Literarischer Verein, 1851).

Standard editions: *Heinrich Wittenwilers Ring: Nach der Meininger Handschrift,* edited by Edmund Wießner (Leipzig: Reclam, 1931); *Heinrich Wittenwiler, Der Ring: In Abbildung der Meininger Handschrift,* edited by Rolf Bräuer, George F. Jones, and Ulrich Müller (Göppingen: Kümmerle, 1990 [i.e., 1991]).

Editions in modern German: *Der Ring: Nach der Ausgabe von Edmund Wießner übertragen,* edited and translated by Helmut Birkhan (Vienna: Braumüller, 1983); *Der Ring oder Wie Bertschi Triefnas um sein Mätzli freite,* edited and translated by Rolf Bräuer (Berlin: Rütten & Loening, 1983); *Der Ring,* edited and translated, with commentary, by Bernhard Sowinski (Stuttgart: Helfant, 1988); *Der Ring: Frühneuhochdeutsch/Neuhochdeutsch. Nach dem Text von Edmund Wießner ins Neuhochdeutsche übersetzt,* edited and translated by Horst Brunner (Stuttgart: Reclam, 1991).

Edition in English: *Wittenwiler's Ring, and the Anonymous Scots Poem Colkelbie Sow: Two Comic-Didactic Works from the Fifteenth Century,* translated by George Fenwick Jones (Chapel Hill: University of North Carolina Press, 1956).

Although Heinrich Wittenwiler's didactic verse narrative *Der Ring* (The Ring, circa 1410) has been preserved in only one known manuscript, it is considered one of the most important literary texts of late-medieval German literature. One cannot say how popular it was in its time or even whether it reached an audience beyond the scribe and reader of the only manuscript. It is certain, however, that a highly satiric, if not sarcastic, view of the world comes to the fore in Wittenwiler's encyclopedic masterpiece, which is replete with references to medical, military, and scientific treatises from antiquity and the Middle Ages. Whereas the text seems to present nothing but a peasant satire, it is really intended as an allegory of the late-medieval world in all its ugliness and stupidity. *Der Ring* has many similarities to medieval encyclopedic works such as the anonymous *Lucidarius* (circa 1190); *Der Renner* (The Runner, 1300), by Hugo von Trimberg; and *Edelstein* (Precious Gem, 1350), by Ulrich Bonner. Other sources appear to have been Neidhart von Reuental's thirteenth-century peasant satires, Wernher der Gartenaere's social-critical novella *Helmbrecht* (circa 1265–1280), and the anonymous fourteenth-century peasant tales *Meier Betz* (Farmer Betz) and *Metzen hochzît* (Metzen's Wedding). The author's manipulation of the basic narrative so as not only to depict the lives of the rural protagonists but also to express many of the values and ideals of the late Middle Ages makes *Der Ring* one of the crowning achievements of peasant satire in German literature.

Der Ring can be seen as a forerunner of Sebastian Brant's *Das Narrenschiff* (The Ship of Fools, 1494), François Rabelais's *Gargantua et Pantagruel* (1532–1564), and Johann Fischart's satiric novel *Affentheurelich naupengeheurliche Geschichtklitterung* (Adventuresome Narrative Scribbling, 1582). Though he is steeped in clerical traditions, the author makes full use of the multiple possibilities developed in secular literature to discuss societal woes and describes the world as an illusion in which only fools can place their trust. Wittenwiler confronts the concept of *stultitia* (foolishness) with that of *sapientia* (wisdom) and appeals to his audience to follow the path of sapientia, regardless of how hard doing so might be in a late-medieval world dominated by conflict and a breakdown of morality.

Documents from Constance show that on 30 November 1387 "maister Heinrich von Wittenwile" was registered as a witness for Count Heinrich von Montfort zu Tettnang; on 29 May 1389 "her Heinrich von Wittenwille" was appointed as a mediator in a legal case. In 1390 the *Konstanzer Ratsbuch* (Book of the Constance City Council) mentions that "maister Hainrich Witwile" attacked another citizen and wounded him with a knife. On 4 March 1395 two parties met in the house of "magister Hainricus de Wittenwil advocatus curie" (Master Henry of Wittenwil, lawyer for the bishop) to reach a compromise regarding the parish income; on 29 July—no year is given—"Meister Heinrich von Wittenwil, hoffmeister zuo Kostenz" (court steward in Constance) is reported as having died. This Constance lawyer, who also worked as an administrator for the bishop, emerges as the most likely author of *Der Ring*. It is not known whether Wittenwiler was a nobleman or a burgher, but *Der Ring* would have appealed to both classes; the peasants, on the other hand, are satirized and ridiculed.

The work, which is almost ninety-seven hundred verses in length, portrays the entire world of the late Middle Ages—the conflict between peasants and knights, love affairs, letter writing, medical science, sex, food and its preparation, weddings, pregnancy, astronomy, astrology, and warfare—while seeming to focus on a single village. In the manuscript the sections of the work that are to be regarded as seriously intended or as true are marked with red lines, while those that are to be considered foolishness or untrue are marked with green lines; but some passages that are obviously serious are marked in green. The reasoning behind this strategy has not been fully understood, but a likely assumption is that the author intended to challenge the reader's skill in distinguishing between veracity and sophistry.

Wittenwiler says in the prologue that he calls his text *Der Ring* "Wan es ze ring umb uns beschait / Der welte lauff und lert auch wol, / Was man tuon und lassen schol" (because it informs us about everything around us, / Especially the way the world

Illustration from the manuscript for Heinrich Wittenwiller's Der Ring *(Staatsarchiv, Meiningen, Nr. 502, Hs. 29, fol. 1ʳ)*

operates and teaches us / What to do and what not to do). He goes on to say that the book is divided into three sections: the first deals with proper behavior at court, pertaining to jousting and swordplay, eloquence and song; the second deals with the temporal and spiritual aspects of human life; the third deals with questions of how to cope in times of war. The author declares that the purpose of *Der Ring* is to show the reader how to gain an education and how to woo ladies. To make his wide-ranging and serious discourse more palatable, he has introduced entertaining pieces from the world of peasants.

The narrative begins with a description of the village of Lappenhausen, where many "esler pauren" (donkey peasants) live. Among them is Bertschi Triefnas, whose surname means "Dripping Nose." Although he is just a simple farmer, he demands to be addressed as "junkherr" (young lord), and he enjoys the favor of all the women. His real love, though, is Mätzli Rüerenzumph (Touch the Penis), whom he describes in a parody of the rhetorical tradition: her teeth and hands are as black as coal; her lips are as red as the sand on the beach; her braid is like a rat's tail; she has a goiter that hangs down to her belly; her feet are flat and fat, so that no wind can knock her down; her breath smells like sulphur; and her behavior is that of a three-year-old child.

To win her favor, Bertschi is willing to "die" in mock battles he holds with his peasant friends on the village tournament field. Their clumsy imitation of knightly armor is improvised from crude objects that are available to them. Needless to say, their humble arms are no match for their first and only opponent, the knight Neidhart, modeled after the early-thirteenth-century character of that name who appears in satiric poems by Neidhart von Reuental. Neidhart devised two types of songs, the *Sommerlied* (summer song), in which the knight is attractive to the peasant girls, and the *Winterlied* (winter song), in which the knight realizes that the peasants have better accommodations and food and are, therefore, advantaged in the battle for love. Wittenwiler apparently had the knightly figure from the summer songs in mind when he wrote *Der Ring*.

Neidhart accepts the peasants' challenge, and Bertschi approaches the knight and asks for instructions as to how to conduct the tournament. Neidhart complies with the request; his instructions are marked in the manuscript with red lines and are, therefore, supposed to be considered factual. The responses by the peasants, which reveal their foolishness and inability to understand anything that he is saying, are marked with green. Neidhart's actions are, however, no more honorable than those of the peasants: he fights them with an iron club covered with straw, whereas they, unaware of the trick, use simple straw clubs and are, thus, placed at a great disadvantage. In their foolishness the peasants maim and kill each other, either deliberately or by accident. Two peasants who are lying badly wounded on the ground confess their sins to Neidhart, who pretends to be a priest: one had made love to his wife after he made her fall off a bench; the other had used a cow to cross a river. They are told to go to their bishop and to the Pope, respectively, and do penance, as if they were guilty of grave moral depravities. Having had enough fun with the villagers, Neidhart rides away.

His tournament scheme having failed to win Mätzli, Bertschi hires a musician to serenade her; but both of them have to flee from angry neighbors awakened by the music. Later Bertschi tries to surprise Mätzli in the cow shed, but he is mistaken for a thief and chased away. On the third night he climbs onto the roof of Mätzli's parents' house, but he falls through the chimney and causes havoc. Her father, Fritz, locks his daughter in the attic, assuming her to be the cause of the disruption. Alone, the young woman discovers the joy of masturbation, which causes her to fall in love with Bertschi.

Bertschi hires the village scribe to write a love letter for him and in the process receives instructions in the art of love as laid down by Ovid and Andreas Capellanus—though these instructions are undermined through irony and parody. The scribe attaches the letter to a stone and throws it through Mätzli's window; it hits her in the head and knocks her out. Waking up, she finds the letter; but she can neither read nor write, so she goes to Doctor Chrippenchra (Grabbing Crow) for help. As a reward for reading the letter to her and writing a response to it, the doctor demands and receives sexual favors. Mätzli quickly learns to enjoy intercourse and demands more of it, but the doctor is exhausted after the second time. Mätzli has become pregnant and must get married to preserve her honor. The doctor provides her with advice on how to fake virginity by putting blood in a pigeon bladder and concealing it in her vagina. He also writes a highly sophisticated allegorical love letter for Mätzli in which she offers to marry her lover.

When the letter reaches Bertschi, he convenes his large family for a consultation on the value of married life. His relatives—including Schlingdenspeck (Gobble up the Bacon), Nabelreiber (He Who Touches the Navel), and Scheißindieblumen (Shits in the Flowers)—contribute various viewpoints on marriage, women, love, sex, and children. Wittenwiler here follows the traditional Scholastic debate format of pro and contra, finally allowing the defenders of marriage to win the argument.

A similar debate takes place at Mätzli's father's house, where the men quickly reach an agreement to test and instruct Bertschi about marriage before he will be allowed to marry Mätzli. Bertschi is called in and is able to recite the basic prayers of the liturgy, such as the Paternoster and the Credo—which are rendered in prose—and to present himself as a successful farmer. Lastersack (Bag of Vices), however, is not satisfied and gives the young man his own set of instructions about the soul, fear of God, moderation, proper behavior, readiness, and the ability to listen and learn. He also teaches Bertschi the meaning of the Holy Trinity, the Ten Commandments, and the rules of fasting. Despite his name, Lastersack turns out to be a highly learned theologian.

Bertschi asks the pharmacist, Straub, to give him a detailed lesson on medicines and their effects on the human body. These teachings are based on popular medical instruction books, such as the thirteenth-century pseudo-Aristotelian *Secretum secre-*

torum (Secrets of Secrets), Arnald of Villanova's *Regimen sanitatis Salernitanum* (Salernian Book on Health, circa 1300), and treatises by Konrad von Eichstätt and Pseudo-Arnaldus. Crude peasant satire and obscene descriptions are combined with learned discourses on topics such as baths, saunas, and hygiene that were relevant to urban, not rural, life.

At their wedding Bertschi and Mätzli receive gifts of tools, animals, and other objects important to a peasant existence; but most of the gifts are worn out from use or are of little value: roots and berries, needles, moldy gloves, a broomstick, and an old hat. The wedding feast is described in the most disgusting terms, as the guests greedily swallow everything that is placed in front of them. It soon becomes apparent that Bertschi has not provided enough food for all his guests, and fights break out in which the host himself is badly beaten. Some of the guests die because of their greediness; others commit gross indecencies; still others expose themselves; and most of them get beastly drunk.

When the dancing begins, the peasants make an attempt to copy the courtly lifestyle; but the refinement quickly gives way to "Ochsendringen, kelberspringen" (pushing of oxen, jumping of calves). The girls are ironically described as dancing so chastely that one could see their legs up to the knees; some women expose their breasts, which leads to general lewdness. During the dance, which, like the meal, results in violence, sexual innuendos lead to erotic acts. Finally, Eisengrein (Crying Loon), who is in love with Gredul, clumsily tries to indicate his feelings to her, scratching her hand until it bleeds. In comparison with the mayhem that has already taken place, this tiny wound hardly seems worth mentioning; but Schindennack (Beat the Neck), Gredul's uncle, observes it and begins to criticize Eisengrein for his rudeness. Eisengrein threatens to rape both Schindennack's niece and his mother if he does not shut up. A fistfight breaks out that escalates into a melée with swords and lances, resulting in many casualties. The brawl quickly turns into a war between the host village of Lappenhausen and the guests from Nissingen. The men from Lappenhausen pursue those from Nissingen to their gates and then are chased back to Lappenhausen, where they find the Nissingen girls and rape them.

In Nissingen the village council meets to deliberate the course of action to be pursued. The mayor, Straub, advises trying to bring their women home safely and declares that war should only be used as a last resort. The council sends a messenger, Schieleinwenig (He Who Squints a Little), to Lappenhausen; he proves to be a bad diplomat and threatens war instead of offering peace. The villagers from Nissingen call for help from all over Switzerland and along the Rhine Valley and prepare for war.

In the meantime, the Lappenhausen peasants continue with the wedding celebration, and Bertschi and Mätzli consummate their marriage. Even in their bedroom a war is being waged: she pretends to be a virgin, and he tries to force himself on her to prove his virility. Finally, he manages to sleep with her, first with the help of clever rhetoric supported by Bible quotations about progeny being the purpose of marriage, and then by raping her. Afterward they receive food and drink from their friends; alone again, they resume their sexual intercourse—this time by mutual agreement. Concurrently, the village girls make love with the young men until the morning dawns.

Realizing that they have to defend themselves against the Nissingen villagers, the inhabitants of Lappenhausen hold a war council. The village elder, Riffian (Brothel Keeper), presents a lecture on the reasons why the feudal class structure would prevent them, as peasants, from waging a war, but Lienhart mit dem Flegel (Lionhart with the Thresher) declares the village independent and appoints his friends as emperor, king, duke, margrave, and so on—a parody of the Swiss struggle to free themselves from Hapsburg rule and perhaps an allusion to the self-ennoblement of the citizens of Zurich in 1386. Ruprecht advises against war because it would not be a just war. His lecture on the principles of war is based on Saint Augustine's concept of the *bellum iustum* (just war) in *De civitate Dei* (City of God, circa 413) and on Giovanni da Legnano's *De Bello, de Represaliis et De Duello* (On War, Repressions, and Duels, circa 1360). He touches on the various types of war—the spiritual war of God against the devil or the clergy against the laypeople through church bans; and worldly wars, of one people or nation against another or an individual against another individual or against society—and the causes of war. Pilian explains the strategies of warfare in factual terms and asserts that the goals of the Lappenhausen peasants are futile because of their lack of professional fighters. Heinz objects, citing the wars of Alexander the Great and the Trojan War, in which the actual number of fighters had never been counted, as examples; he does not realize that he is not really responding to Pilian's argument. In apocalyptic terms borrowed from the Bible, Dame Laichdenman (Cheat the Man) warns that the mayor is a weak leader who will be the downfall of all of them. The younger peasants chase her away because they yearn to prove themselves in a war.

Lappenhausen requests military aid from all the major cities in Europe, including Rome, Bruges, Palermo, Genoa, Constantinople, Florence, Paris, Montpellier, Cologne, Basel, Constance, Würzburg, Prague, Regensburg, Salzburg, Munich, Passau, and Krakow. A council of the cities convenes and decides not to get involved because the various members have friends on both sides of the dispute. The mayor of Constance presents a lecture on how to give advice to neighbors and what sort of aid to offer them, and recommends that the council should mediate between the parties and try to settle the conflict. The speech is rational and balanced; the "glerte amman von der stat" (educated city administrator) might be a self-projection of the author, since Wittenwiler once settled a dispute between the city of Radolfzell and the monastery of Reichenau.

The peasants are too obstinate and ignorant to listen to such good advice; for them, violence is the only solution. The Lappenhausen peasants appeal for help to their friends and relatives in other villages, places with fictional names such as Narrenhäm (Home of the Fools) and Torenhofen (Idiot Farm). They also ask witches, dwarfs, and giants to come to their aid but dismiss Jews and Greeks as too weak to help. Heroes of ancient Germanic epics, including Dietrich von Bern, at first want to join the Lappenhausen side; but then they remember their old hatred of the giants, who are already on that side, and switch their loyalty to Nissingen. The giants have significant names from literary history, such as Sigen, Golias (Goliath), and Roland. The narrator says that the knights of the Round Table would have joined the fight but are too busy defending their castles against attacks by urban armies and that Sir Burckhart of Ellerbach would have liked to participate in the fighting but has not yet been born. The peasants of Mätzendorf (Village of Prostitutes) arrive on the battlefield to avenge a crime committed against their forefathers a hundred years ago by the ancestors of the Lappenhausen peasants.

Several instructions follow pertaining to practical aspects of warfare: how to sit on a horse, how to throw lances, and so on. The actual battle is described in both excessively gruesome and ridiculous terms. Wittenwiler reports the scores of casualties in a detached, cold-blooded manner and mentions that the warriors wade through knee-deep blood—features reminiscent of Crusade epics such as Pfaffe Konrad's *Das Rolandslied* (The Song of Roland, circa 1172) and Wolfram von Eschenbach's *Willehalm* (circa 1210–1220).

Eventually the Lappenhausen forces are defeated; only Bertschi escapes, taking refuge in a barn that is impregnable to his enemies. They try to lure him from his fortress with threats and promises, but he retorts with farts. When they try to starve him out, he demonstrates that he can eat hay. This sight leads his opponents to believe that he has turned into a beast, and, filled with fear, they flee. Bertschi returns to Lappenhausen and discovers that everybody has been killed, including his wife. Realizing that he has wasted his life, he withdraws into the Black Forest and becomes a hermit. Under these conditions he gains eternal life, and the narrative concludes with a short prayer that God will give the readers the same promise of Paradise that Bertschi received for his pious life in the wilderness.

Wittenwiler skillfully weaves a multitude of literary threads to create an amazing textual image of his world. *Der Ring* is a monumental achievement, combining parody, sarcasm, moral teaching, and practical instruction. The author's deliberate strategy of undermining the actions and speeches of his protagonists, his many allusions to the literary past, and his highly negative view of human affairs made it hard, however, for his contemporaries to appreciate the work. It may be for this reason that the text is preserved in only one manuscript, while modern scholarship has hailed it as a milestone in the history of late-medieval literature.

References:

Arpad Stephan Andreànsky, *Topos und Funktion: Probleme der literarischen Transformation in Heinrich Wittenwilers "Ring"* (Bonn: Bouvier, 1977);

Jürgen Belitz, *Studien zur Parodie in Heinrich Wittenwilers "Ring"* (Göppingen: Kümmerle, 1978);

Helmut Birkhan, *Das Historische im "Ring" des Heinrich von Wittenwiler* (Vienna: Österreichische Akademie der Wissenschaften, 1973);

Bruno Boesch, "Bertschis Weltflucht: Zum Schluß von Wittenwilers 'Ring,'" in *Studien zur deutschen Literatur und Sprache des Mittelalters: Festschrift für Hugo Moser zum 65. Geburtstag,* edited by Werner Besch and others (Berlin: Schmidt, 1974), pp. 228–237;

Boesch, "Phantasie und Wirklichkeitsfreude in Heinrich Wittenwilers 'Ring,'" *Zeitschrift für deutsche Philologie,* 67 (1942): 139–161;

Richard Brinkmann, "Zur Deutung von Wittenwilers 'Ring,'" *Deutsche Vierteljahresschrift zur Geistesgeschichte und Literaturwissenschaft,* 30, no. 2/3 (1956): 57–87;

Albrecht Classen, "Wort und Gemeinschaft: Sprachliche Apokalypse in Heinrich Wittenwilers 'Ring,'" in *Jahrbuch der Oswald von*

Wolkenstein Gesellschaft, 8 (1994-1995): 141-157;

John Michael Clifton-Everest, "Wittenwiler's Marriage Debate," *Modern Language Notes,* 90 (1975): 629-642;

Christa Wolf Cross, *Magister ludens: Der Erzähler in Heinrich Wittenwilers "Ring"* (Chapel Hill: University of North Carolina Press, 1984);

Ulrich Gaier, *Satire: Studien zu Neidhart, Wittenwiler, Brant und zur satirischen Schreibart* (Tübingen: Niemeyer, 1967), pp. 97-214;

George T. Gillespie, "Helden und Bauern: Beziehungen zur Heldendichtung bei Neidhart, Wernher dem Gartenaere und Wittenwiler," in *Studien zur deutschen Dichtung des Mittelalters (Festschrift für Gerhart Lohse),* edited by Ulrich Fellmann and Rudolf Schützeichel (Bonn: Bouvier, 1979), pp. 485-500;

Christoph Gruchot, *Heinrich Wittenwilers "Ring": Konzept und Konstruktion eines Lehrbuches* (Göppingen: Kümmerle, 1988);

George Fenwick Jones, "Late-Medieval 'Realism' as Exemplified in Heinrich Wittenwiler's 'Ring,'" in *Helen Adolf Festschrift,* edited by Sheema Zeben Buehne and others (New York: Ungar, 1968), pp. 86-98;

Jones, "Sartorial Symbols in Mediaeval Literature," *Medium Aevum,* 25 (1956-1957): 63-70;

Jones, "The Tournaments of Tottenham and Lappenhausen," *PMLA,* 66 (1951): 1123-1140;

Kristina Jürgens-Lochthove, *Heinrich Wittenwilers "Ring" im Kontex hochhöfischer Epik* (Göppingen: Kümmerle, 1980);

Elisabeth de Kadt, "er ist ein gpaur in meinem muot, Der unrecht lept und läppisch tuot: Zur Bauernsatire in Heinrich Wittenwilers 'Ring,'" *Daphnis,* 15 (1986): 1-29;

Raimund Kemper, "Diätetik des Schreckens: Zum 'Ring' Heinrich Wittenwilers," *Jahrbuch der Oswald von Wolkenstein Gesellschaft,* 4 (1986-1987): 3-23;

Birgit Knühl, *Die Komik in Heinrich Wittenwilers 'Ring' im Vergleich zu den Fastnachtspielen des 15. Jahrhunderts* (Göppingen: Kümmerle, 1981);

Eckart Conrad Lutz, *Spiritualis Fornicatio: Heinrich Wittenwiler, seine Welt und sein "Ring"* (Sigmaringen: Thorbecke, 1990);

Fritz Martini, "Heinrich Wittenwilers Ring," *Deutsche Vierteljahresschrift für Literaturwissenschaft und Geistesgeschichte,* 20 (1942): 200-235;

Rolf R. Mueller, *Festival and Fiction in Heinrich Wittenwiler's "Ring": A Study of the Narrative in its Relation to the Traditional Topoi of Marriage, Folly, and Play* (Amsterdam: Benjamins, 1977);

Jutta Nanninga, *Realismus in mittelalterlicher Literatur: Untersucht an ausgewählten Großformen spätmittelalterlicher Epik* (Heidelberg: Winter, 1980);

Bernward Plate, *Heinrich Wittenwiler* (Darmstadt: Wissenschaftliche Buchgesellschaft, 1977);

Christa Maria Puchta-Mähl, *Wan es ze ring umb uns beschait: Studien zur Narrenterminologie, zum Gattungsproblem und zur Adressatenschicht in Heinrich Wittenwilers "Ring"* (Heidelberg: Winter, 1986);

Ortrun Riha, *Die Forschung zu Heinrich Wittenwilers "Ring" 1851-1988* (Würzburg: Königshausen & Neumann, 1990);

Kurt Ruh, "Ein Laiendoktrinal in Unterhaltung verpackt: Wittenwilers 'Ring,'" in *Literatur und Laienbildung im Spätmittelalter und in der Reformationszeit: Symposion Wolfenbüttel 1981,* edited by Ludger Grenzmann and Karl Stackmann (Stuttgart: Metzler, 1984), pp. 344-355;

Winfried Schlaffke, *Heinrich Wittenweilers [sic] Ring: Komposition und Gehalt* (Berlin: Schmidt, 1969);

Elisabeth Schmid, "Leben und Lehre in Heinrich Wittenwilers 'Ring,'" *Jahrbuch der Oswald von Wolkenstein Gesellschaft,* 4 (1986-1987): 273-292;

Bernhard Sowinski, *Lehrhafte Dichtung des Mittelalters* (Stuttgart: Metzler, 1971);

Rudolf Voss, "Weltanschauung und poetische Totalität in Heinrich Wittenwilers 'Ring,'" *Beiträge zur Geschichte der deutschen Sprache und Literatur,* 93 (1971): 351-365;

Edmund Wießner, *Kommentar zu Heinrich Wittenwilers "Ring"* (Leipzig: Reclam, 1936).

Niklas von Wyle

(circa 1415 – 13 April 1479)

John L. Flood
University of London Institute of Germanic Studies

WORKS: *Translationen* (Esslingen: Konrad Fyner, 1478);

"Colores rethoricales," in *Rhetorica und teutsch Formulare,* by Alexander Huge (Tübingen, 1528), fols. XXIX^r–XXXIII^v;

"Oratio nycoli de Wile," edited by J. Baechtold, in his "Zu Niklaus Von Wyle," *Zeitschrift für Vergleichende Litteraturgeschichte und Renaissance-Litteratur,* new series 1 (1887–1888): 348–350.

Editions: *Transzlatzion oder Tütschungen des hochgeachten Nicolai von wyle* (Strasbourg: Johann Prüss the Elder, 1510);

Translation oder Deütschungen des hochgeachten Nicolai von Weil (Augsburg: Heinrich Steiner, 1536);

Translationen von Niclas von Wyle, edited by Adelbert von Keller (Stuttgart: Litterarischer Verein, 1861).

OTHER: Enea Silvio Piccolomini (Pope Pius II), *Epistole Enee siluii Poete lauriati,* edited by Wyle (Reutlingen: Michael Greyff, 1479).

Niklas von Wyle, one of the earliest German humanists, was responsible for introducing awareness of important Italian writers into Germany. He is remembered, above all, for his experimental theory of translation, which advocated close adherence to the Latin source so as to promote a gradual improvement in German style. This word-for-word approach distinguishes him sharply from his contemporaries Heinrich Steinhöwel and Albrecht von Eyb, who saw it as the translator's prime task to convey the sense, rather than the style, of a passage.

Niklas von Wyle was born at Bremgarten, Aargau, Switzerland, around 1415 (some authorities suggest 1410). He spent the years 1430 to 1433 studying at the University of Vienna, after which he taught and served as a notary in Zurich, where Felix Hemmerli was his mentor. He then became *Stadtschreiber* (town clerk) at Radolfzell on Lake Constance. In 1447 he held an appointment as clerk to the city council of Nuremberg for a short period, which brought him into contact with the circle around the humanist and jurist Gregor Heimburg. Either that year or the next he moved to Esslingen, near Stuttgart, where, in addition to running a private school for the training of chancery clerks and teaching young people stylish expression in speech and writing, he was to serve as town clerk for almost twenty-two years.

In spite of his heavy administrative and training duties, Wyle found time to cultivate contacts with aristocrats and scholars and to realize his intellectual ambitions. He claimed that the only leisure time he had was at Shrovetide and at the wine harvest, and, indeed, it seems that it was precisely those periods that he used for working on his translations. One of the products of his years in Esslingen was "Colores rethoricales" (Colors of Rhetoric), written between 1464 and 1469 and left unfinished even though it is prefaced by a dedication to his brother-in-law, Dr. Georg Ehinger of Ulm. It covers only the first six *colores* of the system of the *Rhetorica ad Herennium* (Rhetoric for Herennius, circa 85 B.C.), a work that was considered in the Middle Ages to be by Cicero: *repetitio, conversio, complexio, traductio, contentio,* and *exclamatio*. Franz Josef Worstbrock has shown that Wyle's work is not a translation of the *Rhetorica ad Herennium*, as many scholars had thought. Each of the six chapters has two sections: the first gives a definition of the color and then illustrates it with examples in the form of German translations of excerpts from the writings of Nikolaus von Dybin; the second section provides a model letter that further exemplifies the use of the color. The letters in the second section are in some cases of Wyle's own devising, though the one in the third chapter is by Enea Silvio Piccolomini, who later became Pope Pius II. "Colores rethoricales" shows clearly that Wyle had one foot in the camp of the late-medieval *Ars dictandi* (the art of using good prose style in composing letters and documents) tradition and the other in that of the Italian humanists.

The years in Esslingen were the most fruitful of Wyle's life, for they brought him into contact with people who were receptive to humanistic endeavors—among them Steinhöwel, Jakob Püterich von Reichertshausen, Antonius von Pforr, the Württemberg counselor Dr. Georg von Absberg, and the chancellor Johann Fünfer. Furthermore, being responsible for the conduct of all of Esslingen's official legal and diplomatic correspondence and negotiations, he was frequently required to travel. His extensive journeys allowed him to meet all the princes in Baden, Stuttgart, Rottenburg, and Heidelberg and took him eight times to the imperial court in Vienna. In 1455 he established official and then literary connections with Mechthild, countess Palatine; she, her son Count Eberhard the Bearded of Württemberg, and her sister-in-law Margaret of Savoy all became Wyle's patrons. Beginning in 1459 he repeatedly received official commissions from Margrave Charles I of Baden; he represented Charles in November of that year at the Diet of Mantua, where he delivered a speech of welcome to Pope Pius II. In 1463, in his capacity as chancellor of Katharina, margravine of Baden, the sister of Emperor Frederick III, he spent several months at the imperial court at Wiener Neustadt. In 1469, accused of damaging the interests of Esslingen in his dealings over the patronage of the monastery at Weil, Wyle, availing himself of his influential contacts, quickly found new employment as deputy to Count Ulrich of Württemberg's chancellor, Johann Fünfer, in Stuttgart. His last years were uneventful, and he died on 13 April 1479 (not 1478, as sometimes said).

Among Wyle's many literary acquaintances, two stand out. The first is Piccolomini, who had worked at the imperial chancery at Wiener Neustadt. Among the more than one hundred surviving letters by Wyle—some in German, others in Latin, some personal, others official correspondence—there are several that reveal his profound admiration of Piccolomini. Their correspondence began in July 1452 after Piccolomini saw a letter Wyle had written to Michael Pfullendorf, a mutual friend; Piccolomini wrote to congratulate Wyle on the rounded (humanistic) hand in which the letter had been written and rejoiced to note that Germany was regaining its classical eloquence. Wyle responded that Piccolomini's writings were more precious to him than gold. Shortly before his death Wyle published the first collection of Piccolomini's letters to be issued in Germany: *Epistole Enee siluii Poete lauriati* (Letters of Enea Silvio, Poet Laureate). The collection, which was to form the basis of several later editions in the sixteenth century, was intended as a model for students of Latin style. The correspondence with Piccolomini reveals that Wyle was also a painter: he sent Piccolomini a painting of Saint Michael in 1452 and one of Saint Christopher in 1453.

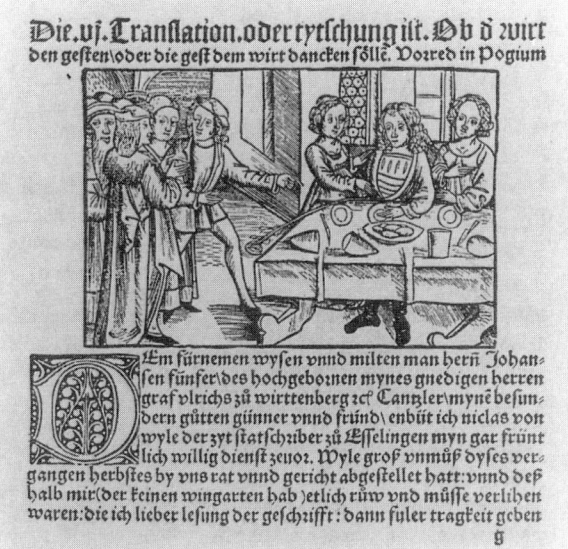

Page from the 1510 edition of Wyle's Translationen

Wyle's second significant literary acquaintance was Mechthild, countess Palatine, the pious and learned lady who had helped found the University of Freiburg im Breisgau in 1460 and, with her son Eberhard, the University of Tübingen in 1477. Her court at Rottenburg on the Neckar, near Tübingen, was a flourishing center of literary culture until her death in 1482. Wyle praises her as "ain grosse liebhaberin aller künste" (a great admirer of all the arts), and several of his translations are dedicated to her.

It is above all for his collection *Translationen* (Translations, 1478), also called *Translatzen* and *Tütschungen,* that Wyle is remembered today. The translations, done mostly in Esslingen but partly in Stuttgart between 1461 and 1478, were intended to provide outstanding examples of humanistic texts. The collection comprises, in order: Piccolomini's "Eurialus und Lucretia"; "Guiscard und Sigismunda," based on Leonardo Bruni's Latin version of the story from Giovanni Boccaccio's *Decameron* (1351–1353); Piccolomini's "De remedio amoris"; Gian Francesco Poggio Bracciolini's consolation to Cosimo de Medici, "On the Fickleness of Fortune," his "Whether the Guest or the Host Should Be the One to Thank," and his "Whether an Old Man Should Marry"; Bruni's version of the story of Alexander the Great and the deliverance of the twenty-four Elders of Athens; Pseudo-Bernard of Clairvaux's "Epistola de cura domestica ad Raimundum militem"; Wyle's mentor Hemmerli's treatise "Contra validos mendicantes," on the Lollards and the Beguines; Piccolomini's letter of 5 December 1443 to Duke Sigismund of Tirol on the subject of humanistic education; Pog-

Title page for the 1478 edition of Niklas von Wyle's Translationen

gio Bracciolini's letter of 30 May 1416 to Bruni on the burning of Jerome of Prague at Constance; Piccolomini's letter of 26 June 1444 to Procopius of Rabenstein on the Dream of Fortune; Lucian's *The Golden Ass,* after Poggio Bracciolini's Latin version; "Whether Nobility of Birth or Nobility of Spirit Is More Valuable," based on Buonaccorso da Montemagno's *De nobilitate;* a consolation for a man who is persecuted though innocent (there is an autobiographical dimension here, since Wyle claimed to have been unjustly persecuted in Esslingen) and one for a man whose wife has died, both based on Petrarch's *De remediis utriusque fortunae* (The Remedies of Fortune, 1360); "In Praise of Women," claimed by Wyle to be an original piece of his own, though half of it is a close translation of an address by Nicolosia Sanuda; Poggio Bracciolini's speech before the College of Cardinals on the occasion of the election of Pope Nicholas V; and "Wie man aim yeden in sinem stande ain gebürlich überschrift setzen sölt" (How Each Person Should Be Addressed According to His Rank), Wyle's own advice, originally intended for his pupils, on rhetoric, style, and letter writing, incorporating a paraphrase of the rules of word order from Gasparino Barzizza's *De compositione* (On Composition, 1420). The wide range of topics considered and the variety of different forms represented—letter, dialogue, speech, treatise, dream account, novella—mark the collection as characteristic of German humanism of the period. Wyle's personal predilections are found, perhaps, only in the piece by his erstwhile mentor Hemmerli and the passage from Petrarch in which he found a parallel to his misfortune in Esslingen.

One of Wyle's principal aims in producing the translations was to use them to train chancery scribes; suitable stylistic models could, in his view, be found only among Latin writers, whether classical or humanist. He strove to provide German renderings that were as faithful as possible to the Latin originals, even though doing so might introduce peculiarities of Latin syntax and word order into German at the risk of sacrificing intelligibility. But he appeals to the authority of such stylists as Bruni, Piccolomini, and Heimburg in support of his assertion that perseverance and growing familiarity with the best style will result in greater awareness, appreciation, and emulation of it. He shares Heimburg's view "daz ain yetklich tütsch, daz usz guotem zierlichem und wol gesatzten latine gezogen und recht und wol getran[s]feryeret wer ouch guot zierlich tütsche und lobes wirdig baissen und sin müste, und nit wol verbessert werden möcht" (that any German deriving from good, elegant, and well-formulated Latin and correctly and well translated must perforce be good, elegant German and appreciated as such, and could not be improved upon). This approach to translation, which Eric John Morrall declares to be "misguided and eccentric," is radically different from that of his contemporaries Steinhöwel and Eyb. Eyb, for instance, translates, as he himself puts it, "nit als gar von worten zu worten ... sunder nach dem synn und mainung der materien als sy am verstendlichisten und besten lauten mügen" (not word for word ... but according to the sense and meaning of the matter in the way that they sound most intelligible and best), striving after intelligibility and popular idiom; this practice has earned him a reputation as one of the best German prose writers before Martin Luther. Wyle, however, believed that through close, though not slavish, imitation of the original the style of the target language—German—would gradually be enhanced. It is important to remember that his advice was intended for chancery scribes rather than for literary practitioners in the modern sense. The peculiar style of his writings is inherently untranslatable, which is why none of his works can be made available in modern translations.

Wyle's translations seem to have been well received at the courts of Rottenburg, Baden, and Stutt-

Title page for the 1536 edition of Wyle's major work (courtesy of the Lilly Library, Indiana University)

gart, whose members had been brought up on medieval romances and the like. For them, the attraction of Wyle's writings doubtless lay less in their style than in their novel subject matter and their literary qualities. From the point of view of posterity, his main importance lies in the fact that he made some of the literary monuments of Renaissance Italy available to a wider public north of the Alps. In the dedicatory prefaces to his translations Wyle draws attention to what should make the texts particularly interesting to the reader, and this information affords considerable insight into the literary tastes of the courts of the time. Originally the translations would have been presented to their respective dedicatees as manuscripts; the collected edition of the *Translationen* printed in 1478 was intended not for small, sophisticated court circles but for a wider public. When, later, printers in Strasbourg, Ulm, Augsburg, and Cologne brought out editions of individual texts from the collection, they chose the first, second, third, and thirteenth—the piquant novellas. The fascination of "Eurialus und Lucretia," a psychological description of an illicit love impeded by social barriers, is evident from the story's subsequent popularity: eleven separate editions of this translation appeared between 1478 and 1594.

In letters to Georg von Absberg and Hans Harscher written on 18 February and 5 April 1478, respectively, Wyle outlined his plans for preparing several works for publication: his *Translationen,* including the Latin originals, the aim being to ensure that his disciples might thereby be "in wolgelert latinisch manne gerâtent" (transformed into learned Latinists) themselves; his translation, not yet completed, of the "Colores rethoricales"; "etwas nutzlichs und guotes daz notariate antreffend" (something useful and good concerning the work of a notary); and his translation of *De consolatione philosophiae* (The Consolation of Philosophy, circa 524) of Boethius, as yet unfinished. Of these projects only the first was realized, and even that only in part, for when *Translationen* appeared in 1478 the Latin texts were not included. Otherwise, only a portion of the "Colores rethoricales" appeared, and those half a century after his death. The Boethius translation, which apparently was highly praised by Absberg, has not survived at all.

Niklas von Wyle's influence as a writer is somewhat intangible, though it is clear that from about 1450 to 1470 he played an important role as a focus for humanistic endeavors in Swabia and northern Switzerland. On Piccolomini's advice he had cultivated a wide circle of like-minded friends, including Bernhard Schöfferlin, later professor of history at the University of Mainz and translator of the works of Livy; and Matteus Hummel, first rector of the University of Freiburg. Scattered remarks in his correspondence, such as those relating to the Boethius translation, suggest that he and his friends were actively engaged in copying and exchanging manuscripts of classical and humanist texts: he is known, for instance, to have lent books by Quintilian and Poggio Bracciolini to Michael Christan and other works by Poggio Bracciolini to Ludwig Rad—both men were clerical friends in Switzerland. Two autograph manuscripts of Wyle's are known that include texts of works by Antonius Panormita, Piccolomini, Virgil's *Aeneid* books 1 through 6, and excerpts from Valerius Maximus. Wyle was a pioneer in the translation of humanist authors such as Piccolomini, and his example was emulated by others, such as Christan in Constance and Wilhelm von Hirnkofen in Nuremberg. Wyle's translation of "Eurialus und Lucretia" was one of the most widely read pieces of narrative prose in Germany for several decades. His Latinizing style influenced Heinrich Österreicher, the abbot of Schussenried, who translated Columella's *De re rustica* (On Agricultural Matters) into German in 1491 and who has recently been credited, albeit tentatively, with the earliest translation of Boccaccio's *Decameron* into German; Johann Gottfried, the translator of works by Cicero and Lucian; and Wilhelm Salzmann, whose *Kaiser Octavianus* (Emperor Octavian, 1535) is a translation from the late-thirteenth- or early-fourteenth-century French work *Florent et Lyon*. Furthermore, Wyle influenced not only the clerks who worked directly under him in Esslingen but also subsequent generations of chancery scribes, for whom his letters in the *Translationen*—through reproductions in various sixteenth-century handbooks on scribal practice such as the anonymous *Formulare und deutsche Rhethorica* (Formulary and German Rhetoric, 1501), Alexander Huge's *Rethorica und Formularium Teütsch* (Rhetoric and German Formulary, 1528), and Johann Elias Meichsner's *Hoch oder gemainer Teütscher Nation Formular* (Formulary of the Upper or General German Nation, circa 1560)—provided models for imitation.

References:

Cecilia M. Ady, *Pius II (Aeneas Silvius Piccolomini), the Humanist Pope* (London: Methuen, 1913);

Eckhard Bernstein, *Die Literatur des deutschen Frühhumanismus* (Stuttgart: Metzler, 1978), pp. 43-62;

Heinrich Gebhard Butz, "Niklaus von Wile," *Jahrbuch für Geschichte der oberdeutschen Reichsstädte, Esslinger Studien,* 16 (1970): 21-105;

C. D. M. Cossar, *The German Translations of the Pseudo-Bernhardine "Epistola de cura rei familiaris"* (Göppingen: Kümmerle, 1978);

Irene Erfen-Hänsch, *Historia Sigismunde: Abbildungen zu einer Boccaccio-Novelle im deutschen Frühdruck: Leonardo Bruni, Arigo, Niklas von Wyle, Albrecht von Eyb* (Göppingen: Kümmerle, forthcoming 1997);

Erfen-Hänsch, *Historia Sigismunde: Zur Rezeption einer Boccaccio-Novelle im deutschen Frühhumanismus: Leonardo Bruni, Arigo, Niklas von Wyle, Albrecht von Eyb* (Göppingen: Kümmerle, forthcoming 1997);

Xenja von Ertzdorff, *Romane und Novellen des 15. und 16. Jahrhunderts in Deutschland* (Darmstadt: Wissenschaftliche Buchgesellschaft, 1989), pp. 22–33;

Frank Fürbeth, "Wyle, Niklas von," in *Literaturlexikon: Autoren und Werke deutscher Sprache*, volume 12, edited by Walther Killy (Gütersloh & Munich: Bertelsmann, 1992), pp. 455–456;

Bodo Gotzkowsky, *"Volksbücher": Prosaromane, Renaissancenovellen, Versdichtungen und Schwankbücher. Bibliographie der deutschen Drucke. Teil I: Drucke des 15. und 16. Jahrhunderts*, Bibliotheca Bibliographica Aureliana, no. 125 (Baden-Baden: Koerner, 1991), pp. 194–203;

Curt Sigmar Gutkind, "Poggio Bracciolinis geistige Entwicklung," *Deutsche Vierteljahrsschrift für Literaturwissenschaft und Geistesgeschichte*, 10 (1932): 548–596;

Konrad Haebler, "Die Drucke der Briefsammlungen des Aeneas Silvius," *Gutenberg-Jahrbuch*, 14 (1939): 138–152;

Margaret Ann Jackson, "Niklas von Wyle, Guiscardus und Sigismunda," thesis, Durham University, 1981;

Paul Joachimsohn, "Aus der Vorgeschichte des 'Formulare und deutsch Rhetorica,'" *Zeitschrift für deutsches Altertum*,

Joachimsohn, "Frühhumanismus in Schwaben," in his *Gesammelte Aufsätze*, volume 1, edited by Notker Hammerstein (Aalen: Scientia, 1970), pp. 149–248;

Joachim Knape, *Die ältesten deutschen Übersetzungen von Petrarcas 'Glücksbuch': Texte und Untersuchungen* (Bamberg: Kaiser, 1986), pp. 61–64, 277–294;

Eric John Morrall, *Aeneas Sylvius Piccolomini (Pius II) und Niklas von Wyle: The Tale of Two Lovers Eurialus and Lucretia* (Amsterdam: Rodopi, 1988);

Morrall, "The Tale of Eurialus and Lucretia by Aeneas Sylvius Piccolomini and Niklas von Wyle," *Neuphilologische Mitteilungen*, 81 (1980): 428–438;

Werner Schwarz, "Translation into German in the Fifteenth Century," *Modern Language Review*, 39 (1944): 368–373;

Rolf Schwenk, *Vorarbeiten zu einer Biographie des Niklas von Wyle und zu einer kritischen Ausgabe seiner ersten Translatze* (Göppingen: Kümmerle, 1978);

Philipp Strauch, *Pfalzgräfin Mechthild in ihren litterarischen Beziehungen: Ein Bild aus der schwäbischen Litteraturgeschichte des 15. Jahrhunderts* (Tübingen: Laupp, 1883);

Bruno Strauss, *Der Übersetzer Nicolaus von Wyle* (Berlin: Mayer & Müller, 1912);

J. H. Tisch, *Fifteenth Century German Courts and Renaissance Literature* (Hobart: University of Tasmania Press, 1971);

Tisch, "The Rise of the *Novella* in German Early Humanism: The Translator Niclas von Wyle (c. 1410–1478)," in *Proceedings and Papers of the Twelfth Congress Held at the University of Western Australia, 5–11 February 1969* (Sydney: Australian Universities Language and Literature Association, 1970), pp. 477–499;

Morimichi Watanabe, "Gregor Heimburg and Early Humanism in Germany," in *Philosophy and Humanism: Renaissance Essays in Honor of Paul Oskar Kristeller*, edited by Edward P. Mahoney (Leiden: Brill, 1976), pp. 406–422;

Franz Josef Worstbrock, "Die 'Colores rethoricales' des Niklas von Wyle," in *Respublica Guelpherbytana: Wolfenbütteler Beiträge zur Renaissance- und Barockforschung. Festschrift für Paul Raabe*, edited by August Buck and Martin Bircher (Amsterdam: Rodopi, 1987), pp. 189–209;

Worstbrock, "Niklas von Wyle," in *Die deutsche Literatur des Mittelalters: Verfasserlexikon*, volume 6, second edition, edited by Kurt Ruh (Berlin & New York: De Gruyter, 1978), cols. 1016–1035;

Worstbrock, "Zur Einbürgerung der Übersetzung antiker Autoren im deutschen Humanismus," *Zeitschrift für deutsches Altertum*, 99 (1970): 45–81.

Papers:

A manuscript written by Niklas von Wyle in 1463, including texts by Antonius Panormita and Enea Silvio Piccolomini, is in the Zentralbibliothek, Zurich (cod. Car. C 158). A manuscript written by Wyle in 1460, including books 1 through 6 of Virgil's *Aeneid*, an excerpt from Valerius Maximus, and two minor pieces, is in the library of the Dominican College, Washington, D.C.

Huldrych Zwingli
(1 January 1484 - 11 October 1531)

J. Wayne Baker
University of Akron

BOOKS: *Von Erkiesen und Freiheit der Speisen* (Zurich: Christoph Froschauer, 1522);

Supplicatio ad Hugonem Episcopum Constantiensem, by Zwingli and others (Zurich: Christoph Froschauer, 1522); translated into German by Zwingli; as *Eine freundliche Bitte und Ermahnung an die Eidgenossen* (Zurich: Christoph Froschauer, 1522);

Apologeticus Archeteles (Zurich: Christoph Froschauer, 1522);

Von Klarheit und Gewissheit des Wortes Gottes (Zurich: Christoph Froschauer, 1522); translated by G. W. Bromiley as "Of the Clarity and Certainty or Power of the Word of God," in *Zwingli and Bullinger,* Library of Christian Classics, volume 25 (Philadelphia: Westminster, 1953), pp. 59-95;

Eine göttliche Vermanung an die Eidgnossen zu Schwytz (Zurich: Christoph Froschauer, 1522);

Auslegen und Grunde der Schlussreden (Zurich: Christoph Froschauer, 1523); translated by E. J. Furcha as "Exposition and Basis of the Conclusions," in *Huldrych Zwingli: Writings,* volume 1: *The Defense of the Reformed Faith,* edited by Furcha (Allison Park, Pa.: Pickwick, 1984), pp. 1-373;

Von göttlicher und menschlicher Gerechtigkeit (Zurich: Christoph Froschauer, 1523); translated by Furcha as "On Divine and Human Righteousness," in *Huldrych Zwingli: Writings,* volume 2: *In Search of True Religion,* edited by H. Wayne Pipkin (Allison Park, Pa.: Pickwick, 1984), pp. 1-41;

Eine kurze christliche Einleitung (Zurich: Christoph Froschauer, 1523); translated by H. Wayne Pipkin as "Short Christian Introduction," in *Huldrych Zwingli: Writings,* volume 2: *In Search of True Religion,* pp. 43-76;

Der Hirt (Zurich: Christoph Froschauer, 1524); translated by Pipkin as "The Shepherd," in *Huldrych Zwingli: Writings,* volume 2: In Search of True Religion, pp. 77-125;

Ad Matthaeum Alberum de coena dominica epistola (Zu-

Huldrych Zwingli; portrait by Hans Asper (Zentralbibliothek, Zurich)

rich: Christoph Froschauer, 1524); translated by Pipkin and Henry Preble as "Letter to Matthew Alber Concerning the Lord's Supper, November 1524," in *Huldrych Zwingli: Writings,* volume 2: *In Search of True Religion,* pp. 127-145;

De vera et falsa religione commentarius (Zurich: Christoph Froschauer, 1525); translated by Preble as "Commentary on True and False Religion," in *The Latin Works of Huldreich Zwingli,* volume

3, edited by Samuel Macauley Jackson and Clarence N. Heller (Philadelphia: Heidelberg, 1929);

Von der Taufe, von der Wiedertaufe und von der Kindertaufe (Zurich: Johannsen Hager, 1525); translated by Bromiley as "Of Baptism," in *Zwingli and Bullinger*, pp. 129-175;

Antwort uber Balthasar Hubmaiers Taufbuchlein (Zurich: Christoph Froschauer, 1525);

Eine klare Unterrichtung vom Nachtmahl Christi (Zurich: Johannsen Hager, 1526); translated by Bromiley as "On the Lord's Supper," in *Zwingli and Bullinger*, pp. 185-238;

In catabaptistarum strophas elenchus (Zurich: Christoph Froschauer, 1527); translated by Preble and George W. Gilmore as "A Refutation of the Tricks of the Catabaptists, 1527," in *Ulrich Zwingli (1484-1531): Selected Works*, edited by Jackson (Philadelphia: University of Pennsylvania Press, 1901), pp. 123-258;

Amica exegesis, id est, expositio Eucharistiae negocii, ad Martinum Lutherum (Zurich: Christoph Froschauer, 1527); translated by Preble and Pipkin as "Friendly Exegesis, That Is, Exposition of the Matter of the Eucharist to Martin Luther," in *Huldrych Zwingli: Writings*, volume 2: *In Search of True Religion*, pp. 233-385;

Ad Carolum Romanorum Imperatorem Germaniae comitia Augustae celebrantem, fidei Huldrychi Zwinglii ratio (Zurich: Christoph Froschauer, 1530); translated anonymously as *The Rekening and declaration of the faith and beleif of Huldrik Zwingly, bischoppe of Züryk the cheif town of Heluetia, sent to Charles. v. that nowe is Emprowr of Rome: holdinge a Parlemente or Cownsaill at Ausbrough with the cheif Lordis and lerned men of Germanye* (Zurich, 1543);

Ad illustrissimum Cattorum principem Philippum sermonis de providentia Dei Anamnema (Zurich: Christoph Froschauer, 1530); translated by Preble and Hinke as "Reproduction from Memory of a Sermon on the Providence of God, Dedicated to His Highness, Philip of Hesse," in *The Latin Works of Huldreich Zwingli*, volume 2, edited by Hinke (Philadelphia: Heidelberg, 1922), pp. 128-234;

Christianae fidei a Hudlrycho Zwinglio praedicatae, brevis et clara expositio (Zurich: Christoph Froschauer, 1536); translated by Preble and Hinke as "A Short and Clear Exposition of the Christian Faith Preached by Huldreich Zwingli," in *The Latin Works of Huldreich Zwingli*, volume 2, pp. 235-393.

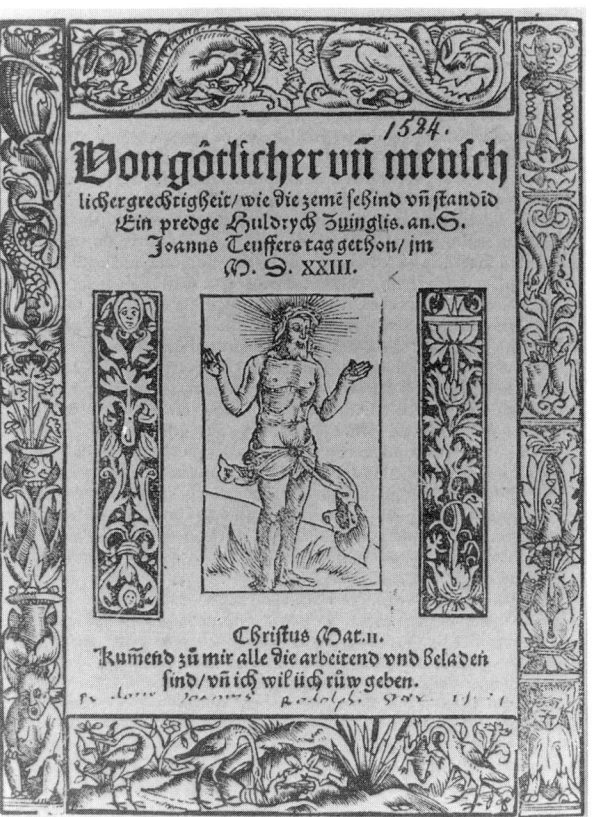

Title page for Zwingli's work on divine and human righteousness

Collections: *Opera d. Hvldrychi Zvingli,* 4 volumes, edited by Rudolph Walther (Zurich: Christoph Froschauer, 1545);

Huldreich Zwingli's Werke: Erste vollständige Ausgabe, 9 volumes, edited by Melchior Schuler and Johannes Schulthess (Zurich: Schulthess, 1828-1842);

Huldreich Zwinglis sämtliche Werke, edited by Emil Egli and Georg Finsler (Berlin: Schwetschke, 1905-).

Huldrych Zwingli was the originator of the Reformed branch of Protestantism. Independently of Martin Luther, Zwingli came to a reforming posture early in the 1520s. Under his leadership the Zurich church established its independence from Rome, created a new church order and discipline, and developed an evangelical theology and worship. Zwingli was a Swiss patriot, a humanist, and a theologian. First and foremost, however, he was a Reformer.

Zwingli was born in Wildhaus, in the Toggenburg Valley fifty-five miles east of Zurich, on 1 January 1484, the third of ten children. His father, also named Huldrych, was a successful farmer and local magistrate; his mother was Margaretha Meili. At the age of five Zwingli went to study with his uncle Bar-

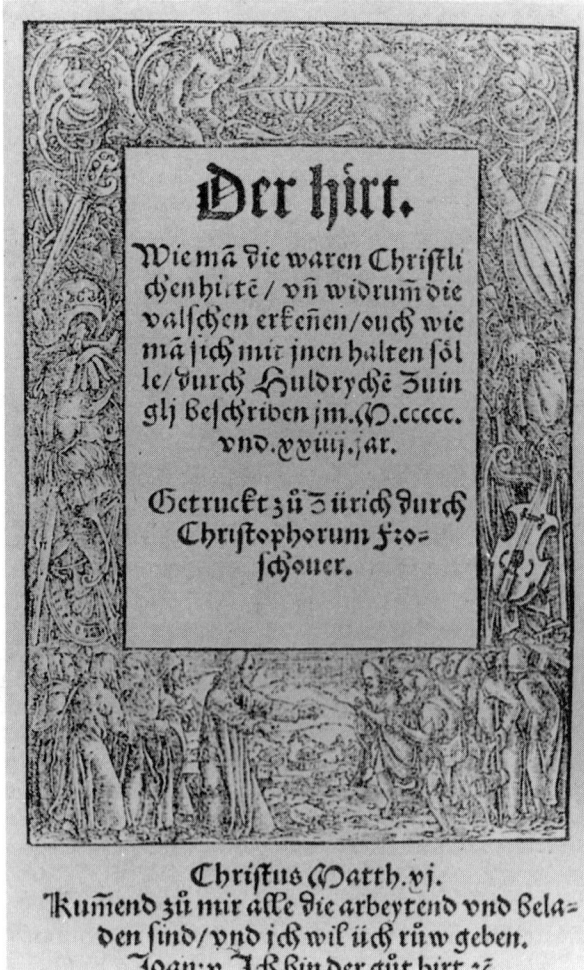

Title page for the work in which Zwingli points out the differences between the unreformed priest and the Reformed pastor

tholomew, a cleric in the village of Weesen on Lake Wallen, southwest of Wildhaus. In 1494 he went to Basel for further schooling; three years later he studied at Bern for a short period under the humanist Heinrich Wölfflin.

In the autumn of 1498 Zwingli entered the University of Vienna. In the spring of 1502 he transferred to the University of Basel. His university education was founded on the thorough absorption of Latin and the ability to write and speak convincingly; he was immersed in the *via antiqua* (Scholastic curriculum), especially the tradition of Duns Scotus, and he adopted the Aristotelian worldview. He received his baccalaureate in 1504 and early in 1506 was promoted to *Magister* (master of arts). After his promotion to Magister, Zwingli remained in Basel, studying theology, until the summer of 1506.

In September 1506 Zwingli was ordained in Constance. Soon thereafter he undertook the duties of his first pastorate, at Glarus, the capital of the Swiss Confederation state of the same name, near Weesen and not far from Wildhaus. During his years at Glarus, Zwingli continued his education by reading widely in classical, patristic, and Scholastic works and by learning Greek on his own. Thus began his development as a humanist. He corresponded with humanist friends, particularly Joachim Vadianus at the University of Vienna and Henry Loriti (Glarean) in Cologne. Around 1515 Zwingli began to read Desiderius Erasmus's works; he met the celebrated humanist in 1516.

Zwingli's humanistic aspirations are evident in three writings he produced in Glarus, all of which evidence his Swiss patriotism; none of them was published during his lifetime. The first was "Das Fabelgedicht vom Ochsen" (The Fable of the Ox), written in 1510 in elegant Latin and then translated into Swiss German; its purpose was to urge his Swiss confederates not to aid the papacy, the French, or the Hapsburgs with mercenary service. Each party is represented by an animal: the ox is the simple Swiss; the leopard represents the French; the lion is the Hapsburgs; and the prey, the fox, is Venice. Though even the good shepherd, the Pope, has ulterior motives, the confederates should go to his aid if he is attacked by the leopard or the lion.

Two years later Zwingli wrote an account of the military campaign in which the Swiss mercenaries drove the French from Lombardy and captured Pavia. "De gestis inter Gallos et Helvetios relatio" (An Account of the Military Conflicts between the French and the Swiss) not only demonstrates the elaborate humanist style Zwingli had developed by 1512 but also clarifies his political loyalty to the Pope: he describes the Swiss as the liberators of the papacy and the punishers of the enemies of the church.

Zwingli took part in a battle near Novara in 1513, and he participated, as chaplain for the troops from Glarus, in the disastrous battle at Marignano in 1515 in which ten thousand Swiss were killed. During this period, probably in 1516, he wrote "Das Labyrinth" (The Labyrinth). Its message is that action without reason is like attempting to traverse a labyrinth without a guide. One might wander, lost forever, without God's help in saving humans from their desires to fight with their neighbors. *Das Labyrinth* reflects Zwingli's disillusionment with war and the mercenary trade and his movement toward an Erasmian sort of pacifism.

Late in November 1516 Zwingli left Glarus to become priest at the Benedictine Abbey at Einsiedeln in Schwyz, south of Zurich. With its shrine to Mary, the monastery at Einsiedeln was a popular destination for pilgrimages. During his two years at Einsiedeln, Zwingli focused his energies on scholarship and preaching. Already an accomplished Greek scholar, he learned Hebrew. His sermons are moral admonitions based on biblical texts. He criticizes reliance on ceremonies and outward piety and promotes a simple, active Christianity. He was a dynamic supporter of the new biblical humanism during his two years at Einsiedeln.

In December 1518 Zwingli was offered the position of priest and preacher (people's priest) at the Great Minster in Zurich. He assumed his new duties on 1 January 1519. Erasmus's influence on him is particularly evident in the biblical and Christocentric nature of his sermons. Beginning with his first sermon in Zurich, Zwingli preached systematically through the Gospels.

It is not certain exactly when Zwingli developed his evangelical understanding of the Christian message. The date has been placed as early as 1516 and as late as 1522; Zwingli himself claimed the earlier date, but it seems clear that the process actually began late in 1519. A severe bout with the plague that year and opposition to his preaching in Zurich in 1520 began to erode Zwingli's Erasmian optimism. During the same period he was powerfully attracted to the Gospel of John and the writings of Saint Augustine. By late 1520 he had come to a Pauline understanding of human nature and divine grace and had moved beyond the humanism of Erasmus, which preserved the traditional authorities of the papacy, church dogma, and councils in its struggle for reform of the church. Zwingli rejected the authority of the Pope and the councils and became convinced that Scripture is the only basis for Christian teaching and living. Zwingli did not know about Luther's new theological ideas until late 1520, and he seems not to have been aware of Luther's three great Reformation writings of that year. Luther had little, if any, influence on Zwingli's transition from Erasmian humanist to evangelical Reformer.

In 1522 several laymen and clergymen broke the Lenten fast by eating an evening meal that included sausage. This act occasioned Zwingli's first explicit act as a Reformer and his first publication. Though Zwingli himself did not eat, he preached a sermon defending those who had participated. The sermon was published in an expanded form in April. In *Von Erkiesen und Freiheit der Speisen* (Of Choice and Freedom in the Matter of Food) he argues that ecclesiastical rules cannot supersede the freedom granted to Christians in Scripture; freedom can only be limited by a threat of public disturbance.

The Zurich city council asked the clergy of Zurich to give an opinion on the matter of fasting; they

Detail of the Zwingli Door of the Great Cathedral in Zurich, sculpted by Otto Münch, showing Zwingli translating the Bible

agreed with Zwingli that fasting is a matter of custom. But they went on to say that breaches of the fasting rules should be punished until the community came to an agreement on the issue. The bishop of Constance sent a delegation to Zurich to try to persuade the council to enforce the fasting regulations, and Zwingli was also allowed to appear. Though the council condemned violations of the fast, it also requested from the bishop a justification based on Scripture of the practice of fasting. In doing so, the council asserted its own authority in religious matters and recognized Zwingli as the equal of the bishop's representatives.

In May 1522 Zwingli returned to his old concern with mercenary service. *Eine göttliche Vermanung an die Eydgnossen zu Schwytz* (A Divine Admonition to the Confederates at Schwyz) argues for the cessation of the trade in mercenary soldiers, urges unity among the confederates, and warns that the mercenary trade will result in foreign control of the confederation and punishment from God. Many of the confederates, however, were more concerned about Zwingli's "heresy" than about the mercenary trade. In July the Diet condemned all the new teachings coming from Zurich; later in the year the Diet went even further, accusing Zurich of heresy and treason.

Nineteenth-century lithograph showing Zwingli disputing with Martin Luther at the Marburg Colloquy in 1529

In July 1522 Zwingli and ten other priests published *Supplicatio ad Hugonem Episcopum Constantiensem* (Petition to Hugo Bishop of Constance), appealing to Scripture to demand the abolition of celibacy. Two weeks later the petition was republished in German as *Eine freundliche Bitte und Ermahnung an die Eidgenossen* (A Friendly Petition and Admonition to the Confederates). For Zwingli himself it was a moot point, for he had publicly married Anna Reinhard in April.

In August the bishop responded to the petition with a mandate demanding that the Zurich council protect the church and maintain ecclesiastical order. Zwingli responded two weeks later with his *Apologeticus Archeteles* (The First and Last Word), in which he defended himself against the charges of dissension, schism, and heresy and condemned the bishop for depending on human law and opposing reform. Because of its degenerate state, Zwingli denied that the church hierarchy had any authority over matters of doctrine or church order. Erasmus wrote to Zwingli, severely criticizing his censure of the hierarchy.

In September, Zwingli published *Von Klarheit und Gewissheit des Wortes Gottes* (translated as "On the Clarity and Certainty of the Word of God," 1953), in which he defined his position on Scripture for the first time. Though the church fathers and councils may be useful, he says, they can only corroborate, and never add to, the authority of Scripture, for the Bible is God's Word. Only the individual believer, taught by God through the Spirit, can interpret the Bible correctly.

The First Zurich Disputation, called by the Zurich council to settle the question of Zwingli's orthodoxy, occurred on 29 January 1523. There were about six hundred participants; a delegation from the bishop attended but was under orders to object to the meeting and not to participate in the debate. Zwingli had prepared sixty-seven articles that summarized his teaching that salvation through Christ alone could only be found in Scripture. Since no one refuted Zwingli's articles, the council not only allowed him to continue his teaching but also ordered other preachers to teach only in accordance with Scripture.

After the First Disputation Zwingli began to write treatises clarifying his position on important theological issues. In mid July 1523 he published *Auslegen und Grunde der Schlussreden* (translated as "Exposition and Basis of the Conclusions," 1984), in which he expands on the sixty-seven articles. Most of Zwingli's Reformed theology is present in this treatise. He asserts that the authority of Scripture stands alone, without confirmation by the Church, that Scripture is inspired by God, and that the Holy Spirit is active in interpreting Scripture. He declares that salvation is found only in Christ, by God's grace through faith. He presents the church as both a spiritual body of all the faithful and as the local congregation. He views the Eucharist as a memorial of Christ. Finally, he affirms the sovereignty

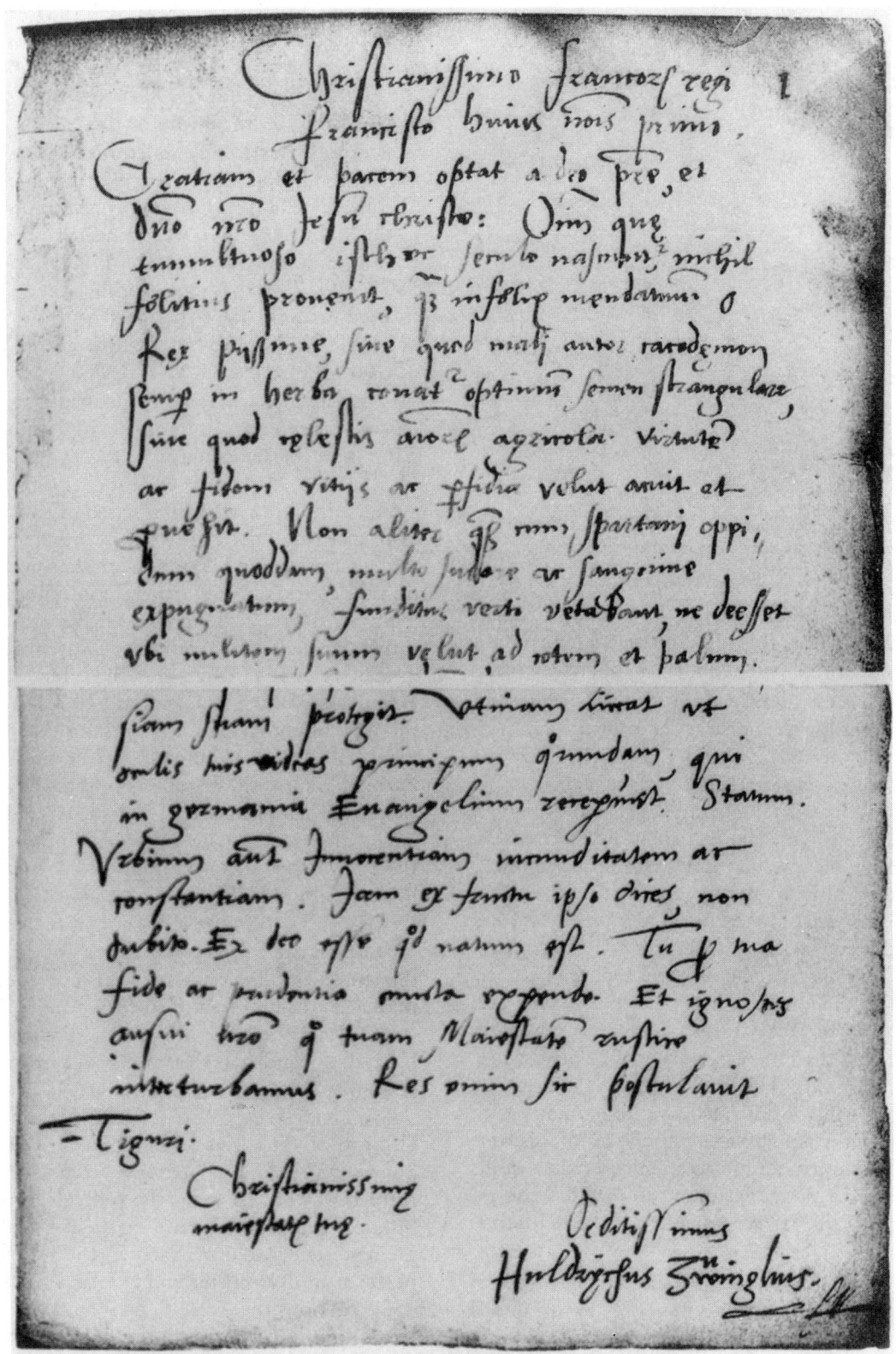

Page from the manuscript for Zwingli's confession of faith, written for King Francis I of France (Paris, Bibliothèque Nationale, Département des Manuscrits, fonds latin 36 73 A, folio 33ʳ)

Medallion by Jacob Stampfer bearing Zwingli's likeness (Zurich, Schweizerisches Landesmuseum)

of the civil government over the entire Christian community. With this document no one could doubt that Zwingli had gone far beyond Erasmus.

At the end of July, radicals in Zurich complained about the slow process of reform. Their agitation precipitated Zwingli's *Von göttlicher und menschlicher Gerechtigkeit* (1523; translated as "On Divine and Human Righteousness," 1984), in which he argues that divine righteousness, as expressed in the commandment to love one's neighbor as oneself, has to do with the inner person. Since humans cannot keep that part of the law, God gave the second part of the law, which includes all the commandments forbidding specific sins and crimes. This second part of the law concerns the outer person and human righteousness and is embodied in the laws and justice of the civil magistracy. The magistrate, however, must listen to divine righteousness and, as much as possible, bring his laws into harmony with the law of God. Applying the principles of this treatise, Zwingli criticizes the economic practices of his day and urges the government to prohibit the exploitation of the farmers through abusive interest rates.

By early autumn 1523 religious images and the mass had become important issues. The city council called the Second Disputation to meet on 26 October to discuss these matters; afterward the council decreed that the images should be kept and the Mass should be retained temporarily. The council also asked Zwingli to write a short introduction to Christian doctrine. Within three weeks Zwingli completed *Eine kurze christliche Einleitung* (1523; translated as "Short Christian Introduction," 1984), which was distributed to the Zurich clergy. In the work Zwingli deals with sin, the gospel, the law, abolition of the law, images, and the Mass; he does not, however, add anything new to the discussion.

Another relatively short treatise resulted from the Second Disputation: *Der Hirt* (translated as "The Shepherd," 1984) was originally a sermon preached to the 350 priests who were among the 900 people who attended the disputation. Published in March 1524, *Der Hirt* distinguishes between the unreformed priest or false shepherd and the true shepherd—the Reformed pastor—who preaches the Word of God without fear.

Zwingli continued this focus in *De vera et falsa religione commentarius* (translated as "Commentary on True and False Religion," 1929), published in March 1525. Dedicated to Francis I of France, this systematic work is the culmination of Zwingli's criticism of Rome: the Pope is the Antichrist and Catholicism is a false religion. Catholicism is superstition, in contrast to the true religion that is derived from Scripture. Zwingli here clearly states the Reformed principle of salvation by faith through God's grace, rejecting what he considers the semi-Pelagianism of the Roman Catholic Church. Along the way he touches on every issue that was being disputed. Toward the end of the lengthy treatise Zwingli assures the French king that the Reformed gospel does not promote civil disorder and disobedience; rather, the true religion supports a godly ruler. Writing in elegant Latin, Zwingli clearly hoped to impress the French humanists.

In June 1524 the city council ordered the removal and destruction of pictures and images from the churches. The following year, however, was the real year of action; within a few months Zurich became a Reformed city and canton. The council secularized the monasteries and reapportioned their revenues for education and welfare. It also created a new marriage court to replace the bishop's court in Constance. The Mass was replaced by the Lord's Supper on Maundy Thursday. Even so, the pace of reform was too slow for the radicals, and they rebuked Zwingli for depending on political arrangements to effect reform. Early in 1525 they began to perform adult baptisms and to form self-disciplining congregations that were to be free of governmental control. In late May, Zwingli answered the radicals with an important treatise, *Von der Taufe, von der Wiedertaufe und von der Kindertaufe* (translated as "On Baptism, Rebaptism, and Infant Baptism," 1953). He makes two principal arguments. First, he rejects the idea that baptism confers grace on the individual; baptism is a sign that the infant belongs to God. Second, he argues that infant baptism replaces circumcision as a sacrament of the New Covenant. He makes similar arguments in his *Antwort uber Balthasar Hubmaiers Taufbuchlein* (Reply to Balthasar Hubmaier's Little Book on Baptism), published in November 1525, in which he elaborates on his notion of the covenant. Finally, in 1527, he attacked the Anabaptist position in *In catabaptistarum strophas elenchus* (translated as "A Refutation of the Tricks of the Catabaptists, 1527," 1901). He refutes their teachings point by point, embellishing his covenantal idea. He says that God's covenant with Christians is simply a renewal of the old covenant that God made with Abraham. Zwingli's use in the title of the terms *elenchus* (refutation) and *strophas* (tricks)—rarely used words derived from Greek—reveals him as a humanist and shows that he is writing for scholars. Throughout these three works, Zwingli emphasizes the unity of the Christian community under the authority of the Christian government.

Controversy also surrounded Zwingli's view of the Eucharist, which was not fully formed until the latter part of 1524. In *Ad Matthaeum Alberum de coena dominica epistola* (translated as "Letter to Matthew Alber Concerning the Lord's Supper, November 1524," 1984) he says that the elements of the sacrament are signs pointing to salvation but not the means of grace themselves. In contrast to Luther's view that Christ is really present in the elements of the Eucharist, Zwingli affirms the spiritual presence of Christ. When Jesus said, "This is my body, this is my blood," he meant that the elements signify his body and blood. As Zwingli published other works on the Eucharist, his differences with Luther became more and more apparent. Then, in February 1526, he published *Eine klare Unterrichtung vom Nachtmahl Christi* (A Clear Explanation of the Supper of Christ; translated as "On the Lord's Supper," 1953), a work addressed to the laity in which he attacks Luther's teaching of the real presence and explains his own symbolic understanding. He also emphasizes his understanding of the Lord's Supper as a communal meal that brings the congregation together in memory and thanksgiving under the covenant, in the same manner as the Passover feast in the Old Testament. This publication resulted in a literary controversy over the Eucharist, involving Zwingli, Luther, and other theologians from upper Germany, that lasted until 1529. The least confrontational of Zwingli's works during this controversy was his *Amica exegesis, id est, expositio Eucharistiae negocii, ad Martinum Lutherum* (1527; translated as "Friendly Exegesis, That Is, Exposition of the Matter of the Eucharist to Martin Luther," 1984), where

Zwingli's grave in Kappel, where he was killed in battle on 11 October 1531

he says that he hopes that he and Luther can find some harmony on this matter—if only Luther would recognize his error. Zwingli uses classical allusions and figures of speech, such as synecdoche and metonomy, to fortify his argument for the symbolic understanding. Finally, at the Marburg Colloquy, convened by Philip of Hesse and held on the first three days of October 1529, Zwingli and Luther debated the issues that separated them. They were able to agree on all matters except the Eucharist. This was the only time that the two met in person. After Marburg, during the final two years of his life, Zwingli combined his roles of Swiss patriot and Reformer as he worked to create an alliance of south German cities and states with the Swiss Reformed states. In November such an agreement was reached between Philip of Hesse, Zurich, Basel, and Strasbourg. During the late 1520s and the 1530s the majority of the south German cities became Zwinglian.

Zwingli also refined his theology during the last two years of his life. Except for his agreement with Luther and against Erasmus in denying the freedom of the will in the matter of salvation, Zwingli took every chance to point out the differences between himself and Luther. *Ad Carolum Romanorum Im-*

peratorem Germaniae comitia Augustae celebrantem, fidei Huldrychi Zwinglii ratio (An Account of the Faith of Huldrych Zwingli Submitted to the German Emperor Charles V, at the Diet of Augsburg, 1530; translated as *The Rekening and declaration of the faith and beleif of Huldrik Zwingly, bischoppe of Züryk the cheif town of Heluetia, sent to Charles. v. that nowe is Emprowr of Rome: holdinge a Parlemente or Cownsaill at Ausbrough with the cheif Lordis and lerned men of Germanye*, 1543) is a bold personal statement that clearly differentiates Reformed Protestantism from both Lutheranism and Catholicism. Zwingli's answer to the Augsburg Confession, he naively hoped that it would persuade the emperor to abandon his Catholicism.

In August 1530, at the request of Philip of Hesse, Zwingli published a sermon he had preached in Marburg the previous year. In *Ad illustrissimum Cattorum principem Philippum sermonis de providentia Dei Anamnema* (translated as "Reproduction from Memory of a Sermon on the Providence of God, Dedicated to His Highness, Philip of Hesse," 1922) Zwingli draws heavily on classical and humanist sources; for instance, he turns to Seneca and to Seneca's use of Plato in defining the supreme deity and master builder of the universe. Later in the treatise he hints that outstanding virtuous pagans, such as Socrates and Seneca, might be granted salvation. Throughout this work, as in the confession for Charles V earlier in 1530, Zwingli's tone is extremely anti-Luther.

By 1530 political tensions were running high within the Swiss Confederation. War between the Catholic states and the Reformed states of Zurich and Bern had narrowly been averted in June 1529 by the First Peace of Kappel. It was in this context that Zwingli wrote the final summary of his theology. The French envoy to Switzerland, Lambert Maigret, was trying to promote an alliance between the two countries, but King Francis I had serious misgivings about the Reformed faith. Maigret urged Zwingli to send a clear statement of his theology to the king to clarify any misunderstandings Francis might have. In July 1531 Zwingli wrote *Christianae fidei a Hudlrycho Zwinglio praedicatae, brevis et clara expositio* (A Brief and Clear Exposition of the Faith Preached by Huldrych Zwingli; translated as "An Exposition of the Faith," 1953) and sent it to Francis; it was not published until 1536. The work shows Zwingli as a humanist: he makes many classical allusions, uses Greek words throughout, and alludes to ancient philosophical concepts. Here again he includes virtuous pagans—Socrates, Aristides, Antigonus, Numa, Camillus, the Catos, and the Scipios—among those whom God will save for eternity.

Zwingli's *Christianae fidei expositio* did not result in an alliance with France, and the agreement with Philipp of Hesse and the south German cities proved to be worthless when war broke out. Nor did the other Reformed states of Switzerland, notably Bern and Basel, come to Zurich's aid when the Catholic Swiss states declared war on Zurich on 9 October 1531. Two days later the Catholic forces attacked at Kappel, south of Zurich. The battle lasted less than an hour; the Protestants were defeated, and five hundred Zurichers were killed. Zwingli was among the dead.

Zwinglianism did not, however, die with Zwingli. Under the leadership of Heinrich Bullinger, Zwingli's successor at Zurich, Reformed Protestantism spread and flourished in Switzerland, southern Germany, England, Scotland, and elsewhere. After 1560, however, the Calvinist branch of Reformed Protestantism increasingly challenged Zwinglianism. By the early seventeenth century Calvinism had virtually subsumed Zwinglianism to become the dominant expression of the Reformed tradition.

Biographies:

Walther Kohler, *Huldrych Zwingli* (Leipzig: Koehler & Amelang, 1943);

Oskar Farner, *Huldrych Zwingli,* 4 volumes (Zurich: Zwingli Verlag, 1943-1960); translated by D. G. Sear as *Zwingli the Reformer: His Life and Work* (Hamden, Conn.: Archon, 1968);

Jean Rilliet, *Zwingle: Le troisième homme de la Reforme* (Paris: Fayand, 1959); translated by Harold Knight as *Zwingli: Third Man of the Reformation* (Philadelphia: Westminster, 1964);

Martin Haas, *Huldrych Zwingli und seine Zeit* (Zurich: Zwingli Verlag, 1969);

Fritz Busser, *Huldrych Zwingli: Reformation als prophetischer Auftrag* (Göttingen, Zurich & Frankfurt am Main: Musterschmidt, 1973);

G. R. Potter, *Zwingli* (Cambridge: Cambridge University Press, 1976);

Francesco Erasmo Sciuto, *Ulrico Zwingli: La vita–il pensio–il suo tempo* (Naples: Giannini, 1980);

Ulrich Gabler, *Huldrych Zwingli: Eine Einführung in sein Leben und sein Werk* (Munich: Beck, 1983); translated by Ruth C.L. Gritsch as *Huldrych Zwingli: His Life and Work* (Philadelphia: Fortress, 1986).

References:

Oskar Farner, *Die Lehre von Kirche und Staat bei Zwingli* (Tübingen: Mohr, 1930);

E. J. Furcha, *Huldrych Zwingli, 1484-1531: A Legacy of Radical Reform,* ARC Supplement no. 2, Faculty of Religious Studies, McGill University

(Montreal: McGill University Press, 1985);

Furcha and H. Wayne Pipkin, *Prophet, Pastor, Protestant: The Work of Huldrych Zwingli after Five Hundred Years* (Allison Park, Pa.: Pickwick, 1984);

Charles Garside, *Zwingli and the Arts* (New Haven: Yale University Press, 1966);

Rene Hauswirth, *Landgraf Philipp von Hessen und Zwingli: Voraussetzungen und Geschichte der politischen Beziehungen zwischen Hessen, Strassburg, Konstanz, Ulrich von Wurttemberg und reformierten Eidgenossen, 1526–1531* (Tübingen: Osiander/Basel: Basileia, 1968);

Walther Kohler, *Zwingli und Luther: Ihr Streit über das Abendmahl nach seinen politischen und religiösen Beziehungen*, 2 volumes (Gutersloh: Heinsius, 1924);

Roger Ley, *Kirchenzucht bei Zwingli* (Zurich: Zwingli Verlag, 1948);

Gottfried W. Locher, *Huldrych Zwingli in neuer Sicht: Zehn Beiträge zur Theologie der Zürcher Reformation* (Zurich: Zwingli Verlag, 1969); translated by Milton Aylor and Stuart Casson as *Zwingli's Thought: New Perspectives* (Leiden: Brill, 1981);

Paul Meyer, *Zwinglis Sociallehren* (Linz: Oberösterreichisches Verlagsgesellschaft, 1921);

Jacques V. Pollet, *Huldrych Zwingli et la Reforme en Suisse d'apres les recherches recentes* (Paris: Presses Universitaires de France, 1963);

Arthur Rich, *Die Anfänge der Theologie Huldrych Zwinglis* (Zurich: Zwingli Verlag, 1949);

Heinrich Schmid, *Zwinglis Lehre von der göttlichen und menschlichen Gerechtigkeit* (Zurich: Zwingli Verlag, 1959);

W. P. Stephens, *The Theology of Huldrych Zwingli* (Oxford: Clarendon Press, 1986);

Robert C. Walton, *Zwingli's Theocracy* (Toronto: Toronto University Press, 1967).

Papers:

Huldrych Zwingli's papers are in the Staatsarchiv and the Zentralbibliothek, Zurich.

Checklist of Further Readings

Albrecht, Günter, and others. *Deutsche Literaturgeschichte in Bildern: Eine Darstellung von den Anfängen bis zur Gegenwart,* volume 1. Leipzig: VEB Bibliographisches Institut, 1969.

Bacon, Tom Ivey. *Martin Luther and the Drama.* Amsterdam: Rodopi, 1976.

Bahr, Ehrhard, ed. *Geschichte der deutschen Literatur: Kontinuität und Veränderung. Vom Mittelalter bis zur Gegenwart,* volume 1: *Vom Mittelalter bis zum Barock.* Tübingen: Francke, 1987.

Bainton, Roland H. *Women of the Reformation in Germany and Italy.* Minneapolis: Augsburg, 1971.

Becker-Cantarino, Barbara. *Der lange Weg zur Mündigkeit: Frau und Literatur (1500–1800).* Stuttgart: Metzler, 1987.

Bernstein, Eckhard. *German Humanism.* Boston: Twayne, 1983.

Bernstein. *Die Literatur des deutschen Frühhumanismus.* Stuttgart: Metzler, 1978.

Beutin, Wolfgang, and others. *A History of German Literature: From the Beginnings to the Present Day,* fourth edition, translated by Clare Krojzl. London & New York: Routledge, 1993.

Bietenholz, Peter C., and Thomas B. Deutscher, eds. *Contemporaries of Erasmus: A Biographical Register of the Renaissance and Reformation,* 3 volumes. Toronto: University of Toronto Press, 1985–1987.

Boesch, Bruno, ed. *Deutsche Literaturgeschichte in Grundzügen: Die Epochen deutscher Dichtung,* third edition. Bern & Munich: Francke, 1967.

Borchardt, Frank L. *German Antiquity in Renaissance Myth.* Baltimore: Johns Hopkins University Press, 1971.

Brink, Jean R., Allison P. Coudert, and Maryanne C. Horowitz, eds. *The Politics of Gender in Early Modern Europe.* Kirksville, Mo.: Sixteenth Century Journal Publishers, 1989.

Brinkler-Gabler, Gisela, ed. *Deutsche Literatur von Frauen,* volume 1: *Vom Mittelalter bis zum Ende des 18. Jahrhunderts.* Munich: Beck, 1988.

Buck, August, ed. *Die Rezeption der Antike: Zum Problem der Kontinuität zwischen Mittelalter und Renaissance.* Hamburg: Hauswedell, 1978.

Burdach, Konrad. *Reformation, Renaissance, Humanismus: Zwei Abhandlungen über die Grundlage moderner Bildung und Sprachkunst.* Darmstadt: Wissenschaftliche Buchgesellschaft, 1978.

Burger, Heinz Otto, ed. *Annalen der deutschen Literatur: Geschichte der deutschen Literatur von den Anfängen bis zur Gegenwart.* Stuttgart: Metzler, 1952.

Burger. *Renaissance, Humanismus, Reformation: Deutsche Litertur im europäischen Kontext.* Bad Homburg, Berlin & Zurich: Gehlen, 1969.

Burns, J. H., ed. *The Cambridge History of Political Thought 1450–1700.* Cambridge, U.K. & New York: Cambridge University Press, 1991.

Catholy, Eckehard. *Das deutsche Lustpiel*. Stuttgart: Kohlhammer, 1969.

Catholy. *Fastnachtspiel*. Stuttgart: Metzler, 1966.

Davidson, N. S. *The Counter-Reformation*. Oxford & New York: Blackwell, 1987.

Davies, Oliver. *God Within: The Mystical Tradition of Northern Europe*. London: Darton, Longman & Todd, 1988; New York: Paulist Press, 1988.

Dilthey, Wilhelm. *Gesammelte Schriften,* volume 2: *Weltanschauung and Analyse des Menschen seit Renaissance und Reformation*. Stuttgart: Teubner / Göttingen: Vandenhoeck & Ruprecht, 1957.

Ellinger, Georg. *Geschichte der neulateinischen Literatur Deutschlands im sechzehnten Jahrhundert,* 3 volumes. Berlin & Leipzig: De Gruyter, 1929–1933.

Ertzdorff, Xenja von. *Romane und Novellen des 15. und 16. Jahrhunderts in Deutschland*. Darmstadt: Wissenschaftliche Buchgesellschaft, 1989.

Fleischer, Manfred P., ed. *The Harvest of Humanism in Central Europe*. Saint Louis: Concordia, 1992.

Frenzel, Herbert A., *Daten Deutscher Dichtung,* volume 1. Cologne: Kiepenheuer & Witsch, 1953.

Füssel, Stephan, ed. *Deutsche Dichter der frühen Neuzeit 1450–1600*. Berlin: Erich Schmidt, 1993.

Grant, W. Leonard. *Neo-Latin Literature and the Pastoral*. Chapel Hill: University of North Carolina Press, 1965.

Grimminger, Rolf, ed. *Hansers Sozialgeschichte der deutschen Literatur vom 16. Jahrhundert bis zur Gegenwart,* volume 3. Munich: Hanser, 1980.

Hardison, O. B. *Christian Rite and Christian Drama in the Middle Ages*. Baltimore: Johns Hopkins University Press, 1965.

Heger, Hedwig, ed. *Spätmittelalter, Humanismus, Reformation: Texte und Zeugnisse,* 2 volumes. Munich: Beck, 1975, 1978.

Henkel, Arthur, and Albrecht Schöne. *Emblemata: Handbuch zur Sinnbildkunst des 16. und 17. Jahrhunderts,* second edition. Stuttgart: Metzler, 1976.

Hillerbrand, Hans, ed. *The Oxford Encyclopedia of the Reformation,* 4 volumes. New York: Oxford University Press, 1996.

Hirsch, Rudolf. *The Printed Word: Its Impact and Diffusion*. London: Variorum, 1978.

Hoffmeister, Gerhart, ed. *The Renaissance and Reformation in Germany: An Introduction*. New York: Ungar, 1977.

Huizinga, Johan. *The Waning of the Middle Ages*. London: Arnold, 1924; New York: Saint Martin's Press, 1985.

Huppert, George. *After the Black Death: A Social History of Early Modern Europe*. Bloomington & Indianapolis: Indiana University Press, 1986.

IJsewijn, Jozef. *Companion to Neo-Latin Studies,* part 1: *History and Diffusion of Neo-Latin Literature,* second edition. Louvain: Louvain University Press & Peeters Press, 1990.

Jaumann, Herbert. *Critica: Untersuchungen zur Geschichte der Literaturkritik zwischen Quintilian und Thomasius*. Leiden & New York: Brill, 1995.

Kemper, Hans Georg. *Deutsche Lyrik der frühen Neuzeit,* volume 1: *Epochen- und Gattungsprobleme: Reformationszeit.* Tübingen: Niemeyer, 1987.

Könneker, Barbara. *Wesen und Wandlung der Narrenidee im Zeitalter des Humanismus: Brant. Murner. Erasmus.* Wiesbaden: Steiner, 1966.

Könneker and Conrad Wiedemann. *Deutsche Literatur in Humanismus und Barock.* Frankfurt am Main: Athenaion, 1973.

Michael, Wolfgang F. *Das deutsche Drama der Reformationszeit.* Bern & New York: Peter Lang, 1984.

Michael. *Frühformen der deutschen Bühne.* Berlin: Selbstverlag der Gesellschaft für Theatergeschichte, 1963.

Nagel, Bert. *Meistersang,* second edition. Stuttgart: Metzler, 1971.

Nauert, Charles G. *Humanism and the Culture of Renaissance Europe.* New York: Cambridge University Press, 1995.

Oberman, Heiko. *The Dawn of the Reformation: Essays in Late Medieval and Early Reformation Thought.* Edinburgh: Clark, 1986; Grand Rapids, Mich.: Eerdmans, 1992.

Ozment, Steven. *The Age of Reform (1250-1550): An Intellectual and Religious History of Late Medieval and Reformation Europe.* New Haven & London: Yale University Press, 1980.

Parker, Patricia, and David Quint, eds. *Literary Theory/Renaissance Texts.* Baltimore & London: Johns Hopkins University Press, 1986.

Pascal, Roy. *German Literature in the Sixteenth and Seventeenth Centuries: Renaissance–Reformation–Baroque.* London: Cresset, 1968 ; New York: Barnes & Noble, 1968.

Pascal. *The Social Basis of the German Reformation: Martin Luther and His Times.* New York: Kelley, 1971.

Pasley, Malcolm, ed. *Germany: A Companion to German Studies,* second edition. London & New York: Methuen, 1982.

Post, R. R. *The Modern Devotion: Confrontation with Reformation and Humanism.* Leiden: Brill, 1968.

Reinhart, Max, and Jeannine Blackwell, eds. "Cultural Contentions in Early Modern Germany." Special double issue of *Colloquia Germanica,* 28, nos. 3-4 (1995).

Roloff, Hans-Gert. "Neulateinische Literatur," in *Renaissance und Barock 1400-1700,* volume 3 of *Propyläen Geschichte der Literatur: Literatur und Gesellschaft der westlichen Welt.* Berlin: Propyläen, 1984, pp. 196-230.

Rupprich, Hans. *Die deutsche Literatur vom späten Mittelalter bis zum Barock,* volume 1: *Das ausgehende Mittelalter, Humanismus und Renaissance (1370-1520).* Munich: Beck, 1970.

Schade, Richard Erich. *Studies in Early German Comedy: 1500-1650.* Columbia, S.C.: Camden House, 1988.

Schmidt, Josef, ed. *Renaissance, Humanismus, Reformation.* Stuttgart: Reclam, 1983.

Schmitt, Charles B., and Quentin Skinner, eds. *The Cambridge History of Renaissance Philosophy.* Cambridge & New York: Cambridge University Press, 1988.

Spitz, Lewis W. *The Religious Renaissance of the German Humanists.* Cambridge, Mass.: Harvard University Press, 1963.

Checklist of Further Readings

Spriewald, Ingeborg, and others. *Grundpositionen der deutschen Literatur im 16. Jahrhundert.* Berlin & Weimar: Aufbau, 1972.

Stammler, Wolfgang. *Von der Mystik zum Barock, 1400–1600,* revised and enlarged edition. Stuttgart: Metzler, 1950.

Suppan, Wolfgang. *Volkslied,* second edition. Stuttgart: Metzler, 1978.

Taylor, Archer. *Problems in German Literary History of the Fifteenth and Sixteenth Centuries.* New York: Kraus, 1966.

Troeltsch, Ernst. *Die Soziallehren der christlichen Kirchen und Grupppen,* volume 1 of his *Gesammelte Schriften,* edited by Hans Baron. Aalen: Scientia, 1961.

Trunz, Erich. "Der deutsche Späthumanismus um 1600 als Standeskultur," in *Deutsche Barockforschung: Dokumentation einer Epoche,* second edition, edited by Richard Alewyn. Cologne: Kiepenheuer & Witsch, 1970, pp. 147–181.

Vivian, Kim, ed. *A Concise History of German Literature to 1900.* Columbia, S.C.: Camden House, 1992.

Walz, Herbert. *Deutsche Literatur der Reformationszeit: Eine Einführung.* Darmstadt: Wissenschaftliche Buchgesellschaft, 1988.

Wilson, Katharina M., ed. *An Encyclopedia of Continental Women Writers,* volume 1. New York & London: Garland, 1991.

Contributors

J. Wayne Baker	*University of Akron*
Paula Datsko Barker	*Seabury-Western Theological Seminary*
Frank Baron	*University of Kansas*
Eckhard Bernstein	*College of the Holy Cross*
David Blamires	*University of Manchester*
Paul F. Casey	*University of Missouri*
Albrecht Classen	*University of Arizona*
Joe G. Delap	*Kansas Wesleyan University*
Glenn Ehrstine	*University of Iowa*
John L. Flood	*University of London Institute of Germanic Studies*
Linda L. Gaus	*University of California, Berkeley*
Pricilla A. Hayden-Roy	*University of Nebraska–Lincoln*
Jeffrey Jaynes	*Methodist Theological School in Ohio*
Hermina Joldersma	*University of Calgary*
James V. Mehl	*Missouri Western State College*
Wanda Merchant	*University of Texas at Austin*
James H. Overfield	*University of Vermont*
David Price	*University of Texas at Austin*
Richard E. Schade	*University of Cincinnati*
Peter Schaeffer	*University of California, Davis*
Debra L. Stoudt	*University of Toledo*
John Van Cleve	*Augsburg College*
Derk Visser	*Ursinus College*
Harry Vredeveld	*Ohio State University*
Elisabeth Wåghäll	*Växjö University*
Stephen L. Wailes	*Indiana University*
Gerhild Scholz Williams	*Washington University, Saint Louis*
Anne Winston-Allen	*Southern Illinois University*

Cumulative Index

Dictionary of Literary Biography, Volumes 1-179
Dictionary of Literary Biography Yearbook, 1980-1996
Dictionary of Literary Biography Documentary Series, Volumes 1-14

Cumulative Index

DLB before number: *Dictionary of Literary Biography*, Volumes 1-179
Y before number: *Dictionary of Literary Biography Yearbook*, 1980-1996
DS before number: *Dictionary of Literary Biography Documentary Series*, Volumes 1-14

A

Abbey Press DLB-49

The Abbey Theatre and Irish Drama, 1900-1945 . . . . DLB-10

Abbot, Willis J. 1863-1934 . . . . DLB-29

Abbott, Jacob 1803-1879 . . . . DLB-1

Abbott, Lee K. 1947- DLB-130

Abbott, Lyman 1835-1922 . . . . DLB-79

Abbott, Robert S. 1868-1940 . . . . DLB-29, 91

Abelard, Peter circa 1079-1142 . . . . . DLB-115

Abelard-Schuman DLB-46

Abell, Arunah S. 1806-1888 . . . . DLB-43

Abercrombie, Lascelles 1881-1938 . . . DLB-19

Aberdeen University Press Limited DLB-106

Abish, Walter 1931- DLB-130

Ablesimov, Aleksandr Onisimovich 1742-1783 . . . . DLB-150

Abraham à Sancta Clara 1644-1709 . . . . DLB-168

Abrahams, Peter 1919- DLB-117

Abrams, M. H. 1912- DLB-67

Abrogans circa 790-800 . . . . DLB-148

Abschatz, Hans Aßmann von 1646-1699 . . . . DLB-168

Abse, Dannie 1923- DLB-27

Academy Chicago Publishers DLB-46

Accrocca, Elio Filippo 1923- DLB-128

Ace Books DLB-46

Achebe, Chinua 1930- DLB-117

Achtenberg, Herbert 1938- DLB-124

Ackerman, Diane 1948- DLB-120

Ackroyd, Peter 1949- DLB-155

Acorn, Milton 1923-1986 . . . . DLB-53

Acosta, Oscar Zeta 1935?- DLB-82

Actors Theatre of Louisville DLB-7

Adair, James 1709?-1783? DLB-30

Adam, Graeme Mercer 1839-1912 . . . DLB-99

Adame, Leonard 1947- DLB-82

Adamic, Louis 1898-1951 . . . . DLB-9

Adams, Alice 1926- Y-86

Adams, Brooks 1848-1927 . . . . DLB-47

Adams, Charles Francis, Jr. 1835-1915 . . . . DLB-47

Adams, Douglas 1952- Y-83

Adams, Franklin P. 1881-1960 . . . . . . DLB-29

Adams, Henry 1838-1918 . . . . DLB-12, 47

Adams, Herbert Baxter 1850-1901 . . . DLB-47

Adams, J. S. and C. [publishing house] DLB-49

Adams, James Truslow 1878-1949 . . . DLB-17

Adams, John 1735-1826 . . . . DLB-31

Adams, John Quincy 1767-1848 . . . . . DLB-37

Adams, Léonie 1899-1988 . . . . DLB-48

Adams, Levi 1802-1832 . . . . DLB-99

Adams, Samuel 1722-1803 . . . . DLB-31, 43

Adams, Thomas 1582 or 1583-1652 . . . . DLB-151

Adams, William Taylor 1822-1897 . . . DLB-42

Adamson, Sir John 1867-1950 . . . . . . DLB-98

Adcock, Arthur St. John 1864-1930 . . . . DLB-135

Adcock, Betty 1938- DLB-105

Adcock, Betty, Certain Gifts DLB-105

Adcock, Fleur 1934- DLB-40

Addison, Joseph 1672-1719 . . . . DLB-101

Ade, George 1866-1944 . . . . DLB-11, 25

Adeler, Max (see Clark, Charles Heber)

Adonias Filho 1915-1990 . . . . DLB-145

Advance Publishing Company DLB-49

AE 1867-1935 . . . . DLB-19

Ælfric circa 955-circa 1010 . . . . DLB-146

Aeschines circa 390 B.C.-circa 320 B.C. DLB-176

Aeschylus 525-524 B.C.-456-455 B.C. DLB-176

Aesthetic Poetry (1873), by Walter Pater DLB-35

After Dinner Opera Company Y-92

Afro-American Literary Critics: An Introduction DLB-33

Agassiz, Jean Louis Rodolphe 1807-1873 . . . . DLB-1

Agee, James 1909-1955 . . . . . . DLB-2, 26, 152

The Agee Legacy: A Conference at the University of Tennessee at Knoxville Y-89

Aguilera Malta, Demetrio 1909-1981 . . . . DLB-145

Ai 1947- DLB-120

Aichinger, Ilse 1921- DLB-85

Aidoo, Ama Ata 1942- DLB-117

Aiken, Conrad 1889-1973 . . . . DLB-9, 45, 102

Aiken, Joan 1924- DLB-161

Aikin, Lucy 1781-1864 . . . . DLB-144, 163

Ainsworth, William Harrison 1805-1882 . . . . DLB-21

Aitken, George A. 1860-1917 . . . . . . DLB-149

Aitken, Robert [publishing house] . . . DLB-49

Akenside, Mark 1721-1770 . . . . DLB-109

Akins, Zoë 1886-1958 . . . . DLB-26

Alabaster, William 1568-1640 . . . . . . DLB-132

Alain-Fournier 1886-1914 . . . . DLB-65

Alarcón, Francisco X. 1954- DLB-122

Alba, Nanina 1915-1968 . . . . DLB-41

Albee, Edward 1928- DLB-7

Albert the Great circa 1200-1280 . . . DLB-115

Alberti, Rafael 1902- DLB-108

Albertinus, Aegidius circa 1560-1620 . . . . DLB-164

Alcaeus born circa 620 B.C. DLB-176

Alcott, Amos Bronson 1799-1888 . . . . . DLB-1

Alcott, Louisa May 1832-1888 ......DLB-1, 42, 79; DS-14

Alcott, William Andrus 1798-1859 ....DLB-1

Alcuin circa 732-804 ....DLB-148

Alden, Henry Mills 1836-1919 ......DLB-79

Alden, Isabella 1841-1930 ....DLB-42

Alden, John B. [publishing house] ...DLB-49

Alden, Beardsley and Company DLB-49

Aldington, Richard 1892-1962 ....DLB-20, 36, 100, 149

Aldis, Dorothy 1896-1966 ....DLB-22

Aldiss, Brian W. 1925- DLB-14

Aldrich, Thomas Bailey 1836-1907 ....DLB-42, 71, 74, 79

Alegría, Ciro 1909-1967 ....DLB-113

Alegría, Claribel 1924- DLB-145

Aleixandre, Vicente 1898-1984 .....DLB-108

Aleramo, Sibilla 1876-1960 ....DLB-114

Alexander, Charles 1868-1923 ......DLB-91

Alexander, Charles Wesley [publishing house] DLB-49

Alexander, James 1691-1756 ....DLB-24

Alexander, Lloyd 1924- DLB-52

Alexander, Sir William, Earl of Stirling 1577?-1640 ....DLB-121

Alexie, Sherman 1966- DLB-175

Alexis, Willibald 1798-1871 ....DLB-133

Alfred, King 849-899 ....DLB-146

Alger, Horatio, Jr. 1832-1899 ....DLB-42

Algonquin Books of Chapel Hill DLB-46

Algren, Nelson 1909-1981 ...DLB-9; Y-81, 82

Allan, Andrew 1907-1974 ....DLB-88

Allan, Ted 1916- DLB-68

Allbeury, Ted 1917- DLB-87

Alldritt, Keith 1935- DLB-14

Allen, Ethan 1738-1789 ....DLB-31

Allen, Frederick Lewis 1890-1954 ...DLB-137

Allen, Gay Wilson 1903-1995 ....DLB-103; Y-95

Allen, George 1808-1876 ....DLB-59

Allen, George [publishing house] ...DLB-106

Allen, George, and Unwin Limited ...DLB-112

Allen, Grant 1848-1899 .....DLB-70, 92, 178

Allen, Henry W. 1912- Y-85

Allen, Hervey 1889-1949 ....DLB-9, 45

Allen, James 1739-1808 ....DLB-31

Allen, James Lane 1849-1925 ....DLB-71

Allen, Jay Presson 1922- DLB-26

Allen, John, and Company DLB-49

Allen, Paula Gunn 1939- DLB-175

Allen, Samuel W. 1917- DLB-41

Allen, Woody 1935- DLB-44

Allende, Isabel 1942- DLB-145

Alline, Henry 1748-1784 ....DLB-99

Allingham, Margery 1904-1966 .....DLB-77

Allingham, William 1824-1889 .....DLB-35

Allison, W. L. [publishing house] DLB-49

The *Alliterative Morte Arthure* and the *Stanzaic Morte Arthur* circa 1350-1400 ....DLB-146

Allott, Kenneth 1912-1973 ....DLB-20

Allston, Washington 1779-1843 ......DLB-1

Almon, John [publishing house] DLB-154

Alonzo, Dámaso 1898-1990 ....DLB-108

Alsop, George 1636-post 1673 ....DLB-24

Alsop, Richard 1761-1815 ....DLB-37

Altemus, Henry, and Company DLB-49

Altenberg, Peter 1885-1919 ....DLB-81

Altolaguirre, Manuel 1905-1959 ....DLB-108

Aluko, T. M. 1918- DLB-117

Alurista 1947- DLB-82

Alvarez, A. 1929- DLB-14, 40

Amadi, Elechi 1934- DLB-117

Amado, Jorge 1912- DLB-113

Ambler, Eric 1909- DLB-77

America: or, a Poem on the Settlement of the British Colonies (1780?), by Timothy Dwight.....................DLB-37

American Conservatory Theatre DLB-7

American Fiction and the 1930s DLB-9

American Humor: A Historical Survey East and Northeast South and Southwest Midwest West......................DLB-11

The American Library in Paris.........Y-93

American News Company..........DLB-49

The American Poets' Corner: The First Three Years (1983-1986) Y-86

American Proletarian Culture: The 1930s....................DS-11

American Publishing Company DLB-49

American Stationers' Company DLB-49

American Sunday-School Union.....DLB-49

American Temperance Union DLB-49

American Tract Society DLB-49

The American Trust for the British Library Y-96

The American Writers Congress (9-12 October 1981)...............Y-81

The American Writers Congress: A Report on Continuing Business Y-81

Ames, Fisher 1758-1808............DLB-37

Ames, Mary Clemmer 1831-1884 ....DLB-23

Amini, Johari M. 1935- DLB-41

Amis, Kingsley 1922-1995 ....DLB-15, 27, 100, 139, Y-96

Amis, Martin 1949- DLB-14

Ammons, A. R. 1926- DLB-5, 165

Amory, Thomas 1691?-1788........DLB-39

Anaya, Rudolfo A. 1937- DLB-82

Ancrene Riwle circa 1200-1225 ......DLB-146

Andersch, Alfred 1914-1980 ....DLB-69

Anderson, Margaret 1886-1973 ...DLB-4, 91

Anderson, Maxwell 1888-1959 ....DLB-7

Anderson, Patrick 1915-1979 ....DLB-68

Anderson, Paul Y. 1893-1938 ....DLB-29

Anderson, Poul 1926- DLB-8

Anderson, Robert 1750-1830.......DLB-142

Anderson, Robert 1917- DLB-7

Anderson, Sherwood 1876-1941..........DLB-4, 9, 86; DS-1

Andreae, Johann Valentin 1586-1654 ....DLB-164

Andreas-Salomé, Lou 1861-1937 ....DLB-66

Andres, Stefan 1906-1970 ....DLB-69

Andreu, Blanca 1959- DLB-134

Andrewes, Lancelot 1555-1626..............DLB-151, 172

Andrews, Charles M. 1863-1943.....DLB-17

Andrews, Miles Peter ?-1814........DLB-89

Andrian, Leopold von 1875-1951 ....DLB-81

Andrić, Ivo 1892-1975 ....DLB-147

Andrieux, Louis (see Aragon, Louis)

Andrus, Silas, and Son............DLB-49

Angell, James Burrill 1829-1916 .....DLB-64

Angell, Roger 1920- DLB-171

Angelou, Maya 1928- DLB-38

Anger, Jane flourished 1589 ....DLB-136

Angers, Félicité (see Conan, Laure)

Anglo-Norman Literature in the Development of Middle English Literature....DLB-146

The Anglo-Saxon Chronicle circa 890-1154.............DLB-146

The "Angry Young Men".........DLB-15

Angus and Robertson (UK) Limited...................DLB-112

Anhalt, Edward 1914-..........DLB-26

Anners, Henry F. [publishing house]...DLB-49

Annolied between 1077 and 1081....DLB-148

Anselm of Canterbury 1033-1109...DLB-115

Anstey, F. 1856-1934.........DLB-141, 178

Anthony, Michael 1932-........DLB-125

Anthony, Piers 1934-...........DLB-8

Anthony Burgess's *99 Novels:* An Opinion Poll................Y-84

Antin, David 1932-.............DLB-169

Antin, Mary 1881-1949...........Y-84

Anton Ulrich, Duke of Brunswick-Lüneburg 1633-1714..............DLB-168

Antschel, Paul (see Celan, Paul)

Anyidoho, Kofi 1947-............DLB-157

Anzaldúa, Gloria 1942-..........DLB-122

Anzengruber, Ludwig 1839-1889...DLB-129

Apess, William 1798-1839........DLB-175

Apodaca, Rudy S. 1939-..........DLB-82

Apollonius Rhodius third century B.C. DLB-176

Apple, Max 1941-...............DLB-130

Appleton, D., and Company......DLB-49

Appleton-Century-Crofts..........DLB-46

Applewhite, James 1935-.........DLB-105

Apple-wood Books...............DLB-46

Aquin, Hubert 1929-1977.........DLB-53

Aquinas, Thomas 1224 or 1225-1274...............DLB-115

Aragon, Louis 1897-1982..........DLB-72

Aratus of Soli circa 315 B.C.-circa 239 B.C. DLB-176

Arbor House Publishing Company..................DLB-46

Arbuthnot, John 1667-1735.......DLB-101

Arcadia House...................DLB-46

Arce, Julio G. (see Ulica, Jorge)

Archer, William 1856-1924........DLB-10

Archilochhus mid seventh century B.C.E. DLB-176

The Archpoet circa 1130?-?......DLB-148

Archpriest Avvakum (Petrovich) 1620?-1682.................DLB-150

Arden, John 1930-..............DLB-13

Arden of Faversham.............DLB-62

Ardis Publishers..................Y-89

Ardizzone, Edward 1900-1979....DLB-160

Arellano, Juan Estevan 1947-.....DLB-122

The Arena Publishing Company....DLB-49

Arena Stage....................DLB-7

Arenas, Reinaldo 1943-1990.......DLB-145

Arensberg, Ann 1937-.............Y-82

Arguedas, José María 1911-1969....DLB-113

Argueta, Manilio 1936-..........DLB-145

Arias, Ron 1941-................DLB-82

Aristophanes circa 446 B.C.-circa 386 B.C.................DLB-176

Aristotle 384 B.C.-322 B.C........DLB-176

Arland, Marcel 1899-1986.........DLB-72

Arlen, Michael 1895-1956...DLB-36, 77, 162

Armah, Ayi Kwei 1939-..........DLB-117

Der arme Hartmann ?-after 1150.................DLB-148

Armed Services Editions..........DLB-46

Armstrong, Richard 1903-.......DLB-160

Arndt, Ernst Moritz 1769-1860......DLB-90

Arnim, Achim von 1781-1831.......DLB-90

Arnim, Bettina von 1785-1859......DLB-90

Arno Press.....................DLB-46

Arnold, Edwin 1832-1904..........DLB-35

Arnold, Edwin L. 1857-1935.......DLB-178

Arnold, Matthew 1822-1888.....DLB-32, 57

Arnold, Thomas 1795-1842.........DLB-55

Arnold, Edward [publishing house]............DLB-112

Arnow, Harriette Simpson 1908-1986.....................DLB-6

Arp, Bill (see Smith, Charles Henry)

Arpino, Giovanni 1927-1987.......DLB-177

Arreola, Juan José 1918-.........DLB-113

Arrian circa 89-circa 155........DLB-176

Arrowsmith, J. W. [publishing house]............DLB-106

Arthur, Timothy Shay 1809-1885........DLB-3, 42, 79; DS-13

The Arthurian Tradition and Its European Context....................DLB-138

Artmann, H. C. 1921-............DLB-85

Arvin, Newton 1900-1963.........DLB-103

As I See It, by Carolyn Cassady.....DLB-16

Asch, Nathan 1902-1964.........DLB-4, 28

Ash, John 1948-.................DLB-40

Ashbery, John 1927-......DLB-5, 165; Y-81

Ashendene Press................DLB-112

Asher, Sandy 1942-..............Y-83

Ashton, Winifred (see Dane, Clemence)

Asimov, Isaac 1920-1992........DLB-8; Y-92

Askew, Anne circa 1521-1546......DLB-136

Asselin, Olivar 1874-1937.........DLB-92

Asturias, Miguel Angel 1899-1974.................DLB-113

Atheneum Publishers.............DLB-46

Atherton, Gertrude 1857-1948....DLB-9, 78

Athlone Press...................DLB-112

Atkins, Josiah circa 1755-1781.....DLB-31

Atkins, Russell 1926-............DLB-41

The Atlantic Monthly Press........DLB-46

Attaway, William 1911-1986......DLB-76

Atwood, Margaret 1939-..........DLB-53

Aubert, Alvin 1930-.............DLB-41

Aubert de Gaspé, Phillipe-Ignace-François 1814-1841...................DLB-99

Aubert de Gaspé, Phillipe-Joseph 1786-1871...................DLB-99

Aubin, Napoléon 1812-1890.......DLB-99

Aubin, Penelope 1685-circa 1731....DLB-39

Aubrey-Fletcher, Henry Lancelot (see Wade, Henry)

Auchincloss, Louis 1917-.....DLB-2; Y-80

Auden, W. H. 1907-1973........DLB-10, 20

Audio Art in America: A Personal Memoir........................Y-85

Auerbach, Berthold 1812-1882.....DLB-133

Auernheimer, Raoul 1876-1948.....DLB-81

Augustine 354-430...............DLB-115

Austen, Jane 1775-1817...........DLB-116

Austin, Alfred 1835-1913..........DLB-35

Austin, Mary 1868-1934.........DLB-9, 78

Austin, William 1778-1841........DLB-74

Author-Printers, 1476–1599........DLB-167

The Author's Apology for His Book (1684), by John Bunyan........DLB-39

An Author's Response, by Ronald Sukenick..................Y-82

Cumulative Index

Authors and Newspapers
   Association DLB-46

Authors' Publishing Company DLB-49

Avalon Books DLB-46

Avancini, Nicolaus 1611-1686 ..... DLB-164

Avendaño, Fausto 1941- DLB-82

Averroës 1126-1198 .... DLB-115

Avery, Gillian 1926- DLB-161

Avicenna 980-1037 .... DLB-115

Avison, Margaret 1918- DLB-53

Avon Books DLB-46

Awdry, Wilbert Vere 1911- DLB-160

Awoonor, Kofi 1935- DLB-117

Ayckbourn, Alan 1939- DLB-13

Aymé, Marcel 1902-1967 .... DLB-72

Aytoun, Sir Robert 1570-1638 .... DLB-121

Aytoun, William Edmondstoune
   1813-1865 .... DLB-32, 159

B

B. V. (see Thomson, James)

Babbitt, Irving 1865-1933 .... DLB-63

Babbitt, Natalie 1932- DLB-52

Babcock, John [publishing house] DLB-49

Babrius circa 150-200 .... DLB-176

Baca, Jimmy Santiago 1952- DLB-122

Bache, Benjamin Franklin
   1769-1798 .... DLB-43

Bachmann, Ingeborg 1926-1973 ..... DLB-85

Bacon, Delia 1811-1859 .... DLB-1

Bacon, Francis 1561-1626 .... DLB-151

Bacon, Roger circa
   1214/1220-1292 .... DLB-115

Bacon, Sir Nicholas
   circa 1510-1579 .... DLB-132

Bacon, Thomas circa 1700-1768 ..... DLB-31

Badger, Richard G.,
   and Company DLB-49

Bage, Robert 1728-1801 .... DLB-39

Bagehot, Walter 1826-1877 .... DLB-55

Bagley, Desmond 1923-1983 .... DLB-87

Bagnold, Enid 1889-1981 ...... DLB-13, 160

Bagryana, Elisaveta 1893-1991 .... DLB-147

Bahr, Hermann 1863-1934 ..... DLB-81, 118

Bailey, Alfred Goldsworthy
   1905- DLB-68

Bailey, Francis [publishing house] ... DLB-49

Bailey, H. C. 1878-1961 .... DLB-77

Bailey, Jacob 1731-1808 .... DLB-99

Bailey, Paul 1937- DLB-14

Bailey, Philip James 1816-1902 ..... DLB-32

Baillargeon, Pierre 1916-1967 ...... DLB-88

Baillie, Hugh 1890-1966 .... DLB-29

Baillie, Joanna 1762-1851 .... DLB-93

Bailyn, Bernard 1922- DLB-17

Bainbridge, Beryl 1933- DLB-14

Baird, Irene 1901-1981 .... DLB-68

Baker, Augustine 1575-1641 .... DLB-151

Baker, Carlos 1909-1987 .... DLB-103

Baker, David 1954- DLB-120

Baker, Herschel C. 1914-1990 ..... DLB-111

Baker, Houston A., Jr. 1943- DLB-67

Baker, Samuel White 1821-1893 .... DLB-166

Baker, Walter H., Company
   ("Baker's Plays") DLB-49

The Baker and Taylor Company DLB-49

Balaban, John 1943- DLB-120

Bald, Wambly 1902- DLB-4

Balde, Jacob 1604-1668 .... DLB-164

Balderston, John 1889-1954 .... DLB-26

Baldwin, James
   1924-1987 .... DLB-2, 7, 33; Y-87

Baldwin, Joseph Glover
   1815-1864 .... DLB-3, 11

Baldwin, Richard and Anne
   [publishing house] DLB-170

Baldwin, William
   circa 1515-1563 .... DLB-132

Bale, John 1495-1563 .... DLB-132

Balestrini, Nanni 1935- DLB-128

Ballantine Books DLB-46

Ballantyne, R. M. 1825-1894 .... DLB-163

Ballard, J. G. 1930- DLB-14

Ballerini, Luigi 1940- DLB-128

Ballou, Maturin Murray
   1820-1895 .... DLB-79

Ballou, Robert O.
   [publishing house] DLB-46

Balzac, Honoré de 1799-1855 ...... DLB-119

Bambara, Toni Cade 1939- DLB-38

Bancroft, A. L., and
   Company DLB-49

Bancroft, George
   1800-1891 .... DLB-1, 30, 59

Bancroft, Hubert Howe
   1832-1918 .... DLB-47, 140

Bangs, John Kendrick
   1862-1922 .... DLB-11, 79

Banim, John 1798-1842 ... DLB-116, 158, 159

Banim, Michael 1796-1874 .... DLB-158, 159

Banks, John circa 1653-1706 .... DLB-80

Banks, Russell 1940- DLB-130

Bannerman, Helen 1862-1946 ...... DLB-141

Bantam Books DLB-46

Banti, Anna 1895-1985 .... DLB-177

Banville, John 1945- DLB-14

Baraka, Amiri
   1934- DLB-5, 7, 16, 38; DS-8

Barbauld, Anna Laetitia
   1743-1825 .... DLB-107, 109, 142, 158

Barbeau, Marius 1883-1969 .... DLB-92

Barber, John Warner 1798-1885 ..... DLB-30

Bàrberi Squarotti, Giorgio
   1929- DLB-128

Barbey d'Aurevilly, Jules-Amédée
   1808-1889 .... DLB-119

Barbour, John circa 1316-1395 ..... DLB-146

Barbour, Ralph Henry
   1870-1944 .... DLB-22

Barbusse, Henri 1873-1935 .... DLB-65

Barclay, Alexander
   circa 1475-1552 .... DLB-132

Barclay, E. E., and Company DLB-49

Bardeen, C. W.
   [publishing house] DLB-49

Barham, Richard Harris
   1788-1845 .... DLB-159

Baring, Maurice 1874-1945 .... DLB-34

Baring-Gould, Sabine 1834-1924 .... DLB-156

Barker, A. L. 1918- DLB-14, 139

Barker, George 1913-1991 .... DLB-20

Barker, Harley Granville
   1877-1946 .... DLB-10

Barker, Howard 1946- DLB-13

Barker, James Nelson 1784-1858 .... DLB-37

Barker, Jane 1652-1727 .... DLB-39, 131

Barker, Lady Mary Anne
   1831-1911 .... DLB-166

Barker, William
   circa 1520-after 1576 .... DLB-132

Barker, Arthur, Limited DLB-112

Barkov, Ivan Semenovich 1732-1768 .... DLB-150

Barks, Coleman 1937- DLB-5

Barlach, Ernst 1870-1938 ...... DLB-56, 118

Barlow, Joel 1754-1812 .... DLB-37

Barnard, John 1681-1770 .... DLB-24

Barne, Kitty (Mary Catherine Barne) 1883-1957 .... DLB-160

Barnes, Barnabe 1571-1609 .... DLB-132

Barnes, Djuna 1892-1982 ...... DLB-4, 9, 45

Barnes, Jim 1933- DLB-175

Barnes, Julian 1946- Y-93

Barnes, Margaret Ayer 1886-1967 .... DLB-9

Barnes, Peter 1931- DLB-13

Barnes, William 1801-1886 .... DLB-32

Barnes, A. S., and Company DLB-49

Barnes and Noble Books DLB-46

Barnet, Miguel 1940- DLB-145

Barney, Natalie 1876-1972 .... DLB-4

Barnfield, Richard 1574-1627 ..... DLB-172

Baron, Richard W., Publishing Company DLB-46

Barr, Robert 1850-1912 .... DLB-70, 92

Barral, Carlos 1928-1989 .... DLB-134

Barrax, Gerald William 1933- DLB-41, 120

Barrès, Maurice 1862-1923 .... DLB-123

Barrett, Eaton Stannard 1786-1820 .... DLB-116

Barrie, J. M. 1860-1937 .... DLB-10, 141, 156

Barrie and Jenkins DLB-112

Barrio, Raymond 1921- DLB-82

Barrios, Gregg 1945- DLB-122

Barry, Philip 1896-1949 .... DLB-7

Barry, Robertine (see Françoise)

Barse and Hopkins DLB-46

Barstow, Stan 1928- DLB-14, 139

Barth, John 1930- DLB-2

Barthelme, Donald 1931-1989 .... DLB-2; Y-80, 89

Barthelme, Frederick 1943- Y-85

Bartholomew, Frank 1898-1985 .... DLB-127

Bartlett, John 1820-1905 .... DLB-1

Bartol, Cyrus Augustus 1813-1900 .... DLB-1

Barton, Bernard 1784-1849 .... DLB-96

Barton, Thomas Pennant 1803-1869 .... DLB-140

Bartram, John 1699-1777 .... DLB-31

Bartram, William 1739-1823 .... DLB-37

Basic Books DLB-46

Basille, Theodore (see Becon, Thomas)

Bass, T. J. 1932- Y-81

Bassani, Giorgio 1916- DLB-128, 177

Basse, William circa 1583-1653 ..... DLB-121

Bassett, John Spencer 1867-1928 ..... DLB-17

Bassler, Thomas Joseph (see Bass, T. J.)

Bate, Walter Jackson 1918- DLB-67, 103

Bateman, Christopher [publishing house] DLB-170

Bateman, Stephen circa 1510-1584 .... DLB-136

Bates, H. E. 1905-1974 .... DLB-162

Bates, Katharine Lee 1859-1929 ..... DLB-71

Batsford, B. T. [publishing house] DLB-106

Battiscombe, Georgina 1905- DLB-155

The Battle of Maldon circa 1000 ...... DLB-146

Bauer, Bruno 1809-1882 .... DLB-133

Bauer, Wolfgang 1941- DLB-124

Baum, L. Frank 1856-1919 .... DLB-22

Baum, Vicki 1888-1960 .... DLB-85

Baumbach, Jonathan 1933- Y-80

Bausch, Richard 1945- DLB-130

Bawden, Nina 1925- DLB-14, 161

Bax, Clifford 1886-1962 .... DLB-10, 100

Baxter, Charles 1947- DLB-130

Bayer, Eleanor (see Perry, Eleanor)

Bayer, Konrad 1932-1964 .... DLB-85

Baynes, Pauline 1922- DLB-160

Bazin, Hervé 1911- DLB-83

Beach, Sylvia 1887-1962 .... DLB-4

Beacon Press DLB-49

Beadle and Adams DLB-49

Beagle, Peter S. 1939- Y-80

Beal, M. F. 1937- Y-81

Beale, Howard K. 1899-1959 .... DLB-17

Beard, Charles A. 1874-1948 .... DLB-17

A Beat Chronology: The First Twenty-five Years, 1944-1969 .... DLB-16

Beattie, Ann 1947- Y-82

Beattie, James 1735-1803 .... DLB-109

Beauchemin, Nérée 1850-1931 ...... DLB-92

Beauchemin, Yves 1941- DLB-60

Beaugrand, Honoré 1848-1906 ...... DLB-99

Beaulieu, Victor-Lévy 1945- DLB-53

Beaumont, Francis circa 1584-1616 and Fletcher, John 1579-1625 .... DLB-58

Beaumont, Sir John 1583?-1627 .... DLB-121

Beaumont, Joseph 1616–1699 ...... DLB-126

Beauvoir, Simone de 1908-1986 .... DLB-72; Y-86

Becher, Ulrich 1910- DLB-69

Becker, Carl 1873-1945 .... DLB-17

Becker, Jurek 1937- DLB-75

Becker, Jurgen 1932- DLB-75

Beckett, Samuel 1906-1989 .... DLB-13, 15; Y-90

Beckford, William 1760-1844 .... DLB-39

Beckham, Barry 1944- DLB-33

Becon, Thomas circa 1512-1567 .... DLB-136

Beddoes, Thomas 1760-1808 .... DLB-158

Beddoes, Thomas Lovell 1803-1849 .... DLB-96

Bede circa 673-735 .... DLB-146

Beecher, Catharine Esther 1800-1878 .... DLB-1

Beecher, Henry Ward 1813-1887 .... DLB-3, 43

Beer, George L. 1872-1920 .... DLB-47

Beer, Johann 1655-1700 .... DLB-168

Beer, Patricia 1919- DLB-40

Beerbohm, Max 1872-1956 ..... DLB-34, 100

Beer-Hofmann, Richard 1866-1945 .... DLB-81

Beers, Henry A. 1847-1926 .... DLB-71

Beeton, S. O. [publishing house] DLB-106

Bégon, Elisabeth 1696-1755 .... DLB-99

Behan, Brendan 1923-1964 .... DLB-13

Behn, Aphra 1640?-1689 .... DLB-39, 80, 131

Behn, Harry 1898-1973 .... DLB-61

Behrman, S. N. 1893-1973 .... DLB-7, 44

Belaney, Archibald Stansfeld (see Grey Owl)

Belasco, David 1853-1931 .... DLB-7

Belford, Clarke and Company DLB-49

Belitt, Ben 1911- DLB-5

Belknap, Jeremy 1744-1798 ...... DLB-30, 37

Bell, Clive 1881-1964 .... DS-10

Bell, Gertrude Margaret Lowthian 1868-1926 .... DLB-174

Bell, James Madison 1826-1902......DLB-50

Bell, Marvin 1937- DLB-5

Bell, Millicent 1919- DLB-111

Bell, Quentin 1910- DLB-155

Bell, Vanessa 1879-1961............DS-10

Bell, George, and Sons............DLB-106

Bell, Robert [publishing house]......DLB-49

Bellamy, Edward 1850-1898........DLB-12

Bellamy, John [publishing house]...DLB-170

Bellamy, Joseph 1719-1790.........DLB-31

Bellezza, Dario 1944- DLB-128

La Belle Assemblée 1806-1837........DLB-110

Belloc, Hilaire 1870-1953........DLB-19, 100, 141, 174

Bellow, Saul 1915- DLB-2, 28; Y-82; DS-3

Belmont Productions DLB-46

Bemelmans, Ludwig 1898-1962......DLB-22

Bemis, Samuel Flagg 1891-1973.....DLB-17

Bemrose, William [publishing house]............DLB-106

Benchley, Robert 1889-1945........DLB-11

Benedetti, Mario 1920- DLB-113

Benedictus, David 1938- DLB-14

Benedikt, Michael 1935- DLB-5

Benét, Stephen Vincent 1898-1943.............DLB-4, 48, 102

Benét, William Rose 1886-1950 .....DLB-45

Benford, Gregory 1941- Y-82

Benjamin, Park 1809-1864 ....DLB-3, 59, 73

Benlowes, Edward 1602-1676......DLB-126

Benn, Gottfried 1886-1956..........DLB-56

Benn Brothers Limited............DLB-106

Bennett, Arnold 1867-1931..........DLB-10, 34, 98, 135

Bennett, Charles 1899- DLB-44

Bennett, Gwendolyn 1902- DLB-51

Bennett, Hal 1930- DLB-33

Bennett, James Gordon 1795-1872...DLB-43

Bennett, James Gordon, Jr. 1841-1918..................DLB-23

Bennett, John 1865-1956............DLB-42

Bennett, Louise 1919- DLB-117

Benoit, Jacques 1941- DLB-60

Benson, A. C. 1862-1925............DLB-98

Benson, E. F. 1867-1940 ......DLB-135, 153

Benson, Jackson J. 1930- DLB-111

Benson, Robert Hugh 1871-1914 ...DLB-153

Benson, Stella 1892-1933.......DLB-36, 162

Bent, James Theodore 1852-1897...DLB-174

Bent, Mabel Virginia Anna ?-?.....DLB-174

Bentham, Jeremy 1748-1832...DLB-107, 158

Bentley, E. C. 1875-1956...........DLB-70

Bentley, Richard [publishing house]............DLB-106

Benton, Robert 1932- and Newman, David 1937- DLB-44

Benziger Brothers DLB-49

Beowulf circa 900-1000 or 790-825..................DLB-146

Beresford, Anne 1929- DLB-40

Beresford, John Davys 1873-1947............DLB-162; 178

Beresford-Howe, Constance 1922- DLB-88

Berford, R. G., Company DLB-49

Berg, Stephen 1934- DLB-5

Bergengruen, Werner 1892-1964 ....DLB-56

Berger, John 1926- DLB-14

Berger, Meyer 1898-1959..........DLB-29

Berger, Thomas 1924- DLB-2; Y-80

Berkeley, Anthony 1893-1971......DLB-77

Berkeley, George 1685-1753....DLB-31, 101

The Berkley Publishing Corporation DLB-46

Berlin, Lucia 1936- DLB-130

Bernal, Vicente J. 1888-1915........DLB-82

Bernanos, Georges 1888-1948......DLB-72

Bernard, Harry 1898-1979..........DLB-92

Bernard, John 1756-1828..........DLB-37

Bernard of Chartres circa 1060-1124?..............DLB-115

Bernari, Carlo 1909-1992..........DLB-177

Bernhard, Thomas 1931-1989.................DLB-85, 124

Bernstein, Charles 1950- DLB-169

Berriault, Gina 1926- DLB-130

Berrigan, Daniel 1921- DLB-5

Berrigan, Ted 1934-1983........DLB-5, 169

Berry, Wendell 1934- DLB-5, 6

Berryman, John 1914-1972........DLB-48

Bersianik, Louky 1930- DLB-60

Berthelet, Thomas [publishing house] DLB-170

Berto, Giuseppe 1914-1978 ....DLB-177

Bertolucci, Attilio 1911- DLB-128

Berton, Pierre 1920- DLB-68

Besant, Sir Walter 1836-1901 ......DLB-135

Bessette, Gerard 1920- DLB-53

Bessie, Alvah 1904-1985 ....DLB-26

Bester, Alfred 1913-1987 ....DLB-8

The Bestseller Lists: An Assessment Y-84

Betham-Edwards, Matilda Barbara (see Edwards, Matilda Barbara Betham-)

Betjeman, John 1906-1984......DLB-20; Y-84

Betocchi, Carlo 1899-1986.........DLB-128

Bettarini, Mariella 1942- DLB-128

Betts, Doris 1932- Y-82

Beveridge, Albert J. 1862-1927 ......DLB-17

Beverley, Robert circa 1673-1722............DLB-24, 30

Beyle, Marie-Henri (see Stendhal)

Bianco, Margery Williams 1881-1944 ....DLB-160

Bibaud, Adèle 1854-1941............DLB-92

Bibaud, Michel 1782-1857..........DLB-99

Bibliographical and Textual Scholarship Since World War II................Y-89

The Bicentennial of James Fenimore Cooper: An International Celebration......................Y-89

Bichsel, Peter 1935- DLB-75

Bickerstaff, Isaac John 1733-circa 1808.................DLB-89

Biddle, Drexel [publishing house]....DLB-49

Bidermann, Jacob 1577 or 1578-1639.............DLB-164

Bidwell, Walter Hilliard 1798-1881 ....DLB-79

Bienek, Horst 1930- DLB-75

Bierbaum, Otto Julius 1865-1910 ....DLB-66

Bierce, Ambrose 1842-1914?.......DLB-11, 12, 23, 71, 74

Bigelow, William F. 1879-1966......DLB-91

Biggle, Lloyd, Jr. 1923- DLB-8

Bigiaretti, Libero 1905-1993 ....DLB-177

Biglow, Hosea (see Lowell, James Russell)

Bigongiari, Piero 1914- DLB-128

Billinger, Richard 1890-1965.......DLB-124

Billings, John Shaw 1898-1975 .....DLB-137

Billings, Josh (see Shaw, Henry Wheeler)

Binding, Rudolf G. 1867-1938....... DLB-66

Bingham, Caleb 1757-1817 .... DLB-42

Bingham, George Barry
   1906-1988 .... DLB-127

Bingley, William
   [publishing house] DLB-154

Binyon, Laurence 1869-1943....... DLB-19

Biographia Brittanica DLB-142

Biographical Documents I............ Y-84

Biographical Documents II Y-85

Bioren, John [publishing house] DLB-49

Bioy Casares, Adolfo 1914- DLB-113

Bird, Isabella Lucy 1831-1904...... DLB-166

Bird, William 1888-1963 .... DLB-4

Birken, Sigmund von 1626-1681.... DLB-164

Birney, Earle 1904- DLB-88

Birrell, Augustine 1850-1933........ DLB-98

Bisher, Furman 1918- DLB-171

Bishop, Elizabeth 1911-1979..... DLB-5, 169

Bishop, John Peale 1892-1944... DLB-4, 9, 45

Bismarck, Otto von 1815-1898 ..... DLB-129

Bisset, Robert 1759-1805.......... DLB-142

Bissett, Bill 1939- DLB-53

Bitzius, Albert (see Gotthelf, Jeremias)

Black, David (D. M.) 1941- DLB-40

Black, Winifred 1863-1936 .... DLB-25

Black, Walter J.
   [publishing house] DLB-46

The Black Aesthetic: Background DS-8

The Black Arts Movement, by
   Larry Neal.................... DLB-38

Black Theaters and Theater Organizations in
   America, 1961-1982:
   A Research List DLB-38

Black Theatre: A Forum
   [excerpts]..................... DLB-38

Blackamore, Arthur 1679-? DLB-24, 39

Blackburn, Alexander L. 1929- Y-85

Blackburn, Paul 1926-1971 .... DLB-16; Y-81

Blackburn, Thomas 1916-1977 ...... DLB-27

Blackmore, R. D. 1825-1900 .... DLB-18

Blackmore, Sir Richard
   1654-1729 .... DLB-131

Blackmur, R. P. 1904-1965 .... DLB-63

Blackwell, Basil, Publisher......... DLB-106

Blackwood, Algernon Henry
   1869-1951 .... DLB-153, 156, 178

Blackwood, Caroline 1931- DLB-14

Blackwood, William, and
   Sons, Ltd. DLB-154

Blackwood's Edinburgh Magazine
   1817-1980 .... DLB-110

Blair, Eric Arthur (see Orwell, George)

Blair, Francis Preston 1791-1876 .... DLB-43

Blair, James circa 1655-1743 .... DLB-24

Blair, John Durburrow 1759-1823 ... DLB-37

Blais, Marie-Claire 1939- DLB-53

Blaise, Clark 1940- DLB-53

Blake, Nicholas 1904-1972.......... DLB-77
   (see Day Lewis, C.)

Blake, William
   1757-1827............ DLB-93, 154, 163

The Blakiston Company DLB-49

Blanchot, Maurice 1907- DLB-72

Blanckenburg, Christian Friedrich von
   1744-1796 .... DLB-94

Blaser, Robin 1925- DLB-165

Bledsoe, Albert Taylor
   1809-1877 .... DLB-3, 79

Blelock and Company DLB-49

Blennerhassett, Margaret Agnew
   1773-1842 .... DLB-99

Bles, Geoffrey
   [publishing house] DLB-112

Blessington, Marguerite, Countess of
   1789-1849 .... DLB-166

The Blickling Homilies
   circa 971 .... DLB-146

Blish, James 1921-1975............. DLB-8

Bliss, E., and E. White
   [publishing house] DLB-49

Bliven, Bruce 1889-1977 .... DLB-137

Bloch, Robert 1917-1994 .... DLB-44

Block, Rudolph (see Lessing, Bruno)

Blondal, Patricia 1926-1959........ DLB-88

Bloom, Harold 1930- DLB-67

Bloomer, Amelia 1818-1894 .... DLB-79

Bloomfield, Robert 1766-1823....... DLB-93

Bloomsbury Group DS-10

Blotner, Joseph 1923- DLB-111

Bloy, Léon 1846-1917 .... DLB-123

Blume, Judy 1938- DLB-52

Blunck, Hans Friedrich 1888-1961 ... DLB-66

Blunden, Edmund
   1896-1974 .... DLB-20, 100, 155

Blunt, Lady Anne Isabella Noel
   1837-1917 .... DLB-174

Blunt, Wilfrid Scawen
   1840-1922 .... DLB-19, 174

Bly, Nellie (see Cochrane, Elizabeth)

Bly, Robert 1926- DLB-5

Blyton, Enid 1897-1968 .... DLB-160

Boaden, James 1762-1839 .... DLB-89

Boas, Frederick S. 1862-1957 ...... DLB-149

The Bobbs-Merrill Archive at the
   Lilly Library, Indiana University ... Y-90

The Bobbs-Merrill Company DLB-46

Bobrov, Semen Sergeevich
   1763?-1810 .... DLB-150

Bobrowski, Johannes 1917-1965 ..... DLB-75

Bodenheim, Maxwell 1892-1954... DLB-9, 45

Bodenstedt, Friedrich von
   1819-1892 .... DLB-129

Bodini, Vittorio 1914-1970 .... DLB-128

Bodkin, M. McDonnell
   1850-1933 .... DLB-70

Bodley Head DLB-112

Bodmer, Johann Jakob 1698-1783.... DLB-97

Bodmershof, Imma von 1895-1982... DLB-85

Bodsworth, Fred 1918- DLB-68

Boehm, Sydney 1908- DLB-44

Boer, Charles 1939- DLB-5

Boethius circa 480-circa 524 .... DLB-115

Boethius of Dacia circa 1240-? DLB-115

Bogan, Louise 1897-1970 ...... DLB-45, 169

Bogarde, Dirk 1921- DLB-14

Bogdanovich, Ippolit Fedorovich
   circa 1743-1803................ DLB-150

Bogue, David [publishing house] ... DLB-106

Böhme, Jakob 1575-1624 .... DLB-164

Bohn, H. G. [publishing house] DLB-106

Bohse, August 1661-1742.......... DLB-168

Boie, Heinrich Christian
   1744-1806 .... DLB-94

Bok, Edward W. 1863-1930 .... DLB-91

Boland, Eavan 1944- DLB-40

Bolingbroke, Henry St. John, Viscount
   1678-1751 .... DLB-101

Böll, Heinrich 1917-1985...... Y-85, DLB-69

Bolling, Robert 1738-1775.......... DLB-31

Cumulative Index

Bolotov, Andrei Timofeevich 1738-1833 .... DLB-150

Bolt, Carol 1941- DLB-60

Bolt, Robert 1924- DLB-13

Bolton, Herbert E. 1870-1953 .... DLB-17

Bonaventura DLB-90

Bonaventure circa 1217-1274 ...... DLB-115

Bonaviri, Giuseppe 1924- DLB-177

Bond, Edward 1934- DLB-13

Bond, Michael 1926- DLB-161

Bonnin, Gertrude Simmons (see Zitkala-Ša)

Boni, Albert and Charles [publishing house] DLB-46

Boni and Liveright DLB-46

Robert Bonner's Sons DLB-49

Bonsanti, Alessandro 1904-1984 .... DLB-177

Bontemps, Arna 1902-1973 ...... DLB-48, 51

The Book Arts Press at the University of Virginia Y-96

The Book League of America DLB-46

Book Reviewing in America: I Y-87

Book Reviewing in America: II Y-88

Book Reviewing in America: III Y-89

Book Reviewing in America: IV Y-90

Book Reviewing in America: V Y-91

Book Reviewing in America: VI Y-92

Book Reviewing in America: VII Y-93

Book Reviewing in America: VIII Y-94

Book Reviewing in America and the Literary Scene Y-95

Book Reviewing and the Literary Scene Y-96

Book Supply Company DLB-49

The Book Trade History Group Y-93

The Booker Prize Y-96

The Booker Prize
Address by Anthony Thwaite, Chairman of the Booker Prize Judges Comments from Former Booker Prize Winners................... Y-86

Boorde, Andrew circa 1490-1549 ... DLB-136

Boorstin, Daniel J. 1914- DLB-17

Booth, Mary L. 1831-1889........ DLB-79

Booth, Philip 1925- Y-82

Booth, Wayne C. 1921- DLB-67

Borchardt, Rudolf 1877-1945 ..... DLB-66

Borchert, Wolfgang 1921-1947 .... DLB-69, 124

Borel, Pétrus 1809-1859 .... DLB-119

Borges, Jorge Luis 1899-1986 .... DLB-113; Y-86

Börne, Ludwig 1786-1837 .... DLB-90

Borrow, George 1803-1881 .... DLB-21, 55, 166

Bosch, Juan 1909- DLB-145

Bosco, Henri 1888-1976........... DLB-72

Bosco, Monique 1927- DLB-53

Boston, Lucy M. 1892-1990 ...... DLB-161

Boswell, James 1740-1795 ..... DLB-104, 142

Botev, Khristo 1847-1876 .... DLB-147

Bote, Hermann circa 1460-circa 1520 .... DLB-179

Botta, Anne C. Lynch 1815-1891 ..... DLB-3

Bottomley, Gordon 1874-1948 ...... DLB-10

Bottoms, David 1949- DLB-120; Y-83

Bottrall, Ronald 1906- DLB-20

Boucher, Anthony 1911-1968 .... DLB-8

Boucher, Jonathan 1738-1804 .... DLB-31

Boucher de Boucherville, George 1814-1894 .... DLB-99

Boudreau, Daniel (see Coste, Donat)

Bourassa, Napoléon 1827-1916...... DLB-99

Bourget, Paul 1852-1935 .... DLB-123

Bourinot, John George 1837-1902 ... DLB-99

Bourjaily, Vance 1922- DLB-2, 143

Bourne, Edward Gaylord 1860-1908 .... DLB-47

Bourne, Randolph 1886-1918 .... DLB-63

Bousoño, Carlos 1923- DLB-108

Bousquet, Joë 1897-1950 .... DLB-72

Bova, Ben 1932- Y-81

Bovard, Oliver K. 1872-1945 .... DLB-25

Bove, Emmanuel 1898-1945 .... DLB-72

Bowen, Elizabeth 1899-1973 .... DLB-15, 162

Bowen, Francis 1811-1890........ DLB-1, 59

Bowen, John 1924- DLB-13

Bowen, Marjorie 1886-1952........ DLB-153

Bowen-Merrill Company DLB-49

Bowering, George 1935- DLB-53

Bowers, Claude G. 1878-1958....... DLB-17

Bowers, Edgar 1924- DLB-5

Bowers, Fredson Thayer 1905-1991 .... DLB-140; Y-91

Bowles, Paul 1910- DLB-5, 6

Bowles, Samuel III 1826-1878 .... DLB-43

Bowles, William Lisles 1762-1850 ... DLB-93

Bowman, Louise Morey 1882-1944 .... DLB-68

Boyd, James 1888-1944 .... DLB-9

Boyd, John 1919- DLB-8

Boyd, Thomas 1898-1935 .... DLB-9

Boyesen, Hjalmar Hjorth 1848-1895.......... DLB-12, 71; DS-13

Boyle, Kay 1902-1992........ DLB-4, 9, 48, 86; Y-93

Boyle, Roger, Earl of Orrery 1621-1679 .... DLB-80

Boyle, T. Coraghessan 1948- Y-86

Brackenbury, Alison 1953- DLB-40

Brackenridge, Hugh Henry 1748-1816 .... DLB-11, 37

Brackett, Charles 1892-1969 .... DLB-26

Brackett, Leigh 1915-1978........ DLB-8, 26

Bradburn, John [publishing house] DLB-49

Bradbury, Malcolm 1932- DLB-14

Bradbury, Ray 1920- DLB-2, 8

Bradbury and Evans............ DLB-106

Braddon, Mary Elizabeth 1835-1915............. DLB-18, 70, 156

Bradford, Andrew 1686-1742 .... DLB-43, 73

Bradford, Gamaliel 1863-1932 ...... DLB-17

Bradford, John 1749-1830 .... DLB-43

Bradford, Roark 1896-1948........ DLB-86

Bradford, William 1590-1657 .... DLB-24, 30

Bradford, William III 1719-1791 .... DLB-43, 73

Bradlaugh, Charles 1833-1891 ...... DLB-57

Bradley, David 1950- DLB-33

Bradley, Marion Zimmer 1930- DLB-8

Bradley, William Aspenwall 1878-1939 .... DLB-4

Bradley, Ira, and Company......... DLB-49

Bradley, J. W., and Company....... DLB-49

Bradstreet, Anne 1612 or 1613-1672 .... DLB-24

Bradwardine, Thomas circa 1295-1349 .... DLB-115

Brady, Frank 1924-1986.......... DLB-111

Brady, Frederic A. [publishing house] DLB-49

Bragg, Melvyn 1939- DLB-14

Brainard, Charles H.
  [publishing house] DLB-49

Braine, John 1922-1986 ....DLB-15; Y-86

Braithwait, Richard 1588-1673 ....DLB-151

Braithwaite, William Stanley
  1878-1962 ....DLB-50, 54

Braker, Ulrich 1735-1798.........DLB-94

Bramah, Ernest 1868-1942.........DLB-70

Branagan, Thomas 1774-1843.......DLB-37

Branch, William Blackwell
  1927- DLB-76

Branden Press DLB-46

Brant, Sebastian 1457-1521 ....DLB-179

Brassey, Lady Annie (Allnutt)
  1839-1887 ....DLB-166

Brathwaite, Edward Kamau
  1930- DLB-125

Brault, Jacques 1933- DLB-53

Braun, Volker 1939- DLB-75

Brautigan, Richard
  1935-1984 ....DLB-2, 5; Y-80, 84

Braxton, Joanne M. 1950- DLB-41

Bray, Anne Eliza 1790-1883 .....DLB-116

Bray, Thomas 1656-1730..........DLB-24

Braziller, George
  [publishing house] DLB-46

The Bread Loaf Writers'
  Conference 1983 ....Y-84

The Break-Up of the Novel (1922),
  by John Middleton Murry.......DLB-36

Breasted, James Henry 1865-1935 ...DLB-47

Brecht, Bertolt 1898-1956 ......DLB-56, 124

Bredel, Willi 1901-1964 ....DLB-56

Breitinger, Johann Jakob
  1701-1776 ....DLB-97

Bremser, Bonnie 1939- DLB-16

Bremser, Ray 1934- DLB-16

Brentano, Bernard von
  1901-1964 ....DLB-56

Brentano, Clemens 1778-1842......DLB-90

Brentano's DLB-49

Brenton, Howard 1942- DLB-13

Breton, André 1896-1966..........DLB-65

Breton, Nicholas
  circa 1555-circa 1626 ....DLB-136

The Breton Lays
  1300-early fifteenth century DLB-146

Brewer, Warren and Putnam DLB-46

Brewster, Elizabeth 1922- DLB-60

Bridgers, Sue Ellen 1942- DLB-52

Bridges, Robert 1844-1930 ......DLB-19, 98

Bridie, James 1888-1951..........DLB-10

Briggs, Charles Frederick
  1804-1877 ....DLB-3

Brighouse, Harold 1882-1958 ....DLB-10

Bright, Mary Chavelita Dunne
  (see Egerton, George)

Brimmer, B. J., Company DLB-46

Brines, Francisco 1932- DLB-134

Brinley, George, Jr. 1817-1875 .....DLB-140

Brinnin, John Malcolm 1916- DLB-48

Brisbane, Albert 1809-1890 ....DLB-3

Brisbane, Arthur 1864-1936.........DLB-25

British Academy DLB-112

The British Library and the Regular
  Readers' Group Y-91

The British Critic 1793-1843.........DLB-110

*The British Review and London
  Critical Journal* 1811-1825.......DLB-110

Brito, Aristeo 1942- DLB-122

Broadway Publishing Company DLB-46

Broch, Hermann 1886-1951 ....DLB-85, 124

Brochu, André 1942- DLB-53

Brock, Edwin 1927- DLB-40

Brockes, Barthold Heinrich
  1680-1747 ....DLB-168

Brod, Max 1884-1968..............DLB-81

Brodber, Erna 1940- DLB-157

Brodhead, John R. 1814-1873 ....DLB-30

Brodkey, Harold 1930- DLB-130

Broeg, Bob 1918- DLB-171

Brome, Richard circa 1590-1652.....DLB-58

Brome, Vincent 1910- DLB-155

Bromfield, Louis 1896-1956 ....DLB-4, 9, 86

Broner, E. M. 1930- DLB-28

Bronk, William 1918- DLB-165

Bronnen, Arnolt 1895-1959........DLB-124

Brontë, Anne 1820-1849 ....DLB-21

Brontë, Charlotte 1816-1855....DLB-21, 159

Brontë, Emily 1818-1848........DLB-21, 32

Brooke, Frances 1724-1789 ......DLB-39, 99

Brooke, Henry 1703?-1783 ....DLB-39

Brooke, L. Leslie 1862-1940 ......DLB-141

Brooke, Margaret, Ranee of Sarawak
  1849-1936 ....DLB-174

Brooke, Rupert 1887-1915..........DLB-19

Brooker, Bertram 1888-1955.......DLB-88

Brooke-Rose, Christine 1926- DLB-14

Brookner, Anita 1928- Y-87

Brooks, Charles Timothy
  1813-1883 ....DLB-1

Brooks, Cleanth 1906-1994 ....DLB-63; Y-94

Brooks, Gwendolyn
  1917- DLB-5, 76, 165

Brooks, Jeremy 1926- DLB-14

Brooks, Mel 1926- DLB-26

Brooks, Noah 1830-1903.....DLB-42; DS-13

Brooks, Richard 1912-1992 ....DLB-44

Brooks, Van Wyck
  1886-1963.............DLB-45, 63, 103

Brophy, Brigid 1929- DLB-14

Brossard, Chandler 1922-1993 .....DLB-16

Brossard, Nicole 1943- DLB-53

Broster, Dorothy Kathleen
  1877-1950 ....DLB-160

Brother Antoninus (see Everson, William)

Brougham and Vaux, Henry Peter
  Brougham, Baron
  1778-1868 ....DLB-110, 158

Brougham, John 1810-1880 ....DLB-11

Broughton, James 1913- DLB-5

Broughton, Rhoda 1840-1920 ....DLB-18

Broun, Heywood 1888-1939 ....DLB-29, 171

Brown, Alice 1856-1948............DLB-78

Brown, Bob 1886-1959...........DLB-4, 45

Brown, Cecil 1943- DLB-33

Brown, Charles Brockden
  1771-1810 ....DLB-37, 59, 73

Brown, Christy 1932-1981..........DLB-14

Brown, Dee 1908- Y-80

Brown, Frank London 1927-1962....DLB-76

Brown, Fredric 1906-1972 ....DLB-8

Brown, George Mackay
  1921- DLB-14, 27, 139

Brown, Harry 1917-1986...........DLB-26

Brown, Marcia 1918- DLB-61

Brown, Margaret Wise
  1910-1952 ....DLB-22

Brown, Morna Doris (see Ferrars, Elizabeth)

Brown, Oliver Madox
  1855-1874 ....DLB-21

Brown, Sterling
  1901-1989 ....DLB-48, 51, 63

Brown, T. E. 1830-1897 . . . . DLB-35

Brown, William Hill 1765-1793 . . . . . DLB-37

Brown, William Wells
1814-1884 . . . . DLB-3, 50

Browne, Charles Farrar
1834-1867 . . . . DLB-11

Browne, Francis Fisher
1843-1913 . . . . DLB-79

Browne, Michael Dennis
1940- DLB-40

Browne, Sir Thomas 1605-1682 . . . . DLB-151

Browne, William, of Tavistock
1590-1645 . . . . DLB-121

Browne, Wynyard 1911-1964 . . . . DLB-13

Browne and Nolan DLB-106

Brownell, W. C. 1851-1928 . . . . DLB-71

Browning, Elizabeth Barrett
1806-1861 . . . . DLB-32

Browning, Robert
1812-1889 . . . . DLB-32, 163

Brownjohn, Allan 1931- DLB-40

Brownson, Orestes Augustus
1803-1876 . . . . DLB-1, 59, 73

Bruccoli, Matthew J. 1931- DLB-103

Bruce, Charles 1906-1971 . . . . DLB-68

Bruce, Leo 1903-1979 . . . . DLB-77

Bruce, Philip Alexander
1856-1933 . . . . DLB-47

Bruce Humphries
[publishing house] DLB-46

Bruce-Novoa, Juan 1944- DLB-82

Bruckman, Clyde 1894-1955 . . . . DLB-26

Bruckner, Ferdinand 1891-1958 . . . . DLB-118

Brundage, John Herbert (see Herbert, John)

Brutus, Dennis 1924- DLB-117

Bryant, Arthur 1899-1985 . . . . DLB-149

Bryant, William Cullen
1794-1878 . . . . DLB-3, 43, 59

Bryce Echenique, Alfredo
1939- DLB-145

Bryce, James 1838-1922 . . . . DLB-166

Brydges, Sir Samuel Egerton
1762-1837 . . . . DLB-107

Bryskett, Lodowick 1546?-1612 . . . . DLB-167

Buchan, John 1875-1940 . . . . DLB-34, 70, 156

Buchanan, George 1506-1582 . . . . . DLB-132

Buchanan, Robert 1841-1901 . . . . DLB-18, 35

Buchman, Sidney 1902-1975 . . . . DLB-26

Buchner, Augustus 1591-1661 . . . . . DLB-164

Büchner, Georg 1813-1837 . . . . DLB-133

Bucholtz, Andreas Heinrich
1607-1671 . . . . DLB-168

Buck, Pearl S. 1892-1973 . . . . DLB-9, 102

Bucke, Charles 1781-1846 . . . . DLB-110

Bucke, Richard Maurice
1837-1902 . . . . DLB-99

Buckingham, Joseph Tinker 1779-1861 and
Buckingham, Edwin
1810-1833 . . . . DLB-73

Buckler, Ernest 1908-1984 . . . . DLB-68

Buckley, William F., Jr.
1925- DLB-137; Y-80

Buckminster, Joseph Stevens
1784-1812 . . . . DLB-37

Buckner, Robert 1906- DLB-26

Budd, Thomas ?-1698 . . . . DLB-24

Budrys, A. J. 1931- DLB-8

Buechner, Frederick 1926- Y-80

Buell, John 1927- DLB-53

Buffum, Job [publishing house] DLB-49

Bugnet, Georges 1879-1981 . . . . DLB-92

Buies, Arthur 1840-1901 . . . . DLB-99

Building the New British Library
at St Pancras Y-94

Bukowski, Charles
1920-1994 . . . . DLB-5, 130, 169

Bulger, Bozeman 1877-1932 . . . . DLB-171

Bullein, William
between 1520 and 1530-1576 . . . DLB-167

Bullins, Ed 1935- DLB-7, 38

Bulwer-Lytton, Edward (also Edward Bulwer)
1803-1873 . . . . DLB-21

Bumpus, Jerry 1937- Y-81

Bunce and Brother DLB-49

Bunner, H. C. 1855-1896 . . . . DLB-78, 79

Bunting, Basil 1900-1985 . . . . DLB-20

Bunyan, John 1628-1688 . . . . DLB-39

Burch, Robert 1925- DLB-52

Burciaga, José Antonio 1940- DLB-82

Bürger, Gottfried August
1747-1794 . . . . DLB-94

Burgess, Anthony 1917-1993 . . . . DLB-14

Burgess, Gelett 1866-1951 . . . . DLB-11

Burgess, John W. 1844-1931 . . . . DLB-47

Burgess, Thornton W.
1874-1965 . . . . DLB-22

Burgess, Stringer and Company DLB-49

Burick, Si 1909-1986 . . . . DLB-171

Burk, John Daly circa 1772-1808 . . . . DLB-37

Burke, Edmund 1729?-1797 . . . . DLB-104

Burke, Kenneth 1897-1993 . . . . . . DLB-45, 63

Burlingame, Edward Livermore
1848-1922 . . . . DLB-79

Burnet, Gilbert 1643-1715 . . . . DLB-101

Burnett, Frances Hodgson
1849-1924 . . . . . . DLB-42, 141; DS-13, 14

Burnett, W. R. 1899-1982 . . . . DLB-9

Burnett, Whit 1899-1973 and
Martha Foley 1897-1977 . . . . DLB-137

Burney, Fanny 1752-1840 . . . . DLB-39

Burns, Alan 1929- DLB-14

Burns, John Horne 1916-1953 . . . . Y-85

Burns, Robert 1759-1796 . . . . DLB-109

Burns and Oates DLB-106

Burnshaw, Stanley 1906- DLB-48

Burr, C. Chauncey 1815?-1883 . . . . . DLB-79

Burroughs, Edgar Rice 1875-1950 . . . DLB-8

Burroughs, John 1837-1921 . . . . DLB-64

Burroughs, Margaret T. G.
1917- DLB-41

Burroughs, William S., Jr.
1947-1981 . . . . DLB-16

Burroughs, William Seward
1914- DLB-2, 8, 16, 152; Y-81

Burroway, Janet 1936- DLB-6

Burt, Maxwell S. 1882-1954 . . . . DLB-86

Burt, A. L., and Company DLB-49

Burton, Hester 1913- DLB-161

Burton, Isabel Arundell
1831-1896 . . . . DLB-166

Burton, Miles (see Rhode, John)

Burton, Richard Francis
1821-1890 . . . . DLB-55, 166

Burton, Robert 1577-1640 . . . . DLB-151

Burton, Virginia Lee 1909-1968 . . . . . DLB-22

Burton, William Evans
1804-1860 . . . . DLB-73

Burwell, Adam Hood 1790-1849 . . . . . DLB-99

Bury, Lady Charlotte
1775-1861 . . . . DLB-116

Busch, Frederick 1941- DLB-6

Busch, Niven 1903-1991 . . . . DLB-44

Bushnell, Horace 1802-1876 . . . . DS-13

Bussieres, Arthur de 1877-1913 . . . . . DLB-92

Butler, Juan 1942-1981 . . . . DLB-53

Butler, Octavia E. 1947- DLB-33

Butler, Robert Olen 1945- DLB-173

Butler, Samuel 1613-1680 .....DLB-101, 126

Butler, Samuel 1835-1902 ...DLB-18, 57, 174

Butler, William Francis
1838-1910 ....DLB-166

Butler, E. H., and Company DLB-49

Butor, Michel 1926- DLB-83

Butter, Nathaniel
[publishing house] DLB-170

Butterworth, Hezekiah 1839-1905 ...DLB-42

Buttitta, Ignazio 1899- DLB-114

Buzzati, Dino 1906-1972 ....DLB-177

Byars, Betsy 1928- DLB-52

Byatt, A. S. 1936- DLB-14

Byles, Mather 1707-1788 ....DLB-24

Bynneman, Henry
[publishing house] DLB-170

Bynner, Witter 1881-1968 ....DLB-54

Byrd, William circa 1543-1623 .....DLB-172

Byrd, William II 1674-1744 ....DLB-24, 140

Byrne, John Keyes (see Leonard, Hugh)

Byron, George Gordon, Lord
1788-1824 ....DLB-96, 110

C

Caballero Bonald, José Manuel
1926- DLB-108

Cabañero, Eladio 1930- DLB-134

Cabell, James Branch
1879-1958 ....DLB-9, 78

Cabeza de Baca, Manuel
1853-1915 ....DLB-122

Cabeza de Baca Gilbert, Fabiola
1898- DLB-122

Cable, George Washington
1844-1925..........DLB-12, 74; DS-13

Cabrera, Lydia 1900-1991 ....DLB-145

Cabrera Infante, Guillermo
1929- DLB-113

Cadell [publishing house] DLB-154

Cady, Edwin H. 1917- DLB-103

Caedmon flourished 658-680 .....DLB-146

Caedmon School circa 660-899 .....DLB-146

Cahan, Abraham
1860-1951.............DLB-9, 25, 28

Cain, George 1943- DLB-33

Caldecott, Randolph 1846-1886 ....DLB-163

Calder, John
(Publishers), Limited DLB-112

Caldwell, Ben 1937- DLB-38

Caldwell, Erskine 1903-1987......DLB-9, 86

Caldwell, H. M., Company DLB-49

Calhoun, John C. 1782-1850.........DLB-3

Calisher, Hortense 1911- DLB-2

A Call to Letters and an Invitation
to the Electric Chair,
by Siegfried Mandel...........DLB-75

Callaghan, Morley 1903-1990.......DLB-68

Callahan, S. Alice 1868-1894.......DLB-175

Callaloo............................Y-87

Callimachus circa 305 B.C.-240 B.C.
...........................DLB-176

Calmer, Edgar 1907- DLB-4

Calverley, C. S. 1831-1884 ....DLB-35

Calvert, George Henry
1803-1889 ....DLB-1, 64

Cambridge Press.................DLB-49

Cambridge Songs (Carmina Cantabrigensia)
circa 1050 ....DLB-148

Cambridge University Press DLB-170

Camden, William 1551-1623.......DLB-172

Camden House: An Interview with
James Hardin Y-92

Cameron, Eleanor 1912- DLB-52

Cameron, George Frederick
1854-1885 ....DLB-99

Cameron, Lucy Lyttelton
1781-1858 ....DLB-163

Cameron, William Bleasdell
1862-1951 ....DLB-99

Camm, John 1718-1778 ....DLB-31

Campana, Dino 1885-1932 ....DLB-114

Campbell, Gabrielle Margaret Vere
(see Shearing, Joseph, and Bowen, Marjorie)

Campbell, James Dykes
1838-1895 ....DLB-144

Campbell, James Edwin
1867-1896 ....DLB-50

Campbell, John 1653-1728..........DLB-43

Campbell, John W., Jr.
1910-1971 ....DLB-8

Campbell, Roy 1901-1957 ....DLB-20

Campbell, Thomas
1777-1844 ....DLB-93, 144

Campbell, William Wilfred
1858-1918 ....DLB-92

Campion, Edmund 1539-1581.......DLB-167

Campion, Thomas
1567-1620 ....DLB-58, 172

Camus, Albert 1913-1960 ....DLB-72

The Canadian Publishers' Records
Database......................Y-96

Canby, Henry Seidel 1878-1961 .....DLB-91

Candelaria, Cordelia 1943- DLB-82

Candelaria, Nash 1928- DLB-82

Candour in English Fiction (1890),
by Thomas Hardy DLB-18

Canetti, Elias 1905-1994 ....DLB-85, 124

Canham, Erwin Dain
1904-1982 ....DLB-127

Canitz, Friedrich Rudolph Ludwig von
1654-1699 ....DLB-168

Cankar, Ivan 1876-1918..........DLB-147

Cannan, Gilbert 1884-1955 ....DLB-10

Cannell, Kathleen 1891-1974.........DLB-4

Cannell, Skipwith 1887-1957........DLB-45

Canning, George 1770-1827 ....DLB-158

Cannon, Jimmy 1910-1973 ....DLB-171

Cantwell, Robert 1908-1978 ....DLB-9

Cape, Jonathan, and Harrison Smith
[publishing house] DLB-46

Cape, Jonathan, Limited DLB-112

Capen, Joseph 1658-1725..........DLB-24

Capes, Bernard 1854-1918.........DLB-156

Capote, Truman
1924-1984.............DLB-2; Y-80, 84

Caproni, Giorgio 1912-1990 ....DLB-128

Cardarelli, Vincenzo 1887-1959 ....DLB-114

Cárdenas, Reyes 1948- DLB-122

Cardinal, Marie 1929- DLB-83

Carew, Jan 1920- DLB-157

Carew, Thomas
1594 or 1595-1640 ....DLB-126

Carey, Henry
circa 1687-1689-1743 ....DLB-84

Carey, Mathew 1760-1839 ......DLB-37, 73

Carey and Hart..................DLB-49

Carey, M., and Company DLB-49

Carell, Lodowick 1602-1675........DLB-58

Carleton, William 1794-1869 ......DLB-159

Carleton, G. W.
[publishing house] DLB-49

Carlile, Richard 1790-1843....DLB-110, 158

Carlyle, Jane Welsh 1801-1866......DLB-55

Carlyle, Thomas 1795-1881 ....DLB-55, 144

Carman, Bliss 1861-1929 ....DLB-92

367

Carmina Burana circa 1230 . . . . DLB-138

Carnero, Guillermo 1947- DLB-108

Carossa, Hans 1878-1956 . . . . DLB-66

Carpenter, Humphrey 1946- DLB-155

Carpenter, Stephen Cullen
?-1820? DLB-73

Carpentier, Alejo 1904-1980 . . . . . . DLB-113

Carrier, Roch 1937- DLB-53

Carrillo, Adolfo 1855-1926 . . . . DLB-122

Carroll, Gladys Hasty 1904- DLB-9

Carroll, John 1735-1815. . . . . DLB-37

Carroll, John 1809-1884. . . . . DLB-99

Carroll, Lewis
1832-1898. . . . . DLB-18, 163, 178

Carroll, Paul 1927- DLB-16

Carroll, Paul Vincent 1900-1968 . . . . DLB-10

Carroll and Graf Publishers DLB-46

Carruth, Hayden 1921- DLB-5, 165

Carryl, Charles E. 1841-1920 . . . . . . DLB-42

Carswell, Catherine 1879-1946. . . . . . DLB-36

Carter, Angela 1940-1992 . . . . DLB-14

Carter, Elizabeth 1717-1806 . . . . . . DLB-109

Carter, Henry (see Leslie, Frank)

Carter, Hodding, Jr. 1907-1972 . . . . DLB-127

Carter, Landon 1710-1778. . . . . DLB-31

Carter, Lin 1930- Y-81

Carter, Martin 1927- DLB-117

Carter and Hendee. DLB-49

Carter, Robert, and Brothers DLB-49

Cartwright, John 1740-1824 . . . . . . DLB-158

Cartwright, William circa
1611-1643 . . . . DLB-126

Caruthers, William Alexander
1802-1846 . . . . DLB-3

Carver, Jonathan 1710-1780 . . . . DLB-31

Carver, Raymond
1938-1988. . . . . DLB-130; Y-84, 88

Cary, Joyce 1888-1957. . . . . DLB-15, 100

Cary, Patrick 1623?-1657 . . . . DLB-131

Casey, Juanita 1925- DLB-14

Casey, Michael 1947- DLB-5

Cassady, Carolyn 1923- DLB-16

Cassady, Neal 1926-1968. . . . . DLB-16

Cassell and Company DLB-106

Cassell Publishing Company. DLB-49

Cassill, R. V. 1919- DLB-6

Cassity, Turner 1929- DLB-105

Cassius Dio circa 155/164-post 229
. . . . DLB-176

Cassola, Carlo 1917-1987 . . . . DLB-177

The Castle of Perserverance
circa 1400-1425. . . . . DLB-146

Castellano, Olivia 1944- DLB-122

Castellanos, Rosario 1925-1974 . . . . DLB-113

Castillo, Ana 1953- DLB-122

Castlemon, Harry (see Fosdick, Charles Austin)

Caswall, Edward 1814-1878 . . . . DLB-32

Catacalos, Rosemary 1944- DLB-122

Cather, Willa
1873-1947 . . . . DLB-9, 54, 78; DS-1

Catherine II (Ekaterina Alekseevna), "The
Great," Empress of Russia
1729-1796 . . . . DLB-150

Catherwood, Mary Hartwell
1847-1902 . . . . DLB-78

Catledge, Turner 1901-1983 . . . . . . DLB-127

Cattafi, Bartolo 1922-1979. . . . . DLB-128

Catton, Bruce 1899-1978 . . . . DLB-17

Causley, Charles 1917- DLB-27

Caute, David 1936- DLB-14

Cavendish, Duchess of Newcastle,
Margaret Lucas 1623-1673. . . . . DLB-131

Cawein, Madison 1865-1914 . . . . DLB-54

The Caxton Printers, Limited. DLB-46

Caxton, William
[publishing house] DLB-170

Cayrol, Jean 1911- DLB-83

Cecil, Lord David 1902-1986 . . . . . . DLB-155

Celan, Paul 1920-1970 . . . . DLB-69

Celaya, Gabriel 1911-1991 . . . . DLB-108

Céline, Louis-Ferdinand
1894-1961 . . . . DLB-72

The Celtic Background to Medieval English
Literature DLB-146

Celtis, Conrad 1459-1508 . . . . DLB-179

Center for Bibliographical Studies and
Research at the University of
California, Riverside. Y-91

The Center for the Book in the Library
of Congress. Y-93

Center for the Book Research Y-84

Centlivre, Susanna 1669?-1723. . . . . DLB-84

The Century Company DLB-49

Cernuda, Luis 1902-1963. . . . . DLB-134

Cervantes, Lorna Dee 1954- DLB-82

Chacel, Rosa 1898- DLB-134

Chacón, Eusebio 1869-1948 . . . . DLB-82

Chacón, Felipe Maximiliano
1873-? DLB-82

Chadwyck-Healey's Full-Text Literary Databases: Editing Commercial Databases of
Primary Literary Texts. Y-95

Challans, Eileen Mary (see Renault, Mary)

Chalmers, George 1742-1825 . . . . . . DLB-30

Chaloner, Sir Thomas
1520-1565 . . . . DLB-167

Chamberlain, Samuel S.
1851-1916 . . . . DLB-25

Chamberland, Paul 1939- DLB-60

Chamberlin, William Henry
1897-1969 . . . . DLB-29

Chambers, Charles Haddon
1860-1921 . . . . DLB-10

Chambers, W. and R.
[publishing house] DLB-106

Chamisso, Albert von
1781-1838 . . . . DLB-90

Champfleury 1821-1889. . . . . DLB-119

Chandler, Harry 1864-1944. . . . . DLB-29

Chandler, Norman 1899-1973. . . . . DLB-127

Chandler, Otis 1927- DLB-127

Chandler, Raymond 1888-1959 . . . . . . DS-6

Channing, Edward 1856-1931. . . . . . DLB-17

Channing, Edward Tyrrell
1790-1856 . . . . DLB-1, 59

Channing, William Ellery
1780-1842 . . . . DLB-1, 59

Channing, William Ellery, II
1817-1901 . . . . DLB-1

Channing, William Henry
1810-1884 . . . . DLB-1, 59

Chaplin, Charlie 1889-1977. . . . . DLB-44

Chapman, George
1559 or 1560 - 1634. . . . . . . DLB-62, 121

Chapman, John. DLB-106

Chapman, William 1850-1917. . . . . . DLB-99

Chapman and Hall DLB-106

Chappell, Fred 1936- DLB-6, 105

Chappell, Fred, A Detail
in a Poem. DLB-105

Charbonneau, Jean 1875-1960 . . . . . DLB-92

Charbonneau, Robert 1911-1967 . . . DLB-68

Charles, Gerda 1914- DLB-14

Charles, William
[publishing house] DLB-49

The Charles Wood Affair:
  A Playwright Revived Y-83

Charlotte Forten: Pages from
  her Diary................... DLB-50

Charteris, Leslie 1907-1993 .... DLB-77

Charyn, Jerome 1937- Y-83

Chase, Borden 1900-1971 .... DLB-26

Chase, Edna Woolman
  1877-1957 .... DLB-91

Chase-Riboud, Barbara 1936- DLB-33

Chateaubriand, François-René de
  1768-1848 .... DLB-119

Chatterton, Thomas 1752-1770 .... DLB-109

Chatto and Windus DLB-106

Chaucer, Geoffrey 1340?-1400 ..... DLB-146

Chauncy, Charles 1705-1787 .... DLB-24

Chauveau, Pierre-Joseph-Olivier
  1820-1890 .... DLB-99

Chávez, Denise 1948- DLB-122

Chávez, Fray Angélico 1910- DLB-82

Chayefsky, Paddy
  1923-1981 .... DLB-7, 44; Y-81

Cheever, Ezekiel 1615-1708......... DLB-24

Cheever, George Barrell
  1807-1890 .... DLB-59

Cheever, John
  1912-1982......... DLB-2, 102; Y-80, 82

Cheever, Susan 1943- Y-82

Cheke, Sir John 1514-1557 .... DLB-132

Chelsea House DLB-46

Cheney, Ednah Dow (Littlehale)
  1824-1904 .... DLB-1

Cheney, Harriet Vaughn
  1796-1889 .... DLB-99

Cherry, Kelly 1940 .... Y-83

Cherryh, C. J. 1942- Y-80

Chesnutt, Charles Waddell
  1858-1932................ DLB-12, 50, 78

Chester, Alfred 1928-1971 .... DLB-130

Chester, George Randolph
  1869-1924 .... DLB-78

The Chester Plays circa 1505-1532;
  revisions until 1575 .... DLB-146

Chesterfield, Philip Dormer Stanhope,
  Fourth Earl of 1694-1773 ..... DLB-104

Chesterton, G. K. 1874-1936
  .... DLB-10, 19, 34, 70, 98, 149, 178

Chettle, Henry
  circa 1560-circa 1607 .... DLB-136

Chew, Ada Nield 1870-1945 .... DLB-135

Cheyney, Edward P. 1861-1947 ..... DLB-47

Chiara, Piero 1913-1986 .... DLB-177

Chicano History DLB-82

Chicano Language DLB-82

Child, Francis James
  1825-1896 .... DLB-1, 64

Child, Lydia Maria
  1802-1880 .... DLB-1, 74

Child, Philip 1898-1978 .... DLB-68

Childers, Erskine 1870-1922 .... DLB-70

Children's Book Awards
  and Prizes DLB-61

Children's Illustrators,
  1800-1880 .... DLB-163

Childress, Alice 1920-1994 .... DLB-7, 38

Childs, George W. 1829-1894 ...... DLB-23

Chilton Book Company........... DLB-46

Chinweizu 1943- DLB-157

Chitham, Edward 1932- DLB-155

Chittenden, Hiram Martin
  1858-1917 .... DLB-47

Chivers, Thomas Holley
  1809-1858 .... DLB-3

Chopin, Kate 1850-1904 .... DLB-12, 78

Chopin, Rene 1885-1953 .... DLB-92

Choquette, Adrienne 1915-1973 .... DLB-68

Choquette, Robert 1905- DLB-68

The Christian Publishing
  Company.................... DLB-49

Christie, Agatha 1890-1976...... DLB-13, 77

Christus und die Samariterin
  circa 950 .... DLB-148

Chulkov, Mikhail Dmitrievich
  1743?-1792 .... DLB-150

Church, Benjamin 1734-1778 ...... DLB-31

Church, Francis Pharcellus
  1839-1906 .... DLB-79

Church, William Conant
  1836-1917 .... DLB-79

Churchill, Caryl 1938- DLB-13

Churchill, Charles 1731-1764 ..... DLB-109

Churchill, Sir Winston
  1874-1965 .... DLB-100

Churchyard, Thomas
  1520?-1604 .... DLB-132

Churton, E., and Company........ DLB-106

Chute, Marchette 1909-1994 ...... DLB-103

Ciardi, John 1916-1986 .... DLB-5; Y-86

Cibber, Colley 1671-1757 .... DLB-84

Cima, Annalisa 1941- DLB-128

Cirese, Eugenio 1884-1955 .... DLB-114

Cisneros, Sandra 1954- DLB-122, 152

City Lights Books................ DLB-46

Cixous, Hélène 1937- DLB-83

Clampitt, Amy 1920-1994 .... DLB-105

Clapper, Raymond 1892-1944....... DLB-29

Clare, John 1793-1864 .... DLB-55, 96

Clarendon, Edward Hyde, Earl of
  1609-1674 .... DLB-101

Clark, Alfred Alexander Gordon
  (see Hare, Cyril)

Clark, Ann Nolan 1896- DLB-52

Clark, Catherine Anthony
  1892-1977 .... DLB-68

Clark, Charles Heber
  1841-1915 .... DLB-11

Clark, Davis Wasgatt 1812-1871 .... DLB-79

Clark, Eleanor 1913- DLB-6

Clark, J. P. 1935- DLB-117

Clark, Lewis Gaylord
  1808-1873 .... DLB-3, 64, 73

Clark, Walter Van Tilburg
  1909-1971 .... DLB-9

Clark, C. M., Publishing
  Company.................... DLB-46

Clarke, Austin 1896-1974 .... DLB-10, 20

Clarke, Austin C. 1934- DLB-53, 125

Clarke, Gillian 1937- DLB-40

Clarke, James Freeman
  1810-1888 .... DLB-1, 59

Clarke, Pauline 1921- DLB-161

Clarke, Rebecca Sophia
  1833-1906 .... DLB-42

Clarke, Robert, and Company DLB-49

Clarkson, Thomas 1760-1846 ...... DLB-158

Claudius, Matthias 1740-1815....... DLB-97

Clausen, Andy 1943- DLB-16

Claxton, Remsen and
  Haffelfinger.................. DLB-49

Clay, Cassius Marcellus
  1810-1903 .... DLB-43

Cleary, Beverly 1916- DLB-52

Cleaver, Vera 1919- and
  Cleaver, Bill 1920-1981 .... DLB-52

Cleland, John 1710-1789 .... DLB-39

Clemens, Samuel Langhorne
  1835-1910 ...... DLB-11, 12, 23, 64, 74

Clement, Hal 1922- DLB-8

Clemo, Jack 1916- DLB-27	Coleridge, Samuel Taylor 1772-1834 .... DLB-93, 107	Conference on Modern Biography Y-85
Cleveland, John 1613-1658 .... DLB-126	Colet, John 1467-1519 .... DLB-132	Congreve, William 1670-1729 .... DLB-39, 84
Cliff, Michelle 1946- DLB-157	Colette 1873-1954 .... DLB-65	Conkey, W. B., Company DLB-49
Clifford, Lady Anne 1590-1676 .... DLB-151	Colette, Sidonie Gabrielle (see Colette)	Connell, Evan S., Jr. 1924- DLB-2; Y-81
Clifford, James L. 1901-1978 .... DLB-103	Colinas, Antonio 1946- DLB-134	Connelly, Marc 1890-1980 ..... DLB-7; Y-80
Clifford, Lucy 1853?-1929 .... DLB-135, 141	Collier, John 1901-1980 .... DLB-77	Connolly, Cyril 1903-1974 .... DLB-98
Clifton, Lucille 1936- DLB-5, 41	Collier, Mary 1690-1762 .... DLB-95	Connolly, James B. 1868-1957 ...... DLB-78
Clode, Edward J. [publishing house] DLB-46	Collier, Robert J. 1876-1918 .... DLB-91	Connor, Ralph 1860-1937 .... DLB-92
Clough, Arthur Hugh 1819-1861 .... DLB-32	Collier, P. F. [publishing house] DLB-49	Connor, Tony 1930- DLB-40
Cloutier, Cécile 1930- DLB-60	Collin and Small DLB-49	Conquest, Robert 1917- DLB-27
Clutton-Brock, Arthur 1868-1924 .... DLB-98	Collingwood, W. G. 1854-1932 .... DLB-149	Conrad, Joseph 1857-1924 .... DLB-10, 34, 98, 156
Coates, Robert M. 1897-1973 .... DLB-4, 9, 102	Collins, An floruit circa 1653 ...... DLB-131	Conrad, John, and Company DLB-49
Coatsworth, Elizabeth 1893- DLB-22	Collins, Merle 1950- DLB-157	Conroy, Jack 1899-1990 .... Y-81
Cobb, Charles E., Jr. 1943- DLB-41	Collins, Mortimer 1827-1876 .... DLB-21, 35	Conroy, Pat 1945- DLB-6
Cobb, Frank I. 1869-1923 .... DLB-25	Collins, Wilkie 1824-1889 ... DLB-18, 70, 159	The Consolidation of Opinion: Critical Responses to the Modernists DLB-36
Cobb, Irvin S. 1876-1944 .... DLB-11, 25, 86	Collins, William 1721-1759 .... DLB-109	Constable, Henry 1562-1613 .... DLB-136
Cobbett, William 1763-1835 .... DLB-43, 107	Collins, William, Sons and Company DLB-154	Constable and Company Limited DLB-112
Cobbledick, Gordon 1898-1969 .... DLB-171	Collins, Isaac [publishing house] DLB-49	Constable, Archibald, and Company DLB-154
Cochran, Thomas C. 1902- DLB-17	Collyer, Mary 1716?-1763? DLB-39	Constant, Benjamin 1767-1830 ..... DLB-119
Cochrane, Elizabeth 1867-1922 ..... DLB-25	Colman, Benjamin 1673-1747 .... DLB-24	Constant de Rebecque, Henri-Benjamin de (see Constant, Benjamin)
Cockerill, John A. 1845-1896 .... DLB-23	Colman, George, the Elder 1732-1794 .... DLB-89	Constantine, David 1944- DLB-40
Cocteau, Jean 1889-1963 .... DLB-65	Colman, George, the Younger 1762-1836 .... DLB-89	Constantin-Weyer, Maurice 1881-1964 .... DLB-92
Coderre, Emile (see Jean Narrache)	Colman, S. [publishing house] DLB-49	Contempo Caravan: Kites in a Windstorm Y-85
Coffee, Lenore J. 1900?-1984 ..... DLB-44	Colombo, John Robert 1936- DLB-53	
Coffin, Robert P. Tristram 1892-1955 .... DLB-45	Colquhoun, Patrick 1745-1820 ..... DLB-158	A Contemporary Flourescence of Chicano Literature Y-84
Cogswell, Fred 1917- DLB-60	Colter, Cyrus 1910- DLB-33	
Cogswell, Mason Fitch 1761-1830 .... DLB-37	Colum, Padraic 1881-1972 .... DLB-19	The Continental Publishing Company DLB-49
Cohen, Arthur A. 1928-1986 .... DLB-28	Colvin, Sir Sidney 1845-1927 ...... DLB-149	
Cohen, Leonard 1934- DLB-53	Colwin, Laurie 1944-1992 .... Y-80	A Conversation with Chaim Potok Y-84
Cohen, Matt 1942- DLB-53	Comden, Betty 1919- and Green, Adolph 1918- DLB-44	Conversations with Editors Y-95
Colden, Cadwallader 1688-1776 .... DLB-24, 30	Comi, Girolamo 1890-1968 .... DLB-114	Conversations with Publishers I: An Interview with Patrick O'Connor Y-84
Cole, Barry 1936- DLB-14	The Comic Tradition Continued [in the British Novel] DLB-15	Conversations with Publishers II: An Interview with Charles Scribner III Y-94
Cole, George Watson 1850-1939 .... DLB-140	Commager, Henry Steele 1902- DLB-17	Conversations with Publishers III: An Interview with Donald Lamm Y-95
Colegate, Isabel 1931- DLB-14	The Commercialization of the Image of Revolt, by Kenneth Rexroth DLB-16	Conversations with Publishers IV: An Interview with James Laughlin Y-96
Coleman, Emily Holmes 1899-1974 .... DLB-4	Community and Commentators: Black Theatre and Its Critics DLB-38	Conversations with Rare Book Dealers I: An Interview with Glenn Horowitz Y-90
Coleman, Wanda 1946- DLB-130	Compton-Burnett, Ivy 1884?-1969 .... DLB-36	
Coleridge, Hartley 1796-1849 .... DLB-96	Conan, Laure 1845-1924 .... DLB-99	Conversations with Rare Book Dealers II: An Interview with Ralph Sipper Y-94
Coleridge, Mary 1861-1907 ..... DLB-19, 98	Conde, Carmen 1901- DLB-108	

Conversations with Rare Book Dealers (Publishers) III: An Interview with Otto Penzler Y-96

The Conversion of an Unpolitical Man, by W. H. Bruford DLB-66

Conway, Moncure Daniel 1832-1907 ..... DLB-1

Cook, Ebenezer circa 1667-circa 1732 ..... DLB-24

Cook, Edward Tyas 1857-1919 ..... DLB-149

Cook, Michael 1933- DLB-53

Cook, David C., Publishing Company DLB-49

Cooke, George Willis 1848-1923 ..... DLB-71

Cooke, Increase, and Company DLB-49

Cooke, John Esten 1830-1886 ..... DLB-3

Cooke, Philip Pendleton 1816-1850 ..... DLB-3, 59

Cooke, Rose Terry 1827-1892 ..... DLB-12, 74

Cook-Lynn, Elizabeth 1930- DLB-175

Coolbrith, Ina 1841-1928 ..... DLB-54

Cooley, Peter 1940- DLB-105

Cooley, Peter, Into the Mirror DLB-105

Coolidge, Susan (see Woolsey, Sarah Chauncy)

Coolidge, George [publishing house] DLB-49

Cooper, Giles 1918-1966 ..... DLB-13

Cooper, James Fenimore 1789-1851 ..... DLB-3

Cooper, Kent 1880-1965 ..... DLB-29

Cooper, Susan 1935- DLB-161

Cooper, William [publishing house] DLB-170

Coote, J. [publishing house] DLB-154

Coover, Robert 1932- DLB-2; Y-81

Copeland and Day DLB-49

Copland, Robert 1470?-1548 ..... DLB-136

Coppard, A. E. 1878-1957 ..... DLB-162

Coppel, Alfred 1921- Y-83

Coppola, Francis Ford 1939- DLB-44

Copway, George (Kah-ge-ga-gah-bowh) 1818-1869 ..... DLB-175

Corazzini, Sergio 1886-1907 ..... DLB-114

Corbett, Richard 1582-1635 ..... DLB-121

Corcoran, Barbara 1911- DLB-52

Corelli, Marie 1855-1924 ..... DLB-34, 156

Corle, Edwin 1906-1956 ..... Y-85

Corman, Cid 1924- DLB-5

Cormier, Robert 1925- DLB-52

Corn, Alfred 1943- DLB-120; Y-80

Cornish, Sam 1935- DLB-41

Cornish, William circa 1465-circa 1524 ..... DLB-132

Cornwall, Barry (see Procter, Bryan Waller)

Cornwallis, Sir William, the Younger circa 1579-1614 ..... DLB-151

Cornwell, David John Moore (see le Carré, John)

Corpi, Lucha 1945- DLB-82

Corrington, John William 1932- DLB-6

Corrothers, James D. 1869-1917 ..... DLB-50

Corso, Gregory 1930- DLB-5, 16

Cortázar, Julio 1914-1984 ..... DLB-113

Cortez, Jayne 1936- DLB-41

Corvinus, Gottlieb Siegmund 1677-1746 ..... DLB-168

Corvo, Baron (see Rolfe, Frederick William)

Cory, Annie Sophie (see Cross, Victoria)

Cory, William Johnson 1823-1892 ..... DLB-35

Coryate, Thomas 1577?-1617 ..... DLB-151, 172

Cosin, John 1595-1672 ..... DLB-151

Cosmopolitan Book Corporation DLB-46

Costain, Thomas B. 1885-1965 ..... DLB-9

Coste, Donat 1912-1957 ..... DLB-88

Costello, Louisa Stuart 1799-1870 ..... DLB-166

Cota-Cárdenas, Margarita 1941- DLB-122

Cotter, Joseph Seamon, Sr. 1861-1949 ..... DLB-50

Cotter, Joseph Seamon, Jr. 1895-1919 ..... DLB-50

Cottle, Joseph [publishing house] DLB-154

Cotton, Charles 1630-1687 ..... DLB-131

Cotton, John 1584-1652 ..... DLB-24

Coulter, John 1888-1980 ..... DLB-68

Cournos, John 1881-1966 ..... DLB-54

Cousins, Margaret 1905- DLB-137

Cousins, Norman 1915-1990 ..... DLB-137

Coventry, Francis 1725-1754 ..... DLB-39

Coverdale, Miles 1487 or 1488-1569 ..... DLB-167

Coverly, N. [publishing house] DLB-49

Covici-Friede DLB-46

Coward, Noel 1899-1973 ..... DLB-10

Coward, McCann and Geoghegan DLB-46

Cowles, Gardner 1861-1946 ..... DLB-29

Cowles, Gardner ("Mike"), Jr. 1903-1985 ..... DLB-127, 137

Cowley, Abraham 1618-1667 ..... DLB-131, 151

Cowley, Hannah 1743-1809 ..... DLB-89

Cowley, Malcolm 1898-1989 ..... DLB-4, 48; Y-81, 89

Cowper, William 1731-1800 ..... DLB-104, 109

Cox, A. B. (see Berkeley, Anthony)

Cox, James McMahon 1903-1974 ..... DLB-127

Cox, James Middleton 1870-1957 ..... DLB-127

Cox, Palmer 1840-1924 ..... DLB-42

Coxe, Louis 1918-1993 ..... DLB-5

Coxe, Tench 1755-1824 ..... DLB-37

Cozzens, James Gould 1903-1978 ..... DLB-9; Y-84; DS-2

Crabbe, George 1754-1832 ..... DLB-93

Crackanthorpe, Hubert 1870-1896 ..... DLB-135

Craddock, Charles Egbert (see Murfree, Mary N.)

Cradock, Thomas 1718-1770 ..... DLB-31

Craig, Daniel H. 1811-1895 ..... DLB-43

Craik, Dinah Maria 1826-1887 ..... DLB-35, 136

Cranch, Christopher Pearse 1813-1892 ..... DLB-1, 42

Crane, Hart 1899-1932 ..... DLB-4, 48

Crane, R. S. 1886-1967 ..... DLB-63

Crane, Stephen 1871-1900 ..... DLB-12, 54, 78

Crane, Walter 1845-1915 ..... DLB-163

Cranmer, Thomas 1489-1556 ..... DLB-132

Crapsey, Adelaide 1878-1914 ..... DLB-54

Crashaw, Richard 1612 or 1613-1649 ..... DLB-126

Craven, Avery 1885-1980 ..... DLB-17

Crawford, Charles 1752-circa 1815 ..... DLB-31

Crawford, F. Marion 1854-1909 ..... DLB-71

Crawford, Isabel Valancy 1850-1887 ..... DLB-92

Crawley, Alan 1887-1975 ..... DLB-68

Crayon, Geoffrey (see Irving, Washington)

Creamer, Robert W. 1922- DLB-171

Creasey, John 1908-1973 .... DLB-77
Creative Age Press DLB-46
Creech, William
  [publishing house] DLB-154
Creede, Thomas
  [publishing house] DLB-170
Creel, George 1876-1953 .... DLB-25
Creeley, Robert 1926- DLB-5, 16, 169
Creelman, James 1859-1915 .... DLB-23
Cregan, David 1931- DLB-13
Creighton, Donald Grant
  1902-1979 .... DLB-88
Cremazie, Octave 1827-1879 .... DLB-99
Crémer, Victoriano 1909?- DLB-108
Crescas, Hasdai
  circa 1340-1412? DLB-115
Crespo, Angel 1926- DLB-134
Cresset Press DLB-112
Cresswell, Helen 1934- DLB-161
Crèvecoeur, Michel Guillaume Jean de
  1735-1813 .... DLB-37
Crews, Harry 1935- DLB-6, 143
Crichton, Michael 1942- Y-81
A Crisis of Culture: The Changing Role
  of Religion in the New Republic
  .... DLB-37
Crispin, Edmund 1921-1978 .... DLB-87
Cristofer, Michael 1946- DLB-7
"The Critic as Artist" (1891), by
  Oscar Wilde DLB-57
"Criticism In Relation To Novels" (1863),
  by G. H. Lewes DLB-21
Crnjanski, Miloš 1893-1977 .... DLB-147
Crockett, David (Davy)
  1786-1836 .... DLB-3, 11
Croft-Cooke, Rupert (see Bruce, Leo)
Crofts, Freeman Wills
  1879-1957 .... DLB-77
Croker, John Wilson
  1780-1857 .... DLB-110
Croly, George 1780-1860 .... DLB-159
Croly, Herbert 1869-1930 .... DLB-91
Croly, Jane Cunningham
  1829-1901 .... DLB-23
Crompton, Richmal 1890-1969 ..... DLB-160
Crosby, Caresse 1892-1970 .... DLB-48
Crosby, Caresse 1892-1970 and Crosby,
  Harry 1898-1929 .... DLB-4
Crosby, Harry 1898-1929 .... DLB-48

Cross, Gillian 1945- DLB-161
Cross, Victoria 1868-1952 .... DLB-135
Crossley-Holland, Kevin
  1941- DLB-40, 161
Crothers, Rachel 1878-1958 .... DLB-7
Crowell, Thomas Y., Company DLB-49
Crowley, John 1942- Y-82
Crowley, Mart 1935- DLB-7
Crown Publishers DLB-46
Crowne, John 1641-1712 .... DLB-80
Crowninshield, Edward Augustus
  1817-1859 .... DLB-140
Crowninshield, Frank 1872-1947 ... DLB-91
Croy, Homer 1883-1965 .... DLB-4
Crumley, James 1939- Y-84
Cruz, Victor Hernández 1949- DLB-41
Csokor, Franz Theodor
  1885-1969 .... DLB-81
Cuala Press DLB-112
Cullen, Countee 1903-1946 ... DLB-4, 48, 51
Culler, Jonathan D. 1944- DLB-67
The Cult of Biography
  Excerpts from the Second Folio Debate:
  "Biographies are generally a disease of
  English Literature" – Germaine Greer,
  Victoria Glendinning, Auberon Waugh,
  and Richard Holmes............ Y-86
Cumberland, Richard 1732-1811 ... DLB-89
Cummings, Constance Gordon
  1837-1924 .... DLB-174
Cummings, E. E. 1894-1962 ...... DLB-4, 48
Cummings, Ray 1887-1957 .... DLB-8
Cummings and Hilliard DLB-49
Cummins, Maria Susanna
  1827-1866 .... DLB-42
Cundall, Joseph
  [publishing house] DLB-106
Cuney, Waring 1906-1976 .... DLB-51
Cuney-Hare, Maude 1874-1936 ..... DLB-52
Cunningham, Allan
  1784-1842 .... DLB-116, 144
Cunningham, J. V. 1911- DLB-5
Cunningham, Peter F.
  [publishing house] DLB-49
Cunqueiro, Alvaro 1911-1981 ..... DLB-134
Cuomo, George 1929- Y-80
Cupples and Leon DLB-46
Cupples, Upham and Company DLB-49
Cuppy, Will 1884-1949 .... DLB-11

Curll, Edmund
  [publishing house] DLB-154
Currie, James 1756-1805 .... DLB-142
Currie, Mary Montgomerie Lamb Singleton,
  Lady Currie (see Fane, Violet)
Cursor Mundi circa 1300 .... DLB-146
Curti, Merle E. 1897- DLB-17
Curtis, Anthony 1926- DLB-155
Curtis, Cyrus H. K. 1850-1933 .... DLB-91
Curtis, George William
  1824-1892 .... DLB-1, 43
Curzon, Robert 1810-1873 .... DLB-166
Curzon, Sarah Anne 1833-1898 .... DLB-99
Cynewulf circa 770-840 .... DLB-146
Czepko, Daniel 1605-1660 .... DLB-164

D

D. M. Thomas: The Plagiarism
  Controversy Y-82
Dabit, Eugène 1898-1936 .... DLB-65
Daborne, Robert circa 1580-1628 .... DLB-58
Dacey, Philip 1939- DLB-105
Dacey, Philip, Eyes Across Centuries:
  Contemporary Poetry and "That
  Vision Thing" DLB-105
Dach, Simon 1605-1659 .... DLB-164
Daggett, Rollin M. 1831-1901 ..... DLB-79
D'Aguiar, Fred 1960- DLB-157
Dahl, Roald 1916-1990 .... DLB-139
Dahlberg, Edward 1900-1977 ...... DLB-48
Dahn, Felix 1834-1912 .... DLB-129
Dale, Peter 1938- DLB-40
Daley, Arthur 1904-1974 .... DLB-171
Dall, Caroline Wells (Healey)
  1822-1912 .... DLB-1
Dallas, E. S. 1828-1879 .... DLB-55
The Dallas Theater Center DLB-7
D'Alton, Louis 1900-1951 .... DLB-10
Daly, T. A. 1871-1948 .... DLB-11
Damon, S. Foster 1893-1971 ...... DLB-45
Damrell, William S.
  [publishing house] DLB-49
Dana, Charles A. 1819-1897 ..... DLB-3, 23
Dana, Richard Henry, Jr
  1815-1882 .... DLB-1
Dandridge, Ray Garfield DLB-51
Dane, Clemence 1887-1965 .... DLB-10

Danforth, John 1660-1730 .... DLB-24
Danforth, Samuel, I 1626-1674 ...... DLB-24
Danforth, Samuel, II 1666-1727 ..... DLB-24
Dangerous Years: London Theater, 1939-1945 .... DLB-10
Daniel, John M. 1825-1865 .... DLB-43
Daniel, Samuel 1562 or 1563-1619 .... DLB-62
Daniel Press..................... DLB-106
Daniells, Roy 1902-1979 .... DLB-68
Daniels, Jim 1956- DLB-120
Daniels, Jonathan 1902-1981 .... DLB-127
Daniels, Josephus 1862-1948 .... DLB-29
Dannay, Frederic 1905-1982 and Manfred B. Lee 1905-1971 ..... DLB-137
Danner, Margaret Esse 1915- DLB-41
Danter, John [publishing house] DLB-170
Dantin, Louis 1865-1945 .... DLB-92
Danzig, Allison 1898-1987......... DLB-171
D'Arcy, Ella circa 1857-1937....... DLB-135
Darley, George 1795-1846........... DLB-96
Darwin, Charles 1809-1882..... DLB-57, 166
Darwin, Erasmus 1731-1802 .... DLB-93
Daryush, Elizabeth 1887-1977....... DLB-20
Dashkova, Ekaterina Romanovna (née Vorontsova) 1743-1810.... DLB-150
Dashwood, Edmée Elizabeth Monica de la Pasture (see Delafield, E. M.)
Daudet, Alphonse 1840-1897 ...... DLB-123
d'Aulaire, Edgar Parin 1898- and d'Aulaire, Ingri 1904- DLB-22
Davenant, Sir William 1606-1668................DLB-58, 126
Davenport, Guy 1927- DLB-130
Davenport, Robert ?-? DLB-58
Daves, Delmer 1904-1977 .... DLB-26
Davey, Frank 1940- DLB-53
Davidson, Avram 1923-1993......... DLB-8
Davidson, Donald 1893-1968 .... DLB-45
Davidson, John 1857-1909.......... DLB-19
Davidson, Lionel 1922- DLB-14
Davie, Donald 1922- DLB-27
Davie, Elspeth 1919- DLB-139
Davies, Sir John 1569-1626 .... DLB-172
Davies, John, of Hereford 1565?-1618 .... DLB-121
Davies, Rhys 1901-1978........... DLB-139

Davies, Robertson 1913- DLB-68
Davies, Samuel 1723-1761......... DLB-31
Davies, Thomas 1712?-1785... DLB-142, 154
Davies, W. H. 1871-1940 ...... DLB-19, 174
Davies, Peter, Limited DLB-112
Daviot, Gordon 1896?-1952 .... DLB-10 (see also Tey, Josephine)
Davis, Charles A. 1795-1867........ DLB-11
Davis, Clyde Brion 1894-1962 ...... DLB-9
Davis, Dick 1945- DLB-40
Davis, Frank Marshall 1905-?....... DLB-51
Davis, H. L. 1894-1960 .... DLB-9
Davis, John 1774-1854 .... DLB-37
Davis, Lydia 1947- DLB-130
Davis, Margaret Thomson 1926- ... DLB-14
Davis, Ossie 1917- DLB-7, 38
Davis, Paxton 1925-1994............. Y-94
Davis, Rebecca Harding 1831-1910 .... DLB-74
Davis, Richard Harding 1864-1916 .... DLB-12, 23, 78, 79; DS-13
Davis, Samuel Cole 1764-1809 ...... DLB-37
Davison, Peter 1928- DLB-5
Davys, Mary 1674-1732........... DLB-39
DAW Books DLB-46
Dawson, Ernest 1882-1947 .... DLB-140
Dawson, Fielding 1930- DLB-130
Dawson, William 1704-1752 .... DLB-31
Day, Angel flourished 1586........ DLB-167
Day, Benjamin Henry 1810-1889 .... DLB-43
Day, Clarence 1874-1935.......... DLB-11
Day, Dorothy 1897-1980 .... DLB-29
Day, Frank Parker 1881-1950 ...... DLB-92
Day, John circa 1574-circa 1640 ..... DLB-62
Day, John [publishing house] DLB-170
Day Lewis, C. 1904-1972 .... DLB-15, 20 (see also Blake, Nicholas)
Day, Thomas 1748-1789 .... DLB-39
Day, The John, Company DLB-46
Day, Mahlon [publishing house]..... DLB-49
Deacon, William Arthur 1890-1977 .... DLB-68
Deal, Borden 1922-1985........... DLB-6
de Angeli, Marguerite 1889-1987 .... DLB-22
De Angelis, Milo 1951- DLB-128

De Bow, James Dunwoody Brownson 1820-1867 .... DLB-3, 79
de Bruyn, Günter 1926- DLB-75
de Camp, L. Sprague 1907- DLB-8
The Decay of Lying (1889), by Oscar Wilde [excerpt] DLB-18
Dedication, *Ferdinand Count Fathom* (1753), by Tobias Smollett............. DLB-39
Dedication, *The History of Pompey the Little* (1751), by Francis Coventry..... DLB-39
Dedication, *Lasselia* (1723), by Eliza Haywood [excerpt]............. DLB-39
Dedication, *The Wanderer* (1814), by Fanny Burney DLB-39
Dee, John 1527-1609 .... DLB-136
Deeping, George Warwick 1877-1950 .... DLB 153
Defense of *Amelia* (1752), by Henry Fielding DLB-39
Defoe, Daniel 1660-1731.... DLB-39, 95, 101
de Fontaine, Felix Gregory 1834-1896 .... DLB-43
De Forest, John William 1826-1906 .... DLB-12
DeFrees, Madeline 1919- DLB-105
DeFrees, Madeline, The Poet's Kaleidoscope: The Element of Surprise in the Making of the Poem................. DLB-105
de Graff, Robert 1895-1981 .... Y-81
de Graft, Joe 1924-1978 .... DLB-117
De Heinrico circa 980? DLB-148
Deighton, Len 1929- DLB-87
DeJong, Meindert 1906-1991........ DLB-52
Dekker, Thomas circa 1572-1632 .... DLB-62, 172
Delacorte, Jr., George T. 1894-1991 .... DLB-91
Delafield, E. M. 1890-1943 .... DLB-34
Delahaye, Guy 1888-1969 .... DLB-92
de la Mare, Walter 1873-1956............ DLB-19, 153, 162
Deland, Margaret 1857-1945........ DLB-78
Delaney, Shelagh 1939- DLB-13
Delany, Martin Robinson 1812-1885 .... DLB-50
Delany, Samuel R. 1942- DLB-8, 33
de la Roche, Mazo 1879-1961 .... DLB-68
Delbanco, Nicholas 1942- DLB-6
De León, Nephtal 1945- DLB-82
Delgado, Abelardo Barrientos 1931- DLB-82

De Libero, Libero 1906-1981 ...... DLB-114

DeLillo, Don 1936- DLB-6, 173

de Lisser H. G. 1878-1944 .... DLB-117

Dell, Floyd 1887-1969 .... DLB-9

Dell Publishing Company DLB-46

delle Grazie, Marie Eugene
  1864-1931 .... DLB-81

Deloney, Thomas died 1600 .... DLB-167

Deloria, Ella C. 1889-1971 .... DLB-175

Deloria, Vine, Jr. 1933- DLB-175

del Rey, Lester 1915-1993 .... DLB-8

Del Vecchio, John M. 1947- DS-9

de Man, Paul 1919-1983 .... DLB-67

Demby, William 1922- DLB-33

Deming, Philander 1829-1915 ...... DLB-74

Demorest, William Jennings
  1822-1895 .... DLB-79

De Morgan, William 1839-1917 .... DLB-153

Demosthenes 384 B.C.-322 B.C. DLB-176

Denham, Henry
  [publishing house] DLB-170

Denham, Sir John
  1615-1669 .... DLB-58, 126

Denison, Merrill 1893-1975 .... DLB-92

Denison, T. S., and Company DLB-49

Dennie, Joseph
  1768-1812 .... DLB-37, 43, 59, 73

Dennis, John 1658-1734 .... DLB-101

Dennis, Nigel 1912-1989 ...... DLB-13, 15

Dent, Tom 1932- DLB-38

Dent, J. M., and Sons DLB-112

Denton, Daniel circa 1626-1703 .... DLB-24

DePaola, Tomie 1934- DLB-61

De Quincey, Thomas
  1785-1859 .... DLB-110, 144

Derby, George Horatio
  1823-1861 .... DLB-11

Derby, J. C., and Company DLB-49

Derby and Miller DLB-49

Derleth, August 1909-1971 .... DLB-9

The Derrydale Press DLB-46

Derzhavin, Gavriil Romanovich
  1743-1816 .... DLB-150

Desaulniers, Gonsalve
  1863-1934 .... DLB-92

Desbiens, Jean-Paul 1927- DLB-53

des Forêts, Louis-Rene
  1918- DLB-83

DesRochers, Alfred
  1901-1978 .... DLB-68

Desrosiers, Léo-Paul 1896-1967 .... DLB-68

Dessì, Giuseppe 1909-1977 .... DLB-177

Destouches, Louis-Ferdinand
  (see Céline, Louis-Ferdinand)

De Tabley, Lord 1835-1895 .... DLB-35

Deutsch, Babette 1895-1982 .... DLB-45

Deutsch, Niklaus Manuel (see Manuel, Niklaus)

Deutsch, André, Limited DLB-112

Deveaux, Alexis 1948- DLB-38

The Development of the Author's Copyright
  in Britain DLB-154

The Development of Lighting in the Staging
  of Drama, 1900-1945 .... DLB-10

de Vere, Aubrey 1814-1902 .... DLB-35

Devereux, second Earl of Essex, Robert
  1565-1601 .... DLB-136

The Devin-Adair Company DLB-46

De Voto, Bernard 1897-1955 .... DLB-9

De Vries, Peter 1910-1993 ..... DLB-6; Y-82

Dewdney, Christopher 1951- DLB-60

Dewdney, Selwyn 1909-1979 .... DLB-68

DeWitt, Robert M., Publisher DLB-49

DeWolfe, Fiske and Company DLB-49

Dexter, Colin 1930- DLB-87

de Young, M. H. 1849-1925 .... DLB-25

Dhlomo, H. I. E. 1903-1956 ...... DLB-157

Dhuoda circa 803-after 843 .... DLB-148

The Dial Press DLB-46

Diamond, I. A. L. 1920-1988 ...... DLB-26

Di Cicco, Pier Giorgio 1949- DLB-60

Dick, Philip K. 1928-1982 .... DLB-8

Dick and Fitzgerald DLB-49

Dickens, Charles
  1812-1870 ..... DLB-21, 55, 70, 159, 166

Dickey, James
  1923-1997 .... DLB-5; Y-82, 93; DS-7

James Dickey, American Poet Y-96

Dickey, William 1928-1994 .... DLB-5

Dickinson, Emily 1830-1886 .... DLB-1

Dickinson, John 1732-1808 .... DLB-31

Dickinson, Jonathan 1688-1747 ..... DLB-24

Dickinson, Patric 1914- DLB-27

Dickinson, Peter 1927- DLB-87, 161

Dicks, John [publishing house] DLB-106

Dickson, Gordon R. 1923- DLB-8

*Dictionary of Literary Biography
  Yearbook* Awards Y-92, 93

The Dictionary of National Biography
  .... DLB-144

Didion, Joan 1934- ... DLB-2, 173; Y-81, 86

Di Donato, Pietro 1911- DLB-9

Die Fürstliche Bibliothek Corvey Y-96

Diego, Gerardo 1896-1987 .... DLB-134

Digges, Thomas circa 1546-1595 ... DLB-136

Dillard, Annie 1945- Y-80

Dillard, R. H. W. 1937- DLB-5

Dillingham, Charles T.,
  Company DLB-49

The Dillingham, G. W.,
  Company DLB-49

Dilly, Edward and Charles
  [publishing house] DLB-154

Dilthey, Wilhelm 1833-1911 ...... DLB-129

Dingelstedt, Franz von
  1814-1881 .... DLB-133

Dintenfass, Mark 1941- Y-84

Diogenes, Jr. (see Brougham, John)

Diogenes Laertius circa 200 .... DLB-176

DiPrima, Diane 1934- DLB-5, 16

Disch, Thomas M. 1940- DLB-8

Disney, Walt 1901-1966 .... DLB-22

Disraeli, Benjamin
  1804-1881 .... DLB-21, 55

D'Israeli, Isaac 1766-1848 .... DLB-107

Ditzen, Rudolf (see Fallada, Hans)

Dix, Dorothea Lynde 1802-1887 ..... DLB-1

Dix, Dorothy (see Gilmer,
  Elizabeth Meriwether)

Dix, Edwards and Company DLB-49

Dixie, Florence Douglas
  1857-1905 .... DLB-174

Dixon, Paige (see Corcoran, Barbara)

Dixon, Richard Watson
  1833-1900 .... DLB-19

Dixon, Stephen 1936- DLB-130

Dmitriev, Ivan Ivanovich
  1760-1837 .... DLB-150

Dobell, Sydney 1824-1874 .... DLB-32

Döblin, Alfred 1878-1957 .... DLB-66

Dobson, Austin
  1840-1921 .... DLB-35, 144

Doctorow, E. L.
  1931- DLB-2, 28, 173; Y-80

Documents on Sixteenth-Century
    Literature DLB-167, 172

Dodd, William E. 1869-1940........ DLB-17

Dodd, Anne [publishing house]..... DLB-154

Dodd, Mead and Company DLB-49

Doderer, Heimito von 1896-1968.... DLB-85

Dodge, Mary Mapes
    1831?-1905.......... DLB-42, 79; DS-13

Dodge, B. W., and Company DLB-46

Dodge Publishing Company DLB-49

Dodgson, Charles Lutwidge
    (see Carroll, Lewis)

Dodsley, Robert 1703-1764 .... DLB-95

Dodsley, R. [publishing house] DLB-154

Dodson, Owen 1914-1983 .... DLB-76

Doesticks, Q. K. Philander, P. B.
    (see Thomson, Mortimer)

Doheny, Carrie Estelle
    1875-1958 .... DLB-140

Domínguez, Sylvia Maida
    1935- DLB-122

Donahoe, Patrick
    [publishing house] DLB-49

Donald, David H. 1920- DLB-17

Donaldson, Scott 1928- DLB-111

Doni, Rodolfo 1919- DLB-177

Donleavy, J. P. 1926- DLB-6, 173

Donnadieu, Marguerite (see Duras,
    Marguerite)

Donne, John 1572-1631 .... DLB-121, 151

Donnelley, R. R., and Sons
    Company.................... DLB-49

Donnelly, Ignatius 1831-1901 .... DLB-12

Donohue and Henneberry......... DLB-49

Donoso, José 1924- DLB-113

Doolady, M. [publishing house] DLB-49

Dooley, Ebon (see Ebon)

Doolittle, Hilda 1886-1961 .... DLB-4, 45

Doplicher, Fabio 1938- DLB-128

Dor, Milo 1923- DLB-85

Doran, George H., Company DLB-46

Dorgelès, Roland 1886-1973 .... DLB-65

Dorn, Edward 1929- DLB-5

Dorr, Rheta Childe 1866-1948 ...... DLB-25

Dorris, Michael 1945-1997 .... DLB-175

Dorset and Middlesex, Charles Sackville,
    Lord Buckhurst,
    Earl of 1643-1706............. DLB-131

Dorst, Tankred 1925- DLB-75, 124

Dos Passos, John
    1896-1970............. DLB-4, 9; DS-1

John Dos Passos: A Centennial
    Commemoration Y-96

Doubleday and Company DLB-49

Dougall, Lily 1858-1923............ DLB-92

Doughty, Charles M.
    1843-1926............. DLB-19, 57, 174

Douglas, Gavin 1476-1522......... DLB-132

Douglas, Keith 1920-1944 .... DLB-27

Douglas, Norman 1868-1952....... DLB-34

Douglass, Frederick
    1817?-1895.......... DLB-1, 43, 50, 79

Douglass, William circa
    1691-1752 .... DLB-24

Dourado, Autran 1926- DLB-145

Dove, Rita 1952- DLB-120

Dover Publications................ DLB-46

Doves Press..................... DLB-112

Dowden, Edward 1843-1913.... DLB-35, 149

Dowell, Coleman 1925-1985 .... DLB-130

Dowland, John 1563-1626 .... DLB-172

Downes, Gwladys 1915- DLB-88

Downing, J., Major (see Davis, Charles A.)

Downing, Major Jack (see Smith, Seba)

Dowriche, Anne
    before 1560-after 1613......... DLB-172

Dowson, Ernest 1867-1900 ..... DLB-19, 135

Doxey, William
    [publishing house] DLB-49

Doyle, Sir Arthur Conan
    1859-1930........ DLB-18, 70, 156, 178

Doyle, Kirby 1932- DLB-16

Drabble, Margaret 1939- DLB-14, 155

Drach, Albert 1902- DLB-85

The Dramatic Publishing
    Company.................... DLB-49

Dramatists Play Service DLB-46

Drant, Thomas
    early 1540s?-1578............. DLB-167

Draper, John W. 1811-1882........ DLB-30

Draper, Lyman C. 1815-1891 .... DLB-30

Drayton, Michael 1563-1631....... DLB-121

Dreiser, Theodore
    1871-1945 .... DLB-9, 12, 102, 137; DS-1

Drewitz, Ingeborg 1923-1986 ...... DLB-75

Drieu La Rochelle, Pierre
    1893-1945 .... DLB-72

Drinkwater, John 1882-1937
    .... DLB-10, 19, 149

Droste-Hülshoff, Annette von
    1797-1848 .... DLB-133

The Drue Heinz Literature Prize
    Excerpt from "Excerpts from a Report
    of the Commission," in David
    Bosworth's *The Death of Descartes*
    An Interview with David
    Bosworth Y-82

Drummond, William Henry
    1854-1907 .... DLB-92

Drummond, William, of Hawthornden
    1585-1649 .... DLB-121

Dryden, Charles 1860?-1931....... DLB-171

Dryden, John 1631-1700... DLB-80, 101, 131

Držić, Marin circa 1508-1567 ...... DLB-147

Duane, William 1760-1835 .... DLB-43

Dubé, Marcel 1930- DLB-53

Dubé, Rodolphe (see Hertel, François)

Dubie, Norman 1945- DLB-120

Du Bois, W. E. B.
    1868-1963............. DLB-47, 50, 91

Du Bois, William Pène 1916- DLB-61

Dubus, Andre 1936- DLB-130

Ducharme, Réjean 1941- DLB-60

Dučić, Jovan 1871-1943.......... DLB-147

Duck, Stephen 1705?-1756......... DLB-95

Duckworth, Gerald, and
    Company Limited DLB-112

Dudek, Louis 1918- DLB-88

Duell, Sloan and Pearce........... DLB-46

Dürer, Albrecht 1471-1528 .... DLB-179

Duff Gordon, Lucie 1821-1869..... DLB-166

Duffield and Green............... DLB-46

Duffy, Maureen 1933- DLB-14

Dugan, Alan 1923- DLB-5

Dugard, William
    [publishing house] DLB-170

Dugas, Marcel 1883-1947 .... DLB-92

Dugdale, William
    [publishing house] DLB-106

Duhamel, Georges 1884-1966 ...... DLB-65

Dujardin, Edouard 1861-1949...... DLB-123

Dukes, Ashley 1885-1959.......... DLB-10

Du Maurier, George
    1834-1896............... DLB-153, 178

Dumas, Alexandre, père
    1802-1870 .... DLB-119

Dumas, Henry 1934-1968 .... DLB-41

Dunbar, Paul Laurence 1872-1906 .... DLB-50, 54, 78

Dunbar, William circa 1460-circa 1522 ..... DLB-132, 146

Duncan, Norman 1871-1916 .... DLB-92

Duncan, Quince 1940- DLB-145

Duncan, Robert 1919-1988 .... DLB-5, 16

Duncan, Ronald 1914-1982 .... DLB-13

Duncan, Sara Jeannette 1861-1922 .... DLB-92

Dunigan, Edward, and Brother DLB-49

Dunlap, John 1747-1812 .... DLB-43

Dunlap, William 1766-1839 .... DLB-30, 37, 59

Dunn, Douglas 1942- DLB-40

Dunn, Stephen 1939- DLB-105

Dunn, Stephen, The Good, The Not So Good DLB-105

Dunne, Finley Peter 1867-1936 .... DLB-11, 23

Dunne, John Gregory 1932- Y-80

Dunne, Philip 1908-1992 .... DLB-26

Dunning, Ralph Cheever 1878-1930 .... DLB-4

Dunning, William A. 1857-1922 .... DLB-17

Duns Scotus, John circa 1266-1308 .... DLB-115

Dunsany, Lord (Edward John Moreton Drax Plunkett, Baron Dunsany) 1878-1957 .... DLB-10, 77, 153, 156

Dunton, John [publishing house] ... DLB-170

Dupin, Amantine-Aurore-Lucile (see Sand, George)

Durand, Lucile (see Bersianik, Louky)

Duranty, Walter 1884-1957 .... DLB-29

Duras, Marguerite 1914- DLB-83

Durfey, Thomas 1653-1723 .... DLB-80

Durrell, Lawrence 1912-1990 .... DLB-15, 27; Y-90

Durrell, William [publishing house] DLB-49

Dürrenmatt, Friedrich 1921-1990 .... DLB-69, 124

Dutton, E. P., and Company DLB-49

Duvoisin, Roger 1904-1980 .... DLB-61

Duyckinck, Evert Augustus 1816-1878 .... DLB-3, 64

Duyckinck, George L. 1823-1863 .... DLB-3

Duyckinck and Company DLB-49

Dwight, John Sullivan 1813-1893 .... DLB-1

Dwight, Timothy 1752-1817 .... DLB-37

Dybek, Stuart 1942- DLB-130

Dyer, Charles 1928- DLB-13

Dyer, George 1755-1841 .... DLB-93

Dyer, John 1699-1757 .... DLB-95

Dyer, Sir Edward 1543-1607 .... DLB-136

Dylan, Bob 1941- DLB-16

E

Eager, Edward 1911-1964 .... DLB-22

Eames, Wilberforce 1855-1937 ..... DLB-140

Earle, James H., and Company DLB-49

Earle, John 1600 or 1601-1665 ..... DLB-151

Early American Book Illustration, by Sinclair Hamilton DLB-49

Eastlake, William 1917- DLB-6

Eastman, Carol ?- DLB-44

Eastman, Charles A. (Ohiyesa) 1858-1939 .... DLB-175

Eastman, Max 1883-1969 .... DLB-91

Eaton, Daniel Isaac 1753-1814 ..... DLB-158

Eberhart, Richard 1904- DLB-48

Ebner, Jeannie 1918- DLB-85

Ebner-Eschenbach, Marie von 1830-1916 .... DLB-81

Ebon 1942- DLB-41

Ecbasis Captivi circa 1045 .... DLB-148

Ecco Press DLB-46

Eckhart, Meister circa 1260-circa 1328 .... DLB-115

The Eclectic Review 1805-1868 .... DLB-110

Edel, Leon 1907- DLB-103

Edes, Benjamin 1732-1803 .... DLB-43

Edgar, David 1948- DLB-13

Edgeworth, Maria 1768-1849 .... DLB-116, 159, 163

The Edinburgh Review 1802-1929 .... DLB-110

Edinburgh University Press DLB-112

The Editor Publishing Company DLB-49

Editorial Statements DLB-137

Edmonds, Randolph 1900- DLB-51

Edmonds, Walter D. 1903- DLB-9

Edschmid, Kasimir 1890-1966 .... DLB-56

Edwards, Amelia Anne Blandford 1831-1892 .... DLB-174

Edwards, Jonathan 1703-1758 .... DLB-24

Edwards, Jonathan, Jr. 1745-1801 .... DLB-37

Edwards, Junius 1929- DLB-33

Edwards, Matilda Barbara Betham- 1836-1919 .... DLB-174

Edwards, Richard 1524-1566 .... DLB-62

Edwards, James [publishing house] DLB-154

Effinger, George Alec 1947- DLB-8

Egerton, George 1859-1945 .... DLB-135

Eggleston, Edward 1837-1902 .... DLB-12

Eggleston, Wilfred 1901-1986 .... DLB-92

Ehrenstein, Albert 1886-1950 .... DLB-81

Ehrhart, W. D. 1948- DS-9

Eich, Günter 1907-1972 .... DLB-69, 124

Eichendorff, Joseph Freiherr von 1788-1857 .... DLB-90

1873 Publishers' Catalogues DLB-49

Eighteenth-Century Aesthetic Theories DLB-31

Eighteenth-Century Philosophical Background DLB-31

Eigner, Larry 1927- DLB-5

Eikon Basilike 1649 .... DLB-151

Eilhart von Oberge circa 1140-circa 1195 .... DLB-148

Einhard circa 770-840 .... DLB-148

Eisenreich, Herbert 1925-1986 .... DLB-85

Eisner, Kurt 1867-1919 .... DLB-66

Eklund, Gordon 1945- Y-83

Ekwensi, Cyprian 1921- DLB-117

Eld, George [publishing house] DLB-170

Elder, Lonne III 1931- DLB-7, 38, 44

Elder, Paul, and Company DLB-49

Elements of Rhetoric (1828; revised, 1846), by Richard Whately [excerpt] DLB-57

Elie, Robert 1915-1973 .... DLB-88

Elin Pelin 1877-1949 .... DLB-147

Eliot, George 1819-1880 ..... DLB-21, 35, 55

Eliot, John 1604-1690 .... DLB-24

Eliot, T. S. 1888-1965 ..... DLB-7, 10, 45, 63

Eliot's Court Press DLB-170

Elizabeth I 1533-1603 .... DLB-136

Elizabeth von Nassau-Saarbrücken after 1393-1456 .... DLB-179

Elizondo, Salvador 1932- DLB-145

Elizondo, Sergio 1930- DLB-82

Elkin, Stanley 1930- DLB-2, 28; Y-80

Elles, Dora Amy (see Wentworth, Patricia)

Ellet, Elizabeth F. 1818?-1877 .... DLB-30

Elliot, Ebenezer 1781-1849 .... DLB-96

Elliot, Frances Minto (Dickinson) 1820-1898 .... DLB-166

Elliott, George 1923- DLB-68

Elliott, Janice 1931- DLB-14

Elliott, William 1788-1863 .... DLB-3

Elliott, Thomes and Talbot DLB-49

Ellis, Edward S. 1840-1916 .... DLB-42

Ellis, Frederick Staridge [publishing house] DLB-106

The George H. Ellis Company DLB-49

Ellison, Harlan 1934- DLB-8

Ellison, Ralph Waldo 1914-1994 .... DLB-2, 76; Y-94

Ellmann, Richard 1918-1987 .... DLB-103; Y-87

The Elmer Holmes Bobst Awards in Arts and Letters Y-87

Elyot, Thomas 1490?-1546 .... DLB-136

Emanuel, James Andrew 1921- DLB-41

Emecheta, Buchi 1944- DLB-117

The Emergence of Black Women Writers DS-8

Emerson, Ralph Waldo 1803-1882 .... DLB-1, 59, 73

Emerson, William 1769-1811 .... DLB-37

Emin, Fedor Aleksandrovich circa 1735-1770 .... DLB-150

Empedocles fifth century B.C. DLB-176

Empson, William 1906-1984 .... DLB-20

The End of English Stage Censorship, 1945-1968 .... DLB-13

Ende, Michael 1929- DLB-75

Engel, Marian 1933-1985 .... DLB-53

Engels, Friedrich 1820-1895 .... DLB-129

Engle, Paul 1908- DLB-48

English Composition and Rhetoric (1866), by Alexander Bain [excerpt] DLB-57

The English Language: 410 to 1500 .... DLB-146

The English Renaissance of Art (1908), by Oscar Wilde DLB-35

Enright, D. J. 1920- DLB-27

Enright, Elizabeth 1909-1968 .... DLB-22

L'Envoi (1882), by Oscar Wilde..... DLB-35

Epictetus circa 55-circa 125-130 .... DLB-176

Epicurus 342/341 B.C.-271/270 B.C. DLB-176

Epps, Bernard 1936- DLB-53

Epstein, Julius 1909- and Epstein, Philip 1909-1952 .... DLB-26

Equiano, Olaudah circa 1745-1797 .... DLB-37, 50

Eragny Press DLB-112

Erasmus, Desiderius 1467-1536 .... DLB-136

Erba, Luciano 1922- DLB-128

Erdrich, Louise 1954- DLB-152, 178

Erichsen-Brown, Gwethalyn Graham (see Graham, Gwethalyn)

Eriugena, John Scottus circa 810-877 .... DLB-115

Ernest Hemingway's Toronto Journalism Revisited: With Three Previously Unrecorded Stories Y-92

Ernst, Paul 1866-1933 .... DLB-66, 118

Erskine, Albert 1911-1993 .... Y-93

Erskine, John 1879-1951 .... DLB-9, 102

Ervine, St. John Greer 1883-1971 .... DLB-10

Eschenburg, Johann Joachim 1743-1820 .... DLB-97

Escoto, Julio 1944- DLB-145

Eshleman, Clayton 1935- DLB-5

Espriu, Salvador 1913-1985 .... DLB-134

Ess Ess Publishing Company DLB-49

Essay on Chatterton (1842), by Robert Browning DLB-32

Essex House Press DLB-112

Estes, Eleanor 1906-1988 .... DLB-22

Estes and Lauriat DLB-49

Etherege, George 1636-circa 1692 ... DLB-80

Ethridge, Mark, Sr. 1896-1981 ..... DLB-127

Ets, Marie Hall 1893- DLB-22

Etter, David 1928- DLB-105

Ettner, Johann Christoph 1654-1724 .... DLB-168

Eudora Welty: Eye of the Storyteller ... Y-87

Eugene O'Neill Memorial Theater Center DLB-7

Eugene O'Neill's Letters: A Review Y-88

Eupolemius flourished circa 1095 .... DLB-148

Euripides circa 484 B.C.-407/406 B.C. DLB-176

Evans, Caradoc 1878-1945 .... DLB-162

Evans, Donald 1884-1921 .... DLB-54

Evans, George Henry 1805-1856 .... DLB-43

Evans, Hubert 1892-1986 .... DLB-92

Evans, Mari 1923- DLB-41

Evans, Mary Ann (see Eliot, George)

Evans, Nathaniel 1742-1767 .... DLB-31

Evans, Sebastian 1830-1909 .... DLB-35

Evans, M., and Company DLB-46

Everett, Alexander Hill 790-1847 .... DLB-59

Everett, Edward 1794-1865 ...... DLB-1, 59

Everson, R. G. 1903- DLB-88

Everson, William 1912-1994 ..... DLB-5, 16

Every Man His Own Poet; or, The Inspired Singer's Recipe Book (1877), by W. H. Mallock DLB-35

Ewart, Gavin 1916- DLB-40

Ewing, Juliana Horatia 1841-1885 .... DLB-21, 163

The Examiner 1808-1881 .... DLB-110

Exley, Frederick 1929-1992 .... DLB-143; Y-81

Experiment in the Novel (1929), by John D. Beresford DLB-36

von Eyb, Albrecht 1420-1475 ..... DLB-179

Eyre and Spottiswoode DLB-106

Ezzo ?-after 1065 .... DLB-148

F

"F. Scott Fitzgerald: St. Paul's Native Son and Distinguished American Writer": University of Minnesota Conference, 29-31 October 1982 .... Y-82

Faber, Frederick William 1814-1863 .... DLB-32

Faber and Faber Limited DLB-112

Faccio, Rena (see Aleramo, Sibilla)

Fagundo, Ana María 1938- DLB-134

Fair, Ronald L. 1932- DLB-33

Fairfax, Beatrice (see Manning, Marie)

Fairlie, Gerard 1899-1983 .... DLB-77

Fallada, Hans 1893-1947 .... DLB-56

Falsifying Hemingway Y-96

Fancher, Betsy 1928- Y-83

Fane, Violet 1843-1905 .... DLB-35

Fanfrolico Press DLB-112

Fanning, Katherine 1927 .... DLB-127

Fanshawe, Sir Richard 1608-1666 .... DLB-126

Fantasy Press Publishers DLB-46

Fante, John 1909-1983 .... DLB-130; Y-83

Al-Farabi circa 870-950 .... DLB-115

Farah, Nuruddin 1945- DLB-125

Farber, Norma 1909-1984 .... DLB-61

Farigoule, Louis (see Romains, Jules)

Farjeon, Eleanor 1881-1965 .... DLB-160

Farley, Walter 1920-1989 .... DLB-22

Farmer, Penelope 1939- DLB-161

Farmer, Philip José 1918- DLB-8

Farquhar, George circa 1677-1707 ... DLB-84

Farquharson, Martha (see Finley, Martha)

Farrar, Frederic William
    1831-1903 .... DLB-163

Farrar and Rinehart DLB-46

Farrar, Straus and Giroux DLB-46

Farrell, James T.
    1904-1979 .... DLB-4, 9, 86; DS-2

Farrell, J. G. 1935-1979 .... DLB-14

Fast, Howard 1914- DLB-9

Faulkner, William 1897-1962
    .... DLB-9, 11, 44, 102; DS-2; Y-86

Faulkner, George
    [publishing house] DLB-154

Fauset, Jessie Redmon 1882-1961 .... DLB-51

Faust, Irvin 1924- DLB-2, 28; Y-80

Fawcett Books DLB-46

Fearing, Kenneth 1902-1961 .... DLB-9

Federal Writers' Project DLB-46

Federman, Raymond 1928- Y-80

Feiffer, Jules 1929- DLB-7, 44

Feinberg, Charles E. 1899-1988 .... Y-88

Feind, Barthold 1678-1721 .... DLB-168

Feinstein, Elaine 1930- DLB-14, 40

Feldman, Irving 1928- DLB-169

Felipe, Léon 1884-1968 .... DLB-108

Fell, Frederick, Publishers DLB-46

Felltham, Owen 1602?-1668 ... DLB-126, 151

Fels, Ludwig 1946- DLB-75

Felton, Cornelius Conway
    1807-1862 .... DLB-1

Fennario, David 1947- DLB-60

Fenno, John 1751-1798 .... DLB-43

Fenno, R. F., and Company DLB-49

Fenoglio, Beppe 1922-1963 .... DLB-177

Fenton, Geoffrey 1539?-1608 ..... DLB-136

Fenton, James 1949- DLB-40

Ferber, Edna 1885-1968 ...... DLB-9, 28, 86

Ferdinand, Vallery III (see Salaam, Kalamu ya)

Ferguson, Sir Samuel 1810-1886 ..... DLB-32

Ferguson, William Scott
    1875-1954 .... DLB-47

Fergusson, Robert 1750-1774 ...... DLB-109

Ferland, Albert 1872-1943 .... DLB-92

Ferlinghetti, Lawrence 1919- DLB-5, 16

Fern, Fanny (see Parton, Sara Payson Willis)

Ferrars, Elizabeth 1907- DLB-87

Ferré, Rosario 1942- DLB-145

Ferret, E., and Company DLB-49

Ferrier, Susan 1782-1854 .... DLB-116

Ferrini, Vincent 1913- DLB-48

Ferron, Jacques 1921-1985 .... DLB-60

Ferron, Madeleine 1922- DLB-53

Fetridge and Company DLB-49

Feuchtersleben, Ernst Freiherr von
    1806-1849 .... DLB-133

Feuchtwanger, Lion 1884-1958 ...... DLB-66

Feuerbach, Ludwig 1804-1872 ..... DLB-133

Fichte, Johann Gottlieb
    1762-1814 .... DLB-90

Ficke, Arthur Davison 1883-1945 .... DLB-54

Fiction Best-Sellers, 1910-1945 .... DLB-9

Fiction into Film, 1928-1975: A List of Movies
    Based on the Works of Authors in
    British Novelists, 1930-1959 .... DLB-15

Fiedler, Leslie A. 1917- DLB-28, 67

Field, Edward 1924- DLB-105

Field, Edward, The Poetry File DLB-105

Field, Eugene
    1850-1895 ...... DLB-23, 42, 140; DS-13

Field, John 1545?-1588 .... DLB-167

Field, Marshall, III 1893-1956 ...... DLB-127

Field, Marshall, IV 1916-1965 ...... DLB-127

Field, Marshall, V 1941- DLB-127

Field, Nathan 1587-1619 or 1620 .... DLB-58

Field, Rachel 1894-1942 .... DLB-9, 22

A Field Guide to Recent Schools of American
    Poetry Y-86

Fielding, Henry
    1707-1754 .... DLB-39, 84, 101

Fielding, Sarah 1710-1768 .... DLB-39

Fields, James Thomas 1817-1881 ..... DLB-1

Fields, Julia 1938- DLB-41

Fields, W. C. 1880-1946 .... DLB-44

Fields, Osgood and Company DLB-49

Fifty Penguin Years Y-85

Figes, Eva 1932- DLB-14

Figuera, Angela 1902-1984 .... DLB-108

Filmer, Sir Robert 1586-1653 ...... DLB-151

Filson, John circa 1753-1788 .... DLB-37

Finch, Anne, Countess of Winchilsea
    1661-1720 .... DLB-95

Finch, Robert 1900- DLB-88

Findley, Timothy 1930- DLB-53

Finlay, Ian Hamilton 1925- DLB-40

Finley, Martha 1828-1909 .... DLB-42

Finn, Elizabeth Anne (McCaul)
    1825-1921 .... DLB-166

Finney, Jack 1911- DLB-8

Finney, Walter Braden (see Finney, Jack)

Firbank, Ronald 1886-1926 .... DLB-36

Firmin, Giles 1615-1697 .... DLB-24

Fischart, Johann
    1546 or 1547-1590 or 1591 ..... DLB-179

First Edition Library/Collectors'
    Reprints, Inc. Y-91

First International F. Scott Fitzgerald
    Conference Y-92

First Strauss "Livings" Awarded to Cynthia
    Ozick and Raymond Carver
    An Interview with Cynthia Ozick
    An Interview with Raymond
    Carver Y-83

Fischer, Karoline Auguste Fernandine
    1764-1842 .... DLB-94

Fish, Stanley 1938- DLB-67

Fishacre, Richard 1205-1248 .... DLB-115

Fisher, Clay (see Allen, Henry W.)

Fisher, Dorothy Canfield
    1879-1958 .... DLB-9, 102

Fisher, Leonard Everett 1924- DLB-61

Fisher, Roy 1930- DLB-40

Fisher, Rudolph 1897-1934 ..... DLB-51, 102

Fisher, Sydney George 1856-1927 ... DLB-47

Fisher, Vardis 1895-1968 .... DLB-9

Fiske, John 1608-1677 .... DLB-24

Fiske, John 1842-1901 .... DLB-47, 64

Fitch, Thomas circa 1700-1774 ..... DLB-31

Fitch, William Clyde 1865-1909 ..... DLB-7

FitzGerald, Edward 1809-1883 ...... DLB-32

Fitzgerald, F. Scott
    1896-1940 ..... DLB-4, 9, 86; Y-81; DS-1

F. Scott Fitzgerald Centenary Celebrations Y-96

Fitzgerald, Penelope 1916- DLB-14

Fitzgerald, Robert 1910-1985 .... Y-80

Fitzgerald, Thomas 1819-1891 ...... DLB-23

Fitzgerald, Zelda Sayre 1900-1948 ...... Y-84

Fitzhugh, Louise 1928-1974 .... DLB-52

Fitzhugh, William
circa 1651-1701 .... DLB-24

Flanagan, Thomas 1923- Y-80

Flanner, Hildegarde 1899-1987 ...... DLB-48

Flanner, Janet 1892-1978 .... DLB-4

Flaubert, Gustave 1821-1880 .... DLB-119

Flavin, Martin 1883-1967 .... DLB-9

Fleck, Konrad (flourished circa 1220)
.... DLB-138

Flecker, James Elroy 1884-1915 .. DLB-10, 19

Fleeson, Doris 1901-1970 .... DLB-29

Fleißer, Marieluise 1901-1974 ... DLB-56, 124

Fleming, Ian 1908-1964 .... DLB-87

Fleming, Paul 1609-1640 .... DLB-164

The Fleshly School of Poetry and Other
Phenomena of the Day (1872), by Robert
Buchanan DLB-35

The Fleshly School of Poetry: Mr. D. G.
Rossetti (1871), by Thomas Maitland
(Robert Buchanan) DLB-35

Fletcher, Giles, the Elder
1546-1611 .... DLB-136

Fletcher, Giles, the Younger
1585 or 1586-1623 .... DLB-121

Fletcher, J. S. 1863-1935 .... DLB-70

Fletcher, John (see Beaumont, Francis)

Fletcher, John Gould 1886-1950 ... DLB-4, 45

Fletcher, Phineas 1582-1650 .... DLB-121

Flieg, Helmut (see Heym, Stefan)

Flint, F. S. 1885-1960 .... DLB-19

Flint, Timothy 1780-1840 .... DLB-73

Florio, John 1553?-1625 .... DLB-172

Foix, J. V. 1893-1987 .... DLB-134

Foley, Martha (see Burnett, Whit, and Martha Foley)

Folger, Henry Clay 1857-1930 ..... DLB-140

Folio Society DLB-112

Follen, Eliza Lee (Cabot) 1787-1860 ... DLB-1

Follett, Ken 1949- Y-81, DLB-87

Follett Publishing Company DLB-46

Folsom, John West
[publishing house] DLB-49

Folz, Hans
between 1435 and 1440-1513 ... DLB-179

Fontane, Theodor 1819-1898 ...... DLB-129

Fonvisin, Denis Ivanovich
1744 or 1745-1792 .... DLB-150

Foote, Horton 1916- DLB-26

Foote, Samuel 1721-1777 .... DLB-89

Foote, Shelby 1916- DLB-2, 17

Forbes, Calvin 1945- DLB-41

Forbes, Ester 1891-1967 .... DLB-22

Forbes and Company DLB-49

Force, Peter 1790-1868 .... DLB-30

Forché, Carolyn 1950- DLB-5

Ford, Charles Henri 1913- DLB-4, 48

Ford, Corey 1902-1969 .... DLB-11

Ford, Ford Madox
1873-1939 .... DLB-34, 98, 162

Ford, Jesse Hill 1928- DLB-6

Ford, John 1586-? DLB-58

Ford, R. A. D. 1915- DLB-88

Ford, Worthington C. 1858-1941 .... DLB-47

Ford, J. B., and Company DLB-49

Fords, Howard, and Hulbert DLB-49

Foreman, Carl 1914-1984 .... DLB-26

Forester, Frank (see Herbert, Henry William)

Fornés, María Irene 1930- DLB-7

Forrest, Leon 1937- DLB-33

Forster, E. M.
1879-1970 .. DLB-34, 98, 162, 178; DS-10

Forster, Georg 1754-1794 .... DLB-94

Forster, John 1812-1876 .... DLB-144

Forster, Margaret 1938- DLB-155

Forsyth, Frederick 1938- DLB-87

Forten, Charlotte L. 1837-1914 ...... DLB-50

Fortini, Franco 1917- DLB-128

Fortune, T. Thomas 1856-1928 ..... DLB-23

Fosdick, Charles Austin
1842-1915 .... DLB-42

Foster, Genevieve 1893-1979 .... DLB-61

Foster, Hannah Webster
1758-1840 .... DLB-37

Foster, John 1648-1681 .... DLB-24

Foster, Michael 1904-1956 .... DLB-9

Foulis, Robert and Andrew / R. and A.
[publishing house] DLB-154

Fouqué, Caroline de la Motte
1774-1831 .... DLB-90

Fouqué, Friedrich de la Motte
1777-1843 .... DLB-90

Four Essays on the Beat Generation,
by John Clellon Holmes DLB-16

Four Seas Company DLB-46

Four Winds Press DLB-46

Fournier, Henri Alban (see Alain-Fournier)

Fowler and Wells Company DLB-49

Fowles, John 1926- DLB-14, 139

Fox, John, Jr. 1862 or
1863-1919 .... DLB-9; DS-13

Fox, Paula 1923- DLB-52

Fox, Richard Kyle 1846-1922 .... DLB-79

Fox, William Price 1926- DLB-2; Y-81

Fox, Richard K.
[publishing house] DLB-49

Foxe, John 1517-1587 .... DLB-132

Fraenkel, Michael 1896-1957 .... DLB-4

France, Anatole 1844-1924 .... DLB-123

France, Richard 1938- DLB-7

Francis, Convers 1795-1863 .... DLB-1

Francis, Dick 1920- DLB-87

Francis, Jeffrey, Lord 1773-1850 .... DLB-107

Francis, C. S. [publishing house] DLB-49

François 1863-1910 .... DLB-92

François, Louise von 1817-1893 .... DLB-129

Franck, Sebastian 1499-1542 .... DLB-179

Francke, Kuno 1855-1930 .... DLB-71

Frank, Bruno 1887-1945 .... DLB-118

Frank, Leonhard 1882-1961 .... DLB-56, 118

Frank, Melvin (see Panama, Norman)

Frank, Waldo 1889-1967 .... DLB-9, 63

Franken, Rose 1895?-1988 .... Y-84

Franklin, Benjamin
1706-1790 .... DLB-24, 43, 73

Franklin, James 1697-1735 .... DLB-43

Franklin Library DLB-46

Frantz, Ralph Jules 1902-1979 .... DLB-4

Franzos, Karl Emil 1848-1904 ...... DLB-129

Fraser, G. S. 1915-1980 .... DLB-27

Fraser, Kathleen 1935- DLB-169

Frattini, Alberto 1922- DLB-128

Frau Ava ?-1127 .... DLB-148

Frayn, Michael 1933- DLB-13, 14

Frederic, Harold
1856-1898 .... DLB-12, 23; DS-13

Freeling, Nicolas 1927- DLB-87

Freeman, Douglas Southall
1886-1953 .... DLB-17

Freeman, Legh Richmond
1842-1915 .... DLB-23

Freeman, Mary E. Wilkins
1852-1930 .... DLB-12, 78

Freeman, R. Austin 1862-1943 ...... DLB-70

Freidank circa 1170-circa 1233 ..... DLB-138

Freiligrath, Ferdinand 1810-1876 ... DLB-133

French, Alice 1850-1934 ..... DLB-74; DS-13

French, David 1939- DLB-53

French, James [publishing house] DLB-49

French, Samuel [publishing house] ... DLB-49

Samuel French, Limited DLB-106

Freneau, Philip 1752-1832 .... DLB-37, 43

Freni, Melo 1934- DLB-128

Freshfield, Douglas W.
1845-1934 .... DLB-174

Freytag, Gustav 1816-1895 .... DLB-129

Fried, Erich 1921-1988 .... DLB-85

Friedman, Bruce Jay 1930- DLB-2, 28

Friedrich von Hausen
circa 1171-1190 .... DLB-138

Friel, Brian 1929- DLB-13

Friend, Krebs 1895?-1967? DLB-4

Fries, Fritz Rudolf 1935- DLB-75

Fringe and Alternative Theater
in Great Britain DLB-13

Frisch, Max 1911-1991 .... DLB-69, 124

Frischlin, Nicodemus 1547-1590 .... DLB-179

Frischmuth, Barbara 1941- DLB-85

Fritz, Jean 1915- DLB-52

Fromentin, Eugene 1820-1876 ...... DLB-123

From *The Gay Science*, by
E. S. Dallas DLB-21

Frost, A. B. 1851-1928 .... DS-13

Frost, Robert 1874-1963 ...... DLB-54; DS-7

Frothingham, Octavius Brooks
1822-1895 .... DLB-1

Froude, James Anthony
1818-1894 .... DLB-18, 57, 144

Fry, Christopher 1907- DLB-13

Fry, Roger 1866-1934 .... DS-10

Frye, Northrop 1912-1991 .... DLB-67, 68

Fuchs, Daniel
1909-1993 .... DLB-9, 26, 28; Y-93

Fuentes, Carlos 1928- DLB-113

Fuertes, Gloria 1918- DLB-108

The Fugitives and the Agrarians:
The First Exhibition Y-85

Fulbecke, William 1560-1603? DLB-172

Fuller, Charles H., Jr. 1939- DLB-38

Fuller, Henry Blake 1857-1929 ...... DLB-12

Fuller, John 1937- DLB-40

Fuller, Roy 1912-1991 .... DLB-15, 20

Fuller, Samuel 1912- DLB-26

Fuller, Sarah Margaret, Marchesa
D'Ossoli 1810-1850 .... DLB-1, 59, 73

Fuller, Thomas 1608-1661 .... DLB-151

Fullerton, Hugh 1873-1945 .... DLB-171

Fulton, Len 1934- Y-86

Fulton, Robin 1937- DLB-40

Furbank, P. N. 1920- DLB-155

Furman, Laura 1945- Y-86

Furness, Horace Howard
1833-1912 .... DLB-64

Furness, William Henry 1802-1896 ... DLB-1

Furthman, Jules 1888-1966 .... DLB-26

The Future of the Novel (1899), by
Henry James DLB-18

Fyleman, Rose 1877-1957 .... DLB-160

G

The G. Ross Roy Scottish Poetry
Collection at the University of
South Carolina Y-89

Gadda, Carlo Emilio 1893-1973 .... DLB-177

Gaddis, William 1922- DLB-2

Gág, Wanda 1893-1946 .... DLB-22

Gagnon, Madeleine 1938- DLB-60

Gaine, Hugh 1726-1807 .... DLB-43

Gaine, Hugh [publishing house] DLB-49

Gaines, Ernest J.
1933- DLB-2, 33, 152; Y-80

Gaiser, Gerd 1908-1976 .... DLB-69

Galarza, Ernesto 1905-1984 .... DLB-122

Galaxy Science Fiction Novels DLB-46

Gale, Zona 1874-1938 .... DLB-9, 78

Galen of Pergamon 129-after 210 ... DLB-176

Gall, Louise von 1815-1855 .... DLB-133

Gallagher, Tess 1943- DLB-120

Gallagher, Wes 1911- DLB-127

Gallagher, William Davis
1808-1894 .... DLB-73

Gallant, Mavis 1922- DLB-53

Gallico, Paul 1897-1976 .... DLB-9, 171

Galsworthy, John
1867-1933 .... DLB-10, 34, 98, 162

Galt, John 1779-1839 .... DLB-99, 116

Galton, Sir Francis 1822-1911 ...... DLB-166

Galvin, Brendan 1938- DLB-5

Gambit DLB-46

Gamboa, Reymundo 1948- DLB-122

Gammer Gurton's Needle DLB-62

Gannett, Frank E. 1876-1957 ...... DLB-29

Gaos, Vicente 1919-1980 .... DLB-134

García, Lionel G. 1935- DLB-82

García Lorca, Federico
1898-1936 .... DLB-108

García Márquez, Gabriel
1928- DLB-113

Gardam, Jane 1928- DLB-14, 161

Garden, Alexander
circa 1685-1756 .... DLB-31

Gardiner, Margaret Power Farmer (see
Blessington, Marguerite, Countess of)

Gardner, John 1933-1982 ...... DLB-2; Y-82

Garfield, Leon 1921- DLB-161

Garis, Howard R. 1873-1962 .... DLB-22

Garland, Hamlin
1860-1940 .... DLB-12, 71, 78

Garneau, Francis-Xavier
1809-1866 .... DLB-99

Garneau, Hector de Saint-Denys
1912-1943 .... DLB-88

Garneau, Michel 1939- DLB-53

Garner, Alan 1934- DLB-161

Garner, Hugh 1913-1979 .... DLB-68

Garnett, David 1892-1981 .... DLB-34

Garnett, Eve 1900-1991 .... DLB-160

Garraty, John A. 1920- DLB-17

Garrett, George
1929- DLB-2, 5, 130, 152; Y-83

Garrick, David 1717-1779 .... DLB-84

Garrison, William Lloyd
1805-1879 .... DLB-1, 43

Garro, Elena 1920- DLB-145

Garth, Samuel 1661-1719 .... DLB-95

Garve, Andrew 1908- DLB-87	Genevoix, Maurice 1890-1980.......DLB-65	Gibson, Charles Dana 1867-1944 .....DS-13
Gary, Romain 1914-1980..........DLB-83	Genovese, Eugene D. 1930- DLB-17	Gibson, Graeme 1934- DLB-53
Gascoigne, George 1539?-1577.....DLB-136	Gent, Peter 1942- Y-82	Gibson, Margaret 1944- DLB-120
Gascoyne, David 1916- DLB-20	Geoffrey of Monmouth circa 1100-1155................DLB-146	Gibson, Margaret Dunlop 1843-1920 ....DLB-174
Gaskell, Elizabeth Cleghorn 1810-1865............DLB-21, 144, 159	George, Henry 1839-1897 ....DLB-23	Gibson, Wilfrid 1878-1962 ....DLB-19
Gaspey, Thomas 1788-1871 ....DLB-116	George, Jean Craighead 1919- DLB-52	Gibson, William 1914- DLB-7
Gass, William Howard 1924- DLB-2	*Georgslied* 896?....................DLB-148	Gide, André 1869-1951 ....DLB-65
Gates, Doris 1901- DLB-22	Gerhardie, William 1895-1977 ......DLB-36	Giguère, Diane 1937- DLB-53
Gates, Henry Louis, Jr. 1950- DLB-67	Gerhardt, Paul 1607-1676 ....DLB-164	Giguère, Roland 1929- DLB-60
Gates, Lewis E. 1860-1924.........DLB-71	Gérin, Winifred 1901-1981 ....DLB-155	Gil de Biedma, Jaime 1929-1990 ....DLB-108
Gatto, Alfonso 1909-1976 ....DLB-114	Gérin-Lajoie, Antoine 1824-1882 ....DLB-99	Gil-Albert, Juan 1906- DLB-134
Gaunt, Mary 1861-1942..........DLB-174	German Drama 800-1280.........DLB-138	Gilbert, Anthony 1899-1973 ....DLB-77
Gautier, Théophile 1811-1872.....DLB-119	German Drama from Naturalism to Fascism: 1889-1933 ....DLB-118	Gilbert, Michael 1912- DLB-87
Gauvreau, Claude 1925-1971 ....DLB-88	German Literature and Culture from Charlemagne to the Early Courtly Period DLB-148	Gilbert, Sandra M. 1936- DLB-120
The *Gawain*-Poet flourished circa 1350-1400 .....DLB-146		Gilbert, Sir Humphrey 1537-1583 ....DLB-136
Gay, Ebenezer 1696-1787 ....DLB-24	German Radio Play, The..........DLB-124	Gilchrist, Alexander 1828-1861 ....DLB-144
Gay, John 1685-1732 ....DLB-84, 95	German Transformation from the Baroque to the Enlightenment, The DLB-97	Gilchrist, Ellen 1935- DLB-130
The Gay Science (1866), by E. S. Dallas [excerpt] DLB-21	The Germanic Epic and Old English Heroic Poetry: *Widseth*, *Waldere*, and *The Fight at Finnsburg*..............DLB-146	Gilder, Jeannette L. 1849-1916 ......DLB-79
Gayarré, Charles E. A. 1805-1895 ...DLB-30		Gilder, Richard Watson 1844-1909 ....DLB-64, 79
Gaylord, Edward King 1873-1974 ....DLB-127	Germanophilism, by Hans Kohn DLB-66	Gildersleeve, Basil 1831-1924 ....DLB-71
Gaylord, Edward Lewis 1919- DLB-127	Gernsback, Hugo 1884-1967.....DLB-8, 137	Giles, Henry 1809-1882 ....DLB-64
Gaylord, Charles [publishing house] DLB-49	Gerould, Katharine Fullerton 1879-1944 ....DLB-78	Giles of Rome circa 1243-1316 .....DLB-115
Geddes, Gary 1940- DLB-60	Gerrish, Samuel [publishing house] ..DLB-49	Gilfillan, George 1813-1878........DLB-144
Geddes, Virgil 1897- DLB-4	Gerrold, David 1944- DLB-8	Gill, Eric 1882-1940 ....DLB-98
Gedeon (Georgii Andreevich Krinovsky) circa 1730-1763................DLB-150	The Ira Gershwin Centenary Y-96	Gill, William F., Company DLB-49
Geibel, Emanuel 1815-1884........DLB-129	Gersonides 1288-1344 ....DLB-115	Gillespie, A. Lincoln, Jr. 1895-1950 ....DLB-4
Geiogamah, Hanay 1945- DLB-175	Gerstäcker, Friedrich 1816-1872....DLB-129	Gilliam, Florence ?-?...............DLB-4
Geis, Bernard, Associates..........DLB-46	Gerstenberg, Heinrich Wilhelm von 1737-1823 ....DLB-97	Gilliatt, Penelope 1932-1993 ....DLB-14
Geisel, Theodor Seuss 1904-1991 ....DLB-61; Y-91	Gervinus, Georg Gottfried 1805-1871 ....DLB-133	Gillott, Jacky 1939-1980............DLB-14
Gelb, Arthur 1924- DLB-103	Geßner, Salomon 1730-1788 ....DLB-97	Gilman, Caroline H. 1794-1888 ...DLB-3, 73
Gelb, Barbara 1926- DLB-103	Geston, Mark S. 1946- DLB-8	Gilman, W. and J. [publishing house] DLB-49
Gelber, Jack 1932- DLB-7	Al-Ghazali 1058-1111 ....DLB-115	Gilmer, Elizabeth Meriwether 1861-1951 ....DLB-29
Gelinas, Gratien 1909- DLB-88	Gibbon, Edward 1737-1794........DLB-104	Gilmer, Francis Walker 1790-1826 ....DLB-37
Gellert, Christian Füerchtegott 1715-1769 ....DLB-97	Gibbon, John Murray 1875-1952 ....DLB-92	Gilroy, Frank D. 1925- DLB-7
Gellhorn, Martha 1908- Y-82	Gibbon, Lewis Grassic (see Mitchell, James Leslie)	Gimferrer, Pere (Pedro) 1945- DLB-134
Gems, Pam 1925- DLB-13	Gibbons, Floyd 1887-1939..........DLB-25	Gingrich, Arnold 1903-1976 ....DLB-137
A General Idea of the College of Mirania (1753), by William Smith [excerpts] DLB-31	Gibbons, Reginald 1947- DLB-120	Ginsberg, Allen 1926- DLB-5, 16, 169
	Gibbons, William ?-? DLB-73	Ginzburg, Natalia 1916-1991.......DLB-177
Genet, Jean 1910-1986 ....DLB-72; Y-86	Gibson, Charles Dana 1867-1944 .....DS-13	Ginzkey, Franz Karl 1871-1963......DLB-81

Gioia, Dana 1950- DLB-120

Giono, Jean 1895-1970 ....DLB-72

Giotti, Virgilio 1885-1957 ....DLB-114

Giovanni, Nikki 1943- DLB-5, 41

Gipson, Lawrence Henry 1880-1971 ....DLB-17

Girard, Rodolphe 1879-1956........DLB-92

Giraudoux, Jean 1882-1944 ....DLB-65

Gissing, George 1857-1903 .....DLB-18, 135

Giudici, Giovanni 1924- DLB-128

Giuliani, Alfredo 1924- DLB-128

Gladstone, William Ewart 1809-1898 ....DLB-57

Glaeser, Ernst 1902-1963..........DLB-69

Glancy, Diane 1941- DLB-175

Glanville, Brian 1931- DLB-15, 139

Glapthorne, Henry 1610-1643?......DLB-58

Glasgow, Ellen 1873-1945 ....DLB-9, 12

Glaspell, Susan 1876-1948......DLB-7, 9, 78

Glass, Montague 1877-1934.........DLB-11

The Glass Key and Other Dashiell Hammett Mysteries......................Y-96

Glassco, John 1909-1981 ....DLB-68

Glauser, Friedrich 1896-1938 ....DLB-56

F. Gleason's Publishing Hall DLB-49

Gleim, Johann Wilhelm Ludwig 1719-1803 ....DLB-97

Glendinning, Victoria 1937- DLB-155

Glover, Richard 1712-1785 ....DLB-95

Glück, Louise 1943- DLB-5

Glyn, Elinor 1864-1943 ....DLB-153

Gobineau, Joseph-Arthur de 1816-1882 ....DLB-123

Godbout, Jacques 1933- DLB-53

Goddard, Morrill 1865-1937 ....DLB-25

Goddard, William 1740-1817 ....DLB-43

Godden, Rumer 1907- DLB-161

Godey, Louis A. 1804-1878.........DLB-73

Godey and McMichael.............DLB-49

Godfrey, Dave 1938- DLB-60

Godfrey, Thomas 1736-1763 ....DLB-31

Godine, David R., Publisher DLB-46

Godkin, E. L. 1831-1902 ....DLB-79

Godolphin, Sidney 1610-1643......DLB-126

Godwin, Gail 1937- DLB-6

Godwin, Mary Jane Clairmont 1766-1841 ....DLB-163

Godwin, Parke 1816-1904........DLB-3, 64

Godwin, William 1756-1836 ...DLB-39, 104, 142, 158, 163

Godwin, M. J., and Company.....DLB-154

Goering, Reinhard 1887-1936......DLB-118

Goes, Albrecht 1908- DLB-69

Goethe, Johann Wolfgang von 1749-1832 ....DLB-94

Goetz, Curt 1888-1960............DLB-124

Goffe, Thomas circa 1592-1629 .....DLB-58

Goffstein, M. B. 1940- DLB-61

Gogarty, Oliver St. John 1878-1957 ....DLB-15, 19

Goines, Donald 1937-1974 ....DLB-33

Gold, Herbert 1924- DLB-2; Y-81

Gold, Michael 1893-1967..........DLB-9, 28

Goldbarth, Albert 1948- DLB-120

Goldberg, Dick 1947- DLB-7

Golden Cockerel Press............DLB-112

Golding, Arthur 1536-1606 ....DLB-136

Golding, William 1911-1993 ....DLB-15, 100

Goldman, William 1931- DLB-44

Goldsmith, Oliver 1730?-1774 ...DLB-39, 89, 104, 109, 142

Goldsmith, Oliver 1794-1861 ....DLB-99

Goldsmith Publishing Company.....DLB-46

Gollancz, Victor, Limited DLB-112

Gómez-Quiñones, Juan 1942- DLB-122

Gomme, Laurence James [publishing house] DLB-46

Goncourt, Edmond de 1822-1896...DLB-123

Goncourt, Jules de 1830-1870 ......DLB-123

Gonzales, Rodolfo "Corky" 1928- DLB-122

González, Angel 1925- DLB-108

Gonzalez, Genaro 1949- DLB-122

Gonzalez, Ray 1952- DLB-122

González de Mireles, Jovita 1899-1983 ....DLB-122

González-T., César A. 1931- DLB-82

Goodbye, Gutenberg? A Lecture at the New York Public Library, 18 April 1995 ....Y-95

Goodison, Lorna 1947- DLB-157

Goodman, Paul 1911-1972 ....DLB-130

The Goodman Theatre DLB-7

Goodrich, Frances 1891-1984 and Hackett, Albert 1900- DLB-26

Goodrich, Samuel Griswold 1793-1860 ....DLB-1, 42, 73

Goodrich, S. G. [publishing house]...DLB-49

Goodspeed, C. E., and Company....DLB-49

Goodwin, Stephen 1943- Y-82

Googe, Barnabe 1540-1594 ....DLB-132

Gookin, Daniel 1612-1687..........DLB-24

Gordon, Caroline 1895-1981 ....DLB-4, 9, 10^2; Y-81

Gordon, Giles 1940- DLB-14, 139

Gordon, Lyndall 1941- DLB-155

Gordon, Mary 1949- DLB-6; Y-81

Gordone, Charles 1925- DLB-7

Gore, Catherine 1800-1861 ....DLB-116

Gorey, Edward 1925- DLB-61

Gorgias of Leontini circa 485 B.C.-376 B.C. DLB-176

Görres, Joseph 1776-1848 ....DLB-90

Gosse, Edmund 1849-1928 .....DLB-57, 144

Gosson, Stephen 1554-1624.........DLB-172

Gotlieb, Phyllis 1926- DLB-88

Gottfried von Straßburg died before 1230...............DLB-138

Gotthelf, Jeremias 1797-1854 ......DLB-133

Gottschalk circa 804/808-869 ......DLB-148

Gottsched, Johann Christoph 1700-1766 ....DLB-97

Götz, Johann Nikolaus 1721-1781 ....DLB-97

Gould, Wallace 1882-1940..........DLB-54

Govoni, Corrado 1884-1965 ....DLB-114

Gower, John circa 1330-1408 ......DLB-146

Goyen, William 1915-1983 .....DLB-2; Y-83

Goytisolo, José Augustín 1928- DLB-134

Gozzano, Guido 1883-1916 ....DLB-114

Grabbe, Christian Dietrich 1801-1836 ....DLB-133

Gracq, Julien 1910- DLB-83

Grady, Henry W. 1850-1889........DLB-23

Graf, Oskar Maria 1894-1967 ....DLB-56

Graf Rudolf between circa 1170 and circa 1185 ....DLB-148

Grafton, Richard [publishing house] DLB-170

Graham, George Rex 1813-1894.....DLB-73

Graham, Gwethalyn 1913-1965 .....DLB-88

Graham, Jorie 1951- DLB-120

Graham, Katharine 1917- DLB-127

Graham, Lorenz 1902-1989........DLB-76

Graham, Philip 1915-1963........DLB-127

Graham, R. B. Cunninghame
  1852-1936...........DLB-98, 135, 174

Graham, Shirley 1896-1977........DLB-76

Graham, W. S. 1918- DLB-20

Graham, William H.
  [publishing house] DLB-49

Graham, Winston 1910- DLB-77

Grahame, Kenneth
  1859-1932...........DLB-34, 141, 178

Grainger, Martin Allerdale
  1874-1941......................DLB-92

Gramatky, Hardie 1907-1979.......DLB-22

Grand, Sarah 1854-1943...........DLB-135

Grandbois, Alain 1900-1975.......DLB-92

Grange, John circa 1556-?........DLB-136

Granich, Irwin (see Gold, Michael)

Grant, Duncan 1885-1978...........DS-10

Grant, George 1918-1988..........DLB-88

Grant, George Monro 1835-1902....DLB-99

Grant, Harry J. 1881-1963........DLB-29

Grant, James Edward 1905-1966....DLB-26

Grass, Günter 1927- DLB-75, 124

Grasty, Charles H. 1863-1924.....DLB-25

Grau, Shirley Ann 1929- DLB-2

Graves, John 1920- Y-83

Graves, Richard 1715-1804........DLB-39

Graves, Robert
  1895-1985..........DLB-20, 100; Y-85

Gray, Asa 1810-1888 ....DLB-1

Gray, David 1838-1861............DLB-32

Gray, Simon 1936- DLB-13

Gray, Thomas 1716-1771..........DLB-109

Grayson, William J. 1788-1863....DLB-3, 64

The Great Bibliographers Series........Y-93

The Great War and the Theater, 1914-1918
  [Great Britain]................DLB-10

Greeley, Horace 1811-1872.......DLB-3, 43

Green, Adolph (see Comden, Betty)

Green, Duff 1791-1875............DLB-43

Green, Gerald 1922- DLB-28

Green, Henry 1905-1973...........DLB-15

Green, Jonas 1712-1767...........DLB-31

Green, Joseph 1706-1780..........DLB-31

Green, Julien 1900- DLB-4, 72

Green, Paul 1894-1981 ......DLB-7, 9; Y-81

Green, T. and S.
  [publishing house] DLB-49

Green, Timothy
  [publishing house] DLB-49

Greenaway, Kate 1846-1901 .....DLB-141

Greenberg: Publisher DLB-46

Green Tiger Press................DLB-46

Greene, Asa 1789-1838 ....DLB-11

Greene, Benjamin H.
  [publishing house] DLB-49

Greene, Graham 1904-1991
  ....DLB-13, 15, 77, 100, 162; Y-85, Y-91

Greene, Robert 1558-1592......DLB-62, 167

Greenhow, Robert 1800-1854.......DLB-30

Greenough, Horatio 1805-1852......DLB-1

Greenwell, Dora 1821-1882........DLB-35

Greenwillow Books................DLB-46

Greenwood, Grace (see Lippincott, Sara Jane Clarke)

Greenwood, Walter 1903-1974......DLB-10

Greer, Ben 1948- DLB-6

Greflinger, Georg 1620?-1677....DLB-164

Greg, W. R. 1809-1881 ....DLB-55

Gregg Press DLB-46

Gregory, Isabella Augusta
  Persse, Lady 1852-1932.........DLB-10

Gregory, Horace 1898-1982 ....DLB-48

Gregory of Rimini
  circa 1300-1358................DLB-115

Gregynog Press..................DLB-112

Greiffenberg, Catharina Regina von
  1633-1694 ....DLB-168

Grenfell, Wilfred Thomason
  1865-1940 ....DLB-92

Greve, Felix Paul (see Grove, Frederick Philip)

Greville, Fulke, First Lord Brooke
  1554-1628 ....DLB-62, 172

Grey, Lady Jane 1537-1554.......DLB-132

Grey Owl 1888-1938 ....DLB-92

Grey, Zane 1872-1939 ....DLB-9

Grey Walls Press DLB-112

Grier, Eldon 1917- DLB-88

Grieve, C. M. (see MacDiarmid, Hugh)

Griffin, Bartholomew
  flourished 1596................DLB-172

Griffin, Gerald 1803-1840 ....DLB-159

Griffith, Elizabeth 1727?-1793 ...DLB-39, 89

Griffith, George 1857-1906 .....DLB-178

Griffiths, Trevor 1935- DLB-13

Griffiths, Ralph
  [publishing house] DLB-154

Griggs, S. C., and Company DLB-49

Griggs, Sutton Elbert 1872-1930..DLB-50

Grignon, Claude-Henri 1894-1976...DLB-68

Grigson, Geoffrey 1905- DLB-27

Grillparzer, Franz 1791-1872....DLB-133

Grimald, Nicholas
  circa 1519-circa 1562.........DLB-136

Grimké, Angelina Weld
  1880-1958 ....DLB-50, 54

Grimm, Hans 1875-1959 ....DLB-66

Grimm, Jacob 1785-1863 ....DLB-90

Grimm, Wilhelm 1786-1859 ....DLB-90

Grimmelshausen, Johann Jacob Christoffel
  von 1621 or 1622-1676 ....DLB-168

Grimshaw, Beatrice Ethel
  1871-1953 ....DLB-174

Grindal, Edmund
  1519 or 1520-1583 ....DLB-132

Griswold, Rufus Wilmot
  1815-1857 ....DLB-3, 59

Gross, Milt 1895-1953 ....DLB-11

Grosset and Dunlap DLB-49

Grossman Publishers DLB-46

Grosseteste, Robert
  circa 1160-1253...............DLB-115

Grosvenor, Gilbert H. 1875-1966....DLB-91

Groth, Klaus 1819-1899...........DLB-129

Groulx, Lionel 1878-1967 ....DLB-68

Grove, Frederick Philip 1879-1949...DLB-92

Grove Press DLB-46

Grubb, Davis 1919-1980 ....DLB-6

Gruelle, Johnny 1880-1938 ....DLB-22

von Grumbach, Argula
  1492-after 1563?.............DLB-179

Grymeston, Elizabeth
  before 1563-before 1604 ......DLB-136

Gryphius, Andreas 1616-1664......DLB-164

Gryphius, Christian 1649-1706....DLB-168

Guare, John 1938- DLB-7

Guerra, Tonino 1920- DLB-128

Guest, Barbara 1920- DLB-5

Guèvremont, Germaine 1893-1968 ... DLB-68

Guidacci, Margherita 1921-1992 ... DLB-128

Guide to the Archives of Publishers, Journals, and Literary Agents in North American Libraries ... Y-93

Guillén, Jorge 1893-1984 ... DLB-108

Guilloux, Louis 1899-1980 ... DLB-72

Guilpin, Everard circa 1572-after 1608? ... DLB-136

Guiney, Louise Imogen 1861-1920 ... DLB-54

Guiterman, Arthur 1871-1943 ... DLB-11

Günderrode, Caroline von 1780-1806 ... DLB-90

Gundulić, Ivan 1589-1638 ... DLB-147

Gunn, Bill 1934-1989 ... DLB-38

Gunn, James E. 1923- ... DLB-8

Gunn, Neil M. 1891-1973 ... DLB-15

Gunn, Thom 1929- ... DLB-27

Gunnars, Kristjana 1948- ... DLB-60

Günther, Johann Christian 1695-1723 ... DLB-168

Gurik, Robert 1932- ... DLB-60

Gustafson, Ralph 1909- ... DLB-88

Gütersloh, Albert Paris 1887-1973 ... DLB-81

Guthrie, A. B., Jr. 1901- ... DLB-6

Guthrie, Ramon 1896-1973 ... DLB-4

The Guthrie Theater ... DLB-7

Guthrie, Thomas Anstey (see Anstey, FC)

Gutzkow, Karl 1811-1878 ... DLB-133

Guy, Ray 1939- ... DLB-60

Guy, Rosa 1925- ... DLB-33

Guyot, Arnold 1807-1884 ... DS-13

Gwynne, Erskine 1898-1948 ... DLB-4

Gyles, John 1680-1755 ... DLB-99

Gysin, Brion 1916- ... DLB-16

H

H. D. (see Doolittle, Hilda)

Habington, William 1605-1654 ... DLB-126

Hacker, Marilyn 1942- ... DLB-120

Hackett, Albert (see Goodrich, Frances)

Hacks, Peter 1928- ... DLB-124

Hadas, Rachel 1948- ... DLB-120

Hadden, Briton 1898-1929 ... DLB-91

Hagedorn, Friedrich von 1708-1754 ... DLB-168

Hagelstange, Rudolf 1912-1984 ... DLB-69

Haggard, H. Rider 1856-1925 ... DLB-70, 156, 174, 178

Haggard, William 1907-1993 ... Y-93

Hahn-Hahn, Ida Gräfin von 1805-1880 ... DLB-133

Haig-Brown, Roderick 1908-1976 ... DLB-88

Haight, Gordon S. 1901-1985 ... DLB-103

Hailey, Arthur 1920- ... DLB-88; Y-82

Haines, John 1924- ... DLB-5

Hake, Edward flourished 1566-1604 ... DLB-136

Hake, Thomas Gordon 1809-1895 ... DLB-32

Hakluyt, Richard 1552?-1616 ... DLB-136

Halbe, Max 1865-1944 ... DLB-118

Haldane, J. B. S. 1892-1964 ... DLB-160

Haldeman, Joe 1943- ... DLB-8

Haldeman-Julius Company ... DLB-46

Hale, E. J., and Son ... DLB-49

Hale, Edward Everett 1822-1909 ... DLB-1, 42, 74

Hale, Janet Campbell 1946- ... DLB-175

Hale, Kathleen 1898- ... DLB-160

Hale, Leo Thomas (see Ebon)

Hale, Lucretia Peabody 1820-1900 ... DLB-42

Hale, Nancy 1908-1988 ... DLB-86; Y-80, 88

Hale, Sarah Josepha (Buell) 1788-1879 ... DLB-1, 42, 73

Hales, John 1584-1656 ... DLB-151

Haley, Alex 1921-1992 ... DLB-38

Haliburton, Thomas Chandler 1796-1865 ... DLB-11, 99

Hall, Anna Maria 1800-1881 ... DLB-159

Hall, Donald 1928- ... DLB-5

Hall, Edward 1497-1547 ... DLB-132

Hall, James 1793-1868 ... DLB-73, 74

Hall, Joseph 1574-1656 ... DLB-121, 151

Hall, Samuel [publishing house] ... DLB-49

Hallam, Arthur Henry 1811-1833 ... DLB-32

Halleck, Fitz-Greene 1790-1867 ... DLB-3

Haller, Albrecht von 1708-1777 ... DLB-168

Hallmann, Johann Christian 1640-1704 or 1716? ... DLB-168

Hallmark Editions ... DLB-46

Halper, Albert 1904-1984 ... DLB-9

Halperin, John William 1941- ... DLB-111

Halstead, Murat 1829-1908 ... DLB-23

Hamann, Johann Georg 1730-1788 ... DLB-97

Hamburger, Michael 1924- ... DLB-27

Hamilton, Alexander 1712-1756 ... DLB-31

Hamilton, Alexander 1755?-1804 ... DLB-37

Hamilton, Cicely 1872-1952 ... DLB-10

Hamilton, Edmond 1904-1977 ... DLB-8

Hamilton, Elizabeth 1758-1816 ... DLB-116, 158

Hamilton, Gail (see Corcoran, Barbara)

Hamilton, Ian 1938- ... DLB-40, 155

Hamilton, Patrick 1904-1962 ... DLB-10

Hamilton, Virginia 1936- ... DLB-33, 52

Hamilton, Hamish, Limited ... DLB-112

Hammett, Dashiell 1894-1961 ... DS-6

Dashiell Hammett: An Appeal in *TAC* ... Y-91

Hammon, Jupiter 1711-died between 1790 and 1806 ... DLB-31, 50

Hammond, John ?-1663 ... DLB-24

Hamner, Earl 1923- ... DLB-6

Hampton, Christopher 1946- ... DLB-13

Handel-Mazzetti, Enrica von 1871-1955 ... DLB-81

Handke, Peter 1942- ... DLB-85, 124

Handlin, Oscar 1915- ... DLB-17

Hankin, St. John 1869-1909 ... DLB-10

Hanley, Clifford 1922- ... DLB-14

Hannah, Barry 1942- ... DLB-6

Hannay, James 1827-1873 ... DLB-21

Hansberry, Lorraine 1930-1965 ... DLB-7, 38

Hapgood, Norman 1868-1937 ... DLB-91

Happel, Eberhard Werner 1647-1690 ... DLB-168

Harcourt Brace Jovanovich ... DLB-46

Hardenberg, Friedrich von (see Novalis)

Harding, Walter 1917- ... DLB-111

Hardwick, Elizabeth 1916- ... DLB-6

Hardy, Thomas 1840-1928 ... DLB-18, 19, 135

Hare, Cyril 1900-1958 ... DLB-77

Hare, David 1947- ... DLB-13

Hargrove, Marion 1919- ... DLB-11

Häring, Georg Wilhelm Heinrich (see Alexis, Willibald)

Harington, Donald 1935- ... DLB-152

Harington, Sir John 1560-1612 ... DLB-136

Harjo, Joy 1951- ... DLB-120, 175

Harlow, Robert 1923- DLB-60

Harman, Thomas
   flourished 1566-1573 ....DLB-136

Harness, Charles L. 1915- DLB-8

Harnett, Cynthia 1893-1981 ....DLB-161

Harper, Fletcher 1806-1877 ....DLB-79

Harper, Frances Ellen Watkins
   1825-1911 ....DLB-50

Harper, Michael S. 1938- DLB-41

Harper and Brothers DLB-49

Harraden, Beatrice 1864-1943......DLB-153

Harrap, George G., and Company
   Limited DLB-112

Harriot, Thomas 1560-1621 ....DLB-136

Harris, Benjamin ?-circa 1720....DLB-42, 43

Harris, Christie 1907- DLB-88

Harris, Frank 1856-1931 ....DLB-156

Harris, George Washington
   1814-1869 ....DLB-3, 11

Harris, Joel Chandler
   1848-1908 ....DLB-11, 23, 42, 78, 91

Harris, Mark 1922- DLB-2; Y-80

Harris, Wilson 1921- DLB-117

Harrison, Charles Yale
   1898-1954 ....DLB-68

Harrison, Frederic 1831-1923 ......DLB-57

Harrison, Harry 1925- DLB-8

Harrison, Jim 1937- Y-82

Harrison, Mary St. Leger Kingsley (see Malet, Lucas)

Harrison, Paul Carter 1936- DLB-38

Harrison, Susan Frances
   1859-1935 ....DLB-99

Harrison, Tony 1937- DLB-40

Harrison, William 1535-1593 .....DLB-136

Harrison, James P., Company........DLB-49

Harrisse, Henry 1829-1910 ....DLB-47

Harsdörffer, Georg Philipp
   1607-1658 ....DLB-164

Harsent, David 1942- DLB-40

Hart, Albert Bushnell 1854-1943 ...DLB-17

Hart, Julia Catherine 1796-1867 ....DLB-99

The Lorenz Hart Centenary..........Y-95

Hart, Moss 1904-1961 ....DLB-7

Hart, Oliver 1723-1795 ....DLB-31

Hart-Davis, Rupert, Limited DLB-112

Harte, Bret 1836-1902....DLB-12, 64, 74, 79

Harte, Edward Holmead 1922- DLB-127

Harte, Houston Harriman 1927- DLB-127

Hartlaub, Felix 1913-1945 ....DLB-56

Hartlebon, Otto Erich
   1864-1905 ....DLB-118

Hartley, L. P. 1895-1972 ....DLB-15, 139

Hartley, Marsden 1877-1943........DLB-54

Hartling, Peter 1933- DLB-75

Hartman, Geoffrey H. 1929- DLB-67

Hartmann, Sadakichi 1867-1944 .....DLB-54

Hartmann von Aue
   circa 1160-circa 1205 ....DLB-138

Harvey, Gabriel 1550?-1631 ......DLB-167

Harvey, Jean-Charles 1891-1967.....DLB-88

Harvill Press Limited DLB-112

Harwood, Lee 1939- DLB-40

Harwood, Ronald 1934- DLB-13

Haskins, Charles Homer
   1870-1937 ....DLB-47

Hass, Robert 1941- DLB-105

The Hatch-Billops Collection DLB-76

Hathaway, William 1944- DLB-120

Hauff, Wilhelm 1802-1827 ....DLB-90

A Haughty and Proud Generation (1922),
   by Ford Madox Hueffer DLB-36

Haugwitz, August Adolph von
   1647-1706 ....DLB-168

Hauptmann, Carl
   1858-1921 ....DLB-66, 118

Hauptmann, Gerhart
   1862-1946 ....DLB-66, 118

Hauser, Marianne 1910- Y-83

Hawes, Stephen
   1475?-before 1529 ....DLB-132

Hawker, Robert Stephen
   1803-1875 ....DLB-32

Hawkes, John 1925- DLB-2, 7; Y-80

Hawkesworth, John 1720-1773 .....DLB-142

Hawkins, Sir Anthony Hope (see Hope, Anthony)

Hawkins, Sir John
   1719-1789 ....DLB-104, 142

Hawkins, Walter Everette 1883-?....DLB-50

Hawthorne, Nathaniel
   1804-1864 ....DLB-1, 74

Hay, John 1838-1905 ....DLB-12, 47

Hayden, Robert 1913-1980 .....DLB-5, 76

Haydon, Benjamin Robert
   1786-1846 ....DLB-110

Hayes, John Michael 1919- DLB-26

Hayley, William 1745-1820.....DLB-93, 142

Haym, Rudolf 1821-1901..........DLB-129

Hayman, Robert 1575-1629........DLB-99

Hayman, Ronald 1932- DLB-155

Hayne, Paul Hamilton
   1830-1886 ....DLB-3, 64, 79

Hays, Mary 1760-1843 ....DLB-142, 158

Haywood, Eliza 1693?-1756 ....DLB-39

Hazard, Willis P. [publishing house]...DLB-49

Hazlitt, William 1778-1830....DLB-110, 158

Hazzard, Shirley 1931- Y-82

Head, Bessie 1937-1986...........DLB-117

Headley, Joel T. 1813-1897 ..DLB-30; DS-13

Heaney, Seamus 1939- DLB-40

Heard, Nathan C. 1936- DLB-33

Hearn, Lafcadio 1850-1904 ......DLB-12, 78

Hearne, John 1926- DLB-117

Hearne, Samuel 1745-1792 ....DLB-99

Hearst, William Randolph
   1863-1951 ....DLB-25

Hearst, William Randolph, Jr
   1908-1993...................DLB-127

Heath, Catherine 1924- DLB-14

Heath, Roy A. K. 1926- DLB-117

Heath-Stubbs, John 1918- DLB-27

Heavysege, Charles 1816-1876 .....DLB-99

Hebbel, Friedrich 1813-1863.......DLB-129

Hebel, Johann Peter 1760-1826......DLB-90

Hébert, Anne 1916- DLB-68

Hébert, Jacques 1923- DLB-53

Hecht, Anthony 1923- DLB-5, 169

Hecht, Ben 1894-1964
   ....DLB-7, 9, 25, 26, 28, 86

Hecker, Isaac Thomas 1819-1888.....DLB-1

Hedge, Frederic Henry
   1805-1890 ....DLB-1, 59

Hefner, Hugh M. 1926- DLB-137

Hegel, Georg Wilhelm Friedrich
   1770-1831 ....DLB-90

Heidish, Marcy 1947- Y-82

Heißenbüttel 1921- DLB-75

Hein, Christoph 1944- DLB-124

Heine, Heinrich 1797-1856 ....DLB-90

Heinemann, Larry 1944- DS-9

Heinemann, William, Limited......DLB-112

Heinlein, Robert A. 1907-1988 .... DLB-8

Heinrich Julius of Brunswick
  1564-1613 .... DLB-164

Heinrich von dem Türlîn
  flourished circa 1230 .... DLB-138

Heinrich von Melk
  flourished after 1160 .... DLB-148

Heinrich von Veldeke
  circa 1145-circa 1190 .... DLB-138

Heinrich, Willi 1920- DLB-75

Heiskell, John 1872-1972 .... DLB-127

Heinse, Wilhelm 1746-1803 .... DLB-94

Heinz, W. C. 1915- DLB-171

Hejinian, Lyn 1941- DLB-165

Heliand circa 850 .... DLB-148

Heller, Joseph 1923- DLB-2, 28; Y-80

Heller, Michael 1937- DLB-165

Hellman, Lillian 1906-1984 ..... DLB-7; Y-84

Hellwig, Johann 1609-1674 .... DLB-164

Helprin, Mark 1947- Y-85

Helwig, David 1938- DLB-60

Hemans, Felicia 1793-1835 .... DLB-96

Hemingway, Ernest 1899-1961
  .... DLB-4, 9, 102; Y-81, 87; DS-1

Hemingway: Twenty-Five Years
  Later Y-85

Hémon, Louis 1880-1913 .... DLB-92

Hemphill, Paul 1936- Y-87

Hénault, Gilles 1920- DLB-88

Henchman, Daniel 1689-1761 .... DLB-24

Henderson, Alice Corbin
  1881-1949 .... DLB-54

Henderson, Archibald
  1877-1963 .... DLB-103

Henderson, David 1942- DLB-41

Henderson, George Wylie
  1904- DLB-51

Henderson, Zenna 1917-1983 .... DLB-8

Henisch, Peter 1943- DLB-85

Henley, Beth 1952- Y-86

Henley, William Ernest
  1849-1903 .... DLB-19

Henniker, Florence 1855-1923 ..... DLB-135

Henry, Alexander 1739-1824 .... DLB-99

Henry, Buck 1930- DLB-26

Henry VIII of England
  1491-1547 .... DLB-132

Henry, Marguerite 1902- DLB-22

Henry, O. (see Porter, William Sydney)

Henry of Ghent
  circa 1217-1229 - 1293 .... DLB-115

Henry, Robert Selph 1889-1970 ..... DLB-17

Henry, Will (see Allen, Henry W.)

Henryson, Robert
  1420s or 1430s-circa 1505 ...... DLB-146

Henschke, Alfred (see Klabund)

Hensley, Sophie Almon 1866-1946 ... DLB-99

Henson, Lance 1944- DLB-175

Henty, G. A. 1832?-1902 .... DLB-18, 141

Hentz, Caroline Lee 1800-1856 ...... DLB-3

Heraclitus flourished circa 500 B.C.
  .... DLB-176

Herbert, Agnes circa 1880-1960 .... DLB-174

Herbert, Alan Patrick 1890-1971 .... DLB-10

Herbert, Edward, Lord, of Cherbury
  1582-1648 .... DLB-121, 151

Herbert, Frank 1920-1986 .... DLB-8

Herbert, George 1593-1633 .... DLB-126

Herbert, Henry William
  1807-1858 .... DLB-3, 73

Herbert, John 1926- DLB-53

Herbert, Mary Sidney, Countess of Pembroke
  (see Sidney, Mary)

Herbst, Josephine 1892-1969 .... DLB-9

Herburger, Gunter 1932- DLB-75, 124

Hercules, Frank E. M. 1917- DLB-33

Herder, Johann Gottfried
  1744-1803 .... DLB-97

Herder, B., Book Company DLB-49

Herford, Charles Harold
  1853-1931 .... DLB-149

Hergesheimer, Joseph
  1880-1954 .... DLB-9, 102

Heritage Press DLB-46

Hermann the Lame 1013-1054 ..... DLB-148

Hermes, Johann Timotheus
  1738-1821 .... DLB-97

Hermlin, Stephan 1915- DLB-69

Hernández, Alfonso C. 1938- DLB-122

Hernández, Inés 1947- DLB-122

Hernández, Miguel 1910-1942 ..... DLB-134

Hernton, Calvin C. 1932- DLB-38

"The Hero as Man of Letters: Johnson,
  Rousseau, Burns" (1841), by Thomas
  Carlyle [excerpt] DLB-57

The Hero as Poet. Dante; Shakspeare (1841),
  by Thomas Carlyle DLB-32

Herodotus circa 484 B.C.-circa 420 B.C.
  .... DLB-176

Heron, Robert 1764-1807 .... DLB-142

Herrera, Juan Felipe 1948- DLB-122

Herrick, Robert 1591-1674 .... DLB-126

Herrick, Robert 1868-1938 .... DLB-9, 12, 78

Herrick, William 1915- Y-83

Herrick, E. R., and Company DLB-49

Herrmann, John 1900-1959 .... DLB-4

Hersey, John 1914-1993 .... DLB-6

Hertel, François 1905-1985 .... DLB-68

Hervé-Bazin, Jean Pierre Marie (see Bazin, Hervé)

Hervey, John, Lord 1696-1743 ..... DLB-101

Herwig, Georg 1817-1875 .... DLB-133

Herzog, Emile Salomon Wilhelm (see Maurois, André)

Hesiod eighth century B.C. DLB-176

Hesse, Hermann 1877-1962 .... DLB-66

Hessus, Eobanus
  1488-1540 .... DLB-179

Hewat, Alexander
  circa 1743-circa 1824 .... DLB-30

Hewitt, John 1907- DLB-27

Hewlett, Maurice 1861-1923 .... DLB-34, 156

Heyen, William 1940- DLB-5

Heyer, Georgette 1902-1974 .... DLB-77

Heym, Stefan 1913- DLB-69

Heyse, Paul 1830-1914 .... DLB-129

Heytesbury, William
  circa 1310-1372 or 1373 .... DLB-115

Heyward, Dorothy 1890-1961 .... DLB-7

Heyward, DuBose
  1885-1940 .... DLB-7, 9, 45

Heywood, John 1497?-1580? DLB-136

Heywood, Thomas
  1573 or 1574-1641 .... DLB-62

Hibbs, Ben 1901-1975 .... DLB-137

Hichens, Robert S. 1864-1950 ..... DLB-153

Hickman, William Albert
  1877-1957 .... DLB-92

Hidalgo, José Luis 1919-1947 ..... DLB-108

Hiebert, Paul 1892-1987 .... DLB-68

Hierro, José 1922- DLB-108

Higgins, Aidan 1927- DLB-14

Higgins, Colin 1941-1988 .... DLB-26

Higgins, George V. 1939- DLB-2; Y-81

Higginson, Thomas Wentworth 1823-1911 .... DLB-1, 64

Highwater, Jamake 1942?- ... DLB-52; Y-85

Hijuelos, Oscar 1951- DLB-145

Hildegard von Bingen 1098-1179 .... DLB-148

Das Hildesbrandslied circa 820 .... DLB-148

Hildesheimer, Wolfgang 1916-1991 .... DLB-69, 124

Hildreth, Richard 1807-1865 .... DLB-1, 30, 59

Hill, Aaron 1685-1750 .... DLB-84

Hill, Geoffrey 1932- DLB-40

Hill, "Sir" John 1714?-1775 .... DLB-39

Hill, Leslie 1880-1960 .... DLB-51

Hill, Susan 1942- DLB-14, 139

Hill, Walter 1942- DLB-44

Hill and Wang DLB-46

Hill, George M., Company DLB-49

Hill, Lawrence, and Company, Publishers DLB-46

Hillberry, Conrad 1928- DLB-120

Hilliard, Gray and Company DLB-49

Hills, Lee 1906- DLB-127

Hillyer, Robert 1895-1961 .... DLB-54

Hilton, James 1900-1954 .... DLB-34, 77

Hilton, Walter died 1396 .... DLB-146

Hilton and Company DLB-49

Himes, Chester 1909-1984 .... DLB-2, 76, 143

Hindmarsh, Joseph [publishing house] DLB-170

Hine, Daryl 1936- DLB-60

Hingley, Ronald 1920- DLB-155

Hinojosa-Smith, Rolando 1929- DLB-82

Hippel, Theodor Gottlieb von 1741-1796 .... DLB-97

Hippocrates of Cos flourished circa 425 B.C. DLB-176

Hirsch, E. D., Jr. 1928- DLB-67

Hirsch, Edward 1950- DLB-120

The History of the Adventures of Joseph Andrews (1742), by Henry Fielding [excerpt] DLB-39

Hoagland, Edward 1932- DLB-6

Hoagland, Everett H., III 1942- DLB-41

Hoban, Russell 1925- DLB-52

Hobbes, Thomas 1588-1679 .... DLB-151

Hobby, Oveta 1905- DLB-127

Hobby, William 1878-1964 .... DLB-127

Hobsbaum, Philip 1932- DLB-40

Hobson, Laura Z. 1900- DLB-28

Hoby, Thomas 1530-1566 .... DLB-132

Hoccleve, Thomas circa 1368-circa 1437 .... DLB-146

Hochhuth, Rolf 1931- DLB-124

Hochman, Sandra 1936- DLB-5

Hodder and Stoughton, Limited DLB-106

Hodgins, Jack 1938- DLB-60

Hodgman, Helen 1945- DLB-14

Hodgskin, Thomas 1787-1869 ..... DLB-158

Hodgson, Ralph 1871-1962 .... DLB-19

Hodgson, William Hope 1877-1918 .... DLB-70, 153, 156, 178

Hoffenstein, Samuel 1890-1947 ...... DLB-11

Hoffman, Charles Fenno 1806-1884 .... DLB-3

Hoffman, Daniel 1923- DLB-5

Hoffmann, E. T. A. 1776-1822 ..... DLB-90

Hoffmanswaldau, Christian Hoffman von 1616-1679 .... DLB-168

Hofmann, Michael 1957- DLB-40

Hofmannsthal, Hugo von 1874-1929 .... DLB-81, 118

Hofstadter, Richard 1916-1970 ..... DLB-17

Hogan, Desmond 1950- DLB-14

Hogan, Linda 1947- DLB-175

Hogan and Thompson DLB-49

Hogarth Press DLB-112

Hogg, James 1770-1835 .... DLB-93, 116, 159

Hohberg, Wolfgang Helmhard Freiherr von 1612-1688 .... DLB-168

von Hohenheim, Philippus Aureolus Theophrastus Bombastus (see Paracelsus)

Hohl, Ludwig 1904-1980 .... DLB-56

Holbrook, David 1923- DLB-14, 40

Holcroft, Thomas 1745-1809 .... DLB-39, 89, 158

Holden, Jonathan 1941- DLB-105

Holden, Jonathan, Contemporary Verse Story-telling DLB-105

Holden, Molly 1927-1981 .... DLB-40

Hölderlin, Friedrich 1770-1843 ...... DLB-90

Holiday House DLB-46

Holinshed, Raphael died 1580 ..... DLB-167

Holland, J. G. 1819-1881 .... DS-13

Holland, Norman N. 1927- DLB-67

Hollander, John 1929- DLB-5

Holley, Marietta 1836-1926 .... DLB-11

Hollingsworth, Margaret 1940- DLB-60

Hollo, Anselm 1934- DLB-40

Holloway, Emory 1885-1977 .... DLB-103

Holloway, John 1920- DLB-27

Holloway House Publishing Company DLB-46

Holme, Constance 1880-1955 .... DLB-34

Holmes, Abraham S. 1821?-1908 .... DLB-99

Holmes, John Clellon 1926-1988 .... DLB-16

Holmes, Oliver Wendell 1809-1894 .... DLB-1

Holmes, Richard 1945- DLB-155

Holroyd, Michael 1935- DLB-155

Holst, Hermann E. von 1841-1904 .... DLB-47

Holt, John 1721-1784 .... DLB-43

Holt, Henry, and Company DLB-49

Holt, Rinehart and Winston DLB-46

Holthusen, Hans Egon 1913- DLB-69

Hölty, Ludwig Christoph Heinrich 1748-1776 .... DLB-94

Holz, Arno 1863-1929 .... DLB-118

Home, Henry, Lord Kames (see Kames, Henry Home, Lord)

Home, John 1722-1808 .... DLB-84

Home, William Douglas 1912- DLB-13

Home Publishing Company DLB-49

Homer circa eighth-seventh centuries B.C. DLB-176

Homes, Geoffrey (see Mainwaring, Daniel)

Honan, Park 1928- DLB-111

Hone, William 1780-1842 ..... DLB-110, 158

Hongo, Garrett Kaoru 1951- DLB-120

Honig, Edwin 1919- DLB-5

Hood, Hugh 1928- DLB-53

Hood, Thomas 1799-1845 .... DLB-96

Hook, Theodore 1788-1841 .... DLB-116

Hooker, Jeremy 1941- DLB-40

Hooker, Richard 1554-1600 .... DLB-132

Hooker, Thomas 1586-1647 .... DLB-24

Hooper, Johnson Jones 1815-1862 .... DLB-3, 11

Hope, Anthony 1863-1933 .... DLB-153, 156

Hopkins, Gerard Manley
 1844-1889 .... DLB-35, 57

Hopkins, John (see Sternhold, Thomas)

Hopkins, Lemuel 1750-1801 .... DLB-37

Hopkins, Pauline Elizabeth
 1859-1930 .... DLB-50

Hopkins, Samuel 1721-1803 .... DLB-31

Hopkins, John H., and Son DLB-46

Hopkinson, Francis 1737-1791 ...... DLB-31

Horgan, Paul 1903- DLB-102; Y-85

Horizon Press DLB-46

Horne, Frank 1899-1974 .... DLB-51

Horne, Richard Henry (Hengist)
 1802 or 1803-1884 .... DLB-32

Hornung, E. W. 1866-1921 .... DLB-70

Horovitz, Israel 1939- DLB-7

Horton, George Moses
 1797?-1883? DLB-50

Horváth, Ödön von
 1901-1938 .... DLB-85, 124

Horwood, Harold 1923- DLB-60

Hosford, E. and E.
 [publishing house] DLB-49

Hoskyns, John 1566-1638 .... DLB-121

Hotchkiss and Company DLB-49

Hough, Emerson 1857-1923 .... DLB-9

Houghton Mifflin Company DLB-49

Houghton, Stanley 1881-1913 ..... DLB-10

Household, Geoffrey 1900-1988 .... DLB-87

Housman, A. E. 1859-1936 .... DLB-19

Housman, Laurence 1865-1959 ..... DLB-10

Houwald, Ernst von 1778-1845 .... DLB-90

Hovey, Richard 1864-1900 .... DLB-54

Howard, Donald R. 1927-1987 .... DLB-111

Howard, Maureen 1930- Y-83

Howard, Richard 1929- DLB-5

Howard, Roy W. 1883-1964 .... DLB-29

Howard, Sidney 1891-1939 .... DLB-7, 26

Howe, E. W. 1853-1937 .... DLB-12, 25

Howe, Henry 1816-1893 .... DLB-30

Howe, Irving 1920-1993 .... DLB-67

Howe, Joseph 1804-1873 .... DLB-99

Howe, Julia Ward 1819-1910 .... DLB-1

Howe, Percival Presland
 1886-1944 .... DLB-149

Howe, Susan 1937- DLB-120

Howell, Clark, Sr. 1863-1936 ...... DLB-25

Howell, Evan P. 1839-1905 .... DLB-23

Howell, James 1594?-1666 .... DLB-151

Howell, Warren Richardson
 1912-1984 .... DLB-140

Howell, Soskin and Company DLB-46

Howells, William Dean
 1837-1920 .... DLB-12, 64, 74, 79

Howitt, William 1792-1879 and
 Howitt, Mary 1799-1888 ...... DLB-110

Hoyem, Andrew 1935- DLB-5

Hoyers, Anna Ovena 1584-1655 .... DLB-164

Hoyos, Angela de 1940- DLB-82

Hoyt, Palmer 1897-1979 .... DLB-127

Hoyt, Henry [publishing house] DLB-49

Hrabanus Maurus 776?-856 ...... DLB-148

Hrotsvit of Gandersheim
 circa 935-circa 1000 .... DLB-148

Hubbard, Elbert 1856-1915 .... DLB-91

Hubbard, Kin 1868-1930 .... DLB-11

Hubbard, William circa 1621-1704 ... DLB-24

Huber, Therese 1764-1829 .... DLB-90

Huch, Friedrich 1873-1913 .... DLB-66

Huch, Ricarda 1864-1947 .... DLB-66

Huck at 100: How Old Is
 Huckleberry Finn? Y-85

Huddle, David 1942- DLB-130

Hudgins, Andrew 1951- DLB-120

Hudson, Henry Norman
 1814-1886 .... DLB-64

Hudson, W. H.
 1841-1922 .... DLB-98, 153, 174

Hudson and Goodwin DLB-49

Huebsch, B. W.
 [publishing house] DLB-46

Hughes, David 1930- DLB-14

Hughes, John 1677-1720 .... DLB-84

Hughes, Langston
 1902-1967 .... DLB-4, 7, 48, 51, 86

Hughes, Richard 1900-1976 .... DLB-15, 161

Hughes, Ted 1930- DLB-40, 161

Hughes, Thomas 1822-1896 .... DLB-18, 163

Hugo, Richard 1923-1982 .... DLB-5

Hugo, Victor 1802-1885 .... DLB-119

Hugo Awards and Nebula Awards DLB-8

Hull, Richard 1896-1973 .... DLB-77

Hulme, T. E. 1883-1917 .... DLB-19

Humboldt, Alexander von
 1769-1859 .... DLB-90

Humboldt, Wilhelm von
 1767-1835 .... DLB-90

Hume, David 1711-1776 .... DLB-104

Hume, Fergus 1859-1932 .... DLB-70

Hummer, T. R. 1950- DLB-120

Humorous Book Illustration DLB-11

Humphrey, William 1924- DLB-6

Humphreys, David 1752-1818 ..... DLB-37

Humphreys, Emyr 1919- DLB-15

Huncke, Herbert 1915- DLB-16

Huneker, James Gibbons
 1857-1921 .... DLB-71

Hunold, Christian Friedrich
 1681-1721 .... DLB-168

Hunt, Irene 1907- DLB-52

Hunt, Leigh 1784-1859 .... DLB-96, 110, 144

Hunt, Violet 1862-1942 .... DLB-162

Hunt, William Gibbes 1791-1833 .... DLB-73

Hunter, Evan 1926- Y-82

Hunter, Jim 1939- DLB-14

Hunter, Kristin 1931- DLB-33

Hunter, Mollie 1922- DLB-161

Hunter, N. C. 1908-1971 .... DLB-10

Hunter-Duvar, John 1821-1899 .... DLB-99

Huntington, Henry E.
 1850-1927 .... DLB-140

Hurd and Houghton DLB-49

Hurst, Fannie 1889-1968 .... DLB-86

Hurst and Blackett DLB-106

Hurst and Company DLB-49

Hurston, Zora Neale
 1901?-1960 .... DLB-51, 86

Husson, Jules-François-Félix (see Champfleury)

Huston, John 1906-1987 .... DLB-26

Hutcheson, Francis 1694-1746 ..... DLB-31

Hutchinson, Thomas
 1711-1780 .... DLB-30, 31

Hutchinson and Company
 (Publishers) Limited DLB-112

von Hutten, Ulrich 1488-1523 .... DLB-179

Hutton, Richard Holt 1826-1897 .... DLB-57

Huxley, Aldous
 1894-1963 .... DLB-36, 100, 162

Huxley, Elspeth Josceline 1907- DLB-77

Huxley, T. H. 1825-1895 .... DLB-57

Huyghue, Douglas Smith
 1816-1891 .... DLB-99

Huysmans, Joris-Karl 1848-1907....DLB-123

Hyman, Trina Schart 1939- DLB-61

I

Iavorsky, Stefan 1658-1722........DLB-150

Ibn Bajja circa 1077-1138..........DLB-115

Ibn Gabirol, Solomon
    circa 1021-circa 1058..........DLB-115

The Iconography of Science-Fiction
    Art...........................DLB-8

Iffland, August Wilhelm
    1759-1814....................DLB-94

Ignatow, David 1914- DLB-5

Ike, Chukwuemeka 1931- DLB-157

Iles, Francis (see Berkeley, Anthony)

The Illustration of Early German
    Literary Manuscripts,
    circa 1150-circa 1300..........DLB-148

Imbs, Bravig 1904-1946.............DLB-4

Imbuga, Francis D. 1947- DLB-157

Immermann, Karl 1796-1840.......DLB-133

Inchbald, Elizabeth 1753-1821...DLB-39, 89

Inge, William 1913-1973...........DLB-7

Ingelow, Jean 1820-1897........DLB-35, 163

Ingersoll, Ralph 1900-1985........DLB-127

The Ingersoll Prizes..................Y-84

Ingoldsby, Thomas (see Barham, Richard
    Harris)

Ingraham, Joseph Holt 1809-1860.....DLB-3

Inman, John 1805-1850............DLB-73

Innerhofer, Franz 1944- DLB-85

Innis, Harold Adams 1894-1952.....DLB-88

Innis, Mary Quayle 1899-1972......DLB-88

International Publishers Company...DLB-46

An Interview with David Rabe.........Y-91

An Interview with George Greenfield,
    Literary Agent...................Y-91

An Interview with James Ellroy.......Y-91

An Interview with Peter S. Prescott.....Y-86

An Interview with Russell Hoban......Y-90

An Interview with Tom Jenks..........Y-86

Introduction to Paul Laurence Dunbar,
    Lyrics of Lowly Life (1896),
    by William Dean Howells.......DLB-50

Introductory Essay: Letters of Percy Bysshe
    Shelley (1852), by Robert
    Browning....................DLB-32

Introductory Letters from the Second Edition
    of Pamela (1741), by Samuel
    Richardson...................DLB-39

Irving, John 1942- DLB-6; Y-82

Irving, Washington
    1783-1859.....DLB-3, 11, 30, 59, 73, 74

Irwin, Grace 1907- DLB-68

Irwin, Will 1873-1948..............DLB-25

Isherwood, Christopher
    1904-1986...............DLB-15; Y-86

The Island Trees Case: A Symposium on
    School Library Censorship
    An Interview with Judith Krug
    An Interview with Phyllis Schlafly
    An Interview with Edward B. Jenkinson
    An Interview with Lamarr Mooneyham
    An Interview with Harriet
    Bernstein.......................Y-82

Islas, Arturo 1938-1991...........DLB-122

Ivers, M. J., and Company..........DLB-49

Iyayi, Festus 1947- DLB-157

J

Jackmon, Marvin E. (see Marvin X)

Jacks, L. P. 1860-1955.............DLB-135

Jackson, Angela 1951- DLB-41

Jackson, Helen Hunt
    1830-1885.................DLB-42, 47

Jackson, Holbrook 1874-1948.......DLB-98

Jackson, Laura Riding 1901-1991....DLB-48

Jackson, Shirley 1919-1965.........DLB-6

Jacob, Piers Anthony Dillingham (see Anthony,
    Piers)

Jacobi, Friedrich Heinrich
    1743-1819....................DLB-94

Jacobi, Johann Georg 1740-1841.....DLB-97

Jacobs, Joseph 1854-1916..........DLB-141

Jacobs, W. W. 1863-1943..........DLB-135

Jacobs, George W., and Company...DLB-49

Jacobson, Dan 1929- DLB-14

Jaggard, William
    [publishing house]...........DLB-170

Jahier, Piero 1884-1966...........DLB-114

Jahnn, Hans Henny
    1894-1959................DLB-56, 124

Jakes, John 1932- Y-83

James, C. L. R. 1901-1989.........DLB-125

James, George P. R. 1801-1860.....DLB-116

James, Henry
    1843-1916.......DLB-12, 71, 74; DS-13

James, John circa 1633-1729........DLB-24

The James Jones Society..............Y-92

James, M. R. 1862-1936..........DLB-156

James, P. D. 1920- DLB-87

James Joyce Centenary: Dublin, 1982...Y-82

James Joyce Conference..............Y-85

James VI of Scotland, I of England
    1566-1625...............DLB-151, 172

James, U. P. [publishing house].....DLB-49

Jameson, Anna 1794-1860......DLB-99, 166

Jameson, Fredric 1934- DLB-67

Jameson, J. Franklin 1859-1937......DLB-17

Jameson, Storm 1891-1986..........DLB-36

Janés, Clara 1940- DLB-134

Jaramillo, Cleofas M. 1878-1956....DLB-122

Jarman, Mark 1952- DLB-120

Jarrell, Randall 1914-1965.......DLB-48, 52

Jarrold and Sons..................DLB-106

Jasmin, Claude 1930- DLB-60

Jay, John 1745-1829................DLB-31

Jefferies, Richard 1848-1887....DLB-98, 141

Jeffers, Lance 1919-1985............DLB-41

Jeffers, Robinson 1887-1962........DLB-45

Jefferson, Thomas 1743-1826........DLB-31

Jelinek, Elfriede 1946- DLB-85

Jellicoe, Ann 1927- DLB-13

Jenkins, Elizabeth 1905- DLB-155

Jenkins, Robin 1912- DLB-14

Jenkins, William Fitzgerald (see Leinster,
    Murray)

Jenkins, Herbert, Limited..........DLB-112

Jennings, Elizabeth 1926- DLB-27

Jens, Walter 1923- DLB-69

Jensen, Merrill 1905-1980..........DLB-17

Jephson, Robert 1736-1803.........DLB-89

Jerome, Jerome K.
    1859-1927............DLB-10, 34, 135

Jerome, Judson 1927-1991.........DLB-105

Jerome, Judson, Reflections: After a
    Tornado....................DLB-105

Jerrold, Douglas 1803-1857....DLB-158, 159

Jesse, F. Tennyson 1888-1958.......DLB-77

Jewett, Sarah Orne 1849-1909....DLB-12, 74

Jewett, John P., and Company......DLB-49

The Jewish Publication Society......DLB-49

Jewitt, John Rodgers 1783-1821.....DLB-99

Jewsbury, Geraldine 1812-1880 ..... DLB-21

Jhabvala, Ruth Prawer 1927- DLB-139

Jiménez, Juan Ramón 1881-1958.... DLB-134

Joans, Ted 1928- DLB-16, 41

John, Eugenie (see Marlitt, E.)

John of Dumbleton
circa 1310-circa 1349 .... DLB-115

John Edward Bruce: Three
Documents DLB-50

John O'Hara's Pottsville Journalism Y-88

John Steinbeck Research Center....... Y-85

John Webster: The Melbourne
Manuscript Y-86

Johns, Captain W. E. 1893-1968.... DLB-160

Johnson, B. S. 1933-1973....... DLB-14, 40

Johnson, Charles 1679-1748 .... DLB-84

Johnson, Charles R. 1948- DLB-33

Johnson, Charles S. 1893-1956... DLB-51, 91

Johnson, Denis 1949- DLB-120

Johnson, Diane 1934- Y-80

Johnson, Edgar 1901- DLB-103

Johnson, Edward 1598-1672 .... DLB-24

Johnson E. Pauline (Tekahionwake)
1861-1913 .... DLB-175

Johnson, Fenton 1888-1958...... DLB-45, 50

Johnson, Georgia Douglas
1886-1966 .... DLB-51

Johnson, Gerald W. 1890-1980...... DLB-29

Johnson, Helene 1907- DLB-51

Johnson, James Weldon
1871-1938 .... DLB-51

Johnson, John H. 1918- DLB-137

Johnson, Linton Kwesi 1952- DLB-157

Johnson, Lionel 1867-1902 .... DLB-19

Johnson, Nunnally 1897-1977...... DLB-26

Johnson, Owen 1878-1952 .... Y-87

Johnson, Pamela Hansford
1912- DLB-15

Johnson, Pauline 1861-1913........ DLB-92

Johnson, Ronald 1935- DLB-169

Johnson, Samuel 1696-1772 .... DLB-24

Johnson, Samuel
1709-1784........ DLB-39, 95, 104, 142

Johnson, Samuel 1822-1882......... DLB-1

Johnson, Uwe 1934-1984 .... DLB-75

Johnson, Benjamin
[publishing house] DLB-49

Johnson, Benjamin, Jacob, and
Robert [publishing house] DLB-49

Johnson, Jacob, and Company DLB-49

Johnson, Joseph [publishing house] ... DLB-154

Johnston, Annie Fellows 1863-1931 .. DLB-42

Johnston, Basil H. 1929- DLB-60

Johnston, Denis 1901-1984 .... DLB-10

Johnston, George 1913- DLB-88

Johnston, Sir Harry 1858-1927 ..... DLB-174

Johnston, Jennifer 1930- DLB-14

Johnston, Mary 1870-1936.......... DLB-9

Johnston, Richard Malcolm
1822-1898 .... DLB-74

Johnstone, Charles 1719?-1800?..... DLB-39

Johst, Hanns 1890-1978 .... DLB-124

Jolas, Eugene 1894-1952 .... DLB-4, 45

Jones, Alice C. 1853-1933 .... DLB-92

Jones, Charles C., Jr. 1831-1893..... DLB-30

Jones, D. G. 1929- DLB-53

Jones, David 1895-1974........ DLB-20, 100

Jones, Diana Wynne 1934- DLB-161

Jones, Ebenezer 1820-1860 .... DLB-32

Jones, Ernest 1819-1868........... DLB-32

Jones, Gayl 1949- DLB-33

Jones, Glyn 1905- DLB-15

Jones, Gwyn 1907- DLB-15, 139

Jones, Henry Arthur 1851-1929 ..... DLB-10

Jones, Hugh circa 1692-1760........ DLB-24

Jones, James 1921-1977 .... DLB-2, 143

Jones, Jenkin Lloyd 1911- DLB-127

Jones, LeRoi (see Baraka, Amiri)

Jones, Lewis 1897-1939 .... DLB-15

Jones, Madison 1925- DLB-152

Jones, Major Joseph (see Thompson, William
Tappan)

Jones, Preston 1936-1979........... DLB-7

Jones, Rodney 1950- DLB-120

Jones, Sir William 1746-1794 ...... DLB-109

Jones, William Alfred 1817-1900 .... DLB-59

Jones's Publishing House........... DLB-49

Jong, Erica 1942- DLB-2, 5, 28, 152

Jonke, Gert F. 1946- DLB-85

Jonson, Ben 1572?-1637........ DLB-62, 121

Jordan, June 1936- DLB-38

Joseph, Jenny 1932- DLB-40

Joseph, Michael, Limited DLB-112

Josephson, Matthew 1899-1978....... DLB-4

Josephus, Flavius 37-100 .... DLB-176

Josiah Allen's Wife (see Holley, Marietta)

Josipovici, Gabriel 1940- DLB-14

Josselyn, John ?-1675 .... DLB-24

Joudry, Patricia 1921- DLB-88

Jovine, Giuseppe 1922- DLB-128

Joyaux, Philippe (see Sollers, Philippe)

Joyce, Adrien (see Eastman, Carol)

Joyce, James
1882-1941......... DLB-10, 19, 36, 162

Judd, Sylvester 1813-1853 .... DLB-1

Judd, Orange, Publishing
Company.................... DLB-49

Judith circa 930 .... DLB-146

Julian of Norwich
1342-circa 1420............. DLB-1146

Julian Symons at Eighty Y-92

June, Jennie (see Croly, Jane Cunningham)

Jung, Franz 1888-1963 .... DLB-118

Jünger, Ernst 1895- DLB-56

Der jüngere Titurel circa 1275 .... DLB-138

Jung-Stilling, Johann Heinrich
1740-1817 .... DLB-94

Justice, Donald 1925- Y-83

The Juvenile Library (see Godwin, M. J., and
Company)

K

Kacew, Romain (see Gary, Romain)

Kafka, Franz 1883-1924 .... DLB-81

Kahn, Roger 1927................ DLB-171

Kaiser, Georg 1878-1945 .... DLB-124

Kaiserchronik circca 1147 .... DLB-148

Kalechofsky, Roberta 1931- DLB-28

Kaler, James Otis 1848-1912 .... DLB-12

Kames, Henry Home, Lord
1696-1782 .... DLB-31, 104

Kandel, Lenore 1932- DLB-16

Kanin, Garson 1912- DLB-7

Kant, Hermann 1926- DLB-75

Kant, Immanuel 1724-1804 .... DLB-94

Kantemir, Antiokh Dmitrievich
1708-1744 .... DLB-150

Kantor, Mackinlay 1904-1977.... DLB-9, 102

Kaplan, Fred 1937- DLB-111

Kaplan, Johanna 1942- DLB-28

Kaplan, Justin 1925- DLB-111

Kapnist, Vasilii Vasilevich 1758?-1823 ....DLB-150

Karadžić, Vuk Stefanović 1787-1864 ....DLB-147

Karamzin, Nikolai Mikhailovich 1766-1826 ....DLB-150

Karsch, Anna Louisa 1722-1791 .....DLB-97

Kasack, Hermann 1896-1966........DLB-69

Kaschnitz, Marie Luise 1901-1974 ...DLB-69

Kaštelan, Jure 1919-1990 ....DLB-147

Kästner, Erich 1899-1974...........DLB-56

Kattan, Naim 1928- DLB-53

Katz, Steve 1935- Y-83

Kauffman, Janet 1945- Y-86

Kauffmann, Samuel 1898-1971 .....DLB-127

Kaufman, Bob 1925- DLB-16, 41

Kaufman, George S. 1889-1961.......DLB-7

Kavanagh, P. J. 1931- DLB-40

Kavanagh, Patrick 1904-1967....DLB-15, 20

Kaye-Smith, Sheila 1887-1956.......DLB-36

Kazin, Alfred 1915- DLB-67

Keane, John B. 1928- DLB-13

Keary, Annie 1825-1879 ....DLB-163

Keating, H. R. F. 1926- DLB-87

Keats, Ezra Jack 1916-1983 ....DLB-61

Keats, John 1795-1821 ....DLB-96, 110

Keble, John 1792-1866...........DLB-32, 55

Keeble, John 1944- Y-83

Keeffe, Barrie 1945- DLB-13

Keeley, James 1867-1934 ....DLB-25

W. B. Keen, Cooke and Company.................DLB-49

Keillor, Garrison 1942- Y-87

Keith, Marian 1874?-1961 ....DLB-92

Keller, Gary D. 1943- DLB-82

Keller, Gottfried 1819-1890........DLB-129

Kelley, Edith Summers 1884-1956 ....DLB-9

Kelley, William Melvin 1937- DLB-33

Kellogg, Ansel Nash 1832-1886......DLB-23

Kellogg, Steven 1941- DLB-61

Kelly, George 1887-1974 ....DLB-7

Kelly, Hugh 1739-1777 ....DLB-89

Kelly, Robert 1935- DLB-5, 130, 165

Kelly, Piet and Company..........DLB-49

Kelmscott Press.................DLB-112

Kemble, Fanny 1809-1893 ....DLB-32

Kemelman, Harry 1908- DLB-28

Kempe, Margery circa 1373-1438................DLB-146

Kempner, Friederike 1836-1904 ....DLB-129

Kempowski, Walter 1929- DLB-75

Kendall, Claude [publishing company]...........DLB-46

Kendell, George 1809-1867 ....DLB-43

Kenedy, P. J., and Sons DLB-49

Kennedy, Adrienne 1931- DLB-38

Kennedy, John Pendleton 1795-1870 ...DLB-3

Kennedy, Leo 1907- DLB-88

Kennedy, Margaret 1896-1967 ......DLB-36

Kennedy, Patrick 1801-1873 ....DLB-159

Kennedy, Richard S. 1920- DLB-111

Kennedy, William 1928- DLB-143; Y-85

Kennedy, X. J. 1929- DLB-5

Kennelly, Brendan 1936- DLB-40

Kenner, Hugh 1923- DLB-67

Kennerley, Mitchell [publishing house] DLB-46

Kenny, Maurice 1929- DLB-175

Kent, Frank R. 1877-1958 ....DLB-29

Kenyon, Jane 1947- DLB-120

Keough, Hugh Edmund 1864-1912 .DLB-171

Keppler and Schwartzmann.........DLB-49

Kerner, Justinus 1776-1862 ....DLB-90

Kerouac, Jack 1922-1969....DLB-2, 16; DS-3

The Jack Kerouac Revival.............Y-95

Kerouac, Jan 1952- DLB-16

Kerr, Orpheus C. (see Newell, Robert Henry)

Kerr, Charles H., and Company.....DLB-49

Kesey, Ken 1935- DLB-2, 16

Kessel, Joseph 1898-1979...........DLB-72

Kessel, Martin 1901- DLB-56

Kesten, Hermann 1900- DLB-56

Keun, Irmgard 1905-1982 ....DLB-69

Key and Biddle DLB-49

Keynes, John Maynard 1883-1946.....DS-10

Keyserling, Eduard von 1855-1918 ..DLB-66

Khan, Ismith 1925- DLB-125

Khemnitser, Ivan Ivanovich 1745-1784 ....DLB-150

Kheraskov, Mikhail Matveevich 1733-1807 ....DLB-150

Khvostov, Dmitrii Ivanovich 1757-1835 ....DLB-150

Kidd, Adam 1802?-1831............DLB-99

Kidd, William [publishing house] DLB-106

Kiely, Benedict 1919- DLB-15

Kieran, John 1892-1981 ....DLB-171

Kiggins and Kellogg DLB-49

Kiley, Jed 1889-1962................DLB-4

Kilgore, Bernard 1908-1967........DLB-127

Killens, John Oliver 1916- DLB-33

Killigrew, Anne 1660-1685 ....DLB-131

Killigrew, Thomas 1612-1683.......DLB-58

Kilmer, Joyce 1886-1918 ....DLB-45

Kilwardby, Robert circa 1215-1279................DLB-115

Kincaid, Jamaica 1949- DLB-157

King, Clarence 1842-1901 ....DLB-12

King, Florence 1936..................Y-85

King, Francis 1923- DLB-15, 139

King, Grace 1852-1932 ....DLB-12, 78

King, Henry 1592-1669 ....DLB-126

King, Stephen 1947- DLB-143; Y-80

King, Thomas 1943- DLB-175

King, Woodie, Jr. 1937- DLB-38

King, Solomon [publishing house] ...DLB-49

Kinglake, Alexander William 1809-1891 ....DLB-55, 166

Kingsley, Charles 1819-1875.........DLB-21, 32, 163, 178

Kingsley, Mary Henrietta 1862-1900 ....DLB-174

Kingsley, Henry 1830-1876.........DLB-21

Kingsley, Sidney 1906- DLB-7

Kingsmill, Hugh 1889-1949........DLB-149

Kingston, Maxine Hong 1940- DLB-173; Y-80

Kingston, William Henry Giles 1814-1880 ....DLB-163

Kinnell, Galway 1927- DLB-5; Y-87

Kinsella, Thomas 1928- DLB-27

Kipling, Rudyard 1865-1936........DLB-19, 34, 141, 156

Kipphardt, Heinar 1922-1982 ......DLB-124

Kirby, William 1817-1906 .... DLB-99

Kircher, Athanasius 1602-1680 ..... DLB-164

Kirk, John Foster 1824-1904 .... DLB-79

Kirkconnell, Watson 1895-1977 ..... DLB-68

Kirkland, Caroline M.
1801-1864 .... DLB-3, 73, 74; DS-13

Kirkland, Joseph 1830-1893 .... DLB-12

Kirkman, Francis
[publishing house] DLB-170

Kirkpatrick, Clayton 1915- DLB-127

Kirkup, James 1918- DLB-27

Kirouac, Conrad (see Marie-Victorin, Frère)

Kirsch, Sarah 1935- DLB-75

Kirst, Hans Hellmut 1914-1989 ..... DLB-69

Kitcat, Mabel Greenhow
1859-1922 .... DLB-135

Kitchin, C. H. B. 1895-1967 .... DLB-77

Kizer, Carolyn 1925- DLB-5, 169

Klabund 1890-1928 .... DLB-66

Klaj, Johann 1616-1656 .... DLB-164

Klappert, Peter 1942- DLB-5

Klass, Philip (see Tenn, William)

Klein, A. M. 1909-1972 .... DLB-68

Kleist, Ewald von 1715-1759 .... DLB-97

Kleist, Heinrich von 1777-1811 .... DLB-90

Klinger, Friedrich Maximilian
1752-1831 .... DLB-94

Klopstock, Friedrich Gottlieb
1724-1803 .... DLB-97

Klopstock, Meta 1728-1758 .... DLB-97

Kluge, Alexander 1932- DLB-75

Knapp, Joseph Palmer 1864-1951 .... DLB-91

Knapp, Samuel Lorenzo
1783-1838 .... DLB-59

Knapton, J. J. and P.
[publishing house] DLB-154

Kniazhnin, Iakov Borisovich
1740-1791 .... DLB-150

Knickerbocker, Diedrich (see Irving, Washington)

Knigge, Adolph Franz Friedrich Ludwig, Freiherr von 1752-1796 .... DLB-94

Knight, Damon 1922- DLB-8

Knight, Etheridge 1931-1992 .... DLB-41

Knight, John S. 1894-1981 .... DLB-29

Knight, Sarah Kemble 1666-1727 .... DLB-24

Knight, Charles, and Company DLB-106

Knight-Bruce, G. W. H.
1852-1896 .... DLB-174

Knister, Raymond 1899-1932 .... DLB-68

Knoblock, Edward 1874-1945 .... DLB-10

Knopf, Alfred A. 1892-1984 .... Y-84

Knopf, Alfred A.
[publishing house] DLB-46

Knorr von Rosenroth, Christian
1636-1689 .... DLB-168

Knowles, John 1926- DLB-6

Knox, Frank 1874-1944 .... DLB-29

Knox, John circa 1514-1572 .... DLB-132

Knox, John Armoy 1850-1906 .... DLB-23

Knox, Ronald Arbuthnott
1888-1957 .... DLB-77

Kober, Arthur 1900-1975 .... DLB-11

Kocbek, Edvard 1904-1981 .... DLB-147

Koch, Howard 1902- DLB-26

Koch, Kenneth 1925- DLB-5

Koenigsberg, Moses 1879-1945 ..... DLB-25

Koeppen, Wolfgang 1906- DLB-69

Koertge, Ronald 1940- DLB-105

Koestler, Arthur 1905-1983 .... Y-83

Kokoschka, Oskar 1886-1980 ...... DLB-124

Kolb, Annette 1870-1967 .... DLB-66

Kolbenheyer, Erwin Guido
1878-1962 .... DLB-66, 124

Kolleritsch, Alfred 1931- DLB-85

Kolodny, Annette 1941- DLB-67

Komarov, Matvei
circa 1730-1812 .... DLB-150

Komroff, Manuel 1890-1974 .... DLB-4

Komunyakaa, Yusef 1947- DLB-120

Konigsburg, E. L. 1930- DLB-52

Konrad von Würzburg
circa 1230-1287 .... DLB-138

Konstantinov, Aleko 1863-1897 ... DLB-147

Kooser, Ted 1939- DLB-105

Kopit, Arthur 1937- DLB-7

Kops, Bernard 1926?- DLB-13

Kornbluth, C. M. 1923-1958 .... DLB-8

Körner, Theodor 1791-1813 .... DLB-90

Kornfeld, Paul 1889-1942 .... DLB-118

Kosinski, Jerzy 1933-1991 ...... DLB-2; Y-82

Kosovel, Srečko 1904-1926 .... DLB-147

Kostrov, Ermil Ivanovich
1755-1796 .... DLB-150

Kotzebue, August von 1761-1819 .... DLB-94

Kotzwinkle, William 1938- DLB-173

Kovačić, Ante 1854-1889 .... DLB-147

Kraf, Elaine 1946- Y-81

Kranjčević, Silvije Strahimir
1865-1908 .... DLB-147

Krasna, Norman 1909-1984 .... DLB-26

Kraus, Karl 1874-1936 .... DLB-118

Krauss, Ruth 1911-1993 .... DLB-52

Kreisel, Henry 1922- DLB-88

Kreuder, Ernst 1903-1972 .... DLB-69

Kreymborg, Alfred 1883-1966 .... DLB-4, 54

Krieger, Murray 1923- DLB-67

Krim, Seymour 1922-1989 .... DLB-16

Krleža, Miroslav 1893-1981 ...... DLB-147

Krock, Arthur 1886-1974 .... DLB-29

Kroetsch, Robert 1927- DLB-53

Krutch, Joseph Wood 1893-1970 .... DLB-63

Krylov, Ivan Andreevich
1769-1844 .... DLB-150

Kubin, Alfred 1877-1959 .... DLB-81

Kubrick, Stanley 1928- DLB-26

Kudrun circa 1230-1240 .... DLB-138

Kuffstein, Hans Ludwig von
1582-1656 .... DLB-164

Kuhlmann, Quirinus 1651-1689 .... DLB-168

Kuhnau, Johann 1660-1722 .... DLB-168

Kumin, Maxine 1925- DLB-5

Kunene, Mazisi 1930- DLB-117

Kunitz, Stanley 1905- DLB-48

Kunjufu, Johari M. (see Amini, Johari M.)

Kunnert, Gunter 1929- DLB-75

Kunze, Reiner 1933- DLB-75

Kupferberg, Tuli 1923- DLB-16

Kürnberger, Ferdinand
1821-1879 .... DLB-129

Kurz, Isolde 1853-1944 .... DLB-66

Kusenberg, Kurt 1904-1983 .... DLB-69

Kuttner, Henry 1915-1958 .... DLB-8

Kyd, Thomas 1558-1594 .... DLB-62

Kyffin, Maurice
circa 1560?-1598 .... DLB-136

Kyger, Joanne 1934- DLB-16

Kyne, Peter B. 1880-1957 .... DLB-78

L

L. E. L. (see Landon, Letitia Elizabeth)

Laberge, Albert 1871-1960.........DLB-68

Laberge, Marie 1950- DLB-60

Lacombe, Patrice (see Trullier-Lacombe, Joseph Patrice)

Lacretelle, Jacques de 1888-1985 ....DLB-65

Lacy, Sam 1903- DLB-171

Ladd, Joseph Brown 1764-1786 .....DLB-37

La Farge, Oliver 1901-1963..........DLB-9

Lafferty, R. A. 1914- DLB-8

La Flesche, Francis 1857-1932......DLB-175

La Guma, Alex 1925-1985........DLB-117

Lahaise, Guillaume (see Delahaye, Guy)

Lahontan, Louis-Armand de Lom d'Arce, Baron de 1666-1715?..........DLB-99

Laing, Kojo 1946- DLB-157

Laird, Carobeth 1895- Y-82

Laird and Lee DLB-49

Lalonde, Michèle 1937- DLB-60

Lamantia, Philip 1927- DLB-16

Lamb, Charles 1775-1834...........DLB-93, 107, 163

Lamb, Lady Caroline 1785-1828 ...DLB-116

Lamb, Mary 1764-1874 ....DLB-163

Lambert, Betty 1933-1983 ....DLB-60

Lamming, George 1927- DLB-125

L'Amour, Louis 1908?- Y-80

Lampman, Archibald 1861-1899.....DLB-92

Lamson, Wolffe and Company......DLB-49

Lancer Books....................DLB-46

Landesman, Jay 1919- and Landesman, Fran 1927- DLB-16

Landolfi, Tommaso 1908-1979.....DLB-177

Landon, Letitia Elizabeth 1802-1838 .DLB-96

Landor, Walter Savage 1775-1864 ....DLB-93, 107

Landry, Napoléon-P. 1884-1956.....DLB-92

Lane, Charles 1800-1870 ....DLB-1

Lane, Laurence W. 1890-1967 .....DLB-91

Lane, M. Travis 1934- DLB-60

Lane, Patrick 1939- DLB-53

Lane, Pinkie Gordon 1923- DLB-41

Lane, John, Company DLB-49

Laney, Al 1896-1988 ....DLB-4, 171

Lang, Andrew 1844-1912 ......DLB-98, 141

Langevin, André 1927- DLB-60

Langgässer, Elisabeth 1899-1950 ....DLB-69

Langhorne, John 1735-1779.......DLB-109

Langland, William circa 1330-circa 1400 ....DLB-146

Langton, Anna 1804-1893 ....DLB-99

Lanham, Edwin 1904-1979 ....DLB-4

Lanier, Sidney 1842-1881 ....DLB-64; DS-13

Lanyer, Aemilia 1569-1645 ....DLB-121

Lapointe, Gatien 1931-1983.........DLB-88

Lapointe, Paul-Marie 1929- DLB-88

Lardner, John 1912-1960 ....DLB-171

Lardner, Ring 1885-1933 ....DLB-11, 25, 86, 171

Lardner, Ring, Jr. 1915- DLB-26

Lardner 100: Ring Lardner Centennial Symposium............Y-85

Larkin, Philip 1922-1985 ....DLB-27

La Roche, Sophie von 1730-1807 ....DLB-94

La Rocque, Gilbert 1943-1984 ......DLB-60

Laroque de Roquebrune, Robert (see Roquebrune, Robert de)

Larrick, Nancy 1910- DLB-61

Larsen, Nella 1893-1964 ....DLB-51

Lasker-Schüler, Else 1869-1945 ....DLB-66, 124

Lasnier, Rina 1915- DLB-88

Lassalle, Ferdinand 1825-1864 .....DLB-129

Lathrop, Dorothy P. 1891-1980 .....DLB-22

Lathrop, George Parsons 1851-1898 ....DLB-71

Lathrop, John, Jr. 1772-1820 ....DLB-37

Latimer, Hugh 1492?-1555 ....DLB-136

Latimore, Jewel Christine McLawler (see Amini, Johari M.)

Latymer, William 1498-1583........DLB-132

Laube, Heinrich 1806-1884 ....DLB-133

Laughlin, James 1914- DLB-48

Laumer, Keith 1925- DLB-8

Lauremberg, Johann 1590-1658 ....DLB-164

Laurence, Margaret 1926-1987 ......DLB-53

Laurentius von Schnüffis 1633-1702 ....DLB-168

Laurents, Arthur 1918- DLB-26

Laurie, Annie (see Black, Winifred)

Laut, Agnes Christiana 1871-1936 ...DLB-92

Lavater, Johann Kaspar 1741-1801...DLB-97

Lavin, Mary 1912- DLB-15

Lawes, Henry 1596-1662.........DLB-126

Lawless, Anthony (see MacDonald, Philip)

Lawrence, D. H. 1885-1930 ......DLB-10, 19, 36, 98, 162

Lawrence, David 1888-1973 ....DLB-29

Lawrence, Seymour 1926-1994.........Y-94

Lawson, John ?-1711 ....DLB-24

Lawson, Robert 1892-1957 ....DLB-22

Lawson, Victor F. 1850-1925 ....DLB-25

Layard, Sir Austen Henry 1817-1894 ....DLB-166

Layton, Irving 1912- DLB-88

LaZamon flourished circa 1200 ....DLB-146

Lazarević, Laza K. 1851-1890 ......DLB-147

Lea, Henry Charles 1825-1909 ......DLB-47

Lea, Sydney 1942- DLB-120

Lea, Tom 1907- DLB-6

Leacock, John 1729-1802...........DLB-31

Leacock, Stephen 1869-1944 ....DLB-92

Lead, Jane Ward 1623-1704 ....DLB-131

Leadenhall Press..................DLB-106

Leapor, Mary 1722-1746 ....DLB-109

Lear, Edward 1812-1888...DLB-32, 163, 166

Leary, Timothy 1920-1996 ....DLB-16

Leary, W. A., and Company........DLB-49

Léautaud, Paul 1872-1956 ....DLB-65

Leavitt, David 1961- DLB-130

Leavitt and Allen DLB-49

Le Blond, Mrs. Aubrey 1861-1934 ....DLB-174

le Carré, John 1931- DLB-87

Lécavelé, Roland (see Dorgeles, Roland)

Lechlitner, Ruth 1901- DLB-48

Leclerc, Félix 1914- DLB-60

Le Clézio, J. M. G. 1940- DLB-83

Lectures on Rhetoric and Belles Lettres (1783), by Hugh Blair [excerpts] DLB-31

Leder, Rudolf (see Hermlin, Stephan)

Lederer, Charles 1910-1976.........DLB-26

Ledwidge, Francis 1887-1917 ....DLB-20

Lee, Dennis 1939- DLB-53

Lee, Don L. (see Madhubuti, Haki R.)

Lee, George W. 1894-1976 ....DLB-51

Lee, Harper 1926- DLB-6

Lee, Harriet (1757-1851) and Lee, Sophia (1750-1824) DLB-39

Lee, Laurie 1914- DLB-27

Lee, Li-Young 1957- DLB-165

Lee, Manfred B. (see Dannay, Frederic, and Manfred B. Lee)

Lee, Nathaniel circa 1645 - 1692..... DLB-80

Lee, Sir Sidney 1859-1926 .... DLB-149

Lee, Sir Sidney, "Principles of Biography," in *Elizabethan and Other Essays*...... DLB-149

Lee, Vernon 1856-1935 ... DLB-57, 153, 156, 174, 178

Lee and Shepard DLB-49

Le Fanu, Joseph Sheridan 1814-1873......... DLB-21, 70, 159, 178

Leffland, Ella 1931- Y-84

le Fort, Gertrud von 1876-1971 ..... DLB-66

Le Gallienne, Richard 1866-1947 ..... DLB-4

Legaré, Hugh Swinton 1797-1843............... DLB-3, 59, 73

Legaré, James M. 1823-1859 .... DLB-3

The Legends of the Saints and a Medieval Christian Worldview.......... DLB-148

Léger, Antoine-J. 1880-1950 .... DLB-88

Le Guin, Ursula K. 1929- DLB-8, 52

Lehman, Ernest 1920- DLB-44

Lehmann, John 1907- DLB-27, 100

Lehmann, Rosamond 1901-1990..... DLB-15

Lehmann, Wilhelm 1882-1968 ...... DLB-56

Lehmann, John, Limited DLB-112

Leiber, Fritz 1910-1992 .... DLB-8

Leibniz, Gottfried Wilhelm 1646-1716 .... DLB-168

Leicester University Press DLB-112

Leinster, Murray 1896-1975 .... DLB-8

Leisewitz, Johann Anton 1752-1806 .... DLB-94

Leitch, Maurice 1933- DLB-14

Leithauser, Brad 1943- DLB-120

Leland, Charles G. 1824-1903....... DLB-11

Leland, John 1503?-1552 .... DLB-136

Lemay, Pamphile 1837-1918 .... DLB-99

Lemelin, Roger 1919- DLB-88

Lemon, Mark 1809-1870 .... DLB-163

Le Moine, James MacPherson 1825-1912 .... DLB-99

Le Moyne, Jean 1913- DLB-88

L'Engle, Madeleine 1918- DLB-52

Lennart, Isobel 1915-1971 .... DLB-44

Lennox, Charlotte 1729 or 1730-1804 .... DLB-39

Lenox, James 1800-1880 .... DLB-140

Lenski, Lois 1893-1974 .... DLB-22

Lenz, Hermann 1913- DLB-69

Lenz, J. M. R. 1751-1792 .... DLB-94

Lenz, Siegfried 1926- DLB-75

Leonard, Elmore 1925- DLB-173

Leonard, Hugh 1926- DLB-13

Leonard, William Ellery 1876-1944 .... DLB-54

Leonowens, Anna 1834-1914 ... DLB-99, 166

LePan, Douglas 1914- DLB-88

Leprohon, Rosanna Eleanor 1829-1879 .... DLB-99

Le Queux, William 1864-1927 ...... DLB-70

Lerner, Max 1902-1992 .... DLB-29

Lernet-Holenia, Alexander 1897-1976 .... DLB-85

Le Rossignol, James 1866-1969...... DLB-92

Lescarbot, Marc circa 1570-1642 .... DLB-99

LeSeur, William Dawson 1840-1917 .... DLB-92

LeSieg, Theo. (see Geisel, Theodor Seuss)

Leslie, Frank 1821-1880......... DLB-43, 79

Leslie, Frank, Publishing House DLB-49

Lesperance, John 1835?-1891 .... DLB-99

Lessing, Bruno 1870-1940 .... DLB-28

Lessing, Doris 1919- DLB-15, 139; Y-85

Lessing, Gotthold Ephraim 1729-1781 .... DLB-97

Lettau, Reinhard 1929- DLB-75

Letter from Japan.................... Y-94

Letter from London................. Y-96

Letter to [Samuel] Richardson on *Clarissa* (1748), by Henry Fielding....... DLB-39

Lever, Charles 1806-1872 .... DLB-21

Leverson, Ada 1862-1933 .... DLB-153

Levertov, Denise 1923- DLB-5, 165

Levi, Peter 1931- DLB-40

Levi, Primo 1919-1987 .... DLB-177

Levien, Sonya 1888-1960.......... DLB-44

Levin, Meyer 1905-1981 .... DLB-9, 28; Y-81

Levine, Norman 1923- DLB-88

Levine, Philip 1928- DLB-5

Levis, Larry 1946- DLB-120

Levy, Amy 1861-1889 .... DLB-156

Levy, Benn Wolfe 1900-1973 .... DLB-13; Y-81

Lewald, Fanny 1811-1889 .... DLB-129

Lewes, George Henry 1817-1878 .... DLB-55, 144

Lewis, Agnes Smith 1843-1926 ..... DLB-174

Lewis, Alfred H. 1857-1914......... DLB-25

Lewis, Alun 1915-1944 .... DLB-20, 162

Lewis, C. Day (see Day Lewis, C.)

Lewis, C. S. 1898-1963 .... DLB-15, 100, 160

Lewis, Charles B. 1842-1924........ DLB-11

Lewis, Henry Clay 1825-1850........ DLB-3

Lewis, Janet 1899- Y-87

Lewis, Matthew Gregory 1775-1818............ DLB-39, 158, 178

Lewis, R. W. B. 1917- DLB-111

Lewis, Richard circa 1700-1734 ..... DLB-24

Lewis, Sinclair 1885-1951............ DLB-9, 102; DS-1

Lewis, Wilmarth Sheldon 1895-1979 .... DLB-140

Lewis, Wyndham 1882-1957........ DLB-15

Lewisohn, Ludwig 1882-1955............. DLB-4, 9, 28, 102

Lezama Lima, José 1910-1976...... DLB-113

The Library of America............ DLB-46

The Licensing Act of 1737.......... DLB-84

Lichfield, Leonard I [publishing house] DLB-170

Lichtenberg, Georg Christoph 1742-1799 .... DLB-94

Lieb, Fred 1888-1980 .... DLB-171

Liebling, A. J. 1904-1963........ DLB-4, 171

Lieutenant Murray (see Ballou, Maturin Murray)

Lighthall, William Douw 1857-1954 .... DLB-92

Lilar, Françoise (see Mallet-Joris, Françoise)

Lillo, George 1691-1739............. DLB-84

Lilly, J. K., Jr. 1893-1966........... DLB-140

Lilly, Wait and Company DLB-49

Lily, William circa 1468-1522...... DLB-132

Limited Editions Club DLB-46

Lincoln and Edmands DLB-49

Lindsay, Jack 1900- Y-84

Lindsay, Sir David circa 1485-1555............... DLB-132

Lindsay, Vachel 1879-1931 ....DLB-54

Linebarger, Paul Myron Anthony (see Smith, Cordwainer)

Link, Arthur S. 1920- DLB-17

Linn, John Blair 1777-1804 ....DLB-37

Lins, Osman 1924-1978 ....DLB-145

Linton, Eliza Lynn 1822-1898.......DLB-18

Linton, William James 1812-1897....DLB-32

Lintot, Barnaby Bernard
  [publishing house] DLB-170

Lion Books DLB-46

Lionni, Leo 1910- DLB-61

Lippincott, Sara Jane Clarke
  1823-1904 ....DLB-43

Lippincott, J. B., Company DLB-49

Lippmann, Walter 1889-1974 ....DLB-29

Lipton, Lawrence 1898-1975........DLB-16

Liscow, Christian Ludwig
  1701-1760 ....DLB-97

Lish, Gordon 1934- DLB-130

Lispector, Clarice 1925-1977.......DLB-113

The Literary Chronicle and Weekly Review
  1819-1828 ....DLB-110

Literary Documents: William Faulkner
  and the People-to-People
  Program Y-86

Literary Documents II: *Library Journal*
  Statements and Questionnaires from
  First Novelists Y-87

Literary Effects of World War II
  [British novel]..................DLB-15

Literary Prizes [British] DLB-15

Literary Research Archives: The Humanities
  Research Center, University of
  Texas...........................Y-82

Literary Research Archives II: Berg
  Collection of English and American
  Literature of the New York Public
  Library Y-83

Literary Research Archives III:
  The Lilly Library.................Y-84

Literary Research Archives IV:
  The John Carter Brown Library Y-85

Literary Research Archives V:
  Kent State Special Collections Y-86

Literary Research Archives VI: The Modern
  Literary Manuscripts Collection in the
  Special Collections of the Washington
  University Libraries Y-87

Literary Research Archives VII:
  The University of Virginia
  Libraries Y-91

Literary Research Archives VIII:
  The Henry E. Huntington
  Library Y-92

"Literary Style" (1857), by William
  Forsyth [excerpt] DLB-57

Literatura Chicanesca: The View From Without
  DLB-82

Literature at Nurse, or Circulating Morals (1885),
  by George Moore..............DLB-18

Littell, Eliakim 1797-1870 ....DLB-79

Littell, Robert S. 1831-1896.........DLB-79

Little, Brown and Company DLB-49

Littlewood, Joan 1914- DLB-13

Lively, Penelope 1933- DLB-14, 161

Liverpool University Press DLB-112

The Lives of the Poets...............DLB-142

Livesay, Dorothy 1909- DLB-68

Livesay, Florence Randal
  1874-1953 ....DLB-92

Livings, Henry 1929- DLB-13

Livingston, Anne Howe
  1763-1841 ....DLB-37

Livingston, Myra Cohn 1926- DLB-61

Livingston, William 1723-1790......DLB-31

Livingstone, David 1813-1873 .....DLB-166

Liyong, Taban lo (see Taban lo Liyong)

Lizárraga, Sylvia S. 1925- DLB-82

Llewellyn, Richard 1906-1983.......DLB-15

Lloyd, Edward
  [publishing house] DLB-106

Lobel, Arnold 1933- DLB-61

Lochridge, Betsy Hopkins (see Fancher, Betsy)

Locke, David Ross 1833-1888....DLB-11, 23

Locke, John 1632-1704 ....DLB-31, 101

Locke, Richard Adams 1800-1871 ...DLB-43

Locker-Lampson, Frederick
  1821-1895 ....DLB-35

Lockhart, John Gibson
  1794-1854 ....DLB-110, 116 144

Lockridge, Ross, Jr.
  1914-1948 ....DLB-143; Y-80

Locrine and *Selimus*.................DLB-62

Lodge, David 1935- DLB-14

Lodge, George Cabot 1873-1909 ....DLB-54

Lodge, Henry Cabot 1850-1924 .....DLB-47

Lodge, Thomas 1558-1625 ....DLB-172

Loeb, Harold 1891-1974 ....DLB-4

Loeb, William 1905-1981..........DLB-127

Lofting, Hugh 1886-1947..........DLB-160

Logan, James 1674-1751 ....DLB-24, 140

Logan, John 1923- DLB-5

Logan, William 1950- DLB-120

Logau, Friedrich von 1605-1655....DLB-164

Logue, Christopher 1926- DLB-27

Lohenstein, Daniel Casper von
  1635-1683 ....DLB-168

Lomonosov, Mikhail Vasil'evich
  1711-1765 ....DLB-150

London, Jack 1876-1916 ......DLB-8, 12, 78

The London Magazine 1820-1829 .....DLB-110

Long, Haniel 1888-1956............DLB-45

Long, Ray 1878-1935.............DLB-137

Long, H., and Brother DLB-49

Longfellow, Henry Wadsworth
  1807-1882 ....DLB-1, 59

Longfellow, Samuel 1819-1892 ....DLB-1

Longford, Elizabeth 1906- DLB-155

Longinus circa first century........DLB-176

Longley, Michael 1939- DLB-40

Longman, T. [publishing house]....DLB-154

Longmans, Green and Company DLB-49

Longmore, George 1793?-1867......DLB-99

Longstreet, Augustus Baldwin
  1790-1870 ....DLB-3, 11, 74

Longworth, D. [publishing house] ...DLB-49

Lonsdale, Frederick 1881-1954 ......DLB-10

A Look at the Contemporary Black Theatre
  Movement....................DLB-38

Loos, Anita 1893-1981.....DLB-11, 26; Y-81

Lopate, Phillip 1943- Y-80

López, Diana (see Isabella, Ríos)

Loranger, Jean-Aubert 1896-1942....DLB-92

Lorca, Federico García 1898-1936 ..DLB-108

Lord, John Keast 1818-1872 ....DLB-99

The Lord Chamberlain's Office and Stage
  Censorship in England DLB-10

Lorde, Audre 1934-1992 ....DLB-41

Lorimer, George Horace
  1867-1939 ....DLB-91

Loring, A. K. [publishing house].....DLB-49

Loring and Mussey................DLB-46

Lossing, Benson J. 1813-1891 ....DLB-30

Lothar, Ernst 1890-1974 ....DLB-81

Lothrop, Harriet M. 1844-1924......DLB-42

Lothrop, D., and Company........DLB-49

Cumulative Index

Loti, Pierre 1850-1923 .... DLB-123

Lotichius Secundus, Petrus
  1528-1560 .... DLB-179

Lott, Emeline ?-? DLB-166

The Lounger, no. 20 (1785), by Henry
  Mackenzie DLB-39

Lounsbury, Thomas R. 1838-1915 ... DLB-71

Louÿs, Pierre 1870-1925 .... DLB-123

Lovelace, Earl 1935- DLB-125

Lovelace, Richard 1618-1657 ...... DLB-131

Lovell, Coryell and Company DLB-49

Lovell, John W., Company DLB-49

Lover, Samuel 1797-1868 .... DLB-159

Lovesey, Peter 1936- DLB-87

Lovingood, Sut (see Harris,
  George Washington)

Low, Samuel 1765-? DLB-37

Lowell, Amy 1874-1925 .... DLB-54, 140

Lowell, James Russell
  1819-1891 .... DLB-1, 11, 64, 79

Lowell, Robert 1917-1977 ...... DLB-5, 169

Lowenfels, Walter 1897-1976 .... DLB-4

Lowndes, Marie Belloc 1868-1947 ... DLB-70

Lownes, Humphrey
  [publishing house] DLB-170

Lowry, Lois 1937- DLB-52

Lowry, Malcolm 1909-1957 .... DLB-15

Lowther, Pat 1935-1975 .... DLB-53

Loy, Mina 1882-1966 .... DLB-4, 54

Lozeau, Albert 1878-1924 .... DLB-92

Lubbock, Percy 1879-1965 .... DLB-149

Lucas, E. V. 1868-1938 .... DLB-98, 149, 153

Lucas, Fielding, Jr.
  [publishing house] DLB-49

Luce, Henry R. 1898-1967 .... DLB-91

Luce, John W., and Company DLB-46

Lucian circa 120-180 .... DLB-176

Lucie-Smith, Edward 1933- DLB-40

Lucini, Gian Pietro 1867-1914 .... DLB-114

Luder, Peter circa 1415-1472 ..... DLB-179

Ludlum, Robert 1927- Y-82

Ludus de Antichristo circa 1160 ..... DLB-148

Ludvigson, Susan 1942- DLB-120

Ludwig, Jack 1922- DLB-60

Ludwig, Otto 1813-1865 .... DLB-129

Ludwigslied 881 or 882 .... DLB-148

Luera, Yolanda 1953- DLB-122

Luft, Lya 1938- DLB-145

Luke, Peter 1919- DLB-13

Lupton, F. M., Company DLB-49

Lupus of Ferrières
  circa 805-circa 862 .... DLB-148

Lurie, Alison 1926- DLB-2

Luther, Martin 1483-1546 .... DLB-179

Luzi, Mario 1914- DLB-128

L'vov, Nikolai Aleksandrovich
  1751-1803 .... DLB-150

Lyall, Gavin 1932- DLB-87

Lydgate, John circa 1370-1450 .... DLB-146

Lyly, John circa 1554-1606 .... DLB-62, 167

Lynch, Patricia 1898-1972 .... DLB-160

Lynch, Richard
  flourished 1596-1601 .... DLB-172

Lynd, Robert 1879-1949 .... DLB-98

Lyon, Matthew 1749-1822 .... DLB-43

Lysias circa 459 B.C.-circa 380 B.C.
  .... DLB-176

Lytle, Andrew 1902-1995 ...... DLB-6; Y-95

Lytton, Edward (see Bulwer-Lytton, Edward)

Lytton, Edward Robert Bulwer
  1831-1891 .... DLB-32

M

Maass, Joachim 1901-1972 .... DLB-69

Mabie, Hamilton Wright
  1845-1916 .... DLB-71

Mac A'Ghobhainn, Iain (see Smith, Iain
  Crichton)

MacArthur, Charles
  1895-1956 .... DLB-7, 25, 44

Macaulay, Catherine 1731-1791 .... DLB-104

Macaulay, David 1945- DLB-61

Macaulay, Rose 1881-1958 .... DLB-36

Macaulay, Thomas Babington
  1800-1859 .... DLB-32, 55

Macaulay Company DLB-46

MacBeth, George 1932- DLB-40

Macbeth, Madge 1880-1965 .... DLB-92

MacCaig, Norman 1910- DLB-27

MacDiarmid, Hugh 1892-1978 .... DLB-20

MacDonald, Cynthia 1928- DLB-105

MacDonald, George
  1824-1905 .... DLB-18, 163, 178

MacDonald, John D.
  1916-1986 .... DLB-8; Y-86

MacDonald, Philip 1899?-1980 ..... DLB-77

Macdonald, Ross (see Millar, Kenneth)

MacDonald, Wilson 1880-1967 ...... DLB-92

Macdonald and Company
  (Publishers) DLB-112

MacEwen, Gwendolyn 1941- DLB-53

Macfadden, Bernarr
  1868-1955 .... DLB-25, 91

MacGregor, John 1825-1892 .... DLB-166

MacGregor, Mary Esther (see Keith, Marian)

Machado, Antonio 1875-1939 .... DLB-108

Machado, Manuel 1874-1947 .... DLB-108

Machar, Agnes Maule 1837-1927 .... DLB-92

Machen, Arthur Llewelyn Jones
  1863-1947 .... DLB-36, 156, 178

MacInnes, Colin 1914-1976 .... DLB-14

MacInnes, Helen 1907-1985 .... DLB-87

Mack, Maynard 1909- DLB-111

Mackall, Leonard L. 1879-1937 .... DLB-140

MacKaye, Percy 1875-1956 .... DLB-54

Macken, Walter 1915-1967 .... DLB-13

Mackenzie, Alexander 1763-1820 ... DLB-99

Mackenzie, Compton
  1883-1972 .... DLB-34, 100

Mackenzie, Henry 1745-1831 .... DLB-39

Mackey, Nathaniel 1947- DLB-169

Mackey, William Wellington
  1937- DLB-38

Mackintosh, Elizabeth (see Tey, Josephine)

Mackintosh, Sir James
  1765-1832 .... DLB-158

Maclaren, Ian (see Watson, John)

Macklin, Charles 1699-1797 .... DLB-89

MacLean, Katherine Anne 1925- DLB-8

MacLeish, Archibald
  1892-1982 .... DLB-4, 7, 45; Y-82

MacLennan, Hugh 1907-1990 .... DLB-68

Macleod, Fiona (see Sharp, William)

MacLeod, Alistair 1936- DLB-60

Macleod, Norman 1906-1985 .... DLB-4

Macmillan and Company DLB-106

The Macmillan Company DLB-49

Macmillan's English Men of Letters,
  First Series (1878-1892) DLB-144

MacNamara, Brinsley 1890-1963 .... DLB-10

MacNeice, Louis 1907-1963 ..... DLB-10, 20

MacPhail, Andrew 1864-1938 .... DLB-92

Macpherson, James 1736-1796 ..... DLB-109

Macpherson, Jay 1931- DLB-53

Macpherson, Jeanie 1884-1946 ...... DLB-44

Macrae Smith Company DLB-46

Macrone, John
[publishing house] DLB-106

MacShane, Frank 1927- DLB-111

Macy-Masius DLB-46

Madden, David 1933- DLB-6

Maddow, Ben 1909-1992 .... DLB-44

Maddux, Rachel 1912-1983 .... Y-93

Madgett, Naomi Long 1923- DLB-76

Madhubuti, Haki R.
1942- DLB-5, 41; DS-8

Madison, James 1751-1836 .... DLB-37

Maginn, William 1794-1842 ... DLB-110, 159

Mahan, Alfred Thayer 1840-1914 .... DLB-47

Maheux-Forcier, Louise 1929- DLB-60

Mahin, John Lee 1902-1984 .... DLB-44

Mahon, Derek 1941- DLB-40

Maikov, Vasilii Ivanovich
1728-1778 .... DLB-150

Mailer, Norman
1923- DLB-2, 16, 28; Y-80, 83; DS-3

Maillet, Adrienne 1885-1963 .... DLB-68

Maimonides, Moses 1138-1204 ..... DLB-115

Maillet, Antonine 1929- DLB-60

Maillu, David G. 1939- DLB-157

Main Selections of the Book-of-the-Month
Club, 1926-1945 .... DLB-9

Main Trends in Twentieth-Century
Book Clubs DLB-46

Mainwaring, Daniel 1902-1977 ...... DLB-44

Mair, Charles 1838-1927 .... DLB-99

Mais, Roger 1905-1955 .... DLB-125

Major, Andre 1942- DLB-60

Major, Clarence 1936- DLB-33

Major, Kevin 1949- DLB-60

Major Books DLB-46

Makemie, Francis circa 1658-1708 ... DLB-24

The Making of a People, by
J. M. Ritchie DLB-66

Maksimović, Desanka 1898-1993 ... DLB-147

Malamud, Bernard
1914-1986 ..... DLB-2, 28, 152; Y-80, 86

Malet, Lucas 1852-1931 .... DLB-153

Malleson, Lucy Beatrice (see Gilbert, Anthony)

Mallet-Joris, Françoise 1930- DLB-83

Mallock, W. H. 1849-1923 ...... DLB-18, 57

Malone, Dumas 1892-1986 .... DLB-17

Malone, Edmond 1741-1812 .... DLB-142

Malory, Sir Thomas
circa 1400-1410 - 1471 .... DLB-146

Malraux, André 1901-1976 .... DLB-72

Malthus, Thomas Robert
1766-1834 .... DLB-107, 158

Maltz, Albert 1908-1985 .... DLB-102

Malzberg, Barry N. 1939- DLB-8

Mamet, David 1947- DLB-7

Manaka, Matsemela 1956- DLB-157

Manchester University Press DLB-112

Mandel, Eli 1922- DLB-53

Mandeville, Bernard 1670-1733 .... DLB-101

Mandeville, Sir John
mid fourteenth century DLB-146

Mandiargues, André Pieyre de
1909- DLB-83

Manfred, Frederick 1912-1994 ..... DLB-6

Mangan, Sherry 1904-1961 .... DLB-4

Mankiewicz, Herman 1897-1953 ..... DLB-26

Mankiewicz, Joseph L. 1909-1993 ... DLB-44

Mankowitz, Wolf 1924- DLB-15

Manley, Delarivière
1672?-1724 .... DLB-39, 80

Mann, Abby 1927- DLB-44

Mann, Heinrich 1871-1950 ..... DLB-66, 118

Mann, Horace 1796-1859 .... DLB-1

Mann, Klaus 1906-1949 .... DLB-56

Mann, Thomas 1875-1955 .... DLB-66

Mann, William D'Alton
1839-1920 .... DLB-137

Manning, Marie 1873?-1945 .... DLB-29

Manning and Loring DLB-49

Mannyng, Robert
flourished 1303-1338 .... DLB-146

Mano, D. Keith 1942- DLB-6

Manor Books DLB-46

Mansfield, Katherine 1888-1923 .... DLB-162

Manuel, Niklaus circa 1484-1530 ... DLB-179

Manzini, Gianna 1896-1974 .... DLB-177

Mapanje, Jack 1944- DLB-157

March, William 1893-1954 .... DLB-9, 86

Marchand, Leslie A. 1900- DLB-103

Marchant, Bessie 1862-1941 .... DLB-160

Marchessault, Jovette 1938- DLB-60

Marcus, Frank 1928- DLB-13

Marden, Orison Swett
1850-1924 .... DLB-137

Marechera, Dambudzo
1952-1987 .... DLB-157

Marek, Richard, Books DLB-46

Mares, E. A. 1938- DLB-122

Mariani, Paul 1940- DLB-111

Marie-Victorin, Frère 1885-1944 ..... DLB-92

Marin, Biagio 1891-1985 .... DLB-128

Marincović, Ranko 1913- DLB-147

Marinetti, Filippo Tommaso
1876-1944 .... DLB-114

Marion, Frances 1886-1973 .... DLB-44

Marius, Richard C. 1933- Y-85

The Mark Taper Forum DLB-7

Mark Twain on Perpetual Copyright ... Y-92

Markfield, Wallace 1926- DLB-2, 28

Markham, Edwin 1852-1940 .... DLB-54

Markle, Fletcher 1921-1991 .... DLB-68; Y-91

Marlatt, Daphne 1942- DLB-60

Marlitt, E. 1825-1887 .... DLB-129

Marlowe, Christopher 1564-1593 .... DLB-62

Marlyn, John 1912- DLB-88

Marmion, Shakerley 1603-1639 ..... DLB-58

Der Marner
before 1230-circa 1287 .... DLB-138

The *Marprelate* Tracts 1588-1589 .... DLB-132

Marquand, John P. 1893-1960 ... DLB-9, 102

Marqués, René 1919-1979 .... DLB-113

Marquis, Don 1878-1937 .... DLB-11, 25

Marriott, Anne 1913- DLB-68

Marryat, Frederick 1792-1848 .. DLB-21, 163

Marsh, George Perkins
1801-1882 .... DLB-1, 64

Marsh, James 1794-1842 .... DLB-1, 59

Marsh, Capen, Lyon and Webb DLB-49

Marsh, Ngaio 1899-1982 .... DLB-77

Marshall, Edison 1894-1967 .... DLB-102

Marshall, Edward 1932- DLB-16

Marshall, Emma 1828-1899 .... DLB-163

Marshall, James 1942-1992 .... DLB-61

Marshall, Joyce 1913- DLB-88

397

Marshall, Paule 1929- DLB-33, 157

Marshall, Tom 1938- DLB-60

Marsilius of Padua
  circa 1275-circa 1342 .... DLB-115

Marson, Una 1905-1965 .... DLB-157

Marston, John 1576-1634 ...... DLB-58, 172

Marston, Philip Bourke 1850-1887 ... DLB-35

Martens, Kurt 1870-1945 .... DLB-66

Martien, William S.
  [publishing house] DLB-49

Martin, Abe (see Hubbard, Kin)

Martin, Charles 1942- DLB-120

Martin, Claire 1914- DLB-60

Martin, Jay 1935- DLB-111

Martin, Johann (see Laurentius von Schnüffis)

Martin, Violet Florence (see Ross, Martin)

Martin du Gard, Roger 1881-1958 ... DLB-65

Martineau, Harriet
  1802-1876 .... DLB-21, 55, 159, 163, 166

Martínez, Eliud 1935- DLB-122

Martínez, Max 1943- DLB-82

Martyn, Edward 1859-1923 .... DLB-10

Marvell, Andrew 1621-1678 .... DLB-131

Marvin X 1944- DLB-38

Marx, Karl 1818-1883 .... DLB-129

Marzials, Theo 1850-1920 .... DLB-35

Masefield, John
  1878-1967 .... DLB-10, 19, 153, 160

Mason, A. E. W. 1865-1948 .... DLB-70

Mason, Bobbie Ann
  1940- DLB-173; Y-87

Mason, William 1725-1797 .... DLB-142

Mason Brothers DLB-49

Massey, Gerald 1828-1907 .... DLB-32

Massinger, Philip 1583-1640 ...... DLB-58

Masson, David 1822-1907 .... DLB-144

Masters, Edgar Lee 1868-1950 ..... DLB-54

Mastronardi, Lucio 1930-1979 .... DLB-177

Mather, Cotton
  1663-1728 .... DLB-24, 30, 140

Mather, Increase 1639-1723 .... DLB-24

Mather, Richard 1596-1669 .... DLB-24

Matheson, Richard 1926- DLB-8, 44

Matheus, John F. 1887- DLB-51

Mathews, Cornelius
  1817?-1889 .... DLB-3, 64

Mathews, John Joseph
  1894-1979 .... DLB-175

Mathews, Elkin
  [publishing house] DLB-112

Mathias, Roland 1915- DLB-27

Mathis, June 1892-1927 .... DLB-44

Mathis, Sharon Bell 1937- DLB-33

Matoš, Antun Gustav 1873-1914 ... DLB-147

The Matter of England
  1240-1400 .... DLB-146

The Matter of Rome
  early twelfth to late fifteenth
  century DLB-146

Matthews, Brander
  1852-1929 .... DLB-71, 78; DS-13

Matthews, Jack 1925- DLB-6

Matthews, William 1942- DLB-5

Matthiessen, F. O. 1902-1950 .... DLB-63

Maturin, Charles Robert
  1780-1824 .... DLB-178

Matthiessen, Peter 1927- DLB-6, 173

Maugham, W. Somerset
  1874-1965 ..... DLB-10, 36, 77, 100, 162

Maupassant, Guy de 1850-1893 .... DLB-123

Mauriac, Claude 1914- DLB-83

Mauriac, François 1885-1970 .... DLB-65

Maurice, Frederick Denison
  1805-1872 .... DLB-55

Maurois, André 1885-1967 .... DLB-65

Maury, James 1718-1769 .... DLB-31

Mavor, Elizabeth 1927- DLB-14

Mavor, Osborne Henry (see Bridie, James)

Maxwell, William 1908- Y-80

Maxwell, H. [publishing house] DLB-49

Maxwell, John [publishing house] ... DLB-106

May, Elaine 1932- DLB-44

May, Karl 1842-1912 .... DLB-129

May, Thomas 1595 or 1596-1650 .... DLB-58

Mayer, Bernadette 1945- DLB-165

Mayer, Mercer 1943- DLB-61

Mayer, O. B. 1818-1891 .... DLB-3

Mayes, Herbert R. 1900-1987 ...... DLB-137

Mayes, Wendell 1919-1992 .... DLB-26

Mayfield, Julian 1928-1984 ... DLB-33; Y-84

Mayhew, Henry 1812-1887 ...... DLB-18, 55

Mayhew, Jonathan 1720-1766 ...... DLB-31

Mayne, Jasper 1604-1672 .... DLB-126

Mayne, Seymour 1944- DLB-60

Mayor, Flora Macdonald
  1872-1932 .... DLB-36

Mayrocker, Friederike 1924- DLB-85

Mazrui, Ali A. 1933- DLB-125

Mažuranić, Ivan 1814-1890 .... DLB-147

Mazursky, Paul 1930- DLB-44

McAlmon, Robert 1896-1956 ..... DLB-4, 45

McArthur, Peter 1866-1924 .... DLB-92

McBride, Robert M., and
  Company DLB-46

McCaffrey, Anne 1926- DLB-8

McCarthy, Cormac 1933- DLB-6, 143

McCarthy, Mary 1912-1989 .... DLB-2; Y-81

McCay, Winsor 1871-1934 .... DLB-22

McClane, Albert Jules 1922-1991 ... DLB-171

McClatchy, C. K. 1858-1936 .... DLB-25

McClellan, George Marion
  1860-1934 .... DLB-50

McCloskey, Robert 1914- DLB-22

McClung, Nellie Letitia 1873-1951 ... DLB-92

McClure, Joanna 1930- DLB-16

McClure, Michael 1932- DLB-16

McClure, Phillips and Company DLB-46

McClure, S. S. 1857-1949 .... DLB-91

McClurg, A. C., and Company DLB-49

McCluskey, John A., Jr. 1944- DLB-33

McCollum, Michael A. 1946 .... Y-87

McConnell, William C. 1917- DLB-88

McCord, David 1897- DLB-61

McCorkle, Jill 1958- Y-87

McCorkle, Samuel Eusebius
  1746-1811 .... DLB-37

McCormick, Anne O'Hare
  1880-1954 .... DLB-29

McCormick, Robert R. 1880-1955 ... DLB-29

McCourt, Edward 1907-1972 .... DLB-88

McCoy, Horace 1897-1955 .... DLB-9

McCrae, John 1872-1918 .... DLB-92

McCullagh, Joseph B. 1842-1896 .... DLB-23

McCullers, Carson
  1917-1967 .... DLB-2, 7, 173

McCulloch, Thomas 1776-1843 ..... DLB-99

McDonald, Forrest 1927- DLB-17

McDonald, Walter
  1934- DLB-105, DS-9

McDonald, Walter, Getting Started: Accepting the Regions You Own— or Which Own You DLB-105

McDougall, Colin 1917-1984 .... DLB-68

McDowell, Obolensky DLB-46

McEwan, Ian 1948- DLB-14

McFadden, David 1940- DLB-60

McFall, Frances Elizabeth Clarke (see Grand, Sarah)

McFarlane, Leslie 1902-1977 .... DLB-88

McFee, William 1881-1966 .... DLB-153

McGahern, John 1934- DLB-14

McGee, Thomas D'Arcy 1825-1868 .... DLB-99

McGeehan, W. O. 1879-1933 ... DLB-25, 171

McGill, Ralph 1898-1969 .... DLB-29

McGinley, Phyllis 1905-1978 .... DLB-11, 48

McGirt, James E. 1874-1930 .... DLB-50

McGlashan and Gill DLB-106

McGough, Roger 1937- DLB-40

McGraw-Hill DLB-46

McGuane, Thomas 1939- DLB-2; Y-80

McGuckian, Medbh 1950- DLB-40

McGuffey, William Holmes 1800-1873 .... DLB-42

McIlvanney, William 1936- DLB-14

McIlwraith, Jean Newton 1859-1938 .... DLB-92

McIntyre, James 1827-1906 .... DLB-99

McIntyre, O. O. 1884-1938 .... DLB-25

McKay, Claude 1889-1948 .... DLB-4, 45, 51, 117

The David McKay Company DLB-49

McKean, William V. 1820-1903 ..... DLB-23

The McKenzie Trust Y-96

McKinley, Robin 1952- DLB-52

McLachlan, Alexander 1818-1896 ... DLB-99

McLaren, Floris Clark 1904-1978 .... DLB-68

McLaverty, Michael 1907- DLB-15

McLean, John R. 1848-1916 .... DLB-23

McLean, William L. 1852-1931 ...... DLB-25

McLennan, William 1856-1904 ...... DLB-92

McLoughlin Brothers DLB-49

McLuhan, Marshall 1911-1980 ...... DLB-88

McMaster, John Bach 1852-1932 .... DLB-47

McMurtry, Larry 1936- DLB-2, 143; Y-80, 87

McNally, Terrence 1939- DLB-7

McNeil, Florence 1937- DLB-60

McNeile, Herman Cyril 1888-1937 .... DLB-77

McNickle, D'Arcy 1904-1977 ...... DLB-175

McPherson, James Alan 1943- DLB-38

McPherson, Sandra 1943- Y-86

McWhirter, George 1939- DLB-60

McWilliams, Carey 1905-1980 ..... DLB-137

Mead, L. T. 1844-1914 .... DLB-141

Mead, Matthew 1924- DLB-40

Mead, Taylor ?- DLB-16

Meany, Tom 1903-1964 .... DLB-171

Mechthild von Magdeburg circa 1207-circa 1282 .... DLB-138

Medill, Joseph 1823-1899 .... DLB-43

Medoff, Mark 1940- DLB-7

Meek, Alexander Beaufort 1814-1865 .... DLB-3

Meeke, Mary ?-1816? DLB-116

Meinke, Peter 1932- DLB-5

Mejia Vallejo, Manuel 1923- DLB-113

Melanchthon, Philipp 1497-1560 ... DLB-179

Melançon, Robert 1947- DLB-60

Mell, Max 1882-1971 .... DLB-81, 124

Mellow, James R. 1926- DLB-111

Meltzer, David 1937- DLB-16

Meltzer, Milton 1915- DLB-61

Melville, Elizabeth, Lady Culross circa 1585-1640 .... DLB-172

Melville, Herman 1819-1891 ...... DLB-3, 74

Memoirs of Life and Literature (1920), by W. H. Mallock [excerpt] DLB-57

Menander 342-341 B.C.-circa 292-291 B.C. DLB-176

Menantes (see Hunold, Christian Friedrich)

Mencke, Johann Burckhard 1674-1732 .... DLB-168

Mencken, H. L. 1880-1956 .... DLB-11, 29, 63, 137

Mencken and Nietzsche: An Unpublished Excerpt from H. L. Mencken's *My Life as Author and Editor* Y-93

Mendelssohn, Moses 1729-1786 ..... DLB-97

Méndez M., Miguel 1930- DLB-82

The Mercantile Library of New York Y-96

Mercer, Cecil William (see Yates, Dornford)

Mercer, David 1928-1980 .... DLB-13

Mercer, John 1704-1768 .... DLB-31

Meredith, George 1828-1909 .... DLB-18, 35, 57, 159

Meredith, Louisa Anne 1812-1895 .... DLB-166

Meredith, Owen (see Lytton, Edward Robert Bulwer)

Meredith, William 1919- DLB-5

Mergerle, Johann Ulrich (see Abraham ä Sancta Clara)

Mérimée, Prosper 1803-1870 .... DLB-119

Merivale, John Herman 1779-1844 .... DLB-96

Meriwether, Louise 1923- DLB-33

Merlin Press DLB-112

Merriam, Eve 1916-1992 .... DLB-61

The Merriam Company DLB-49

Merrill, James 1926-1995 .... DLB-5, 165; Y-85

Merrill and Baker DLB-49

The Mershon Company DLB-49

Merton, Thomas 1915-1968 ... DLB-48; Y-81

Merwin, W. S. 1927- DLB-5, 169

Messner, Julian [publishing house] ... DLB-46

Metcalf, J. [publishing house] DLB-49

Metcalf, John 1938- DLB-60

The Methodist Book Concern DLB-49

Methuen and Company DLB-112

Mew, Charlotte 1869-1928 ..... DLB-19, 135

Mewshaw, Michael 1943- Y-80

Meyer, Conrad Ferdinand 1825-1898 .... DLB-129

Meyer, E. Y. 1946- DLB-75

Meyer, Eugene 1875-1959 .... DLB-29

Meyer, Michael 1921- DLB-155

Meyers, Jeffrey 1939- DLB-111

Meynell, Alice 1847-1922 .... DLB-19, 98

Meynell, Viola 1885-1956 .... DLB-153

Meyrink, Gustav 1868-1932 .... DLB-81

Michaels, Leonard 1933- DLB-130

Micheaux, Oscar 1884-1951 .... DLB-50

Michel of Northgate, Dan circa 1265-circa 1340 .... DLB-146

Micheline, Jack 1929- DLB-16

Michener, James A. 1907?- DLB-6

Micklejohn, George circa 1717-1818 .... DLB-31

Middle English Literature: An Introduction DLB-146

The Middle English Lyric DLB-146

Middle Hill Press DLB-106

Middleton, Christopher 1926- DLB-40

Middleton, Richard 1882-1911 .... DLB-156

Middleton, Stanley 1919- DLB-14

Middleton, Thomas 1580-1627 .... DLB-58

Miegel, Agnes 1879-1964 .... DLB-56

Miles, Josephine 1911-1985 .... DLB-48

Milius, John 1944- DLB-44

Mill, James 1773-1836 .... DLB-107, 158

Mill, John Stuart 1806-1873 .... DLB-55

Millar, Kenneth 1915-1983 .... DLB-2; Y-83; DS-6

Millar, Andrew [publishing house] DLB-154

Millay, Edna St. Vincent 1892-1950 .... DLB-45

Miller, Arthur 1915- DLB-7

Miller, Caroline 1903-1992 .... DLB-9

Miller, Eugene Ethelbert 1950- DLB-41

Miller, Heather Ross 1939- DLB-120

Miller, Henry 1891-1980 .... DLB-4, 9; Y-80

Miller, J. Hillis 1928- DLB-67

Miller, James [publishing house] DLB-49

Miller, Jason 1939- DLB-7

Miller, May 1899- DLB-41

Miller, Paul 1906-1991 .... DLB-127

Miller, Perry 1905-1963 .... DLB-17, 63

Miller, Sue 1943- DLB-143

Miller, Vassar 1924- DLB-105

Miller, Walter M., Jr. 1923- DLB-8

Miller, Webb 1892-1940 .... DLB-29

Millhauser, Steven 1943- DLB-2

Millican, Arthenia J. Bates 1920- DLB-38

Mills and Boon DLB-112

Milman, Henry Hart 1796-1868 .... DLB-96

Milne, A. A. 1882-1956 .... DLB-10, 77, 100, 160

Milner, Ron 1938- DLB-38

Milner, William [publishing house] DLB-106

Milnes, Richard Monckton (Lord Houghton) 1809-1885 .... DLB-32

Milton, John 1608-1674 .... DLB-131, 151

The Minerva Press DLB-154

Minnesang circa 1150-1280 .... DLB-138

Minns, Susan 1839-1938 .... DLB-140

Minor Illustrators, 1880-1914 .... DLB-141

Minor Poets of the Earlier Seventeenth Century DLB-121

Minton, Balch and Company DLB-46

Mirbeau, Octave 1848-1917 .... DLB-123

Mirk, John died after 1414? DLB-146

Miron, Gaston 1928- DLB-60

A Mirror for Magistrates DLB-167

Mitchel, Jonathan 1624-1668 .... DLB-24

Mitchell, Adrian 1932- DLB-40

Mitchell, Donald Grant 1822-1908 .... DLB-1; DS-13

Mitchell, Gladys 1901-1983 .... DLB-77

Mitchell, James Leslie 1901-1935 .... DLB-15

Mitchell, John (see Slater, Patrick)

Mitchell, John Ames 1845-1918 .... DLB-79

Mitchell, Joseph 1908-1996 .... Y-96

Mitchell, Julian 1935- DLB-14

Mitchell, Ken 1940- DLB-60

Mitchell, Langdon 1862-1935 .... DLB-7

Mitchell, Loften 1919- DLB-38

Mitchell, Margaret 1900-1949 .... DLB-9

Mitchell, W. O. 1914- DLB-88

Mitchison, Naomi Margaret (Haldane) 1897- DLB-160

Mitford, Mary Russell 1787-1855 .... DLB-110, 116

Mittelholzer, Edgar 1909-1965 .... DLB-117

Mitterer, Erika 1906- DLB-85

Mitterer, Felix 1948- DLB-124

Mitternacht, Johann Sebastian 1613-1679 .... DLB-168

Mizener, Arthur 1907-1988 .... DLB-103

Modern Age Books DLB-46

"Modern English Prose" (1876), by George Saintsbury DLB-57

The Modern Language Association of America Celebrates Its Centennial Y-84

The Modern Library DLB-46

"Modern Novelists – Great and Small" (1855), by Margaret Oliphant DLB-21

"Modern Style" (1857), by Cockburn Thomson [excerpt] DLB-57

The Modernists (1932), by Joseph Warren Beach DLB-36

Modiano, Patrick 1945- DLB-83

Moffat, Yard and Company DLB-46

Moffet, Thomas 1553-1604 .... DLB-136

Mohr, Nicholasa 1938- DLB-145

Moix, Ana María 1947- DLB-134

Molesworth, Louisa 1839-1921 .... DLB-135

Möllhausen, Balduin 1825-1905 .... DLB-129

Momaday, N. Scott 1934- DLB-143, 175

Monkhouse, Allan 1858-1936 .... DLB-10

Monro, Harold 1879-1932 .... DLB-19

Monroe, Harriet 1860-1936 .... DLB-54, 91

Monsarrat, Nicholas 1910-1979 .... DLB-15

Montagu, Lady Mary Wortley 1689-1762 .... DLB-95, 101

Montague, John 1929- DLB-40

Montale, Eugenio 1896-1981 .... DLB-114

Monterroso, Augusto 1921- DLB-145

Montgomerie, Alexander circa 1550?-1598 .... DLB-167

Montgomery, James 1771-1854 .... DLB-93, 158

Montgomery, John 1919- DLB-16

Montgomery, Lucy Maud 1874-1942 .... DLB-92; DS-14

Montgomery, Marion 1925- DLB-6

Montgomery, Robert Bruce (see Crispin, Edmund)

Montherlant, Henry de 1896-1972 .... DLB-72

The Monthly Review 1749-1844 .... DLB-110

Montigny, Louvigny de 1876-1955 .... DLB-92

Montoya, José 1932- DLB-122

Moodie, John Wedderburn Dunbar 1797-1869 .... DLB-99

Moodie, Susanna 1803-1885 .... DLB-99

Moody, Joshua circa 1633-1697 .... DLB-24

Moody, William Vaughn 1869-1910 .... DLB-7, 54

Moorcock, Michael 1939- DLB-14

Moore, Catherine L. 1911- DLB-8

Moore, Clement Clarke 1779-1863 .... DLB-42

Moore, Dora Mavor 1888-1979 .... DLB-92

Moore, George 1852-1933 .... DLB-10, 18, 57, 135

Moore, Marianne 1887-1972 . . . . DLB-45; DS-7

Moore, Mavor 1919- DLB-88

Moore, Richard 1927- DLB-105

Moore, Richard, The No Self, the Little Self, and the Poets DLB-105

Moore, T. Sturge 1870-1944 . . . . DLB-19

Moore, Thomas 1779-1852 . . . . . DLB-96, 144

Moore, Ward 1903-1978 . . . . DLB-8

Moore, Wilstach, Keys and Company. DLB-49

The Moorland-Spingarn Research Center DLB-76

Moorman, Mary C. 1905-1994 . . . . . DLB-155

Moraga, Cherríe 1952- DLB-82

Morales, Alejandro 1944- DLB-82

Morales, Mario Roberto 1947- . . . DLB-145

Morales, Rafael 1919- DLB-108

Morality Plays: *Mankind* circa 1450-1500 and *Everyman* circa 1500 . . . . DLB-146

Morante, Elsa 1912-1985 . . . . DLB-177

Morata, Olympia Fulvia 1526-1555 . . . . DLB-179

Moravia, Alberto 1907-1990 . . . . DLB-177

Mordaunt, Elinor 1872-1942 . . . . DLB-174

More, Hannah 1745-1833 . . . . DLB-107, 109, 116, 158

More, Henry 1614-1687 . . . . DLB-126

More, Sir Thomas 1477 or 1478-1535 . . . . DLB-136

Moreno, Dorinda 1939- DLB-122

Morency, Pierre 1942- DLB-60

Moretti, Marino 1885-1979 . . . . DLB-114

Morgan, Berry 1919- DLB-6

Morgan, Charles 1894-1958 . . . . DLB-34, 100

Morgan, Edmund S. 1916- DLB-17

Morgan, Edwin 1920- DLB-27

Morgan, John Pierpont 1837-1913 . . . . DLB-140

Morgan, John Pierpont, Jr. 1867-1943 . . . . DLB-140

Morgan, Robert 1944- DLB-120

Morgan, Sydney Owenson, Lady 1776?-1859 . . . . DLB-116, 158

Morgner, Irmtraud 1933- DLB-75

Morhof, Daniel Georg 1639-1691 . . . . DLB-164

Morier, James Justinian 1782 or 1783?-1849 . . . . DLB-116

Mörike, Eduard 1804-1875 . . . . DLB-133

Morin, Paul 1889-1963 . . . . DLB-92

Morison, Richard 1514?-1556 . . . . . . DLB-136

Morison, Samuel Eliot 1887-1976 . . . . DLB-17

Moritz, Karl Philipp 1756-1793 . . . . . DLB-94

Moriz von Craûn circa 1220-1230 . . . . DLB-138

Morley, Christopher 1890-1957 . . . . . DLB-9

Morley, John 1838-1923 . . . . DLB-57, 144

Morris, George Pope 1802-1864 . . . . DLB-73

Morris, Lewis 1833-1907 . . . . DLB-35

Morris, Richard B. 1904-1989 . . . . . . DLB-17

Morris, William 1834-1896 . . . . . DLB-18, 35, 57, 156, 178

Morris, Willie 1934- Y-80

Morris, Wright 1910- DLB-2; Y-81

Morrison, Arthur 1863-1945 . . . . DLB-70, 135

Morrison, Charles Clayton 1874-1966 . . . . DLB-91

Morrison, Toni 1931- DLB-6, 33, 143; Y-81

Morrow, William, and Company DLB-46

Morse, James Herbert 1841-1923 . . . . DLB-71

Morse, Jedidiah 1761-1826 . . . . DLB-37

Morse, John T., Jr. 1840-1937 . . . . DLB-47

Morselli, Guido 1912-1973 . . . . DLB-177

Mortimer, Favell Lee 1802-1878 . . . . DLB-163

Mortimer, John 1923- DLB-13

Morton, Carlos 1942- DLB-122

Morton, John P., and Company DLB-49

Morton, Nathaniel 1613-1685 . . . . . . DLB-24

Morton, Sarah Wentworth 1759-1846 . . . . DLB-37

Morton, Thomas circa 1579-circa 1647 . . . . DLB-24

Moscherosch, Johann Michael 1601-1669 . . . . DLB-164

Moseley, Humphrey [publishing house] DLB-170

Möser, Justus 1720-1794 . . . . DLB-97

Mosley, Nicholas 1923- DLB-14

Moss, Arthur 1889-1969 . . . . DLB-4

Moss, Howard 1922-1987 . . . . DLB-5

Moss, Thylias 1954- DLB-120

The Most Powerful Book Review in America [*New York Times Book Review*] Y-82

Motion, Andrew 1952- DLB-40

Motley, John Lothrop 1814-1877 . . . . DLB-1, 30, 59

Motley, Willard 1909-1965 . . . . . DLB-76, 143

Motte, Benjamin Jr. [publishing house] DLB-154

Motteux, Peter Anthony 1663-1718 . . . . DLB-80

Mottram, R. H. 1883-1971 . . . . DLB-36

Mouré, Erin 1955- DLB-60

Mourning Dove (Humishuma) between 1882 and 1888?-1936 . . . . DLB-175

Movies from Books, 1920-1974 . . . . . . DLB-9

Mowat, Farley 1921- DLB-68

Mowbray, A. R., and Company, Limited DLB-106

Mowrer, Edgar Ansel 1892-1977 . . . . DLB-29

Mowrer, Paul Scott 1887-1971 . . . . . . DLB-29

Moxon, Edward [publishing house] DLB-106

Moxon, Joseph [publishing house] DLB-170

Mphahlele, Es'kia (Ezekiel) 1919- DLB-125

Mtshali, Oswald Mbuyiseni 1940- DLB-125

Mucedorus DLB-62

Mudford, William 1782-1848 . . . . . . DLB-159

Mueller, Lisel 1924- DLB-105

Muhajir, El (see Marvin X)

Muhajir, Nazzam Al Fitnah (see Marvin X)

Mühlbach, Luise 1814-1873 . . . . DLB-133

Muir, Edwin 1887-1959 . . . . DLB-20, 100

Muir, Helen 1937- DLB-14

Mukherjee, Bharati 1940- DLB-60

Mulcaster, Richard 1531 or 1532-1611 . . . . DLB-167

Muldoon, Paul 1951- DLB-40

Müller, Friedrich (see Müller, Maler)

Müller, Heiner 1929- DLB-124

Müller, Maler 1749-1825 . . . . DLB-94

Müller, Wilhelm 1794-1827 . . . . DLB-90

Mumford, Lewis 1895-1990 . . . . DLB-63

Munby, Arthur Joseph 1828-1910 . . . . DLB-35

Munday, Anthony 1560-1633 . . . DLB-62, 172

Mundt, Clara (see Mühlbach, Luise)

Mundt, Theodore 1808-1861 . . . . DLB-133

Munford, Robert circa 1737-1783 . . . . DLB-31

Mungoshi, Charles 1947- DLB-157

Munonye, John 1929- DLB-117

Munro, Alice 1931- DLB-53

Munro, H. H. 1870-1916....... DLB-34, 162

Munro, Neil 1864-1930 .... DLB-156

Munro, George
 [publishing house] DLB-49

Munro, Norman L.
 [publishing house] DLB-49

Munroe, James, and Company DLB-49

Munroe, Kirk 1850-1930 .... DLB-42

Munroe and Francis DLB-49

Munsell, Joel [publishing house] DLB-49

Munsey, Frank A. 1854-1925 .... DLB-25, 91

Munsey, Frank A., and
 Company.................... DLB-49

Murav'ev, Mikhail Nikitich
 1757-1807 .... DLB-150

Murdoch, Iris 1919- DLB-14

Murdoch, Rupert 1931- DLB-127

Murfree, Mary N. 1850-1922 .... DLB-12, 74

Murger, Henry 1822-1861........ DLB-119

Murger, Louis-Henri (see Murger, Henry)

Murner, Thomas 1475-1537 .... DLB-179

Muro, Amado 1915-1971.......... DLB-82

Murphy, Arthur 1727-1805..... DLB-89, 142

Murphy, Beatrice M. 1908- DLB-76

Murphy, Emily 1868-1933.......... DLB-99

Murphy, John H., III 1916- DLB-127

Murphy, John, and Company DLB-49

Murphy, Richard 1927-1993 .... DLB-40

Murray, Albert L. 1916- DLB-38

Murray, Gilbert 1866-1957 .... DLB-10

Murray, Judith Sargent 1751-1820 ... DLB-37

Murray, Pauli 1910-1985.......... DLB-41

Murray, John [publishing house] ... DLB-154

Murry, John Middleton
 1889-1957 .... DLB-149

Musäus, Johann Karl August
 1735-1787 .... DLB-97

Muschg, Adolf 1934- DLB-75

The Music of *Minnesang* DLB-138

Musil, Robert 1880-1942....... DLB-81, 124

Muspilli circa 790-circa 850 .... DLB-148

Mussey, Benjamin B., and
 Company.................... DLB-49

Mwangi, Meja 1948- DLB-125

Myers, Gustavus 1872-1942 .... DLB-47

Myers, L. H. 1881-1944............ DLB-15

Myers, Walter Dean 1937- DLB-33

N

Nabbes, Thomas circa 1605-1641.... DLB-58

Nabl, Franz 1883-1974............ DLB-81

Nabokov, Vladimir
 1899-1977...... DLB-2; Y-80, Y-91; DS-3

Nabokov Festival at Cornell.......... Y-83

The Vladimir Nabokov Archive
 in the Berg Collection Y-91

Nafis and Cornish................. DLB-49

Naipaul, Shiva 1945-1985 .... DLB-157; Y-85

Naipaul, V. S. 1932- DLB-125; Y-85

Nancrede, Joseph
 [publishing house] DLB-49

Naranjo, Carmen 1930- DLB-145

Narrache, Jean 1893-1970 .... DLB-92

Nasby, Petroleum Vesuvius (see Locke, David Ross)

Nash, Ogden 1902-1971........... DLB-11

Nash, Eveleigh
 [publishing house] DLB-112

Nashe, Thomas 1567-1601?........ DLB-167

Nast, Conde 1873-1942 .... DLB-91

Nastasijević, Momčilo 1894-1938 ... DLB-147

Nathan, George Jean 1882-1958 .... DLB-137

Nathan, Robert 1894-1985.......... DLB-9

The National Jewish Book Awards Y-85

The National Theatre and the Royal
 Shakespeare Company: The
 National Companies DLB-13

Naughton, Bill 1910- DLB-13

Naylor, Gloria 1950- DLB-173

Nazor, Vladimir 1876-1949........ DLB-147

Ndebele, Njabulo 1948- DLB-157

Neagoe, Peter 1881-1960 .... DLB-4

Neal, John 1793-1876........... DLB-1, 59

Neal, Joseph C. 1807-1847.......... DLB-11

Neal, Larry 1937-1981 .... DLB-38

The Neale Publishing Company..... DLB-49

Neely, F. Tennyson
 [publishing house] DLB-49

Negri, Ada 1870-1945 .... DLB-114

"The Negro as a Writer," by
 G. M. McClellan DLB-50

"Negro Poets and Their Poetry," by
 Wallace Thurman DLB-50

Neidhart von Reuental
 circa 1185-circa 1240 .... DLB-138

Neihardt, John G. 1881-1973 ..... DLB-9, 54

Neledinsky-Meletsky, Iurii Aleksandrovich
 1752-1828 .... DLB-150

Nelligan, Emile 1879-1941.......... DLB-92

Nelson, Alice Moore Dunbar
 1875-1935 .... DLB-50

Nelson, Thomas, and Sons [U.S.].... DLB-49

Nelson, Thomas, and Sons [U.K.] .. DLB-106

Nelson, William 1908-1978........ DLB-103

Nelson, William Rockhill
 1841-1915 .... DLB-23

Nemerov, Howard 1920-1991... DLB-5, 6; Y-83

Nesbit, E. 1858-1924 ..... DLB-141, 153, 178

Ness, Evaline 1911-1986 .... DLB-61

Nestroy, Johann 1801-1862........ DLB-133

Neukirch, Benjamin 1655-1729..... DLB-168

Neugeboren, Jay 1938- DLB-28

Neumann, Alfred 1895-1952 .... DLB-56

Neumark, Georg 1621-1681 .... DLB-164

Neumeister, Erdmann 1671-1756 ... DLB-168

Nevins, Allan 1890-1971 .... DLB-17

Nevinson, Henry Woodd
 1856-1941 .... DLB-135

The New American Library DLB-46

New Approaches to Biography: Challenges
 from Critical Theory, USC Conference
 on Literary Studies, 1990 .... Y-90

New Directions Publishing
 Corporation DLB-46

A New Edition of *Huck Finn* Y-85

New Forces at Work in the American Theatre:
 1915-1925 .... DLB-7

New Literary Periodicals:
 A Report for 1987 .... Y-87

New Literary Periodicals:
 A Report for 1988 .... Y-88

New Literary Periodicals:
 A Report for 1989 .... Y-89

New Literary Periodicals:
 A Report for 1990 .... Y-90

New Literary Periodicals:
 A Report for 1991 .... Y-91

New Literary Periodicals:
 A Report for 1992 .... Y-92

New Literary Periodicals:
 A Report for 1993 .... Y-93

The New Monthly Magazine
  1814-1884 .... DLB-110

The New *Ulysses* Y-84

The New Variorum Shakespeare Y-85

A New Voice: The Center for the Book's First
  Five Years Y-83

The New Wave [Science Fiction] DLB-8

New York City Bookshops in the 1930s and
  1940s: The Recollections of Walter
  Goldwater Y-93

Newbery, John
  [publishing house] DLB-154

Newbolt, Henry 1862-1938 .... DLB-19

Newbound, Bernard Slade (see Slade, Bernard)

Newby, P. H. 1918- DLB-15

Newby, Thomas Cautley
  [publishing house] DLB-106

Newcomb, Charles King 1820-1894 ... DLB-1

Newell, Peter 1862-1924 .... DLB-42

Newell, Robert Henry 1836-1901 .... DLB-11

Newhouse, Samuel I. 1895-1979 .... DLB-127

Newman, Cecil Earl 1903-1976 ..... DLB-127

Newman, David (see Benton, Robert)

Newman, Frances 1883-1928 .... Y-80

Newman, John Henry
  1801-1890 .... DLB-18, 32, 55

Newman, Mark [publishing house]... DLB-49

Newnes, George, Limited DLB-112

Newsome, Effie Lee 1885-1979 ...... DLB-76

Newspaper Syndication of American
  Humor DLB-11

Newton, A. Edward 1864-1940 ..... DLB-140

Ngugi wa Thiong'o 1938- DLB-125

Niatum, Duane 1938- DLB-175

The *Nibelungenlied* and the *Klage*
  circa 1200 .... DLB-138

Nichol, B. P. 1944- DLB-53

Nicholas of Cusa 1401-1464 .... DLB-115

Nichols, Dudley 1895-1960 .... DLB-26

Nichols, Grace 1950- DLB-157

Nichols, John 1940- Y-82

Nichols, Mary Sargeant (Neal) Gove
  1810-1884 .... DLB-1

Nichols, Peter 1927- DLB-13

Nichols, Roy F. 1896-1973 .... DLB-17

Nichols, Ruth 1948- DLB-60

Nicholson, Norman 1914- DLB-27

Nicholson, William 1872-1949 ..... DLB-141

Ní Chuilleanáin, Eiléan 1942- DLB-40

Nicol, Eric 1919- DLB-68

Nicolai, Friedrich 1733-1811 .... DLB-97

Nicolay, John G. 1832-1901 and
  Hay, John 1838-1905 .... DLB-47

Nicolson, Harold 1886-1968 ... DLB-100, 149

Nicolson, Nigel 1917- DLB-155

Niebuhr, Reinhold 1892-1971 ...... DLB-17

Niedecker, Lorine 1903-1970 ...... DLB-48

Nieman, Lucius W. 1857-1935 ..... DLB-25

Nietzsche, Friedrich 1844-1900 ..... DLB-129

Niggli, Josefina 1910- Y-80

Nightingale, Florence 1820-1910 .... DLB-166

Nikolev, Nikolai Petrovich
  1758-1815 .... DLB-150

Niles, Hezekiah 1777-1839 .... DLB-43

Nims, John Frederick 1913- DLB-5

Nin, Anaïs 1903-1977 .... DLB-2, 4, 152

1985: The Year of the Mystery:
  A Symposium Y-85

Nissenson, Hugh 1933- DLB-28

Niven, Frederick John 1878-1944 .... DLB-92

Niven, Larry 1938- DLB-8

Nizan, Paul 1905-1940 .... DLB-72

Njegoš, Petar II Petrović
  1813-1851 .... DLB-147

Nkosi, Lewis 1936- DLB-157

Nobel Peace Prize
The 1986 Nobel Peace Prize
  Nobel Lecture 1986: Hope, Despair and
  Memory
  Tributes from Abraham Bernstein,
  Norman Lamm, and
  John R. Silber Y-86

The Nobel Prize and Literary Politics ... Y-86

Nobel Prize in Literature
The 1982 Nobel Prize in Literature
  Announcement by the Swedish Academy
  of the Nobel Prize Nobel Lecture 1982:
  The Solitude of Latin America Excerpt
  from *One Hundred Years of Solitude* The
  Magical World of Macondo A Tribute
  to Gabriel García Márquez Y-82

The 1983 Nobel Prize in Literature
  Announcement by the Swedish Academy
  Nobel Lecture 1983 The Stature of
  William Golding Y-83

The 1984 Nobel Prize in Literature
  Announcement by the Swedish Academy
  Jaroslav Seifert Through the Eyes of the
  English-Speaking Reader
  Three Poems by Jaroslav Seifert Y-84

The 1985 Nobel Prize in Literature
  Announcement by the Swedish Academy
  Nobel Lecture 1985 .... Y-85

The 1986 Nobel Prize in Literature
  Nobel Lecture 1986: This Past Must Address Its Present Y-86

The 1987 Nobel Prize in Literature
  Nobel Lecture 1987 .... Y-87

The 1988 Nobel Prize in Literature
  Nobel Lecture 1988 .... Y-88

The 1989 Nobel Prize in Literature
  Nobel Lecture 1989 .... Y-89

The 1990 Nobel Prize in Literature
  Nobel Lecture 1990 .... Y-90

The 1991 Nobel Prize in Literature
  Nobel Lecture 1991 .... Y-91

The 1992 Nobel Prize in Literature
  Nobel Lecture 1992 .... Y-92

The 1993 Nobel Prize in Literature
  Nobel Lecture 1993 .... Y-93

The 1994 Nobel Prize in Literature
  Nobel Lecture 1994 .... Y-94

The 1995 Nobel Prize in Literature
  Nobel Lecture 1995 .... Y-95

Nodier, Charles 1780-1844 .... DLB-119

Noel, Roden 1834-1894 .... DLB-35

Nolan, William F. 1928- DLB-8

Noland, C. F. M. 1810?-1858 ...... DLB-11

Nonesuch Press DLB-112

Noonday Press DLB-46

Noone, John 1936- DLB-14

Nora, Eugenio de 1923- DLB-134

Nordhoff, Charles 1887-1947 .... DLB-9

Norman, Charles 1904- DLB-111

Norman, Marsha 1947- Y-84

Norris, Charles G. 1881-1945 .... DLB-9

Norris, Frank 1870-1902 .... DLB-12

Norris, Leslie 1921- DLB-27

Norse, Harold 1916- DLB-16

North, Marianne 1830-1890 .... DLB-174

North Point Press DLB-46

Nortje, Arthur 1942-1970 .... DLB-125

Norton, Alice Mary (see Norton, Andre)

Norton, Andre 1912- DLB-8, 52

Norton, Andrews 1786-1853 .... DLB-1

Norton, Caroline 1808-1877 .... DLB-21, 159

Norton, Charles Eliot 1827-1908 .. DLB-1, 64

Norton, John 1606-1663 .... DLB-24

Norton, Mary 1903-1992 .... DLB-160

Norton, Thomas (see Sackville, Thomas)

Norton, W. W., and Company......DLB-46

Norwood, Robert 1874-1932........DLB-92

Nossack, Hans Erich 1901-1977.....DLB-69

Notker Balbulus circa 840-912.....DLB-148

Notker III of Saint Gall circa 950-1022................DLB-148

Notker von Zweifalten ?-1095......DLB-148

A Note on Technique (1926), by Elizabeth A. Drew [excerpts]....DLB-36

Nourse, Alan E. 1928- DLB-8

Novak, Vjenceslav 1859-1905......DLB-147

Novalis 1772-1801................DLB-90

Novaro, Mario 1868-1944.........DLB-114

Novás Calvo, Lino 1903-1983......DLB-145

"The Novel in [Robert Browning's] 'The Ring and the Book'" (1912), by Henry James................DLB-32

The Novel of Impressionism, by Jethro Bithell..............DLB-66

Novel-Reading: *The Works of Charles Dickens, The Works of W. Makepeace Thackeray* (1879), by Anthony Trollope....DLB-21

The Novels of Dorothy Richardson (1918), by May Sinclair...............DLB-36

Novels with a Purpose (1864), by Justin M'Carthy DLB-21

Noventa, Giacomo 1898-1960......DLB-114

Novikov, Nikolai Ivanovich 1744-1818..................DLB-150

Nowlan, Alden 1933-1983..........DLB-53

Noyes, Alfred 1880-1958...........DLB-20

Noyes, Crosby S. 1825-1908........DLB-23

Noyes, Nicholas 1647-1717.........DLB-24

Noyes, Theodore W. 1858-1946.....DLB-29

N-Town Plays circa 1468 to early sixteenth century............DLB-146

Nugent, Frank 1908-1965 ....DLB-44

Nugent, Richard Bruce 1906- DLB-151

Nušić, Branislav 1864-1938........DLB-147

Nutt, David [publishing house].....DLB-106

Nwapa, Flora 1931- DLB-125

Nye, Edgar Wilson (Bill) 1850-1896................DLB-11, 23

Nye, Naomi Shihab 1952- DLB-120

Nye, Robert 1939- DLB-14

O

Oakes, Urian circa 1631-1681.......DLB-24

Oates, Joyce Carol 1938- DLB-2, 5, 130; Y-81

Ober, William 1920-1993 ....Y-93

Oberholtzer, Ellis Paxson 1868-1936....................DLB-47

Obradović, Dositej 1740?-1811.....DLB-147

O'Brien, Edna 1932- DLB-14

O'Brien, Fitz-James 1828-1862......DLB-74

O'Brien, Kate 1897-1974 ....DLB-15

O'Brien, Tim 1946- DLB-152; Y-80; DS-9

O'Casey, Sean 1880-1964 ....DLB-10

Occom, Samson 1723-1792 ....DLB-175

Ochs, Adolph S. 1858-1935.........DLB-25

Ochs-Oakes, George Washington 1861-1931 ....DLB-137

O'Connor, Flannery 1925-1964 .....DLB-2, 152; Y-80; DS-12

O'Connor, Frank 1903-1966.......DLB-162

Octopus Publishing Group DLB-112

Odell, Jonathan 1737-1818 ......DLB-31, 99

O'Dell, Scott 1903-1989 ....DLB-52

Odets, Clifford 1906-1963.........DLB-7, 26

Odhams Press Limited...........DLB-112

O'Donnell, Peter 1920- DLB-87

O'Donovan, Michael (see O'Connor, Frank)

O'Faolain, Julia 1932- DLB-14

O'Faolain, Sean 1900- DLB-15, 162

Off Broadway and Off-Off Broadway.DLB-7

Off-Loop Theatres DLB-7

Offord, Carl Ruthven 1910- DLB-76

O'Flaherty, Liam 1896-1984..........DLB-36, 162; Y-84

Ogilvie, J. S., and Company DLB-49

Ogot, Grace 1930- DLB-125

O'Grady, Desmond 1935- DLB-40

Ogunyemi, Wale 1939- DLB-157

O'Hagan, Howard 1902-1982.......DLB-68

O'Hara, Frank 1926-1966 ....DLB-5, 16

O'Hara, John 1905-1970....DLB-9, 86; DS-2

Okara, Gabriel 1921- DLB-125

O'Keeffe, John 1747-1833 ....DLB-89

Okes, Nicholas [publishing house] DLB-170

Okigbo, Christopher 1930-1967 ....DLB-125

Okot p'Bitek 1931-1982...........DLB-125

Okpewho, Isidore 1941- DLB-157

Okri, Ben 1959- DLB-157

Olaudah Equiano and Unfinished Journeys: The Slave-Narrative Tradition and Twentieth-Century Continuities, by Paul Edwards and Pauline T. Wangman................DLB-117

Old English Literature: An Introduction DLB-146

Old English Riddles eighth to tenth centuries DLB-146

Old Franklin Publishing House DLB-49

Old German Genesis and *Old German Exodus* circa 1050-circa 1130..........DLB-148

Old High German Charms and Blessings DLB-148

The *Old High German Isidor* circa 790-800..................DLB-148

Older, Fremont 1856-1935.........DLB-25

Oldham, John 1653-1683..........DLB-131

Olds, Sharon 1942- DLB-120

Olearius, Adam 1599-1671 ....DLB-164

Oliphant, Laurence 1829?-1888................DLB-18, 166

Oliphant, Margaret 1828-1897 ......DLB-18

Oliver, Chad 1928- DLB-8

Oliver, Mary 1935- DLB-5

Ollier, Claude 1922- DLB-83

Olsen, Tillie 1913?- DLB-28; Y-80

Olson, Charles 1910-1970........DLB-5, 16

Olson, Elder 1909- DLB-48, 63

Omotoso, Kole 1943- DLB-125

"On Art in Fiction "(1838), by Edward Bulwer............DLB-21

On Learning to Write Y-88

On Some of the Characteristics of Modern Poetry and On the Lyrical Poems of Alfred Tennyson (1831), by Arthur Henry Hallam.................DLB-32

"On Style in English Prose" (1898), by Frederic Harrison.............DLB-57

"On Style in Literature: Its Technical Elements" (1885), by Robert Louis Stevenson DLB-57

"On the Writing of Essays" (1862), by Alexander Smith............DLB-57

Ondaatje, Michael 1943- DLB-60

O'Neill, Eugene 1888-1953 ....DLB-7

Onetti, Juan Carlos 1909-1994 .....DLB-113

Onions, George Oliver 1872-1961 ... DLB-153
Onofri, Arturo 1885-1928 ... DLB-114
Opie, Amelia 1769-1853 ... DLB-116, 159
Opitz, Martin 1597-1639 ... DLB-164
Oppen, George 1908-1984 ... DLB-5, 165
Oppenheim, E. Phillips 1866-1946 ... DLB-70
Oppenheim, James 1882-1932 ... DLB-28
Oppenheimer, Joel 1930- ... DLB-5
Optic, Oliver (see Adams, William Taylor)
Orczy, Emma, Baroness 1865-1947 ... DLB-70
Origo, Iris 1902-1988 ... DLB-155
Orlovitz, Gil 1918-1973 ... DLB-2, 5
Orlovsky, Peter 1933- ... DLB-16
Ormond, John 1923- ... DLB-27
Ornitz, Samuel 1890-1957 ... DLB-28, 44
Ortese, Anna Maria 1914- ... DLB-177
Ortiz, Simon J. 1941- ... DLB-120, 175
Ortnit and *Wolfdietrich* circa 1225-1250 ... DLB-138
Orton, Joe 1933-1967 ... DLB-13
Orwell, George 1903-1950 ... DLB-15, 98
The Orwell Year ... Y-84
Ory, Carlos Edmundo de 1923- ... DLB-134
Osbey, Brenda Marie 1957- ... DLB-120
Osbon, B. S. 1827-1912 ... DLB-43
Osborne, John 1929-1994 ... DLB-13
Osgood, Herbert L. 1855-1918 ... DLB-47
Osgood, James R., and Company ... DLB-49
Osgood, McIlvaine and Company ... DLB-112
O'Shaughnessy, Arthur 1844-1881 ... DLB-35
O'Shea, Patrick [publishing house] ... DLB-49
Osipov, Nikolai Petrovich 1751-1799 ... DLB-150
Oskison, John Milton 1879-1947 ... DLB-175
Osofisan, Femi 1946- ... DLB-125
Ostenso, Martha 1900-1963 ... DLB-92
Ostriker, Alicia 1937- ... DLB-120
Osundare, Niyi 1947- ... DLB-157
Oswald, Eleazer 1755-1795 ... DLB-43
Oswald von Wolkenstein 1376 or 1377-1445 ... DLB-179

Otero, Blas de 1916-1979 ... DLB-134
Otero, Miguel Antonio 1859-1944 ... DLB-82
Otero Silva, Miguel 1908-1985 ... DLB-145
Otfried von Weißenburg circa 800-circa 875? ... DLB-148
Otis, James (see Kaler, James Otis)
Otis, James, Jr. 1725-1783 ... DLB-31
Otis, Broaders and Company ... DLB-49
Ottaway, James 1911- ... DLB-127
Ottendorfer, Oswald 1826-1900 ... DLB-23
Ottieri, Ottiero 1924- ... DLB-177
Otto-Peters, Louise 1819-1895 ... DLB-129
Otway, Thomas 1652-1685 ... DLB-80
Ouellette, Fernand 1930- ... DLB-60
Ouida 1839-1908 ... DLB-18, 156
Outing Publishing Company ... DLB-46
Outlaw Days, by Joyce Johnson ... DLB-16
Overbury, Sir Thomas circa 1581-1613 ... DLB-151
The Overlook Press ... DLB-46
Overview of U.S. Book Publishing, 1910-1945 ... DLB-9
Owen, Guy 1925- ... DLB-5
Owen, John 1564-1622 ... DLB-121
Owen, John [publishing house] ... DLB-49
Owen, Robert 1771-1858 ... DLB-107, 158
Owen, Wilfred 1893-1918 ... DLB-20
Owen, Peter, Limited ... DLB-112
The Owl and the Nightingale circa 1189-1199 ... DLB-146
Owsley, Frank L. 1890-1956 ... DLB-17
Oxford, Seventeenth Earl of, Edward de Vere 1550-1604 ... DLB-172
Ozerov, Vladislav Aleksandrovich 1769-1816 ... DLB-150
Ozick, Cynthia 1928- ... DLB-28, 152; Y-82

P

Pace, Richard 1482?-1536 ... DLB-167
Pacey, Desmond 1917-1975 ... DLB-88
Pack, Robert 1929- ... DLB-5
Packaging Papa: *The Garden of Eden* ... Y-86
Padell Publishing Company ... DLB-46
Padgett, Ron 1942- ... DLB-5
Padilla, Ernesto Chávez 1944- ... DLB-122

Page, L. C., and Company ... DLB-49
Page, P. K. 1916- ... DLB-68
Page, Thomas Nelson 1853-1922 ... DLB-12, 78; DS-13
Page, Walter Hines 1855-1918 ... DLB-71, 91
Paget, Francis Edward 1806-1882 ... DLB-163
Paget, Violet (see Lee, Vernon)
Pagliarani, Elio 1927- ... DLB-128
Pain, Barry 1864-1928 ... DLB-135
Pain, Philip ?-circa 1666 ... DLB-24
Paine, Robert Treat, Jr. 1773-1811 ... DLB-37
Paine, Thomas 1737-1809 ... DLB-31, 43, 73, 158
Painter, George D. 1914- ... DLB-155
Painter, William 1540?-1594 ... DLB-136
Palazzeschi, Aldo 1885-1974 ... DLB-114
Paley, Grace 1922- ... DLB-28
Palfrey, John Gorham 1796-1881 ... DLB-1, 30
Palgrave, Francis Turner 1824-1897 ... DLB-35
Palmer, Joe H. 1904-1952 ... DLB-171
Palmer, Michael 1943- ... DLB-169
Paltock, Robert 1697-1767 ... DLB-39
Pan Books Limited ... DLB-112
Panamaa, Norman 1914- and Frank, Melvin 1913-1988 ... DLB-26
Pancake, Breece D'J 1952-1979 ... DLB-130
Panero, Leopoldo 1909-1962 ... DLB-108
Pangborn, Edgar 1909-1976 ... DLB-8
"Panic Among the Philistines": A Postscript, An Interview with Bryan Griffin ... Y-81
Panneton, Philippe (see Ringuet)
Panshin, Alexei 1940- ... DLB-8
Pansy (see Alden, Isabella)
Pantheon Books ... DLB-46
Paperback Library ... DLB-46
Paperback Science Fiction ... DLB-8
Paquet, Alfons 1881-1944 ... DLB-66
Paracelsus 1493-1541 ... DLB-179
Paradis, Suzanne 1936- ... DLB-53
Pareja Diezcanseco, Alfredo 1908-1993 ... DLB-145
Pardoe, Julia 1804-1862 ... DLB-166
Parents' Magazine Press ... DLB-46
Parise, Goffredo 1929-1986 ... DLB-177

Parisian Theater, Fall 1984: Toward
A New Baroque Y-85

Parizeau, Alice 1930- DLB-60

Parke, John 1754-1789 .... DLB-31

Parker, Dorothy
1893-1967 .... DLB-11, 45, 86

Parker, Gilbert 1860-1932 .... DLB-99

Parker, James 1714-1770 .... DLB-43

Parker, Theodore 1810-1860 .... DLB-1

Parker, William Riley 1906-1968 ... DLB-103

Parker, J. H. [publishing house] DLB-106

Parker, John [publishing house] DLB-106

Parkman, Francis, Jr.
1823-1893 .... DLB-1, 30

Parks, Gordon 1912- DLB-33

Parks, William 1698-1750 .... DLB-43

Parks, William [publishing house] ... DLB-49

Parley, Peter (see Goodrich, Samuel Griswold)

Parmenides late sixth-fith century B.C.
.... DLB-176

Parnell, Thomas 1679-1718 .... DLB-95

Parr, Catherine 1513?-1548 .... DLB-136

Parrington, Vernon L.
1871-1929 .... DLB-17, 63

Parronchi, Alessandro 1914- DLB-128

Partridge, S. W., and Company DLB-106

Parton, James 1822-1891 .... DLB-30

Parton, Sara Payson Willis
1811-1872 .... DLB-43, 74

Pasinetti, Pier Maria 1913- DLB-177

Pasolini, Pier Paolo 1922- DLB-128, 177

Pastan, Linda 1932- DLB-5

Paston, George 1860-1936 .... DLB-149

The *Paston Letters* 1422-1509 ..... DLB-146

Pastorius, Francis Daniel
1651-circa 1720 .... DLB-24

Patchen, Kenneth 1911-1972 ..... DLB-16, 48

Pater, Walter 1839-1894 .... DLB-57, 156

Paterson, Katherine 1932- DLB-52

Patmore, Coventry 1823-1896 ... DLB-35, 98

Paton, Joseph Noel 1821-1901 ...... DLB-35

Paton Walsh, Jill 1937- DLB-161

Patrick, Edwin Hill ("Ted")
1901-1964 .... DLB-137

Patrick, John 1906- DLB-7

Pattee, Fred Lewis 1863-1950 ...... DLB-71

Pattern and Paradigm: History as
Design, by Judith Ryan DLB-75

Patterson, Alicia 1906-1963 .... DLB-127

Patterson, Eleanor Medill
1881-1948 .... DLB-29

Patterson, Eugene 1923- DLB-127

Patterson, Joseph Medill
1879-1946 .... DLB-29

Pattillo, Henry 1726-1801 .... DLB-37

Paul, Elliot 1891-1958 .... DLB-4

Paul, Jean (see Richter, Johann Paul Friedrich)

Paul, Kegan, Trench, Trubner and Company
Limited DLB-106

Paul, Peter, Book Company DLB-49

Paul, Stanley, and Company
Limited DLB-112

Paulding, James Kirke
1778-1860 .... DLB-3, 59, 74

Paulin, Tom 1949- DLB-40

Pauper, Peter, Press DLB-46

Pavese, Cesare 1908-1950 ..... DLB-128, 177

Paxton, John 1911-1985 .... DLB-44

Payn, James 1830-1898 .... DLB-18

Payne, John 1842-1916 .... DLB-35

Payne, John Howard 1791-1852 ..... DLB-37

Payson and Clarke DLB-46

Peabody, Elizabeth Palmer
1804-1894 .... DLB-1

Peabody, Elizabeth Palmer
[publishing house] DLB-49

Peabody, Oliver William Bourn
1799-1848 .... DLB-59

Peace, Roger 1899-1968 .... DLB-127

Peacham, Henry 1578-1644? DLB-151

Peacham, Henry, the Elder
1547-1634 .... DLB-172

Peachtree Publishers, Limited DLB-46

Peacock, Molly 1947- DLB-120

Peacock, Thomas Love
1785-1866 .... DLB-96, 116

Pead, Deuel ?-1727 .... DLB-24

Peake, Mervyn 1911-1968 ...... DLB-15, 160

Pear Tree Press DLB-112

Pearce, Philippa 1920- DLB-161

Pearson, H. B. [publishing house] DLB-49

Pearson, Hesketh 1887-1964 .... DLB-149

Peck, George W. 1840-1916 ..... DLB-23, 42

Peck, H. C., and Theo. Bliss
[publishing house] DLB-49

Peck, Harry Thurston
1856-1914 .... DLB-71, 91

Peele, George 1556-1596 ...... DLB-62, 167

Pegler, Westbrook 1894-1969 ...... DLB-171

Pellegrini and Cudahy DLB-46

Pelletier, Aimé (see Vac, Bertrand)

Pemberton, Sir Max 1863-1950 ..... DLB-70

Penguin Books [U.S.] DLB-46

Penguin Books [U.K.] DLB-112

Penn Publishing Company DLB-49

Penn, William 1644-1718 .... DLB-24

Penna, Sandro 1906-1977 .... DLB-114

Penner, Jonathan 1940- Y-83

Pennington, Lee 1939- Y-82

Pepys, Samuel 1633-1703 .... DLB-101

Percy, Thomas 1729-1811 .... DLB-104

Percy, Walker 1916-1990 ... DLB-2; Y-80, 90

Percy, William 1575-1648 .... DLB-172

Perec, Georges 1936-1982 .... DLB-83

Perelman, S. J. 1904-1979 ...... DLB-11, 44

Perez, Raymundo "Tigre"
1946- DLB-122

Peri Rossi, Cristina 1941- DLB-145

Periodicals of the Beat Generation ... DLB-16

Perkins, Eugene 1932- DLB-41

Perkoff, Stuart Z. 1930-1974 .... DLB-16

Perley, Moses Henry 1804-1862 ..... DLB-99

Permabooks DLB-46

Perrin, Alice 1867-1934 .... DLB-156

Perry, Bliss 1860-1954 .... DLB-71

Perry, Eleanor 1915-1981 .... DLB-44

Perry, Sampson 1747-1823 .... DLB-158

"Personal Style" (1890), by John Addington
Symonds DLB-57

Perutz, Leo 1882-1957 .... DLB-81

Pesetsky, Bette 1932- DLB-130

Pestalozzi, Johann Heinrich
1746-1827 .... DLB-94

Peter, Laurence J. 1919-1990 .... DLB-53

Peter of Spain circa 1205-1277 ..... DLB-115

Peterkin, Julia 1880-1961 .... DLB-9

Peters, Lenrie 1932- DLB-117

Peters, Robert 1924- DLB-105

Peters, Robert, Foreword to
Ludwig of Bavaria DLB-105

Petersham, Maud 1889-1971 and Petersham, Miska 1888-1960 ....DLB-22

Peterson, Charles Jacobs 1819-1887 ....DLB-79

Peterson, Len 1917- DLB-88

Peterson, Louis 1922- DLB-76

Peterson, T. B., and Brothers DLB-49

Petitclair, Pierre 1813-1860 ....DLB-99

Petrov, Gavriil 1730-1801 ....DLB-150

Petrov, Vasilii Petrovich 1736-1799 ....DLB-150

Petrović, Rastko 1898-1949 ....DLB-147

Petruslied circa 854? DLB-148

Petry, Ann 1908- DLB-76

Pettie, George circa 1548-1589 .....DLB-136

Peyton, K. M. 1929- DLB-161

Pfaffe Konrad flourished circa 1172 ....DLB-148

Pfaffe Lamprecht flourished circa 1150 ....DLB-148

Pforzheimer, Carl H. 1879-1957 ....DLB-140

Phaer, Thomas 1510?-1560 ....DLB-167

Phaidon Press Limited DLB-112

Pharr, Robert Deane 1916-1992 .....DLB-33

Phelps, Elizabeth Stuart 1844-1911 ....DLB-74

Philander von der Linde (see Mencke, Johann Burckhard)

Philip, Marlene Nourbese 1947- DLB-157

Philippe, Charles-Louis 1874-1909 ....DLB-65

Philips, John 1676-1708 ....DLB-95

Philips, Katherine 1632-1664.......DLB-131

Phillips, Caryl 1958- DLB-157

Phillips, David Graham 1867-1911 ....DLB-9, 12

Phillips, Jayne Anne 1952- Y-80

Phillips, Robert 1938- DLB-105

Phillips, Robert, Finding, Losing, Reclaiming: A Note on My Poems DLB-105

Phillips, Stephen 1864-1915.........DLB-10

Phillips, Ulrich B. 1877-1934........DLB-17

Phillips, Willard 1784-1873.........DLB-59

Phillips, William 1907- DLB-137

Phillips, Sampson and Company DLB-49

Phillpotts, Eden 1862-1960.........DLB-10, 70, 135, 153

Philo circa 20-15 B.C.-circa A.D. 50 ....DLB-176

Philosophical Library............DLB-46

"The Philosophy of Style" (1852), by Herbert Spencer DLB-57

Phinney, Elihu [publishing house] ...DLB-49

Phoenix, John (see Derby, George Horatio)

PHYLON (Fourth Quarter, 1950), The Negro in Literature: The Current Scene............DLB-76

Physiologus circa 1070-circa 1150 ....DLB-148

Piccolo, Lucio 1903-1969..........DLB-114

Pickard, Tom 1946- DLB-40

Pickering, William [publishing house] DLB-106

Pickthall, Marjorie 1883-1922.......DLB-92

Pictorial Printing Company.........DLB-49

Piel, Gerard 1915- DLB-137

Piercy, Marge 1936- DLB-120

Pierro, Albino 1916- DLB-128

Pignotti, Lamberto 1926- DLB-128

Pike, Albert 1809-1891............DLB-74

Pilon, Jean-Guy 1930- DLB-60

Pinckney, Josephine 1895-1957.......DLB-6

Pindar circa 518 B.C.-circa 438 B.C. DLB-176

Pindar, Peter (see Wolcot, John)

Pinero, Arthur Wing 1855-1934 .....DLB-10

Pinget, Robert 1919- DLB-83

Pinnacle Books DLB-46

Piñon, Nélida 1935- DLB-145

Pinsky, Robert 1940- Y-82

Pinter, Harold 1930- DLB-13

Piontek, Heinz 1925- DLB-75

Piozzi, Hester Lynch [Thrale] 1741-1821 ....DLB-104, 142

Piper, H. Beam 1904-1964..........DLB-8

Piper, Watty DLB-22

Pirckheimer, Caritas 1467-1532 ....DLB-179

Pirckheimer, Willibald 1470-1530 ....DLB-179

Pisar, Samuel 1929- Y-83

Pitkin, Timothy 1766-1847 ....DLB-30

The Pitt Poetry Series: Poetry Publishing Today Y-85

Pitter, Ruth 1897- DLB-20

Pix, Mary 1666-1709 ....DLB-80

Plaatje, Sol T. 1876-1932..........DLB-125

The Place of Realism in Fiction (1895), by George Gissing................DLB-18

Plante, David 1940- Y-83

Platen, August von 1796-1835.......DLB-90

Plath, Sylvia 1932-1963.......DLB-5, 6, 152

Plato circa 428 B.C.-348-347 B.C. DLB-176

Platon 1737-1812 ....DLB-150

Platt and Munk Company.........DLB-46

Playboy Press DLB-46

Playford, John [publishing house] DLB-170

Plays, Playwrights, and Playgoers ...DLB-84

Playwrights and Professors, by Tom Stoppard.................DLB-13

Playwrights on the Theater DLB-80

Der Pleier flourished circa 1250 ....DLB-138

Plenzdorf, Ulrich 1934- DLB-75

Plessen, Elizabeth 1944- DLB-75

Plievier, Theodor 1892-1955........DLB-69

Plomer, William 1903-1973.....DLB-20, 162

Plotinus 204-270 ....DLB-176

Plumly, Stanley 1939- DLB-5

Plumpp, Sterling D. 1940- DLB-41

Plunkett, James 1920- DLB-14

Plutarch circa 46-circa 120.........DLB-176

Plymell, Charles 1935- DLB-16

Pocket Books...................DLB-46

Poe, Edgar Allan 1809-1849............DLB-3, 59, 73, 74

Poe, James 1921-1980............DLB-44

The Poet Laureate of the United States Statements from Former Consultants in Poetry.......................Y-86

Pohl, Frederik 1919- DLB-8

Poirier, Louis (see Gracq, Julien)

Polanyi, Michael 1891-1976 ....DLB-100

Pole, Reginald 1500-1558 ....DLB-132

Poliakoff, Stephen 1952- DLB-13

Polidori, John William 1795-1821 ....DLB-116

Polite, Carlene Hatcher 1932- DLB-33

Pollard, Edward A. 1832-1872 ......DLB-30

Pollard, Percival 1869-1911.........DLB-71

Pollard and Moss DLB-49

Pollock, Sharon 1936- DLB-60

Polonsky, Abraham 1910- DLB-26

Polotsky, Simeon 1629-1680 ....DLB-150

Polybius circa 200 B.C.-118 B.C. DLB-176

Pomilio, Mario 1921-1990 ....DLB-177

Ponce, Mary Helen 1938- DLB-122

Ponce-Montoya, Juanita 1949- DLB-122

Ponet, John 1516?-1556 ....DLB-132

Poniatowski, Elena 1933- DLB-113

Ponsonby, William
    [publishing house] DLB-170

Pony Stories DLB-160

Poole, Ernest 1880-1950 ....DLB-9

Poole, Sophia 1804-1891 ....DLB-166

Poore, Benjamin Perley
    1820-1887 ....DLB-23

Pope, Abbie Hanscom
    1858-1894 ....DLB-140

Pope, Alexander 1688-1744 .....DLB-95, 101

Popov, Mikhail Ivanovich
    1742-circa 1790 ....DLB-150

Popular Library DLB-46

Porlock, Martin (see MacDonald, Philip)

Porpoise Press DLB-112

Porta, Antonio 1935-1989 ....DLB-128

Porter, Anna Maria
    1780-1832 ....DLB-116, 159

Porter, Eleanor H. 1868-1920 ....DLB-9

Porter, Gene Stratton (see Stratton-Porter, Gene)

Porter, Henry ?-? DLB-62

Porter, Jane 1776-1850 ....DLB-116, 159

Porter, Katherine Anne
    1890-1980 ...DLB-4, 9, 102; Y-80; DS-12

Porter, Peter 1929- DLB-40

Porter, William Sydney
    1862-1910 ....DLB-12, 78, 79

Porter, William T. 1809-1858 .....DLB-3, 43

Porter and Coates DLB-49

Portis, Charles 1933- DLB-6

Posey, Alexander 1873-1908 ....DLB-175

Postans, Marianne
    circa 1810-1865 ....DLB-166

Postl, Carl (see Sealsfield, Carl)

Poston, Ted 1906-1974 ....DLB-51

Postscript to [the Third Edition of] *Clarissa* (1751), by Samuel Richardson ...DLB-39

Potok, Chaim 1929- DLB-28, 152; Y-84

Potter, Beatrix 1866-1943 ....DLB-141

Potter, David M. 1910-1971 ....DLB-17

Potter, John E., and Company DLB-49

Pottle, Frederick A.
    1897-1987 ....DLB-103; Y-87

Poulin, Jacques 1937- DLB-60

Pound, Ezra 1885-1972 ....DLB-4, 45, 63

Povich, Shirley 1905- DLB-171

Powell, Anthony 1905- DLB-15

Powers, J. F. 1917- DLB-130

Pownall, David 1938- DLB-14

Powys, John Cowper 1872-1963 .....DLB-15

Powys, Llewelyn 1884-1939 ....DLB-98

Powys, T. F. 1875-1953 ....DLB-36, 162

Poynter, Nelson 1903-1978 ....DLB-127

The Practice of Biography: An Interview with Stanley Weintraub Y-82

The Practice of Biography II: An Interview with B. L. Reid Y-83

The Practice of Biography III: An Interview with Humphrey Carpenter Y-84

The Practice of Biography IV: An Interview with William Manchester Y-85

The Practice of Biography V: An Interview with Justin Kaplan Y-86

The Practice of Biography VI: An Interview with David Herbert Donald Y-87

The Practice of Biography VII: An Interview with John Caldwell Guilds Y-92

The Practice of Biography VIII: An Interview with Joan Mellen Y-94

The Practice of Biography IX: An Interview with Michael Reynolds Y-95

Prados, Emilio 1899-1962 ....DLB-134

Praed, Winthrop Mackworth
    1802-1839 ....DLB-96

Praeger Publishers DLB-46

Praetorius, Johannes 1630-1680 ....DLB-168

Pratolini, Vasco 1913—1991 ....DLB-177

Pratt, E. J. 1882-1964 ....DLB-92

Pratt, Samuel Jackson 1749-1814 ....DLB-39

Preface to *Alwyn* (1780), by
    Thomas Holcroft DLB-39

Preface to *Colonel Jack* (1722), by
    Daniel Defoe....................DLB-39

Preface to *Evelina* (1778), by
    Fanny Burney..................DLB-39

Preface to *Ferdinand Count Fathom* (1753), by
    Tobias Smollett.................DLB-39

Preface to *Incognita* (1692), by
    William Congreve DLB-39

Preface to *Joseph Andrews* (1742), by
    Henry Fielding DLB-39

Preface to *Moll Flanders* (1722), by
    Daniel Defoe....................DLB-39

Preface to *Poems* (1853), by
    Matthew Arnold................DLB-32

Preface to *Robinson Crusoe* (1719), by
    Daniel Defoe....................DLB-39

Preface to *Roderick Random* (1748), by
    Tobias Smollett DLB-39

Preface to *Roxana* (1724), by
    Daniel Defoe....................DLB-39

Preface to *St. Leon* (1799), by
    William Godwin................DLB-39

Preface to Sarah Fielding's *Familiar Letters* (1747), by Henry Fielding
    [excerpt]........................DLB-39

Preface to Sarah Fielding's *The Adventures of David Simple* (1744), by
    Henry Fielding DLB-39

Preface to *The Cry* (1754), by
    Sarah Fielding.................DLB-39

Preface to *The Delicate Distress* (1769), by
    Elizabeth Griffin DLB-39

Preface to *The Disguis'd Prince* (1733), by
    Eliza Haywood [excerpt] DLB-39

Preface to *The Farther Adventures of Robinson Crusoe* (1719), by Daniel Defoe ...DLB-39

Preface to the First Edition of *Pamela* (1740), by
    Samuel Richardson DLB-39

Preface to the First Edition of *The Castle of Otranto* (1764), by
    Horace Walpole DLB-39

Preface to *The History of Romances* (1715), by
    Pierre Daniel Huet [excerpts] DLB-39

Preface to *The Life of Charlotta du Pont* (1723), by Penelope Aubin DLB-39

Preface to *The Old English Baron* (1778), by
    Clara Reeve DLB-39

Preface to the Second Edition of *The Castle of Otranto* (1765), by Horace
    Walpole.......................DLB-39

Preface to *The Secret History, of Queen Zarah, and the Zarazians* (1705), by Delariviere
    Manley........................DLB-39

Preface to the Third Edition of *Clarissa* (1751), by Samuel Richardson
    [excerpt]........................DLB-39

Preface to *The Works of Mrs. Davys* (1725), by
    Mary Davys DLB-39

Preface to Volume 1 of *Clarissa* (1747), by
    Samuel Richardson DLB-39

Preface to Volume 3 of *Clarissa* (1748), by
    Samuel Richardson DLB-39

Préfontaine, Yves 1937- DLB-53

Prelutsky, Jack 1940- DLB-61

Premisses, by Michael Hamburger...DLB-66

Prentice, George D. 1802-1870......DLB-43

Prentice-Hall.....................DLB-46

Prescott, Orville 1906-1996............Y-96

Prescott, William Hickling
1796-1859...............DLB-1, 30, 59

The Present State of the English Novel (1892),
by George Saintsbury..........DLB-18

Prešeren, France 1800-1849........DLB-147

Preston, Thomas 1537-1598........DLB-62

Price, Reynolds 1933-..............DLB-2

Price, Richard 1723-1791..........DLB-158

Price, Richard 1949-.................Y-81

Priest, Christopher 1943-..........DLB-14

Priestley, J. B. 1894-1984
........DLB-10, 34, 77, 100, 139; Y-84

Primary Bibliography: A
Retrospective....................Y-95

Prime, Benjamin Young 1733-1791..DLB-31

Primrose, Diana
floruit circa 1630.............DLB-126

Prince, F. T. 1912-...............DLB-20

Prince, Thomas 1687-1758.....DLB-24, 140

The Principles of Success in Literature (1865), by
George Henry Lewes [excerpt]...DLB-57

Printz, Wolfgang Casper
1641-1717....................DLB-168

Prior, Matthew 1664-1721..........DLB-95

Prisco, Michele 1920-.............DLB-177

Pritchard, William H. 1932-......DLB-111

Pritchett, V. S. 1900-.........DLB-15, 139

Procter, Adelaide Anne 1825-1864...DLB-32

Procter, Bryan Waller
1787-1874...............DLB-96, 144

The Profession of Authorship:
Scribblers for Bread.............Y-89

The Progress of Romance (1785), by Clara Reeve
[excerpt]......................DLB-39

Prokopovich, Feofan 1681?-1736...DLB-150

Prokosch, Frederic 1906-1989......DLB-48

The Proletarian Novel..............DLB-9

Propper, Dan 1937-................DLB-16

The Prospect of Peace (1778), by
Joel Barlow...................DLB-37

Protagoras circa 490 B.C.-420 B.C.
..............................DLB-176

Proud, Robert 1728-1813..........DLB-30

Proust, Marcel 1871-1922..........DLB-65

Prynne, J. H. 1936-...............DLB-40

Przybyszewski, Stanislaw
1868-1927....................DLB-66

Pseudo-Dionysius the Areopagite floruit
circa 500....................DLB-115

The Public Lending Right in America
Statement by Sen. Charles McC.
Mathias, Jr. PLR and the Meaning
of Literary Property Statements on
PLR by American Writers.........Y-83

The Public Lending Right in the United Kingdom Public Lending Right: The First Year
in the United Kingdom............Y-83

The Publication of English
Renaissance Plays..............DLB-62

Publications and Social Movements
[Transcendentalism]..............DLB-1

Publishers and Agents: The Columbia
Connection.....................Y-87

A Publisher's Archives: G. P. Putnam...Y-92

Publishing Fiction at LSU Press........Y-87

Pückler-Muskau, Hermann von
1785-1871....................DLB-133

Pufendorf, Samuel von
1632-1694....................DLB-168

Pugh, Edwin William 1874-1930...DLB-135

Pugin, A. Welby 1812-1852.........DLB-55

Puig, Manuel 1932-1990...........DLB-113

Pulitzer, Joseph 1847-1911..........DLB-23

Pulitzer, Joseph, Jr. 1885-1955......DLB-29

Pulitzer Prizes for the Novel,
1917-1945......................DLB-9

Pulliam, Eugene 1889-1975........DLB-127

Purchas, Samuel 1577?-1626.......DLB-151

Purdy, Al 1918-..................DLB-88

Purdy, James 1923-................DLB-2

Purdy, Ken W. 1913-1972.........DLB-137

Pusey, Edward Bouverie
1800-1882....................DLB-55

Putnam, George Palmer
1814-1872..................DLB-3, 79

Putnam, Samuel 1892-1950..........DLB-4

G. P. Putnam's Sons [U.S.].........DLB-49

G. P. Putnam's Sons [U.K.]........DLB-106

Puzo, Mario 1920-.................DLB-6

Pyle, Ernie 1900-1945.............DLB-29

Pyle, Howard 1853-1911.....DLB-42; DS-13

Pym, Barbara 1913-1980......DLB-14; Y-87

Pynchon, Thomas 1937-........DLB-2, 173

Pyramid Books....................DLB-46

Pyrnelle, Louise-Clarke 1850-1907...DLB-42

Pythagoras circa 570 B.C.-?.......DLB-176

Q

Quad, M. (see Lewis, Charles B.)

Quarles, Francis 1592-1644........DLB-126

The Quarterly Review
1809-1967....................DLB-110

Quasimodo, Salvatore 1901-1968...DLB-114

Queen, Ellery (see Dannay, Frederic, and
Manfred B. Lee)

The Queen City Publishing House...DLB-49

Queneau, Raymond 1903-1976......DLB-72

Quennell, Sir Peter 1905-1993......DLB-155

Quesnel, Joseph 1746-1809.........DLB-99

The Question of American Copyright
in the Nineteenth Century
Headnote
Preface, by George Haven Putnam
The Evolution of Copyright, by Brander
Matthews
Summary of Copyright Legislation in
the United States, by R. R. Bowker
Analysis of the Provisions of the
Copyright Law of 1891, by
George Haven Putnam
The Contest for International Copyright,
by George Haven Putnam
Cheap Books and Good Books,
by Brander Matthews........DLB-49

Quiller-Couch, Sir Arthur Thomas
1863-1944...............DLB-135, 153

Quin, Ann 1936-1973..............DLB-14

Quincy, Samuel, of Georgia ?-?.....DLB-31

Quincy, Samuel, of Massachusetts
1734-1789....................DLB-31

Quinn, Anthony 1915-.............DLB-122

Quintana, Leroy V. 1944-..........DLB-82

Quintana, Miguel de 1671-1748
A Forerunner of Chicano
Literature....................DLB-122

Quist, Harlin, Books...............DLB-46

Quoirez, Françoise (see Sagan, Francçise)

R

Raabe, Wilhelm 1831-1910........DLB-129

Rabe, David 1940-.................DLB-7

Raboni, Giovanni 1932-...........DLB-128

Rachilde 1860-1953...............DLB-123

Racin, Kočo 1908-1943...........DLB-147

Rackham, Arthur 1867-1939.......DLB-141

Radcliffe, Ann 1764-1823 . . . . . . DLB-39, 178

Raddall, Thomas 1903- DLB-68

Radiguet, Raymond 1903-1923 . . . . . . DLB-65

Radishchev, Aleksandr Nikolaevich
   1749-1802 . . . . DLB-150

Radványi, Netty Reiling (see Seghers, Anna)

Rahv, Philip 1908-1973 . . . . DLB-137

Raimund, Ferdinand Jakob
   1790-1836 . . . . DLB-90

Raine, Craig 1944- DLB-40

Raine, Kathleen 1908- DLB-20

Rainolde, Richard
   circa 1530-1606 . . . . DLB-136

Rakić, Milan 1876-1938 . . . . DLB-147

Ralegh, Sir Walter 1554?-1618 . . . . . DLB-172

Ralph, Julian 1853-1903 . . . . DLB-23

Ralph Waldo Emerson in 1982 . . . . Y-82

Ramat, Silvio 1939- DLB-128

Rambler, no. 4 (1750), by Samuel Johnson
   [excerpt] DLB-39

Ramée, Marie Louise de la (see Ouida)

Ramírez, Sergío 1942- DLB-145

Ramke, Bin 1947- DLB-120

Ramler, Karl Wilhelm 1725-1798 . . . . DLB-97

Ramon Ribeyro, Julio 1929- DLB-145

Ramous, Mario 1924- DLB-128

Rampersad, Arnold 1941- DLB-111

Ramsay, Allan 1684 or 1685-1758 . . . DLB-95

Ramsay, David 1749-1815 . . . . DLB-30

Ranck, Katherine Quintana
   1942- DLB-122

Rand, Avery and Company DLB-49

Rand McNally and Company DLB-49

Randall, David Anton
   1905-1975 . . . . DLB-140

Randall, Dudley 1914- DLB-41

Randall, Henry S. 1811-1876 . . . . . . DLB-30

Randall, James G. 1881-1953 . . . . . . DLB-17

The Randall Jarrell Symposium: A Small
   Collection of Randall Jarrells
   Excerpts From Papers Delivered at
   the Randall Jarrell
   Symposium Y-86

Randolph, A. Philip 1889-1979 . . . . . DLB-91

Randolph, Anson D. F.
   [publishing house] DLB-49

Randolph, Thomas 1605-1635 . . DLB-58, 126

Random House DLB-46

Ranlet, Henry [publishing house] DLB-49

Ransom, John Crowe
   1888-1974 . . . . DLB-45, 63

Ransome, Arthur 1884-1967 . . . . DLB-160

Raphael, Frederic 1931- DLB-14

Raphaelson, Samson 1896-1983 . . . . . DLB-44

Raskin, Ellen 1928-1984 . . . . DLB-52

Rastell, John 1475?-1536 . . . . . . DLB-136, 170

Rattigan, Terence 1911-1977 . . . . DLB-13

Rawlings, Marjorie Kinnan
   1896-1953 . . . . DLB-9, 22, 102

Raworth, Tom 1938- DLB-40

Ray, David 1932- DLB-5

Ray, Gordon Norton
   1915-1986 . . . . DLB-103, 140

Ray, Henrietta Cordelia
   1849-1916 . . . . DLB-50

Raymond, Henry J. 1820-1869 . . . DLB-43, 79

Raymond Chandler Centenary Tributes
   from Michael Avallone, James Elroy, Joe
   Gores,
   and William F. Nolan Y-88

Reach, Angus 1821-1856 . . . . DLB-70

Read, Herbert 1893-1968 . . . . . . DLB-20, 149

Read, Herbert, "The Practice of Biography," in
   *The English Sense of Humour and Other
   Essays* DLB-149

Read, Opie 1852-1939 . . . . DLB-23

Read, Piers Paul 1941- DLB-14

Reade, Charles 1814-1884 . . . . DLB-21

Reader's Digest Condensed
   Books DLB-46

Reading, Peter 1946- DLB-40

Reading Series in New York City Y-96

Reaney, James 1926- DLB-68

Rebhun, Paul circa 1500-1546 . . . . . . DLB-179

Rèbora, Clemente 1885-1957 . . . . . . DLB-114

Rechy, John 1934- DLB-122; Y-82

The Recovery of Literature: Criticism in the
   1990s: A Symposium Y-91

Redding, J. Saunders
   1906-1988 . . . . DLB-63, 76

Redfield, J. S. [publishing house] DLB-49

Redgrove, Peter 1932- DLB-40

Redmon, Anne 1943- Y-86

Redmond, Eugene B. 1937- DLB-41

Redpath, James [publishing house] . . . DLB-49

Reed, Henry 1808-1854 . . . . DLB-59

Reed, Henry 1914- DLB-27

Reed, Ishmael
   1938- DLB-2, 5, 33, 169; DS-8

Reed, Sampson 1800-1880 . . . . DLB-1

Reed, Talbot Baines 1852-1893 . . . . . DLB-141

Reedy, William Marion 1862-1920 . . . DLB-91

Reese, Lizette Woodworth
   1856-1935 . . . . DLB-54

Reese, Thomas 1742-1796 . . . . DLB-37

Reeve, Clara 1729-1807 . . . . DLB-39

Reeves, James 1909-1978 . . . . DLB-161

Reeves, John 1926- DLB-88

Regnery, Henry, Company DLB-46

Rehberg, Hans 1901-1963 . . . . DLB-124

Rehfisch, Hans José 1891-1960 . . . . . DLB-124

Reid, Alastair 1926- DLB-27

Reid, B. L. 1918-1990 . . . . DLB-111

Reid, Christopher 1949- DLB-40

Reid, Forrest 1875-1947 . . . . DLB-153

Reid, Helen Rogers 1882-1970 . . . . . DLB-29

Reid, James ?-? DLB-31

Reid, Mayne 1818-1883 . . . . DLB-21, 163

Reid, Thomas 1710-1796 . . . . DLB-31

Reid, V. S. (Vic) 1913-1987 . . . . DLB-125

Reid, Whitelaw 1837-1912 . . . . DLB-23

Reilly and Lee Publishing
   Company DLB-46

Reimann, Brigitte 1933-1973 . . . . DLB-75

Reinmar der Alte
   circa 1165-circa 1205 . . . . DLB-138

Reinmar von Zweter
   circa 1200-circa 1250 . . . . DLB-138

Reisch, Walter 1903-1983 . . . . DLB-44

Remarque, Erich Maria 1898-1970 . . . DLB-56

"Re-meeting of Old Friends": The Jack
   Kerouac Conference Y-82

Remington, Frederic 1861-1909 . . . . . DLB-12

Renaud, Jacques 1943- DLB-60

Renault, Mary 1905-1983 . . . . Y-83

Rendell, Ruth 1930- DLB-87

Representative Men and Women: A Historical
   Perspective on the British Novel,
   1930-1960 . . . . DLB-15

(Re-)Publishing Orwell Y-86

Rettenbacher, Simon 1634-1706 . . . . DLB-168

Reuchlin, Johannes 1455-1522 . . . . . DLB-179

Reuter, Christian 1665-after 1712 . . . DLB-168

Reuter, Fritz 1810-1874 . . . . DLB-129

Reuter, Gabriele 1859-1941 .... DLB-66

Revell, Fleming H., Company DLB-49

Reventlow, Franziska Gräfin zu
1871-1918 .... DLB-66

Review of Reviews Office DLB-112

Review of [Samuel Richardson's] *Clarissa*
(1748), by Henry Fielding DLB-39

The Revolt (1937), by Mary Colum
[excerpts] DLB-36

Rexroth, Kenneth
1905-1982 .... DLB-16, 48, 165; Y-82

Rey, H. A. 1898-1977 .... DLB-22

Reynal and Hitchcock DLB-46

Reynolds, G. W. M. 1814-1879 ..... DLB-21

Reynolds, John Hamilton
1794-1852 .... DLB-96

Reynolds, Mack 1917- DLB-8

Reynolds, Sir Joshua 1723-1792 .... DLB-104

Reznikoff, Charles 1894-1976 .... DLB-28, 45

"Rhetoric" (1828; revised, 1859), by
Thomas de Quincey [excerpt] ... DLB-57

Rhett, Robert Barnwell 1800-1876 ... DLB-43

Rhode, John 1884-1964 .... DLB-77

Rhodes, James Ford 1848-1927 ...... DLB-47

Rhys, Jean 1890-1979 ..... DLB-36, 117, 162

Ricardo, David 1772-1823 ..... DLB-107, 158

Ricardou, Jean 1932- DLB-83

Rice, Elmer 1892-1967 .... DLB-4, 7

Rice, Grantland 1880-1954 ..... DLB-29, 171

Rich, Adrienne 1929- DLB-5, 67

Richards, David Adams 1950- DLB-53

Richards, George circa 1760-1814 ... DLB-37

Richards, I. A. 1893-1979 .... DLB-27

Richards, Laura E. 1850-1943 ..... DLB-42

Richards, William Carey
1818-1892 .... DLB-73

Richards, Grant
[publishing house] DLB-112

Richardson, Charles F. 1851-1913 ... DLB-71

Richardson, Dorothy M.
1873-1957 .... DLB-36

Richardson, Jack 1935- DLB-7

Richardson, John 1796-1852 .... DLB-99

Richardson, Samuel
1689-1761 .... DLB-39, 154

Richardson, Willis 1889-1977 ...... DLB-51

Riche, Barnabe 1542-1617 .... DLB-136

Richler, Mordecai 1931- DLB-53

Richter, Conrad 1890-1968 .... DLB-9

Richter, Hans Werner 1908- DLB-69

Richter, Johann Paul Friedrich
1763-1825 .... DLB-94

Rickerby, Joseph
[publishing house] DLB-106

Rickword, Edgell 1898-1982 .... DLB-20

Riddell, Charlotte 1832-1906 ...... DLB-156

Riddell, John (see Ford, Corey)

Ridge, John Rollin 1827-1867 ...... DLB-175

Ridge, Lola 1873-1941 .... DLB-54

Ridge, William Pett 1859-1930 ..... DLB-135

Riding, Laura (see Jackson, Laura Riding)

Ridler, Anne 1912- DLB-27

Ridruego, Dionisio 1912-1975 ...... DLB-108

Riel, Louis 1844-1885 .... DLB-99

Riemer, Johannes 1648-1714 .... DLB-168

Riffaterre, Michael 1924- DLB-67

Riggs, Lynn 1899-1954 .... DLB-175

Riis, Jacob 1849-1914 .... DLB-23

Riker, John C. [publishing house] DLB-49

Riley, John 1938-1978 .... DLB-40

Rilke, Rainer Maria 1875-1926 ..... DLB-81

Rimanelli, Giose 1926- DLB-177

Rinehart and Company DLB-46

Ringuet 1895-1960 .... DLB-68

Ringwood, Gwen Pharis
1910-1984 .... DLB-88

Rinser, Luise 1911- DLB-69

Ríos, Alberto 1952- DLB-122

Ríos, Isabella 1948- DLB-82

Ripley, Arthur 1895-1961 .... DLB-44

Ripley, George 1802-1880 ..... DLB-1, 64, 73

The Rising Glory of America:
Three Poems DLB-37

The Rising Glory of America: Written in 1771
(1786), by Hugh Henry Brackenridge and
Philip Freneau DLB-37

Riskin, Robert 1897-1955 .... DLB-26

Risse, Heinz 1898- DLB-69

Rist, Johann 1607-1667 .... DLB-164

Ritchie, Anna Mowatt 1819-1870 .... DLB-3

Ritchie, Anne Thackeray
1837-1919 .... DLB-18

Ritchie, Thomas 1778-1854 .... DLB-43

Rites of Passage
[on William Saroyan] Y-83

The Ritz Paris Hemingway Award Y-85

Rivard, Adjutor 1868-1945 .... DLB-92

Rive, Richard 1931-1989 .... DLB-125

Rivera, Marina 1942- DLB-122

Rivera, Tomás 1935-1984 .... DLB-82

Rivers, Conrad Kent 1933-1968 ..... DLB-41

Riverside Press DLB-49

Rivington, James circa 1724-1802 .... DLB-43

Rivington, Charles
[publishing house] DLB-154

Rivkin, Allen 1903-1990 .... DLB-26

Roa Bastos, Augusto 1917- DLB-113

Robbe-Grillet, Alain 1922- DLB-83

Robbins, Tom 1936- Y-80

Roberts, Charles G. D. 1860-1943 ... DLB-92

Roberts, Dorothy 1906-1993 .... DLB-88

Roberts, Elizabeth Madox
1881-1941 .... DLB-9, 54, 102

Roberts, Kenneth 1885-1957 .... DLB-9

Roberts, William 1767-1849 .... DLB-142

Roberts Brothers DLB-49

Roberts, James [publishing house] .. DLB-154

Robertson, A. M., and Company DLB-49

Robertson, William 1721-1793 ..... DLB-104

Robinson, Casey 1903-1979 .... DLB-44

Robinson, Edwin Arlington
1869-1935 .... DLB-54

Robinson, Henry Crabb
1775-1867 .... DLB-107

Robinson, James Harvey
1863-1936 .... DLB-47

Robinson, Lennox 1886-1958 .... DLB-10

Robinson, Mabel Louise
1874-1962 .... DLB-22

Robinson, Mary 1758-1800 .... DLB-158

Robinson, Richard
circa 1545-1607 .... DLB-167

Robinson, Therese
1797-1870 .... DLB-59, 133

Robison, Mary 1949- DLB-130

Roblès, Emmanuel 1914- DLB-83

Roccatagliata Ceccardi, Ceccardo
1871-1919 .... DLB-114

Rochester, John Wilmot, Earl of
1647-1680 .... DLB-131

Rock, Howard 1911-1976 .... DLB-127

Rodgers, Carolyn M. 1945- DLB-41

Rodgers, W. R. 1909-1969 .... DLB-20

Rodríguez, Claudio 1934- DLB-134	Ross, Martin 1862-1915..........DLB-135	Royston, Richard [publishing house] ..DLB-170
Rodriguez, Richard 1944- DLB-82	Ross, Sinclair 1908- DLB-88	Ruark, Gibbons 1941- DLB-120
Rodríguez Julia, Edgardo 1946- DLB-145	Ross, W. W. E. 1894-1966 ....DLB-88	Ruban, Vasilii Grigorevich 1742-1795 ....DLB-150
Roethke, Theodore 1908-1963 ....DLB-5	Rosselli, Amelia 1930- DLB-128	Rubens, Bernice 1928- DLB-14
Rogers, Pattiann 1940- DLB-105	Rossen, Robert 1908-1966.........DLB-26	Rudd and Carleton................DLB-49
Rogers, Samuel 1763-1855..........DLB-93	Rossetti, Christina Georgina 1830-1894 ....DLB-35, 163	Rudkin, David 1936- DLB-13
Rogers, Will 1879-1935 ....DLB-11	Rossetti, Dante Gabriel 1828-1882...DLB-35	Rudolf von Ems circa 1200-circa 1254 ....DLB-138
Rohmer, Sax 1883-1959............DLB-70	Rossner, Judith 1935- DLB-6	Ruffin, Josephine St. Pierre 1842-1924 ....DLB-79
Roiphe, Anne 1935- Y-80	Rosten, Leo 1908- DLB-11	Ruganda, John 1941- DLB-157
Rojas, Arnold R. 1896-1988 ....DLB-82	Rostenberg, Leona 1908- DLB-140	Ruggles, Henry Joseph 1813-1906 ...DLB-64
Rolfe, Frederick William 1860-1913 ....DLB-34, 156	Rostovsky, Dimitrii 1651-1709 .....DLB-150	Rukeyser, Muriel 1913-1980........DLB-48
	Bertram Rota and His Bookshop.......Y-91	Rule, Jane 1931- DLB-60
Rolland, Romain 1866-1944 ....DLB-65	Roth, Gerhard 1942- DLB-85, 124	Rulfo, Juan 1918-1986 ....DLB-113
Rolle, Richard circa 1290-1300 - 1340.........DLB-146	Roth, Henry 1906?- DLB-28	Rumaker, Michael 1932- DLB-16
Rölvaag, O. E. 1876-1931 ....DLB-9	Roth, Joseph 1894-1939 ....DLB-85	Rumens, Carol 1944- DLB-40
Romains, Jules 1885-1972 ....DLB-65	Roth, Philip 1933- DLB-2, 28, 173; Y-82	Runyon, Damon 1880-1946.............DLB-11, 86, 171
Roman, A., and Company..........DLB-49	Rothenberg, Jerome 1931- DLB-5	
Romano, Lalla 1906- DLB-177	Rotimi, Ola 1938- DLB-125	*Ruodlieb* circa 1050-1075..........DLB-148
Romano, Octavio 1923- DLB-122	Routhier, Adolphe-Basile 1839-1920 ....DLB-99	Rush, Benjamin 1746-1813 ....DLB-37
Romero, Leo 1950- DLB-122		Rusk, Ralph L. 1888-1962 ....DLB-103
Romero, Lin 1947- DLB-122	Routier, Simone 1901-1987 ....DLB-88	Ruskin, John 1819-1900........DLB-55, 163
Romero, Orlando 1945- DLB-82	Routledge, George, and Sons DLB-106	Russ, Joanna 1937- DLB-8
Rook, Clarence 1863-1915.........DLB-135	Roversi, Roberto 1923- DLB-128	Russell, B. B., and Company.......DLB-49
Roosevelt, Theodore 1858-1919 .....DLB-47	Rowe, Elizabeth Singer 1674-1737 ....DLB-39, 95	Russell, Benjamin 1761-1845........DLB-43
Root, Waverley 1903-1982 ....DLB-4	Rowe, Nicholas 1674-1718 ....DLB-84	Russell, Bertrand 1872-1970 ....DLB-100
Root, William Pitt 1941- DLB-120	Rowlands, Samuel circa 1570-1630...............DLB-121	Russell, Charles Edward 1860-1941 ....DLB-25
Roquebrune, Robert de 1889-1978...DLB-68		Russell, George William (see AE)
Rosa, João Guimarāres 1908-1967 ....DLB-113	Rowlandson, Mary circa 1635-circa 1678 ....DLB-24	Russell, R. H., and Son DLB-49
Rosales, Luis 1910-1992...........DLB-134	Rowley, William circa 1585-–1626...DLB-58	Rutherford, Mark 1831-1913........DLB-18
Roscoe, William 1753-1831........DLB-163	Rowse, A. L. 1903- DLB-155	Ryan, Michael 1946- Y-82
Rose, Reginald 1920- DLB-26	Rowson, Susanna Haswell circa 1762-1824................DLB-37	Ryan, Oscar 1904- DLB-68
Rose, Wendy 1948- DLB-175	Roy, Camille 1870-1943............DLB-92	Ryga, George 1932- DLB-60
Rosegger, Peter 1843-1918 ....DLB-129	Roy, Gabrielle 1909-1983 ....DLB-68	Rymer, Thomas 1643?-1713 ....DLB-101
Rosei, Peter 1946- DLB-85	Roy, Jules 1907- DLB-83	Ryskind, Morrie 1895-1985.........DLB-26
Rosen, Norma 1925- DLB-28	The Royal Court Theatre and the English Stage Company................DLB-13	Rzhevsky, Aleksei Andreevich 1737-1804 ....DLB-150
Rosenbach, A. S. W. 1876-1952 ....DLB-140		
Rosenberg, Isaac 1890-1918 ....DLB-20	The Royal Court Theatre and the New Drama DLB-10	
Rosenfeld, Isaac 1918-1956 ....DLB-28		# S
Rosenthal, M. L. 1917- DLB-5	The Royal Shakespeare Company at the Swan.....................Y-88	The Saalfield Publishing Company....................DLB-46
Ross, Alexander 1591-1654 ....DLB-151	Royall, Anne 1769-1854 ....DLB-43	
Ross, Harold 1892-1951 ....DLB-137	The Roycroft Printing Shop DLB-49	Von Saaz, Johannes (see von Tepl, Johannes)
Ross, Leonard Q. (see Rosten, Leo)	Royster, Vermont 1914- DLB-127	Saba, Umberto 1883-1957 ....DLB-114

Sábato, Ernesto 1911- DLB-145

Saberhagen, Fred 1930- DLB-8

Sacer, Gottfried Wilhelm 1635-1699 .... DLB-168

Sachs, Hans 1494-1576 .... DLB-179

Sackler, Howard 1929-1982 .... DLB-7

Sackville, Thomas 1536-1608 .... DLB-132

Sackville, Thomas 1536-1608 and Norton, Thomas 1532-1584 .... DLB-62

Sackville-West, V. 1892-1962 .... DLB-34

Sadlier, D. and J., and Company DLB-49

Sadlier, Mary Anne 1820-1903 .... DLB-99

Sadoff, Ira 1945- DLB-120

Saenz, Jaime 1921-1986 .... DLB-145

Saffin, John circa 1626-1710 .... DLB-24

Sagan, Françoise 1935- DLB-83

Sage, Robert 1899-1962 .... DLB-4

Sagel, Jim 1947- DLB-82

Sagendorph, Robb Hansell 1900-1970 .... DLB-137

Sahagún, Carlos 1938- DLB-108

Sahkomaapii, Piitai (see Highwater, Jamake)

Sahl, Hans 1902- DLB-69

Said, Edward W. 1935- DLB-67

Saiko, George 1892-1962 .... DLB-85

St. Dominic's Press DLB-112

Saint-Exupéry, Antoine de 1900-1944 .... DLB-72

St. Johns, Adela Rogers 1894-1988 .... DLB-29

St. Martin's Press DLB-46

St. Omer, Garth 1931- DLB-117

Saint Pierre, Michel de 1916-1987 .... DLB-83

Saintsbury, George 1845-1933 .... DLB-57, 149

Saki (see Munro, H. H.)

Salaam, Kalamu ya 1947- DLB-38

Salas, Floyd 1931- DLB-82

Sálaz-Marquez, Rubén 1935- DLB-122

Salemson, Harold J. 1910-1988 .... DLB-4

Salinas, Luis Omar 1937- DLB-82

Salinas, Pedro 1891-1951 .... DLB-134

Salinger, J. D. 1919- DLB-2, 102, 173

Salkey, Andrew 1928- DLB-125

Salt, Waldo 1914- DLB-44

Salter, James 1925- DLB-130

Salter, Mary Jo 1954- DLB-120

Salustri, Carlo Alberto (see Trilussa)

Salverson, Laura Goodman 1890-1970 .... DLB-92

Sampson, Richard Henry (see Hull, Richard)

Samuels, Ernest 1903- DLB-111

Sanborn, Franklin Benjamin 1831-1917 .... DLB-1

Sánchez, Luis Rafael 1936- DLB-145

Sánchez, Philomeno "Phil" 1917- DLB-122

Sánchez, Ricardo 1941- DLB-82

Sanchez, Sonia 1934- DLB-41; DS-8

Sand, George 1804-1876 .... DLB-119

Sandburg, Carl 1878-1967 .... DLB-17, 54

Sanders, Ed 1939- DLB-16

Sandoz, Mari 1896-1966 .... DLB-9

Sandwell, B. K. 1876-1954 .... DLB-92

Sandy, Stephen 1934- DLB-165

Sandys, George 1578-1644 .... DLB-24, 121

Sangster, Charles 1822-1893 .... DLB-99

Sanguineti, Edoardo 1930- DLB-128

Sansom, William 1912-1976 .... DLB-139

Santayana, George 1863-1952 .... DLB-54, 71; DS-13

Santiago, Danny 1911-1988 .... DLB-122

Santmyer, Helen Hooven 1895-1986 .... Y-84

Sapidus, Joannes 1490-1561 .... DLB-179

Sapir, Edward 1884-1939 .... DLB-92

Sapper (see McNeile, Herman Cyril)

Sappho circa 620 B.C.-circa 550 B.C. DLB-176

Sarduy, Severo 1937- DLB-113

Sargent, Pamela 1948- DLB-8

Saro-Wiwa, Ken 1941- DLB-157

Saroyan, William 1908-1981 .... DLB-7, 9, 86; Y-81

Sarraute, Nathalie 1900- DLB-83

Sarrazin, Albertine 1937-1967 .... DLB-83

Sarris, Greg 1952- DLB-175

Sarton, May 1912- DLB-48; Y-81

Sartre, Jean-Paul 1905-1980 .... DLB-72

Sassoon, Siegfried 1886-1967 .... DLB-20

Saturday Review Press DLB-46

Saunders, James 1925- DLB-13

Saunders, John Monk 1897-1940 .... DLB-26

Saunders, Margaret Marshall 1861-1947 .... DLB-92

Saunders and Otley DLB-106

Savage, James 1784-1873 .... DLB-30

Savage, Marmion W. 1803?-1872 .... DLB-21

Savage, Richard 1697?-1743 .... DLB-95

Savard, Félix-Antoine 1896-1982 .... DLB-68

Saville, (Leonard) Malcolm 1901-1982 .... DLB-160

Sawyer, Ruth 1880-1970 .... DLB-22

Sayers, Dorothy L. 1893-1957 .... DLB-10, 36, 77, 100

Sayles, John Thomas 1950- DLB-44

Sbarbaro, Camillo 1888-1967 .... DLB-114

Scannell, Vernon 1922- DLB-27

Scarry, Richard 1919-1994 .... DLB-61

Schaeffer, Albrecht 1885-1950 .... DLB-66

Schaeffer, Susan Fromberg 1941- DLB-28

Schaff, Philip 1819-1893 .... DS-13

Schaper, Edzard 1908-1984 .... DLB-69

Scharf, J. Thomas 1843-1898 .... DLB-47

Schede, Paul Melissus 1539-1602 .... DLB-179

Scheffel, Joseph Viktor von 1826-1886 .... DLB-129

Scheffler, Johann 1624-1677 .... DLB-164

Schelling, Friedrich Wilhelm Joseph von 1775-1854 .... DLB-90

Scherer, Wilhelm 1841-1886 .... DLB-129

Schickele, René 1883-1940 .... DLB-66

Schiff, Dorothy 1903-1989 .... DLB-127

Schiller, Friedrich 1759-1805 .... DLB-94

Schirmer, David 1623-1687 .... DLB-164

Schlaf, Johannes 1862-1941 .... DLB-118

Schlegel, August Wilhelm 1767-1845 .... DLB-94

Schlegel, Dorothea 1763-1839 .... DLB-90

Schlegel, Friedrich 1772-1829 .... DLB-90

Schleiermacher, Friedrich 1768-1834 .... DLB-90

Schlesinger, Arthur M., Jr. 1917- DLB-17

Schlumberger, Jean 1877-1968 .... DLB-65

Schmid, Eduard Hermann Wilhelm (see Edschmid, Kasimir)

Schmidt, Arno 1914-1979 .... DLB-69

Schmidt, Johann Kaspar (see Stirner, Max)

Schmidt, Michael 1947- DLB-40

Schmidtbonn, Wilhelm August 1876-1952 ....DLB-118

Schmitz, James H. 1911- DLB-8

Schnabel, Johann Gottfried 1692-1760 ....DLB-168

Schnackenberg, Gjertrud 1953- ...DLB-120

Schnitzler, Arthur 1862-1931 ...DLB-81, 118

Schnurre, Wolfdietrich 1920- DLB-69

Schocken Books DLB-46

Scholartis Press.................DLB-112

The Schomburg Center for Research in Black Culture DLB-76

Schönbeck, Virgilio (see Giotti, Virgilio)

Schönherr, Karl 1867-1943 ....DLB-118

Schoolcraft, Jane Johnston 1800-1841 ....DLB-175

School Stories, 1914-1960 ....DLB-160

Schopenhauer, Arthur 1788-1860....DLB-90

Schopenhauer, Johanna 1766-1838...DLB-90

Schorer, Mark 1908-1977..........DLB-103

Schottelius, Justus Georg 1612-1676 ....DLB-164

Schouler, James 1839-1920 ....DLB-47

Schrader, Paul 1946- DLB-44

Schreiner, Olive 1855-1920.....DLB-18, 156

Schroeder, Andreas 1946- DLB-53

Schubart, Christian Friedrich Daniel 1739-1791 ....DLB-97

Schubert, Gotthilf Heinrich 1780-1860 ....DLB-90

Schücking, Levin 1814-1883 ....DLB-133

Schulberg, Budd 1914- DLB-6, 26, 28; Y-81

Schulte, F. J., and Company DLB-49

Schulze, Hans (see Praetorius, Johannes)

Schupp, Johann Balthasar 1610-1661 ....DLB-164

Schurz, Carl 1829-1906 ....DLB-23

Schuyler, George S. 1895-1977...DLB-29, 51

Schuyler, James 1923-1991 .....DLB-5, 169

Schwartz, Delmore 1913-1966....DLB-28, 48

Schwartz, Jonathan 1938- Y-82

Schwarz, Sibylle 1621-1638 ....DLB-164

Schwerner, Armand 1927- DLB-165

Schwob, Marcel 1867-1905 ....DLB-123

Sciascia, Leonardo 1921-1989 ......DLB-177

Science Fantasy..................DLB-8

Science-Fiction Fandom and Conventions DLB-8

Science-Fiction Fanzines: The Time Binders......................DLB-8

Science-Fiction Films DLB-8

Science Fiction Writers of America and the Nebula Awards..................DLB-8

Scot, Reginald circa 1538-1599 .....DLB-136

Scotellaro, Rocco 1923-1953 ....DLB-128

Scott, Dennis 1939-1991...........DLB-125

Scott, Dixon 1881-1915 ....DLB-98

Scott, Duncan Campbell 1862-1947 ....DLB-92

Scott, Evelyn 1893-1963 ....DLB-9, 48

Scott, F. R. 1899-1985 ....DLB-88

Scott, Frederick George 1861-1944 ....DLB-92

Scott, Geoffrey 1884-1929 ....DLB-149

Scott, Harvey W. 1838-1910 ....DLB-23

Scott, Paul 1920-1978.............DLB-14

Scott, Sarah 1723-1795............DLB-39

Scott, Tom 1918- DLB-27

Scott, Sir Walter 1771-1832 ...DLB-93, 107, 116, 144, 159

Scott, William Bell 1811-1890.......DLB-32

Scott, Walter, Publishing Company Limited DLB-112

Scott, William R. [publishing house] DLB-46

Scott-Heron, Gil 1949- DLB-41

Scribner, Charles, Jr. 1921-1995........Y-95

Charles Scribner's Sons......DLB-49; DS-13

Scripps, E. W. 1854-1926...........DLB-25

Scudder, Horace Elisha 1838-1902 ....DLB-42, 71

Scudder, Vida Dutton 1861-1954 ....DLB-71

Scupham, Peter 1933- DLB-40

Seabrook, William 1886-1945 ....DLB-4

Seabury, Samuel 1729-1796.........DLB-31

Seacole, Mary Jane Grant 1805-1881 ....DLB-166

The Seafarer circa 970 ....DLB-146

Sealsfield, Charles 1793-1864 .....DLB-133

Sears, Edward I. 1819?-1876........DLB-79

Sears Publishing Company DLB-46

Seaton, George 1911-1979 ....DLB-44

Seaton, William Winston 1785-1866 ....DLB-43

Secker, Martin, and Warburg Limited DLB-112

Secker, Martin [publishing house] ..DLB-112

Second-Generation Minor Poets of the Seventeenth Century DLB-126

Sedgwick, Arthur George 1844-1915 ....DLB-64

Sedgwick, Catharine Maria 1789-1867 ....DLB-1, 74

Sedgwick, Ellery 1872-1930.........DLB-91

Sedley, Sir Charles 1639-1701......DLB-131

Seeger, Alan 1888-1916 ....DLB-45

Seers, Eugene (see Dantin, Louis)

Segal, Erich 1937- Y-86

Seghers, Anna 1900-1983...........DLB-69

Seid, Ruth (see Sinclair, Jo)

Seidel, Frederick Lewis 1936- Y-84

Seidel, Ina 1885-1974 ....DLB-56

Seigenthaler, John 1927- DLB-127

Seizin Press DLB-112

Séjour, Victor 1817-1874 ....DLB-50

Séjour Marcou et Ferrand, Juan Victor (see Séjour, Victor)

Selby, Hubert, Jr. 1928- DLB-2

Selden, George 1929-1989 ....DLB-52

Selected English-Language Little Magazines and Newspapers [France, 1920-1939]....................DLB-4

Selected Humorous Magazines (1820-1950) DLB-11

Selected Science-Fiction Magazines and Anthologies....................DLB-8

Self, Edwin F. 1920- DLB-137

Seligman, Edwin R. A. 1861-1939 ...DLB-47

Selous, Frederick Courteney 1851-1917 ....DLB-174

Seltzer, Chester E. (see Muro, Amado)

Seltzer, Thomas [publishing house] DLB-46

Selvon, Sam 1923-1994 ....DLB-125

Senancour, Etienne de 1770-1846...DLB-119

Sendak, Maurice 1928- DLB-61

Senécal, Eva 1905- DLB-92

Sengstacke, John 1912- DLB-127

Senior, Olive 1941- DLB-157

Šenoa, August 1838-1881..........DLB-147

"Sensation Novels" (1863), by H. L. Manse DLB-21

Sepamla, Sipho 1932- DLB-157

Seredy, Kate 1899-1975 .... DLB-22

Sereni, Vittorio 1913-1983 .... DLB-128

Seres, William
[publishing house] DLB-170

Serling, Rod 1924-1975 .... DLB-26

Serote, Mongane Wally 1944- DLB-125

Serraillier, Ian 1912-1994 .... DLB-161

Serrano, Nina 1934- DLB-122

Service, Robert 1874-1958 .... DLB-92

Seth, Vikram 1952- DLB-120

Seton, Ernest Thompson
1860-1942 .... DLB-92; DS-13

Settle, Mary Lee 1918- DLB-6

Seume, Johann Gottfried
1763-1810 .... DLB-94

Seuse, Heinrich 1295?-1366 .... DLB-179

Seuss, Dr. (see Geisel, Theodor Seuss)

The Seventy-fifth Anniversary of the Armistice:
The Wilfred Owen Centenary and the
Great War Exhibit at the University of
Virginia Y-93

Sewall, Joseph 1688-1769 .... DLB-24

Sewall, Richard B. 1908- DLB-111

Sewell, Anna 1820-1878 .... DLB-163

Sewell, Samuel 1652-1730 .... DLB-24

Sex, Class, Politics, and Religion [in the
British Novel, 1930-1959] DLB-15

Sexton, Anne 1928-1974 .... DLB-5, 169

Seymour-Smith, Martin 1928- DLB-155

Shaara, Michael 1929-1988 .... Y-83

Shadwell, Thomas 1641?-1692 ...... DLB-80

Shaffer, Anthony 1926- DLB-13

Shaffer, Peter 1926- DLB-13

Shaftesbury, Anthony Ashley Cooper,
Third Earl of 1671-1713 .... DLB-101

Shairp, Mordaunt 1887-1939 .... DLB-10

Shakespeare, William
1564-1616 .... DLB-62, 172

The Shakespeare Globe Trust Y-93

Shakespeare Head Press DLB-112

Shakhovskoi, Aleksandr Aleksandrovich
1777-1846 .... DLB-150

Shange, Ntozake 1948- DLB-38

Shapiro, Karl 1913- DLB-48

Sharon Publications DLB-46

Sharp, Margery 1905-1991 .... DLB-161

Sharp, William 1855-1905 .... DLB-156

Sharpe, Tom 1928- DLB-14

Shaw, Albert 1857-1947 .... DLB-91

Shaw, Bernard 1856-1950 .... DLB-10, 57

Shaw, Henry Wheeler 1818-1885 .... DLB-11

Shaw, Joseph T. 1874-1952 .... DLB-137

Shaw, Irwin 1913-1984 .... DLB-6, 102; Y-84

Shaw, Robert 1927-1978 .... DLB-13, 14

Shaw, Robert B. 1947- DLB-120

Shawn, William 1907-1992 .... DLB-137

Shay, Frank [publishing house] DLB-46

Shea, John Gilmary 1824-1892 ...... DLB-30

Sheaffer, Louis 1912-1993 .... DLB-103

Shearing, Joseph 1886-1952 .... DLB-70

Shebbeare, John 1709-1788 .... DLB-39

Sheckley, Robert 1928- DLB-8

Shedd, William G. T. 1820-1894 .... DLB-64

Sheed, Wilfred 1930- DLB-6

Sheed and Ward [U.S.] DLB-46

Sheed and Ward Limited [U.K.] DLB-112

Sheldon, Alice B. (see Tiptree, James, Jr.)

Sheldon, Edward 1886-1946 .... DLB-7

Sheldon and Company DLB-49

Shelley, Mary Wollstonecraft
1797-1851 .... DLB-110, 116, 159, 178

Shelley, Percy Bysshe
1792-1822 .... DLB-96, 110, 158

Shelnutt, Eve 1941- DLB-130

Shenstone, William 1714-1763 ...... DLB-95

Shepard, Ernest Howard
1879-1976 .... DLB-160

Shepard, Sam 1943- DLB-7

Shepard, Thomas I,
1604 or 1605-1649 .... DLB-24

Shepard, Thomas II, 1635-1677 ..... DLB-24

Shepard, Clark and Brown DLB-49

Shepherd, Luke
flourished 1547-1554 .... DLB-136

Sherburne, Edward 1616-1702 ..... DLB-131

Sheridan, Frances 1724-1766 ..... DLB-39, 84

Sheridan, Richard Brinsley
1751-1816 .... DLB-89

Sherman, Francis 1871-1926 .... DLB-92

Sherriff, R. C. 1896-1975 .... DLB-10

Sherry, Norman 1935- DLB-155

Sherwood, Mary Martha
1775-1851 .... DLB-163

Sherwood, Robert 1896-1955 ..... DLB-7, 26

Shiel, M. P. 1865-1947 .... DLB-153

Shiels, George 1886-1949 .... DLB-10

Shillaber, B.[enjamin] P.[enhallow]
1814-1890 .... DLB-1, 11

Shine, Ted 1931- DLB-38

Ship, Reuben 1915-1975 .... DLB-88

Shirer, William L. 1904-1993 .... DLB-4

Shirinsky-Shikhmatov, Sergii Aleksandrovich
1783-1837 .... DLB-150

Shirley, James 1596-1666 .... DLB-58

Shishkov, Aleksandr Semenovich
1753-1841 .... DLB-150

Shockley, Ann Allen 1927- DLB-33

Short, Peter
[publishing house] DLB-170

Shorthouse, Joseph Henry
1834-1903 .... DLB-18

Showalter, Elaine 1941- DLB-67

Shulevitz, Uri 1935- DLB-61

Shulman, Max 1919-1988 .... DLB-11

Shute, Henry A. 1856-1943 .... DLB-9

Shuttle, Penelope 1947- DLB-14, 40

Sibbes, Richard 1577-1635 .... DLB-151

Sidgwick and Jackson Limited DLB-112

Sidney, Margaret (see Lothrop, Harriet M.)

Sidney, Mary 1561-1621 .... DLB-167

Sidney, Sir Philip 1554-1586 .... DLB-167

Sidney's Press DLB-49

Siegfried Loraine Sassoon: A Centenary Essay
Tributes from Vivien F. Clarke and
Michael Thorpe Y-86

Sierra, Rubén 1946- DLB-122

Sierra Club Books DLB-49

Siger of Brabant
circa 1240-circa 1284 .... DLB-115

Sigourney, Lydia Howard (Huntley)
1791-1865 .... DLB-1, 42, 73

Silkin, Jon 1930- DLB-27

Silko, Leslie Marmon
1948- DLB-143, 175

Silliman, Ron 1946- DLB-169

Silliphant, Stirling 1918- DLB-26

Sillitoe, Alan 1928- DLB-14, 139

Silman, Roberta 1934- DLB-28

Silva, Beverly 1930- DLB-122

Silverberg, Robert 1935- DLB-8

Silverman, Kenneth 1936- DLB-111

Simak, Clifford D. 1904-1988 .... DLB-8

Simcoe, Elizabeth 1762-1850 .... DLB-99

Cumulative Index

Simcox, George Augustus 1841-1905 .... DLB-35

Sime, Jessie Georgina 1868-1958 ..... DLB-92

Simenon, Georges 1903-1989 .... DLB-72; Y-89

Simic, Charles 1938- DLB-105

Simic, Charles, Images and "Images" DLB-105

Simmel, Johannes Mario 1924- DLB-69

Simmes, Valentine [publishing house] DLB-170

Simmons, Ernest J. 1903-1972 ...... DLB-103

Simmons, Herbert Alfred 1930- DLB-33

Simmons, James 1933- DLB-40

Simms, William Gilmore 1806-1870 .... DLB-3, 30, 59, 73

Simms and M'Intyre DLB-106

Simon, Claude 1913- DLB-83

Simon, Neil 1927- DLB-7

Simon and Schuster DLB-46

Simons, Katherine Drayton Mayrant 1890-1969 .... Y-83

Simpkin and Marshall [publishing house] DLB-154

Simpson, Helen 1897-1940 .... DLB-77

Simpson, Louis 1923- DLB-5

Simpson, N. F. 1919- DLB-13

Sims, George 1923- DLB-87

Sims, George Robert 1847-1922 .... DLB-35, 70, 135

Sinán, Rogelio 1904- DLB-145

Sinclair, Andrew 1935- DLB-14

Sinclair, Bertrand William 1881-1972 .... DLB-92

Sinclair, Catherine 1800-1864 .... DLB-163

Sinclair, Jo 1913- DLB-28

Sinclair Lewis Centennial Conference Y-85

Sinclair, Lister 1921- DLB-88

Sinclair, May 1863-1946 .... DLB-36, 135

Sinclair, Upton 1878-1968 .... DLB-9

Sinclair, Upton [publishing house] ... DLB-46

Singer, Isaac Bashevis 1904-1991 .... DLB-6, 28, 52; Y-91

Singmaster, Elsie 1879-1958 .... DLB-9

Sinisgalli, Leonardo 1908-1981 ..... DLB-114

Siodmak, Curt 1902- DLB-44

Sissman, L. E. 1928-1976 .... DLB-5

Sisson, C. H. 1914- DLB-27

Sitwell, Edith 1887-1964 .... DLB-20

Sitwell, Osbert 1892-1969 .... DLB-100

Skármeta, Antonio 1940- DLB-145

Skeffington, William [publishing house] DLB-106

Skelton, John 1463-1529 .... DLB-136

Skelton, Robin 1925- DLB-27, 53

Skinner, Constance Lindsay 1877-1939 .... DLB-92

Skinner, John Stuart 1788-1851 ...... DLB-73

Skipsey, Joseph 1832-1903 .... DLB-35

Slade, Bernard 1930- DLB-53

Slater, Patrick 1880-1951 .... DLB-68

Slaveykov, Pencho 1866-1912 ...... DLB-147

Slavitt, David 1935- DLB-5, 6

Sleigh, Burrows Willcocks Arthur 1821-1869 .... DLB-99

A Slender Thread of Hope: The Kennedy Center Black Theatre Project DLB-38

Slesinger, Tess 1905-1945 .... DLB-102

Slick, Sam (see Haliburton, Thomas Chandler)

Sloane, William, Associates DLB-46

Small, Maynard and Company DLB-49

Small Presses in Great Britain and Ireland, 1960-1985 .... DLB-40

Small Presses I: Jargon Society Y-84

Small Presses II: The Spirit That Moves Us Press Y-85

Small Presses III: Pushcart Press Y-87

Smart, Christopher 1722-1771 ..... DLB-109

Smart, David A. 1892-1957 .... DLB-137

Smart, Elizabeth 1913-1986 .... DLB-88

Smellie, William [publishing house] DLB-154

Smiles, Samuel 1812-1904 .... DLB-55

Smith, A. J. M. 1902-1980 .... DLB-88

Smith, Adam 1723-1790 .... DLB-104

Smith, Alexander 1829-1867 ..... DLB-32, 55

Smith, Betty 1896-1972 .... Y-82

Smith, Carol Sturm 1938- Y-81

Smith, Charles Henry 1826-1903 .... DLB-11

Smith, Charlotte 1749-1806 .... DLB-39, 109

Smith, Chet 1899-1973 .... DLB-171

Smith, Cordwainer 1913-1966 .... DLB-8

Smith, Dave 1942- DLB-5

Smith, Dodie 1896- DLB-10

Smith, Doris Buchanan 1934- DLB-52

Smith, E. E. 1890-1965 .... DLB-8

Smith, Elihu Hubbard 1771-1798 .... DLB-37

Smith, Elizabeth Oakes (Prince) 1806-1893 .... DLB-1

Smith, F. Hopkinson 1838-1915 .... DS-13

Smith, George D. 1870-1920 ...... DLB-140

Smith, George O. 1911-1981 .... DLB-8

Smith, Goldwin 1823-1910 .... DLB-99

Smith, H. Allen 1907-1976 ...... DLB-11, 29

Smith, Hazel Brannon 1914- DLB-127

Smith, Henry circa 1560-circa 1591 .... DLB-136

Smith, Horatio (Horace) 1779-1849 .... DLB-116

Smith, Horatio (Horace) 1779-1849 and James Smith 1775-1839 .... DLB-96

Smith, Iain Crichton 1928- DLB-40, 139

Smith, J. Allen 1860-1924 .... DLB-47

Smith, John 1580-1631 .... DLB-24, 30

Smith, Josiah 1704-1781 .... DLB-24

Smith, Ken 1938- DLB-40

Smith, Lee 1944- DLB-143; Y-83

Smith, Logan Pearsall 1865-1946 .... DLB-98

Smith, Mark 1935- Y-82

Smith, Michael 1698-circa 1771 ..... DLB-31

Smith, Red 1905-1982 .... DLB-29, 171

Smith, Roswell 1829-1892 .... DLB-79

Smith, Samuel Harrison 1772-1845 .... DLB-43

Smith, Samuel Stanhope 1751-1819 .... DLB-37

Smith, Sarah (see Stretton, Hesba)

Smith, Seba 1792-1868 .... DLB-1, 11

Smith, Sir Thomas 1513-1577 ...... DLB-132

Smith, Stevie 1902-1971 .... DLB-20

Smith, Sydney 1771-1845 .... DLB-107

Smith, Sydney Goodsir 1915-1975 ... DLB-27

Smith, Wendell 1914-1972 .... DLB-171

Smith, William flourished 1595-1597 .... DLB-136

Smith, William 1727-1803 .... DLB-31

Smith, William 1728-1793 .... DLB-30

Smith, William Gardner 1927-1974 .... DLB-76

Smith, William Henry 1808-1872 .... DLB-159

Smith, William Jay 1918- DLB-5	Southern, Terry 1924- DLB-2	Spinrad, Norman 1940- DLB-8
Smith, Elder and Company DLB-154	Southern Writers Between the Wars DLB-9	Spires, Elizabeth 1952- DLB-120
Smith, Harrison, and Robert Haas [publishing house] DLB-46	Southerne, Thomas 1659-1746 ..... DLB-80	Spitteler, Carl 1845-1924 .... DLB-129
Smith, J. Stilman, and Company DLB-49	Southey, Caroline Anne Bowles 1786-1854 .... DLB-116	Spivak, Lawrence E. 1900- DLB-137
Smith, W. B., and Company DLB-49	Southey, Robert 1774-1843 .... DLB-93, 107, 142	Spofford, Harriet Prescott 1835-1921 .... DLB-74
Smith, W. H., and Son DLB-106	Southwell, Robert 1561?-1595 ..... DLB-167	Squibob (see Derby, George Horatio)
Smithers, Leonard [publishing house] DLB-112	Sowande, Bode 1948- DLB-157	The St. John's College Robert Graves Trust Y-96
Smollett, Tobias 1721-1771 ..... DLB-39, 104	Sowle, Tace [publishing house] DLB-170	Stacpoole, H. de Vere 1863-1951 .... DLB-153
Snellings, Rolland (see Touré, Askia Muhammad)	Soyfer, Jura 1912-1939 .... DLB-124	Staël, Germaine de 1766-1817 ...... DLB-119
Snodgrass, W. D. 1926- DLB-5	Soyinka, Wole 1934- DLB-125; Y-86, 87	Staël-Holstein, Anne-Louise Germaine de (see Staël, Germaine de)
Snow, C. P. 1905-1980 .... DLB-15, 77	Spacks, Barry 1931- DLB-105	Stafford, Jean 1915-1979 .... DLB-2, 173
Snyder, Gary 1930- DLB-5, 16, 165	Spalding, Frances 1950- DLB-155	Stafford, William 1914- DLB-5
Sobiloff, Hy 1912-1970 .... DLB-48	Spark, Muriel 1918- DLB-15, 139	Stage Censorship: "The Rejected Statement" (1911), by Bernard Shaw [excerpts] DLB-10
The Society for Textual Scholarship and TEXT Y-87	Sparke, Michael [publishing house] DLB-170	
The Society for the History of Authorship, Reading and Publishing Y-92	Sparks, Jared 1789-1866 .... DLB-1, 30	Stallings, Laurence 1894-1968 ..... DLB-7, 44
Soffici, Ardengo 1879-1964 .... DLB-114	Sparshott, Francis 1926- DLB-60	Stallworthy, Jon 1935- DLB-40
Sofola, 'Zulu 1938- DLB-157	Späth, Gerold 1939- DLB-75	Stampp, Kenneth M. 1912- DLB-17
Solano, Solita 1888-1975 .... DLB-4	Spatola, Adriano 1941-1988 .... DLB-128	Stanford, Ann 1916- DLB-5
Soldati, Mario 1906- DLB-177	Spaziani, Maria Luisa 1924- DLB-128	Stanković, Borisav ("Bora") 1876-1927 .... DLB-147
Sollers, Philippe 1936- DLB-83	*The Spectator* 1828- DLB-110	Stanley, Henry M. 1841-1904 .... DS-13
Solmi, Sergio 1899-1981 .... DLB-114	Spedding, James 1808-1881 .... DLB-144	Stanley, Thomas 1625-1678 .... DLB-131
Solomon, Carl 1928- DLB-16	Spee von Langenfeld, Friedrich 1591-1635 .... DLB-164	Stannard, Martin 1947- DLB-155
Solway, David 1941- DLB-53	Speght, Rachel 1597-after 1630 .... DLB-126	Stansby, William [publishing house] DLB-170
Solzhenitsyn and America Y-85	Speke, John Hanning 1827-1864 .... DLB-166	Stanton, Elizabeth Cady 1815-1902 .. DLB-79
Somerville, Edith Œnone 1858-1949 .... DLB-135	Spellman, A. B. 1935- DLB-41	Stanton, Frank L. 1857-1927 .... DLB-25
Song, Cathy 1955- DLB-169	Spence, Thomas 1750-1814 .... DLB-158	Stanton, Maura 1946- DLB-120
Sontag, Susan 1933- DLB-2, 67	Spencer, Anne 1882-1975 .... DLB-51, 54	Stapledon, Olaf 1886-1950 .... DLB-15
Sophocles 497/496 B.C.-406/405 B.C. DLB-176	Spencer, Elizabeth 1921- DLB-6	Star Spangled Banner Office DLB-49
	Spencer, Herbert 1820-1903 .... DLB-57	Starkey, Thomas circa 1499-1538 ... DLB-132
Sorge, Reinhard Johannes 1892-1916 .... DLB-118	Spencer, Scott 1945- Y-86	Starkweather, David 1935- DLB-7
Sorrentino, Gilbert 1929- DLB-5, 173; Y-80	Spender, J. A. 1862-1942 .... DLB-98	Statements on the Art of Poetry DLB-54
	Spender, Stephen 1909- DLB-20	Stationers' Company of London, The DLB-170
Sotheby, William 1757-1833 .... DLB-93	Spener, Philipp Jakob 1635-1705 ... DLB-164	
Soto, Gary 1952- DLB-82	Spenser, Edmund circa 1552-1599 .. DLB-167	Stead, Robert J. C. 1880-1959 ...... DLB-92
Sources for the Study of Tudor and Stuart Drama DLB-62	Sperr, Martin 1944- DLB-124	Steadman, Mark 1930- DLB-6
Souster, Raymond 1921- DLB-88	Spicer, Jack 1925-1965 .... DLB-5, 16	The Stealthy School of Criticism (1871), by Dante Gabriel Rossetti DLB-35
The *South English Legendary* circa thirteenth-fifteenth centuries DLB-146	Spielberg, Peter 1929- Y-81	
	Spielhagen, Friedrich 1829-1911 .... DLB-129	Stearns, Harold E. 1891-1943 .... DLB-4
Southerland, Ellease 1943- DLB-33	"Spielmannsepen" (circa 1152-circa 1500) DLB-148	Stedman, Edmund Clarence 1833-1908 .... DLB-64
Southern Illinois University Press Y-95	Spier, Peter 1927- DLB-61	Steegmuller, Francis 1906-1994 ..... DLB-111

Steel, Flora Annie 1847-1929 .... DLB-153, 156

Steele, Max 1922- Y-80

Steele, Richard 1672-1729 ...... DLB-84, 101

Steele, Timothy 1948- DLB-120

Steele, Wilbur Daniel 1886-1970 .... DLB-86

Steere, Richard circa 1643-1721 ..... DLB-24

Stegner, Wallace 1909-1993 .... DLB-9; Y-93

Stehr, Hermann 1864-1940 .... DLB-66

Steig, William 1907- DLB-61

Stein, Gertrude 1874-1946 .... DLB-4, 54, 86

Stein, Leo 1872-1947 .... DLB-4

Stein and Day Publishers DLB-46

Steinbeck, John 1902-1968 ... DLB-7, 9; DS-2

Steiner, George 1929- DLB-67

Steinhoewel, Heinrich 1411/1412-1479 .... DLB-179

Stendhal 1783-1842 .... DLB-119

Stephen Crane: A Revaluation Virginia Tech Conference, 1989 .... Y-89

Stephen, Leslie 1832-1904 ...... DLB-57, 144

Stephens, Alexander H. 1812-1883 ... DLB-47

Stephens, Ann 1810-1886 .... DLB-3, 73

Stephens, Charles Asbury 1844?-1931 .... DLB-42

Stephens, James 1882?-1950 .... DLB-19, 153, 162

Sterling, George 1869-1926 .... DLB-54

Sterling, James 1701-1763 .... DLB-24

Sterling, John 1806-1844 .... DLB-116

Stern, Gerald 1925- DLB-105

Stern, Madeleine B. 1912- ... DLB-111, 140

Stern, Gerald, Living in Ruin DLB-105

Stern, Richard 1928- Y-87

Stern, Stewart 1922- DLB-26

Sterne, Laurence 1713-1768 .... DLB-39

Sternheim, Carl 1878-1942 ..... DLB-56, 118

Sternhold, Thomas ?-1549 and John Hopkins ?-1570 .... DLB-132

Stevens, Henry 1819-1886 .... DLB-140

Stevens, Wallace 1879-1955 .... DLB-54

Stevenson, Anne 1933- DLB-40

Stevenson, Lionel 1902-1973 ...... DLB-155

Stevenson, Robert Louis 1850-1894 ...... DLB-18, 57, 141, 156, 174; DS-13

Stewart, Donald Ogden 1894-1980 .... DLB-4, 11, 26

Stewart, Dugald 1753-1828 .... DLB-31

Stewart, George, Jr. 1848-1906 ..... DLB-99

Stewart, George R. 1895-1980 .... DLB-8

Stewart and Kidd Company DLB-46

Stewart, Randall 1896-1964 .... DLB-103

Stickney, Trumbull 1874-1904 ..... DLB-54

Stieler, Caspar 1632-1707 .... DLB-164

Stifter, Adalbert 1805-1868 .... DLB-133

Stiles, Ezra 1727-1795 .... DLB-31

Still, James 1906- DLB-9

Stirner, Max 1806-1856 .... DLB-129

Stith, William 1707-1755 .... DLB-31

Stock, Elliot [publishing house] DLB-106

Stockton, Frank R. 1834-1902 .... DLB-42, 74; DS-13

Stoddard, Ashbel [publishing house] DLB-49

Stoddard, Richard Henry 1825-1903 .... DLB-3, 64; DS-13

Stoddard, Solomon 1643-1729 ..... DLB-24

Stoker, Bram 1847-1912 .... DLB-36, 70, 178

Stokes, Frederick A., Company DLB-49

Stokes, Thomas L. 1898-1958 .... DLB-29

Stokesbury, Leon 1945- DLB-120

Stolberg, Christian Graf zu 1748-1821 .... DLB-94

Stolberg, Friedrich Leopold Graf zu 1750-1819 .... DLB-94

Stone, Herbert S., and Company DLB-49

Stone, Lucy 1818-1893 .... DLB-79

Stone, Melville 1848-1929 .... DLB-25

Stone, Robert 1937- DLB-152

Stone, Ruth 1915- DLB-105

Stone, Samuel 1602-1663 .... DLB-24

Stone and Kimball DLB-49

Stoppard, Tom 1937- DLB-13; Y-85

Storey, Anthony 1928- DLB-14

Storey, David 1933- DLB-13, 14

Storm, Theodor 1817-1888 .... DLB-129

Story, Thomas circa 1670-1742 ...... DLB-31

Story, William Wetmore 1819-1895 ... DLB-1

Storytelling: A Contemporary Renaissance Y-84

Stoughton, William 1631-1701 ...... DLB-24

Stow, John 1525-1605 .... DLB-132

Stowe, Harriet Beecher 1811-1896 .... DLB-1, 12, 42, 74

Stowe, Leland 1899- DLB-29

Stoyanov, Dimitŭr Ivanov (see Elin Pelin)

Strabo 64 or 63 B.C.-circa A.D. 25 .... DLB-176

Strachey, Lytton 1880-1932 .... DLB-149; DS-10

Strachey, Lytton, Preface to Eminent Victorians DLB-149

Strahan and Company DLB-106

Strahan, William [publishing house] DLB-154

Strand, Mark 1934- DLB-5

The Strasbourg Oaths 842 .... DLB-148

Stratemeyer, Edward 1862-1930 ..... DLB-42

Strati, Saverio 1924- DLB-177

Stratton and Barnard DLB-49

Stratton-Porter, Gene 1863-1924 ..... DS-14

Straub, Peter 1943- Y-84

Strauß, Botho 1944- DLB-124

Strauß, David Friedrich 1808-1874 .... DLB-133

The Strawberry Hill Press DLB-154

Streatfeild, Noel 1895-1986 .... DLB-160

Street, Cecil John Charles (see Rhode, John)

Street, G. S. 1867-1936 .... DLB-135

Street and Smith DLB-49

Streeter, Edward 1891-1976 .... DLB-11

Streeter, Thomas Winthrop 1883-1965 .... DLB-140

Stretton, Hesba 1832-1911 .... DLB-163

Stribling, T. S. 1881-1965 .... DLB-9

Der Stricker circa 1190-circa 1250 .. DLB-138

Strickland, Samuel 1804-1867 .... DLB-99

Stringer and Townsend DLB-49

Stringer, Arthur 1874-1950 .... DLB-92

Strittmatter, Erwin 1912- DLB-69

Strode, William 1630-1645 .... DLB-126

Strother, David Hunter 1816-1888 .... DLB-3

Strouse, Jean 1945- DLB-111

Stuart, Dabney 1937- DLB-105

Stuart, Dabney, Knots into Webs: Some Autobiographical Sources DLB-105

Stuart, Jesse 1906-1984 .... DLB-9, 48, 102; Y-84

Stuart, Lyle [publishing house] DLB-46

Stubbs, Harry Clement (see Clement, Hal)

Stubenberg, Johann Wilhelm von 1619-1663 .... DLB-164

Studio DLB-112

The Study of Poetry (1880), by Matthew Arnold DLB-35

Sturgeon, Theodore 1918-1985 .... DLB-8; Y-85

Sturges, Preston 1898-1959 .... DLB-26

"Style" (1840; revised, 1859), by Thomas de Quincey [excerpt].... DLB-57

"Style" (1888), by Walter Pater DLB-57

Style (1897), by Walter Raleigh [excerpt] DLB-57

"Style" (1877), by T. H. Wright [excerpt] DLB-57

"Le Style c'est l'homme" (1892), by W. H. Mallock DLB-57

Styron, William 1925- DLB-2, 143; Y-80

Suárez, Mario 1925- DLB-82

Such, Peter 1939- DLB-60

Suckling, Sir John 1609-1641? .. DLB-58, 126

Suckow, Ruth 1892-1960 .... DLB-9, 102

Sudermann, Hermann 1857-1928 ... DLB-118

Sue, Eugène 1804-1857 .... DLB-119

Sue, Marie-Joseph (see Sue, Eugène)

Suggs, Simon (see Hooper, Johnson Jones)

Sukenick, Ronald 1932- DLB-173; Y-81

Suknaski, Andrew 1942- DLB-53

Sullivan, Alan 1868-1947 .... DLB-92

Sullivan, C. Gardner 1886-1965 ..... DLB-26

Sullivan, Frank 1892-1976 .... DLB-11

Sulte, Benjamin 1841-1923 .... DLB-99

Sulzberger, Arthur Hays 1891-1968 .... DLB-127

Sulzberger, Arthur Ochs 1926- DLB-127

Sulzer, Johann Georg 1720-1779 ..... DLB-97

Sumarokov, Aleksandr Petrovich 1717-1777 .... DLB-150

Summers, Hollis 1916- DLB-6

Sumner, Henry A. [publishing house] DLB-49

Surtees, Robert Smith 1803-1864 .... DLB-21

A Survey of Poetry Anthologies, 1879-1960 .... DLB-54

Surveys of the Year's Biographies

A Transit of Poets and Others: American Biography in 1982 .... Y-82

The Year in Literary Biography ... Y-83–Y-96

Survey of the Year's Book Publishing

The Year in Book Publishing Y-86

Survey of the Year's Children's Books

The Year in Children's Books Y-92–Y-96

Surveys of the Year's Drama

The Year in Drama Y-82–Y-85, Y-87–Y-96

The Year in London Theatre Y-92

Surveys of the Year's Fiction

The Year's Work in Fiction: A Survey Y-82

The Year in Fiction: A Biased View Y-83

The Year in Fiction...... Y-84–Y-86, Y-89, Y-94–Y-96

The Year in the Novel Y-87, Y-88, Y-90–Y-93

The Year in Short Stories Y-87

The Year in the Short Story........... Y-88, Y-90–Y-93

Survey of the Year's Literary Theory

The Year in Literary Theory Y-92–Y-93

Surveys of the Year's Poetry

The Year's Work in American Poetry Y-82

The Year in Poetry ... Y-83–Y-92, Y-94–Y-96

Suso, Henry (see Seuse, Heinrich)

Sutherland, Efua Theodora 1924- DLB-117

Sutherland, John 1919-1956......... DLB-68

Sutro, Alfred 1863-1933............ DLB-10

Swados, Harvey 1920-1972 .... DLB-2

Swain, Charles 1801-1874 .... DLB-32

Swallow Press DLB-46

Swan Sonnenschein Limited DLB-106

Swanberg, W. A. 1907- DLB-103

Swenson, May 1919-1989 .... DLB-5

Swerling, Jo 1897- DLB-44

Swift, Jonathan 1667-1745............ DLB-39, 95, 101

Swinburne, A. C. 1837-1909..... DLB-35, 57

Swineshead, Richard floruit circa 1350 .... DLB-115

Swinnerton, Frank 1884-1982 .... DLB-34

Swisshelm, Jane Grey 1815-1884 .... DLB-43

Swope, Herbert Bayard 1882-1958 ... DLB-25

Swords, T. and J., and Company DLB-49

Swords, Thomas 1763-1843 and Swords, James ?-1844 .... DLB-73

Sykes, Ella C. ?-1939 .... DLB-174

Sylvester, Josuah 1562 or 1563 - 1618 .... DLB-121

Symonds, Emily Morse (see Paston, George)

Symonds, John Addington 1840-1893 .... DLB-57, 144

Symons, A. J. A. 1900-1941........ DLB-149

Symons, Arthur 1865-1945............ DLB-19, 57, 149

Symons, Julian 1912-1994........... DLB-87, 155; Y-92

Symons, Scott 1933- DLB-53

A Symposium on *The Columbia History of the Novel*........................ Y-92

Synge, John Millington 1871-1909 .... DLB-10, 19

Synge Summer School: J. M. Synge and the Irish Theater, Rathdrum, County Wiclow, Ireland......................... Y-93

Syrett, Netta 1865-1943 .... DLB-135

Szymborska, Wisława 1923- Y-96

T

Taban lo Liyong 1939?- DLB-125

Taché, Joseph-Charles 1820-1894.... DLB-99

Tafolla, Carmen 1951- DLB-82

Taggard, Genevieve 1894-1948...... DLB-45

Tagger, Theodor (see Bruckner, Ferdinand)

Tait, J. Selwin, and Sons DLB-49

Tait's Edinburgh Magazine 1832-1861 .... DLB-110

The Takarazaka Revue Company Y-91

Talander (see Bohse, August)

Tallent, Elizabeth 1954- DLB-130

Talvj 1797-1870 .... DLB-59, 133

Tan, Amy 1952- DLB-173

Tapahonso, Luci 1953- DLB-175

Taradash, Daniel 1913- DLB-44

Tarbell, Ida M. 1857-1944 .... DLB-47

Tardivel, Jules-Paul 1851-1905 ...... DLB-99

Targan, Barry 1932- DLB-130

Tarkington, Booth 1869-1946.... DLB-9, 102

Tashlin, Frank 1913-1972 .... DLB-44

Tate, Allen 1899-1979 .... DLB-4, 45, 63

Tate, James 1943- DLB-5, 169

Tate, Nahum circa 1652-1715 .... DLB-80

Tatian circa 830 .... DLB-148

Tauler, Johannes circa 1300-1361 ... DLB-179

Tavčar, Ivan 1851-1923 . . . . DLB-147

Taylor, Ann 1782-1866 . . . . DLB-163

Taylor, Bayard 1825-1878 . . . . DLB-3

Taylor, Bert Leston 1866-1921 . . . . . . DLB-25

Taylor, Charles H. 1846-1921 . . . . DLB-25

Taylor, Edward circa 1642-1729 . . . . . DLB-24

Taylor, Elizabeth 1912-1975 . . . . DLB-139

Taylor, Henry 1942- DLB-5

Taylor, Sir Henry 1800-1886 . . . . DLB-32

Taylor, Jane 1783-1824 . . . . DLB-163

Taylor, Jeremy circa 1613-1667 . . . . DLB-151

Taylor, John
  1577 or 1578 - 1653 . . . . DLB-121

Taylor, Mildred D. ?- DLB-52

Taylor, Peter 1917-1994 . . . . Y-81, Y-94

Taylor, William, and Company DLB-49

Taylor-Made Shakespeare? Or Is
  "Shall I Die?" the Long-Lost Text
  of Bottom's Dream? Y-85

Teasdale, Sara 1884-1933 . . . . DLB-45

The Tea-Table (1725), by Eliza Haywood [excerpt] DLB-39

Telles, Lygia Fagundes 1924- DLB-113

Temple, Sir William 1628-1699 . . . . DLB-101

Tenn, William 1919- DLB-8

Tennant, Emma 1937- DLB-14

Tenney, Tabitha Gilman
  1762-1837 . . . . DLB-37

Tennyson, Alfred 1809-1892 . . . . DLB-32

Tennyson, Frederick 1807-1898 . . . . . DLB-32

von Tepl, Johannes
  circa 1350-1414/1415 . . . . DLB-179

Terhune, Albert Payson 1872-1942 . . . DLB-9

Terhune, Mary Virginia 1830-1922 . . . . DS-13

Terry, Megan 1932- DLB-7

Terson, Peter 1932- DLB-13

Tesich, Steve 1943- Y-83

Tessa, Delio 1886-1939 . . . . DLB-114

Testori, Giovanni 1923-1993 . . . DLB-128, 177

Tey, Josephine 1896?-1952 . . . . DLB-77

Thacher, James 1754-1844 . . . . DLB-37

Thackeray, William Makepeace
  1811-1863 . . . . DLB-21, 55, 159, 163

Thames and Hudson Limited DLB-112

Thanet, Octave (see French, Alice)

The Theater in Shakespeare's Time DLB-62

The Theatre Guild DLB-7

Thegan and the Astronomer
  flourished circa 850 . . . . DLB-148

Thelwall, John 1764-1834 . . . . . . DLB-93, 158

Theocritus circa 300 B.C.-260 B.C.
  . . . . DLB-176

Theodulf circa 760-circa 821 . . . . . . DLB-148

Theophrastus circa 371 B.C.-287 B.C.
  . . . . DLB-176

Theriault, Yves 1915-1983 . . . . DLB-88

Thério, Adrien 1925- DLB-53

Theroux, Paul 1941- DLB-2

Thibaudeau, Colleen 1925- DLB-88

Thielen, Benedict 1903-1965 . . . . . . DLB-102

Thiong'o Ngugi wa (see Ngugi wa Thiong'o)

Third-Generation Minor Poets of the
  Seventeenth Century DLB-131

Thoma, Ludwig 1867-1921 . . . . DLB-66

Thoma, Richard 1902- DLB-4

Thomas, Audrey 1935- DLB-60

Thomas, D. M. 1935- DLB-40

Thomas, Dylan
  1914-1953 . . . . DLB-13, 20, 139

Thomas, Edward
  1878-1917 . . . . DLB-19, 98, 156

Thomas, Gwyn 1913-1981 . . . . DLB-15

Thomas, Isaiah 1750-1831 . . . . . . DLB-43, 73

Thomas, Isaiah [publishing house] . . . DLB-49

Thomas, Johann 1624-1679 . . . . DLB-168

Thomas, John 1900-1932 . . . . DLB-4

Thomas, Joyce Carol 1938- DLB-33

Thomas, Lorenzo 1944- DLB-41

Thomas, R. S. 1915- DLB-27

Thomasîn von Zerclære
  circa 1186-circa 1259 . . . . DLB-138

Thomasius, Christian 1655-1728 . . . DLB-168

Thompson, David 1770-1857 . . . . . . DLB-99

Thompson, Dorothy 1893-1961 . . . . . DLB-29

Thompson, Francis 1859-1907 . . . . . . DLB-19

Thompson, George Selden (see Selden, George)

Thompson, John 1938-1976 . . . . DLB-60

Thompson, John R. 1823-1873 . . . . DLB-3, 73

Thompson, Lawrance 1906-1973 . . . DLB-103

Thompson, Maurice
  1844-1901 . . . . DLB-71, 74

Thompson, Ruth Plumly
  1891-1976 . . . . DLB-22

Thompson, Thomas Phillips
  1843-1933 . . . . DLB-99

Thompson, William 1775-1833 . . . . . DLB-158

Thompson, William Tappan
  1812-1882 . . . . DLB-3, 11

Thomson, Edward William
  1849-1924 . . . . DLB-92

Thomson, James 1700-1748 . . . . DLB-95

Thomson, James 1834-1882 . . . . DLB-35

Thomson, Joseph 1858-1895 . . . . DLB-174

Thomson, Mortimer 1831-1875 . . . . . DLB-11

Thoreau, Henry David 1817-1862 . . . . DLB-1

Thorpe, Thomas Bangs
  1815-1878 . . . . DLB-3, 11

Thoughts on Poetry and Its Varieties (1833),
  by John Stuart Mill DLB-32

Thrale, Hester Lynch (see Piozzi, Hester
  Lynch [Thrale])

Thucydides circa 455 B.C.-circa 395 B.C.
  . . . . DLB-176

Thümmel, Moritz August von
  1738-1817 . . . . DLB-97

Thurber, James
  1894-1961 . . . . DLB-4, 11, 22, 102

Thurman, Wallace 1902-1934 . . . . . . DLB-51

Thwaite, Anthony 1930- DLB-40

Thwaites, Reuben Gold
  1853-1913 . . . . DLB-47

Ticknor, George
  1791-1871 . . . . DLB-1, 59, 140

Ticknor and Fields DLB-49

Ticknor and Fields (revived) DLB-46

Tieck, Ludwig 1773-1853 . . . . DLB-90

Tietjens, Eunice 1884-1944 . . . . DLB-54

Tilney, Edmund circa 1536-1610 . . . DLB-136

Tilt, Charles [publishing house] DLB-106

Tilton, J. E., and Company DLB-49

Time and Western Man (1927), by Wyndham
  Lewis [excerpts] DLB-36

Time-Life Books DLB-46

Times Books DLB-46

Timothy, Peter circa 1725-1782 . . . . . DLB-43

Timrod, Henry 1828-1867 . . . . DLB-3

Tinker, Chauncey Brewster
  1876-1963 . . . . DLB-140

Tinsley Brothers DLB-106

Tiptree, James, Jr. 1915-1987 . . . . DLB-8

Titus, Edward William 1870-1952 . . . DLB-4

Tlali, Miriam 1933- DLB-157

Todd, Barbara Euphan
  1890-1976 . . . . DLB-160

Tofte, Robert
1561 or 1562-1619 or 1620 ..... DLB-172

Toklas, Alice B. 1877-1967 .... DLB-4

Tolkien, J. R. R. 1892-1973 .... DLB-15, 160

Toller, Ernst 1893-1939 .... DLB-124

Tollet, Elizabeth 1694-1754 .... DLB-95

Tolson, Melvin B. 1898-1966 .... DLB-48, 76

Tom Jones (1749), by Henry Fielding
[excerpt].................... DLB-39

Tomalin, Claire 1933- DLB-155

Tomasi di Lampedusa, Giuseppe 1896-1957
.... DLB-177

Tomlinson, Charles 1927- DLB-40

Tomlinson, H. M. 1873-1958 ... DLB-36, 100

Tompkins, Abel [publishing house] .. DLB-49

Tompson, Benjamin 1642-1714 ...... DLB-24

Tonks, Rosemary 1932- DLB-14

Tonna, Charlotte Elizabeth
1790-1846 .... DLB-163

Tonson, Jacob the Elder
[publishing house] DLB-170

Toole, John Kennedy 1937-1969 .... Y-81

Toomer, Jean 1894-1967 .... DLB-45, 51

Tor Books DLB-46

Torberg, Friedrich 1908-1979 .... DLB-85

Torrence, Ridgely 1874-1950 .... DLB-54

Torres-Metzger, Joseph V.
1933- DLB-122

Toth, Susan Allen 1940- Y-86

Tottell, Richard
[publishing house] DLB-170

Tough-Guy Literature DLB-9

Touré, Askia Muhammad 1938- DLB-41

Tourgée, Albion W. 1838-1905 ...... DLB-79

Tourneur, Cyril circa 1580-1626 .... DLB-58

Tournier, Michel 1924- DLB-83

Tousey, Frank [publishing house] ... DLB-49

Tower Publications................. DLB-46

Towne, Benjamin circa 1740-1793 ... DLB-43

Towne, Robert 1936- DLB-44

The Townely Plays
fifteenth and sixteenth
centuries DLB-146

Townshend, Aurelian
by 1583 - circa 1651 .... DLB-121

Tracy, Honor 1913- DLB-15

Traherne, Thomas 1637?-1674 ..... DLB-131

Traill, Catharine Parr 1802-1899 ... DLB-99

Train, Arthur 1875-1945 .... DLB-86

The Transatlantic Publishing
Company.................... DLB-49

Transcendentalists, American DS-5

Translators of the Twelfth Century:
Literary Issues Raised and Impact
Created DLB-115

Travel Writing, 1837-1875 .... DLB-166

Travel Writing, 1876-1909 .... DLB-174

Traven, B.
1882? or 1890?-1969? DLB-9, 56

Travers, Ben 1886-1980 .... DLB-10

Travers, P. L. (Pamela Lyndon)
1899- DLB-160

Trediakovsky, Vasilii Kirillovich
1703-1769 .... DLB-150

Treece, Henry 1911-1966 .... DLB-160

Trejo, Ernesto 1950- DLB-122

Trelawny, Edward John
1792-1881 .... DLB-110, 116, 144

Tremain, Rose 1943- DLB-14

Tremblay, Michel 1942- DLB-60

Trends in Twentieth-Century
Mass Market Publishing DLB-46

Trent, William P. 1862-1939........ DLB-47

Trescot, William Henry
1822-1898 .... DLB-30

Trevelyan, Sir George Otto
1838-1928 .... DLB-144

Trevisa, John
circa 1342-circa 1402 .... DLB-146

Trevor, William 1928- DLB-14, 139

Trierer Floyris circa 1170-1180 ...... DLB-138

Trilling, Lionel 1905-1975....... DLB-28, 63

Trilussa 1871-1950 .... DLB-114

Trimmer, Sarah 1741-1810 .... DLB-158

Triolet, Elsa 1896-1970 .... DLB-72

Tripp, John 1927- DLB-40

Trocchi, Alexander 1925- DLB-15

Trollope, Anthony
1815-1882............. DLB-21, 57, 159

Trollope, Frances 1779-1863.... DLB-21, 166

Troop, Elizabeth 1931- DLB-14

Trotter, Catharine 1679-1749 ...... DLB-84

Trotti, Lamar 1898-1952 .... DLB-44

Trottier, Pierre 1925- DLB-60

Troupe, Quincy Thomas, Jr.
1943- DLB-41

Trow, John F., and Company....... DLB-49

Truillier-Lacombe, Joseph-Patrice
1807-1863 .... DLB-99

Trumbo, Dalton 1905-1976 .... DLB-26

Trumbull, Benjamin 1735-1820 ..... DLB-30

Trumbull, John 1750-1831.......... DLB-31

Tscherning, Andreas 1611-1659 .... DLB-164

T. S. Eliot Centennial Y-88

Tucholsky, Kurt 1890-1935......... DLB-56

Tucker, Charlotte Maria
1821-1893 .... DLB-163

Tucker, George 1775-1861 .... DLB-3, 30

Tucker, Nathaniel Beverley
1784-1851 .... DLB-3

Tucker, St. George 1752-1827....... DLB-37

Tuckerman, Henry Theodore
1813-1871 .... DLB-64

Tunis, John R. 1889-1975 ...... DLB-22, 171

Tunstall, Cuthbert 1474-1559 ...... DLB-132

Tuohy, Frank 1925- DLB-14, 139

Tupper, Martin F. 1810-1889 .... DLB-32

Turbyfill, Mark 1896- DLB-45

Turco, Lewis 1934- Y-84

Turnbull, Andrew 1921-1970 ...... DLB-103

Turnbull, Gael 1928- DLB-40

Turner, Arlin 1909-1980 .... DLB-103

Turner, Charles (Tennyson)
1808-1879 .... DLB-32

Turner, Frederick 1943- DLB-40

Turner, Frederick Jackson
1861-1932 .... DLB-17

Turner, Joseph Addison
1826-1868 .... DLB-79

Turpin, Waters Edward
1910-1968 .... DLB-51

Turrini, Peter 1944- DLB-124

Tutuola, Amos 1920- DLB-125

Twain, Mark (see Clemens,
Samuel Langhorne)

Tweedie, Ethel Brilliana
circa 1860-1940............... DLB-174

The 'Twenties and Berlin, by
Alex Natan DLB-66

Tyler, Anne 1941- DLB-6, 143; Y-82

Tyler, Moses Coit 1835-1900 .... DLB-47, 64

Tyler, Royall 1757-1826 .... DLB-37

Tylor, Edward Burnett 1832-1917 ... DLB-57

Tynan, Katharine 1861-1931....... DLB-153

Tyndale, William
circa 1494-1536................ DLB-132

U

Udall, Nicholas 1504-1556 .... DLB-62

Uhland, Ludwig 1787-1862 .... DLB-90

Uhse, Bodo 1904-1963 .... DLB-69

Ujević, Augustin ("Tin") 1891-1955 .... DLB-147

Ulenhart, Niclas flourished circa 1600 .... DLB-164

Ulibarrí, Sabine R. 1919- DLB-82

Ulica, Jorge 1870-1926 .... DLB-82

Ulizio, B. George 1889-1969 .... DLB-140

Ulrich von Liechtenstein circa 1200-circa 1275 .... DLB-138

Ulrich von Zatzikhoven before 1194-after 1214 .... DLB-138

Unamuno, Miguel de 1864-1936 .... DLB-108

Under the Microscope (1872), by A. C. Swinburne DLB-35

Unger, Friederike Helene 1741-1813 .... DLB-94

Ungaretti, Giuseppe 1888-1970 ..... DLB-114

United States Book Company DLB-49

Universal Publishing and Distributing Corporation DLB-46

The University of Iowa Writers' Workshop Golden Jubilee Y-86

The University of South Carolina Press Y-94

University of Wales Press DLB-112

"The Unknown Public" (1858), by Wilkie Collins [excerpt] DLB-57

Unruh, Fritz von 1885-1970 .... DLB-56, 118

Unspeakable Practices II: The Festival of Vanguard Narrative at Brown University Y-93

Unwin, T. Fisher [publishing house] DLB-106

Upchurch, Boyd B. (see Boyd, John)

Updike, John 1932- DLB-2, 5, 143; Y-80, 82; DS-3

Upton, Bertha 1849-1912 .... DLB-141

Upton, Charles 1948- DLB-16

Upton, Florence K. 1873-1922 ..... DLB-141

Upward, Allen 1863-1926 .... DLB-36

Urista, Alberto Baltazar (see Alurista)

Urzidil, Johannes 1896-1976 .... DLB-85

Urquhart, Fred 1912- DLB-139

The Uses of Facsimile Y-90

Usk, Thomas died 1388 .... DLB-146

Uslar Pietri, Arturo 1906- DLB-113

Ustinov, Peter 1921- DLB-13

Uttley, Alison 1884-1976 .... DLB-160

Uz, Johann Peter 1720-1796 .... DLB-97

V

Vac, Bertrand 1914- DLB-88

Vadianus, Joachim 1484-1551 ...... DLB-179

Vail, Laurence 1891-1968 .... DLB-4

Vailland, Roger 1907-1965 .... DLB-83

Vajda, Ernest 1887-1954 .... DLB-44

Valdés, Gina 1943- DLB-122

Valdez, Luis Miguel 1940- DLB-122

Valduga, Patrizia 1953- DLB-128

Valente, José Angel 1929- DLB-108

Valenzuela, Luisa 1938- DLB-113

Valeri, Diego 1887-1976 .... DLB-128

Valgardson, W. D. 1939- DLB-60

Valle, Víctor Manuel 1950- DLB-122

Valle-Inclán, Ramón del 1866-1936 .... DLB-134

Vallejo, Armando 1949- DLB-122

Vallès, Jules 1832-1885 .... DLB-123

Vallette, Marguerite Eymery (see Rachilde)

Valverde, José María 1926- DLB-108

Van Allsburg, Chris 1949- DLB-61

Van Anda, Carr 1864-1945 .... DLB-25

Van Doren, Mark 1894-1972 ...... DLB-45

van Druten, John 1901-1957 .... DLB-10

Van Duyn, Mona 1921- DLB-5

Van Dyke, Henry 1852-1933 .... DLB-71; DS-13

Van Dyke, Henry 1928- DLB-33

van Itallie, Jean-Claude 1936- DLB-7

Van Loan, Charles E. 1876-1919 ... DLB-171

Van Rensselaer, Mariana Griswold 1851-1934 .... DLB-47

Van Rensselaer, Mrs. Schuyler (see Van Rensselaer, Mariana Griswold)

Van Vechten, Carl 1880-1964 ...... DLB-4, 9

van Vogt, A. E. 1912- DLB-8

Vanbrugh, Sir John 1664-1726 ..... DLB-80

Vance, Jack 1916?- DLB-8

Vane, Sutton 1888-1963 .... DLB-10

Vanguard Press DLB-46

Vann, Robert L. 1879-1940 .... DLB-29

Vargas, Llosa, Mario 1936- DLB-145

Varley, John 1947- Y-81

Varnhagen von Ense, Karl August 1785-1858 .... DLB-90

Varnhagen von Ense, Rahel 1771-1833 .... DLB-90

Vásquez Montalbán, Manuel 1939- DLB-134

Vassa, Gustavus (see Equiano, Olaudah)

Vassalli, Sebastiano 1941- DLB-128

Vaughan, Henry 1621-1695 .... DLB-131

Vaughan, Thomas 1621-1666 ...... DLB-131

Vaux, Thomas, Lord 1509-1556 .... DLB-132

Vazov, Ivan 1850-1921 .... DLB-147

Vega, Janine Pommy 1942- DLB-16

Veiller, Anthony 1903-1965 .... DLB-44

Velásquez-Trevino, Gloria 1949- DLB-122

Veloz Maggiolo, Marcio 1936- DLB-145

Venegas, Daniel ?-? DLB-82

Vergil, Polydore circa 1470-1555 ... DLB-132

Veríssimo, Erico 1905-1975 .... DLB-145

Verne, Jules 1828-1905 .... DLB-123

Verplanck, Gulian C. 1786-1870 .... DLB-59

Very, Jones 1813-1880 .... DLB-1

Vian, Boris 1920-1959 .... DLB-72

Vickers, Roy 1888?-1965 .... DLB-77

Victoria 1819-1901 .... DLB-55

Victoria Press DLB-106

Vidal, Gore 1925- DLB-6, 152

Viebig, Clara 1860-1952 .... DLB-66

Viereck, George Sylvester 1884-1962 .... DLB-54

Viereck, Peter 1916- DLB-5

Viets, Roger 1738-1811 .... DLB-99

Viewpoint: Politics and Performance, by David Edgar DLB-13

Vigil-Piñon, Evangelina 1949- DLB-122

Vigneault, Gilles 1928- DLB-60

Vigny, Alfred de 1797-1863 .... DLB-119

Vigolo, Giorgio 1894-1983 .... DLB-114

The Viking Press DLB-46

Villanueva, Alma Luz 1944- DLB-122

Villanueva, Tino 1941- DLB-82

Villard, Henry 1835-1900 .... DLB-23

Villard, Oswald Garrison 1872-1949 ... DLB-25, 91

Villarreal, José Antonio 1924- ... DLB-82

Villegas de Magnón, Leonor 1876-1955 ... DLB-122

Villemaire, Yolande 1949- ... DLB-60

Villena, Luis Antonio de 1951- ... DLB-134

Villiers de l'Isle-Adam, Jean-Marie Mathias Philippe-Auguste, Comte de 1838-1889 ... DLB-123

Villiers, George, Second Duke of Buckingham 1628-1687 ... DLB-80

Vine Press ... DLB-112

Viorst, Judith ?- ... DLB-52

Vipont, Elfrida (Elfrida Vipont Foulds, Charles Vipont) 1902-1992 ... DLB-160

Viramontes, Helena María 1954- ... DLB-122

Vischer, Friedrich Theodor 1807-1887 ... DLB-133

Vivanco, Luis Felipe 1907-1975 ... DLB-108

Viviani, Cesare 1947- ... DLB-128

Vizenor, Gerald 1934- ... DLB-175

Vizetelly and Company ... DLB-106

Voaden, Herman 1903- ... DLB-88

Voigt, Ellen Bryant 1943- ... DLB-120

Vojnović, Ivo 1857-1929 ... DLB-147

Volkoff, Vladimir 1932- ... DLB-83

Volland, P. F., Company ... DLB-46

Volponi, Paolo 1924- ... DLB-177

von der Grün, Max 1926- ... DLB-75

Vonnegut, Kurt 1922- ... DLB-2, 8, 152; Y-80; DS-3

Voranc, Prežihov 1893-1950 ... DLB-147

Voß, Johann Heinrich 1751-1826 ... DLB-90

Vroman, Mary Elizabeth circa 1924-1967 ... DLB-33

W

Wace, Robert ("Maistre") circa 1100-circa 1175 ... DLB-146

Wackenroder, Wilhelm Heinrich 1773-1798 ... DLB-90

Wackernagel, Wilhelm 1806-1869 ... DLB-133

Waddington, Miriam 1917- ... DLB-68

Wade, Henry 1887-1969 ... DLB-77

Wagenknecht, Edward 1900- ... DLB-103

Wagner, Heinrich Leopold 1747-1779 ... DLB-94

Wagner, Henry R. 1862-1957 ... DLB-140

Wagner, Richard 1813-1883 ... DLB-129

Wagoner, David 1926- ... DLB-5

Wah, Fred 1939- ... DLB-60

Waiblinger, Wilhelm 1804-1830 ... DLB-90

Wain, John 1925-1994 ... DLB-15, 27, 139, 155

Wainwright, Jeffrey 1944- ... DLB-40

Waite, Peirce and Company ... DLB-49

Wakoski, Diane 1937- ... DLB-5

Walahfrid Strabo circa 808-849 ... DLB-148

Walck, Henry Z. ... DLB-46

Walcott, Derek 1930- ... DLB-117; Y-81, 92

Waldegrave, Robert [publishing house] ... DLB-170

Waldis, Burkhard circa 1490-1556? ... DLB-179

Waldman, Anne 1945- ... DLB-16

Waldrop, Rosmarie 1935- ... DLB-169

Walker, Alice 1944- ... DLB-6, 33, 143

Walker, George F. 1947- ... DLB-60

Walker, Joseph A. 1935- ... DLB-38

Walker, Margaret 1915- ... DLB-76, 152

Walker, Ted 1934- ... DLB-40

Walker and Company ... DLB-49

Walker, Evans and Cogswell Company ... DLB-49

Walker, John Brisben 1847-1931 ... DLB-79

Wallace, Dewitt 1889-1981 and Lila Acheson Wallace 1889-1984 ... DLB-137

Wallace, Edgar 1875-1932 ... DLB-70

Wallace, Lila Acheson (see Wallace, Dewitt, and Lila Acheson Wallace)

Wallant, Edward Lewis 1926-1962 ... DLB-2, 28, 143

Waller, Edmund 1606-1687 ... DLB-126

Walpole, Horace 1717-1797 ... DLB-39, 104

Walpole, Hugh 1884-1941 ... DLB-34

Walrond, Eric 1898-1966 ... DLB-51

Walser, Martin 1927- ... DLB-75, 124

Walser, Robert 1878-1956 ... DLB-66

Walsh, Ernest 1895-1926 ... DLB-4, 45

Walsh, Robert 1784-1859 ... DLB-59

Waltharius circa 825 ... DLB-148

Walters, Henry 1848-1931 ... DLB-140

Walther von der Vogelweide circa 1170-circa 1230 ... DLB-138

Walton, Izaak 1593-1683 ... DLB-151

Wambaugh, Joseph 1937- ... DLB-6; Y-83

Waniek, Marilyn Nelson 1946- ... DLB-120

Warburton, William 1698-1779 ... DLB-104

Ward, Aileen 1919- ... DLB-111

Ward, Artemus (see Browne, Charles Farrar)

Ward, Arthur Henry Sarsfield (see Rohmer, Sax)

Ward, Douglas Turner 1930- ... DLB-7, 38

Ward, Lynd 1905-1985 ... DLB-22

Ward, Lock and Company ... DLB-106

Ward, Mrs. Humphry 1851-1920 ... DLB-18

Ward, Nathaniel circa 1578-1652 ... DLB-24

Ward, Theodore 1902-1983 ... DLB-76

Wardle, Ralph 1909-1988 ... DLB-103

Ware, William 1797-1852 ... DLB-1

Warne, Frederick, and Company [U.S.] ... DLB-49

Warne, Frederick, and Company [U.K.] ... DLB-106

Warner, Charles Dudley 1829-1900 ... DLB-64

Warner, Rex 1905- ... DLB-15

Warner, Susan Bogert 1819-1885 ... DLB-3, 42

Warner, Sylvia Townsend 1893-1978 ... DLB-34, 139

Warner, William 1558-1609 ... DLB-172

Warner Books ... DLB-46

Warr, Bertram 1917-1943 ... DLB-88

Warren, John Byrne Leicester (see De Tabley, Lord)

Warren, Lella 1899-1982 ... Y-83

Warren, Mercy Otis 1728-1814 ... DLB-31

Warren, Robert Penn 1905-1989 ... DLB-2, 48, 152; Y-80, 89

Die Wartburgkrieg circa 1230-circa 1280 ... DLB-138

Warton, Joseph 1722-1800 ... DLB-104, 109

Warton, Thomas 1728-1790 ... DLB-104, 109

Washington, George 1732-1799 ... DLB-31

Wassermann, Jakob 1873-1934 ... DLB-66

Wasson, David Atwood 1823-1887 ... DLB-1

Waterhouse, Keith 1929- ... DLB-13, 15

Waterman, Andrew 1940- ... DLB-40

Waters, Frank 1902- Y-86	Weigl, Bruce 1949- DLB-120	West, Nathanael 1903-1940 .... DLB-4, 9, 28
Waters, Michael 1949- DLB-120	Weinbaum, Stanley Grauman 1902-1935 .... DLB-8	West, Paul 1930- DLB-14
Watkins, Tobias 1780-1855........ DLB-73	Weintraub, Stanley 1929- DLB-111	West, Rebecca 1892-1983 ..... DLB-36; Y-83
Watkins, Vernon 1906-1967 .... DLB-20	Weise, Christian 1642-1708........ DLB-168	West and Johnson................. DLB-49
Watmough, David 1926- DLB-53	Weisenborn, Gunther 1902-1969 .... DLB-69, 124	Western Publishing Company DLB-46
Watson, James Wreford (see Wreford, James)	Weiß, Ernst 1882-1940............. DLB-81	*The Westminster Review* 1824-1914 ... DLB-110
Watson, John 1850-1907 .... DLB-156	Weiss, John 1818-1879............. DLB-1	Weston, Elizabeth Jane circa 1582-1612................ DLB-172
Watson, Sheila 1909- DLB-60	Weiss, Peter 1916-1982 .... DLB-69, 124	Wetherald, Agnes Ethelwyn 1857-1940 .... DLB-99
Watson, Thomas 1545?-1592 ...... DLB-132	Weiss, Theodore 1916- DLB-5	Wetherell, Elizabeth (see Warner, Susan Bogert)
Watson, Wilfred 1911- DLB-60	Weisse, Christian Felix 1726-1804 ... DLB-97	Wetzel, Friedrich Gottlob 1779-1819 .... DLB-90
von Watt, Joachim (see Vadianus, Joachim)	Weitling, Wilhelm 1808-1871 ...... DLB-129	Weyman, Stanley J. 1855-1928 .... DLB-141, 156
Watt, W. J., and Company DLB-46	Welch, James 1940- DLB-175	Wezel, Johann Karl 1747-1819 ...... DLB-94
Watterson, Henry 1840-1921 .... DLB-25	Welch, Lew 1926-1971?............ DLB-16	Whalen, Philip 1923- DLB-16
Watts, Alan 1915-1973............. DLB-16	Weldon, Fay 1931- DLB-14	Whalley, George 1915-1983 .... DLB-88
Watts, Franklin [publishing house]... DLB-46	Wellek, René 1903- DLB-63	Wharton, Edith 1862-1937 ...... DLB-4, 9, 12, 78; DS-13
Watts, Isaac 1674-1748 .... DLB-95	Wells, Carolyn 1862-1942 .... DLB-11	Wharton, William 1920s?- Y-80
Waugh, Auberon 1939- DLB-14	Wells, Charles Jeremiah circa 1800-1879................ DLB-32	Whately, Mary Louisa 1824-1889 .... DLB-166
Waugh, Evelyn 1903-1966 ..... DLB-15, 162	Wells, Gabriel 1862-1946 .... DLB-140	What's Really Wrong With Bestseller Lists........................... Y-84
Way and Williams DLB-49	Wells, H. G. 1866-1946......... DLB-34, 70, 156, 178	Wheatley, Dennis Yates 1897-1977 .... DLB-77
Wayman, Tom 1945- DLB-53	Wells, Robert 1947- DLB-40	Wheatley, Phillis circa 1754-1784 .... DLB-31, 50
Weatherly, Tom 1942- DLB-41	Wells-Barnett, Ida B. 1862-1931 ..... DLB-23	Wheeler, Anna Doyle 1785-1848? DLB-158
Weaver, Gordon 1937- DLB-130	Welty, Eudora 1909- DLB-2, 102, 143; Y-87; DS-12	Wheeler, Charles Stearns 1816-1843 .... DLB-1
Weaver, Robert 1921- DLB-88	Wendell, Barrett 1855-1921......... DLB-71	Wheeler, Monroe 1900-1988......... DLB-4
Webb, Frank J. ?-? DLB-50	Wentworth, Patricia 1878-1961 ..... DLB-77	Wheelock, John Hall 1886-1978 ..... DLB-45
Webb, James Watson 1802-1884 .... DLB-43	Werder, Diederich von dem 1584-1657 .... DLB-164	Wheelwright, John circa 1592-1679................. DLB-24
Webb, Mary 1881-1927 .... DLB-34	Werfel, Franz 1890-1945 .... DLB-81, 124	Wheelwright, J. B. 1897-1940 .... DLB-45
Webb, Phyllis 1927- DLB-53	The Werner Company............. DLB-49	Whetstone, Colonel Pete (see Noland, C. F. M.)
Webb, Walter Prescott 1888-1963 ... DLB-17	Werner, Zacharias 1768-1823 .... DLB-94	Whetstone, George 1550-1587 ..... DLB-136
Webbe, William ?-1591 .... DLB-132	Wersba, Barbara 1932- DLB-52	Whicher, Stephen E. 1915-1961 .... DLB-111
Webster, Augusta 1837-1894........ DLB-35	Wescott, Glenway 1901- DLB-4, 9, 102	Whipple, Edwin Percy 1819-1886 .... DLB-1, 64
Webster, Charles L., and Company................ DLB-49	Wesker, Arnold 1932- DLB-13	Whitaker, Alexander 1585-1617..... DLB-24
Webster, John 1579 or 1580-1634? DLB-58	Wesley, Charles 1707-1788 .... DLB-95	Whitaker, Daniel K. 1801-1881 ..... DLB-73
Webster, Noah 1758-1843 .... DLB-1, 37, 42, 43, 73	Wesley, John 1703-1791 .... DLB-104	Whitcher, Frances Miriam 1814-1852 .... DLB-11
Weckherlin, Georg Rodolf 1584-1653 .... DLB-164	Wesley, Richard 1945- DLB-38	White, Andrew 1579-1656........... DLB-24
Wedekind, Frank 1864-1918 .... DLB-118	Wessels, A., and Company DLB-46	
Weeks, Edward Augustus, Jr. 1898-1989 .... DLB-137	*Wessobrunner Gebet* circa 787-815..................... DLB-148	
Weems, Mason Locke 1759-1825............. DLB-30, 37, 42	West, Anthony 1914-1988.......... DLB-15	
Weerth, Georg 1822-1856 .... DLB-129	West, Dorothy 1907- DLB-76	
Weidenfeld and Nicolson DLB-112	West, Jessamyn 1902-1984 ..... DLB-6; Y-84	
Weidman, Jerome 1913- DLB-28	West, Mae 1892-1980............. DLB-44	

White, Andrew Dickson
  1832-1918 .... DLB-47

White, E. B. 1899-1985 .... DLB-11, 22

White, Edgar B. 1947- DLB-38

White, Ethel Lina 1887-1944. ...... DLB-77

White, Henry Kirke 1785-1806. ..... DLB-96

White, Horace 1834-1916 .... DLB-23

White, Phyllis Dorothy James
  (see James, P. D.)

White, Richard Grant 1821-1885 .... DLB-64

White, T. H. 1906-1964. .... DLB-160

White, Walter 1893-1955. .... DLB-51

White, William, and Company DLB-49

White, William Allen
  1868-1944 .... DLB-9, 25

White, William Anthony Parker (see Boucher, Anthony)

White, William Hale (see Rutherford, Mark)

Whitechurch, Victor L.
  1868-1933 .... DLB-70

Whitehead, Alfred North
  1861-1947 .... DLB-100

Whitehead, James 1936- Y-81

Whitehead, William
  1715-1785 .... DLB-84, 109

Whitfield, James Monroe
  1822-1871 .... DLB-50

Whitgift, John circa 1533-1604 ..... DLB-132

Whiting, John 1917-1963. .... DLB-13

Whiting, Samuel 1597-1679. .... DLB-24

Whitlock, Brand 1869-1934. .... DLB-12

Whitman, Albert, and Company DLB-46

Whitman, Albery Allson
  1851-1901 .... DLB-50

Whitman, Alden 1913-1990 .... Y-91

Whitman, Sarah Helen (Power)
  1803-1878 .... DLB-1

Whitman, Walt 1819-1892 .... DLB-3, 64

Whitman Publishing Company. DLB-46

Whitney, Geoffrey
  1548 or 1552?-1601 .... DLB-136

Whitney, Isabella
  flourished 1566-1573 .... DLB-136

Whitney, John Hay 1904-1982 ..... DLB-127

Whittemore, Reed 1919- DLB-5

Whittier, John Greenleaf 1807-1892... DLB-1

Whittlesey House DLB-46

Who Runs American Literature? Y-94

Wickram, Georg
  circa 1505-circa 1561 .... DLB-179

Wideman, John Edgar 1941- DLB-33, 143

Widener, Harry Elkins 1885-1912.... DLB-140

Wiebe, Rudy 1934- DLB-60

Wiechert, Ernst 1887-1950 .... DLB-56

Wied, Martina 1882-1957 .... DLB-85

Wiehe, Evelyn May Clowes (see Mordaunt, Elinor)

Wieland, Christoph Martin
  1733-1813 .... DLB-97

Wienbarg, Ludolf 1802-1872. ...... DLB-133

Wieners, John 1934- DLB-16

Wier, Ester 1910- DLB-52

Wiesel, Elie 1928- DLB-83; Y-87

Wiggin, Kate Douglas 1856-1923 .... DLB-42

Wigglesworth, Michael 1631-1705 ... DLB-24

Wilberforce, William 1759-1833. ... DLB-158

Wilbrandt, Adolf 1837-1911 .... DLB-129

Wilbur, Richard 1921- DLB-5, 169

Wild, Peter 1940- DLB-5

Wilde, Oscar
  1854-1900. ... DLB-10, 19, 34, 57, 141, 156

Wilde, Richard Henry
  1789-1847 .... DLB-3, 59

Wilde, W. A., Company DLB-49

Wilder, Billy 1906- DLB-26

Wilder, Laura Ingalls 1867-1957 .... DLB-22

Wilder, Thornton 1897-1975 .... DLB-4, 7, 9

Wildgans, Anton 1881-1932 .... DLB-118

Wiley, Bell Irvin 1906-1980. .... DLB-17

Wiley, John, and Sons DLB-49

Wilhelm, Kate 1928- DLB-8

Wilkes, George 1817-1885. .... DLB-79

Wilkinson, Anne 1910-1961 .... DLB-88

Wilkinson, Sylvia 1940- Y-86

Wilkinson, William Cleaver
  1833-1920 .... DLB-71

Willard, Barbara 1909-1994 .... DLB-161

Willard, L. [publishing house]. DLB-49

Willard, Nancy 1936- DLB-5, 52

Willard, Samuel 1640-1707 .... DLB-24

William of Auvergne 1190-1249.... DLB-115

William of Conches
  circa 1090-circa 1154 .... DLB-115

William of Ockham
  circa 1285-1347. .... DLB-115

William of Sherwood
  1200/1205 - 1266/1271. .... DLB-115

The William Chavrat American Fiction
  Collection at the Ohio State University Libraries Y-92

Williams, A., and Company DLB-49

Williams, Ben Ames 1889-1953 .... DLB-102

Williams, C. K. 1936- DLB-5

Williams, Chancellor 1905- DLB-76

Williams, Charles
  1886-1945 .... DLB-100, 153

Williams, Denis 1923- DLB-117

Williams, Emlyn 1905- DLB-10, 77

Williams, Garth 1912- DLB-22

Williams, George Washington
  1849-1891 .... DLB-47

Williams, Heathcote 1941- DLB-13

Williams, Helen Maria
  1761-1827 .... DLB-158

Williams, Hugo 1942- DLB-40

Williams, Isaac 1802-1865. .... DLB-32

Williams, Joan 1928- DLB-6

Williams, John A. 1925- DLB-2, 33

Williams, John E. 1922-1994 .... DLB-6

Williams, Jonathan 1929- DLB-5

Williams, Miller 1930- DLB-105

Williams, Raymond 1921- DLB-14

Williams, Roger circa 1603-1683 .... DLB-24

Williams, Samm-Art 1946- DLB-38

Williams, Sherley Anne 1944- DLB-41

Williams, T. Harry 1909-1979 ..... DLB-17

Williams, Tennessee
  1911-1983. .... DLB-7; Y-83; DS-4

Williams, Ursula Moray 1911- DLB-160

Williams, Valentine 1883-1946. ..... DLB-77

Williams, William Appleman
  1921- DLB-17

Williams, William Carlos
  1883-1963. .... DLB-4, 16, 54, 86

Williams, Wirt 1921- DLB-6

Williams Brothers. DLB-49

Williamson, Jack 1908- DLB-8

Willingham, Calder Baynard, Jr.
  1922- DLB-2, 44

Williram of Ebersberg
  circa 1020-1085. .... DLB-148

Willis, Nathaniel Parker
  1806-1867 ..... DLB-3, 59, 73, 74; DS-13

Willkomm, Ernst 1810-1886 .... DLB-133

Wilmer, Clive 1945- DLB-40

Wilson, A. N. 1950- DLB-14, 155

Wilson, Angus
1913-1991...........DLB-15, 139, 155

Wilson, Arthur 1595-1652.........DLB-58

Wilson, Augusta Jane Evans
1835-1909 ....DLB-42

Wilson, Colin 1931- DLB-14

Wilson, Edmund 1895-1972 ....DLB-63

Wilson, Ethel 1888-1980 ....DLB-68

Wilson, Harriet E. Adams
1828?-1863? DLB-50

Wilson, Harry Leon 1867-1939 ......DLB-9

Wilson, John 1588-1667............DLB-24

Wilson, John 1785-1854...........DLB-110

Wilson, Lanford 1937- DLB-7

Wilson, Margaret 1882-1973.........DLB-9

Wilson, Michael 1914-1978.........DLB-44

Wilson, Mona 1872-1954..........DLB-149

Wilson, Thomas
1523 or 1524-1581 ....DLB-132

Wilson, Woodrow 1856-1924 ....DLB-47

Wilson, Effingham
[publishing house] DLB-154

Wimpfeling, Jakob 1450-1528......DLB-179

Wimsatt, William K., Jr.
1907-1975 ....DLB-63

Winchell, Walter 1897-1972 ....DLB-29

Winchester, J. [publishing house] DLB-49

Winckelmann, Johann Joachim
1717-1768 ....DLB-97

Winckler, Paul 1630-1686 ....DLB-164

Wind, Herbert Warren 1916- DLB-171

Windet, John [publishing house]....DLB-170

Windham, Donald 1920- DLB-6

Wingate, Allan [publishing house] ..DLB-112

Winnemucca, Sarah 1844-1921.....DLB-175

Winnifrith, Tom 1938- DLB-155

Winsloe, Christa 1888-1944 ....DLB-124

Winsor, Justin 1831-1897...........DLB-47

John C. Winston Company.........DLB-49

Winters, Yvor 1900-1968..........DLB-48

Winthrop, John 1588-1649 .....DLB-24, 30

Winthrop, John, Jr. 1606-1676 ......DLB-24

Wirt, William 1772-1834...........DLB-37

Wise, John 1652-1725 ....DLB-24

Wiseman, Adele 1928- DLB-88

Wishart and Company............DLB-112

Wisner, George 1812-1849 ....DLB-43

Wister, Owen 1860-1938.........DLB-9, 78

Wither, George 1588-1667 ....DLB-121

Witherspoon, John 1723-1794........DLB-31

Withrow, William Henry 1839-1908...DLB-99

Wittenwiler, Heinrich
before 1387-circa 1414?........DLB-179

Wittig, Monique 1935- DLB-83

Wodehouse, P. G.
1881-1975 ....DLB-34, 162

Wohmann, Gabriele 1932- DLB-75

Woiwode, Larry 1941- DLB-6

Wolcot, John 1738-1819...........DLB-109

Wolcott, Roger 1679-1767..........DLB-24

Wolf, Christa 1929- DLB-75

Wolf, Friedrich 1888-1953.........DLB-124

Wolfe, Gene 1931- DLB-8

Wolfe, John [publishing house].....DLB-170

Wolfe, Reyner (Reginald)
[publishing house] DLB-170

Wolfe, Thomas
1900-1938 ......DLB-9, 102; Y-85; DS-2

Wolfe, Tom 1931- DLB-152

Wolff, Helen 1906-1994 ....Y-94

Wolff, Tobias 1945- DLB-130

Wolfram von Eschenbach
circa 1170-after 1220 ....DLB-138

Wolfram von Eschenbach's *Parzival*:
Prologue and Book 3 ....DLB-138

Wollstonecraft, Mary
1759-1797...........DLB-39, 104, 158

Wondratschek, Wolf 1943- DLB-75

Wood, Benjamin 1820-1900 ....DLB-23

Wood, Charles 1932- DLB-13

Wood, Mrs. Henry 1814-1887 ......DLB-18

Wood, Joanna E. 1867-1927 ....DLB-92

Wood, Samuel [publishing house] ...DLB-49

Wood, William ?-? DLB-24

Woodberry, George Edward
1855-1930 ....DLB-71, 103

Woodbridge, Benjamin 1622-1684 ...DLB-24

Woodcock, George 1912- DLB-88

Woodhull, Victoria C. 1838-1927....DLB-79

Woodmason, Charles circa 1720-?...DLB-31

Woodress, Jr., James Leslie
1916- DLB-111

Woodson, Carter G. 1875-1950 .....DLB-17

Woodward, C. Vann 1908- DLB-17

Woodward, Stanley 1895-1965.....DLB-171

Wooler, Thomas
1785 or 1786-1853 ....DLB-158

Woolf, David (see Maddow, Ben)

Woolf, Leonard 1880-1969 ....DLB-100; DS-10

Woolf, Virginia
1882-1941 .....DLB-36, 100, 162; DS-10

Woolf, Virginia, "The New Biography," *New York Herald Tribune*, 30 October 1927
...........................DLB-149

Woollcott, Alexander 1887-1943 ....DLB-29

Woolman, John 1720-1772 ....DLB-31

Woolner, Thomas 1825-1892 ....DLB-35

Woolsey, Sarah Chauncy
1835-1905 ....DLB-42

Woolson, Constance Fenimore
1840-1894 ....DLB-12, 74

Worcester, Joseph Emerson
1784-1865 ....DLB-1

Worde, Wynkyn de
[publishing house] DLB-170

Wordsworth, Christopher
1807-1885 ....DLB-166

Wordsworth, Dorothy
1771-1855 ....DLB-107

Wordsworth, Elizabeth
1840-1932 ....DLB-98

Wordsworth, William
1770-1850 ....DLB-93, 107

The Works of the Rev. John Witherspoon
(1800-1801) [excerpts] DLB-31

A World Chronology of Important Science
Fiction Works (1818-1979) DLB-8

World Publishing Company DLB-46

World War II Writers Symposium at the
University of South Carolina,
12–14 April 1995................Y-95

Worthington, R., and Company.....DLB-49

Wotton, Sir Henry 1568-1639......DLB-121

Wouk, Herman 1915- Y-82

Wreford, James 1915- DLB-88

Wren, Percival Christopher
1885-1941 ....DLB-153

Wrenn, John Henry 1841-1911.....DLB-140

Wright, C. D. 1949- DLB-120

Wright, Charles 1935- DLB-165; Y-82

Wright, Charles Stevenson 1932- DLB-33

Wright, Frances 1795-1852 ....DLB-73

Wright, Harold Bell 1872-1944.......DLB-9

Wright, James 1927-1980 .... DLB-5, 169

Wright, Jay 1935- DLB-41

Wright, Louis B. 1899-1984 .... DLB-17

Wright, Richard
  1908-1960 .... DLB-76, 102; DS-2

Wright, Richard B. 1937- DLB-53

Wright, Sarah Elizabeth 1928- DLB-33

Writers and Politics: 1871-1918,
  by Ronald Gray DLB-66

Writers and their Copyright Holders:
  the WATCH Project.............. Y-94

Writers' Forum..................... Y-85

Writing for the Theatre, by
  Harold Pinter DLB-13

Wroth, Lady Mary 1587-1653 ..... DLB-121

Wurlitzer, Rudolph 1937- DLB-173

Wyatt, Sir Thomas
  circa 1503-1542................ DLB-132

Wycherley, William 1641-1715...... DLB-80

Wyclif, John
  circa 1335-31 December 1384... DLB-146

von Wyle, Niklas 1415-1479....... DLB-179

Wylie, Elinor 1885-1928 .... DLB-9, 45

Wylie, Philip 1902-1971............. DLB-9

Wyllie, John Cook 1908-1968...... DLB-140

X

Xenophon circa 430 B.C.-circa 356 B.C.
  .... DLB-176

Y

Yates, Dornford 1885-1960..... DLB-77, 153

Yates, J. Michael 1938- DLB-60

Yates, Richard 1926-1992 ... DLB-2; Y-81, 92

Yavorov, Peyo 1878-1914 .... DLB-147

Yearsley, Ann 1753-1806.......... DLB-109

Yeats, William Butler
  1865-1939......... DLB-10, 19, 98, 156

Yep, Laurence 1948- DLB-52

Yerby, Frank 1916-1991............ DLB-76

Yezierska, Anzia 1885-1970........ DLB-28

Yolen, Jane 1939- DLB-52

Yonge, Charlotte Mary
  1823-1901 .... DLB-18, 163

The York Cycle
  circa 1376-circa 1569 .... DLB-146

A Yorkshire Tragedy DLB-58

Yoseloff, Thomas
  [publishing house] DLB-46

Young, Al 1939- DLB-33

Young, Arthur 1741-1820 .... DLB-158

Young, Dick 1917 or 1918 - 1987... DLB-171

Young, Edward 1683-1765 .... DLB-95

Young, Stark 1881-1963.......... DLB-9, 102

Young, Waldeman 1880-1938....... DLB-26

Young, William [publishing house] .. DLB-49

Young Bear, Ray A. 1950- DLB-175

Yourcenar, Marguerite
  1903-1987 .... DLB-72; Y-88

"You've Never Had It So Good," Gusted by
  "Winds of Change": British Fiction in the
  1950s, 1960s, and After......... DLB-14

Yovkov, Yordan 1880-1937........ DLB-147

Z

Zachariä, Friedrich Wilhelm
  1726-1777 .... DLB-97

Zamora, Bernice 1938- DLB-82

Zand, Herbert 1923-1970........... DLB-85

Zangwill, Israel 1864-1926 ..... DLB-10, 135

Zanzotto, Andrea 1921- DLB-128

Zapata Olivella, Manuel 1920- DLB-113

Zebra Books DLB-46

Zebrowski, George 1945- DLB-8

Zech, Paul 1881-1946.............. DLB-56

Zepheria........................ DLB-172

Zeidner, Lisa 1955- DLB-120

Zelazny, Roger 1937-1995........... DLB-8

Zenger, John Peter 1697-1746.... DLB-24, 43

Zesen, Philipp von 1619-1689...... DLB-164

Zieber, G. B., and Company........ DLB-49

Zieroth, Dale 1946- DLB-60

Zigler und Kliphausen, Heinrich Anselm von
  1663-1697 .... DLB-168

Zimmer, Paul 1934- DLB-5

Zingref, Julius Wilhelm
  1591-1635 .... DLB-164

Zindel, Paul 1936- DLB-7, 52

Zinzendorf, Nikolaus Ludwig von
  1700-1760 .... DLB-168

Zitkala-Ša 1876-1938 .... DLB-175

Zola, Emile 1840-1902............ DLB-123

Zolotow, Charlotte 1915- DLB-52

Zschokke, Heinrich 1771-1848 ...... DLB-94

Zubly, John Joachim 1724-1781 ..... DLB-31

Zu-Bolton II, Ahmos 1936- DLB-41

Zuckmayer, Carl 1896-1977 .... DLB-56, 124

Zukofsky, Louis 1904-1978...... DLB-5, 165

Župančič, Oton 1878-1949 .... DLB-147

zur Mühlen, Hermynia 1883-1951 ... DLB-56

Zweig, Arnold 1887-1968........... DLB-66

Zweig, Stefan 1881-1942 .... DLB-81, 118

Zwingli, Huldrych 1484-1531 ...... DLB-179

ISBN 0-7876-1068-2

90000